D1552355

LUKE

Smyth & Helwys Bible Commentary: Luke

Publication Staff

President & CEO
Cecil P. Staton

Publisher & Executive Vice President
Lex Horton

Vice President, Production
Keith Gammons

Book Editor
Leslie Andres

Graphic Designers
Wesley Crook
Dave Jones

Assistant Editors
Kelley F. Land
Rachel Stancil

Smyth & Helwys Publishing, Inc.
6316 Peake Road
Macon, Georgia 31210-3960
1-800-747-3016
© 2008 by Smyth & Helwys Publishing
All rights reserved.
Printed in the United States of America.

The paper used in this publication meets the minimum
requirements of American National Standard for Information
Sciences—Permanence of Paper for Printed Library Materials.
ANSI Z39.48–1984 (alk. paper)

Library of Congress Cataloging-in-Publication Data

Vinson, Richard B.
Luke / Richard B. Vinson.
p. cm. — (Smyth & Helwys Bible commentary, 21)
Includes bibliographical references and indexes.
ISBN 978-1-57312-078-4
CIP information on file.

SMYTH & HELWYS BIBLE COMMENTARY

LUKE

RICHARD B. VINSON

SMYTH&HELWYS
PUBLISHING INCORPORATED   MACON, GEORGIA

PROJECT EDITOR
R. SCOTT NASH
Mercer University
Macon, Georgia

OLD TESTAMENT
GENERAL EDITOR
SAMUEL E. BALENTINE
Union Theological Seminary and
Presbyterian School of
Christian Education
Richmond, Virginia

NEW TESTAMENT
GENERAL EDITOR
R. ALAN CULPEPPER
McAfee School of Theology
Mercer University
Atlanta, Georgia

AREA
OLD TESTAMENT EDITORS
MARK E. BIDDLE
Baptist Theological Seminary
at Richmond, Virginia

AREA
NEW TESTAMENT EDITORS
R. SCOTT NASH
Mercer University
Macon, Georgia

KANDY QUEEN-SUTHERLAND
Stetson University
Deland, Florida

RICHARD B. VINSON
Salem College
Winston-Salem, North Carolina

PAUL REDDITT
Georgetown College
Georgetown, Kentucky

Baptist Seminary of Kentucky
Lexington, Kentucky

ADVANCE PRAISE

With this commentary, Richard Vinson proves himself to be not only a sensitive reader of the Gospel of Luke but also an adventurous and sure guide through its pages. His engaging style of writing and his prophetic comments on the ongoing significance of Luke's message make this a welcome edition to any pastor's library.

—*Joel B. Green*
Professor of New Testament Interpretation
Fuller Theological Seminary

Richard B. Vinson writes in a style that is socially and theologically relevant, always aware of his primary audience—pastors and teachers. Supporting, sustaining, and engaging Vinson's commentary and applications are sound, critical scholarship, knowledge of relevant primary sources, and an awareness of contemporary culture that sorely needs a fresh hearing of Luke's good news.

—*J. Bradley Chance*
Professor of Religion and Chair
William Jewell College

Vinson offers a remarkably wide-ranging and cutting-edge commentary on Luke's Gospel as valuable to seasoned scholars as it is accessible to thoughtful ministers and laypersons. This volume attractively combines exegetical precision, social-historical insight, and theological conviction with prophetic challenge, cultural engagement, and pastoral sensitivity: no mean achievement, as Luke himself might put it.

—*F. Scott Spencer*
Professor of New Testament and Preaching
Baptist Theological Seminary at Richmond

Richard Vinson's commentary on Luke's Gospel is both accessible and engaging. It shows his strengths as a scholar, thinker, teacher and preacher. He has combined an easily readable approach with excellent provocative research. Those of us who are constantly in need of solid Biblical study that challenges our own thinking, and helps us to prepare in instructing our congregations, will benefit from his work on Luke. Richard makes learning fun, and this commentary confirms what I thought I knew, with what I had never thought of before in reading Luke's Gospel.

—Elizabeth Pugh Mills
Pastor, Grace Baptist Church
Richmond, Virginia

CONTENTS

DEDICATION

To my parents,

Richard and Betty Vinson,

"servants of the Word."

ABBREVIATIONS USED IN THIS COMMENTARY

Books of the Old Testament, Apocrypha, and New Testament are generally abbreviated in the Sidebars, parenthetical references, and notes according to the following system.

The Old Testament

Genesis	Gen
Exodus	Exod
Leviticus	Lev
Numbers	Num
Deuteronomy	Deut
Joshua	Josh
Judges	Judg
Ruth	Ruth
1–2 Samuel	1–2 Sam
1–2 Kings	1–2 Kgs
1–2 Chronicles	1–2 Chr
Ezra	Ezra
Nehemiah	Neh
Esther	Esth
Job	Job
Psalm (Psalms)	Ps (Pss)
Proverbs	Prov
Ecclesiastes	Eccl
or Qoheleth	Qoh
Song of Solomon	Song
or Song of Songs	Song
or Canticles	Cant
Isaiah	Isa
Jeremiah	Jer
Lamentations	Lam
Ezekiel	Ezek
Daniel	Dan
Hosea	Hos
Joel	Joel
Amos	Amos
Obadiah	Obad
Jonah	Jonah
Micah	Mic

Nahum	Nah
Habakkuk	Hab
Zephaniah	Zeph
Haggai	Hag
Zechariah	Zech
Malachi	Mal

The Apocrypha

1–2 Esdras	1–2 Esdr
Tobit	Tob
Judith	Jdt
Additions to Esther	Add Esth
Wisdom of Solomon	Wis
Ecclesiasticus or the Wisdom of Jesus Son of Sirach	Sir
Baruch	Bar
Epistle (or Letter) of Jeremiah	Ep Jer
Prayer of Azariah and the Song of the Three	Pr Azar
Daniel and Susanna	Sus
Daniel, Bel, and the Dragon	Bel
Prayer of Manasseh	Pr Man
1–4 Maccabees	1–4 Macc

The New Testament

Matthew	Matt
Mark	Mark
Luke	Luke
John	John
Acts	Acts
Romans	Rom
1–2 Corinthians	1–2 Cor
Galatians	Gal
Ephesians	Eph
Philippians	Phil
Colossians	Col
1–2 Thessalonians	1–2 Thess
1–2 Timothy	1–2 Tim
Titus	Titus
Philemon	Phlm
Hebrews	Heb
James	Jas
1–2 Peter	1–2 Pet
1–2–3 John	1–2–3 John
Jude	Jude
Revelation	Rev

Other commonly used abbreviations include:

AD	*Anno Domini* ("in the year of the Lord") (also commonly referred to as CE = the Common Era)
BC	Before Christ (also commonly referred to as BCE = Before the Common Era)
C.	century
c.	*circa* (around "that time")
cf.	*confer* (compare)
ch.	chapter
chs.	chapters
d.	died
ed.	edition or edited by or editor
eds.	editors
e.g.	*exempli gratia* (for example)
et al.	*et alii* (and others)
f./ff.	and the following one(s)
gen. ed.	general editor
Gk.	Greek
Heb.	Hebrew
ibid.	*ibidem* (in the same place)
i.e.	*id est* (that is)
Lat.	Latin
LCL	Loeb Classical Library
lit.	literally
n.d.	no date
rev. and exp. ed.	revised and expanded edition
sg.	singular
trans.	translated by or translator(s)
vol(s).	volume(s)
v.	verse
vv.	verses

Selected additional written works cited by abbreviations include the following. A complete listing of abbreviations can be referenced in *The SBL Handbook of Style* (Peabody MA: Hendrickson, 1999):

AB	Anchor Bible
ABD	*Anchor Bible Dictionary*
ACCS	Ancient Christian Commentary on Scripture
ANF	*Ante-Nicene Fathers*
ANTC	Abingdon New Testament Commentaries
BA	*Biblical Archaeologist*
BAR	*Biblical Archaeology Review*
CBQ	*Catholic Biblical Quarterly*

HTR	*Harvard Theological Review*
HUCA	*Hebrew Union College Annual*
ICC	International Critical Commentary
IDB	*Interpreters Dictionary of the Bible*
JBL	*Journal of Biblical Literature*
JSJ	*Journal for the Study of Judaism in the Persian, Hellenistic, and Roman Periods*
JSNT	*Journal for the Study of the New Testament*
JSOT	*Journal for the Study of the Old Testament*
KJV	King James Version
LXX	Septuagint = Greek Translation of Hebrew Bible
MDB	*Mercer Dictionary of the Bible*
MT	Masoretic Text
NASB	New American Standard Bible
NEB	New English Bible
NICNT	New International Commentary on the New Testament
NIV	New International Version
NovT	*Novum Testamentum*
NRSV	New Revised Standard Version
NTS	*New Testament Studies*
OGIS	*Orientis graeci inscriptiones selectae*
OTL	Old Testament Library
PRSt	*Perspectives in Religious Studies*
RevExp	*Review and Expositor*
RSV	Revised Standard Version
SBLSP	*Society of Biblical Literature Seminar Papers*
SP	Sacra pagina
TDNT	*Theological Dictionary of the New Testament*
TEV	Today's English Version
WBC	Word Biblical Commentary

ACKNOWLEDGMENTS

Writing this commentary has been lots of fun, much more so than I expected when I agreed to do it. I'm grateful to Alan Culpepper and to the other members of the editorial board who issued the invitation. Thanks also go to the many churches who graciously received my ideas on these texts; being able to field-test my notions in the context of sermons or Bible studies was crucial, and I'm indebted for all the suggestions and comments, and most of all the patience, these groups gave me. Two groups were regularly subjected to my interpretations and so substantially influenced the way things took shape: the congregation of Grace Baptist Church in Richmond, Virginia, and the youth of Knollwood Baptist Church in Winston-Salem, North Carolina. Various classes at Baptist Theological Seminary at Richmond also heard and read parts of this Commentary in earlier drafts. My wife, B. Diane Lipsett, who teaches New Testament at the School of Divinity at Wake Forest University, has been my most constant conversation partner and first reader. Thank you, brothers and sisters, for all you gave me; if I'd listened to you better, this would be a better book.

This is dedicated to my parents, Richard G. Vinson and Betty B. Vinson. They have taught the Bible in Sunday school classes for as long as I can remember, and their example of patient study and dedication to teaching the Word surely left its mark on me.

Richard B. Vinson
September 2008

SERIES PREFACE

The *Smyth & Helwys Bible Commentary* is a visually stimulating and user-friendly series that is as close to multimedia in print as possible. Written by accomplished scholars with all students of Scripture in mind, the primary goal of the *Smyth & Helwys Bible Commentary* is to make available serious, credible biblical scholarship in an accessible and less intimidating format.

Far too many Bible commentaries fall short of bridging the gap between the insights of biblical scholars and the needs of students of God's written word. In an unprecedented way, the *Smyth & Helwys Bible Commentary* brings insightful commentary to bear on the lives of contemporary Christians. Using a multimedia format, the volumes employ a stunning array of art, photographs, maps, and drawings to illustrate the truths of the Bible for a visual generation of believers.

The *Smyth & Helwys Bible Commentary* is built upon the idea that meaningful Bible study can occur when the insights of contemporary biblical scholars blend with sensitivity to the needs of lifelong students of Scripture. Some persons within local faith communities, however, struggle with potentially informative biblical scholarship for several reasons. Oftentimes, such scholarship is cast in technical language easily grasped by other scholars, but not by the general reader. For example, lengthy, technical discussions on every detail of a particular scriptural text can hinder the quest for a clear grasp of the whole. Also, the format for presenting scholarly insights has often been confusing to the general reader, rendering the work less than helpful. Unfortunately, responses to the hurdles of reading extensive commentaries have led some publishers to produce works for a general readership that merely skim the surface of the rich resources of biblical scholarship. This commentary series incorporates works of fine art in an accurate and scholarly manner, yet the format remains "user-friendly." An important facet is the presentation and explanation of images of art, which interpret the biblical material or illustrate how the biblical material has been understood and interpreted in the past. A visual generation of believers deserves a commentary series that contains not only the all-important textual commentary on Scripture, but images, photographs, maps, works of fine art, and drawings that bring the text to life.

The *Smyth & Helwys Bible Commentary* makes serious, credible biblical scholarship more accessible to a wider audience. Writers and editors alike present information in ways that encourage readers to gain a better understanding of the Bible. The editorial board has worked to develop a format that is useful and usable, informative and pleasing to the eye. Our writers are reputable scholars who participate in the community of faith and sense a calling to communicate the results of their scholarship to their faith community.

The *Smyth & Helwys Bible Commentary* addresses Christians and the larger church. While both respect for and sensitivity to the needs and contributions of other faith communities are reflected in the work of the series authors, the authors speak primarily to Christians. Thus the reader can note a confessional tone throughout the volumes. No particular "confession of faith" guides the authors, and diverse perspectives are observed in the various volumes. Each writer, though, brings to the biblical text the best scholarly tools available and expresses the results of their studies in commentary and visuals that assist readers seeking a word from the Lord for the church.

To accomplish this goal, writers in this series have drawn from numerous streams in the rich tradition of biblical interpretation. The basic focus is the biblical text itself, and considerable attention is given to the wording and structure of texts. Each particular text, however, is also considered in the light of the entire canon of Christian Scriptures. Beyond this, attention is given to the cultural context of the biblical writings. Information from archaeology, ancient history, geography, comparative literature, history of religions, politics, sociology, and even economics is used to illuminate the culture of the people who produced the Bible. In addition, the writers have drawn from the history of interpretation, not only as it is found in traditional commentary on the Bible but also in literature, theater, church history, and the visual arts. Finally, the *Commentary* on Scripture is joined with *Connections* to the world of the contemporary church. Here again, the writers draw on scholarship in many fields as well as relevant issues in the popular culture.

This wealth of information might easily overwhelm a reader if not presented in a "user-friendly" format. Thus the heavier discussions of detail and the treatments of other helpful topics are presented in special-interest boxes, or Sidebars, clearly connected to the passages under discussion so as not to interrupt the flow of the basic interpretation. The result is a commentary on Scripture that focuses on the theological significance of a text while also offering the reader a rich array of additional information related to the text and its interpretation.

An accompanying CD-ROM offers powerful searching and research tools. The commentary text, Sidebars, and visuals are all reproduced on a CD that is fully indexed and searchable. Pairing a text version with a digital resource is a distinctive feature of the *Smyth & Helwys Bible Commentary.*

Combining credible biblical scholarship, user-friendly study features, and sensitivity to the needs of a visually oriented generation of believers creates a unique and unprecedented type of commentary series. With insight from many of today's finest biblical scholars and a stunning visual format, it is our hope that the *Smyth & Helwys Bible Commentary* will be a welcome addition to the personal libraries of all students of Scripture.

The Editors

HOW TO USE
THIS COMMENTARY

The *Smyth & Helwys Bible Commentary* is written by accomplished biblical scholars with a wide array of readers in mind. Whether engaged in the study of Scripture in a church setting or in a college or seminary classroom, all students of the Bible will find a number of useful features throughout the commentary that are helpful for interpreting the Bible.

Basic Design of the Volumes

Each volume features an Introduction to a particular book of the Bible, providing a brief guide to information that is necessary for reading and interpreting the text: the historical setting, literary design, and theological significance. Each Introduction also includes a comprehensive outline of the particular book under study.

Each chapter of the commentary investigates the text according to logical divisions in a particular book of the Bible. Sometimes these divisions follow the traditional chapter segmentation, while at other times the textual units consist of sections of chapters or portions of more than one chapter. The divisions reflect the literary structure of a book and offer a guide for selecting passages that are useful in preaching and teaching.

An accompanying CD-ROM offers powerful searching and research tools. The commentary text, Sidebars, and visuals are all reproduced on a CD that is fully indexed and searchable. Pairing a text version with a digital resource also allows unprecedented flexibility and freedom for the reader. Carry the text version to locations you most enjoy doing research while knowing that the CD offers a portable alternative for travel from the office, church, classroom, and your home.

Commentary and Connections

As each chapter explores a textual unit, the discussion centers around two basic sections: *Commentary* and *Connections*. The analysis of a passage, including the details of its language, the history reflected in the text, and the literary forms found in the text, are the main focus of the *Commentary* section. The primary concern of the *Commentary* section is to explore the theological issues presented by the Scripture passage. *Connections* presents potential applications of the insights provided in the *Commentary* section. The *Connections* portion of each chapter considers what issues are relevant for teaching and suggests useful methods and resources. *Connections* also identifies themes suitable for sermon planning and suggests helpful approaches for preaching on the Scripture text.

Sidebars

The *Smyth & Helwys Bible Commentary* provides a unique hyperlink format that quickly guides the reader to additional insights. Since other more technical or supplementary information is vital for understanding a text and its implications, the volumes feature distinctive Sidebars, or special-interest boxes, that provide a wealth of information on such matters as:

• Historical information (such as chronological charts, lists of kings or rulers, maps, descriptions of monetary systems, descriptions of special groups, descriptions of archaeological sites or geographical settings).

• Graphic outlines of literary structure (including such items as poetry, chiasm, repetition, epistolary form).

• Definition or brief discussions of technical or theological terms and issues.

• Insightful quotations that are not integrated into the running text but are relevant to the passage under discussion.

• Notes on the history of interpretation (Augustine on the Good Samaritan, Luther on James, Stendahl on Romans, etc.).

• Line drawings, photographs, and other illustrations relevant for understanding the historical context or interpretive significance of the text.

• Presentation and discussion of works of fine art that have interpreted a Scripture passage.

Each Sidebar is printed in color and is referenced at the appropriate place in the *Commentary* or *Connections* section with a color-coded title that directs the reader to the relevant Sidebar. In addition, helpful icons appear in the Sidebars, which provide the reader with visual cues to the type of material that is explained in each Sidebar. Throughout the commentary, these four distinct hyperlinks provide useful links in an easily recognizable design.

ΑΩ

Alpha & Omega Language

This icon identifies the information as a language-based tool that offers further exploration of the Scripture selection. This could include syntactical information, word studies, popular or additional uses of the word(s) in question, additional contexts in which the term appears, and the history of the term's translation. All non-English terms are transliterated into the appropriate English characters.

Culture/Context

This icon introduces further comment on contextual or cultural details that shed light on the Scripture selection. Describing the place and time to which a Scripture passage refers is often vital to the task of biblical interpretation. Sidebar items introduced with this icon could include geographical, historical, political, social, topographical, or economic information. Here, the reader may find an excerpt of an ancient text or inscription that sheds light on the text. Or one may find a description of some element of ancient religion such as Baalism in Canaan or the Hero cult in the Mystery Religions of the Greco-Roman world.

Interpretation

Sidebars that appear under this icon serve a general interpretive function in terms of both historical and contemporary renderings. Under this heading, the reader might find a selection from classic or contemporary literature that illuminates the Scripture text or a significant quotation from a famous sermon that addresses the passage. Insights are drawn from various sources, including literature, worship, theater, church history, and sociology.

Additional Resources Study

Here, the reader finds a convenient list of useful resources for further investigation of the selected Scripture text, including books, journals, websites, special collections, organizations, and societies. Specialized discussions of works not often associated with biblical studies may also appear here.

Additional Features

Each volume also includes a basic Bibliography on the biblical book under study. Other bibliographies on selected issues are often included that point the reader to other helpful resources.

Notes at the end of each chapter provide full documentation of sources used and contain additional discussions of related matters.

Abbreviations used in each volume are explained in a list of abbreviations found after the Table of Contents.

Readers of the *Smyth & Helwys Bible Commentary* can regularly visit the Internet support site for news, information, updates, and enhancements to the series at **www.helwys.com/commentary**.

Several thorough indexes enable the reader to locate information quickly. These indexes include:

- An *Index of Sidebars* groups content from the special-interest boxes by category (maps, fine art, photographs, drawings, etc.).

- An *Index of Scriptures* lists citations to particular biblical texts.

- An *Index of Topics* lists alphabetically the major subjects, names, topics, and locations referenced or discussed in the volume.

- An *Index of Modern Authors* organizes contemporary authors whose works are cited in the volume.

INTRODUCTION

Author

The document we call the Gospel of Luke carries no author's name, and chances are that the author never intended to put his or her name on it. The author knew Theophilus (1:3), and presumably Theophilus knew the author and expected to receive this book; thus there was no need for biographical details. As for other readers who might not know "Luke," the author must have felt that a name would add nothing—no extra authority, no greater credibility—beyond what he or she claims anonymously in the preface (1:1-4).

Yet the name "Luke" comes to us from early Christian tradition. The earliest known copy of the Gospel of Luke, dating from AD 175–225, had the title "according to Luke" at the end of the text.[1] Around 185, Irenaeus wrote, "Luke also, the companion of Paul, recorded in a book the Gospel preached by him."[2] The collection of four Gospels that Irenaeus knows was probably already circulating by the middle of the second century (Justin Martyr, a Christian in Rome who died around 150, writes of "the memoirs of the apostles," as if there were more than one known to him). We presume that when somebody put Matthew, Mark, Luke, and John together and called the collection "the Gospels," somebody also assigned names to the four: "according to Matthew," etc. The great and ultimately irresolvable question is how that collector knew the names. Since the originals were all anonymous, were the traditions about the authors passed down orally, or did second-century Christians take their best guesses about who wrote them?

Whoever wrote the Gospel of Luke also wrote the Acts of the Apostles, and there are sections of Acts written in the first person: "We set sail from Troas," etc. These sections cover parts of Paul's ministry, and one would naturally think of trying to look in Paul's letters to see who, from the list of Paul's companions, would be the most likely author of our two volumes. The name "Luke" appears in three places:

• Colossians 4:14: "Luke, the beloved physician, and Demas greet you."

- Philemon 23–24: "Epaphras, my fellow prisoner in Jesus Christ, sends greetings to you, and so do Mark, Aristarchus, Demas, and Luke, my fellow workers."
- 2 Timothy 4:9-11: "Do your best to come to me soon, for Demas, in love with this present world, has deserted me and gone off to Thessalonica; Crescens has gone to Galatia; Titus to Dalmatia. Only Luke is with me."

Someone could have reasoned this way: "Luke" is a Greek rather than a Jewish name, fitting better the Gentile tone of the Gospel. Luke is identified as a physician, and whoever wrote Luke-Acts was educated. The 2 Timothy passage indicates a person who was loyal to Paul, and that fits with the way Paul is the hero of the last half of Acts. In fact, Irenaeus makes that final point the thrust of an argument against the heretics. He writes, "But that this Luke was inseparable from Paul, and his fellow-laborer in the gospel, he himself clearly evinces." Irenaeus then narrates a number of episodes from the "we" sections of Acts, arguing that Luke saw it all and wrote it all down. He then quotes 2 Timothy 4:10-11 and Colossians 4:4, concluding that Luke "always preached in company with Paul and is called by him 'the beloved,' and with him performed the work of an evangelist, and was entrusted to hand down to us a Gospel . . . ."[3] Irenaeus did this exegetical work to prove that Paul never taught any secret doctrines to anyone, and that Luke was always there to write down what Paul said. Irenaeus himself was transmitting what he was taught, not creating this chain of reasoning; but his close readings of the New Testament show how the name "Luke" could have been deduced from the letters of Paul.

On the other hand, our evidence does not prove that "Luke" was a deduction rather than a tradition. Maybe the second-century collector who named the third part of his Gospel collection "According to Luke" did so because the author's name had been part of early Christian oral tradition passed along from the first recipients of the Gospel of Luke, who knew the author personally. The arguments for and against this scenario—that Paul's friend Luke wrote the Gospel and Acts, and that the church remembered this—are mostly based on comparisons between Acts and Paul's letters, which we will not take up in this commentary. One's position on this question does not affect interpretations of the Gospel, since Paul never knew Jesus personally and could not have added any eyewitness testimony. As a matter of convenience, I will use the name "Luke" and the male pronoun for the author of the Gospel of

Luke and the Acts of the Apostles, not drawing any conclusions about the validity of the ancient tradition.

"Luke" read the Old Testament in Greek, rather than in Hebrew, and he knew it well. He imitates the style of the Septuagint (the Greek translation of the Old Testament), especially in his first two chapters, and cites or alludes to it in many places. In contrast to Matthew, however, Luke does not devote much space to the interpretation of the Old Testament, and does not assume that his audience keeps kosher or worships on Sabbath. I presume, then, that neither Luke nor the audience he kept in mind as he wrote was Jewish. Luke shows no greater knowledge of Palestinian geography than he could have read in Mark, so I presume that he lived outside Palestine. Luke knows the rules of speech-making and can shift from a more colloquial style to a more elevated one; this is a sign of having had a good education, so I presume that Luke was either wealthy or well-born or both. I will also presume that he lived in a city; his education and the publication of his Gospel would have been more easily obtained there than in some rural setting.

Although some, most notably William K. Hobart (*The Medical Language of St. Luke* [Dublin: Hodges, Figgis, 1882]), have argued that Luke's vocabulary was laced with specialized medical terms, this has been shown not to be the case. Luke's words for illnesses and cures were common ones, found "in the Septuagint, Josephus, Plutarch, and Lucian, all non-medical writings."[4] Maybe the author of this Gospel was a physician, but we could not prove it by his language.

Audience

The Gospel is addressed to Theophilus, whom I assume to have been a real person, and a Christian who wanted (or who was going to get, whether he wanted it or not!) further instruction in the life and teachings of Jesus. (This argument is elaborated in the commentary on 1:1-4.)

I presume that the author hoped or knew his book would be heard by more than just Theophilus. Luke may have expected that the congregation where Theophilus worshiped would hear the Gospel read aloud to them and would then share it with others. The New Testament indicates that congregations shared letters (Col 4:16, "when this letter has been read among you, have it read also in the church of the Laodiceans, and see that you read also the letter from Laodicea"). If Theophilus was a wealthy or influential person—a plausible guess, but only a guess—Luke may have expected or hoped that Theophilus would use his contacts and networks to encourage the Gospel's spread.[5]

Luke's Gospel is very much concerned with wealth and poverty, specifically with how the wealthy should give to the poor. Although he records that Jesus met people who were poor—the blind beggar in 18:35, for instance, was certainly poor—the text never identifies them by the term "poor." While Jesus speaks about the poor (e.g., 6:20), and while the fictive character Lazarus is called "a poor man" (16:20), Jesus is not pictured interacting with folks labeled "poor." On the other hand, Jesus does meet two men described as "rich": the "ruler" or "leader," who is described as "very rich" after he refuses to sell his possessions and give the money to the poor (18:23), and Zacchaeus, who promises to give away half his possessions and restore four-fold what he had taken by fraud. This combination of factors suggests that Luke's audience—that is, the people he had in mind as he wrote—included rich people.

Sources

Luke writes that "many" had written narratives before he started his work (1:1)—don't we wish he had named them! But for many years, most students of the New Testament have concluded, based on comparisons of Mark, Matthew, and Luke, that Luke used Mark and another source—now commonly called "Q"—to provide him with most of his material, and that Matthew's author did the same. "Q" (an abbreviation of the German word *Quelle*, "source"), according to the standard theory, was a collection of sayings and stories that existed in the 50s; Luke and Matthew, independently of each other, knit together sections of Mark, of Q, and of other materials known to them.

Luke and Matthew's Sources

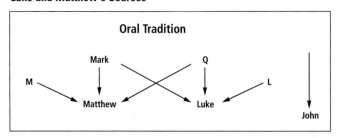

Here is the data that any theory about the relationship between Mark, Matthew, and Luke must explain:

• Mark, Matthew, and Luke (when we speak of them as a group, we call them the Synoptics, meaning that you can align their contents in three parallel columns and see that the three mostly tell one story) share the same basic outline, if you leave off the birth narratives on the front end (Mark has none) and the resurrection appearances on the back end (the oldest copies of Mark have none). Sometimes Luke disagrees with the order of Matthew and Mark. Sometimes Matthew disagrees with the order of Luke and Mark. But the order of the stories in Mark always (or almost always, depending on how small you slice up the stories) agrees either with Matthew or Luke. Mark's order is the middle term, somehow explaining why Luke and Matthew are as much alike as they are.

- The Synoptics share a great many words in common. Some passages are word-for-word the same in all three. Some of these word-for-word passages are in editorial or narrative material. Thus, one can't explain the Synoptics' close similarities by appealing to how early Christians memorized the sayings of Jesus. Our theory must involve one or two of them copying from one or two of the others.

- To complicate things, Matthew and Luke also share some word-for-word identical passages in places where Mark has nothing parallel. This material includes things like the story of Jesus' three temptations—narrative and editorial material as well as sayings of Jesus. Once again, the evidence demands that either Luke read Matthew, or Matthew read Luke, or they both read the same source independently of each other. This body of material is the so-called "Q" material, and it includes significant teachings by Jesus: the Lord's Prayer; the parable of the lost sheep; some of the Beatitudes; "love your enemies," "turn the other cheek," etc. It seems unlikely to most New Testament interpreters that Mark, had he read Matthew and Luke, would have omitted that material. Thus, most conclude that Mark came first and that Matthew and Luke read and edited Mark.

- Finally, when Mark is absent, Matthew and Luke tend to go their own way. They each have birth narratives, but they are very different, as are their stories of the resurrected Jesus. The "Q" material also falls mostly in different places relative to the outline of Mark; for instance, Matthew puts the Lord's Prayer early, as a part of his Sermon on the Mount. Luke has a parallel sermon early on, but saves the prayer until Jesus has begun his journey to Jerusalem. This sort of thing encourages most New Testament interpreters to think that Matthew and Luke independently used Mark and Q. It also is the main reason most New Testament interpreters do not think that Matthew read Luke or vice-versa: why would one change the other's order so often, and leave out so much good stuff?

To repeat, the most common theory has Matthew and Luke independently editing Mark and Q. My own opinion is that

Matthew and Luke used Mark, but I am much less certain about Q.[6] However, since this commentary is designed mostly to be used by pastors and other Bible teachers, it is not the place for the kind of detailed source analysis that would be necessary to argue for or against the standard theory. So I will content myself with the occasional "if Q really exists" and worry about more important issues. Generally speaking, even if we could know for certain that there was a Q, we cannot be certain about the exact words it contained, since we have to reconstruct it from Matthew and Luke. To do redaction criticism (tracking an author's emphases by noting how he changes his sources) on the Q passages in Luke, we'd need to know what Q read so that we could track Luke's changes. But we can't. Take for instance Luke 3:7, "John said to the crowds," and Matthew 3:7, "When he saw many Pharisees and Sadducees, [John] said to them." Luke has a demonstrable interest in "crowds" as an audience for the gospel, while it can also be shown that Matthew increases the number of places where somebody, usually Jesus, blasts the Pharisees. Which evangelist changed Q to suit his own setting? We can't be certain. So I mostly steer clear of conclusions drawn from Luke's putative editing of Q.

Ministers and others who teach the Bible in a church context will sometimes encounter the possibility or presumption that Mary the mother of Jesus was Luke's principle source for the material in Luke 1–2. Luke never claims this, and never gives any hints of what his special sources might have been.

Date

The short answer is "no later than the middle of the second century." The standard date assigned in textbooks and commentaries is between 70 and 150. Luke cannot have been written earlier than AD 70 because it used Mark, which is usually dated 65–70. It cannot have been written much later than 150, since Irenaeus, quoted earlier, knew it as a part of a four-fold Gospel collection. Most commentators tend to narrow the range to 85–100, putting it well after the destruction of Jerusalem and the temple and well after Nero's brief persecution of Christians in Rome, but before the persecutions of Christians under Trajan. Under this standard scnario, Luke writes during a brief period of relative calm for the church, trying to push the comfortably wealthy into a more rigorously ascetic faith.

Some recent commentators have argued for an early second-century date, when the church was trying to come to grips with its place in the empire.[7] During this period, when Christians were identified as such and when the magistrate was interested enough to arrest them, they could be executed if they would not recant (see [Pliny's Letter to Trajan]). By the mid-second century, Justin Martyr and the anonymous author of the *Epistle to Diognetus* wrote apologies, treatises arguing that Christians posed no danger to theempire and should not be punished unless they were actual criminals. In those same years, some wrote martyrologies urging Christians to hold fast to their faith even if death might be the result.

By AD 150 or so, Christianity was a fairly diverse movement. Some sectors allowed women to function as prophets, deacons, and apostles, while other sectors prohibited this, ruling that women could not teach or lead men. Christians debated whether Jesus was truly or only seemingly human; more precisely, those who thought Christ was truly human cursed those who did not and tried to exclude them from congregations. All of these strands—martyrdom, imperial values, roles of women, diverse christologies—can be seen in Luke-Acts, and so the early second-century date is as plausible as the late first-century date. In the commentary sections within each chapter, I will attempt to keep both possible contexts as options open to the interpreter.

Structure of the Gospel

If one looks at large-scale units, then Luke seems to have taken Mark's outline and expanded it, in some places by inserting blocks of non-Markan material, and in others by weaving together Markan and non-Markan verses.

Mark		Luke	
1:1	Superscription	1:1-4	Prologue
		1:5–2:52	Birth Narratives
1:2-11	John's Preaching, Baptism	3:1-22	John's Preaching, Baptism
		3:23-38	Genealogy
1:12-13	Temptation	4:1-13	Temptation
1:14–9:50	Ministry in Galilee	4:14–9:50	Ministry in Galilee
10:1-52	Journey	9:51–19:28	Journey
11:1–13:37	Entry; Teaching in Jerusalem	19:29–21:38	Entry, Teaching in Jerusalem
14:1–15:47	Passion Narrative	22:1–23:56	Passion Narrative
16:1-8	Empty Tomb	24:1-11	Empty Tomb
		24:12-52	Resurrection Narratives

This outline oversimplifies things, but it probably gives an accurate picture of Luke's overall writing plan. One way to think of Luke is as a revised and expanded Mark. He had access to material—birth stories, resurrection accounts, parables, sayings—that Mark either did not know or chose not to include. Luke, believing that this extra material was important for understanding what Jesus was about, produced what he no doubt felt was a "new and improved" Mark.

A closer look at the way Luke deals with Mark, however, shows that things are more complex than the outline above indicates. Look, for instance, at "John's Preaching, Baptism."

Mark		**Luke**	
1:2-3	Citations from Isaiah and Malachi	3:4-5	Citation from Isaiah
1:4	"Baptism of repentance"	3:3	"Baptism of repentance"
1:5	Popular response	3:10-15	More detailed popular response
1:6	John's dress	No parallel	
1:7-8	"More powerful/ baptize with water"	3:16	"More powerful/ baptize with water"
1:9-11	Baptism of Jesus	3:21-22	Baptism of Jesus

Note that Luke reverses the order of Mark's first two items; substitutes a more detailed account of the public response to John; omits the hairy coat, locusts, and wild honey; and, in 3:4-9 and 17-20, inserts material not found in Mark. This section exhibits more complicated editing than most, but it demonstrates that Luke felt free to add, to delete, to change order, and to insert new material—in short, to make whatever changes he felt would improve his source. For example, Luke has no parallel to Mark 6:45–8:26 (called the "Great Omission") or to Mark 9:41–10:12 (the "Little Omission"), and most of Luke 9:51–18:14 has no parallel in Mark. Scholars wonder whether Luke really left out that much of Mark, or whether perhaps his copy of Mark was shorter than ours.

A brief outline of Luke looks something like this:

1:1–2:52	Prologue and Birth Narratives
3:1–4:13	Baptism and Temptation
4:14–9:50	Ministry in Galilee
9:51–19:28	Journey to Jerusalem
19:29–21:38	Teaching in Jerusalem
22:1–23:56	Passion Narrative
24:1-53	Resurrection Narratives

Within each section, and sometimes across sections, Luke has ways of tying one episode to another. In the birth narratives, he lines up two sets of events, one for John and one for Jesus, inviting the reader to compare and contrast what God was doing in each man. At the beginning of the "Ministry in Galilee" section, Jesus announces themes for his ministry in his opening sermon. Luke then narrates examples of those activities, and repeats the list in 7:22, this time challenging the readers to recognize what they "have seen and heard." In 8:1-3 Jesus is on mission, supported by some women, and the twelve are with him; in 9:1-6, the Twelve go on mission; in 10:1-20, a larger group of seventy (or seventy-two) disciples go on mission. In 5:29-32, Jesus attends the first of seven banquets. Luke uses these events to illustrate the great banquet that symbolizes the kingdom of God; there are two meals in the "Ministry in Galilee" section, three in the "Journey" section, one in the Passion Narrative, and one in Luke's final chapter, so it is a theme that helps to unify the whole work.

The longest section by far is the Journey to Jerusalem. While some scholars find a pattern in the arrangement of the stories, others do not; as explained in the commentary on 9:51-62, Luke gives regular reminders that Jesus is on a journey, but they do not seem to me to fall into predictable patterns. Instead, the journey itself is how Luke organized the teaching material he found in his other source(s): Jesus was on a mission for God, heading resolutely toward Jerusalem and his destiny. But God's mission required him to preach the good news, heal, exorcise, and share food with people in every village and town along the way. For most of the Journey section, you could not plot Jesus' progress on a map, and you never get any sense of the passage of time. The point is that the gospel is moving, always moving, and nobody—not Herod Antipas, nor the Romans, nor the Pharisees—will turn Jesus around.

In a surprising move, Luke also erases most of the chronological notes in Mark that give us the tradition of Holy Week. Luke's Jesus enters the temple and then "day by day" teaches there for an indeterminate period. Luke keeps most of Mark's sequence of stories intact, so it isn't the outline he wants to disrupt. Instead, Luke's structure emphasizes the difference between the period of Jesus' teaching, when the people gathered to hear him, shielding him from the anger of the temple authorities, and the time after Satan entered Judas, when the people agreed with the temple authorities in demanding Jesus' crucifixion.

Luke's final chapter begins, like Mark's, with women finding the empty tomb. But then things change: the women, prompted by heavenly messengers to remember Jesus' teachings, believe he is alive. Two disciples walk with the risen Jesus but fail to recognize him until he breaks bread with them. Finally, he appears to the whole group, apostles and disciples, opening their minds to understand how the Scriptures apply to him and sending them on mission one more time.

Themes

The Kingdom of God. The Old Testament, especially the Psalms, frequently refers to God as King of all creation, reigning over everything and everyone. But the phrase "kingdom of God," as a marker for a future age when God's will would prevail everywhere, does not appear in the Old Testament (although 1 Chr 28:5 and 2 Chr 13:8 use "kingdom of YHWH"). *Psalms of Solomon* 17:3 (usually dated to the first century BC) is the earliest pre-Christian use of the phrase: "But we hope in God our savior, for the strength of our God is forever with mercy, and the Kingdom of our God is forever over the nations in judgment." The author of *Psalms of Solomon* 17 hopes for God to raise up the Messiah, who will "destroy the unlawful nations with the word of his mouth" and gather the tribes of Israel together (*Pss. Sol.* 17:21-26). The resulting kingdom will be absolutely righteous: "There will be no unrighteousness among them in his days, for all shall be holy, and their king shall be the Lord Messiah" (*Pss. Sol.* 17:32).

Luke's Jesus says that his purpose is to proclaim the good news of the kingdom of God (4:43); he also gives this task to the twelve apostles (9:2) and to the seventy(-two) (10:9). His primary symbol for the kingdom is a banquet, where "people will come from east and west, from north and south, and will eat in the kingdom of God" (13:29); where beggars like Lazarus will recline on the couch with patriarchs like Abraham (16:23); where the banquet hall will be filled with "the poor, the crippled, the blind, and the lame" (14:21), but where some who expected to be there will be excluded. The feast can be imagined as a wedding party (5:34), or as a meal served by the new bridegroom to his household slaves (12:35-37), but unlike Matthew, Luke never uses the image of a king throwing a party.

Luke seems to waste no chance to capitalize on this banqueting image. Jesus is constantly eating with someone, and conspicuously eats with Pharisees and tax collectors (not at the same time!), illustrating the wideness of God's mercy. Jesus' followers are sent out with nothing, not even a bag, so that the success of the mission to spread the gospel depends on the hospitality of the people they encounter. Eat with anyone, eat whatever they offer: do this in imitation of life in the kingdom of God.

God's kingdom also means relief from disease. Luke's Jesus heals and exorcises, releasing those "bound by Satan" (13:16), as do the apostles (9:1, 6) and disciples (10:9, 17). Satan, who claimed authority over all the kingdoms of the world (4:6), was being pushed out, overmastered by the emissaries of God's kingdom (10:18; 12:20-22).

This raises the question of timing: did Luke think that the kingdom was present in Jesus' ministry or that it was still to come? Yes—Luke's eschatology is paradoxical, insisting that Jesus' exorcisms are proof that the kingdom had taken (or retaken) ground from Satan (12:20) and that the kingdom could be granted by Jesus to his followers (22:29). The famous "the kingdom of God is among (or within) you" (17:21) may express the same idea: in the healing, exorcising, preaching, and sharing of food that characterize the ministry of Jesus and his followers, the kingdom has drawn near (see my commentary on that passage for alternate interpretations). On the other side of the ledger, his disciples are to pray, "Let your kingdom come" (11:2); Jesus vows that he will not again eat Passover or drink wine until he can do it in the kingdom (22:15-18); believers can endure much in this life because they can look forward to rewards in the kingdom (14:14; 18:29-30). Despite being a generation or two beyond Jesus' promise to return soon, Luke-Acts still anticipates the Parousia as the moment when God's kingdom will be fully realized.

Luke's Jesus anticipates the kingdom and preaches its nearness but never calls himself "king," nor does he respond positively when others do. For Luke, "king" is not a positive rubric. Kings rule over others and like to be called benefactor, but among Jesus' followers, things should be different (22:25-26). Kings would like to see what the disciples have seen, but they cannot (10:24). Kings will be part of the group that persecutes Jesus' followers in the future (21:12). The actual kings who have some active role in Luke-Acts are all sorry specimens. Herod Antipas imprisons and beheads John and mocks Jesus. Herod Agrippa I executes James the son of Zebedee and imprisons Peter, and is then struck down by God—eaten, like Jonah's gourd vine, by worms—when he accepts the crowd's acclamation that he sounds like a god. Herod Agrippa II wants to hear Paul's case but cannot make up his mind about it; he admits that in any case he has no authority to change his situation. The king in the parable of the pounds (19:11-27) is Jesus' opposite number: he draws his authority from Rome and exercises it ruthlessly in pursuit of wealth and revenge.

Luke has constructed his narrative to disrupt the widespread expectation among early Christians that Jesus would return to rule as king over a reconstituted Israel (Luke 19:11; Acts 1:6). Gabriel predicts that Jesus will sit on David's throne, ruling over the house of Jacob forever (1:32-33), and unwary readers may expect something like the scenario in *Psalms of Solomon* 17. But then Luke piles up examples of real-life kings—why would we want more of this?—and repeated sayings of Jesus that make "servant" the proper goal for Christian leaders. Jesus is falsely accused of claiming to be king, and then even though Pilate knows the charge is false, he is forced to crucify Jesus. What use is a kingdom or an empire that cannot do right even when it has the lawful authority to enforce justice? Luke presents the "King of the Jews" theme as a cruel joke, something that led only to Jesus' murder, in order to get readers to see that God's kingdom is something entirely different. God raises Jesus from the dead, enthroning him at God's right hand, fulfilling Gabriel's prediction, and releasing the church from needing to emulate any form of earthly empire.

Empire? Seems like we've heard a lot about that lately, debates about how America, being the world's only superpower, should exercise its *imperium*. Paying attention to Luke will help us question Christian involvement in empire, or Christian assumption of imperial values.

Wealth and Poverty. In order to enter the kingdom of God, people must divest themselves of their possessions (12:32-33; 18:24-25), receiving the kingdom as God's gift. Luke's Jesus hammers at this throughout the Gospel:

• Blessed are you who are poor/Woe to you who are rich (6:20, 24)
• The seeds choked by thorns are those who hear the word, but "are choked by the cares and riches and pleasures of life" (8:14)
• Take nothing for your journey (9:3)
• Carry no purse, no bag, no sandals (10:4)
• But give the inner things for alms (11:41)
• Parable of the Rich Fool (12:13-21)
• Sell your possessions, and give alms (12:33)
• When you give a banquet, invite the poor (14:13)
• None of you can be my disciple if you do not give up all your possessions (14:33)
• You cannot serve God and mammon (16:13)

• Parable of the rich man and Lazarus (16:19-31)
• How hard it is for the wealthy to enter the kingdom of God! (18:24-25)
• Zacchaeus repents, giving away most or all of his wealth (19:1-10)

Because of its uncompromising stance against wealth and its insistence that disciples divest themselves of their stuff, Luke is both ideally suited to speak to modern American Christians and practically guaranteed to be ignored by the same folks. Luke's message is so counter-cultural that interpreters must face the urge to make it easier for church members to swallow. "Luke doesn't mean that we have to give away our possessions; we just have to be willing to do it if God ever asked us," we might say, although how God could make things clearer than Luke does is beyond me. "Luke means spiritual poverty; he means that we shouldn't put money or things ahead of God." That's true, but he also clearly means that we are supposed to feed the hungry, which if we took seriously would mean sacrificing much of what separates us from the poor. Zacchaeus didn't just promise to put God first in his life; he gave half his money to the poor and then gave back four times what he had overcharged.

Readers will probably grow tired of this commentary's regular harangues against American Christianity's acceptance of materialism. It's just that if we don't listen to Luke, we're unlikely to hear a similarly steely-eyed critique anywhere else. Our whole culture is designed to reinforce the drive to accumulate more stuff, and too often we're seduced into praying, "Thank you, Lord, for blessing me with all this stuff" when we should be praying, "Lord, be merciful to me, the sinner, for buying more stuff when I should have been saving somebody's life."

A Prophet's Work. Luke's favorite category for the good guys in his two volumes is "prophet." Elizabeth, Mary, Zechariah, Simeon, and Anna preview the type: a person filled by the Holy Spirit who speaks the word under divine inspiration. With John the Baptist, Luke elaborates the type:

• He preaches repentance of sins.
• He warns of the coming judgment on the wicked.
• He urges people to share their possessions.
• He promises the gift of the Holy Spirit.
• He opposes the wicked actions of a king.

• He suffers the prophet's fate, being killed by the king he criticized.

Luke characterizes Jesus as a prophet: the Spirit of the Lord has anointed him for his work (4:18-21), and like John, he preaches the coming of God's kingdom, judgment for the wealthy and the wicked, and good news for the poor. When he does miracles that resemble the deeds of Elijah and Elisha, the crowd responds, "A great prophet has risen among us!" (7:1-17). Simon the Pharisee doubts that Jesus is truly a prophet (7:39), but this is because he cannot see what Jesus sees, a woman who has shown great love and whose sins are forgiven (7:44-50). Jesus predicts that he will die as all prophets do, that Jerusalem will not see him until they say, "Blessed is the one who comes in the name of the Lord," and that Jerusalem will be destroyed (13:32-35); the first two predictions are fulfilled in the narrative, and the third had come true before Luke composed his Gospel.

Thus, "prophet" gives Luke a hook by which to explain how various parts of Jesus' life, especially his death, could have fit into God's plan. It also gives him a way to present Jesus as a model for church leaders to imitate. In Acts, Peter, members of the Seven, and Paul speak prophetically, advocate for the poor, do prophetic-type miracles, and are hauled up before governors and kings. While "Messiah" and "Son of God" are also true characterizations of Luke's Jesus, Luke emphasizes "prophet," probably because it helps him connect Jesus' story to the story of the early church.

Repentance and Forgiveness. These are some of Luke's favorite terms, appearing over and over in both volumes. They are connected so often that one must assume that when Luke speaks of forgiveness he presumes repentance, and vice-versa:

Luke 3:3	Baptism of repentance for the forgiveness of sins
3:8	Bear fruits worthy of repentance
5:8	Go away from me—I'm a sinner man, O Lord
5:32	I have not come to call the righteous, but sinners to repentance
6:21b	Blessed are you who weep now, for you will laugh
7:29	The people, even tax collectors, acknowledge God's justice, since they were baptized with John's baptism [of repentance]
10:13-16	Chorazin and Bethsaida are cursed because they did not repent when they saw deeds of power

11:4	Forgive us our sins, as we ourselves forgive our debtors
11:32	The people of Nineveh condemn this generation because they repented
13:3, 5	Unless you repent, you'll all likewise perish
13:6-9	Give the fig tree one more year, more manure, etc.; if it bears fruit, fine; if not, cut it down
15:7,10	More joy in heaven (with God) over one sinner who repents
15:11ff.	Prodigal son (if "coming to his senses" is the equivalent of repentance)
16:30	"if someone goes to them from the dead, they will repent"
17:3-4	If someone repents seven times a day, you must forgive
18:13	Tax collector: "Lord, be merciful to me, the sinner."
23:39-43	Penitent thief
24:47	Repentance and forgiveness of sins is to be proclaimed in Jesus' name to all nations
Acts 2:38	Repent, and be baptized every one of you in the name of Jesus Christ so that your sins may be forgiven; and you will receive the gift of the Holy Spirit.
3:19	Repent therefore, and turn to God so that your sins may be wiped out
5:31	God exalted him at his right hand as Leader and Savior that he might give repentance to Israel and forgiveness of sins.
8:22	Repent therefore of this wickedness of yours
11:18	God has given even to the Gentiles the repentance that leads to life.
13:24	before his coming John had already proclaimed a baptism of repentance to all the people of Israel.
17:30	While God has overlooked the times of human ignorance, now he commands all people everywhere to repent
19:4	John baptized with the baptism of repentance, telling the people to believe in the one who was to come after him, that is, in Jesus.
26:20	. . . that the Gentiles should repent and turn to God and do deeds consistent with repentance.

"Repentance and forgiveness of sins" can therefore function as a sort of shorthand for what Luke means when he writes that characters preach the good news or the gospel (24:47).

Jesus not only speaks about God's forgiveness of the penitent's sins, but requires his disciples to forgive each other (11:4), even if a fellow disciple wrongs us the same way seven times daily (17:4). More than that, we are to love our enemies, not only forgiving them but finding ways to do them good (6:27-38). The unforgiving elder brother who refused to join his brother's welcome-home party; the Pharisee who held the penitent tax collector in contempt; the rich ruler whose wealth kept him from repenting and entering the kingdom; the rich fool (12:16-21); Dives (16:19-31); the unfruitful fig tree (13:6-9)—all these are negative examples demonstrating the consequences of non-repentance (13:3, 5). Levi (5:27-28), Zacchaeus (19:1-10), and the disciples (18:28-30) are all examples of repenting from one's possessions; the prodigal son, the penitent tax collector, and the penitent thief all realize their sins and repent. Repentance, in fact, is Luke's model for how one begins discipleship (5:8).

Apostles, Disciples, Crowds, and Enemies. During the Journey section, these four groups are always around Jesus. Luke seems to expect us to remember this; sometimes he will have Jesus speak to one group and then to another. For instance, note the rapid change of audience in chapter 12. There's a large crowd stepping over each other, but Jesus speaks to the disciples about the Pharisees (12:1). He is interrupted by a member of the crowd (12:13) and answers him (12:14), but then speaks to "them" (12:15-21)—probably the crowds, since he next turns back to the disciples (12:22). In 13:22-30 he answers a question from "someone" and then immediately responds to a warning from the Pharisees (13:31-35). Luke seems to think of these four groups sort of milling around Jesus as he travels, since he rarely explains where they came from.

The apostles are the twelve men named in 6:12-16, sent out on mission in 9:1-6, at table with Jesus for the Last Supper in 22:14, and appearing as witnesses to the resurrection in the first six chapters of Acts. The disciples are a larger group—70 (or 72) in chapter 10 and 120 in Acts 1—that includes women who began following him in Galilee and who supported him with their own resources (8:1-3). Luke writes that "all who knew him, including the women who had followed him from Galilee," saw the crucifixion (23:49). These women were the first to believe the resurrection, while two disciples who were not part of the Twelve were the first to see Jesus alive, or at least their story is narrated before the report that Jesus had appeared also to Peter. Jesus' final appearance in the Gospel is to the apostles and disciples together (24:33-53). Luke's disciples are given the same authority and commissions as the Twelve (cf. 9:1-6 to 10:1-20, and note that 24:44-49 is given to the larger group), and are no less witnesses to the resurrection.

The Pharisees, sometimes paired with scribes, fill the role of Jesus' enemies up to Jesus' entry into Jerusalem. They object to Jesus' healings on Sabbath; they criticize him for eating with tax collectors and sinners; they treat him inhospitably (7:44-46) and mock his teachings on possessions (16:14). Yet they invite him to dinner three times, and they deliver what they seem to regard as a legitimate warning about Herod Antipas's plans to murder him. Jesus rips into them twice (11:39-52; 20:45-47), but he keeps accepting their dinner invitations. "Love your enemies," says Jesus, and when it turns out that some Pharisees are members of the church (Acts 15:5), we can see how that pays off.

After Jesus gets to Jerusalem, his enemies are the chief priests, scribes, and elders: the temple leadership, the heads of non-priestly families, and their secretaries and advisers. They immediately decide that Jesus must be put to death but are afraid to seize him openly because he is a favorite with the crowds. Once Satan takes over Judas, however, they are able to arrest Jesus in the dark, away from the city. In the first five chapters of Acts, the apostles accuse these men of murdering the Son of God by the hands of the Gentiles, and offer them the chance to repent. While Luke says that many priests became obedient to the faith (Acts 6:7), he does not claim that any of those who arrested Jesus ever repented. Instead, they become the chief opponents of the apostles in Acts 1–6; they arrest and stone Stephen (Acts 7:1–8:1) and begin a persecution of the church in Jerusalem (8:2-3); and they urge the death of Paul on baseless charges (Acts 21–24).

Luke's crowds are a variable element in the story. They try to interfere with Jesus' mandate to preach to every village (4:42-44), but they correctly identify him as God's prophet (7:16). They ask questions indicating that they are not willing to give up everything to follow him (12:13) and are rebuked as hypocrites (12:56), but they are enthralled by Jesus' teachings (19:48) and thus prevent Jesus' immediate arrest once he enters Jerusalem. They come daily to listen to him teach in the temple (21:38), but then join the temple leaders to clamor for Jesus to be crucified. Peter blames them, too, for murdering Jesus (Acts 2:22-23; 4:27); he tells them to repent, and thousands do and are baptized. Luke's account prepares for this mass conversion by depicting the crowds watching Jesus die, but not joining in the mocking (23:35-37), and then leaving the killing grounds "beating their breasts" in mourning or repentance or both (23:48).

Luke and Women. The current state of opinion about Luke's attitude toward women in the Christian movement is divided. This may come as a surprise to those who have read books celebrating Luke as the Gospel that liberated women, but there are those who consider Luke a dangerous work for women. In the opinion of these scholars, Luke is all the more damaging because it does not simply treat women as invisible, but spotlights them in order to domesticate them.[8]

When one compares Luke to Matthew or Mark, there is no question that "the author of Luke-Acts appears to have deliberately multiplied representations of women within the narrative."[9] There are women paired with men at numerous points:

- Annunciations to Zechariah and to Mary
- Mary's Magnificat, Zechariah's Benedictus
- Simeon and Anna, two prophets in the temple
- Jesus heals the centurion's slave and the widow's son
- Healings of the bent-over woman (13:10-17) and the man with dropsy (14:1-6)
- Twin parables: male shepherd loses sheep, female loses coin; man plants mustard seed, woman puts leaven in dough; unjust judge and widow, Pharisee and tax collector (first female, then male as righteous characters)
- Twelve male apostles, seven named female disciples (see commentary at 8:1-3)

There are also women who stand alone, whose stories are not (or at least not obviously) paired with any man's story: Elizabeth's prophecy, the woman who anoints Jesus' feet, the hospitality of Mary and Martha. The point is that Luke has taken pains to make women visible in his Gospel—thus far, everyone agrees. But some argue that if we set Mary and Elizabeth aside—they act before Jesus appears on the scene, and so might be taken to belong to the period of the law and the prophets[10]—then women generally do not have important things to say, and are often put into more traditional roles compared to Mark. For instance, the woman who anoints Jesus' feet (7:36-50) is probably a variant of the story of the woman who anoints Jesus' head in Mark 14:3-9. Mark's woman, alone in that Gospel, believes Jesus when he says he will die and does something to try to prepare him for his death. She anoints Jesus' head—as a prophet might—and is singled out for the monetary sacrifice she makes. Luke's woman anoints Jesus' feet, weeps over them, and wipes them with her hair. These are not prophetic acts, but quasi-erotic acts, and the question becomes why Jesus, as a prophet, allows her to do this.

In another example, Luke takes Mark's note about women who provided for Jesus (Mark 15:40-41) and moves it from the Passion Narrative to an early point in Jesus' ministry (Luke 8:1-3). Luke also says that Jesus had cured these women of demon possession and diseases. Luke, so the argument goes, is moving the women from Mark's category of disciple into the more respectable category of patron, and providing a reason—gratitude for healing—for why they might have provided for Jesus.[11]

In the commentary on relevant sections, I will argue that it does not appear plausible to me that Luke is, in these sections, trying to relegate women to safe, respectable roles. The women in Luke 8:1-3 are traipsing around Galilee with Jesus and the Twelve—not a traditional role for wealthy Roman matrons. Martha receives Jesus into her house—Luke bats not an eyelash over the potential scandal. The woman who anoints Jesus' feet is taking charge, doing what hospitality demands, making up for Simon the inhospitable Pharisee who invited Jesus but then snubbed him. I will argue that Luke means for us to imagine women constantly with Jesus from 8:2 on, always among the disciples even when they are not specifically mentioned. [Resources on Luke]

Nevertheless, we must pay attention to the suspicious readings of Luke, listening carefully to those who find Luke's treatment of women dangerous or damaging. Those of us who believe that patriarchy is a systemic and systematic evil cannot ignore such readings, because they stem, unfortunately, from real experiences. For some believers, it is important to admit that stories like Martha and Mary are dangerous because they can be used to exclude women from pastoral ministries. But many others cannot abandon Luke and the women of the Third Gospel; for those it is necessary to find a way to read these stories that supports the desire to be open and affirming of anyone who feels the call to ministry. Call it an ethics, or a pragmatics, of interpretation: it is part of the goal of this commentary's interpretation of Luke to offer readings that support the full participation of women in ministry.

Resources on Luke

Bovon, François. *Luke 1: A Commentary on the Gospel of Luke 1:1–9:50*. Hermeneia. Edited by Helmut Koester. Minneapolis: Fortress, 2002. [Technical, but readable for those who know Greek. Bovon proposes many new ways to interpret familiar passages]

Craddock, Fred B. *Luke*. Interpretation. Louisville: Westminster/John Knox, 1990. [Insights from redaction-critical approaches, homiletic suggestions]

Culpepper, R. Alan. *The Gospel of Luke*. Volume 9 of *The New Interpreter's Bible*. Nashville: Abingdon, 1995. [Especially good insights from literary analysis]

Danker, Frederick W. *Jesus and the New Age: A Commentary on St. Luke's Gospel*. Revised edition. Philadelphia: Fortress, 1988. [Valuable citations of Greek and Roman authors from antiquity]

Fitzmyer, Joseph A. *The Gospel According to Luke*. Volumes 28 and 28A of Anchor Bible. Garden City NY: Doubleday, 1981. [Technical; comments on syntax, grammar, and etymology, as well as insights from source and redaction criticism]

Green, Joel B. *The Gospel of Luke*. New International Commentary on the New Testament. Grand Rapids: Eerdmans, 1997. [Very thorough close reading, with use of discourse theory and theories of intertextuality]

Hornik, Heidi J., and Mikeal C. Parsons. *Illuminating Luke: The Infancy Narrative in Italian Renaissance Painting*. Harrisburg PA: Trinity, 2003. [Parsons is an expert on Luke; Hornik is an expert on Italian Renaissance art; their books demonstrate how art interprets text and how text affects art]

———. *Illuminating Luke: The Public Ministry of Christ in Italian Renaissance and Baroque Painting*. New York: Trinity, 2005.

Johnson, Luke Timothy. *The Gospel of Luke*. Volume 3 of SP. Collegeville MN: Liturgical Press, 1991. [Valuable insights from literary analysis]

Just, Jr., Arthur A., editor. *Luke*. Ancient Christian Commentary on Scripture: New Testament, volume 3. Downer's Grove IL: Intervarsity Press, 2003. [A compendium of quotations from ancient Christians on Luke, excerpted and ordered by the chapters and verses on which they comment]

Parsons, Mikeal C. *Luke: Storyteller, Interpreter, Evangelist*. Peabody MA: Hendrickson, 2007. [A brief introduction to the Gospel of Luke and its author]

Schaberg, Jane. "Luke." In *The Women's Bible Commentary*, edited by Carol Newsome and Sharon H. Ringe. Louisville: Westminster/John Knox, 1992. [A valuable and "suspicious" feminist reading of Luke]

Talbert, Charles H. *Reading Luke: A Literary and Theological Commentary on the Third Gospel*. Revised edition. Macon GA: Smyth and Helwys, 2002. [A thorough analysis of the structure of Luke, with particular attention to chiasm and parallelism]

Tannehill, Robert C. *Luke*. Abingdon New Testament Commentaries. Nashville: Abingdon, 1996. [Both this volume and *The Narrative Unity of Luke-Acts* are extremely helpful guides to Luke's literary methods and themes]

———. *The Narrative Unity of Luke-Acts: A Literary Intepretation*. Volume 1 of *The Gospel According to Luke*. Philadelphia: Fortress, 1986.

NOTES

[1] This is Bodmer Papyrus P[75], which contains "parts of Luke 3–24 and all of John 1–15" (Jack Finegan, *Encountering New Testament Manuscripts* [Grand Rapids: Eerdmans, 1974], 104). All assume that the "Luke" meant was the Luke from Paul's letters. Although this is not a necessary conclusion, it is probably correct, since there is no other famous "Luke" from early Christianity. See Mikeal C. Parsons, *Luke: Storyteller, Interpreter, Evangelist* (Peabody MA: Hendrickson, 2007), 4; Alan R. Culpepper, *The Gospel of Luke* (NIB, vol. 9; Nashville: Abingdon, 1995), 4.

[2] Irenaeus, *Adv. Haer.* III.1.1 (*ANF* 1:414).

[3] Irenaeus, *Adv. Haer* III.14.1 (*ANF* 1:438).

[4] Parsons, *Luke*, 6. Parsons is summarizing the work of H. J. Cadbury's monumental *The Style and Literary Method of Luke* (Cambridge: Harvard University Press, 1920).

[5] Loveday Alexander, *The Preface to Luke's Gospel: Literary Convention and Social Context In Luke 1.1-4 and Acts 1.1* (Cambridge: Cambridge University Press, 1993), 194–200.

[6] My main objections to the standard theory are the places where, according to the theory, Matthew and Luke make the same corrections of Mark. In my opinion, this happens too often for the standard theory to be true. The truly curious (or obsessive) should read my article, "How Minor? Assessing the Significance of the Minor Agreements as an Argument against the Two-Source Hypothesis," in *Questioning Q*, ed. Mark Goodacre and Nicholas Perrin (London: SPCK, 2004).

[7] Joseph B. Tyson, *Marcion and Luke-Acts: A Defining Struggle* (Columbia: University of South Carolina, 2006), argues that Luke and Acts were both composed in the first quarter of the second century. He thinks that in AD 70–90, an early version of Luke was constructed depending on Mark, containing approximately the material in Luke 3–23. Marcion edited this into what more orthodox Christians called a "mutilated version of Luke" around 115–120. The final, anti-Marcionite version of Luke is what we know as the Gospel of Luke. See especially Tyson, pp. 79–120. Tyson's arguments are intriguing, and I will take up some of them in my treatment of the passion and resurrection accounts.

[8] For example, Mary Rose D'Angelo, "(Re)Presentations of Women in the Gospel of Matthew and Luke-Acts," in Ross Shepard Kraemer and Mary Rose D'Angelo, eds., *Women and Christian Origins* (New York: Oxford University Press, 1999); Kathleen E. Corley, *Private Women, Public Meals: Social Conflict in the Synoptic Tradition* (Peabody MA: Hendrickson, 1993); Jane Schaberg, "Luke," *The Woman's Bible Commentary*, ed. Carol A. Newsome and Sharon H. Ringe (Louisville KY: Westminster/John Knox, 1992); Turid Karlsen Seim, *The Double Message: Patterns of Gender in Luke-Acts* (Nashville: Abingdon, 1994).

[9] D'Angelo, "(Re)Presentations," 181.

[10] Ibid., 186.

[11] Corley, *Private Women*, 145.

NATIVITY STORIES, PART 1

Luke 1

COMMENTARY

Preface, Luke 1:1-4

The first four verses of Luke are one long sentence in Greek, lauded by some scholars as the best in the New Testament: "a model of precisely crafted prose" or "a perfectly constructed Greek period."[1] Others are not so impressed: "In a sense, Luke writes with exaggerated artistry; the long sentence in 1:1-4 illustrates effort as much as ability."[2] However we judge its sublimity [(Pseudo)-Longinus's Preface to *On the Sublime*], the sentence gives us more information about the writer, his sources, his audience, and his purpose than do the introductory sentences of Matthew or Mark. At the end of it, however, the reader is still left with more questions than answers.

> **(Pseudo)-Longinus's Preface to *On the Sublime***
>
> As I am writing for you, Terentianus, who are a man of some erudition, I almost feel I can dispense with a long preamble showing that sublimity consists in a certain excellence. . . . For the effect of elevated language is, not to persuade the hearers, but to entrance them; and at all times, and in every way, what transports us with wonder is more telling than what merely persuades or gratifies us.
>
> Longinus, *Subl.*, 1.3-4, *Classical Literary Criticism*, trans. T. S. Dorsch (New York: Penguin, 1965).

Greek authors of the period sometimes, but not always, provided the reader with a preface. Because narratives were still produced as scrolls, the preface helpfully served as a brief introduction, giving the reader a peek at what could not be thumbed through.[3] Prefaces often included the author's name, a dedication, remarks about others who had written on this subject, claims to authenticity, and a description of the contents of the volume.[4] Luke's preface does not name the author; perhaps he was following the example of the Gospel of Mark or of the anonymous editor of 2 Maccabees ("all this, which has been set forth by Jason of Cyrene in five volumes, we shall attempt to condense into a single book" [2 Mac 2:23]).

As to the other expected elements, they are present, but only as suggestions. There were "many" who had come before Luke. How many? Whom did he mean? Luke writes in the first verse that they had "set their hands to compose a narrative." Does he mean that these earlier efforts were admirable failures, so that "set their hands" means "tried, but did not succeed"?[5] There is a claim to have "followed all things closely" and to "write an orderly account," but the author is unclear about what makes him an authority on the matters he covers in his Gospel. He does not claim to be an eyewitness or even a "servant of the word." Such people handed on narratives of "the things accomplished among us" to "us," in which group Luke includes himself, but this is no claim for special knowledge or for expert status. There is a dedication—"to write to you, most excellent Theophilus"—but who this person was, what his relation was to Luke, or even whether he was a real person is famously debated (see discussion below). And finally, there is no actual description of the work. Others wrote narrative (*diēgēsis*), but Luke does not name his own effort. The adverb "orderly" goes with the infinitive "to write," so that a literal translation of v. 3 would be, "it also seemed well for me, having investigated everything carefully from the beginning, to write in an orderly way to you, most excellent Theophilus." Would Luke call his project a narrative, like the others that came before him? And why not name Jesus somewhere in the four verses—"an account of the things accomplished among us by our Lord"?

Everything in order! We cannot know which written narratives Luke had in mind, but as noted in the introduction, this commentary follows the standard view that Luke copied from Mark and either from Q or from Matthew. Luke, as a practicing Christian, was also exposed to the reading and interpretation of Scripture in worship—perhaps Luke was a preacher himself—and those "oral traditions" no doubt influenced his work. But in v. 1, he focuses on the written accounts, the "narratives," because that is what he is providing, and because he wants his work to be seen in relation to these other written accounts. It is not so surprising that he does not name them. If Luke used Mark, for example, he almost certainly knew it by some other name—"the gospel of Jesus Christ, the Son of God," for example—since the current titles were most likely not in use until after all four Gospels were circulated together (Justin Martyr, around 150, calls the Gospels "the memoirs of the apostles"). Perhaps in Luke's circles, "narratives of the things accomplished among us" is as much of a name as Luke's predecessors had. [Early Christians Read the Gospels]

Early Christians Read the Gospels

Justin, *1 Apol.* 67: "On the day called Sunday there is a meeting in one place of those who live in the cities or the country, and the memoirs of the apostles or the writings of the prophets are read as long as time permits. When the reader has finished, the president in a discourse urges and invites us to the imitation of these noble things."

"The First Apology of Justin, the Martyr," ed. and trans. Edward Rochie Hardy, in Cyril C. Richardson, ed., *Early Christian Fathers* (New York: MacMillan, 1970), 287.

If Luke is making a critique of these earlier Gospels, it is quite oblique. Contemporary prefaces tended to be less subtle and more caustic. Here are two examples of how authors writing near the end of the first century took a whack at rivals in their prefaces.

- Longinus, *On the Sublime*: "You know, my dear Postumius Terentianus, that when we were studying together Caecilius' little treatise on the Sublime it appeared to us to fall below the level of its subject and to fail to address the main points . . ." (1.1).
- Josephus, *Jewish War*: "While those that were present [during the War] have given false accounts of things, and this either out of a humor of flattery to the Romans, or out of hatred to the Jews, and while their writings contain sometimes accusations, and sometimes encomiums, but nowhere the accurate truth of the facts . . ." (Preface, 1.2)

If Luke's preface intends to criticize his predecessors, he only implies this by the nuances of his words: "they set their hands" may imply "they did not succeed"; the use of "closely" and "orderly" in v. 3 may mean that Luke found the other narratives to be disorganized and inaccurate; and the whole of v. 4, "so that you may know the certainty of the things about which you have been instructed," may be meant to contrast the certainty of this Gospel with the inaccuracy of what Theophilus has learned up to this point.[6] More likely Luke means to engender the reader's trust in this narrative, to characterize it as organized, accurate, and reliable, and has no great interest in what the reader, who may never have read or heard the other narratives, thinks about the earlier works.

Luke positions himself, first, as part of the community who has received the testimony of eyewitnesses and "ministers of the word." The word translated "minister" means an assistant of some kind; Luke uses it in Acts 5:22, 26 for the men who assisted the captain of the temple guards and in Luke 4:20 for the person in the synagogue service who handed Jesus the scroll to read. The word also appears in one of Paul's speeches as his self-characterization (Acts 26:16)—Jesus, who appeared to him, appointed him as "minister" and "martyr" (or witness). It is not as clear to me, then, as it is to others, that Luke thinks of "eyewitness" and "minister of the word" as separate, serial categories, as if Luke were describing first- and second-generation Christians and putting himself in a third generation.[7] Rather, he seems to want to connect the whole Christian community of his day to those who saw Jesus. Perhaps Luke would think of himself as a "minister of the word," but perhaps he, like

Paul, would have claimed to have seen Jesus; since we do not have his personal testimony, we cannot say.

As we can see from the citation from Josephus just above, eyewitness testimony was no proof of veracity in Luke's day. Luke claims no special sources of information about Jesus, but he does claim to be especially diligent. The verb he uses to describe his research often means "follow," but ancient writers of history often used it to mean "investigated" or "informing oneself."[8] The object of the verb is "everything," and the two adverbs attached to the verb are "from the first" and "accurately" or "carefully." This, then, is not so much a claim about his qualifications as his commitment.

And what has he written? The balanced structure of the preface would imply another "narrative" (*diēgēsis*), a word that covered written or oral recitals of events. They wrote narratives; it seemed good to Luke also to write . . . well, there is no other choice but "narrative." This sort of ellipsis is not uncommon in Luke's Gospel, as we will see in later passages.[9] Perhaps Luke avoids calling his book a "narrative" because he does not want to say that it is just like the others. Readers can supply their own designation. He does, however, claim that it was written "in an orderly manner" so that Theophilus, or anyone else who reads it, may know the reliability of the contents of their instruction. Verse 4 presumes that most readers will not be coming to the topic of Jesus *de novo*, as neophytes who have previously heard nothing about Jesus; they will have heard something, and reading Luke's Gospel will give them an orderly treatment that will affirm what they have heard. Perhaps "orderly" implies that what Theophilus and the others may have heard lacked organization, but v. 4 argues that Luke presumed that his book would be largely consonant with what had come before.

Finally, we know nothing of "most excellent Theophilus" except that the name is repeated at the beginning of Acts. Christian interpreters from the time of Origen have wondered if the name, which means "God's friend," were symbolic, as if Luke had written "dear Christian reader,"[10] but most scholars now believe that Luke was addressing a real person. ["Theophilus" as the Ideal Reader] The name is Greek, used by Jews and Gentiles, found in inscriptions and literature from the third century BC. The courtesy title "most excellent" was used in the first century for persons in official positions but also in prefaces as a way to honor the person to

---

"Theophilus" as the Ideal Reader

Origen, *Hom. Luc* 1.6: "Someone might think that Luke addressed the Gospel to a specific man named Theophilus. But if you are the sort of people God can love, then all of you who hear us speaking are Theophiluses, and the Gospel is addressed to you."

Ambrose, *Exp. Luc.* 1.12: "So the Gospel was written to Theophilus, that is, to him whom God loves. If you love God, it was written to you."

Both are cited in Arthur A. Just Jr., ed., *Luke* (ACCS: NT, vol. 3; Downer's Grove IL: Intervarsity Press, 2003), 4.

whom the work was dedicated.[11] Unfortunately, then, we cannot use this dedication as a window into the social world of Luke. Perhaps Theophilus was a wealthy Christian supporting a church in his house, and Luke was providing a written account of Jesus' life for his library, knowing that other Christians would thereby have access to it.[12] Perhaps Theophilus was Luke's patron, supporting him financially in return for being immortalized in this way. Perhaps Theophilus was a wealthy man and a new Christian, needing some assurance that this new sect that emphasized ministry to the poor and sharing of property was the group for him.[13] Perhaps Theophilus was a Christian and a person of some standing in the city where he lived, and this Gospel is intended to demonstrate to him and to others that the Way could be a respectable option for the well born and well placed. All of these, and more, are possible.

[How Did Luke Get Published?]

The preface gives us no clarity about the author's sources or the dedicatee, and it does not describe the work to be undertaken. It does, however, indicate that the author knew how prefaces to important works were supposed to sound. The fact that he took the trouble to write a long, balanced sentence full of polysyllabic words means that he wanted this book to be taken seriously.[14] He does not claim first-hand knowledge of Jesus, but asserts his own diligence, and promises that the Christian reader will be the more assured for having read his book. He does not clear the ground for his own work by impugning those who came before him, and for his own work does not claim inerrancy but orderliness. All in all, and especially in comparison to writers of his period, this is a serious but understated beginning. Luke no doubt agreed with the author of 2 Maccabees: "At this point therefore let us begin our narrative, without adding anything more to what has already been said; for it would be foolish to lengthen the preface while cutting short the history itself."

How Did Luke Get Published?

 In our modern world, there are authors and publishers and booksellers. Everyone in the chain hopes to make money in the process. You get book advertisements by direct mail, through the Internet, through magazines, through book reviews in newspapers and journals, and by physical displays of books in stores. Harry Gamble, who has written the definitive treatment of bookmaking and distribution during ancient times, states flatly, "In these matters modern conceptions of publication, edition, and book trade are irrelevant and misleading" (83).

First, an author wrote and then often showed the work or read parts of it aloud to a select group of friends, who made comments. Next, the author might arrange a public reading in a larger setting and for a bigger group. If the author had an influential and wealthy patron, the reading might be organized by the patron. In this way, both would benefit: the author, by the patron's wider and more prestigious circle of friends; the patron, by the public standing that comes from giving help to brilliant authors. The author might, at the same time or later, have copies made of the manuscript, to give to the patron and his friends. If the public reading went well, and if the patron and friends talked up the excellence of the work, then other people would want to make their own copies, either for their own use or to give away to friends or to their own patrons. "In principle the work became public property: copies were disseminated without regulation through an informal network composed of people who learned of the work, were interested enough to have a copy made, and knew someone who possessed the text and would permit it to be duplicated" (85).

Harry Gamble, *Books and Readers in the Early Church: A History of Early Christian Texts* (New Haven: Yale, 1995).

Annunciation 1: Gospel Rejected, 1:5-25

Poor Zechariah. His story was going so well: the narrator calls him righteous before God and a blameless follower of the Torah. The lot falls to him and he gets a chance to shine, to fulfill his duty and bring credit to himself and his family. Then the angel Gabriel appears to him—surely this must be a sign of God's favor? Sure enough, his prayers have been answered, and all that faithful service and dutiful obedience has been rewarded; like Abraham, he will have a child in his old age!

After Gabriel shows up, things begin to fall apart, but we're getting ahead of ourselves. Let us first pay attention to how Luke sets the scene: the descriptions of the characters involved, the setting, and the parts played offstage and on.

Elizabeth and Zechariah, the Gospel's first characters, are described in ways that make them familiar character types for a first-century audience, and especially for an audience familiar with the Old Testament. He was a priest, and she was from a priestly family. In Judaism, only the members of certain family groups could act as priests. Most Roman or Greek priesthoods were offices that the more well-to-do individuals sought out, in order to demonstrate their piety. In general, the whole first-century world thought of the priesthood as an honorable, desirable position. Verse 5 describes good people from good families, and v. 6 shifts the focus to the way they conducted their lives. They were both "righteous before God, walking blamelessly in all the commandments and ordinances of the Lord." Luke uses phrases from the LXX to describe his two characters. For example, Deuteronomy 5:28-33 speaks of the "commandments and ordinances" that God gives Moses as a path, and God warns Moses not to stray from it. [LXX] This is old-fashioned language, deliberately echoing the sacred text, and Luke employs it to give his characters weight and dignity, and to get his readers thinking of the connections between his characters and the ones in their Bible. But the words also look ahead, to the time when Jesus' teaching becomes known as "the Way."

Elizabeth and Zechariah were good people from good families who lived godly lives, but they had no child because Elizabeth was barren. Here Luke quotes Genesis 29:31, where Rachel's barren state is described as God's justice: Leah, whom Jacob "hated," was given sons to make her more valued, while Rachel, the favorite

LXX

"LXX" is the standard abbreviation for the Septuagint, the ancient Greek version of the Old Testament, used by non-Palestinian Jews (and later by Christians) who read Greek rather than Hebrew. There were actually several different Greek translations made at different times—we have no idea which one Luke would have used, but clearly he read the Old Testament in Greek. The LXX included books not in the Hebrew Scriptures, and Luke seems to have been familiar with some of them.

wife, was barren. Luke thereby sets up a dilemma: we know these are good guys, but we also know that infertility could be God's judgment. If they are so righteous, why are they childless?

The next line, "and both were far along in their years," both shows how desperate the situation is and lets the attentive reader know how it will all work out. This time Luke quotes Genesis 18:11, where the phrase describes Abraham and Sarah. Their story in Genesis is a classic—God keeps promising that they will have more progeny than they can count, but year after year, the number of cribs in the nursery is zero. They resort to adoption and then to a surrogate mother, but finally, when Abraham is 100 and his lovely wife is 90, "Chuckles" (also known as Isaac, from the Hebrew for "he laughs") is born. The reader is supposed to know this, and think that God will work things out for Elizabeth and Zechariah.

All of this is character description, not action; the story has reached v. 7, and so far nothing has happened. Finally, in v. 8 we are given a specific place—the temple in Jerusalem—and a specific time—the incense offering, which was made twice daily (Exod 30:7-8). Luke probably has the late afternoon offering in mind, because he describes the "whole multitude of the people" gathered for prayer, and knows that the "hour of prayer" was the ninth hour, according to the Roman reckoning, or around 3:00 P.M. in our system (see Acts 3:1). Off camera, and earlier in the afternoon, Zechariah had been chosen by lot to offer the incense; God had marked him for this task on this day. According to the Mishnah, there were so many priests eligible to serve in the temple that they had to be divided into sections (these are all listed in 1 Chr 23:6). Each section rotated into Jerusalem for a week twice a year; that is only fourteen days of active service, with only twenty-eight chances to perform the sacrifice or offer the incense. The Mishnah says that within each section, priests who had never offered incense would cast lots to see who would take the turn.[15] If this correctly describes what happened in the Second Temple, and if Luke knew of it, then we're to imagine that Zechariah, the righteous, aging priest, had been waiting for the lot to fall on him for years, probably just as long as he had been waiting for a child. [The Mishnah]

The Mishnah

The Mishnah is a collection of traditions from the very early rabbis, put together near the end of the second century AD. The editor, Rabbi Judah the Prince, was the great-grandson of the Gamaliel who gives a speech in Acts 5:34-39.

We can imagine the scene in the Court of Israel, the wide space just in front of the balustrade marking the area reserved for priests [Diagram of the Inner Courts]. There is a congregation of worshipers praying; Luke describes them in vv. 10 and

Diagram of the Inner Courts

The Court of Israel is the wide space (labeled #5 in the diagram) just in front of the area reserved for priests; there would also be a congregation of praying worshipers.

1. Holy of Holies
2. Holy Place
3. Altar of Incense
4. Court of Priests
5. Court of Israel (Men)
6. Altar of Burnt Offerings

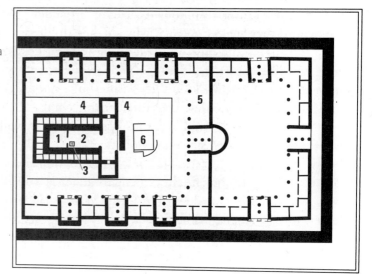

21, so they are in view. As the Mishnah describes the incense ceremony, there was more than one priest involved, but Luke has chosen to show us only Zechariah, walking up the steps to the great door of the temple and stepping inside, holding the golden incense ladle.[16] If the Mishnah describes the way things were done in Zechariah's day, then he would have been preceded by three other priests, one who would have cleared the morning's ashes from the altar, another who would have made certain that the proper oil lamp was burning, and another who would have prepared the coals to receive the incense.[17] "He that offered the incense did not offer it until the officer said to him, 'Offer the incense!' . . . When all were gone away he offered the incense and prostrated himself and came away."[18] Maybe Luke did not know exactly how the temple service worked (since he may never have been in Jerusalem to see it), but from the way he describes the temple courts in Luke and Acts, he must have known that there would have been a sizable group of clerics needed to run the place. Picturing Zechariah alone is a deliberate narrowing of focus, making this aged priest the center of the story and the one standing between the people and their God.

Imagine, then, as Luke wants us to, this old priest, righteous and blameless, standing with the dish of incense before the altar of God, ready to offer it as a token of the prayers of the people. Gabriel's appearance disrupts all that—did Zechariah ever perform his duty? By the time the story is over, it is beside the point.

When Zechariah saw the angel, he was overcome by terror. The phrasing of v. 12 is interesting: "and when he saw, Zechariah was terrified [*etarachthē*, from a root that means to be unsettled or thrown into confusion] and fear fell on him." On the one hand, this is a pretty standard reaction to an angel; when Raphael reveals himself as an angel to Tobit and Tobias, "the two of them were terrified [*etarachthēsan*] and fell face down, because they were afraid" (Tob 12:16). On the other hand, his reaction is surely meant to contrast with Mary's (1: 29) and is at odds with his question to Gabriel (1:18). When Zechariah's son John is finally born, the fear returns to all who hear about him (1:65).

Zechariah in the Temple

Jacopo della Quercia (c.1367–1438). *Annunciation to Zacharias*. Bronze relief from the baptismal font. 1417–1418. Baptistery, Siena, Italy. (Credit: Scala/Art Resource, NY)

As Luke uses the word "fear" (*phobos*), it is not always good or always bad. Sometimes it indicates a negative emotion: "'Where is your faith?' But, being afraid, they were amazed, saying to each other, 'Who then is this, that he commands the winds and waters and they obey him?'" (Luke 8:25). In this example, the disciples' fear is linked to their lack of faith. But in 7:16, the crowds who see Jesus raise the dead are taken by fear and begin to praise God; their faith seems to increase. Zechariah's fear, then, does not make him more or less faithful or godly; perhaps Luke understood it as an intermediate step on the way to something else.

Gabriel's speech to the priest is rather long and includes announcements of good news, specific commands for the parents-to-be, and predictions about how the child will impact the world. You can almost see the angel pausing and saying, "You might want to write some of this down."

Verse 13: Your prayer has been heard: *announcement of good news*
Your wife, Elizabeth will bear you a son: *announcement of good news*
You shall call his name "John": *command*

Verse 14: You will have joy and happiness: *announcement of good news*
Many will rejoice at his birth: *prediction*

Verse 15: He will be great before the Lord: *prediction*
He must never drink wine or beer: *command* ["Beer"]
He shall be filled with the Holy Spirit from his
mother's womb: *prediction*

Verse 16: He will turn many of the sons of Israel to the Lord
their God: *prediction*

Verse 17: He will go before him in the spirit and power of
Elijah, to turn the hearts of the fathers to their children and the disobedient in the wisdom of the
righteous; *prediction* to prepare for the Lord a prepared people: *prediction*

From this, we are to conclude that Zechariah and Elizabeth have
been praying for God to resolve the dilemma set up in vv. 5-7. If
Gabriel had delivered only the good news in vv. 13-14, then this
story would be mostly about God's care for these
two righteous people. But the rest of the angel's
message speaks to a wider role and a greater
impact for John. John will be a composite hero,
combining aspects of several important figures
from Israel's past. Verse 15b quotes Numbers
6:3, where a person wanting to take a special
Nazirite vow of devotion to God was required to
abstain from anything alcoholic. Samuel's
mother Hannah vowed that if God would give her a son, she
would never let him drink anything alcoholic, and Luke appears to
have drawn v. 15a (*estai gar megs enōpion tou kyriou*, he shall be
great before the Lord) from 1 Samuel 3:21b, which in the LXX
reads "*kai emegalynthē to paidarion Samouēl enōpion kyriou* [the
child Samuel became great (or grew up) before the Lord]." John,
then, will be especially holy, dedicated to the Lord, and, like
Samuel, will not stand for hypocrisy in the worship of God.

Verses 15c-17a put John in the roles of Elijah and Elisha.
Malachi 4:5-6 (in the LXX, 3:22-23) predicts that God will send
Elijah before the Day of Judgment, and that "he will turn the heart
of a father to his son." Sirach 48:1-11 celebrates Elijah in this role
of reformer, and Luke seems to have quoted 48:10 in v. 16, and to
have drawn v. 15c from 48:12, "Elisha was filled with his spirit
[that is, with Elijah's spirit]." John will be a great prophet, like
Elijah, who was to purify the worship of Israel and start a process of
repentance. Like all the prophets, John will be driven by God's
Spirit, yet he will be greater than any of them (Luke 7:26, 28), and

"Beer"

The word translated "beer" only appears
in the New Testament in this verse. It is
often translated "strong drink" in English versions.
The Greek word *sikera* means some sort of alcoholic beverage other than wine, and may be
related to the Akkadian word for "barley beer."
See BAGD, 923.

one marker of that will be that the Spirit controls him while he is still in his mother's womb.

The final part of v. 17 comes from David's prayer in 2 Samuel 7:24. David thanks God "for preparing your people Israel for yourself as your own people." Gabriel's message to Zechariah thus melds recollections of Samuel, Elijah, Elisha, and David.[19] What a marvelous thing for a future father to hear about his son, especially when the father is an elderly, childless priest. Finally, this righteous couple can be vindicated when God grants their prayer for a child, and they can know that their son will be part of something amazingly good for their people. Surely Zechariah can hardly believe his ears, can hardly wait to go home and tell his wife the good news! [I can wade Grief—]

Here we hit a bump in the road. Zechariah asks the angel for proof, stating the obvious: he and his wife are too old to have children. His answer is biblical; "how shall I know this?" was what Abram asked God when God promised him the land, and "for I am old and my wife is getting on in years" repeats the quote from Genesis 18:11 already cited in v. 7. With all due respect, this is a dumb question; I know, the correct teacherly point of view is there are no dumb questions, but this is dumb. An angel of the Lord stands before him and says, "Your prayer has been answered." What sort of evidence would have convinced him if the appearance of an angel was not enough? (This is a question that will come up again in the final chapter of the Gospel.) And if Zechariah can quote from the story of Abraham, can he not remember how the story turned out? Luke's use of the quotation helps us see why Zechariah gets disciplined— for being a schoolboy who did not pay attention to the daily lesson.

Gabriel offers him no proof of his good news, beyond the fact of his own identity (maybe Zechariah did not know who it was?). He also apparently does not even raise his voice—v. 19 begins "Answering, the angel said to him"—but matter-of-factly says he was sent from God's presence with good news to speak to Zechariah. The order of things in v. 20 is important: "And behold, you will be silent and unable to speak until the day these things happen, because you did not believe my words, which will be fulfilled at their proper time." The curse comes first: Zechariah spoke imprudently, so he will speak no more for a while. Then the reason for the curse: he did not believe Gabriel's testimony, which was God's good news for him. Last of all, so that the emphasis falls here, is the promise: all these things will happen in their proper time, Zechariah's doubts notwithstanding. Since Zechariah and

Elizabeth are going to have a baby in the ordinary way (except for their age), Gabriel's statement that these things will happen is as much a statement of faith in Zechariah's willingness to be a part of God's plan as about God's ability to make things happen. Gabriel zaps him for doubting, but is confident that the old priest will not take a vow of celibacy out of spite. And his speechless condition, therefore, is "both punitive and propaedeutic—both a judgment upon unbelief and an education for belief."[20] Zechariah will learn something about the way God works in the world while he quietly watches and listens to his wife and to her kinswoman Mary.

The scene ends with a little comic relief. Everyone outside—all the congregation who had been praying while Zechariah was inside—is puzzled at the delay, but as soon as he comes out speechless, they know that he had seen a vision in the temple. They grasp immediately what has happened and do not need any further explanation, while he, rendered silent by the angel's curse, keeps waving his arms in an attempt to communicate. Luke is a master of these kinds of ironic moments. [Speechless!]

When his section's two weeks were over, Zechariah went home, and in due course, Elizabeth conceived. Surprisingly, she hid herself, when one might have expected that she would make sure all her friends and relations saw that God had blessed her with a child. Her words may be another example of Lukan irony: "for thus the Lord has done to me in the days when he saw fit to take away my public shame." Her seclusion may simply be a plot device, so that Gabriel could be the one to break the news of Elizabeth's pregnancy to Mary.[21] Some ancient Christian interpreters suggested that she was embarrassed over being pregnant at such an advanced age.[22] But given how Luke stresses that her deliverance from the undeserved shame of childlessness came late in her life, and that it was accompanied by the corresponding curse on her husband, perhaps he means for her seclusion to give an ironic tone to her words: "So this is how the Lord rescues the faithful?" Whatever the case, her seclusion will be resolved, first by Gabriel's announcement to Mary, then by Mary's visit, and finally by the way John's birth is treated as a miracle.

Speechless!

📖 "Zacharias was speechless, instead of being silent. Had he accepted the revelation, he may perhaps have come out of the temple not dumb but silent."

Ernest Hello, quoted by Dietrich Bonhoeffer, *Life Together*, trans. John W. Doberstein (New York: Harper, 1954), 78.

Annunciation 2: Gospel Accepted, 1:26-38

The annunciation to Mary has been a favorite subject for artists through the centuries, and it is interesting to note how differently artists pose Gabriel and Mary (The Web Gallery of Art [www.wga.hu] has an extensive collection searchable by a keyword such as "annunciation.") Many early illustrated manuscripts and icons have them both standing, but beginning in the High Middle Ages and Renaissance periods, Gabriel often kneels to show respect to Mary, who is frequently seated, sometimes in a throne or elaborate chair, as befits the Queen of Heaven. Other artists, trying to show the human reaction of a girl stunned by such an announcement, will often have Gabriel standing or hovering above Mary, who either looks up at the angel or (as in Caravaggio's painting from 1608) kneels, head bowed, eyes closed, apparently crushed by the news. Another issue: What does Mary look like? In da Vinci's version (1472–1475), she is young, blonde, well-dressed, seated at an elaborately carved desk,

her finger holding her place in the book she has been reading; she is a fragile beauty from the upper classes, innocent but educated. In Henry O. Tanner's version (1898), she is no less beautiful, but with dark hair and eyes, dressed in clothes that look more homespun and more first-century Palestinian. The room makes us think of poorer circumstances— the rough rugs on the floor and the wall, the single jug and plate. Her expression is harder to place; compared to Rossetti's

The Annunciation

Henry Ossawa Tanner (1859–1937). *The Annunciation*. 1898. Oil on canvas, Philadelphia Museum of Art, Philadelphia, PA. (Credit: The Philadelphia Museum of Art/Art Resource, NY)

red-haired Mary (1850), who shrinks back on her bed, stunned, frightened, Tanner's Mary looks up at the beam of light that is the angel and seems to be thinking, "You've got to be kidding—and this is going to start *when*?"

Luke gives us a few clues on how he imagines things. This scene, as commentators frequently note, is based on the episode just finished, the annunciation to Zechariah. But whereas Zechariah and Elizabeth are typical characters in a stock plot—the aging righteous childless couple longing for a baby—Mary is not. There are no biblical examples of young unmarried women who get the happy news that they will have a baby through God's direct intervention. So

Luke composes this second annunciation on the model of the first one, letting us first see the similarities between the two situations, all the better to feel their differences.

First, notice the parallels between the two scenes

Zechariah	**Mary**
He is "terrified [*etarachthē*]"	She is "troubled [*dietarachthē*]"
"Do not be afraid"	"Do not be afraid"
"Elizabeth will bear you a son"	"You will bear a son"
"You will name him John"	"You will name him Jesus"
"He will be great"	"He will be great"
"How will I know that this is so?"	"How can this be, since I have no husband?"

But there are also many differences between the two scenes. Zechariah is old, a priest, on duty in the temple when the vision comes. Mary's age is not given, but since she is called "virgin" (*parthenos*) twice without any sort of qualifying phrase, we assume that Luke thinks of her as young. We do not know her precise age. The figure of twelve years that often appears in commentaries is based on a Mishnah passage that says a girl's vows are valid in her twelfth year. Actual evidence of Jewish practice from the first century is scarce, but what there is demonstrates that the ages of brides ranged from thirteen to early twenties.[23] The most we can say for sure is that certainly by contrast with Zechariah and Elizabeth, Mary is a more normal age for having her first baby; the obstacle that requires suspension of disbelief in her case is that she is single.

Mary is also in no place as significant as the temple. She is in a small village in the north. And until the end of the episode, when we learn she is related to Elizabeth, we have no idea of her family. Even then, we assume she is also a descendant of Aaron, but we do not know her clan, as we do for Zechariah. We also do not know her social or economic status. Commentaries frequently presume that she is poor ("dirt poor," as one puts it[24]), but we actually have no information about her status at this point. (When Mary and Joseph make an offering at the temple, they offer two doves, meaning that they are not wealthy [2:24]; but had they been truly destitute, they could have offered meal instead.) The point is that Luke wants us to take Mary as an unknown quantity: we know her name, her marital status, and the name of the village where she lives, so that God's choice of her comes as something of a surprise to the reader as well as to Mary herself.

The two greatest contrasts with Zechariah are the nature of the promise to Mary and the nature of her response. Gabriel promised Mary that she would have a son, just as he promised Zechariah that Elizabeth would, too. But whereas John will be great before the Lord, Jesus will be great and will be called "Son of the Most High." John will turn the people back to the Lord, but Jesus will be granted David's throne and will "rule over the house of Jacob forever." This is the beginning of the motif of kingship in Luke, and for Luke's readers past and present it creates many questions. Nowhere in Luke does Jesus claim the title "King" or "Messiah" (in 23:3 he gets the chance to do so, but passes it up), but others proclaim him king (19:38), accuse him of saying he is king (23:2), and crucify him under that title (23:38). This commentary will argue that Luke is aware of how some of Jesus' followers know him as Messiah and understand him to have been Israel's rejected King, but that Luke undercuts the title, preferring instead to present Jesus as a prophet. In many ways, as we will see later, Luke treats the whole notion of kingship as something to be ridiculed.

Luke's first readers may have wrestled with how to square Gabriel's prophecy with their reality: when has Jesus ruled over the Jews, the descendants of Jacob? By the time Luke wrote, the temple lay in ruins and Christianity had developed branches that no longer believed that Jewish piety—keeping Sabbath, obeying the dietary laws—was necessary or helpful for Christians. Some believed Christians had replaced Jews as the chosen people of God; for such readers, what meaning did Gabriel's promise hold? For modern Christians, faced with the church's consistently anti-Jewish behavior since the time of Constantine, the question becomes whether proclaiming Jesus as the future ruler of Jacob's descendants is not one more act of virulent triumphalism. Why would they want to be ruled by the founder of another religion? And if we Christians believe that the promises God made to Abraham, Isaac, and Jacob are still valid—if we do not, then we will have problems understanding Jesus and Paul—then we need to consider carefully how we can proclaim the coming kingship of Jesus without sounding like we are condemning the house of Jacob to the outer darkness.

The last part of v. 35 can be translated "the holy one to be born will be called the Son of God," or "the one to be born, the holy one, will be called the Son of God."[25] In either case, Jesus is set apart for God (holy) and is God's Son by the action of God's Spirit descending on Mary. The emphasis is on God's action, and nothing is said about Mary's status as a virgin contributing or being necessary to Jesus' status as holy Son of God. Gabriel emphasizes God's action throughout his oracle: the Lord is with you; you have found favor with God; God will give him the throne; the Holy Spirit will come upon you; the power of the Most High will overshadow you; nothing shall be impossible with God. To keep us focused on "the Lord God" who is doing all this through Mary, Luke suppresses Gabriel's name; he never says it, Mary never asks it, and after mentioning it once, the narrator drops it for "the angel." On the other hand, Luke does not make Mary passive: "you will conceive in your womb," "you will bear a son," "you will call his name Jesus." A young girl from no place special, she has been chosen by God to do a very important task, and everything hinges on whether she will accept it. [John Donne's *Annunciation*]

John Donne's *Annunciation*

From John Donne, *Annunciation*:

Ere by the spheres time was created, thou
Wast in his mind, who is thy Son, and Brother;
Whom thou conceiv'st, conceived; yea thou are now
Thy Maker's maker, and thy Father's mother;
Thou hast light in dark; and shut'st in little room,
Immensity cloistered in thy dear womb.

The Complete Poetry and Selected Prose of John Donne, ed. Charles M. Coffin (New York: Modern Library), 231.

Mary's response "How can this be?" does not sound so terribly different from Zechariah's "How will I know that this is so?"; yet Mary is not struck mute, so we surmise that Luke considered it significantly different. Zechariah's question is a request for proof, which colors him absurdly recalcitrant: if a priest is not going to believe an angel, then what would he believe? Besides, he is quoting Abraham; does he not remember the story? Mary's question is more of a question of method: does Gabriel mean that she will marry Joseph, and their baby will be heir to David's throne through Joseph? Or perhaps it's more general still: "I'm not now sexually active; how will this happen?" Her question has struck some commentators as odd, for that very cause: why would a young woman about to be married need to ask an angel how she would become pregnant? But Gabriel has said nothing about Joseph, and has only spoken about what God has done or will do for her or for her son, and just as the "hail, graced one, the Lord is with you" puzzled her, so must the rest of Gabriel's speech. Mary is not looking for proof, but for clarity.

The simplest explanation for "you will conceive in your womb and bear a son" would have been that Mary and Joseph would have a baby, and some commentators have argued that Luke understood it that way. "Mary's question . . . is then a simple human request for reassurance that all will happen in due time and in due order, in keeping with the commitments made in her betrothal. The messenger's reply to Mary's question . . . need not be read as referring to anything but a conception involving human parents."[26] While this is possible, it seems unlikely; Mary is pregnant in the very next episode, when she meets Elizabeth, and Luke is still calling her Joseph's betrothed in 2:5.

Luke's readers will have been familiar with many different stories of how male gods had children by women. Plutarch, for example, narrates several versions of the divine origin of Alexander the Great, including one in which his mother was impregnated by a lightning bolt from Zeus on the eve before her marriage to Philip of Macedon.[27] Zeus/Jupiter's sexual dalliances with women were the stuff of both serious myth and bawdy comedy. The Roman comic playwright Plautus's *Amphitryon* has Jupiter impersonate a general from Thebes in order to spend one night in bed with his wife; time stands still while the god takes his pleasure, and the wife gives birth to the god's child the very next day. Luke is careful not to use language that will at all sound sexual but that nonetheless emphasizes Jesus' divine origin.[28]

Luke uses two images for how Mary conceived, images that recur in his narrative. "The Holy Spirit will come upon you" has parallels in Acts 1:8, where it predicts the Pentecost event. There the Spirit descended upon each believer in visible form as flames resting on each of them. One is also reminded of Jesus' baptism where the Spirit descended visibly upon Jesus. The second metaphor is overshadowing, which is described quite literally in Acts 5:15—when Peter's shadow fell on the sick, they were healed. There is likewise a literal, physical overshadowing in Luke's transfiguration story, when the cloud of God's presence surrounded Peter, James, and John. One suspects, then, that Luke imagined (although he does not narrate it, so we cannot be certain) that the descent of the Spirit on Mary felt as real to her as the transfiguration cloud did to Peter. Commentators often point to how the Greek word for "overshadow" appears in Exodus 40:35, when God's Spirit fills the tabernacle in the desert.[29] It would appear, however, that Luke was thinking more about the experience of Jesus and the early church, as they were filled and empowered by God's Spirit; Mary's conception was a prototype for the way God would be manifest in all believers.[30] [Overshadow]

Mary's second response heightens the sense that Luke is composing her as a model believer: "Behold the Lord's servant; may it happen to me just as you said." In Greek, the believing acceptance is amplified by the wordplay: Gabriel says, "No event [*rēma*, lit., "word," but here it means "thing" or "event"] will be impossible with God," and she says, "May it happen to me according to your *rēma*." That was Zechariah's line, or it should have been; what is a priest but the servant of the Lord, whose very life is dedicated to

Overshadow

Gabriel addresses his majestic words in an unlikely setting to an unlikely person, someone poor and powerless, extremely vulnerable in her place and time, a young peasant woman about to find herself pregnant before her wedding. . . . When a time or place seems touched by God, it is an over-shadowing, a sudden eclipsing of my priorities and plans. But even in terrible circumstances and calamities, in matters of life and death, if I sense that I am in the shadow of God, I find light, so much light that my vision improves dra-matically. I know that holiness is near.

And it is not robed in majesty. It does not assert itself with the raw power of empire (not even the little empire of the self in which I all too often reside), but it waits in puzzlement, it hesitates. Coming from Galilee, as it were, from a place of little hope, it reveals the ordinary cir-cumstances of my life to be full of mystery, and gospel, which means "good news."

Kathleen Norris, *Amazing Grace: A Vocabulary of Faith* (New York: Riverhead, 1998), 30–31.

doing what God's word commands? Mary's *fiat* is echoed in Luke by other exemplary characters: Simeon, who waited at God's command to see the Messiah and called himself God's servant; the centurion who knew that Jesus' word would be enough to heal his servant, because he, too, had masters to whom he submitted; and Jesus himself, who set God's will above his own.

How would you illustrate all this? If Gabriel's head is higher than Mary's, we emphasize her sub-mission to God's will, but how do we capture her bold faith in God's plan? If Mary's face shows fear or grief or shock, we are reminded that the story begins that way, but the painters who gave her a placid smile point us to the end, where Mary has the last word. A halo around her head would be true to her status as model believer, but not to Luke's theme of how the least likely persons respond most favorably to God's good news. Luke has given us a rich text to think on, and since it comes first—since Mary comes before all the other exemplary men and silent women—we must think seriously about whether we are to carry her image forward into the Gospel, allowing it to ameliorate the disappoint-ment we feel when other women do not speak prophetically, as she is about to do. That is, will Mary's strong colors, especially since she can be sketched in so many different ways in this story, be allowed to sum up, in advance, what Luke really hopes for women as leaders in the church, or are we to read chronologically, con-cluding that Luke could only tolerate the strong women at the beginning, while Jesus was offstage, and that the silent, more sub-servient women who appear later in the Gospel are actually more his model for how women should behave?

Mary Visits Elizabeth; the Magnificat, 1:39-56

This episode always puts me in mind of *The Sound of Music*, where the movie characters are forever breaking into song; not an opera, where everything is sung, but a musical, where the plot is carried sometimes by conversation and sometimes by songs. In one scene Maria goes to see the head of her convent for advice, and is treated to "Climb Every Mountain." In another, the von Trapp children are performing the good-night song, and at the end, the crowd below echoes, in perfect harmony, the "good-bye" of the children. Marvelous, unforgettable entertainment; not very much like real life.

In our scene, the infant John leaps for joy in Elizabeth's womb; Elizabeth, filled with the Spirit, offers prophetic blessing and oracles that may be poetry[31]; and then Mary tilts back her head and belts out a Handelian recitative whose libretto is drawn from all over the Old Testament.[32] According to v. 56, Mary stays there three months, almost until time for John to be born, but we do not get to see any of the everyday things that two kinswomen who find themselves unexpectedly expecting must have done. This is high drama, done for theological effect; it is not meant to tell us anything about the way first-century Palestinian women actually behaved. Realism is not the point, so we will take no time looking for explanations for how Mary could have memorized so much Torah or for what this story says about the social location of the two women.

The episode also is a sort of crux in the flow of the narrative. There are two birth announcements, two birth stories, and two childhood stories (both about Jesus), but only one story of the two mothers getting together. Mary's Magnificat, at first glance, would be naturally paired with Zechariah's Benedictus, except that Zechariah prophesies after John is born, and so that might make a better parallel to Simeon's predictions while the baby Jesus is in the temple, or to the much shorter song of the angels just after Jesus' birth. Some commentators, impressed by the structure of three paired stories, call this one a transitional episode.[33] Others see it as more pivotal, as it merges the two story lines, puts the two mothers on stage together, and thereby previews for the reader how Jesus and John will relate.[34] Even more important, Elizabeth and Mary are the first examples of roles that will be enormously significant for Luke-Acts. Luke uses them to set the standard for what is about to come.

Elizabeth has already been introduced to us as a member of a priestly family, the wife of a priest, an elderly barren woman, and a person of conspicuous virtue, righteous before God, walking blamelessly in all the commandments and ordinances of the Lord. She is now six months pregnant. Would it not make sense for Mary, the young unmarried girl, to seek advice from her older, wiser, godly kinswoman?[35] Other texts suggest such behavior: Uzziah, elder of Bethulia, remarks that the people of his town were accustomed to asking the godly Judith for advice (Jdt 8:29); Proverbs 31:26 praises the ideal wife for being a wise teacher; and

Lady Wisdom herself invites anyone to her school to learn insight and maturity (Prov 1:20-33). Luke turns the tables in this scene, however, because Elizabeth praises Mary.

When Elizabeth first hears Mary's voice, the baby "leaps"—described as an objective event, not as something Elizabeth felt—and then she is filled with the Holy Spirit. John's leap is first of all his testimony to Jesus, as he is overjoyed to be in the presence of the Lord. Second, it is Luke's sign to the reader that Gabriel's prediction that John would be filled with the Spirit *in utero* has been fulfilled (1:15). Elizabeth's reception of the Spirit, followed by a great cry, signals that she is speaking prophetically, although Luke chooses not to use the word "prophesy." She first blesses Mary, and then interprets what is happening to them both. When Judith returns from saving her village, Uzziah the elder says, "Blessed are you, O daughter, beyond all the women of the earth, and blessed is the Lord God, who created the heavens and the earth" (Jdt 13:18). Luke echoes this in Elizabeth's two lines: "Blessed are you among women, and blessed is the fruit of your womb," who Luke understands to be the Lord. "Why should the mother of my Lord come to me" honors Mary and the child she carries, and is the first narrative hint that Mary has already conceived.[36] Verse 45 also praises Mary for her faith in what was promised; the praise of believing Mary is also a critique of doubting Zechariah. "Blessed is she who believed" could also describe Elizabeth herself, since it is God who revealed to her that Mary was pregnant with God's Son.

Elizabeth is thus the prototype for the Lukan prophet, speaking by the inspiration of the Spirit, pointing to God's mighty acts of salvation offered to those who believe. She is the first character to call Jesus "Lord" and the first woman to offer a beatitude in the Gospel (the second comes at Luke 11:27). She is without question a noteworthy character; however, Mary, the younger kinswoman, overshadows her.

Robert Tannehill's description of the structure of the Magnificat, based on his analysis of the rhythm of the Greek text, is convincing.[37] The poem has two sections (or strophes), vv. 46-50 and 51-55. In the first, Mary focuses on what God has done for her, and in the second she speaks more broadly of what God has done for all, especially for Israel. What follows translates the poem literally, keeping the Greek word order, and trying to emphasize the parallels between the strophes.

> Magnifies my soul the Lord, ["my soul" is the subject of "magnifies"]
> And rejoices my spirit in God my savior, ["my spirit" is the subject of "rejoices"]

Because he looked carefully at the lowliness of his servant-girl.
For behold, from now on, will bless me all generations, ["all generations will bless"]
Because did for me magnificent things The Mighty One. ["The Mighty One did"]
> And holy (is) his name,
> And his mercy (is) to generations and generations
> > For those who fear him.

Did a strong thing with his arm,
Scattered the proud in the ideas of their hearts,
Unseated the mighty from their thrones,
And lifted the lowly
The poor (he) filled with good things,
And the rich (he) sent away empty.
Helped Israel his servant-boy,
> In order to remember his mercy,
Just as (he) said to our ancestors,
> To Abraham and his seed forever.

This is a terribly wooden translation of a beautiful poem, and to make up for it, there is a better rendering below. But notice, if you will, some elements that show how the poem is constructed. First, most of the lines begin with verbs, and God is the subject of all of them except the first two, where Mary is the subject (of "magnifies" and "rejoices") and God the object, and the fourth, where the generations will bless Mary even as she is now blessing the Lord. In the first strophe, Mary's actions and God's are fairly balanced: she magnifies the Lord because the Mighty One has done the same for her (the verb *megalynei*, "magnify," in v. 46 is the same root as "great things," *megala* [thus "magnificent things"]); all generations will bless her because of what God has done for her, even as God's mercy rests on those who live devotedly. This is a rather remarkable thing, when you think of it; Mary offers herself as a sign of God's salvation, greatness, and attitude toward the lowly.

The first stanza ends with praise for God's mercy on God's devotees, and the second stanza elaborates that theme. The first two lines are parallel, each line explaining the other: God did/God scattered (like sowing seeds); a strong thing/to the "uppity" ones; with God's arm/in their characteristic ways of thinking (the considerations of their hearts). The next four lines are in ABBA form: "unseated the mighty" is parallel to "and the rich he sent away empty," while "and lifted the lowly" matches up with "the poor he filled with good things." "Lowly" at the end of line 4, stanza 2, is the same root Mary uses to describe herself in line 3, stanza 1, and "servant-girl" and "servant-boy" are an obvious connection; in this way, Mary both shows up in the wider plan of God in stanza 2 and stands as a representative of the righteous poor of Israel in stanza 1. The "mercy" at the ends of both stanzas is God's *ḥesed*, God's unswerving commitment to the covenant with Israel. Mentioning it in both stanzas means that we are to see God's choice of Mary as part of the covenant, part of the plan to do right by the promises made to Abraham, Isaac, and Jacob.

Mary's words are drawn from a range of LXX passages. Like her son, she can "begin with Moses and all the prophets" and rattle off the themes of God's salvation: mercy to the poor, judgment on the wealthy; honor to the humble, confusion to the proud; faithfulness to the promises made to Israel through Abraham and the patriarchs. These, of course, are also the essentials of Jesus' message in Luke: "Blessed are you poor/Woe to you who are rich," etc. And like Jesus, Peter, Stephen, and Paul, Mary takes the first opportunity after her inauguration into God's plan to offer a speech laying out the plan of God in relation to Israel, to Jesus, and to her own role. Like all those men, she is first called by God, then goes on the road, and then stands and delivers the gospel.[38] The only thing they do that she does not is heal someone, and one could argue that the life growing inside her should count as a miracle as much as any other in Luke-Acts. [Mary's Pregnancy as Miracle]

Mary's Pregnancy as Miracle

She knew the planet tilts on its axis to nearly the same degree that a woman's womb is tilted outward, that we are all walking into and out of the light, every day, and a thousand million times, more than we can ever count or claim to recognize, all the elements converge toward what can only be called a miracle, so often it happens that it must be the very nature of the world.

Haven Kimmel, *The Solace of Leaving Early* (New York: Random House, 2002), 6.

Mary, then, is even more than Elizabeth the prototypical prophet, the first example of the heroic protagonist that will carry Luke's story along. The careful reader will notice that Luke never qualifies this positive image of Mary. In 8:19-21, Jesus does not indicate that the crowd around him is his true family; instead, he says that his mother and brothers are those who hear the word of God and do it, as Mary has done in this first chapter. In 11:27-28, Jesus does not deny that his mother is blessed, but explains why: not because she gave birth to him and raised him, but because she heard God's word and guarded it in her heart (2:51).[39] Luke uses Mary to set a pattern for the kind of hero we are to expect. [Mary as Ideal Disciple]

More than that, as Tannehill notes, Luke uses Mary and her song to begin the characterization of God. God is Lord, Savior, Mighty One, Holy. God takes careful notice of a girl in Galilee, choosing her out of all the families of the earth to make her a blessing to all the earth. God disperses and unseats the powerful, but lifts up and fills the poor. God stands by God's promises. Mary voices the authoritative, authorial point of view: this is the God of the Gospel of Luke, whose actions are often couched in the "divine passive" and who is not often directly described. Mary's song inscribes God in more concrete (and in the end, more reliable) terms than even Gabriel. The angel gets the first word, but his God will put Jesus on David's throne to rule over Israel forever; when has that happened, either in the narrative or in the witness of any of Luke's readers? Mary gets the last word: her God will use Jesus to bless the poor, undo the rich, and be faithful to the promise to Abraham ("I will make of you a great nation; I will make your name a blessing; all the families of the earth will be blessed by you").

> **Mary as Ideal Disciple**
>
> Mary is a "prototype of the Church," and this for two reasons: she is the place of the real and bodily indwelling of the Word in the most intimate union of mother and child sharing the same flesh; and, in the spiritual sphere, she is—and to this the former is due—a servant, in her entire person, body and soul, one who knows no law of her own, but only conformity to the word of God. . . . She is the model which should govern contemplation, if it is to keep clear of two dangers: one, that of seeing the word only as something external, instead of the profoundest mystery within our own being, that in which we live, move, and are; the other, that of regarding the word as so interior to us that we confuse it with our own being, with a natural wisdom given to us once for all, and ours to use as we will.
>
> Hans Urs von Balthasar, *Prayer* (trans. A. V. Littledale; New York: Paulist, 1961), 22–23.

Here we begin the theme of God's choice of the poor, and Jesus' salvation of the poor and condemnation of the rich. No educated American like me, sitting at a word processor in an air-conditioned office, has the full experience of either, for I have never been poor in the way that Mary means, and so far God has not crushed me for my wealth as she predicts. Luke's Gospel, Mary's God, and Mary's Son will not prove easy for me or for my readers, or else we are not paying attention. This year, Americans gave less to the poor than the year before; in fact, we Americans spent more on dog food, or chewing gum, or many other single convenience items, than we gave to the poor. We must face the truth: we are the bad guys in this story we're reading. If God chooses the poor, we are doomed. If God scatters the rich, the proud, and the powerful, we will be dust in the wind.

Is the Magnificat good news? That will inevitably depend on how we structure our lives in response to the calls of Mary, John the Baptist, and Jesus to do right by the poor. Listen to it again, this time in a more fluid translation:

My soul proclaims the greatness of the Lord,
My spirit rejoices in God my Savior,
Who has looked with favor on me, a lowly servant.
From this day all generations shall call me blessed:
The Almighty has done great things for me
And holy is the name of the Lord,

Whose mercy is on those who fear God
From generation to generation.

The arm of the Lord is strong,
And has scattered the proud in their conceit.
God has cast down the mighty from their thrones
And lifted up the lowly.
God has filled the hungry with good things,
And sent the rich away empty.
God has come to the aid of Israel, the chosen servant,
Remembering the promise of mercy,
The promise made to our forebears,
To Abraham and to his children forever.[40]

Birth of John; the Benedictus, 1:57-80

"God is an iron," according to a Spider Robinson story[41]; certainly Luke was, a lover and practitioner of irony. This story is a great example of how he can blend comic and tragic elements into the same episode, and of how wry, how ironic, was his comic sense. Irony happens when someone in the story knows less than someone else. Usually the reader is also in the know, giving the reader a sort of insider's perspective and creating feelings of pity or ridicule for the poor sap. Luke sometimes uses a crowd as the ignorant actor, as he does in this story; it is a technique he uses elsewhere both for comic effect (Acts 28:1-6) and for tragic (Luke 23:18-25, 27-30, 48).

Elizabeth's due date arrives, and she gives birth, and when they hear about it, her neighbors and kinspeople come to rejoice with her and to "magnify the Lord for his mercy," just as Mary had done. Gabriel had predicted "many will rejoice at his birth," and so they do, and that John would turn people to the Lord, and that, too, seems to be happening. All is well until the eighth day, at John's circumcision: "they," the neighbors and relations, began to call him "Zechariah."[42] "No, indeed," says Elizabeth, "but he will be called John." This naming business is a conundrum for commentators. In Old Testament birth stories, sometimes the mother and sometimes the father named the child, but it always happened at birth. We know that Luke was thinking of Abraham and Sarah and other biblical characters as he wrote these episodes; those stories are supposed to be in the back of the reader's mind, so that we can tell when the characters are acting in surprising ways. In Luke's imagination, then, either parent can name the child, and Elizabeth probably had already done so when she gave birth—we are not supposed to imagine that she spent the first eight days of his life calling him Roscoe. How did she know the baby's name was John? Had Zechariah or God told Elizabeth the name of the child? Luke leaves that silent, so that we can understand it either way. Given that the crowd at the temple knew Zechariah had seen a vision (1:22) and that the couple has been at home together for at least nine months after Zechariah's revelation (1:23-24), it seems reasonable to think that Zechariah could have written her a note. But it is also reasonable to think that, since Elizabeth is a prophet (1:41-45), the Holy Spirit gave her the name. Either way, the name comes from God's command, and both parents know it; there is nothing particularly remarkable about that, given what we know of the characters.

The crowd of relatives, however, thinks that they have the right to name the baby. Because none of them, Elizabeth's relatives, has the name "John," they try to veto her choice. Turning to Zechariah for support, they make hand motions to him—do they think he is deaf as well as mute?—and somehow communicate that they want to know his choice for a name—have they lost their powers of speech, since they, too, are disobeying the angel's command? Zechariah solves the problem, asking for a writing tablet, and writing, "John is his name." And they are all amazed—at what? That the mother and father had already agreed on a name? Or that they were not able to carry the day by trying to name him "Zechariah"? The point is that they are clueless to God's plan and to how God has already been working, and because of their ignorance, they are trying to create problems. But—and this is one of Luke's major themes—nothing can thwart God's plan. Gabriel said "You will name him John," and so that is what the aged couple does.

If the friends and relations were amazed by the name, they are floored by what happens next. Zechariah, mute for nine months, now lets fly, praising God with his newly opened mouth and tongue. The crowd's reaction is instructive: they are afraid. Of what? Surely not of Zechariah's words, since only moments before they, too, had been praising God for divine mercy to Elizabeth. They are afraid of this demonstration of power, of God's ability to strike a man mute or to loose his tongue, realizing that it could happen to them. Had they been able to enforce their will, and to hijack the naming of the baby, they never would have seen this small miracle. Perhaps they are hearing the whiff, the near miss of God's judgment; do they realize that Elizabeth's and Zechariah's faithfulness to the angel's command has saved them, possibly, from being struck mute themselves?

The crowd, then, switches quickly from being joyous co-celebrants of God's mercy to being parochial obstructionists, insisting that the future prophet must be named after one of them, to being amazed by Elizabeth and Zechariah for following God's command rather than their suggestion, to being afraid once they had seen God's power and mercy exercised on someone in their line of sight. It all happens so fast, and it is all so understated (Luke knows not to explain a joke), and their exit lines leave them still clueless, wondering what this child would become, wandering all over the hill country of Judea talking about their incomprehension. Had they stuck around for the song, they could have learned something.

Zechariah's song is not as clearly organized as Mary's. It does not have the same patterns of paired lines and parallel phrases, and the lines are not as balanced, but it is not quite fair to call it "ramshackle," because it has not been carelessly constructed.[43] Rather than working by parallelism, as is typical for the psalms, this one works more by a series of resumptions, where a theme is stated and then picked up and elaborated later in the poem.[44]

> Blessed be the Lord, the God of Israel,
> Because he visited and made redemption for his people,
> And raised a horn of salvation for us in the house of David his son/servant-boy,
> Just as he said through the mouth of his holy prophets from long ago,
> Salvation from our enemies and from the hand of all who hate us,
> To do mercy to our fathers and to remember his holy covenant,
> The oath he swore to Abraham our father, to appoint us fearlessly,
> Who are rescued from the hand of our enemies,
> to serve him in piety and righteousness before him all our days.
>
> And you, child, will be called Prophet of the Most High,
>   for you will go before the Lord to prepare his way,
> In order to give the knowledge of salvation to his people in the forgiveness of their sins,
> Because of the bowels of mercy of our God,
> In which the dawn from on high will visit us,
> To shine upon those dwelling in darkness and in the shadow of death,
> To direct our feet into the way of peace.

The first strophe begins as a hymn of praise, stating the intent to bless God, and then following with motive clauses, or reasons for the praise. There are three verbs stating what God has done: God visited, God made, and God raised. The first and second verbs share the indirect object "for his people," and the second verb takes "redemption" as its direct object. The third verb has a direct object, "horn of salvation," as well as an indirect object, "for us," and a prepositional phrase, "in the house of David his son," clarifying "horn of salvation." The effect is to have phrases of increasing length and complexity: God

Visited			
Made	redemption	for his people	
Raised	a horn of salvation	for us	in the house of David his son.

Verse 70 introduces the messianic promise, further elaborating what God has done by explaining that it is all according to God's words spoken through the prophets.

The resumptions begin in v. 71. "Salvation" is reprised and inverted: salvation *for* us becomes salvation *from* our enemies and from the hand of all who hate us. "Made" is repeated in v. 72; in v. 68, God made redemption for his people, and in v. 72 makes mercy with our fathers (that is, God acts in *ḥesed*, covenant mercy, when God is faithful to the promises made to the patriarchs). "Makes" is an infinitive, the first of three that give the purpose or the result (or both) of God's actions described in the first three verbs. God's aim in acting, or the result of God's actions, is

To make mercy with the fathers (to act in *ḥesed* as God promised to the patriarchs)
To remember his holy covenant, the oath he swore to Abraham our father,
To grant to us, who are rescued from the hands of our enemies, fearlessly to serve him.

The emphasis on God's faithfulness to the covenant repeats the thrust of v. 70, and the salvation from the enemies repeats v. 71. The only new idea is that God's salvation from our enemies and in accord with the promises has the aim of giving us the chance to serve God without fear.

Thus far, then, the hymn praises God for salvation, and with every line the salvation is narrowed, both in its object and in the description of what sort of salvation is in mind. This is not salvation generally, but for Israel, for us, and from our enemies who hate us. It is salvation through David's line—an expectation for a Davidic redeemer—and to accomplish the promise made to Abraham. Zechariah, like Gabriel and unlike Mary, specifies David, but notice that he does not mention ruling anyone, nor does he recount the Abrahamic promises of being a great nation or gaining possession of a land. Instead, God's aim is to produce a worshiping people who could serve without fear of enemies. Nothing is said about the destruction of the enemies or about the form God's rescue would take. Nothing is said about Jesus, either, and nothing from the context would indicate that Zechariah knows about the birth of God's Son. We should assume that as Mary's song celebrates God's action to her, and then through her to the wider world, Zechariah's song also celebrates what is being done through John, but in reverse order, first in the wider world, and then through John specifically.

The second strophe begins with the turn to John. God's actions are still present in this stanza, but are mediated through John, the Prophet of the Most High. John will prepare the Lord's way and will give knowledge of salvation, defined (in very Lukan terms) as forgiveness of sins. All of this, like everything in the first stanza, is in keeping with God's faithfulness to the covenant. Verses 78b-79 appear to be a metaphorical way of describing how God's salvation will come to the people through John, like the sun dawning, shining in the darkness, illuminating those in the shadow, and putting them onto the path of peace. The object of John's ministry is consistent with the first stanza: God's people, us.

So much for the structure of the poem. The real genius of the poem, and of Luke's use of it in his narrative, comes when one notices how it sits against the story of John's birth and against the ministries of John and Jesus. First, recall how Luke uses the crowds in 1:57-66; they are fickle and obstructionist, ignorant of God's true purposes, beginning in praise and ending in fear. Zechariah's song hopes for better days for these people, for fearlessness, enlightenment, and faithful service to God in the right paths. The priest's song blesses God for redemption tailor-made for the crowd of neighbors and relatives who just left his house! Second, notice how his song anticipates John's ministry. John will prepare the Lord's way (3:4), will preach repentance for the forgiveness of sins (3:3), and will certainly bring the clarity of light to those who hear him preach. And when John mentions the promise to Abraham, it is to caution his listeners that Abrahamic descent is not enough (3:8). This helps to make sense of Zechariah's mention of Abraham: the covenant promise is to rescue "us" so that "we" can serve him in holiness and righteousness and without fear.

The verbal links to Jesus' ministry are much more tragic. Zechariah twice uses the rare word "visit": in v. 68, God visited the people, and in v. 78, the dawn from on high will visit us. That word shows up again in 19:44, when Jesus pronounces doom on Jerusalem because they did not recognize the visitation. Zechariah predicts that John will set "our" feet on the path of peace, but Jesus says that destruction will come on Jerusalem because they were ignorant of the things that lead to peace (19:42). Zechariah's continual use of "us" as the category for those who will receive the blessings of redemption and salvation is particularly tragic. Mary spoke of how God blessed her, but her other categories were not "us" and "them," Israel and "our enemies." Instead, she spoke of rich and poor, powerful and lowly. Jesus' divisions are much more like his mother's than his uncle's: "Blessed are you poor/woe to you rich."[45] Luke's irony, which at first worked to put the reader in sync with God and Elizabeth and Zechariah, feeling superior to the foolish pack of kinfolk, now works to make the reader doubt the security of Zechariah's "us."

Luke's readers, knowing that the temple and Jerusalem had been laid waste some decades before, could have seen the irony. Zechariah is speaking as a prophet filled with God's Spirit, but he has no idea who the "us," the recipients of redemption and salvation and forgiveness of sins, will be. He has much more insight into God's plan for John, but with respect to how this will play out among God's people, he is as clueless as the crowds rehashing their confusion on the hills of Judea. Zechariah sings that John's ministry will bring God's visitation as a light from on high. There will be a glorious light, but it will shine on very few in Judea (2:8-9); there will be a call to walk the path of peace (6:27-31), but very few takers. And in the end, although John and Jesus are sent to enable people to know God's salvation, Jesus will pray, "Father, forgive them; they do not know what they are doing."

The episode ends with an understated summary of John growing up and with the tantalizing note that he was in the wilderness until he began his public ministry. Since the discovery of the Dead Sea Scrolls and the community at Qumran, scholars have wondered if John spent his adolescent years as an Essene, learning from their teachings. Possible—the Essenes practiced immersion, as did John, they looked forward to the near end of the present age, as he did, and they were offering an alternative to sacrifice and worship at the temple in Jerusalem, as he was. But the adult John was certainly not an Essene; he was not out recruiting for Qumran, and they were not hosting him and his followers for Friday night Sabbath meals. Further, the ideas they had in common were also shared with other Jewish groups of the Second Temple period. Finally, Luke likely knew nothing about the Essenes, unless he had read about them in Josephus. Luke probably means for the reader to connect John's desert sojourn with Elijah or Moses, and to make sure that we know John has never been a part of the Jerusalem temple complex.

CONNECTIONS

Luke has given us such wonderful characters in his first chapter. In Zechariah, we have the good, devout man who cannot quite believe that God would bless him as God blessed other people in the past. He knows the story of Abraham and Sarah, and he has been praying that God would bless him and Elizabeth in the same way, but when Gabriel gives him the good news, he cannot simply open his heart to it. This first annunciation story can be fairly called "the gospel rejected," introducing a recurring storyline for Luke: often the people who got the good news first could not accept it.

As Christian interpreters, we must be careful when we preach and teach this to make certain that our hearers do not take this as one more proof of the superiority of Christianity to Judaism: namely, they did not believe God's Son, but we have. It is more likely the case, if your congregation is like me and mine, that much of Jesus' message found in Luke does not strike us as good news, and that we have found ways to duck, dodge, and deconstruct it. "Love your enemies," provided they are not threats to national security. "Give to those who ask," but not to actual beggars—that's what the United Way is for. "Lend, expecting nothing in return"— Jesus must have meant books or cups of sugar, but there's no way he would expect Christians to opt out of the money-making possibilities of investments. No, Zechariah may be much more our photograph than we care to admit—good people who say they want to serve God but balk at God's good news.

In Mary, we get a character to imitate. She calls herself God's slave, and submits to God's good news, although it must have gone through her mind that this "good news" would shake up her world and leave her current plans in tatters. A miracle, yes, but at what cost to her? We do not hear any of this sort of adding up the pros and cons, just "let it be with me according to your word." But lest we think she is naïve, Luke lets her sing an amazing hymn of praise to God. The Magnificat shows that Mary understands how the world works, and understands that Jesus will turn it on its head. When we preach and teach this part of Luke, where the gospel is wholeheartedly accepted and celebrated, we can look in hope to how we would like to serve God and thank God for the invitation. And we can hear the song of Mary for what it is—a statement of faith in God's choice for the poor, against all the evidence of our world, and a statement of personal commitment to be on God's side in this matter.

Elizabeth also accepts God's blessing, as does Mary, and if you connect 1:21-25, 41-45, and 59-60, you get the impression of a spunky woman who can stand up for herself but who does not insist on her own prestige. Her "this is what the Lord has done" may be somewhat ironic—look, God, at the disgrace I have endured; was it really necessary?—and her insistence that the baby be named John are a nice balance to how she defers to Mary and her son. Elizabeth, Luke's first prophet, is perhaps also a good example of how "meek" does not mean "doormat."

The chapter closes with Zechariah getting a second chance. This time he obeys exactly, regains his voice, and gets to sing his own song of praise to God. If we preach Zechariah as an example of the consequences of failing to accept God's revelation, then we can point to the end of Zechariah's story as an illustration of grace after judgment.

NOTES

[1] Frederick W. Danker, *Jesus and the New Age: A Commentary on St. Luke's Gospel* (rev. ed.; Philadelphia: Fortress, 1988), 23; John Nolland, *Luke* (WBC, vols. 35A-C; Dallas TX: Word, 1989-93), 1.4.

[2] François Bovon, *Luke 1: A Commentary on the Gospel of Luke 1:1–9:50*, ed. Helmut Koester (Hermeneia; Minneapolis: Fortress, 2002), 16.

[3] Joel B. Green, *The Gospel of Luke* (NICNT; Grand Rapids: Eerdmans, 1997), 33.

[4] Charles H. Talbert, *Reading Luke: A Literary and Theological Commentary on the Third Gospel* (rev. ed.; Macon GA: Smyth and Helwys, 2002), 7–11; Green, *Luke*, 34.

[5] So Luke Timothy Johnson, *The Gospel of Luke* (SP, vol. 3; Collegeville MN: Liturgical Press, 1991), 30, who notes that the verb can be read neutrally or as criticism of the predecessors. His point, "why should Luke write if the previous work was satisfactory," leaves out of consideration all sorts of motives one might have to write. Perhaps Luke wrote because Theophilus asked him to, or because he enjoyed it, or because he had new ideas. Green's point, that Luke's absorption of much of Mark proves that he had no real problems with it, is well put (Green, *Luke*, 37, n. 20).

[6] Johnson, *Luke*, 27–30; Bovon, *Luke 1*, 19–25; and Joseph A. Fitzmyer, *The Gospel According to Luke* (AB 28 and 28A; Garden City NY: Doubleday, 1981), 1.291-92, suggest readings that understand Luke to be offering mild criticism.

[7] For example, Wayne Meeks, "Assisting the Word by Making (Up) History: Luke's Project and Ours," *Int* 57 (April 2003): 154.

[8] BAGD, 767; Bovon, *Luke 1*, 21; Loveday Alexander, *The Preface to Luke's Gospel: Literary Convention and Social Context In Luke 1.1-4 and Acts 1.1* (Cambridge: Cambridge University Press, 1993), 127–31.

[9] For example, Luke ends the section on John the Baptist by writing about how Herod Antipas put him in prison. In the next verse, Luke writes, "when Jesus had been baptized," leaving the reader to surmise that John did it. In the case of Jesus' baptism, one might think that Luke avoided writing about it because it was problematic to think of the Lord being baptized by someone else.

[10] Fitzmyer, *Luke 1*, 299–300.

[11] Bovon, *Luke 1*, 23.

[12] Alexander, *Preface*, 187–200.

[13] Darrell Bock, *Luke* (Grand Rapids MI: Baker, 1994), 63–64.

[14] Loveday Alexander's work has shown that the language and style of Luke's preface does not match up well with prefaces to Greek histories, and so it seems unlikely Luke intended the Gospel to be received as history. However, she has also shown that Luke's use of Greek that imitates the style of the Septuagint was a "prestige code"—a strategy for getting readers to take his work as informed and important. See Alexander, *Acts in Its Ancient Literary Context* (London: T & T Clark, 2007).

[15] *m. Tamid* 5:2: "[The officer] said to them, 'Ye that are new to the incense preparation, come and cast lots,' and they cast lots, and the lot fell on whom it fell."

[16] *m. Tamid* 5:4: "He to whom fell the lot of [offering] the incense took the ladle. The ladle was like a large golden three-*kab* measure, holding three *kabs*; within was a dish, heaped up full of incense. It had a lid and over this a kind of covering."

[17] *m. Tamid* 6:1-2.

[18] *m. Tamid* 6:3.

[19] The question of how many LXX allusions there are in Gabriel's announcement is vexed; Mark Coleridge finds parallels to Gen 16:11-12; 17:19; Num 6:3; Lev 10:9; Judg 13:4; 2 Kgs 2:9-10; 1 Sam 1:11; Dan 10:12; Mal 2:6; 3:1, 24; Sir 48:10. Coleridge identifies this as Luke's attempt to cover the breadth of the Old Testament—Torah, Prophets, and Writings—to impress upon readers that God is bringing all things to fulfillment in this story. See Coleridge, *The Birth of the Lukan Narrative: Narrative as Christology in Luke 1–2* (Sheffield UK: Sheffield Academic Press, 1993), 35–36.

[20] Coleridge, *Birth*, 43.

[21] So Coleridge, *Birth*, 48; Raymond E. Brown, *The Birth of the Messiah: A Commentary on the Infancy Narratives in the Gospels of Matthew and Luke* (Garden City NY: Doubleday, 1993), 282.

[22] So Ambrose, "For there is a prescribed age for each duty, and what is fitting at one time is unseemly at another" (Exposition of the Gospel of Luke, 1.46), or Maximus of Turin, "Elizabeth, conscious of her old age, blushes that her womb is heavy with the one she has conceived" (Sermon 5.4), cited in Arthur A. Just Jr., ed., *Luke* (ACCS: NT, vol. 3; Downer's Grove IL: Intervarsity Press, 2003), 10–11.

23 *m. Niddah* 5:6: "A girl eleven years old and one day—her vows must be examined; if she is twelve years old and one day her vows are valid, but they must be examined throughout the twelfth year"; see Tal Ilan, *Jewish Women in Greco-Roman Palestine* (Peabody MA: Hendrickson, 1996), 65–69.

24 James F. Kay, "Mary's Song—And Ours," *ChrCent* 114/35 (10 December 1997): 1157.

25 C. F. D. Moule, *An Idiom Book of New Testament Greek* (Cambridge: Cambridge University Press, 1959), 107 allows that either translation is possible, but calls the first "distinctly irregular" since the placement of the definite article does not clearly make the participle into an adjective.

26 Sharon Ringe, *Luke* (Louisville KY: Westminster/John Knox, 1995), 32; so also an earlier article by Fitzmyer ("The Virginal Conception of Jesus in the New Testament," *Theological Studies* 34 [1973]: 541–75), who later agrees with the judgment of Raymond Brown that such a line of interpretation is an unlikely reading of Luke's understanding; see Fitzmyer, *Luke*, 1.338; Brown, *Birth*, 303–309.

27 Plutarch, *Parallel Lives, Life of Alexander* 2.1-5.

28 Talbert, *Reading Luke*, 22–23; Bovon, *Luke 1*, 52.

29 Fitmyer, *Luke*, 1.351; Nolland, *Luke*, 1.54.

30 So Green, *Luke*, 90.

31 Fitzmyer, *Luke*, 1.258, identifies two prophetic, poetic oracles in vv. 42 and 45, with intervening prose; Brown, *Birth*, 342, calls it a canticle.

32 Robert C. Tannehill, *The Narrative Unity of Luke-Acts: A Literary Intepretation, vol. 1 of The Gospel According to Luke* (Philadelphia: Fortress, 1986), 1.31, likens it to an operatic aria, but I think the pastiche of Old Testament quotations sounds more like Handel.

33 Talbert, *Reading Luke*, 25, uses this term; Brown calls it an epilogue (*Birth*, 252).

34 Green, *Luke*, 92–93; Alan R. Culpepper, *The Gospel of Luke* (*NIB*, vol. 9; Nashville: Abingdon, 1995), 54.

35 Ringe, *Luke*, 33; Green, *Luke*, 94.

36 It is possible to interpret this episode as if Mary is not pregnant (so Coleridge, *Birth*, 79–83), but if she is not, then Elizabeth is not correct to call her a mother.

37 Tannehill, *Narrative Unity*, 1.26-32. His analysis agrees in large measure with that of Brown (*Birth*, 355–65), Fitzmyer (*Luke*, 1.356-369), and Eben Scheffler, *Suffering in Luke's Gospel* (Zürich: Theologischer Verlag, 1993), 49–54. Stephen Farris (*The Hymns of Luke's Infancy Narratives: Their Origin, Meaning and Significance* [Sheffield UK: Sheffield, 1985], 113–14) arguing that it has the form of a hymn of praise, divides it into introductory word of praise (46–47), two motive clauses (48, 49a), amplification of the second motive clause (49–53), and summary (54–55). He is disinclined to divide the poem into strophes because he finds the shifts in the poem to be more gradual than stanzas would imply. This analysis, in my view, underestimates the shift from Mary's self-focus in the first stanza to the world-focus in the second.

38 Green, *Luke*, 95, notes the link to the journey theme, pointing out that Mary's trip is not commanded by God and seems extremely implausible for a young unmarried Palestinian girl.

39 Talbert, *Reading Luke*, 25–26.

[40] See *The Chalice Hymnal* (Atlanta: Chalice, 1995), 131.

[41] Spider Robinson, *God Is an Iron and Other Stories* (Waterville ME: Gale Group, 2002), 103–26. The full line is "If a person who indulges in gluttony is a glutton, and a person who commits a felony is a felon, then God is an iron. Or else He's the dumbest designer that ever lived."

[42] The verb *ekaloun* is in the imperfect tense, so it can mean "they were calling him" or "they wanted to call him."

[43] Farris writes, "It is true that certain themes are reiterated but the hymn gives the impression of a rather ramshackle construction" (*Hymns*, 133).

[44] So Tannehill, *Narrative Unity*, 1.33.

[45] Tannehill, *Narrative Unity*, 1.35–36, develops this line of interpretation.

NATIVITY STORIES, PART 2

Luke 2

COMMENTARY

Birth of Jesus, 2:1-20

We all know how the birth of Jesus looked. First, there was the stall, made of rough wood, with straw strewn on the floor. We probably imagine it as part of a larger wooden barn filled with the friendly beasts, the cattle looking over the edge of their stall into the one where the Holy Family was gathered. Then there was the manger—a feedbox or a freestanding trough also filled with hay, the infant Jesus nestled into it, wrapped in a blanket. Mary and Joseph leaned over him, their eyes filled with love and wonder. The shepherds were there, in their striped bathrobes and head cloths, each holding a long shepherd's crook, with one or two sheep that declined to be left in the fields. The magi came, too, parking their camels outside, bringing in jars of incense and boxes of gold coins. The whole scene was lit by the soft but brilliant light of the star hanging over the manger. We have seen it so many times; if we grew up in church, we probably played one of those roles or helped to organize the annual pageant. We have arranged the figures on our mantels, have given and received cards decorated with this scene, and have sung carols that reinforce the picture. Too bad it isn't what we find in the Gospel.

The reader may know that there is no evidence that the church celebrated the birth of Christ until the fourth century, when the date of Christmas, December 25, was set as a feast day by the Western church—probably to counter the popular celebration of the feast of the winter solstice. The Eastern churches celebrated Jesus' birth and baptism on January 6, on the Feast of Epiphany. After the christological controversies, when it became important to make clear that Jesus in no sense became the Son of God at his baptism, the Eastern churches (excepting the Armenian Orthodox, who still retain January 6 as the date to celebrate Christ's birth) began to shift toward the Western practice. Christians began to put on Nativity pageants during the high Middle Ages, during the time of St. Francis, who thought illiterate peasants needed to see the story of Christ's birth. He organized people to stand as tableaux, dramatizing the words of the Gospels.[1]

All this is simply to point out a contrast. In our day, the birth of Jesus may be, after the crucifixion, the Gospel scene most easily visualized by the general public. In Luke's day, and for centuries thereafter, it was not nearly so familiar. Other scenes—the baptism of Jesus, the feeding of the 5,000, stilling the tempest—were more frequent scenes of early Christian art. On the other hand, what moderns "know" is not the biblical account, but an account stemming from and nourished by American culture, an account harnessed to an enormous marketing campaign for spending large sums of money. It would not be terribly useful for us to ask modern readers to replace their image with what we imagine Luke's to have been. Instead, we can ask about the ethics of our readings: what can we do to use the power of this symbol more responsibly, in the service of goals more in keeping with Luke's?

Luke crafts his account to be not an ageless story—a nativity set that will fit in any home at any time—but as a drama taking place within an emphatically political environment. He begins with Caesar Augustus and his decision to enroll the populated world. To be blunt and brief, we cannot identify the census Luke has in mind; it is likely that he was thinking of the one that happened a few years after Jesus' birth.[2] It is also hard to imagine why the Roman government would have been interested in requiring male Jews who claimed Davidic descent to return to Bethlehem, David's hometown. We can find no parallel to such a census method, and with good reason: governments want to list people at their current addresses, at the spot where they make the money the government wants to collect. Luke and Luke's readers would have known this, so it would appear that Luke is being sarcastic—typical, is it not, of the stupid Romans to move people around for no good reason—and ironic—convenient, is it not, for the stupid Romans to make a rule that gets the Messiah's mother into the city predicted for his birth.

In keeping both with this sense of parody and with later Roman usage, Luke calls Octavian "Caesar Augustus." Octavian himself, modest chap that he was, wrote that Augustus was a cognomen assigned to him "by the Senate and the Roman people to commemorate my virtue, clemency, justice, and piety."[3] In his own day, Augustus was celebrated as a divine savior, the beginning of a new era; a contemporary inscription states, "Not only has he outstripped all benefactors who have gone before him, but he will leave posterity no hope of surpassing him. The birthdate of our God has signaled the beginning of good news for the world."[4] Augustus was also the self-proclaimed inaugurator of the Pax Romana, the so-called era of world peace guaranteed by the might of the Roman legions. It was a complete fiction, of course; there were wars and military campaigns, but it played well to be seen as the savior, the peace-giver:

> I extended the frontiers of all the provinces of the Roman people on whose boundaries were peoples not subject to our empire. I restored peace to the Gallic and Spanish provinces and likewise to Germany. . . . I caused peace to be restored in the Alps . . . without undeservedly making war against any people. . . . By my command and under my auspices two armies were led almost at the same time into Ethiopia and into Arabia which is called Felix, and very large forces of the enemy belonging to both peoples were killed in battle, and many towns were captured.[5]

Augustus was also celebrated, not surprisingly, by poets to whom he acted as patron. Virgil's *Aeneid* calls him "son of a god, who will once again establish the golden age,"[6] while Horace promises, "as long as Caesar is guardian of the state, neither civil dissension nor violence shall banish peace, nor wrath that forges swords and brings discord and misery to cities."[7] This was state-supported propaganda, a first-century advertising campaign among the literate in defense of the benevolent rule of the emperor.[8]

Luke and his readers knew all the puffery that lay behind the title "Augustus," and knew that emperors after Octavian had delighted in using the same title. One suspects that in Luke's mind, "Caesar Augustus" sounded something like "Emperor Godly" rather than "our revered Emperor."

Luke also names Quirinius the governor of Syria. Publius Sulpicius Quirinius was appointed legate of Syria in AD 6, after Herod the Great's son Archelaus proved incapable of ruling Judea. Thereafter, Judeans

The Census at Bethlehem

Pieter Bruegel, the Elder (c.1525–1569). *The Census at Bethlehem*. Musee d'Art Ancien, Musees Royaux des Beaux-Arts, Brussels, Belgium. (Credit: Scala/Art Resource, NY)

Bruegel's painting gets at the insignificance of the Holy Family, almost lost in the hum of activity in a small village. Bruegel also paints Mary and Joseph to look much like all the other figures in the scene—very true to the Lukan account.

were ruled by prefects or procurators who reported to the legate. Luke's mention of him may be, as some suggest, to relate the birth of Jesus to world events,[9] but his name also would remind the audience of Rome's colonial policies that brought so much misery to Palestine.

Joseph went, says Luke, from Galilee to Bethlehem. As this is his only role in Luke's story, we should note that it puts him, too, in the role of a traveler just as Mary has been and Jesus will be. Luke calls Mary "his betrothed," as if the marriage had not yet happened.[10] If he is serious, then Jesus was not only born to a virgin, but also born out of wedlock, and the whole notion of Mary and Joseph traveling together would have been a scandal. Most commentators suggest that Luke wrote "betrothed" to indicate that Joseph and Mary had not yet consummated their marriage.[11] In either case—whether Mary was not yet married, or married but not yet Joseph's wife in all senses—the first-century audience would understand the unsettled, ambiguous position Mary occupied.

Generations of painters and Christmas pageant organizers have pictured Mary giving birth in a barn surrounded by animals, but these are American or European features; so far as we can tell, first-century Palestinians did not keep their animals in barns. The poor seem to have brought them into the house at night, separated from the rest of the family by having the sleeping area raised above the dirt floor.[12] Luke says that Jesus was laid in a feeding trough, but does not say where the manger was. We also cannot be certain what Luke meant by "inn," since the same word (κατάλυμα, *katalyma*) can mean a room of a house (as it does in Luke 22:11) or a place where travelers could spend the night—a large room or "flophouse" providing sleeping space and not much else. Scholars are divided on which reading is most likely to have been the way Luke imagined the scene. In the first, Mary and Joseph are in a spare room in someone's home, but as it is a small home and the room is full, the only place to put the baby is in a feed trough, outside the house.[13] In the second, Mary and Joseph are in the Bethlehem equivalent of a homeless shelter, and again, the only room for the baby is in the feed trough, located inside the shelter but away from the sleeping platform.[14] Ancient Christian tradition as early as AD 150 located the manger in a cave in Bethlehem, but this may well have been a guess based on the supposition that Mary needed a private place to give birth, and that the place was where animals were ordinarily kept.[15] In any case the image of a hotel with a "no vacancy" sign and a heartless innkeeper who turns away a pregnant woman is based on modern understandings of an "inn."

So Jesus is born under the following conditions. First, Emperor Godly, in his infinite wisdom, decides to enroll the whole world. Second, for no better reason than that, Joseph must leave his home in Nazareth to go about seventy miles south to Bethlehem to participate in the census. Third, for no reason given in the text whatsoever, Mary—still not Joseph's wife in some sense, pregnant, and close to term—travels with him, and while there gives birth. There is not enough space wherever they are staying for the baby Jesus to lie next to his mother, so she lays him in the trough where the animals feed. Could she not have stayed with kinfolk in Nazareth? Whose decision was it for her to travel with him— Caesar's, or Joseph's, or her own? We don't know. Thus far, this is a story about the powers that be, the emperors and their lackeys who depose rulers and send in tax collectors and who, if they wish, can cook up a crazy scheme to move Galilean carpenters around like checkers. [St. Jerome on the Manger]

Birth stories of famous people are supposed to be predictive. The infant Heracles strangled a python with his bare baby hands when it appeared in his crib. When Alexander the Great was born, according to Plutarch, a new star appeared in the heavens. "When John Henry was a little baby, sitting on his daddy's knee/ he picked up a hammer and a little piece of steel/ said This hammer's going to be the death of me, Lord, Lord." You get the picture—what does Jesus' birth tell us about who he would be?

Part of the answer may come when the scene shifts to shepherds on nightly guard duty. "Shepherd" is rich with nuances: David was a shepherd who became a king, so the new baby born in David's city should rightly be acclaimed first to and then by shepherds. Ezekiel prophesied against the false shepherds of the flock of Israel, warning that when the true shepherd came, he would protect the flock and punish the false shepherds who harmed it. Shepherds were peasants, performing unskilled labor, and were on the other end of the power scale from Emperor Godly. The message comes to the shepherds, rather than to Augustus or to any other person of power, because Jesus' destiny is to unseat the powerful. The baby born in unsettled circumstances is the real Savior, the bringer of peace, rather than Augustus or any subsequent emperor.

The angel calls the baby's birth "a great joy to all the people" and calls the child "a Savior, who is the Lord Christ." Gabriel predicted great joy at John's birth, so this announcement brings the two in line. "Savior," as noted above, was used for Augustus and for other

St. Jerome on the Manger

He was found in no Holy of Holies that shone with gold, precious stones, pure silk and silver. He was not born in the midst of gold and riches, but in the midst of dung, in a stable where our sins were filthier than the dung.

Jerome, *On the Nativity of the Lord*, cited in Arthur A. Just Jr., ed., *Luke* (ACCS: NT, vol. 3; Downer's Grove IL: Intervarsity Press, 2003), 39.

emperors. It was applied to gods such as Asclepius, god of healing, and to "personalities who are active in the world's affairs," such as philosophers and generals.[16] "Savior," in other words, marks Jesus as a doer of good, but does not specify what form that good will take. "Lord Christ" or "Christ the Lord" is an unusual form. Christ, or Messiah, refers to the person from David's line who would restore the fortunes of Israel. "Lord" denotes superior rank, and was used by slaves for masters, wives and children for husbands and fathers, lower-born for nobility, and everyone for God. Since this is the only place in the New Testament where the two nouns are stuck together like this, it would appear that Luke is contrasting this baby with the divine Augustus; whereas Octavian got his title of "revered Emperor" by Senate decree, Jesus was acclaimed "Lord Christ" by God's angels at his birth and by God's act of resurrection after his death (Acts 2:36).

The angel tells the shepherds how they will pick Jesus out from any other infant in Bethlehem: he will be the one in the feed trough. When they arrive, they find it just as the angel has predicted. This seems to have been enough to convince them that the baby was worth talking about, so like Elizabeth's relatives, they spread the word around. But unlike the relatives, who speak about what they do not know, the shepherds praise God for what they have seen and heard. The narrator describes them imitating the angels, who likewise give glory and praise to God.[17] Contrary to our usual tableaux, the shepherds do not linger over the manger; they come in haste, and then leave to go spread the news. Like Mary, they seem more than a little unlikely to have been chosen to be first recipients and then bearers of God's good news, but they take to their job with enthusiasm. [Shepherds and Ministers]

As for Mary, Joseph, and the baby, this story places them in the middle, between Augustus and the shepherds. Augustus decrees, and they move, and all the world with them, and so they find themselves in a place without enough room for them and their baby. Barbara Robinson describes them this way: "They looked like the people you see on the six o'clock news—refugees, sent to wait in some strange ugly place, with all their boxes and sacks around them."[18] But the shepherds hear the voices of the angels in the night, and go "with haste" to look them up—can you picture this? If the Holy Family is

Shepherds and Ministers

AΩ The term "shepherd" has rich connotations not only backward, in the history of Israel, but forward, in the history of the church. First Peter urges the elders of the churches of Asia Minor to act like good shepherds towards those in their charge, imitating Jesus, the "chief shepherd" (1 Pet 5:1-4). Likewise, Eph 4:11 uses the term "shepherd" in a list of Christian leadership roles enabled by gifts of the spirit; the Latin word for shepherd, "pastor," quickly became one of the main titles for Christian ministers. As many ancient interpreters note, God's good news was delivered to "pastors," not just for their own salvation, but so that they could deliver it to others who needed to hear the good news.

squeezed into some guest room or flophouse, having to resort to putting the baby in the manger, where are the shepherds standing while they look? We need to imagine them crowding in, straining to get a look—at an infant, wrapped in cloth like any other, lying in a makeshift crib—and then gasping with wonder, explaining to all the other grumpy lodgers why they are making such a fuss over the newborn. Whose version of the story makes most sense: are Mary, Joseph, and Jesus government-manufactured refugees or the instruments of God's revelation to the world?

In the last three verses, Luke, like an on-the-street reporter, gives us three sample reactions. The crowds who hear the shepherds are, predictably, "amazed," neither believing nor unbelieving, but shaken. Mary stores up all that happens and turns everything over in her heart; not an unquestionably positive response, either, since the verb can mean "think about" or "argue with."[19] But Mary, by not letting go of the episodes, is more in line with God's will than are the crowds. The shepherds, though, are the ideal responders, praising God and repeating what God had shown them.

The popular image of Christmas in twenty-first-century American culture is manifestly non-Christian, although it is thoroughly infused with elements of Luke's nativity story. In John Irving's *A Prayer for Owen Meany*, there is a wonderful demonstration of how the hymn "Away in a Manger" exerts more control over the traditional Christmas pageant than the Gospel of Luke:

> It was only our second rehearsal of the Christmas Pageant when Owen decided that the crib, in which he could fit—but tightly—was unnecessary and even incorrect. Dudley Wiggin based his entire view of the behavior of the Christ Child on the Christmas carol "Away in a Manger," of which there are only two verses.
>
> It was this carol that convinced the Rev. Wiggin that the Baby Jesus mustn't cry:
>> The cattle are lowing, the baby awakes
>> But little Lord Jesus, no crying he makes.
>
> If Mr. Wiggin put such stock in the second verse of "Away in a Manger," Owen argued that we should also be instructed by the very first verse.
>> Away in a manger, no crib for his bed
>> The little Lord Jesus lay down his sweet head.
>
> "IF IT SAYS THERE WAS NO CRIB, WHY DO WE HAVE A CRIB?" Owen asked. Clearly, he found the crib restraining.[20]

The Lukan birth narrative and especially the Virgin Birth underlie Irving's plot and the character of Owen Meany in much more direct ways than it informs Rev. Wiggin's production, an irony that works only if Irving can presume both the verisimilitude (with some license for parody) of the pageant episode and the reader's knowledge of the rudiments of the nativity story. Barbara Robinson's *The Best Christmas Pageant Ever* exaggerates the awfulness of the Herdmans ("absolutely the worst kids in the history of the world") who invade a church's nativity pageant, but not the essential sameness of those pageants, endlessly exhibiting the characters of Luke's story without ever explaining their motivations. Cigar-smoking, worldly-wise Imogene Herdman, who has never heard the story at all, has serious problems with its credibility when she first hears it read:

> When Mother read about there being no room at the inn, Imogene's jaw dropped and she sat up in her seat. "My God!" she said. "Not even for Jesus . . . ." "Well, now, after all," Mother explained, "nobody knew the baby was going to turn out to be Jesus." "You said Mary knew," Ralph said. "Why didn't she tell them?" "I would have told them!" Imogene put in. "Boy, would I have told them! What was the matter with Joseph that he didn't tell them? Her pregnant and everything," she grumbled.[21]

In Robinson's story, the church girl who always plays Mary is Alice Wendleken, "because she's so smart, so neat and clean, and most of all, so holy-looking."[22] But when Imogene gets the part, she plays it quite differently:

> Imogene, for instance, didn't know that Mary was supposed to be acted out in one certain way—sort of quiet and dreamy and out of this world. The way Imogene did it, Mary was a lot like Mrs. Santoro at the Pizza Parlor. Mrs. Santoro is a big fat lady with a little skinny husband and nine children and she yells and hollers and hugs her kids and slaps them around. That's how Imogene's Mary was—loud and bossy. "Get away from the baby!" she yelled at Ralph, who was Joseph. And she made the Wise Men keep their distance.[23]

Irving's and Robinson's accounts of Christmas pageants show us that while it may not be possible to eradicate the American cultural reading of Luke's nativity, it is certainly possible to use it as a hermeneutical foil. Imogene Herdman seems the more outlandish character at the beginning of Robinson's book, but by the end the reader is convinced that she has caught the spirit of the real Mary. By means of parody—parody suggested by the Lukan account—interpreters may be able to persuade their audiences to rethink their beliefs and practices.

Giotto's *Nativity*

The artist includes shepherds and angels from the Lukan text, and puts the whole scene outdoors, under a wooden shelter, with the feeding trough in the left foreground. Joseph is napping, as is customary for nativity paintings from this era. This one also has a midwife assisting Mary. The painting illustrates how believers always read the stories in light of their own culture: what Italian noblewoman of the 1300s would have given birth without a midwife, or what Italian husband of the same period would have stayed awake for the delivery?

Giotto di Bondone (1266–1336). *The Nativity*. Scrovegni Chapel, Padua, Italy. (Credit: Cameraphoto/Art Resource, NY)

The greatest challenge to the interpreter, however, is the commercialism that defines the American holiday. Leigh Eric Schmidt argues persuasively that there is "whispered ambivalence" about Christmas: "the suspicion that the holidays have somehow been worked up by Hallmark or Macy's, that the holidays are not our own, hangs like a shadow over the modern American celebration."[24] This fear is not without warrant, since the irony of buying sweatshirts or mugs reading "Keep Christ in Christmas," or of watching innumerable television specials paid for by commercials purporting to address "the true meaning of Christmas," regularly escapes the American public. Commercialism, like a faceless Caesar Augustus, seems to drive us all slouching toward Bethlehem, forced by social mores and the expectations of others to celebrate by spending, lest we be considered unloving. The interpreter can count on a church audience's agreement that Christmas is far too commercial, that children expect too many presents, and that we would all be better off with less. But would the church, for example, be able to get away with teaching that the whole myth of Santa bringing presents to good children all over the world is materialist propaganda that blinds us to the real needs of the poor? Can we use Luke's story to point out that Jesus was the only gift given that night, that God gave him to the poor, and that the wealthy and powerful were excluded? [Christmas and the Poor]

Christmas and the Poor

. . . that it should ever have been possible for anyone to doubt that the church of Jesus Christ is the friend and champion of the little people is enough to make Christmas angels weep. . . . Let your mind dwell upon Bethlehem, and your Christmas festivity can include every bereaved and suffering family in our land. And in every third world country, every country traumatized by war, the only kind of God who makes sense is the one who is never on the side of the big battalions and knows nothing of that sort of power, but can say with literal age-long truth, I was hungry, I was naked, I was in prison. . . . Let your mind dwell upon Bethlehem, and the weakness of God will command your worship more than the images of his omnipotence ever did.

John V. Taylor, *The Incarnate God*, (New York: Continuum, 2004), 10, 16.

Jesus in the Temple, Act I, 2:21-40

In the next two sections (2:21-40 and 2:41-52), Jesus and his family appear in the temple, obediently following the Law, connected firmly to the priestly and prophetic traditions of Israel. This first act is composite: Jesus' naming and circumcision; the sacrifice for purification; Simeon's appearance and oracles; and Anna's testimony.

The first episode begins at an unspecified spot; in 2:21, Luke most likely thinks that the Holy Family is still in Bethlehem, since v. 22 spells out their movement to Jerusalem. True to the command laid down in Genesis 17:12, Mary and Joseph see that Jesus is circumcised on the eighth day after his birth; in this way, Jesus becomes a participant in the covenant with Abraham, following the practice of Jews "throughout your generations" (Gen 17:9). The infant is named Jesus, just as Gabriel had instructed Mary, but interestingly, Luke does not specify who named him; in contrast with the naming of John, where both mother and father must override the objections of their friends and relations, this naming happens quietly. The passive "he was called" matches "when Jesus was baptized" (3:21). In both cases, we must assume that Luke expects the readers to think of human agency: one or both of his parents named him; John baptized him. But the passive voice in the Bible is often a way to imply God's activity, and Luke's phrasing may be intended to remind us of the overarching plan of God behind what happens to Jesus.

In the next scene, the Holy Family goes to Jerusalem "for their purification." More specifically, they need to do at least two things to be obedient to the Law. First, they must redeem Jesus, their first-born son. Exodus 34:19-20 declares that every firstborn belongs to God. Clean animals, such as sheep or goats, would be sacrificed, but unclean animals, like donkeys, would be redeemed by offering a different animal instead. Sons, according to Numbers 18:16, were redeemed with a monetary payment of five shekels. Philo and Josephus both say the same; Philo notes that it is one of the few offerings that was fixed, rather than scaled according to wealth or poverty.[25]

The second task in the temple was Mary's purification. Childbirth rendered women unclean, and the duration of the uncleanness depended on the sex of the child. Bearing a son meant that for seven days, Mary was unclean to the same degree as during her normal menstrual period: she, her clothes, her bed, and wherever she sat would transmit uncleanness by contact. Now, this was not a fatal condition, either for the woman or for the persons rendered unclean through contact, since anyone who contracted secondary uncleanness by sitting on her bed could wash and wait until evening and be clean again. One imagines that in some households, the woman could stay to herself in a separate room, but in poor, one-room, one-bed households, her husband either stayed unclean until his wife's week was up, or went daily to the *miqveh* where he could immerse himself and be clean again [Miqveh; miqvaoth]. For another thirty-three days, she was also forbidden to enter the temple or to touch "holy things"—for example, food that had been set aside as a gift to the temple or as payment of tithes. At the end of this period, the woman could come to the temple with an animal offering. The two doves that Mary brought were the required offering for the poor (all of these rules are in Lev 12:1-8).

> **Miqveh; miqvaoth**
>
> A *miqveh* (pl., *miqvaoth*) was an immersion pool, usually dug into the ground and then lined with something so that the water did not seep away. There would be steps cut into one side so that people could climb in and out. The water in it was to be "natural"—either water diverted from a stream or lake, or rainwater caught and channeled into the pool. Most sorts of uncleanness could be remedied by immersing oneself completely in the pool (or in a river or lake or ocean).

The drawings of the temple courts help us visualize the scene Luke is describing. The first shows the many entrances into the temple, all of them feeding into the huge open courtyard surrounded by colonnaded spaces. This was the Court of the Gentiles, and anyone, Jew or Gentile, was welcome to enter. The animal vendors were probably either located in stalls or shops built into the outside walls of the Temple, close to the various staircases

Temple Complex

(Credit: Barclay Burns)

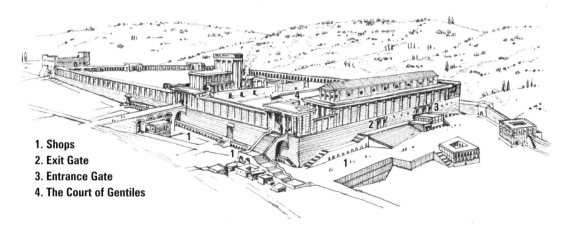

1. Shops
2. Exit Gate
3. Entrance Gate
4. The Court of Gentiles

Inner Courts

1. **First eastern gate, through which the male Israelites entered.**
2. **Court of Women.**
3. **Wall Separating Court of Women from the male area.**
4. **Second eastern gate, through which male Israelites entered.**
5. **Court of the (ordinary, male) Israelites.**

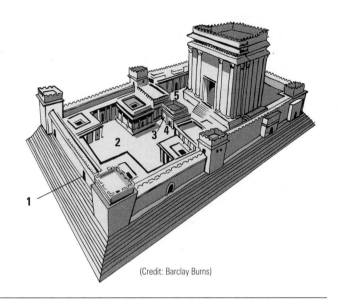

(Credit: Barclay Burns)

leading in, or in the Court of the Gentiles itself, in the colonnaded areas. The second drawing shows the inner courts in more detail (see also [Diagram of the Inner Courts]). Mary and Joseph would have stopped to buy two doves and then walked through the Court of the Gentiles, past the low wall through which only Jews were permitted, and up the steps to the inner courts. Mary, taking her two doves, would have entered the Court of the Women through one of the side doors. According to Leviticus 12:6, she would have given the doves to the priest at the door. Either the priest came out of the Court of the Priests to receive the offering, which seems unlikely because of the concern for his state of purity; or a Levite took it from the woman to the priest; or the woman handed it to the priest through one of the side doors that led into the Court of the Priests. Joseph would have come through the men's door through the Court of the Women into the very narrow Court of Israel, where he could give his monetary payment to a priest. Which parent held baby Jesus? The Law does not specify, so we are free to imagine either Mary, baby in one arm, doves in the other hand, showing the priest the reason for the sacrifice, or Joseph, proudly holding up his son as he paid his redemption price, or maybe one and then the other. [Philo on the Meaning of the Redemption of the First-born]

Philo on the Meaning of the Redemption of the First-born

[Moses] consecrates also their own first-born male children after the fashion of other first fruits, as a sort of thanks-offering for fertility, and a number of children both existing and hoped for, and wishing at the same time that their marriages should be not only free from blame, but even very deserving of praise, the first fruit arising from which is consecrated to God; and keeping this in their minds, both husbands and wives ought to cling to modesty, and to attend to their household concerns, and to cherish unanimity, agreeing with one another, so that what is called a communion and a partnership may be so in solid truth, not only in word, but likewise in deed.

Philo, *Spec. Laws*, I.138.

Luke describes all this dispassionately: they brought him up to Jerusalem, they offered a sacrifice. Luke does not name the priest or describe the scene with either parent; unlike the encounter between Gabriel and Zechariah, there are no details of place or setting in this part of the story. Mary and Joseph are obedient, but Luke does not tell us if they are anxious or excited or worried about the money they are spending, and he does not put a human face on the priests who help the two of them at this important moment. They are obedient, everything functions normally, no big deal.

All that changes when we come to v. 25, to the prophetic side of the story. Simeon is said to be righteous, just like Zechariah and Elizabeth, and devout (a word that only appears in Luke and Acts in the New Testament). "Expecting the consolation [*paraklēsis*] of Israel" echoes Isaiah 40:1-3 LXX: "'Comfort [*parakaleite*], comfort my people,' God, says. 'O priest, speak to the heart of Jerusalem, comfort her, because her humiliation is fulfilled, her sin has been released, because she has received from the Lord's hand double her sins.'" Simeon, like John the Baptist after him, believes that Israel's sins have put her in danger of God's judgment, but that God will send relief. "The Holy Spirit was upon him," like Elizabeth and John and Mary and Zechariah (after John's birth), and so what he will say will be the words of God. Simeon, in other words, is a prophet. Luke tells us that Simeon had been given an oracle, a prediction that he would not die until he saw the Messiah.

Have you been counting the predictions in the first two chapters that have already come true in the narrative? Zechariah and Elizabeth would have a child and would name him John; his birth would bring great joy and would turn many to God; Zechariah would be mute until all these things took place; Mary would conceive and give birth by God's direct creative act; the shepherds would find the baby in the manger; and now Simeon will see what he was promised. Like the "divine passive" in v. 21, this thread of prediction fulfillment is a Lukan reminder that everything is happening according to God's plan.

Under the Spirit's leadership, Simeon is in the temple on the same day Joseph and Mary come to make their offerings. He meets them as they enter the temple—so before the episode just narrated in vv. 22-24—and begins to prophesy. By ordering the stories this way, Luke avoids making the purification simply an anticlimax, but the attentive reader realizes that as they went to do as the Law required, they went with Simeon's words ringing in their ears.

Simeon's first oracle is called the *Nunc Dimittis*, from the first two words of the poem in Latin. It is a blessing, a type of Hebrew prayer called a *berakah*, of which there are many examples: for instance, "Blessed art thou, O Lord our God, King of the universe, because you bring forth bread from the earth." Simeon, holding Jesus in his arms, praises God for this moment:

> Now send away your slave, master, according to your word, in peace.
> Because my eyes have seen your salvation,
> Which you have prepared before the face of all peoples,
> Light for revelation for the nations (Gentiles),
> And for glory for your people Israel.

Commentators note how this short poem both complements and complicates the two longer hymns in the first chapter. It begins with peace, where Zechariah's prayer ended (1:79); but whereas Zechariah anticipated movement back from the shadow of death into peace, Simeon is poised to depart, probably to die, in peace. What Simeon is experiencing is "according to your word": he sees the deliverance, and he knows that salvation, light, and glory are coming, but he also knows that he will not be around for that. Zechariah's prediction also reminds God of the promises to Israel through the prophets (1:70) and to Abraham (1:73) that they would be preserved and rescued from their enemies. Luke's reader, who knows that the Romans destroyed Jerusalem in AD 70, is likely to think that Simeon is the more accurate prophet in this case. There would be consolation for Israel, but not for those alive in the temple on that day.

Simeon's prayer also understands God's work in Jesus to be on behalf of all the world: light for the Gentiles, glory for Israel. Despite "before the face of all peoples," his prayer is not for even-handed treatment, since "your people Israel" puts them in a special position that the Gentiles do not have, and since "light for revelation" speaks of access to salvation, and "glory" speaks of the results of salvation. Nevertheless, Simeon's prayer blesses God for providing salvation for everyone, whereas Zechariah's thanks God for rescuing Israel from their enemies. Again, Simeon would seem the more perspicacious, especially since Jesus will predict the destruction of the city and the "times of the Gentiles."

Simeon's song begins where Mary's does, with the actions of God for a slave and with praise for God's salvation. The Magnificat mentions no Gentiles directly, but does describe God scattering the proud, the powerful, and the rich, and helping the lowly and hungry. Mary and Simeon both call themselves God's slaves, a title Zechariah applies only to David, and both speak directly of what God has done for them: "all generations will call me blessed, for the

Holy One has done great things for me" and "my eyes have seen your salvation."

Simeon, who recognizes that God has fulfilled the promise to him and that his dismissal is now at hand, sends Mary and Joseph away with a blessing, and with a cryptic oracle to Mary:

Look, this one is set
for the falling and rising of many in Israel and
for a disputed sign
and your own soul will be pierced through with a sword
so that the reasonings of the hearts of many may be revealed.

The terms of the oracle are sufficiently general that the reader can see it fulfilled over and over in Luke. Some people respond favorably to Jesus, while others do not. Some who listen to him teach want to kill him afterward (4:29), while others are amazed and want to prevent his ever leaving them (4:42). Some will be healed or literally raised from the dead, resulting in the word spreading that Jesus is a prophet (7:11-17). Others, hearing the same news, will have only more questions (7:18-19); Jesus' deeds are certainly "disputed signs." ["Disputed Sign"] Jesus often knows the intents and internal disputes of his opponents (5:22; 6:8) and reveals them by his teachings and actions, sometimes even seeming deliberately to provoke angry reactions.

The last two lines—which in Greek appear in the order given in the translation above, but which are often inverted by translators—are the head-scratcher parts of the oracle. If "your own soul will be pierced through with a sword" is to be related to the lines that surround it, then it should say something about how the disputes over Jesus and his way of revealing people's hidden thoughts are like a sword through Mary's heart.[26] Perhaps we are to imagine that Jesus' mother is hurt by the cruel things others say about him. Some suggest that she is cast here as the personification of Israel, so that the sword through her heart is a more personal version of the sort of division Jesus brings to the people (13:51); she suffers as her people suffer when they are unable or unwilling to hear God's word through Jesus.[27] A third possibility relates to Jesus' death. Luke describes Mary as a faithful believer (8:21) who stuck by Jesus and who, with his brothers, was a charter member of the Jerusalem church (Acts 1:14). This being the case, the reader could also take the "sword" statement to refer to the grief Mary

"Disputed Sign"

AΩ The phrase translated "disputed sign" in the commentary (2:34) is itself debatable. "Sign" is clear enough—the Greek word means an event that marks something or points to divine intervention [BAGD, 920]. Luke often uses it to mean "miracle" (11:16) or to mean "noteworthy event that points to something else" (2:12). The word translated "disputed" can mean "contradicted" or "argued against." The phrase could mean "a sign that causes arguments" or "a sign that people argue about or against" or "a sign of an argument." Any of these could describe Luke's Jesus.

John of Damascus on "a sword shall pierce your soul"

When she saw him put to death as a criminal—the man she knew to be God when she gave birth to him—her heart was torn from maternal compassion and she was rent by her thoughts as by a sword.

John of Damascus, *Orthodox Faith*, 4.14, cited in Arthur A. Just Jr., ed., *Luke* (ACCS: NT, vol. 3; Downer's Grove IL: Intervarsity Press, 2003), 50.

suffered when Jesus' enemies conspired to have him crucified. Perhaps, like most oracles, this is meant to be subject to many readings and to being fulfilled on several levels. [John of Damascus on "a sword shall pierce your soul"]

Simeon is joined this day by Anna, a prophet, who is identified to the reader by her father's name and by her tribe. Contrast this with the way Mary is earlier introduced, where we only know her name, the name of her town, and her fiancé's name; there, Luke was making the point that Mary's credentials were not her family line but her willingness to be obedient to God's call. Anna, on the other hand, is given all the markers of respectability to increase the effect of her testimony to Jesus. By naming Anna's tribe as Asher, Luke also lets the reader know that Anna was not from a priestly family, although she was very devoted to the temple. She remained unmarried after her husband's death, devoting herself for her long life to the worship of God in the temple, and like the shepherds, became a witness to the great thing that God was doing through Jesus.

Let us take a moment to review some of the characters who function as prophets in the birth narratives.

<u>Elizabeth—Old</u>
  Priestly family
  Righteous
  Recognizes Jesus in Mary's womb
  Pronounces blessing on Mary
  Names her son John in obedience to God's command, despite
    opposition

<u>Mary—Young</u>
  Elizabeth's kinswoman—priestly family also?
  Righteous—the point of the visit to the temple
  Receptive to God's commands
  Leaves her home after receiving the good news
  Thanks God for blessing her
  Predicts that through Jesus, God will overthrow the powerful and
    bless the poor
  Predicts that through Jesus, God is helping Israel
  Is told by another prophet that her son will be opposed and that
    she will be hurt

<u>Zechariah—Old</u>
  Priest

Righteous, but then doesn't receive the good news and is cursed
Once cursed, goes back to being obedient, and curse is lifted
Predicts God will, through Jesus, rescue Israel from its enemies
Predicts that John will pave the way for Jesus

Simeon—Old
    Righteous
    Hopes for Israel's consolation
    Predicts his own death
    Predicts that Jesus will be good news for Israel and for the
        Gentiles
    Predicts that Jesus will divide Israel
    Predicts that Mary will be hurt

Anna—Old
    From a specific, but non-priestly, family
    Widow
    Pious: fasting, praying, worshiping at temple
    Praises God
    Speaks of Jesus to all who hope for redemption of Israel

Momentarily setting Mary aside, you have four old people, two men and two women, all called righteous or pious; two from priestly lines, two not. One of the older women is pregnant, one a widow of long standing and most assuredly not pregnant. The priest, who has been praying for a child for years, cannot believe the good news when it is given to him by an angel and is cursed for it; the other old man, who has waited for years to see a child, sees and believes immediately, and blesses the Holy Family. Zechariah's curse is lifted by his obedience to the angel's command; Simeon's obedience leads to his grateful acceptance of his own portending death, not as a curse, but as God's dismissal. Mary, who is not part of a pair—unless we count her son in her womb—is young, single, and at first, of uncertain lineage and piety. Because of the way Luke introduces Mary, we judge her first by her actions in accepting the revelation, rather than by epithets like "righteous" applied to her by the narrator. Whereas Zechariah doubts, Mary accepts; whereas Elizabeth blesses Mary for her belief, Mary blesses God for God's favor on her; whereas Simeon speaks of a sword piercing Mary's heart and of the falling and rising of many, Mary speaks of God's justice dividing rich and poor, powerful and lowly—her criteria are much more specific. And whereas Anna speaks of Jesus to anyone hoping for Israel's restoration, Mary keeps all these things in her heart. So many ways to be a prophet! In Luke's second volume, Peter quotes the text from Joel 2 on Pentecost, saying that the Spirit of the Lord will fall on young and old, on men and women, so that all can hear and call upon the name of the Lord for salvation (Acts 2:17-21). Luke has populated the infancy story of Jesus with a variety of prophets as a preview of what will come.

Luke sums up this story with a reprise of several themes. Mary and Joseph, like all the others, are devout and obedient, completing "everything according to the law of the Lord." They are not wealthy or important or powerful: they go back to rural Nazareth. And most importantly, everything is going according to God's plan: "the child grew and became strong, full of wisdom, and God's grace was upon him" (2:40).

Jesus in the Temple, Act II, 2:41-52

This story was a lot easier to preach or to teach before my own sons were born, and before I had any experience of the overwhelming grief and panic that comes when a child is lost, even very briefly. I can scarcely imagine what the story might feel like to parents who have lost children in tragic circumstances. Luke gives us this story to show us Jesus' understanding of his mission, but I always want to preface it with "please don't try this at home."

This story wraps up the birth narratives, and is the companion piece to the presentation story in 2:21-39. Luke's outline seems to have been two annunciations; then the bridge story where the two mothers visit; two birth stories, each with some sort of sign for what the baby will become; and finally, two childhood stories. In the first two pairs, the reader gets a John story followed by a Jesus story. This pair of stories is only about Jesus, but it is also about how others respond to Jesus. Simeon and Anna are matched by the temple teachers and Jesus' own parents—how do they interact with Jesus, and what do we learn from that?

Commentators often draw attention to two other sorts of stories. In non-Christian literature, people told stories like this in order to show that the famous wise man was also a precocious boy. Plutarch, writing about Alexander the Great, tells a story of how ambassadors from Persia came to visit King Philip, who happened to be away. In the king's absence, the young prince entertained the guests, and "charmed them with his gracious hospitality and his inquiring manner . . . . The envoys were impressed and concluded that Philip's reputed shrewdness was nothing compared to the young lad's aspiration for greatness."[28] Josephus, never one to withhold self-praise, says that when he was a chap of fourteen, "high priests and leading men of the city came to me in a body, to determine my view about precise interpretations of the law."[29] Sure they did. Luke's story sounds like the "amazing child" stories of other famous people, and if there were only the part about the temple teachers being amazed, one would say that it had the same function. But the fact that Jesus did this without permission and that his parents searched desperately for him puts a different twist to the tale. Sure, this kid is smart, but according to the Torah, the first step in learning wisdom is learning to be submissive to those in authority, beginning with one's parents (Prov 4:1-9).

The other interesting comparison is to the noncanonical Christian infancy stories, all of which seem to have been written down later than Luke. But they circulated orally before they were written down, and we have no idea how early that process began, so it is worthwhile at least to have them in one's head while reading Luke's account. In the *Infancy Gospel of Thomas*, Jesus is a child who, very much like a normal child, dams up a little creek to make a pool and plays in the mud and then pitches a fit when another kid knocks down his mud dam. Unlike a normal child, however, Jesus' divine powers allow him to clap his hands and turn his mud birds into real ones and to curse his tormentor so that he dies. [A Story from the *Infancy Gospel of Thomas*] The imaginative spark behind such stories seems to be "boy, if I had been Jesus as a kid, what could I have done with all that power?" In comparison to those, Luke's story is restrained—no magic powers, no fits of anger. Jesus is no Wonderboy, but someone very bright and very focused on what he believes God wants him to do. If Christians were already telling Thomas-type stories about Jesus in Luke's day, then we can be grateful for Lukan restraint.

Luke's story begins where the last one ended, with Mary and Joseph practicing their faith, going to Jerusalem for the feast of Passover, "as they did every year," notes Luke (cf. "as his custom was" in 4:16— his parents raised him right, in other words). The requirement of Deuteronomy 16:16 that all male Jews make a pilgrimage to the temple three times annually was, in practice, too hard for most poor people—how can you be away from your home and farm or business for a couple of weeks three times a year and expect to make a living? Most scholars of ancient Judaism do presume that

A Story from the *Infancy Gospel of Thomas*

After this [Jesus] again went through the village, and a child ran and knocked against his shoulder. Jesus was angered and said to him, "You shall not go further on your way," and immediately he fell down and died. But some, who saw what took place, said, "From where was this child born, since his every word is an accomplished deed?" And the parents of the dead child came to Joseph and blamed him and said, "Since you have such a child, you cannot dwell with us in the village; teach him to bless and not to curse. For he is killing our children."

Gosp. Thom. 4.1-2; text in *The Apocryphal Jesus*, ed. J. K. Elliott (New York: Oxford University Press, 1996), 21.

most Palestinian Jews in the first century "made at least one pilgrimage a year, the most popular being Passover."[30] If that is correct, then Mary and Joseph were being normally, but not conspicuously, pious by their habits.

The tale Luke tells happens when Jesus is twelve. According to a rabbinic passage about the age of accountability for vows, boys aged twelve years and one day may take vows, but the vow must be examined—presumably by an adult, to make sure everyone understands the consequences (perhaps a bit like a parent co-signing a loan). A boy's vows are not accepted without examination until he is past his thirteenth year.[31] By this standard, the twelve-year-old Jesus was not an adult, but was capable of making decisions with adult consequences. Sounds about right for this story!

The syntax of vv. 42-43 is important: "When he was twelve years old, and after they went up for the festival (as their custom was), and after the feast-days were finished, while they were returning home, Jesus, the boy, remained behind in Jerusalem, but his parents did not know." Luke sets up the sentence so that traveling to Jerusalem, attending the festival, and leaving for home are circumstantial clauses, so that the main action of the sentence is "Jesus stayed behind"—something he does deliberately—"and his parents were clueless"—the consequence of something he chooses not to do. Not *Home Alone*, then, because Jesus is not forgotten by distracted adults, nor *Huckleberry Finn*, because Jesus does not run away, but somewhere in between—he decides to stay, and he deliberately or carelessly does not inform his parents of his plan; they assume that he is somewhere in the crowd of travelers—but do not actually check.

How many parents reading this are remembering losing sight of a child at a mall or in a big department store and searching until you found her or him? Luke has a pair of stories like that—the lost sheep and lost coin (15:1-10). The awful combined feelings of worry, shame, dread, and anger wash over you, even if the child is missing only for a few minutes. Imagine, or remember, how much worse it feels when the child does this deliberately; Luke has a story like this, too, the parable of the prodigal son (15:11-32). He allows the tension to build in this one by asking us to think about Mary and Joseph missing Jesus for three days—the day's journey out, the return trip, and then a frantic day looking high and low in Jerusalem, until finally they find him in the temple.

Now, recall, the temple was a huge rectangle the size of several football fields, mostly open courtyard, with colonnaded spaces around the perimeter. We think that teachers more than likely held classes in the colonnaded areas, sitting on benches under the shade of the roof. As we imagine Mary and Joseph looking for Jesus, the mall or a crowded football stadium is not a bad image to suggest to an audience, rather than church. Luke says they found him, not frantically looking for them, but calmly sitting in a crowd of teachers doing Q and A. The teachers are amazed at his insight and his answers, but his parents are shocked or dumbfounded[32] at the way he has treated them: "Child, why have you treated us so? Your father and I have been in distress looking for you."

It is a story simply told, but far from simplistic, and part of its complexity is illustrated by two paintings of this moment in the story. In Duccio's *Christ among the Doctors*, Jesus is the central figure, and in control of the moment. Although he is child-sized, he is seated so that his head is higher than any of the teachers; he wears his cloak like a philosopher, and his hand is raised in blessing or to make a point to them. The teachers are arranged so that they make an inverted "V" with Christ at the center point. Mary and Joseph, arms outstretched, are separated from him by the bodies of the teachers, and although Jesus is facing them, the main feeling the painting gives the viewer is the distance between parents and son. The Jesus of this painting is already a teacher, an adult in a child-sized body.

Luke, by using "his parents" in 2:41 and 2:43, and by having "his mother" say "your father and I" in 2:48, lets us feel all the normal ties between parents and children. Of course they love him, and they have been going crazy looking for him for three days; of course they are proud of him, but they are also ashamed for having "lost" him, and ashamed and angry at him for having put them in this predicament. When Jesus says, "Why were you searching for me? Didn't you know that I must be in my Father's things?"[33] Luke lets us feel the sword cutting Mary to the quick of her soul (2:35). One part of this story, then, is

Christ among the Doctors

Duccio (di Buoninsegna) (c.1260–1319). *Christ among the Doctors*. From the predella of the Maesta altarpiece. Museo dell'Opera Metropolitana, Siena, Italy. (Credit: Scala/Art Resource, NY)

the conscious choice by Jesus to go where God leads, even if that will be hurtful to his parents, and to choose to serve God above all else.

But the story ends with a reconciliation of sorts. His parents did not understand what he said to them, but he nonetheless went with them back to Galilee and was obedient to them. Rembrant's etching, depicting Jesus between his parents—Joseph's hand rather firmly over Jesus'—is of an adolescent in need of parental advise and protection. Luke's Jesus, at the end of the birth narrative, needs to grow up, and so he does, in the safety of a family who would not stop looking until they found him.

Theologically, the two strands of the story are related to the intersection of humanity and divinity in Jesus. He knows, and only God knows how he knows, that he must be about God's business; did Mary tell him, or, like Mary, did he hear the voice of an angel telling him about his special role in God's plan? He can amaze the teachers with his perception, and can fail to tell his parents what he is up to, causing them days of unnecessary grief. That is pure teenager, that wonderful and maddening mixture of quick perceptiveness and

The Return of Christ and His Parents From the Temple

Rembrandt Harmensz van Rijn (1606–1669). *The Return of Christ and His Parents From the Temple.* 1654. Etching and drypoint on Japanese paper. Kupferstichkabinett, Staatliche Museen zu Berlin, Berlin, Germany (Credit: Bildarchiv Preussischer Kulturbesitz/Art Resource, NY)

utter self-absorption. Onstage, he never apologizes, and the way he talks to Mary, under normal circumstances, would probably only increase the length of his grounding ("Didn't we *know*? Worry us sick, and then he says we *should have known*? I'll tell you what *you're* going to know, young man! You're going to know the inside of your father's workshop like the back of your hand, and you're *not* going to know much else until Elijah comes back or you grow up, whichever comes first!"). But what he says is true: he must be in his Father's . . . whatever—places, tasks, people, plans. This is not a miracle story, like the later Christian infancy tales of Jesus making clay birds fly and bullies drop dead—thanks be to God! Instead, it is a tale of the wonder of how God's Son grew up listening for God's voice, taught by caring adults, protected by loving parents, nourished in a safe place so he could mature to be strong and wise.

CONNECTIONS

The commentary section on the birth of Jesus addressed the issue of how to approach the story of Jesus' birth, mindful of how hard it is for present-day Americans to separate what they hear and read from what they know, which is Christmas as an American icon. I am not certain that we can hear the duplicity in our own Christmas practices—a holiday that sells itself as a season of giving, generosity, and good will, using Christian terms and concepts to reinforce the American cultural values of conspicuous consumption, personal excess, and owning and spending as a means of defining self. Have we ever stopped to reflect theologically on the story of Santa Claus delivering toys to all the children of the world all in one night? Suppose we change the terms of the story slightly; suppose Santa gave out food instead of toys, and we told our children that the world's children got all the food they wanted on Christmas Eve, provided they had been good that year. Such a myth would be no less cruelly hypocritical, but slightly less American: Santa still doesn't come, but what he isn't delivering to the world's poor is something they could really use, rather than the excess that we can enjoy because we're rich and greedy.

But you probably cannot preach that, or at least not often. Let's focus on what Luke says: the world's only superpower in the first century concocted a brainless idea to move people around to their ancestral homes—as if everybody could locate the old home place, as if the Jews, like many other people groups conquered by various empires over the centuries, had not been refugees many times over. Mary and Joseph must travel to Bethlehem from Nazareth to take part in the census, even though she is almost ready to give birth. So God's Son winds up being born in the right spot—Bethlehem—as the result of what seem like stupid decisions. Although Caesar thinks he is pulling the strings, God bypasses him and all his cronies to send the birth announcement to shepherds, down near the bottom of the social hierarchy. Who are we most like in this story? Who, in our world, has the power to decide to overthrow regimes and move people around for what turn out to be poorly conceived reasons? And who might get the good news that God is doing something amazing in our world?

The story of the presentation is of Mary and Joseph participating in the requirements of their faith, but being surprised by two prophets, one male and one female, who recognize what God is doing through Jesus. This story is nicely balanced: law-directed ritual and spirit-driven ecstatic speech are both affirmed; the joy of perceiving God's hand at work sits alongside the prediction of pain, disappointment, and sorrow; one prophet speaks to the couple and to God while the other speaks to all who will listen. One could see in this pericope the ministry of the church in brief sketch.

The final story of the birth narratives is a challenge, as it shows so clearly the trouble with preaching that God can speak to anybody regardless of age or gender. Would God really encourage a young adolescent to stay behind in the big city and worry his parents to death? But suppose Jesus had come to Mary and Joseph with a plan to stay behind for some extra instruction; could they have agreed with him that it was absolutely necessary for him to do this now? We all struggle to hear God's voice clearly, and parents struggle doubly to see God's hand at work in children, especially as they grow older and their inner lives become more and more opaque to us. Mary, who said, "Behold the handmaid of the Lord; let it be to me according to your will," did not know what to say when Jesus told her that he had to be about his Father's stuff. Praise God for the blessings of children, and praise God for grace that works with parents and children alike, but it is all sometimes a mystery.

In Haven Kimmel's *The Solace of Leaving Early*, the male and female protagonists struggle to make sense of how three young children who have been through an unspeakable tragedy hear the voice of the Virgin Mary. In one scene, the eldest is explaining the sorts of things Mary tells them: "I'm waiting for her to tell me something to do," Immaculata continues, "you know, like she told Bernadette to dig. But so far all she's said is Pray, Forgive, Say Your

Rosary, and Eat Fruit. Stuff like that."[34] God's revelations are unpredictable, both in terms of who hears them and how they come. Jesus' life with his parents is described by Luke in blandly positive terms in vv. 39-40 and 52, but punctuated by this one radical moment of stepping out. He, too, must have been directed by God through his parents to Eat Fruit and Pray; but then, like the girls, there must have been moments where he heard the voice of God in a way that confounded even those closest to him. Luke gives us no seven-step process for clarifying the call of God—just a vivid description of how wonderfully complicated it can be.

NOTES

[1] "The popular understanding of Luke 2:1-20 has been shaped, not only by preaching and storytelling, but also by art and especially by the custom of the Christmas crèche or crib scene. This custom was popularized by St. Francis of Assisi, beginning at midnight mass in Greccio in 1223" (Raymond E. Brown, *The Birth of the Messiah: A Commentary on the Infancy Narratives in the Gospels of Matthew and Luke* [Garden City NY: Doubleday, 1993], 491, n. 34).

[2] Joseph A. Fitzmyer shows how easily it could have been confused: Herod the Great died around 4 BC; about ten years later, Judea was annexed after Herod's son proved ineffectual as a ruler. Both events were marked by civil disturbances; in the first, Varus had to come in with an army, destroying cities, crucifying thousands (according to Josephus); in the second, Rome again intervened and imposed heavy taxes. Thus it is likely that many thought of the death of Herod and the beginning of Roman rule happening at about the same time In *The Gospel According to Luke* (AB 28 and 28A; Garden City NY: Doubleday, 1981), 1.401-405, Fitzmeyer discusses all the attempts to reconcile things.

[3] *Res Gestae Divi Augusti* 34, in C. K. Barrett, ed., *The New Testament Background: Writings from Ancient Greece and the Roman Empire* (San Francisco: HarperSanFrancisco, 1987), 3.

[4] Frederick W. Danker, *Jesus and the New Age: A Commentary on St. Luke's Gospel* (rev. ed.; Philadelphia: Fortress, 1988), 54, citing the Asian decree of 9 BC that reorganized the calendar so that Augustus's birthday would be New Year's Day.

[5] *Res Gestae Divi Augusti*, 26, in Naphtali Lewis and Meyer Reinhold, *The Empire*, vol. 2 of *Roman Civilization* (New York: Harper and Row, 1966), 17. Obviously "peace" in Gaul, Germany, and the two Spains did not come without an occupying force that goes unmentioned in the official listing of deeds.

[6] Virgil, Aeneid, 6.793-94.

[7] Horace, *Ode* 4.15, cited in Lewis and Reinhold, *The Empire*, 20–21.

[8] Karl Christ, *The Romans* (Berkeley: University of California, 1984), 137–40.

[9] Alan R. Culpepper, *The Gospel of Luke* (*NIB*, vol. 9; Nashville: Abingdon, 1995), 63; John Nolland, *Luke* (WBC, vols. 35A-C; Dallas TX: Word, 1989–93), 1.111.

[10] There are manuscripts that read "wife," but most interpreters follow the weight of the external evidence; the oldest and best-attested reading is "betrothed."

[11] So Nolland, *Luke*, 1.111.

[12] Nolland, *Luke*, 1.105.

[13] Danker, *Jesus and the New Age*, 55; Joel B. Green, *The Gospel of Luke* (NICNT; Grand Rapids: Eerdmans, 1997), 128; Culpepper, *Luke*, 63.

[14] Nolland, *Luke*, 1.105, although he admits the possibility of the first interpretation. Brown, *Birth*, 400, concludes that there is not enough information to choose, and translates *katalyma* as "lodgings" to preserve the ambiguity.

[15] The tradition dates to Justin Martyr (*Dial.* 78.5), who would have been thinking of Roman habits, not Palestinian. The *Protevangelion of James* also put the manger in a cave, but incorrectly states that Bethlehem was in a desert. Origen, writing about a hundred years later, says that he had been shown the cave and strips of the swaddling cloths. See Brown, *Birth*, 401.

[16] BAGD, 985. Josephus, *Vita* 259, says that the Galileans called him Savior after he exposed his rival generals as liars.

[17] Mark Coleridge, *The Birth of the Lukan Narrative: Narrative as Christology in Luke 1–2* (Sheffield UK: Sheffield Academic Press, 1993), 148; Fitzmyer, *Luke*, 1.413.

[18] Barbara Robinson, *The Best Christmas Pageant Ever* (New York: Harper and Row, 1972), 72.

[19] BAGD, 956.

[20] John Irving, *A Prayer for Owen Meany* (New York: William Morrow, 1989), 153.

[21] Robinson, *Pageant*, 43.

[22] Ibid., 18.

[23] Ibid., 55.

[24] Leigh Eric Schmidt, "Christianity in the Marketplace: Christmas and the Consumer Culture," *Cross Currents* 42/3 (Fall 1992): 342ff. Available online: www.crosscurrents.org/schmidt.htm.

[25] Josephus, *Ant.* 4.71; Philo, *Special Laws* 1.139-40. Philo argues that since all children are valuable, the fixed amount is appropriate, and also argues that Moses picked a low amount that everyone should be able to pay.

[26] Green, *Luke*, 149, notes this as a possible reading of the phrase.

[27] Luke Timothy Johnson, *The Gospel of Luke* (SP, vol. 3; Collegeville MN: Liturgical Press, 1991), 57; so also Green, *Luke*, 149.

[28] Plutarch, *Alexander* 5; cited in Danker, *Jesus and the New Age*, 75.

[29] Josephus, *Life* 2; cited in Danker, *Jesus and the New Age*, 75–76.

[30] E. P. Sanders, *Judaism: Practice and Belief, 63 BCE–66 CE* (Philadelphia: Trinity, 1992), 127. He cites Josephus, *Ant.* 17.214, which speaks of an "innumerable multitude" that came to Jerusalem from all over Palestine and beyond for Passover.

[31] *m. Niddah* 5:6: "A boy twelve years old and one day—his vows are examined; if he is thirteen years old and one day, his vows are valid, but they must be examined throughout the thirteenth year." The same passage, interestingly, sets the threshold ages for girls at a year younger in each case. The passage is noted by Johnson, *Luke*, 58–59.

[32] BAGD, 308 s.v. ἐκπλήσσω.

[33] This is a fairly literal translation of v. 49. There is no noun for "house" or "business," only a plural definite article. It is fairly common in Greek to leave out a word that the author thinks the readers can fill in, but here the noun that must be supplied is not obvious. "House" seems unlikely, since the definite article is plural—one would have to read "in my Father's houses." "Places" would work grammatically, but since he is only in one place, the temple, it would not make much sense as an answer. "Things" is vague, perhaps implying that Jesus' business is not just the temple but any activity involving God.

[34] Haven Kimmel, *The Solace of Leaving Early* (New York: Anchor, 2003), 204.

JOHN'S MINISTRY, JESUS' BAPTISM

Luke 3

COMMENTARY

John the Baptist, 3:1-17

The first six verses of this chapter reintroduce the grown-up John the Baptist by naming current power brokers, from the emperor through the high priest, and one famous personality from Israel's past: the prophet Isaiah, whose word about a voice in the wilderness frames what John is up to.

We recall the first two verses of chapter 2, where Augustus and Quirinius are named but then forgotten as the story unfolds. Three of these six people also vanish: we will not hear of Tiberius again, although he was the emperor when Jesus was crucified, nor of Philip, whose territories to the north of Galilee Jesus probably never went through. The name "Lysanias, ruler of Abilene," only appears here in all of Greek literature, so there is nothing more to say about him. But the other three characters—Pontius Pilate, Herod Antipas, and Joseph Caiaphas—are crucial for how Luke's story progresses.

Pilate was "governor" of Judea, Samaria, and Idumea, having direct responsibility for the area south of Galilee and west of the Jordan-Dead Sea line. (Pilate's title is more correctly "prefect," an army or civilian position that has to do with making sure that the troops are well provisioned. But Josephus also uses the term *hēgemōn*, "governor," for Pilate.) After the death of Herod the Great in 4 BC, the Romans had at first given authority over Judea to Archelaus, one of Herod's sons, but in AD 6 he was removed and replaced with a Roman who reported to the governor of Syria. Pilate was the fifth of these officials, and he was in office for at least ten years, possibly more (see commentary on 23:1-25). Josephus criticizes him for a number of rash actions:

- When he took first office and brought the troops into Jerusalem from Caesarea Maritima, he allowed the army to bring in its standards, topped with the busts of the emperor. Josephus says Pilate knew of the Jewish restrictions against idols, and so had the army bring them in at night. But the standards were discovered, the citizens protested, and Pilate was ready to break up the demonstration by force. But when he saw their resolve, says Josephus, he changed his mind and removed the standards. (See [Pilate and Caesar's Images].)
- Then he built the aqueduct with money taken from the temple treasury, which provoked more protests. This time, Pilate went through with his threat to beat the protesters, and many were killed or injured. (See [The Abuse of a Mob].)
- Finally, a Samaritan prophet appeared, promising to reveal certain treasures hidden by Moses on Mt. Gerizim. When his movement grew to include armed men, Pilate ordered in cavalry and infantry, who killed some and captured others, whom Pilate then executed. This led to protests by the leading citizens of the Samaritans, and Pilate was ordered to come to Rome to explain himself.

Luke's Pilate will be a bit of a puzzle. In 13:1, he is reported to have murdered some Galileans who were in the temple, which would indicate a person who cared little for justice for those he governed, who acted first and sorted things out later. But in 23:1-25, Pilate investigates the charges against Jesus, concludes they are baseless, and announces his intention to set Jesus free—and then fails to follow through, overcome by the voices of the people and the temple leaders.

Herod Antipas was lambasted by Josephus for killing John the Baptist and for marrying his brother's wife in clear disobedience to Jewish legal custom. In Luke, Antipas also arrests and kills John the Baptist. He tries to see Jesus (9:9), and the Pharisees report to Jesus that Antipas wants him dead (13:31). But in his brief appearance in the Passion Narrative, Herod interrogates Jesus, but then finds no reason to kill him. Like Pilate, Antipas will not be an admirable character in Luke, but is also not clearly a villain, and there is the curious note in the Passion Narrative testifying to Pilate's friendship with Antipas and its beginning with Jesus' trial (23:12).

Joseph Caiaphas was high priest from AD 18–37, so he began when Valerius Gratus was prefect, continued in his office for all of Pilate's term, and then was deposed just after Pilate's own removal from office. He was from a wealthy family, probably living in a grand house like the ones excavated by Nahman Avigad in the Upper City of old Jerusalem. (See [Reconstructed Upper-class Home].) He was a Sadducee, a religious conservative, denying the existence of angels and the resurrection of the body.

Luke tells us none of this in the Gospel, and indeed, never again mentions Caiaphas by name until Acts 4:5. The high priest is mostly hidden within the "chief priests," who tend in Luke to act as a unit, collectively questioning Jesus and then handing him over to Pilate. Luke cites Caiaphas's Sadducean membership in Acts 5:17, and has the high priest act as an individual in the trials of the Twelve (Acts 5:17-42) and Stephen (Acts 7), so his choices in the Gospel represent editorial strategy, not a lack of information. Luke's chief priests are Jesus' intransigent opponents, so submerging Caiaphas into a group was not a sympathetic move; rather, it must be seen as a way to reduce his individual status, so that those who oppose Jesus and insist on his crucifixion are faceless enemies. [Caiaphas's Burial Box]

Of these, only Antipas will have direct connection with John the Baptist, so introducing them all at this point is a subtle way to link John's ministry and fate with Jesus'.

The last name, and the only truly friendly name in the bunch, is Isaiah, whose prediction of the voice in the wilderness prepares the way for John's ministry. Isaiah says nothing about a baptism of repentance for the forgiveness of sins, but lifts up several important features of John's work:

Caiaphas's Burial Box

In the Israel Museum in Jerusalem, visitors can see the beautiful ossuary that held the bones of Joseph Caiaphas, the high priest named by Luke. For a couple of centuries, including the first, wealthier Jews began using carved boxes to hold the bones of dead family members. The person was first buried on a shelf, and then after the flesh had decayed, the bones were collected into these boxes. The one that held Caiaphas's bones has careful and delicate decorative carvings on the front and top—obviously it was meant to be art in the same way that elaborate burial monuments are in our time. The box shows both the wealth of the family and its willingness to adopt a new trend or fad in burial practices.

(Credit: Barclay Burns)

• He was a voice in the wilderness: Luke 1:80 named the wilderness as the place where John matured, and 7:24 confirms that the crowds gathered to him in the wilderness.

- His role is to prepare the Lord's way: Luke's John is a precursor for Jesus and a model for discipleship. He not only prepares the crowds for the Coming One, who will baptize with the Spirit, but begins to introduce them to the themes of Jesus' ministry.
- He begins the process of revealing God's salvation: in Acts, the ministry of John is consistently set as the beginning of the gospel (Acts 1:21-22; 10:36-37; 13:23-25), and Jesus will say that from John forward, the gospel has been proclaimed (16:16).

By anchoring all these aspects of John's ministry in Isaiah's prophecy, Luke starts to show how it is possible for his readers to understand the Baptist, who led a popular ministry parallel to Jesus', as a part of the Christian movement. This is part of the process, in other words, of how John the Baptist became a Christian saint.

Verses 7-9 are also found in Matthew 3:7-10, almost word for word the same. The standard source theory says that these verses come from Q, the second source (in addition to Mark) behind Matthew and Luke. Alternatively, we could imagine Luke reading Matthew or vice-versa, but that still would not explain the origin of the verses, because it is hard to imagine that either Luke or Matthew created them. We must reckon, then, with a source earlier than Matthew and Luke, independent of Mark, that contained not only some of Jesus' teachings, but some of John's as well.

Matthew's version of v. 7 has it addressed to the Pharisees and Sadducees. Matthew is famously polemical in his treatment of the Pharisees, so more than likely "crowds" was not a Lukan alteration, but was the way the verse read when it came to him. John's preaching presumed that all Israel was under the threat of God's imminent judgment. Like most prophets of the Hebrew Bible, he does not single out some as less guilty, but insists that everyone must repent in order to escape the fire and the axe. "The wrath to come" was the Day of Judgment, here described as a landowner cutting down unfruitful trees and burning them. John warns that the covenant with Abraham will not be enough to escape judgment; instead, his audience must bear "fruits worthy of repentance."

Luke uses "repentance for the forgiveness of sin" as a summary of the gospel taught by Jesus to the apostles, to be spread to all nations (Luke 24:47), so John's preaching and baptism are completely in accord with the way Luke will describe Jesus. According to v. 8, John's expectation was that people would change their lives, demonstrating the proof of their repentance, prior to being baptized. Josephus says the same: John insisted that baptism was "a consecration of the body implying that the soul was already thoroughly cleansed by right behavior" (*Ant.* 18.117). In vv. 10-14, we have some examples of the sort of changed behavior John had in mind, according to Luke. We also learn, from Luke 5:33 (taken from Mark) and 7:33 (taken from Q) that John fasted to such a degree that some people thought he was crazy, and that he taught his disciples to fast. Fasting is a sign of mourning and repentance in the Old Testament; furthermore, stringent fasting is something that, if one does it, is obvious to others. It seems likely, then, that one of the "fruits of repentance" that John demanded was fasting as a sign of repentance from and mourning for the sins of the nation. [Josephus on John the Baptist]

Luke does not describe the way John performed baptisms. The word "baptize" normally means to immerse, although it can mean to dip or to wash. Immersions, either in running water or in water naturally collected in a pool deep enough for an adult to be fully submerged, were a normal part of Jewish practice (see [Miqveh; miqvaoth]). When a person became "unclean"— meaning that in that condition, they were not to enter the temple or other places sacred to God, or touch food or other items that had been set apart for God—most of the time, all that was required was for the person to immerse and wait until sundown. But John's practice differed from these sorts of ritual immersions in three significant ways.

First, when a person immersed to be ritually clean again, he or she did it solo; John performed the immersion, from which we deduce that he believed he was an essential part of the process. This was his ministry as God's prophet, to call Israel to repentance and to immerse those who followed through. Second, immersions to be clean were to be repeated as often as necessary. All sorts of normal and ordinary life processes made one unclean, and archaeologists have found plenty of immersion pools (*miqvaoth*) throughout Jewish settlements in Galilee. John's immersion, however, seems to have been singular; people traveled to him, making a pilgrimage as if to the temple, convinced him that they

Josephus on John the Baptist

But to some of the Jews, it seemed that the destruction of Herod's army by God was indeed very just, God exacting satisfaction for John who was named "the Baptist." For Herod killed him, although he was a good man and commanded the Jews to come together by using baptism, if they were practicing virtue, [namely] deeds both of righteousness toward others and piety towards God. For in this way baptism would appear acceptable to [God], if they used it not as a pardon for some [of their] sins, but as a purification for the body, the soul having previously been made clean by righteous deeds. And when others were gathered around [John], lifted to ecstasy by listening to his words, Herod—worried lest such great persuasion might lead to some instance of rebellion (for they seemed to be doing everything according to [John's] counsel)—thought it much better to destroy him, seizing John before some innovation arose from the changes happening on his account, than to change his mind later after falling into difficulties. So John, having been brought in chains to the aforementioned Machaerus, was there executed for the suspicions of Herod; but to the Jews, the verdict on John was that God willed destruction to come upon the army as retribution, by ruining Herod.

Author's translation of the Greek text in Josephus, *Ant* 18.116-119, trans. Louis H. Feldman (Cambridge MA: Harvard University Press, 1965).

had truly repented, immersed, and then went home. John was not creating an alternative community in the wilderness, as did the sectarians at Qumran. Third, and most significantly, immersion in a *miqveh* and sundown took away the ritual impurities that life's ordinary situations created. John's baptism would have done that, too, since the Jordan was running water. But John claimed that his baptism not only cleansed, but atoned; that is, it not only took away ritual impurities, but also the effects of sin. What John was offering, in other words, was a service providing what temple sacrifices provided, except that one did not have to buy an animal. Come to John; fast a while (which, if you were poor, you might be doing anyway); accept his baptism; and the result was that you were ritually clean and guilt-free, ready for Judgment Day. [Unclean, Sinful] No wonder he drew crowds!

Unclean, Sinful

A person is made unclean by all sorts of natural events—childbirth, menstruation—things that involve no ethical choice and that are not sinful in any way. While unclean, a person may not enter a holy place, like the temple, nor touch holy things, like a Torah scroll. Being unclean was more than a metaphor; since one had to immerse in clean water and wait until sundown to be clean again, the "uncleanness" was understood to be a physical condition, as if it were a film or residue on the body. A person who did things prohibited by the law of Moses, whether deliberately or not, was guilty of sin, which also left "guilt" as a sort of residue on the person. In Jesus' day, most Jews believed that guilt could be removed only by repentance followed by animal sacrifice in the temple.

Verses 10-14 are found only in Luke, and sound very much like sayings of Jesus found later in the Gospel. In this scene, John responds to three audiences who want more specific instruction on how to live. To the crowds, he says that anyone with more than enough food or clothing should share with those who have nothing. Jesus' version will be "give to everyone who begs from you" or "lend, expecting nothing in return" (6:29, 35). John's version sounds more like equity, while Jesus' version sounds more like sacrifice, but both sayings are moving in the same direction: one of the fruits of repentance is divesting oneself of wealth and providing for the poor.

The second audience is tax collectors. The Romans required provinces like Judea to pay tribute annually. So for the privilege of having Roman troops permanently stationed in their territory and a Roman governor having final say on what went on, Judeans would have to cough up a certain amount of cash. Ultimately the senate and emperor were responsible for setting the amount they expected the provinces to pay and for deciding how to collect the money; from time to time, the provinces would complain of abuse and corruption, and there would be a reform of the methods. During Jesus' lifetime, the collection of taxes in a province was sold to wealthy people, who would then collect the amount owed to the Romans, plus whatever bribes had to be paid in order to keep the contract, plus whatever profit the tax contractor and all his employees were going to make. So we should imagine a network of people, with some wealthy tax-franchise owners at the top and the actual tax collectors—the people who assessed taxes on things that crossed the borders or on property or on crops—being much closer to ordinary people in their wealth, but still wealthier than average. It is these bottom-level people who are meant in v. 12.

John's word for them is to collect "nothing beyond what has been set for you," which could refer either to an amount of money that they needed to collect, or to the orders given them by their superiors. We wonder, then, whether the low-level tax collector could make a living by only collecting what his bosses required, or whether anyone would want to take the job under those conditions. When John says, "Only follow orders," is he actually saying, "Rethink your priorities—there is no way to do this job ethically and profitably"? Even if he were only trying to prohibit graft at the bottom level of tax collection, the change would have been a step away from the abuse inherent in the Roman system, and a fruit of real repentance. In 19:1-10, we will see how a chief tax collector, upon meeting Jesus, addressed this very issue.

The third audience was soldiers. There were several different sorts of soldiers in Judea, but unfortunately Luke does not specify which sort he meant. The Judean prefects had two wings of cavalry and four cohorts of infantry, according to Josephus, and most of these troops were recruited locally. The temple also had guards whose job was to keep order and provide some security for the large amounts of money in the treasury. There were also soldiers under the command of Antipas, who arrested John (3:19) and who might have had reason to want a report on his activities. Whatever sort of soldiers Luke has in mind were likely to have been Jews, not Gentiles, seeking advice from the prophet.

John's advice to them was to live within their means and to avoid using their power as soldiers to extort more money than was due them. Again, we want to know whether this sort of behavior was tacitly expected of soldiers—was the system set up to encourage pilfering or extortion? If so, then John's request to refrain from shaking people down or blackmailing them would have sounded more radical to Luke's readers than it may to us.

There is evidence aplenty to show that in Luke's time, people expected tax collectors to overcharge [The Story of a Wicked Tax Collector] and soldiers to "requisition" what they wanted from the local populations. [Soldiers Extorting Money] John's advice to them is perhaps a bit like Jesus' line "give to Caesar . . . give to God " (20:25). One can understand John to be saying, live within the system; do not cheat, but you can be an honorable person and still work as a tax collector

The Story of a Wicked Tax Collector

Not long ago a certain man who had been appointed a collector of taxes in our country, when some of those who appeared to owe such tribute fled out of poverty, from a fear of intolerable punishment if they remained without paying, carried off their wives, and their children, and their parents, and their whole families by force, beating and insulting them, and heaping every kind of contumely and ill treatment upon them, to make them either give information as to where the fugitives had concealed themselves, or pay the money instead of them . . . .

[Philo then describes how the tax collector tortured his victims.] But perhaps it is not wonderful if men, barbarians by nature, utterly ignorant of all gentleness and under the command of a despotic authority, which compelled them to give an account of the yearly revenue, should, in order to enforce the payment of the taxes, extend their severities, not merely to properties but also to the person, and even to the lives, of those from whom they thought they could exact a vicarious payment.

Philo, *Spec. Laws* 3.159-63.

Soldiers Extorting Money

Josephus records what he claims is a decree of Julius Caesar published in Judea, wherein Caesar exempts Judea from the tribute due Rome during the sabbatical year. He says that otherwise the Judeans "are to pay the same tithes to Hyrcanus and his sons which they paid to their forefathers. And that no one, neither president, nor lieutenant, nor ambassador, raise auxiliaries within the bounds of Judea, nor may soldiers exact money of them for winter quarters, or under any other pretense, but that they may be free from all sorts of injuries."

Josephus, *Ant.* 14.204.

John the Baptist, Muckraker

John's simple phrasing cuts through the roots of graft, cost overruns, the payoff, the kickback, the torn-up ticket—all the tentacles that reach out to destroy the health and substance, the moral fiber, and the ethical backbone of individuals and their nation.

From Frederick W. Danker, *Jesus and the New Age: A Commentary on St. Luke's Gospel* (rev. ed.; Philadelphia: Fortress, 1988), 89.

or a soldier for the colonial power that holds your people in thrall. John, after all, believed that the age to come was close to hand, and so, like Paul, he may have thought that large-scale social change was irrelevant. But one can also understand John to be saying, be a tax collector or a soldier, but only if you can live free of corruption; and since you cannot, you should think about a new line of work. Either way, John demands specific behaviors as fruit of repentance. [John the Baptist, Muckraker]

Verse 15 is a transition that appears only in Luke. There is no hint in Mark or Q that some people thought John was the Messiah, but it makes more sense in Luke, since John is something of a full-service prophet, not only criticizing how things are done but offering concrete suggestions for how they should be done. Verses 16-17 are John's implicit "no" to the question "are you the Messiah?," but in Acts 13:25, John is quoted as denying it directly. Luke's concern over John's messianic status probably results from the continued existence of a group of disciples of John the Baptist (Acts 19:1-6), whom Luke would like to see folded into the church.

John's "answer" is an indirect but forceful denial of any messianic pretensions: "I baptize you with water, but he who is mightier than I is coming . . . he will baptize you with the Holy Spirit and fire." The Coming One—Luke clearly thought of the Messiah rather than God—will clear the threshing floor, gathering into the granary all the seed beaten from the stalks and then burning the remainder. John's vision for the Coming One—axe-wielder (v. 9), winnower (v. 17), and trash-burner (both verses)—sounds more destructive than constructive, but his role as Spirit-baptizer carries with it the whole range of prophetic descriptions of the age to come, when the Spirit would be poured out on all people (Joel 2), granting the ability to live by God's law (Ezek 36:26-27).

"Baptize with the Holy Spirit and fire" could mean that Jesus would bring blessing (spirit) and judgment (fire), and the two uses of fire in v. 9 and v. 17 would support this reading. It is also possible to read it as one baptism considered from two angles, where the Spirit-baptism of the righteous is preceded by purifying judgment; the description of Pentecost, where the Spirit falls as tongues of fire, would support this reading. Either way, John's predictions are fulfilled within Luke-Acts: Jesus receives the Spirit at his own baptism (Luke 3:22), promises the disciples that they will receive the Spirit after his ascension into heaven (Luke 24:49; Acts 1:5, 8), and then delivers on that promise on Pentecost (Acts 2). Luke's readers are assured that anyone who asks for the Spirit will receive (11:13), and Acts gives example after example of how that works out. Luke's Jesus also preaches plenty of fiery judgment (10:13-15; 12:49; 16:19-31), confirming that part of the prediction.

Excursus: St. Luke's Portrait of John the Baptist

Luke writes a lot about John the Baptist (JB). Because it is spread throughout his two volumes, and because Luke skillfully directs the reader's attention to Jesus, we do not always get the sense of how big a role JB plays in the Gospel of Luke. What follows is a synopsis of the material in the order it appears in Luke and Acts.

- 1:5-25 is the story of the annunciation to Zechariah and of Elizabeth's conception. In this section, we are told that JB's father is a priest and his mother is from a priestly family, and that both of them are righteous, scrupulously obedient to the Law. Their inability to have a son is thus a theological problem; why would God treat them so? Gabriel tells Zechariah that his prayers have been answered, leading the reader to suppose that the parents have both been asking for God's help. Gabriel describes the baby as one who will do great things: he will be great in God's sight; he must be a Nazirite, staying away from alcohol; he will be filled with the Spirit even before birth; and he will be the fulfillment of the prediction that Elijah will return, fulfilling that prophet's role of preparing Israel for the coming of the Lord. Zechariah asks the angel how senior citizens will be able to have a baby and is struck dumb because he doubted. Elizabeth, by contrast, takes the news of her conception as proof that God is acting on her behalf, removing the shame of her barrenness.

- 1:39-56 puts Mary and Elizabeth together. Mary has just learned that she will bear God's child, and before she can tell her kinswoman, Elizabeth is filled with the Holy Spirit and JB leaps in his mother's womb "for joy." This fulfills Gabriel's prediction that JB would be filled with the Spirit *in utero*, and marks JB (as well as Elizabeth) as a prophet.

- 1:57-66 narrates the story of JB's birth. The narrator interprets JB's birth as an act of God motivated by God's great mercy, the same terms Mary used to speak of Jesus' coming birth in 1:54. When the neighbors rejoice with Elizabeth, this fulfills another prediction by Gabriel (1:14, "many will rejoice at his birth"). When Zechariah confirms Elizabeth's choice of the name John for their son, the curse of silence is lifted, Zechariah praises God, and the fear of God spreads throughout Judea. This, too, fulfills Gabriel's word that the baby would turn many toward God, and that Zechariah would remain mute until everything began to occur. JB's appearance, then, does not merely fulfill the prediction of Elijah's coming, but also fulfills all the special predictions made by Gabriel.

- JB's birth is followed by 1:67-79, Zechariah's long prayer of blessing (the "Benedictus"). The first part of it is about the Messiah, but vv. 76-79 speak to JB's mission. He will be a prophet; he will prepare the way of the Lord; all of this restates what Luke found in Mark. But 1:77 states that JB will do all these things "in order to give knowledge of salvation to his people in the forgiveness of their sins." This phrase could easily serve as a Lukan summary of Jesus' message (Luke 24:47; Acts 2:38-40), and shows that Luke does not imagine that JB's message was trumped or superseded by Jesus. Instead, Jesus continued what the Baptist began.

- 1:80 is the only note about JB's childhood; then JB is absent from the stage while Luke narrates Jesus' birth, presentation in the temple, and the story of Jesus in the temple as a boy.

- 3:1-6 introduces JB again to the reader, noting all the political and temple authorities of the time. JB, however, as a true prophet is under the direction of no secular or religious authority, but acts in accord with the word that came to him and in fulfillment of the prophet Isaiah. He is the voice in the wilderness preparing the way of the Lord.

- 3:7-9 reproduces Q material and gives us JB's apocalyptic preaching. Whereas Matthew has this word of warning and condemnation addressed to the Pharisees and Sadducees, Luke has it addressed to the crowds. Luke's JB, like Luke's Jesus, is thus not as hostile to the Pharisees as Matthew's JB and Jesus. Nevertheless, the Pharisees and scribes later come under the narrator's condemnation for rejecting JB's baptism and thus rejecting "the plan of God" (7:30).

- 3:10-14 is material found only in Luke that shows JB to be teaching a way of life with many close ties to Jesus' teaching. People who have more than they need should share with those who have nothing (6:30, 35, 38). Tax collectors should collect no more than the prescribed amount; Jesus does not ever say anything like that, but his encounter with Zacchaeus leads to a promise both to give to the poor and to refund, with interest, what was taken by fraud (19:8). Soldiers likewise should refrain from extortion and be satisfied with their pay. Jesus tells everyone to love their enemies and to avoid doing evil (6:27-36), and Jesus praises the faith of a centurion as being greater than any in Israel (7:9).

- 3:15-17 begins with the narrator's note that some who heard JB preach wondered if he were the Messiah, a question never raised in Mark, Q (so far as we know), or Matthew. JB does not answer that question directly here, although Paul (Acts 13:25) will later say that JB said, "I am not he." Instead, JB gives the answer found in Mark and Q: I baptize you with water, but the Coming One will baptize with Holy Spirit and fire. The filling with the Holy Spirit and fire is fulfilled in Acts 2, at Pentecost, when the Spirit comes with tongues of fire. The risen Jesus reminds the readers of JB's word in Acts 1:5 so that we can be prepared for it. Luke, then, provides a way for readers to see JB's prediction fulfilled in the narrative, so that by definition JB is a true prophet of God.

- 3:18-20 narrates JB's imprisonment. Luke omits the whole business about Antipas's oath and Herodias's daughter's dance, laying the whole blame on Herod's evil response to JB's prophetic indictment of marrying his brother's wife.

- 3:21-22, where Jesus is baptized, tells us nothing whatsoever about JB, because JB is not mentioned. Curiously, Luke puts Jesus' baptism in the passive voice immediately after the verse where Herod shuts JB up in prison. It is hard to imagine that Luke wants the readers to conclude that someone other than JB baptized Jesus, or that Jesus baptized himself. As we will note below, Acts 1:21-22 is phrased so one has to presume that Luke knows, and thinks the readers know, that JB baptized Jesus. But Luke is equally consistent to avoid simply stating that JB baptized Jesus, something that did not seem to be a problem for Mark or Matthew. Luke's caution here is probably related to the question in 3:15 about whether JB was Messiah. Luke knows of disciples of JB in Ephesus (Acts 19:1-7), and he may have been trying to avoid giving any impression that Jesus was JB's disciple.

- At 5:33-39, Luke reproduces the question about fasting. Like Mark, the question comes from an unnamed group, unless the reader is to carry over the "Pharisees and their scribes" from 5:30 to be the subject of "they said to him" in 5:33. That is possible, but an anonymous "they" seems more likely; had Luke's narrator meant to specify the Pharisees as the interrogators, then the text would have read, "John's disciples, like ours, frequently fast and pray . . . ." So others link JB's disciples and their practice with what the Pharisees and their disciples do; an unsavory connection, but not enough to make JB a bad guy.

- Luke includes the "are you the one to come?" question at 7:18-23. Luke's version has several differences from Matthew's. JB's disciples go to JB (still in prison, we presume) to give him a report about Jesus. JB then sends them with instructions to ask, "Are you the Coming One, or should we wait for another?" The narrator then has the disciples ask that exact question, so that the reader sees it twice. While they are waiting for an answer, Jesus cures many sick, casts out demons, and heals the blind, and tells the disciples to go repeat what they just saw. All of this reminds the attentive reader of the sermon at Nazareth, where many of the same elements—preaching the good news, healing the sick, sight to the blind—are read from the scroll of Isaiah. JB's question, then, becomes a reminder to the reader of why Jesus is the Coming One: he fulfills the Scriptures that predict he will bring healing to the sick, release to captives, good news to the poor, etc.

- Since Luke does not narrate the baptism, there is no moment where the adult JB introduces Jesus, hears a voice from heaven, or sees the heavenly dove. He is therefore not guilty of doubt when he sends his disciples to ask, "Are you the Coming One?"; it is a legitimate question, based on the reports that JB got from his own disciples about what Jesus was doing.

- Like Matthew, Luke then follows with the encomium on JB (7:24-30). He is a true prophet, and more, because he fulfills Malachi's prediction that Elijah would precede the Messiah. Verse 7:28 states that no human is greater than JB, but anyone in the kingdom—which in Luke is both coming and present—is greater than he. 7:29-30, which only appears in Luke, puts anyone baptized by JB in the kingdom, and the Pharisees and scribes, who refused JB's baptism, outside the "plan of God" and thus outside the kingdom. JB, too, will be in the kingdom come Judgment Day, with "Abraham and Isaac and Jacob and all the prophets" (13:28).

- Then comes the parable of the children in the marketplace (7:31-35). In Luke's version, when Jesus says he is the friend of tax collectors and sinners, the reader is reminded that JB baptized tax collectors (3:12; 7:29), and so the contrast between JB and Jesus is limited to their position on asceticism. JB is also the "friend of tax collectors and sinners."

- Luke reproduces Mark 6:14-16, where Antipas and the crowds claim that JB had been raised from the dead (9:7-9). This comes as something of a surprise, since JB was alive in 7:18-19, and since Luke had not informed the reader of JB's demise. In 9:9, Herod says, "John I beheaded," so Luke imagines that the reader already knows the facts of JB's martyrdom before reading the Gospel.

- Jesus soon thereafter asks the disciples "Who do the crowds say I am?" They repeat what the narrator had just reported in 9:7, that the populace thinks of Jesus as the risen JB or Elijah or another prophet. Interestingly, Luke does not add "or the Messiah," although 3:15 pictured all the crowds wondering if JB were the Coming One.

- Luke introduces the model prayer with a question from the disciples: "Lord, teach us to pray, as John taught his disciples" (11:1). This is the only text connecting JB to prayer, and so it is of little use for reconstructing history, but it does expand Luke's portrait of John as a teacher.

- JB is then absent from the story for quite some time; the next mention of him is at 16:16: "The law and the prophets were in effect until John; since then the good news of the kingdom of God is proclaimed, and everyone tries to enter it by force." This verse clearly puts JB as the pivot between the ages, and includes JB as the beginning of the point where the kingdom is preached as good news. Luke, then, is able to picture JB not yet in the kingdom in 7:28, proleptically in the kingdom in 13:28, and as the beginning of the kingdom in 16:16.

- After entering Jerusalem, Jesus is asked about his authority, and he refuses to answer unless the chief priests, scribes, and elders will tell him what they think of JB's authority (20:1-8). They refuse to answer, because the crowd holds him to be a prophet, and so Jesus also refuses.

- In Acts 1:5, the risen Jesus repeats what JB said in Luke 3:16: JB baptized with water, but Jesus will bring the baptism of the Holy Spirit. Jesus predicts that it will happen in just a few days.

- In 1:21-22, "the baptism of John" is named as the beginning point of the ministry of Jesus and his followers. This is most interesting, since the Gospel does not actually say that JB baptized Jesus, or that any of Jesus' disciples were present at Jesus' baptism, or that JB baptized any of the people who later followed Jesus. But the passage implies that JB's baptism was the beginning of "the whole time during which the Lord Jesus was going in and out among us," so we must assume Luke (and Luke's ideal readers) believe that JB baptized Jesus and some of Jesus' followers as well.

- 10:37-38 also makes JB's baptism the start of the gospel message; note how this passage continues Luke's ambiguity about Jesus' own baptism: "That message spread throughout Judea, beginning in Galilee after the baptism that John announced: how God anointed Jesus of Nazareth with the Holy Spirit and with power . . . ." Luke can say that JB's baptism marked the start of the gospel without explicitly saying that JB baptized Jesus.

- In 13:24-25, Paul takes up the same emphasis, stating that JB preached a baptism of repentance to all Israel as part of the preparation for Jesus' coming, but insisting that he, JB, was not the Coming One. In these three sections of Acts, JB is thus a prophet who came before Jesus, who preached repentance and baptism just as Jesus and his followers would, and who never claimed to be a rival to Jesus.

- The final mention of JB comes at Acts 19:1-7, where a group of "disciples" had been baptized by JB but had never been taught about the Holy Spirit; they were rebaptized in the name of Jesus and then received the Spirit when Paul laid hands on them. This section is most likely a witness to the issue of the relationship between JB's group and Jesus' group. However worried Luke may be about the existence of an ongoing JB movement, he does not ever demonize it, in the manner that the Gospels do the Pharisaic movement. Instead, Luke calls JB's followers "disciples," and at the end of the story it is clear that they are disciples of Jesus. In Luke's ideal world, the remainder of the JB movement would merge with the Christians.

Luke's JB is thus "a prophet and more than a prophet," more like Jesus in certain ways than Mark's or Matthew's JB. Luke's JB is Malachi's Elijah *redivivus* and Isaiah's voice in the wilderness, but he is also the fulfillment of Gabriel's direct predictions. He still baptizes great crowds, demanding repentance in view of the Coming One, but he also preaches a way of life that includes fasting, prayer, almsgiving, and right living—much like Jesus or any other Jewish ethical teacher. Most significantly, Luke's JB is part of Jesus' extended family, and that addition to the gospel tradition—whatever its origin—was a major influence on later Christian thinking about John. Luke's blending of themes of kinship and witness shows up in paintings of the Baptist and the Savior as infants: da Vinci's *Madonna of the Rocks* (1506–1508) is a famous example. The painting has Jesus and JB as cherubic toddlers, Jesus with his right hand raised in the three-fingered blessing, and JB kneeling to be blessed, a reed cross resting on his shoulder. The way the figures are positioned, Mary occupies the center of the painting, JB sits under her right hand, and she has her left hand outstretched toward Jesus. But baby Jesus sits facing both of them, so that from his perspective Mary is on the right and JB on the left. It is a brilliant statement of Luke's message: Mary links the two figures, but JB's role is subservient to Jesus'.

Luke's JB does not introduce Jesus by baptizing him, but in many other respects he is Jesus' forerunner. His birth narratives are the foil for Jesus'; Mary's quiet acceptance of Gabriel's prophecy is to be contrasted

Madonna of the Rocks

Leonardo da Vinci (1452–1519). *Madonna of the Rocks.* 1483. Oil on canvas, Louvre, Paris, France. (Credit: Erich Lessing/Art Resource, NY)

with Zechariah's question, and the crowd's amazement at JB's naming is to be contrasted with the way the shepherds receive the good news from the angels. JB was a friend of tax collectors and sinners before Jesus was, and taught prayer before Jesus did. Luke's JB dies as a martyr (9:9) before Jesus, but we hear of it only in passing from Herod's musings about the power Jesus possesses. Since there is no Baptist passion narrative in Luke, Jesus' death stands alone until Stephen dies as this Gospel's first Christian martyr (Acts 7).

Jesus' Baptism, 3:18-22

Baptist churches almost always have a baptistery behind the platform where the pulpit stands, and there is often a picture hanging in it or a mural painted on the wall. Sallman's *The Head of Christ* is a favorite, or the same artist's rendering of Jesus praying in the garden; others have a pastoral scene including a river, evoking the Jordan even if the scenery is more American than Palestinian. Few Baptist churches hang a painting of Jesus' own baptism by John above the baptismal pool. By contrast, ancient baptisteries were typically decorated with a painting or carving of that scene, sometimes also including scenes from John's life. In some treatments, the baptism becomes a miracle, with the water jumping up out of the riverbed to surround Jesus. In most cases, however, the water stays calm but John becomes a Christian saint, complete with halo, as in the painting by Verrocchio and da Vinci.

Perhaps we can see all of these examples as evidence of

Baptism of Christ

Andrea del Verrocchio (1436–1488). *Baptism of Christ*. Painted in collboration with his pupils Leonardo da Vinci and Lorenzo di Credi. Wood, Uffizi, Florence, Italy. (Credit: Erich Lessing/Art Resource, NY)

John the Baptist wears his typical hair shirt, and true to his role as witness to Christ, both baptizes him and holds the crucifer. God's hands send down the Holy Spirit, while angels wait nearby to dress Jesus when he is done. Note that Jesus is praying, as Luke records.

ongoing Christian discomfort with the notion that John, who was God's prophet but who never became Jesus' disciple, baptized the Son of God as if Jesus were any other sinner. Some ancients dealt with their discomfort by making the baptism a miracle or John a Christian, but others—like Luke and many modern Baptists—by treating John's baptism of Jesus obliquely.

Luke 3:18 is a typical Lukan summary and transitional sentence, tying up what John had been doing in the previous section and drawing his ministry to a close. The Baptist is described as "exhorting" or "encouraging" his audiences; Luke uses (*parakaleō*), which can mean to urge or to console or to encourage. John's ministry is summarized with the verb (*euangelizō*), meaning "evangelize" or "preach the gospel." In Luke's thinking, John the Baptist was the beginning of the gospel's presentation to the world. Luke's John was a forerunner, but he was also a Christian preacher, sharing the message of repentance, forgiveness, and the promise of the Spirit.

We jump straight from God's servant John to Herod Antipas, the man who put him to death. Luke calls him "Herod the tetrarch" to distinguish him from his father Herod the Great, who was named "King of the Jews" by the senate in Rome. Herod the Great had three sons whom he did not kill, and after his death, the Romans divided Judea between the three of them: Archelaus got Judea and Samaria, Antipas got Galilee and Perea, and Philip got Gaulinitis and Trachonitis. Archelaus proved unable to control his part, so within a few years the Romans removed him and substituted a Roman official instead. Philip governed the parts that play little role in the New Testament, so you should not feel bad if his name and the location of his realm escape you. Antipas, on the other hand, appears several times in Luke, so it is worth knowing a bit about him.

According to Josephus, Antipas rebuilt Sepphoris, which had been badly damaged in the Roman suppression of the revolt following Herod the

Map of Galilee

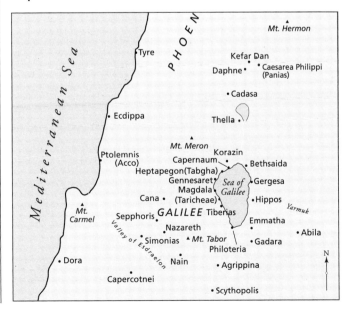

Great's death in 4 BC. Then, to honor the emperor and to give himself a new administrative outpost on the Sea of Galilee, he built Tiberias. Both were sizable cities for the area—populations estimated between 8,000–12,000 for Sepphoris and 6,000–12,000 for Tiberias. Neither was as grand as Caesarea, the port city Herod the Great built on the coast, but both were far more ostentatious than any other city in Galilee, with ornamental and monumental public architectural features. Antipas, then, acted like his father, trying to cement good relations with the Roman emperor by building new cities in his honor and using these same new cities to begin to concentrate the wealth and power of the area.

Antipas was married to the daughter of the king of Nabatea, the kingdom adjoining Perea on its southeast border. The way Josephus tells the story, Antipas fell in love with his half-brother's wife, who in the unbelievably tangled Herodian family tree, was also the daughter of another half-brother. The woman in question, according to Josephus, was Herodias, daughter of Aristobulus (Herod the Great's son by Mariamne I), who married Herod, Herod the Great's son by Mariamne II (I am not making this up!). Mark says she was Philip's wife; Philip, ruler of the aforementioned Gaulinitis and Trachonitis, was also Antipas's half-brother, but his mother was named Cleopatra. Luke just says "his brother's wife," avoiding confusion and cutting right to the main problem: Antipas married Herodias while his half-brother was still alive, which Josephus describes as transgressing the Law.[1] Luke follows Mark in stating that because John the Baptist rebuked the king for his unlawful marriage, Antipas locked him up.

Again, Josephus tells a different story, but this time his version and the biblical version could be complementary. In Josephus's account, Antipas imprisoned and then killed John the Baptist because John was a powerful, popular preacher whose large following would do whatever he told them. Antipas reasoned, wrote Josephus, that he would rather kill John before any problem arose than wish later that he had done it sooner. Although Josephus says nothing about the Baptist criticizing the legitimacy of the king's marriage, such a detail would be compatible with his reasons why Antipas feared John's influence. Both Luke and Josephus consider John's arrest to be Antipas's decision, and do not suggest, as Mark does, that he regretted killing the prophet.

We assume that Luke had the Markan story of John's imprisonment and beheading, the rash oath made by Antipas, the blandishments of his stepdaughter, and the antipathy of his wife. Perhaps Luke did not find the story edifying, or perhaps he wanted to make Jesus' martyrdom the only one narrated in the Gospel; for whatever reason, he reduced the story to two verses here and three in 9:7-9, making the reasons Herod's own evil nature and the criticism John leveled at his marriage. In so doing, Luke also concluded John's activities, with the exception of the episode in chapter 7 where John sends disciples to ask Jesus if he was truly the Coming One. Sometime between that episode and 9:7-9, Antipas beheads John (9:9, "John I beheaded"), but this grisly event is left to our imaginations.

Also left to our imaginations are the specifics of Jesus' baptism in v. 21. Because John is in prison in v. 20 and because "when Jesus also had been baptized" is in the passive voice, Luke seems to raise the possibility that someone other than John baptized Jesus. But what sense would that make? For three chapters, Luke has been putting John the Baptist on a sort of parallel track with Jesus: announcement of birth, birth accompanied by signs, and early ministry. The audience is prepared to see the Baptist immerse Jesus and then to see Jesus inaugurate the ministry John has predicted for the Coming One. So it would be more than passing strange to remove John from that role and plug in someone else just as Jesus was going down into the water.

Part of the explanation for the puzzling diction of v. 21 is that in Luke's day, disciples of John the Baptist still existed as a movement separate from Christianity. Acts 19:1-7 tells the story of twelve "disciples"—Luke does not specify whose disciples until the end of the story—whom Paul discovered in Ephesus. They had been baptized by John, but had never heard of Jesus or of the Spirit. Paul explained things to them, baptized them in Jesus' name, and they received the Spirit and prophesied. This, it seems, is how Luke would prefer things, with the former disciples of John being absorbed into the Christian movement. Their continued separate status may have been an embarrassment, and they may have been competitors to the early church. So perhaps Luke removes John's name and active participation from Jesus' baptism in order to make the story less about Jesus submitting to John and more about God affirming Jesus.

Another reason may be that Luke wants to emphasize how Jesus is the paradigm for believers. The structure of v. 21 makes the people's baptism parallel with Jesus', and the fact that his baptizer is unnamed makes his baptism more parallel with the reader's. Luke's Jesus, following the baptism, will enter the wilderness and fast and face down the devil by quoting Scripture to him. So between that passage and this one, we have Jesus, our example, being baptized, praying, fasting, and meditating on Scripture as a means of overcoming temptation. From this point of view, Jesus is a model believer.

The voice in Luke says, "You are my son," as Mark has it, seemingly a private revelation to Jesus—until you think about the dove visible to all the others being baptized. Luke inserts the word "bodily" to make sure we know that he means something the crowd saw. This, too, connects Jesus to Luke's readers, who have in all likelihood been taught that they received the gift of the Spirit at their baptism (Acts 2:38) or following baptism, in the laying on of hands (Acts 9:18; 19:5-6).

Luke does not often use the title "Son of God" for Jesus, restricting it to the baptism, the temptation (where Satan uses it), an exorcism (where the demons use it), and the interrogation by the high priest. Most of the instances, then, come from the lips of hostile characters. But here at the baptism, from the mouth of God, "you are my son" functions as God's public acknowledgment of Jesus. Others have named him other things: Zechariah predicts he will be a mighty savior (1:69); the angels tell the shepherds that this baby is a savior, the Messiah (2:11); Simeon calls him salvation, light, and glory (2:30-32); John the Baptist has called him the Coming One who would baptize with spirit and fire (3:16-17). God's testimony, "this is my son," fits well with Jesus' testimony in the temple, "I must be in my father's affairs."

Did the voice say "I am well-pleased with you" or "today I have begotten you"? The majority of Greek texts have the first reading, including most of those thought to be reliable, and so most English versions read that way, many without even a footnote to alert the reader that the reading is disputed. "Today I have begotten you" would finish the quote from Psalm 2:7, and so one theory is that "well-pleased" was original and some early scribe wrote "begotten" because he heard the psalm in his head as he was copying. Most professional text critics of the New Testament, however, are convinced that "I have begotten" is earlier, for two reasons. First, although it appears in only one early manuscript, four second-century Christian writers refer to the reading, making it clearly early and widely known. Second, once the arguments over the divine and human nature of Jesus began, only a heretic would have written "today I have begotten you," since that would have given fuel to Christians (called "adoptionists") who thought Jesus was born an ordinary human but then chosen, or adopted, at his baptism. Clearly, with the story of the virgin birth and the episode in the temple at twelve, Luke believed that Jesus was the Son of

God from conception. If he wrote "today I have begotten," it was not meant to be the mark of an "adoptionist" Christology, but a sign that he thought it an appropriate thing for God to say to Jesus at his baptism. Psalm 2 is a coronation psalm, and while Luke surely did not think that Jesus became God's son on that day, Luke did believe that Jesus was anointed by and filled with the Spirit on that day, and may have considered "today I have begotten you" an appropriate marker for that event.

Bottom line: if "today I have begotten you" was the earliest reading, we can explain how "I am well-pleased with you" came about, as later scribes removed a potential theological problem by making Luke sound more like Mark and Matthew. But if "well-pleased" is the earliest reading, then the rise of "begotten" by the early second century is harder to explain. The first option is more plausible.

Luke intended for Jesus' baptism to be a model for the baptism of Jesus' followers, and so he emphasized Jesus praying and waiting with all the others. The early church, drawing on images from Revelation, began the practice of robing the newly baptized in white after they came out of the water. Protestant groups that practice immersion acknowledge this ancient custom with the more modern practice of having people be baptized in white robes. The white robes are also a symbol of the complete cleansing brought about by salvation. Sometimes the reality fails to match the symbolism, as in this wonderful description by Anne Moody of her own baptism:

> When Reverend Tyson and the two deacons were standing in water up to their chests, the first candidate was led out. Everyone continued to sing "Take Me to the Waters" but much lower. . . . I looked down at the water and saw big piles of cow manure floating around. The thought of being dunked under the water made me want to vomit. The water was so muddy, the whole pond looked like a giant mud pie. Then I looked at the girl standing between Reverend Tyson and one of the deacons.
>
> "I baptize you in the name of the Father, in the name of the Son, and in the name of the Holy Ghost, *Amen*," Reverend Tyson said, drawing out the last syllable as he ducked her quickly under the water. She came up coughing and sputtering, her white dress was now dark brown. Her hair was dripping with mud. . . . All the other candidates were aware of the saying that if you coughed when you were being baptized, it meant the Devil was coming out of you. I knew she was embarrassed because she had coughed.
>
> "All dressed in white! Washed clean! Look at that!" I thought looking at her.

As the girl ahead of me was being led out, Jack leaned close and whispered, "'Member, Moody, betta not cough out there. Sister Jones gonna say you were a *sinner*. Hee-hee-hee."

"You got a lot more to cough about than me," I said. I saw two deacons coming for me. As I waded into the water, I could feel the mud sticking to my legs. . . . I was so mad I barely heard Reverend Tyson shouting, "I baptize you in the name of the Father, in the name of the Son, and in the name of the Holy Ghost, A-*men*!" Suddenly a wet hand was slapped over my face and I felt the mud folding over me, sucking me down. Just as I began to feel the heaviness of the mud, I was lifted out of the water. I tried to open my eyes but mud was stuck to my lashes, so I just left them closed. . . . As they were leading me out of the water, I could hear the cows mooing, Jack laughing, and everyone singing, "Take Me to the Waters." Everything sounded far away. It took me a minute to realize that my ears were stuffed full of mud.

After the last candidate was baptized, we were all rushed up to Miss Rose's where we washed off and changed. Even then, I still smelled like wet mud, and the smell lingered for weeks.[2]

Moody's treatment is part satirical inversion—white dresses made brown by mud and cow manure—and part straight-up recognition of how one may be changed by this ancient, powerful rite, but not in the ways one expects. She was pushed down into the mud that might have choked her, but then lifted, as the spiritual has it, out of the miry clay. No dove for Miss Moody, only the lowing of cows; her world stayed the same, but she was changed.

Jesus' Genealogy, 3:23-38

It is unusual for a genealogy to go backwards, as this one does, and one can only surmise that the reason was so that the genealogy could be seen to bridge the baptism, where God declares Jesus Son of God, and the temptation, where the devil says, "If you are the son of God." All three pericopes—the baptism, the genealogy, and the temptation—demonstrate, in different ways, how Jesus is Son of God and how Jesus is an example for believers. In this one, Jesus is the supposed son of Joseph, but the actual Son of God; but then, so was Adam, and by extension, so were all the persons in the list. Jesus' family tree includes some heroic and admirable figures, like Noah and Abraham, but mostly persons whose names are not in the Bible and about whom we know nothing. Luke's genealogy, for example, traces Jesus' line through David's son Nathan, an unknown, rather than through Solomon and the rest of the

Davidic kings (as Matthew has it). Such a collection of named no-names fits well in this Gospel where surprising heroes emerge: shepherds, a Samaritan, a wealthy tax collector, a loose-haired woman with a jar of perfume, and an unscrupulous business manager.

The names between Joseph and Zerubbabel are otherwise unknown, and are different from the names for the same section of the family in Matthew's list, except for Matthat as the name of Joseph's grandfather. The names between Shealtiel and Nathan are likewise unknown and different from Matthew's list. Sometimes I am asked whether Luke gives us Mary's family tree, but as one can see, Mary is nowhere mentioned in it. It is hard to imagine where the authors of Matthew and Luke got this material (excepting the names of biblical characters), since it is unlikely that either of them had interviewed Jesus' parents about their ancestors.

If you count Joseph as name one in Luke's list, then God is name seventy-seven. There are twenty-one names before Abraham, fourteen from Abraham to Jesse, twenty-one from David to Neri (which one would suppose would mark the Babylonian exile), and twenty-one from Shealtiel to Joseph. This is probably the pattern Luke used to give shape to the genealogy: seventy-seven generations from creation to the Savior, between Adam and Jesus.[3] Modern readers should take it in that vein, as part of Luke's argument that Jesus is the culmination of God's plan to redeem the world.

CONNECTIONS

The baptism scene in *O Brother, Where Art Thou?* is a wonderful interpretive foil for many parts of this chapter. Drawn by the ethereal singing of "As I Went Down to the River to Pray," our three miscreants wander down to the water and come upon a host of people lining up to wade into the river to be baptized. Delmar and Pete take the plunge, but Everett stays on the side of the river. Delmar tries to coax him in: "All of my sins have been washed away—come on in, Everett, the water's fine!" Everett won't bite, and later ridicules both of them for being "as dumb as a bag of hammers" for thinking that baptism makes any difference at all. Later in the movie there is an anti-baptism by three "sirens" who wet them all over with river water, get them drunk on white lightning, and then do things left to the audience's imagination. Then, near the movie's conclusion, they are saved from hanging by total immersion in the torrent that comes from flooding the valley where Everett's old house stands.

None of these "baptisms" fit Luke's pattern. Clearly, John's baptism offers no irresistible, accidental deliverance and no pre-dunking seduction, but it also differs from Delmar's spontaneous experience of all-encompassing pardon. John's is a baptism of repentance, and he insists on proof of repentance beforehand. Perhaps this is worth thinking over in church: if our baptism is supposed to be in imitation of Christ, then how is it that we do not impose the disciplines that John did?

John's illustrations of repentance, given in his instructions to the crowds, to the soldiers, and to the tax collectors, take up the Lukan theme of economic justice. As the commentary section notes, it is hard to tell whether John expected the soldiers and tax collectors to keep their jobs but to perform them more ethically, or to recognize that they could not ethically work at those professions. The two ways of reading those sets of instructions could spark an interesting discussion among American believers. Are there jobs that a Christian should not take at all? May a Christian take a job that regularly demands behaviors contrary to the teachings of Jesus? What if the job only indirectly supports ends or uses means of which Jesus would disapprove?

Baptism is practiced so differently by different Christian groups: on infants or "adults" (who often turn out to be children or early adolescents); by sprinkling, dunking, or pouring; at only certain times of the year or at the end of every service where someone professes faith in Christ. Luke's version of Jesus' baptism allows for wide latitude in mode since it is only implied and not actually recounted, but it does depict baptism as a congregational event and as one blessed by the presence of the Spirit. Services will be more Lukan to the degree that they involve the whole congregation in prayer and enhance our understanding of the Spirit's role in incorporating the baptized into the Body of Christ.

NOTES

[1] Josephus, *Ant.* 18.136.

[2] Anne Moody, *Coming of Age in Mississippi* (New York: Delta, 2004), 78–79.

[3] Raymond E. Brown, *The Birth of the Messiah: A Commentary on the Infancy Narratives in the Gospels of Matthew and Luke* (Garden City NY: Doubleday, 1993), chart on 76, discussion 90–94.

TEMPTATION; TWO SABBATHS, TWO SYNAGOGUES

Luke 4

COMMENTARY

Jesus and Satan, 4:1-13

I shake my head furiously, like a dog tormented by wasps. Her very calm infuriates me, and I can hear a kind of buzzing in my head, an unsteadiness that sends the room spinning about me. The creamy smell of chocolate is maddening. For a moment my senses are unnaturally enhanced; I can smell her perfume, a caress of lavender, the warm spicy scent of her skin. Beyond her, a whiff of the marshes, a musky tang of engine oil and sweat and paint from her red-haired friend.[1]

So says Père Reynaud, the beleaguered priest in *Chocolat*, who believes that the woman who came to his village to start a chocolate shop is devil-sent. Whether he is correct or not, he reacts badly to what he views as temptation, committing unchristian acts in misguided and ultimately fruitless attempts to protect himself and his congregation. By contrast, Luke's version of Jesus' temptations, like his version of Jesus' baptism, was meant to give readers a model for discipleship—here is how, as Jesus' follower, you should deal with Satan.

This episode is also found in Matthew, mostly word for word the same, except for the order of the second and third temptations. We

The Purification of the Leper and the Temptation of Christ

Sandro Botticelli (1444–1510). *The Purification of the Leper and the Temptation of Christ.* 1481. Sistine Chapel, Vatican Palace, Vatican State. (Credit: Scala /Art Resource, NY)

presume, then, that it came from Q and that both Luke and Matthew copied it into their Gospels at the point where Mark had his own temptation account. Mark's version is, characteristically, short, violent, and cryptic: "The Spirit immediately drove him out into the wilderness. He was in the wilderness forty days, tempted by Satan; and he was with the wild beasts; and the angels waited on him" (Mark 1:12-13). Luke avoids the image of the Spirit driving Jesus out, opting for a gentler introduction, and then, to give his readers some concrete examples of how to face temptation, puts in the longer version.

It is no surprise to the reader that Luke's Jesus was "filled with the Spirit," and not just "led by the Spirit." His birth came about by the Spirit's creative act (1:35), and the Spirit descended upon him at his baptism (3:22). John predicted that this Coming One would baptize with the Spirit (3:16), and in order to do that, Jesus would need himself to be empowered and directed by the Spirit. The first readers of Luke, attentive as they were to the sounds of the Old Testament, would have heard "full of the Holy Spirit" and thought "prophet," able to do mighty deeds, like outrunning a chariot for several miles (1 Kgs 18:46), or able to speak mighty words from God (Isa 61:1). In this episode, Jesus will do both: he will face down the devil over a forty-day fasting and praying retreat, and in a final showdown, he will speak the word of God to the great enemy of God's people.

Jesus "returned from the Jordan" and his time with John the Baptist, but he did not go back to Nazareth. Instead, he "was led in the wilderness" by the Spirit. Luke read "The Spirit cast him out into the wilderness" in Mark 1:12, and made two changes. Luke's version does not say that he was led *into* the wilderness, but *in* the wilderness; Luke thus makes Jesus like the Israelites under Moses, led by the "pillar of cloud by day and the pillar of fire by night" for forty years in the Sinai. Israel had to wander as punishment for their disobedience to God's command to enter the land of promise. But Jesus chooses to go, in obedience to the Spirit's leadership and in solidarity with the people of Israel; so Luke writes that the Spirit *led* him, rather than *cast* him. Luke must have understood this time in Jesus' life in much the same way that he understood the baptism: Jesus, God's obedient Son, did not need to repent of or be punished for his own sins. But the people of God needed to repent, or face God's wrath on the Day of Judgment. So Jesus, the righteous man, will suffer on their behalf and hope to avert God's punishment thereby.

Luke says that he fasted for forty days, and "ate nothing"—the kind of thing a Spirit-driven man might attempt, and reminiscent of the mighty-mighty Elijah who traveled forty days and nights in the wilderness on the strength of a piece of pita bread and a liter of water.[2] The last part of v. 2, "when they [the forty days] were completed, he was hungry," sounds like Luke understood this as a set period—a vow, perhaps, to seek the Lord's guidance by fasting and prayer for forty days.

The three temptations could be seen as a sort of summary of the kinds of temptations Jesus endured throughout his time in the wilderness. The "stones into bread" would then tell us of his perfectly human struggle with his appetites, and his determination to master them; the other two temptations might be examples of continuing temptations to strike out on a road other than God's. We can also read the temptations as the climax of the retreat, and "when [the forty days] were complete" would point this way. If this is so, then the reader is warned that a godly person is vulnerable to attack just after completing some great work in God's name. Fasting, praying, resisting Satan for forty days would be all for naught if, after the vow was done, Jesus relaxed his guard, congratulated himself on his devotional prowess, and got a little cocky. Maybe we are to see this as the devil's final shot at him, thinking that he will be physically weak and emotionally unprepared. [Abba Macarius on How to Master Satan]

> **Abba Macarius on How to Master Satan**
>
> Macarius, a monk of the 4th-century Egyptian desert tradition, encounters the devil, who complains about why Macarius has greater power than he: "Yet whatever thou dost, I do also, and more. For thou dost fast now and then, but by no food am I ever refreshed. Thou doest often keep vigil; no slumber ever falls upon me. But in one thing thou dost overmaster me . . . . It is thy humility alone," he said, "that masters me." He spoke and the blessed Macarius stretched out his hands in prayer: and the evil spirit vanished into the air.
>
> *Sayings of the Fathers*, sec. 124, cited in Helen Waddell, *The Desert Fathers* (Ann Arbor: University of Michigan Press, 1957), 142.

"If you are the Son of God, command this stone to become a loaf of bread." What would the harm be, when you think of it? The word for "bread" really just means one loaf, so this is not about feeding the multitudes, only about feeding Jesus. Would it have been wrong for him to provide for his own needs? Some early readers saw this as a temptation to gluttony, to put his body's needs ahead of his devotion to God[3]; but in light of "when [the forty days] were complete," Jesus' period of fasting was done. As a human, Jesus needed to eat to survive. If he had completed his vow, then eating would not have been a sin; so gluttony seems to be the wrong category for understanding this temptation. Some early interpreters suggest that the sin is in the way the devil phrases the test: "If you are the Son of God," so that the miracle then becomes a proof of who he is. Had Jesus done a miracle on command to prove to others that he was God's Son, perhaps he would have been guilty of pride—needing to prove to the devil that he really was somebody.[4] Others suggest that the sin would have been using God's power for his personal benefit—a sort of spiritual embezzlement, where Jesus diverts miraculous energy intended for others and uses it to feather his own nest.[5]

The problem with the last two explanations is that they take the devil at his word, and assume that Jesus could have turned a stone into bread just because he wanted to. Maybe Luke thinks this way; in 6:19, power comes out of Jesus to heal others, and this sounds a bit like a holy energy that resides in Jesus. But Jesus claims to be able to cast out demons "by the finger of God," which is to say that he does it as God's agent and not by his own spiritual power (11:19). If God wanted Jesus to turn a stone into bread, he could, but not otherwise; it is a mistake to think that Jesus, by virtue of being Son of God, had supernatural powers residing in him that were unavailable to ordinary mortals. According to Luke, Jesus assigned the disciples the same authority and ability to heal and to cast out demons, so it was not innate to Jesus, but a gift of the Spirit. Luke understood Jesus' own miracle-working ability as he did the abilities of the apostles in Acts, as God's gifts.

W. H. Auden suggests that had Jesus tried to transmogrify the stone, he would have failed, and the very attempt would have been the sin.[6] The temptation was to listen to the devil and to think that because he was the Son of God, he had this sort of magical power reserve. But "the devil is a liar and a conjurer, too, and if you don't mind out he'll conjure you," as the spiritual goes; you cannot take anything Satan says at face value, and Jesus wisely just ignores him. [Satan Is a Liar] "A person does not live by bread alone," says Jesus, implying that he has been sustained through his long fast by God's power and expects to be preserved if he sticks close to God. This proves true, since every meal Jesus eats in Luke (and there are many of them!) is provided by somebody else. He tells the disciples, when they go out on their own, that they should take no money but expect to find food and shelter from those to whom they minister (10:8-9). So Jesus, in this first temptation, exhibits the sort of caution and firmness of spiritual resolve that he expects of his followers.[7]

The second temptation is almost laughable: can anyone imagine any circumstances under which Jesus would really worship the devil? Perhaps that is why Luke moved this episode, as most

Satan Is a Liar

"The devil appeared to a certain brother, transformed into an angel of light, and said to him, 'I am the angel Gabriel and I am sent unto thee.' But he said, 'Look to it that thou was not sent to some other; for I am not worthy that an angel should be sent to me.' And the devil was no more seen."

Sayings of the Fathers, book 15, sec. 68, cited in Helen Waddell, *The Desert Fathers* (Ann Arbor: University of Michigan Press, 1957), 120.

suspect, from the climax to the penult.[8] Jesus' retort, "Worship God only," is a better closing line for the whole temptation narrative, and "I'll give you all the kingdoms of the world" is more grandiose than "throw yourself from the temple." But the premise is utterly weak: why on earth would Jesus want to worship Satan? The temptation would be to the sin of idolatry, worshiping something or someone other than God.

While it is not likely to have been a besetting sin for Jesus, it was a problem for Luke's audience, as it was for all early Christians. Idols and images of the gods were everywhere in the cities, and most people thought it was reasonable to show respect to a multitude of divinities even if one had doubts about whether they all actually existed. At the beginning of the second century, probably a few decades after Luke-Acts was completed, some Roman officials began to put Christians to death if they refused to acknowledge the divinity of the emperor. In Luke's own time, emperor worship seems to have been encouraged but not enforced; cities promoted these rites by holding games in the emperor's honor, having festivals on the emperor's birthday or the date of his accession to office, and ascribing honor to those who served as priests in the emperor cult. Jesus serves as paradigm for Luke's readers: no matter what blandishments they offer, you must worship only God. [Letter from the Emperor Caligula to the Achaean League, AD 37]

"All the kingdoms of the world" echoes 2:1, where the emperor decided that all the world should be enrolled. But not even Augustus, whom Luke pictured as thinking he could write down everyone's name in the whole civilized world, would have imagined he really controlled all the kingdoms of the world. Some commentators grant the devil his boast: the whole world is under the control of the powers of darkness, and Satan is the "dark dumb thing who turns the handle on this idle show." True enough, John the Baptist's apocalyptic message assumes that Israel generally is under the threat of God's judgment and that all need to repent. Galilee, as Jesus walks around in it, seems to be infested with demons, a sign that Satan's dominion is great and that the Strong Man needs to be bound. But does Luke believe, like John the Revelator, that the power behind Rome and the empire is Satan, the great dragon? Were that true, how could Jesus command his followers to "render to Caesar what is Caesar's," and would we not

Letter from the Emperor Caligula to the Achaean League, AD 37

Caligula writes to a group of Greek city-states to thank them for honors paid him by their populations. The letter illustrates how cities held festivals or games to honor the emperors, an aspect of emperor worship that would have been attractive to the general public: "I have read the decree given me by your envoys and perceive that you have omitted no extreme of zeal and reverence for me. You have offered sacrifice each [city] individually and have held a common festival for my safety."

Cited in Naphtali Lewis and Meyer Reinhold, *The Empire*, vol. 2 of *Roman Civilization* (New York: Harper and Row, 1966), 565.

read about Satan entering Pilate rather than Judas? ["A guy named Satan"]

Perhaps Luke thinks that Satan could really have made Jesus the *Pantokrator*, the worldwide potentate, but I suspect that in Luke's mind, Satan is lying again. Jesus gives his followers a kingdom, just as his Father gave him one (22:28-29); only God could do what Satan claims to be able to do. So when Jesus answers that one must worship only God, it is the only sensible answer.

The third and final temptation is for Jesus to make a spectacle of himself: jump from the pinnacle of the temple, and God will catch him. The text reads as if Satan teleported Jesus from the wilderness to Jerusalem, to a very high place; we are not told that Jesus was returned to the wilderness after the testing was over, so perhaps we could read it as a visionary, rather than an actual, experience. Satan quotes the Bible to Jesus to argue that God would never let him fall, taking the words of Psalm 91:11-12 very literally. Jesus, perhaps understanding the verses more metaphorically, declines to jump, quoting Deuteronomy 6:16 and the prohibition against putting God to the test. [Humility Defeats Satan]

Had Jesus jumped, the sin would have been pride, in the form of a big, showy event that would prove he indeed was God's chosen servant. Jesus refuses to do miracles as demonstrations of who he was (4:23-24; 11:29), and he cautions his disciples against crowing about their own power over evil (10:18-20). Pride is insidious, however, as illustrated once again by Père Reynaud:

My sin is that of pettiness, *mon père*. For this reason God is silent in his house. I know it, but I do not know how to cure the ill. I have increased the austerity of my Lenten fast, choosing to continue even on the days when a relaxation is permitted. Today, for instance, I poured my Sunday libation onto the hydrangeas and felt a definite lifting of the spirit. For now water and coffee will be the only accompaniment to my meals, the coffee to be taken black and sugarless to enhance the bitter taste. Today I had a carrot salad with olives—roots and berries in the wilderness. True, I feel a little light-headed now, but the sensation is not unpleasant. I feel a prick of guilt at the thought that even my deprivation gives me pleasure, and I resolve to place myself in the path of temptation. I shall stand for five minutes at the window of the *rôtisserie*, watching the chickens on the spit. If Arnauld taunts me, so much the better. In any case, he should be closed for Lent.[9]

It is important that in Luke's story, Jesus fights Satan in the same ways that the reader might, by resisting the logic of temptation and by turning to Scripture. Jesus is "full of the Spirit" and is "led by the Spirit," just as the Christians in Acts will be. He fasts and prays; forty days with nothing was out of the ordinary, but in principle, Jesus was doing what his followers would do later. His use of Scripture was not subtle or difficult, just straightforward quotes to say that he would not do what the devil was asking. Here, then, was Luke's model for how to resist evil without using evil methods.

Many Christians turn to this passage to begin Lent in Year C of the liturgical cycle, hoping to find guidance for their own lives. Many of us do not experience evil as a visit from Satan, as did Jesus and the monks of the Egyptian desert. For us, the first step in resisting temptation is recognizing it; in this episode, Satan is not disguised but completely open about his identity, rarely the case for us. But in the first temptation, we see something of the ambiguity of the evil we experience, because Satan tempts Jesus to do something that in and of itself is not sinful. Jesus, full of the Spirit, is not fooled; the Spirit gives him the words he needs, just as he promises will be true for his followers (12:11-12). Jesus' example teaches us to study Scripture, to lean on it for guidance under pressure, and to forego any sort of "returning evil for evil"; Jesus endured the temptations, but he took no steps to use Satan's weapons against him.

The Synagogue at Nazareth, 4:14-30

First, a word about the division of the episode: the lectionary cuts the section in two, assigning 4:14-21 to the third Sunday after Epiphany in Year C and 4:22-32 to the fourth Sunday. Although there is an odd and hard-to-explain shift of tone at v. 23, the whole pericope belongs together. The comments below will give some suggestions on treating the halves of the story separately in a sermon, but it is an artificial and unnatural procedure. Luke 4:31-32 also most likely goes with the next pericope, which is likewise a synagogue story, meant by Luke to stand in contrast to this one. If you are free to modify the lectionary selections, then one suggestion would be to preach 4:14-30 on the third Sunday after Epiphany and 4:31-37 or 4:31-44 on the fourth since Luke 4:33-44 is not included in Year C.

Next, a note about sources: Mark 6:1-6 is a much more basic account of a visit to the hometown synagogue at Nazareth. In that episode, the audience is very skeptical of Jesus' abilities, and as a result, he can do no miracles. There are obvious similarities—the place, the saying about "no prophet is without honor," and the negative reaction—and so Luke's version is most likely an expansion of the one in Mark. But there are also dissimilarities. The audience in Mark's version takes offense before Mark's readers get to hear Jesus say a word, whereas Luke's synagogue audience is pleased with Jesus until he starts telling them that God gives all the good stuff to the Gentiles. Once they get riled, the audience in Luke's account wants to kill Jesus, whereas the Markan audience seems basically unresponsive. Most significantly, Luke's account includes a programmatic statement by Jesus based on a reading of Isaiah 61:1-2. Since Luke is the only Gospel that has these elements, one must either attribute them to special material known only to Luke or to his imaginative interpretation.

In these early chapters, Luke wants to drive home the point, by repetition, that Jesus' actions were entirely led by the Spirit. The Spirit descended on him at his baptism (3:22), led him into the desert to be tempted by Satan (4:1), and now goes with him back to Galilee (4:14). Although Luke will not always write that Jesus was filled with the Spirit or spoke under the Spirit's direction, the narrative always assumes it is so.

Jesus' reputation spreads through Galilee, and he teaches in "their" synagogues, enjoying rave reviews. This will be repeated in 4:36-37 and 4:44, so that the episode at Nazareth, which turns out so badly, is sandwiched between reports of continuous success. In Luke, the synagogue is not necessarily a place of conflict or danger for Jesus, but a place where sometimes he can teach and preach and gain a favorable hearing.

This text is one of a few that describe a first-century synagogue service. In Luke's account, the congregation owns a scroll of the prophet Isaiah; if they had that, they almost certainly also had a Torah scroll and scrolls of the prophets and the writings. There is also an attendant (like the modern hazzan) who handed the scroll to Jesus and took it back from him. Jesus stood to read but sat to teach, implying a lectern or table behind which he stood to read, and a chair from which he taught. If a seated man could be the focus of the whole audience, then a logical arrangement for the

Floor Plan of a First-century Synagogue at Gamla

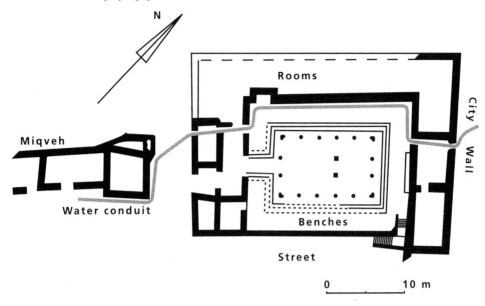

Worshipers in a 1st-century synagogue like the one at Gamla in northern Galilee sat on benches arranged like stadium seats in a rectangle with one open end. If the speaker stood at the south end, in the opening, he would have been the focus of the whole group, who would also have been facing in the general direction of Jerusalem.

room would be stadium-style benches on three sides of the room, with the speaker standing at the open end.

Such evidence as there is—and there is not much—supports Luke's picture as the way synagogue buildings were normally constructed and the way synagogue worship was normally done. The Theodotus inscription from Jerusalem, which many date to the first century, describes the functions of a synagogue as a place for reading the Law (aloud), teaching the commandments, providing hospitality within the Jewish community, and providing the means for purification (i.e., a *miqveh* or immersion pool for cleansing of normal impurities). [The Theodotus Inscription] Such archaeological evidence as there is for synagogue buildings in the first century would suggest that when Jewish communities built a specialized meeting and worship space, they built rectangular rooms with multilevel benches and with a row of decorative columns down each of the long sides. Many of those excavated so far have a *miqveh* attached to the building, connecting Torah-teaching with the observance of the purity codes, and perhaps

The Theodotus Inscription

Theodotus, (son) of Vettenus, priest and *archisynagôgos*, son of an *archisynagôgos*, grandson of an *archisynagôgos*, built the synagogue for the reading of the law and the teaching of the commandments, and the guest-chamber and the rooms and the water installations for lodging for those needing them from abroad, which his fathers, the elders and Simonides founded implying that the worshipers considered the space sacred enough to warrant purification before entry.

There is scholarly debate, as there always is, about the dating of the inscription and of the synagogue buildings upon which that summary view is based.[10] But most would agree that there were, in at least some parts of Palestine, first-century synagogue buildings and services involving reading Torah and commenting on it, just as Luke describes. Luke's picture is realistic, especially if we think of the ways Jews were worshiping in larger cities or in places where the numbers and income levels were great enough to finance a building, expensive scrolls, and specialized officers.

But others doubt that the organization was that complex in a place like Nazareth in the early first century. They assume that the community would have gathered to pray on Sabbath, but not in a synagogue building; rather, outside or in a house or in a facility that structurally looked no different than a house. So far as we can tell, first-century Nazareth was a small Jewish village of 200–400 inhabitants. Some scholars believe the citizens of Nazareth are unlikely to have had a synagogue building, to have owned a Torah scroll, and to have had a literate interpreter. Perhaps Luke is importing details from synagogues in his area, assuming that the situation would have been the same wherever Jews worshiped.

Histories written in the New Testament period always have speeches at important moments, because that was how people in that time imagined things got done. Readers of the New Testament will be familiar with how Acts is filled with speeches, to a degree that often leaves us puzzled: why would Luke choose to have Paul describe his conversion in detail in three different speeches, especially when the reader already had read it as a narrative in chapter 9? We simply must grant that first-century readers of Greek historical narratives expected many speeches. Readers also expected that the historians would compose the speeches based on their knowledge of how events unfolded and of what might have been appropriate to say on such an occasion.

To see one example of how this worked, skim through 2 Maccabees 7:1-42, which dates to the first or second century before Christ, and compare it with 4 Maccabees 8:1–16:25, which is roughly contemporary with Luke. The older text tells the story of seven brothers and their mother who died under torture in the time of Antiochus IV rather than eat pork in disobedience to the Torah. Antiochus's henchmen ask the second brother if he will eat rather than be dismembered; he replies, "No" (2 Macc 7:7-8). In the comparable scene in 4 Maccabees, the brother says,

How sweet is any kind of death for the religion of our ancestors . . . .
Do you not think, you most savage tyrant, that you are being tortured more than I, as you see the arrogant design of your tyranny
being defeated by our endurance for the sake of religion? I lighten my
pain by the joys that come from virtue, but you suffer torture by the
threats that come from impiety. You will not escape, you most abominable tyrant, the judgments of the divine wrath. (4 Macc 9:29-32)

The author of 4 Maccabees, who has no other sources for this story
than 2 Maccabees, not only provides speeches much more satisfying than the short retorts in the earlier story, but also composes
alternative speeches that the brothers might have given had they
been cowards!

Luke, then, in order to write an account of Jesus' life that would
make sense and appeal to his audience, needed to give a more
appropriate beginning for Jesus' ministry than Mark provided.
Jesus needed to make a speech that would set out the themes of his
ministry and lay the groundwork for why that ministry ultimately
failed to win his audience. Luke chose to move the Nazareth speech
from the middle of the Galilee section, where Mark had it, to its
beginning; but he also chose to indicate, with the broad-brush
summary of 4:15-16, that Jesus' speech in the Nazareth synagogue
was not his first outing, but was his first rejection.

The text he read is not exactly an outline of what Jesus does in
the rest of Luke, but the headings cover many of his activities and
major emphases.

The Spirit of the Lord is upon me: Jesus the speaker repeats what
Luke the narrator said about him: he is being led by God's Spirit.
This puts Jesus in the category of "prophet," a point that Luke will
make later in this episode. It also means that Jesus, as a character, is
following the pattern already set in this Gospel by Mary, Elizabeth,
Zechariah, Simeon, and John the Baptist. Throughout this Gospel,
Jesus will be identified as a prophet, by the types of miracles he
does, by the manner in which he champions the poor against the
wealthy, by the way he predicts judgment falling on the disobedient
people of God, and by the way he calls for repentance in view of
the coming kingdom.

Because he has anointed me: The Hebrew word "Messiah" and the
Greek word "Christ" both mean "anointed one." The root idea of
the Messiah was to fulfill God's promise to David that there would
always be a king from his line over Israel (2 Sam 7:8-17). The
"anointed one" would be God's choice to restore that line, to rescue
Israel, and to bring God's salvation. But specifics on the Messiah—

human or angelic? mortal or immortal? king or prophet or priest or some combination?—were all debated in Jesus' day. There was no single "messianic ideal" that Luke was trying to correct; there was, instead, a variety of views, and Luke was fitting Jesus into the mix. But as the Gospel progresses, there are also strong hints that for Luke, "messiah" or "king" is not a straightforwardly positive thing to say about Jesus. Thus, Jesus' inaugural text does not simply say, "because he has anointed me," but "because he has anointed me to evangelize the poor."

To preach the gospel to the poor: Jesus echoes his mother's song when he reads this part of the Isaiah text. Speaking of God's act of creation in herself, she had said, "He has brought down the powerful from their thrones, and lifted up the lowly; he has filled the hungry with good things, and sent the rich away empty" (1:52-53). He echoes his cousin's plainspoken advice to the crowds; when asked what to do in view of God's coming scourge of Israel, John said, "Whoever has two coats must share with anyone who has none, and whoever has food must do likewise." Salvation in Luke is good news for the poor, and Jesus will not only proclaim it so, but also practice it. The company of believers in Luke-Acts does good for the poor, to the point that one begins to wonder if Luke could imagine a wealthy person remaining wealthy for long after joining Jesus' followers.

Release to the captives/to set the oppressed free (lit., to send away the oppressed with release): The word translated "release" here is used often in Luke, but elsewhere is translated "forgiveness." Jesus again sounds like John the Baptist. Luke's Gospel will often use "repentance and forgiveness of sins" as a summary of the good news, and there is a close connection between discipleship and the forgiveness of sins. The first disciples will be so impressed by Jesus' miracles that one of them will say, "Depart from me, for I am a sinful man, Lord" (5:8), and Luke's Jesus will express his mission as calling sinners to repentance (5:32; Mark 2:17, the source for this verse, lacks "to repentance"). Once Jesus describes a healing as a liberation from Satan (13:16); Luke's theology also connects Jesus' ministry of exorcism with this mission to provide "release to the captives." Freedom, then, means freedom from sin and freedom from the oppressive powers of evil.

Recovery of sight to the blind: Jesus does heal the blind, and at 7:21-22 suggests that his miracles and his preaching the good news to the poor should be sufficient proof that he is the Coming One predicted by John the Baptist. Luke does not present Jesus' healing ministry as a distraction from his teaching ministry as Mark sometimes does. Whereas Mark's Jesus never seeks out someone to heal, Luke's Jesus sometimes does (e.g., 13:12); whereas Mark's Jesus gives his disciples authority over demons, Luke's Jesus, in addition, gives them authority to heal and tells them to preach the kingdom of God and to heal (Mark 6:7; Luke 9:1-2).

To preach the favorable year of the Lord: The word "favorable" is an echo of the angels' song at 2:14; Jesus' ministry, now started, begins a time when God shows great favor to humans. In the songs of the birth narratives, it is a time when enemies are routed, when the lowly are lifted up, when promises are kept, when light comes to all in darkness. Jesus' good news will sometimes appear under the heading of the kingdom of God (4:43) or repentance and forgiveness (5:32) or salvation (19:9), but in each case the central idea is of the gracious activity of God for humans.

For Luke, then, the Isaiah text helps to preview the aims and activities of Jesus. Those who read Luke's Gospel or who heard it read aloud would have made connections, as we just did, with material in the first three chapters and with themes throughout the rest of the Gospel. For the readers and the hearers of Luke, this text, and Jesus' words, "Today this scripture has been fulfilled in your hearing," help to give a sense of direction and unity to this long narrative of Jesus' ministry. Those who are following the lectionary and are focusing only on vv. 14-21 could use the Isaiah text as a *précis* of the ministry of Luke's Jesus, and then as a template against which to think about the ministry of a local congregation.

It is possible to read v. 22 in at least three ways. The first part is literally "and everyone bore witness to [or against] him." Elsewhere in Luke, the verb used here (*martyreō*, whence we get the English word "martyr") has the sense of giving testimony to something one has witnessed, so it can be evidence for a position

Jesus in the Synagogue

Alexandre Bida. *Jesus in the Synagogue*. 1874. Illustration. Dover Pictorial Archive Series.

one holds (21:13) or testimony against someone (9:5, 22:71). The second part, "they marveled at the gracious words coming out of his mouth," is a favorable response, but not necessarily indicative of understanding. Being amazed is not the same thing as being convinced or being converted, especially in Luke. "Gracious" can be an adjective meaning "grace-filled, kind, generous," but it can also be more literally "words about God's grace." If the first sense is meant, then the Nazareans are amazed at how well Jesus speaks; if the second, they are amazed at what he is saying about God's grace. In either case, it sounds like a favorable response. The third and final part of v. 22 quotes the crowd saying, "Isn't this Joseph's son?" This may have been meant as a critique, the equivalent of "he's a nobody, so why is he speaking like this?" But there is nothing innately critical, from the point of view of the audience in the story, about calling him Joseph's son, since that was how they knew him. My take on this verse, then, is that since the last two parts are a favorable response, the first part probably is, too: "They all testified to him and were amazed at the gracious words coming out of his mouth, and they said, 'Isn't this Joseph's son?'"

Up to this point, then, the story is positive. Jesus is welcomed home and welcomed into the pulpit at Sabbath services. He reads a nice passage that promises blessings and says that it is even now coming true. The hometown folks are surprised at how he talks and perhaps about the sorts of things he says, but they think he is doing fine.

Jesus' next move is abrupt. He says that they will surely want him to duplicate in his own hometown some of the miracles he has been doing in Capernaum. (The narrator, in fact, has described no mighty deeds done in any particular place, only that he has been teaching in synagogues throughout Galilee.) Jesus then goes on to state that as a prophet, he expected a hostile reception from his hometown; a prophet is never honored in his native place. But, he reminds them, famous prophets from the past ministered to people outside Israel. Elijah helped to feed a widow in Sidon, but none in Israel; Elisha healed a Syrian leper, but none in Israel. Now the congregation reacts abruptly; filled with rage, they cast him out of the city (the verb here is the one used for exorcising demons) and lead him to a nearby cliff intending to throw him to his death. ["Hurl him off a cliff"] Then Jesus inexplicably, and anticlimactically, escapes: "passing through the midst of them, he left." No intervention of God? No

"Hurl him off a cliff"

Ancient Nazareth was built on a hill three and a half miles from Sepphoris, but there are no signs of a cliff such as the one Luke describes in 4:29. Perhaps Luke was thinking of the death of Jezebel, thrown down to her death from a high window (2 Kgs 9:30-33), or of the deaths of faithful Jewish mothers who were killed with their children by being thrown from the walls of Jerusalem as punishment for circumcising their boys (4 Macc 4:25 uses the same verb Luke uses in 4:29).

prophetic word of judgment, something to the effect that the stone rejected will become head of the corner? It is the final abrupt move in a series of sudden mood swings in this story.

Unless we supply some missing steps, it is hard to avoid reading this as Jesus' deliberate provocation of the synagogue audience. Noting the progression of Mark's story makes this clear:

- Jesus goes to the hometown synagogue.
- He teaches—Mark does not say what he teaches.
- Many who hear are amazed—an ambiguous reaction.
- They say, "Is this not the carpenter, the son of Mary, brother of James and Joses and Judah and Simon"—in other words, he is not educated; he has no father; and we know all about all his kinfolk.
- The narrator adds, "They were offended by him." Mark's account of the audience reaction, then, is more clearly and consistently negative, and this comes before Jesus says anything provocative.
- Then, only after they respond badly, Jesus says that a prophet has no honor except among his own people.

By contrast, Luke's Jesus seems to be facing a mostly positive audience reaction. After v. 22, the narrator does not describe their attitudes or reactions until v. 28, where they are in a murderous rage. The synagogue audience goes straight from generally positive amazement to definitely negative actions, but only after Jesus tells them what they doubtless will think or say.

One way to read this story is to say that Luke expects the reader to supply several steps: Jesus has done miracles in Capernaum; the word about them has spread; the townspeople of Nazareth have heard and are jealous; as a prophet, Jesus knows all this and is responding appropriately. On this reading, Jesus opposes a parochial view of the gospel that would restrict it to any particular group. The worshipers at Nazareth want to keep God's blessings for themselves, and Jesus prophetically denounces their attitude. Clearly, Luke does want the reader to supply the miracles at Capernaum; otherwise, the story breaks down at v. 23. Likewise, Luke's Jesus adopts the prophetic persona here and at many subsequent places. So it is possible to imagine that Luke wants us to read this thinking that Jesus already knows how they will react to his ministry and launches a preemptive prophetic strike against this point of view. A similar episode is 13:31-35, where Jesus says he would have gathered the people of Jerusalem to him had they been willing; at that point in the story, he has never preached in

Jerusalem, and so must be thinking ahead to what will happen during Holy Week. On this reading of the Nazareth episode, the congregation's hostility at the end is proof of Jesus' prescience, not a reaction to his provocation.

On the other hand, Jesus does speak provocatively in other parts of Luke. For example, in 11:37-54, Jesus is invited to eat with a Pharisee; the host is amazed to see that Jesus fails to wash before eating, but does not say a word to Jesus. Jesus, on the other hand, denounces the Pharisees and scribes with very caustic language, leading to a plot of sorts against Jesus. Perhaps Luke's understanding of Jesus as a prophet includes the possibility that Jesus could go on the attack like this because this is what prophets do.

Another way to read the episode is to see it as advancing the theme announced in the birth narratives and particularly in the songs of Mary, Zechariah, and Simeon. Each of them, in different ways, said that Jesus' birth was God's blessing to Israel: "he has helped his servant Israel in remembrance of his mercy" (1:54); "he has looked favorably and has made redemption for his people" (1:68); "light for revelation for the Gentiles, and glory for your people Israel" (2:32). Jesus brings the good news to his hometown synagogue—to Israel, as Mary, Zechariah, and Simeon all say he will do—but he insists it is not just for them, but also for the Gentiles, as Simeon said. Jesus, said Simeon, was "set for the falling and rising of many in Israel" (2:34). The Nazareth episode is the "falling," and there will be plenty of examples of "rising" elsewhere in the Gospel.

Yet another way to get an angle on the Nazareth story is to contrast it with 4:31-44. In this section, Jesus does miracles at Capernaum: first a demoniac in the synagogue, then Peter's mother-in-law, and then all the rest of the sick in the city. The demons and demoniacs cry out that he is the Son of God (4:34, 41), but the rest of the population is only amazed (4:36). The next day, the crowds found him in an out-of-the-way place and "held him so that he could not leave them" (4:42). Jesus, however, went on his way, after telling them that it was necessary for him to give the gospel to other towns. In other words, in two successive stories, a crowd tries to prevent Jesus from carrying out his mission, the first because they were angry enough to kill him, the second because they wanted to keep him and his miracle-working in their neighborhood. In Nazareth, he hints that God's power to do good will be shared with others; in Capernaum, he tells them that he must go to other places to share the gospel. In the first case, there is an attempted murder and in the second an attempted binding, but in neither case can Jesus be deflected from his chosen path.

On any reading, the violent reaction of his hometown synagogue is a tragic element in the storyline of Luke. Jesus just walks away from it; as he will say in 13:33, the site of his death has to be Jerusalem. Nevertheless, we are to see this as a real threat. The hostility at Nazareth previews for the reader the mob's voice that prevails in Jesus' trial. This time, "Jesus, passing through the midst of them, went on his way," but his days are numbered.

The Day at Capernaum, 4:31-44

Mark 1:21-39 gave Luke this "busy day" section, and Luke has kept most of it intact, with a few important shifts in emphasis to which we should pay attention. But as several commentators point out, Luke sets this section up to be parallel to 4:16-30.[11] Luke gives us plenty of clues, by the way the two stories begin, that we are supposed to play the one story against the other:

He came into Nazareth	He came into Capernaum
Stood to read	Was teaching them
On Sabbath	On Sabbath
In the synagogue	In the synagogue
All bore witness to him and marveled	They were amazed at his teaching
At his gracious words	His word was with authority

As the two episodes progress, the contrasts matter more than the similarities. At Nazareth, Jesus tells the audience that they will demand that he perform for them the sorts of miracles he had done at Capernaum, but he refuses. In Capernaum, he does a miracle, exorcising a demon from a man who stands up to shout at him. Jesus tells the Nazareth crowd that they will doubtless say to him, "Physician, heal yourself!" While in Capernaum, Jesus heals anyone in town who comes to his door that evening. In Nazareth, Jesus notes that Elijah and Elisha helped two foreigners, feeding a widow and cleansing a leper. At Capernaum, Jesus heals Simon's mother-in-law (who may have been understood to be a widow, since she was living with her son-in-law), who then feeds him; and he cleanses the demoniac in the synagogue. At the conclusion of the Nazareth episode, the crowd, enraged, casts Jesus out of their town and takes him to a cliff to throw him over, but he simply walks away. At Capernaum, Jesus leaves to find a deserted spot, and the crowd seeks him out, wanting to hold him to keep him from leaving them. But again, Jesus leaves, going on his way as God has directed. The two episodes thus begin the same way, with Jesus entering a synagogue to teach, and end the same way, with Jesus successfully overcoming an obstacle to his presentation of the gospel. Luke gives the reader three successive episodes—the temptation, the sermon at Nazareth, and the day at Capernaum—ending with Jesus successfully resisting impediments and staying focused on his mission.

Mark's parallel section (1:21-39) reads like a typical day in the life of Jesus of Nazareth: he heals one man in the synagogue and one woman in a friend's home, and suddenly he is surrounded by people sick and possessed by demons. No wonder, we're supposed to conclude, that Jesus would try to keep the news of his healings from spreading, as he does when he heals the leper (Mark 1:40-45). Luke keeps this connection; he notes in 5:15-16 that the word about Jesus' miracles spread despite his commands to silence, and that consequently crowds continued to come to be healed. But Luke's narrative also presents the spread of the "word" as a positive thing:

- 4:14-15: A report went out through the whole region about him, and he was teaching in their synagogues, praised by many.
- 4:37: A story circulated about him in every place of the region.
- 4:43: He told them, "I must preach the good news of the kingdom of God in the other cities also, because I was sent out for this purpose."

The spread of the "word" thus agrees with Jesus' own mission from God; God sent him to preach, and the spread of the "word" to every place is part of God's plan.

The Capernaum synagogue crowd remarks on the authority (*exousia*) of his words (4:32) and later on their authority and power (*dynamis*; 4:36). Satan had promised to give him all the authority and glory of all the inhabited world, claiming it was his to disburse; Jesus had not fallen for that, nor for any of Satan's other enticements, and as a result Jesus returned to Galilee "in the power of the Spirit" (4:14). Jesus' teachings and his power to cast out demons come from being sent by God "to preach release/forgiveness to the captives . . . to send captives away in release" (4:18), and the two functions of preaching and demon exorcism are related.

It is no accident that this first Lukan miracle is an exorcism, and that it happens in the context of Jesus' synagogue teaching. In the popular understanding of Second Temple Judaism, demons were the result of the illicit intercourse between angels and women described in Genesis 6. The offspring of these unions were giants

(Gen 6:4), and the offspring of the giants were the demons, who were held to be responsible for all sorts of evil (witchcraft, sorcery, necromancy, idolatry) and diseases (*1 En.* 6-16). ["evil spirits upon the earth"] These were expected to continue to afflict people until the coming of God's kingdom, when God would banish them to their prison-houses at the edges of the world. When Jesus teaches the word of God, demons quake, knowing that their doom has arrived, and indeed he silences the demon and prevents it from harming the possessed man (4:35). Jesus is both preaching release and performing it, setting free the captives and clearing the way for the advance of God's word by cleansing those polluted by evil. He is also proving that he was right to ignore Satan's lies; obviously, Jesus' authority is greater than that of the demons. But his "authority and power" cuts no ice in Nazareth; he can out-debate Satan and impress a crowd in Capernaum by his power to exorcise, but in Nazareth, the same authoritative speech only makes his audience want to throw him off a cliff.

"evil spirits upon the earth"
But now the giants who are born from the (union of) the spirits [the angels] and the flesh [the women] shall be called evil spirits upon the earth . . . . Evil spirits have come out of their bodies. (*1 En.* 15:8-9)

Jesus goes straight from the synagogue to Simon's house. In Mark, the call of the first four disciples—Simon and Andrew, James and John—comes earlier, so that Jesus is going to a disciple's house and performing a healing at the request of friends (Mark 1:29-31). But because Luke delays the call of the four until after the "busy day," the effect of the miracle is reversed: now we understand why Simon and his friends might be drawn to Jesus and might be led to trust him. Jesus exorcises a demon in Simon's hometown synagogue, so "they," presumably Simon and his friends and relations, ask Jesus into their home. Once there, "they" ask him about the mother-in-law, and Jesus heals her: they grant him hospitality, and he heals their family member. In the same way, Luke will remark that Jesus had healed women who then contributed from their means to support him (8:2-3), or that the centurion was worthy of having his servant healed because he had built a synagogue for the Jewish people of Capernaum (7:4-5), or that the disciples on mission should "heal the sick" and then expect to eat from the tables of those whom they have helped. Luke's Greco-Roman readers would recognize this sort of reciprocity and webs of indebtedness as the way their world worked (more on this at 5:1-11). [Patrons, Clients, and Reciprocity]

Luke reduces the physical contact between Jesus and Simon's mother-in-law; Jesus, rather than taking her by the hand, stands over her. Luke also treats it as an exorcism: the fever "holds" her;

Patrons, Clients, and Reciprocity

A patron is a person in a position to do a favor for someone, the client, who needs it done: a loan, or a favorable judgment, or a word of introduction. The client would then be obliged to do, in return, whatever the patron needed at the time when he needed it. In this section of Luke, Jesus heals Peter's mother-in-law, making Peter his client; later, Peter is in no position to refuse when Jesus asks to borrow his boat and then tells Peter to let down his nets (5:3, 4-5).

Jesus rebukes the fever, just as he rebuked the demon in the man at the synagogue; the fever "released" her (using the same verbal root as "release" in 4:18).[12] Some suggest that Luke's rewrite is partly motivated by a concern for Jesus' reputation—no unnecessary touching!—but the very suggestive story of the woman weeping over Jesus' feet (7:36-50) makes that unlikely. It seems more probable that Luke is making her healing more like the synagogue exorcism so that Jesus does two of the same sort back to back, healing a man and a woman by rebuking that which bound them. In both cases, the person is restored to normal without any damage; we are frequently told this about demoniacs Jesus helps (8:35; 9:42; 13:13,16), but are warned that other exorcists (11:19) may only make things worse (11:24-26). Jesus' exorcisms, because they are acts of God's release, truly clear the way for the full blessing of God and show that God's kingdom has come (11:20).

One final word about the mother-in-law: as soon as she was released from the grip of the fever, "immediately rising she served them." The word translated "serve," *diakoneō*, is the word from which we get the English word "deacon." Luke takes it from Mark, and so perhaps means nothing special by it,[13] but the fact is that Peter's mother-in-law is the first person in Luke to minister to Jesus. Just as Elizabeth and Mary were the first Spirit-inspired speakers, so this woman is the first to respond, out of gratitude, in service to Jesus.[14]

For the rest of the day, even as evening is coming, Jesus heals and exorcises people in Capernaum. He heals "all" who have various sorts of illnesses by laying hands on them, and drives out demons from "many" by rebuking them as he had done with the man in the synagogue and Peter's mother-in-law. The end of v. 41 gives us our first taste of the question of whether Jesus considered himself a king. This is the most serious of the three charges made against him when he is handed over to Pilate (23:1-2), and the only one Pilate takes seriously. Luke 4:41 would imply that Jesus kept the demons from confessing him to be Messiah not because it was false but because it was true. Luke thus shows Jesus being cautious and responsible. The Sanhedrin will say, "he says he is Messiah, a king" (23:2); in fact, he never says that, and insofar as he is able, prevents others from saying it. Luke is preparing the reader to be able to recognize the charges against Jesus as spurious.

At the end of the episode, Jesus retreats to a desert place. The fact that Luke does not add "to pray," as he will later (5:16; 6:12) makes the connection stronger with the beginning of the temptation story (4:1). The crowds to whom he has been ministering "tracked him down and came to him and held him so that he could not leave them" (4:42). The word translated "held" (also used at 8:15, for "holding" the word in one's heart, and at 14:9, for claiming a seat at a banquet) could also be rendered "they wanted to hold him" or "they tried to hold him." But the more direct translation "they grabbed him" makes a nice parallel with the end of the Nazareth scene and with the last two temptations. Satan takes Jesus up high to show him all the world's glory and up to the top of the temple to urge him to make a spectacle of himself; Jesus declines both, and Satan leaves. The Nazareth congregation frog-walks Jesus out to the edge of town, ready to hurl him to his doom; Jesus just walks away, leaving them standing there. The townspeople of Capernaum, who see Jesus as the free healthcare provider we all wish we could have, hold him to prevent his escape. But Jesus cannot be held; "it is necessary [by which we understand "necessary in God's plan"] for me to preach the good news of the kingdom of God to other cites, because I was sent [by God, he means] for this." So Satan tries to stop him; Jesus sends him away. Nazareth tries to stop him; Jesus walks away. Capernaum tries to stop him; Jesus explains his real purpose, and then goes about his business preaching.

CONNECTIONS

What may look like disparate material—the temptation, the sermon at Nazareth, and the "busy day" at Capernaum—are three episodes meant to be compared and contrasted. The end of all three is the same: no matter who tries to stop Jesus, be it Satan or an angry crowd or a happy bunch of groupies, Jesus cannot be diverted from the path God has set. Satan wants him to jump, Nazareth wants to throw him down, and Capernaum wants to tie him up and keep him; in each case, he walks away—God has other places for him to go.

Our culture has plenty of "dealing with the devil" stories, most of them involving some sort of contest or wager between Satan and a human. Steven Vincent Benet's "The Devil and Daniel Webster" has Jabez Stone sign over his soul in return for a more profitable farm, and then Daniel Webster argue successfully that it was an unconstitutional contract; in Charlie Daniel's "The Devil Went

Down to Georgia," Satan bets a golden fiddle against a young man's soul in a fiddle-playing contest. This Faustian genre probably is in the heads of our audiences, and confuses our readings of Luke's story. The premise in the more modern stories is that Satan could be trusted to make a valid contract; that is unlikely to have been Luke's presumption, for the first-century Satan was the deceiver of the world (Rev 12:9) and the father of lies (John 8:44). If everything out of his mouth is a lie, then Satan presents Jesus with several false choices with the sole hidden aim of getting Jesus to listen to him rather than to God. Where are the false, deceptive voices in our culture? Too many to count, I suspect.

The Nazareth episode gives one of several interpretive choices. Is the crowd initially pleased with Jesus, or just impressed, not necessarily favorably? Does Jesus respond to negative vibes from the crowd, or is he prophetically denouncing their hidden thoughts, as Simeon predicted he would? When Jesus tells them that Isaiah's great vision of the kingdom is being fulfilled among them, they may not understand, but they seem pleased. But when he tells them that God may, as in the past, widen the scope of divine mercy to include Gentiles, they blow up and want to kill him. It is a pair of abrupt turns—Jesus from "good news is yours" to "well, maybe not," and the audience from "Isn't that Joseph's boy talking so nice" to "Let's kill him!" But that's what happens sometimes when the Spirit leads in the worship of God. Garrison Keillor's Father Emil, pastor at Our Lady of Perpetual Responsibility, "was inspired by the sight of all the lapsed Catholics" at Christmas Eve Mass, and "gave them a hard homily, strolling right down into the congregation." He gives them a good Lukan tongue-lashing: "Shame. Shame on us . . . to receive a great treasure in our younger days and to abandon it so that we can lie down in the mud with swine." The congregation doesn't care for it: "They came for Christmas, to hear music and see the candles and smell incense and feel hopeful, and here was their old priest with hair in his ears whacking them around."[15] Luke's Jesus whacks the people, and then gets taken to the edge of a cliff before he simply walks away to the next thing God has for him.

The busy day turns all this around: Jesus heals, he finds attentive and grateful crowds, he is swarmed by well-wishers who only want him to do them good. Jesus is having none of this, either: I have to go to other places and preach the good news of the kingdom. When Dwight L. Moody held revival meetings in Brooklyn in 1875, the city built extra street-car tracks to the auditorium where the services were held.[16] But Jesus would not stay long enough in one place to accommodate the crowds—success in drawing a crowd is no more a sign of God's blessing than failure is a sign of God's displeasure.

NOTES

1 Joanne Harris, *Chocolat* (New York: Viking, 1999), 99.

2 Josephus, *Ant.* 3.99, says that Moses ate nothing during the 40 days and nights he spent on Sinai.

3 Origen, *Fragments on Luke* 96, cited in Arthur A. Just Jr., ed., *Luke* (ACCS: NT, vol. 3; Downer's Grove IL: Intervarsity Press, 2003), 74: "He approaches Jesus and introduces the first temptation, that of gluttony, through which he had also captured the first Adam. Since there was no food anywhere . . . He thought that Christ . . . would yield to his stomach, since he was very hungry."

4 Luke Timothy Johnson, *The Gospel of Luke* (SP, vol. 3; Collegeville MN: Liturgical Press, 1991), 74.

5 Joel B. Green, *The Gospel of Luke* (NICNT; Grand Rapids: Eerdmans, 1997), 193, notes that this is singular—turn this stone into a loaf—so it really is about Jesus' own personal needs, rather than a temptation to feed the whole world. Joseph A. Fitzmyer, *The Gospel According to Luke* (AB 28 and 28A; Garden City NY: Doubleday, 1981), 1.511: he is tempted to use his divine power for his own benefit.

6 "Satan knows that the miracle is impossible, and hopes by persuading Jesus to attempt it, to destroy his faith in the shock of failure" (W. H. Auden, from "The Prolific and the Devourer," cited in David Curzon, *The Gospels in Our Image: An Anthology of Twentieth-Century Poetry Based on Biblical Texts* [New York: Harcourt Brace, 1995], 55–58).

7 "All the same, when temptation first appears, we must be especially alert, because it is easier to defeat the enemy if we do not allow him to set foot inside the door of the mind but meet him on the step as he knocks" (Thomas à Kempis, *The Imitation of Christ* 13 [trans. Betty I. Knott; London: Collins, 1963], 54).

8 So James M. Robinson, et. al., eds., *The Critical Edition of Q* (Minneapolis: Fortress: 2000), 28–39; Kloppenborg, *Q Parallels* (Sonoma CA: Polebridge, 1988), 20.

9 Harris, *Chocolat*, 61.

10 John S. Kloppenborg, "The Theodotos Synagogue Inscription and the Problem of First-Century Synagogue Buildings," in Charlesworth, ed., *Jesus and Archaeology* (Grand Rapids MI: Eerdmans, 2006), 236–82, is a detailed examination of the arguments, mostly advanced by H. C. Kee, against a first-century dating. Kloppenborg concludes that the inscription is most likely Herodian, indicating the existence of at least one synagogue in Jerusalem in Jesus' time.

11 Alan R. Culpepper, *The Gospel of Luke* (NIB, vol. 9; Nashville: Abingdon, 1995), 110; Green, *Luke*, 220.

12 Culpepper, *Luke*, 111.

13 So Green, *Luke*, 225.

[14] Culpepper, *Luke*, 111, says that "she serves as a pattern for all who would subsequently be delivered by Jesus' word and then express their gratitude through serving."

[15] Garrison Keillor, "Exiles," in *Leaving Home* (New York: Penguin, 1997), 188–89.

[16] Bernard Weisberger, *They Gathered at the River* (Boston: Little, Brown, and Co., 1958), 203.

GATHERING DISCIPLES

Luke 5

COMMENTARY

The Call of the First Four Disciples, 5:1-11

Here we begin Luke's account of how Jesus attracted and taught disciples, and how these men (and women, although none appear in this episode) fared in their attempts to follow him. Much of the raw material for this subplot comes from Mark; the boats, the detail that the fishermen were washing their nets, the names of the four fishermen, and Jesus' word at the end about fishing for people are all present in Mark 1:16-20. But the miraculous catch of fish sounds more like the resurrection story in John 21:4-6, leading some commentators to suspect that Luke's version of the call of the four blends the Markan call tradition with a story of the appearance of the risen Christ.[1] Whether or not this is so, this call story is very Lukan, echoing themes from the birth narratives and previewing themes to be developed further. This story gives us the essence of how Luke defines discipleship.

It begins with the crowds—a pushy group in this part of Luke! The mention of the lake and the presence of Simon and his partners means that even though Luke said Jesus was in Judea in 4:44, he is, in this story, by the lake near Capernaum, and thus this is the same crowd mentioned in 4:42. There they wanted to hold Jesus to keep him from leaving; here they push against him, so that to get some space from them, he gets into a boat and asks to row a little distance out.

The boat belongs to Simon, introduced to the reader in 4:38-39. Jesus healed his mother-in-law, so of course he would not refuse a request to let Jesus sit in his boat and teach a while, even if he was busy washing out his nets from a long, unproductive night of fishing (avid anglers may see [Fishing] for more details). Jesus turns the boat into a lectern, teaching this crowd who had come to hear the word of God. We may gather, incidentally, that Peter, Andrew, James, and

John were not part of that pushy crowd, since they were busy with their nets. It speaks to the ambivalent nature of miracles that the crowd wants to hear more, but that Simon, who also saw one close up, is not yet inclined to jump into the Master's net.

Simon sits there in his boat until Jesus finishes teaching, and then Jesus gives him an order; in 5:3, Jesus *asked* for the use of the boat, but in 5:4 says directly, "Push out into the deep water and let down your nets for a catch." Simon the fisherman has worked all night and knows the fish are someplace else that day; letting down the big net is hard, time-consuming work, and it will come to nothing. "Yet at your word I will let down the net"; Simon owes him this much, anyway, for the healing Jesus has already performed. Simon sounds a bit like Mary at the Annunciation, puzzled about how things might work, but willing to submit to the Lord's will.[2] Jesus, for his part, reminds the reader of Gabriel revealing what is about to happen; later he will say what an angel always says ("do not be afraid," 5:10).

Like Mary, Simon has a choice, but if he wants to be part of the larger plan of God, he must follow Jesus' instructions. Simon addresses Jesus as "master" (*epistata*), a word only Luke uses for Jesus. The disciples use it when they are scared or confused (8:24, 45; 9:33, 49), and once lepers use it to get Jesus' attention (17:13). In this scene, it denotes a less perfect faith than the "Lord" (*kyrios*) of v. 8. His experience, then, is a sort of conversion. He hears the word as the crowd hears it, but it has no effect on him; he hears Jesus' specific word to him, is dubious, but decides to obey. Then, confronted by God's presence, he repents and receives a different commission.

Once Simon obeys, he becomes party to a miraculous catch of fish, so large that first the nets begin to tear and then the boats begin to sink. This is sometimes explained as a naturalistic sort of phenomenon: Jesus spots a large shoal of fish and talks Simon into giving it one more try. But the fisherman's reaction shows it to be a theophany, a revelation of the presence of the divine: he falls to his knees, seized by a great sense of awe, and begs Jesus to leave him, because he is afraid of what might happen to a sinful person like himself. [Theophany] Thus Peter begins his discipleship by repenting, and Jesus calls his first disciple by leading him to repent. There will be others who follow the same pattern—Levi (5:32), Zacchaeus (19:8), the prodigal son (15:17-21), etc. The very last disciple Jesus makes, from the cross, will also be a penitent (23:39-43). At his opening sermon, Jesus, quoting Isaiah, says that God sent him to proclaim "release to the captives" (4:18); the word translated "release" is normally translated "forgiveness," and "repentance and forgiveness of sins" is how the risen Jesus summarizes the gospel in his last bit of instruction to the disciples (24:47). The motif of repentance and forgiveness thus frames Jesus' ministry; for Luke, this is how one begins to follow Jesus. [Repenting]

Luke's version of the call of the first four disciples also emphasizes the theme of reciprocity, and how people whom Jesus helps then help him as well. The contrast with Mark is instructive. In Mark's version, Peter and Andrew, James and John meet Jesus when he calls them to follow him; there is no network, no web of relations to explain why they leave their family to spend their lives with a man they have only seen once. In Luke's version, Jesus has been in Peter's house, healed his mother-in-law, eaten at his table. Jesus has sat in Peter's boat to teach the crowd while Peter listened, and then Jesus has given Peter a miraculous boost to his income. Luke's readers would more readily understand why Peter would feel indebted to Jesus, and why he might then leave his family to follow him.

Luke's version also makes discipleship more of a process than an immediate and sudden change; more descriptive, perhaps, of how Luke's readers might have come to faith. In Mark's version of the call of Peter and Andrew, the apostles respond immediately, without protest or request for explanation, enjoying a brief moment as exemplary characters. In Luke, Peter's conversion happens in stages. First, he observes Jesus healing his mother-in-law and eats with him. Next, he does Jesus a favor and listens to him teach. Next, although he doubts Jesus knows anything about

Theophany

Our discovery of God is, in a way, God's discovery of us. . . . He comes down from heaven and finds us. He looks at us from the depths of his own infinite actuality, which is everywhere, and his seeing us gives us a new being and a new mind in which we also discover him. We only know him in so far as we are known by him. . . . We become contemplatives when God discovers himself in us.

Thomas Merton, *New Seeds of Contemplation* (New York: New Directions, 1972), 39.

Repenting

Larry Sorenson came forward weeping buckets and crumpled up at the communion rail, to the amazement of the minister, who had delivered a dry sermon about stewardship, and who now had to put his arm around this limp soggy individual and pray with him and see if he had a ride home. . . . Granted, we're born in original sin and are worthless and vile, but twelve conversions is too many. . . . There comes a point when you should dry your tears and join the building committee and start grappling with the problems of the church furnace and the church roof and make church coffee and be of use, but Larry kept on repenting and repenting.

Garrison Keillor, "Exiles," in *Leaving Home* (New York: Penguin, 1997), 190.

fishing, he obeys the command to fish—something he already knows how to do—and experiences the miracle in the context of his own livelihood. Only then is he ready to repent and to launch out into the truly deep waters of full-time discipleship.

The end of Luke's story returns to its roots in Mark. Jesus tells Simon that he will be catching people, and he and the other three beach their boats in order to abandon them and to follow Jesus.

Jesus, the Leper, and the Crowds, 5:12-16

The word translated "leprosy" described, in Jesus' day, a skin rash or swelling or boil, especially one that turned the body hair white, with or without itching. Leviticus 13:1-59 gives a fairly detailed set of instructions for priests on how to recognize leprosy on different parts of men's and women's bodies and on clothing; you should read it, especially to see how much attention is given to distinguishing conditions that are problematic but not leprosy (my favorite: "if anyone loses the hair from his head, he is bald, but he is clean," Lev 13:40). Modern readers would do better to think of biblical leprosy not so much as a physical disease but as a religious condition, or an "illness" as opposed to a "disease." [Illness and Disease, Curing and Healing] In the first place, Leviticus gives no thought to the cause of the symptoms. Our understanding of disease is founded on the notion that there is always a physical cause that must be identified and treated, and Leviticus says nothing about that. In the second place, the condition that leprosy presents—it makes a person unclean in a way that cannot be easily remedied—actually goes away if the skin condition spreads until it covers the whole body (Lev 13:12-13). That flies in the face of the way we think of disease: "if the disease has covered all his body, [the priest] shall pronounce him clean of the disease; since [his skin] has all turned white, he is clean" (Lev 13:13).

Lepers were instructed to stay away from anywhere people lived, and to warn away anyone who came too close. Hear the word of the Lord:

Illness and Disease, Curing and Healing

Medical anthropologists distinguish between different ways that we think about unhealthy states and the approaches taken to make things better. "Disease . . . describes abnormalities in the structure and/or function of human organs and organ systems," and is "the arena of biomedicine and the biomedical model." Diseases are "cured" by modern biomedical approaches when the affected organs or systems are restored to proper functioning. "Illness" is a different way of looking at the same set of issues: "the human perception, experience, and interpretation of certain socially disvalued states including but not limited to disease." A person covered with a skin rash might be diagnosed by a physician with the "disease" eczema, but the Bible would define it as "leprosy"—a cultural interpretation of the same physical condition, so an "illness" rather than a "disease." Illnesses may be "healed": "the attempt to provide personal and social meaning for the life problems created by sickness." A person who no longer had the symptoms of the skin rash was not yet "healed" or "cleansed" until he/she had gone through the weeklong process that resulted in restoration to the community.

Quotes from John Pilch, *Healing in the New Testament: Insights from Medical and Mediterranean Anthropology* (Minneapolis: Fortress, 2000), 24–25.

The person who has the leprous disease shall wear torn clothes and let the hair of his head be disheveled; and he shall cover his upper lip and cry out, "Unclean, unclean." He shall remain unclean as long as he has the disease; he is unclean. He shall live alone; his dwelling shall be outside the camp. (Lev 13:45-46)

To understand the purpose of the quarantine, we need to review the concepts of holy, unclean, and clean. A holy place, such as the temple in Jerusalem or a synagogue, is set aside as a place where one may approach God. An unclean person is one who cannot enter a holy place, because the uncleanness would be transmitted to the holiness of the place, polluting it and defeating the purpose for which the place was set aside. Uncleanness is contagious, transmitted by touch or by secondary touching. If an unclean person touches a clean person, or in some cases if a clean person sits on a chair or bed where an unclean person sat, then the clean person contracts uncleanness. In most cases, the original source of the uncleanness is temporary. For example, a woman is unclean so long as she is having her menstrual period, but as soon as her flow stops, so does the contagion. Her husband, who becomes unclean if he sleeps in the same bed with her, can go to the local *miqveh* and immerse every evening if he cares to, and be clean again; or he might just stay unclean until her flow stopped and then go to the *miqveh*. Either way, it would have been a temporary condition that in no way hampered daily household life.

Leprosy, however, was considered a more virulent contagion, perhaps because it was longer lasting. Lepers, when their skin condition went away, had to go through an eight-day purification process that included more than one immersion, shaving all the hair off the body, washing the clothes, and a ceremony with two doves; the house where the leper previously lived also had to be purified (Lev 14:1-57). For this reason, lepers were commanded to stay away from towns, because that was the only way to make sure that the virulent uncleanness they carried was not accidentally passed to another person who in turn could infect something or someplace dedicated to God. Lepers had to stay in limbo until they were no longer lepers, lest they render all holy places unclean. [Misconceptions about Leprosy]

Luke takes this story from Mark, and so by looking at the places where Luke alters the text

Misconceptions about Leprosy

The leprosy germ is a bacillus . . . about one six-thousandth of an inch long. Several misconceptions about leprosy (Hansen's disease) persist in modern perception, but the disease is only mildly contagious. Rarely do spouses or children contract it, and it is not transmitted sexually. No one has ever died from leprosy; those who contract it have the same life-expectancy as anyone else. Nor do the fingers and toes rot and drop off. Rather, the disease deadens nerve endings, and with a lack of feeling, cuts and other sources of infection often go undetected until the infection spreads to the bones, which in turn are gradually destroyed. Physical deformations do not occur unless the disease is untreated for fifteen or twenty years.

John Pilch, *Healing in the New Testament: Insights from Medical and Mediterranean Anthropology* (Minneapolis: Fortress, 2000), 45.

of Mark, we can see some of Luke's particular emphases. Mark's introduction to the story has Jesus roaming Galilee, preaching in synagogues and casting out demons (Mark 1:39). The leper then meets Jesus somewhere in Galilee, perhaps in between towns in one of the "desert places" that he resorted to after the leper spread the word of his healing to the whole region (1:40, 45). Luke, curiously, specifies that the leper met Jesus in one of the cities (5:12).[3] Luke knows the Levitical regulation; in 17:12, lepers meet Jesus just as he is entering a village, yelling at him from a distance. The Lukan leper in 5:12-16 breaks the law twice, first by being in the village and second by approaching Jesus to ask for help rather than warning Jesus away. And he is not just a leper (Mark 1:40 uses *lepros*, the noun for "leper"; he was "*anēr plērēs lepras*" (a man full of leprosy), so Luke clearly does not think that his disease is a secret. Perhaps Luke did not mean to create this element of disobedience; perhaps he was only thinking about the end of the story, where Jesus leaves the city for the desert places (5:16), and so needs Jesus to be in so he can go out. Intentional or not, this story is more interestingly complicated by the questions of obedience to Torah. The leper has not obeyed the Law about leprosy, and nor has the town; the way Luke frames the story, others transgress the Law, but Jesus does not, as we will see.

The leper does not see Jesus and then enter the town, but is there, and sees Jesus, and then moves to adopt the posture of a supplicant. He "falls upon his face," stretching out to show his submission and his tenacity; Jesus will have either to step over him or stop to hear his request. "O Lord, if you wish, you are able to make me clean." How does he know that? One supposes that from the reports about Jesus circulating (4:37) or from Jesus' own preaching (4:44), the leper has learned of Jesus' power and now just hopes that Jesus is willing. To judge from Luke's narrative so far, one never knows: Jesus will not perform a miracle for Satan, nor for the Nazareth congregation, and he will not agree to be Capernaum's designated healer. On the other hand, he exorcises a demon in the synagogue, heals Simon's mother-in-law, spends a long afternoon healing the sick at Capernaum, and fills Simon's nets to the breaking point. The reader, if not the leper, knows that the odds are in the petitioner's favor.

Sure enough, Jesus reaches out to touch the leper, saying, "I will; be clean." The leprosy "left him," like the demon (4:35) and the fever (4:39). Touching the leper made one unclean, but was not forbidden by Leviticus 13–14, and so was not an act of deliberate disobedience to the Law.[4] Had the miracle not happened, Jesus would have contracted secondary uncleanness; the Bible does not specify the nature of the purification procedures, but at most, he would have been unclean for a week before he could have immersed and been clean again (Lev 15:24). By touching the leper, Jesus is in danger of becoming temporarily unclean; but by being in the town, the leper has put everyone in the same danger, and by allowing the leper to stay, the towns-people are risking the contamination of holy places—their synagogue, if they have one, and the temple, if someone were to go there while still in a polluted state.[5] Luke's specification "in one of their cities," intentionally or not, has changed Jesus' action from an encounter between two individuals to one with much wider social implications. "I will; be clean," says Jesus, and thereby rescues the whole town from danger. [Praying for Healing]

When the man's leprosy left him, he was not yet clean, according to Leviticus. The man had to go before a priest; Josephus wrote that the priests were dispersed throughout Judea and Galilee, so the man would not have needed to travel too far to find one. The priest had to examine him and pronounce him disease-free, but before the man could be pronounced "clean," he had to be sprinkled with two different sorts of water, spend seven days in isolation, shave all his body hair, wash his clothes, and immerse himself. Jesus' command that the man keep quiet until he has seen the priest and has done everything commanded in the Law is sensible; the former leper is not completely clean until all the steps are complete, and only then can he truly testify to the whole extent of the miracle.

But "the word went out all the more concerning him"—gee, how did that happen? Luke's use of the passive leaves open the question of whether the former leper disobeyed Jesus, but emphasizes that the message could not be hidden. The result is the same as in 4:42, when the Capernaum crowds wanted to keep Jesus to themselves, or in 5:1, when the same group was pushing to get close enough to hear him teach. Jesus did not stay long in any one place as a healer; his practice was to depart for "deserts" (Luke uses the same word in 5:16 as in 4:1 and 4:41) to pray.

Healing the Paralytic, 5:17-26

Verse 17 includes an odd construction: *kai dynamis kyriou ēn eis to iasthei auton* (and the power of the Lord was for him to heal). First, does "Lord" mean Jesus or God? Second, does the "him" of the

---

Praying for Healing

If your approach to . . . healing is less ideological and more empirical, you can always give it a try. Pray for it. If it's somebody else's healing you're praying for, you can try at the same time laying your hands on him as Jesus sometimes did. If his sickness involves his body as well as his soul, then God may be able to use your inept hands as well as your inept faith to heal him. If you feel like a fool as you are doing this, don't let it throw you.

Frederick Buechner, *Wishful Thinking: A Theological ABC* (New York: Harper and Row, 1973), 36–37.

purpose clause function as object or subject of the infinitive? "And the Lord's power was for him to heal" might then mean "Jesus' power was oriented towards healing," or "God's power was enabling Jesus to heal"; the alternative, "and the Lord's power was for healing him," would have to mean that Jesus' power was aimed at healing a specific person, and that would make no sense in context. Most commentators argue that "Lord" is equivalent here to "God," noting that Luke has used this terminology often in the first four chapters.[6] While Luke certainly does use "Lord" to mean "God," he also uses "Lord" to mean "Jesus"; the first time is when Elizabeth calls Mary "the mother of my Lord" and, more to the point, "Lord" means "Jesus" in the previous two pericopes (5:8; 5:12). Luke's narrator can use "the Lord" without any further identification to mean Jesus (7:19; 10:1, etc.). Allowing, then, that "Lord" can mean God, and that however we translate this verse, Luke always believes that God's power enabled Jesus to heal, let us consider the possibility that here it means "Jesus," and that this phrase is meant to tell us something about Jesus' intentions that day. After all, Luke has shown the reader in the previous few sections that Jesus is not always or automatically interested in healing. He healed many in Capernaum, but only as many as he could see in one day, and then he left. He healed the leper in the story just prior, but withdrew when confronted by crowds. Luke's implication is that while Jesus could heal scores of people, healing was not always his intent or his primary mission, and on some days he would leave rather than deal with more requests for healing. On this day, however, he had his mind set on healing and teaching.

On that day, too, Jesus was surrounded by "Pharisees and teachers of the law who had come from every village of Galilee and Judea and Jerusalem." This is not an unfamiliar posture for Luke's Jesus. Looking backwards, this scene recalls the temple scene in 2:41-51; on that day, the twelve-year-old Jesus was seated in the midst of the teachers, amazing them with his insight. Looking forward, Jesus will dine with Pharisees on three occasions, and each time there will be elements of questioning and examination that go both ways (7:36-50; 11:37-54; 14:1-24). On this occasion, they are on Jesus' turf; we are not told whose house they are in, but clearly he is the teacher and they the audience. This episode will show how the Pharisees act when they are guests, and will serve as the first salvo in the ongoing skirmishes between Jesus and the legal experts of Judaism.

Who were the Pharisees? Wary interpreters of the New Testament will realize that the historical questions—who were they, really?—

and the questions about who the Pharisees are in Luke are connected but not identical. The sidebar "Who Were the Pharisees?" deals with the historical reconstruction; what follows in this section deals with Luke's portrait, without raising the questions of historicity. [Who Were the Pharisees?]

Luke takes over almost everything Mark wrote about the Pharisees, and almost all of that material casts them in a negative light. In fact, the first four appearances by the Pharisees show them opposing or accusing Jesus: first of blasphemy (5:21), then of eating and drinking with sinners (5:30), and then twice of breaking Sabbath rules (6:2, 6-11); all of these episodes come from Mark. But then Luke begins to tell stories about Jesus eating with the Pharisees (7:36-50; 11:37-54; 14:1-24), where Jesus is invited to

---

Who Were the Pharisees?

We find information about the Pharisees in the New Testament, where they are mostly bad guys; in Josephus, where they are sometimes described as political opportunists and sometimes as very popular interpreters of the Law; in the Mishnah, where they are pictured as the forerunners of the rabbis whose opinions make up the bulk of the volume; and in the Dead Sea Scrolls, where their opinions are ridiculed by the Essenes as weak and wishy-washy. So far as we know, we have no first-hand accounts by Pharisees. We have, instead, first-hand materials written by two former Pharisees: Paul, who writes as a Pharisee who now believes that Jesus is the key to all things, and Josephus, whose claim to have been a Pharisee is widely doubted (he also claims to have been a Sadduccee and an Essene, as well as a member of a very small sect begun by a man named Banus, all before he was 19; he also was the greatest general of the war of 66–70, and at age 14 all the legal experts came to ask him for advice—well, you get the picture).

It is impossible to say when the Pharisees originated. Josephus first mentions them in his account of the reign of John Hyrcanus I (135–104 BC), so some believe their movement began during the Hasmonean period, in reaction to the Hellenizing impulse among some Jews. Others trace the roots of the movement to the Exilic period and to the attempt to protect Jewish religion and culture from being swallowed up under foreign influences.

An older view treated Pharisees as the dominant religious party within Judaism during the first century. This view, which relies heavily on some passages in Josephus and on the negative characterization of the Pharisees in the New Testament, sees the Pharisees as so popular that they were able to force other Jews, including the high priests, to follow their interpretations of the Torah. When Jesus opposed them, under this interpretation, he was making enemies of a group with the clout to arrange his death.

Another view sees the Pharisees as a religious sect with little actual influence over the temple leaders. In this reading, the Pharisees concentrated on religious observance, trying to live their whole lives as if they were priests in the temple. To keep this level of purity, they ate and interacted mostly only with others of their group.

Yet a third interpretation sees them as a sort of political interest group—a sort of midpoint view between the first and second—who were educated but not members of the aristocracy or ruling class. They were professionals who worked for the upper classes as secretaries, teachers, judges, and clerks.

Josephus says there were about 6,000 Pharisees. One cannot put too much stock in Josephus's numerical estimates, but this one would mean that they were a much smaller group than the priests and only slightly larger than the Essenes. His stories about them mostly place them in Jerusalem, whereas the Gospels mostly place them in Galilee.

Most interpreters would agree that the available evidence allows us to say that Pharisees believed in some form of life beyond death, as opposed to the more traditional Jewish view that death is the end of life; that they believed in angels and in angelic revelations to humans; that in their quest to be especially obedient to the Torah, they tended to stretch biblical rules to cover new situations; and that they tended to be more scrupulous about certain areas of Torah such as tithing and avoiding uncleanness.

eat, accepts, and then criticizes his hosts. Jesus warns the disciples about the hypocrisy of the Pharisees (12:1), but then the Pharisees warn him of Herod Antipas's wish to kill him (13:31). They ridicule his teaching about money (16:14), and he tells a parable making them the butt of the joke (18:9-14). Luke pictures the Pharisees trying to catch Jesus in some misdeed (6:7; 14:1) or misstatement (11:53-54), but Luke's Pharisees are not named in any plot against Jesus' life (as at Mark 3:6), nor do they ask Jesus questions in order to test him (as at Mark 10:2; cf. Luke 17:20, where they ask a straight-up question).

This is clearly a more complicated picture than Mark's, where the Pharisees are intransigent foes, hard-headed bad guys who only want to trick, trap, and destroy Jesus. Interpreters of Luke should be wary of reading Luke's Pharisees as if they were Mark's, or even worse, as if they were Matthew's or John's. In Luke's account, they behave boorishly when they are hosts or guests, but then Jesus is not exactly the exemplary dinner-party guest, either. Luke's account, although it never shows Jesus bested by the Pharisees and never gives their opinion without censuring it, nevertheless opens the way to avoid demonizing Jesus' opponents, with all the ethical consequences that brings. [Luke's Character]

The "teachers of the Law" are apparently the same as the "scribes"; Luke uses the first term in 5:17 and the second in 5:21. My guess is that Luke thinks of "teacher of the Law," "lawyer," and "scribe" as synonyms. The term "scribe" appears quite often in Luke, usually connected with the Pharisees, and the Lukan Pharisees include scribes among them (5:30). Jesus chastises the Pharisees in 11:37-44, and a lawyer speaks up to say that an attack on the Pharisees is an attack on them (11:45). All of this would argue that, as some think, Luke blends all the bad guys into one big mushy ball of evil. But scribes get their own separate "woe" in 20:45-47, just after the "chief priests, elders, and scribes" have taken over the role of Jesus' chief opponents (20:1, 19; 22:2). In addition, only the Pharisees invite Jesus to dinner, and they alone warn Jesus about Herod Antipas. While the Pharisees are angry with Jesus, they are never said to be plotting to kill him; that role is reserved for the "chief priests, scribes, and elders." One suggestion that might explain all the data is that Luke considered scribe/lawyer/law-teacher a profession and Pharisee a religious sect. He thought the Pharisees were wealthy (16:14) and were given the

Luke's Character

Luke shows he was a man who believed that you shouldn't let the fact that a person is jail-bait keep you from treating him like a human being, and that if you pray hard enough, there's no telling what may happen, and that if you think you've got Heaven made but don't let it worry you that there are children across the tracks who are half starving to death, then you're kidding yourself.

Frederick Buechner, *Peculiar Treasures: A Biblical Who's Who* (New York: Harper and Row, 1979), 95.

best seats in synagogue and respectful greetings in public places (11:43); in other words, Luke thought of the Pharisees as aristocrats, who would naturally have scribes around as secretaries and legal advisors—no self-respecting big shot would have been without them. Likewise, the chief priests and elders, who were also aristocrats, would have employed scribes, but not the Pharisaic scribes—Luke knew that the high priest and his chief advisors were members of the Sadducees (Acts 5:17) and that they and the Pharisees did not see eye to eye (Acts 23:6-10).

On this day, Jesus was surrounded by Pharisees and law-teachers who had come from "every village of Galilee and Judea and Jerusalem"; this sounds like Mark's description of the crowds that came to John the Baptist (Mark 1:5), a descriptive phrase Luke left off there (Luke 3:7) and added here. The reader already knew that Jesus was attracting crowds of the sick (4:40) and the curious (5:1), and that this was beginning to lead him to withdraw from center stage, at least from time to time (5:15-16). Now Luke constructs a crowd of the pious and the learned; how will they compare to the Nazareth synagogue audience or to the Capernaum synagogue audience or to the crowds around the lake?

Some English translations of 5:17 (e.g., the NRSV) give the reader the impression of a crowd gathered around Jesus with the Pharisees sitting nearby. The Greek text only mentions the experts: "And so it was that one day he was teaching and there were Pharisees and law-teachers sitting there who had come from every village of Galilee and Judea and Jerusalem; and the Lord's power was aimed at healing." Healing whom? Well, it is not exactly clear. There are at least four options. The first is that even though the text only names the Pharisees and law-teachers in 5:17, we are supposed to think of a separate crowd and read them back in from 5:19. Jesus heals some of them while the Pharisees watch. My objection to this reading is that it is perfectly clear in Mark, so that if that was what Luke wanted, he could have copied Mark verbatim. The second option is to read 5:17 as "the Lord's power was for the purpose of healing him," namely the paralytic. On this reading, there is no healing until 5:25, and Luke has put in 5:17 so we can know that a miracle will happen in due course. Possible, but not plausible; Luke tends not to give away the ending of the story. The third option is to read 5:17 to mean that Jesus was healing some of the scribes and Pharisees that day—some of them had ailments that they brought to Jesus, and he was helping them out. The fourth option is that 5:17 means only that Jesus was in a healing mood, but not that anyone was actually being healed; the

Pharisees and scribes sat there with their bum knees and fluttery hearts and could have had help, but never asked. These last two options fit Luke's language and theology better, and put the conflict later in the story in a new light.

In the next verse some men arrive, carrying a paralytic on his bed, trying to find a way to enter (here is where we discover Jesus is in a house) and set the paralyzed man in front of Jesus: "And when they could not find how to bring him in because of the crowd, going up upon the roof, they set him down through the roof-tiles with his bed into the middle (of the crowd) in front of Jesus" (5:19). This is a "hole in the bottom of the sea" sort of sentence: "because of the crowd upon the roof through the tiles with his bed into the middle in front of Jesus." Luke opts for this string of prepositional phrases as a sort of rhetorical flourish; this is *pleonasm*, using more words than is necessary in order to make the scene more vivid. You can almost see the caption balloons next to the heads of the guys carrying the bed: "Those sorry #@*s won't move over—now what?" "Let's try the roof!" "Wait, you're going to drop him!!" "Yank those things off—you're going to have to make the hole bigger." "OK, on three—down you go." "Yo, Jesus—can you give us a hand here?"

As many commentators note, the roof is tiled, not thatched, which is another indication that Luke is thinking of larger, nicer, and more generally Mediterranean homes and not of the smaller Galilean homes with mud-and-straw roofs. And unless we readers are supposed to supply a larger non-Pharisaic crowd, Luke has created an all-expert audience who begin as recipients of Jesus' teaching and who now function both as barriers and witnesses to the miracle. Picture, then, a nice house filled with well-educated aristocratic people and their advisers; they will not move to let in the rabble, and are no doubt rolling their eyes at the impudence of the group that cuts the hole in the roof.

The story in Mark is more like the "Jesus Mafa" painting—mixed crowd of people that includes some elders and teachers, and a rough hole in a mud-and-stick roof. The illustration by Julius Schnorr von Carolsfeld is much more like Luke's image, if you ignore the women: a finer house, and a crowd of Pharisees and teachers who are put off by the appearance of the man on the mat.

Jesus saw "their faith"—vague enough that it can include the paralytic and those who carried him—and said, "Man, your sins have been forgiven" (5:20). Technically, Jesus does not forgive his sins, but pronounces forgiveness. As God's prophet, Jesus has been sent to announce God's release/forgiveness to the captives (4:18), but if he announces that it has been done, speaking not just about what God is willing to do but what God has done, he risks being a false prophet. Does Jesus in fact know God's heart so well that he can say what God's decision is about a particular sinner?

The Pharisees have their doubts: "Who is this who speaks blasphemy? Who is able to forgive sins except God alone?" "Blasphemy" when used technically means speaking disrespectfully or

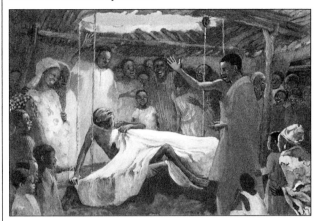

Jesus Heals the Paralyzed Man

inappropriately of God, which Jesus has not done. But it is also used more loosely in the Gospels to mean "insult" or "slander," and perhaps we should think Luke has that in mind for this scene. His Pharisees and scribes object to Jesus' announcement because they do not see how Jesus could know such a thing, and they presume that he is speaking lightly of very serious matters.

In Mark's version the scribes are turning these things over in their minds, but in Luke's, they are arguing among themselves. So imagine the scene now: Jesus, surrounded by a crowd of experts in the law and in piety, sitting under a hole in the roof, with some men up there looking in and one man on a bed right in front of him. The righteous intelligentsia are having a sidebar discussion of whether Jesus has gone too far; the guys on the roof and the man in the bed are no doubt complaining that they could have gone to the temple if they were worried about sin—can Jesus please do something about the fact that he can't walk?

Healing the Paralytic

Julius Schnorr von Carolsfeld. *Jesus heals the paralytic*. Illustration. Dover Pictorial Archive Series.

Did Jesus Call Himself the Son of Man?

The term "Son of Man" appears in the Gospels and almost nowhere else in the New Testament. Paul and the rest of the epistle-writers call Jesus "Lord," "Christ," "Son of God," and all sorts of other things, but except for Rev 1:13 (and possibly Rev 14:14), none but the evangelists calls Jesus "Son of Man." Even in the Gospels, nobody but Jesus uses the term. He tends to use it in three contexts: to predict his death, to speak of his current mission or authority, and to speak of the One coming at the end of time to judge the wicked and reward the righteous.

This last category is derived from Dan 7:13, with the "son of man" coming on the clouds of heaven. In Daniel, the figure is moving up to heaven, and in Jesus' prediction, the figure is moving down from heaven, but the words Jesus uses are clearly drawn from Daniel. Some interpreters believe that Jesus did use the term "Son of Man" to predict the Judge who will preside at the Last Day, but that he meant someone else, and that all the other "Son of Man" sayings are later adjustments by Christians who believed that Jesus was the Son of Man, the apocalyptic Judge and Savior. Others believe he probably used the term to refer to himself when speaking of his mission—it literally means "human,"

so he could have used it to mean himself as an ordinary human or as one whose life was dedicated to others ("son of humanity," as some new translations put it). Still others think that none of the "Son of Man" references were authentic, and that they were read into the Jesus tradition by those who wanted to identify him with the Judge for the Last Day.

It seems to me that the odds favor Jesus having used it. Since it was not a term widely used for Jesus by Christians, the scenario where it gets inserted into the gospel tradition is implausible: who would do that, and what would they have gained by it? We have plenty of evidence that early Christians expected Jesus to return soon as Apocalyptic Judge, but when they prayed for his near return and sang hymns to his future role as Judge and Savior, they did not (so far as we can tell) use the term "Son of Man." The term is an artifact—something they remembered Jesus called himself, even though they called him by other names. This does not rule out the possibility that early Christians or the Gospel writers inserted it where it seemed to them Jesus might have said it; this theory only rejects as implausible the idea that some early Christian community invented the usage.

Jesus' question, "Which is easier?" is the typical double-bind remark we hear from Jesus, especially in situations of conflict and particularly with the Pharisees and scribes. Theologically, saying "get up and walk!" is easier than "your sins are forgiven," because it does not claim to speak for God; but practically, "your sins are forgiven" is easier, because none can tell what God has or has not forgiven until Judgment Day, but "get up and walk" has an immediate test of validity. The way the scene is set, we are to conclude that the one implies the other, and that Jesus' ability to heal the paralytic shows that he is a true prophet, able to speak as well for God's gracious forgiveness. Both healing and forgiving are part of his commission (4:18-19).

This pericope not only introduces the Pharisees, but also the term "Son of Man." New Testament scholars argue over whether Jesus truly used this term for himself and if he did, what he meant by it. [Did Jesus Call Himself the Son of Man?]. What follows will focus on how Luke uses the term. Jesus calls himself "Son of Man" throughout Luke: the Son of Man

• Has authority on earth to forgive sins (5:24)
• Is Lord of the Sabbath (6:5)

- Eats and drinks rather than fasts (7:34)
- Will return in glory and with the angels on the Last Day (9:26)
- Will be betrayed (9:44)
- Is homeless (9:57)
- Is to his generation as Jonah was to the people of Nineveh (11:30)
- Will acknowledge his followers before God on the Last Day (12:8)
- Can be blasphemed without eternal consequences (12:10)
- Is coming at an unexpected hour (12:40)
- Will appear like lightning at his return (17:24)
- Will bring catastrophic judgment at his return (17:30)
- May not find any faithful when he returns (18:8)
- Has come to seek and to save the lost (19:10)
- Is being betrayed in accord with God's plan (22:22)
- Will be granted a seat at God's right hand (22:69)

The term "son of man" in Hebrew or Aramaic means "human," as in Psalm 8:4, where "man" and "son of man" are parallel to each other. In Daniel 7, the prophet first sees visions of fantastic monsters made of part one thing and part another, and then sees a figure "like a son of man," meaning "looking like a human being rather than one of those Godzilla things." Daniel's "son of man" comes from the earth to heaven to receive from God the authority to rule the earth after God has destroyed the last and worst of the monsters.

"Son of Man" is a tricky title, and it's hard to get the nuances right for modern congregations. Some churchgoers tend to think of "Son of Man" as a title representing the human nature of Jesus, as "Son of God" sums up Christ's divine nature. As one can see from the previous list of verses, "Son of Man" often has an apocalyptic function, designating Jesus as the one who will appear on the Last Day to commence the Judgment, the punishment of the wicked and the rewarding of the faithful. Even in some contexts where Jesus is speaking of his present role and authority, it does not sound like a title expressing humility. To say "the son of man has authority on earth to forgive sins" is to claim that, because he will be the executor of God's justice at the Last Day, he can start to execute it now.

On the other hand, in verses like 9:44, where he says he has no place to lay his head, and 9:57, where he predicts his betrayal, there is no explicit claim of authority or power. Some commentators suggest that in these cases, "Son of Man" may simply be a way for

Jesus to speak of himself either as an ordinary human or as a representative human. Luke 12:8-9 shows that "Son of Man" can be parallel to "me," and we should presume, whatever Jesus meant by it, Luke understood Jesus to be speaking of himself whenever he used the phrase. But it is possible, and in my view likely, that Luke did not consider "Son of Man" simply to be a self-reference. The primary backdrop for the term—the figure who, at the Last Day, rises to receive from God the right to administer God's justice on the earth—should prompt the interpreter to ask how the apocalyptic function of "Son of Man" connects with its use in each context.

Back to our story: the Pharisees and scribes question among themselves whether Jesus has gone too far in announcing the forgiveness of the paralytic's sins, and the friends who brought him are doubtless wondering if Jesus has missed the point and will fail to heal him. "Which is easier?" asks Jesus, confronting both groups, but then instead of answering that question, he heals the paralytic, stating that his action should prove to them that he, the Son of Man, has authority on earth to forgive sins. Note that he does not touch the man, but commands him to take his bed and go home; his healing power, like his authority over sins, operates in this scene in his words alone. Like Mark, Luke gives us no details to explain when the paralytic was healed: did it happen as he rose, or did he first feel himself healed and then rise? This gap reminds us of Mark's version of the call of the first four disciples, and sets up the call of Levi (the next pericope), which Luke takes over mostly unchanged from Mark; Jesus calls, and the true believer simply responds. In v. 25, the paralytic does exactly what Jesus commands—stands up in front of them, picks up his bed, and goes to his home—and glorifies God, which Jesus had not commanded, but which is the obvious and proper response to what had just happened to him. Luke often notes that the result of Jesus' ministry is that people praise or glorify God; this is both a way to remind the reader that frequent praise of God is part of following Jesus and a way to build the case that Jesus' ministry, far from leading people astray (one of the accusations made against him in 23:2), brought people closer to God.

In this episode, even the Pharisees and scribes are bowled over and praise God just as the former paralytic did. The words Luke uses here all have more than one sense to them; *ekstasis* can mean astonishment or confusion; *phobos* connotes fear or awe; *paradoxa* means a strange or wonderful thing. This group began and ended by listening to Jesus' words; his instructional techniques on that day have apparently included straight lecture at the beginning, controversy and discussion, open-ended questioning, visual aids, and discovery learning. The Pharisees and scribes, who voice some objections, appear to have had those met on this day, but Luke's words for their experience leave room for some confusion, which may help the reader understand why their good feelings do not last long in the narrative.

Jesus, whose mission is to preach forgiveness/release to the captives, has done that today. The crowd of curious experts in law and piety sat as a physical barrier to the man's healing, and their doubts about Jesus' competence were a mental or emotional barrier to the offer of forgiveness. The paralytic and those who carried him came seeking healing, showing faith in finding a way to get to Jesus despite barriers, but were likely surprised by the offer of forgiveness. In the end all of them, from the seated crowd to the healed man walking home, agreed that something amazing had happened that day. "Today this scripture has been fulfilled in your hearing," Jesus told the Nazareth crowd, but they could not hear, and wanted to kill him. "Today we have seen an amazing thing," the Pharisees say to each other; on this day, at least, they can see and hear for themselves, and praise God for release and salvation.

Levi's Banquet, 5:27-39

In this section, Jesus finds a new disciple (the fourth named so far in Luke), has a party to attend, and gets involved in a couple of arguments over table guests and overeating. Although Luke has dropped occasional notes about food in what has come before this story—Mary's song said the poor would be fed while the rich went hungry, Jesus fasted for forty days, and Simon's mother-in-law probably fed Jesus after he fixed her fever—with Levi's party, he really sets the theme of food on the table.

Verse 27 allows the reader to think either that Jesus called Levi on the same day he healed the paralytic or sometime later. Either way, this episode continues to work with the themes of Jesus' responses to sinners, to faith, and to opposition. The section includes a call story and two controversy stories that Luke takes over from Mark. In Mark, the stories are part of the controversy cycle (Mark 2:1–3:6) that begins with Jesus confronting the scribes over what was in their hearts and ends with the Pharisees and Herodians plotting to kill him. Luke has the same stories in the same order, but his grouping works differently. For one thing, Luke stitches together the controversy in Levi's house with the controversy over fasting, making one continuous episode from Mark's two peri-copes.[7] For another, Luke's version of the Sabbath healing controversy, the last story in the cycle, does not climax with a plot to kill Jesus; instead, the scribes and Pharisees, filled with fury, begin a dialogue (think of the People's Liberation Front in *The Life of Brian*).

Luke uses three stock character sets already at play in the narrative—Pharisees, scribes, and tax collectors—and introduces two more: sinners and disciples. The "Pharisees and their scribes" (to summarize the earlier discussion at 5:17-26) in Luke's Gospel are wealthy aristocrats who are concerned with Jesus' lax attitude about certain issues of religious practice. "Their scribes" would be, for Luke, their secretaries and legal advisers. Tax collectors first show up in 3:12-13, responding to John's preaching. In real life, as well as in the Gospel, tax collectors ranged from very wealthy men who owned the tax franchise for a given area to guys who sat at a border toll booth making assessments and collecting the loot. Levi is this latter sort: Jesus finds him at his tax-collection spot, and even though Levi throws Jesus a big party, Luke never labels him "rich."

One could argue that sinners make their first appearance earlier in Luke, either when the crowds come to John the Baptist or when Peter confesses that he is *hamartōlos*, a sinner (5:8). But although John the Baptist calls on the crowds to repent, they are not labeled "sinners." Peter is a sinner, by his own admission, but he is an individual, and the term "sinners" will be used in Luke to name an anonymous herd of persons who, with tax collectors, frequently gather around Jesus. When Luke writes "sinner," he means someone who has done things for which he or she needs to repent, which includes pretty much everyone. The strange episode in 13:1-5 makes this clear: sudden tragedy does not prove that those who suffer are worse sinners than those who do not. Instead, unless everyone repents, they will perish in God's judgment. For Luke, "sinner" is an ethical or religious rather than a social, political, or economic category. It is not equivalent to "poor" or to "Gentile," and sinners in Luke are not equivalent to the oppressed or the disadvantaged.[8] The poor are blessed with the kingdom of God (6:20), but sinners must repent (5:32) and in that way enter the kingdom.

The other stock group making their debut in this passage, the disciples, appear rather abruptly, but have no active role in the story. In 5:11, Peter, James, and John follow Jesus; in 5:28, Levi follows him; and in 5:30, the Pharisees complain to Jesus' disciples, whom we must assume to be those four. They say nothing in this episode—the Pharisees complain to them, and Jesus answers—but Luke needs them in order for the controversy over fasting to make sense.

Jesus, having healed the man on the mat in front of a crowd of scribes and Pharisees (5:21; see earlier discussion), now spots Levi the tax collector. Jesus approaches him at work, as he did Simon, but his recruitment technique is much more direct, more Markan: "Follow me." Levi obeys: "Rising, abandoning everything, he followed him" (5:28). Luke's insertion of "abandoning everything" connects Levi with Peter, James, and John, who did the same (5:11).

Jesus ate with Peter's family before Peter began following Jesus, but with Levi the call comes first, then the dinner. Luke borrows a phrase from the Septuagint: Levi "made a great banquet," just like Kings Belshazzar (Dan 5:1) and Ahasuerus (Esth 1:3). He did it "in his house," which makes the next part pretty interesting. One can imagine him inviting all his rowdy friends and ending up with a "crowd" of tax collectors, but why were the Pharisees and their scribes there? They call Levi and his friends "tax collectors and sinners" (5:30), whereas Luke's narrator calls them "tax collectors and others" (5:29). The Pharisees and their lackeys also "murmur," the famous word from the wilderness stories of Exodus, where the Israelites whine and complain like kids in the back seat on a twelve-hour drive to Florida. Clearly, we're supposed to think that the Pharisees disapprove of Levi and his guests and of Jesus' presence there. So how do we explain the presence of Pharisees as guests in the house of a tax collector?

The banquet table is Luke's great location for bringing together surprising groups of people for Jesus' instruction and sometimes for Jesus' offer of forgiveness and salvation. There are seven formal meals or banquets in Luke:

- 5:27-39: Jesus eats with Levi, tax collectors, and others in Levi's house; the Pharisees and their scribes complain.
- 7:36-50: Jesus eats with Simon the Pharisee; a sinner woman drenches Jesus' feet with perfume and tears and wipes them with her hair; Simon complains.
- 11:37-54: Jesus eats with another Pharisee, who is offended by Jesus not washing; Jesus verbally chastises his guests, other Pharisees and scribes, who react in anger.
- 14:1-24: Jesus eats with a third Pharisee and his guests, scribes and Pharisees; Jesus heals a man and tells controversial parables, offending the guests.

- 19:1-10: Jesus eats with Zacchaeus the chief tax collector; the whole town is offended.
- 22:7-38: Jesus eats with his disciples, who are explicitly designated as sinners during the meal.
- 24:13-35: Jesus breaks bread with two disciples in their house.

Many commentators note how much Luke's meals sound like Greek *symposia*: that is, like meals followed by extensive table talk. The meals in chapters 11 and 14 are explicitly set out that way, with Jesus responding to the actions or words of other table guests, silencing everyone by his repartee. Likewise, Luke's Last Supper keeps Jesus and the Twelve at table much longer than Matthew or Mark, and although the discourse is less polemical than in chapters 11 and 14, there is some of the same verbal struggle, with Jesus winning the war of words. This present scene is, of the six, the least clearly drawn if Luke means for us to read it as table talk following dinner.[9] Are we to understand that the Pharisees and scribes are also at table, objecting to Jesus' presence? Or, as some suggest, should we think of this as a village festival, and thus more public, with the Pharisees as observers and critics rather than as participants?[10]

We probably do not have to choose. If Luke imagined Levi's house as one with a large decorative peristyle (courtyard) and ample triclinium (dining room), all on a sight-line with the front gate, then he could have imagined the Pharisees in the house, which seems to be demanded by v. 29, yet not necessarily at table or as invited guests. [Banquet Space in Luke's World] We should also recall that in Acts 15, the believers who belonged to the sect of the Pharisees were part of the discussion over how Gentiles would be incorporated into the church. Thus Luke has no difficulties picturing Pharisees as the most conservative part of the Jesus movement—in the house, as it were, but unwilling to sit at table with all of the others.

So let us imagine the scene this way. Levi the tax collector has a large house, with dining arrangements suitable for a "great banquet." Jesus and his disciples are "reclining" (5:29)

Banquet Space in Luke's World

By Luke's time, wealthy persons in the empire, especially in Greek and Roman cities, were building houses that put the dining area, the central courtyard, and the front gate all in the same line of sight. The triclinium—the formal dining area—was so named because the traditional arrangement for banquets had three rows of diners in a U-shape. Each diner reclined, leaning on the left arm on dining couches or cushions, and used the right hand to eat from the food arranged on a low table or rug in front of him. The U of the dining area opened onto the central courtyard, the peristyle, often decorated with statues, mosaics, greenery, etc. Beyond the peristyle was more open space—the atrium (a small open courtyard), the impluvium (a pool to collect rainwater diverted to it by gutters and drainpipes), and the entrance hall. During banquets, the host could open the large front doors so that passers-by could see inside and be impressed, or even wander in and admire the spread.

See Carolyn Osiek and David Balch, *Families in the New Testament World* (Louisville: Westminster/John Knox, 1997), 6–17.

with Levi and his guests, including other tax collectors as well as "others." There are Pharisees and their scribes present; perhaps they have been invited, or perhaps they just wandered in the open gate to check out the party. Their question, "Why are you eating and drinking with tax collectors and sinners?" is addressed to the disciples, as the "you" is plural and is a comment on what they are doing at that moment—a sort of shocked "what are you thinking!?" The

Atrium and Impluvium at the House of the Vettii
House of the Vettii atrium, Via dei Fortuna, Pompeii, Italy

(Credit: Vladimir Khirman, iStock.com)

issue, as Luke constructs the scene, is almost certainly not impurity. The actual historical Pharisees seem to have tended to eat with each other in an attempt to maintain a practice of purity stricter than the average Judean, but if Luke knew that, he ignores it in his Gospel. Remember, after this meal, Jesus' next three dinner invitations come from Pharisees! Luke simply cannot have had a mental image of Pharisees avoiding eating with non-Pharisees since they regularly invite Jesus to their table.

The issue under discussion is sin, not impurity. The Pharisees and scribes want to know why Jesus and his disciples are eating and drinking with sinners, accepting their hospitality and thereby giving public acceptance of the sinners themselves. Do Jesus and his disciples have such a flexible view of sin that they can ignore it or endorse it by eating with a whole gang of prodigals? No, says Jesus. He explains his presence at Levi's table through the metaphor of a doctor making a house call: " The healthy need no physician, but the sick; I have not come to call the righteous but the sinners to repentance."[11] Luke, by adding "to repentance" to Mark's "I did not come to call the righteous, but the sinners," makes it clear that he did not understand Jesus to be loose on morality or soft on sin. Jesus, in Luke's understanding, was not endorsing sin by accepting Levi's invitation to dinner, but offering healing, in the form of repentance. Levi, in fact, has already shown typical Lukan signs of repentance: he abandoned a profitable business siphoning off money from rich and poor, and his first act of following Jesus is providing generous hospitality to Jesus, to other sinners, and perhaps even to cranky Pharisees and scribes. Levi's banquet, like

Food and Repentance

One dispute when I was a boy had to do with the question of hospitality toward those in error . . . . Uncle Al had family and friends on both sides of the so-called Cup of Cold Water debate, and it broke his heart. . . . He arranged for them to meet at his and Aunt Flo's one Sunday, a few Millerites and a few Johnsonians, not to discuss the hospitality-to-error doctrine but simply to enjoy a dinner of Aunt Flo's famous fried chicken. . . .

Al the peacemaker, concerned lest one brother take prayer and beat the others over the head with it, said, "Let us bow our heads in silent prayer, giving thanks for the meal," and they bowed their heads and closed their eyes and—a long time passed . . . soon it was clear that neither side wanted to stop before the other: they were seeing who could pray the longest. . . .

Al said "Amen" to offer them a way out of the deadlock, and said it again: "*Amen.*" Brother Miller looked up and saw Johnson still bowed, so he went back down just as Johnson put his periscope up and saw Brother Miller submerged, so down he went. It was becoming the longest table grace in history, it ground on and on and on, and then Aunt Flo slid her chair back, rose, went to the kitchen, and brought out the food that they were competing to see who could be more thankful for. She set the hay down where the goats could get it. Tears ran down Brother Johnson's face. His eyes were clamped shut, and tears streamed down, and so was Brother Miller weeping. . . . the stony hearts of the two giants melted; they raised their heads and filled their plates and slowly peace was made over that glorious chicken.

Garrison Keillor, "Brethren," in *Leaving Home* (New York: Penguin, 1997), 164–66.

the sinner woman's anointing of Jesus' feet, is proof that he has repented and thus proof that Jesus' technique is effective. [Food and Repentance]

"They"[12] raise another objection: "John's disciples fast and make their prayers all the time, as do the Pharisees' disciples, but yours are eating and drinking" (5:33). The reader knows that Jesus also sometimes fasted (4:2) and prayed (5:16), so the objection might assume that the interrogators are uninformed, or, more probably, that this is another comment on what was going on at Levi's banquet. In Second Temple Judaism, fasting was associated with mourning and repentance. John the Baptist, convinced that Israel was going to hell in a handbasket for their gross national immorality, called on everyone to fast and repent and only then to come to the waters for cleansing and forgiveness. Jesus has just said he is all about repentance, and so "their" remark is actually on point: if you came to call sinners to repentance, why are you stuffing yourself? Why aren't you fasting as a sign of your mourning over the corruption of this present age?

Jesus switches metaphors, from a doctor's visit to a wedding dinner. In their culture, the groom went to his father-in-law's house to retrieve his bride and returned to have a big feast. Imagine how it would be, says Jesus, to have the groom and the bride and all the guests standing around the full table but not eating—you, my offended interrogators, could not make them keep a fast under such conditions. Here is the Lukan theme of joy over those who repent: "we had to celebrate and rejoice, because this brother of yours was dead and is alive, was lost and is found" (15:32). On one level, then, the metaphor is simply a way to explain why banqueting and calls to repentance could both be part of Jesus' ministry: once they repent, you could no more keep them from rejoicing than you could keep wedding guests from grazing at the buffet.

But like most commentators, I wonder if Luke wanted to suggest that Levi's banquet was, or was like, the messianic banquet.[13] Such a connection shows up in at least two of the other banquets Jesus attends. At 14:15, a dinner guest at a Pharisee's house exclaims, "Blessed is anyone who will eat bread in the kingdom of God." In response, Jesus tells the parable of the great banquet, where the invited guests snub the host and the table is then filled with the poor and the disabled. At the last banquet, Jesus vows to abstain from eating and drinking until he can celebrate with them in the kingdom (22:15-18, 29-30). If Levi's house, filled with tax collectors and sinners, Pharisees and scribes, and the first handful of Jesus' disciples, can be compared to or equated with the kingdom, then the command to follow, Levi's obedient renunciation of the pursuit of wealth, Levi's extravagant hospitality, and the announcement of repentance and healing all come together seamlessly. In God's kingdom, there is salvation for the penitent and healing for the sick, a place at the welcome table, hallelujah! [Why Party—Why Not Fast?]

Verse 35 notes what the reader already knows, that Jesus' followers from Luke's day until the present have fasted as a Christian practice. "The days will come" foreshadows Jesus' prediction of the destruction of Jerusalem (19:43), and the passive voice of "will be taken from them" is the first veiled passion prediction in this Gospel. There will be plenty of reasons for Christians to mourn, in other words, and plenty of time to fast.

Verses 36-39 are labeled a parable, the first in Luke. The verses, however, do not tell a continuous story, as do most of the sections Luke calls "parables," and v. 39 seems to be pulling in a different direction than the others. The section is really three loosely connected metaphors: mending an old garment with new cloth; putting new wine into used wineskins; and the superiority of old wine over new. The last is found in Luke alone, and the first, although built on Mark's picture, works in a different way. In order to see the two levels at play in these parables, we begin with the third, v. 39: "No one drinking old [wine] wants new, for he says,

---

Why Party—Why Not Fast?

"Yes, Clarissa thinks, it's time for the day to be over. We throw our parties . . . . We live our lives, do whatever we do, and then we sleep—it's as simple and ordinary as that. A few jump out of windows or drown themselves or take pills; more die by accident; and most of us, the vast majority, are slowly devoured by some disease or, if we're very fortunate, by time itself. There's just this consolation: an hour here or there when our lives seem, against all odds and expectations, to burst open and give us everything we've ever imagined, though everyone but children (and perhaps even they) knows these hours will inevitably be followed by others, far darker and more difficult.

"Heaven only knows why we love it so.

"Here, then, is the party, still laid; here are the flowers, still fresh; everything is ready for the guests . . . . It is a party for the not-yet-dead; for the relatively undamaged; for those who for mysterious reasons have the fortune to be alive.

"It is, in fact, great good fortune."

Michael Cunningham, *The Hours* (New York: Farrar, Straus, and Giroux, 1998), 225–26.

'The old is good [or "of good quality"].'" Luke uses a tiny bit of internal dialogue as a characterization device to make us imagine the person who drinks the older wine; who would this have been? Well, a person of means, who could afford the good quality stuff and would not have to drink the cheap vinegary wine consumed by the poor. We hear this man's voice in other places in Luke: for example, "I will say to my soul, 'Soul, you have ample good laid up for many years; relax, eat, drink, and be merry'" (11:19).

Now look at the first metaphor: nobody tears up new clothes to patch something old, since you then wind up with a torn new garment and an old one with a mismatched piece on it. Who would do such a foolish thing as that? Nobody, of course, but only a wealthy person could even conceive of ripping up a new tunic to patch an old one; for a person who had ever actually mended something, the image would be so ludicrous that it would not work. Then the second metaphor: no one puts new wine into old wineskins. That turns out to be truer than most commentators know, since wine was allowed to ferment in barrels or jars before being put into wineskins. The real danger in putting new wine into old wineskins was that the wine would take up a bad taste from the residue left behind in the old skin and thus be ruined. Only a person who had no concept of viticulture could make the mistake implied by v. 37, that the fermenting wine would burst the old skin; it would burst any skin, new or old, and so that is why fermenting wine was stored in jars with a hole to release the gasses.[14]

All of this suggests strongly that Luke's Jesus is needling the Pharisees on two levels. First, he offers two metaphors suggesting that it would be foolish for him to modify his new way of operating to please the Pharisees, as foolish as tearing a new tunic to patch an old one or as pouring unfermented wine into old wineskins. On this same level, he offers an image suggesting why the Pharisees remain unconvinced by Jesus' rhetoric; naturally, they like the old wine better than the new.[15] But on the second level, Jesus lampoons them as rich people; they own new, unmended clothes; they have never stained their hands and feet processing wine; and they would never offend their palates with the cheap smelly stuff the masses call "wine." Only Luke calls the Pharisees "lovers of money" (16:14), and this bit is Jesus' opening salvo in his broadsides against the wealthy.

As the first banquet, this episode also sets up some of the patterns and themes for the others that come later. All six have elements of controversy, mostly with Pharisees criticizing Jesus and Jesus giving it right back to them. That is more muted here than it will be later;

they criticize him, first indirectly and then directly, and he responds with parables rather than with polemic. In this one, Jesus is a guest of a tax collector, and the Pharisees behave boorishly, criticizing the host and Jesus for their choice of guests and their eating habits. Later, Jesus will turn on his hosts over the same issues. In this scene, the Pharisees call some of the guests "sinners," but not to their faces; later, Jesus will call fellow guests fools, unmarked graves, murderers, etc.

All six banquets also illustrate different aspects of hospitality. In this one, Levi leaves the toll booth, where he extracts money for himself, his masters, and for Rome, and opens up his house, generously providing a feast to mark his transition from Roman leech to follower of Jesus. The Pharisees cannot accept his invitation to the table, and prove poor guests, grumbling and name-calling. Yet no one expels them, as in Matthew's version of the parable of the Great Banquet ("friend, how did you get in here? . . . Bind him hand and foot, and throw him into the outer darkness," Matt 22:12-13). Luke's banquets are not placid, and dinner conversations are not always civil, but no one is ever ejected—not even Judas—and that serves both as an embodiment of Jesus' teachings on love, forgiveness, and hospitality and as a hint of how Luke understands the kingdom of God. If Jesus and Pharisees can eat together even when they are swearing at each other, and if Jesus and the tax collectors can eat together even though Jesus pronounces dire woes on the rich, then maybe God's welcome table really is big enough for all the world.

CONNECTIONS

This chapter gives us a little bit of everything. There are several miracles: the huge catch of fish, the cleansing of the leper, the healing of the paralytic, and the conversion of a tax collector (Luke's readers probably thought it was pretty miraculous). There are several arguments: is it blasphemous for Jesus to pronounce a man's sins forgiven? Is it right for Jesus to eat with tax collectors and sinners? Is it right for Jesus and his disciples to avoid fasting? There are the calls of Peter, James, John, and Levi, beginning the theme of discipleship. And there is the first of the banquets, Jesus' coming-out party, complete with postprandial verbal sparring between Jesus and the Pharisees.

The miracles continue to be controversial. The leper, who should not have been in a town to begin with, is ordered to keep mum even if he must show himself to the priest, but the word about the healing spreads, leading to more crowds from whom Jesus retreats. The paralytic, let down through the roof into a room filled with religious teachers who would not scoot over to accommodate a sick man, has his sins forgiven first, prompting murmurs about blasphemy. Jesus squashes that one by healing the man and amazing his critics, but it is only the first round in several stories where Jesus must go toe to toe with the ever-vigilant Pharisees. Let the reader note: Jesus' good works do not guarantee his good reception. Christians and churches who try to do good in their communities learn this quickly, and learn to do good whether anyone appreciates it or not.

The arguments continue to be one-sided, with his opponents announcing the theme and then never getting to rebut Jesus' proofs. Is it blasphemous to pronounce forgiveness of sins? No, because God gave Jesus that authority, just as God gave Jesus the power to heal. Is it wrong for Jesus to eat with sinners? No, it is a means for them to repent. Why won't Jesus and the boys fast? Because it is inappropriate to fast when you are celebrating something as amazing as salvation coming to a tax collector.

It has never been easy to follow Jesus: Thomas à Kempis calls it "a great art to know how to keep company with Jesus, and great wisdom to know how to hold him."[16] Mark's account sometimes makes discipleship almost inconceivable, because the disciples jump up and run off with Jesus, leaving their families and professions. Luke's account of Peter's conversion and of the beginning of his discipleship makes it more of a process—but no less a sacrifice. Peter still must give up what he is doing to follow, still must submit to Jesus' instructions when Peter thinks they are foolish. But in Luke's account, we see more of the steps that may have gone into Peter's decision to join up with Jesus: Jesus' ministry to Peter's family, Jesus' vigorous teaching, Jesus' transformation of Peter's own profession into something miraculous.

By contrast, the call of Levi is sudden and direct, and his decision to follow Jesus instant. Perhaps Luke is demonstrating that finding the beginning of the Jesus road happens differently to various people, and suggesting that as the church recruits and evangelizes, it should be flexible.

NOTES

[1] So Raymond E. Brown, *Gospel According to John* (New York: Doubleday, 1970), 2:1090; Alan R. Culpepper, *The Gospel of Luke* (NIB, vol. 9; Nashville: Abingdon, 1995), 117.

[2] Luke Timothy Johnson, *The Gospel of Luke* (SP, vol. 3; Collegeville MN: Liturgical Press, 1991), 90.

[3] Johnson, *Luke*, 92, suggests that Luke puts in the detail about the city only to make sense of why Jesus withdrew to the deserted places at the end of the story.

[4] Contra most interpreters: Culpepper, *Luke*, 120; Joel B. Green, *The Gospel of Luke* (NICNT; Grand Rapids: Eerdmans, 1997), 237 (but see n. 40).

[5] The detail about the town also tends to undercut the common interpretation of the man as an outcast, and Jesus' ministry as providing "concern for those who are ritually outcast from the people of Israel and therefore from full participation in its life" (so Johnson, *Luke*, 95–96, and similarly most other commentators). The lepers in ch. 17 can work that way, but not this leper, who is already in a town.

[6] Green, *Luke*, 240; Culpepper, *Luke*, 123; Joseph A. Fitzmyer, *The Gospel According to Luke* (AB 28 and 28A; Garden City NY: Doubleday, 1981), 1:582.

[7] So Johnson, *Luke*, 98–99.

[8] Contra John Nolland, *Luke* (WBC, vols. 35A-C; Dallas TX: Word, 1989-93), 1.246, who takes it to mean "those publicly known to be unsavory types who lived beyond the edge of respectable society"; Robert C. Tannehill, *Luke* (ANTC; Nashville: Abingdon, 1996), 108, who thinks of them as "the outcasts of Jewish society"; Green, *Luke*, 247, who includes them among the poor; E. E. Ellis, *The Gospel of Luke* (London: Oliphants, 1974), 107, who reads them, following J. Jeremias, as "people who did not keep the ceremonial regulations laid down by the rabbis." The last spin on "sinner" has largely been discredited for Historical Jesus research by E. P. Sanders (e.g., in his chapter "The Sinners" in *Jesus and Judaism* [Philadelphia: Fortress, 1985], 174–209). Sanders makes the point forcefully (and in my judgment, convincingly) that Jesus' association with the sinners had nothing to do with purity laws. But since our question in this commentary is what Luke expected his readers to understand by the term "sinner," we should agree that it is all the more unlikely that Luke, writing for a Gentile audience, was terribly concerned about purity issues. Consider this episode, where Jesus, Levi and his tax collector cronies, and the Pharisees are all in Levi's house discussing the rightness of eating with tax collectors. Had the purity issue been the main point, would not the narrator have made it clearer that the Pharisees were outside the house yelling through the open gate?

[9] Green, *Luke*, 244–50, reads it that way, based on the pattern of meal, discourse, protest, and response that is found elsewhere in Luke. He imagines the Pharisees present "to monitor legal observance" (247), but he understands their objections to Jesus as complaints raised during table talk.

[10] So Culpepper, *Luke*, 127–28.

[11] Green, *Luke,* 247–48, suggests this way of reading. Johnson, *Luke*, 99, notes that Jesus' metaphor is "the standard medical imagery of the Hellenistic philosopher."

[12] The closest antecedent would be the Pharisees and their scribes, held over from the previous complaint, and the only real objection to this is the awkwardness of having the Pharisees talk about the disciples of the Pharisees; so Green, *Luke*, 249, and

Culpepper, *Luke*, 130. Others assume the Pharisees are continuing their criticism of Jesus' practice; so Nolland, *Luke*, 1.247; Fitzmyer, *Luke*, 1.597; Johnson, *Luke*, 98.

[13] So Tannehill, *Luke*, 109; Green, *Luke*, 249.

[14] John J. Rousseau and Rami Arav, *Jesus and His World* (Minneapolis: Fortress, 1995), 329; Pheme Perkins, "Patched Garments and Ruined Wine: Whose Folly?" in Mary Ann Beavis, ed., *The Lost Coin: Parables of Women, Work, and Wisdom* (Sheffield: Sheffield Academic Press, 2002), 124–35.

[15] Tannehill, *Luke*, 109; Culpepper, *Luke*, 131; Johnson, *Luke*, 99–100.

[16] Thomas à Kempis, *The Imitation of Christ* 13 (trans. Betty I. Knott; London: Collins, 1963), 94.

CHOOSING TWELVE; SERMON ON THE PLAIN

Luke 6

COMMENTARY

Sabbath Controversies, 6:1-11

Maybe some readers remember the "blue laws" that made it illegal to do certain things on Sunday. In rural Alabama when I was growing up, most stores were closed, so that one either had to buy what one needed—gas, milk, eggs, whatever—on Saturday, or know how to sweet-talk the store owner into making a "Sabbath sale" for "emergency purposes." My people were okay with going to restaurants on Sunday, but not to the movies; some relatives avoided playing cards on Sunday, but dominoes were fine, or Rook cards, since they are not normally used for gambling; I got to watch *Ed Sullivan* and Disney's *Wonderful World of Color* on Sunday nights so long as it did not interfere with Training Union and Sunday evening worship, but I had friends whose families thought that was unchristian. As a child, I chafed at restrictions to having fun on Sundays; as an adult, I now think a law requiring a Sunday afternoon nap would be a fine idea.

The Sabbath is not Sunday, of course; the Sabbath goes from sundown on Friday until sundown on Saturday. The blue laws had their roots in the Christian sabbatarianism that was part of a general pietist and holiness strain in Southern religion, and part of their motivation—Christians should be separate from the world—is the same as the motivation behind Sabbath laws—Jews should also be separate, so that it is clear that they belong to God alone. The Mishnah exhibits the same kind of diversity of opinion about what was lawful on Sabbath as my examples above illustrate about Christian sabbatarian practice. "Is it lawful to eat an egg laid on Sabbath?" seems to me not terribly different from "is it lawful to watch television on Sunday?" So let us begin our consideration of these stories by purging our interpretive vocabulary of all words like "petty" or "nit-picking," inasmuch as those sorts of attitudes about holiness/pietist codes of behavior prevent us from ever understanding them.

Luke treats these as two separate incidents happening on different Sabbaths at least a week apart[1] (6:1, "And so it happened on the Sabbath," and 6:6, "And so it happened on another Sabbath"), yet we do no harm to the structure by considering them together. The first episode in 6:1-5, which takes up the issue of the disciples plucking and eating grain on Sabbath, is connected to 5:27-39, Levi's banquet, by the theme of eating (although eating is not really the issue here); the second, in 6:6-11, is connected to the first by the Sabbath question. Luke takes them over in Mark's order, so he did not invent the connections, but in Luke's Gospel, with its heavy use of eating and meal imagery, the thread of food and feeding the hungry stands out more in the narrative weave than it does in Mark.

There are several important structural parallels between these two pericopes and earlier ones. The grain-field episode is a typical controversy or pronouncement story, like 5:29-32 and 5:33-35: very brief description of setting; accusation or accusatory question by the Pharisees; response by Jesus to end the episode. The sequence is also parallel to the controversy section of the healing of the paralyzed man, 5:21-24: accusatory question; response from Jesus in the form of rhetorical questions; pronouncement about the extent of the authority of the Son of Man. Again, Luke has not invented any of this, but is accepting it from his source, Mark, recognizing the value of repeated structures for reinforcing the reader's understanding of Jesus' nature and mission.

The episode in 6:6-11 puts Jesus in a synagogue for the third time, healing an individual for the fifth time, and healing in front of critical Pharisees for the second time. Looking at the three synagogue episodes, we notice that the reactions to Jesus go from amazement (4:22) to murderous rage (4:28-29) in the first one, from astonishment (4:32) to further amazement and news-spreading (4:36-37) in the second, and in the third, from close scrutiny with hostile intent (6:7) to rage and discussion of what they might do with/to Jesus (6:11). The scribes and the Pharisees in this synagogue act more like the worshipers in Nazareth than like the worshipers in Capernaum; doing the miracle in front of them makes them no less hostile than the Nazareans, for whom Jesus refused to do a miracle. Yet it isn't clear that the miracle at Capernaum did Jesus any real favors; that crowd did not want to kill him, but they liked the miracle so much that they wanted to prevent Jesus from leaving them (4:42). On the other hand, Pharisees and scribes who saw the healing of the paralytic, and who were initially scandalized by Jesus' announcement, "your sins are forgiven," were moved to the praise of God by what they saw. The Pharisees and scribes are not completely beyond redemption in Luke, nor are miracles either absolute proofs or completely worthless testimony of Jesus' relation to God.

The issue, at least on the surface of both episodes, is what one may lawfully do on Sabbath. In order to read these correctly, modern American Protestants must clear their heads of certain misperceptions.

First, the Sabbath was regarded by Jews and non-Jews everywhere as a marker of Jewish identity. It was commonplace information about Jews, like the prohibition against pork, that they kept the seventh day sacred to their God. Philo, the Alexandrian Jew who lived between 20 BC and AD 50, argues in one place that nations everywhere have begun to imitate the Jewish practice because they recognize the value of a day free from labor. [Philo on the Universality of Sabbath Practice] This is a big chunk of rhetorical overstatement. Josephus lists various decrees from Julius Caesar and various other Roman and local officials protecting the rights of Jews to practice Sabbath and other elements of their faith. These decrees show that sometimes the Sabbath was resented in places where Jews lived and that they had to appeal for government protection of their right to abstain from work once in seven days. For example,

Philo on the Universality of Sabbath Practice

Philo, *Moses* 2.4.20-21: "[our laws] influence all nations, barbarians and Greeks, the inhabitants of continents and islands, the eastern nations and the western, Europe and Asia; in short, the whole habitable world from one extremity to the other. For what man is there who does not honor that sacred seventh day, granting in consequence a relief and relaxation from labor . . . ."

The decree of the Ephesians . . . Since the Jews that dwell in this city have petitioned Marcus Julius Pomperus, the son of Brutus, the proconsul, that they might be allowed to observe their Sabbaths, and to act in all things according to the customs of their forefathers, without impediment from anybody, the praetor has granted their petition. Accordingly, it was decreed by the senate and people, that in this affair that concerned the Romans, no one of them should be hindered from keeping the Sabbath day, or be fined for so doing, but that they may be allowed to do all things according to their own laws.[2]

Second, the evidence from the first century, such as it is, shows that Jews by and large observed the Sabbath and did not think it burdensome to do so. Again, Philo:

Is it not a most beautiful recommendation, and one most admirably adapted to the perfecting of, and leading man to, every virtue, and above all to piety? The commandment, in effect, says: Always imitate

God; let that one period of seven days in which God created the world, be to you a complete example of the way in which you are to obey the law, and an all-sufficient model for your actions.[3]

In another place, Philo called the Sabbath "the birthday of the world, as the day in which the work of the Father, being exhibited as perfect with all its parts perfect, was commanded to rest and abstain from all works."[4] Josephus writes as if he and the others involved in the War of 66–70 observed the Sabbath rest and the Sabbath meal; that gives us some notion of how deeply committed people were to its observance. [Josephus on Sabbath-keeping during the War]

[Josephus on Sabbath-keeping during the War]

And for most people most of the time, what would be the burden of a day when you were required not to work? If one's workdays were filled mostly with hard physical labor, and if grocery stores and entertainment media were not available on any day, the prospect of a day where one's only obligations were to rest, to eat, to think about Scripture, and to be with one's family would be liberating and welcome.

Josephus on Sabbath-keeping during the War

Josephus, *Life* 2.275, 279: "However, they desired me to lodge somewhere else, because the next day was Sabbath; and that it was not fit the city of Tiberias should be disturbed [on that day].

"But the multitude were not pleased with what was said, and had certainly gone into a tumult, unless the sixth hour, which was now come, had dissolved the assembly, at which hour our laws require us to go to dinner on Sabbath days."

The point for reading our stories is this: Luke, a Gentile, and his Gentile readers were unlikely to have practiced Sabbath, but they would have known that Jesus, like all Jews, did. Luke and his readers would have assumed that Jesus and his followers observed the Sabbath as a duty and as a joy, and the idea that Jesus was freeing them from restrictive and oppressive regulations would have been doubly absent from their minds. First, Luke's readers would not have felt obliged to obey the Torah, and second, they would not have presumed that obedience to Sabbath laws was a problem for those who observed it. They might, like some other Gentiles, have considered Sabbath a nuisance, because of the problems it created for integrating Jews into Greco-Roman city life, but those issues are not at all in view for these stories. So whatever else we make of these episodes, we should not read them as acts of liberation from oppressive legalism.

In the first episode, Luke adds to Mark's description of what the disciples were doing, adding "rubbing" and "eating" to Mark's "plucking." One wonders if Luke thinks that his readers would need a bit more help that Mark provides in order to visualize the scene: first you pluck the kernels, then you rub them in your hands to remove the chaff, then you pop them in your mouth for a tasty snack. The greater specificity of the scene also makes clearer why the Pharisees were griped: not only were Jesus' disciples reaping on Sabbath, but they were threshing as well, at least according to the Pharisees. [The Mishnah Defines Work on Sabbath]

To have been such an important marker of the Jewish faith, the Sabbath is defined in Scripture in a rather minimalist way. Hear the word of the Lord from Exodus 20:8-11:

> Remember the Sabbath day, and keep it holy. Six days you shall labor and do all your work. But the seventh day is a Sabbath to the LORD your God; you shall not do any work—you, your son or your daughter, your male or female slave, your livestock, or the alien resident in your towns. For in six days the LORD made heaven and earth, the sea, and all that is in them, but rested the seventh day; therefore the LORD blessed the Sabbath day and consecrated it. (NRSV)

The parallel passage in Deuteronomy 5:12-15 has the same command with a different motive clause: do this because you, too, were a slave in Egypt, and God delivered you from your bondage. In both cases, then, Israel is to imitate God—either God's rest following creation or God's delivery from overwork—by not working on Sabbath. But what counts as work? Scripture gives only a few specifics: you may not kindle a fire (Exod 35:3) nor plow nor reap (Exod 34:21) nor gather food (Exod 16:27-30) nor firewood (Num 15:32). Technically, the disciples were not reaping, since they were only using their hands, but they were gathering food. So the line of defense offered by some interpreters—this was a dispute over the interpretation of Torah, pitting Jesus the liberal versus the conservative Pharisees—is probably not correct. Philo wrote that "there is no shoot, and no branch, and not leaf even which it is allowed to cut or to pluck on that day, nor any fruit which it is lawful to gather."[5] The disciples probably were breaking the Law as it was generally understood in Jesus' day.[6]

In addition, Jesus' defense does not argue that what the disciples did was not work; by not arguing against the Pharisees' accusation directly, he appears to concede their point. In rebuttal, he offers an example from 1 Samuel 21; David, on the run from King Saul, lies to Ahimelech the priest, telling him that he is on a secret mission for the king and needs whatever food the priest has on hand for himself and some young men he says he is meeting.[7] The priest replies that he only has holy bread, the bread of the Presence—

The Mishnah Defines Work on Sabbath

The main classes of work are forty save one: sowing, ploughing, reaping, binding sheaves, threshing, winnowing, cleansing crops, grinding, sifting, kneading, baking, shearing wool, washing or beating or dyeing it, spinning, weaving, making two loops, weaving two threads, separating two threads, tying [a knot], loosening [a knot], sewing two stitches, tearing in order to sew two stitches, hunting a gazelle, slaughtering or flaying or salting it or curing its skin, scraping it or cutting it up, writing two letters [of the alphabet], erasing in order to write two letters, building, pulling down, putting out a fire, lighting a fire, striking with a hammer and taking out anything from one domain into another.

m. Šabb. 7:2.

loaves baked and set out weekly by priests as offerings to God, which priests were to eat in the sanctuary as "most holy portions for him from the offerings by fire to the LORD" (Lev 24:5-9). Ahimelech asks if David and his friends are currently celibate; David assures him that they are, and he takes the bread and the sword of Goliath (kept as a war trophy in the sanctuary) and heads for the hills. The reader wonders whether David lied about the companions, too, as a way to get more bread.

It is not a story about Sabbath, but about non-priests eating holy things. Jesus appears to offer it to make the general point that sometimes God's laws can be set aside for good reason. And then Jesus offers the reason: he, the Son of Man, is Lord of the Sabbath, and so he can decide what is permissible.

Dire Human Needs Override the Sabbath

If a man has a pain in his throat they may drop medicine into his mouth on the Sabbath, since there is doubt whether his life is in danger, and whenever there is doubt whether life is in danger, this overrides the Sabbath. If a building fell down upon a man and there is doubt whether he is there or not, or whether he is alive or dead, or whether he is a gentile or an Israelite, they may clear away the ruin from above him.

m. Yoma 8:6-7.

There are a couple of issues of logic to be faced. First, the story about David might argue that dire human need overrides any law, including Sabbath laws. The Pharisees might even have agreed with that; the rabbis who put together the Mishnah taught that one might break Sabbath in order to save a life, and that even if one was not certain that the situation was life or death, one could still break Sabbath blamelessly. [Dire Human Needs Override the Sabbath] But in the story of the disciples in the grain field, there is no apparent dire need; the disciples seem to be snacking, not dealing with desperate hunger. Could they not have waited? Second, once Jesus says, "I am in charge of Sabbath law," then any other reason is superfluous, and the whole "David and the showbread" incident is beside the point. What we are left with is a story that shows the disciples being a bit careless or cavalier about Sabbath observance; the Pharisees catch them red-handed, and Jesus says, "I'm in charge—I decide what's lawful." [Maybe the Disciples Were Starving]

Maybe the Disciples Were Starving

Scott Spencer suggests that we read this story in light of the disciples' decision to abandon everything to follow Jesus. This makes them broke and homeless, dependent on what they can gather up from day to day, much like the Israelites in the wilderness: "These are men on the move with an urgent mission, without land, home, or resources to call their own. They are not harvesting on the Sabbath for sale or trade or even to stock their own cupboards; they gather what they can on the fly to meet the day's hunger."

Scott Spencer, *What Did Jesus Do?: Gospel Profiles of Jesus' Personal Conduct* (Harrisburg PA: Trinity, 2003), 183.

It is a story that makes little sense in Jesus' own time, but that makes much more sense in Luke's story world and in the putative world of Luke's readers. Within Luke, Jesus has compared himself to Elijah, who made sure that the widow at Zarephath had enough to eat; he has filled Peter's nets with fish; he has told the Pharisees that he and his disciples eat and drink like guests at a wedding banquet. He refused to turn stones to bread at Satan's suggestion, but he has no ethical issues eating what Peter's mother-in-law fixed for him or what Levi the tax collector laid out in his honor. This teacher loves to eat! So is it any wonder that his boys nosh on grain kernels as they wander through a field on Sabbath? It isn't so much an issue of disrespect for the Sabbath—notice that Luke removes Mark's "the Sabbath was made for humanity, not humanity for the Sabbath"—as an issue of ministry style, where Jesus sort of eats his way through Galilee, eating with sinners, eating with Pharisees, eating on Sabbath, using food and table as a strategy for extending the offer of repentance and salvation.

For the world of Luke's readers, we imagine few people actually keeping Sabbath or worrying about what counted as work. To them, the Lukan Jesus' defense—God's holy bread was taken to feed the hungry, and that was a good thing—and the Lukan Jesus' self-identification—"The Son of Man is Lord of the Sabbath"— may well have sounded like an exhortation to charity. Recall Paul's word to the Corinthians: "Now concerning the collection for the saints: . . . on the first day of every week, each of you is to put aside and save whatever extra you earn, so that collections need not be taken when I come" (1 Cor 16:1-2). And as Luke describes the normal practices of these same disciples in the early days following Jesus' ascension, he writes, "They devoted themselves to the apostle's teaching and fellowship, to the breaking of bread and to prayers . . . they would sell their possessions and goods and distribute the proceeds to all, as any had need . . . they broke bread from house to house and ate their food with glad and generous hearts" (Acts 2:42-46). Here is Jesus defending the practices of his disciples and through them the habits that Luke hopes his readers will cultivate.

The second episode opens with Jesus, on another Sabbath, entering a synagogue and teaching; as noted earlier, this is the third time so far in Luke, bearing out 4:16, "he went to the synagogue on Sabbath, as his custom was." There was a man whose right hand—his dominant hand, so Luke's readers would assume—was withered.[8] Despite the presence of the Pharisees, there is no suggestion that the man was a plant, but the fact that they were scrutinizing Jesus to see if he would heal is meant to suggest that by now they know what he is like. So they know the disabled man normally attends this synagogue; they know Jesus is teaching here that day; they watch, then, to see if their suspicions are borne out and to find "grounds for accusing him."

Jesus "knew their thinking"—the word here, *dialogismos*, can mean inner reasoning or verbal arguments or discussions, and it is a word already associated with the Pharisees and scribes. In 5:21, they began to do this in response to Jesus' word to the paralyzed man, "Your sins are forgiven," and Jesus knew then what they were thinking/saying. This running theme in Luke starts with Simeon's prediction in 2:34-35: "Behold, this one is set for the falling and rising of many in Israel and for a sign that will be opposed [lit., "spoken against"] . . . so that he may reveal the *dialogismoi*, the reasonings/arguments/discussions of their hearts."[9] In this scene, several elements of Simeon's prediction come to pass: the opposition to Jesus, the "rising" of the one he is helping (Luke uses the same word for the paralyzed man and Levi), and the exposure of what his enemies were considering.

What Jesus exposes, by his rhetorical question in 6:9, was a disagreement with the scribes and Pharisees over the purpose of the Sabbath. As in the previous episode, there is an unreality to this pericope if we think of it only in terms of Jesus' own environment. Having just said that he was master of the Sabbath, why does he need to justify his decision to heal to the Pharisees? And the decision to heal or not to heal a man with a withered hand is hardly a decision "to save life or to destroy." We know nothing of the circumstances of the man's illness, but if he was present in synagogue for Sabbath services, it would not appear that he was dying or in danger of dying. Had he been, the Pharisees and scribes likely would have agreed with Jesus that the need to save life overrode the command to refrain from work on Sabbath (see [Dire Human Needs Override the Sabbath]). If we think of this as a real argument between Jesus and the Pharisees over the interpretation of Sabbath law, then Jesus loses: he could have waited until Sabbath was past to heal the man's hand, and everyone, including God who gave the Sabbath commandments, would have been happy. But as noted above, Luke's readers were not likely to have been debating what they might or might not do on Sabbath—that's not the burning question for Luke or his audience. [Christian Sabbatarianism]

The way Jesus frames his challenge to the Pharisees begs the question; of course it is lawful to do good on Sabbath and unlawful to do evil (*kakopoiēsai* in v. 9 could mean "do harm," as in physical harm to the man, or "do evil," which I think is the better and broader contrast to *agathopoiēsai*, "do good" or "do a good deed"). The Pharisees would, in real life, have doubtless argued that waiting until sundown to heal the man was a greater good, since it preserved the Law and balanced reverence for the Law with concern for the man. Jesus' action argues that the greater good is the care of the individual, and that meeting any need is a good that God would approve for the Sabbath. As Spencer points out, the man's disability is likely to have prevented him from working, making every day a Sabbath; why would God be honored by delaying the man's restoration even one more minute?[10] ["Stretch out your hand"]

In this case and in the case of the grain field, Jesus' teaching argues that God is honored when God's people meet the needs of others. The word "save" in v. 9 not only means "heal," but was in the first century a political claim by the emperors. Rome, in the person of its dictators, was claiming that its occupation of foreign territory, taxation, building military bases and quartering troops, domination of international trade, etc., was salvation for the world. Jesus, in this tiny Galilean house of prayer, demonstrates that he thinks salvation begins by meeting the needs of the anonymous man with the crippled hand, and that it can happen no matter who objects, because he is the Son of Man, the Lord of the Sabbath.

In this synagogue scene, the enemies are at first watching to find something they can use against Jesus. When Jesus challenges them with his analysis of their reasoning, they are silent. But at the end, when the man is healed, they are enraged. What sense is there in their reaction? The healing took no effort, apparently, on Jesus' part; the man reached out his hand and it "was restored," a divine passive indicating that God, in this sacred space, has done the healing. But they, like the Nazareth crowd, were filled with fury. Unlike Jesus' hometown audience, this group does not grab him and try to kill him; Luke even tones down Mark's "they had a meeting about how they might destroy him" (3:6). Instead, for all their fury, all they do is talk about what they might do to/with Jesus. As we go forward in the narrative, what they do is invite him to dinner three times, warn him about Herod Antipas's plans to kill him, and criticize and mock him occasionally, but never actually participate in the plot to put him to death. Luke is saving a place at the table for some of the Pharisees, who will turn up in Acts as the conservative wing of Jesus' followers. In Luke, loving your enemies actually works.

"Stretch out your hand"

Then you heard the words of the Lord, saying, "Stretch forth your hand." That is the common and universal remedy. You who think that you have a healthy hand beware lest it is withered by greed or by sacrilege. Hold it out often. Hold it out to the poor person who begs you. Hold it out to help your neighbor, to give protection to a widow, to snatch from harm one whom you see subjected to unjust insult. Hold it out to God for your sins. The hand is stretched forth; then it is healed.

Ambrose, *Exp. Luc.* 5.40, cited in Arthur A. Just Jr., ed., *Luke* (ACCS: NT, vol. 3; Downer's Grove IL: Intervarsity Press, 2003), 100.

Choosing Twelve, 6:12-16

Here is another list, like the genealogy in 3:23-38, but with some framing that makes it pretty interesting. We tackle the list first:

these are the apostles drawn from the disciples, according to 6:13, implying that somewhere between 5:11 and 6:12 the group has grown to more than a dozen people. There are other lists in the other Gospels (John does not have a list; his names appear in a few places in the Gospel):

Luke 6:14-16	Mark 3:16-19	Matthew 10:2-4	John
Simon, AKA Peter	Simon, AKA Peter	Simon, AKA Peter	Simon Peter
Andrew his brother	Andrew (diff. order)	Andrew his brother	Andrew his brother
James	James son of Zebedee	James son of Zebedee	The sons of Zebedee
John	John, brother of James, AKA Boanerges	John his brother	
Philip	Philip (diff. order)	Philip	Philip
Bartholomew Matthew	Bartholomew Matthew	Bartholomew Matthew the tax collector (diff. order)	
Thomas	Thomas	Thomas (diff. order)	Thomas
James son of Alphaeus	James son of Alphaeus	James son of Alphaeus	
Simon, AKA the Zealot	Simon the Cananaean (diff. order)	Simon the Cananaean (diff. order)	
Judas son of James	Thaddeus (diff. order)	Thaddeus (diff. order)	Judas, not Iscariot
Judas Iscariot, who betrayed him	Judas Iscariot, who betrayed him	Judas Iscariot, who betrayed him	Judas Iscariot, who betrayed him
			Nathanael

Luke's list is mostly the same as Mark's, but there are a couple of differences. The difference between "Simon the Zealot" and "Simon the Cananaean" has sometimes been explained as a translation variant; the Greek word Mark used, *kananaion*, "Cananaean," may actually be an Aramaic word written out in Greek, meaning "the zealous one."[11] Does Luke know enough Aramaic to be able to translate Mark's term with the correct Greek equivalent? We either have to think he does, or conclude that his Mark is different from Matthew's, or that he had another list alongside the one from Mark. Luke has "Judas son of James" for Mark's "Thaddeus," which seems thin grounds for positing a variant list until one notes that John also has a "Judas not Iscariot." Luke's order is also slightly different from Mark's. His list keeps the brothers together—the way they appear in John 1:40-42, in Matthew's list and Mark 1:16. Possibly, then, Luke has modified Mark's list by a second list he had, or else his copy of Mark was different from ours at this place.

Most of the names in the Synoptics are the same, and John's Gospel, which knows of the Twelve but never names all of them, has only one name (Nathanael) that appears in none of the Synoptics. The overall impression, then, is of a list of names that was mostly, but not entirely, stable, as if the ancient church knew that there were twelve, knew for certain the majority of the names, but was fuzzier on the rest. As some note, this probably indicates that the concept of the Twelve, and their role as the base for the kingdom of God, was more important than the actual names of twelve persons.[12] While this was likely true for Jesus, it was important for Luke to have twelve actual persons occupying twelve spots, and so he alone recounts the story of the replacement of Judas Iscariot[13] after his death (Acts 1:16-26). For Luke, then, "apostle" is a title Jesus chose to apply to a dozen men from among the larger number of disciples. At this point in the narrative, he says nothing about the function of the apostles; he will assign them duties and give them authority in 9:1-6, but then give the same authority and slightly expanded duties to seventy (or seventy-two) others in 10:1-12. "Apostle" is thus an important title, but one that grants no exclusive rights or privileges.

The frame for the naming of the Twelve continues Luke's depiction of Jesus' own spiritual practices. He went to a mountain to pray, as he had gone to deserted places earlier (4:1; 4:42; 5:16), and "was in prayer to God right through the night." Like his forty-day fast, an all-night prayer vigil was a sign of his piety and devotion to God. [Jesus in Prayer] Coming right on the heels of stories emphasizing his willingness to eat with sinners, to leave off fasting, and to disregard Sabbath restrictions, this verse reminds the reader that Jesus was seriously religious. It also was surely meant to help the reader think that his choice of the Twelve, including Judas the traitor, was directed by God.

Jesus in Prayer

No one can safely go among [people] but the [one] who loves solitude. No one can safely speak, but the [one] who loves silence. No one can safely be in command, but the [one] who has learned complete obedience.

Thomas à Kempis, *The Imitation of Christ*, book 1, sec. 20 (trans. Betty I. Knott; London: Collins, 1963), 65.

The Sermon on the Plain, 6:20-49

The Sermon on the Plain is not nearly as long as Matthew's Sermon on the Mount. Because most of Luke 6:20-49 finds a parallel in Matthew 5–7, most modern Gospel commentators assume that both Luke and Matthew drew their material from Q. The first, second, and fourth Lukan beatitudes closely parallel the first, fourth, and last beatitudes in Matthew; Matthew 7:1-5 is very close to Luke 6:37, 41-42; Matthew 7:21 is similar to Luke 6:46, and both sermons end with the parable of the two houses (Matt 7:24-27; Luke 6:47-49). So perhaps there was a "great sermon" in Q from which each author drew some material; opinions differ as to whether the parts in Luke that are not in Matthew were in Q, or whether Luke added them to his source. Opinions also differ about whether the organizational scheme of Matthew's sermon was original to Q or was contributed by Matthew; if we knew the former to be true, then it would be worthwhile to ask about how and why Luke changed the structure. Luke may well have redacted his source, but since we cannot with confidence reconstruct his source, we will employ other interpretive strategies.

Luke's sermon does not have a linear flow from a proposition to arguments for it to a dramatic conclusion. [Luke Gets Poor Marks for Organization] It has few indications of movement and structure. The beatitudes and woes are introduced by "lifting up his eyes . . . he said," and v. 27, which begins "But I say to you who are listening," marks the beginning of another section. I take 6:39, "And he told them a parable," to introduce a new heading or topic, but many commentators include it in the "don't judge" section. In my division, 6:48-49 is included in the last section; it also functions as the conclusion to the sermon, and could be set apart in the outline. We should admit, then, that no one's division of the sermon will be universally persuasive.[14]

Here is how I will treat it:

6:17-20a—Audience and Setting
6:20b-26—Beatitudes and Woes
6:27-35—Topic One: Love Your Enemies
6:36-38—Topic Two: Be Merciful, as God Is Merciful
6:39-42—Topic Three: Sight and Blindness, Teaching and Learning
6:43-49—Topic Four: Walk Like You Talk

In this division, the four beatitudes and four woes are matched by the four topics; the narrator's intrusion at 6:39 is accounted for as a section break; and the shift to direct address in 6:42b is treated as an appeal to passion[15] to end the section.

Audience and Setting, 6:17-20a

Jesus was on the mountain for prayer and for the selection of the Twelve from the larger group of disciples. Now he descends to a level place; it is hard to resist the comparison to Moses, who went up on the mountain as God came down to receive God's message (Exod 19:20; 34:4) and then descended to deliver it to the people (Exod 32:15; 34:29-35).[16] The power that came out from Jesus to heal is perhaps Luke's reflection on the glory of God that suffused Moses' face, making the Israelites afraid; Jesus' power, far from needing to be hidden by a veil, goes out to heal all those troubled by disease or demons. The setting also ensures that, in order to be heard, Jesus will have been standing while his audience was seated; although Luke does not specify their posture, that must have been how they were arranged. This arrangement is more typical for Greek or Roman speech-makers, and contrasts with the setting in Luke 4, where Jesus sits to teach—the Jewish cultural pattern.[17]

On three previous occasions, Jesus has taught synagogue audiences, but the better parallels are the two other times when Luke specifies a crowd clustered around Jesus. On the first occasion, he was teaching the same crowd from Capernaum that wanted to hold him physically, keeping him in the city; on that occasion, he borrowed a boat to put out to water so that he could teach them as they lined the shore (5:1-3). On the second occasion, he was in a house, and the crowd—composed of Pharisees and scribes—was a barrier that the paralytic's friends had to get around. Crowds, then, are not necessarily good things for Luke's Jesus: Jesus borrows a boat to teach without being crushed (5:1-3), goes to deserted places to escape them (5:16), and confronts their criticisms of his approach to physical and spiritual healing (5:17-26).

Luke's syntax is a bit wobbly in v. 17, but he appears to mean that there was a crowd of disciples at the bottom of the hill as well as a crowd, period, who included the sick and demon-possessed, and who came from all over Palestine. The apostles, just named in 6:12-16, must be assumed to be present as well, but they are not directly addressed. So for the purposes of the discourse, we think of "disciples"—gathered in large numbers, and probably including the twelve apostles—who are directly addressed in 6:20, and "non-disciples," the larger crowd whose loyalties go unremarked, directly addressed in 6:27. This dual audience helps to explain how Luke can have Jesus say "you poor" and "you rich," etc., without being careful to sort which tag belongs to which listener. Jesus will later pronounce and then repeat a curse on Jerusalem (13:35, "your house is left [desolate] to you"; 19:41-44); he will use Tyre and Sidon as examples of cities where God's Day of Judgment will fall

No Easy Consciences

So I cannot rest my hopes or put my trust in anything except the great mercy of God and the hope of heavenly grace. Even if I have around me good men, devout brethren, faithful friends, holy books, fine treatises, sweet chants and hymns, all of these are of little help and give little pleasure when I am abandoned by grace and left to my own poverty. Then there is no better remedy than patience and self-denial in the will of God.

Thomas à Kempis, *The Imitation of Christ* II.9 (trans. Betty I. Knott; London: Collins, 1963, p. 98).

hard; some of Jesus' auditors, Luke supposes, were those under the doom of the woes Jesus pronounced in the sermon.[18] But even when Jesus is said to speak directly to disciples, he mixes blessings and woes; perhaps the strategy is to leave no one with a completely easy conscience. After all, included among the Twelve are both those who have left everything to follow Jesus (5:11, 28) and one who will betray him (6:16). [No Easy Consciences]

The Beatitudes and Woes, 6:20b-26

This first section, like the beatitudes in Matthew's Sermon on the Mount, functions as an introduction to the speech. Rhetorical theory (and common sense) insists that at the beginning of a speech, a speaker must establish his or her personal credentials and obtain the interest and sympathy of the audience. Luke's Jesus makes immediate and direct personal contact with the audience through his repeated use of the second-person pronouns and second-person verb forms: "yours," "you will be sated," "you will laugh," etc. Since the rest of the speech does not move in a systematic or linear fashion, perhaps we should think of this opening less as a traditional proem in a speech—setting up speaker and audience in such a way that the argument will be effective—and more as the opening movement of a tone poem, setting the mood, displaying colors that will be elaborated more than argued in what follows.

The beatitudes and woes are poetry, much like the psalms or the poetic sections of the Hebrew prophets, so we should begin by paying close attention to form and structure. Beatitudes are fairly common forms in the Old Testament; the following examples all come from the LXX, the form in which Luke most probably would have known them. I cite the Greek so that those who can follow the Greek text of Luke can see the formal similarities and differences between Luke's beatitudes and his Old Testament models:

- Psalm 1:1: "Blessed is the man who does not walk by the counsel of the wicked." (μακάριος ἀνὴρ ὃς οὐκ ἐπορεύθη ἐν βουλῇ ἀσεβῶν, *makarios anēr hos ouk eporeuthē en boulē asebōn.*)
- Psalm 31:2-3: "Blessed is the man to whom the Lord never reckons sin, nor in whose mouth is deceit." (μακάριος ἀνὴρ οὗ οὐ μὴ λογίσηται κύριος ἁμαρτίαν οὐδέ. ἔστιν ἐν τῷ στόματι αὐτοῦ δόλος, *makarios anēr hou ou mē logisētai kyrios hamartian oude. estinen tō stomati autou dolos.*)

- Psalm 34:9 (LXX 33:9): "Blessed is the man who hopes upon him." (μακάριος ἀνὴρ ὃς ἐλπίζει ἐπ᾽ αὐτόν, *makarios anēr hos elpizei ep᾽ auton.*)
- Tobit 13:14 (LXX 13:15): "And blessed are all people who grieve with you for all your beatings, because they will rejoice with you and will see all your joy forever." (καὶ μακάριοι πάντες οἱ ἄνθρωποι οἳ ἐπὶ σοὶ λυπηθήσονται ἐπὶ πάσαις ταῖς μάστιξίν σου ὅτι ἐν σοὶ χαρήσονται καὶ ὄψονται πᾶσαν τὴν χαράν σου εἰς τὸν αἰῶνα, *kai makarioi pantes hoi anthrōpoi hoi epi soi lypēthēsontai epi pasais tais mastixin sou hoti en soi charēsontai kai opsontai pasan tēn charan sou eis ton aiōna.*)
- Sirach 25:8-9: "Blessed is he who lives with a wise wife, and who does not slip with his tongue and who does not serve one unworthy of himself. Blessed is the one who finds insight and who relates it into the ears of listeners." (μακάριος ὁ συνοικῶν γυναικὶ συνετῇ καὶ ὃς ἐν γλώσσῃ οὐκ ὠλίσθησεν καὶ ὃς οὐκ ἐδούλευσεν ἀναξίῳ ἑαυτοῦ. 9 μακάριος ὃς εὗρεν φρόνησιν καὶ ὁ διηγούμενος εἰς ὦτα ἀκουόντων, *makapios ho synoikōn gynaiki synetē kai hos en glōssē ouk ōlisthēsen kai hos ouk enouleusen anaxiō eautou. 9 makarios hos heuren phronēsin kai ho diēgoumenos eis ōta akouontōn.*)

This is only a representative sampling, but it demonstrates a formal difference between the Gospel beatitude and its Old Testament roots: Jesus' beatitudes always include a second line introduced by a causal particle that structurally, if not actually, gives a reason for the first line. This form is fairly rare in the Psalms and Wisdom literature; there, the authors mostly just announce the blessedness of the person who is doing the right thing. The example from Tobit 13:14, which is more like the Gospel form, illustrates the reason for the difference in Luke's form. Since it is a surprising move to say that the one who shares the grief and pain of Jerusalem is blessed, the second clause of the Tobit beatitude is a necessary explanation—otherwise, who would believe that a sad person is blessed? In the same way, Jesus' beatitudes, because they announce a reversal of fortunes, need the second clause. Tobit's beatitude also demonstrates how this sort of "reversal beatitude" necessarily presupposes belief in the certainty of God's good future; it is not immediately apparent that those who share Jerusalem's present troubles would rejoice in the future, unless one already believed that God's justice demanded a future reversal.[19]

Woes are a common prophetic speech form, but they also appear in Wisdom literature as judgments on those who fail to do God's will. Here are a few examples:

- Sirach 2:12-13: Woe to timid hearts and idle hands and to the sinner who sets out upon two paths. Woe to the heart at present that does not believe, because it will have no shelter. (¹² οὐαὶ καρδίαις δειλαῖς καὶ χερσὶν παρειμέναις καὶ ἁμαρτωλῷ ἐπιβαίνοντι ἐπὶ δύο τρίβους ¹³ οὐαὶ καρδίᾳ παρειμένῃ ὅτι οὐ πιστεύει διὰ τοῦτο οὐ σκεπασθήσεται, ¹² *ouai kardies deilais kai chersin pareimenais kai hamatōlō epibainonti epi dyo tribous* ¹³ *ouai kardia pareimenē hoti ou pisteuei dia touto ou skepasthēsetai.*)

- Amos 5:18: "Woe to the ones who desire the day of the Lord; for what is this day of the Lord to you? It is darkness, and not light. (¹⁸ οὐαι οἱ ἐπιθυμοῦντες τὴν ἡμέραν κυρίου ἵνα τί αὕτη ὑμῖν ἡ ἡμέρα τοῦ κυρίου καὶ αὐτή ἐστιν σκότος καὶ οὐ φῶς, ¹⁸ *ouai hoi epithymountes tēn hēmeran kyriou hina ti hautē hymin hē hēmera tou kyriou kai autē estin skotos kai ou phōs.*)

- Isaiah 1:24: "Therefore, thus says the Sovereign Lord of Hosts, Woe, O mighty ones of Israel, for my wrath will not stop on my opponents and I will make judgment upon my enemies." (διὰ τοῦτο τάδε λέγει ὁ δεσπότης κύριος σαβαωθ οὐαὶ οἱ ἰσχύοντες Ισραηλ οὐ παύσεται γάρ μου ὁ θυμὸς ἐν τοῖς ὑπεναντίοις καὶ κρίσιν ἐκ τῶν ἐχθρῶν μου ποιήσω, *dia touto tade legei ho despotēs kyrios sabaōth ouai hoi ischyontes Ispaēl ou pausetai gar mou ho thymos en tois hypenantiois kai krisin ek tōn echthrōn mou poiēsō.*)

The first two, from Sirach, show the same grammatical form as Luke's examples, where the object of the woe is set in the dative case. Sirach 2:13 and Isaiah 1:24 also have, like Luke, causal second lines, announcing not the reason for the curse but the nature of it: the unbelieving heart will, in the future, find no shelter from God; God's opponents will feel the full and unrelenting force of God's wrath.

Each beatitude starts with the word *makarioi*, better translated "blessed" than "happy"[20]—an adjective to be applied to different categories or circumstances of person. The first three have the same structure: blessed are X, because Y, where Y is a statement about what God is doing or will do. Each "woe" also starts with the same word, *ouai*, "woe," an onomatopoeic word that pronounces the curse or the judgment of God on some person or category of person. The first three woes also have the same structure: woe to X, because Y, where Y is something that will happen to X because of God's judgment. In both cases, the blessings and the woes, the last one is longer and has a structure different from the other three in the category, but similar to each other: You are blessed/cursed whenever people do X; (the beatitude puts in a motive clause here) their ancestors did the same to the prophets/false prophets.

Each blessing is also structurally parallel to its corresponding woe, so we will work through each pair together, rather than doing all the blessings and then all the woes, so that we can more easily see how Luke's strategies of parallel structures work in both directions at once. Again, I cite the Greek text so that the reader can see the way the poetic forms work—even if you don't read Greek, you can notice how the similar words line up.

Μακάριοι οἱ πτωχοί,	Πλὴν οὐαὶ ὑμῖν τοῖς πλουσίοις
ὅτι ὑμετέρα ἐστὶν ἡ βασιλεία τοῦ θεοῦ.	ὅτι ἀπέχετε τὴν παράκλησιν ὑμῶν.
Macharioi hoi ptōchoi,	*Plēn ouai hymin tois*
hoti hymetera esin hē	*plousiois*
basileia toū theou.	*hoti apechete tēn*
	paraklēsin hymōn.
Blessed the poor	(but) Woe to you rich
Because yours is the Kingdom of God	Because you have your consolation.

In both cases, there is a pronoun, not strictly necessary, but used for emphasis; the "yours" appears in the second line of the beatitude and the first line of the woe. In the woe, the "you" appears before "the rich ones," so that "rich" in effect is a category of the immediate audience—those of you listening to me who are rich. But in the blessing, delaying "yours" until line 2 makes "the poor" wider than just the immediate audience: the poor, including those listening to me. In other words, the blessing is cast with a wider net than the curse. And in the beatitude, saving the "yours" until the second line means that the reader's first translation has to be revised; you read "blessed (are) the poor," but then when you get to the "yours," you go back and read "blessed (are you) poor." Unconscious or deliberate, this forces the reader, from the very first line, to wrestle with which category he or she belongs to.[21]

Another point of grammar: "blessed" is an adjective agreeing with "poor" in case, gender, and number, so that we translate it as a predicate—that is, as a statement about the poor: The poor are blessed. But "woe" is an interjection applied to the noun by the use of the dative case: not "woe are the rich," but "woe to you, the rich." God's judgment or curse is not a characteristic of the wealthy, but is a definite decision applied to them.

And another point, this time about verb tenses: in both the blessing and the curse, the verb is in the present tense—the kingdom has been assigned to the poor already, in the same way that those enjoying this world's wealth have already enjoyed its "consolation" and comfort. In the middle two pairs of blessings and curses, the verb tenses shift to future: you will be satisified/you will go hungry, you will laugh/you will mourn and weep. Then, in good chiastic fashion, the last pair returns to the present: your reward is great in heaven (more below on the nature of the reward and punishment implied by the fourth pair).

Each second line begins with ὅτι, *hoti*, "because," as if it were a reason for the first statement. In fact, it is simply a restatement of the first line. The "blessing" that falls to the poor *is* the kingdom of God, and the curse falling to the rich is that their only consolation for the future *is* their current wealth; they will have no share in the kingdom when it arrives.

The parallelism of the beatitudes and woes sets up a paradox, where the same audience, all addressed with "you" or "your," is alternately blessed and cursed. As stated above, Luke has noted the presence of disciples and non-disciples, and probably expects the readers to imagine that among both groups are those who might be hostile to Jesus. But even without the preparation, Luke's readers can think back to Jesus' inaugural sermon, where after receiving a favorable reaction, Jesus offers provocative criticisms, predicting— and so possibly encouraging—the audience's negative response, if not their violence. Readers who know both Luke and Acts can think of sermons in Luke's second volume, too, that show Christian speakers being anything but conciliatory even in situations where, as the rhetorical handbooks would have put it, a more indirect approach would have been appropriate. Think of Stephen, for example, accusing Moses' parents of exposing him, characterizing God's response to the Israelites as "turning away" and "handing them over," and describing Solomon's temple as a theological error, before calling his judges and jury "stiff-necked" and "uncircumcised in heart and ears," "betrayers," and "murderers." Luke's image of Jesus and his apostolic followers included a fair measure of Amos and Jeremiah, excoriating their audiences in true prophetic fashion.

Luke's unmodified use of "poor" is sometimes contrasted with Matthew's "poor in spirit," with the conclusion that Luke is concerned about economics and Matthew about piety. Since we cannot be certain what Q said, assuming there was a Q, then we cannot know if Luke deleted "in spirit" or Matthew added it.[22] What we can say for certain is that Luke was, indeed, concerned with the economically poor; the imperatives that follow in the sermon make it plain that Jesus' followers were duty-bound to give away any excess money, food, or clothing they had, and to be completely responsive to those in need. We can also say for certain that Luke was also concerned for piety; his "poor" includes the "poor in spirit," as we will see in the parable of the Pharisee and the tax collector. The latter man goes down to his house redeemed by his humility and his repentance; whether he gave away his money is left unsaid. Likewise, the father in the parable of the Good Samaritan has rings and fine clothes and fatted calves and servants to spare, but can stand in, at least in part, for God because he has a forgiving and generous heart.

What we can also say for certain is that for Luke, the rich cannot be sure of God's blessings of salvation unless and until they begin to obey the imperatives in the section that follows. In Luke there is no comfort for the pious rich who are not also living by Jesus' commands to give to anyone who asks; Levi and Zacchaeus are exemplars for how to give up/give away excess wealth, as are the members of the church in Acts. [The Poor Are Still with Us]

Christians have since very early in the game been troubled by this resolute preference for the poor and against the rich. Generous Christians have been duped by unscrupulous beggars, leading the author of the *Didache* to warn that those who beg and receive without a real need will receive God's judgment. Although the *Didache* urges generous giving, it also says that one should be a cautious giver: "Let your alms sweat in your hands until you know to whom to give it" (*Did.* 1.6).

The Poor Are Still with Us

"There are an estimated 40 million more hungry people in the world today than there were ten years ago" (7). According to a study conducted by the Fordham University Institute for Innovation in Social Policy, in several key areas such as "the number of children in poverty, the number of people with health insurance, the affordability of housing, the buying power of the average paycheck, and especially disparities of income, the national report card has gotten worse" over the past thirty years (5).

ChrCent 121/1 (13 January 2004).

μακάριοι οἱ πεινῶντες νῦν,
ὅτι χορτασθήσεσθε.

οὐαὶ ὑμῖν, οἱ
ἐμπεπλησμένοι νῦν,
ὅτι πεινάσατε.

Macharioi hoi peinōtes nyn,
hoti chortasthēsesthe.

ouai hymin, hoi
empeplēsmenoi nyn,
hoti peinasate.

Blessed the hungry now,
Because you will be sated.

Woe to you who are full now,
Because you will be hungry.

The first lines of both blessing and curse have the word "now," and the verb in the second line in both cases is future tense; we have future consequences of present behavior. The blessing and curse are exactly parallel except for the emphatic "you" in the first line of the curse. In the beatitude, there is no pronoun; the only "you" is embedded in the verb. But the "you" is again emphatic in the curse: "Woe to *you*, the ones who now are full."

In this pair, in form the two first lines match and the two second lines match, but in content, the parallelism is chiastic, so that "hungry" is in blessing line 1 and curse line 2, and "full"/"sated" are similarly inverted. These are also clearly statements about what will happen in the future; you cannot be hungry and sated at the same time, so God's blessing on the hungry is that they will be fed, and the curse on the full is that they will go hungry.

Up to this point in the narrative, Jesus has fasted once for forty days, but mostly has been eating. He and his disciples get criticized for dining with sinners, for Sabbath snacking, and for eating and drinking rather than fasting—this last jab comes while he is at the banquet table with his disciples. While the reader probably identifies Jesus with "the poor," given his humble origins, his call to leave everything to follow him, and the fact that others must support him (8:3), the Lukan Jesus cannot be labeled "hungry"—he eats too often and too well in the narrative, even if in real life as an itinerant preacher he may have missed many meals. For Luke, the crime is not in eating well—Jesus and his boys have just had a great party at Levi's house, and he will banquet with Pharisees three times before the Gospel ends. For Luke, the crime is in eating well with your friends, family, and social equals while you exclude the poor from your table: this is part of his critique of the Pharisees in chapter 14, and the reason Dives wakes up roasting in chapter 16. [Food, Friendship, and God's Blessing] So as with rich and poor, the definition of hungry and full is not as simple as people who do not eat and people who do. Luke's "hungry" includes the

Food, Friendship, and God's Blessing

There was a certain old man in Egypt, and before the abbot Poemen came to that place, he was held in great worship by all. But when the abbot Poemen came down thither from Scete, many abandoned the old man and came to him, and because of this the old man began to envy him and carp at him. And hearing of it, the abbot Poemen was saddened and said to his brethren, "What shall we do? These men have brought trouble upon us, for they have deserted so holy an old man, and look to us that are naught. How shall we heal this great man of his hurt? Come, let us make a little food and make our way to him carrying it, and a little wine, and sup with him, and perchance in this way we might soothe his soul." So they set out and knocked at his door. But the old man's disciple, hearing them, said, "Who be ye?" And they answered, "Tell thy abbot that Poemen hath come to seek a blessing from him." But when the old man heard it from his disciple, he answered him, "Go and say to them, 'Go your ways, for I am not at leisure.'" Nevertheless they stayed there sorrowful, saying, "We shall not go from hence, till we have been found worthy to kneel before him." And when he saw their humility and their patience, he was sorry and opened the door and they kissed one another and did sup together. And the old man said to him, "in truth it is not only the works that I have heard of thee, but I have seen in thee a hundredfold more." And from that day he was made his dearest friend.

Sayings of the Fathers, sec. 93, cited in Helen Waddell, *The Desert Fathers* (Ann Arbor: University of Michigan Press, 1957), 141–42.

poor who cannot provide food for themselves. But his term is broader than that, and includes the spiritually hungry as well. The prodigal son in the far country is hungry, but we can scarcely call him poor; he has no money, but that is a temporary condition. His bigger problem is sin; he needs to repent and "hunger and thirst for righteousness," as Matthew has the beatitude.

μακάριοι οἱ κλαίοντες νῦν, ὅτι γελάσετε.	οὐαί, οἱ γελῶντες νῦν ὅτι πενθήσετε καὶ κλαύσατε.
Macharioi hoi klaiontes nyn, hoti gelasete.	*ouai, hoi gelōntes nyn hoti penthēsete kai klausate.*
Blessed the weepers now, Because you will laugh.	Woe the laughers now, Because you will mourn and weep.

In this pair, the first lines are exactly parallel; Luke omits the pronoun "you" in both and has the corresponding words in the same order. But the second line of the curse, by comparison to the blessing, is elaborated: you will mourn and weep, rather than the expected "you will weep." Like the second pair, these are statements about what will happen in the future: the blessing falling on the weepers is that they will laugh, and the curse on the laughers is that they will mourn and weep. If this were not in the sermon, one would think it was simply a proverb stating that tears always eventually turn to laughter and vice versa.[23]

But Luke, as always, complicates the categories. In the Old Testament, laughter is often associated with the fool (Sir 21:20, "A fool raises his voice when he laughs, but the wise smile silently"). The crowd at Jairus's house laughed at Jesus for saying that the little girl was only sleeping (8:53), one of several places where Jesus is mocked or ridiculed (16:14; 23:35-36, 39). Here we do find foolish laughter, the sneers of those who think they have won, but who will find out soon enough that they have not. But not all laughter is bad. Sarah's laugh may be the most famous in the Bible (Gen 18:9-15), and was at first a sign of her disbelief, but then a sign of how God had changed her fortunes (Gen 21:6: "The Lord has made laughter [*gelōta moi epoiēsen kyrios*] for me; for whoever hears of this will rejoice with me [*synchareitai moi*]"). The connection of laughter with rejoicing reminds us that while few Lukan people laugh, many rejoice, and uniformly for the right reasons:

John the Baptist, *in utero*, at the prospect of meeting Jesus (1:44); Elizabeth and her friends and relations, at the birth of John (1:58); the defamed for Jesus' sake, on the Day of Judgment, when God rewards them (6:23); the seventy (or seventy-two), at the success of their mission (10:17); etc.

The Lukan Jesus weeps for Jerusalem, prophetic tears shed over the coming destruction of the city (19:41), but for the most part is not a weeper; he is associated with eating and drinking, not with fasting and mourning. He told a grieving mother (7:13) and two grieving parents (8:52) to stop weeping and then gave life to their dead children, but he told the women of Jerusalem, who were weeping for him, to save their tears for themselves and their children in the judgment of God coming on their city (23:28). The woman who wept over his feet did so as a sign of her repentance (7:38), while Peter wept from shame and grief (22:62), and Jesus predicts that all those excluded in the judgment will weep and gnash their teeth (13:28). Lukan weeping is therefore motivated by more than one cause, and not all weepers are good guys.

Thus Luke's curse on those who laugh now and blessing on those who weep now is not as simple as connecting poor=hungry= weepers or rich=well-fed=laughers. [Laughing and Weeping] Not all weepers in Luke are on the side of the angels, nor are all those currently rejoicing destined to join the teeth-gnashers. Luke's beatitude promises that those who weep will rejoice, but his narrative limits the promise to those who weep in penitence or as part of a petition for Jesus' help. Luke's curse surely means that the self-satisfied sneerers will get their comeuppance, but because Jesus is out raising the dead and doing other things normally associated with the age to come, some who rejoice now are, like Sarah and Elizabeth, enjoying a God-given reversal of fortunes.

So far, the curses have been slightly more elaborate in form than the blessings. But with the fourth and final example in this series, the blessing becomes far more detailed.

Laughing and Weeping

The good man can find plenty to cause him sorrow and tears. He has only to consider himself or think of his neighbor, to realize that no one lives on this earth without distress; and the more closely he looks at himself, the more his grief increases. Our sins and failings give us good cause for sorrow and inner compunction because we are so bound down by them that we are hardly ever able to raise our eyes to heavenly things.

Thomas à Kempis, *The Imitation of Christ*, I.21 (trans. Betty I. Knott; London: Collins, 1963, 68–69).

μακάριοις ἐστε
ὅταν μισήσωσιν ὑμᾶς οἱ ἄνθρωποι
καὶ ὅταν ἀφορίσωσιν ὑμᾶς
καὶ ὀνειδίσωσιν
καὶ ἐκβάλωσιν τὸ ὄνομα ὑμῶν ὡς
   πονηρὸν
ἕνεκα τοῦ υἱοῦ τοῦ ἀνθρώπου·
χάρητε ἐν ἐκείνῃ τῇ ἡμέρᾳ καὶ
   σκιρτήσατε,
ἰδοὺ γὰρ ὁ μισθὸς ὑμῶν πολὺς ἐν
   τῷ οὐρανῷ·
κατὰ τὰ αὐτὰ γὰρ ἐποίουν
τοῖς προφήταις οἱ πατέρες αὐτῶν.

οὐαι
ὅταν ὑμᾶς καλῶς εἴπωσιν πάντες
   οἱ ἄνθρωποι

κατὰ τὰ αὐτὰ γὰρ ἐποίουν
τοῖς ψευδοπροφήταις οἱ πατέρες
   αὐτῶν.

makarioi eeste
hotan misēsōsin humas hoi anthrōpoi
kai hotan aphorisōsin hymas
kai oneidisōsin
kai ekbalōsin to onoma hymōn hōs
ponēron
heneka tou huiou tou anthrōpou
charēte en ekeinē tē hēmera kai skirtēate,
idou gar ho misthos hymōn polys en tō
*   ouranō;*
kata ta auta gar epoioun
tois prophētais hoi pateres autōn.

ouai
hotan hymas kalōs eipōsin pantes hoi
*   anthrōpoi*

kata ta auta gar epoioun
tois psuedoprophētais hoi pateres autōn.

Blessed are you
Whenever people hate you
Or whenever they exclude you
Or (whenever they) revile (you)
Or (whenever they) cast out your name
   as evil
On account of the son of man;
Rejoice in that day, and leap,
Because your reward is great in heaven.
Because (they) did the same
To the prophets. (their ancestors)

Woe
Whenever all people speak well of you

Because (they) did the same
To the false prophets. (their ancestors)

The final beatitude, but not the final curse, gets "you are" for emphasis in the first line, and this is only the beginning of how this final beatitude is elaborated more than its corresponding curse. Both curse and blessing have "whenever" clauses that are in effect conditional sentences: if these things should happen to you, then you are blessed or cursed. The blessing is whenever "you" are persecuted in various ways; if hate, exclusion, and slander happen to "you" on Jesus' account, then celebrate, because "you" have gained a great reward with God. The conjunction in the list is καί, *kai*, normally translated "and," but since it is hard to imagine that Luke thinks of the blessing only falling to the person who experiences all of these things in sequence, we should translate "or," so that the blessing is promised to any of "you" who undergo any of those conditions.

Notice how the parallel to "hate you . . . exclude you . . . revile you . . . cast out your name as evil" is "speak well of you." Those are formally parallel, but Luke has deliberately made one side completely outweigh the other in gravity and seriousness; you are blessed if all hell falls on your head; you are cursed if people say nice things about you. What's so awful about having a good reputation, and what's so great about being slandered or excluded or hated? The unbalanced lines also point to what is missing on the curse side—there is nothing to correspond to "on account of the Son of Man." The person of stellar reputation is not known for any particular virtue; his good reputation is only self-referential.

The same imbalance applies to the "reward" or "reversal" part of the beatitude, which in the first three is introduced by ὅτι, *hoti*, because. The first part is so elaborated by the "whenever" clauses that Luke has Jesus do a sort of reprise of the statement of blessing: "rejoice in that day, and leap" repeats the substance of "Blessed are you" in order to set up the "because," which is doubled and introduced by a repeated γάρ: Because your reward is great in heaven; (and) because they, their ancestors, did the same to the prophets.

What sort of reward is this? In the first three beatitudes, the reward is an explicit reversal: if you are poor, you will be given God's kingdom; if you are hungry, you will be fed; if you are weeping, you will laugh. But if you are hated or excluded or reviled or slandered, what is the corresponding blessing? Because of the connection to the fate of the prophets, we can guess that Jesus is promising God's words of affirmation on the Day of Judgment. Just as the reader of Luke can expect that the great prophets of old—Abraham, Moses, Elijah, etc.—will be in the kingdom, so can the reader guess that he or she will receive the "well done" from God in the kingdom, reversing the slander that he or she is now receiving for following Christ. The somewhat surprising "rejoice and leap" may point in the same direction: that is what John the Baptist, another prophet, did when he first met Jesus. So because "their ancestors" persecuted and killed the prophets (11:48-51), and because they will do the same to Jesus the prophet (13:33-34), Jesus' followers can expect the same treatment from them and from God. But that is left implicit; the reader must piece it out. Even more implicit is the nature of the reversal on the curse side. Those with good reputations and nothing else will be condemned, we assume, just as we expect those who rejected true and praised false prophets will be condemned on that day.

The reader has already seen some of this in action. John, God's prophet, who offered the ritual of repentance and forgiveness, has been jailed for his preaching against sin. Jesus, God's prophet, has been man-handled and nearly killed by a furious crowd; we have seen Pharisees begin to show up regularly to object and to murmur about his ministry, and to begin to discuss what they might do to him. Yet whose side would the reader of Luke prefer, the more dangerous and painful side of the Son of Man or the side of his enemies? Which side would the reader identify as blessed by God?

Luke's readers may have experienced similar treatment themselves; "casting out your name as evil on account of the Son of Man" sounds like people whose affiliation with Jesus has caused others to slander them. Perhaps some have been excluded, or have excluded themselves, from full participation in the civic or religious life of their city because of their exclusive commitment to Jesus. But it is equally likely that the terms in the curse, "when all speak well of you," describe the situation of some of Luke's intended readers. That is, one can well imagine that in the last two decades of the first century, before Roman persecution of Christians became standard practice, some Christians were, from Luke's point of view, all too comfortable in their society. Luke may be playing both sides of the net: for those who suffered for their association with Christ, there is good news; for those who are quite at home in their culture, there is impending doom. [The *Epistle to Diognetus* on Persecution of Christians]

The *Epistle to Diognetus* on Persecution of Christians

For Christians are no different from other people in terms of their country, language, or customs. Nowhere do they inhabit cities of their own, or use a strange dialect, or live life out of the ordinary . . . . They live in their respective countries, but only as resident aliens; they participate in all things as citizens, and they endure all things as foreigners . . . . They love everyone and are persecuted by all. They are not understood and they are condemned. They are put to death and made alive. They are impoverished and make many rich. They lack all things and abound in everything. They are dishonored and they are exalted in their dishonors. They are slandered and they are acquitted. They are reviled and they bless, mistreated and they bestow honor. They do good and are punished as evil; when they are punished they rejoice as those who have been made alive. They are attacked by Jews as foreigners and persecuted by Greeks. And those who hate them cannot explain the cause of their enmity.

[Note: *Diognetus* is an apology for the Christian faith, probably dating to the 2d century AD.]

Diog. 5.1-2, 5, 11-17.

Topic One: Love Your Enemies, 6:27-35

Following the curses, Jesus turns again to those inclined to listen to him, and gives them a string of eight imperatives, four short and four more elaborated.

Short:
Love your enemies
Do good to those who hate you
Bless those who curse you
Pray for those who mistreat you

Elaborated:
To the one who strikes you on the cheek, turn also the other one
From the one who takes your coat do not withhold your undergarment
Give to everyone who asks you and from the one who takes your stuff do not demand it
As you wish that people should treat you, do the same to them

This section is nicely balanced. The short clauses each include an imperative, an object, and the second-person pronoun, always in the same order; the only breaks in the sequence are in the second one, where the adverb *kalōs* had to be added to the verb (otherwise, it would have been "do those who hate you," which is something else entirely), and in the last one, where the beneficiary of "pray" must be identified by the preposition *peri*. The first and last of the more elaborated clauses have imperative followed by object in the second half of the verse, whereas the middle two save the imperative until the last, emphatic position in the sentence.

The imperatives are followed by three motive clauses, each presented as a rhetorical question, and each presuming that the reader will obviously want to do better than the "sinners," who love, do good deeds, and lend. The section is rounded out by v. 35, containing three imperatives, repeating the three verbs that were the basis of the motive clauses (love, do good, lend), and three clauses that describe the reward coming to those who do these things. Verse 35 also repeats language from earlier in the sermon: "love your enemies" repeats part of v. 27, and "your reward will be great" repeats part of v. 23.

The final beatitude and final woe focus on being hated, or not, by the wider world, so the turn to "love your enemy" makes sense.[24] The noun "enemies" in v. 27 is elaborated by a series of participles detailing what enemies might do: hate you, curse you, mistreat you, strike your cheek, and take your coat. These are all clearly hostile actions, and the command "love" is likewise elaborated by what one does in all those specific situations: do good, bless, pray, turn, and let go (lit., "not withhold"). This is a remarkable list for its variety of more active and more passive behaviors, behaviors that match or do not match the nature of the hostile act. Bless is an active and opposite response to curse: if your enemy pronounces a curse on you, pronounce a blessing on him or her. Prayer offered for those who mistreat you is an active but not opposite response, whereas not withholding your undergarment is a passive and opposite response. Since this is scarcely a catalog of all the ways one can be persecuted, the lists of responses are also only examples, and the variety shows that evil must be opposed by many different means.

"Do good" is broad, but it also probably sounded more specific in Luke's day than in ours: more like "do good deeds" than "have a good attitude." Those who hate you, in Luke's thinking, are not just harboring ill will; they are your enemies, those people who populate the psalms who are always trying to trip you up, who laugh at your misfortune, who rub salt in your wounds by saying that you suffer because you are sinful. Your responsibility to them is not simply to have a good attitude, but to find ways to do them good—on the whole, a much more practical goal for the follower of Jesus than the goal of trying to work up what we think of as the emotion of love. That is, once we realize that we have an adversary who is actively trying to do us harm, our responsibilities are to pray for him or her, to look for opportunities to do him or her a good turn, and to avoid any sort of retaliation. We are not required to feel about them the way we feel about our circle of friends and family, but we are required to act toward them in the way defined here. The moment when we decide, "You are my enemy, and so I must act in love toward you" can actually be a clarifying and liberating point when we cease pretending that this person is a friend or colleague and turn to doing what a Christian must for an enemy. [Loving and Hating]

The blow to the cheek is more for humiliation than for injury; it means that the Christian response to attempts to humiliate is active nonretaliation. To turn the other cheek is to show that one is not humiliated and that one does not need to strike back. The verse does not preclude taking nonretaliatory actions that would prevent further abuse.

Loving and Hating

I had no time to Hate—
Because
The Grave would hinder Me—
And Life was not so
Ample I
Could finish—enmity—

Nor had I time to Love—
But since
Some Industry must be—
The little toil of Love—
I thought
Be large enough for me—

Emily Dickinson, 478, *The Complete Poems of Emily Dickinson*, ed. Thomas H. Johnson (Boston: Little, Brown, 1960).

(Credit: www.wikipedia.org)

Give to Everyone who Asks

I have had a certain acquaintance with a kind of holy poverty. My grandfather never kept anything that was worth giving away, or let us keep it, either, so my mother said. . . . He lacked patience for anything but the plainest interpretations of the starkest commandments, "To him who asks, give," in particular. . . . He really would give anything away. My father would go looking for a box of nails and it would be gone.

Marilynne Robinson, *Gilead* (New York: Farrar, Straus, Giroux, 2004), 31–32.

Pastors and Bible teachers must make clear, every time this verse shows up in church, that Jesus was not asking anyone to submit to regular beatings or verbal abuse without trying to make it stop.

The one who takes your cloak may be a thief or a creditor calling in a loan or a tax collector taking your property if you had no money or a Roman soldier requisitioning your property. The one who asks might be a beggar, or might also be the tax collector or soldier, and the one who takes could be any of those. What we have, then, are three commands that cover a fairly broad range of circumstances in which we might lose personal property, whether legally or illegally, whether through violence or begging, whether through a request or a demand or a seizure. Think about how you feel when your bills are high, your taxes are coming due, the fundraisers keep calling during your supper, and the church wants you to make a pledge to the building campaign—you may find yourself feeling oppressed even by the legitimate requests for aid. The command is that we give, that we let go, that we do not demand back. We give to whoever asks—straight up, no mixed motives—but to the one who seizes, we again engage in active nonretaliation: "You want to take my coat? Okay, take my undergarment as well," so that the one who is seizing, in whatever context, is brought to shame. [Give to Everyone who Asks]

All of the short imperatives are addressed to the plural "you," to the whole community: "Y'all love your enemies," etc. The first three of the elaborated imperatives shift to the singular "you": each of you, as individuals, must turn the other cheek, not withhold your underclothes, give, and not seek the return of goods taken. The final imperative—the Lukan form of the golden rule—is again plural, to wrap everything up. Luke thereby clearly thinks that this standard of nonretaliation and active care of persecutors applies to Christians as individuals and as groups; it is no good trying to dodge our individual responsibility by claiming what our church does on our behalf, nor to say that "love your enemies" only applies to personal and individual behavior. "When Jesus said to love your enemies, he probably didn't mean kill them" is bumper-sticker theology, but how can Christians read this passage and then support military retaliation in the name of national defense? [Learning Not to Hate]

The three motive clauses are deliciously ironic. Think of how Jesus, so far, has behaved with "sinners": he eats with them, he invites them to be his disciples, he structures his ministry so as to give them the opportunity to repent. They are used as the baseline behavior in the motive clauses: sinners love those who love them, sinners do good deeds to those who have done them well, and sinners lend to those from whom they expect to get a return. Now, if a person did those three things conscientiously over a lifetime, then that person would be widely regarded as pious, not sinful. Check out Tobit, that eminently pious man, who gave charitably, made sure the dead were buried honorably, invited the poor to his dinner table, etc. He did good deeds for his "neighbors," not for those who persecuted him, and nobody would call him "sinner." By saying "even sinners do that," Luke's Jesus is reducing standard piety to a least-common denominator and urging his readers to try for something greater: "That's fine, but you can do better than that."

The conclusion of this section begins by repeating "love your enemies and do good and lend, expecting nothing back," repeating the opening line from v. 27 as well as the topic of each of the motive clauses. Then we get to the reward for all the hard things commanded in these verses: you will be sons [and daughters] of the Most High. In Hebrew, "son of X" is sometimes a way to make a noun into an adjective; a "son of perdition" is a wicked man, for example. So "sons and daughters of the Most High" is a way of saying "godly people"—people who imitate God's character, since God is kind to the ungrateful and the wicked. But "God's sons and daughters" was also meant literally, and was one common way to express the reward of living as God commands (Wis 5:5; Sir 4:10). [The Ability to Love Enemies Is a Divine Gift]

Topic Two: Be Merciful, as God Is Merciful, 6:36-38

This part of the sermon could admittedly be divided in different ways. Verse 36 can either be taken to introduce a new section, as I have, or it could be connected with what went before.[25] The sentence has no conjunction or connecting particle, so that the first

---

Learning Not to Hate

I was fifteen years old when I began to hate people. I hated the white men who murdered Emmett Till and I hated all the other whites who were responsible for the countless murders Mrs. Rice had told me about and those I vaguely remembered from childhood. But I also hated Negroes. I hated them for not standing up and doing something about the murders.

After the sit-in, all I could think of was how sick Mississippi whites were. They believed so much in the segregated Southern way of life, they would kill to preserve it. I sat there in the NAACP office and thought of how many times they had killed when this way of life was threatened. . . . Before the sit-in, I had always hated the whites in Mississippi. Now I knew it was impossible for me to hate sickness. The whites had a disease, an incurable disease in its final stage. What were our chances against such a disease?

Anne Moody, *Coming of Age in Mississippi* (New York: Delta, 2004), 136, 292.

The Ability to Love Enemies Is a Divine Gift

There are two marks, both of which are one and the same thing, that manifest the difference between spiritual and human love: Human love cannot tolerate the dissolution of a fellowship that has become false for the sake of genuine fellowship, and human love cannot love an enemy, that is, one who seriously and stubbornly resists it. Both spring from the same source: human love is by its very nature desire—desire for human community. So long as it can satisfy this desire in some way, it will not give it up, even for the sake of truth, even for the sake of genuine love for others. But where it can no longer expect its desire to be fulfilled, there it stops short—namely, in the face of an enemy. There it turns into hatred, contempt, and calumny.

Dietrich Bonhoeffer, *Life Together*, trans. John W. Doberstein (New York: Harper, 1954), 34.

Dietrich Bonhoeffer, 1924. (Credit: Bildarchiv Preussischer Kulturbesitz/Art Resource, NY)

word in the sentence is the imperative "Be," which perhaps argues slightly for thinking of this as a new unit.

Verse 36 states the principle of the section—be merciful, in imitation of God. This is followed by four imperatives, two with warnings, two with promises; in each, the imperative and the warning/promise use matching verb stems, so that the two clauses would have had lots of sounds in common. The final promise is amplified in a rhetorical figure called *phantasia*: "passages where, inspired by strong emotion, you seem to see what you describe and bring it vividly before the eyes of your audience."[26] This particular bit of amplification imitates the pattern of the whole section by having a basic statement ("good measure") then amplified by four more. The whole section is drawn together by another statement of principle, but this time, pulling in a different direction from v. 38, and meant as a counterweight to it. This concluding summary uses the stem –μετ three times in succession: μέτρω μετρεῖτε ἀντιμετρηθήσεται, met*rō* met*reite anti*met*rēthēsetai*, with what measure you measure it shall be measured back (to you).

That God is kind and merciful is a commonplace in the Old Testament. Exodus 34:6, "The Lord God is *oiktirmōn* [the same root as the word Luke uses for "merciful" and meaning "compassionate" or "merciful"] and *eleēmon* [also meaning "merciful"]" is one famous example. Jesus uses "your Father" to describe God, the first of many times he will use that expression. At twelve he had claimed God as his father (2:49), but his first teaching use of "father" posits that sort of relationship with God for everyone. In fact, "Father" was not an unusual way to describe God in Jesus' day; there are plenty of references to God as Father in the Old Testament, as well as in Jewish literature written closer to the first century: Tobit 13:4, "He is our Lord and God, he is our Father forever [*autos patēr hēmōn eis pantes tous aiōnas*]"; Sirach 23:1, "O Lord, Father and Master of my life"; 1QH 17.36-41: "For Thou are a father/to all the sons of thy truth/and as a woman who tenderly loves her babe,/so dost Thou rejoice in them;/and as a foster-father bearing a child in his lap/so carest Thou for all Thy creatures."[27] The last quote, from one of the hymns used at Qumran, is particularly striking: God is a parent tenderly caring for all who cleave to truth, as tender as a mother or as protective as a father. Luke's Jesus urges his audience to be the same way.

This is made more specific or graphic in the four imperatives that follow. Do not judge, lest you be judged: "One is not to be a fault-finder, a nitpicker, creating the impression that one shares none of the flaws of humanity."[28] Jesus' command, obviously, does not preclude his calling someone a hypocrite (6:42) or criticizing Simon the Pharisee's hospitality (7:44-46) or even condemning Chorazin, Bethsaida, and Capernaum, whole villages, to God's judgment (10:13-15). But then Jesus is the Son of Man, who is to be entrusted with the role of judge at the Last Day; in this instance, we are to imitate God's kindness and patience rather than God's judgment as exercised through Jesus. Do not condemn lest you be condemned: this is an even more pointed version of "do not judge." Our role as Jesus' disciples is not to be the judge pronouncing the verdict or even the prosecuting attorney, but to be a witness. God remains the judge: lest you be judged/lest you be condemned both assume that God would be the one who brought down the gavel.

Be merciful, then, precludes deciding who stands condemned under God's justice and who may receive mercy. Those are negative commands—avoid these things. The next two are positive aspects of "be merciful." First, forgive, and you will be forgiven. Jesus included this, in inverted form, in the Lord's Prayer as well, so it was obviously an important principle with him. Theologians argue over whether Jesus meant this as a quid pro quo: God will forgive you if you forgive others and will not if you will not. Surely God's mercy extends beyond our own; that is what the amplification of the last promise means, that if we give, God gives back far more. Further, the basis for God's forgiveness of us is not our kindness, but God's; that is what is meant by "just as your father is merciful" and "he is kind to the ungrateful and the wicked." But "forgive and you will be forgiven" has to mean something, and it probably means that the person who refuses to forgive others cannot expect God's mercy in the Judgment.

The amplification of "good measure" describes how a very generous employer pays his field hands with the grain that they just harvested, threshed, and winnowed for him. He scoops up the grain into his measuring jar; shakes it to make more room; puts more in; packs it down with his hand to make still more room; puts more in until it runs over; and then pours it out into the

Give Generously

Meanwhile, the sermon ended and Pastor Ingqvist launched into prayer. Clarence tried to tear the check quietly out of the checkbook. There's no worse sound in the sanctuary than a check ripping . . . . At prayer's end, as they said the Lord's Prayer, he eased the check out . . . and when Elmer passed the basket, Clarence laid the check folded neatly in half in the basket and bowed his head and suddenly realized he had written it for three hundred dollars. He had written it with his eyes averted and he knew he had written three-zero-zero on the short line and three-zero-zero on the long line. Could a man sneak downstairs after church and find the deacons counting the collection and say, "Fellows, there's been a mistake. I gave more than I really wanted to"? He now felt fully alive for the first time all day. He felt terrifically awake. He had given all he had in the checking account and a little more.

Garrison Keillor, "Collection," in *Leaving Home* (New York: Penguin, 1997), 91.

(Credit: Barclay Burns)

worker's bag, or if the worker is too poor to own a sack, into his tunic, which he holds out to form a sack.[29] If that is how God means to respond to us—if that is the measure we would get back—then why would we ever fail to be merciful, nonjudgmental, noncondemning, forgiving, and generous? Yet we all know too well how easy it is to take advantage of God's mercy and forgiveness and to be unforgiving ourselves. So this last bit is the counterweight to v. 36: Be merciful, as God is merciful, and know that whatever you dole out, you can expect in return. [Give Generously]

Topic Three: Sight and Blindness, Teaching and Learning, 6:39-42

"He told them a parable" is, frankly, an inelegant intrusion into a speech, and probably indicates that Luke, who was a pretty fair speech writer when he set his mind to it, really did not think of the Sermon on the Plain as a speech—at least not in the same way as some of the speeches in Acts. But the awkward phrase does have the value of marking a turn in the text. This section begins with two rhetorical questions, followed by a two-part maxim, followed by two more rhetorical questions, and concluding with a two-part command. None of the material is a story, but the images are vivid enough, and the imagined dialogue in v. 42 helps to create a sense of character and movement, even without the typical framework of a story.

The first pair of questions considers the issue of finding the right teacher or guide for one's life: "It is impossible for the blind to lead the blind, is it not? Will not both fall into a pit?" These two lines are well balanced, each having five words in Greek, each beginning with the negative particle and ending with a verb.[30] Is this a comic image—slapstick, clowning, the audience knowing exactly what is about to happen and laughing when it does—or a tragic image of people with disabilities lost in the world with no one to help them to safety? Luke's audience will have known the image in both contexts—from the philosophers, it is a stock complaint about poor teachers and incorrigible students,[31] but from Second Isaiah, it is a lament about the fate of Israel:

> Listen, you who are deaf
> And you that are blind, look up and see!
> Who is blind but my servant,
> Or deaf like my messenger that I send?
> Who is blind like my dedicated one,
> Or blind like the servant of the Lord?
> He sees many things, but does not observe them;
> His ears are open, but he does not hear.
> The Lord was pleased, for the sake of his righteousness,
> To magnify his teaching and make it glorious.
> But this is a people robbed and plundered,
> All of them trapped in holes and hidden in prisons
> They have become a prey with no one to rescue,
> A spoil with no one to say, "Restore!" (Isa 42:18-22 LXX)

For the prophet, the image of the blind guide is deeply troubling: where are those, the servants of the Lord, who can save the Lord's people from their own dark prisons? Could it be that God's servants are just as blind as those they were sent to rescue?

The next verse reads like another proverbial saying, this time set as a statement rather than a question: "The disciple is not above the teacher; but everyone who is trained [or everyone, when trained] will be like his/her teacher." *Katērtismenos* means to be mended—Luke had this word in Mark 1:19—and in this context, it means "put into proper condition" by a trainer.[32] It is usually taken to be a good thing, Jesus commending his disciples for how they will be once they are trained, and Luke refusing to let the "blind" label stick to Jesus and his disciples. But it can be understood simply as a restatement of the first part of v. 39. If the teacher is blind, then the disciple can do no better, but once trained, will have absorbed all the teacher's limitations.[33] Let us leave it ambivalent for a bit, and go on to the next pair of rhetorical questions.

The log and the speck is unquestionably satire, and is meant to be at least a little funny; if you have ever seen this acted out, in *Godspell* or other Christian dramas, you know how comical it is. The bizarre image of a man with a log in his eye trying to help a poor brother wipe away a speck—rich imagery, and it may blind us to a couple of interesting features of this parody of teaching. In v. 41, the question is "why do you see the speck?"—not "how can you possibly claim to see a speck with this great honking log in your eye?" In other words, the log-jammed brother really does see the speck that is really in the eye of the second brother. And brother, let me tell you, specks in the eye are a pain, both in your own eye and in the eye, say, of your small child while you are in some public place—the child suddenly begins to wail and rub his or her eyes and fall to the ground and beg for help, and to get it out, you first have to calm a child who is in real distress. It's no picnic. Also notice that at the end of v. 42, the expectation is that both the log and the speck are coming out. Luke uses the same word here, *ekbalō*, that he uses to describe exorcisms (again, appropriate word for the small child eye-speck scenario). So the issue comes down to this: since the teacher can't see the log in his own eye, he also can't adequately remove the speck from the brother's eye.

Here, then, is how the whole section fits together. A blind teacher can only lead a blind pupil into disaster; we all know how that goes from Isaiah 42. In fact, a student can (normally) do no better than he or she is taught; so if the teacher is poor, the student may in fact adopt all the bad habits of the teacher. What the teacher must do first, then, is learn to see his or her own deficiencies and correct them before passing them on, willy-nilly, to the student. And despite the "hypocrite!" thrown in v. 42, the parable ends on a positive note, holding out hope that in fact, both log and speck can be cast out to the betterment of all concerned.

This section would have fit many situations in the early churches to whom Luke was writing. It urges caution in selecting teachers and leaders, so we might see it as Luke's equivalent to the sections of the Pastorals and 1 Peter that describe the ideal church leader. It can be taken, in Luke's narrative world, as another indirect dig at the Pharisees and scribes, who are accused of hindering people from entering the kingdom (11:52). The Pharisees in the narrative may serve Luke's audience as a sort of stand-in for their own inept leaders or for leaders of rival sectarian groups, but in the narrative, they need not represent anything except the growing opposition to Jesus and illustrate how he dealt with it. Like the broad commands of 6:36-38, one could imagine these being applicable in almost any setting.

The advice to learners—be careful who teaches you—and to teachers—address your own issues before you try to help others—sounds curiously modern. Before we see it as a dominical endorsement of the self-help/self-care trend in ministry, let us remember that at the end of the section, the log and the mote are cast out through the intervention of the teacher. Self-understanding or self-differentiation is never the greatest good for

Bearing with Your Brother

We thank God for giving us brethren who live by his call, by his forgiveness, and his promise. We do not complain of what God does not give us; we rather thank God for what He does give us daily. And is not what has been given us enough: brothers, who will go on living with us through sin and need under the blessing of his grace? Is the divine gift of Christian fellowship any less than this, any day, even the most difficult and distressing day? Even when sin and misunderstanding burden the communal life, is not the sinning brother still a brother, with whom I, too, stand under the Word of Christ? Will not his sin be a constant occasion for me to give thanks that both of us may live in the forgiving love of God in Jesus Christ?

Dietrich Bonhoeffer, *Life Together*, trans. John W. Doberstein (New York: Harper, 1954), 28.

Luke, but a means to the greater good of ministering to others. [Bearing with Your Brother]

Topic Four: Walk Like You Talk, 6:43-49

Note the progression of the four topics: love your enemies; be merciful; learn to see your own faults before you correct others; and now, flowing from the issue of hypocrisy, do what you say.

Structurally, the section is arranged like this:

• Verse 43: A proverb, with its two parts antithetically parallel; the metaphor is fruit. The two parts of the proverb are almost identical:

Οὐ γάρ ἐστιν	δένδρον καλὸν ποιοῦν καρπὸν σαπρόν,
οὐδὲ πάλιν	δένδρον σαπρὸν ποιοῦν καρπὸν καλόν.
Ou gar estin	*dendron kalon poioun karpon sapron*
oude palin	*dendron sapron poioun karpon kalon*

Each half has the same number of syllables, and in the five-word strings at the end of each half, the words rhyme, are two syllables each, and are accented so that each word in each half puts the stress in the same place. It is a bit of a tonguetwister: the first line has "*den*-dron ka-*lon* poi-*oun* kar-*pon* sa-*pron*" and the second "*den*-dron sa-*pron* poi-*oun* kar-*pon* ka-*lon*," which you might try saying five times fast.

• Verse 44: Another proverb, in three parts: first the principle, then two examples in synonymous parallelism; continues the fruit metaphor.

• Verse 45a: Another proverb, in two parts: two examples in synonymous parallelism, with the metaphor being the heart as soil producing good fruit. This one, like v. 43, relies on lots of similar words with similar sounds:

ὁ ἀγαθὸς ἄνθρωπος   ἐκ τοῦ ἀγαθοῦ θησαυροῦ τῆς καρδίας
                                  προφέρει τό ἀγαθόν,
ho agathos anthrōpos   *ek tou agathou thēsaurou tēs kardis
                                  propherei   to agathon,*

καὶ ὁ πονηρὸς   ἐκ τοῦ πονηροῦ
                                  προφέρει τὸ πονηρὸν
kai ho ponēros   *ek tou pnoērou*
                                  propherei to ponēron

- Verse 45b: Bridge statement, moving from heart to mouth.
- Verse 46: Rhetorical question about the relationship between speech and actions.
- Verse 47: Introduction to the parable, setting the focus on the successful disciple as one who hears and does. The first part of v. 47 is another example, though not as spectacular as v. 38, of amplification by spelling out things in a series: "the one who comes to me, hears my words, and does them."
- Verse 48: Positive example: the metaphor is building and natural disasters. The image is amplified by describing all the steps of building in order and by using vivid words for the flood.
- Verse 49: Negative example: the descriptions of the building process and the arrival of the flood are diminished, which is consistent with v. 47 and its focus on the good disciple.

Good—the word can mean "sound" and "beautiful"—trees do not bear poor quality fruit, nor do poor quality trees bear good fruit. Any farmer or weekend gardener knows that—stunted, blighted, wilted, or otherwise diseased plants will not produce good quality fruit. Jesus sounds much like his cousin John, who urged his hearers "bear fruits worthy of repentance," warning them that if they didn't, they'd end up being used for fuel for the fires of Judgment Day (3:8-9). But Jesus does not go immediately to Judgment, but to judgment: you can tell which trees are good by their fruit. Take note of the progression in the sermon: we are to love our enemies and do good to them, and we are not to play judge, condemning others as if we were the Son of Man. But neither are we to imitate poor teachers, and if we are teachers ourselves, we must be careful to be self-critical before we criticize others. So on what basis do we discriminate between good and poor teachers, and on what basis do we judge our own spiritual acuity? By fruit—by the sorts of good works Jesus has been and will be doing. [On Overlooking Others' Faults]

Verse 45 grafts the image of the heart as a treasury for good and bad motives onto the growing/fruit-producing image, in a manner that presages the parable of the four soils. After "the good man from the good treasury of his heart," we would expect a verb like "bring forth"—Matthew 13:52, which may be a distant cousin to Luke's verse, uses *ekballō* ("cast out"), which Luke has already used in v. 42. But Luke uses *propherō* ("bring forth"), an agricultural term for production of fruit.[34]

> **On Overlooking Others' Faults**
>
> Once a brother in Scete was found guilty, and the older brethren came in assembly and sent to the abbot Moses, asking him to come, but he would not. Then the priest sent to him, saying: "Come, for the assembly of the brethren awaits thee." And he rose up and came. But taking with him a very old basket, he filled it with sand and carried it behind him. And they went out to meet him, asking, "Father, what is this?" And the old man said to them, "My sins are running behind me and I do not see them, and I am come today to judge the sins of another man." And they heard him, and said naught to the brother, but forgave him.
>
> *Sayings of the Fathers* book 9, sec. 4, cited in Helen Waddell, *The Desert Fathers* (Ann Arbor: University of Michigan Press, 1957), 96.

Good deeds arise from good character, and good character draws from the treasury of the heart, the heart made good by good teaching, good habits, and above all, by submission to God: all this is straightforward Jewish ethical teaching.

The bridge at the end of v. 45 connects "heart" to "mouth" in order to put verbal claims of discipleship and obedience into consideration. How can you claim Jesus as master and not obey his teachings? Yes, well, we know how—we see it done, and we do it ourselves, over and over. Shall we have a show of hands: who among us would claim truly to be obedient to "give to everyone who asks" or to "do not judge" or to "first, take the log out of your own eye"?

Verse 47 introduces the parable with a three-step discipleship process—come, hear, do—matched by the three-step building preparation done by the first man: "he dug, dug deeper, and set the foundation upon the rock." Commentators note that neither deeply dug foundation trenches nor the river rising against the house were particularly Palestinian features,[35] but the language and the image is biblical. God laid the foundations for the earth (Job 38:4; Pss 18:15; 80[LXX 81]:5: *salevthēsontai panta ta themelia tēs gēs*), which guard the land against the waves of the vasty deep (Job 38:8-11; Ps 18:16). A river's flood is often a metaphor for the trials from which God redeems God's people (Isa 43:2; Ps 69:2; Jonah 2:3). So the person who digs and sets his or her life on the flood-proof foundation imitates God and receives God's salvation from the flood—not even shaken. The one who hears but fails to act builds a house doomed to fall; *hrēgma*, means "wreck" or "collapse," a vivid word for a building smashed to pieces by the force of the rising river.

Jesus' words in this sermon have been words mostly about what one does for others—give, forgive, etc.—and the parts that are focused on self are mostly about self-scrutiny—taking the log out of one's eye, e.g. A builder needs to accumulate supplies in order to complete the job, and as Paul uses the metaphor, the builder's choices are to use fine or shoddy materials in building on the foundation of faith (1 Cor 3:12-15). The ideal builder, by the standards of the Sermon on the Plain, gives away possessions and casts off bad habits, forgives loans and ignores calumnies. The result would not be a fine house of "gold, silver, and precious stones," but a simple building well-anchored to the unshakeable bedrock. Perhaps that is why Luke stresses foundation-setting to the exclusion of all the other necessary steps in building a house; the imperatives in Jesus' sermon are more like excavation than construction.

The Sermon on the Plain undercut many presumptions, overturned much commonsense wisdom. It is better to be wealthy than poor, and for those who have it, wealth is a shelter against an uncertain future (Prov 10:15). Love your friends and your neighbors, but curse your enemies (Pss 3:7; 72:9; 92:11; 137:9; 139[LXX 138]:22: *teleion misos emisoun autous, eis echthrous egenonto moi*, I [customarily] hate them with perfect hatred; they have become as enemies for me). Do favors for those beneath you in status so that they will owe you favors, and in that way build up a network of clients; do favors for those above you in status so that they will protect you, and thus acquire at least one patron. Jesus flips all those first-century values, urging people to do the opposite of many habits encouraged by their culture. Ours too, yes? Plan your charitable giving with an eye to tax benefits and to having your name published on donor lists, but most importantly, with an eye to how the group to which you give matches up with your values. Invest your money for the best return possible; take your enemies to court, or let your government go to war with them and watch the triumph on television. The poor and the hungry are mostly lazy or careless, those who weep need therapy, and if you are defamed, hire a lawyer to protect your good name. The rich—who are never us, but people with more than we have—enjoy life, eat well, laugh a lot, and are popular.

The sermon confronts all that, and by skillful use of poetic devices, encourages us to begin the process of wrestling with our own desires and sensibilities to become strong enough to walk away from what our culture teaches and reinforces on every hand. The

Sermon on the Plain is strong medicine, and only the brave can live by it.

CONNECTIONS

The first three sections of the chapter—the two Sabbath controversies, treated together in this commentary, and the choice of the Twelve—are much more like a continuation of chapter 5 than like the sermon that follows. Jesus, Son of Man, Lord of the Sabbath, tells the Pharisees why they are wrong to criticize how his disciples eat or how he heals. The Sabbath, Jesus argues, was not meant to prevent the doing of good. One suspects that Luke's churches, who most likely did not keep Sabbath, found the Sabbath controversies an encouragement for their programs of charity and help for the poor. Perhaps this gives us an angle on these stories as well; Lord knows that modern American Christians do not need to be persuaded that Sabbath observance is a matter of little consequence. So rather than reinforcing the notion that it's all the same to God whether or not we worship regularly in a congregation, perhaps we could use the stories to focus on how Jesus fed the hungry and healed the sick on his Sabbath, and that maybe we should consider using our leisure time to do the same things.

The Sermon on the Plain, as noted at the end of the commentary section above, is mostly countercultural, counterintuitive advice disguised as common wisdom. Jesus' commands and parables are clothed with the form of proverbs and other wisdom sayings, but their contents are much more like the radical words from the mouths of Mary and John the Baptist. Marilynne Robinson's narrator in *Gilead*, himself a minister, describes his grandfather as a man who took literally Jesus' command to give to anyone who asks, and who consequently was a pain to live with: "When he left us, we all felt his absence bitterly. But he did make things difficult."[36] He gave things away that were not extras, bringing extra hardship to an already poor family: ". . . he would actually give away the blankets off his bed. He did that several times, and my mother was at a good deal of trouble to replace them."[37] The narrator's mother raised chickens to sell eggs for money, and tried to hide her earnings in the baking powder or on her person:

> I remember once he came into the kitchen while she was doing her ironing. He said, "Daughter, some folks have come to us for help."

"Well," she said, "I hope they can wait a minute. I hope they can wait till this iron is cool." After a few minutes she put the iron on the stove and went into the pantry and came out with a can of baking powder. She delved around in it with a fork until she drew up a quarter. She did this again until she had a quarter and two dimes lying there on the table. She picked them up and polished the powder off with a corner of her apron and held them out to him. Now, forty-five cents represented a good many eggs in those days—she was not an ungenerous woman. He took them, but it was clear enough he knew she had more. . . . That day, though, he stood there with those three coins in his drastic old mummified hand and watched her with that terrible eye, and she crossed her arms right over the handkerchief with the hidden money in it, as he clearly knew, and watched him right back, until he said, "Well, the Lord bless and keep you," and went out the door.[38]

The rules of the sermon are not easy, and as this exchange shows, even godly, generous people may disagree on their extent. But before we let ourselves off the hook, saying "you can never give enough" and "God doesn't expect us to give away everything," let us remember that few of us have ever gotten close to that. The choices many of us face—if I give more to the poor, will I have enough for our vacation, or for the monthly payments on my second car—are so far from Jesus' teachings that we ought to spend some time with the one-eyed grandfather of *Gilead*, thinking about how much closer we might come to Jesus' standards: "He thought we should all be living at a dead run. I don't say he was wrong. That would be like contradicting John the Baptist."[39]

NOTES

[1] There is a very strange textual variant in 6:1 that appears to have been a botched scribal attempt to sort out the two Sabbaths; some manuscripts read "on the second-first Sabbath," which no modern reader has yet to elucidate.

[2] Josephus, *Ant.* 14.262-64.

[3] Philo, *On the Decalogue* 20.100.

[4] Philo, *Special Laws* 2.15.59.

[5] Philo, *Life of Moses* 2.4.21-22.

[6] Many commentators argue that Jesus was not breaking the Law, but engaging in actions that the Pharisees would have considered unlawful: Alan R. Culpepper, *The Gospel of Luke* (NIB, vol. 9; Nashville: Abingdon, 1995), 133; John Nolland, *Luke* (WBC, vols. 35A-C; Dallas TX: Word, 1989-93), 1.256.

[7] Luke probably knows the story from the LXX and not just from Mark, since he drops Mark's inaccurate "When Abiathar was high priest." The priest in the story is Ahimelech, not Abiathar, and since there was yet no temple, there was also no high priest; Ahimelech was priest at the sanctuary at Nob.

[8] F. Scott Spencer, *What Did Jesus Do?: Gospel Profiles of Jesus' Personal Conduct* (Harrisburg PA: Trinity, 2003), 184, reminds us of the tradition from the Gospel of the Nazarenes, where the man is a mason and has lost the ability to work.

[9] Joel B. Green, *The Gospel of Luke* (NICNT; Grand Rapids: Eerdmans, 1997), 255, points this out.

[10] Spencer, *What Did Jesus Do*, 184.

[11] Joseph A. Fitzmyer, *The Gospel According to Luke* (AB 28 and 28A; Garden City NY: Doubleday, 1981), 1.619; I. Howard Marshall, *The Gospel of Luke* (Grand Rapids MI: Eerdmans, 1978), 240; BAGD, 507, s.v. κανανaîος.

[12] E. P. Sanders makes this argument in *Jesus and Judaism* (Philadelphia: Fortress, 1985), 98–106.

[13] We do not know for certain what "Iscariot" means. Some suggest it is a corruption of Kerioth—"Judas from Kerioth." Some suggest a variant of "sicarius," which means "assassin"; some suggest it derives from the Aramaic word for falsehood; see Marshall, *Luke*, 240; BAGD, 480.

[14] Green, *Luke*, 260–80, divides it into three parts: 6:20-26, 27-38, 39-49. Fitzmyer, *Luke*, 1.629, divides it into five: 6:20-26, 27-36, 37-42, 43-45, 46-49.

[15] "Passion" in the sense of Aristotle's categories of rhetoric: the logic of the argument (logos), the character of the speaker (ethos), and the emotions or passions of the audience (pathos).

[16] Frederick W. Danker, *Jesus and the New Age: A Commentary on St. Luke's Gospel* (rev. ed.; Philadelphia: Fortress, 1988), 136–37.

[17] George Kennedy, *New Testament Interpetation through Rhetorical Criticism* (Chapel Hill: University of North Carolina Press, 1984), 65.

[18] Ibid., 64–65.

[19] Similarly, Fitzmyer, *Luke*, 1.633: "Here [in the Gospels] the beatitudes only rarely express practical wisdom, since they usually stress a reversal of values that people put on earthly things in view of the kingdom now being preached by Jesus."

[20] Whether to translate *macharios* as "happy" or "lucky" or "blessed" depends on context. Maybe this is gnat-straining, but the emphasis in the Sermon on the Mount is on what God is doing for or to various groups. Nobody would argue with "happy" as the result of God's blessing—if God feeds you, makes you laugh, etc., then you are happy. But it seems to me that the emphasis falls on God's actions rather than on the recipient's feelings, and so "blessed" is a better translation.

[21] Hans Dieter Betz, *The Sermon on the Mount* (Minneapolis: Fortress, 1995), 572, agrees with the conclusion, but on the basis of the conditional nature of the sentences, and not because of the rereading strategy I am proposing.

[22] Many commentators argue that Matthew has adapted the original (Culpepper, *Luke*, 143–44; Fitzmyer, *Luke*, 1.632; Robert W. Funk et. al, eds., *The Five Gospels* [New York: MacMillan, 1993], 290; Betz, *Sermon on the Mount*, 575).

[23] This pair of beatitudes and woes exemplifies the futility of trying to decide whether Matthew or Luke has altered Q. Because Matthew's "blessed are those who mourn, for

they shall be comforted" is closer to the language of Isa 61:2, Fitzmyer judges it the more original. The Jesus Seminar judged the Lukan version to be more original and in fact dominical (Funk, *Five Gospels*, 290). Betz, *Sermon on the Mount*, 577–78, despairs of demonstrating how one gets from Luke's version, if it were more original, to Matthew's, and declares them to be independent traditions.

[24] Robert C. Tannehill, *The Narrative Unity of Luke-Acts: A Literary Intepretation vol. 1: The Gospel According to Luke*. Philadelphia: Fortress, 1986), 1.209.

[25] Betz, *Sermon on the Mount*, 67, takes it as the conclusion of the preceding section, as does Fitzmyer; Danker, *Jesus and the New Age*, 151, divides this part as I have.

[26] Longinus, *On the Sublime* 15.2 (trans. W. H. Fyfe; Cambridge MA: Harvard University Press, 1995), 217.

[27] Citations drawn from a longer list in James D. G. Dunn, *Jesus Remembered* (Grand Rapids MI: Eerdmans, 2003), 548, n. 30 and 31; translation of the quote from 1QH from Geza Vermes, *The Complete Dead Sea Scrolls in English* (New York: Penguin, 1997), 284.

[28] Danker, *Jesus and the New Age*, 151.

[29] Some commentators imagine buying grain in the market, but such practices on the part of a seller would be unprofitable. But we actually get a narrative description of something approaching this verse in Ruth 2 and 3.

[30] Betz, *Sermon on the Mount*, 620, also notes that they have the same number of syllables in Greek.

[31] Betz, *Sermon on the Mount*, 620, and Danker, *Jesus and the New Age*, 153, give some examples: for example, Horace, *Epistle* 1.17.3, "I have still much to learn, but listen to me anyway, even if I appear to be a blind man giving directions."

[32] BAGD, 526.

[33] So Nolland, *Luke*, 1.307.

[34] BAGD, 889.

[35] Arlen Hultgren, *The Parables of Jesus: A Commentary* (Grand Rapids MI: Eerdmans, 2000), 135; Culpepper, *Luke*, 152; Nolland, *Luke*, 1.310.

[36] Marilynne Robinson, *Gilead* (New York: Farrar, Straus, Giroux, 2004), 31.

[37] Ibid., 32.

[38] Ibid., 32–33.

[39] Ibid., 32.

PROPHETIC IDENTITY

Luke 7

COMMENTARY

Healing the Centurion's Servant, 7:1-10

Following the long Sermon on the Plain, where Jesus tells his audience of disciples and others that they must give, forgive, and love their enemies, Luke places a story where Jesus gets a chance to put his money where his mouth is. Luke's readers, even if they were Roman, would have known that the Jews of Palestine considered Rome their enemy, not their benefactor. Despite all the Roman propaganda about how Roman intervention into the affairs of other nations was actually salvation for them, the facts were plain: the Jews of Palestine had revolted against their so-called saviors in AD 66 and had consequently suffered terribly at the hands of the Roman armies. To put this in our terminology, imagine Jesus as an Iraqi and the centurion as an American soldier; even we Americans would probably see the irony of the conqueror asking for help from the colonized. Will Jesus turn the other cheek? Will he love his nation's enemies?

The centurion's assignment in Capernaum is not specified, in the same way that Luke was vague about the soldiers of 3:14. In Jesus' day, Galilee was under the direct supervision of Herod Antipas, son of Herod the Great; his security force was organized in Roman fashion, so one possibility is that Luke means for us to think of the centurion as a soldier in Antipas's outfit.[1] This would make him no less an enemy—Antipas killed John the Baptist and may want to kill Jesus (9:9, 13:31). And even if he works for Antipas, the centurion is a Gentile, as 7:4 and 7:9 make clear. But we have to wonder if Luke uses "centurion" without any other designation because he knows that his readers will first think "Roman"—in other words, what job he may have done "in real life" is less important than the imperial overtones his title brings to the story. As one commentator suggests, "The drama lies in the focus on two powerful political figures: Jesus, representative of the Kingdom of God, and a centurion, representative of Eternal Rome."[2]

The episode begins when Jesus "finished all his words in the hearing of the people" and "entered Capernaum." The people fade out of focus just for a bit, but they come back in v. 9, when they are present to witness the conclusion of the story. This is important for Luke's sequence, because once the crowd sees this miracle followed by the raising of the widow's son (7:11-15), they will conclude that Jesus is God's prophet and that his deeds are a sign of God's favor (7:16). This in turn is crucial for Luke's version of Jesus' arrest and trial; one of the charges against him will be that he leads the people astray (23:2), but the reader can clearly see that the opposite is true—Jesus' actions lead people to praise God.

This is a miracle story, but the miracle is only a small part of what makes the story work. The plot unfolds through the gradual revealing of a set of interconnected relationships, a family system of sorts that, true to its first-century context, includes a patron, his clients, his friends, and his slave. The snarl in the web is Jesus, of course: how will he relate to these people? Will he be client or patron to the Roman; will he own the obligations owed by "his people"; will he be sucked into the Roman system or opt out?

In Capernaum lived a centurion who had a slave—of course he had a slave!—whom he valued. Luke uses a word here, ἔντιμος, that can mean "precious" or "held in high esteem,"[3] so he wants to paint this first relationship of master-slave as an affectionate one. The slave was very ill, about to die; Luke gives us no description of the centurion's inner state, but the fact that he calls on Jesus implies that he is worried, perhaps even desperate.

The next relationship introduced in the story is between the centurion and Jesus—the centurion has heard about Jesus. Heard what? That he healed a leper (5:15), or that he held himself superior to the rules of Sabbath (6:11)? Had he heard that people came to him from all over to be healed (6:17-19), or had he heard something of Jesus' teachings (7:1)? We do not know, but whatever he heard led him to spring into action. From the beginning of the story, then, the centurion thinks of Jesus as someone who is able to help his dying slave.

The story's third relationship is between the centurion and the Jewish elders. Luke 7:3 says that the centurion "sent to [Jesus] elders of the Jews to ask him to come heal his slave"; perhaps Luke is being economical with words, but the relationship described here is of a patron ordering his clients to do his bidding. What they say about him reinforces that judgment: "He is worthy that you would grant him this [favor], for he loves our ethnic group and he built our synagogue for us" (7:4-5). The centurion has done favors for the Jews of Capernaum, and so he is their benefactor. He may have used his own funds to pay for their building, as was customary for persons trying to climb the ladder of success in the first century, or he may have been the intermediary whose word in the right ear caused the money to flow in their direction. Either way, they became his clients when they accepted his largesse, and they are therefore obligated to do him favors when he needs them done, such as interceding with a man who can heal his sick slave. [Praise for a Benefactor]

There is a scene in *Patton* where the general orders his chaplain to write a prayer for good weather so that his soldiers can have their air cover again. The movie incident was loosely based on a historical incident—the chaplain who wrote the prayer gives his account of the incident in [The True Story of the Patton Prayer]. General Patton's order to Chaplain O'Neill operated on the same sort of principles as the centurion's order to the Jewish elders: I need God's intervention, and so I need help from someone better placed than I to influence the Almighty.

The story's fourth relationship is between Jesus and the Jewish embassy from the centurion. He and they must know each other,

Praise for a Benefactor

This is from an inscription dating from the early 1st century. It is located in a Jewish community in the town of Berenike in Cyrenaica, modern-day Libya.

Whereas Marcus Titius of Sestos, son of Aimilia and a man of exceptional merit, after his assumption of office as procurator carried out his public responsibilities in a generous and distinguished manner and in all his conduct continues to display such a conciliatory attitude that his presence is no burden either to the people in general or to anyone in particular; and whereas, in the course of his administration that affects our Jewish community he has sought our best interests both publicly and privately, and does many things for us that are worthy of his reputation for exceptional nobility . . . .

The inscription goes on to say that the resolution would be put on a marble pillar and that he would be publicly praised during Jewish worship.

Citation in Frederick W. Danker, *Jesus and the New Age: A Commentary on St. Luke's Gospel* (rev. ed.; Philadelphia: Fortress, 1988), 158–59.

The True Story of the Patton Prayer

The incident of the now famous Patton Prayer commenced with a telephone call to the Msgr. James H. O'Neill, Third Army Chaplain on the morning of December 8, 1944, when the Third Army Headquarters were located in the Caserne Molifor in Nancy, France. Msgr. O'Neill describes the phone call and his response as follows:

"This is General Patton; do you have a good prayer for weather? We must do something about those rains if we are to win the war." My reply was that I know where to look for such a prayer, that I would locate, and report within the hour. As I hung up the telephone receiver, about eleven in the morning, I looked out on the steadily falling rain, "immoderate" I would call it—the same rain that had plagued Patton's Army throughout the Moselle and Saar Campaigns

from September until now, December 8. The few prayer books at hand contained no formal prayer on weather that might prove acceptable to the Army Commander. Keeping his immediate objective in mind, I typed an original and an improved copy on a 5" x 3" filing card.

Almighty and most merciful Father, we humbly beseech Thee, of Thy great goodness, to restrain these immoderate rains with which we have had to contend. Grant us fair weather for Battle. Graciously hearken to us as soldiers who call upon Thee that, armed with Thy power, we may advance from victory to victory, and crush the oppression and wickedness of our enemies and establish Thy justice among men and nations.

"The True Story of the Patton Prayer," http://www.pattonhq.com/prayer.html.

given how much time he has already spent in Capernaum. They "exhorted" or "beseeched" Jesus, depending on how one translates *parakaleō*, which can mean to beg or to urge; they put their hearts into it, indicating that they believe he can do it. Their use of "our *ethnos*," which means "us Jews" as opposed to "those Gentiles," is intended to make Jesus feel obligated to help; after all, while the centurion has done nothing directly to help Jesus, he has helped all the Jewish inhabitants of the town, including Jesus, by building the synagogue. Won't Jesus come to help? But they do not order Jesus, as the centurion orders them. Jesus is neither their client nor the centurion's, and nobody is clear yet on where his loyalties stand.

But off they go, Jesus with them. At this point, it seems clear that Luke wants us to think that Jesus was not only willing to help, but willing to go into the centurion's house and lay hands on the dying slave. These "elders of the Jews" are curiously quiet about that—no criticisms about going in to a Gentile, even though the centurion is part of the same system that put tax collectors in place, and even though Jesus has already been scolded for eating with them (5:30). If the story had gone without the second embassy from the centurion, and Jesus had entered the house to do the miracle, what might they have said? Touching a Gentile was not a sin; the scandal would have come if, out of gratitude for the healing, the centurion had invited Jesus to a meal and Jesus had accepted. That, of course, is the nature of the argument in Acts 10-11: may Jewish Christians eat with Gentile Christians? But Luke isn't ready for that yet.

The story now introduces another strand in the web of relationships, the centurion's friends. The elders are his clients, and they do his bidding out of a sense of obligation. In Luke's world, as in ours, friends cannot be ordered, and the basis for friendship is mutual affection, not obligation. Thus, when they quote the centurion directly, we are probably supposed to think that they state his intent more accurately: "Sir, don't trouble yourself, for I am not worthy for you to come under my roof; but say a word, and let my 'boy' be healed." The friends, then, introduce a new complication into the scene, since they give us a new view of how the centurion is operating. He says he is not worthy, contradicting the elders; while this may be polite self-deprecation (Southerners used to call it "mush-mouthing"), it may be his way of saying that his first embassy did not represent him correctly. ["Lord, do not trouble yourself"] One way of reading him is that "I am not worthy" means "I really am, but I'm willing to play the game, since I'm sure that the elders

"Lord, do not trouble yourself"

Readers may remember Abraham's greeting to the angelic visitors: "My lord, if I find favor with you, do not pass by your servant. Let a little water be brought, and wash your feet, and rest yourselves under the tree. Let me bring a little bread, that you may refresh yourselves, and after that you may pass on—since you have come to your servant" (Gen 18:3-5). The "little water" and "little bread" turned out to be a feast, of course.

told you how much your people owe me." Jesus' reaction to him, however, indicates that we are supposed to take him at his word: "You owe me nothing, and I want to ask from you the smallest possible favor—just say a word." The quote from the friends puts the centurion's request into a new light: this isn't a man pulling strings, calling in favors, but a man pleading for a tiny favor.

What the centurion says through the friends alters the shape of his relationship with Jesus, or, more precisely, begins to give that relationship shape. The elders' request had left us wondering whether Jesus might be patron or client; the friends' request clearly puts the centurion in the position of supplicant, if not penitent. He thinks of Jesus as operating in a situation analogous to his own: "I am also a man ordered under authority." The centurion's authority comes from Rome, ultimately, as Jesus' authority comes from God; both of them can give orders and expect them to be carried out. The centurion makes no attempt to link his world with Jesus' world, nor to give any reason why Jesus should be inclined to grant the request. In this respect, he is most like the other supplicant encountered so far in Luke, the leper of 5:12-16, who begs Jesus, saying, "Lord, if you will, you can make me clean." Both men have full confidence in Jesus' ability; neither man voices any particular claim on Jesus' generosity; they just ask, and they receive.

On hearing this, Jesus is "amazed"—the only time in the Gospels that this word is used of him. Here it is a role reversal, since Jesus is usually the one amazing the crowds or the Pharisees by doing a miracle. Here, the man's faith is a miracle; Jesus is a bit stunned by it, and declares that he has never seen faith of this sort in Israel. Hmm—the elders also thought Jesus could and would heal the slave, and seem willing to believe that Jesus will go to whatever lengths to do it. The disciples have had faith enough in Jesus to leave everything to follow him. What is unique about the centurion's faith? It must be that he has the combination of humility—Lord, I am not worthy—and confidence—Lord, you can do this—that is a clearer model of ideal faith than Jesus has so far encountered. Peter said, "We've toiled all night and have caught nothing, but at your word I will let down the nets"—a faith that says "I'm not sure it will work, but I'll do it if you say so." The centurion's request has no such caveats—"Lord, don't trouble yourself—just say a word."

At the end of the story, all those who have been sent—the elders and the friends—return home to find the slave healthy again. All their relationships stay the same: slave and master, Roman official and Jewish clients, centurion and his pals. The crowd following

Jesus, silent throughout this incident, hears and marks the event and Jesus' affirmation of the centurion's faith. But what about Jesus and the centurion? The story, unfortunately, stops before we learn whether the centurion learns more about Jesus' teaching or becomes his disciple. All we know for certain is that Jesus moves on, neither client nor patron to anyone in the story, not really even broker for God's blessings. Jesus never claimed to have healed the slave, and could not have taught the centurion to have such faith in a man he'd never seen. Jesus will not be captive to the client-patron reciprocity system of his culture, and will answer a request for help from a representative of his people's great enemy. "Give to anyone who asks," he teaches, and so he does.

As you prepare to teach or preach this passage, look ahead to the next one and to its conclusion in 7:16: "A great prophet has risen among us!" This miracle is something like Elisha's healing of Naaman. Both stories involve a Jewish prophet who heals and a non-Jewish army officer; in both cases there is an intervention from a Jewish intermediary; and in both cases the healing happens without the prophet touching the Gentile.[4] Luke, who loves to take stock stories and put a little twist on them, has seriously inverted this model. Naaman himself was sick, and it was his Jewish slave who first told him of Elisha. Naaman comes to Elisha to ask for help and is offended at the cure offered by the prophet; his slaves, presumably Gentiles, talk him into doing what the prophet suggests, and so he is cleansed, not because of his faith, but because of the faith of his servant girl, who first pointed him to Elisha, and of his manservants, who nudge him into taking the plunge. In Luke's version, "Elisha" is willing to come to "Naaman" to cure the officer's slave, and it's "Naaman's" faith that results in the cure—the same way the faith of the paralytic's friends are part of his cure. In Luke's version, "Naaman's" Jewish servants—the elders of Capernaum—do not point him to "Elisha"—he already knows who Jesus is—but carry, and maybe miscarry, the message asking for help. And perhaps most interestingly, in 2 Kings 5, Naaman uses the "I am under authority" argument to get a special dispensation from the prophet that allows him to worship in a pagan temple, even though he knows that Israel's God is the true one. By contrast, Luke's centurion correctly assumes that Jesus' relation to God is something like his own authority structure.

Luke, then, presents Jesus as a prophet like Elisha who can and will heal Gentiles as well as Jews, but with a twist: this prophet is willing to go to them, if need be. And in turn, Luke presents the Gentile who is healed as a model of how to respond to a prophet's willingness to help in God's name.

The Widow's Son, 7:11-17

To go from the previous story, the healing of the centurion's slave, to this one, the raising of the widow's son, is to experience Luke's gifts at connecting themes and creating atmosphere with a minimum of words. There are so many overtones to this story that the interpreter would do well to read it more than once, listening for different things: connections to Elijah and Elisha traditions; connections to the three stories in Luke where children are healed or resuscitated; connections to Luke's understanding of John the Baptist; connections to what the reader already knows of Jesus from the narrative so far; and connections to the development of the role of prophet as one of Luke's primary ways of interpreting Jesus to the reader. We begin with a close reading of the text, and then the comments will work back over it, developing these thematic touches.

Soon after healing the centurion's slave, Jesus left there and went to a "city" called Nain. Capernaum, where he was in 7:1-10, was on the northwest shore of the Sea of Galilee, and was not a large place (population estimate of 1,000 based on the roughly 25-acre size of the area known to be inhabited in the first century[5]); Nain, located southwest of the Sea of Galilee, almost on the Samaritan border, was a rural village. Jesus was accompanied by his disciples, making their first appearance since 6:20, and the large crowd named at 7:9. They therefore knew about the centurion's slave and had heard Jesus' remark that the centurion had a faith unmatched in Israel.

Verse 12, however, narrows focus to Jesus—"as he drew near the gate of the city"—so we are to imagine Jesus at the head of a crowd, with Jesus nearing the border of the village first. The reader's attention is now directed to a procession coming out of the village: "look, a man who had just died was being carried out, the only son of his mother (and she a widow!), and a large crowd from the city was with her." In other words, Jesus is at the head of one crowd, and the woman and her dead son at the head of another. Everything on the Nain side of the meeting is oriented toward the woman—she's the dead man's mother, she's a widow, the crowd is with her—just as everything on the Capernaum side of the meeting is oriented toward Jesus—his disciples and the crowd are accompanying him.

In vv. 13-14, we see all three principal characters at the same time, but from Jesus' perspective: "And seeing her, the Lord was overcome with compassion for her and said to her, 'Stop crying.' And going over he touched the bier, and those who carried it held

Jesus Resurrecting the Son of the Widow of Naim

This painting captures the position of the figures Luke imagines—Jesus' apostles to one side, townspeople to the other, with Jesus, the dead boy, and the mother in the center.

Pierre Bouillon (1776–1831). *Jesus Resurrecting the Son of the Widow of Naim*. Musee de Tesse, Le Mans, France. (Credit: Réunion des Musées Nationaux/Art Resource, NY)

their place, and he said, 'Boy, I say to you, Rise.'" Note that the narrator, who has not used Jesus' name so far in the story, now calls him *kyrios*, "Lord"; this is the first time the narrator has called Jesus that in the course of a story, but it is no surprise to the reader, because Elizabeth, Peter, the leper, and the centurion have all called him by that term. The narrator of Luke also does not often name Jesus' emotions; indeed, Luke usually omits them when he copies Mark.[6] Like Jesus' amazement at the centurion's faith, his flood of concern ["He had compassion for her"] for the widow is a special event.

"He had compassion for her"

ΑΩ The Greek word translated "he had compassion" or "he was filled with pity" is σπλαγχνίζομαι, *splanchnizomai*, which literally refers to a flutter in a person's viscera; that is, the feeling you have when you say that your heart turned over or your insides did a flip-flop. It is supposed to be a strong emotion but a generally positive one, so that "overcome with compassion" is probably a good paraphrase.

BAGD, 938.

Upon Jesus' word, "the dead man sat up and started to talk, and he [that is, Jesus] gave him [the son] back to his mother." I had a classmate in graduate school who would go to sleep in class and wake up talking—in the case of the dead son, it is probably not supposed to be as funny as I found my classmate's behavior, but it is still an interesting first thing to do, and we will come back to it shortly.

The story closes with a focus on crowd reactions: "Fear took hold of them all, and they gave glory to God, saying, 'A great prophet has been raised among us,' and 'God has visited God's people.' And this word about him spread throughout Judea and in all the region." "All" of them would mean that both crowds—the one following Jesus and the one following the widow and her dead son—as well as the disciples are saying these things. These are correct observations to make about Jesus and about God's intentions for Jesus: he is a great prophet and a sign of God's visitation upon God's people.

The judgment "A great prophet has been raised among us" connects us to the Elijah and Elisha traditions. The healing of the centurion's servant, as noted in the commentary section on that story, was told in a way that is supposed to remind the reader of how Elisha cured Naaman the leper. If you think of Luke's story as a retelling of the Elisha-Naaman miracle, then Jesus/Elisha goes to centurion/Naaman and heals the servant based on Naaman's faith, rather than healing Naaman based on the servant's faith. Luke recasts 2 Kings 5 to make it much more pro-Gentile.

But the story of the widow's son, contrary to the expectations raised in Luke 4:25-26, has nothing to say about Gentiles. So far as we know, everyone in the story is Jewish, and the conclusion "God has visited God's people" will bear that out. But, like the retelling of 2 Kings 5, Luke puts some new wrinkles into his retelling of 1 Kings 17.

Elijah, scourge of the idolatrous King Ahab of Israel, is sent by God to the widow's house as a safe place to stay during the drought brought on by Elijah's curse. She offers him her meager hospitality, and in return, her food multiplies to feed her, her son, and the prophet for as long as Elijah stays with her. But then the son dies, and the widow complains to Elijah that he was responsible—a logical complaint, if he could cause a three-year drought or an endless supply of oil and grain. He in turn accuses God of killing the boy, and prays that God will bring his breath back to him. God listens, the boy revives, and Elijah "gave him to his mother"—Luke quotes 1 Kings 17:23 in 7:15. Then the woman says, "Now I know that you are a man of God."

Luke's treatment, in effect, moves the woman's anger at the prophet to other places in the Gospel, to the sermon at Nazareth, for example. There, a prophet is held without honor for telling the truth about what God had done for others and might do for others in the future. Here, the community appreciates Jesus' actions and honors him as a great prophet. Elijah's complaint against God is replaced by Jesus' strong emotion of compassion or pity; he has told his disciples that they should be merciful as God has been merciful to them (6:36), and so he is.[7]

This episode also has none of the elements of patron-client reciprocity that marked the earlier healing. Rather than a meeting between the "Kingdom of God" and "Eternal Rome" (see earlier discussion), this one is more like a meeting between Resurrection and Death, especially with the two processions meeting at the city limits. Neither the widow nor her town has any claim on Jesus. Instead, Jesus is struck by the widow's need: having no husband and having lost her only son, she was going to have a hard time making a living. Biblical law required that a portion of the tithe be set aside in towns for relief of resident aliens, orphans, and widows

Early Christian Ministry to Widows

"Instead of fields, then, purchase souls that have been afflicted, insofar as you can, and take care of widows and orphans and do not neglect them"; "taste nothing but bread and water on the day you fast. Then estimate the cost of the food you would have eaten on that day and give that amount to a widow or orphan or someone in need." (Shepherd of Hermas, *Similitudes* 1.8, 5, 3, 7)

"Do not allow the widows to be neglected. After the Lord, it is you [he is writing to a local bishop] who must be mindful of them." (Ignatius to Polycarp, 4.1)

"The presbyters also should be compassionate, merciful to all, turning back those who have gone astray, caring for all who are sick, not neglecting the widow, the orphan, or the poor, but always taking thought for what is good before both God and others." (Pol. *Phil.*, 6.1)

(Deut 14:28-29), so we should not assume that the villagers in places like Nain would have let her starve. But their economy, just like ours, was structured so that single elderly women without strong family support were vulnerable. Luke's readers would have assumed that the woman would be in need, and one wonders what this story might have said to them about the responsibility of the church to provide a "son" for widows. Did Luke's readers see Jesus' miracle symbolically reproduced whenever they took widows into their homes, treating them as family? [Early Christian Ministry to Widows]

As noted earlier, there are three other Lukan stories where children are healed or revived: the centurion's slave (because the centurion calls him "boy," we assume he is young); Jairus's daughter (8:40-56); and the epileptic boy (9:37-43). There are points of connection between all of them. The widow's son, Jairus's daughter, and the epileptic boy are all said to be only children, while the centurion's slave is said to be precious to him. Jesus says "stop crying" to the widow and to Mr. and Mrs. Jairus; he gives the epileptic boy back to his father as he does the widow's son; he tells the little girl "rise" just as he does the dead son; and there are double messages to Jesus in the Jairus and centurion stories. The connections are sparse enough to keep us from thinking "I just read this," but numerous enough to make us wonder what the similarities mean. Certainly the widow is the social and economic inverse of Jairus the synagogue leader, and yet both of them are equally devastated, and Jesus treats them the same. The centurion is the only Gentile in the mix, and the only one whose faith Jesus finds remarkable; yet he heals all of them, even when Jairus's friends laugh at him and his disciples fail to heal the epileptic boy.[8]

There is also a faint connection between the story of the widow's son and the John the Baptist material. The clearest is "God has visited his people," quoting Zechariah's Benedictus: "Blessed be the LORD, the God of Israel, who has visited and has worked redemption for his people" (1:68). Jesus is God's prophet just as John was, but as we will see shortly in this chapter, Luke will explain how Jesus' ministry goes beyond John's. John, too, was fulfilling the role of Elijah by coming to purify a people to make them ready for God's visitation; Jesus takes up Elijah's role but in a bigger way, bringing not just repentance but resurrection. And, like Zechariah, when the curse of death is lifted from the boy, the first thing he does is talk, and then the talk about this event spreads through the land, as it did about John's name and Zechariah's newfound voice. Here, too, is a subtle theological point: Zechariah finds his voice when he obeys the angel's word; John brings the word of repentance and forgiveness of sins; but only Jesus can heal or bring to life with just a word: "Speak the word, Lord" (7:7); "I say to you, Rise!"

The last set of connections to note is to the role of prophet in Luke. If you have been reading Luke in sequence, you'll recall that there have already been a bunch of prophets: Elizabeth, Mary, Zechariah, Simeon, Anna, and John the Baptist. Jesus took up the prophetic roles in his first sermon by reading from Isaiah and claiming that the words were being fulfilled. He has been filled with the Spirit and led by the Spirit, and he has thundered against the rich and for the poor as prophets are wont to do. So Luke, to make sure you notice, has the crowds draw your attention to the prophetic nature of these two miracles and to the growing consensus in Palestine that Jesus was a prophet.

Moses famously predicted a prophet like himself who would arise (Deut 18:15-22, quoted by Luke at Acts 3:22-23). Luke includes far more references to Jesus as prophet than any other Gospel or New Testament writer. For him, Jesus is no less Son of God for being a prophet; remember, in this same episode the narrator calls him "Lord," echoing what Luke's prototypical prophet Elizabeth calls him. The rhetorical benefit for Luke of using "prophet" is that it includes and explains so many aspects of Jesus' life, death, and ministry. Why was Jesus so riled up over the plight of the poor? Why did Jesus' own village and own temple leaders want to kill him? Being a prophet not only explains why he was rejected, but links the predictions he made (that Luke carefully documents as fulfilled) and the miracles he did. Prophet, in other words, can serve Luke as both a theological and literary character type, unifying his presentation of Jesus. And, as a bonus, prophets were a ubiquitous religious phenomenon in the first-century empire— even the senate and the emperor consulted collections of prophetic oracles from time to time—so stressing Jesus's prophetic identity would have helped Luke's readers to understand him.

The pericope's end is one of Luke's typical "all's well" summaries—the word is spreading, things are going fine. In the next episode, Luke modifies this rosy picture by naming criticism of Jesus floating around the same countryside, and by having Jesus' cousin and closest parallel question his authenticity.

Jesus and John the Baptist, 7:18-35

In order to keep all the John the Baptist material together, this commentary section bites off a big chunk of verses, including material of different forms: a controversy story (7:18-23), an encomium (7:24-28), commentary by the narrator (7:29-30), and a parable (7:31-32) followed by commentary by Jesus (7:33-35). Since Matthew has everything Luke has (except 7:29-30, which is clearly something Luke added to make a point to his readers) and in the same order (Matt 11:2-19), then either the material existed in this form in Q—which is what most New Testament professionals think—or Luke is copying Matthew or Matthew is copying Luke. In my opinion, the first two options—Luke got it from Q or from Matthew—are more likely. The greatest difference between Matthew and Luke in the way this section is structured is that Matthew puts the saying about the kingdom of God suffering violence (Matt 11:12) and the judgment that John is Elijah (11:13-14) here, while Luke saves them for later in the Gospel. In my opinion, it is impossible to judge whether Matthew or Luke changed the text of Q (if there was a Q), since there are plausible reasons for either to have put the material where they did. But whether Luke was reading Q or Matthew, Luke 7:29-30 is a Lukan addition to the text, so we will think about what that decision tells us about Luke's purposes.

John the Baptist was a legitimate phenomenon in the first century, a name that would have been widely known among those living in Palestine in the first century. Josephus writes about him (see [Josephus on John the Baptist]) and confirms much of what the Gospels say: John attracted large numbers of people through his preaching of repentance and his offer of baptism following repentance. Josephus says that the crowds who followed him were so inspired that Herod Antipas worried that John's powers of persuasion might lead to rebellion, so he had John arrested and later executed. Mark 6:14-29 also names Antipas, but says that he arrested John for preaching against the legality of his marriage, and then executed him when his stepdaughter beguiled him with a dance on his birthday. [Machaerus] Josephus also corroborates the fact that according to Jewish law, Antipas's marriage was suspect, since he married his brother's former wife while his brother was still living. The two stories, then, could both be true—Antipas's fear of popular uprisings would be compatible with anger over a prophetic denunciation of his marriage. Furthermore, although Mark's statement that John criticized Antipas's marriage as adultery stands alone without corroboration (Matthew and Luke copied Mark, so they don't count), it also fits with John's general call for repentance. If he thought that Israel in his day was "a wicked and adulterous generation," then he could well have pointed to the king's marriage as exhibit A.

Machaerus

Machaerus was a palace/fortress kept by Herod Antipas as a safe retreat. It is likely the place where he kept John the Baptist in prison, and the traditional site of John's execution.

Machaerus Palace/Fortress. Image courtesy of Mark Connally and www.holylandphotos.org.

All of that happened in the late 20s or early 30s, or some fifty to seventy years before Luke wrote. He surely knew what he read in Mark and in his other source (Q or Matthew), but he may have known nothing else about the Baptist. His readers, mostly Gentile Christians living outside Palestine, probably only knew about John from reading Luke. So far in the narrative, they had learned that John and Jesus were family and that both had been born through God's intervention. John's elderly parents were divinely enabled to have a child in the normal way—Elizabeth's barrenness lifted—while Jesus' mother was divinely enabled to have a child in a most unusual way. Both John and Jesus preached repentance, and both taught that the change of life God required involved giving to the poor and avoiding violence; both taught that there was judgment and reward coming soon, and that listeners had better be ready. Jesus went further, asking his hearers to forgive their enemies and to pray for their persecutors, and at Nazareth, he claimed that God's blessings of the Age to Come were fulfilled in his ministry. The reader probably thought that John baptized Jesus, although the syntax of 3:21-22 uses a bit of indirection to soft-pedal the troublesome aspects of Jesus submitting to anyone but God.

By the time the reader gets to 7:18, in other words, he or she already thinks of John as God's prophet, closer in style and vocabulary to Jesus than anyone else in the story. The reader also knows that there were disciples of John who were independent of the Jesus movement (5:33); Luke thinks these folks ought to get over that and join the Christian movement (Acts 19:1-7). So the appearance of disciples of John at 7:18 creates an interesting dynamic for the reader. John is a God-sent prophet, but his role is to point people to Jesus—"Prepare the way of the Lord!" If he still has disciples of his own, then he has not become Jesus' disciple, and the followers of John, though not hostiles like the Pharisees, are not insiders either. The very existence of such people in Luke's day was a question about Jesus' validity—if he was so great, how come John never signed on?

The section opens with a follow-up to the general report of 7:16-17, where the word about Jesus is spreading, with people saying that he is a great prophet and that his miracles are God's visitation upon Israel. Recall that the two miracles of 7:1-15 were modeled after Elisha and Elijah, and that Elijah is John's role, too (1:76, where Zechariah quotes Malachi's prediction of Elijah's return to prepare the way of the Lord). So when John's disciples see these things and hear the reports that Jesus is a great prophet, they take the news to their teacher, who is locked up in Antipas's prison (3:20). John then picks two of them and sends them "to the Lord"—the narrator is already making the point about who is greater—to ask, "Are you the Coming One or must we expect another?" The reader will recall that John himself spoke of "the one who is mightier than I" who was coming, armed with a winnowing fork to separate the wheat from the chaff. John sends two disciples so that each can testify to Jesus as to the legitimacy of the question and to the accuracy of the answer they take back. The two questioners are an ironic contrast to various Lukan pairs who witness to Jesus' standing with God: Simeon and Anna, the centurion and widow of 7:1-15, the two angels at the tomb, etc. The narrator plays with this a bit, calling them "disciples" at 7:18—foils for the Lord's disciples—and "angels"—properly translated "messengers," but it's the same word—in verse 24. [John Sends Two Disciples]

John Sends Two Disciples

John sent them to him not to interrogate him, but rather that the Lord might confirm those former things that John had proclaimed to them. John was directing the minds of his disciples toward the Lord.

Ephrem the Syrian, *Commentary on Tatian's Diatessaron* 9.2, cited in Arthur A. Just Jr., ed., *Luke* (ACCS: NT, vol. 3; Downer's Grove IL: Intervarsity Press, 2003), 120.

We can read this question "in real life"—that is, against the background of what we think we know about John the Baptist, drawing on all our sources—or against the background of what we have read so far in Luke. In the first case, the existence of John's disciples during John's life and afterward makes it extremely improbable that John the Baptist ever considered Jesus to be the Coming One. In my opinion, the historical John the Baptist baptized Jesus in the Jordan, but then continued to baptize until his arrest and execution. When he baptized Jesus, he must have believed that Jesus fulfilled what John considered to be the conditions for baptism, and having baptized him, he must have believed that Jesus would be included among the righteous on Judgment Day. But John's continued teaching (implied by having disciples) and baptizing ministry means that he thought that the Coming One had not yet appeared. The New Testament indicates that John's disciples continued after his death; probably, then, John never "converted" to the Jesus Movement. The question "Are you the Coming One?" only appears in Q, and one can never be completely confident about a "fact" appearing in only one source; on the other hand, there is nothing implausible about it, and the question itself advances no Christian purpose, so it is hard to imagine that an early Christian invented the scene. Bottom line: in real life, John may well have asked the question, and if he did, our best guess is that whatever answer he got did not persuade him to give up his own ministry and disciples.

The case is a bit different when we read this against the background of Luke, however. As a "prophet and more than a prophet," John would have a seat at the banquet table in the kingdom with "Abraham and Isaac and Jacob and all the prophets" (13:28). For Luke to be consistent, we should read 7:18-23 knowing that Luke considered John to be the beginning of the Christian gospel (Acts 1:21-22; 10:37-38). That does not rule out a reading where the Baptist doubts Jesus, but does rule out reading Jesus' answer in a way that leaves his cousin off the roll to be called up yonder.

Luke not only gives the question in v. 19, but has the messengers repeat it word for word in v. 20—a clear sign that we are supposed to read it carefully and take it seriously: "Are you the Coming One, or must we expect another?" The standard way to read John's question is to point to the differences between his description of the Coming One and Jesus' ministry thus far. He said, "The ax is already laid at the root of the trees, so every tree that does not produce good fruit is being cut down and thrown into the fire" (3:9), and "he will baptize you with the Holy Spirit and fire. His winnowing fork is in his hand to clear his threshing floor and gather the wheat into his granary, but he will burn the chaff with unquenchable fire" (3:16-17). If one contrasts this description— ax-wielder, wheat-thresher, chaff-burner—with the accounts of Jesus' healing, or with Jesus' application of Isaiah 61:1-2 to himself, then there is a gap. One reading, then, is to say that John has been looking for someone to come to clean house, and he is concerned or confused or disillusioned by Jesus' conduct thus far. If Jesus

Woodcut of John Sending the Two Disciples

Eduard von Gebhardt. *John Sends Disciples to Jesus.*

really is to be the Coming One, why has he not burned up the wicked?[9]

Another way to read the question is to see it as the question of a seeker, not a doubter: not, "You're so different from what I expected—can you *really* be the Coming One?" but "I've heard such amazing things about you—can you *really* be the Coming One?"[10] This reading is more in keeping with the strong similarities Luke draws between Jesus and John: the similar calls for reform of character and economic justice, and the use of the word *prosdokeō*, "expect" or "wait for," to describe John's audience (3:15) and John's question.

Another reading makes John's question more like his dad's—perhaps more incredulity than doubt. Zechariah, you will recall, had prayed for a son, but when the angel showed up to give him the good news, he asked for proof. The Baptist has heard the good news also, but he cannot quite believe it yet. The answer Jesus offers does not give him any new data, really; he is still going to have to make up his mind based on the testimony of others. But instead of a curse like the one that left his father speechless, John gets a blessing, leading us to think that he will make the right choice.

Verse 21 begins "in that hour," a phrase Luke regularly uses to mean "at that very moment" (10:21; 12:12; 13:31; 20:19; 24:33), so that we are to imagine that Jesus performs the miracles while the two Baptistians watch. The reader has already seen Jesus heal "diseases" and "plagues" (Luke uses a word elsewhere translated "whip" to mean serious illness[11]) and cast out demons, but v. 21 is the first account of sight being restored to the blind. Verse 22 is a list of types of miracles to this point in the narrative, except for "the deaf hear"—Luke does not describe the healing of a deaf person specifically; more on this below. [Do Miracles Make the Messiah?]

The benediction in 7:23, "Blessed is the one who is not caused to stumble by me," is best read as Jesus truly blessing John. Think of the symmetry in how blessings and curses work with John and his family. First, Zechariah gets good news, but wants proof, and so is cursed with speechlessness. When his curse is lifted, he blesses God for God's gracious acts to Israel. Second, Elizabeth, filled with the Spirit, blesses Mary for not doubting the angel as did Zechariah. Even though at the outset of the story John sounds more like Zechariah—this can't be true, can it?—Jesus blesses him for *not* stumbling; in the end John is more like his mother than his father!

Jesus' miracle-working stretches in several directions. First, John's testimony about the Coming One was that while John baptized with water, the Coming One would baptize with fire and Spirit. It was the Spirit who overshadowed Mary to begin Jesus' journey (1:35); the Spirit who prompted John to leap for joy when, *in utero*, he was in Jesus' presence (1:41-44); the Spirit who descended on Jesus at his baptism (3:22), who led Jesus in the wilderness like Israel of old (4:1), and who led Jesus to return to Galilee for a preaching and healing mission (4:14-15). Now, through the Spirit's power, Jesus is making the words of Isaiah 61:1-2 come to life, just as he said to the Nazareth crowd. Jesus' miracles are a continuation of God's gracious deeds for God's people: "a light for those who sit in darkness," as Zechariah had sung (1:78-79).

Second, the link to the Nazareth scene, through the connections between 7:22 and 4:18-19 (good news to poor, sight to blind), also reminds us that Jesus has not actually avoided preaching harsh words of judgment. He told his hometown synagogue that God's miracles might go to the Gentiles instead of to them, and he got them so riled up they wanted to kill him. True, he eats with sinners, but he also pronounces curses on the rich, the full, the laughers, and the popular (6:24-26), and warns those who listen to him but do not keep his teachings of their eventual destruction (6:49). Jesus' miracles, like

Do Miracles Make the Messiah?

In Michael Chabon's *The Yiddish Policemen's Union*, two Jewish detectives are investigating the murder of a man who, in his youth, was reported to have done miracles; some believed he would be revealed as the Messiah. The detectives are skeptical:

"That stuff the maven was telling us about Mendel. The wonders and miracles. Berko, you believe any of that?"

"You know it's not about believing for me, Meyer. It never has been."

"But do you—I'm curious—do you really feel like you're waiting for Messiah?"

Berko shrugs, uninterested in the question, keeping his eyes on the track of the black galoshes in the snow. "It's Messiah," he says. "What else can you do but wait?"

"And then when he comes, what? Peace on earth?"

"Peace, prosperity. Plenty to eat. Nobody sick or lonely. Nobody selling anything. I don't know."

"And Palestine? When Messiah comes, all the Jews move back there? To the promised land? Fur hats and all?"

"I heard Messiah cut a deal with the beavers," Berko says. "No more fur."

Michael Chabon, *The Yiddish Policemen's Union* (New York: HarperCollins, 2007), 20.

Gabriel's announcement, are only good news to those who are willing to receive them; for those who stumble at Jesus (7:23), there is judgment coming.

Third, the mention of the blind getting their sight and the deaf hearing connects this episode with a couple of others. Zechariah, once he got his voice back, predicted that John would prepare the way for the Lord, who would break like the dawn upon Israel (1:76-79). The Lord has come, and some have seen the light: "Go away from me, Lord, for I am a sinful man"; "amazement seized all of them and they glorified God and were filled with fear, saying, 'We saw marvels today'"; "A great prophet has risen among us!"; "God has visited God's people!" Others have not: "they got up and drove him out of town and led him to the brow of the hill on which their town was built, so that they might hurl him off the cliff"; "why do you eat with tax collectors and sinners?"; "they were filled with fury and discussed with one another what they might do to Jesus." In his Sermon on the Plain, Jesus used the images of the blind leading the blind and of the teacher with the log in his eye trying to remove a speck from a student's eye. The scene of the two Baptist disciples watching Jesus perform miracles and then reporting what they had "seen and heard" puts them at a crossroads. Can they draw the right conclusion from what they have witnessed? Can they choose the right teacher and avoid stumbling and falling into the ditch? Luke hopes so, but as noted above, he knows of disciples of John yet to be folded into the church, and so he leaves this scene open-ended. Jesus pronounces the benediction, opening the door as wide as possible, and we get the Acts 19 scene of a group of them coming in, so the reader has reason to feel hopeful. [Jesus Heals while John's Disciples Watch]

After John's "angels" leave, Jesus "began to speak to the crowds concerning John." What follows is a brief encomium, an address praising John. According to the narrative, John is alive and in prison, but somewhere between 7:18 and 9:9, Herod Antipas beheads him. In the reader's time, of course, John is dead; as Jesus speaks these words, the reader knows, and probably assumes that Jesus knows, that John will never leave prison alive. So though this is not technically a funerary speech or eulogy, functionally it is—Jesus reflecting on God's work through John, praising him to the crowds, berating those who failed to listen to him.

Jesus Heals while John's Disciples Watch

Here see, I ask, the beautiful art of the Savior's management. He does not simply say, "I am." If he had spoken this, it would have been true. He leads them to the proof given by the works themselves.

Cyril of Alexandria, *Commentary on Luke*, homily 37; cited by Arthur A. Just Jr., ed., *Luke* (ACCS: NT, vol. 3; Downer's Grove IL: Intervarsity Press, 2003), 121.

Again, we can read this either "in real life" or in the context of Luke's narrative. In Jesus' Galilean ministry, I suspect that he explained his connections to John the Baptist often, perhaps every time he moved into a new area and sent out the troops to spread the message of the kingdom of God. The gospel tradition includes a surprising amount of material on John, all of it favorable, and in a couple of clusters, Jesus argues for his own authority from John's status as a prophet sent by God—something that the Gospels and Josephus agree was popular opinion. Furthermore, John's movement and Jesus' movement resembled each other in many important ways, not the least of which is that both used baptism to mark a person's repentance and readiness for the coming of the kingdom. It was John who was known as "the baptizer," so the appearance of another prophet who preached John's message of repentance in view of the coming kingdom and followed that with baptism would

John in Prison

Gerrit van Honthorst (1590–1656). *Decapitation of Saint John the Baptist.* S. Maria della Scala, Rome, Italy. (Credit: Scala/Art Resource, NY)

have required some explanation—how are you the same as and different from John? Since all the gospel material about John is favorable (or neutral—"why don't your disciples fast like John's?"), our best guess about "real life" is that Jesus probably began his preaching in a new area by praising John and explaining their relationship.

Luke's Gospel laid out the relationship between the two from the start of the Gospel. John is most definitely God's prophet and is also most definitely Jesus' forerunner. He explicitly leaps for joy at the presence of his Lord (1:44) and only implicitly baptizes Jesus (3:21), so there can be no mistaking John's willingness, to paraphrase the Fourth Gospel, to decrease while Jesus increases. While in real life Jesus' movement and John's movement may well have looked like (and perhaps may have been) competitors for converts among the poor of Galilee, in Luke's Gospel there is no contest. Thus Jesus' praise for John can be effusive without fear of lifting up the Baptist too high; Luke's narrative has already solved that problem by this point in the story.

Luke would have heard encomia at funerals or at public festivals, where speeches in praise of heroes and the event's patrons would have been offered. He no doubt read Sirach's "let us now sing the praises of famous men" section (Sir 44–50), and so had plenty of models to draw on, which were mostly longer and more flowery than this brief section. [Sirach's Encomium for Elijah] Yet he apparently chose to leave it mostly as he found it; Luke 7:24-28 is nearly identical to Matthew 11:7-11. Whoever composed it, this miniencomium agrees with much of the advice given in a popular rhetorical handbook of the period. The anonymous author of *Ad Herennium* states that a speech of praise should begin either with the speaker's connection to the subject, with the hearer's connection, or with the person or subject under praise (III.vi.11); Jesus chooses to start with the crowd's connection to John: "When the Introduction is drawn from the person of the hearers: if we speak in praise, we shall say that since we are not delivering an encomium amongst people unacquainted with the man, we shall speak but briefly, to refresh their memories" (III.vi.12). Jesus' beginning focuses on what the crowds knew for themselves: "what did you go out into the desert to see?" The repeated use of rhetorical questions is a strategy designed to build passion in an address; it is unusual to do so at the beginning of a speech, but in this case the whole speech is so short that it works.

Ad Herennium recommends that after the introduction one will need to set out the virtues of the person being praised, following the order of external circumstances (descent, education), physical attributes, and virtues and defects of character. In each case, one either praises the subject for what he has—illustrious ancestors, physical beauty or strength—or for making good despite the lack of those advantages: "Has he been rich or poor? What kinds of power has he wielded? What have been his titles to fame? What his

Sirach's Encomium for Elijah

NRS **Sirach 48:1** Then Elijah arose, a prophet like fire, and his word burned like a torch. [2] He brought a famine upon them, and by his zeal he made them few in number. [3] By the word of the Lord he shut up the heavens, and also three times brought down fire. [4] How glorious you were, Elijah, in your wondrous deeds! Whose glory is equal to yours? [5] You raised a corpse from death and from Hades, by the word of the Most High. [6] You sent kings down to destruction, and famous men, from their sickbeds. [7] You heard rebuke at Sinai and judgments of vengeance at Horeb. [8] You anointed kings to inflict retribution, and prophets to succeed you. [9] You were taken up by a whirlwind of fire, in a chariot with horses of fire. [10] At the appointed time, it is written, you are destined to calm the wrath of God before it breaks out in fury, to turn the hearts of parents to their children, and to restore the tribes of Jacob. [11] Happy are those who saw you and were adorned with your love! For we also shall surely live.

friendships?" (III.vii.13-14; quote from III.vii.14.3).[12] John, of course, had no money, no powerful friends, no titles—none of his culture's marks of success or prestige. But Jesus, rather than apologizing for these, forcefully and artfully puts the crowd into the position of agreeing that John was just what God wanted and just what they needed.

"A reed shaken by the wind" is, on the surface, an image of a weak, fragile thing; Luke, who draws so regularly on Isaiah, will have expected his audiences to recall Isaiah 42:3, "a bruised reed he will not break" and the comparison of Egypt to a "broken reed" (Isa 36:6). Third Maccabees 2:22 compares God's punishment of Ptolemy IV to the way a reed is shaken by the wind (*kradanas auton kōs kalamon hypo anemou*); since Herod Antipas, who killed John, minted coins with a reed on them to commemorate his new city of Tiberias,[13] it is not hard to imagine attentive readers making the connections. John had no political clout, and was killed by a wicked king who did, but in the end, who was the weak reed shaken by the wind and who was the voice of God inspired by the Spirit, the wind of God?

The second image of soft clothes and fine apparel is explicitly a contrast between John and the palace; they live in luxury, while he lived in the desert. Luke never gives us Mark's line about John wearing camel's hair and leather, so his readers may not have imagined John in a hair tunic. But they certainly would not have imagined him wearing fine or expensive clothes while living in the desert, and the word translated "soft," *malakos*, was often used to mean "effeminate,"[14] an adjective that none of Luke's readers would associate with John. This, then, is not only praise of John but indirect censure of Antipas, his murderer. Who was the prophet, and who the rich soft worthless scoundrel who killed him?

Having established what John was not, Jesus now turns to what he was: "a prophet? Yes, I say to you, even more than a prophet; he is the one about whom it stands written, Behold I will send my messenger ["angel"] before your face, who will prepare your way before you" (7:26-27). In Jesus' opinion, John was the fulfillment of Malachi's promise that Elijah would return before the Day of Judgment (Mal 4:5-6) to cause the people to repent in preparation for the Lord's coming. "More than a prophet" can simply mean "the greatest of all prophets," but by Luke's day, John was already on the way to being understood to be a Christian saint and martyr, so the phrase carried more and more freight as time passed.

Verse 28, "I say to you, no one born among women is greater than John, but the least in the kingdom of God is greater than he," can be read in more than one way. As an isolated saying, it could mean that John was the greatest of all persons in the present age, but was excluded from the Age to Come, so that the least in God's kingdom would be better off than he, since he would not be there.[15] As noted earlier, that would not be a consistent reading within Luke, since he identifies John as the greatest prophet and anticipates the prophets being present in the Age to Come. Luke's understanding of 7:28 must have been more a contrast between the two ages: one would rather be the least person in the kingdom, once it fully begins, than the greatest person in the present age.

Luke's narrator draws the Lukan moral from the saying in an editorial insertion, 7:29-30. The crowd listening to the encomium, including tax collectors, "justified God, since they had been baptized with John's baptism." "Justify" in this sense means to declare something just or righteous; the people and tax collectors are saying "amen!" to Jesus' speech, agreeing that he has correctly described how God acted through John. Well, naturally, since they had all accepted John's baptism, you would expect them to agree that he was God's prophet and more. But the scene puts them agreeing with Jesus—they are modeling the transfer of allegiance from John to Jesus that Luke believes is appropriate for all John's disciples. The Pharisees and teachers of law, on the other hand, refused John's baptism, disagreed with Jesus, and so rejected *tēn boulēn tou theou*, the plan or the will of God. If any remaining Baptistians refuse to follow Jesus, then they are joining ranks with Pharisees and lawyers and stepping outside God's great plan for bringing in the Age to Come.

Jesus now turns from praise of John to a rebuke of "the people of this generation." Since the narrator has just split the audience for us into "the people listening, including the tax collectors," who approve of John and Jesus' message, and "the Pharisees and the lawyers," who reject John and God's plan, "this generation" in Luke's context has to refer to the latter group, as it appears to in 11:50-51. ["This Generation"]

The "real-life" implications of this section are pretty significant. Jesus contrasts himself with John on the issue of fasting: John did, Jesus did not. The same point is made in 5:33 in a text Luke gets from Mark, so both Q (if there was a Q, or Matthew's non-Markan source if there wasn't) and Mark agree on this point. More than likely, the historical John expected those whom he baptized to fast in advance of baptism as part of their showing "the

"This Generation"

AΩ In general, "this generation" seems to be Luke's way of referring to an audience that does not respond in faith to Jesus. In 9:41, it refers to the disciples when they could not cast out a demon; at 11:29, to a crowd that wants a miracle; in 11:50-51, to Pharisees and lawyers who will be charged with the death of the prophets.

fruits of repentance," and since John baptized Jesus, we may assume that Jesus fasted according to John's directions before his baptism. The Markan saying about fasting (copied by Luke in 5:33-35) also notes that Jesus' disciples resumed fasting after Jesus' death and resurrection ("the days will come when the bridegroom is taken away from them"). Thus, Jesus' rejection of fasting was a temporary measure, one I believe was connected to his decision to become an itinerant preacher relying on the hospitality of those to whom he preached. Later in Luke he will tell the disciples to eat whatever is set before them (10:7); Jesus' followers will heal, exorcise, and give the good news, and those to whom they minister will give the preachers food and shelter. From this pericope, then, we see that Jesus' ministry thus differed from John's in two significant respects: Jesus took John's message of repentance in view of the coming kingdom to the villages of Galilee, rather than expecting the villagers to make a pilgrimage to him; Jesus ceased fasting as John did for the duration of his ministry. If we reach ahead to 9:1-6 and 10:1-12, we can add a third major difference. John did all the baptizing himself, so far as we know, and so reserved the most significant part of his prophetic ministry for himself alone. Jesus, on the other hand, empowered his disciples to do everything he did.

In Luke's context, Jesus berates the Pharisees and lawyers for being willfully blind to God's purpose. He compares them to children—an insult then, just as much as calling somebody "infantile" or "childish" is now.[16] Jesus' parable asks us to imagine a group of children "in the marketplace"—in Luke's readers' cities, these would be crowded squares in city centers jammed with people selling things from carts or rugs spread on the paving stones. One group complains to the other that they piped a dance tune, but the others would not dance, and then wailed like professional mourners at a funeral, but the others would not weep. One reading of this is that the first group is criticizing the second for not knowing how to behave at weddings and funerals; they cannot learn what is appropriate behavior.[17] Another reading has the first group criticizing the second for never joining in the game: "We tried to get you to play weddings, but you wouldn't dance; we tried to get you to play funerals, but you wouldn't weep." This second reading makes the criticism more about how the second group is impossible to please.[18] As one commentator notes, Luke's v. 32 actually says *prosphōnousin allēlos*, "they yell at each other," so that the scene is really of a melee where nobody is happy and everyone is complaining.[19]

This last reading fits well with 7:33-34. John habitually fasted, and "this generation" (the Pharisees) says "He has a demon"—he's crazy, and not only that, but his asceticism, preaching, and baptism are leading people away from God. Jesus, the Son of Man, habitually eats and drinks, and "this generation" says, "He's a glutton and a drunkard, a friend of tax collectors and sinners." They are willfully deaf, in other words, incapable of hearing God's truth no matter whose voice speaks it.

The last verse in this section sounds like an aphorism or proverb; it may well be, although we have no source for it. In this setting, though, it connects to v. 29 to round out the section. The people and tax collectors justified God—that is, agreed with Jesus' analysis of God's actions through John, and demonstrated their commitment by accepting both John's baptism and Jesus' preaching. They are "wisdom's children," where Wisdom has its sense from Proverbs as the personified Word of God reaching out to draw all who are willing to life in obedience to God. The Pharisees and lawyers, on the other hand, have rejected God's plan; they have no place in v. 35, and they neither think of God correctly nor are justified by God for their choices.[20]

This section, which begins with John's question to Jesus, "Are you the Coming One?" works in part to clarify the relationship between John and Jesus. John becomes aware of Jesus' mighty deeds and of the word spreading about him, and wonders if Jesus can be the One he expected. Jesus does not say, "Yes, I am, and if you don't believe it, wait 'til Judgment Day!" Instead, he keeps doing what he has been doing and invites John's "angels" to watch and then report what they have seen.

In Luke's view, John was Elijah who came to prepare the way for Jesus and the kingdom by turning people's hearts toward God. Luke saw that Jesus and John were on the same team, and that while their places in the mission and their approach to ministry differed, those who wanted to be on side with God would accept both of them. In this pericope, the crowds and the tax collectors do just that, while Pharisees and lawyers reject John, Jesus, and God's wise plan for the world. In the middle stand John's disciples—loyal to their first teacher, who was God's true prophet, but not as yet committed to the Lord whose precedence John acknowledged as an unborn babe. Thus the episode that begins with a question about John and Jesus ends by quizzing the interrogators: what do you conclude about what you have seen and heard?

Before we leave this section, let us hear clearly the profound respect Jesus had for John: "no one born among women is greater than John." Sure, in an encomium, and particularly in a eulogy, you never speak badly of the subject, and you might use superlatives where an ordinary adjective might be more precise: "she made the world's best banana pudding," you might say, and nobody will ask for proof. But take Jesus at his word; he includes himself as one "born of woman," so Jesus is not too proud to take his place at the feet of God's greatest prophet. No reed he, bending with the wind; John took his stand against the evil that mighty people do and paid for it with his life. No palace preacher, either; he lived hard and talked plain and there was nothing soft about him. A prophet? Yes, more than a prophet, and probably because Jesus spoke this way about him, John was given several traditional and important spots in visual representations of Jesus. In scenes where Christ is enthroned as judge of the world, John is usually on his left hand, the Virgin on his right. In many crucifixion scenes, John stands below the cross, pointing his finger toward Jesus. In both of these, John is the eternal witness to Christ, answering his own question with an emphatic "yes, he is the Coming One."

The Party at Simon's House, 7:36-50

This episode is the second of seven banquets Jesus attends, first of three at a Pharisee's house. The first of the seven is in 5:27-39, at Levi's house, where Jesus gets raked over the coals by Pharisees for eating with tax collectors and sinners. There, Levi the tax collector is the host who invites Jesus, and the Pharisees are intruders. Here Jesus is invited by a Pharisee and a sinner is the intruder; here the criticism is all in Simon's head, but the reader gets to hear it, and Jesus reacts to it as he did the earlier criticism, with parables and counter-critiques.

Each of the four Gospels has a story in which a woman pours oil on Jesus, but the relationships between the four are puzzling. Mark and Matthew share one version—most of us assume that Matthew 26:6-13 is copied from Mark 14:3-9. John 12:1-8 is like Luke in some respects, but mostly like Mark. The chart below illustrates some of the points of connection and difference:

Mark	John	Luke
Unnamed Woman	Mary, sister of Martha and Lazarus	Unnamed Woman
House of Simon the leper	Lazarus' house	House of Simon the Pharisee
Reclined to eat	Not specified	Reclined to eat
Alabaster jar	A pound	Alabaster jar
"Pure nard, very costly"	"Pure nard, very costly"[21]	Myrrh
300 denarii	300 denarii	
Anoints Jesus' head	Anoints Jesus' feet	Anoints Jesus' feet
		Weeps on feet
	Wipes feet with hair	Wipes feet with hair
		Kisses feet
Disciples respond	Judas responds	Pharisee responds
Why not sold and money given to poor?	Why not sold and money given to poor?	Jesus is no prophet; Why let a sinner touch him?
Scolding woman		Internal critique
Let her alone; why trouble her?	Let her alone	Parable
You always have the poor	You always have the poor	Her many sins are forgiven
You will not always have me	You will not always have me	
She anointed my body for burial	She bought it for my burial	Go in peace

Scholars are divided over how the source-lines ought to be drawn. If Luke had Mark, as most of us assume, that would explain the similarities between their two Gospels, but the similarities between Luke and John raise the possibility of another version of the story known to those two authors. In other words, maybe John and Luke had Mark plus another version of the story where the woman anointed Jesus' feet, and each combined the two versions, adding their own touches as well.

The variation between head and feet—which may strike modern readers as bizarre—could be the result that different cultural practices make on imagination. In Greek and Roman practice, diners typically were led to the dining room, where a servant would remove the guests' shoes and wash their feet. The guests then reclined, and servants brought water for washing their hands. While most of the evidence from the first century points to Jewish adoption of this same practice, some texts describe a two-stage process for Jews. In the first stage, they sat on chairs or benches in a room other than the dining room, where servants brought water so that they could wash the hand they used to eat. While there, they ate an appetizer. Then they adjourned to the dining room and reclined to eat the rest of the meal.[22] As the story of the anointing was repeated, Jesus' assumed posture—sitting or reclining—could have influenced whether the teller imagined that the woman would more easily reach his head (if he was sitting) or his feet (if he was reclining).

In Luke's version—whatever his sources were—he clearly imagines Jesus reclining in the home of one of the Pharisees, whom Luke identifies as lovers of money (16:14) and as people who are accorded seats of honor at synagogue (11:43). Luke's Pharisees, then, were wealthy men of power, and so we imagine Simon the Pharisee as a man with a fine house who can spread a nice table. Sirach, writing roughly 200 years before Jesus' ministry, was full of helpful advice about how to behave in such a setting:

> Are you seated at the table of the great? Do not be greedy at it, and do not say, "How much food there is here!" . . . Do not reach out your hand for everything you see, and do not crowd your neighbor at the dish. . . . Eat what is set before you like a well brought-up person, and do not chew greedily, or you will give offense. Be the first to stop, as befits good manners, and do not be insatiable, or you will give offense. If you are seated among many persons, do not help yourself before they do.
>
> Wine drunk at the proper time and in moderation is rejoicing of heart and gladness of soul. Wine drunk to excess leads to bitterness of spirit, to quarrels and stumbling. Drunkenness increases the anger of a fool to his own hurt, reducing his strength and adding wounds. Do not reprove your neighbor at a banquet of wine, and do not despise him in his merrymaking; speak no word of reproach to him, and do not distress him by making demands of him.
>
> Where there is entertainment, do not pour out talk; do not display your cleverness at the wrong time. . . . Speak, you who are young, if you are obliged to, but no more than twice, and only if asked. Be brief; say much in few words; be as one who knows and can still hold his tongue. Among the great do not act as their equal; and when another is speaking, do not babble. . . . Leave in good time and do

not be the last; go home quickly and do not linger. (Sir 31:12-18, 28-31; 32:1-13)

Jesus does not always abide by these rules, especially the ones about not talking too much and not talking to others as if he were their equal. More importantly for this story, however, is that it comes immediately after the accusation by the Pharisees (see the commentary section arguing that in 7:31-35, "this generation" = Pharisees) that Jesus is an uncouth dinner guest. The Pharisees say of Jesus, "Look, a glutton and a drunkard, the friend of tax collectors and sinners" (7:34). Perhaps that is why Simon the Pharisee does not provide even the rudimentary elements of hospitality for Jesus: water to wash his hands and feet, oil to anoint his head, and (Simon's most offensive omission of custom) the kiss of greeting. If the Pharisees, on the basis of Jesus' dinner conduct at Levi's party, have decided that Jesus is an uncultured rural lout unworthy of proper hospitality, then Simon's slights are deliberate insults. It's as if you invited someone to your home for dinner, and then deliberately made them as uncomfortable as possible—dirty dishes, burned or molding food, watching television instead of talking to the guest, etc. And since we know from 7:49 that there were other guests at the table, these slights to Jesus were not just deliberate, but public. Being deliberately inhospitable to an invited guest was one of the worst offenses in all Mediterranean cultures—something Jews, Greeks, and Romans would all have noted, and something that would have seemed intolerably rude to all Luke's readers.[23] [The Gracious Host]

Jesus, on the other hand, appears at first to be minding his p's and q's. The reader does not get all this information until the end of the story, but once you do, then you reconstruct the night in question like this: Simon the Pharisee invites Jesus to dinner, and Jesus comes. Simon fails to meet Jesus at the door ("I entered your house," rather than "you welcomed me to your house" in 7:44), fails to

The Gracious Host

In the following excerpt from *The Odyssey*, Telemachus, Odysseus's son, demonstrates the role of a good host to the goddess Athena, who appears at his door in disguise. Keep in mind that he is standing in for his father, who is far away and feared dead, and that his house is already full of boorish "Suitors" who are very unpleasant houseguests.

No one noticed her at first but Telemachus, who was sitting disconsolate among the Suitors, dreaming of how his noble father might come back from out of the blue, drive all these gallants pell-mell from the house . . . . he caught sight of Athene and set off at once for the porch, thinking it a shame that a stranger should be kept standing at the gates. He went straight up to his visitor, shook hands, relieved him of his bronze spear and gave him cordial greetings. "Welcome, sir, to our hospitality!" he said. "You can tell us what has brought you when you have had some food." With this he led the way and Pallas Athene followed. . . . He conducted her to a carved chair, over which he spread a rug, and seated her there with a stool for her feet. . . . Presently a maid came with water in a handsome golden jug and poured it out over a silver basin so that they could rinse their hands. She then drew a polished table to their side, and the staid housekeeper brought some bread and set it by them with a choice of dainties, helping them liberally to all she could offer . . . .

From *The Odyssey*, l.105-81 (trans. E. V. Rieu; New York: Penguin, 1946), 28–29.

greet him with a kiss, fails to give him water for his feet or oil for his head. Jesus says nothing about how rude his host is being, but takes his place at table with the other invited guests. In fact, according to the narrative, Jesus is silent until after the woman's appearance and after Simon's inner dialogue. This story, then, is an escalation of Pharisaic hostility and inhospitality toward Jesus. At Levi's house, Jesus was busy eating when the Pharisees—perhaps uninvited guests—challenged his behavior; very rude, but at least Levi the host was making Jesus feel welcome. In the interim, the Pharisees begin spreading the word that Jesus eats like a pig and drinks like a horse. At Simon's house, Jesus swallows his host's insults and remains silent until his behavior is attacked for the second time. They started it, Luke wants us to see; when we get to 11:37-54 and Jesus is an unruly and impolite dinner guest, we are supposed to recall these first two scenes.

The woman's entrance and behavior is the stick that stirs the pot; what she does leads to Jesus' revealing the "inner thoughts" of his host (2:34-35). Simon, according to v. 39, knew that some considered Jesus a prophet; the word spreading in 7:17 had come to him as well. His inner dialogue appears to base his decision that Jesus is no prophet on the fact that Jesus let the woman touch him, but that is simply a rationalization. Had Simon considered Jesus a prophet sent from God, or had Simon been of divided mind on the matter, he would have been properly hospitable to Jesus; clearly, Simon's inhospitality shows that he had made up his mind already, and that the incident with the woman was only further confirmation of his opinion

Luke describes the woman as *gynē hētis ēn en tē polei*, "a woman, a sinner, who was in the city." A "sinner woman" is the parallel to a "sinner man," making this woman the counterpart to Simon Peter (5:8, where he calls himself *hamartōlos*, lit., "a man, a sinner"). The phrase "in the city" has led many interpreters to call the woman a prostitute,[24] but there is no evidence that Luke's readers would have read "a woman in the city" and thought "streetwalker"; there were other direct and euphemistic terms in first-century Greek for "prostitute," and this is not one of them. Luke 18:3, reading *chēra de ēn en tē polei ekeinē*, is the closest parallel in Luke-Acts: "and there was a widow in that city," where "city" is purely a place locator, not a comment on her occupation or moral status.[25] True, the sinner woman in chapter 7 does engage in activity that can be interpreted as erotic, and Luke perhaps lets us think we know what her "sin" is. But, as we will see, Jesus' interpretation of her actions pulls our imaginations out of the gutter and reveals her true intent, much as he revealed Simon's. "A sinner-woman in the city" is a way for Luke to indicate that the anonymous woman was not a stranger to Simon. Simon sees her in his house, and Simon says, "she's a sinner." But Simon is no prophet and cannot see the woman's heart as Jesus can; he concludes that Jesus is no prophet, but only because Simon truly sees neither the woman nor Jesus.

As noted earlier in this commentary, "sinner" is not a social or economic category for Luke, but a theological one. Calling this woman a "sinner" does not give us any information on what she did for a living, nor on whether she was wealthy or poor. "Sinner" means that she needs to repent in order to receive forgiveness and salvation; in Luke's theology, that is true of everyone (13:3, 5), even of those who think they have little from which to repent.

The Pharisees have spread the word that Jesus is a "friend of tax collectors and sinners" (7:34), and the Lukan Jesus would have agreed wholeheartedly. He had already accepted an invitation from Levi the tax collector, after inviting him to be one of his disciples, and he now accepts the affection of a sinner woman. Here is what she does: "when she learned that he was reclining in the Pharisee's house, she bought an alabaster flask of perfume and standing behind [Jesus], by his feet, weeping, began to rain her tears on his feet and wiped [them] with the hair of her head and kissed his feet and anointed them with the perfume." Now, everybody knew about so-called "flute girls" at parties; some hosts provided male and female entertainers, who made music and who could be persuaded to have sex with the guests. ["Flute Girls"] These characters were in enough accounts of banquets that we can assume that Luke's readers might have thought "flute girl" when this woman came in, in the same way that we might think "stripper" if Jesus were at a bachelor party and the woman had jumped out of a cake.

Along the same lines, Luke has clearly sexed up the story with double entendres that "tempt you with the pleasures that the flesh does surely hold."[26] "Feet" in Hebrew are sometimes a euphemism for the genitals, but readers would not have to know Hebrew to catch the pun, because it is all dramatized in the famous third chapter of Ruth. Ruth washes and anoints herself, and when Boaz had drunk lots and was reclining, Ruth uncovered his "feet" and lay down with him. Any reader would think, "Okay, was it his feet or his *feet* [wink-wink, nudge-nudge]?" A woman's unbound hair was

"Flute Girls"

"Do not dally with a singing girl, or you will be caught by her tricks" (Sir 9:4). Dennis Smith, in his description of ancient banqueting practices, says that the flute girls are consistently represented in ancient literature and art as either prostitutes or as poor, lower-class women of whom the upper-class male guests felt free to take advantage. The image is a stereotype, but because it is so common it must have reflected either common practice or the common mental image people had, or both.

See Smith's *From Symposium to Eucharist: The Banquet in the Early Christian World* (Minneapolis: Fortress, 2003), 35–36.

similarly erotic, to be reserved for the bedroom and her husband (see Paul's nervous comments in 1 Cor 11:2-16). Anointing with perfume is part of a woman's self-preparation for receiving her lover (Song 5:5). And kisses—well, a properly hospitable greeting was a kiss on both cheeks. The woman's numerous kisses on Jesus feet—his *feet*—went beyond mere hospitality.[27] By doing all that the host should have done, but in an exaggerated fashion, with lots of touching and hair flying and foot-smooching, she is making him *really* welcome, right? [Hair and Kisses and Tears]

Beyond mere hospitality comes . . . what? Is the woman trying to seduce Jesus right in the Pharisee's dining room? And is she really trying to entice him by weeping buckets? We are supposed to think that the woman shed enough tears to wet Jesus' feet sufficiently to get the dust off, since Luke uses the word *brechein*, which describes how rain gets things wet. Copious weeping was not seductive behavior, and should give the reader the first clue that Luke is setting us up. The more obvious cultural context for a weeping disheveled woman was, of course, mourning:

- "The priest shall set the woman before the LORD, dishevel the woman's hair, and place in her hands the grain offering of remembrance, which is the grain offering of jealousy. In his own hand the priest shall have the water of bitterness that brings the curse." (Num 5:10)
- "She took off her splendid apparel and put on the garments of distress and mourning, and instead of costly perfumes she covered her head with ashes and dung, and she utterly humbled her body; every part that she loved to adorn she covered with her tangled hair." (Greek Esther 14:2)
- "Young women who had been secluded in their chambers rushed out with their mothers, sprinkled their hair with dust, and filled the streets with groans and lamentations." (3 Macc 1:18)
- "And young women who had just entered the bridal chamber to share married life exchanged joy for wailing, their myrrh-perfumed hair sprinkled with ashes, and were carried away unveiled, all together raising a lament instead of a wedding song,

Hair and Kisses and Tears

In the Greek novel *An Ephesian Tale* (probably 2d century AD), the hero and heroine fall in love and are too proud/shy/afraid to tell each other. Love makes them sick, and so when they finally marry and are alone in their bed,

their bodies trembled and their hearts quivered. And at last Habrocomes recovered and took Anthia in his arms. And she wept, as she poured forth the tears that symbolized her inward desire . . . . [She says] "But look, here are my tears; let your beautiful hair drink a cup of love; and as we lock together, let us embrace and wet the garlands [decorating the bridal bed] with each others' tears so that these too may share our love." With this she kissed him all over his face, pressed all his hair to her own eyes . . . .

Clearly, tears, unbound hair, and kisses can all be elements in a love scene!

Xenophon of Ephesus, *An Ephesian Tale*, trans. Graham Anderson, in B. P. Reardon, *Collected Ancient Greek Novels* (Berkeley: University of California Press, 1989), 133.

as they were torn by the harsh treatment of the heathen."
(3 Macc 4:6)

The weeping widow of 7:12-13, weeping mother and father of
8:52, and weeping women of 23:27, as well as Jesus' own weeping
at 19:41, make grief a likely Lukan context for the woman's tears.
Luke, then, has given us an ambiguous scene, and then has Jesus
reveal first the Pharisee's interpretation and then the woman's true
motives. But by making the woman's behavior so equivocal, Luke
allows us to read the woman like the Pharisee does—to see her
through Simon's eyes—and then pulls us back once Jesus begins his
interpretation.

Verse 39 begins with the word "seeing"—"But when the Pharisee
who had invited him saw, he spoke to himself, saying. . . ." Whom
did he see? First, he saw Jesus: "If this one were a prophet, he
would know . . . ." Second, he saw the woman: "who and what sort
is this woman who touched him, for she is a sinner." As stated
above, Simon's rudeness shows that he did not think Jesus was a
prophet when he invited him, or else Simon would have given him
a more proper welcome. Simon's observation of the scene only confirms his judgment that Jesus is no prophet. The reader, however,
knows this is wrong, having just read of Jesus' prophetic acts and of
his interaction with John. The crowds know that Jesus is a great
prophet raised up by God, just as they also recognized John as a
true prophet. The Pharisees, on the other hand, have already been
labeled as those who rejected God's purpose by rejecting John
(7:30) and by slandering the Son of Man (7:33-35). Jesus is a
prophet, the reader knows, and so we suspect that Simon's point of
view on the woman is also flawed. But since he agrees with the narrator that she is a sinner, and since she has just done some sketchy
stuff with Jesus' feet, we are not certain. For sure, Jesus is a prophet,
but maybe Simon is right about this woman; why would Jesus let
her slobber all over him like that?

Jesus interrupts Simon's interior conversation—he would like to
speak to him, replacing "Simon says" with a word from the Lord.
In an unusual syntactical move, Luke lets Simon's "Teacher, speak"
introduce the parable that Jesus tells; without the typical "and so
Jesus said," Jesus' words seem almost to appear in Simon's head.
The story is of a man who had loaned money to two others, neither
of whom could pay. If a denarius was about what a day laborer
could expect to be paid for a day's work, then 500 denarii is a lot of
money. A day laborer could also expect to spend most of his day's
wage feeding his family, and since he could not count on working

every day, then 500 days' wages was an almost unreachable sum. Fifty would be hard enough, but easier to imagine. The creditor forgave both men their debts, an act both generous and righteous; generous, because it was a lot of money simply to release, and righteous, because forgiving debts was something law-abiding Jews were supposed to do every seventh year. This moneylender, for no reason other than that the two debtors had no means to repay him, forgave them both.

Which former debtor loved the lender more? In our culture, love is not supposed to be driven by gratitude or a sense of obligation, so the word "love" may not be so easy for us to assimilate. In Luke's culture (and Jesus' real-world culture as well), love is as much an expected set of actions and commitments as an emotion. Read Deuteronomy 15:12-17, describing the case of a master and slave, both Hebrews. The Hebrew master must emancipate his Hebrew slave at the end of seven years, and must send him out with the means to sustain himself as a freedman. "But if he says to you, 'I will not go out from you,' because he loves you and your household, since he is well off with you," then there is a procedure for making his slavery permanent. Love includes gratitude, takes account of how well the master has treated the slave and of the slave's relative security; it is perhaps less "romantic" than our understanding of love, but also perhaps more realistic. So when a debtor receives forgiveness from a generous and righteous creditor, of course he loves him in response, and would be honor bound to demonstrate that mix of love/gratitude/indebtedness in public and extravagant ways.[28]

Jesus focuses the Pharisee's attention on the two debtors rather than on the righteous, generous, forgiving moneylender. "Which one loved more" presumes that both loved—we are not being asked to judge one of the two deficient. The one who was forgiven for a fifty-denarius debt "loves," but not to the extent or to the degree that the larger debtor "loves." Simon picks the larger debtor to love more, and Jesus agrees, and then begins to contrast Simon's behavior with the woman's. He failed to be hospitable, but she has gone out of her way to make up for that, says Jesus. Simon—"the Pharisee who had invited him"—fails to be a gracious host, but the woman throws her whole body into making up for Simon's failure. Jesus' point-for-point analysis of how Simon and the woman have acted makes it clear that if Simon "loves" Jesus, it is scarcely recognizable as love. The woman's actions, by contrast, are clearly both acts of penitence and demonstrations of love all rolled into one. She weeps for her sins, but she also weeps in order to wash Jesus'

Joseph and Aseneth

Joseph and Aseneth is a love story from ancient times (variously dated from the 1st century BC to the 2d century AD), expanding on the biblical reference to Joseph's marriage to an Egyptian princess (Gen 41:45). As the tale begins, Aseneth lives by herself in a tower, by her own choice, because she hates men. But one sight of the Hebrew Joseph turns her insides to mush; he, however, refuses to be kissed by an idolater, and prays for her conversion. She then undergoes a process of fasting, visions, and acts of penitence culminating in her conversion to the worship of Joseph's God. When next they meet, Joseph knows he has found his future bride. He blesses her in the name of God and invites her into his arms:

> And Joseph stretched out his hands and called Aseneth by a wink of his eyes. And Aseneth also stretched out her hands and ran up to Joseph and fell on his breast. And Joseph put his arms around her, and Aseneth put hers around Joseph, and they kissed each other for a long time and both came to life in their spirit. [There's more kissing, and then Aseneth invites him in to dinner:]
>
> And Aseneth said to Joseph, Come, my Lord, and enter our house, because I have prepared our house and made a great dinner. And she grasped his right hand and led him into her house and seated him on Pentephres her father's throne. And she brought water to wash his feet. And Joseph said, Let one of the virgins come and wash my feet. And Aseneth said, No, my lord, because you are my lord from now on, and I am your maidservant. And why do you say this that another virgin is to wash your feet? For your feet are my feet, and your hands are my hands, and your soul my soul, and your feet another woman will never wash. And she urged him and washed his feet. [There's more kissing, and then they plan the wedding.]

From "Joseph and Aseneth," trans. Joseph Burchard, in James H. Charlesworth, *The Old Testament Pseudepigrapha* (2 vols; New York: Doubleday, 1985), 2.233-34.

feet, reminding many commentators of how Aseneth washed Joseph's feet in order to show him how she adored him: "Your feet are my feet, and your hands are my hands, and your soul my soul, and your feet another woman will never wash" (*Joseph and Aseneth* 20:3). [Joseph and Aseneth]. She kisses his feet continuously, a sign of her affection but also of her supplicant status; like the leper of 5:12, she is at Jesus' feet rather than looking him in the eyes.

Notice also Jesus' posture for this exchange. Luke will likely have thought of Simon's dining room having a typical arrangement: couches arranged in a U-shape, with small tables in front of each one. Jesus will have been reclining on one of them, resting on his left elbow, facing the table in front of him as well as the faces of the other diners. He "turns toward the woman," which would require him to turn his back to his host and the rest of the diners, and then he "says to Simon," over his shoulder, "Do you see this woman?" Luke will have presumed that Simon, as host, will have occupied a seat in the center of the U. If Jesus had been treated as an honorable guest, he would also have been in the middle, in the place where he could talk to everybody and be the center of attention at the dinner party. But since Simon has treated him ungraciously, we should probably picture Jesus at one of the least desirable seats, at the ends of one of the legs of the U. When he asks, "do you see this woman," it is not a rhetorical question; Simon has seen her, according to v. 39, but since she is at Jesus' feet and at the end of the dining space, Simon cannot see her face the way Jesus can. What he judges as lewd behavior from "that sort of woman," Jesus sees more truly as repentance and love. [Unbound Hair and Feet-kissing as Acts of Worship]

"Her many sins have been forgiven her, because she loved much, but the one forgiven little loved little." Here Jesus concludes the teaching moment, exposing the hearts of Simon and the woman. Simon felt no obligation to ask for Jesus' forgiveness, even though he invited him only to treat him badly; Jesus' words do not stir him to repent or to apologize or to demonstrate his true affection in some other way. Instead, Simon's other invited guests echo the sentiment of the scribes and Pharisees at 5:21: Who is this that forgives sins? The readers already know Jesus' answer to this objection; Simon the Pharisee should know it, too, if he has been paying attention. So the Pharisee's status in this story moves from open-minded host (v. 39) to scandalized host (v. 39) to shabby host (vv. 44-47) to being closed-minded, unobservant, unforgiven, and judgmental (v. 49). The woman, on the other hand, moves from being a sinner (v. 37) who appears at first to be acting out her sinfulness (v. 38) to being an extravagantly generous substitute host (vv. 44-47) to being forgiven and "saved," an exemplar of great love and great faith.

> **Unbound Hair and Feet-kissing as Acts of Worship**
>
> At the end of the ancient Greek novel *Chaereas and Callirhoe* (probably either 1st century BC or 1st century AD), the heroine is finally reunited with her husband, and expresses her gratitude to Aphrodite, to whom she gives credit for her good fortune:
>
> > Callirhoe went to Aphrodite's temple before entering her house. She put her hands on the goddess's feet, placed her face on them, let down her hair, and kissed them. "Thank you, Aphrodite!" she said. "You have shown Chaereas to me once more . . . . I do not blame you, my lady, for what I have suffered; it was my fate. Do not separate me again from Chaereas, I beg of you; grant us a happy life together, and let us die together!"
>
> Chariton, *Chareeas and Callirhoe*, trans. B. P. Reardon, in Reardon, *Collected Ancient Greek Novels* (Berkeley: University of California Press, 1989), 124.

Later, in 18:9-14, Luke will use the same sort of setup—the Pharisee who prays a self-satisfied, self-righteous prayer and the tax collector who humbles himself—to trap the reader into being as judgmental of the Pharisee as the Pharisee is of the tax collector. By using deliberately lurid language for the woman's actions, and by delaying the narration of the Pharisee's rude treatment of Jesus, Luke makes it possible for us to judge the woman as harshly as Simon does. Do we then end the story by saying to ourselves, "If there's one thing I can't stand, it's a closed-minded, unobservant, judgmental Pharisee," and if we do, do we need Jesus to tell us a parable about two debtors?

CONNECTIONS

In this chapter, Luke works hard at Jesus' role as a prophet. Jesus heals a Gentile army officer's slave, a retelling of one of Elisha's mighty deeds. Then he raises a widow's son from the dead, reprising Elijah's miracle for the widow at Zarephath. When the crowds say "a great prophet has risen among us" and "God has looked with favor on God's people," they are only voicing what the reader should conclude by connecting the dots from chapter 4 to chapter 7. Jesus, preaching in Nazareth, told the crowd that Elijah and Elisha show us that God's mighty deeds are not always done for the benefit of the Jews, and that he, as a prophet, did not expect to be treated with respect at home.

The crowds of Nazareth believe he is a prophet, but others are not so sure. John the Baptist sends his disciples to ask whether Jesus is the Coming One, a question that may be read as an expression of doubt, but that is more likely to be read as a question of beginning faith—a seeker's question, if you will. In order to show John's disciples who he is, Jesus heals many, and then sends them back to tell John that the words of Isaiah 61:1-2, Jesus' sermon text at Nazareth, are being fulfilled in Jesus' ministry.

The crowds believe, the seekers question, but the Pharisees have made up their minds. John was no prophet, and neither is Jesus; the former was demon-possessed, and the latter is an uncultured party animal, chugging and scarfing his way through Galilee. And to dramatize the difference between crowds and Pharisees, Luke puts Jesus at dinner in a Pharisee's house where a woman from the crowds comes to give him a tear-drenched, hair-wiped, and well-oiled foot massage and toe-kissing. Who loves you, baby? Well, not the Pharisee, whose opinion of Jesus was so low that he treated his guest contemptuously. Simon the Pharisee is not fooled by Jesus' miracles or his connections with John the Baptist; all he needs to know is that Jesus is the friend of tax collectors and sinners, and no true prophet would be friends with such folk. But the woman loves him well enough to burst into a room where she is clearly not invited and engage in lavish, perhaps even outrageous, expressions of love, gratitude, and penitence.

We know where the crowds stand, and if the woman is their exemplar, then they receive Jesus' benediction: Go in peace; your faith has saved you. We know where the Pharisees stand: they accept neither John nor Jesus as prophet. Yet the reader knows well that Jesus is a prophet, and that Jesus' prophetic insight into both Simon and the woman shows both his power and their true natures. But at the end of the chapter, we do not know where the seekers stand. John is in prison; his disciples are on their way back to him, having seen all they need to see to be converted. Will that be enough? "Blessed is the one who finds no cause for stumbling in me" (7:23). "Wisdom is justified by all her children" (7:35). In other words, John's followers are more than welcome to join up with Jesus, to accept him as God's spokesperson, and to receive the "go in peace" just as the woman did.

When we look at the marks of Jesus' prophetic office in this chapter, we are struck again by how much he sounds and acts like his mother. Jesus "scatters the proud in the thoughts of their hearts"

(1:51) and "lifts up the lowly" (1:52). He goes without hesitation to the centurion's home, he has compassion for a grieving widow, and he sees the sinner woman's affection for what it is, not what it may seem to be. His prophetic ministry heals the sick, relieves those beset with evil spirits, grants forgiveness and dignity to those who ask. Is that not what people come to Jesus' followers hoping to receive as well? Then perhaps Luke 7:22 is a good checklist or measuring stick for a congregation; can people, once they get to know you, go away saying, "The blind receive their sight; the lame walk; the lepers are cleansed; the deaf hear; the dead are raised; the poor have good news brought to them"?

NOTES

[1] Alan R. Culpepper, *The Gospel of Luke* (NIB, vol. 9; Nashville: Abingdon, 1995), 155; Frederick W. Danker, *Jesus and the New Age: A Commentary on St. Luke's Gospel* (rev. ed.; Philadelphia: Fortress, 1988), 157.

[2] Danker, *Jesus and the New Age*, 158.

[3] BAGD, 340.

[4] Joel B. Green, *The Gospel of Luke* (NICNT; Grand Rapids: Eerdmans, 1997), 284, makes a good case for the correspondences between the two stories.

[5] John D. Crossan and Jonathan L. Reed, *Excavating Jesus* (San Francisco: HarperSanFrancisco, 2001), 81.

[6] Culpepper, *Luke*, 158.

[7] Luke Timothy Johnson, *The Gospel of Luke* (SP, vol. 3; Collegeville MN: Liturgical Press, 1991), 118.

[8] Culpepper, *Luke*, 158, also treats the connection between these stories.

[9] Culpepper, *Luke*, 160, who opts for this reading from several options; Danker, *Jesus and the New Age*, 163; E. E. Ellis, *The Gospel of Luke* (London: Oliphants, 1974), 119; Joseph A. Fitzmyer, *The Gospel According to Luke* (AB 28 and 28A; Garden City NY: Doubleday, 1981), 1.664-65; Green, *Luke*, 295.

[10] Robert C. Tannehill, *Luke* (ANTC; Nashville: Abingdon, 1996), 129–31; Luke Timothy Johnson, *The Gospel of Luke* (SP, vol. 3; Collegeville MN: Liturgical Press, 1991), 124; M. Eugene Boring and Fred L. Craddock, *The People's New Testament Commentary* (Louisville KY: Westminster/John Knox, 2004), 205.

[11] John Nolland, *Luke* (WBC, vols. 35A-C; Dallas TX: Word, 1989-93), 329.

[12] All citations from *Rhetorica Ad Herennium* (trans. Harry Caplan; Cambridge: Harvard University Press, 1964).

[13] John J. Rousseau and Rami Arav, *Jesus and His World* (Minneapolis: Fortress, 1995), 58; John D. Crossan, *The Historical Jesus* (San Francisco: HarperSanFrancisco, 1991), 236–37, also reads the saying as a critique of Antipas following John's arrest.

[14] BAGD, 613.

[15] Culpepper, *Luke*, 164; Crossan, *Historical Jesus*, 237–38.

[16] Bruce Malina and Richard L. Rohrbach, *Social Science Commentary on the Synoptic Gospels* (Minneapolis: Fortress, 1992), 331.

[17] Ibid.

[18] Danker, *Jesus and the New Age*, 168; Johnson, *Luke*, 123.

[19] Johnson, *Luke*, 123.

[20] Green's analysis of the chiastic relationship between 7:29 and 7:35 is incisive; *Luke*, 302–304.

[21] The phrase shared by Mark and John is very odd: μύρου νάρδου πιστικῆς πολυτελοῦς (John reads πολυτίμου). The first word, "myron," means a fragrant oil or salve. "Nard" is another word for perfume or oils made from the spikenard plant. No one is certain what "pistic" means, although many translations guess that it means something like "pure." The final word means "very costly."

[22] Dennis Smith, *From Symposium to Eucharist* (Minneapolis: Fortress, 2003), 27–28, 137, 145.

[23] David B. Gowler, *Host, Guest, Enemy, and Friend: Portraits of the Pharisees in Luke and Acts* (New York: Peter Lang, 1991), 224–25.

[24] James Malcolm Arlandson, *Women, Class, and Society in Early Christianity: Models from Luke-Acts* (Peabody MA: Hendrickson, 1997), 152; Culpepper, *Luke*, 169; Green, *Luke*, 309.

[25] Kathleen Corley, *Private Women, Public Meals* (Peabody MA: Hendrickson, 1993), 124, argues that Luke used the phrase to connote "streetwalker," but offers no examples in Greek literature where the phrase means "prostitute"; ditto Jane Schaberg, "Luke," in *The Women's Bible Commentary*, ed. Carol Newsome and Sharon H. Ringe (Louisville: Westminster/John Knox, 1992), 286; Nolland, *Luke*, 1.353, who takes "in the city" as an adjectival phrase, the equivalent of "public"; Green, *Luke*, 309; Culpepper, *Luke*, 169. In view of Luke's use of "in the city" as a simple place locator, one would need counter examples in Greek to support the interpretation "harlot." The phrase ἐν τῇ πόλει is not used to mean "streetwalker" in any New Testament or LXX text. There are a couple of examples where "in the city" is paired with "woman" or "women," but the women in question are manifestly not prostitutes: in 1 Macc 13:45, a group of men, women, and children "in the city" are gathered to plead for mercy, and in 3 Macc 1:19, young virgins betrothed and close to being married appear in public "in the city" because of their consternation over a Gentile king's threat to enter the temple. In all its other uses, "in the city" means, well, "in the city" as opposed to somewhere else. When Proverbs or Sirach wants to label a woman a prostitute, the euphemism is *en plateiais*, "in the streets," not "in the city"; see Prov 7:12; 9:14; Sir 9:7 (uses a cognate word for street).

[26] Bruce Springsteen, "Pink Cadillac," 1984.

[27] Scott Spencer, "Passions and Passion: the 'Loose' Lady, Woman Wisdom, and the Lukan Jesus," in *Dancing Girls, Loose Ladies, and Women of the Cloth* (New York: Continuum, 2004), 114–20, is an entertaining discussion of the innuendo in Luke's language.

[28] So Danker, *Jesus and the New Age*, 170.

PARABLES, MIRACLES, AND REACTIONS

Luke 8

COMMENTARY

Luke 8:1-21 Those Who Hear and Do The Word

> The people I love the best
> jump into work head first . . .
> I want to be with people who submerge
> in the task, who go into the fields to harvest
> and work in a row and pass the bags along . . .
> The work of the world is common as mud.[1]

In this chapter we will see some great examples of those who dive into the work, giving it their all, who "pass the bags along" to make sure that the work of sowing the word of God gets done. It isn't rocket science, this work; anyone can do it, but not everyone will.

This long section is marked off by similar phrases: *kai egento en tō kathexēs*, "and so it was in what followed" (8:1), and *egeneto de en mia hēmepōn*, "and so it was on one day" (8:22). The section includes a summary and transitional verse (8:1), a note about women who traveled with Jesus (8:2-3), the parable of the sower (8:4-8), instruction to the disciples about the parable's interpretation (8:9-15), further instruction about listening carefully (8:16-18), and an encounter with Jesus' family (8:19-20). The theme tying all this material together is how one responds to the word of God, and Luke gives us several different types of responses.

Luke uses summary verses like 8:1 at different points to let the reader know that all is going well: 4:44, "And he was preaching in the synagogues in Judea," and 7:17, "the word (*no logos*) about him [that he was God's prophet] went out in all Judea and in the whole region," are echoed in this verse. Luke 8:1 implies that Jesus is going town by town and village by village, preaching (the word of God) and spreading the good news of the kingdom of God. It is just what he said he would be doing in 4:18-19 and what he demonstrated to John's messengers in 7:21-22. Okay, Luke, we get it: Jesus talks the talk and then walks the walk.

Verses 1-3 mention Jesus, the Twelve, and some women, and to understand the women, we need to sort out "apostles" and "disciples." In 6:12-16, Jesus chooses the Twelve apostles, who are all named and all male. Luke 6:13 makes it clear that Luke imagines a larger group, named "disciples," from which the Twelve were chosen. Luke 6:17 refers to *ochlos polys mathētōn autou*, "a great crowd of his disciples"—many more than twelve, in other words. Both groups are present for the Sermon on the Plain (as well as other people from all over), and both seem to be present for the raising of the widow's son (7:11, "his disciples and a great crowd went with him").

Up to 8:2-3, Luke has allowed the larger group of disciples to remain nameless, but in these verses he gives us three names, all women. Both 8:2-3 and 23:49, 55 imply that these are just examples of a larger group of women who had been with Jesus throughout his work in Galilee and who followed him to Jerusalem. There were others, in other words, and I think Luke gives us the names of seven of them: Mary Magdalene, Joanna the wife of Chuza, Susanna (all from 8:2-3), Martha and Mary of Bethany (10:38-42), Mary the mother of James (24:10), and Mary the mother of Jesus (8:21; Acts 1:14). The number seven could be a coincidence, but I think not. First, Mary the mother of Jesus is both the beginning and the end of the list, appearing in chapter 1, prefiguring Jesus' own preaching in her Magnificat, accepted as a disciple in 8:21, and present at the beginning of the church in Acts 1:14. Second, Luke has three women named at 8:2-3 and three at 24:10; Mary Magdalene and Joanna are the same, but he changes the name of the third woman from Susanna to Mary the mother of James. Keeping the third woman the same would have actually served one of his theological interests, providing a group who had been steadily present "beginning from the baptism of John until the day when he was taken up from us." Switching the third name, then, mostly just brings the number of named women disciples to seven. Third, Luke has a pattern of prefiguring later church structures with earlier examples. Elizabeth—who cannot be presumed from the narrative to have been part of the Jesus movement—is the first prophet, and then Mary's prophetic poem prefigures the work and preaching of John, Jesus, and the apostles in Acts. I will argue below that the women who minister in 8:2-3 prefigure the work of the church in Acts 2–4. And fourth, Luke also has a well-established pattern of pairing male and female actors, like Simeon and Anna, or the centurion and the widow. These seven women, collectively, "deaconize" from their resources, witness his death and burial, testify to the empty tomb, and are present among the 120 who install the twelfth apostle and receive the Spirit. They, as much as the apostles, are the foundation for the church.

The women are people "whom Jesus had healed from evil spirits and sicknesses." The first named is "Mary called Magdalene, from whom he cast out seven demons." This is her first appearance in Luke; she appears again at 23:49-56, 24:1-10 as part of the group that sees Jesus crucified and buried by Joseph, sees the empty tomb and the angels, and then becomes the first witnesses to the resurrection. [Mary Magdalene] Joanna is likewise named here and at the crucifixion account. Here we are told that her husband works for Herod Antipas; since Antipas is a bad guy in Luke, we are left to wonder whether Chuza knows about Joanna's attachment to Jesus' movement. The third woman, Susanna, is not named again; at 24:10, the third name is "Mary the mother of James."

These women are, like the Twelve, "with Jesus." There are others so designated in Luke, and not all are women: the blind beggar of 18:35-43 follows Jesus after receiving his sight, and the penitent thief is promised that he will be with Jesus in Paradise (23:43). Not all faithful responders are given the chance to follow or to be with Jesus: the paralytic (5:24), the sinful woman (7:50), the Gerasene demoniac (8:38-39), and the woman with the issue of blood (8:48) are all told to *go* rather than to *follow*. So in Luke, not everyone who responds positively to Jesus is therefore a "disciple," but only those who are invited to follow him or to be with him. These women, who have been healed and/or exorcised, are not only recipients of Jesus' healing power, like the crowds at Capernaum (4:40-41) and the crowds on the level plain (6:18-19), but have received Jesus' invitation to follow him and have responded, not only by following but by serving. They, like Peter's mother-in-law, from whom Jesus cast out a fever, "serve"— *diēkonoun*, from the verb *diakoneō*, from which we get the word

Mary Magdalene

Ancient Christians connected the sinner woman of 7:36-50 with Mary Magdalene, who could have been presumed to be extremely grateful after being exorcised of seven demons (8:2). Gregory the Great, bishop of Rome 540–604, considered the seven demons to be the seven deadly sins, and speculated that the perfume used to anoint Jesus' feet had been previously used to anoint her body, "to perfume her flesh in forbidden acts." Later Christian art often pictured her with unbound hair, or grasping the feet of the crucified Jesus (or the dead Jesus as he is being taken from the cross), or standing below the cross as the counterpart to John the Baptist (he calls for repentance, she is the model penitent)—all features that result from the identification of the sinner woman and Mary Magdalene. None of this has much to do with Luke: the sinner woman is not a prostitute and is not identified with Mary Magdalene. She, rather than being a model penitent, is in Luke a model disciple, ministering from her possessions and faithfully testifying to the resurrection of the Lord. Luke doubtless believes her to have been present among "the certain women" in the 120 persons who were the core of the Jerusalem church, but does not name her.

Quotation from Gregory, *Homily* 33, cited in Jane Schaberg, *The Resurrection of Mary Magdalene: Legends, Apocrypha, and the Christian Testament* (New York: Continuum, 2002), 82.

"deacon." The women, named and unnamed, "'deaconize' them from their own property." "Them" is usually taken to mean Jesus and the apostles, but it could refer to all the persons presumed in the back story behind 8:1-3: Jesus, the Twelve, the rest of the disciples, and the people to whom Jesus is preaching and evangelizing in every town and village.

Many interpreters do equate "them" with "Jesus and the apostles," and read this as Luke's domestication of the early Jesus movement.[2] Luke is the only Gospel to have these verses at this place, but Luke was drawing on Mark 15:40-41 for his material. Mark names Mary Magdalene, Mary mother of James and Joseph, and Salome, and then says, "who had followed him while he was still in Galilee and had 'deaconized him,' and many other women had gone up with him to Jerusalem." Luke keeps Mark's use of *diēkonoun* but drops the "followed him" and adds "from their property." Luke, so the argument goes, changes Mark's female disciples ("followed him") into patrons, who support Jesus and the apostles monetarily, and/or into more typical women's roles—the gals do the cooking and cleaning while the guys do the preaching and healing. [On Serving]

The last part—Luke is trying to rescue the tradition by reimposing gendered division of labor—is unlikely. First, only Jesus is preaching and evangelizing in 8:1; the Twelve do not get their chance until 9:1-6. Second, Luke and Luke's readers would have a hard time imagining women who were both wealthy enough to provide for the group and willing to do household chores for a bunch of men. They could be patrons or servants, but not both, and since Luke puts "out of their property" into the mix, it is unlikely that he is thinking of these women as Merry Maids. Third, whatever we make of the story of Martha and Mary—and there are some translation difficulties that make it hard to work with—it is hard to come away from that story thinking that Luke wants to put women back in the kitchen. Fourth, Luke's purported anti-feminist agenda can only be read in the Gospel (Acts is another matter) by contrast to Mark, and only if we grant that Mark assigns women greater public roles. I'm not convinced that Mark 15:40-41 does that.

On Serving

You don't go into Reynaldo's to buy tamales. You knock at the side door and speak with Lupe. . . . If you are smart you will ask for one and eat it right on the spot. At first you will not be able to speak. When you can speak, your words will be given by the Holy Spirit. "Oh my God" seems to be the most common utterance among Anglos. "Madre de Dios" among Hispanics. Lupe has been making tamales at Reynaldo's for forty years . . . she makes and serves tamales. That is her life. Do you think her life is less fulfilling than yours or mine, less interesting or actualized? You wouldn't think so if you ate her tamales with your closest friends. If you let the jalapeno arouse and the masa soothe you, if you felt the endorphins release into the buzz from your beer and felt your passion for your friends rise until you could not contain your laughter, then you would not think so. You would praise the name of Lupe and marvel at what she gives the world. There would not be tamales if there were not people like Lupe. The women who make tamales in our town are some of the most Christ-like people I know. They give their lives away so that something good may come into the world.

Gordon Atkinson, *RealLivePreacher.com* (Grand Rapids: Eerdmans, 2004), 7–8.

But if Luke wants them to be seen as patrons, it might be because he does not want them confused with preachers and evangelists. He describes them as previously sick or demon-ridden, some say, because he wants the reader to think of their faith as mere reciprocity. Jesus cured the women, and they, in gratitude, provide the money to sustain his movement. Following just after the encounter with the sinful woman, who does her acts of love and penitence at Jesus' feet, like a servant, Luke is pigeon-holing these women: they were sick or possessed, Jesus rescued them, and now their role is to bankroll the Jesus movement.

Luke does make reciprocity an element of Jesus' call to his disciples, but not just to the women. When he calls Simon Peter in 5:1-11, it is only after an exchange of favors: Jesus healed Simon's mother-in-law, and she ministered to—"deaconized"—them. Then Jesus borrowed Simon's boat to use as a preaching platform; in return, Jesus directed Simon to catch a month's worth of fish at one whack. Luke's readers would be better able to understand how a man could legitimately leave his family and his business to follow Jesus once they read the whole story. In the same way, Luke has offered his readers a clue to why these women—at least one of them married to an important and powerful man, and therefore higher in class and status than the fishermen and tax collectors in Jesus' party—would be attracted to Jesus. But Luke resists putting Jesus into patron-client relationships. He heals all sorts of people— a leper, a Gentile's slave, a widow's dead son—but he will not be kept in Capernaum as their special healer. Luke's Jesus, heading off to heal the centurion's servant, is a man unlimited by the obligations of clan or family; far from choosing patrons, he honors a sinner woman and embarrasses his host, the wealthy Pharisee. He teaches his disciples to give freely and to lend, expecting nothing in return, which amounts to the same thing; this is not the basis for patron-client relationships.[3]

The women give, not as patronesses, but as members of Jesus' fictive family. The proper context against which to read their behavior is Acts 2:44-45 and 4:32-37, where all the believers hold all their property in common.[4] What they own (Luke uses the same word for "property" or "possessions" in Acts 4:32 as in 8:3) is used to provide for the Christian fellowship, but also for the needs of the poor in Jerusalem. I would argue that in 8:1-3, Luke is giving us a preview of how the Jerusalem church will work: Jesus is ministering to every town and village of Galilee, and these women are playing the role of the church, providing the means not just for Jesus to survive, but also the means by which he can bring good news to the poor. I would also argue that it would be hard for Luke's readers to see "deaconize" and not think "perform the ministry of a deacon," which at the end of the first century tended to include a wide range of word and sacramental functions. [Ignatius of Antioch on Deacons] In short, Luke is not by this passage restricting ministry to Jesus and the boys—the Twelve, in fact, are the only ones in 8:1-3 who have no active role—but is using them as prototypes for the church, in the same way that Mary and Elizabeth were prototypes for John the Baptist, Jesus, and all the other prophetic leaders.

Would Luke's motive, then, be to discourage women from taking leadership roles in church, by saying "give your money, if you have any, but leave the work of ministry to us men"? If it were, would it not have been simpler to keep the women out of the picture altogether, or to use a word other than "deaconize" to describe their activity? The Gospel of Luke does in fact restrict the term "twelve" and "apostle" to these twelve men, and it appears to matter to him that there were twelve men named apostles who were chosen by Jesus and were part of the earliest church in Jerusalem. But it also matters to Luke that there were others, including women, who were there, too, from the beginning, doing the work of ministry in imitation of Jesus.

As we move to the parable of the sower, note the sequence of material. When Jesus is poorly treated by his host Simon the Pharisee, a woman comes to provide for him from her means and with her own hands, tears, lips, and hair. When Jesus is preaching town by town in Galilee, a large number of women are with him; he has helped them previously by healing them, and they are now providing the means for his ministry, as prototypes for the church. Now he tells a story about how the word of God is cast upon four sorts of soil; guess who should be in the reader's mind as the most fruitful receptors for the word?

The parable of the sower is found in Mark, whence it was copied and edited by Matthew and Luke, and in the *Gospel of Thomas*, which some think is dependent on the Synoptics and others believe is an independent version of Jesus' teachings. The four accounts have many common features, and yet each one has some individual touches. Mark's version of the parable is the longest and most detailed; Matthew's version is only a little shorter than Mark's, and

Ignatius of Antioch on Deacons

And those who are deacons of the mysteries of Jesus Christ must also be pleasing in every way to all people. For they are not deacons dealing with food and drink; they are servants of the church of God, and so they must guard themselves against accusations as against fire. So too let everyone respect the deacons like Jesus Christ . . . . (*Trallians* 2.3-3.1)

I urge you to hasten to do all things in the harmony of God, with the bishop presiding in the place of God and the presbyters in the place of the council of the apostles, and the deacons, who are especially dear to me, entrusted with the ministry of Jesus Christ, who was with the Father before the ages and has been manifest at the end. (*Magnesians* 6.1) adds no new details, though it smooths Mark's grammar just a bit. The version in Thomas is shorter even than Luke's, but Thomas also adds a worm to eat the seeds in the thorns. Scholars of the historical Jesus mostly think that Jesus really told this parable, but are divided about what the original version would have included. In what follows, I will focus only on Luke's version. [The Parable of the Sower in the *Gospel of Thomas*]

The audience for the parable is mixed. First there is the "great crowd" being gathered by Jesus' town-by-town ministry (8:4), and then there are his disciples, who (as described above) include the Twelve but who also include the larger group of men and women who are following him. The story is fairly simple. A "sower" sows seed: Luke takes Mark's opening line (Mark 4:3) and enhances the alliteration (*exēlthen ho **sp**eirōn tou **sp**eirai ton **sp**oron auton*) to give a little more punch to the opening, and, as we will see, to focus our minds on this one action in particular.

In Luke's version, the sower sows "his seed, and in his sowing, one [part] fell by [or upon] the path and was trampled down, and the birds of the air gobbled it down." One way of reading the parable is to take it as a description of ordinary processes; this was the great contribution of Joachim Jeremias, whose book *The Parables of Jesus* still influences many Gospel interpreters. Jeremias proposed that the farmer in this parable sows first, then turns the seed under, so that what looks like wasteful seeding is really standard farming practice.[5] Jeremias may or may not have been correct in his description of what a first-century Galilean farmer normally did; the evidence is mixed.[6] But what is more to the point, Luke, following Mark, calls the actor in the parable a "sower," rather than a farmer or a landowner. The central character is not a farmer, and Luke only wants the readers to think about this one specific action, leaving all the other necessary steps for crop growing, cultivating, and harvesting to the side.

So the sower sows, and as a result of his sowing, one part of the seeds gets trampled (*katepatēthē*; note the *kat-* prefix) and gobbled (*katephagen*, same prefix). Here Luke expands upon Mark's narrative a little, adding the stomping feet—whose feet? The sower's? The crowd's? "Another part fell down [*katepesen*] upon the rock, and as it grew, it withered because there was no moisture." Here

The Parable of the Sower in the *Gospel of Thomas*

 The *Gospel of Thomas* is a collection of 114 sayings of Jesus. It was written in Greek and then translated into Coptic; some Greek fragments survive, but the majority of the text is available only in Coptic. Scholars are divided on whether it depends on the canonical Gospels or is independent of them. Thomas's version of the Sower goes like this:

> Jesus said: See, the sower went out, he filled his hand, he threw. Some seeds fell on the road; the birds came, they gathered them. Others fell on the rock and did not strike root in the earth and did not produce ears. And others fell on the thorns; they choked the seed and the worm ate them. And others fell on good earth; and it brought forth good fruit; it bore sixty per measure and one hundred twenty per measure.

A. Guillaumont et al., eds., *The Gospel According to Thomas: Coptic Text Established and Translated* (New York: Harper and Row, 1959), 7.

Van Gogh's *The Sower*

Vincent van Gogh (1853–1890). *The Sower*. 1888. Rijksmuseum Kroeller-Mueller, Otterlo, The Netherlands. (Credit: Erich Lessing/Art Resource, NY)

Luke prunes Mark substantially, cutting out Mark's detailed explanation for why and how the rocky seeds perish. Luke's seeds die from lack of moisture—an interesting feature to which we return in a bit. "And another part fell in the midst of thorns, and as they grew up together, the thorns choked it." Bummer. Luke edits Mark by leaving out a statement about the weedy seeds ceding no fruit. The overall result in these first three stages is a tighter story, with few details of setting or atmosphere to distract us from the plot: sower sowing, seeds falling, seeds dying. It puts one in mind of nature shows where the piranhas swarm the water buffalo or the great white sharks shoot out of the water to chomp the seals in one great bite. Nature red in tooth and claw; seeds are sown, seeds die, life is hard. Does the sower care that some of *his* seeds die? Do the seeds feel regret for a life they never experienced? There is no emotion in this parable; no sorrow over the loss of seeds nor, for that matter, joy over the harvest in the next verse.

After going 0 for 3, part of the seed "'fell into good earth, and growing it produced fruit one hundred fold.' And having said these things, he said, 'Let the one with ears to hear, hear.'" Commentators on the parables debate whether we are to take the hundred-fold yield as miraculous, remarkable, or ordinary. In Genesis 26:12 Isaac "sowed [*espeiren*] in that land and in that same year he reaped barley one hundred fold, and the Lord blessed him." The hundred-fold harvest is part of God's blessing, but that does not make it necessarily miraculously abundant. Instead, the parable's ending in a good, but not outrageously good, harvest is more in line with the dispassionate tone of its first three parts. Certainly, God brings the good harvest; but just as certainly, God can tell you that if you sow seed, some of that seed will be foot-trampled, bird-gobbled, drought-withered, and thorn-choked. Does God cause that, too? [Some Seeds Die—Is that Fair?]

If we only had the parable and not its interpretation, what might we make of it? The structure of the parable makes you notice that the sower sows his seed, and that it—the seed—falls either to death or to life, without further interference from the sower. Thus far, it is Jesus who has been ministering—preaching, teaching, healing, spreading the good news of the kingdom from town to town and village to village. When he takes an invitation to a Pharisee's house, the inquiring reader might wonder why, given that the Pharisees have not been particularly open; and when the Pharisee proves to be a dry, prickly host—no water for his feet, no embrace, no oil for his head—the reader might think Jesus is wasting his time. But then, from the same soil, a woman of that city comes to soak Jesus' feet with her tears and her perfume as she soaks in his words of forgiveness. Simon the Pharisee needs no help from Jesus: is he a rock, or what? But the woman, good soil that she is, even provides her own rainfall. The Twelve, including at least one Rock and one thorn, are with Jesus, thus far passive and inactive; but the women are already bearing fruit, ministering from their possessions. We might then take the parable as interpretation of Jesus' ministry thus far, and as a prediction of what will happen with the town-by-town and village-by-village sweep; these great

Some Seeds Die—Is that Fair?

 The example of losing some seeds during planting is found in 2 Esdras (*4 Ezra*) 8:37-62. Ezra asks God to bless the righteous and not punish them for the sins of the wicked. God (through an angel) replies that he is on the right track: "For just as the farmer sows many seeds in the ground and plants a multitude of seedlings, and yet not all that have been sown will come up in due season, and not all that were planted will take root; so also those who have been sown in the world will not all be saved" (2 Esd 8:41). Ezra complains that his is not a fair analogy:

If the farmer's seed does not come up, because it has not received your rain in due season, or if it has been ruined by too much rain, it perishes. But people, who have been formed by your hands and are called your own image because they are made like you, and for whose sake you have formed all things—have you also made them like the farmer's seed? Surely not, O Lord above! But spare your people and have mercy on your inheritance, for you have mercy on your own creation. (2 Esd 8:43-45)

crowds may look impressive, but we should not expect them to persist.

The disciples—including the Twelve, but also including many others in Luke—ask Jesus what this parable might be. Note that Luke omits Mark 4:13, which comments on the disciples' lack of comprehension; in Luke's version, they ask for an explanation and he gives it. Otherwise, Luke stays pretty close to Mark. "To you [plural, meaning to the disciples] it has been given [by God, that is] to know the mysteries [or secrets] of the kingdom of God, but to the rest—in parables, so that 'seeing they may not see and hearing they may not understand.'" Luke omits the verb that connects "to the rest" with "in parables," leaving us to supply something. The NRSV has "I speak," but the first part of the verse is not about what Jesus does, but what God does. If God has given the disciples the ability to penetrate the mysteries of Jesus' teaching, then what "the rest" lack is God-given comprehension. Of course, the disciples have the gift but still do not understand the parable until Jesus explains it. So having the gift does not mean that one comprehends everything, but that one is capable of being taught; the others, lacking the gift, can look and listen but never really comprehend.

We've been on this ground before. At the synagogue in Nazareth, the crowd hears the words of the prophet fulfilled in their ears, but then they want to kill the messenger. The Pharisees observe him doing miracles and can be amazed (5:26), but they still conclude that because he is a friend to tax collectors and sinners, he is a glutton and a drunkard. Simon the Pharisee can see neither Jesus as a true prophet nor the woman as a grateful penitent. They would all be examples of Lukan characters who can look without ever seeing. The disciples of John, watching Jesus do miracles and then being sent back to report on what they had seen and heard, are on the knife's edge of decision. Will they understand what they see? Blessed are they if they can avoid stumbling over Jesus, blind guides leading one another straight into the ditch.

In 8:11-15, Luke trims Mark's explanation of the parable (Mark 4:13-20). Luke omits the rebuke of the disciples' failure to understand (Mark 4:13), the identification of the sower (Mark 4:14), and the reference to persecution on account of the word (Mark 4:17). But Luke also adds words here and there, sowing seeds of his own into the minds of the readers, to make the interpretation better fit the intent of his Gospel.

"This is the parable": this is the way Luke wants his readers to think about it, in other words. Practically speaking, that cannot preclude other readings of the parable, since readings of narratives always change according to readers and their contexts. But what follows is Luke's take on it. "The seed is the word of God": so far in Luke, the word of God has been delivered by the angel Gabriel, Mary, Zechariah, Simeon, John the Baptist, Jesus, and anonymous crowds who pass along the "word" that Jesus was healing people (5:15) and that he was God's prophet (7:16-17). Neither disciples nor apostles have spread the word yet, but that will change in the next two chapters. So in Luke's reading, the sower need not be identified; once you know that the seed is the word, then anyone who spreads the word plays the role of the sower.

"Those on (or by) the path are those who hear; then the devil comes and takes the word from their hearts, lest they should be saved by believing." The clearest example in Luke of someone like this would be Judas Iscariot, who was called and empowered by Jesus, but because Satan entered his heart, he plotted with the chief priests and temple officers about how to hand Jesus over (22:3-6). In Luke's theology, Satan has extensive power to possess people, causing illness and erratic behavior. The Twelve, when they are sent out, are assigned authority over demons (9:1), and the seventy-two who are sent out report great success over demons (10:17). But this power was not limited to Jesus' disciples (11:19), nor was an exorcism a once-for-all event; Jesus said that a person could be exorcised and then reinfested (11:24-26). At the Last Supper, after Satan had possessed Judas, Jesus tells Peter and the rest that his prayers were protecting them from Satan's attack on them. In Luke's narrative world, then, the image of Satan snatching the gospel from an inquirer's heart is not just a metaphor.

Following the lead of theologians like Walter Wink, modern interpreters may appreciate Luke's understanding of Satan by reflecting on the power of the powers-that-be in our world. [Corporate Evil] It is not difficult to imagine a scenario like this: a young person in your congregation goes on a mission trip to do hands-on ministry to the desperately poor in some part of the world. While there, the youth is angered by American consumerism and how our economic/military/political power conspires with normal human selfishness to produce the conditions for hunger, poverty, disease, etc. The youth comes back full of plans to change the world. What happens when he/she gets back home, turns on the TV, opens the closet or the

Corporate Evil

We go about our lives largely oblivious to the demon, kissing our children before school, patting the dog, being polite to the bus driver. We are sane, civilized, perhaps a bit too given to violence and sadism on TV, but by common national consent still the most genial people on the face of the globe. We do not see that the demonic has been installed at the heart of national policy. The nation (administration, Congress, armed forces, CIA) carries out for us the dirty work required to maintain American political and economic dominance in the world. Most of us would rather not know the bloody tale of deeds performed on our behalf. We are content to be beneficiaries.

Walter Wink, *Unmasking the Powers* (Philadelphia: Fortress, 1986), 52.

fridge, starts to IM with friends? How long until the powers gobble down every bit of that passion to change?

"Those upon the rock are they who, when they hear, receive the word with joy, but they have no root; they believe for a short time and then fall away in a time of testing/temptation." Perhaps Peter is the best example in Luke, since we know the story of his falling away "in a time of testing." The same word in Greek means both "temptation," implying evil intent behind the choice offered, and "testing," which can be a way to characterize how God stretches our faith. In Peter's case, although Jesus predicts his apostasy, Jesus also says that his failure is connected to Satan's attacks on him, and that after he has repented from his failure, he should help to restore the other disciples (22:31-32). In Luke's theology, a person can be in Jesus' movement and fall away and then be restored, meaning that the parable's plot line is not the only way to imagine these seeds' fate.

"And the part that fell into the weeds—these are those who hear and, as they go about their life, are choked by cares and riches and pleasures of life and do not bear mature fruit." The Gospel has many examples of this sort of failure. Three would-be disciples in 9:57-62 are prevented from maturing by the needful things of home and family responsibilities. The rich man of 18:18-25 is prevented by his wealth, as are the Lukan Pharisees, who are "lovers of money" (16:14). The rich men of 12:13-21 and 16:19-31 both love the pleasures that come from wealth too much to do the right thing. And the rather spectacular example of Ananias and Sapphira (Acts 5:1-11) is meant to say that possessiveness, evil in and of itself, can lead one to do something so foolish as to try to lie to the Spirit of God, with fatal results.

"And the part [that fell] in the good soil, these are they who, hearing the word with a fine, good heart hold onto it and bear fruit with patience." Luke uses two words for "good" to describe the heart that hears the word and keeps it; both emphasize the "integrity" side of "good," like a "good" tree that produces "good" fruit. These ideal hearers listen and then construct their lives around what they hear, and in time, bear fruit. "Patience" is meant to indicate that life is not always easy, nor the results of a life of integrity immediately obvious. Luke's examples here would include Mary, who hears a hard word from God but accepts it and bears all that comes her way. In Luke, she sticks with the word God has given her, clear through until she becomes a part of the first church in Acts.

There are a couple of interesting switches from parable to interpretation. First, in the parable, the seeds fall here and there, and have no choice in the matter, so that when the rocky seeds wither and the weedy seeds are choked, the reader's first thought is not, "Bad seed! You should have been more careful." But the interpretation makes the rocky and weedy places into metaphors for poor decisions; falling away under temptation and getting drawn away by riches are both morally reprehensible. The seeds don't just fall, they fall away, and no one would blame the seed-sower—the preacher of the word of God—for the death of a seed who chooses to live among the weeds or who refuses to develop a deeply rooted faith. Second, because the parable begins with the sower, it can serve as a boost for the minister's morale. Sure, not so many people respond when they hear the word. But some do, so don't give up. But the interpretation mostly works as a cautionary tale: watch out for the devil, yield not to temptation, don't be choked by riches, and your life will bear fruit.

The tone of warning continues into 8:16-18, which amplifies the seeing and hearing theme woven into this whole section. Luke follows Mark in putting these verses immediately after the interpretation of the sower, but Matthew separates the material into four bits and puts them in four different contexts. One could therefore take the separate parts individually, as Matthew has done, and read them in many different ways; Luke repeats the lamp saying at 11:33-36, and the hidden/revealed saying at 12:1-3, and in both cases the meaning is slightly different than here. In this context, these verses appear to conclude Jesus' answer to the disciples' question about the meaning of the parable of the sower, and so we will read them that way.

The illustration of the lamp works off what was customary in Luke's world. Lamps for indoor use burned oil (olive oil, mostly, with salt added to make the flame brighter), and ranged from simple clay bowls with pinched corners to hold the wick to decorative pieces shaped more like a shallow teapot, with spouts, handles, and designs on the body. None of them put out much light, and so the examples Luke gives—putting the lamp inside a vessel or under a bed—are meant to be obviously absurd. Why go to the trouble and expense of lighting a lamp and then put it where it does no good? Instead, one puts a lamp in a place where it can be visible. Poorer homes probably put the lamp on a table or in a niche in the wall, or hung the lamp from a chain; archaeologists have found decorative iron stands of the sort Luke mentions, some made to stand on the floor and lift the lamp to eye level, while others were

Lamps and Lampstands

A lamp purchased in the Holy Land. It is similar to lamps used in first-century Palestine.

(Credit: David Claassen, iStock.com)

Lampstand

(Credit: Kelsey Museum of Archaeology)

only 3–4 inches high and were intended for tabletops. Luke's assumption that anyone would use a stand probably tells us something about the audience he has in mind.

The purpose of the lamp, according to 8:16, is "so that those who enter may see the light." Not really—Matthew's "and it gives light to all in the house" is more accurate, since lamps are to illumine other things, not to attract the gaze of the visitors. Luke's version sets up a connection between 8:16 and 8:4, where a great crowd is gathering town by town and coming out to Jesus. Jesus, Luke has said, is God's dawn breaking, giving light to those in darkness (1:78-79), and Jesus has literally done that by giving sight to the blind (7:21-22). Metaphorically Jesus has also illumined others by sharing the word of God, and has warned his followers to beware of following a blind guide (6:39). Thus, we are probably supposed to read 8:16 as a comment on Jesus' ministry so far, and as an explanation in advance for his motives in sending out the apostles and the larger group of disciples. Even if many do not respond to the word, for the reasons given in the parable and its explanation, and even if spreading the word puts the sower in danger (that will become apparent in a few chapters), Jesus in any event cannot keep it hidden. Like Jeremiah's image of fire in the bones making silence impossible, the image of the lamp here is meant to say that one cannot keep the gospel a secret.

The next verse continues this thought: "For there is nothing hidden that will not become visible, nothing covered up that will not surely become known and come into visibility." The terms "hidden" and "covered" connote intent, the act of putting something out of sight and trying to keep others from seeing it.[7] These two words are matched by three versions of "hidden things will be exposed": *phaneron genēsetai*, "it will become visible"; *gnōsthē*, "it will be made known"; and *eis phaneron elthē*, "it may come into visibility." The passive voice of the first two make one think of the action of God—by God's hand or God's will secrets will always be revealed; this is the warning in 12:1-3, where what is covered is the hypocrisy of the Pharisees, which God will reveal in judgment. Here, we might think more of the way in which Jesus' message and ministry cannot be hidden. Even when Jesus commands the leper to keep quiet, "the word about him went around all the more" (5:15). We may also think about Jesus' promise to the disciples in 8:10: it has been given to you (by God) to know the mystery of the kingdom of God. Everyone else will never see and never hear, but to the disciples, no divine mystery will be held hidden for long.

Verses 16-17 also work as warnings to Jesus' followers. If Jesus cannot keep a lid on the spread of the word, then Jesus' followers should not even try. Jesus' mission to the villages of Galilee will be matched by the mission of the Twelve and then by the mission of the seventy, and then in Acts by the sending of missionaries in all directions. Those followers who might not be too excited about taking the message to potentially hostile audiences should be warned that they will not be able to keep the faith a secret.

Verse 18 is clearly a warning: "So beware of how you listen; for whoever has, it will be given to him/her; whoever does not have, even what he/she seems to have will be snatched from him/her." If you cut off the "whoever has/whoever has not" part, it can be understood as a sardonic comment on the life of the poor, on par with "the rich get richer." But the "be careful how you listen" introduction means that the having/not having is about possession of the word, and this in turn connects us to 8:15: "these are they who, hearing the word with a fine, good heart, hold onto it." Those who, with patience, hear the word and live it out will be given more—more understanding, more of the word from God. But those who listen poorly will lose what they seem to have. Verse 18, in other words, is in this context a more cryptic version of the parable of the wise and foolish builders (6:46-49).

Verses 19-21 now return to the setting that began the whole section, with Jesus teaching and attracting a crowd. "His mother and his brothers" came to him, but the crowds got there first, and prevented his family from "joining" him; *syntynchanō* means to come together, not just "reach" as the NRSV translates. The report to Jesus—from the crowd?—puts the family's purpose a little differently, stating that they wish to *see* him. Jesus, however, agrees more with the narrator in v. 19 than with the anonymous voice of v. 20, because he treats his family as disciples: "My mother and my brothers are they who hear and do the word of God." They do see him, in other words, and hear him, too. Mark's version of this scene has Jesus choose the crowd over his family (Mark 3:31-35), which has the effect of naming Jesus' followers as his "fictive family," with the sort of tight-knit, closer-than-family bonds that come from being part of a small, dedicated movement. Luke's version of the saying also means that those who hear and do the will of God are Jesus' family, and in Acts 1–4, Luke shows us how the first believers live like family, sharing everything with each other. But in Luke's view, the core of that first congregation, Jesus' fictive family, included Jesus' actual family, his mother and his brothers (Acts 1:14). So Luke edits Mark in such a way that Jesus can create the larger family without rejecting his mother and brothers.

In 8:1-21, Jesus dispenses the word of God like a sower broadcasting seed, spreading it all over. The parable of the sower and its interpretation teaches us not to expect too much mature fruit from this crowd; many will listen, but few will understand. But some do. So far, the best examples of seeds growing in fruitful soil are the women who serve as deacons, using their resources, and Jesus' mother and brothers, who are held up by Jesus as ideal disciples. As for the rest—the Twelve, the other disciples, and the members of the crowd—they are warned that those who listen casually to Jesus without practicing his teachings will see their faith gobbled down by Satan or dried up in a time of temptation or choked out by life's cares and pleasures. If you fail to listen carefully—putting what you hear into action—you stand to lose what you think you have. And if you try to hide what you have been given by God—the word, and your ability to understand the will of God—then you will be as useless as a light under a bed, and the truth will come out anyway.

Calming the Storm, 8:22-25

This is Luke's second boat story; in the first, he used Peter's boat as a teaching platform and then ordered his host to put out his nets. On that day, the boat was filled with fish and began to sink; on this day, it is ordinary lake water that threatens the safety of the sailors. Mark, Luke's source for this story, has three boat scenes, all of which show both Jesus' power and the disciples' lack of faith and comprehension (Mark 4:35-41, parallel to this Lukan story; Mark 6:45-52 and 8:14-21 have no parallel in Luke).

Luke intensifies the connections already present in Mark between Jesus' miracle and the story of Jonah. The storm comes up with a big wind and great waves, and the boat "is in peril" (same verb in Luke and the LXX text of Jonah). The central character is asleep, and the sailors are rightly worried that they will "perish" (again, same verb). After the water calms, the sailors are afraid. The parallels only serve to highlight the differences, making it clear that the Gospel story is an inversion of Jonah 1. The disciples are saved, not by throwing their prophet overboard, but by his command of the storm. The storm comes, not to force the prophet into obedience, since he is already following God's path; in the Gospel story, it's the sailors who fail to have faith, so perhaps we should ask whether the storm was meant to expose their lack of faith and comprehension.

Many biblical texts use the images of strong winds and high waves as metaphors. Wherever the word *lailaps* (whirlwind or gale) appears in the LXX, it connotes God's judgment: "[the ungodly] shall be as chaff before the wind or as dust caught up by the whirlwind" (Job 21:18 LXX; see also the LXX texts of Wis 5:22-23 and Jer 32:32). The word Luke uses for the waves (*klydōni*) is used to signify the temptation presented by a "strange woman" (Prov 23:34), human passions generally (4 Macc 7:5, 15:31), and the depression experienced by a wicked ruler just before his death (1 Macc 6:11). Not these words precisely, but the word picture of the waves of the sea is often a metaphor for sickness (Ps 69:1-2) or death (Ps 69:15). And since it is God, either through direct intervention or through the Torah, who rescues persons from judgment, temptation, the passions, sickness, and death, we can presume that Luke's readers would understand this scene as a theophany:

Peace Be Still

Hanna Cheriyan Varghese. *Peace Be Still*. In Ron O'Grady, *Christ for All People* (Asian Christian Art Assn., 2001), 94.

Jesus, as God's Son, brings God's power to bear on a dangerous situation.

Luke treats the miracle as an exorcism, much as he did the healing of Peter's mother-in-law. Jesus "rebuked the wind and the waves of water, and they were silent and there was calm." The demons want to come out shouting, but he can silence them (4:21) and send them away. Some of the female disciples have themselves been "cured of evil spirits" (8:2-3), and Peter witnessed the rebuke of his mother-in-law's fever, so Jesus' ability to exorcise a storm should not have been a great surprise.

The response of the disciples is thus altogether curious. First, they wake Jesus: "Master, master, we perish!" Luke softens Mark's "Teacher, is it no concern to you that we perish?" His disciples are not sarcastic, but neither are they ideal believers at this moment; they do not call him κύριος (*kyrios*, "Lord"), but ἐπιστάτα (*epistata*, "Master"). Peter called Jesus this as he doubted whether throwing his nets in would do any good (5:5), and the ten lepers later called him this before he sent them on their way to be healed (17:13). It is not a term that connotes faith, and so we are not surprised to hear Jesus ask, "Where is your faith?" [Christ Calms the Disciples' Doubt]

Why is this curious? Well, consider who is in the boat. "Disciple" includes the Twelve, but also the larger group from which the Twelve were drawn. Maybe, as some commentators suggest, Luke is thinking only of the Twelve and Jesus fitting into one of the small fishing boats that were normal for the Lake of Galilee. [The Magdala Boat] But it is also possible that he means "disciple" to be broad and vague, so that any or all of Jesus' would-be followers are included. Peter, James, and John had already seen a miracle in a boat, and Peter at least had treated it as a theophany: "Depart from me, Lord, for I'm a sinner man." Luke has in this chapter been careful to note how disciples such as Mary Magdalene, Joanna, Susanna, and many other women had been "deaconizing" from their resources. Thus far in Luke, disciples have been successful followers of Jesus. In this story, however, they all take a step back.

Christ Calms the Disciples' Doubt

Cyril of Alexandria reads Jesus' rebuke of the disciples somewhat differently than this Commentary does: "When Christ calmed the storm, he also changed the faith of the holy disciples that was shaken along with the ship into confidence. He no longer permitted it to be in doubt. He worked a calm in them, smoothing the waves of their weak faith."

Commentary on Luke, Homily 43; cited in Arthur A. Just Jr., ed., *Luke* (ACCS: NT, vol. 3; Downer's Grove IL: Intervarsity Press, 2003), 136–37.

The Magdala Boat

In 1986, during a drought that lowered the level of the Sea of Galilee substantially, the wreck of a 1st-century fishing boat was discovered "buried in mud near ancient Magdala . . . . Nearly two thousand years ago, the dilapidated 8-by-26 foot boat was stripped of its usable parts and pushed offshore to sink" (Crossan and Reed, 85–86). The boat could have been handled by a crew of five, but was long enough to have carried as many as sixteen (Rousseau and Arav, 26–27).

John D. Crossan and Jonathan L. Reed, *Excavating Jesus* (San Francisco: HarperSanFrancisco, 2001).

John J. Rousseau and Rami Arav, *Jesus and His World* (Minneapolis: Fortress, 1995).

To put this in perspective, look at how various characters in Luke 4–8 have responded to Jesus' miracles:

- 4:22—The people in the synagogue at Nazareth, having heard of Jesus miracles and having heard Jesus preach, ask "Is this not Joseph's son?"
- 4:34, 41—Demons say, "I know who you are, the Holy One of God."
- 5:21, 26—Scribes and Pharisees say, "Who is this who speaks blasphemies?" until they see the miracle, and then say, "We have seen riddles today!"
- 7:16—The crowds, seeing miracles, say that Jesus is a great prophet.

So when the disciples in 8:25 say "Who, then, is this?" they are more like the Pharisees or the synagogue crowd; the demons and the crowds, at least, know who Jesus is without having to puzzle over it. "Who is this that the winds and the waters obey him" has a pretty clear answer—haven't they read the Torah? God makes paths in the trackless sea. God sends the storm to put Jonah in a corner, and then rescues him from drowning. God saves the authors of the lament psalms who say that illness or hard times have swept over them like the waves of the ocean. If Jesus can do this too, then he is the presence of God in their midst.

They fail their first big test, then, and Luke makes it a sort of broad-brush failure. It was not just the Twelve, but the disciples, who had their chance and whiffed. What would have counted as "faith" in that moment? That's always a dangerous way to read a story, since the ways it was not written are infinite, but just for a moment, let us speculate about what Luke presumes the correct response might have been. First, Luke may have thought that the disciples could have rebuked the storm themselves. After all, in just a few verses Jesus will give them authority over demons, and in a later episode he will show his disappointment in them when they cannot exorcise a demon without his help (9:41). And second, while Jesus elsewhere teaches the disciples to ask for what they need and trust that God will provide (11:9), and while the disciples do turn to him for help in their tight spot, their cry is not a request for help but a shriek of despair—"Master, master, we perish!" Matthew's version of this is more an orthodox prayer: "Save us, Lord, we are perishing!"

So they fail—where is your faith? who is this?—but Jesus does not throw them overboard or send them back home as incorrigibles. On this day, they cannot do what he expects, but on other

The True Nature of the Miracle

I don't know about Will Rogers, but I grew up deciding the world was nothing but a sad, dangerous junk pile heaped with shabby geegaws, the bullies who peddled them, and the broken-up human beings who worked the line. Some good people came along, and they softened my opinion. So I'm open to any evidence they can show me that God's not asleep at the wheel, barreling blind down the highway with all us dumb scared creatures screaming in the back seat.

Michael Malone, *Time's Witness* (New York: Little, Brown, and Co., 1989), 3.

days they will. Those two things—Jesus' patient presence and the disciples' eventual progress in imitating Christ—are much more important miracles than the calming of a storm. [The True Nature of the Miracle]

Legion, 8:26-39

Luke draws this story from Mark and keeps most of it, including many of the details of the demoniac's plight; we begin our examination by looking at a few specific instances where Luke changed Mark or kept his source intact.

Geography

The manuscript tradition is divided on the place name: Gergasa, Gadara, or Gerasa. The same options also appear at Mark 5:1, and are notoriously hard to figure out. Gadara was a town in the Decapolis, located about six miles southeast of the coast of the Sea of Galilee. Gerasa, also part of the Decapolis, was more than thirty miles from the lake in the same direction. If the original text of Mark said "region of the Gerasenes," then perhaps some later scribe, troubled by the thirty-mile jog the pigs took in order to drown themselves in the sea, changed it to "region of the Gadarenes" in order to make it more plausible.[8] Luke has almost certainly copied Mark, having no better geographical information (witness 17:11 and the "region between Samaria and Galilee"). So as we begin the episode, there is a certain amount of suspension of disbelief involved; but if we, like most of Luke's readers, have only a vague knowledge of the location of Gerasa, the distance to the lake is not an interpretive issue.

Ethnicity

Neither Mark nor Luke clearly labels the demoniac, the swineherds, or the townspeople as Jews or Gentiles. Again, we know that Gerasa was part of the Decapolis, an originally independent confederation of ten cities that in the first century was, like everything else in Palestine, under Roman control. The population of most of the cities was mostly Gentile, but would Luke or Luke's readers have known that? A safer bet is to think that any ancient reader would know that Jews did not eat pork or raise pigs, and would have assumed that the swineherds and townspeople were Gentile. Probably, then, Luke and Luke's readers also assumed that the demoniac was Gentile, but since the narrator makes no special point about this being the first instance of Jesus being a light to the Gentiles (2:32), we should not press it hard, either.

Social Location

Luke specifies that the man was "from the city," even though he had lived for a long time among the tombs and was driven by demons into deserted places. By adding this bit to Mark's account, Luke makes it clear that the city to which Jesus sends the man is the man's place of residence. Luke also states that the man had been naked for a long time; perhaps that is implied in Mark's account, but Luke makes it clear. Luke also has, "and he did not live in a house but among the grave-markers." This man, like Jesus, is homeless (9:58), and like Jesus and the disciples, he has no extra clothes (9:3).

Character

The demons often "seized him," writes Luke, using a verb that he uses twice in Acts to mean "arrest" (6:12) or "compel with bodily force" (19:29). Although the vocabulary differs, we should remember other "seizures" thus far in Luke: the crowd at Nazareth "threw him out of the city and led him up to the edge of the hill upon which their city is built, so that they could throw him off the cliff" (4:29), while the crowd at Capernaum wanted to hold Jesus to prevent his leaving them (4:42). Legion's demonic captors are at war, seemingly, with the would-be human captors: the demons seize him—successfully, it seems; the humans "put him in chains and fetters as a way of imprisoning him," but "breaking the bonds, he was driven by the demons into deserted places." Jesus chooses to withdraw to deserted places when pressed by crowds, and the Spirit led him there to be tempted. Jesus' would-be human captors also don't succeed until the very end of the Gospel. Is Legion, then, Jesus' opposing number, driven by demons instead of by the Spirit—a sort of inverse Christ-figure? [Legion as Metaphor for Delivery from Despair]

Legion as Metaphor for Delivery from Despair

Veasey tries to get Inman to talk, but he is silent. You're about as bad off as Legion, I believe, Veasey finally said. And he told Inman the story of the man whose wounded spirit Jesus comforted. How Jesus found him naked, fleeing mankind, hiding in the wilderness, gnashing his teeth on tomb rocks, cutting himself with stones. Turned wild by some ill fortune. What few thoughts Legion had just rampant.

Always, night and day, he was in the mountains and in the tombs, crying and wailing like a dog, Veasey said. And Jesus heard of him and went to him and straightened him right out quicker than a dose of salts running through you. Legion went home a new self.

Charles Frazier, *Cold Mountain* (New York: Atlantic Monthly, 1997), 123.

Plot

Like Mark, Luke has Legion cry to Jesus first, even though "in real life" Jesus has the first word. The inversion of the actual order of things makes the reader's first impression that this miracle follows the general pattern established early and often in Luke, that almost all of Jesus' miracles are done in response to a request. In fact, once you realize that Jesus initiated the contact, you connect this miracle with the only one so far where that was the case—the raising of the widow's son at Nain, where Jesus encounters a situation and acts rather than responding to a request. Perhaps the reason is the same in both cases: Jesus acts on his own because no one intercedes for the needy person.

In "real life," then, we are to imagine Jesus coming to Legion and commanding the demons to come out, and then Legion responding, "What concern am I to you, Jesus, Son of God most High? I beg you, do not torture me!" Luke sticks closely to Mark's wording here, and we presume that the voice is the demon's, and not the man's. Elsewhere, it is the demons that come out saying "you are the son of God!" (4:34, 41), and in this story the demons are concerned about being sent into the abyss (8:31). We will explore Luke's understanding of demons shortly, but for the moment, let's notice that the demons know who Jesus truly is— something that the man by himself would not have known—and that they fear Jesus' authority will lead to their hurt. In fact, Jesus in his ministry is stronger than Satan's kingdom, attacking and overpowering him and stripping his armor from him (11:22). The demons have good reason to be afraid!

Thus, it is the demons that respond in terror to Jesus' command to come out, the demons that answer "Legion" when Jesus asks their name, and the demons that ask Jesus to allow them to enter the pigs. We still have not heard from the man—we don't know his name, how he feels about what is happening, or what he thinks of Jesus. Like the widow, the man with the Legion of demons is in a vulnerable place in his world; as Mark Twain once remarked, a naked man has surprisingly little influence in society, and this one is alternatively imprisoned by the citizens of his town or driven into inhospitable places by the demons. Jesus "had compassion" for the widow and gave her son back to her; the narrator tells us nothing about Jesus' emotions in this story, but we do find him restoring the man to his clothes and to his right mind and, eventually, to his community. This is a story, then, of liberation and restoration.

Ministers often find themselves confronted by persons with mental illnesses, whose needs for treatment far surpass what one can typically offer in an office counseling session, and whose issues far exceed the counseling expertise one normally gains in seminary. Evidence of multiple personality disorder, or anything approaching that level of psychological complexity, should lead caring ministers to take immediate steps to put the person into the care of qualified medical professionals. The issue is not whether you, the minister, believe in demonic possession, nor whether God could miraculously heal the troubled soul through your intervention. It is not an either-or choice; treatment of mental illness can combine bio-, psycho-, or neuro-medicine with faith-directed ministry, thereby reducing suffering and increasing the odds for recovery.

In Jesus' day, some Jews—perhaps many Jews—attributed many of life's ills to demonic attack or possession. *First Enoch* illustrates how some Jews—perhaps many Jews—in the Second Temple period accounted for the existence of evil spirits who caused disease. *First Enoch* begins with Genesis 6:1-4, the story of how angels lusted and consorted with women, resulting in a race of giants; *1 Enoch* goes on to say that these wicked angels taught humans all sorts of harmful things, and that the giants themselves produced evil spirits who corrupt and torment humans endlessly (*1 En.* 6–16). On Judgment Day, however, the fallen angels, the giants, and the demons will all be rounded up and put into "a deep pit with heavenly fire on its pillars" (*1 En.* 18:11–19:3). While Luke never cites *1 Enoch*, his understanding of demons as a major source for illness and disability, the demons' fearful reaction in this story, and 11:24-26, which pictures demons as restless and always on the lookout for a human to infest, are all compatible with *1 Enoch*'s cosmology.

Everyone in the ancient world understood that Jews do not eat pork. So the desire of unclean spirits for the herd of swine would have made sense to Luke's readers—unclean spirits would naturally choose an unclean animal if they get thrown out of a human. The crazed behavior of the porkers is probably meant to convey to the reader the true sense of the burden this anonymous man had been carrying: look what happened to all those pigs—no wonder he ran around naked in the graveyard!

There is also the overtone in this story that the name "Legion" created. What person in ancient times hearing this story would not have made the connection to the Roman legions who possessed Palestine, and much of the rest of the Mediterranean world, often making life as miserable for the general public as these demons did for their victim? That the soldiers of the legions used their power to extort money from the general public was a fact of life (3:14). That they also were from time to time the sharp end of Rome's rule, rounding up enemies of Rome and crucifying them or destroying villages deemed dangerous to Rome, was no secret either. So the idea of the legion cowering in fright before Jesus, then dismissed into pigs that drown themselves, must have been a pleasant one for many of Luke's readers.

The Gerasenes are afraid when they hear what has happened; the detail about the swineherds fleeing and preaching this "in the city and in the fields" reminds us a bit of the responses of the shepherds to the birth of Jesus and of the friends and relations to the naming of John the Baptist. The Gerasenes come and see the man seated at Jesus' feet—to learn, probably—clothed and sane, and their reaction is not joy, but fear. Maybe we are to presume that they are scared because of the dead pigs and the loss of income, but their fear comes when they see that Jesus can release and restore a man that they could not keep locked up. They all ask him to leave their region, which he does, true to his instructions in 9:5 and 10:11. [Why Object to a Miracle?]

The newly healed man wants "to be with him," but Jesus refuses, and instead makes this man the first person sent out to preach on Jesus' behalf. Think about that: in 6:13-16, the apostles are named, but are given no commission; at 8:1, they are with Jesus, but do not have an active role; at 8:39, with the apostles nowhere in sight, Jesus commissions some anonymous former demoniac to go and tell, which he does; and then, in 9:1-6, we finally get a set of instructions for what apostles are supposed to do. "Return to your house," says Jesus, "and tell the story of the things God has done for you." You will recall the house from 8:27; he has not lived in a house for a long time, but apparently he still owns one, and his commission is not to give up his house to follow Jesus, but to return to it and spread the good news in his city.

Paul Simon's song "I Am A Rock" creates the unforgettable image of the solitary person in perhaps self-imposed exile because of hurts suffered at the hands of others. The song ends "And a rock feels no pain/and an island never cries."[9] But people, people who seek the safety of isolation or who have it thrust upon them because of mental illness or social awkwardness, do suffer from it. As Veasey tells Inman (see [Legion as Metaphor for Delivery from Despair]), "Jesus heard of him and went to him and straightened him right out quicker

---

Why Object to a Miracle?

In Leif Enger's novel *Peace Like a River*, the protagonist's father heals the face of the man, his supervisor, who has just fired him for no good reason: "He roared a few words, and Dad became a former janitor." But then the father puts his hand on the supervisor's face:

It was the oddest little slap you ever saw. Holgren quailed back a step, hunching defensively, but Dad turned and walked off; and the superintendent stood with his fingers strangely awonder over his chin, cheeks, and forehead. Then I saw that his bedeviled complexion—that face set always at a rolling boil—had changed. I saw instead skin of a healthy tan, a hale blush spread over cheekbones, that suddenly held definition; and above his eyes the shine of constant seepage had vanished, and light lay at rest upon his brow.

Listen: There are easier things than witnessing a miracle of God. For his part, Mr. Holmgren didn't know what to make of it; he looked horrified; the new peace in his hide didn't sink deep; he covered his face from view and slunk from the cafeteria.

Leif Enger, *Peace Like a River* (New York: Grove, 2001), 79–80.

than a dose of salts running through you."[10] We should not expect instant cures like Legion's, but we who follow Jesus should work to bring healing and restoration to situations of deep pain and isolation.

Life and Death, 8:40-56

Clyde Edgerton's novel *Lunch at the Piccadilly* introduces us to the memorable L. Ray Flowers, a preacher who "seems to have a little personality—I guess that means he's a Pentecostal"[11] and who is temporarily at the Rosehaven Nursing Home to receive therapy for his bad knee. In conversation with two women residents, he comes up with what he considers a revolutionary idea:

> . . . a worldwide movement that will work to makes churches and nursing homes interchangeable. Think about it: why should Christians, or anybody else, go to church on Sunday morning when they can go down the street to a nursing home and gladden these wrecks of old women lining the grim halls of nursing homes? . . . Look at all those ramps and empty rooms in every church in the nation—empty rooms all week long. Why shouldn't a few needy old people be staying there with church members taking care of them, in shifts? . . . This notion—this very simple idea—is where every religion on earth can intersect. Something every decent human being can believe in. I'm talking nursing homes interchangeable with synagogues, too, and temples, mosques, whatever else.[12]

Predictably, this scheme comes to pieces just as it comes to light. L. Ray is more than a little off-kilter, with a shady past; his first audience of female nursing home residents has no power, no influence, and only a slippery hold on reality; and the only person with real power in the story, the owner of the nursing home, decides L. Ray is a menace and has him evicted. But you can't help but admire the power of his idea to give life and relieve suffering among his small congregation of nursing-home porch-sitters: "Listen. Old people are still alive. Alive. Their corpuscles breathe and move like little tiny white things in tomato sauce. It's all any of us are given at the outset: life. It's all any of us lose: life."[13]

In this pericope, Luke mostly copies from Mark, but structures the story so that it connects with several other Lukan stories. First, it has Jesus healing a child and restoring her to her parents, like the raising of the widow's son, the healing of the epileptic boy, and (although the familial connection is different) the healing of the centurion's servant. Jairus's daughter, the widow's son, and the epileptic boy are only children; by the time Jesus gets to them, Jairus's daughter and the widow's son are both dead, and Jesus tells each of them to rise. The four episodes all tug at the hearts of Luke's readers, who know or can imagine how hard it is to lose a child; "don't be afraid," he tells Jairus, and "stop crying," he tells Jairus and his wife, just as he told the grieving widow at Nain. Here is Jesus, restoring life and exchanging sorrow for joy.

There is another thread, the plot element where a petitioner asks Jesus to do something; in this respect, the episode of Jairus's daughter is like the centurion's servant and the epileptic boy, but unlike the widow's son. Jairus's posture—on the ground before Jesus—makes him like the leper of 5:12 or the Gerasene demoniac (8:28). Jairus, as a "ruler" of a synagogue, could have sent others to ask Jesus to come, like the centurion, but instead he humbles himself before the Galilean prophet to ask sincerely for his help.

Yet in another way, Jairus is more like the sinful woman of 7:36-50 or Mary of Bethany in 10:38-42. Luke 8:40 tells us that the crowds "welcomed" and "were waiting expectantly" for Jesus, fulfilling temporarily the role of host. Jairus interrupts that welcome by his prostration at Jesus' feet, just as the sinful woman and Mary disturbed the dinner plans of Simon and Martha, who had each received Jesus. The crowd posed no initial barrier to Jairus's approach, but then, characteristically, inhibited Jesus' movement away from them to go minister to the needs of someone else.

All in all, then, this story is written so that we have a web of possible connections to other stories in our heads as the words flow over us. Even stronger, however, are the internal connections between the story of the twelve-year-old girl and the story of the woman with the twelve-year disease. Jairus asks Jesus to heal his daughter; Jesus calls the woman "daughter." "Your faith has saved you," he tells the woman, and tells the grieving father, "Have faith, and she will be saved." The woman tries to remain secret; Jesus orders the parents to keep their good news secret. And in both cases, a touch—the woman's grasp of Jesus' tassels and Jesus' touch on the girl's hand—brings healing.

Jairus's position as synagogue "ruler" (*archōn*) likely means that he was the patron of the local synagogue, more like the chairman of the board than like a worship leader. ["Ruler" of the Synagogue] In his need, he does not hesitate to bow down to Jesus to beg him for a favor. Jesus is completely willing to go to Jairus's house, and Jairus is

"Ruler" of the Synagogue

AΩ The Theodotus inscription (see [The Theodotus Inscription]) names an *archisynagogos* who gave to money to build the synagogue and who, like most patrons, then exercised some authority about its operation. Other texts seem to indicate that the *archon* was the leader of a group of elders who performed a whole range of leadership functions: "And then some priest who is present, or some one of the elders, reads the sacred laws to them, and interprets each of them separately till eventide."

Philo, *Hypothetica* 7.12.

equally willing, if not to say anxious, for Jesus to be there. There is, then, no hint of issues of impurity seeping into the text of the framing story; Jairus is not concerned about where Jesus has been and is not worried that Jesus may not have washed (cf. 11:38). No one in the story seems worried about being in the room with the dead girl, or worried about Jesus touching her.

In the same way, no one in the crowd seems concerned about the impurity of the woman with the flow of blood. As many commentators note, the phrase *en hrusei haimatos* is drawn from Leviticus 15:19-30. A woman's menstrual blood makes her unclean for seven days. Her uncleanness is contagious, spreading to everything upon which she sits or lies. Her husband, should he have sex with her, is either unclean for the remainder of her period and equally contagious (15:24), or guilty, along with the woman, of such an offense that they must both be expelled from the community (20:18). The latter, much more stringent ruling, seems not to have been enforced in Jesus' day, but to have been interpreted by the rabbis (and therefore, perhaps, by their predecessors the Pharisees) as a requirement for a sacrificial offering (*m. Niddah* 2:2, for example, which specifies one of the conditions under which an offering might be waived). [*m. Niddah* 2:2-3] Mishnah tractate *Niddah*, full of helpful case law for determining how far contamination has spread depending on when the woman discovered that her flow had begun, is probably an indication of how seriously some Jews in the Second Temple period tried to avoid becoming unclean through contact with a menstruating woman. The same tractate, however,

> **m. Niddah 2:2-3**
>
> If the blood [assumed to be menstrual blood] is found with him, both are unclean and liable to an offering. If it was found with her at the time itself, both are unclean and liable to an offering; but if it was found with her after a time, their uncleanness remains in doubt and they are exempt from an offering. How long is meant by "after a time"? Time enough for her to get down from bed and wash her "face"; if after this [she suffered a flow] she is deemed to have conveyed uncleanness during the preceding twenty-four hours; but she has not rendered unclean him that has connection with her. But the Sages agree with R. Akiba that if she observes a blood-stain she renders unclean him that has connection with her. [But see Akiba's ruling cited in the text of the commentary.]

gives lots of evidence that even very devout and observant Jews would sometimes (regularly?) find themselves unclean, needing to decide when precisely the uncleanness began and what else, beside the menstruant and her clothes, needed to be cleansed. A certain amount of latitude, then, was expected: "Women may always be assumed clean in readiness for their husbands. When men have come from a journey their wives may be assumed clean in readiness for them [*m. Niddah* 2:4]. . . . A woman once came to Rabbi Akiba and said to him, 'I have found a stain.' He said to her, 'Perhaps thou hast a wound in thee?' She said to him, 'Yea, but it has healed.' He said to her, 'Perhaps it may have opened again and bled?' She said to him, 'Yea.' And Rabbi Akiba declared her clean [8.3]."

Anyone who picked up secondary uncleanness from the woman or from her clothes or her chair or her bed was unclean until sundown. Then he or she could self-immerse in a stream or in the Lake of Galilee or in the local *miqveh* and be clean. The same rule applied to uncleanness transmitted by a woman who had an abnormal flow caused by disease (Lev 15:27). Anyone who touched the woman in Luke's story would have thereby become unclean, but the remedy was dunking oneself in the *miqveh* that evening—which one might have done anyway for other reasons. If one did nothing, one would remain unclean, but such a condition was not fatal, did not prevent daily prayers, and would have posed no "danger" to anyone else—that is, the secondary uncleanness is not itself contagious. Leviticus, in fact, does not prescribe and does not seem to presume any sort of quarantine or seclusion either for a menstruant or for a woman with an abnormally long flow. "Whoever touches her" is repeated in 15:19, 21-23, and 27, and as noted above, 15:24 addresses the issue of sexual contact between a menstruant and her husband.

Summing up: the woman with the flow would make others unclean by touch. She was certainly expected to keep herself away from the temple while she was in her condition. It is possible that some or most Jews considered synagogues to be holy spaces and would expect people to come in a state of cleanness; Josephus's account of the intentional pollution of the synagogue at Caesarea leans this way (*J. W.* 2.284-292), but Gospel accounts that place persons with unclean spirits in synagogue (Luke 4:33, for example) lean the other way. [Were Synagogues Considered Holy Spaces?] So maybe, in a real-live first-century Galilean village, this woman would have been excluded by common understanding from attending synagogue. Or maybe they would have included her so long as she sat alone; or maybe those who sat with her—her family, for example—would have visited the *miqveh* that night and prayed to God for her healing. We do not know.

Were Synagogues Considered Holy Spaces?

Now on the next day, which was the seventh day of the week, when the Jews were crowding apace to their synagogue, a certain man of Caesarea, of a seditious temper, got an earthen vessel and set it, with the bottom upward, at the entrance of that synagogue, and sacrificed birds. This thing provoked the Jews to an incurable degree, because their laws were affronted, and the place was polluted.

Josephus, *J.W.* 2.289.

So the woman is unclean. But notice how nobody in the Lukan narrative pays attention to that. She is in the crowd, behind Jesus, and grabs his tassels, and when Jesus wants to know who did it, Peter notes that the crowds are pressing in on him on all sides. In Luke's mind, the crowd is pushing to get as close to Jesus as possible—how can they do that if they are simultaneously trying to isolate a woman standing right behind him? And in v. 47, when she "realizes she cannot remain hidden," it is because she is blending into the crowd. They know who she is, perhaps, but Jesus does not.

Enough, you say, and perhaps it is. Enough, I hope, that New Testament commentators will cease writing, and biblical inter-preters in the church will cease treating this story as an example of Jesus liberating Jewish women from the demands of the purity codes:

- . . . the woman was excluded from the common life of the people because of purity regulations. By the measure of these remark-ably complex strictures which had the effect of effectively marginalizing the woman . . . Simply entering a crowd was there-fore a bold act of faith, perhaps born of desperation."[14]
- "She is untouchable, forbidden normal human contact (especially sexual contact), and excluded from religious services and cere-monies. If she has ever been married, she is almost certainly now divorced."[15]
- "Although her physical condition was not contagious, her ritual condition was, with the consequence that she had lived in isola-tion from her community these twelve years. . . . Just as the Gerasene demoniac had dwelled among the dead (v 27), so this woman exists outside the boundaries of the socially alive in her community."[16]

Most of this language is exaggeration, unsupported by Leviticus or *m. Niddah*, and highly unlikely to have been the case among poor Galileans. More to the point, it is highly unlikely that Luke, writing for a mostly Gentile audience, would have thought of this as an anti-purity story or would have expected his audience to hear it that way. Jewish purity rules and their applications were simply not an issue for most of Luke's audience.

But sickness and death—those were universal issues, close to the bone for everybody. In Luke's sandwiched story, illness strikes the twelve-year-old daughter of a synagogue leader with servants and prestige, and illness makes miserable the life of a grown woman who could find no cure with anyone.[17] In both cases, the illness drives the person to seek Jesus—Jairus, to beg for Jesus' favor; the woman, to act before asking. When Jesus stops and asks, "Who touched me?" the woman is afraid and tries to hide in the crowds. When the news comes, "Your daughter is dead; don't bother the teacher any longer," the father is afraid. It is even possible that Luke intends us to think that those mocking Jesus in 8:53 are Peter,

John, James, and the father and mother, indicating that Jairus had lost hope entirely. Jesus offers peace, salvation, hope, and life instead of fear and cynicism.

Luke's statement that Jesus knew that power had gone from him (8:46) reminds the reader of 5:17 ("the Lord's power was with him for healing") and 6:19 ("the whole crowd tried to touch him, because power was going out from him and healing everyone"). Luke's view is that Jesus has the Spirit's power (4:14) to do mighty deeds in God's name. In this chapter, we've seen Jesus rebuke a windstorm (8:11), order a legion of demons out of a man and into pigs (8:29-32), raise a young girl from the dead, and heal a woman's flow of blood. Rather than dwelling on how this power resides in Jesus, however, the text will turn immediately to how it is transferred to Jesus' twelve apostles (9:1) and then to seventy others (10:17-20). Jesus' power is not simply an aspect of being Son of God, but is part of being God's prophet—a role that can be filled by any dedicated disciple.

The pericope ends with the command to secrecy, familiar to readers of Mark but not so important to the plot of Luke. Earlier Jesus would not allow demons to reveal his identity (4:35, 41), and he ordered the leper he healed to stay mum (5:14). There's an ironic or fatalistic element in all these secrecy commands. Jesus orders the demons to be silent, but only after they come out shouting that he is Son of God (4:34, 41). He tells the former leper to tell no one, but somehow the word spreads anyway and the crowds increase (5:15). Given that the servant announces the news of the little girl's death publicly (8:49), one wonders how the parents will keep her resuscitation a secret. The secrecy motif, then, is Luke's way of noting how Jesus is not using his power to increase his notoriety. Crowds are increasing (7:17; 8:4; 9:11, etc.), but that is not Jesus' goal. His goal, like L. Ray Flowers's goal, is to bring life, to make the world better for those he meets.

Before he is evicted from the Rosehaven Nursing Home, L. Ray Flowers also helps a young man who comes regularly to visit his Aunt Lil, teaching him to play electric bass, encouraging him to write country lyrics and to sing gospel. When Aunt Lil dies, L. Ray writes the young man, comparing life to "a very long hallway full of thick fog" with a little campfire at the end. Mostly we can't see the fire, but sometimes we get glimpses of it, and realize our lives will end. "To prepare, we think of all the things we need to do before we get there, and one of your aunt Lil's gifts to the world, and to me, is her part in coming up with the idea" of combining churches and nursing homes. "Your aunt brought me hope toward the end of my hallway."[18] This is the kind of life-giving power Jesus demonstrates in this sandwiched pericope. His power exchanges hope for despair, life for death, health for disease, and then he gives that power to others so that they can share it, too.

CONNECTIONS

The chapter begins by describing Jesus trekking through the villages and cities of Galilee, and gives us three examples of the kinds of people he encountered. A man possessed by a legion of demons: Jesus drives out the spirits, sending the man home healed. A synagogue leader whose daughter died while Jesus was on the way to cure her: he raises the girl to life. A poor woman who cannot be cured of a persistent bleeding: she touches his fringes and immediately is better. Whatever else you conclude about Jesus, he made their lives better in obvious ways.

The chapter also speaks briefly to those who were traveling with Jesus. There are the apostles, the twelve men he named in 6:12-16; they are with him, and so far, that's all we can say. When the bleeding woman touched Jesus and he wanted to know who had touched him in faith, Peter unhelpfully pointed out the crowds. Peter, James, and John watched while he resuscitated the girl; perhaps they were part of the crowd who laughed at Jesus for thinking that anything could be done. The Twelve will have more success in the next chapter, but at the moment they are not setting the woods on fire. There are the disciples, the larger group of people attracted to Jesus. They listen to him and ask for more instructions, but a windstorm is enough to make them think they are goners. They will also have their moments later, when in chapter 10 Jesus commissions them as he does the Twelve in chapter 9. And then there are the women, part of the disciples, but the only part at this point actually doing anything. They minister—they perform the service captured by the Greek word for "deacon"—with the result that the good news gets where it needs to go.

The real measure of a disciple or an apostle is that they "hear the word of God and do it." The good soil receives the seed and produces. The newly healed former demoniac is sent to spread the good news in his hometown, whose people previously had chained him. The woman whom no doctor could cure takes matters into her own hands: her faith saves her. The women who follow Jesus from Galilee know him as perhaps the other disciples still do not, and they gladly give what they have. "These are they who, hearing the word with a fine, good heart hold onto it and bear fruit with patience."

NOTES

[1] Marge Piercy, "To be of use," from *Circles on the Water* (New York: Knopf, 1982), 106.

[2] Jane Schaberg, "Luke," in *The Women's Bible Commentary*, ed. Carol Newsome and Sharon H. Ringe (Louisville: Westminster/John Knox, 1992), 286–88; Schaberg, *The Resurrection of Mary Magdalene: Legends, Apocrypha, and the Christian Testament* (New York: Continuum, 2002), 76–80; Joseph A. Fitzmyer, *The Gospel According to Luke* (AB 28 and 28A; Garden City NY: Doubleday, 1981), 1.698; Kathleen Corley, *Private Women, Public Meals* (Peabody MA: Hendrickson, 1993), 111–19: "the 'women who serve' become respectable Greco-Roman patronesses" (119).

[3] Joel B. Green, *The Gospel of Luke* (NICNT; Grand Rapids: Eerdmans, 1997), 318–21.

[4] Luke Timothy Johnson, *The Gospel of Luke* (SP, vol. 3; Collegeville MN: Liturgical Press, 1991), 134.

[5] Joachim Jeremias, *The Parables of Jesus* (3rd ed.; London: SCM, 1972), 11–12.

[6] Arlen Hultgren, *The Parables of Jesus: A Commentary* (Grand Rapids MI: Eerdmans, 2000), 183–87, reviews the evidence and finds that while some relevant texts do seem to imagine sowing and then plowing, most describe the process in the reverse order.

[7] BAGD, 570–71 (s.v. κρυπτός), 114 (s. v. ἀπόκρυφος).

[8] Bruce Metzger, *A Textual Commentary on the Greek New Testament* (New York: United Bible Societies, 1971), 84, 145, suggests that the scribal motive may have been assimilation to Matthew, but comes to the same conclusion.

[9] Paul Simon, "I Am a Rock," 1965.

[10] Charles Frazier, *Cold Mountain* (New York: Atlantic Monthly, 1997), 123.

[11] Clyde Edgerton, *Lunch at the Picadilly* (Chapel Hill NC: Algonquin, 2003), 8.

[12] Ibid., 62–63.

[13] Ibid., 64.

[14] Johnson, *Luke*, 143.

[15] Timothy J. Geddert, *Mark* (Believers Bible Commentary; Scottsdale PA: 2001), 119.

[16] Green, *Luke*, 346, 347.

[17] In some ancient manuscripts, Luke 8:43 reads "And a woman who had a flow of blood for twelve years, who was not able to be healed by anyone," while in other manuscripts the phrase "spent lavishly her whole life-savings on doctors" appears after the second "who." The older texts have the shorter reading, and most textual critics think the longer text came about because of copyists remembering Mark as they copied Luke.

[18] Edgerton, *Lunch at the Picadilly*, 226–27.

BEGINNING THE
JOURNEY TO THE CROSS

Luke 9

COMMENTARY

Ministry and Danger, 9:1-17

From the beginning of Luke's Gospel, people are in motion, being sent, carrying out missions, and fitting these into some larger plan set by God. The angel Gabriel is sent to Mary (1:26); Mary goes to visit Elizabeth (1:39); the friends and relations take the news of John's birth and Zechariah's restored speech throughout the hill country of Judea (1:65); a decree goes out from the emperor that moves the world around (2:1); shepherds spread the news of the child wrapped in baby clothes announced by the angel chorus (2:20); etc. Luke also tracks the progress of "the word" from angel to doubting priest; from angel to willing maiden to the whole world, through her song; from God to baptizing prophet to receptive crowds; from Spirit-inspired Son to synagogue congregations, scattered towns and villages of Galilee, hostile Pharisees, and penitents of all stripes. Since we know that Luke is headed toward Acts, where the gospel message will be taken into all the world, beginning from Jerusalem, and where it will be preached by a whole range of different persons, we are not surprised to find Luke building a case, lining up precedents, citing examples of who was commissioned when to do what, and how those early missions fared. [Evangelism]

 This section is held together by the verbs of sending and returning, giving and receiving. Luke, using Mark's material, weaves together some rather complicated patterns:

9:1—Jesus calls the Twelve together
9:2—Jesus sends the Twelve
9:3—Take nothing on the road
9:4—Some will receive you—stay there and leave from there
9:5—Some will not receive you—leave there

9:10—The apostles return; Jesus, taking the apostles, goes away

9:11—Crowds follow him; he receives them

9:12—The Twelve come to him: "Send the crowd away, so they can go"

9:13—Jesus: "Give them something to eat"; Twelve: "Not enough, unless you want us to go"

9:16—Taking the five loaves and two fish, he gave to the disciples to set before the crowd

9:17—Twelve baskets of leftovers were taken

Jesus sends and gathers the Twelve, and in these parts of the narrative, the Twelve are successful; when Jesus sends them out, they are able to fulfill the mission he assigns them, and when they are gathered back to him, they are able, eventually, to be part of helping Jesus minister to the crowd. He welcomes the crowd, giving them the word as well as food. He is sender, receiver, commissioner, and welcoming host.

The Twelve are sent out with nothing except the authority and power Jesus gives them, and Jesus tells them to expect both welcome and rejection. They come back with good reports about their work, and yet they have not learned to be as hospitable as Jesus or as the anonymous villagers who welcome and feed them. "Send the crowds away," they say, "unless you mean to send us away instead." Jesus dismisses no one. He, the gracious host, feeds the crowd, satisfying them with plenty to spare; he, the patient teacher, includes his recalcitrant apostles in the work of ministry.

Herod Antipas, stuck into this pleasant scene like a splinter in a finger, menaces Jesus with his attempts to "see him." Not likely to be all Herod wants to do, given that he beheaded John; thus all the sending and receiving, giving and taking happens under the threat of danger from Rome's puppet king in Galilee.

Jesus began his ministry by announcing that God was sending him to preach good news to the poor, release to the captives, etc. He later repeated much of this list in answer to the messengers from John the Baptist: "Go tell John what you have seen and heard: the blind see, the lame walk, lepers are cleansed, the deaf hear, the dead are raised, and the poor are given the good news." Jesus has been doing this sort of thing steadily over several chapters—healing, exorcising, teaching, and eating with those who receive him. The Twelve have been named since 6:12-16, and have been with Jesus fairly consistently, but have not had much of a role. They have been criticized by Pharisees for failing to keep the Law, and by Jesus for their lack of faith, but mostly they have been bystanders. Now they are sent with instructions to imitate Jesus both in how they travel and in what they do in the villages.

Jesus gave them "power and authority" (*dynamis kai exousia*). "Power" in Luke has mostly to do with the ability to do miracles. Three times it is used specifically to mean the healing force coming from Jesus (5:17; 6:19; 8:46) and three times it is connected to the ability to overcome demons (4:36; 9:1; 10:19). The Spirit is the source of this power for Jesus (4:14), enabling him to assign the same power to the Twelve. "Authority" is also connected to the ability to exorcise (4:36; 9:1; 10:19, paired with "power"), but Luke uses it as well to speak of the power of Jesus' teaching (4:32) or of his right to pronounce forgiveness of sins (5:24). The chief priests, scribes, and elders ask Jesus what "authority" he has to act as he does (20:2). Taken together, the two words convey both the raw spiritual force that could unseat Satan or drive away a fever and the appointment from God to use that force in God's work. Jesus has both, of course, and in this passage gives both to the Twelve, just as later he will give both to the seventy (10:19).

The Twelve have power and authority "over all the demons and to heal diseases." Luke gives them a good performance review: "Going out, they made their way through village by village preaching the good news and healing everywhere." But compare this to Luke's source: "And going out, they preached that [their audiences] should repent, and they cast out many demons, and they anointed many sick with oil and healed them" (Mark 6:12-13). Did Luke leave out the demons on purpose? We wonder, particularly since later in the same chapter they cannot do it (9:40) and try to keep others from doing what they can't (9:49). In this regard, the seventy get higher marks, since they report power over demons (10:17), and about their ministry Jesus remarks, "I was watching Satan fall from heaven" (10:18).

Take nothing for the road, Jesus says, neither staff nor bag, neither bread nor money, nor have two tunics with you. [Don't Dress like a Cynic?] Hikers know how useful a strong walking stick is, for everything from leaning to reaching to fending off unwanted visitors. "No bag" means no supplies of any sort, since you would have no place to keep them, and the "no bread, no cash, no extra clothes" simply runs out the list of the normal provisions any traveler would take. How will they survive? Just as Jesus has been doing, they will rely on the kindness of strangers. Some "houses"—

Don't Dress like a Cynic?

Many interpreters note that Jesus' instructions not to carry bag, staff, or extra tunic sound like he (or Luke) was trying to avoid confusion between his followers and the Cynics, a lifestyle or philosophy of radical freedom from all social conventions and popular in Greco-Roman cities of the first century. A letter attributed to Diogenes "the Dog," from whom the movement got its name (it derives from the Greek word for dog), describes him this way: "Do not be upset, Father, that I am called a dog and put on a double, coarse cloak, carry a wallet over my shoulders, and have a staff in my hand. It is not worth while getting distressed over such matters, but you should rather be glad that your son is satisfied with little, while being free from popular opinion . . . . As for my clothing, even Homer writes that Odysseus, the wisest of the Greeks, so dressed while he was returning home from Ilium under Athena's direction."

Abraham Malherbe, *The Cynic Epistles* (Atlanta: Scholars Press, 1977), 99.

Vasily Polenov. *What People Think.* 1900. (Credit: www.wikipedia.org)

metonymy for the owners and families who live in them—will receive the Twelve, and when that happens, they should stay put until they leave the village (no casting about for a better invitation). Whenever they are not welcomed, they should leave, dropping off the town's dust at the border to show that they took nothing from inhospitable hosts. Shaking off the dust is also a "witness against them"—in other words, against the Day of Judgment, when people will be called to account for how they have received the word of God (10:13-16).

Speaking of Judgment Day, Herod Antipas, who had imprisoned John the Baptist back in 3:20, now confesses to having beheaded the prophet. Luke omits most of Mark's long story of how a girl's dance, a king's rash oath, and a queen's offended sense of honor combined to decapitate the Baptist. But he keeps the note about John's death here, probably because of the contrast between the ways the crowds, the Twelve, and Herod respond to Jesus. Antipas hears about "everything taking place" and is puzzled. Some reports make Jesus out to be John *redivivus* (whether literally—Jesus was possessed by the spirit of the dead John—or figuratively—Jesus was the "sp[ir]it'n image" of John— is impossible to say). Others think that Jesus embodied the return of Elijah predicted in Malachi 4:5, while others count him as one of the other prophets. All of these guesses would presume that the latter days had come, either because the dead were being raised or because Elijah had returned. Antipas seems not to believe any of these rumors: "John is dead—I know that, because I cut his head off—so who is this new guy?" Luke's audience may have taken "he tried to see him" ironically—see him headless, too, if Jesus is careless. The Pharisees will make this explicit in 13:31: "Herod wants to kill you." But when Herod finally gets his mitts on Jesus in 23:8-11, he is disappointed—Jesus won't do a miracle on command—and bored, and sends him back to Pilate.

Jesus can give the Twelve his power over demons, but he cannot keep himself or his followers safe forever from the political powers. Jesus can send the Twelve out, certain that they will find places to stay where their message will be welcome and where they will be fed. But the mention of Herod reminds the reader that there will come a day when the messengers of Jesus will be treated much as he was.

On this day, however, the apostles return with good reports of what they did, and Jesus takes them all with him on retreat to Bethasaida, a fishing village at the north end of the Sea of Galilee. Luke adds the place name to Mark's account, thus providing some evidence for why Bethsaida could be especially condemned for not repenting when they saw a great miracle (10:13). Jesus and the Twelve withdraw alone, but the crowds learn of it and tag along. Jesus, who could have sent them away or could have withdrawn again to a more remote area, "welcoming them, spoke to them concerning the kingdom of God." He also cured the sick among them, just as he had commanded the Twelve to do in 9:2.

As the day began to "recline"—Luke uses *klinein*, a verb that already gets us thinking about eating—the disciples go to Jesus to tell him what to do: "Dismiss the crowd, so that they may go into surrounding villages and countryside to find lodging and provisions, because here we are in a deserted place." Well, they are not in a deserted place—they are near Bethsaida, by Luke's account a *polis*, a city. [Bethsaida, a *polis*] Not very hospitable; this sounds like the Twelve just want to get rid of the crowds. Jesus has a better suggestion: "You guys give them something to eat" (9:13). Their answer is sarcastic: "In our group, there's no more than five loaves and two fishes, unless perhaps we're supposed to go buy food for all these people." Jesus knows they have no money—he just sent them out on the road without cash—so this is a complaint by the Twelve that Jesus is asking too much of them. Send them away, Jesus, unless you really mean for us to leave.

Instead, Jesus acts as host, inviting his guests to recline (*kataklinein*), which they do, in groups of fifty. The function of the number fifty is unclear; maybe it is meant to give us the sense of a hundred clusters of people, so that the reader can imagine how the food was served. Then, in language meant to remind us of the Last

Bethsaida, a *polis*

According to Josephus, Herod Philip "advanced the village Bethsaida, situated at the lake of Gennesareth [i.e., the Sea of Galilee], unto the dignity of a city, both by the number of inhabitants it contained, and its other grandeur, and called it by the name of Julias, the same name with Caesar's daughter" (*Ant.* 18.29).

Supper, Jesus takes the food, looks up to heaven, blesses and breaks it, and gives it to the disciples (took, blessed, broke, and gave are all the same roots as the words of institution in Luke 22:19). Jesus' act is probably also supposed to remind us of Elisha commanding a man to set food before a multitude (2 Kgs 4:42-44), where a small amount was enough and more besides.[1] Once again, Jesus is acting like a prophet, imitating Elisha while he also predicts, by his actions, what will happen later in the story.

So Jesus hosts a big party on the spur of the moment, giving them first the word, then healing, and then, at day's end, a simple but filling meal of fish and bread. He does not let the sullen Twelve off the hook, but turns them into table servants (except that there are no tables) trundling bread and fish around to one hundred parties of fifty (Yo, Peter, we need more fish over here!) until all those hungry peasants have had their fill. Here, boys, he is saying, this is what you do with crowds. You don't throw up your hands or send them away, nor do you (like Martha in 10:38-42) lose track of preaching and healing in your concern over providing food. But you do feed them; you don't just give them a Bible lesson or a gospel tract, you provide for their physical and spiritual needs at the same time. You don't let Herod buffalo you into running away, either. You stand in there, you give what you have, and you receive what they can give you with gratitude. And, as Mary commented ("he filled the hungry with good things," 1:33) and as Jesus predicted ("blessed are you who hunger now, for you will be filled," 6:21), "everyone ate and was satisfied." [Preaching and Serving]

Once more, Luke uses hospitality and eating as a way of depicting the gospel, how it works and how it spreads. The disciples can just go, taking nothing with them, counting on God to stir up the hearts of others to provide enough for them, seeds cast upon good soil producing a hundredfold.[2] They may not hunt for the best offer—just stay with the first one who invites you in, and be grateful—that's grace, isn't it? Jesus can take a little bit of food and stretch it to satisfy a whole multitude. Even so, the gospel grows like a mustard seed, spread by open hearts and welcome tables.

Preaching and Serving

For the first five years she believed she had done something very important when she delivered a good sermon. In year six she began to realize that sermons aren't so important in the scheme of things. That year she said publicly that the woman watching the children during the service was giving the greater gift.

In year eight she truly began to believe this.

She does everything possible to de-emphasize the sermon. She does not leave printed manuscripts in the foyer. She does not sell tapes. She does not post sermons on the church website. She is not strong enough to withstand that kind of temptation. Every sermon is a sand painting, created with all the energy she can muster and blown away on the winds of her voice.

They love each other, the woman and her people. They are in this together, for the long haul. Her best sermons are like the whispers of dear friends and lovers.

Gordon Atkinson, *RealLivePreacher.com* (Grand Rapids: Eerdmans, 2004), 86.

Who Is Jesus? Who Will Follow Him?, 9:18-27

Of all things said about Jesus, the item we know most assuredly is that the Romans executed him, almost certainly for the crime of claiming to be a king. For ancient Christians, the cross was a tough obstacle to overcome: why should anyone listen to a group of persons who worship a crucified man? In Jesus' time, the cross was an instrument of Roman control over slaves and subject peoples. Crucifixions were part of the legions' strategies to break the will of a besieged city, and part of an imperial governor's methods for humiliating would-be insurgents. No civilized person should even be required to think of crosses or crucifixions, said Cicero, who nevertheless approved of crucifixions for the purposes just named. If Jesus, then, was crucified, as everybody knew he had been, he could not have been the Son of God, since no self-respecting Roman citizen, let alone a divine being, would have allowed himself to be so treated. [Some Ancient Writers on Crucifixion]

Luke, in this pericope, begins to face these issues and to shape a narrative designed to make sense of Jesus' crucifixion. He takes over from Mark three "passion predictions" and adds to them, giving

Some Ancient Writers on Crucifixion

Cicero: "How grievous a thing it is to be disgraced by a public court; how grievous to suffer a fine, how grievous to suffer banishment; and yet in the midst of any such disaster we retain some degree of liberty. Even if we are threatened with death, we may die free men. But the executioner, the veiling of the head and the very word 'cross' should be far removed not only from the person of a Roman citizen but from his thoughts, his eyes, and his ears. For it is not only the actual occurrence of these things or the endurance of them, but liability to the, the expectation, indeed the very mention of them, that is unworthy of a Roman citizen and a free man." (*Pro Rabirio* 16)

Quintilian: "Whenever we crucify the guilty, the most crowded roads are chosen, where the most people can see and be moved by this fear. For penalties related not so much to retribution as to their exemplary effect." (*Declamations* 274)

Josephus: "[During the siege of Jerusalem, some of the Jewish defenders attempted to escape and were captured by the Romans.] They were first whipped, and then tormented with all sorts of tortures, before they died and were then crucified before the wall of the city. Titus [the Roman general, later emperor] felt pity for them, but as their number—given as up to 500 per day—was too great for him to risk either letting them go or putting them under guard, he allowed his soldiers to have their way, especially as he hoped the gruesome sight of the countless corpses might move the besieged to surrender. So the soldiers, out of the rage and hatred they bore the prisoners, nailed those they caught in different postures, to the crosses, by way of jest, and their number was so great that there was not enough room for the crosses and not enough crosses for the bodies. (*J.W.* 5.449-51)

Chariton: "[Theron, a pirate, has been convicted of kidnapping the heroine Callirhoe.] Theron was condemned to death, but Chaereas [Callirhoe's husband] begged that he should not be executed yet, 'so that he can come and show me who bought her,' he said. 'Consider what I am compelled to do—plead for the man who sold my wife.' Hermocrates [the magistrate, and Callirhoe's father] would not allow this. 'It is better,' he said, 'to make our search more laborious than to allow the law to be broken.' . . . As Theron was led away, a great part of the crowd followed. He was crucified in front of Callirhoe's tomb, and from his cross he looked out on that sea over which he had carried as a captive the daughter of Hermocrates. (*Chaereas and Callirhoe* 3.4; in Reardon, *Collected Ancient Greek Novels* [Berkeley: University of California Press, 1989], 57–58) the reader a growing sense of what will happen and what it will mean. In Mark, the three passion predictions are one of the key structural features of the central part of the Gospel (chs. 8–10). In Luke, the predictions do not have this function—they do not mark off a section of Luke as they do Mark—but taken together, they help to answer the question of Jesus' identity and to prepare the reader for Jesus' upcoming death. In Mark, the passion predictions are each connected to the disciples' failure to understand Jesus, which Jesus then follows with a section on the nature of discipleship. Luke's predictions are not always accompanied by stories of the disciples' hard-headedness, but he does tend to link them with discussions of what it means to follow the Lord.

The chart below shows how Luke keeps all of Mark's predictions, adds some of his own, keeps the material about discipleship, but omits Peter's rebuke of Jesus (and the "get behind me, Satan!" comeback by Jesus) and the request for thrones.

Mark		Luke
8:27-30	Who am I? Peter's confession	9:18-21
8:31	First passion prediction	9:22
8:32-33	Peter rebukes and is rebuked	
8:34–9:1	Take up the cross	9:23-27
	"told his departure . . . in Jerusalem"	9:31
9:30-31	Second passion prediction	9:43-44
9:32	The disciples are ignorant and afraid	9:45
9:33-37	The greatest among you is least	9:46-48
	This generation kills all the prophets	11:49-51
	I have a baptism to undergo	12:49-53
	All prophets killed in Jerusalem	13:31-35
	Whoever does not carry the cross and follow me	14:27
	They won't be convinced by a resurrection	16:31
	You will wish for one of the days of the Son of Man	17:22
10:32-34	Third passion prediction	18:31-34
10:35-40	James and John want thrones	
10:41-45	You must be servants	(22:25-27)

If you have access to a Gospel parallel, you will have noticed that Luke skips over everything from Mark 6:45–8:26, leaving out Jesus' walking on water, an account of healings at Gennesaret, the argument with the Pharisees over washing hands, the faith of the Syrophoenician woman, the cure of a deaf and speechless man, the feeding of the four thousand, a request by the Pharisees for a sign, the third of Mark's boat scenes, and the cure of the blind man at Bethsaida ("I see men like trees, walking"). There is no completely satisfactory explanation for such a large omission. Perhaps Luke's copy of Mark was missing that material, or perhaps Luke had reasons for avoiding each pericope. For example, the argument over washing hands is somewhat like the debate at dinner in Luke 11:37-54, and so Luke may have decided not to repeat material. It also may have suited him not to include stories that emphasize the dullness of the apostles, such as the boat scenes and the scene with the Syrophoenician woman.

Whatever his motives, the effect of the omission is that Luke's first passion prediction and Peter's confession come very close to the commissioning of the Twelve and their success and failure, and within a few verses of Herod Antipas's musings over who Jesus might be. The first part of chapter 9 prepares us to think that the Twelve can obey Jesus' commands to go and preach and heal without completely comprehending the nature of his mission; they are capable of accepting the hospitality of villagers while they are preaching and of refusing hospitality to a hungry crowd who has gathered to hear Jesus preach. [Preaching the Gospel without Being Changed] We already know that some who have heard of Jesus think he is somebody other than who he truly is: John the Baptist come back to life, or a returned Elijah or one of the other historical prophets. We are prepared, then, for fuzzy thinking from disciples, crowds, and kings, and that is what Luke gives us.

> ### Preaching the Gospel without Being Changed
>
> Thus the Gospel is not only Good and New but, if you take it seriously, a Holy Terror. Jesus never claimed that the process of being changed from a slob into a human being was going to be a Sunday school picnic. . . . Part of what it means to be a slob is to hang on for dear life to our slobbery.
>
> Frederick Buechner, *Wishful Thinking: A Theological ABC* (New York: Harper and Row, 1973), 33.

Jesus in solitary prayer is a familiar scene (5:16; 6:12), as is the presence of the disciples (8:1; 9:10); but while Acts frequently pictures the apostles and other followers of Jesus knit together in prayer, the Gospel only does at 19:37, when the disciples praise God. The disciples need to be taught how to pray (11:1) and will need to learn a great deal more about who Jesus truly is. Jesus' prayer may be understood in many ways: as a prayer for guidance, as an intercession for the Twelve, or simply as the continuing pattern where Jesus, after intense periods of ministry, steps aside to pray.[3]

"Who do the crowds say I am?" he asks the disciples; note that this is not the Twelve or the apostles, but the larger group of disciples around Jesus, as is clear from the "he said to all" in v. 23. They report the same list of options that Herod had been chewing over in 9:7-8: John the Baptist, Elijah, or one of the other prophets of old. The fact that these were Antipas's ideas does not commend the list, and repeating it at this point links popular opinion with the opinions of Rome's puppet king in Galilee.[4] Great minds think alike, eh? The "crowds" were more perceptive earlier in the narrative, when they recognized Jesus as a prophet, the result of God's favorable attention to Israel (7:16), and when they responded to the preaching of John the Baptist (7:29). That was accurate, but thinking of Jesus as one of the former prophets come back to life—even Elijah, herald of the end times (Mal 4:5-6), or John, the greatest human ever born (7:28)—is inaccurate.

"Who do you say I am?" asks Jesus. Peter answers, "The Christ of God (*ton christon tou Theou*)." In order to evaluate his answer, we need to put it in context, both with respect to how and where the term "Christ" appears elsewhere in Luke, and in the context of this passage:

1:3—Gabriel to Mary: "And the Lord will give to him the throne of his ancestor David, and he will be king over the house of Jacob forever, and his kingdom will never end."
2:11—Angels to shepherds: "To you, today, in David's city is born a savior who is the Messiah, the Lord."
2:26—God to Simeon: He will not die until he has seen "the Lord's Messiah [*ton christon kyriou*]."
2:38—Anna to people: She spoke about the baby Jesus to everyone looking forward to the redemption of Israel.
3:15-17—John to people: When they wondered whether he might be the Messiah, he reported that the Coming One was mightier than he.
4:18—Jesus to Nazareth synagogue, reading Isaiah: "The Lord's Spirit is upon me, because he has anointed [the verbal form of "Christ"] me to preach good news to the poor, [etc.]."
4:41—Jesus to demons: He will not allow them to speak, because they know he is Messiah.

Then nothing for several chapters, until we reach Peter's confession. Luke's readers are thus prepared to think that "Christ" or "The Lord's Messiah" is an acceptable term for Jesus—if an angel calls him that, and if the demons know it's true, then "Christ" is accurate, unlike "Elijah come back to life." But notice in this context, and in all future references to "Christ" or "king," how quickly the narrator will move the reader toward other ways to think about Jesus. Jesus, until the crucifixion, never calls himself "Christ" and only once speaks of his kingdom (22:28-30). But after the resurrection, he twice states that the Messiah must suffer and then rise (24:26, 46). In Luke's understanding, then, "Messiah" is a meaningful term for Jesus only if it includes the cross.

Notice also how Luke rewrites Mark to stress this point of view even more than Mark does. As soon as Peter says "God's Messiah," Jesus, "charging them, orders that they tell this to nobody, saying, 'It is necessary for the Son of Man . . . .'" In Luke's construction, the first passion prediction becomes part of the command to silence about Jesus' Messianic identity. Until the disciples are up to speed on why and how Jesus must die, it would be better that they keep mum on who Jesus is.

So Luke imagines that Jesus sends the Twelve out to preach the kingdom of God, to heal the sick, and to cast out demons (9:1-2) before they and the rest of the disciples get any instruction on Jesus' death. Picture Peter or one of the others going to a village to preach the coming kingdom and to heal: does he do it in the name of Jesus, God's Messiah? The proximity of the stories suggests that Luke thinks they did, and that the command to silence is corrective, not prophylactic; Jesus has to hush up the Twelve, just as he did the demons, because neither group really understands the nature of the cross. [The Disciples Not Understanding the Cross]

In v. 22, Luke follows Mark in having Jesus refer to himself as "Son of Man" when speaking of his coming passion: "It is necessary that the Son of Man suffer many things and be condemned by the elders, chief priests, and scribes, and be killed, and be raised on the third day." As noted earlier in the commentary (see commentary on 5:17-26 and [Did Jesus Call Himself the Son of Man?]), "Son of Man" literally translates a Hebrew or Aramaic phrase meaning "human being." It was used in Daniel 7:13 to refer to a human figure who is lifted up to heaven and appointed judge for the Day of Judgment, which is the sense it has in Luke 9:26. Using it here is a way for Jesus (or Luke, or both) to connect the necessity of suffering with the promise of glorious return; the same figure whom the elders, chief priests, and scribes condemn will someday return as God's Judge to institute God's justice. For the disciples, the point is that the one they expect to rescue Israel and take over David's throne is headed first for a cross and then for a throne in heaven.

The Disciples Not Understanding the Cross

"In the spring we'll go to Jerusalem for Passover, and there I will be judged by the scribes and the priests, and there I will be tortured and put to death. But three days from the day of my death, I shall rise, and be with you again."

As Joshua spoke Maggie had latched onto my arm. By the time he was finished speaking her nails had drawn blood from my biceps. A shadow of grief seemed to pass over the disciples. We looked not at each other, and neither at the ground, but at a place in space a few feet from our faces, where I suppose one looks for a clear answer to appear out of undefined shock.

"Well, that sucks," someone said.

Christopher Moore, *Lamb: The Gospel According to Biff, Christ's Childhood Pal* (New York: HarperCollins, 2002), 357–58.

Are you still up to following this person? Luke, who often seems to avoid repeating material, has no qualms about including more than one version of sayings about taking up the cross:

9:23—If anyone wishes to come after me, they must deny themselves and take up their crosses daily and follow me.
9:24—Whoever wishes to save his soul will lose it; whoever loses her soul on my account, she saves it.
14:26—If anyone comes after me and does not hate his own father, mother, wife, children, brothers and sisters, and even his own soul, that one cannot be my disciple.
14:27—Whoever does not bear his own cross and come after me, that one cannot be my disciple.

The terms "come after me," "follow me," and "be my disciple" all mean the same thing, and they are equated with saving one's *psychē*, which I have chosen to translate with the archaic term "soul." The word means one's whole self—not just the invisible parts, and certainly not just some immortal spark within each human—but it also means more than physical life. As the parallels show, "losing one's soul" is equivalent to denying one's self or despising one's family. To become a follower (9:23) or to remain a follower (14:27), one must renounce normal family ties and even the reasonable human expectation for a self-directed life. [Losing One's Soul]

In Jesus' time, "take up the cross" was no metaphor, but a literal call to follow him on a path that would inevitably lead to crucifixion. A search of Greek literature prior to the first century turns up many references to "cross" and "crucifixion," but only as literal descriptions of how some government threatened or enacted what the Romans called the extreme penalty. Martin Hengel, who demonstrates that ancient writers mostly avoided discussion of crucifixion when possible, cites Seneca where the cross is used as an example of the most degraded form of suffering and death; this is no metaphor, but a vivid literal description of death on the cross that sums up the worst possible death a man could imagine:

Losing One's Soul

A number of spells had to do with the spirit. Swimmer knew a few ways to kill the soul of an enemy and many ways to protect your own. His spells portrayed the spirit as a frail thing, constantly under attack and in need of strength, always threatening to die inside you. Inman found this notion dismal indeed, since he had been taught by sermon and hymn to hold as truth that the soul of man never dies. . . . Inman guessed Swimmer's spells were right in saying a man's spirit could be torn apart and cease and yet his body keep on living. . . . His spirit, he feared, had been blasted away so that he had become lonesome and estranged from all around him as a sad old heron standing pointless watch in the mudflats of a pond lacking frogs. It seemed a poor swap to find that the only way one might keep from fearing death was to act numb and set apart as if dead already, with nothing much left of yourself but a hut of bones.

Charles Frazier, *Cold Mountain* (New York: Atlantic Monthly, 1997), 14, 16.

Can anyone be found who would prefer wasting away in pain dying limb by limb, or letting out his life drop by drop, rather than expiring once for all? Can any man be found willing to be fastened to the accursed tree, long sickly, already deformed, swelling with ugly weals on shoulders and chest, and drawing the breath of life amid long-drawn-out agony? He would have many excuses for dying even before mounting the cross. (Seneca, *Ep.* 101)[5]

But Luke, by adding the word "daily" to the imperative "take up the cross," shows that by his time the cross has become a Christian metaphor for living a life of self-denial, always ready to face death if following Christ demands it. Such a call makes Jesus sound a bit like the narrator of 2 Maccabees:

Eleazar, one of the scribes in high position, a man now advanced in age and of noble presence, was being forced to open his mouth to eat swine's flesh. But he, welcoming death with honor rather than life with pollution, went up to the rack of his own accord, spitting out the flesh, as all ought to go who have the courage to refuse things that it is not right to taste, even for the natural love of life. (2 Macc 6:18-20)

"Therefore, by bravely giving up my life now, I will show myself worthy of my old age and leave to the young a noble example of how to die a good death willingly and nobly for the revered and holy laws." When he had said this, he went at once to the rack. Those who a little before had acted toward him with goodwill now changed to ill will, because the words he had uttered were in their opinion sheer madness. When he was about to die under the blows, he groaned aloud and said: "It is clear to the Lord in his holy knowledge that, though I might have been saved from death, I am enduring terrible sufferings in my body under this beating, but in my soul I am glad to suffer these things because I fear him." So in this way he died, leaving in his death an example of nobility and a memorial of courage, not only to the young but to the great body of his nation. (2 Macc 6:27-31)

One tells gruesome martyr stories, full of details about the implements of torture and how they were applied, to make that sort of death vivid in the hearers' imaginations. Second Maccabees uses these horror stories to call the reader to imagine how one could respond as bravely as the elderly priest, the seven brothers, and their mother if one ever needed to die for the Law. [The Martyrs of 2 and 4 Maccabees] In the same way, Luke asks readers and hearers of his Gospel to think daily upon the passion narrative, to bring it

---

The Martyrs of 2 and 4 Maccabees

Second Maccabees (usually dated in the 2d C. BC) 6–7 describes how an aged Jewish priest named Eleazar, an anonymous Jewish mother, and her seven sons were all tortured in an attempt to make them eat pork. Each suffered bravely and died rather than disobey God's law. In the 1st century CE, in a work now called 4 Maccabees, another author expanded these stories and used them to argue that serious study of the Torah will enable anyone to master his/her passions and live an exemplary life.

---

before their eyes, to be ready to imitate Christ in his death.

Those who do will "save their souls," which is explained in vv. 25-26. On the Day of Judgment, when the Son of Man returns in glory in his role as Judge, he will either confess or deny them before God and the holy angels (in Jewish apocalyptic literature of the Second Temple period, angels are almost always present at the last judgment; see *1 En.* 62:11; 90:21-22; *Sib. Or.* 2.242; *T. Ab.* 12:1-18). So one can either deny oneself, one's family, and one's normal life now, or be denied by the Son of Man when it really counts.

The final verse, many commentators suspect, was originally understood to mean that Jesus would return before all of the original apostles died. The same understanding probably underlies Mark 13:30 (par Luke 21:32), and in John 21:20-23 and 2 Peter 3:1-10 we see Christians wrestling with the disappointment caused when this expectation was not realized. Luke, following Mark, gives an immediate, if partial, fulfillment of Jesus' prediction in the story of the transfiguration, where three of the Twelve get a glimpse of Jesus' future glory in the kingdom of God.

Who is Jesus, then? The Christ of God, appointed to restore the promises to Israel, but only after he has suffered. A prophet, who in the narrative can predict his own death in detail and who will later explain his own death as a prophet's death. The Son of Man, who will be crucified and who someday will return as Judge to impose God's justice on the earth. A martyr for obedience to God, who, like the seven brothers, said, "Imitate me" (4 Macc 9:23).

And who will follow him? Only those who are willing to take up their own crosses, deny their own lives, hate their families, lose everything for Christ's sake. None of us, or very few of us, who take Christianity to be the blueprint for middle-class virtue, affluence, and "family values." Schweitzer said it most memorably:

> Because it is thus preoccupied with the general, the universal, modern theology is determined to find its world-accepting ethic in the teaching of Jesus. Therein lies its weakness. The world affirms itself automatically; the modern spirit cannot but affirm it. But why on that account abolish the conflict between modern life, with the world-affirming spirit which inspires it as a whole, and the world-negating spirit of Jesus? Why spare the spirit of the individual man [sic] its appointed task of fighting its way through the world-negation of Jesus, of contending with Him at every step over the value of

materials and intellectual goods—a conflict in which it may never rest?

He comes to us as One unknown, without a name, as of old, by the lakeside, He came to those men who knew him not. He speaks to us the same word: "Follow thou me!" and sets us to the tasks which He has to fulfill for our time. He commands. And to those who obey Him, whether they be wise or simple, He will reveal Himself in the toils, the conflicts, the sufferings which they shall pass through in His fellowship, and, as an ineffable mystery, they shall learn in their own experience Who He is.[6]

Transfiguration, 9:28-36

"I tell you truly, there are some standing here who will not taste death until they see the kingdom of God." Jesus' promise in 9:27 may originally have been understood to mean that he would return as Son of Man, bringing Judgment Day and the kingdom, before all the apostles died (see commentary on 9:18-27). In the same way, some interpreters believe that the story of Jesus' transfiguration was originally a resurrection story that was transposed back into his ministry, either by Mark or by the tradition Mark was using. Whatever the story's early history, Luke uses it to preview what lies ahead for Jesus—although he will be crucified, he will also be resurrected and ascend to heaven in glory—and to fulfill Jesus' promise in 9:27. Peter, James, and John will see the kingdom of God enacted before them, and, like Mary, who had also seen wondrous things, will keep their impressions to themselves.

"Transfiguration" means to be changed physically, something Flannery O'Connor described in "Revelation":

> Mrs. Turpin eased into the vacant chair, which held her tight as a corset. "I wish I could reduce," she said, and rolled her eyes and gave a comic sigh.
> "Oh, you aren't fat," the stylish lady said.
> "Ooooo I am too," Mrs. Turpin said. "Claud he eats all he wants and never weighs over one hundred and seventy-five pounds, but me I just look at something good to eat and I gain some weight," and her stomach and shoulders shook with laughter.[7]

Americans also seek regular advice on how to look better by changing the way we dress, since clothing places us in a societal niche:

> Without appearing to, Mrs. Turpin always noticed people's feet. The well-dressed lady had on red and gray suede shoes to match her dress.

Mrs. Turpin had on her good black patent leather pumps. The ugly girl had on Girl Scout shoes and heavy socks. The old woman had on tennis shoes and the white-trashy mother had on what appeared to be bedroom slippers, black straw with gold braid threaded through them—exactly what you would have expected her to have on.[8]

Jesus' change comes, not by dieting or by shopping for a new tunic, but through the apparent intervention of God and for no reason given in the text. Taking Peter, James, and John with him, he goes up a mountain to pray. Jesus did this earlier just before he announced the choice of the Twelve (6:12), so the connection of disciples, mountain, and prayer might lead us to expect some pronouncement about the nature of discipleship, or some new commission to give to the Twelve. They had been out preaching with mixed results (9:1-17): while they could heal and preach the good news, they had not caught on either to the possibilities of God's power or to the need for hospitable welcomes for the crowds. Jesus had just presented them with his ultimatum about the cross: either take it up daily, or you cannot be my disciple (9:23-27). Perhaps, then, the trip up the mountain with these three will result in some change in them; perhaps they will descend with more faith or more power or more dedication to Jesus' cause. [Transfigured]

What happens is supposed to remind us of Moses' experiences on the mountain, when God called him up to receive the tablets of the Law. Moses goes up Mt. Sinai, taking Aaron, Nadab, and Abihu and the seventy elders, but he leaves all of them near the base, taking only Joshua (Gk., "Jesus") with him to the top (Exod 24:1-14). As he ascends, a cloud covers the mountain (Exod 24:15). After the incident with the golden calf and Moses' second trip up, when he descends, his face is glowing, and he has to wear a veil to keep from frightening the Israelites (Exod 34:29-35). Jesus' face changes—literally, it becomes "other"—there is the cloud at the end, and Moses' presence with Jesus. Seen from one angle, the transfiguration is a revelatory moment, and we expect some important word from God on the order of the tablets of the Law. The link to Moses' reception of the revelation serves also to temper our

Transfigured

When her doctor took her bandages off and led her into the garden, the girl who was no longer blind saw "the tree with the lights in it." It was for this tree that I searched through the peach orchards of summer, in the forests of fall and down winter and spring for years. Then one day I was walking along Tinker Creek thinking of nothing at all and I saw the tree with the lights in it. I saw the backyard cedar where the mourning doves roost charged and transfigured, each cell buzzing with flame. I stood on the grass with the lights in it, grass that was wholly fire, utterly focused and utterly dreamed. It was less like seeing than like being for the first time seen, knocked breathless by a powerful glance. The flood of fire abated, but I'm still spending the power. Gradually the lights went out in the cedar, the colors died, the cells unflamed and disappeared. I was still ringing. I had been my whole life a bell, and never knew it until at that moment I was lifted and struck. I have since only very rarely seen the tree with the lights in it. The vision comes and goes, mostly goes, but I live for it, for the moment when the mountains open and a new light roars in spate through the crack, and the mountains slam.

Annie Dillard, *Pilgrim at Tinker Creek* (New York: Harper and Row, 1974), 33–34.

expectations for improvement in the disciples—look what happened to Aaron and the others while Moses was talking to God!

But Moses is not the only visitor. He is joined by Elijah, who has already been named twice in this chapter. Elijah was to return before the Day of the Lord, to cleanse the temple and the priesthood and to turn Israel back toward God (Mal 4:5-6). When Jesus' clothes become dazzling, Luke uses a verb that connects the transfiguration to the predictions of what the Son of Man will look like on his return (17:24, where his appearance is compared to lightning). Elijah's appearance, the verbal link to the predictions of the return of the Son of Man, and the prediction about some seeing the kingdom of God, make us read the transfiguration as a preview of the Last Day.

Near the end, God speaks: "This is my Son, the Chosen One; listen to him!" No list of laws or instructions on how to build the tent of meeting and all its furnishings; the word from the mountain is astonishingly brief, but in keeping with the proclamations at his birth and baptism. God's message comes this time in and through God's Son—pay attention to what he says! And the event is also a preview of the day when Jesus will appear as Son of Man, to claim those who have not been ashamed to confess him (9:26; 12:8-9). Clothed with God's glory, surrounded by the angels and the prophets, Jesus will accept some and reject others (9:26; 13:22-30). Again, the voice of God is right on point: listen to Jesus now, so that you'll hear him call your name on that day.

As a christological event, or as a theophany, the transfiguration is pretty easy to read. Jesus is revealed as God's revealer, validated by the voice from above as the One chosen to deliver the word of salvation now and words of judgment when the time comes. For disciples struggling to understand the first passion prediction, it can act like a theatrical trailer, a preview of coming attractions. As a discipleship training event, it is harder to assess. The two heavenly visitors, we are told, speak with Jesus about his upcoming "exodus"—a nice Lukan touch, just in case we missed the reference to Moses and the mountain—his death in Jerusalem, in other words. Moses, forbidden to cross into Canaan, died alone on a mountain, and God buried him in a hitherto-undisclosed location in Moab (Deut 34:6). Elijah was swept up into heaven in a whirlwind (2 Kgs 2:11). The three of them, one might imagine, could exchange interesting perspectives on living and dying for God.

But do the three apostles comprehend any of this? Luke 9:32 says they were "weighed down with sleep." The "weighed down" verb shows up again in a verse about the dangers of not being prepared for the return of the Son of Man (9:34), and the image of sleepy-eyed disciples comes back while Jesus is praying just before his arrest (22:45-46). Neither connection puts them in a good light here, where they seem unready for this brief glimpse of the kingdom or for the discussion of Jesus' upcoming crucifixion. The participle in the middle of v. 32 can either mean "wake up" or "stay awake." On the first reading, they snooze while Jesus, Moses, and Elijah are talking about death, and then wake up in time to peek at Jesus' glory before the cloud rolls in. On the second reading, Peter and the other two are drowsy, but manage to stay awake to see the whole show. The first option keeps the disciples consistent through the episode: like children, they fall asleep while the adults are talking over serious things, and then wake up to suggest something nonsensical. "Let's build tents [like the tent of meeting that Moses learned about on his mountain], one for each of you"—not knowing what Jesus was talking about. The point of the experience is not to locate a specific site for revelation; Jesus is on the move, and shortly will "set his face for Jerusalem." The point of this event, so far as the disciples were concerned, was to validate the predictions Jesus had made to them and to emphasize to them the necessity of listening to him. [*Transfiguration*]

God mercifully pulls down the curtain on Peter, a sudden cloud that isolates them from Jesus and from each other, and terrifies them into silence. The voice speaks—This is my Son, the Chosen

Transfiguration

Fra Angelico, brother of the Benedictine order, captured many of these overtones of discipleship in his painting from around 1440. He painted frescoes on the monks' cells in his monastery in Florence—most of them various images of saints viewing the crucifixion. This one puts the transfigured Christ into a cruciform shape, backlit by what appears to be a flame, while the three apostles cower in fear below his feet. No, Peter obviously did not know what he was saying: did he really mean to compare the living, breathing, glowing Christ in front of him with the ghostly apparitions of Moses (left) and Elijah (right)? He cannot even look Christ in the eye; silence would have been the better choice! Christ's posture, and the proximity of Moses and Elijah to him, puts the conversation about death and departure on the level of the saints, while Peter, James, and John, groveling below, cannot at this point say anything worth hearing. But the two other figures—the Virgin on the left and Saint Benedict on the right—indicate that someday Jesus' followers will be able to receive his teachings and meditate on his transfigured nature.

Fra Angelico (1387–1455). *Transfiguration*. 1440–1445. Fresco. Museo di S. Marco, Florence, Italy. (Credit: Scala/Art Resource, NY)

One; listen to him!—but they have nothing to say in response, then or later. To judge from the next few episodes, if the experience changed them, it was a slow-acting, time-release sort of change, because they come down off the mountain to failures at exorcism and at understanding Jesus' predictions of the cross, to arguments about which one of them is the greatest, and to hostile intent towards disciples not in their group. Sometimes even theophanies and revelatory moments take a while to sink in:

> Until the sun finally slipped behind the tree line, Mrs. Turpin remained there with her gaze bent to them as if she were absorbing some abysmal life-giving knowledge. At last she lifted her head. There was only a purple streak in the sky, cutting through a field of crimson and leading, like an extension of the highway, into the descending dusk. She raised her hands from the side of the pen in a gesture hieratic and profound. A visionary light settled in her eyes. She saw the streak as a vast swinging bridge extending upward from the earth through a field of living fire. Upon it a vast horde of souls were rumbling toward heaven. There were whole companies of white-trash, clean for the first time in their lives, and bands of black niggers [sic] in white robes, and battalions of freaks and lunatics shouting and clapping and leaping like frogs. And bringing up the end of the procession was a tribe of people whom she recognized at once as those who, like herself and Claude, had always had a little of everything and the God-given wit to use it right. She leaned forward to observe them closer. They were marching behind the others with great dignity, accountable as they had always been for good order and common sense and respectable behavior. They alone were on key. Yet she could see by their shocked and altered faces that even their virtues were being burned away. She lowered her hands and gripped the rail of the hog pen, her eyes small but fixed unblinkingly on what lay ahead. In a moment the vision faded but she remained where she was, immobile.[9]

A Father and His Only Son, 9:37-43

According to *The Christian Handbook*, "Advancements in medical science have made it easier to distinguish cases of possession from mental illness." The authors suggest that signs of actual possession include:

> 1. Physical ailments not linked to wounds or direct medical causes. These may include a loss of the ability to speak (Matthew 9:32-34), blindness (Matthew 12:22), seizures (Matthew 4:24), convulsions (Mark 9:14-29), or being disabled for years (Luke 13:11-17)

2. Superhuman strength, self-wounding behavior, and crying out . . . [the example is the Gerasene/Gadarene demoniac]

3. Abrupt personality changes . . . [King Saul]

4. Unprovoked acts of betrayal. The most dramatic example is in Luke 22:3, where Satan possesses Judas, causing the disciple to turn against Jesus. In a typical betrayal, the perpetrator seeks revenge, justice, or to satisfy a growing thirst for power. Yet these enticements do not motivate Judas.[10]

The authors, perhaps not entirely seriously, suggest that biblical descriptions of demoniacs could be used to diagnose a true case of demon possession and to distinguish it from "physical ailments" with "direct medical causes." This is problematic from a number of perspectives: how does one determine that self-wounding behavior, for example, is not an aspect of mental illness? But there is a more surface-level issue: the biblical evidence is not so clear or clean. Mark's version of this story (9:14-29) speaks only of demonic agency: "whenever it seizes him it rips him, and he foams and grinds his teeth and stiffens." Matthew, who names the boy's condition "epilepsy" (17:15), nevertheless describes Jesus casting out a demon that causes the boy's suffering. Mark gives no motive whatsoever for Judas's betrayal, but Matthew suggests the motive was greed, while Luke says that Judas was possessed. It would be a mistake, then, for the modern interpreter to think that one evangelist or another was describing the phenomena of the boy's condition in language objective enough that we could decide "demon" or "medical illness." [Observing Suffering]

Observing Suffering

Because the biomedical model depends too heavily on modern, scientific understandings of human sickness as disease, it is less helpful in interpreting healing accounts from antiquity.

John Pilch, *Healing in the New Testament: Insights from Medical and Mediterranean Anthropology* (Minneapolis: Fortress, 2000), 53.

Thanks be to God, few modern American ministers or Bible teachers will be called on to make such a diagnosis, but most of us will need to think about the connection of evil or sin to illness, and about the proper ministry of the church to persons with physical or mental disabilities. In this pericope, a demon—an unclean spirit—torments the boy. Is the disease, or the diseased person, corrupted or made evil by the spirit? And in this pericope, as in all the others involving Jesus and sick people, Jesus gives the boy complete relief from his condition. We tend to think of this as a cure; Jesus has removed the cause of the illness, and the boy is now free to "be a productive member of society once more."[11] Our cultural perspective on disease causes problems for us in two directions. First, medical anthropologists suggest that we misread how Luke or other ancient authors would have understood the event. For Luke, the boy was healed—restored to complete well-being, a state in which the removal of physical symptoms was only one element. Second, we rightly wonder if our ministry to the sick and to the disabled can have the same effect as Jesus', especially if we cannot promise the same instant physical cure we read in the Gospels.

We begin with a close reading of Luke's text. Luke's chronology is a bit different from Mark's, who has Jesus and the three descend from the mountain straight into a maelstrom where the nine are arguing with some scribes in the midst of a huge crowd, all upset over the disciples' inability to heal the boy. In Luke, the sequence appears to be[12] that Jesus, Peter, James, and John come down and rejoin the disciples—the term Luke often uses for the larger group of followers that includes men and women (8:1-3). Mark's crowd is still there, and meets Jesus on the day after the transfiguration, but they stay quiet until the end, when they are "all amazed at the mighty acts of God" (9:43). Luke's version reduces the number of characters—no scribes, no bustling crowd for most of the episode—and focuses our attention on the father and his son and on Jesus and his disciples.

There are two supplicants, the man who speaks for his son, and the son who is controlled by the demon. The man begins by shouting at Jesus, a sign of his emotional state. Demons come out shouting (4:41, using a form of *krauzein*) and Legion shouts as he approaches Jesus (8:28, also *krauzein*), but so does the blind man of 18:35-43 (using a form of *boaō*, as our present passage does). Against the backdrop of the Greco-Roman ideal of how reason is supposed to control emotion, particularly in males, the father is being portrayed as desperate and frightened, caught up by his natural love for his only son. [A Mother Controls Her Emotions]

On the issue of emotion, Luke seems mostly to share his culture's preference for keeping strong emotions under wraps by the application of reason. He mostly removes Mark's references to Jesus' displays of emotions, but allows them to come through in two, perhaps three, places: Jesus is "filled with compassion" when he meets

The Disciples Fail to Heal a Boy

Raphael (Raffaello Sanzio) (1483–1520). *The Transfiguration* (detail). 1520. Oil on wood, Pinacoteca, Vatican Museums, Vatican State. (Credit: Scala/Art Resource, NY)

In this detail from Raphael's *Transfiguration*, the disciples are unable to heal the demon-possessed boy, who is supported by his father.

A Mother Controls Her Emotions

A helpful contrast to Luke's father is the mother in 4 Maccabees, who although she must watch her seven sons be tortured and killed, remains in control of her emotions:

In what manner might I express the emotions of parents who love their children? We impress upon the character of a small child a wondrous likeness both of mind and of form. Especially is this true of mothers, who because of their birth pangs have a deeper sympathy toward their offspring than do the fathers. Considering that mothers are the weaker sex and give birth to many, they are more devoted to their children. The mother of the seven boys, more than any other mother, loved her children. In seven pregnancies she had implanted in herself tender love toward them, and because of the many pains she suffered with each of them she had sympathy for them; yet because of the fear of God she disdained the temporary safety of her children. Not only so, but also because of the nobility of her sons and their ready obedience to the law, she felt a greater tender-ness toward them. For they were righteous and self-controlled and brave and magnanimous, and loved their brothers and their mother, so that they obeyed her

even to death in keeping the ordinances. Nevertheless, though so many factors influenced the mother to suffer with them out of love for her children, in the case of none of them were the various tortures strong enough to pervert her reason. (4 Macc 15: 4-10)

For as in the council chamber of her own soul she saw mighty advocates—nature, family, parental love, and the rackings of her children—this mother held two ballots, one bearing death and the other deliverance for her children. She did not approve the deliverance that would preserve the seven sons for a short time, but as the daughter of God-fearing Abraham she remembered his fortitude. O mother of the nation, vindicator of the law and champion of religion, who carried away the prize of the contest in your heart! O more noble than males in steadfastness, and more courageous than men in endurance! Just as Noah's ark, carrying the world in the universal flood, stoutly endured the waves, so you, O guardian of the law, overwhelmed from every side by the flood of your emotions and the violent winds, the torture of your sons, endured nobly and withstood the wintry storms that assail religion. (4 Macc 15:25-32)

---

the widow at Nain, who like this father has lost her only son (7:13); he weeps for the coming destruction of Jerusalem, which he foresees clearly as he approaches the city (19:41); and, if we include the disputed text at 22:43-44, Jesus agonizes over his own fate as he prays on the Mount of Olives. Mostly, however, Luke's Jesus is compassionate but not sentimental, more John Wayne than Alan Alda. This fact is important for assessing the father's approach and Jesus' response.

"O teacher, I beg you to take a close look at my son, because he is my one and only. Look, a spirit takes him and immediately cries out [or, "he cries out," meaning the son rather than the demon] and shakes him around with foam [that is, so that the child foams at the mouth] and it hardly ever [or, with great difficulty] leaves him, having crushed him." The father's testimony is heart-rending. What parent can hear descriptions of the pain of children and not be moved? In this account, we get not only the pathos of the child's pain at the hands of the demon, but some sense of the grinding nature of the illness, where something regularly, persistently mauls the child, leaving him—and his father—crushed in body and spirit. And just in case we could not imagine it well enough, Luke gives us a description of an actual seizure: "But while he was still coming, the demon threw him down and sent him into convulsion" (9:42).

By this point in Luke, we have seen Jesus approached by several persons who petition him to help someone else. "They" ask him about Simon's mother-in-law (4:38); the Jewish elders ask him to come heal the centurion's servant, and then the centurion makes his own appeal (7:1-10); Jairus asks Jesus to come to heal his daughter (9:40-42, 49-56). In each case, Jesus does not hesitate to help; only when the crowds of Capernaum want to keep him for themselves does he refuse assistance, but then only after healing all the sick in the town (4:40-43). Jesus gave life back to the dead son of the widow at Nain, the only place where Luke says he was "filled with compassion" (7:13). We readers are therefore prepared for a positive response to the father's request.

But there is a complicating factor. The father has first asked the disciples for help: "I begged your disciples to cast it out, but they were unable." The word "unable" is a form of the word *dynamis*, usually translated "power." The attentive reader will recall that in 9:1 Jesus gave the twelve *dynamis* and *exousia* (authority) over all demons, and that in 9:6 the narrator reported that they went village by village preaching the good news and healing many. Have they ever been able to cast out demons? If so, they have somehow lost the knack. [They Were Unable] The attentive reader will also notice that the failure is not just for the Twelve, but for "disciples." Perhaps Luke means us to think only of the Twelve here, but in my opinion, the larger group mentioned at 9:18 and 9:23 is in view. Jesus took only three up the mountain with him, but when those four came back down, they rejoined the "all" of v. 23. If this is correct, then the disciples who fail to exorcise include not just the Twelve, but also the larger group who include, for example, Mary Magdalene and other women from whom Jesus cast out evil spirits (8:2-3).

One more note: the father says "they were unable," not "they were unwilling." The reader is to imagine not only the boy's long painful disability as brought on by an evil spirit, but also the sad spectacle of repeated failures by the disciples to relieve his suffering. Having been healed themselves, some of them, and others

They Were Unable

"I want to say how very sorry I am that you feel that Carolyn, you, and your family are not welcomed here anymore. There is, however, a problem with Carolyn's coming to Sunday school. First, it is questionable whether this would be the best environment for Carolyn, as there are so many children her age but without her handicap in the class. You must consider how this will affect the other children in the class. Besides, parents are starting to take their children out of this particular Sunday school class.

"Second, the real problem is that there is no one to work and worship with Carolyn; we have no money to hire anyone to be with your daughter during Sunday school. I'm sure you wouldn't want Carolyn to just sit there without receiving any kind of religious instruction. If you or your wife would like to come with Carolyn and work with us in providing Christian instruction to her, that would be marvelous. However, if you are unable or unwilling to provide that, why then do you lay the burden at our feet? Carolyn is your family's responsibility, not ours."

Brett Webb-Mitchell, *Dancing with Disabilities: Opening the Church to All God's Children* (Cleveland OH: United Church Press, 1996), 90.

having been given specific power and authority by Jesus, they cannot help.

When Jesus "answers" in 9:41, we naturally presume he is responding to the father's request, and so "O faithless and perverse generation" sounds inappropriate. But Jesus is commenting on the disciples' lack of faith. In 7:31, he uses "generation" to mean the Pharisees, who accepted neither John the Baptist nor Jesus. In 11:29-32, he uses "this generation" to refer to those who do not respond in faith despite the miracles Jesus has done. In 11:47-51, it means Pharisees again, whose rejection of Jesus makes them also complicit in the deaths of the former prophets of God. Thus, Luke uses it to mean a specific group of people who have all committed the same offense. Here, it is the disciples who have failed to do what Jesus would have done. They are "faithless," as at the moment in the boat in the storm, when they should have either stilled the tempest themselves or rested secure in God's care for them (8:25); they are also "perverse," meaning that they have deliberately turned away from Jesus' instruction.

Taking stock so far, we have two petitioners: the boy, who cannot speak for himself, since the demon holds him in thrall, and the father, whose strong emotions make him shout his request to Jesus. We have two requests, one to the disciples and one to Jesus. And we have two potential benefactors, the whole gang of disciples—who try, but cannot help—and Jesus, whose first move is not to heal but to rebuke: "You no-count, hard-headed people, until when shall I be with you and put up with you?" Well, we know the answer, since he has already predicted his death in Jerusalem; they can expect Jesus to be around until they reach the holy city near the end of the Gospel.

The healing comes rather quickly after such a powerful introduction. Jesus commands the father to bring his son, and although the demon gives the poor child one more convulsion, Jesus commands it to leave. He then "healed the child"—perhaps Luke thinks of Jesus undoing damage left by the evil spirit—and "gave him to his father," an echo of the healing of the dead boy at Nain (7:15).

From Luke's perspective, evil is the source of this disease. We do not know much about Luke's understanding of the origin of evil spirits, but if he shared the views of many ancients, he may have believed that ultimately, evil spirits resulted from the sins of the fallen angels who consorted with women (Gen 6:1-4). Their progeny were terrifying giants, whose offspring were the demons who caused all manner of sickness and suffering. If Luke shared this worldview, then he was unlikely to have believed that the demon infested the boy because of anything he or his parents had done. Under this way of thinking, the boy's condition was the result of cosmic, not personal, evil; evil beings much more powerful than humans infected the cosmos and made living hell for some unfortunate people. God did not create the demons, nor did God send the demon on this boy, but some of God's powerful created beings, in their freedom, chose corruption and we all suffer for it, some of us more than others. Suffering is not distributed fairly, but that's to be expected, since it is distributed by evil beings; for the sufferer, cold comfort. [Suffering Isn't Fair]

Except for the personified view of evil, the view just described is not terribly different from the way some modern theologians think about the suffering of innocents. Creation is incomplete, or it has been corrupted by human selfishness. We know of some specific birth defects that our technology and modern pharmaceuticals and environmental pollution and use of hallucinogens have caused; how many others have we caused unwittingly? Moreover, we spend billions on trivial pursuits and hundreds of billions more destroying others or developing the capacity to do so. Were those assets and energy invested in research to cure diseases, what miracles could we do? Millions die daily, needlessly, from hunger and from diseases that accompany hunger. We who eat well and live well while they die are the origins of their personal evil; we are the demons who torment them, although we and they are only impersonally linked. "Faithless and perverse generation," indeed, to have strayed so far from "blessed are the poor" and to have ignored so thoroughly "he has filled the poor with good things, but the rich he has sent empty away."

In this pericope, the disciples fail. Since Luke takes out Mark's "this kind can only come out by prayer and fasting," their failure is no longer mitigated by the particularly tough nature of the case. And when you put "they were unable" together with "faithless and perverse," you get the odd picture of a group trying to do the right thing being accused of deliberately turning aside from Jesus' teaching. He gave them power over all demons; why could they not exercise it when it was needed and when they were willing? The paradox is unsettling, but also descriptive of where many ministers find themselves when facing persons with mental illnesses or physical disabilities. In this story, the boy, the father, and the disciples

Suffering Isn't Fair

All nondisabled people have a certain probability of involuntarily becoming disabled during their lifetimes. However, this probability is not randomly distributed. Studies reveal a disproportionately higher percentage of persons with disabilities among racial minorities, lower socioeconomic, and rural populations. . . . About twice as many people in families with incomes of less than $20,000 a year are impaired, when compared with the total population.

Nancy L. Eiesland, *The Disabled God: Toward a Liberatory Theology of Disability* (Nashville: Abingdon, 1994), 64–65.

all find themselves disabled by the demon—not equally, of course, because the level of physical, mental, and emotional agony varies greatly between them. The answer, according to the pericope, is to bring the sufferer to Jesus. In the story as we have it, the father comes, bringing the boy, first to the disciples, and then, having failed to receive what he needs, the father brings his son to Jesus. Could we imagine a different scenario where one or two disciples—say, Mary Magdalene and Joanna—bring the boy and the father to Jesus, confessing their inability to help, and asking Jesus to intervene?

Sure, it's an imaginary moment, but we get to it by thinking about what would have been the right thing for the disciples to do. Radical access, or what one theologian calls "copious hosting," is the natural extension of Luke's theme of hospitality: the church must become a place where physical and mental disabilities are not seen as problems for those suffering from them, but as problems that the community of Christ must address: "when bars and supermarkets are more accessible than altars, we all bear the shame."[13]

Our pericope ends with Jesus healing the boy and giving him back to his father, astounding everyone there. Some theologians suggest that the distinction between healing and cure will help make this and other healing passages less a text of terror than it has sometimes been:

> Generally speaking, most interpretations of the disability narratives in the four Gospels are a problem for people with disabilities . . . . First, they create a "fix-it" mentality suggesting the idea that getting rid of a disability is the ideal. Second, they often perpetrate marginalization by portraying people with disabilities as marginalized figures. Finally, within the Christian tradition an unfortunate and harmful "cult of healing" has developed that misinterprets the relationship between faith and healing.[14]

Rather than putting our focus on how the illness was cured—the foaming and other behaviors removed—we could instead focus on how the boy was healed, symbolized by Jesus giving him back to his father, freed from any evil stigma and safe from harm. Such healing, or restoration to spiritual wholeness, is no small gift, and any of us can imagine how our Christian community might carry out such healings regularly: "Our own hearts and spirits can be healed, again and again, in Christ, by the power of the Holy Spirit, often through the experience of the sacramental life of the Christian community. It is this type of healing that should be an ordinary event in the Christian life . . . ."[15]

Read in this way, the point of the story is that the boy and the boy's father found peace, acceptance, welcome, and community. Read imaginatively as a model for ministry, the story could teach us as much about the healing of the community of Jesus' followers as about the healing of a boy. Some congregations have become hospitable, welcome homes for single parents and their emotionally disturbed or mentally or physically disabled children, safe places giving something close to a miracle for everyone. Others, tragically, have not been able to do so:

> She [the pastor] said, "Well, Diane, you can't get in the choir."
> And I said, "Why not?"
> And she said, "Well, for one, there's a step going up to the choir."
> "Yeah," I said, "You could make a ramp. Or, I could be up there already when the choir marches on." . . . And I said, "Carl [the speaker' husband], he's in the choir . . . . Carl would make sure I got up there. People would make sure I got up there."
> "Oh, no," she said. "And plus that, when we all stand, and you're sitting there, that would look so awful. It would look so uneven. And what about your robe? You can't wear a big old robe."
> I said, "I could get one made for me."
> She said, "Oh, it just wouldn't look right."[16]

Who needs healing here, Diane or her pastor? Both, actually, but in different ways. If Diane could be given a "normal" body, her life would be easier, but then so would the pastor's, since she would no longer have to invent ways to keep Diane out of the choir. But if the pastor's sense of what's not "right" could be healed—if she could picture Diane (who was born "without lower limbs and with above-elbow upper extremity stumps"[17]) as a whole person and part of the kingdom of God, then Diane could put on her robe and sing, and maybe we'd all be healed.

Dealing with the issue of disability in the context of the Scriptures will never simply be a matter of sensitizing able-bodied students of ministry about the needs and perspectives of the disabled. Nor is it simply a matter of the community as a whole providing access and inclusion for all its members (as wonderful as that prospect might be). Ultimately it is a matter of learning from and being transformed by the vantage point, experience, and insight into the meaning of human existence and the Christian message that in many instances persons with disabilities can provide. Put quite simply, the challenge for the church ultimately is not so much to learn how to minister to disabled people but to be open to being ministered to and, ultimately, healed by them.[18]

Second Passion Prediction, 9:43b-50

Steve Martin used to do a stand-up routine with a banjo, claiming that the happy plunking sound made sad songs impossible, and he'd sing "death, gloom, murder, despair" with a snappy little tune running underneath to make his point. Luke has given us the transfiguration—Jesus, Elvis-like in glowing robes with clouds and voices and disappearing sidemen—and the very public successful healing of the demonic boy. In both cases, the audience is overwhelmed with God's power demonstrated through Jesus. With this as the background music, how can the disciples take seriously his predictions of betrayal and death? What human hands could seize a man who can light up like a Christmas tree and throw out demons with a word? [Passion Predictions Confusing]

Passion Predictions Confusing

There is nothing unlikely in supposing that the disciples would be troubled. Perhaps in their secret thoughts even they would say, "How is One so glorious, who raised the dead by his godlike power, rebuked the seas and winds, and by a word crushed Satan, now seized as a prisoner and caught in these murderer's traps? Were we mistaken in thinking he is God?"

Cyril of Alexandria, *Commentary on Luke*, Homily 53, cited in Arthur A. Just Jr., ed., *Luke* (ACCS: NT, vol. 3; Downer's Grove IL: Intervarsity Press, 2003), 163.

The material in this section is all Markan: the second prediction, taken from Mark 9:30-32; the argument over who is greatest, from Mark 9:33-37; and the episode of the "strange exorcist," from Mark 9:38-41. Luke, however, is ramping up for the long journey section, which runs from Luke 9:51 to 19:27, and although 9:51 begins a new section, all the material in Luke 9, reaching back to the sending of the Twelve, speaks to the issue of discipleship.

While everyone is busy being amazed at everything Jesus has done—imagine for the soundtrack a gospel choir, singing "Oh Happy Day" or "He Touched Me"—the camera zooms in on Jesus, who is now speaking straight to his disciples, the ones who just now were exposed as incompetent exorcists. The Greek is emphatic: "Hey, you lot, put these words into your ears." In the first passion prediction, Jesus had said that if they were ashamed of him and his words, they would be rejected on Judgment Day, and at the Transfiguration, God ordered Peter, James, and John to listen to Jesus.[19] This is the essence of the gospel, the word that has been spread by Gabriel, Mary, John the Baptist, and now Jesus; if the disciples fail to pay attention to these words, they are in serious trouble.

Luke makes the second passion prediction much shorter than the first: "The Son of Man is about to be handed over into the hands of men." No mention here of crucifixion or resurrection, in part because that can be assumed from the first prediction, but in part because it makes the disciples' incomprehension starker: what part of "I will be betrayed" don't you understand? Luke piles it on: "But they did not comprehend this word, it was hidden from them so that they would not understand it, and they were afraid to ask him about this word." Possibly the passive voice of "they did not comprehend" is meant to suggest that God had hidden the true meaning away, to be revealed after the resurrection (24:45, "then he opened their minds to understand the scriptures"), but inasmuch as Jesus has already spelled out in detail what will happen (9:21-27), it seems unlikely that Luke is letting the disciples off the hook by claiming that God clouded their minds. More likely, the four phrases of v. 45 all add up to "they failed to understand."[20]

Now the camera pans to show the disciples—the larger group, not just the Twelve—scratching their heads, looking puzzled at one another, shrugging their shoulders, and the music behind them is dark and sad. Suddenly, without anything or anyone intervening, an argument starts. Literally, Luke writes, "Now an argument entered among them"—an interesting turn of phrase, as it is both a personification ("Old Man Wrangle just walked in the room") and a euphemism (not "Peter started bragging about how he was the greatest disciple, and James jumped down his throat," but "Hey, that argument just started all by itself"). The disciples zip from "That Jesus, man, he is amazing" to "What's he talking about" to "No, I'm the best disciple" with scarcely a breath, making them much like the crowd at the birth of John the Baptist (see discussion at 1:57-80) or like the Maltese islanders of Acts 28:1-10.

Well, the answer is that none of them is the greatest. Greatest what? Best at disappointing anxious fathers of sick boys? Quickest to misunderstand Jesus' predictions of his death? The argument is probably meant to be about pecking order—which student is closest to Jesus, is the most favored—and following the prediction of his death, has the unsavory overtones of an argument over succession ("Uh, after you're gone, maybe I can be head honcho?"). Since Luke repeats this scene at the Last Supper (22:24), he means for his readers to think of images all too familiar in their time: the worthless sons of the tyrant Herod the Great jockeying for position around their father's deathbed, the endless intrigues in Rome about who would succeed childless emperors. Some of these succession disputes threw the whole world into chaos; think of the wars following Julius Caesar's death, or the eighteen months following the assassination of Nero. [Succession Struggles]

Luke describes Jesus knowing what they were thinking—they cannot understand his spoken words, but he can slice through their words to what they intend—just as Simeon predicted he would ("the disputes [*dialogismoi*, translated "argument" in 9:46 and "thoughts" in 9:47] of many will be revealed"), and just as Jesus did

Succession Struggles

As Herod the Great lay dying from a very painful illness, his son Antipater, already imprisoned by his father's command, tried to bribe the jailer with promises of rewards once he took power. Herod found out and ordered his son's death (Josephus, *Ant.* 17.185-187), and then changed his will: "he appointed Antipas, to whom he had before left the kingdom, to be tetrarch of Galilee and Perea, and granted the kingdom to Archelaus. He also gave Gaulonitis and Trachonitis and Paneas to Philip" (*Ant.* 17.188-89). Both Archelaus and Antipas went to Rome, each wishing to unseat the other; neither got everything he wanted, and in time, both lost what they had through agitating for more. Augustus appointed Archelaus ruler of Judea, then deposed him ten years later, appointing Roman procurators in his place. Antipas ruled Galilee and Perea until AD 39, when he was banished for pestering Gaius ("Caligula") for more territory to rule.

when confronted by the opposition of the Pharisees in 5:22. As many commentators note, this characterization connects the disciples with the behavior of Jesus' opponents—not so good, all things considered! But there is a difference; whereas the Pharisees have accused Jesus in their hearts of blasphemy, the disciples have, by their behavior, repudiated Jesus' teachings. Which is worse, to decide Jesus is a fraud and say so, or to claim to be loyal to him while ignoring his words?

So Jesus takes a child—perhaps even the same child he has just healed, since the Luke runs the scenes together[21]—and says two things. First, "Whoever receives this child [this particular child, not children in general] in my name, receives me, and whoever receives me, receives the One who sent me." Such a clever word! Let this sink into your ears, doofuses: I could send this child out as a disciple if I chose, and the work that God sent me to do would still get done. Whoever goes out in my name represents me and in turn represents God who sent me. This is like John the Baptist's word to the crowds: God could make the nation of Israel out of rocks if God chose. Don't get cocky, thinking that you disciples have a lock on anything.

From Claudius

Tiberius Claudius Caesar Augustus Germanicus [conqueror of the Germans] Imperator [holder of *imperium*, the sort of power a victorious general had on the battlefield—power of life and death, of being able to make war or peace, etc.], Pontifex Maximus [high priest], holder of tribunician power, consul designate, to the city of Alexandria, greeting.

Letter from Claudius to the city of Alexandria (AD 41), in C. K. Barrett, *The New Testament Background* (rev. ed.; New York: Harper and Row, 1987), 47.

Second, Jesus says, "The smallest living among you all, that one is 'The Great.'" Another stinger: Luke and his readers know all about the Roman elites and their paths to glory, ending in honorific names and titles. [From Claudius] Any member of the Jesus movement want to be known as "Magnus"? It's all about shrinkage—get very small! Seriously, the saying is hardly a direction for being the top person as much as a repudiation of the whole notion of "top-ness." Nobody is the greatest; John the Baptist was the greatest (7:28), but even he would gladly trade his spot for entrance into the kingdom of God. If God is King and God gives the kingship to Jesus and he gives it, in turn to all his friends (22:28-30), then there is no one king in charge. And if, in that kingdom, the youngest and smallest is valued just the same as the leader—if the king and the scullery maid have the same status (22:24-27)—then there is no status. As Jesus' mother said,

"He has scattered the proud in the imaginations of their hearts/he unseated the powerful from their thrones/and lifted up the poverty-stricken" (1:51-52).

If we are still filming this scene, the disciples are all gathered around Jesus and the boy. Luke gives us no clues about whether they are puzzled or rejoicing or grief-stricken, so we go from a tight focus on Jesus and the boy—Jesus looking very serious, the boy perhaps looking embarrassed at the attention—to a wide shot showing the whole group of disciples. John raises his hand: "Master [he uses the word *epistata*, which comes up when people are not understanding Jesus very well], we saw someone casting out demons in your name and we stopped him, because he was not following with us."

Oh, good grief—are you serious? You can't exorcise, although you'd like to, and so you prohibit others from doing what you can't? You want to be the greatest, and Jesus refuses to play that game, so you make sure that nobody else can show you up? All of us in congregational ministry are unfortunately familiar with moves like this. Shameful, but not implausible. Another way to read the boundary setting is in terms of Luke's community and the diversity of Christian practice in the late first century. From Acts, we know of arguments between the Hebrews and Hellenists (6:1) and between the circumcision faction and Paul (15:1-2; 21:17-26); there are the disciples of John the Baptist (19:1-7) and the inadequately instructed Apollos (18:24-28). There are strong hints in Luke's resurrection account that he knows of doubts over the truly physical nature of the resurrected Jesus (24:36-43)—perhaps indications of an early version of Docetic Christianity. All of these involve issues of community identity: who is truly Christian, and who is a false believer?

Luke's Jesus replies, "Quit stopping [him], because whoever is not against you is for you." Luke's Jesus will later say, in a different context, "Whoever is not with me is against me, and whoever does not come together with me is scattering" (11:23). There, Jesus is reacting to the accusation by some that he casts out demons through the power of Satan and to the demand by others that he do a miracle to prove his true origins. That is no longer a question of who loves Jesus most or follows him most closely—not a boundary issue; instead, it's a question of Jesus' own identity—a center issue. You cannot be part of the group if you believe that Jesus is possessed by a demon, but you can cast out demons in Jesus' name even if you are not part of the named, preferred circle. "Whoever is not against you is for you" means "make your network

Whoever Is Not against You

[The apostles] imagined that permission to be invested with the authority that he granted them was not given to anyone else but only to them . . . We find something like this also in the ancient sacred scriptures . . . . When those who were chosen assembled at the first tabernacle, except for only two men who remained in the camp, the spirit of prophecy descended on them. Not only did those who assembled in the holy tabernacle prophesy but also those who remained in the camp. It says, "Joshua the son of Nun, the minister of Moses, one of his chosen men, said, 'My lord Moses, forbid them.' But Moses said to him, 'Are you jealous for my sake? Would that all the Lord's people were prophets, that the Lord would put his spirit upon them!'" . . . All who wish to act to his glory are on the side of us who love Christ and are crowned by his grace. This is a law to the churches continuing even to this day.

Cyril of Alexandria, *Commentary on Luke*, Homily 55; cited in Arthur A. Just Jr., ed., *Luke* (ACCS: NT, vol. 3; Downer's Grove IL: Intervarsity Press, 2003), 165–66.

of partners wide," while "whoever is not with me is against me" means that nobody who thinks Jesus is evil can possibly be your partner. [Whoever Is Not against You]

The nameless child, who must be welcomed in Jesus' name, and the anonymous exorcist, who must not be stopped from using Jesus' name, are icons of Christian hospitality. Anyone—even this child—could be Jesus' emissary, sent in his name, to be welcomed as Jesus and as the One who sent Jesus. Anyone—even this faith healer—who is doing the work of Christ in Christ's name deserves respect rather than harassment from Jesus' followers. We have enough real enemies (think of Antipas's glib "Well, I beheaded John") that we must daily face the prospect of the cross; we don't need to make enemies among the followers of the Lord. And for sure we don't need to wrangle over who is the best or the purest or the most authentic or the most ancient or the most enthusiastic or the most correct. Ain't none of us the greatest—except maybe Elvis, and he's gone.[22]

Following Jesus, 9:51-62

Here begins Luke's journey section, wherein Jesus travels from Galilee to Jerusalem, a distance of approximately 85 miles and 408 verses, if you count the journey's end at 19:28. But Jesus does not actually enter Jerusalem until 19:45, when Luke has him going into the temple. If we count that as the end of the journey, it has covered most of 10 chapters and 425 verses. By contrast, Mark's Jesus takes the express train, covering the same distance in one chapter; Luke's Jesus takes the local, stopping at every cattle crossing along the way. [Jesus' Journey]

Jesus' Journey

Jesus just left Chicago and he's bound for New Orleans
Workin' from one end to the other and all points in between

"Jesus Just Left Chicago," ZZ Top, 1973.

Most of the material in this section comes from someplace other than Mark. Luke uses Mark's story of the unnamed exorcist (Mark 9:38-41//Luke 9:49-50) and then picks Mark's narrative back up at the blessing of the children (Mark 10:13-16//Luke 18:15-17). Between Mark 9:41 and 10:13 there are two pericopes: some sayings about being a stumbling block or having your body parts cause you to sin (Mark 9:42-50), from which Luke takes two verses (17:1-2); and the pericope about divorce (Mark 10:1-12), from which Luke takes only one verse (16:18).

Some interpreters see a pattern in the way Luke arranges the material. One theory is that the material forms a chiasm, where the story at the end matches the one at the beginning, the second story matches the penultimate story, and so forth until you get to the middle.[23] Others have argued that the trip is based on the journey of Israel from Egypt to the promised land (more on this below). Most interpreters (including myself) see no particular pattern in the arrangement of the material, but think that the journey itself is the thing; rather than arranging the new non-Markan material into speeches or lectures, as Matthew did, Luke chose to keep Jesus moving, more an itinerant preacher than a classroom teacher.

Here are the mileposts Luke lists; note the vague nature of things until 18:35:

9:51—Sets his face to go to Jerusalem
9:52—Enters a Samaritan village
9:56—Goes into another village
9:57—Traveling along the road
10:1—Sends 70 (72) in pairs to every village he intends to go
10:38—While they were traveling he entered a certain village
11:1—He was in a certain place praying
11:37—Enters the house of a Pharisee
11:53—Goes outside (the house? the village?)
13:10—He was teaching in one of the synagogues
13:22—He was passing through town by town, village by village, teaching, and making his way into Jerusalem
13:33—I must be on my way, because it is impossible for a prophet to be killed outside Jerusalem
14:1—He entered the house of a certain ruler of the Pharisees
14:25—Many crowds were going with him
17:11—While traveling towards Jerusalem, he passed through the region between Samaria and Galilee
18:31—See, we are going up to Jerusalem
18:35—While he was nearing Jericho
19:1—And entering, he passed through Jericho
19:28—And saying these things, he was going ahead, going up into Jerusalem
19:29—And so it was that as he drew near to Bethphage and Bethany, at the mountain called "of Olives"

19:37—While he was already drawing near to the descent of the
Mount of Olives
19:41—As he drew near, seeing the city he wept
19:45—And entering into the temple

Most of the time you cannot tell where Jesus is on a map. At
9:51, he is in Galilee somewhere, and in 9:52 goes into a Samaritan
village—rather like saying he left one state and entered a small
town in the state just south of the first one. That does not locate
him precisely, and from there, things only get worse. When he goes
into "another village," is that still in Samaria, or has he retreated
north a bit to get back into friendly Galilee? In 10:38 he is in
another nameless village, the home of Martha, and between that
story and 13:22 the reader gets no real sense of movement; the
Pharisee's house at 11:37 could be in Martha's village, or might be
somewhere else. Luke 13:22, however, means for us to think that
Jesus is systematically moving south, toward Jerusalem, but with
frequent stops, since he hits every town and village. When we get
to 17:11, however, we are caught up short. In the first place, there
is no region between Samaria and Galilee. They are contiguous
areas, like North and South Dakota. In the second place, if Luke
means that Jesus was hugging the borderlands dividing the two
regions, he was going east or west, not south toward Jerusalem.
Why is he still up in Galilee in 17:11 if his face was set for
Jerusalem at 9:51? Clearly, Luke is not terribly interested in convincing the reader that Jesus is ticking off the miles between Galilee
and Jerusalem. Rather, the journey, while not *simply* a metaphor
and a plot device, is mostly just that: a way for Luke to organize a
treasure trove of non-Markan material and a way to keep Jesus, like
the gospel itself, on the move.

Lots of biblical narratives are journey stories—homecomings,
quests, escape and chase stories, migrations, etc. Sometimes Jesus'
journey has been compared to the Exodus, particularly because of
the use of ἔξοδος (exodus, "departure") in 9:31 to refer to his
death.[24] Maybe we can think of some of the miracles Jesus does as
parallel to the ten plagues Moses brought on Egypt; there is the
pursuit by Herod Antipas in 9:7-9 and 13:31, the rending of the
temple veil to substitute for the parting of the Red Sea, etc. But
Galilee is not equivalent in any real sense to Egypt; if anything,
Jesus is heading toward danger and away from home. That is, if he
has a home; 9:58 will suggest that he does not, and so the journey
to Jerusalem is hard to read as a migration or a homecoming. Jesus
is moving—in circuitous fashion, to be sure—toward his destiny,

accompanied by companions, beset by riddles and obstacles; this is more like a quest than like the other sorts of journey stories. [The Journey of St. Paul the Hermit]

The Jacob narratives are a biblical quest story. The wily Jacob leaves home under duress to go to his uncle's house. On the way he has a visit from God to give him (and the reader) a sense of his destiny. He must struggle in the foreign land to make his way and to demonstrate his wit and strength and patience. He overcomes all the obstacles, must again leave under duress, and as he nears home, face the fears that made him run away—another encounter with God and with his murderous older brother. Jacob does not die, but the storyline assumes that his life hangs in the balance, and that all the great company and treasure he has accumulated will not save him. He must live or die by what he has learned and what he has become. In the fight with the angel, he is wounded, but survives to face and to be reconciled with his brother. The story of Genesis goes on, but Jacob's quest is over when "Jacob journeyed to Succoth, and built himself a house, and made booths for his cattle" (Gen 33:17)—home, safe and sound, and all his family and cattle with him.

Less familiar to some readers, but closer to being contemporaneous with Luke, is the quest undertaken by Tobias, his traveling companion Raphael, and his little dog Spike (just kidding—the dog is in the story, but not the name). Raphael is an angel who keeps his identity under wraps, but who gives the young man Tobias all sorts of helpful advice, like how to keep from being killed by a demon on his wedding night, how to speak politely to his future father-in-law, and what sort of salve might cure his father's blindness. The story of Tobit is much lighter in tone than Luke, but there is still life and death at issue: Tobit wants to die because of the shame of his blindness; Sarah, the demon-plagued seven-time virginal widow, wants to die rather than repeat the experience of watching her new husband be killed; and Tobias, brave young lad that he is, marries Sarah hoping that his friend's demon repellant works. In the end, nobody dies (although Sarah's father digs a grave for Tobias just in case), the newlyweds love each other, the salve solves Tobit's blindness, and everybody is happy.

One more example, at the risk of losing the reader's attention (assuming I ever had it), from the multitude of quest stories in serious and popular literature and movies: the quest of Ulysses

The Journey of St. Paul the Hermit

The boy, far-sighted as he was, had the wit to discern [the decision of his brother-in-law to betray him], and took flight to the mountains . . . . What had been his necessity became his free choice. Little by little he made his way, sometimes turning back and again returning, till at length he came upon a rocky mountain, and at its foot, at no great distance, a huge cave . . . . So then, in this beloved habitation, offered to him as it were by God himself, he lived his life through in prayer and solitude.

From *The Life of St. Paul the First Hermit*, in Helen Waddell, *The Desert Fathers* (Ann Arbor: University of Michigan Press, 1957), 30–31.

Everett McGill for reconciliation with his wife, as told in *O Brother, Where Art Thou?*[25] He is manifestly not a Christ figure, and the script is loosely based on a combination of Homer's *Odyssey* and the lives and legends of various Southern American personalities. McGill is a sneak and a liar, like Odysseus and Jacob, but he does put his life on the line more than once to rescue his two less able companions, Pete and Delmar. They, too, face "many ob-stackles" along the way, including the real threat of death on several occasions, and at movie's end, they seem to have come home to safety and a brighter future.

Jesus' quest, like Jacob's, is for his destiny. Like Tobias, Jesus has companions, much less competent than Raphael, perhaps more intelligent than Delmar and Pete. Like all three heroes, Jesus must face dangers, toils, and snares on his way to the holy city. In all these quest stories, there is a real threat of death, more gravely narrated in Genesis and Luke than in Tobit and the movie, but present in all of them. [Heroic Struggles in Quest Stories] That Jesus actually dies, and that he knows in advance that he must die, increases the seriousness of the quest and changes the nature of the happy ending. Jesus is not nearly killed by an angel or his brother or a demon or a dead-eyed high sheriff; he is actually killed by a whole collection of individuals and institutions who, inspired by Satan, conspire to put him to death. By the time Jesus sets his face to do this, the reader has already heard about it three times: once in detail (9:21-22) and twice in less specific language (9:31, 44).

His death is thus neither a surprise nor a defeat, as the deaths of Jacob, Tobias, or McGill would have been; instead, his death is the last great trial to be mastered before Jesus' quest is complete. Many heroes are wounded in the climactic trial and changed thereby: Jacob walks with a limp, Frodo loses a finger. Fewer quest stories narrate the actual death and rebirth of the hero, and this change darkens the journey, taking the overall narrative much closer to tragedy. This is a long dark highway, and Jesus must walk it to the end.

Luke, who wants the reader to see this moment as a transition, piles up more words than will actually go into a stylish English sentence: "So it was that when the days of his assumption were fulfilled that he set his face to travel to Jerusalem." The construction is much like 2:6: "So it was that while they were there, the

Heroic Struggles in Quest Stories

In his turn, royal Odysseus told [Penelope] of all the discomfiture he had inflicted on his foes and all the miseries which he himself had undergone . . . . He began with his first victory over the Cicones . . . he spoke of what the Cyclops did . . . of his stay with Aeolus . . . and how the gale, since Providence would not let him reach his home so soon, had caught him up once more and driven him in misery down the highways of the fish. Next came his call at Telepylus on the Laestrygonian coast, where the savages destroyed his fleet and all his fighting men . . . . He spoke of Circe and her magic arts. . . .

The Odyssey, 23.308-349 (trans. E. V. Rieu; New York: Penguin, 1946), 348–49.

days were completed for her deliverance," and Luke's resumption at 9:51 of a style more influenced by the Septuagint (as in chs. 1–2) helps to alert the reader to a change of direction. The Greek word here translated "assumption" is from a root that means "take up," and Luke uses another form from the same root at Acts 1:11. In both cases, it refers to Jesus being taken up into heaven by God; we can call it "ascension," but that word loses the stress on God's agency. The journey goes through the cross and the grave, but the end of it is God taking Jesus up to be in God's presence (24:51).

In the meantime, however, Jesus has to go to Jerusalem. His first step along this long road that "goes ever on and on" is to send out messengers "before his face." This again takes us back to the beginning of the Gospel, when God sends Gabriel to announce the good news to Zechariah and to Mary, and then to announce the birth of Jesus to the shepherds. Jesus acknowledges his own sent-ness in 4:18-19, 43, and sends his own messengers in 9:1-6, just as John the Baptist does in 7:18-20. This, then, is the second sending by Jesus; there will be another in 10:1, and yet another at the end of the Gospel, after the resurrection. "Before his face" implies that the messengers are to prepare the hearers to be an audience for Jesus when he arrives—as Elijah was supposed to prepare the hearts of Israelites for the coming of God in judgment (Mal 4:5-6).

But things go badly. "They"—the messengers, who are not identified as disciples (the bigger group) or as the Twelve—go into a Samaritan village to prepare it for him, but the villagers do not receive him, because "his face was traveling [that's what Luke writes—he probably means "set for traveling"] to Jerusalem." This raises several questions that the text does not precisely answer for us, but about which we may make guesses.

Did Jesus send the disciples into Samaria in an attempt to spread the good news there? Based on what happens in chapter 10, I presume so; there, he sends out the seventy into every village where he himself intends to go, and gives them instructions to heal the sick, cast out demons, and preach the good news. I think Luke means that Jesus sent the disciples into Samaria, not just to find lodging for the night, but to find host homes that could be the base for sharing the gospel while on his way south.

Why would the Samaritans reject Jesus simply because his ultimate goal was Jerusalem? As many commentators note, the parallel here with the sermon at Nazareth is helpful. There, Jesus' approval rating goes from "such a nice young man" to "let's kill him" because he tells the audience that God's blessings are often sent to Gentiles rather than to Jews. Here, the Samaritans have similar problems

The Samaritans

The city of Samaria was the site of the palace of many rulers over the ancient kingdom of Israel. It was sacked and destroyed by the Assyrians in 721 BC, and according to the Old Testament and to Assyrian records, close to 30,000 Israelites were deported to other parts of the Assyrian empire. The area passed under the control of the Babylonians (who destroyed Jerusalem and took many Judeans into exile in 587) and then the Persians. In Ezra-Nehemiah we read of the Samaritans resisting the efforts of returned Judean exiles to rebuild Jerusalem, for a mix of religious and political reasons. By the time of Jesus, "Samaria" meant the territory south of Galilee and north of Judea; the

Plain of Esdraelon, just south of Nazareth, was the approximate northern boundary, while a line just north of Jericho was the border in the south; the Jordan and the Mediterranean were the eastern and western edges.

Samaritans worshiped the God of Abraham, read the Pentateuch, and built a temple on Mount Gerizim where they conducted animal sacrifices in much the same fashion as the Jews at Jerusalem. John Hyrcanus, grandson of Mattathias who began the Maccabean revolt, led an expedition that destroyed the Samaritan temple in 128 BC. In Jesus' day, according to Josephus, the two groups hated each other and occasionally acted violently against each other (*Ant.* 20.118-136).

imagining that God would send good news to their religious and ethnic rivals. [The Samaritans]

What is the connection between "they [the disciples] entered the village" and "they [the villagers] did not receive him [Jesus]"? Jesus said, "Whoever receives this child in my name receives me" (9:48); the disciples entered the village as Jesus' messengers, and so by refusing to listen to their message, the villagers refuse Jesus. Luke does not give us a transcript of what the messengers said, but since the villagers know about Jerusalem, perhaps we are to infer that the messengers said something about the ultimate goal: "He is preaching the kingdom of God, healing, and so forth, but he also says he's going up to Jerusalem, where he will be crucified." Nope, not interested, say the Samaritans.

"Seeing this"—were they part of the messenger team, or were they standing with Jesus, watching?—James and John are incensed: "Lord, do you wish that we should command fire to descend from heaven and consume them?" What colors are the clouds in your world, guys? Come on—you could not cast out a demon only about twenty verses ago, so what had made you suddenly become Elijah, roasting idolaters for their impudence? Luke quotes 2 Kings 1:10, 12 in the last few words of 9:54, just so we won't miss the connection, and like most of his uses of Old Testament narratives, this one comes with a twist. King Ahaziah of Samaria lies sick and sends messengers (same words as Luke 9:52) to seek an oracle from Baal-zebub, but Elijah heads them off at the pass, telling them that the real God has decreed that for the sin of idolatry, the king will never rise from his bed. The king then sends a captain and fifty soldiers to order Elijah to appear before the king; Elijah says, "If I am a man of God, fire will descend from heaven and devour you and your fifty," and it does. This happens again (with another fifty-one persons), and then the third captain asks nicely instead of commanding the prophet. Luke, typically, inverts elements of the story: Jesus, the man of God, sends the messengers, rather than the Samaritans; they refuse the invitation, but then the messengers want to call down the fire. The reader is supposed to know not only the story of 2 Kings 1:1-18, where the Samaritan idolaters are really Israelites (AKA the northern kingdom), but also the first-century context, where Samaritans and Jews hate each other.

Which brings us back to the narrative: Jesus, marching to a different cadence, wants to take the story into Samaria, but they will have none of it. The disciples want to speed up Judgment Day, calling down fire on them like was done on Sodom and Gomorrah. But Jesus rebukes them, embodying the commands he will give in 10:10-12: wipe the dust off your feet and move on, and trust God to sort things out on that eventual day. The story also serves to illustrate the continued ability of the disciples to get a few things right—they must have correctly stated Jesus' intention to go to Jerusalem—and many significant things wrong—they must have forgotten "love your enemies, do good to those who hate you, bless those who curse you, pray for those who abuse you"; not a word about "roast those who won't give you the time of day."

They do move on, Jesus and his companions, and encounter three potential recruits on the road. Think here of Everett, Delmar, and Pete meeting Tommy Johnson, George (not Babyface) Nelson, and Big Dan Teague. The first becomes a trusted companion, the second involves them in a bank heist and then abandons them, and the third beats them up and steals their cash. You never can tell about people you encounter on the way to your destiny. [Traveling Companions]

The first says what sounds like the right thing: "I will follow you wherever you may go." That was what Peter, James, John, and Levi did (5:11, 28). Jesus does not refuse him, but warns him about the nature of the journey: there is no home at the end of the day, and the life of an itinerant preacher is not easy. Wild animals have safe places where they can return every night, but not the Son of Man; for him, it will be one village after another, taking what is offered until he gets to Jerusalem, where there will be a cross and a grave. [The Itinerant]

The second gets the equivalent of an engraved invitation: "Follow me!" His request to be allowed to bury his father, as most argue, is to be understood to mean that he must, as a good son, care for his father until his death, and then he will be free to follow Jesus. This responsibility, based on the commandment "Honor

Traveling Companions

On the fourth evening, we made a friend. We were sitting in a nice little clearing beside the trail, our tents pitched, eating our noodles, savoring the exquisite pleasure of just sitting, when a plumpish, bespectacled young woman in a red jacket and the customary outsized pack came along. She regarded us with the crinkled squint of someone who is either chronically confused or can't see very well. We exchanged hellos and the usual banalities about the weather and where we were. Then she squinted at the gathering gloom and announced she would camp with us.

Her name was Mary Ellen. She was from Florida, and she was, as Katz forever after termed her in a special tone of awe, a piece of work. She talked nonstop, except when she was clearing out her Eustachian tubes (which she did frequently) by pinching her nose and blowing out with a series of violent and alarming snorts of a sort that would make a dog leave the sofa and get under a table in the next room. I have long known that it is part of God's plan for me to spend a little time with each of the most stupid people on earth, and Mary Ellen was proof that even in the Appalachian woods I would not be spared.

Bill Bryson, *A Walk in the Woods* (New York: Broadway, 1998), 51.

The Itinerant

"The Road goes ever on and on
Down from the door where it began.
Now far ahead the Road has gone,
And I must follow, if I can . . .

"Certainly it reminds me very much of Bilbo in the last years, before he went away. He used often to say there was only one Road; that it was like a great river: its springs were at every doorstep, and every path was its tributary. 'It's a dangerous business, Frodo, going out of your door,' he used to say. 'You step into the Road, and if you don't keep your feet, there is no knowing where you might be swept off to.'"

J. R. R. Tolkien, *The Lord of the Rings* (Boston: Houghton Mifflin, 1994), 72.

your father and your mother," was a broadly and deeply felt obligation in Jesus' day, and yet he was consistent in asking people to put the call to share his destiny ahead of everything else: "Whoever comes to me and does not hate father and mother, wife and children, brothers and sisters . . . cannot be my disciple" (14:26); "Look, we, abandoning our own, have followed you" (18:28). Even so, "let the dead bury their own dead" was a shocking, offensive way of putting the decision to follow Jesus. The physically dead cannot bury anyone, so if we take this literally, Jesus was suggesting that corpses could stay unburied while sons like this one followed Jesus. If we take the saying more metaphorically, it is only slightly easier: let the [spiritually] dead bury the [physically] dead, meaning that those who stay behind in this man's family would take up his responsibility to his father. In any case, Jesus is calling him to follow now, abandoning his family obligation, treating his father as if he were already dead. The shame accruing to this man and to his extended family would be substantial if he took up Jesus' command to go and preach the kingdom. [Burying the Dead]

The third is another volunteer, but one who has his heart in more than one place: he will follow Jesus, but he begs first to be able to set his household in order for his departure. Luke uses

Burying the Dead

The nearest friends can go
With anyone to death, comes so far short
They might as well not try to go at all.
No, from the time when one is sick to death,
One is alone, and he dies more alone.
Friends make pretence of following to the grave,
But before one is in it, their minds are turned
And are making the best of their way back to life
And living people, and things they understand.

From "Home Burial," by Robert Frost, in Edward Connery Lathem, ed., *The Poetry of Robert Frost* (New York: Henry Holt, 1979), 54.

the verb *apotassō* both to mean "bid farewell" (Acts 18:18) and "renounce" (Luke 14:33), and it probably carries both senses here; the volunteer is a householder who needs to take certain steps to get rid of all the legal obligations and family responsibilities that come with his position. Jesus' answer does not argue with his need to do that, but points out that if he were serious about joining up, he would already have settled his affairs. The metaphor of trying to plow while looking backwards is a vivid image of the unsettled mind: go home until you can decide whether you are in or out. [To Will One Thing]

Luke does not tell us what any of the three decided. These three are often called "would-be" followers of Jesus, but we cannot know that from the text. Luke is perfectly capable of rounding off a story; he gives us three more volunteers in 18:18–19:10, of whom one goes away sadly and two sign up. But he chooses to leave these stories open-ended, so that the reader is confronted at the beginning of Jesus' long dark road with the question of who will walk it with him.

To Will One Thing

Father in Heaven! What is a man without Thee! What is all that he knows, vast accumulation though it be, but a chipped fragment if he does not know Thee! What is all his striving, could it even encompass a world, but a half-finished work if he does not know Thee: Thee the One, who art one thing and who art all! So may Thou give to the intellect, wisdom to comprehend that one thing; to the heart, sincerity to receive this understanding; to the will, purity that wills only one thing. In prosperity may Thou grant perseverance to will one thing; amid distractions, collectedness to will one thing; in suffering, patience to will one thing.

Søren Kierkegaard, *Purity of Heart Is to Will One Thing* (trans. Douglas Steere; New York: Harper and Row, 1956), 31.

CONNECTIONS

This is a transitional chapter: Jesus begins to predict his death and "sets his face" for the hike down to Jerusalem. From this point on, the journey is toward the cross; even if Jesus still wanders around Galilee for a while, he is headed for his "exodus" (9:31), his "being taken up" (9:51). Jesus tells the disciples all this directly and plainly, but they do not, or cannot, understand. This is clearly an everlasting problem for Jesus' followers. American Christians take it for granted that our government should destroy those who take action against us, or those who plan actions against us, or even those who might someday act against us. A recent video game one wins by killing the soldiers of the Antichrist can call itself "Christian"; its designers opine that while Christians are clearly taught to love our enemies, that does not exclude killing an aggressor. "Take up your cross and follow me" remains obscure, not nearly as obvious as "the lessons of September 11" or "winning the war on terror" or "these colors don't run." Good luck preaching that one—it didn't work for Jesus, either.

The ninth is also a chapter about welcoming and rejecting. Herod wants to see Jesus; the Samaritans won't have him. The apostles travel among the villages of Galilee, preaching and healing and being hosted by others, but when faced with 5,000 hungry Galileans, they want to send the crowds back home. The gospel is spread table by table, fish and bread settling into tummies while words sink into ears.

Luke also continues his examination of the nature of discipleship, showing us a range of options in this chapter. Jesus puts up with the "faithless and perverse" disciples, and defends the "unknown exorcist," but appears to discourage three others who want to follow him. The Twelve are given powers over demons, but fail at exorcism and want to ban others from using a power they can't use themselves. James and John get rebuked for wanting to roast the inhospitable Samaritans; Peter is chastised for wanting to build shelters for Jesus, Moses, and Elijah; all of them are scolded for failing to help the demon-possessed boy; all of them squabble about who is greatest, when in fact none of them is. How will anybody ever measure up? Jesus is still hopeful, and in his willingness to keep teaching, keep correcting, keep encouraging, churches have one of their best arguments for not throwing in the towel.

NOTES

[1] Alan R. Culpepper, *The Gospel of Luke* (NIB, vol. 9; Nashville: Abingdon, 1995), 195–96.

[2] Joel B. Green, *The Gospel of Luke* (NICNT; Grand Rapids: Eerdmans, 1997), 359, makes the connection between this episode and the parable of the sower.

[3] Green, *Luke*, 369, suggests that the only reason Peter gets the right answer to Jesus' question is that Jesus has prayed for him.

[4] Culpepper, *Luke*, 199.

[5] Cited by Martin Hengel, *Crucifixion* (Philadelphia: Fortress, 1977), 31.

[6] Albert Schweitzer, *The Quest of the Historical Jesus* (2d ed., trans. W. Montgomery; London: Black, 1931), 400–401.

[7] Flannery O'Connor, "Revelation," in *The Complete Stories* (New York: Farrar, Straus, and Giroux, 1984), 489–90.

[8] Ibid., 490–91.

[9] O'Connor, "Revelation," 508–509.

[10] Kristofer Skrade, ed., *The Christian Handbook* (Minneapolis: Augsburg, 2005), 121–23.

[11] John J. Pilch, *The Cultural Dictionary of the Bible* (Collegeville MN: Liturgical Press, 1999), 73. I am using Pilch's distinction between illness and disease, curing and

healing, as found in his *Healing in the New Testament: Insights from Medical and Mediterranean Anthropology* (Minneapolis: Fortress, 2000), 3–17.

[12] The genitive absolute *katelthontōn autōn* could be translated "after they had come down" or "while they were coming down." The verse might mean that Jesus and the Three spent the night on the mountain and were met by the crowd as soon as they came down, or might mean that they came down, spent the night with the whole band of disciples, and met the crowd the next day.

[13] Ginny Thornburgh, quoted in Jennie Weiss Block, *Copious Hosting: A Theology of Access for People with Disabilities* (New York: Continuum, 2002), 141.

[14] Block, *Copious Hosting*, 102.

[15] Ibid., 104.

[16] Diane DeVries, quoted in Nancy L. Eiesland, *The Disabled God: Toward a Liberatory Theology of Disability* (Nashville: Abingdon, 1994), 35–36.

[17] Eiesland, *Disabled God*, 33.

[18] Donald Senior, "Beware of the Canaanite Woman: Disability and the Bible," in Marilyn E. Bishop, ed., *Religion and Disability* (Kansas City: Sheed and Ward, 1995), 25–26.

[19] Luke Timothy Johnson, *The Gospel of Luke* (SP, vol. 3; Collegeville MN: Liturgical Press, 1991), 160.

[20] Green, *Luke*, 390.

[21] Ibid., 391; Johnson, *Luke*, 159–60.

[22] "Eventually the whole world will be Elvis" (Andrei Codrescu, "Elvis 20/20: Concluding Remarks at the Third International Elvis Conference in Memphis, Tennessee, 1997," in *The Devil Never Sleeps and Other Essays* [New York: St. Martins, 2000], 28).

[23] Charles H. Talbert, *Reading Luke: A Literary and Theological Commentary on the Third Gospel* (rev. ed.; Macon GA: Smyth and Helwys, 2002), 117–19.

[24] Green, *Luke*, 397–99.

[25] Dir. Joel Coen and Ethan Coen, Paramount, 2000.

MISSIONARIES AND HOUSEHOLDERS

Luke 10

COMMENTARY

On the Road Again, 10:1-20

We start this chapter with Jesus on the road again, sending out advance teams, intending future stops, giving his representatives their publicity kits and instructions on how to use them. There is not much in the passage about Jesus' own feelings about this new chapter, so interpreters might read it different ways: the Willie Nelson Jesus, eager to be out there pressing the flesh, looking forward to new chances to spread the word; or the Bob Seeger Jesus, seriously tired of all the travel, the stupid questions, and the negative reactions. [Two Road Songs] Maybe some of both, actually.

> ### Two Road Songs
> On the road again
> I just can't wait to be on the road again
> —Willie Nelson
> Here I am on the road again . . .
> There I go, turn the page
> —Bob Seeger

Much of this material is found in Matthew 10:5-42, the second of Matthew's five great sermons. His version is addressed to the Twelve and includes material found only in Matthew: instructions to avoid Samaritans and Gentiles and to preach only to Jews (Matt 10:5-6) and a list of degrees of hospitality and their rewards (10:40-42). The woes on Galilean cities (Luke 10:13-15) appear at Matthew 11:20-24, and Matthew has no parallel for Luke 10:17-20. If, then, there was a Q document available to Matthew and Luke, then perhaps it contained a section of missionary instructions that looked something like Luke 10:2-12//Matthew 10:7-15. These verses are also parallel in many respects to Mark 6:7-11 and to a few isolated sayings in *Gospel of Thomas.* [Sayings on Mission from *Gospel of Thomas*] If—two big ifs, actually—Q existed, and if

> ### Sayings on Mission from *Gospel of Thomas*
> *Gosp. Thom.*, Logion 73: "Jesus said: The harvest is indeed great, but the laborers are few; but beg the Lord to send laborers into the harvest."
> Logion 14.4: "If you go into any land and wander in the regions, if they receive you, eat what they set before you, heal the sick among them."

Abuses of Hospitality

But act towards the apostles and prophets as the gospel decrees. Let every apostle who comes to you be welcomed as the Lord. But he should not remain more than a day. If he must, he may stay one more. But if he stays three days, he is a false prophet. When an apostle leaves he should take nothing except bread, until he arrives at his night's lodging. If he asks for money, he is a false prophet.

Did. 11.3-6.

the core of the *Gospel of Thomas* was put together independently of the Synoptic Gospels, then Mark, Q, and Thomas each bear witness to a cluster of sayings in which Jesus instructs a group of his followers on how to represent him to others: a strong argument for its historicity.

Even without the argument from multiple independent attestation, these commands of Jesus (1) are understandable in the context of first-century Galilee but not in later urban Greco-Roman contexts; (2) are different from the conduct of many later Christian missionaries, as evidenced by Paul's letters and Acts; (3) show signs of having been adjusted because they were too stringent; (4) were in some circles practiced, where they led to abuses that had to be corrected. [Abuses of Hospitality] In these verses, we are likely to be in touch with the way Jesus and his followers regularly presented themselves and their message in Galilee. One of the questions for the interpreter, on the way to "what does this have to do with me and my congregation?" is "what did Luke think it had to do with him and his congregation?" Luke is the only evangelist to have a section where Jesus sends out a large group with these sorts of instructions, so it is obviously important to him. Yet when you compare these commands to the conduct of Peter and the Twelve, Stephen and Philip and the seven, and Paul and his companions, there is not much correspondence. What were these commands to Luke beyond being a museum exhibit of How They Used to Do Things Back in the Day?

The first verse contains a notoriously difficult textual variant. Was it seventy or seventy-two that Jesus sent out? There are old and generally reliable manuscripts on each side, and since Luke does not use either number symbolically elsewhere in Luke or Acts, we can't argue from the author's typical use of language. Most interpreters think that because seventy is a more frequent symbolic number in the Old Testament (Moses appointed seventy elders, seventy years for the length of the exile, etc.), seventy-two is more likely to have been original, and then copyists corrected it to the more biblical seventy.[1]

Jesus is identified as "the Lord," which Luke does occasionally (7:13; 10:39; 11:39; 12:42; 13:15; 17:6; 18:6; 19:31) and in enough different contexts that it may be simply a matter of Luke wanting to vary the way he refers to Jesus in the narrative. But Luke's choice links Jesus, the Lord sending out the messengers, to the Lord of the Harvest (v. 2), reminding us of 9:48: whoever welcomes this child welcomes me, and whoever welcomes me welcomes the One who sent me (in case we forget, Luke brings this up again in 10:16).

The seventy-two are first "appointed" or "revealed" (Luke uses the same verb in Acts 1:24, where Peter prays for God to reveal which of the two candidates for apostle number 12 God had chosen [Appointed] and then "sent" (the verbal form of "apostle" is used here). The Twelve were "chosen out" of the larger group of disciples (6:13), named "apostles," and then later empowered and sent (9:1-2). This larger group is not named individually or collectively, unless "the seventy-two" is their name, and they are depicted as volunteers, not draftees. One way to read the narrative is to think that this is the entire company of those with Jesus: the Twelve plus sixty others, who would include Mary Magdalene, Joanna wife of Chuza, Susanna (8:2-3), Jesus' own mother and brothers (8:21), and a few dozen others, including among them some other women (8:3). This larger group of disciples never disappears from view in Luke's narrative. It is they who walk with him into Nain (7:11), who ask him about the parable of the sower (8:9), who (some group of them, anyway) are afraid in the storm (8:22), who hear Jesus' predictions of his death (9:23), who fail to heal the boy with the demon (9:40), and who argue over who is the greatest (9:43-46). Luke does not present this larger group as any less fallible than the Twelve, who have their share of poor performances, too (9:12, 33, 49, 54). Both groups fail to live up to Jesus' teachings and fail to understand him. But the larger group, like the Twelve, follows Jesus to Jerusalem, observes his crucifixion and burial from afar (23:49), and is there in Jerusalem to receive the good news of the resurrection. The first narrated resurrection appearance is to Cleopas and another of this group (24:13). Luke's report that the group in the

Jesus Preaching to the Disciples

Bonifacio de' Pitati (1487–1553). *Christ with his Apostles*. Accademia, Venice, Italy. (Credit: Cameraphoto Arte, Venice/Art Resource, NY)

Appointed

AΩ "The Greek verb for 'appointed' (*anadeiknymi*) is common in diplomatic contexts. Luke reserves the term for action by Jesus, as here, and by God at Acts 1:24. The cognate noun (*anadeixis*) appears in Luke 1:80, and the context requires God as the agent. These are the only occurrences in the NT. The implications are clear: Jesus functions as a head of state."

Frederick W. Danker, *Jesus and the New Age: A Commentary on St. Luke's Gospel* (rev. ed.; Philadelphia: Fortress, 1988), 211.

upper room numbered about 120 indicates a few converts between Luke 10:1 and Acts 1:15.

Luke almost certainly thought that the seventy-two included women. Connect the dots: there are women among the disciples in Galilee (8:1-3) who are at the tomb (24:10) and in the upper room (Acts 1:14). These are described as "those who had followed him from Galilee" (23:49, 55). Therefore, although Luke names no names in 10:1-20, I would argue that he means for us to presume the presence of the women he has already named and others he has not. The other way to read it is to assume an all-male seventy-two, on the grounds that not mentioning women would mean that readers would, by default, assume men.[2] This reading, indeed, is likely if one takes this pericope in isolation from the stream of the Lukan narrative. But that sort of reading—looking at only a few verses at a time—is a modern practice. Luke's audience was much more likely to have heard the narrative read (some argue "performed" is more accurate), and in longer chunks at a sitting.[3] In lively readings to an attentive audience, the threads holding the individual episodes together become more apparent: moving town by town, proclaiming the gospel of the kingdom of God, casting out evil spirits, and the use of resources all appear in 8:1-3, 9:1-6, and 10:1-20. If ancient audiences heard these episodes in sequence, and not in isolation, they might have connected things as I have done.

Jesus sends them out two by two, reminding us of other pairs: Mary and Elizabeth, Anna and Simeon, and the two disciples sent from John the Baptist. Two is the magic number for witnesses agreeing in court (Deut 19:15), but since these people are not testifying to a crime, the idea of pairs may be for safety, especially since they go out unarmed. Thirty-six pairs—wonder who buddied up with Peter or Judas or Mary Magdalene? Thirty-six pairs could cover a lot of ground in an area as small as Galilee; in a matter of a few weeks, they might have been able to spend a few days in every village. This raises another question: if they are going and doing what he would do—preaching, healing, casting out demons, eating—why is their work described as preparatory for his arrival? What will he do when he arrives that they have not already done?

Here, perhaps, is the first clue about how these missionary instructions relate to Luke and his church. Luke is prepping his audience for Jesus' departure: when they preach, heal, exorcise, and above all, break bread in his name, Jesus is there (24:35). And on that eventual day, Jesus will return to take account of the reactions of each of these towns (10:12-16). So we can read 10:1 to imply that Jesus visited each of these villages in person on his way to Jerusalem, and to imply that he was there in the presence of his disciples, and to promise that he would be there again at his return.

The first responsibility of these folks is to find more of themselves: "The harvest is big, the workers few; so beg the Lord of the Harvest so that he may send out workers into his harvest." The phrase "Lord of the Harvest" does not appear in the LXX, but it is in Matthew 9:38, and thus in the putative Q. The ultimate source for the phrase may be either Old Testament laws about leaving part of the harvest for the poor (as in Lev 19:9-10) [Leviticus 19:9-10, according to the LXX] or Old Testament uses of the image of the harvest as judgment (as in 2 Sam 24:14-15). [2 Samuel 24:14-15 LXX] The latter example is particularly apt. This is the story of David taking a census and then having to choose a punishment for his presumption. The Lord sends an angel to smite the people, killing 70,000; David sees the angel upon a threshing floor, and prays that God turn the punishment upon himself: "Behold, I, I have been unrighteous; but these sheep, what have they done? Let your hand instead be on me and on my father's house" (2 Sam 24:17 LXX). The prayer of intercession and the harvest image are both there, but inverted; in the Gospel saying, Jesus' appointed pairs are begging God for more "angels" to be sent to bring life, not death, to the people. The Lord, who demands that you leave part of your harvest for the needy, now claims this as his harvest.

Day laborers (which is what the word translated "workers" normally means) have no share in the harvested crops; they work only as long as there are sheaves in the field and grapes on the vines, and when they do not work, they are not paid. Matthew's parable of the workers in the vineyard tells the story from the field owner's perspective: at harvest time, it is in the Lord's best interests to get the crop in as soon as it is ripe, so the master keeps going back to the marketplace to hire more workers. Day laborers, on the other hand, have no incentive to add to the work force—it only decreases their income. Jesus' missioners are thus asked to be more than mere wage earners; although this is the Lord's harvest, the workers are to look at it through the Lord's eyes. Pray for more help, certainly; this will translate into not putting stumbling blocks in front of those the

Leviticus 19:9-10, according to the LXX

And when you harvest out the harvest of your land, you shall not completely harvest out the harvest of your field nor gather up the gleanings of your harvest nor twice-gather your grapes nor gather the remnants of your grapes; you shall leave [it all] for the poor and the stranger; I am the Lord your God.

2 Samuel 24:14-15 LXX

And David chose death (or a plague) as his choice; it was the time of the wheat harvest, and the Lord gave death (or the plague) in Israel from early morning until noon.

Lord calls (9:49-50; 17:1-4) and into being the Lord's recruiting agents (24:44-48).

Verse 3 is one of the many warnings to the thirty-six pairs about the dangers they will face. When Jesus sent out the Twelve, he told them to take no staff; he does not repeat that here, but this verse implies that the seventy-two are unarmed. "Lambs in the midst of wolves" is the epitome of defenselessness in the face of not only danger, but inevitable death. Not every audience will be that hostile, but inasmuch as Jesus' first sermon nearly got him thrown off a cliff (4:29-30), and given the negative response of the first villages the messengers visited (9:51-56), the disciples will do well to be realistic. Facing this danger and not flinching is part of denying themselves and taking up their cross daily (9:23).

Not only unarmed, but unequipped—or unencumbered, depending on your point of view. No "purse" to carry money, no "bag" to carry food, and no sandals; the seventy-two will look like the beggars they are. There are several ways that we can imagine the purpose and/or the meaning of these commands.

• Some suggest that barefoot and unequipped is fine for the short distances between villages in Galilee, and that when the messengers show up, it will be obvious to all that they are no threat to anyone—just poor folks, peasants who stand in start contrast to the tax collectors or soldiers who show up from time to time. In this reading, the commands are part of an itinerant strategy designed to get the message to as many people as possible in as short a time as possible.[4]

• Others, beginning with Albert Schweitzer, believe that the root of the itinerant strategy was Jesus' firm belief that the kingdom of God was about to appear, and that time was very short. In this interpretation, abandoning material goods is not just part of being a traveling preacher, but a response to an imminent Judgment Day—better sell the Caddy, give the money to the poor, and hope God is merciful.[5]

• Some have argued that Jesus is commanding "a symbolic representation of an unbrokered egalitarianism."[6] Jesus is consciously rejecting the pattern of his society to form patron-client relations. Instead, he sends his disciples out to do good and then move on, before any sort of patronage network can be set up.

• Still others read these commands as a form of asceticism: Jesus and his followers are constructing an alternative empire where all the normal markers of power and status have no place. Jesus is disrupting particular households, but more than that, he is creating a network of non-households, where men, women, and children live under quite different social arrangements than any of their peers in these villages.[7]

Each of these readings is plausible for Jesus in Galilee, and since this is not a book about the historical Jesus, I will not pause here to argue the relative merits of each one. The more pressing question now is how Luke understood the commands. His Jesus has no permanent home, but is invited to dinner by Pharisees, tax collectors, and single women; his Jesus is supported financially by women disciples who share their possessions as well as by homeowners who receive him. In Acts, the Jerusalem believers pool their resources and have a common purse from which they feed the poor. Some sell their homes and give the money to the cause, but the text is careful to say that this is not a requirement (Acts 5:4). Luke knows that Paul, Priscilla, and Aquila worked to support themselves (Acts 18:3; cf. 1 Thess 2:9 and 1 Cor 9:14; in 1 Cor 9:6, Paul admits that he and Barnabas do not follow the Lord's command to rely on the gifts of others), and yet Paul is not critiqued for doing missions differently. So Luke probably understood the rules about no supplies and no shoes to have been temporary strategies rather than constitutive principles for the Jesus movement. This becomes clearer in the verses that follow.

The seventy-two are to be peacemakers. When they enter a village and approach a household, their first words are to be "Peace to this house"—"shalom la-bayit ha-zeh," not so different from the normal "peace to you" one still hears from Hebrew speakers. The contrast between "greet no one on the road" and "peace to this house" is striking. For whatever combination of reasons—speed, security, single-minded focus on the task—they are to ignore normal polite greetings on the road, but implement them fully once they arrive at the village [Greet No One on the Road]. This puts the household, not the road, as the locus for sharing the gospel and healing. Once again, think of Jesus in Luke 24, talking to the disciples as they walked from Jerusalem to Emmaus, interpreting Scriptures to them as they traveled. They did not understand, nor did they recognize him, but when he sat at table with them and broke the bread, they did. In Luke's version, the "peace" greeting is extended also as a sort of password challenge: is the householder a "son of peace," a person characterized by peace[8]? If not, well, no harm to you, and at v. 10

Greet No One on the Road

Luke's Jesus has many connections to the characters of Elijah and Elisha (see [Jesus as Elijah]). Once, when a boy had just died, Elisha commanded his servant Gehazi to go to place his staff upon the dead boy, without stopping to greet anyone who spoke to him on the way (2 Kgs 4:29). Jesus' command might have a similar motive: Your message has to get there as quickly as possible.

Jesus takes up what to do when the village has not one single person interested in hearing the good news. But if the householder is a son (or daughter—think ahead to Martha's reception of Jesus later in this chapter) of peace, then continue on to v. 7.

Beyond simple good manners, "peace to this house" is a promise of the blessings of the kingdom. When the angels announced Jesus' birth with "glory in the highest to God, and upon the earth, peace among people of [God's] goodwill," their message was set in the text against the machinations of Caesar Augustus moving people around in his empire. The famous Pax Romana—the peace of Rome—was promoted by Roman propaganda as Rome's gift to the rest of the world. [The Pax Romana] Luke, however, satirizes the Pax: the emperor's order overturned the order of the civilized world, putting everyone on the road, traveling to the birthplaces of their ancestors so that they could be counted. By contrast, God's gift of a son was to bring real peace, of the sort Jesus announced in his Nazareth sermon. God's peace was not enforced by the legions and paid for by over-taxing the peasants, but was freely given, with angelic birth announcements to shepherds. Rome's peace required Galilee to become a subject people; God's peace brought "release to captives, recovery of sight for the blind, setting free the oppressed," and the announcement of the year of God's favor. The seventy-two are peacemakers because they are spreading the news of the arrival of the new kingdom, the anti-empire. No one is required to belong or to contribute or even to listen, and the response of the messengers to rejection is to be firm but nonviolent.

When things go well—when there is a willing listener for the missionary—they are then to focus on settling in with one household, eating and drinking whatever is provided. They are not to move around, giving offense to the householder whose hospitality may not be sumptuous but is freely offered (the Twelve got the same instructions at 9:4). Luke uses the verb "receive" (*dechomai*) in situations where one person offers hospitality to another: 9:5, in the directions to the Twelve; 9:48, in the principle of receiving the messenger = receiving the sender; 10:38 and 19:6 use the compound *hypodechomai*, which is synonymous. "The laborer is worthy of his/her wages" was known to Paul as Jesus' teaching (1 Cor 9:14)

The Pax Romana

Whereas our ancestors have willed that the gateway of Janus Quirinus should be shut [note: the doors of the temple of Janus] whenever victorious peace is secured by sea and by land throughout the empire of the Roman people, and whereas before my birth twice only in all is it on record that the gateway had been shut, three times under my principiate has the Senate decreed that it should be shut . . . . I extended the frontiers of all the provinces of the Roman people, which has as neighbors races not obedient to our empire. I restored peace to all the provinces of Gaul and Spain and to Germany, to all that region washed by the Ocean from Gades to the mouth of the Elbe . . . .

From the *Res Gestae Divi Augusti*, in C. K. Barrett, *The New Testament Background* (rev. ed.; New York: Harper and Row, 1987), 2–3.

and as a sort of general principle supported both by the Torah and by common sense (1 Cor 9:3-12). In the context of Luke 10, it almost certainly does not mean that the seventy-two should expect to be paid for their preaching, healing, and exorcising; they have no purses or wallets in which to store wages. "Wages" here means that they can expect to be housed and fed, and if Jesus' conduct is any indication, they should not expect or encourage elaborate meals—he fed the multitude all the fish and bread they could eat, but provided no appetizers, sides, or desserts.

"Cure the sick" comes after "eat what is set out before you"—they do not heal to attract a crowd or to gain a hearing. Healing is part of God's peace, freely offered and received; it is the disciples' part of the give and take of hospitality, and cannot be separated from it. James and John wanted to use God's fire to burn the inhospitable Samaritan village (9:49-50), but Jesus rebuked them. The disciples' ability to do miracles is limited to charitable acts, and limited as well to persons receptive to the message of the arrival of the kingdom. In a village where they are received, they are to heal the sick—not only in the household feeding them, so this is not merely quid pro quo. But they are given no instructions to heal in unreceptive places; Mark 6:5-6 has Jesus unable to do many miracles in unreceptive Nazareth, and although Luke chose not to copy it, he may well have understood it as a general principle of miracle working.

When things do not go well—when nobody will sit still long enough to listen and nobody will invite them in for coffee and pound cake—then the missionaries are to leave. Jesus' instructions to the seventy-two repeat but elaborate on his commands to the Twelve. First, just leave—no shouting matches in the synagogues, no hiding out in barns, no waiting around to be physically abused or chased out of town. Second, there is the ceremonial shaking off the dust. The Twelve are advised to do it as they are leaving town, but the seventy-two are to make a production of it, going into the broad streets (not the little alleys between houses, but the wider roads that could accommodate vehicles) to announce, "Even the dust from your city clinging to our feet we wipe off for you; but know this: the kingdom of God is near." One can understand this as a protest ("we call heaven and earth—your particular earth, in fact—to witness against you that we have offered you the terms of peace, which you rejected") or as a sarcastic sign of innocence ("we won't take anything from your town, not even your stupid dirt") or as a prophetic act ("you guys are going to get it now, so we don't even want to have your dust on our shoes"), or maybe as some combination of all three. Given the warning of v. 12 and the curses of vv. 13-15, returning the dust may even be the disciples' role in invoking the curse ("when God gets done with you, you're going to look like this"); they may not call down fire on their enemies, but they may, as prophets commissioned by Jesus, announce the certain judgment of God on the unrepentant.

There are interesting connections between Luke 10:5-12 and Deuteronomy 20:10-18. The rules for holy warfare require that the invading Israelites first offer terms of peace ("call out to them with peace," Deut 20:10 LXX). "If they answer peaceably to you and open to you, then every person found in it shall be to you tribute-payers and servants" (20:11 LXX). Those villages that resist the offer of peace are to be put to the sword. If they are villages on the far side of the Jordan, then the Israelites may take war prizes from them, but if they are on the Israelite side of the Jordan, then the Israelites must keep nothing—the LXX says "you must not take alive any breathing thing, but rather let them be anathema" (20:16-17). The missionaries are not warriors, so they will neither kill nor enslave; they bring good news of God's kingdom, broader even than the Deuteronomic vision of the good life in the promised land. But Luke and the Deuteronomic Historian would have agreed that real peace is a gift from God, and that if it is rejected, only bad consequences can result. Better for God's messengers to carry nothing, not even dust, from a town that gets crossways with God.

Verse 12, addressed as a promise to the disciples, introduces a series of curses on some Galilean cities. Any town that rejects the message of the seventy-two will, on Judgment Day, want to trade places with Sodom. Luke expects that his readers will know the basics of the story in Genesis 19:12-29, where God rained "fire from heaven, and he overthrew those cities, and the whole region, and everyone living in the cities, as well as what grew up from the earth" (19:24-25 LXX). This is meant as reassurance for the missionaries: God takes your business seriously and will not let offenses against you go unpunished. Then, as if to illustrate the point, Luke has Jesus pronounce woes on Chorazin, Bethsaida, and Capernaum for failure to repent. Of the three, only Capernaum has been named enough in Luke for the reader to have any sense of a group reaction to Jesus, and up to this point in the narrative, Jesus' experiences in Capernaum have been mostly positive. In fact, if one wanted to pick towns to be zapped for unresponsiveness, so far the leading candidates in Luke would be Nazareth and the unnamed Samaritan village (9:52).

So we are not told why these three Galilean towns are singled out for being unrepentant, nor whether their non-responsiveness to Jesus' message had already happened or would happen during the mission of the seventy-two. This feels more than a little like the sermon at Nazareth, where Jesus seems to predict, and possibly to incite, the congregation's negative response to his saying that God's mercy sometimes reaches Gentile recipients instead of

Map of Galilee Showing the Unrepentant Towns

Israelites. In this little collection of woes, Jesus asserts that Tyre and Sidon—Gentile cities on the Mediterranean coast north of Galilee—would have repented had he given them the chance (so why didn't he?). "If the miracles done among you had been done in Tyre and Sidon, they all would have repented, sitting in sackcloth and ashes"—an allusion to Gentile Nineveh, who dressed similarly after hearing Jonah's laconic prophecy of doom. The mission of the seventy-two is not to Gentiles, but Jesus' words keep the issue alive for Luke's Gentile readers—a teaser that points ahead to Luke's episode 2 in Acts.[9]

Some New Testament scholars believe that the specificity of the town names indicates a memory of some particular incidents of rejection or persecution, either during Jesus' ministry or in the early years after the crucifixion. [Bethsaida] For Luke's audience, they likely functioned as ciphers for other places more real to their own experience, places where they suffered rejection. They hear the lector read out Jesus' curse against Chorazin and think, "then Jonesville will probably get it, too." There is a fine line, I think, between the potentially reassuring function of these verses—don't become discouraged when people reject you, because God will sort it all out on that eventual day—and the way these verses could equally encourage judgmentalism. As a guard against the latter tendency, one could point out that Jesus himself offers the woes, for reasons that the narrative does not make clear. He does not give his

Bethsaida

According to John 1:44 and 12:21, Bethsaida was the home of Philip, Andrew, and Peter. Luke locates it near the place where Jesus fed the multitudes (Luke 9:10), while Mark states that Jesus left the feeding and crossed the Lake to reach Bethsaida (Mark 6:45). Modern excavations locate ancient Bethsaida at et-Tell (Tell Bethsaida), which in biblical times was on the northeast shore of the Sea of Galilee.

During Jesus' lifetime, Bethsaida was in the territory ruled by Philip the tetrarch, son of Herod the Great. In AD 30 he changed its status from village to city, renaming it Julias to honor Livia-Julia, the Emperor Tiberius's mother (Josephus, Ant. 18.28). According to Rami Arav, who excavated the site, Philip also converted a house into a small Roman-style temple; ritual implements recovered from the site—incense shovels and a figurine of a crowned, veiled woman (indicating her status as both a royal and a priestess)—identify the site as a temple. And since Livia-Julia is known to have been a priestess in the imperial cult, it is likely that the temple was dedicated to Augustus (and/or the Augustan family) and to the goddess Roma.

It is possible, then, that the woe against Bethsaida has some connection to this interjection of the imperial cult into the hometown of some of the original apostles. Members of the early Jesus movement in the immediate aftermath of his crucifixion and resurrection may well have condemned this innovation as an outrage, pronouncing woes against Bethsaida in his name.

Rami Arav, "Bethsaida," in James H. Charlesworth, ed., *Jesus and Archaeology* (Grand Rapids MI: Eerdmans, 2006), 145–66.

disciples license to do the same—shake off the dust, but do not call down fire or consign them to hell in Jesus' name.

Here is another place where missionaries in Acts do not conform to the teaching of this chapter. The apostles remain in Jerusalem even after a severe persecution arises against the church (Acts 8:1-3). Paul shakes the dust from his feet at Pisidian Antioch (13:51) and from his clothes at Corinth (18:6), but routinely argues in the synagogues against hostile audiences, escaping Damascus in a basket lowered over the city wall (9:25), being stoned and left for dead in Lystra (14:19), etc. But then Paul's experiences are more mixed than Jesus' missionary instructions imply. At Philippi, for example, he and the rest are given hospitality by Lydia, where they stay for some time (Acts 16:15). Paul then exorcises a slave girl in the city, in accordance with Luke 10:9, but the miracle creates a hostile environment for Paul and his entourage, and they are beaten and imprisoned. At Corinth, Paul's dust-shaking is not against the whole city, but only against the unrepentant parts of his audience; he leaves the synagogue and starts a church next door (Acts 18:6-7). Luke therefore understood 10:1-16 to be strategies appropriate for Jesus' mission in Galilee on his way to Jerusalem, and did not take them as standards by which to judge later missionaries. Paul and the others could accept hospitality or work to support themselves, could leave unrepentant cities quickly or stand and argue until the hammer fell—it all depended on the needs of the situation.

There are a few points that carry over from Luke 10 though Acts, however. Missionaries preach, heal, cast out demons, and enjoy table fellowship with those who listen to them. Meal scenes are moments of revelation (Acts 10:1-23) and miracle working (Acts 20:7-12), are opportunities for conflict resolution (Acts 6:1-7; 11:1-18), and are sometimes the sign that the gospel has been received and God's peace now rests on a new believer (Acts 2:41-42; 16:15, 34). Missionaries do not use healings to advertise the gospel; Paul's experience at Lystra, where he and Barnabas are mistaken for Zeus and Hermes, shows Luke's steady disdain for miracle-as-crowd-teaser.

The missionary sermon ends in 10:16 with a restatement of 9:48: Whoever receives or rejects you is doing the same to Jesus and to God, who sent Jesus who sent you. In a sense, that is the whole ball of wax—everything else is strategy for the moment. Jesus' followers are to go doing as he did and to know that however anyone responds, it is all about God and the kingdom.

Thus, when the disciples return with reports of great victories over demons, Jesus affirms their success but warns them about misplaced pride. "I was watching when Satan fell like lightning from heaven," he says. If one takes this verse away from Luke 10, it could describe a singular moment of revelation for Jesus. In context, it describes how Jesus interprets the work of the seventy-two in their foray into the towns and villages of Galilee. Their work, like his, is part of the invasion of God's kingdom and part of the rolling back of Satan's empire. The closest New Testament parallel to this verse is Revelation 12:10-12, where the saints who refuse to cooperate with the Satan-inspired work of the empire help to bring about Satan's defeat: "they have conquered him by the blood of the Lamb and by the word of their testimony." The disciples are engaged in a larger-than-life enterprise, spreading the word of the kingdom's arrival and of Satan's binding. They have been given extraordinary powers, here described metaphorically as the ability to walk unharmed over snakes and scorpions. Nevertheless, says Jesus, they are not to rejoice at their victories over evil spirits, but over how they will stand at God's side on that day. Their power over Satan is only a gift from God, in other words, and not something they earned or deserved. Be grateful that God has forgiven you, in light of the nearness of the kingdom's arrival; it would be a bad thing to be on the wrong side when it comes for once and all.

Some believers from my part of the world handle snakes and drink poison because they take the promises of Luke 10:19 and Mark 16:18 very literally. But the structure of Luke 10:19 argues for seeing them as examples of Satan's power: "Behold I have given you authority to walk over snakes and scorpions and over all the power of the enemy, and he will never harm [lit., do unrighteous things to] you." Given what happens to Jesus at the end of Luke and what happens to Jesus' followers throughout Acts, one cannot think Luke meant "never harm" literally, and likewise the snakes and scorpions are metaphors for all the ways evil seeks to make our lives miserable. Jesus' followers have his authority, however, and so should act boldly and speak bravely, knowing that by so doing they are doing God's work.

Hidden and Revealed, 10:21-24

This odd little paragraph is sometimes called the "Johannine Thunderbolt," because although it appears in Matthew and Luke (and thus perhaps originally in Q, the hypothetical common second source for Matthew and Luke), it reminds one so much of the language of John, especially v. 22. The text of Matthew 11:25-27 is almost the same as Luke 10:21-22, if one starts at the actual prayer of Jesus. Matthew 11:27 reads "no one knows the son except the father nor does anyone know the father except the son," and Luke's version is a bit less direct: "none knows who the son is except the father or who the father is except the son." Despite the difference in wording, both versions mean the same thing, and one is hard-pressed to explain why either Matthew or Luke would make such a small change in a common written source (or Luke to Matthew, if he had Matthew as a source).

The language is also close to several texts in John:

• Jesus answered, You know neither me nor my Father; if you knew me, you would also know my Father (John 8:19b).
• I am the good shepherd. I know my own and my own know me, just as the Father knows me and I know the Father (John 10:14-15).
• No one comes to the Father except through me. If you know me, you will know my Father also. From now on you do know him and have seen him (John 14:6b-7).
• And this is eternal life, that they may know you, the only true God, and Jesus Christ whom you have sent . . . . I have made your name known to those who you gave me from the world . . . . Righteous Father, the world does not know you, but I know you; and these know that you have sent me. I made your name known to them, and I will make it known, so that the love with which you have loved me may be in them, and I in them (John 17:3, 6, 25–26).

The connections between John and Matthew/Luke are thematic—there are not strings of consecutive identical words. But the similarities are strong enough that we may suppose that versions of this saying were known to various early Christian communities, and were something early Christian preachers turned to as a point of reflection on Jesus' origin and mission.[10] These sayings are not in Luke's customary vocabulary, so we presume that wherever he found it—in Q, in Matthew, or in the preaching of some early follower of Jesus—he took it over more or less intact and unedited.

Luke's "in that hour" means that we are to read these sayings as part of Jesus' response to the return of the seventy-two missionaries. Their joy (10:17) is now matched, and trumped, by his, since he rejoices "in the Holy Spirit" and does not need to be cautioned about hubris. They rejoice in their victories over demons, while he rejoices over the revelation of God that makes salvation possible. And whereas he announced curses on three Galilean cities for non-repentance (10:12-15), he now blesses the disciples for having eyes that see and ears that hear.[11] In Luke, the disciples find themselves closest to ideal when they are preaching, healing, exorcising, and sharing table with others in imitation of Jesus.

As one commentator notes, both Christology and discipleship find their apex in this section.[12] In it, Jesus is connected as Son both to the Holy Spirit and to the Father; he speaks of his role in revealing the true nature of the Father; and he praises the disciples' giftedness, their privileged place as receptors of his revelation, and their ability to see and hear truly.

The Spirit language comes first. Jesus "rejoiced in the Holy Spirit," reminding the reader that the Spirit that overshadowed his mother (1:35), descended upon him at baptism (3:22), led him in the wilderness (4:1), filled him as he began his ministry (4:14), and anointed him for his mission (4:18) was still directing his activities. [Rejoicing in the Holy Spirit] In Acts, believers filled with the Spirit sometimes pray (4:23-31; 13:1-3), and in this text Luke sets a dominical pattern for disciples' praxis. [From George Herbert, *Prayer* (I)]

Jesus' prayer begins like many Jewish prayers from the Second Temple period: "I thank you, Father, Lord of heaven and earth." Tobit's "prayer of rejoicing" calls God "the one who lives for ever . . . our Lord, and God our father for all time . . . the King of heaven" (Tob 13:1, 4, 7); in another passage, God is named "Lord of heaven and earth" (7:18). Sirach 51:1, using

Rejoicing in the Holy Spirit

I have tasted a thrill in fellowship with God which has made anything discordant with God disgusting. This afternoon the possession of God has caught me up with such sheer joy tht I thought I never had known anything like it. God was so close and so amazingly lovely that I felt like melting all over with a strange blissful contentment.

Frank C. Laubach, *Letters by a Modern Mystic* (Westwood NJ: Revell, 1937), 21–22.

the same verb as Luke 10:21, begins, "I will thank you, O Lord, O King." The form of the prayer, then, is not unusual, nor the form of address for God—this is a *berakah*, a blessing or thanksgiving prayer to God, and so Jesus, the Spirit-filled Son, is doing nothing that his disciples could not do in their own prayers. [Prayers from Qumran]

　　The motive clause in the prayer states that Jesus thanks God for having revealed "these things" to "babies" while hiding them from "the wise and intelligent." Jesus, like Paul in 1 Corinthians 1:18-31, does a riff on Isaiah 29:9-21, where God closes the eyes of the prophets and rulers and seals away God's secrets in a book the learned cannot read (Isa 29:10-11). Isaiah predicts a day will come when God "will destroy the wisdom of the wise, and I will hide the intelligence of the intelligent" (29:14 LXX). But "in that day the deaf will hear the words of the book . . . the eyes of the blind will see, and the poor will rejoice with joy because of the Lord." Luke understands that day to have come in Jesus' ministry, where not only those who heard the Lord directly, but those who received the ministry of the Lord's messengers heard the good news of the kingdom's arrival. The wise and intelligent, the prophets and kings of this world, have not been the objects of God's special revelation through Jesus. The emperors Augustus and Tiberius, Governor Quirinius, Herod Antipas, and Pontius Pilate all missed the news bulletins; instead, God sent angels to Zechariah and Mary and the shepherds, sent the word by the Spirit to Elizabeth, Simeon, Anna, and John. As Mary predicted, God "has scattered the proud in their hearts' reasonings; he has unseated the mighty from their thrones/and lifted up the lowly" (1:51-52).

Prayers from Qumran

　　The Essenes, who lived at Qumran near the Dead Sea, and were responsible for the Dead Sea Scrolls, left behind many beautiful hymns and prayers dating from the 2d century BC to the 1st century AD. Two examples:

　　Blessed art Thou, O Lord, God of mercy and abundant grace, for thou hast made known thy wisdom to me that I should recount thy marvelous deeds, keeping silence neither by day nor by night! For I have trusted in thy grace . . . . For thou thyself hast shaped my spirit and established me according to thy will; and thou hast not placed my support in gain, nor does my heart delight in riches . . . . Thou wilt give to the children of thy truth unending joy and everlasting gladness . . . . (from Hymn 20)

　　I thank thee, my God, for thou hast dealt wondrously to dust, and mightily towards a creature of clay! I thank thee, I thank thee! What am I, that thou shouldst teach me the counsel of thy truth, and give me understanding of thy marvelous works? (from Hymn 21)

Geza Vermes, *The Complete Dead Sea Scrolls in English* (New York: Penguin, 1997), 285–87.

　　In v. 22, Jesus claims to have exclusive knowledge of the Father and exclusive rights on revealing what he knows of the Father to others. This is the position of the Gospel of John also, but other Christians, notably Paul, argued that God's nature and will is revealed in the Old Testament and in the created order. Luke also believed that the Hebrew Scriptures reveal God. When the lawyer says that the Law requires one to love God with all one's being and one's neighbor as oneself, Luke's Jesus replies that he has answered correctly—he did not need Jesus to teach him that. The apostles, preaching in Acts, hold their Jewish audiences accountable for not paying attention to the words of the prophets and psalms that predicted the Messiah (3:17-26; 13:26-41). But Luke also believed that correct understanding of the Old Testament was granted by Christ (Luke 24:45), so that the people of Jerusalem were acting in ignorance of the truth, now preached by Spirit-inspired followers of Jesus (3:17; 13:27). The absolute claims of 10:22, in other words, must be tempered by the actual practices of Jesus and his followers in the rest of Luke-Acts. Luke does not mean that Jews, through Torah study, prayer, and worship, are without true knowledge of God. But he clearly does mean that the Christological interpretation of the Old Testament and the Christian understanding of the God-directed life are given by Christ exclusively. No surprise there—interpreting the Old Testament as a preview of Jesus is a Christian invention.

The emphasis on the choices of Father and Son—"you have hidden . . . have revealed" and "all things have been handed over to me by my Father . . . anyone to whom the Son chooses to reveal him" reminds us of 8:10, where Jesus told the disciples "to you it has been given to know the mysteries (or secrets) of the kingdom of God, but to the rest [it has been given to know] in parables, so that seeing they may not see and hearing they may not understand." Jesus sent the seventy-two "before his face into every town and place where he was himself about to come" (10:1)—presumably omitting some places where he was not intending to come—and admitted that Tyre and Sidon, had they been given what Chorazin and Bethsaida got, would have repented (10:13). Not everyone is blessed by hearing the good news. In this text, Jesus does not answer the question of the fates of those who wanted to hear but never did (although he says that Tyre and Sidon will get off easier on Judgment Day than the two Galilean villages who heard but did not repent). Nor does he address the eternally perplexing question of why God would choose one person or one group and not another. In this text, it is only a matter for thanksgiving: praise God that you have seen and heard, and count yourself blessed. Blessed, not deserving or virtuous; vv. 23-24 reprise the warning against pride in v. 20. Be happy you know what you do, but don't get cocky about it.

Interesting that Luke put these election sayings into the context of the large mission effort. Jesus sends out all his disciples—not just

Scorekeeping

By the second decade of the twentieth century, it remained only for cheaper, simpler men with gaudier personalities and fewer scruples to bring the revivalistic movement into disrepute. . . . The growing tendency to emphasize statistics was characteristic of Rodney "Gipsy" Smith, who not only made news on the number of "decisions" he secured, but indicated to his sponsors that he could produce converts for $4.92 apiece. The most spectacular champions of the sawdust trail, however, were the ex-baseball player, Billy Sunday, and his chorister, Homer A. Roadeaver (1880–1955)—a team, incidentally, that cut conversion costs to $2.00 a soul when they finally got their system working.

Sydney E. Ahlstrom, *A Religious History of the American People* (2 vols.; New York: Doubleday, 1975), 2.205.

the Twelve, but all those following him so far in the narrative—to an undisclosed number of places, telling them to do everything he had been doing—preach the arrival of the kingdom, heal the sick, cast out demons, and live in fellowship with those to whom you minister. Not everyone will respond positively, Jesus teaches. So how will you think of these hard cases? Perhaps they choose to be hard-hearted, or perhaps God hardens their hearts; either way, you cannot tell in advance, and so the imperative to go, preach, heal, and share the table has no clear boundaries. Where does Jesus intend to go? The only safe way to be obedient to his command is to go everywhere, leaving the business of election to Father and Son. But knowing that salvation is ultimately God's choice may keep us from attributing their salvation to our great soul-winning techniques; if we took it seriously, maybe it would temper some of the scorekeeping impulses in modern American Christianity. [Scorekeeping]

Good Samaritan, 10:25-36

I hate student essays that begin, "According to Webster's, a parable is . . . ." So, breaking my own rule, I note that the *American Heritage Dictionary* lists "Good Samaritan" along with good-for-nothing, Good Friday, good-sized, and other common compounds of the word "good." The definition: "1. In a New Testament parable, the only passer-by to aid a man who had been beaten and robbed. 2. A compassionate person who unselfishly helps others."[13] Even with current levels of biblical illiteracy, widely agreed to be astonishingly high and pervasive, Americans still use "Good Samaritan" to name auto clubs, charitable agencies, and even, tragically, evacuation strategies for major cities. [The "Good Samaritan Scenario"] Most churchgoers may not be aware that the adjective "good" is nowhere found in the story; in fact, if we remove "good" from our thoughts as we approach the parable, we are less apt to read it as a melodrama involving two Snidely Whiplash characters and one Dudley Do-Right, rescuing Nell once again from railroad tracks just before she gets squashed by the train.

The "Good Samaritan Scenario"

Shortly after Hurricane Katrina devastated the Gulf Coast in 2005, Brian Wolshon, a civil-engineering professor at LSU who served as a consultant on the [Louisiana] state evacuation plan, said that [New Orleans] relied almost entirely on a "Good Samaritan scenario," in which residents would check on elderly and disabled neighbors and drive them out of danger.

Winston-Salem Journal, 4 September 2005.

Luke expects the readers to know a bit about the Samaritans (see also [The Samaritans]). Back in 9:52, they refused to grant Jesus hospitality. Samaritans in Luke, then, are not automatically hospitable, especially to Jews headed for Jerusalem. Beyond that, Luke probably expects his readers to know that Jews and Samaritans tended to avoid each other; he may know, and he may think his audience knows, that groups of Jews and Samaritans had each acted violently toward the other in the past. But Luke did not think that Jews and Samaritans were automatically hostile, or that they had no commerce or communication between them. Luke's Jesus can intend to minister in a Samaritan village, and in the parable, Jews and the Samaritan travel the same road and use the same roadside hostel. So we must not prejudge the Samaritan as "good" or "despised," or assume that Luke thinks of the Samaritan-Jew divide the same way we think of race issues in our culture. This parable may help us think about race, but first-century Jew/Samaritan issues are not very analogous to, say, Caucasian/African American or Israeli/Palestinian tensions.

The parable itself, which only appears in Luke, is introduced by a Q and A session between Jesus and a lawyer. Luke seems to use the terms "lawyer," "law-teacher," and "scribe" interchangeably. "Lawyer" is most often plural and connected to "Pharisees"; the same goes for "scribes," although after Jesus enters Jerusalem in 19:45, "scribes" is linked to "chief priests and elders." Luke probably considered lawyer/scribe to be the same profession—a literate person trained in the Law of Moses who could serve as secretary and advisor to Pharisees or priests or elders. In Luke's culture, powerful men always had such persons to take care of correspondence and to give advice. This "lawyer" who addressed Jesus, then, is an anomaly: he is speaking for himself, not for some other more powerful person, and he is singular, not part of a group of inquisitors.

Where does he come from? The setting in 10:17 is a bit vague; Jesus has turned his face toward Jerusalem and is somewhere on the road; he sent the seventy-two out on mission, and presumably in the meantime he has been visiting villages and towns where they have done advance work for him. But the missionaries come back all in a group, reporting on their great success, and from 10:18-24 Jesus has been speaking to them, then praying, then speaking to them again. Then 10:25: "And behold, a certain lawyer stood, testing him by saying . . . ." Perhaps Luke imagines a scene in a house or the marketplace of one of these nameless Galilean villages. Jesus and the whole gang are sitting around (eating, no doubt) catching up on how everyone has done, and this lawyer is sitting nearby listening in. His question, therefore, has a context: he has heard the missionaries report that the demons submit to them and heard Jesus' responses of praise and caution. He's heard Jesus claim that nobody knows the Father as he and those to whom he, the Son, chooses to teach. The last thing he hears is Jesus' blessing on the disciples for seeing and hearing what many prophets and kings desire to see but cannot. In that context—the Son claiming to choose who gets to know God correctly—the lawyer asks, "Teacher, what must I do to inherit eternal life?"

Luke characterizes the question as *ekpeirazōn*, meaning "testing" or "tempting." Luke uses the root verb (without the preposition *ek*) to mean both being tempted by Satan (4:2) and going through hard or pressured times (22:28). The lawyer's question, then, has an edge to it—at the least, he is pushing Jesus; at worst, he is trying to trip Jesus up. He calls Jesus "teacher," which is an equivocal greeting in Luke, sometimes offered by respectful questioners (3:12; 9:38; 12:13) and sometimes by those already hostile to Jesus (11:45; 19:39). The narrative allows us to choose. We can read the lawyer as a curious interrogator who hears Jesus speaking of his role as revealer and the disciples' status as blessed recipients of special revelation and who wants to push him a bit: OK, Jesus, show me what you got. Or we can read the lawyer as hostile, scandalized by Jesus' high-flown claims, and hoping to show him up as a puffed-up know-it-all: OK, "Teacher"—bet you don't know Genesis from a hole in the ground. In either case, "what must I do to inherit eternal life" may put the stress on the "I"—I, the lawyer, as opposed to your disciples or the peasants to whom they have been preaching. Where is the boundary, in other words, between your movement and the rest of us? What do you think you have that is so special, and what would somebody like me need to do to get hold of it? The difference between pushy and hostile would be whether the lawyer is open to being instructed by this Teacher; does he think there is any chance that he can learn something?

Jesus, using the age-old educational principle that a good teacher never answers a question that the student can answer for himself or herself, turns it around: "What has been written in the law? How do you read it?" Great move—make him show his cards first. If it's a trap, once you see it you can deal with it; if it's a legitimate question, then no need to jump down the man's throat. If the lawyer thinks Jesus really is a teacher, then Jesus' question is respectful and encouraging; if the lawyer thinks Jesus is a fraud, then Jesus may as well hear the lawyer's opinion first, since his mind is closed.

The lawyer quotes Deuteronomy 6:5, a part of the Shema [The Shema], and Leviticus 19:18b, putting them together as if they were one verse. In Mark's version, which Luke is editing, the scribe asks, "What is the most important commandment of all?" and Jesus gives him the Shema as number one and Leviticus 19:18b as number two (Mark 12:28-34). Luke therefore knows that the two verses are separate commands and also knows that combining the two was Jesus' idea. By the time Luke was writing, many Gentile Christians probably did not think of "love the Lord" and "love your neighbor" as Old Testament quotes, but as Jesus' teaching on the most significant teachings from the Torah and the most succinct summary of Christian ethics (Jas 2:8 calls "love your neighbor" "the royal law"). By structuring the story as he does, Luke allows the Jewish legal expert to voice the Christian legal/ethical opinion, giving it a sort

The Shema

The first word of Deut 6:4-6 in Hebrew is "shema," the imperative of the verb "to hear." These verses came to be recited morning and evening; according to the Mishnah (*m. Ber.* 1:1-3), one recites in the evening between sundown and midnight and in the morning "as soon as one can distinguish between blue and white." These verses were also written with others on tiny scrolls and put into boxes that could be fastened onto the hands and forehead (in Heb., *tefillin*; in Gk., *phylacteries*), in literal obedience to Deut 6:8; Matt 23:5 and Josephus (*Ant.* 4.213) attest to the practice in the 1st century. The same sort of scrolls were also put into containers called mezuzot and attached to the doorposts of homes. Sanders wrote, "It seems, then, that Jews generally accepted the biblical requirement to bear in mind the laws of God, and they fulfilled it by saying the Shema', posting mezuzot and wearing tefillin."

E. P. Sanders, *Judaism: Practice and Belief* 63 BCE–66 CE (London: SCM, 1992), 197.

of independent confirmation. It also makes the lawyer's challenge fall flat, because instead of an argument from Jesus, he gets a "Great answer! Go do that, and you will live [that is, God will reward you with eternal life at Judgment Day]."

In this first part of the episode, Jesus and the lawyer apparently wind up on the same side of the issue of how one obtains salvation. They agree that the answer is found in Torah and that obedience to these two biblical commands is enough to put a person on the side of the angels on Judgment Day. The lawyer has not yet gotten an answer to his question about boundaries: if the unique knowledge of God that Jesus has must be revealed to those whom he chooses, how is it that he, the lawyer, already knows the way to inherit eternal life? If the answer is as simple as the Shema, which Jews recited daily as part of their devotion to God, then why does Jesus need to send seventy-two emissaries gallivanting all over Galilee to spread the word? Something is fishy. I'm certain that we disagree somewhere; let's define our terms, shall we?

The lawyer begins at the end, rather than the beginning: "Who is my neighbor," taking up the last noun in the sequence. Why not begin with the verb "love"? Or with the nature of the self? Or with the character of God? Partly, and maybe mostly, the answer is to be found in Luke's need to segue into the parable, which defines "neighbor" rather than any of the other terms.

Another part of the answer is that "who is my neighbor" turned out to be an important question for the early church. One can understand the lawyer to be asking for Jesus to explain where he thought "neighbor" ended: Who is *not* my neighbor, in other words? In Acts, each time the gospel reaches a new group—Hellenistic Jews, Samaritans, Gentiles who already worship God, and finally Gentile converts from Greco-Roman religions—the discomfort and debate among the Christians increases. "Who is my neighbor?" may presage "Why did you go to uncircumcised men and eat with them?" (Acts 11:3). Luke is certain that Christians, under the Spirit's leadership, can overcome the xenophobia common to most humans, but his narrative shows that the church struggled with it at every turn.

But the lawyer's question could also be about not wanting to lose the challenge in the first round. The lawyer wants to test Jesus on the law, to see how he understands it, and Jesus essentially says, "Just like you do—now, go and do what you say." The exhortation at the end puts Jesus in an authoritative role, and the lawyer is not yet willing to admit that Jesus is the better man. Luke describes the lawyer as "wishing to justify himself," which can be understood to mean "wishing to be able to declare himself the winner in this contest of wits." Maybe "who is my neighbor" is the equivalent of "You won't get off that easy, Jesus. Let's see you define 'neighbor' according to the Law." [Fred Craddock and Albert Schweitzer]

The definition of "neighbor" is not as straightforward in Leviticus 19 as one might suppose. Leviticus 19:17-18 speaks of not hating one's own kin or carrying out vengeance against one's own people; but Leviticus 19:33-34 extends this to include resident aliens, non-Jews living in Jewish territory. In the lawyer's day, there were Roman troops stationed in Judea and Galilee, and Jews and non-Jews lived in different sections of cities such as Caesarea Maritima; did the Levitical command mean loving them, too? The LXX translation of v. 33 adds another wrinkle. It

Fred Craddock and Albert Schweitzer

"I think I was twenty years old when I read Albert Schweitzer's *Quest for the Historical Jesus*. I found his Christology woefully lacking—more water than wine. I marked it up, wrote in the margins, raised questions of all kinds. And one day, one day I read in the Knoxville *News-Sentinel* that Albert Schweitzer was going to be in Cleveland, Ohio, to play the dedicatory concert for a big organ in a big church up there. According to the article he would remain afterward in the fellowship hall for conversation and refreshment. . . ."

Craddock bought a bus ticket and worked out his questions, carefully writing them all down against the chance he would have some time to corner Schweitzer during the reception.

". . . I went there; I heard the concert; I rushed into the fellowship hall, got a seat in the front row, and waited with my lap of questions. After a while he came in, shaggy hair, big white mustache, stooped, and seventy-five years old. You know he was master organist, medical doctor, philosopher, biblical scholar, lecturer, writer, everything. He came in with a cup of tea and some refreshments and stood in front of the group, and there I was, close. Dr. Schweitzer thanked everybody: 'You've been very warm, hospitable to me. I thank you for it, and I wish I could stay longer among you, but I must go back to Africa. I must go back to Africa because my people are poor and diseased and hungry and dying, and I have to go. We have a medical station at Lambarene. If there's anyone here in this room who has the love of Jesus, would you be prompted by that love to go with me and help me?'

"I looked down at my questions; they were so absolutely stupid. And I learned, again, what it means to be a Christian and had hopes that I could be that someday."

Fred Craddock, *Craddock Stories* (ed. Mike Graves and Richard F. Ward; St. Louis: Chalice, 2001), 125–26.

reads, "As the native among you shall be the alien who comes to you, and you shall love him as yourself." The Hebrew word for "alien," *ger*, means a non-Israelite who has taken up permanent residence in Israel, but the LXX chose *prosēlytos*, which by Luke's day was sometimes used to mean "convert" (see Matt 23:15). Had Jesus and the lawyer really gotten into the meaning of "neighbor," they could have stood there all day debating which biblical passages controlled its meaning.

Instead, Jesus tells a story to draw out the meaning of "neighbor" and of Leviticus 19:33.[14] "A certain man"—just as the lawyer is "a certain lawyer," meaning a particular individual, but unnamed— "was headed down from Jerusalem to Jericho." All roads, by custom, lead *up to* and *down from* Jerusalem; but as you go north to Jericho from the holy city, you descend from 2500 feet above sea level to 770 feet below. Josephus said that the "150 *stadioi*," or about eighteen miles, led through "desert and stony" country;[15] he also noted that because of the dangers of "bandits" (same word as in the parable), the normally pacifist Essenes carried weapons whenever they went on any significant journey.[16] Nothing improbable, then, about a man traveling solo who got mugged and robbed.

The bandits, "after stripping him and beating him, left, leaving him half-dead." Did they get away with a sack of money? Nothing is said about that—they take his clothes, but maybe that was all he had on him. In fact, if we read this as a completely senseless act of violence, I suspect we come closer to Luke's purpose in the story. These bandits fell on this bloke like a force of nature, leaving him naked, battered, and only a short ride from the cemetery. He is there without family or friends, in the wastelands between inhabited places; at the moment, he has no neighbors, only enemies, and it looks like he may die ungrieved and unburied. Sounds a bit like Jesus on the cross, eh?

"Now, by chance a certain priest was going down that same road, and when he saw [the injured man], he passed by on the other side [of the road]." Just as the bandits are given no motive for pouncing on this man, the priest is given no motive for passing him by. True, a priest was not supposed to handle corpses except those of his birth family (Lev 21:1-4), but in my opinion, it is a mistake to assign that motive to the priest.[17] First, in the actual practice of Judaism in Jesus' day it is likely that priests, like all Jews, believed that the Torah put saving life ahead of keeping any purity regulation. Second, since it was not clear that the man was dead, the priest would not be disobeying the restriction against corpse defilement, since he was not deliberately handling a corpse. And third, he, like the injured man, was heading away from Jerusalem. Luke knew that priests served two-week terms in Jerusalem and then returned home (1:8, 23), and so we may presume he thought this fictional priest was doing the same.[18] If the man were dead, the priest (like righteous Tobit; see Tob 1:18; 2:1-8) would have been doing a righteous act by burying the man, and would in any event have had time to become decontaminated before his next round of temple service. The parable deliberately assigns no motive to the priest, so that his inaction is put in the same category as the violence of the bandits. They fall on the man like floods from broken levees, and the priest fails to help—does it matter what his reason was? Poor organization, bad decision-making, inter-agency squabbling, lack of focus—who cares what the reasons were when an injured man is dying and someone who might make a difference either can't or won't? [Failing to Help vs. Helping]

"Likewise"—equally by chance, in other words—"a Levite, coming to the same place and seeing [him], passed by on the other side." Levites were members of the tribe of Levi but not descendants of Aaron, and so not priests. The Law prescribed that Levites would assist with sacrifices, lead worshipers in prayers and music in the temple, and, like priests, receive portions of the tithes.

We may assume a certain level of Lukan antipathy for the temple leadership, since they were the ones who pushed for Jesus' crucifixion, who empowered Saul to ravage the church in Jerusalem, who ordered Stephen's stoning, and who called for Paul's execution. Thus we might presume that Luke would not expect much from a priest or a Levite. But if we think of Jesus' audience, the question is more complicated. On the one hand, many suspect that poor Galilean peasants resented the tithes and temple taxes that supported the priesthood. One can imagine some of Jesus' listeners, who envied the priest his inherited income prescribed by Torah, thought that Jesus' two clerics were pretty typical of all of them. On the other hand, some rural priests were also poor, and there is no real evidence for a widespread anticlerical sentiment among first-century Galileans. Perhaps some, or many, of Jesus' listeners

Failing to Help vs. Helping

"So I guess you want me to be the superhero that is going to step in there and suddenly take everybody out of New Orleans." Michael Brown, former director of FEMA, to a congressional panel investigating what went wrong in the federal response to Hurricane Katrina.

"It feels good when people call me a hero," says De'Monte. "But I don't know why they do." De'Monte Williams, 6 years old, kept his 5-month-old brother, two cousins, and three neighborhood kids "all ranging in ages from 14 months to 3 years," together and safe when they were put on a helicopter and evacuated from their home in New Orleans. Separated from their parents, they were taken by well-meaning rescue workers to Baton Rouge, while their parents eventually went to San Antonio. De'Monte explained things to the shelter staff in enough detail that within a few days they were reunited with their parents.

Time, 26 December 2005, pp. 27, 107–108.

were shocked or offended by Jesus' characterization of the priest and Levite. Since the narrative neither names the two nor explains why they acted as they did, the listener/reader is apt to fill in the gaps in all sorts of ways, depending on his/her own experiences with clergy.

"But then a certain Samaritan on a journey"—because he would not have been heading to or from the temple—"came upon him and when he saw him, was filled with compassion." Zechariah the priest predicts John's prophetic ministry in these terms: "to give knowledge of salvation to his people in the forgiveness of their sins, through the compassionate mercy of our God" (1:77-78). Luke, who avoids assigning Jesus emotions, once says, "seeing her, he was filled with compassion" when he came upon a widow who had just lost her only son (7:13). The Samaritan, then, is acting in imitation of the Father and the Son when he tenderly cares for the injured man. Jesus' story illustrates how even a non-Israelite may act upon the true knowledge of God if he does mercy to those who need it.

The Samaritan gives the injured man first-century first aid—wine to clean the wounds, oil to soothe them, wrappings to keep them clean—but in doing this he also gives away rations he planned to use on his journey. He put the injured man on his animal (the word used means any sort of transport animal) and took him to an inn, which was a sort of roadhouse or hostel that sold meals, a place to sleep, and a place to shelter animals. There he cared for the man through the night. Next morning, he gave two denarii—two days' wages for a common laborer—to the innkeeper, asking the innkeeper now to take over the role of caregiver and promising to give more money if it were required. Think about that last part for a bit: in Jesus' story, the Samaritan expects the hostel-keeper to continue to provide compassionate care until the injured man is better, and for the hostel-keeper to accept the Samaritan's promise that he would return to repay any debts incurred. What if, as soon as the Samaritan was around the bend, the innkeeper threw the man out on the road and kept the money for himself?

The parable puts an ordinary person in a tragic circumstance—unfortunately, an all-too-commonplace occurrence. Two religious persons, from family groups of whom Torah says "their portion is the Lord," fail to provide the Lord's mercy for the person in need. Two other persons do what it takes to get the man back on his feet. The first, the Samaritan, might or might not be included in the strict definition of "neighbor" according to Leviticus 19, since he was not an Israelite and might not have been a resident alien. As noted earlier, the Samaritans Jesus encountered earlier were most definitely inhospitable, but this man's generosity and hospitality could not be faulted. The second, the innkeeper, we assume to have been an Israelite and assume to have followed the Samaritan's instructions. His acts are not selfless, since he is going to be paid for his troubles, but are the sort of normal human goodness we all count on: people who do their jobs honestly, fairly, even compassionately, so that we don't have to spend all our lives watching our backs. In the world of Jesus' story, as in the real world Luke and we live in, there are senselessly violent acts, acts of immoral indifference, outstandingly compassionate acts, and acts of normal honest commerce. Sometimes the people we would like to count on to be the best of us let us down—that's life.

So how will we live? Jesus puts the question to the lawyer this way: "Which of these three, does it seem to you, became neighbor to the man beaten by the bandits?" The lawyer's question was "Who is *my* neighbor?" Jesus frames a story that, in effect, puts the lawyer in the ditch: if you were the man beaten by bandits, who would you say had been your neighbor? The answer is obvious: "The one doing mercy (or a merciful deed) to him." Commentators normally point out that the lawyer speaks of the man's actions, not his race; perhaps we should read this as reluctance to name a Samaritan as the hero of the story. But it could be that the lawyer gets the point—the issue is not race, class, religion, or status, but behavior. It's the act of mercy, the act in imitation of the nature of God, that defines this person, and so Jesus' words, "Go, and *you* do the same" also defines neighbor in terms of behavior rather than race.[19]

Note what the parable addresses and does not address. By assigning no motives for the crime, it does not address the roots of violence in our society. Were these bandits driven off their lands by the cumulative effects of high taxes, limited markets, bad crop years, and greedy creditors? Acts of mercy to individuals are only part of a Christian response to world violence, particularly government-sponsored violence. [Charity and Structural Injustice]

By assigning no motives for the priestly and Levitical bypassing, the parable does not address the sources of the apathy of religious people toward the plight of hundreds of thousands of people teetering, like this man, on the edge of life and death. How many thousands die daily for lack of food, medicine, and shelter that would cost us less than we spend on fast food in a week? Or cable TV fees? Or video rentals? Or any of a hundred things that would not, for us, spell the difference between life and death? The vast majority of Americans give to charity, and the total sum is impressive, until you think of it as a percentage of our national income. Why don't we care more that we could stop people from dying?

The parable also fails miserably, from the point of view of our modern therapeutic culture, to address the (to us) all-important issue of self-care. Didn't the Samaritan worry about being overcome by compassion fatigue? Was he loving himself enough, or was he foolishly overextending himself by his open-ended offer of help? It is true that some people go into the helping professions in the hopes that by addressing the needs of others they can feel better about themselves; this is an almost sure-fire recipe for burnout and collapse. It is also true that the pressures of ministry combined with our cultural definitions of success produce great strains on the physical and mental health of clergy, and that self-care is a valid concern. My point is that this parable, since it is given by Jesus to define the Great Commandments, goes in a completely opposite direction. If we are looking for a "self-love" text, we should keep looking.

The parable addresses, instead, the definition of "neighbor," and it does so by ignoring territory or race or income. Was the beaten man rich or poor, Jewish or Gentile? Was the Samaritan religious? Were the two days' wages he gave to the innkeeper his whole income for the month, or was he a wealthy man who could have afforded much more? All of that is beside the point. The merciful man, because he was filled with God's compassion, gave what was needed from what he had, and promised to do more if more was needed. That is the definition of neighbor: one who acts from the mercy of the God he or she loves with all of his or her self.

What must I do to inherit eternal life?

What does the Law say? How do you read it?

Love God with all I am and love my neighbor as myself.

Good answer—do this, and you will live.

But who is my neighbor?

Well, who acted like a neighbor to the person who needed a neighbor?

The one doing God's mercy.

You do the same.

Charity and Structural Injustice

The parable of the merciful Samaritan is often accused of banality: It is only an ethical example story without any deeper dimension. But if the hearers of this story begin to reflect on it and to talk with one another about what each needs to do here and now, the specter of supposed superficiality vanishes. What does it mean today to see what is happening with raw materials from poor countries? And if the deed of love is even a tiny one, if it really helps to protect the life of the victim, it is a miracle . . . . As long as the soup kitchens cause us not to make light of the structural injustice of violence to the poor, they are a necessary first step.

Luise Schottrof, *The Parables of Jesus* (trans. Linda M. Maloney; Minneapolis: Fortress, 2006), 136.

Two Sisters and Jesus, 10:38-42

This is a complicated knot of a story: difficult textual variants to resolve, disputed meanings of words, and the intersection of several different important Lukan themes all make it hard to arrive at a single interpretation. The Florentine painter Alessandro Allori painted Christ in the House of Mary and Martha more than once, illustrating how one might understand it differently. In 1578–1580, in a painting for a private chapel in the palatial home of a wealthy patron (not reproduced here), Allori put Christ seated in a chair between Mary, who sits on the floor to his right, and Martha, who stands close to his left knee. Both women are looking intently at Christ; he gestures towards Mary but his head is turned towards Martha, and he gazes intently into Martha's eyes. Mikeal Parsons and Heidi Hornik, reflecting on the picture's composition, write, "[T]he meaning in our particular painting is clear. Allori fits the complementary pattern, with both Martha and Mary's actions—action and contemplation—being commended."[20]

By "complementary pattern," Parsons and Hornik mean a reading of the story that holds together both activity and contemplation as important aspects of discipleship. [Combining Mary and Martha in One Person] Another way to interpret Luke's scene stresses the value judgment Jesus appears to make if one translates 10:42b as "Mary has chosen the better part." In a second take on the Martha and Mary scene (the one reproduced here), Allori put the two sisters side-by-side, and depicts Christ pointing to Mary and looking into her eyes, implying that he prefers her conduct to her sister's. But notice that all three figures are calm; if Jesus indicates his preference for Mary's way, he does not seem to be rebuking Martha. A painting by the Spaniard Diego Rodriguez de Silva y Velazquez (1599–1660) appears to have understood our passage as a choice for Mary and against Martha, and then imagines how Martha might have felt as a result. He put Martha and Mary as figures in a popular style of painting in seventeenth-century Seville, the

Allori's Jesus, Mary, and Martha

Alessandro Allori (1535–1607). Christ in the House of Mary and Martha. Poplar wood, Kunsthistorisches Museum, Vienna, Austria. (Credit: Erich Lessing/Art Resource, NY)

bodegone. In this style, people are arranged in ordinary settings involving eating or food preparation; sometimes the setting is a tavern, other times (as this one) a private home with a kitchen in the foreground. Velazquez focuses the viewer's eye on Martha, who is working on a meal in the foreground. She is in the kitchen, with the makings of a meal on the worktable in front of her, and an older woman leaning over her shoulder. But the viewer can look past Martha to another room (or perhaps the viewer sees the other room in a mirror in the kitchen) where Jesus sits in a chair, Mary at his feet, and another older woman stands behind her. The Savior, Mary, and her chaperone are deep in their conversation; Jesus raises his hand, perhaps to bless Mary; she looks at him with devotion. Martha, however, is staring into space, looking like she is about to burst into tears; the older woman behind her is shaking her finger, and her furrowed brow and tight-lipped face seem to be poised to tell Martha to get her mind back on the cooking if she ever expects to get dinner on the table. [The Angry Martha] This painting interprets Luke's scene as clearly as Allori's, but makes a different point: Martha, in the dark kitchen, realizes she has been left out of something important, while Mary, staring at Jesus in the well-lit sitting room, has been transported to bliss.

Step 1 is to decide what text of the story we will follow. The first significant variant is in v. 38, where some manuscripts read "received him into her house" and others "received him." The shorter reading is found in the oldest manuscripts, and the longer is generally thought to be a secondary addition by Christian scribes sensitive to the issue of a single woman "receiving" Jesus.[21] It seems possible that the shorter reading could have originated from scribes trying to harmonize Luke to John (John 12:1-8 makes Martha and Mary sisters of Lazarus living in their brother's home); either reading means that Martha offered Jesus hospitality, acting as host. In the next verse, manuscripts disagree on the grammatical form of the participle for "seated," but the more important difference is whether Luke wrote "the Lord's feet" or "Jesus' feet." Here the manuscripts are split, and I suspect that "Jesus" was original and that "Lord" was put into v. 39 because it appears in v. 41.[22] The

Combining Mary and Martha in One Person

In the monastic life one could find, according to Bernard [of Clairvaux], three vocations: that of Lazarus the penitent, that of Martha the active and devoted servant of the monastic household, and that of Mary the contemplative . . . . St. Bernard himself . . . [says] that after all Martha and Mary are sisters and they should dwell in the same household in peace. They supplement one another. But in actual fact, true monastic perfection consists above all in the union of all three vocations: that of the penitent, the active worker (in the care of souls above all) and the contemplative.

Thomas Merton, *The Climate of Monastic Prayer* (Spencer MA: Cistercian, 1969), 75–76.

The Angry Martha

Martha may do her work in silence, but it is a sham, a mask for rage. I like to think of her as saying nothing as she bangs around the house, trying to get Mary's attention, or better yet, make her feel guilty for not helping out. At any rate, Martha is so internally noisy that Jesus has to call her by name twice—"Martha, Martha"—before she can hear him and respond. I recognize myself all too clearly in the scene; all the internal—infernal—distractions, the clatter-bang of daily routines and deadlines, that can make me unfit company for anyone.

Kathleen Norris, *Amazing Grace: A Vocabulary of Faith* (New York: Riverhead, 1998, 281–82.

Velazquez's Jesus, Mary, and Martha

Diego Rodriguez Velazquez (1599–1660). *Christ in the House of Martha and Mary*. 1629–1630. National Gallery, London, Great Britain. (Credit: Erich Lessing/Art Resource, NY)

verb for "listen" is aorist in some manuscripts and imperfect in others; the imperfect is usually preferred, and it gives the sense of something Mary had been doing for a while before Martha came into the room.

The biggest and hairiest textual problem is what Jesus says to Martha in vv. 41-42. Some manuscripts read "worried and troubled," using a fairly rare verb for "troubled"—some copyists substituted a more common word. Some manuscripts read "but one thing is needed"; some read "a few things are needed"; still others, "a few, or one, is needed." Some manuscripts start Jesus' words to Martha with "Mary has chosen," perhaps because the copyists could not figure out what v. 42a means. Most commentators think that the "a few, or one" is the most secondary reading, resulting from some scribe looking at manuscripts that differed and taking the safest route of keeping both.[23] But at least one modern scholar has argued for the originality of the longer text,[24] on the grounds that it is the harder reading. In my opinion, the contrast with "many" in the first clause argues for "one thing is needed" in the final clause; the longer reading, "a few or one are needed," is the more flaccid reading, watering down the contrast until it washes away.

Next, we need to take note of how this story connects with several others. The one most often mentioned is the parable of the Samaritan just finished. The lawyer and Martha are both introduced with the indefinite pronoun ("a certain"); the parable of the Samaritan "develops the meaning of the command to love one's neighbor, and the story of Mary and Martha highlights the overriding importance of devotion to the Lord's word as an expression of one's love for God."[25] Another link is to the themes of hospitality and table fellowship. Notice the progression of things in Luke so far:

- After preaching in the Capernaum synagogue and exorcising a demon, Jesus "enters Simon's house," where Simon's mother-in-law is ill. Jesus rebukes the fever, and the woman "rising, served [using the verb *diakoneō*] them."
- After Jesus calls Levi, the former tax collector throws Jesus a great banquet "in his house," and Jesus reclines to eat with many tax collectors and others. The Pharisees and scribes complain, but Jesus states that his mission is to call sinners to repentance.
- At 7:36, Simon the Pharisee invites Jesus to dinner, and Jesus, "entering the house of the Pharisee, reclined to eat." We learn later that Simon has been a poor host when an unnamed woman, a sinner from that city, "standing behind him by his feet," anoints Jesus' feet with perfume, bathing them with her tears, wiping them down with her hair, and kissing them continually.
- In 8:1-3, we learn that several women have been "serving [again, the verb *diakoneō*] Jesus and others with their own money while he and the Twelve are on the road.
- In 9:10-17, the Twelve want to dismiss a big hungry crowd, but Jesus plays host, feeding them though the miracle of the loaves and fishes.
- In 9:51-55, Jesus sends the disciples ahead of him, and "they enter into a village of Samaritans" to prepare for him, but "they would not receive [using the verb *dechomai*] him." Two of the Twelve want God to rain fire on the ingrates, but Jesus rebukes them.
- In the missionary instructions of 9:1-6 and 10:1-16, Jesus expects the Twelve and the seventy-two to find hospitality in the villages and towns where they will go. If they "receive" (*dechomai*) you, eat with them, heal the sick, and give them the good news. If they don't, then shake the dust off your feet as you leave.

The Samaritan in the parable provides care for the wounded man on the road, and we could think of his actions, motivated by compassion and mercy (10:33, 37), as being an illustration of ministry and hospitality. He does what he can to heal, he takes the man to shelter, he provides for immediate and longer-term care. But neither *diakoneō* nor *dechomai* appear in the parable, and the closer verbal parallels are to the other "house" episodes. To read Martha and Mary properly, we need to see it in connection with all the hospitality and ministry pericopes in chapters 1–10.

The story begins with an odd construction that puts "they" and "he" side by side in the sentence for emphasis; to get it in English we have to resort to italics: "Now while *they* were traveling, *he* entered a certain village." The reader knows that Jesus sent the seventy-two off on in pairs (10:1); they come back in 10:17, but if they split up again in 10:38, we are not too surprised. The main thing is that Luke wants to stress that Jesus goes to this place alone. "And a certain woman named Martha received [using the verb *dechomai*] him." Wait just a minute—he went to a village, by himself, and while he was preaching and healing and doing his kingdom of God thing, he met this woman named Martha, who invited him home? And he went with her?

Early Christians connected this Martha and Mary with the sisters of Lazarus in the Gospel of John. [How Many Marys?] John 11:1-57, the miracle of the raising of Lazarus, makes Jesus close friends of the whole family, who live at Bethany (in the south, close to Jerusalem). John 12:1-8 has Mary of Bethany anoint Jesus' feet and wipe them with her hair in Lazarus's house. If we assume that this Johannine information was known to Luke, then it takes away much of the scandal of a single woman inviting the visiting preacher to stay in her home—it wasn't her home, it was Lazarus's home, and maybe he was in the back watching the football game while the girls were fussing over Jesus. But we have no reason to think that Luke knew any of John's information, and less than no reason to think that Luke expected his readers to put all this together. The only Lazarus in Luke is the poor man in the parable of 16:19-31; Martha's village is nowhere close to Jerusalem (he gets to Bethany at 19:29); it is her house, even on the shorter reading of 10:38.

So Luke, then, sets up this story of Jesus going by himself into the house of a woman of recent acquaintance. She is the host, he the missionary, and according to the rules of 10:1-16, he should heal, teach about the kingdom, and eat what is set before him. From that passage, we can only infer the host's responsibilities by

How Many Marys?

Luke writes about three Marys (not including the mother of Jesus):

1. Mary the mother of James (24:10), unless this Mary is also the mother of Jesus;
2. Mary Magdalene, from whom Jesus cast out seven demons, who helped to support Jesus while he was on mission, and who was one of the women at the tomb (8:1-3; 24:10);
3. Mary, sister of Martha, who lived with Martha in a house "in a certain village" of uncertain provenance, although Luke must have assumed it was in Galilee (since in 17:11, Jesus is moving "between" Galilee and Samaria).

Luke also writes of an anonymous woman in ch. 7 who wets Jesus' feet with her tears and dries them with her hair.

John writes about two Marys:

1. Mary of Bethany, sister to Martha and Lazarus, who lived in her brother's house (11:1-57). In John's account, Mary of Bethany washed Jesus' feet and wiped them with her hair in her brother's house;
2. Mary Magdalene, who was the only woman at the tomb and the first witness to the resurrected Jesus (20:1-18).

The early church first combined John's Mary of Bethany with Luke's Mary number 3 and with the anonymous woman in Luke 7. Augustine makes the identification, but knows it was not certain: "Behold this sister of Lazarus (if indeed it was she who anointed the Lord's feet with unguent, and dried with her hair what she had washed with her tears) was raised from the dead more truly than her brother—she was freed from the weight of her bad habits . . . . And of her it has been said, 'For she was a famous sinner.'"

Later Christians also linked Mary of Bethany with Mary Magdalene, and near the end of the 6th century, Pope Gregory made this official. Thus, Allori's painting depicts the seated Mary with unbound long red hair and her jar of ointment, part of the typical iconography for the Magdalene.

Augustine, in *Johannis Evangelium*, PL 35, col. 1748; cited in Heidi J. Hornik and Mikeal C. Parsons, *Illuminating Luke: The Public Ministry of Christ in Italian Renaissance and Baroque Painting* (New York: T & T Clark, 2005), 114.

reading between the lines: receive the missionary in peace; offer food, drink, and lodging; keep him as long as he stays. Luke 10:1-16, since it takes the point of view of the missionary, is less than specific about certain important questions: How much food is a good host supposed to provide one of Jesus' missionaries, and for how long?

"A certain woman named Martha received him," from the immediate and longer-range contexts of Luke-Acts, implies that she gave Jesus room and board. Besides the examples already cited, we can cite Luke 16:4, where the dishonest manager, who is a slave, hopes to find employment and lodging in the houses of one of his master's creditors. Martha is the precursor to Lydia, "a certain woman" who met Paul and his entourage in Philippi, was converted with all her household, and offered the missionaries shelter (Acts 16:15). I make this point emphatically, because of the need to define "service" or "ministry" (*diakonian*) in v. 40; quite apart from the meaning of that word, in this story, Luke imagined Martha was personally preparing food for Jesus. How else could he eat what was set before him, in obedience to his own command?

Enter the sister: "And there was also a sister named Mary, who, seated beside [him] at Jesus' feet, was listening to his word." Both of our painters put Jesus in a chair and Mary on the floor, and many modern interpreters do as well. But what might Luke have imagined? In his culture, men reclined to eat, and Luke uses that word specifically at 7:36, 14:8, and 24:30. The last example is most telling—Jesus is invited in by the two disciples at Emmaus and reclines to eat with them. If Luke assumes that most meals at which Jesus was an invited guest were ones where the guest reclined, then he might well have imagined Jesus on a dining couch and Mary on a chair next to his feet; or if Luke imagines that Martha was poor, as I will argue, perhaps Jesus was on cushions and Mary on the floor next to his feet.[26] Note how her posture is both similar to and different from the anointing woman's; Mary is *parakathestheisa pros tous podas . . . ēkovein* (sitting beside by his feet . . . listening), whereas the anointing woman is *stasa opisō para tous podas . . . klaiousa* (standing behind beside his feet . . . weeping). Luke is not in the habit of picturing women groveling on the floor by Jesus' feet! But of the two, Mary is (admirably, from the standpoint of Luke's culture) in control of her emotions and listening to his word. Note the singular "word"—Luke means that Jesus is teaching/telling/preaching the gospel, and Mary is soaking it in. [Mary Was Eating, Too]

Mary Was Eating, Too

What was Mary enjoying while she was listening? What was she eating? What was she drinking? Do you know? Let's ask the Lord, who keeps such a splendid table for his own people, let's ask him. "Blessed," he says, "are those who are hungry and thirsty for justice, because they shall be satisfied."

Augustine, *Serm.* 179.5, cited in Arthur A. Just Jr., ed., *Luke* (ACCS: NT, vol. 3; Downer's Grove IL: Intervarsity Press, 2003), 182.

So far: Martha meets Jesus in the village and receives him—that's a good thing. Mary meets Jesus in the dining room and listens to him—another good thing. Both could be considered responses appropriate to first-time hearers of the gospel or to long-time disciples of the Lord. Neither woman is part of the group traveling with Jesus; neither one has left home or family to provide for Jesus on the road, as did Mary Magdalene, Joanna, and Susanna, among others. But both Mary and Martha are, up to this point in the narrative, exemplary characters. Having this story follow the parable may be, as some suggest, a way to illustrate the Great Commandment in reverse: love your neighbor/love God, but it also may be a way to illustrate ways to carry out Jesus' missionary commands. The Samaritan is the disciple on the road, doing good wherever he finds a need; Mary and Martha are the disciples in the village, welcoming needy missionaries when they arrive. More kudos to Martha once we notice that there is no servant in the house (since she is doing all the food prep herself). The absence of slaves and her single-handed kitchen labor means that Luke is painting her as a non-elite, relatively poor person, and yet she takes it as her responsibility to take care of Jesus.

No narrative is interesting without some tension to resolve, so Luke disturbs this placid Allorian scene with a good dose of sisterly hard feelings. "But Martha was distracted by [or about] much service [or ministry; the word is *diakonia*]." The verb translated "distracted," when used literally, means to be pulled away; in a more metaphorical sense, as here, it means to have one's attention pulled away or to be overburdened.[27] Martha is being pulled or stretched by a great (or a lot of) service. We can imagine her trying to put together a nice meal on short notice all by herself, rushing between her small house and the courtyard in the rear where the community oven/stove would have been. We've been there—the guests are in your home, and you want to go make them feel welcome, but you also have to finish dinner, and you feel pulled in more than one direction. Luke most certainly does not mean that *diakonia* is a bad thing, or that it is a bad thing for women to do; as noted earlier, Simon's mother-in-law and the women from Galilee in 8:1-3 are commended for doing it.

It also seems unlikely to me that Luke thinks either the noun or verb for "service," applied to women, means only "food preparation." One argument goes like this: Peter's mother-in-law "served" Jesus, Peter, and whoever else was there by feeding them after Jesus raised her from her bed of affliction. The Galilean women "served" Jesus and the Twelve by feeding them and by paying, from their own bank accounts, whatever was needed. In Acts 6, when the Hellenists complain that their widows were neglected in the daily distribution of food, the Twelve say that they will not abandon the "word of God to serve [*diakoneō*] tables," and propose that seven men be picked to do this while the Twelve continue in the ministry (*diakonia*) of the word (Acts 6:2-4). Luke, by putting Martha in the kitchen, distracted by much service, and then scolded by Jesus for not listening to the word, both denigrates table service (in the manner of the Twelve in Acts) and women's suitability for *any* form of official ministry. Luke, according to this reading, domesticates the Galilean women and Martha: it is all well and good for them to be patrons of the Jesus movement, but they may not preach or serve in any official capacity.

There are several problems with this reading. First, while it is likely that "serve" when applied to Peter's mother-in-law meant "feed the minister and his new friends," it is not necessary to read the verb the same way in 8:1-3 (see the commentary at that section), so that there is no clear mandate to read it to mean "cook a meal" in 10:40. We already know from "receive" that Martha has agreed to feed and house Jesus. "Much service" certainly includes her kitchen duties, but "host" would have wider overtones for Luke's audience. Second, Luke writes that "Martha was distracted by her much service." Luke's language assigns her the role of "servant/minister," but then states that she was performing it incorrectly. If he had meant to eliminate women from being ministers or deacons, then he would not have used the word for what Martha was doing. Third, if Luke had meant to say that women could only serve as patrons, then he went at it backwards. He should have pulled in Lazarus from John and had him listening to Jesus rather than sister Mary; or Jesus should have scolded Martha for talking too much rather than "deaconizing" too much. The argument that says Luke wants women as silent, passive students, on the grounds that Mary is commended for silently listening to Jesus, ignores at least two things. First, Mary is commended for choosing, not for being passive; and second, Luke's Jesus never commends anyone for listening and not doing. If Mary is correctly listening to the word, it is with a view to doing the word.

Here's what actually happens. Martha, distracted by too much service/ministry, "coming in [or maybe, bursting in] says, 'O Lord, doesn't it matter to you that my sister abandoned me to serve/minister alone? Tell her to help me out!'" Luke arranges her sentence so that the words for "my," "alone," and "me" in the first sentence are consecutive; they all begin with an "m" sound, and the alliteration is a way to show the emotion in her words. Her question to him expects him to answer yes, it does matter to him, but then she follows it up with a command. Not so many people in Luke get away with ordering Jesus to do anything!

Instead of speaking to Mary, "the Lord" answers Martha. Luke is clever with the use of names, if we're right to read "Jesus" in v. 39. Mary sits next to Jesus' feet; the image is a teacher and a student, but more familiar than "Lord" and "servant girl." Martha wants to use his authority against her sibling: O Lord, tell my sister . . . . So Luke has "the Lord" reply to her, using her name: "Martha, Martha, you are worried and troubled about many things, but only one is needed." The double use of the name may have a bit of rebuke in it, something like your mother using your full name to call you into the kitchen when you were in trouble.[28] But it also seems to be a way of getting someone's attention. In 22:31, Jesus says, "Simon, Simon, look—Satan has demanded you all in order to sift you like wheat." He isn't rebuking Peter, but trying (unsuccessfully) to get him to take this warning seriously. "You are worried and troubled about many things" is not so much a rebuke as an observation that echoes the narrator's "Martha was distracted." "One thing is needed" is not a request for food; if it were, then Jesus is a poor guest and a poorer student of his own teaching, "eat and drink what is set before you." If it were about food, it also demands a change in referent from the first clause to the second: *you* are worried, but one thing is necessary for *me*. We should assume that Jesus is talking about Martha's needs in both clauses, and the one thing she needs, in her current condition, is to take time to listen to the word.

So Jesus will not order Mary into the kitchen; instead, he urges Martha to think about the one thing from which her much service has turned her attention. "For Mary has chosen the good portion which shall not be taken away from her." "Good portion," not "better"—true, in the Greek of the New Testament, the word "good" in some contexts really does mean "better," but not here. There is no comparative function in the sentence. To paraphrase Vince Lombardi, the "one thing" is not "better," it's the only thing—it's the one thing that Martha lacks. And note this: Jesus does not say, "I will not take it away from her," but "it will not be taken away from her." Luke's Jesus forbids anyone from ordering a woman away from the study of the word.

[Mary and Martha as Complementary]

Luke's story has several plausible functions in his narrative. First, it can be read as an illustration of the "love God" part of the Great Commandment, just as the parable of the Samaritan narrates the meaning of "love your neighbor as yourself." Second, it functions as a case study of sorts for the application of the commands in the missionary instructions in the first part of the chapter. When a visiting preacher shows up, what is required of a good host? Third, the story unapologetically puts Jesus into the home of a woman host at her invitation. Whatever concerns such behavior raised in Luke's culture, one must admit that he does not apologize or tone down the situation by introducing chaperones (as did Velazquez) or by pulling in Lazarus (as did the early church). This story acts as if there is no "issue" here, and maybe there was none, or maybe Luke wants to act as if there was none. Fourth, the story has been read by some as a domestication of women in the early church, part of a Lukan program to limit women's roles. Obviously, since it has been read that way, the text has dangerous potential for women in ministry. I have argued above for a reading that pulls in the opposite direction: Martha's participation in ministry/service, *diakonia*, is not being questioned, but assumed, while Mary's participation in learning the

---

Mary and Martha as Complementary

How might the story be told if there were no polarization of "hearing" and "doing"? How would the episode end if there were no tensions over vocal, public ministries for women? What would happen if Mary, Martha, and Jesus interacted in an equal triad, not with Jesus in the center and the two sisters using him as a go-between? What if Mary and Martha, instead of being pitted against each other, were portrayed as mutually supportive of each other, as in the visitation scene with Mary and Elizabeth (Luke 1:39-45)?

Barbara E. Reid, *Choosing the Better Part? Women in the Gospel of Luke* (Collegeville MN: Liturgical Press, 1996), 161.

word, which in Luke's narrative world is a prelude to doing the word, is affirmed by dominical fiat. But since we do not know precisely how women functioned in congregations of Luke's acquaintance, we also do not know whether to think that Luke is arguing against those who want to limit women's participation in ministry, or whether he is affirming the local status quo, or whether in his churches, women actually have much greater roles than this story presumes.

Velazquez's painting captures the emotion we all have felt when it seems to us that our hard service is taken for granted. Allori's version with Christ between the two sisters, pointing to Mary but looking at Martha, is a more hopeful interpretation—the Lord values both the hard work of hospitality and the focused stillness of meditating on the word—and a useful corrective to generous hosts who might be tempted to equate busy service with complete service.[29]

CONNECTIONS

The first section of this chapter spells out how Jesus' missionaries should behave. Don't take anything with you; stay with whoever offers you a roof and a meal; heal, exorcise, and preach. If they don't like you, don't stick around to argue—move on down the road. As noted in the commentary, these rules do not seem to govern the conduct of the missionaries in Acts, nor do they have much connection to Paul's descriptions of his own missionary strategies. Nevertheless, we ought to consider what they have to do with our practices as missionaries.

Come in peace. The first move is not denunciation, but conversation. We are proud of our faith, and rightly so—our relationship with God through Christ has changed our lives. But since our faith in Christ comes to them through the mouths of twenty-first-century Americans—materialistic, nationalistic, militaristic—we will need to overcome some barriers in order to build trust. Wait to see if your peace will return to you in the form of real conversation about things that matter.

Don't bring your stuff. Better yet, be prepared to discard your stuff once you find out what it is. You don't think you can live without it, but you can; odds are, the folks to whom you intend to minister probably live without it. Let go. It doesn't help anyway.

Come to stay. Eat what is set before you. Don't move about from place to place. All these are cautions against doing bungee-jump mission trips ("Jesus loves you, gotta go!") or boutique local missions (the annual cleanup day at the community center in the projects). There is a place for very short-term missions, but they feed our sense that we, with our superior wealth and technology, can fix the needs of the people to whom we minister. Quick-fix missions let us off the hook too easily. "Remain in the same house, eating and drinking what they provide," until you begin to see what God can really do in the community you and your hosts are forming.

The chapter moves on to the amazing parable of the merciful Samaritan. How does the hero of that story match up against Jesus' rules for the road? Well, he does carry money and supplies—good thing, too, or how could he have given first aid to the injured man, or paid for his stay in the inn? He stays a night caring for the man and then goes on his way—he has a job, a family, he cannot stay even until the man is fully recovered. But what he has, he shares. What he can do, he does. The Samaritan pays for health care, food, and lodging for a perfect stranger and promises to come back to make sure things go well. In the missionary sermon, Luke depicts a symbiosis of sorts between the missionaries who go out and the householders who give them hospitality. The Samaritan illustrates how a householder may serve as missionary—healing the sick, feeding the hungry, sheltering the homeless, protecting the vulnerable—and how, if we do so, we exemplify God's mercy.

The chapter concludes with the Martha and Mary story, long taken by Christian interpreters as illustrating the call to active service (Martha) and the call to contemplative prayer (Mary). As the commentary section above argues, Jesus does not call Mary's choice the "better," but also does not order her to cease learning and begin cooking. Think of what Jesus could say, but doesn't: "Martha, you're absolutely right. A woman's place is in the kitchen, making it possible for us men to do the work of real ministry, so Mary, get up and make yourself useful!" Jesus, knowing that Martha is pulled in too many directions at once by her ministry, urges her to reconsider the one thing that she needs. If Jesus will only briefly be available to teach her "the word" because he is moving from town to town, always moving toward his cross, then she needs to soak it up now while she may. Salvation—the good news that sets us free and heals us—is not only for the man in the ditch, but for the busy woman trying to feed the visiting minister.

NOTES

[1] Joseph A. Fitzmyer, *The Gospel According to Luke* (AB 28 and 28A; Garden City NY: Doubleday, 1981), 2.845-46; Bruce Metzger, *A Textual Commentary on the Greek New Testament* (New York: United Bible Societies, 1971), 150–51; Joel B. Green, *The Gospel of Luke* (NICNT; Grand Rapids: Eerdmans, 1997), 409.

[2] Mary Rose D'Angelo, "Women in the Gospel of Matthew and Luke-Acts," in Ross Shepard Kraemer and Mary Rose D'Angelo, eds., *Women and Christian Origins* (New York: Oxford University Press, 1999), 187; Jane Schaberg, "Luke," in *The Women's Bible Commentary*, ed. Carol Newsome and Sharon H. Ringe (Louisville: Westminster/John Knox, 1992), 287; Kathleen Corley, *Private Women, Public Meals* (Peabody MA: Hendrickson, 1993), 142.

[3] Whitney Shiner, *Proclaiming the Gospel: First-Century Performance of Mark* (Harrisburg PA: Trinity, 2003), 37–52.

[4] M. Eugene Boring and Fred Craddock, *The People's New Testament Commentary* (Louisville: Westminster/John Knox, 2004), 212, 218. William E. Arnal, *Jesus and the Village Scribes* (Minneapolis: Fortress, 2001), who investigates not Luke's understanding but the original context of the hypothetical Q, argues from the density of the population in first-century Galilee that the villages were very close together indeed, and that one can hardly think of this "mission" as itinerate (97–133, 172–203).

[5] Albert Schweitzer, *The Quest of the Historical Jesus* (2d ed., trans. W. Montgomery; London: Black, 1931), 355.

[6] John D. Crossan, *The Historical Jesus* (San Francisco: HarperSanFrancisco, 1991), 346.

[7] Halvor Moxnes, *Putting Jesus in His Place* (Louisville KY: Westminster/John Knox, 2003).

[8] Fitzmyer, *Luke*, 2.848; Green, *Luke*, 414.

[9] Green, *Luke*, 411; Luke Timothy Johnson, *The Gospel of Luke* (SP, vol. 3; Collegeville MN: Liturgical Press, 1991), 170.

[10] So Alan R. Culpepper, *The Gospel of Luke* (NIB, vol. 9; Nashville: Abingdon, 1995), 224. The same saying or interpretive tradition may be part of the source for Paul's reflections in 1 Cor 1:18-31: "Where is the wise? Where is the scribe? Where is the debater of this age? Has God not made foolish the world's wisdom? For since in the wisdom of God the world, by its own wisdom, did not know God, it pleased God through the foolishness of what we preach to save those who believe" (1 Cor 1:20-21).

[11] Green, *Luke*, 420–21.

[12] Ibid., 421.

[13] *The American Heritage Dictionary* (2d college ed.; Boston: Houghton Mifflin Company, 1985), s.v. "Good Samaritan."

[14] Green, *Luke*, 426, defines this as "an exposition of a text that takes the form of a story rather than of a prose-oriented argument or presentation."

[15] Josephus, *J.W.* 4.474; Fitzmyer, *Luke*, 2.886.

[16] Josephus, *J.W.* 2.125.

[17] Contra Fitzmyer, *Luke*, 2.887.

[18] So Green, *Luke*, 430; Luise Schottroff, *The Parables of Jesus* (trans. Linda M. Maloney; Minneapolis: Fortress, 2006), 135.

19 Luise Schottrof, *Parables*, 132–37, argues that the lawyer's questions are friendly, that his "testing" is a way of seeing if Jesus will be a teacher he could follow, and that his response at the end indicates that he understands the point of the parable.

20 Heidi J. Hornik and Mikeal C. Parsons, *Illuminating Luke: The Public Ministry of Christ in Italian Renaissance and Baroque Painting* (New York: T & T Clark, 2005), 127.

21 Fitzmyer, *Luke*, 2.893, and John Nolland, *Luke* (WBC, vols. 35A-C; Dallas TX: Word, 1989-93), 2.600, accept the longer reading but note the difficulty of deciding; Metzger, *Commentary*, 153, argues that "the bold and bare [received him] seems to call for some appropriate addition," and notes that scribes added several different versions of "into her house."

22 So Fitzmyer, *Luke*, 2.893, and apparently Nolland, *Luke*, 2.600, although Nolland's comments assume "Lord" is original.

23 So Metzger, *Commentary*, 153–54, who thinks "one is needed" is original, which was softened by "a few," which was then bowdlerized into "a few, or one." So also Nolland, *Luke*, 2.600; Fitzmyer, *Luke*, 2.894.

24 Gordon Fee, "One Thing Is Needful?" in E. J. Epp and Gordon D. Fee, *New Testament Textual Criticism* (Oxford: Clarendon, 1981), 61–75.

25 Culpepper, *Luke*, 231; see also Green, *Luke*, 433–34; Nolland, *Luke*, 2.600-01 lists several more points of comparison.

26 The most traditional form for Greek, Roman, and Jewish banquets was males only. But by the 1st century, sometimes women were present for at least part of the meal. "By the first century AD there is evidence that respectable women of the Roman aristocratic class were increasingly to be found at banquets and would often recline. This represented a change from the well-known earlier custom, identical to that of the Greeks, in which women did not normally appear at the banquet, and when they did, they sat" (Dennis E. Smith, *From Symposium to Eucharist* [Minneapolis: Fortress, 2003], 43).

27 BAGD, 804.

28 So most commentators; Culpepper, *Luke*, 232, for example.

29 Hornik and Parsons, *Illuminating*, 127–28.

ON PRAYER; NEGATIVE
REACTIONS TO JESUS

Luke 11

COMMENTARY

The Model Prayer and Other Advice on Prayer, 11:1-13

Nobody prays the Lukan form of the Lord's Prayer—not even anyone else in Luke, even though Jesus says "pray like this." Christians normally pray the Matthean form, except when those who say "forgive us our trespasses, as we forgive those who trespass against us." Luke has "forgive us our sins [or trespasses, if you prefer] as we forgive our debtors," so even there we are not following Luke very closely. [Variations in the Lord's Prayer] Ironically, many who pursue the historical Jesus think that except for "forgive us our trespasses," Luke's form is more original and that Matthew's form was modified for (and probably by) use in early Christian worship. That Luke preserves this form is curious: is this the way Christians in his part of the empire regularly prayed the model prayer? That is, did they really pray "Father" and not "Our Father," and did they end the prayer so abruptly? Or did Luke think that he was providing a list of topics for prayer, or an individual prayer, never really intended for corporate use? We can't know for sure; what we do know is that no evidence exists to suggest that any church or group of churches ever prayed Luke's version of the Model Prayer liturgically.

Variations in the Lord's Prayer

There is no such thing as a fixed text, a fixed meaning, or a fixed way of using this prayer, as we have seen from the very start of our story. Not only are there significant textual variants . . . but the Latin text of the Roman church produced its own need for vernacular versions and paraphrases. Much later, the technology of printing brought with it important rivals ("trespasses" in England and "debts" in Scotland), so that the common memory occasionally invoked as a reaction to today's multiplicity of texts is not quite as uniform as it is made out to be.

From Kenneth W. Stevenson, *The Lord's Prayer: A Text in Tradition* (Minneapolis: Fortress, 2004), 233.

This commentary section, like the lectionary reading, holds together assorted teachings on prayer. First there is the request for instruction on prayer (vv. 1-2a, found only in Luke); then the model prayer (vv. 2b-4); then the parable of the friend at midnight (vv. 5-8), also found only in Luke; and then the instructions "ask, seek, and knock," with the analogy about the child asking for food, which is found in Matthew also, although not in the context of teachings about prayer (Matt 7:7-11). If there was a Q, then Luke will have drawn the prayer and "ask, seek, and knock," from it, and some scholars think he preserved the order of materials in his source. Others are not so sure—maybe the tidiness of this section is due to Luke's skill as an arranger.

Once again, Jesus is praying (5:16; 6:12; 9:18; 9:29; 10:21); by reminding his audience frequently of Jesus' prayerful habits, Luke no doubt hopes to encourage others to imitate the Lord. [Praying Like Jesus] On this occasion, Jesus' own prayer leads one of the disciples to ask for instruction. This verse is the only reference to John the Baptist as a teacher of prayer. It is not implausible that John taught his disciples to pray in a way that set them apart from other Jews, since both Mark and Q testify to how John and his disciples fasted in their own way (Mark 2:18//Luke 5:33; Luke 7:33//Matt 11:18). If Luke knew anything about the content or style of Baptist-type praying, he gives us no clues, but the impression that we are to get from this scene is that this is common knowledge.

Given that Luke has already often shown Jesus at prayer and has made the point that it was his normal practice, why put in the part about John—what force does it add to the story? Luke considered John the Baptist the beginning of the gospel, and naming him here, in connection to prayer, pulls on elements as far back as the first chapter, where John's father got his angelic message while offering the incense sacrifice at the hour of prayer. In Luke's version of Mark's question about fasting, the Pharisees say, "John's disciples, like the disciples of the Pharisees, frequently fast *and pray* " (5:33; Mark's version lacks "and pray"). Jesus has already explained why his disciples will not fast until after he is gone, but it is entirely appropriate that they learn to pray, and appropriate, from Luke's understanding of God's plan for the gospel, that John was the forerunner in this regard (1:76-77).

Praying Like Jesus

She began to pray.

It would be a lengthy prayer. She thanked the Lord for everything good, including me, "her new friend." She prayed for those who were sick and for those who might become so. She prayed for rain and sun and health and humility and patience, and though I began to worry about the food getting cold I was mesmerized by her voice. Her cadence was low, with thought given to each word. Her diction was perfect, every consonant treated equally, every comma and period honored. I had to peek to make sure I wasn't dreaming. I had never heard such speech from a Southern black, or a Southern white for that matter.

I peeked again. She was talking to her Lord, and her face was perfectly content. For a few seconds, I actually forgot about the food. She squeezed my hands as she petitioned the Almighty with eloquence that came only from years of practice. She quoted Scripture, the King James Version for sure, and it was a bit odd to hear her use words like "thou" and "thine" and "whither" and "goest." But she knew precisely what she was doing. In the clutches of this very holy woman, I had never felt closer to God.

John Grisham, *The Last Juror* (New York: Bantam, 2004), 85.

"Whenever you pray, say" certainly sounds like Jesus offers a prayer to be repeated, and not just topics. But E. P. Sanders points out that the Eighteen Benedictions, which are transmitted as fixed phrases, were considered by the rabbis in the Mishnah [The Eighteen Benedictions] to have been guides to the sorts of things for which one should pray, rather than set texts to be repeated.[1] The history of the transmission of the prayer, from the Gospels down to modern times, is one of fluidity and change; whatever Luke meant, later Christians who read his account did not feel constrained to follow his text precisely.[2]

For every phrase of the prayer we can list parallels in Jewish prayers from the Second Temple period.

The Eighteen Benedictions

The Eighteen Benedictions are Jewish prayers for use by individuals and by congregations in the synagogue. The Mishnah refers to them by titles, in ways that make them seem like set texts that sometimes people had trouble remembering ("Rabban Gamaliel says: A man should pray the Eighteen [Benedictions] every day. R. Joshua says: the substance of the Eighteen. R. Akiba says: If his prayer is fluent in his mouth he should pray the Eighteen, but if not, the substance of the Eighteen" [*m. Ber.* 4:3]). Rabban Gamaliel, cited as the first authority, was the 1st-century teacher named in Acts 5:34. Most scholars think that the prayers in some form go back that early.

Father

He is our father and he is God forever. (Tob 13:4)

I cried out, Lord, you are my father. (Sir 51:10a)

It is your providence, O Father, that steers [a ship's] course, because you have given it a path in the sea. (Wis 14:3)

King of great power, Almighty God Most High, governing all creation with mercy, look upon the descendants of Abraham, O Father. (3 Macc 6:2-3)

May the Lord God be for you and for the people a father always and may you be a firstborn son. (*Jub* 19:29)[3]

My Father and my God, do not abandon me to the hands of the nations. (4Q372)[4]

For Thou art a Father to all the sons of Thy truth, and as a woman who tenderly loves her babe, so dost Thou rejoice in them; and as a foster-father bearing a child in his lap so carest Thou for all thy creatures. (1QH 17.35ff)

Witness my prayer now . . . all-powerful father [Jupiter] and you, his Saturnian wife (kinder now, goddess, I pray), and you renowned Mars, father, who direct all wars under your powers. (Vergil, *Aeneid* 12.176 ff., cited in Mark Kiley, ed. *Prayer from Alexander to Constantine: A Critical Anthology* [London: Routledge, 1997], 147)

Father Mars, I pray and request, that you be willing and propitious to me, my house, and family . . . ." (Cato, *On Agr.* 141)

Zeus the all-giver, wielder of bright lightning in the dark clouds, deliver mankind from its miserable incompetence. Father, disperse this from our soul; give us good judgment, trusting in you to guide all things in justice . . . . (Cleanthes, *Hymn to Zeus* 31–34)

O divine essence of Caesar Augustus, father of his country . . . . (inscription of a prayer to Augustus on an altar in Narbo; cited in Kiley, *Prayer from Alexander to Constantine*, 163)

O divine Penates of my parents, O father Lar of the household (*familiai Lar pater*), to you I commit the fortunes of my parents: guard them well. (Plautus, *Mercator* 833)

Let your name be sanctified

We will praise thy name for ever and ever. (4Q508)

Blessed art thou, O Lord, who art righteous in all thy ways. (4Q408)

Blessed be God who lives forever. (Tob 13:1a)

I give thanks to your name. (Sir 51:1)

Let the whole nation and every tribe know and understand that you are God, the God of all power and might, and that there is no other who protects the people of Israel but you alone. (Jdt 9:14)

O Lord, you are great and glorious, wonderful in strength, invincible. (Jdt 16:13)

Blessed are you, O Lord . . . and blessed is your glorious, holy name. (*Prayer of Azariah* 29–30)

Glorified and sanctified be God's great name throughout the world which he has created according to his will . . . (Opening phrases of the Kaddish prayer[5])

Thou art holy and thy name is awesome, and there is no God beside thee. Blessed art thou, O Lord, the Holy God. (Benediction 3 according to the Cairo Genizah fragments[6])

O Lord, O Lord, king of the heavens and Master of all creation, O Holy One among the holy ones, Sole Ruler, Emperor of all . . . (3 Macc 2:2)

May it be good, auspicious, and favorable to the emperor Caesar Augustus (inscription of a prayer to Augustus on an altar in Narbo; cited in Kiley, *Prayer from Alexander to Constantine*, 163)

Holiest of the Holy, perpetual comfort of mankind, you whose bountiful grace nourishes the whole world . . . (prayer to Isis, in Apuleius, *The Golden Ass* 19)

Let your kingdom come

Because his kingdom lasts throughout all ages . . . (Tob 13:1b)

O Lord, Lord, you rule as king over all things, for the universe is in your power and there is no one who can oppose you when it is your will to save Israel . . . . O Lord, you only are our king. (Add Esth 13:9; 14:3)

Blessed are you on the throne of your kingdom . . . (*Prayer of Azariah* 33)

For you are enthroned forever, and we are perishing forever. (Bar 3:3)

May he give us gladness of heart, and may there be peace in our days in Israel, as in the days of old. May he entrust to us his mercy, and may he deliver us in our days. (Sir 50:23–24)

Give thanks to him who gathers the dispersed of Israel; give thanks to him who makes a horn to sprout for the house of David, for his mercy endures forever . . . . Give thanks to the King of the kings of kings, for his mercy endures forever. (Sir 51:12, Hebrew additions)

For thou art terrible, O God, in the glory of thy kingdom, and the congregation of thy Holy Ones is among us for everlasting succor. We will despise kings, we will mock and scorn the mighty; for our Lord is holy, and the King of Glory is with us together with the Holy Ones. (1QM XII.6-7)

In your kingdom your goodness is upon Israel. May the glory of the Lord be praised, for he is our king. (*Pss. Sol.* 5:18-19)

Lord, you are our king forevermore . . . . We hope in God our savior, for the strength of our God is forever with mercy, and the kingdom of our God is forever over the nations in judgment . . . . See, Lord, and raise up for them their king, the son of David, to rule over your servant Israel. (*Pss. Sol.* 17:1, 3, 21)

Blow the great horn for our liberation, and lift a banner to gather our exiles. . . . Restore our judges as at the first, and our counselors as at the beginning; and reign thou over us, Thou alone. (from Benedictions 10 and 11)[7]

May he make his kingship sovereign in your lifetime and in your days, and in the lifetime of the whole house of Israel speedily, in the near future. (from the Kaddish)[8]

Give us . . . bread

Bless for us, O Lord our God, this year for our welfare, with every kind of produce thereof . . . . (from Benediction 9)

Blessed art thou who createst the fruit of the vine; blessed art thou who bringest forth bread from the earth. (*m. Berakoth* 6:1)

May He give you as your portion the firstfruits of all delectable things. (1Q28b)

For if I am hungry, I will cry out to you, O God, and you will give me something. You feed the birds and the fish, and you send rain to the wilderness that the grass may sprout to provide pasture in the wilderness for every living thing, and if they are hungry, they will lift up their faces to you. You feed kings and rulers and peoples, O God, and who is the hope of the poor and needy, if not you, Lord? (*Pss. Sol.* 5:8-11)

My Father and my God, do not abandon me to the hands of the nations. Execute judgment for me so that the humble and the poor may not perish. (4Q372.16)

Father Mars, I pray and beseech you to be favorable and kind to me, my house, and our household . . . [the pray-er has sacrificed a *suovetaurilia*, which is an offering of a pig, a sheep, and an ox] . . . that you may prevent, ward off, and avert diseases, visible and invisible, dearth and destruction, ruin and storm, and that you permit the crops, corn, vineyards and plantations to grow and flourish. (Cato, *On Agr.* 141)[9]

Forgive us our sins, as we forgive our debtors

We pray Thee, O Lord, do in accordance with Thyself, in accordance with the greatness of Thy might, Thou who didst pardon our fathers when they rebelled against Thy saying. Thou wert angry with them so as to wish to destroy them, but because of Thy love for them and for the sake of Thy covenant—for Moses had atoned for their sin—and in order that Thy great might and the abundance of Thy mercy might be known to everlasting generations, Thou didst take pity on them. So let thine anger and wrath against all their sin turn away from Thy people Israel. Remember the marvels which Thou didst for the poor of the nations . . . . [Thou hast taken away] all our transgressions and hast purified us of our sin for Thine own sake. Thine, Thine is righteousness, O Lord, for it is Thou who hast done all this! Now, on the day when our heart is humbled, we expiate our iniquity and the iniquity of our fathers, together with our unfaithfulness and rebellion . . . we pray thee, O Lord, since thou workest marvels from everlasting to everlasting, to let thine anger and wrath retreat from us. (4Q504)

Our God, hide Thy face from our sins and blot out all our iniquities and create in us a clean spirit, O Lord . . . do not withhold faithfulness . . . and bring back sinners to thee. (4Q393)

Do not punish me for my sins and for my unwitting offenses. (Tob 3:3)

Do not withdraw your mercy from us, for the sake of Abraham your beloved and for the sake of your servant Isaac and Israel your holy one. (*Prayer of Azariah* 12)

Hear, O Lord, and have mercy, for we have sinned before you . . . do not remember the iniquities of our ancestors, but in this crisis remember your power and your name . . . for we have put away from our hearts all the iniquity of our ancestors who sinned against you. (Bar 3:2-7)

Wipe away our sins and disperse our errors, and reveal your mercy at this hour. Speedily let your mercies overtake us, and put praises in the mouth of those who are downcast and broken in spirit, and give us peace. (3 Macc 2:19-20)

Even if our lives have become entangled in impieties in our exile, rescue us from the hand of the enemy. (3 Macc 6:10)

I, like my brothers, give up body and life for the laws of our ancestors, appealing to God to show mercy soon to our nation and by trials and plagues to make you confess that he alone is God, and through me and my brothers to bring to an end the wrath of the Almighty that has justly fallen on our nation. (2 Macc 7:37-38)

Be merciful to your people, and let our punishment suffice for them. Make my blood their purification, and take my life in exchange for theirs. (4 Macc 6:29)

Hear, O Lord . . . do not look on the sins of your people, but on those who serve you in truth. (*4 Ezra* 8:27)

Forgive us, our Father, for we have sinned against thee. Erase and blot out our transgressions from before thine eyes, for thou are abundantly compassionate. Blessed art thou, O Lord, who forgives readily. (Sixth benediction, according to the Cairo Geniza fragment)[10]

Have mercy on me in my extreme distress, restore my shattered fortune, grant me repose and peace after this long series of miseries . . . but if I have offended some god of unappeasable cruelty who is bent on making life impossible for me, at least grant me one sure gift, the gift of death. (Prayer to Isis, *Golden Ass* 17).

You have won, Eros. . . . You have set up a great trophy over the self-possessed Habrocomes; he is your suppliant. In his desperation he has come for refuge to you, the master of all things. Do not abandon me or punish my arrogance too hard; because I had not felt you, Eros, I paid no attention to you as yet. But now give me Anthia. Do not be only a vengeful god against the man who has resisted you, but a help to the man you have conquered. (*Ephesian Tale* 130)

Kindest of the gods, ruler of Egypt, revealer of land and sea to all men; if I, Habrocomes, have done anything wrong, may I perish miserably and incur an even greater penalty if there is one; but if I have been betrayed by a wicked woman, I pray that the waters of the Nile should never be polluted by the body of a man unjustly killed; nor should you look on such a sight, a man who has done no wrong being murdered in your territory. (*Ephesian Tale* 154)

Father Mars, I pray and beseech you to be favorable and kind to me . . . . [the person praying has offered a *suovetaurilia*, namely, a pig, a sheep, and an ox] In respect of these things, in respect of purifying my farm, ground and land, and performing the purification, as I have said, be honored by the sacrifice of the suckling victims of this *suovetaurilia* . . . . If no favorable omens come out at all, make this prayer, "Father Mars, if nothing in the sacrifice of the suckling victims of this *suovetaurilia* has pleased you, I offer you this *suovetaurilia* in expiation." If there is doubt about one or two of the animals, make this prayer: "Father Mars, insofar as you were not pleased with that pig, I offer you this pig in expiation." (Cato, *On Agr.* 141)[11]

Mother Venus, we two girls do tearfully beg you, as we kneel and clasp this altar of yours, to take us in your custody and defend us. Wreak vengeance on the wicked men who have scorned your shrine, and by your good grace let this altar be our refuge. We were both stripped clean last night by Neptune, so be not offended with us, hold us not at fault for this, if there be anything about us which you think unseemly. [the two young women, having just survived a shipwreck, are disheveled and have nothing to offer Venus] (Plautus, *Rud.* 694ff.)

Do not carry us into testing/temptation

Thou wilt save us from sinning against thee. (4Q504)

Remember me and forget me not, and bring me not to unbearable hardships. Put away from me the sin of my youth, and may my sins not be remembered against me. Lord, cleanse me from the evil plague, and let it not return to me. Dry up its roots within me, and permit not its leaves to flourish in me. (11Q5.24.11-14)

Forgive my sins, O Lord, and purify me of my iniquity. Grant me a spirit of faithfulness and knowledge; let me not be dishonored in ruin. Let not Belial dominate me, nor an unclean spirit; let pain and the evil inclination not possess my bones. (11Q5.19.13-16)

[Prevent] your servant from sinning against you, from tripping over all the things of your will. Strengthen [text missing—your servant?] against [fiendish] spirits, [so that] he can walk in all you love . . . . (1QH 4.23-24)[12]

Let no man walk in the stubbornness of his evil heart. (4Q393)

Let no adversary have dominion over me to lead me astray from thy way. (4Q213a)

Do not put us to shame, but deal with us in your patience and in your abundant mercy. (*Prayer of Azariah* 19)

From the earth I raised up my supplication and I begged for salvation from death. I called upon the Lord, the father of my Lord [perhaps this should be "O Father, my Lord, . . ."], "Do not abandon me in days of tribulation, in the time of the proud when [I was] helpless. I will praise your name ceaselessly and in thanksgiving will sing a hymn, for my supplication was accepted. For you saved me from destruction and led me out of an evil time; because of this I will give thanks and praise you and pronounce blessings to the name of the Lord." (Sir 51:9-12 LXX)

Jesus famously addressed God as "Abba," "father" in his native Aramaic. Some of Jesus' followers imitated his practice, even some who spoke Greek or other languages rather than Aramaic. Paul twice mentions praying to God as "Abba":

- "For we did not receive a spirit of slavery again for fear [i.e., to make us fearful again] but we received a spirit of sonship, in which [condition] we cry, Abba; Father" (Rom 8:15).
- "But because you are sons, God sent the sprit of his son into our hearts crying, "Abba; Father" (Gal 4:6).[13]

Whether the single word "Abba" indicates that Paul and others were using the model prayer, we cannot say. Paul's usage ("Abba, the Father") is like neither Matthew's ("Our Father") nor Luke's ("O Father"). If it does refer to Pauline churches using the prayer, then it also points again to the fluid transmission of the prayer among early Christians.

Luke has no pronoun attached to "Father," but his version of the prayer is no more individualistic than Matthew's; we will get "our bread," "our sins," and "those indebted to us." So this is a communal prayer, even when offered by an individual. [Prayer, a Communal Act] In Luke's scene, Jesus has just come from solitary prayer and is answering the question of a single disciple. But his instructions, which we should take to agree with his practice, are to pray thinking of oneself as part of a group. In Luke's context, the group must be the disciples—not the

Prayer, a Communal Act

One who prays never prays alone . . . Always there must be a second person, another, a member of the fellowship, the Body of Christ, indeed, Jesus Christ himself, praying with him, in order that the prayer of the individual may be true prayer.

Dietrich Bonhoeffer, *Life Together*, trans. John W. Doberstein (New York: Harper, 1954), 40.

Twelve, but the larger group—who have been empowered to heal, to cast out demons, to preach the news of the kingdom, and to share table fellowship, all just as Jesus does. This group, then, is being instructed to join Jesus in his prayers, praying not only as he taught, but as he prayed.[14]

"Father," in Jesus' mouth, reaches back to Gabriel's promise to Mary about her son. "He will be called 'Son of the Most High,' and the Lord God will give him the throne of his father David." Jesus is "Son of God" by virtue of his birth and by virtue of God's election of Israel through the promises to Abraham (1:55) and to David (1:32). At twelve, he knew he must be about his Father's affairs, and set this task ahead of his concern for his earthly father and mother (2:48-49). The demons have come out shouting, "You are the Son of God!" (4:41), and he has claimed to have a son's unique knowledge of the Father, whom he reveals to whomever he chooses (10:22). It is therefore a powerful thing for Jesus to teach his disciples to pray to God as he does. When we say "Father," do we in fact aspire to mean what Jesus meant when he said it, to reach to the level of his devotion to God?

"Father" in any language, Aramaic, Greek, or English, cannot be entirely asexual, and Luke's ancient and modern audiences are almost certain to connect the word with their own experiences of having/not having fathers and of being/not being fathers. Interpreters of Luke should be aware of this, and think about how to talk about "Father" with those for whom "father" is not a positive image. In my opinion, there is nothing about this prayer or our participation in it that depends on our addressing God using masculine terms. As described in the paragraph above, "Father" connects Jesus' address to God to promises and events already narrated in Luke, most notably Jesus' own conception. But Luke was careful to avoid sexual language or imagery in describing how Mary came to bear Jesus. Look again at the commentary on that section—the principal registers of language are creation and the experience of the filling of the Spirit, both of which happen to both men and women as asexual acts. The virgin birth is a unique event: since humans can only be born from women, then Mary was female, but Luke is at pains to keep us from thinking about God impregnating her as a male. So God the Father of Jesus, in the sphere of the virgin birth, is not about maleness, even less about Maleness, and if we pray, with Jesus, to the One who created Jesus' life in Mary, we could as correctly, if not as easily, think of a Mother as of a Father. Thus, if Christians want to address God as "Mother" as well as "Father," I cannot think of why, from Luke's frame of reference, that would be problematic. Substituting "parent" makes it less personal than Luke intends; any title is a step away from the intimacy of direct address.

"Father" in Luke's prayer is meant to connote a good parental relationship, where it would be unthinkable for the One petitioned to try to harm or to trick the petitioner (see vv. 11-13). Nevertheless, "let your name be sanctified" keeps "Father" from being so intimate an address that the prayer-maker thinks that God can be wheedled into something. This first petition is a head-scratcher. The psalms are full of statements of praise for God: "Blessed be the Lord God" or "I will exalt you, O Lord," and at first glance this sounds as if it might be a loose equivalent. But to make something holy is to purify it so that it can properly serve God (as in Exod 19:22 or Lev 10:3, where all those who approach God to offer sacrifices must first be made holy). Two verses from Leviticus help to demonstrate the principle:

hoti egō eimi kyrios ho theos hymōn kai hagiasthēsesthe kai hagioi esesthe hoti hagios eimi egō kyrious ho theos hymōn
Because I am the Lord your God, and you shall be sanctified (or you shall sanctify yourselves), and then you shall be holy; I am the Lord your God (Lev 11:44 LXX).

kai phylaxete tas entolas mou kai poiēsete autas kai ou bebēlōsete to onoma tou hagiou kai hagasthēsomai en mesō tōn huiōn Israēl egō kyrious ho hagiazōn hymas, ho exagagōn hymas ek gēs Aigyptou hōste einai hymōn theos egō kyrios
And you shall guard my commandments and do them, and you shall not profane the Holy Name, and I will be sanctified in the midst of the sons of Israel. I am the Lord, who sanctifies you, who leads you out of the land of Egypt, with the result (or for the purpose) that I, the Lord, am your God (Lev 22:31-33 LXX).

There were things, very specific things, that Israel was supposed to do that were said to have the effect of "sanctifying" the name of the Lord: offering the twice-daily sacrifice of the lamb; keeping the kosher requirements; never failing to cleanse oneself before approaching the altar. In other words, keeping God's name holy was the result of actually doing God's commandments. In the context of the prayer, "let your name be made holy" is a prayer for people to do the right thing, and therefore for God to do whatever God can do to make that happen. [Hallowed Be Thy Name]

This makes the first two petitions of the prayer parallel, since if God's name were kept holy everywhere, God's kingdom would have come. In 10:9 the disciples are taught to say "The kingdom of

Hallowed Be Thy Name

To pray for the hallowing, coming, and doing of God is, therefore, to rest in our dependence on him, and only then do we pray for food for the hungry, reconciliation for the unforgiving and unforgiven, and the capacity to move trustingly into an uncertain future—a future in which dominion, power and glory only make sense when they are themselves shot through with the scars of the wounded healer of Nazareth who dared to call God his "Abba."

From Kenneth W. Stevenson, *The Lord's Prayer: A Text in Tradition* (Minneapolis: Fortress, 2004), 234.

God has come near you," not to say "It is here"—the kingdom is still to come, since the beneficial effects of God's rule are not everywhere felt. Despite Luke 17:20-21 ("the kingdom of God is among you"), Luke's Jesus does not teach a kingdom that was fully present in his ministry. It was still to come—it is still to come, just as the Son of Man is yet to return in power and glory. We hope for that day, we pray for that day, and as we do, we fight against the tendrils and vines of the "cares and riches and pleasures of life" that threaten to choke out our ultimate allegiance to Jesus (8:14). If we are faithful disciples, we also announce the near approach of the kingdom (10:9) and we live by its habits and practices, forgiving enemies, healing the sick, casting out demons, sharing generous hospitality. Do we, by those actions, bring the kingdom nearer, or if not quite that, do we make the kingdom more visible or tangible to unbelievers? Jesus' use of the "binding the strong man" image (11:20-22) suggests that our participation in the work of the kingdom pushes back the evil empire so that those in its shadow may see the light and accept the good news. Thus, while the two petitions are truly requests for God to do something, they may also be understood to be self-reminders to do what Christ has commanded us to do.

The third petition is about asking for bread for ourselves—everyone agrees with that. Beyond that, the meaning is disputed. The phrase says, "Give us our [*epiousion*] bread day by day." The word *epiousion* only appears here, in Matthew's text of the prayer, and in the prayer as it appears in *Didache*.[15] [The Lord's Prayer in the *Didache*] Many modern commentators agree with the third-century Christian Origen that whoever first translated the prayer into Greek invented the word from the preposition *epi*, meaning "for," and the verbal form *ousion*, a participial form of the verb "to be." The main theories[16] about what it means are

The Lord's Prayer in the *Didache*

The *Didache* is a 1st-century Christian book of instructions. Some scholars believe it used Matthew as a source, while others think it is independent. Here is what it says about praying the Prayer:

Nor should you pray like the hypocrites, but as the Lord commanded in his gospel, you should pray as follows: Our Father in heaven, may your name be kept holy, may your kingdom come, may your will be done on earth as in heaven. Give us today our daily bread. And forgive us our debt, as we forgive our debtors. And do not bring us into temptation but deliver us from the evil one. For the power and the glory are yours forever. Pray like this three times a day.

Did. 8.2-3.

• "for" + "existence"= "necessary." This theory has the advantage of taking the parts of the word at their most natural meanings, and the resulting meaning of "necessary" would mean that we are praying for God to provide our basic rations on a daily basis. This would be consistent with the missionary instructions—go out there and preach and heal and so forth, and trust that God will provide someone to give you food and shelter. But eat whatever is put before you. You are praying for the bare necessities. The image of gathering the manna comes to mind, where one could gather only enough: "those who gathered much had nothing more, and those who gathered little had no shortage" (Exod 16:18).

• "for" + "the existing [day]"= "daily." This interpretation takes the *ousion* part of the word as a sort of verbal adjective, "existing," to which the reader/prayer-maker is supposed to supply the word "day" from the end of the petition. While this interpretation is possible, it would be more convincing if "existing" had a feminine ending so that it would agree with "day." There is also a perfectly good Greek word for "daily" built of the preposition *epi* and the word "day," used at James 2:15 ("lacking daily food").

• "for" + "the coming [day]"= "tomorrow's [bread]," taken either literally ("give us day by day what we will need for the next day") or as the ancient Christian Jerome suggested, as a request for the bread we will eat in the kingdom of God. Jerome based his theory not so much on the meanings of the Greek words but on a reading in the now-lost *Gospel of the Nazareans*, a reading that supposed that the Hebrew word "machar," "tomorrow," was the original text. Others who derive this meaning from *epiousion* understand *ousion* as a participle of a verb meaning "to come." Again, it would be a more convincing theory if "coming" agreed with the gender of "day," which it is supposed to modify, and it must be admitted that "day by day" provision of "tomorrow's bread" seems not to fit as well with the instructions following the prayer.

As attractive as the third option has been among modern interpreters, the first is the most obvious and has the fewest grammatical difficulties. Praying for daily subsistence rations fits well with the instructions to the missionaries in chapter 10 and with the parable and instructions that follow.

Praying for daily subsistence rations, for most of us reading this commentary, is a bit like praying for a pay cut. We eat more food, surely, than any society has ever eaten. We have more varieties of food available to us, from fresh to frozen to fast, than any society has ever had, more than most societies a few generations back would have believed possible. If we pray, "Give us day by day the food we need," are we prepared to have God slash our incomes or somehow wreck the food production industry? Are we prepared to stand in real solidarity with the poor, whom Mary said God would raise up, while sending the rich, like us, empty away?

Being a New Testament professor, and not a politician or an economist, I have no plan for how to redistribute food or modify food production, and no expertise that would enable me to recommend one plan over another. But it seems plain to me that if American Christians were serious about feeding the hungry worldwide, we could, by doing with less, provide what would keep millions and millions alive. If we thought that's what we were praying—that is, that we, along with other Christians around the world, were asking God to give us, all of us, what we needed—maybe we would change our behaviors. If we thought that we were interceding for the poor, and committing ourselves in prayer to put our surplus in service of their need, maybe fewer people would starve.

Most interpreters think that Luke's "sins" is less original that Matthew's "debts," since both have "debtors" in the second line. Matthew's "debts" are also thought to be metaphors for "sin," so if Luke changed the word, he correctly caught the sense of it. Putting "sins" in the first line links the prayer to Luke's broad themes of repentance and forgiveness, beginning with John the Baptist's "baptism of repentance for the forgiveness of sins" (3:3). In Jesus' opening sermon, he said that God had sent him to preach "release for captives," and the word "release" is the word elsewhere translated "forgiveness." Jesus said he had come to call "sinners to repentance" (5:32) and taught "forgive, and you will be forgiven" (6:37). He has announced the forgiveness of the sins of particular people (5:20; 7:48) and has claimed general authority to forgive sins (5:24). [Forgiving Others]

But while it seems right for Jesus to pronounce forgiveness, or to teach his disciples to pray for forgiveness, it may strike readers as odd to think of Jesus himself praying for forgiveness, and yet we recall, from the first part of this discussion, how Luke introduces the prayer as following the example of Jesus. Frankly, since Luke never addresses the question of Jesus' sinfulness or sinlessness, we do not know what he thought about it. One could interpret this, like

Forgiving Others

There was a meeting at Scetis about a brother who had sinned. The Fathers spoke, but Abba Pior kept silence. Later, he got up and went outside; he took a sack, filled it with sand and carried it on his shoulder. He put a little sand also into a small bag which he carried in front of him. When the Fathers asked him what this meant, he said, "In this sack which contains much sand, are my sins, which are many. I have put them behind me so as not to be troubled about them and so as not to weep; and see here are the little sins of my brother which are right in front of me and I spend my time judging them. This is not right. I ought rather to carry my sins in front of me and concern myself with them, begging God to forgive me for them." The Fathers stood up and said, "Truly, this is the way of salvation."

In Helen Waddell, *The Desert Fathers* (Ann Arbor: University of Michigan Press, 1957), 337–38.

the baptism, as an instance of Jesus standing with sinners while not participating in their misdeeds.

"Forgive us our sins, for we ourselves forgive everyone indebted to us"—it would seem that while Luke wanted "sins" in the first line to connect to one of the great themes of his Gospel, he retained "debtors" in the second line to connect to another, one's treatment of the poor.[17] In Luke's day, as in Jesus' day, there was no such thing as "consumer debt," where people kept monthly balances on their charge cards in order to buy things to make their lives easier. There were no banks; one borrowed from wealthy people. There was no federally regulated system of lending, with controlled interest rates and tax deductions for mortgage interest; you had to pay what the lender demanded and pay your taxes in the bargain. Debt was a scary thing, especially when the poor had to put their land or their personal property as collateral for the loan. If the weather was bad and the crops failed, or if you suffered some other reverses, you lost your home, or you sold yourself or others of your family into slavery to pay the debts. Gee—as the American usury industry grows, enticing people into greater and greater debt, and as foreclosures escalate in many American cities, maybe things aren't so different after all.

Luke, it seems, created the uneven parallelism of the lines—we ask God to forgive our sins, but we forgive anyone indebted to us—perhaps to remind those in his audience with means to lend that Jesus expected his followers to "lend, expecting nothing in return" (6:35) and to "give to everyone who begs" (6:30). That was powerful medicine in Jesus' day; perhaps even more so in Luke's day, when there were some persons of means among Jesus' followers, and certainly even more so in our day in our country, when the vast majority of American church-goers need to be forgiven of the sin of greed and to encourage our governments to forgive the debts of the world's poorest nations. As individuals and churches, we can also live by the prayer we make when we participate in programs (such as Habitat for Humanity) that provide no-interest loans that make housing available to the poor.

The final petition of Luke's prayer can also be understood in more than one way. "Do not lead us into temptation" is a possible translation, but an odd thing to ask God—would God deliberately put us in the path of temptation, and if God would, does asking God to desist do any good? The verb used here (*eispherō*) means to carry something into a place, so it's even more dramatic than the normal word for "lead"—we're asking God not to plunk us down in dangerous territory. In Luke, the Spirit leads Jesus "in" rather than "into" the wilderness, where he is tempted by Satan; in Luke's formulation, God does not lead Jesus into temptation, but is with him while he is being tempted. "Temptation" may also be translated "testing," which removes the notion of evil intent from God. But the second question still remains: if God wants to test us, what good does it do to ask God to lay off? Some commentators argue for "into the testing," meaning the "tribulations" of the last days before the return of Christ. But this seems inconsistent with praying for the kingdom to come; if we truly want God's kingdom to arrive, then we also have to be willing to go through the hard times predicted to come first.

The petition comes up again at the Last Supper and in the arrest. Jesus tells the Twelve that they are "the ones who have stood by me in my temptations/testings" (22:28). Then he tells them, as they get to the Mount of Olives, "Pray that you not enter into temptation" (22:40); he repeats the same words when he has to wake them up, just before Judas and the arresting group arrive (22:46). Luke gives us clues that in these three verses, he means "temptation" and thinks that Satan is battling Jesus and his disciples. First, Satan "enters" Judas—i.e., takes possession of him (22:3), explaining for Luke how one of the Twelve could have done something so awful. Next, Jesus tells Peter and the others that Satan wants them, too, but that Jesus is praying for them that their faith will not fail (22:31-32). Then, when Judas and the arresting party arrive, Jesus tells them, "This is your hour and the authority of darkness," implying that Satan has taken control of their whole group (22:53). In Luke, the disciples do not run away when Jesus is arrested; they do fall asleep, but they do not flee. So Jesus' characterization of them in 22:28 and his admonitions to them in 22:40, 46 are most likely to be understood as warnings against the onslaughts of Satan, and therefore "temptation" is the better translation. If we can put this sense back into the prayer, then perhaps we can understand it as a request for God to protect us from Satan's power. If this is correct, then it is a confession of weakness as well as a prayer for help—we don't think we can stand up to Satan's temptations, so please lead us in another path.

In the parable that follows, there are three persons who act. There is the Guest who arrives at night, the Host who must provide hospitality to the Guest, and the Neighbor whom the Host wakes up. Host calls both Guest and Neighbor "friend," so that we are clear about social relationships—nobody is kin to anybody else, and nobody in the story is client or patron. These are social equals, then, but more than that, the word presumes a level of trust and mutual affection: the centurion's friends quote him to Jesus, rather than talking about him in the third person (7:6); the shepherd who finds the hundredth sheep invites his friends in to celebrate (15:6); when Jesus urges the big wheels to consider doing more for the poor, he lists whom not to invite in the order friends, brothers, relatives, or wealthy neighbors.

Host gets a surprise visit from friend Guest—great news, but a little embarrassing, since Host would have preferred to clean the bathroom, change the sheets, and make sure there was food in the house. As embarrassed as you would be to be caught without anything fit to put before your Guest, so much more embarrassed was Host; in the Palestinian culture of Jesus, you must greet your guests with kisses, wash their feet, and feed them, or you are a no-account uncivilized inhospitable lout who shames your mother. Never mind that it's the middle of the night—a friend can show up any time and expect to find hospitality. After all, it isn't as if you can call ahead, and you can't check into the Dew Drop Inn, and since you're traveling on foot, you may not be able to control how far you'll get in a day. You pretty much have to trust that your network of friends and relatives and relatives' friends will put you up when you get there and knock on the door.

In Host's world, bread was baked daily in ovens used by more than one household. Their small houses backed up to each other, with a common courtyard of sorts, and a community oven. In this setting, Host or Mrs. Host would know that Mrs. Neighbor had baked and had some extra loaves. That's what's required—not scraps of bread, mind you, but whole loaves of flatbread, because people ate by tearing off chunks to dip in sauces and to scoop up stews and veggies. So Host answers the door: "Well, Guest, I declare, how long has it been since I laid eyes on you? Come in, sit down. Kids, wake up, this is your Uncle Guest. Malachi, show him your rock collection while I take care of a few things." Host makes Guest as welcome as possible, begs a thousand pardons, and then nips over to Neighbor's house to bang on the door: "Friend, lend me three loaves, because my friend arrived at my house from the road, and I have nothing to set before him." We recall that Jesus told the Twelve and the seventy-two to hope for hospitality from those to whom they preached, and recall as well the story of Martha receiving Jesus; maybe more than one of those pairs of missionaries caught their potential hosts at a loss, provoking a scene just like this.

Jesus first lets Neighbor give a speech that nobody in a similar position would ever make, ending with "I am unable by rising to give you [anything]." The Neighbor who did this would be even more of a no-account uncivilized inhospitable mother-shaming person, because Neighbor's refusal makes it impossible for Host to do right by Guest. If Neighbor does this, then the whole village will know about it and Neighbor's standing in the village will be in the toilet. So Neighbor gets up, grumbling (that's allowed, between friends, and it *is* the middle of the night), and gives Host what's needed, and probably even a little more ("Take some of these good olives—do you have enough wine?"). This way, Neighbor gets to tell the story of saving Host's bacon; Host has to endure a little good-natured kidding at the central market ("Hey, man, I'm really tired tonight, so I'm leaving your midnight snack in the mailbox"), but everyone's honor is intact.

That's how the parable works. The exact wording of v. 8 is a little puzzling: "I tell you, if he will not give him, rising, what he needs because he is his friend, then on account of his shamelessness, rising, he will give him whatever he needs." It is not clear grammatically if "shamelessness" belongs to Host or Neighbor, but logically, it makes more sense to imagine Neighbor avoiding the charge of "shameless" by getting up and handing over the goods.

The instructions of vv. 9-10, coming right after the parable, urge the audience to ask, to seek, and to knock, just as Guest and Host did, each in turn, and to trust that what they need will be provided. The passives that follow the imperatives assume that God is the one providing, even if friendly neighbors are the means by which the provisions are made. Both Christian missionary and Christian host can follow these rules, as we have just seen. [Ask, and You Will Receive]

Ask, and You Will Receive

Is Heaven an Exchequer?
They speak of what we owe—
But that negotiation
I'm not a Party to—

Emily Dickinson, 1270, *The Complete Poems of Emily Dickinson*, ed. Thomas H. Johnson (Boston: Little, Brown, 1960).

Verses 11-12 are not quite a parable, but use a vivid image to illustrate the imperatives of vv. 9-10. The children are hungry, and ask for a fish or an egg. Would any parent give a snake or a scorpion instead? We know the answer is supposed to be "no," but we also know of plenty of tragic circumstances where parents have deliberately harmed their children physically and emotionally. Jesus' example here assumes normal human parental affection and then asks, in v. 13, that if we evil humans almost always do the best we can by our children, how much more will "the Father from heaven give the Holy Spirit to those who ask?" [Praying as a Child Asks]

The turn to the Holy Spirit right at the end is a bit of a surprise; from context, we might expect "give good things" (Matt 7:11) or even "give whatever is needed." One suspects that Luke has

Praying as a Child Asks

Gordon Atkinson's daughter asked the church for prayer for her sick hermit crab. As heads bowed, Atkinson (the pastor) thought about the other needs in the congregation: a man whose father just died; a woman whose father abused her for years while she prayed that God would make him stop; the family of a little girl who died, painfully, of cancer when she was five.

All the heads were bowed except mine. I was left standing at the front, wondering how you pray for a hermit crab in the presence of a man who prayed that his daddy would live. How do you pray for a hermit crab while looking at the bowed head of a woman who prayed that her daddy would stop?

And what about Julie, God? Exactly what was going on with that situation? . . . Maybe you have complex reasons for taking a hands-off approach. But what grand scheme

would have been derailed if you had let her die without pain? If letting Julie die in peace was outside your self-imposed limits, what will you do for a hermit crab that we hear is a little under the weather? . . .

You know what got me started praying? The heads. Roy's head and Chris's head. All of them. Rows and rows of bowed heads, waiting expectantly . . . . Here were people who would pray for a crab. They loved this little girl that much, and she felt comfortable enough to share the concerns of her heart. Even in the midst of their own unanswered prayers, they were big enough and small enough to pray with their young friend. . . .

I am a man who has become a child again, and I tell you I will pray for just about anything.

Gordon Atkinson, *RealLivePreacher.com* (Grand Rapids: Eerdmans, 2004), 19–21.

introduced the promise of the gift of the Spirit to look ahead to 24:49, where Jesus promises the Spirit, and then to Acts, where the promise is fulfilled. But the verse points backwards as well. Jesus, the Son of God, is filled with the Spirit (3:22; 4:1; 4:14) and is teaching the disciples how to pray as he does. Spirit-filling and prayer are mutually causative; the Spirit's filling both causes and results from fervent prayer (see Acts 4:31). To pray for the Spirit is, again, to pray as Jesus did and as he taught his followers.

Reactions to Jesus, 11:14-36

Miroslav Volf begins *The End of Memory* by describing how, while doing his compulsory military duty in Yugoslavia in 1984, he was interrogated after being denounced for seditious behavior:

I had engaged in religious propaganda on the base—I must therefore be against socialism, which in Yugoslavia was linked officially with atheism. I had praised a Nazarene conscientious objector for acting according to his principles—I was therefore undermining the defense of our country. I had said something unkind about Tito—I was therefore an enemy of the people. . . . The charges should have been embarrassing for the interrogators . . . but the officers were utterly serious: I must be out to overthrow the regime. The real issue, which they sensed rightly, was that the seams holding Yugoslavia together were at their breaking point. An enemy could be hiding under any rock, behind any bush.[18]

In this chapter, Jesus responds to equally ridiculous-sounding charges. He casts a demon from a man; for this he is accused of being the pawn of Satan. But as in the quote above, the charge against Jesus simply lays bare the anxiety felt within Satan's empire as it creaked and groaned under the strain of keeping everyone in line.

Chapter 11 opens with Jesus praying, and one of his disciples asking him for instruction in prayer. The first thirteen verses give Jesus' answer to that request. Although Luke does not specify a change in location, the scene shifts at v. 14, because Luke narrates another event—an exorcism, followed by three different reactions by sections of the "crowd," the non-disciples who appear wherever Jesus goes. Luke then gives Jesus' responses to each of the three reactions, and then (I think) concludes the section with some summary material on how important it is to see God's revelation clearly. The next division in the chapter comes with the introduction in 11:37 of a new audience, the Pharisees, and a new setting, a meal in a Pharisee's home. Almost by process of elimination, then, 11:33-36 concludes the section; its connections to the rest of the material are, admittedly, subtle, and the outline suggested below may owe more to the eye of the interpreter than to Luke's design.[19] With that caveat, here is how the section divides:

Jesus casts out a demon, v. 14a
Some are amazed, v. 14b
Others accuse him of demon-possession, v. 15
Others want a sign from heaven, v. 16
Teaching on Satan/return of the demons, vv. 17-26; response to v. 15
Teaching on blessedness, vv. 27-28; response to v. 14b
Teaching on signs from heaven, vv. 29-32; response to v. 16
Summary comments on seeing correctly, vv. 33-36

Luke's source for this material is debatable. All three Synoptic Gospels have a story where Jesus is accused of being possessed by Beelzebul and an episode where Jesus is asked for a sign from heaven. But Luke and Matthew have material in common with each other not found in Mark: the initial exorcism, the reference to other Jewish exorcists, the statement about the kingdom of God coming on the accusers, the story of the return of the evil spirit, and the material on the sign of Jonah. Many interpreters believe that Mark and Q (the source that many believe Matthew and Luke had in addition to Mark) both had accounts of the Beelzebul accusation and the request for a sign. But even that is not a simple solution, because in some verses Luke is much closer to Matthew than to Mark (Luke 11:17//Matt 12:25; contrast Mark 3:24-25), while at other times Luke is closer to Mark (Luke 11:15//Mark 3:22; contrast Matt 12:24), and at other times Luke is the odd bird, while Mark and Matthew are close (Mark 3:27//Matt 12:29; contrast Luke 11:21-22). Since the source relationships are not clear, the following interpretation will rely less on ideas of how Luke edited Mark or Q (or Matthew, if one adopts that theory) and more on how Luke's internal structure seems to work.

The section begins with good news: a speechless man has a demon driven from him, with the result that he begins to speak. Recall that Zechariah, John the Baptist's father, was rendered speechless by the angel Gabriel as a consequence of not believing the good news. The old priest's speech returned when God's promise was fulfilled, partly through Zechariah's obedience. We do not know how long the man in v. 14 had been speechless, nor why the demon afflicted him, nor why Jesus picked him out to heal. As noted in the commentary on 4:31-37, many Jews in Jesus' day believed that demons were spawned by the giants who were themselves the progeny of the angels and women of Genesis 6:1-4. According to this way of looking at things, demon infestation was ultimately not the result of human misconduct but was the unfortunate result of angelic lust. According to *1 Enoch* (see ["evil spirits upon the earth"]), demons would continue to plague humans until God's kingdom arrived, when they would be rounded up and contained in cells kept at the edges of the world. Luke's setting emphasizes the randomness of evil and the powerlessness that many people felt in the face of it. If you are poor, and if most of the conditions of your life—your taxes, the local economy, droughts, disease, etc.—are all beyond your control, then this worldview makes a lot of sense.

There are crowds around, as there frequently are, who react in three different ways. Some are amazed—a word that connotes a positive, though not necessarily informed, response to Jesus. But some from the crowd opined that Jesus "casts out demons by Beelzebul the ruler of the demons." Mark's sentence reads, "they said, 'He has [that is, he is possessed by] Beelzebul' and 'He casts out demons by the ruler of the demons'" (Mark 3:22). It looks as if Luke blends Mark's two parallel clauses into one, and in the process avoids writing down the charge that Jesus is demon-possessed. Instead, the charge is that Jesus somehow has learned to control Beelzebul and use the demon chief's power for his own purposes.

Luke takes special notice of magic, especially in Acts, and takes pains to show Christianity both different from and superior to magic. Simon the magician of Samaria had long "amazed" the city there through his magic, and when he offered to buy the power of the Spirit, he was rebuked and threatened by the apostles (Acts 8:9-24). In Acts 16:16-18, Paul casts a demon from a slave girl whose owners have profited from her demon-given ability to tell fortunes. In 19:11-20, some Jewish exorcists try to invoke Jesus' name to cast out demons, but to no avail; the demon-possessed man beats them up instead, causing the residents to be amazed and to burn their magical books. In Luke's world, many people wore amulets, consulted books of spells, mixed potions, and recited lists of powerful words in attempts to ward off the attacks of demons, who came on them through Satan's mischief or because of the curses of enemies.[20] [Magic] "He casts out demons by Beelzebul" would have been a plausible charge to Luke's audience, even if it makes little sense to us.

A third section of the crowd wants to see a sign from heaven done by Jesus, offered as evidence of his divine origin. Like Pharaoh, who will not believe Moses' claim to be God's prophet until he (Moses) can perform a miracle that cannot be replicated by his court magicians, this third group wants something definitive. All three groups agree that Jesus can do miracles, but their responses to his ability range from being greatly impressed ("they were amazed") to being skeptical ("they kept seeking a sign from heaven, testing him") to being repulsed ("they said, 'he casts out demons by Beelzebul'"). Luke Johnson makes a good case for how this range of negative opinion inverts Jesus' instruction on prayer:

Now, rather [than] asking and receiving the "Holy Spirit from heaven" (11:13), these opponents seek a "sign from out of heaven" (11:16). Rather than praying to God to deliver them from testing (11:4), they deliberately put Jesus to the test (11:16). Rather than ask forgiveness of sins they in effect accuse Jesus of the sin of collusion with Satan (11:4, 15). Rather than recognize in Jesus the one who

Magic

Ancient people wore amulets to ward off evil and to promote healing. A text in Mishnah (*m. Šabb.* 6:10) reads, "Men may go out [of their houses on Sabbath] with a locust's egg or a jackal's tooth or with a nail of one who was crucified, as a means of healing. So R[abbi] Meir [a teacher from the mid-2d century AD]. But the Sages say: Even on ordinary days this is forbidden as following in the ways of the Amorite." The text proves that many Jews, even observant Jews, wore amulets or carried magical charms, even if many religious teachers considered it sinful.

Some people—it is impossible to tell if these were Christians—wore images of Jesus as amulets. "From the Pereire collection in Paris comes a brown jasper stone, dated to about 200 C.E. It depicts Jesus nailed by his wrists to a cross and sitting on a peg projecting from the upright post. The legs are dangling loose, the feet slightly spread. Around the figure and on the reverse of the stone are the words, 'One Father, Jesus Christ,' followed by seemingly meaningless magical words" (John J. Rousseau and Rami Arav, *Jesus and His World* [Minneapolis: Fortress, 1995], 192).

The largest collection of magical texts from ancient times is in H. D. Betz, ed., *The Greek Magical Papyri in Translation* (Chicago: University of Chicago, 1986). These texts date from the 2d century BC to the 5th century AD. In it are remedies for demon possession involving complicated potions and spells with detailed instructions on how to perform them.

proclaims the kingdom of the Father (11:2), they accuse him of being a minion of Satan's rule (11:15).[21]

Luke has arranged Jesus' responses so that he takes on the most serious criticism first, followed by the uninformed praise, and finishing with the mid-range skeptics who think they need a sign. Jesus' counter-arguments against the Beelzebul [Beelzebul] accusation begin with two reasons why the accusation is not logical. The first reasons from a generally accepted principle, one that could be demonstrated by multiple examples from any period of human history: A kingdom that becomes internally divided falls, and a household divided against itself suffers the same fate.[22] If we accept that (and the argument assumes that all right-thinking persons will), then "if Satan has been divided against himself, how will his kingdom stand?" The argument thus also presumes that anyone would agree that healing a speechless person is a good, not an evil, act. If that be true, and if Satan's intentions are always evil, then why would the evil one permit anyone to use his (or his chief underling's) name to do good? That would deliberately divide his kingdom, and would be deliberate self-destruction, and is thus improbable.

The second argument begins from the common knowledge that there were other Jewish exorcists who were not followers of Jesus. [Jewish Exorcists] "Your sons" in this context means "your people as opposed to mine"; those listening to Jesus and to Luke's account of Jesus' words could probably name local magicians, healers, and/or exorcists who had the reputation for helping people get over illnesses attributed to the power of evil. Jesus grants that they cast out demons as well, and asks about comparable sources of power: if I am doing this by Beelzebul, then what is their source of power? They will be your judges on this matter. This second argument presumes the first, that anyone casting out demons is by necessity doing it without Satan's help. [Satan's Purposes]

So much for their accusation. Jesus now shows them the correct interpretation to draw from his exorcisms—not that he is working

Beelzebul

AΩ Beelzebul derives from *Baal zebul*, the Hebrew equivalent of a name or title given to one of the creation/fertility deities in the ancient Near East. In Hebrew, the word means something like "Baal the Prince" or "Lord of Heaven"; in 2 Kgs 1, the title of a local deity is given as "Baal zebub," which most people think is a deliberate corruption to make "Lord of Heaven" into "Lord of flies." The name the Gospels transmit does not appear in the LXX or in other Jewish literature from the Second Temple period.

Giovanni Stradano (1523–1605). *Lucifer*. S. Gabinetto dei Disegni e delle Stampe, Uffizi, Florence, Italy. (Credit: Scala/Ministero per i Beni e le Attività culturali/Art Resource, NY)

Jewish Exorcists

 Josephus' account of an exorcism:

[45] God also enabled him to learn that skill which expels demons, which is a science useful and wholesome to men. He composed such incantations also by which distempers are alleviated. And he left behind him the manner of using exorcisms, by which they drive away demons, so that they never return; [46] and this method of cure is of great force to this day; for I have seen a certain man of my own country, whose name was Eleazar, releasing people that were demonic in the presence of Vespasian, and his sons, and his captains, and the whole multitude of his soldiers. The manner of the cure was this: [47] he put a ring, that had a root of one of those sorts mentioned by Solomon to the nostrils of the demoniac, after which he drew out the demon through his nostrils; and when the man fell down

immediately, he warned him to return into him no more, making still mention of Solomon, and reciting the incantations which he composed. [48] And when Eleazar would persuade and demonstrate to the spectators that he had such a power, he set a little way off a cup or basin full of water, and commanded the demon, as he went out of the man, to overturn it, and thereby to let the spectators know that he had left the man; [49] and when this was done, the skill and wisdom of Solomon was shown very manifestly: for which reason it is, that all men may know the vastness of Solomon's abilities, and how he was beloved of God, and that the extraordinary virtues of every kind with which this king was endowed, may not be unknown to any people under the sun for this reason, I say, it is that we have proceeded to speak so much of these matters.

Josephus, *Ant.* 8.45-49.

---

to advance Satan's kingdom, but that he is the champion for God's kingdom. Luke uses "finger of God" in v. 20 (Matthew's parallel [Matt 12:28] has "Spirit of God"—one or the other was presumably in Q), which makes the connection to Exodus 8:19 and the contest between Moses and Pharaoh's magicians; after the plague of lice, the magicians say, "This is the finger of God" (Exod 8:19 LXX). If it is true that Satan would not deliberately undermine his own kingdom, and if we agree that an exorcism is an attack on Satan, then Jesus must be working by God's power; and if he is, then "the kingdom of God has arrived upon you" or "has arrived against you." The second translation keeps the sense of *epi* (a preposition meaning against or upon) the same as in vv. 17-18, and makes sense, given the tone of the verses that follow. We might have expected "then the kingdom of God has arrived against him," meaning against Satan; but Jesus' use of "you" makes the point that to confuse Jesus' work with Satan's is to put oneself on the wrong side of the fight between the evil empire and the kingdom of God.

Satan's Purposes

Pleased to meet you
Hope you guess my name
But what's puzzling you
Is the nature of my game

M. Jagger/K. Richards, "Sympathy for the Devil," 1968.

One could well ask whether the exorcisms performed by the other exorcists also proved the arrival of God's kingdom—it was not an "infallible sign," as the teachers of rhetoric put it, that conclusively proved a point. The skeptics, who look for a sign from heaven, will not be convinced by an exorcism. But we who see the healing of the sick as signs of the presence of God's reign need not insist that Jesus' miracles were unique signs, since Luke has already explained that Jesus' apostles, the seventy-two, and an unnamed exorcist not of Jesus' group could also perform God's work in Jesus' name (9:1; 10:17; 9:49-50). The issue is not who heals, or the orthodoxy of the healer, but that healing is done, always, as part of God's work and as a sign of God's kingdom.

Jesus' teaching about the strong man is perhaps a parable, or perhaps, like the saying on a divided kingdom, simply an observation about how the wealthy and powerful operate. "Whenever a strong man in armor guards his space [the word can mean "house" or "courtyard" or "palace"], his possessions are at peace. But whenever a stronger man than he, coming against him, conquers him, he [the stronger] takes his [the original strong man's] armor, upon which he trusted, and his plunder is divided." To the victor go the spoils—is this the good news? Many think so, and interpret the "stronger" as Jesus defeating Satan, taking away his armor, and giving the spoils of his kingdom to the good guys. But another reading is to take it as a sardonic account of why empires always fall, even if they are not divided internally. The strong man must be armored to guard his stuff, but even that is insufficient to protect him, because there is always another tyrant, another empire, a bigger fish to swallow the smaller. No empire can truly promise peace, not even Rome; thus must Jesus' opponents be careful about what they think protects them from evil.

Verse 23 is a negative restatement of 9:50, "whoever is not against you is on your side." The earlier verse encouraged the disciples to be broad-minded when it came to possible friends and partners—if they are not your enemies, then treat them as colleagues. In the context of 11:14-36, when Jesus has been accused of being in league with the Enemy, he makes it clear that on this issue, at least, if one is not with Jesus—agreed that performing exorcisms is part of the arrival of the kingdom—then one is against him, scattering what Jesus is trying to draw together.

The little vignette about the returning demon could also be a parable, but is presented as straight-up teaching about the habits of demons. It assumes that demons, like the boll weevil, are just looking for a home. [Wandering Spirits] Evicted from one person, the demon wanders in the desert (in Lev 16:10, the sin-bearing scapegoat is sent into the desert to Azazel, another name for a demon or Satan) until, tired of the bleak terrain, it decides, "I will return to my house from which I exited." It scouts out the place, and finding it neat as a pin, finds seven other

Wandering Spirits

4 Ezra (=2 Esdras) discusses the fate of the souls of the wicked: "If it is one of those who have shown scorn and have not kept the way of the Most High, who have despised his law and hated those who fear God—such spirits shall not enter into habitations, but shall immediately wander about in torments, always grieving and sad . . ." (2 Esd 7:79-80).

rowdy friends and reinvades the poor victim, leaving him or her worse than before.

Very good—now, how is this supposed to help me, other than satisfying my curiosity? Minimally, the teaching reinforces the assumptions that underlie Jesus' earlier arguments: demons, and so presumably their masters, are real stinkers. You'd never catch a demon doing anyone a good turn. Some interpreters understand these to be extra warnings about complacency; just like the strong man gets whipped by a stronger, so the newly exorcised person needs to fill up the empty space with something, lest the demons come back. The "something" needed would be accepting Jesus' teachings about the arrival of the kingdom and becoming obedient to the word as Jesus teaches it.[23] The context, particularly Jesus' beatitude in v. 28, makes this plausible, but one must admit that there is nothing in vv. 24-26 that sounds like the victim has any choice about the attack. Later in the Gospel, Jesus tells Peter and the others that Satan has wanted to have them (22:31), just as Satan already possessed Judas (22:3), but that Jesus' intercessory prayer would keep the evil one at bay (22:32). Nevertheless, he warns them twice to pray that they not enter into temptation (22:40, 46), presumably to become part of the "authority of darkness" (22:53). Perhaps part of the reason for putting 11:24-26 midway through the Gospel is so Luke's audience will be ready for Satan's attack on the disciples and his victory over Judas. But the reader also knows that seven (8:2) or eight or a Legion (8:30) of demons are no match for Jesus. Maybe part of the point is that while there are others who can chuck out demons, with Jesus, they stay chucked.

Luke now turns to the "amazed" group (11:14b), symbolized by the woman's compliment to him and his mother: "Blessed be the womb that bore you and the breasts which you suckled." "You are a real credit to your mother," in other words—"you've made your mama so proud." The woman's praise, coming just as Jesus was finishing his rebuttal of the Beelzebul charge, takes us to the other end of the spectrum of responses to Jesus. This woman is all for Jesus, and shouts an affirmation of him against the slanders offered by others in the same crowd. [Praising a Person's Mother] Now, Elizabeth had offered a beatitude for Mary: "Blessed are you among women, and blessed is the fruit of your womb" (1:42), and this unnamed woman's blessing is not terribly different.

Praising a Person's Mother

"It was customary to praise the offspring through congratulation of the mother," writes F. W. Danker. "Thus Petronius writes in his Satyricon (94.1): 'How blessed is the mother who bore such an one as you.' And Ovid (Metamorphoses 4.320-24 sings:

O Youth, most worthy
To be named among the gods. If god
You be, then Cupid is your name.
And if a mortal, blessed are those
Who call you son. Blessed is the one
Who boasts you brother, and she who calls
Herself a sister. Blessed is the nurse
Who tendered you her breasts."

Frederick W. Danker, *Jesus and the New Age: A Commentary on St. Luke's Gospel* (rev. ed.; Philadelphia: Fortress, 1988), 234–35.

Jesus' response is a correction, but not a rebuke: "Rather, blessed are those who hear the word of God and keep it." Jesus has already said in 8:21 that his mother and brothers are those who hear and do the word of God, meaning both that his family were true disciples and that all true disciples were his family (see the commentary at 8:1-21). Jesus, then, is not so interested in hearing others praise him (or his mother); he wants to see them live their lives in keeping with the word, the good news about the kingdom of God.

The third group, the skeptics who wanted a sign, are the subject of 11:29-32. Luke characterized those who sought a sign as "testing" or "tempting" Jesus (11:16). Satan tempts Jesus (4:2), but when a compound from the same verb is used at 10:25, it is possible to read it as "testing" or "pushing" Jesus. Jesus' reaction to this crowd, however, is unequivocal: "This generation is an evil (or guilty) generation." As at 7:31, "this generation" lumps together the crowd of skeptics and all others who feel the same way. The word often translated "evil" is used in 11:34 to mean the opposite of "whole," and, significantly, is used to describe demons ("evil spirits") at 7:21 and 8:2. One might even translate it "perverse," since the problem with "this generation" is its failure to repent even after hearing the facts clearly.

"The sign of Jonah" in this pericope turns out to be Jonah himself, the prophet who reluctantly preached repentance, resulting in Nineveh's complete repentance, down to the last man, woman, child, and cow. [Jonah as a Sign of Repentance] Matthew's version of this saying makes the point Jonah's three-day sojourn in the great fish; Jesus' resurrection, for Matthew, is the sign that the ages have turned and the validation of Jesus' message. But Luke's comparison builds on his use of the category "prophet" to describe Jesus. Jonah preached repentance, and Nineveh responded; Jesus is a greater preacher than Jonah ever was (who could argue, since Jonah's whole sermon was "Forty days, and Nineveh is toast!"), and yet "this generation" listening to him will not repent. Luke and

Jonah as a Sign of Repentance

Then Jonah prayed unto the Lord out of the fish's belly. But observe his prayer, and learn a weighty lesson. For sinful as he is, Jonah does not weep and wail for direct deliverance. He feels that his dreadful punishment is just. He leaves all his deliverance to God, contenting himself with this, that in spite of all of his pains and pangs, he will still look towards His holy temple. And here, shipmates, is true and faithful repentance; not clamorous for pardon, but grateful for punishment. And how pleasing to God was this conduct in Jonah, is shown in the eventual deliverance of him from the sea and the whale. Shipmates, I do not place Jonah before you to be copied for his sin but I do place him before you as a model of repentance. Sin not; but if you do, take heed to repent of it like Jonah.

Herman Melville, Moby-Dick, ed. Harrison Hayford and Hershel Parker (New York: Norton, 1967), 49.

"Jonah Released by the Whale." Illustration from *Mirror of Human Salvation*. 15th C. Musée Condé, Chantilly, France. (Credit: Réunion des Musées Nationaux/Art Resource, NY)

Matthew also name "the queen of the South" (the LXX calls her "Queen Saba," taking the Hebrew word "sh'bah" to be a personal or place name rather than a compass direction) as another example that "this generation" fails to live up to. In 1 Kings 10, the queen "heard the name of Solomon and the name of the Lord" and came "to test him [same verb Luke uses] with riddles" (1 Kgs 10:1 LXX). When Solomon answered all her questions to her satisfaction, she blessed his wives and his children who profited from his wisdom, and then blessed the Lord who established Solomon as king (1 Kgs 10:8-9 LXX). She then put her money where her mouth was by donating a small fortune to the wise king (1 Kgs 10:10-12 LXX). Thus, while Jonah is a type for Jesus—the prophet preaching repentance—the queen of Sheba functions as an ideal type for Jesus' audience—the skeptic who is persuaded and converted by the teacher's wisdom, and a woman who both offers praises and does God's will.

The section closes with some reflections on seeing properly. These verses hang together rather loosely, and have an even looser connection with what goes before. Presumably Luke means the images of seeing or not seeing to return us to the beginning of the section, where Jesus had cured a speechless man—the event that the crowd "saw" in three different ways, leading to different responses. The first saying is another version of Mark's "light under a bushel" (Mark 4:21), which Luke transcribed in 8:16. Both Lukan versions of the saying end almost identically: one puts a lighted lamp on a stand, so that those entering may see the light (rather than what the light illuminates).[24]

"The lamp of your body is your eye." The ancients believed that the body emitted light through the eyes, so that they functioned like lamps or flashlights—the opposite of what we now believe to be true.[25] If you have healthy eyes, then your body is enlightened, but if your eyes are "evil" or "damaged," then your body is in darkness. OK so far? Now v. 35: "Consider whether the light in you is darkness," or "Watch out lest the light in you is darkness." Are you seeing correctly, in other words? If your eyes are not healthy, you may be in darkness and be unaware of it. Verse 36 urges the audience to seek to be completely whole, as completely filled with light as the one who looks at a lamp on a stand.

The exhortation to self-examination and to being fully enlightened is another way of putting the conclusions Jesus offers to each of the three responding groups. "Whoever is not with me is against me"; "rather, blessed are those who hear the word of God and keep it"; "the people of Nineveh will condemn this generation, because they repented and this generation will not." Some say he's great; some say he's in Satan's corner; some have not made up their minds, and want more proof. None of these is a completely satisfactory response. The proper way to see Jesus is to be completely committed and made whole, so that one's seeing, speaking, and doing can all be consistent with the gospel.

Dining with Pharisees, Round 2, 11:37-54

Jesus clearly skipped the courses on pastoral care and cultural sensitivity in seminary. He accepts the Pharisee's invitation to eat, but does not practice the Pharisee's habit of (hand?) washing, not even at the Pharisee's table. Instead of eating what is set before him, Jesus chews on the host instead for what Jesus terms the hypocrisy of the host's religious practice. When one of the guests sticks up for the host, claiming to be insulted along with him, Jesus slams him, too, accusing him and all his kind of murdering God's prophets. Bad day? A migraine? Over-fatigue? Too much stress? If you saw your pastor do something like this, wouldn't you want the personnel committee to find out what's up?

Luke appears to have blended material from a couple of different places to construct this scene. The issue of washing may have come from Mark 7:1-23; there, the Pharisees ask Jesus why his disciples do not keep "the tradition of the elders" and wash their hands, and Jesus blasts them for hypocrisy. The woes against the Pharisees and lawyers are close (in some cases word-for-word) to the woes in Matthew 23:1-36, so most interpreters assign the bulk of 11:39-52 to Q. The banquet scene, however, is purely Lukan. This is the second of three instances where Jesus eats in the home of a Pharisee (7:36-50; 14:1-24) and the third of at least seven formal meals Jesus attends.

Luke's depiction of banquets where guests insulted each other would not have surprised his readers. Literary descriptions of banquets often include elements of competition and sometimes outright fights. Banqueters often played a game where they flung the last few drops of wine in their cup at a bowl placed in the center of the room, with prizes (including sexual favors) given to the one who hit the target (think of it as an ancient version of beer pong).[26] Plato's famous *Symposium* has a group of friends of Socrates agree to an after-dinner round of speeches on love. It is not set up as a contest, but each speaker begins by naming the mistake made by the previous speaker:

"Phaedrus," [Pausanias] said, "the argument has not been set before us, I think, quite in the right form: we should not be called upon to praise Love in such an indiscriminate manner. If there were only one Love, then what you said would be well enough; but since there are more Loves than one, you should have begun by determining which of them was to be the theme of our praises. I will amend this defect . . . ."

Eryximachus spoke as follows: "Seeing that Pausanias made a fair beginning, but a lame ending, I must endeavor to supply his deficiency . . . ."

[Agathon says] "The previous speakers, instead of praising the god Love, or unfolding his nature, appear to have congratulated mankind on the benefits which he confers upon them. But I would rather praise the god first, and then speak of his gifts; this is always the right way of praising everything . . . ."[27]

These are friendly jabs among men who are comfortable with each other, but they belong on the pleasant end of the spectrum of competition, "a theme that inheres in the symposium [genre] for much of its history."[28] Petronius's first-century *Satyricon* includes a banquet scene that, after too much eating and drinking, dissolves into name-calling: "sheep's head . . . you can see the lice on others, but not the bugs on yourself . . . You are a child just weaned, you cannot squeak out *mu* or *ma* . . . you curly-headed onion . . . you rat, you puff-ball."[29] Juvenal, in his *Satire 5* (probably dating between 100–117), says that when a patron invites a client to dinner, "Insults open the hostilities, but once you're hit it won't be long before you're hurling cups, too, and mopping your wounds with a reddened napkin."[30] [On Boorish Dinner Guests]

The frequency with which these kinds of scenes appear in the literature of the period says something about how Greco-Roman banquets were contests of honor, occasions for people to demonstrate their power or wealth or knowledge. [Parties as Contests of Honor] These values were shared widely across the Mediterranean, and are evident in some Jewish writings from the same period. Sirach warns the reader

On Boorish Dinner Guests

Now an unsavory dish can be declined, and, if the wine be poor, one may find refuge with the water-sprites; but a guest at dinner who gives the others a headache, and is churlish and uncivil, ruins and spoils the enjoyment of any wines and viands or of any girl's music.

Plutarch, "Dinner of the Seven Wise Men," 147F, in Plutarch's Moralia (trans. Frank Cole Babbitt; 14 vols. New York: G. P. Putnam, 1928), 2.357.

When an influential person invites you, be reserved, and he will invite you more insistently. Do not be forward, or you may be rebuffed; do not stand aloof, or you will be forgotten. Do not try to treat him as an equal, or trust his lengthy conversations; for he will test you by prolonged talk, and while he smiles he will be examining you. (Sir 13:9-11)

Sirach has an extended section about etiquette at formal meals, and most of the advice seems geared toward keeping harmony:

Do not reprove your neighbor at a banquet of wine, and do not despise him in his merry-making; speak no word of reproach to him, and do not distress him by making demands of him (Sir 31:31).

Speak, you who are older, for it is your right, but with accurate knowledge, and do not interrupt the music . . . . Speak, you who are young, if you are obliged to, but no more than twice, and only if asked. Be brief; say much in few words; be as one who knows and can still hold his tongue. Among the great do not act as their equal; and when another is speaking, do not babble. (Sir 32:3, 7-9)

Thus an audience reading (or hearing) Jesus rip into his host and guests might well have thought, "Well, people do that at dinner parties, don't they," but that does not mean that they would necessarily have considered his behavior admirable or reasonable. To gain some perspective on why Jesus goes off like this, let us remind ourselves of Luke's banqueting sequence thus far:

• The first banquet is at Levi's house; Jesus is an invited guest, and the Pharisees show up to criticize Jesus for accepting the invitation. In this episode, they are the ones acting rudely, and they may well have been uninvited guests giving unsolicited opinions. Very bad form all around (see commentary on 5:27-39).
• Because Jesus eats with people like Levi, the Pharisees—whom Luke describes as wealthy (16:14) men with positions of honor and influence (11:43)—decide that Jesus is low-class: "a glutton and a drunkard, friend of tax collectors and sinners" (7:31-35; see commentary for the argument that Luke understands this as the Pharisees' opinion).

Parties as Contests of Honor

"Hi, there, Mr. Swallow, mighty glad to see you." He ushered Philip into the spacious living-room, where forty or more people were already assembled, and helped him to a gin and tonic of giant proportions. "Now, who would you like to meet? Nearly all English Department folk here, I guess."

Only one name would come into Philip's head. "I haven't met Mr. Kroop yet."

Hogan went slightly green about the jowls. "Kroop?"

"I've read so much about him, in buttonholes," Philip quipped, to cover what was evidently a *faux pas*.

"Yeah? Oh yeah. Ha, ha. I'm afraid you won't see Karl at many cocktail parties—Howard!" Hogan's enormous paw fell heavily on the shoulder of a sallow, bespectacled young man cruising past with a tumbler of Scotch held to pursed lips. He staggered slightly, but skifully avoided spilling the drink. Philip was introduced to Howard Ringbaum. "I was telling Mr. Swallow," said Hogan, "that you don't often see Karl Kroop at faculty social gatherings."

"I hear," said Ringbaum, "that Karl has totally rethought his course on 'The Death of the Book?' He's removing the query mark this quarter."

David Lodge, *Changing Places* (New York: Penguin, 1975), 75–76.

• The second banquet is the dinner Jesus attends at the house of Simon the Pharisee. Jesus' host treats him disrespectfully by failing to provide water for washing or the kiss of greeting or the fragrant oil poured on the hair of honored guests. Acting on the Pharisaic opinion about Jesus' poor breeding and low status, Simon invites Jesus to dinner in order to humiliate him, but the nameless woman with the perfume and the unbound hair steps in to take over as host, providing Jesus the respectful treatment he deserves (see commentary on 7:36-50).

In addition, some other encounters between Jesus and the Pharisees are supposed to be in the backs of our minds as we start this pericope:

• When Jesus tells the paralyzed man, "Your sins are forgiven," the Pharisees think Jesus is being blasphemous; after watching the miracle, they are amazed, but not converted (5:21, 26).
• When Jesus' disciples pluck grain on a Sabbath, the Pharisees accuse him of doing something unlawful; Jesus justifies his behavior by appeal to Scripture (6:1-5).
• When Jesus heals a man in a synagogue on Sabbath, they are first wanting to accuse him and then filled with fury, wanting to destroy him (6:6-11).
• We also know that the Pharisees and lawyers refused John's baptism and thereby put themselves outside God's will (7:29-30).

So the reader has already been conditioned to think that the Pharisees have a poor opinion of Jesus and have acted rudely in the past. They are not his friends, and the ungracious behavior of Simon only exemplifies this. Meal invitations from Pharisees are not innocent events; they mean to do him harm.

This banquet scene begins "While he was speaking"; in the section just finished, Jesus had been addressing the reactions to his exorcism, which ranged from "Blessed the womb that bore you!" to "We need a sign that proves you came from God" to "He's in cahoots with Satan." The host Pharisee, we presume, was listening to the exchange, and knows that Jesus thinks he casts out demons by the finger of God, but refuses to do signs on command to prove his God-sent status. But the Pharisee is amazed that Jesus did not wash before he reclined to eat; who does this "curly-headed onion" think he is to treat *us* that way?

"Wash" is the translation of *ebaptisthē*, which could mean "wash the hands" or "immerse" (by dipping oneself in a *miqveh*, an immersion pool). Since we presume that Luke is copying from Mark and does not have better historical information about the Pharisees than Mark has, commentators normally assume that Luke means hand washing—Jesus did not immerse his hands in water before eating.[31] Although Pharisees may have done this out of concern to remove ritual impurities before eating, it was not an uncommon practice at banquets generally: "At last we sat down, and boys from Alexandria poured water cooled with snow over our hands."[32] Luke, then, could have assumed Pharisees washed hands before eating either because he associated that habit with Pharisees or all Jews (based on Mark 7:3) or because he assumed that all well-born people washed their hands before dining. It is possible, however, that Luke means "bathe" or "immerse," either because it was customary in the Greco-Roman banquet tradition to bathe and get spruced up before arriving at the host's house or (less probably) because Luke assumed or knew that Pharisees immersed in a *miqveh* before the evening meal.[33]

Miqveh

"Miqveh" (Credit: Todd Bolen, BiblePlaces.com)

Nothing Luke has written up to this point would lead a reader to expect Jesus to observe Pharisaic purity traditions.[34] So what does Luke intend by "When the Pharisee saw, he was amazed that [Jesus] did not first wash [or immerse] before dinner"? One possibility is that we are to imagine that this Pharisee provided water for Jesus to wash his hands, but that Jesus deliberately abstained—an insult, and a provocation, but also an honest act that brought Pharisaic hostilities into the light. In support of this alternative, we remember that Jesus similarly said provocative things to the Nazareth synagogue before they reacted negatively to him, and that story, like this one, ends in a hostile reaction to Jesus (4:16-30). Jesus, as Simeon predicted, is continuing to expose the inner wranglings of others (2:35). But in order for this reading to work, we have to supply the Pharisee's hospitality and Jesus' snub, and in my opinion, the flow of the narrative works against this reading. This Pharisee's "seeing" takes us back to Simon's vision problems in 7:39 and his incorrect judgment that Jesus was not a true prophet, since he allowed a sinner to touch him. We may presume that this Pharisee—who is not named so that he can stand as a part that represents the whole—acts no better toward Jesus than did Simon, since Pharisaic myopia has not improved since the dinner in 7:36-50.

Another plausible reading is that the Pharisee expected Jesus to bathe before he came, and was surprised when Jesus treated the dinner as a "come as you are" occasion. Luke's Pharisees, as we will see below, are persons of high status and wealth whom Jesus accuses of mistreating the poor. The issues the Lukan Jesus highlights in his woes are not purity issues, but economic ones. So while it is possible that Luke understands Jesus' conduct to be a rejection of the purity codes, or of Pharisaic purity practices, it seems more plausible to me that those are really non-issues for Luke and his Gentile audience. After all, Luke had a Markan parallel (Mark 7:1-23) in which Jesus rejects handwashing and the distinction between clean and unclean food, and chose to omit most of it. What matters more to Luke is that Jesus deliberately snubs wealthy influential high-status persons at a banquet. [Bathing before a Banquet] The Pharisees think Jesus is a glutton and a drunkard, a friend of tax collectors and sinners—a low-class, ill-bred person—and they have already tried public humiliation of him. Well, this time he rubs their noses in it by showing up dirty and stinky instead of freshly washed and perfumed, and as he spreads himself out on the dining couch, you can imagine Pharisaic noses wrinkling and eyebrows knitting. The host's amazement—again, probably meant to reflect the attitude of the whole group—is over why this no-account preacher from the sticks does not act more deferentially to them. Doesn't he know who they are?

Bathing before a Banquet

Two quotations from Greek writers illustrate the custom of bathing before reclining for a formal meal. Plato, *Symp.* 174a: "[Apollodorus] said that he met Socrates fresh from the bath and sandaled; and as the sight of the sandals was unusual, he asked him whither he was going that he had been converted into such a beau. 'To a banquet at Agathon's,' he replied" (*The Works of Plato*, trans. R. Jowett; ed. I. Edman [New York: Modern Library, 1965], 335).

Plutarch, "Dinner of the Seven Wise Men," 148C: "As for the other guests, each one, after enjoying a rub-down or a bath, was conducted by the servants to the dining-room through the open colonnade" (359).

Although Jesus addresses the host directly, he is speaking to "you Pharisees" in the plural: "You [plural] cleanse the outside of the cup and the platter, but your [plural] insides are full of greed and evil." The beginning of the second clause, *to de esōthen hymōn*, "y'all's insides," shows that "cup and platter" is a metaphor for the person. These Pharisees are examples of persons Jesus describes in 11:35-36; they cannot see correctly, and so their whole bodies are full of darkness, here described very broadly as "greed" or "acquisitiveness" and "evil." Both terms are made more pointed in the woes. "Fools (or Ignoramuses)!" he calls them; the Maker is responsible for inside as well as outside, and is naturally concerned with both.

The way to be clean, in and out, is to "give as alms what is inside." It is not surprising to see almsgiving presented this way; admonitions to be charitable and thereby to receive God's blessings or forgiveness show up frequently in Jewish literature of the period. [What Almsgiving Does] But even with those texts as background, this word from Jesus makes little sense until we link it to Luke 16:14: "The Pharisees, who were money-lovers [*philargyrioi*] . . . ." This is a sin roundly condemned in the Jewish ethical literature of the period. In 2 Maccabees 10:18-23, Judas Maccabeus executes two of his lieutenants for accepting bribes to allow some of the enemy to escape; the traitors are called "money-lovers," the same word Luke used. Fourth Maccabees 2:26 lists "money-loving" (same word, often translated "avarice") as one of the excesses of the soul, akin to gluttony as a bodily excess. Through obedience to the Law, even a money-lover "is forced to act contrary to natural ways and to lend without interest to the needy and to cancel the debt when the seventh year arrives" (4 Macc 2:8). Sirach 31:5 is pretty blunt: "The one who loves gold will not be justified, and the one who pursues money will be led astray by it." Luke's Pharisees need to repent of their money-loving, which will result in alms-giving and in a life free of acquisitiveness and evil.

Jesus continues by pronouncing three woes on the Pharisees. First, they are diligent tithers (every pastor's dream!) but are neglectful of "the justice [or judgment] and love of God." The last phrase of v. 42 ("it is necessary to do these things without neglecting the others") indicates that Luke's Jesus has no objection to tithing. But God's love—either our love for God, or God's love for us that we imitate by loving others as God loves us—includes using wealth to help the needy. The merciful Samaritan and Zacchaeus are Luke's examples of how to do this well; the rich man who ignored poor Lazarus and the wealthy ruler who would not distribute his goods to the poor are examples of how to fail at it. The rich, money-loving Pharisees fail to use their power to do justice to the poor, and fall under the same sorts of condemnation.

What Almsgiving Does

Tobit 4:6b-11: To all those who practice righteousness [7] give alms from your possessions, and do not let your eye begrudge the gift when you make it. Do not turn your face away from anyone who is poor, and the face of God will not be turned away from you. [8] If you have many possessions, make your gift from them in proportion; if few, do not be afraid to give according to the little you have. [9] So you will be laying up a good treasure for yourself against the day of necessity. [10] For almsgiving delivers from death and keeps you from going into the Darkness. [11] Indeed, almsgiving, for all who practice it, is an excellent offering in the presence of the Most High.

Sirach 12:2-3: [2] Do good to the devout, and you will be repaid—if not by them, certainly by the Most High. [3] No good comes to one who persists in evil or to one who does not give alms.

Sirach 29:12-13: [12] Store up almsgiving in your treasury, and it will rescue you from every disaster; [13] better than a stout shield and a sturdy spear, it will fight for you against the enemy.

The Best Seats in Synagogue

AΩ Matthew 23:2 refers to "Moses' seat," which many scholars believe refers to a wooden or stone chair given as a seat of honor to the teacher or other visiting dignitaries. Stone chairs, decorated and inscribed, have been found in excavations of synagogues at the Greek island of Delos (dates to the first or 2d century AD) and at Chorazin in Galilee (3rd–4th century AD). Such furniture may have been used in synagogue buildings known to Matthew. Luke's *prōtokathedrian* literally means "first chair" and might also refer to a nicely decorated chair at the front of the building. But it might just as well refer to a favored spot on the benches where most of the congregation sat. One can imagine that the seats nearest the front, closest to where the speaker was located, would have been considered best.

The second woe takes up the issue of status: the Pharisees love status markers such as the best seats in synagogue and respectful greetings in public. [The Best Seats in Synagogue] Josephus's descriptions of the Pharisees make them the most popular party among ordinary people, but Luke is thinking more of the deference that the poor and lowerclass are supposed to give to wealthy, upperclass people.

The first and second woes describe moral failings—ignoring God's values but pursuing wealth and prestige—while the third describes the effect of their lifestyles: they are corrupting people, but their victims do not realize it. Touching a corpse was defiling, and by extension, so was walking over a grave. The Pharisees, according to Luke's Jesus, are imitating Herod Antipas, who built his new city Tiberias over a graveyard, making it, in the eyes of many observant Jews, a permanently defiled and defiling place. Similarly, because the Pharisees have refused to repent at John's preaching, have written Jesus off because of his eating habits, and have acted toward the poor like any other group of wealthy, powerful aristocrats, they are doing harm even when they appear harmless.

It is important for the interpreter to remember that Luke's Pharisees are a literary construct. Scholars of Second Temple Judaism believe that the Pharisees who encountered Jesus were unlikely to have been aristocrats; more likely, they were a professional class, like lawyers or clerks, who worked for the wealthy. Luke's portrait was shaded by his understanding of what was problematic or dangerous for the followers of Jesus in his own day. In James and 1 Corinthians, we see examples of wealthy Christians who expect deference from the poor and who love their own status more than justice and mercy. Quite possibly Luke models these Pharisees after rich Christians of his acquaintance; perhaps, when these parts were read aloud to Luke's original congregations, it was the wealthier members reclining on their couches who were supposed to squirm as they recognized themselves in the conduct of the Pharisees. [The Best Seats in Sunday School]

At this point in the story, one of the other dinner guests, a lawyer, speaks up. Luke imagines that Pharisees, being wealthy and influential, would have people like this working for them: educated and literate men, who could give them advice and do correspondence. If this reads Luke correctly, the lawyer is the host Pharisee's client, and is obligated to come to his patron's defense; "Teacher, by saying these things you are also attacking us," where "us" now stands for the scribes and lawyers who work for the Pharisees. Yep, says Jesus, you're just as guilty as your masters. This is an interesting move for Luke to make. The seven woes of Matthew 23 are all aimed at "scribes and Pharisees, hypocrites!" By dividing the imprecations into three for Pharisees and three for lawyers, Luke may be protecting Jesus a bit against the feeling of rhetorical overkill one gets when reading through Matthew 23. But maybe not; the lawyer's statement equating the two groups also links them, so whatever Jesus said about one group applies to the other. Possibly Luke is thinking about the Christian equivalent of "lawyers": while the rich Christians squirm on their couches as they listen to the first part of this story, perhaps their client-advisors sitting in the cheap seats squirm when they hear the latter part.

Lawyers are guilty, says Jesus, of three things. First, they overburden people and refuse to make things easier. Since the "burden" is not specified, it could be anything. Many commentators take it to mean the Pharisaic expansion of the Torah, as in the thirty-nine categories of work forbidden on Sabbath.[35] Maybe, but it seems unlikely, for two reasons. First, Pharisaic interpretations of Torah were not legally obligating, neither in Jesus' day nor in Luke's; their views of Torah were obligatory for members of their sect, but membership in the sect was voluntary. Second, even if we take "binding" as a metaphor for "highly influential," why should a poor person object if the Pharisees want to define more kinds of activity as "work"? If Pharisaic opinion held sway in the Jewish community, then nobody could force me to do

The Best Seats in Sunday School

The visitors were given the highest seat of honor, and as soon as [Sunday school superintendent] Mr. Walters' speech was finished, he introduced them to the school. The middle-aged man turned out to be a prodigious personage—no less a one than the county judge—altogether the most august creation these children had ever looked upon . . . .

Mr. Walters fell to "showing off," with all sorts of official bustlings and activities, giving orders, delivering judgments, discharging directions here, there, everywhere that he could find a target. The librarian "showed off"—running hither and thither with his arms full of books and making a deal of the splutter and fuss that insect authority delights in. The young lady teachers "showed off"—bending sweetly over pupils that were lately being boxed, lifting pretty warning fingers at bad little boys and patting good ones lovingly. The young gentleman teachers "showed off" with small scoldings and other little displays of authority and fine attention to discipline—and most of the teachers, of both sexes, found business up at the library, by the pulpit, and it was business that frequently had to be done over again two or three times (with much seeming vexation). The little girls "showed off" in various ways, and the little boys "showed off" with such diligence that the air was thick with paper wads and the murmur of scufflings. And above it all the great man sat and beamed a majestic judicial smile upon all the house, and warmed himself in the sun of his own grandeur—for he was "showing off," too.

Mark Twain, *The Adventures of Tom Sawyer* (1876; repr., New York: Barnes and Noble Classics, 2003), 37–38.

Mark Twain (Credit: Library of Congress Prints and Photographs Division, Washington, D.C.)

any of those things on Sabbath—that's a good thing! So perhaps the burdens Luke has in mind are economic, taking the form of predatory loans where the lender hopes the borrower defaults so that he can foreclose on the property put up as collateral. In favor of this reading, recall that in Luke's version of the model prayer, we ask God to forgive our sins while we forgive the debts we're owed; we could also look ahead to the conduct of the steward in the parable of 16:1-9. Jesus, who by God's finger casts out demons (11:20), now fingers the heavy-handed lending practices of the wealthy and powerful.

Second, the lawyers are accomplices to the murders of the prophets. The argument presumes several things:

- That all the prophets were murdered by audiences who did not want to listen to the word of the Lord. A bit later in Luke, Jesus will say that prophets are always killed in Jerusalem (13:33-34); the idea that prophets are always destined to die is important to Luke's plot and to his characterization of Jesus as a prophet.
- That Abel and Zechariah should be considered prophets. Perhaps we can understand this as a combination of two ideas. Abel and Zechariah were the first and last murders recorded in the Hebrew Bible (Gen 4:10; 2 Chr 24:20-22—in the Hebrew Bible, 1–2 Chronicles comes last), and the gift of prophecy, it was believed, was given to persons about to be martyred for their obedience to God (e.g., Mark 13:11).
- That those who built monuments to the memory of the prophets also agreed that they should have been killed. No doubt the monument-builders believed they were honoring the prophets, but this saying accuses the lawyers and Pharisees of preferring dead prophets to live ones.[36]
- That "this generation," by which Luke means the lawyers and Pharisees (as at 7:31-35), should be held uniquely accountable for the deeds of their ancestors. Why blame them and not other Jews? The explanation comes in vv. 49-51; God's Wisdom promises to send "apostles and prophets to them," but expects "this generation" to kill them, too. Because "this generation," who are not Wisdom's children (7:35), rejected John the Baptist (7:30) and Jesus and will reject Jesus' followers, they show that they are the true heirs of the prophet-killers of old.

This section recalls 10:13-15 and 11:29-32, and repeats a theme Luke has been steadily reinforcing since Zechariah's reaction to Gabriel: God sends the good news, but if those who receive it reject it, the good news becomes a curse.

The final woe is a variant on the first one against the lawyers. They are not only wrong, but are problems to sincere seekers after truth. The "key" that they hide from others would be the key to Wisdom's house (Prov 9:1-6); they do not enter, and try to prevent others. But since Jesus can speak for Wisdom—he knows who are Wisdom's children, and he knows Wisdom's plans—the lawyers' plans will come to nothing.

Having blasted the host and other guests, Jesus takes his leave, but this group will not leave him alone. They "began to act with hostility and to pester him about many things" (the verb translated "pester" normally means something like "teach by dictation," with the implication that his enemies constantly harp on the same topics), hoping to catch him in a misstatement. That is not hard to understand; Jesus has whacked a hornets' nest, and we should expect them to come right back with more of the same. But note, first, that Luke says nothing about a plot to kill Jesus, as we find in Mark 3:6, and second, that Jesus will accept a third dinner invitation from a Pharisee in chapter 14. However hard the words between Jesus and the Pharisees and lawyers, he has not yet written them off.

CONNECTIONS

Nobody prays Luke's version of the Lord's Prayer. It seems too short and rough, compared to Matthew's form, and it ends rather abruptly. My guess is that introducing it into a worship service would require people to slow down and read it aloud, rather than repeating from memory the form we all memorized long ago. That might be a good thing for a church or Sunday school class to do sometime, especially if then we think hard about what the prayer commits us to do: to hope for the inbreaking of God's kingdom; to limit ourselves to daily rations, thereby feeding the hungry; to forgive others, even our enemies; and to be humble enough to admit that a time of testing/temptation might trip us up.

Nobody prays Luke's version of the Lord's Prayer, but everybody prays—desperate prayers to get out of trouble, even more desperate prayers that a loved one's life be spared or health returned. "Ask and it will be given" opens the door of heaven really wide, giving us all sorts of anxiety. Jesus (and Luke) knew well that "you can't always get what you want"; after hearing the Lord's Prayer, we're not supposed to be praying for ponies and pocketknives, but for justice and daily rations. Pray boldly, like a child who trusts the parent to give only good things. And as we pray, we should remember the parable of the guest at midnight: the needy who knock are hoping we will open our doors to them.

I have had fun asking church groups to imagine themselves as each of the three characters in the parable of the guest at midnight. The neighbor is asked to give alms—to share from his pantry what someone at some remove needs to meet his immediate hunger. The host is asked to welcome his guest—bringing the hungry, tired man into his home and providing hospitality. The guest simply asks, and trusts that his host will give him what he needs. Probably almost all American churches practice the first form, the neighborly charitable-giving form, of meeting the needs of the world. The distance between us and those we help is something of a problem, but on the other hand, we Americans need, really need, to redistribute what we accumulate, and alms-giving is probably the only way to send our surplus to the world's neediest people. Many American churches also practice hosting in some form or other—feeding the hungry in their churches and homes, providing shelter for those who need it, advocating for them in various ways. This decreases the distance between them and us, but can put us into the very patron-client relations that Luke's Jesus tries to disrupt. The third form is probably least familiar to us. If we move beyond hosting toward being hosted, toward a relationship that is truly reciprocal, then perhaps we arrive at Luke's construction of the earliest Christian community in Acts, wherein all property was held in common, meals were shared, and nobody went without.

The middle section of the chapter is constructed around different reactions to Jesus. Some are amazed (11:14), some skeptical (11:16), some antagonistic (11:15), some laudatory (but for the wrong reasons, 11:27), and some apathetic (11:29-32). That's ministry, right? You try to do your best, and there will always be some who misunderstand or misrepresent you. Jesus mostly issues dire warnings in this part: you could be reinfested with even more demons; you are missing what Nineveh and Sheba saw; beware lest your blindness fill your whole body with darkness. But note the one beatitude, standing in v. 28 like a daffodil in the mud: Blessed are those who hear the word of God and obey it! Focus on that, both as the essence of your own responsibility and as a reminder that your ministry will bear fruit. As you make the word of God plain to others, some will hear and obey, and find life.

The final section of the chapter describes a most unpleasant dinner where Jesus gnaws on some Pharisees and lawyers. It starts badly when Jesus shows up unbathed, goes off the rails when he rips into them for hypocrisy and pride, and crashes and burns when he accuses them of murdering all the prophets. Here we see, rather spectacularly, that the Lukan Jesus, when he says "love your enemies," doesn't mean "be nice." Loving them means telling them the truth, even if that's painful, just as much as it means sharing food with them. "Bless those who curse you" is harder to rationalize; in this chapter, Jesus is pronouncing woes, prophetic curses, on them. But he is speaking to them rather than about them, and neither side has yet written the other off, since there will be another dinner in chapter 14.

NOTES

[1] E. P. Sanders, *Jesus and Judaism* (Philadelphia: Fortress, 1985), 203.

[2] Kenneth W. Stevenson, *The Lord's Prayer: A Text in Tradition* (Minneapolis: Fortress, 2004) provides a full and fascinating tradition history for the prayer.

[3] Translations from the Old Testament Pseudepigrapha are from James H. Charlesworth, ed., *The Old Testament Pseudepigrapha* (2 vols; New York: Doubleday, 1983).

[4] Translations from the Dead Sea Scrolls are from Geza Vermes, *The Complete Dead Sea Scrolls in English* (New York: Penguin, 1997).

[5] As given in Philip Birnbaum, *Daily Prayer Book* (New York: Hebrew Publishing, 1949), 50. The earliest written text of the Kaddish prayer is much later than the first century, but most think the use of the prayer is much earlier. As Joseph A. Fitzmyer, *The Gospel According to Luke* (AB 28 and 28A; Garden City NY: Doubleday, 1981), 2.901 notes, even if the text of the prayer is later than the first century and even if it had been influenced by Christian practice, the point still stands that the Kaddish is a Jewish prayer, and the parallels show that Jesus' formulations are at home in Judaism. See also Joseph Heinemann and Jakob J. Petuchowski, *Literature of the Synagogue* (New York: Behrman House, 1975), 81–84.

[6] Joseph Heinemann, *Prayer in the Talmud: Forms and Patterns* (New York: de Gruyter, 1977), 26–27.

[7] As cited in M. Eugene Boring et al., eds., *Hellenistic Commentary to the New Testament* (Nashville: Abingdon, 1995), 211. The history of the transmission of the Eighteen Benedictions is tremendously complicated. The Mishnah sometimes refers to them as if they had a standard form in the Second Temple period (e.g., *m. Ta'an.* 2:2), but most historians doubt that this was the case. The basic themes of the Eighteen and some of their wording do appear in Second Temple prayers (e.g., in the Hebrew version of Sir 51). So a plausible theory is that some Jews in the Second Temple period prayed benedictions that resemble early versions of what was made into the standard liturgy after the destruction of the temple. See Heinemann, *Prayer in the Talmud*; Shaye J. D. Cohen, "The Temple and the Synagogue," in William Horbury et al., eds., *The Cambridge History of Judaism* (Cambridge: Cambridge University Press, 1999), 3.298-325; Stefan C. Reif, "The Early Liturgy of the Synagogue," *CHJ* 3.331-32.

[8] Boring, *Hellenistic Commentary*, 212.

[9] Mary Beard et al., eds., *Religions of Rome* (2 vols; Cambridge: Cambridge University Press, 1998), 2.152.

[10] Sixth benediction from the Cairo Geniza fragment, reflecting what some feel is an old Palestinian version of the Eighteen Benedictions. See Heinemann, *Prayer in the Talmud*, 26–27; Charlesworth, "Forgiveness (Early Judaism)," *ADB* 2.834, judges it to reflect pre-70 tradition.

[11] Cited in Beard et al., eds., *Religions of Rome*, 2.152-53.

[12] Translation according to Florentino Garcia Martinez and Eibert J. C. Tigchelaar, *The Dead Sea Scrolls Study Edition* (Leiden: Brill, 1997), 1.149. Vermes' translation reads, "[Preserve] thy servant, [O God], lest he sin against Thee, or stagger aside from any word of Thy will. Strengthen the [loins of thy servant that he may] resist the spirits [of falsehood, that] he may walk in all Thou lovest" (Vermes, *Dead Sea Scrolls in English*, 245–46).

[13] In both cases, Paul writes the Aramaic word *Abba* followed by the nominative form of the Greek word for "father," including the definite article. Since a prayer beginning "Abba, (the) Father" makes little sense (if "Abba! Father!" were meant, then "father" would either be in the vocative case or be anarthrous), we may deduce that Paul writes the Greek form of the word to explain the Aramaic. If that is correct, then these two verses show that some Christians other than Paul use *Abba* in prayer, but that Paul knows well that not all do.

[14] So Alan R. Culpepper, *The Gospel of Luke* (*NIB*, vol. 9; Nashville: Abingdon, 1995), 234; contra Fitzmyer, *Luke*, 2.898.

[15] BAGD, 376–77.

[16] See the discussions and evidence cited at Fitzmyer, *Luke*, 2.904-906 (Fitzmyer opts for "necessary" or "bread for subsistence." So Joel B. Green, *The Gospel of Luke* (NICNT; Grand Rapids: Eerdmans, 1997), 442–43, with a nod to "bread for tomorrow," and Culpepper, *Luke*, 234.

[17] John Nolland, *Luke* (WBC, vols. 35A-C; Dallas TX: Word, 1989-93), 2.617; Fitzmyer, *Luke*, 2.897, suggests that "debt" as a metaphor for "sin" might not be comprehensible to Luke's audience.

[18] Miroslav Volf, *The End of Memory: Remembering Rightly in a Violent World* (Grand Rapids: Eerdmans, 2006), 5.

[19] Robert C. Tannehill, *Luke* (ANTC; Nashville: Abingdon, 1996), 191–96, suggests the division I follow, for slightly different reasons; Charles H. Talbert, *Reading Luke: A Literary and Theological Commentary on the Third Gospel* (rev. ed.; Macon GA: Smyth and Helwys, 2002), 141–42, also argues for 11:14-36 being the unit, but counts two responses to Jesus rather than three. Green, *Luke*, 450–51, argues that 11:14-54 all belongs together under the heading of responses to criticism.

[20] Howard Clark Kee, *Miracle in the Early Christian World* (New Haven: Yale University, 1983), 214; John P. Meier, *A Marginal Jew* (New York: Doubleday, 1994), 2.541-51.

[21] Luke Timothy Johnson, *The Gospel of Luke* (SP, vol. 3; Collegeville MN: Liturgical Press, 1991), 183.

[22] At least, I think that's what v. 17b means. Luke writes "every kingdom being divided against itself is laid waste, and house against house falls." I presume, with many others, that Luke's use of "house" means the household, rather than the building,

and that we are supposed to supply the participle "divided" from the first part of the saying.

[23] So Culpepper, *Luke*, 242; Fitzmyer, *Luke*, 2.924-25; Green, *Luke*, 459.

[24] There is a textual variant in 11:33. Some old manuscripts add read "in a cellar or under a basket," while others read "in a cellar." Text critics are divided on whether the longer text is earlier or represents a scribal assimilation to Mark and Matthew; the second explanation makes most sense to me. So Nolland, *Luke*, 2.656; see Bruce Metzger, *A Textual Commentary on the Greek New Testament* (New York: United Bible Societies, 1971), 159.

[25] Dale C. Allison, Jr., "The Eye is the Lamp of the Body (Matthew 6.22-23=Luke 11.34-36)," *NTS* 33 (1987): 61–83.

[26] Dennis Smith, *From Symposium to Eucharist* (Minneapolis: Fortress, 2003), 34.

[27] Plato, *Symposium* (trans. B Jowett; Roslyn NY: Walter Black, 1942), 169, 175, 184.

[28] Smith, *From Symposium to Eucharist*, 35.

[29] Petronius, *Satyricon* (trans. Michael Heseltine; Cambridge MA: Harvard University, 1939), sections 57–58 (pp. 101–105).

[30] Juvenal, *Satire* 5.25-29 (trans. Susanna Morton Braund [Cambridge MA: Harvard University Press, 2004], 217).

[31] So Green, *Luke*, 470; Frederick W. Danker, *Jesus and the New Age: A Commentary on St. Luke's Gospel* (rev. ed.; Philadelphia: Fortress, 1988), 239; Fitzmyer, *Luke*, 2.947, and Nolland, *Luke*, 2.663, allow for the possibility that "immerse" is intended.

[32] Petronius, *Satyricon* 31 (trans. Heseltine, 47).

[33] Most forms of Levitical impurity may be cleansed, according to Torah, by immersing and waiting until sundown. So if Pharisees, as many think, tried to eat their evening meals "in purity," meaning that they were Levitically clean when they ate, they would likely have immersed just before sundown and then begun the meal just after dark.

[34] David B. Gowler, *Host, Guest, Enemy, and Friend: Portraits of the Pharisees in Luke and Acts* (New York: Peter Lang, 1991), 227: "The host Pharisee is astonished that Jesus did not wash, and the reader should be surprised at the Pharisee's astonishment!"

[35] So Fitzmyer, *Luke*, 2.949.

[36] So Danker, *Luke*, 242; Green, *Luke*, 474.

TEACHINGS ON HYPOCRISY, POSSESSIONS, AND SERVANTHOOD

Luke 12

COMMENTARY

The Leaven of Hypocrisy, 12:1-12

Many understand this section to be a crazy quilt rather than a tapestry, with subsections connected by key words but no overriding theme. The previous section (11:37-54) had Jesus butting heads with Pharisees over saying one thing and doing another, so 12:1 uses the words "Pharisees" and "hypocrisy," which is apparently how Luke understood 12:2-3. The link between 12:2-3 and 12:4-10 seems to be the promise (or threat) that secrets will be revealed. Luke 12:10 mentions the Holy Spirit; 12:11-12 does as well. Perhaps Luke stitched together diverse material from Mark and Q through link words only, but in what follows, I shall argue that he understood it all to be about hypocrisy, how foolish and how dangerous it is.

[The Danger of Hypocrisy]

Jesus' growing popularity, evident in 11:29, is not presented by Luke as a positive thing. Luke's sentence says that a "myriad-sized crowd," which can mean "ten thousand" or "a whopping big number," had all come together around Jesus, so many folks trying to get close that they were stepping on each other. But Jesus speaks directly to the disciples—not the Twelve, but the larger group that included women (8:1-3) and that Jesus sent out two by two on the mission in 10:1-20. The crowds will show up again in this chapter (12:13, 54), but only to be warned about the dangers of riches (12:14-21) and to be called "hypocrites" (12:54-59). Luke puts the big crowd in this scene, not as

> **The Danger of Hypocrisy**
>
> When a man is virtuous enough to be able to delude himself that he is almost perfect, he may enter into a dangerous condition of blindness in which all his violent efforts finally to grasp perfection strengthen his hidden imperfections and confirm him in his attachment to his own judgment and his own will.
>
> Thomas Merton, *New Seeds of Contemplation* (New York: New Directions, 1972), 257.

a sign of Jesus' success, but as a foil for the disciples; the crowds may be fooled by the Pharisees, but the disciples should be better informed and more wary.

Leaven was made by leaving dough or bread to turn sour and mold.[1] The bit of decaying material could then be mixed with other dough, and as the molds multiplied, they also made the dough rise by releasing gas. Leaven was a symbol of something that, though small, affected a much larger quantity. The image is almost always negative, as it is here, where the disciples are warned against how the Pharisees' hypocrisy may change them for the worse. In Mark's version of the story, Jesus warns the disciples against "the leaven of the Pharisees and the leaven of Herod," recalling for the reader the plot to kill Jesus that was announced in Mark 3:6. Mark's disciples do not understand, and Jesus chews them out (Mark 7:14-21). But Luke's Pharisees are not in league with Herod (see 13:31) and are not trying to kill Jesus, so their "leaven" needs to be specified. Hypocrisy—saying one thing but doing another—is a nice one-word summary of Jesus' woes against the Pharisees; interesting, then, that Luke's Jesus never calls the Pharisees hypocrites, but instead warns the readers against it.[2] Rhetorically, Luke is shifting from an epithet slung at an enemy to a warning against a virus infecting the audience; Luke's audience cannot sit back and gloat while Jesus tears down a straw man, but must wonder, "Is it I, Lord?" [Warnings against Hypocrisy]

Warnings against Hypocrisy

Someone steals, deals unjustly, robs, cheats, but yet has pity on the poor. This also has two aspects, but is evil as a whole. He who cheats his neighbor provokes God's wrath; he who serves falsely before the Most High, and yet has mercy on the poor, disregards the Lord who uttered the Law's commands; he provokes him, and yet he alleviates the plight of the poor day laborer. He defiles the soul and takes pride in his own body; he kills many, yet has pity on a few . . . Someone else commits adultery and is sexually promiscuous, yet is abstemious in his eating. While fasting, he is committing evil deeds. Through the power of his wealth he ravages many, and yet in spite of his excessive evil, he performs the commandments. . . . But you, children, do not be two-faced like them, one good and the other evil; rather, cling only to goodness, because in it the Lord God is at rest, and men aspire to it. Flee from the evil tendency, destroying the devil by your good works. For those who are two-faced are not of God, but they are enslaved to their evil desires, so that they might be pleasing to Beliar and to persons like themselves.

Testament of Asher (usually dated in the 2d century BC) 2:5–3:2; translation by H. C. Kee, in James H. Charlesworth, *The Old Testament Pseudepigrapha* (2 vols; New York: Doubleday, 1985), 1.817.

Verses 2-3 introduce a section found in Matthew 10:26-33, but not in Mark, so it is usually assigned to Q. These two verses have an interesting kind of parallel structure:

> Nothing has been covered up
> which will not be uncovered,
> Nor hidden
> which will not be made known.
> Therefore, whatever you say in the darkness
> will be heard in the light,
> And whatever you spoke into the ear in secret rooms
> will be preached from the roofs.

The first line of all four couplets uses images of secrecy; the second line, of revelation. The first four lines are all passives without a specified subject, inviting the listener to wonder whether God is involved in the hiding or the revealing or both: is this a promise that all divine secrets will be revealed someday? But because the secret-speaker in v. 3 is specified as "you," Luke more likely thought of a human hider and divine revealer, and considered vv. 2-3 to be a critique of and warning against hypocrisy. The divine revelation will certainly happen at Judgment Day, as we will see in vv. 8-9, but may happen sooner (for example, at the dinner table in 7:36-50 and 11:37-54); recall Simeon's prediction that Jesus would be the rising and falling of many, revealing their inner thoughts.

But the audience for these verses is the disciples, not the Pharisees; the plural "you" who whisper things in the dark are Jesus' followers, not his enemies. The scenario in v. 3 imagines disciples who are up to no good, plotting things that will be embarrassing once they come to light. If we keep that in mind, then vv. 4-5 make more sense, where the disciples are warned against fearing a magistrate more than God. Luke writes about some of the persecutions of early believers in Acts, and describes Peter and the apostles standing firm under threats, saying, "We must obey God rather than humans" (Acts 5:29). Whether Luke's audience was in any current danger is harder to say. Nero's execution of Christians in mid-60s Rome was apparently both localized and short-lived, and after that we have no firm evidence of Roman magistrates killing people for being Christians until the famous letter of Pliny, governor of Bithynia, to the Emperor Trajan in AD 112. [Pliny's Letter to Trajan] Luke, who likely wrote between 70–100, may well have addressed an audience who felt fairly comfortable and safe in their environment. If that is correct, then the repeated, emphatic "fear him" and the image of God killing and casting into Gehenna is meant to alert complacent Christians to the dangers of becoming too cozy in their society.

We probably need only a brief reminder of all the scandals associated with Christians and clergy of all denominations in our young century. Lots of things done behind closed doors make for lurid headlines. Perhaps in our time, we could read these two verses as "Don't be afraid of those who will defrock you or put your picture above the fold on page 1; all they can do is ruin your life and reputation. The one you should really fear is the One who can do all that plus make you suffer eternally."

Pliny's Letter to Trajan

Around AD 112, Pliny the Younger, who was serving as governor of Bithynia, wrote to Emperor Trajan to make certain that he was following proper procedures with respect to Christians. He begins by explaining why he is asking for advice: "I was never present at any trial of Christians; therefore I do not know what are the customary penalties or investigations, and what limits are observed." Most think that this shows that there was no established policy or standard practice, or Pliny, a member of the senatorial class who had served in the Roman bureaucracy, would have known about it. Pliny continues,

> I have hesitated a great deal on the question of whether there should be any distinction of ages; whether the weak should have the same treatment as the more robust; whether those who recant should be pardoned; or whether a man who has ever been a Christian should gain nothing by ceasing to be such; whether the name itself, even if innocent of crime, should be punished, or only the crimes attaching to that name.

This last part indicates that Pliny was uncertain whether Christianity alone was a crime; all this probably implies that persecution of Christians simply for being Christians was not yet standard policy or practice in his day. Pliny then says that publicity surrounding the trials produced a wave of accusations:

> An anonymous pamphlet was issued, containing many names. All who denied that they were or had been

Christians I considered should be discharged, because they called upon the gods at my dictation and did reverence, with incense and wine, to your image which I had ordered to be brought forward for this purpose, together with the statues of the deities; and especially because they cursed Christ, a thing which, it is said, genuine Christians cannot be induced to do.

Governor Pliny then describes testimony given by Christians who recanted their faith:

> Others named by the informer first said that they were Christians and then denied it; declaring that they had been but were so no longer, some having recanted three years or more before and one or two as long ago as twenty years. They all worshipped your image and the statues of the gods and cursed Christ. But they declared that the sum of their guilt or error had amounted to only this, that on an appointed day they had been accustomed to meet before daybreak and to recite a hymn antiphonally to Christ, as to a god, and to bind themselves by an oath, not for the commission of any crime but to abstain from theft, robbery, adultery and breach of faith, and not to deny a deposit when it was claimed. After the conclusion of this ceremony it was their custom to depart and meet again to take food; but it was ordinary and harmless food, and they had ceased this practice after my edict in which, in accordance with your orders, I had forbidden secret societies.

Translation from Henry Bettenson, ed., *Documents of the Christian Church* (2d ed; New York: Oxford, 1977), 3–4.

But immediately after Luke makes this argument—if the threat of exposure won't keep you faithful, then perhaps the threat of hell will—he shifts the tone, from threatening to consoling. God keeps up with the sparrows that sell very cheaply; God keeps count of the hairs of your head. Don't be afraid—you matter more to God than many sparrows! So, fear God in v. 5, but don't be afraid in v. 7? Two sides of the same coin, actually. "Every breath you take . . . every vow you break . . . I'll be watching you"[3] is both promise and threat, and most of all, proof of the utter futility of hypocrisy. If God knows how many hairs you have (for some of us, fewer all the time, alas), then God knows your "secret" loyalties; if God keeps up with how many sparrows get sold for dinners, and thinks your lives are much more interesting than theirs, then God is not going to lose track of your hypocrisies.

"Whoever acknowledges me" and "whoever denies me" could be in a setting of potential martyrdom. "We gave you strict orders not to teach in this name," says Caiaphas to Peter and the apostles (Acts 5:28), orders that the Twelve say they must disobey. Pliny's letter states that when people were accused of being Christians, he first gave them several chances to recant, and then executes them if they refuse:

> Meanwhile, this is the course that I have adopted in the case of those brought before me as Christians. I ask them if they are Christians. If they admit it I repeat the question a second and a third time, threatening capital punishment; if they persist I sentence them to death. For I do not doubt that, whatever kind of crime it may be to which they have confessed, their pertinacity and inflexible obstinacy should certainly be punished.[4]

The letter, and the policy Governor Pliny describes, dates to AD 112, and we cannot assume it was in effect in Luke's time and location. More likely, owning up to being a Christian was more a matter of possible social embarrassment. The new cult honored a crucified man, encouraged masters and slaves to think of themselves as equals, and shared Judaism's negative attitude toward the gods. If "acknowledging me" translates into "refuse to participate in religious ceremonies honoring the emperor or the patron gods of your city," then there may have been many Lukan Christians guilty of keeping quiet and thus "denying me." [Denying Me]

Once again, Luke reaches for eternal consequences. Even if the human settings are not necessarily judicial, the divine setting is. The "Son of Man" is the title Jesus wears as judge of humanity, and the presence of the angels identifies this scene as Judgment Day. Jesus is giving testimony for some and against others, based on how they spoke for or against him during their lives. The ones whom the Son of Man will deny before the angels are presumably "cast into Gehenna " (12:5) and shut out of the kingdom banquet (13:24-30). [Gehenna]

The "unpardonable sin" saying appears in Mark 3:28-30, but in several respects Luke 12:10 is closer to Matthew 12:32 than to Mark, so many commentators believe that the saying appeared in Q. There is also a version in the *Gospel of Thomas* 44, and 1 John 5:16-17 also distinguishes between an ordinary sin and a "sin unto death," for which it would do no good to pray. Thus, the idea of an unforgivable sin has broad support in early Christianity, even

Denying Me

And back of that failure [to remain focused on the presence of God] there was something else. A crowd of people arrived who, when they are in a crowd, wish to talk or think nothing of religion. I fear I have not wanted some of them to think me religious for fear I might cease to be interesting.

Fellowship with God is something one dare not cover, for it smothers to death.

Frank C. Laubach, *Letters by a Modern Mystic* (Westwood NJ: Revell, 1937), 24.

Gehenna

AΩ The word *Gehenna* comes from the Hebrew for "Valley of Hinnom," referring to a valley west of Jerusalem. It had been a place of terror in the past, according to Jeremiah, who said that in the past people burned their children there as sacrifices (7:30-34; 19:1-13). Because the entrance to the valley was in later times known as the Dung Gate (Neh 2:13), most scholars presume that the valley was used as a garbage dump; Jer 19:2 calls the same spot "the Potsherd Gate," implying that it was the place to throw out trash and broken dishes. Both associations—the place to dispose of refuse, and the place where children were sacrificed by fire to foreign gods—would have made it a natural symbol of God's judgment. Being tossed into Gehenna, then, was to be abandoned like garbage or like those poor children. 12:5 is Luke's only use of the word.

Hinnom Valley with Sultan's Pool from south.

(Credit: Todd Bolen, BiblePlaces.com)

though none of these documents defines it with any precision. To blaspheme means to curse or slander; in what circumstances would one curse the Holy Spirit? It is hard to imagine how one would commit this sin if we take "blaspheme" literally, so many interpret it more broadly. Mark, who places the saying right after the scribes accuse Jesus of partnership with Beelzebul, probably thought that the scribes' slander was not just against Jesus but against the Spirit of God, by whose power Jesus cast out demons. But since Luke chooses a different setting, it seems likely that he understood the sin differently. In Luke's case, it is actually easier to say what the unpardonable sin is not than what it is. It is not apostasy, denying Jesus under pressure, since Peter does that and is subsequently restored to his leadership role in the church. It is not cursing, torturing, or killing Jesus (or by extension, anyone else), since Jesus asks God to forgive the ones who did that to him; Peter specifically offers forgiveness to those who preferred Barabbas to Jesus (Acts 3:19). It is not idolatry; Luke's Paul calls that a sin of ignorance and offers repentance and forgiveness (Acts 17:30-31). Although there is a certain logic to the theory that blasphemy against the Spirit means failing to respond to the call to repent and believe in the gospel (how could you be forgiven if you never repent?), it does not explain all the evidence. Luke's Pharisees are Jesus' steadfast enemies, harassing him and trying to catch him in a misstatement (11:53-54); yet there were Pharisees in the early church, according to Acts 15:5.

This present context suggests that Luke considered hypocrisy, particularly when it involves lying to God, to be blasphemy against the Spirit; recall that when Ananias and Sapphira pretend to give away the full price from the sale of a piece of property, Peter tells them that they have lied to the Holy Spirit, and they are struck dead (Acts 5:1-11). That episode, and this saying, are meant to be warnings against trying to fake devotion to God: eventually what you whisper in your heart will be evident before everyone. Luke put this saying into this section to show that the leaven of hypocrisy, once it pervades a person's whole being, leads that one to a tragic end.

The foil for the Spirit-blasphemer is the martyr-prophet, to whom the Spirit gives just the right words for the moment. Luke was probably familiar with stories of Jewish martyrs like Eleazar and the seven brothers and their mother (2 Macc 6–7). In these gruesome but stirring episodes, each character refused to disobey the Torah, even under torture, and gave a final brave testimony to his or her faith: for example, "It is clear to the Lord in his holy knowledge that, though I might have been saved from death, I am enduring terrible sufferings in my body under this beating, but in my soul I am glad to suffer these things because I fear him" (2 Macc 6:30). In Acts, Luke gives us several speeches of believers seized by the temple authorities (Acts 4:5-12; 5:29-32; 7:2-53; 23:1-10) or Roman magistrates (24:10-21; 26:2-29). Stephen's speech is the only one followed immediately by the speaker's martyrdom, and so it is not accidental that Luke tells us that his opponents "could not withstand the wisdom and the Spirit with which he spoke" (Acts 6:10); that his face was like an angel's (Acts 6: 15; probably shining, as at Luke 24:4); that just before he was killed, he was filled with the Spirit and given a vision of Jesus (Acts 7:55-56); and that as he died, his last words echoed Jesus' (Acts 7:59-60; cf. Luke 23:34, 46). No sane person craves martyrdom, but the promise of Luke 12:11-12 and the example of Stephen's death were meant to reassure Luke's audience that they could be faithful unto death if need be.

The Rich Fool and Commandments on Wealth, 12:13-21

At the beginning of Tom Wolfe's *Bonfire of the Vanities*, Sherman McCoy, the Wall Street bond salesman, is riding high on a string of big financial successes: "He was part of the pulverizing might of Pierce & Pierce, Masters of the Universe . . . . To risk $6 billion in one afternoon to make *two ticks*—six and a quarter cents per one hundred dollars—and then to make four ticks—*four ticks!*—the audacity! The audacity! Was there any more exciting power on the face of the earth?"[5] McCoy's success makes him crave things, and the exercise of power makes him assume that he deserves them—fine clothes, expensive sports car, the best school for his daughter, apartment featured in *Architectural Digest* for his wife, and a beautiful young mistress for himself. You know when you begin the novel that he will fall hard, and that you will not be sad to see him knocked off his high horse. Nobody likes a man who calls himself "Master of the Universe."

Luke's parable of the rich fool is the first of three "rich man" parables (the other two are 16:1-9, the rich man's steward, and 16:19-31, the rich man and Lazarus), but the reader already knows about the dangers of wealth. Mary's song celebrated God tipping the mighty from their thrones and sending the rich away empty, while lifting up the lowly and feeding the hungry (1:32-33). "Woe to you rich," said Jesus, as he commanded his disciples to give to beggars, to lend without expecting repayment, and to give as generously as God gives (6:24, 30, 35, 38). Luke's audience, then, if they have been paying attention, would have expected the rich man to fall as hard as Sherman McCoy, Master of the Universe.

It's an old plot, actually, and a cross-cultural one. "The wealthy never stop wanting more" and "death comes to everyone, rich and poor" were commonplace lessons in Luke's day:

• "Neither silver nor gold abates the love of money, nor does greed [*pleonexia*, the same word as in Luke 12:15] cease with the purchase of something new, but one says to wealth as to a foolish doctor, 'Your medicine is making the sickness greater.'" (Plutarch, "On Love of Wealth," *Moralia* 7 523.E)

• "Another peculiarity of the love of money is this: it is a desire that opposes its own satisfaction." (Plutarch, "On Love of Wealth," 524.F)

• "Guard yourselves therefore, my children, against sexual promiscuity and love of money; listen to Judah, your father, for these things distance you from the Law of God, blind the direction of the soul, and detach arrogance. They do not permit a man to show mercy to his neighbor. They deprive his soul of all goodness, and oppress him with hardships and grief, they take away sleep from him and utterly waste his flesh. They impede the sacrifices to God, he does not remember the blessings of God, he does not obey the prophet when he speaks, and he is offended by a pious word. For two passions contrary to God's commands enslave him, so that he is unable to obey God: They blind his soul, and he goes about in the day as though it were night." (*T. Jud.* 18:2-6)

- "One becomes rich through diligence and self-denial, and the reward allotted to him is this: when he says, 'I have found rest, and how I shall feast on my goods!' he does not know how long it will be until he leaves them to others and dies." (Sir 11:18-19)
- "O death, how bitter is the thought of you to the one at peace among possessions, who has nothing to worry about and is prosperous in everything, and still is vigorous enough to enjoy food." (Sir 41:1)
- "Do not fear death's decree for you; remember those who went before you and those who will come after. This is the Lord's decree for all flesh; why then should you reject the will of the Most High? Whether life lasts for ten years or a hundred or a thousand, there are no questions asked in Hades." (Sir 41:3-4)
- "Woe unto you who gain silver and gold by unjust means; you will then say, 'We have grown rich and accumulated good, we have acquired everything that we have desired. So now let us do whatever we like; for we have gathered silver, we have filled our treasuries with money like water. And many are the laborers in our houses.' Your lies flow like water. For your wealth shall not endure but it shall take off from you quickly for you have acquired it all unjustly, and you shall be given over to a great curse." (*1 En.* 97:8-10)

All of these references predate the first century, and even if they had no direct influence on Luke or Jesus, they demonstrate how the parable's story line—a wealthy man who wants more and who fails to account for God's control of things—would have been familiar, understandable, and predictable. [Anacharsis to Croesus]

Luke frames the parable with a question from the crowd. Recall that the chapter began with Luke's note that the crowds around Jesus had grown so large that they were stepping on each other (12:1), but then Jesus' instructions are aimed at the disciples (12:1-12). The crowds, stomping around in the background while Jesus spoke of how loyalty to him would be recognized on Judgment Day, now speak up through an unnamed person who wants help with his personal finances. "Teacher, tell my brother to

Anacharsis to Croesus

Anacharsis was a nobleman from Scythia, a land considered barbaric by Greeks and Romans, who visited Greece in the 6th century BC. A collection of letters attributed to him circulated in the 1st or 2d century BC; they were almost certainly written by someone else pretending to be Anacharsis, and are an example of what one Greek writer, perhaps influenced by an early form of the Cynic philosophy, thought about the dangers of wealth. Croesus was the legendary Greek king whose lust for gold was turned into a curse on him.

I have heard that this evil which befalls most men has befallen you, too. From this evil, others follow. For neither great wealth nor possession of fields has ever bought wisdom. . . . Because of your immoderate enjoyment of pleasure you have physicians for your bodies, but not for your souls. It would be wise for you to renounce pleasure. When much gold flows toward you, the fame that attaches to gold and the envy and desire of those who wish to rob you of your gold have flowed toward you, too, together with the gold. If, therefore, you had purified yourself of the disease, you would have become healthy, speaking and ruling freely. . . . But the disease, laying hold of you in your incontinence, plunged you into ruin and made you a slave instead of a free man.

Translation in Abraham J. Malherbe, *The Cynic Epistles* (Atlanta: Scholars Press, 1977), 47–49. See also the introductory comments, pp. 6–7.

divide the inheritance with me." Not a great opening line. First, Jesus does not respond well to orders from others (see 10:40b, "tell my sister to help me!"). Second, the man calls Jesus "teacher," the term used by Pharisees (7:40; 19:39), lawyers (10:25; 11:45), temple leaders (20:21, 39), Sadducees (20:28), and the rich "ruler" (18:18); only once do Jesus' disciples call him "teacher" (21:7), mostly preferring "Lord." Third, Luke's audience knows that Jesus and the disciples have left homes, families, and businesses behind, and that those who wanted to follow him had to abandon their normal family obligations (9:57-62). If this guy needs resolution of an inheritance, he is clearly not a disciple.

The person's question could have implied a property dispute in which the oldest sibling was failing to divide the inheritance with a younger; on this reading, Luke would be giving us the counterpart to the prodigal son, who asks for his share of the inheritance early. But Jesus is uninterested in the facts of the case; he will not hear it at all, claiming that he has no jurisdiction: "Who set me up as judge or arbitrator over you [plural you, meaning you and your sibling]?" In other words, God did not call me to this task, and you're not the boss of me!

The New Testament gives us plenty of examples, sadly, of how members of the Christian family fall out over property. Paul scolds the Corinthians for taking each other to court, most likely over property issues, and recommends that they should either just drop the argument or appoint an arbiter within the congregation to rule on such issues (1 Cor 6:1-8). James is much closer to Jesus' attitude when the letter locates the source of disputes among Christians in the desire for things and tells the readers to fight their covetousness instead of each other (4:1-10).

Jesus then warns "them," probably meaning the crowd as well as the disciples, against greed (*pleonexia*, which is also translated as avarice, covetousness, or other synonyms for wanting more and more[6]). Greed is often included in vice lists in the New Testament (Rom 1:29; Col 3:5) and in early Christian literature (*1 Clem.* 35:5; *Epistle of Polycarp* 2:2; *Did.* 5:1), but Luke fleshes it out, illustrating it first by a proverb and then by the parable.

The proverb in the last half of v. 15 reads literally, "His life is not in the multiplying of his possessions," where the "his" refers back to the person who asked the question as a representative of all who have not sufficiently guarded themselves against greed. Verse 15 uses the word *zōē*, which normally means "life" in the biological sense. Luke 12:23, using the word *psychē*, says "Life is more than food"; that word for "life" is sometimes translated "soul," and it is how the rich man addresses himself in v. 19. The point is that the accumulation of things beyond what is necessary for subsistence does not define "life" or "self" and guarantees neither the persistence of physical existence nor the wholeness of the self. Things won't keep you alive, and things won't make you a real, full self. [Life Is Not Possessions]

Life Is Not Possessions

It is the vice of a vulgar mind to be thrilled by bigness, to think that a thousand square miles are a thousand times more wonderful than one square mile, and that a million square miles are almost the same as heaven.

E. M. Forster, *Howards End* (New York: Penguin, 1980), 43.

So this rich man's land produced bountifully—nothing wrong with that whatsoever. Unlike the *1 Enoch* passage quoted above, this is not a story about ill-gotten gain. But note the contrast between "the land of a rich man produced bountifully" and what follows, where the rich man's internal dialogue is all about his actions and his property: "What will I do, because I have no place where I may gather my produce? . . . I will do this: I will pull down my barns and build bigger ones, and there I will gather all my grain and good things." Again, let us be clear: so far, the rich man has done nothing illegal. The land is his, and the produce of his crops belongs to him. If he failed to tithe it—setting aside the portions that went to the priests and the portions that were to be held in his village for relief of the poor—or if he failed to allow the poor to come and glean in his fields, orchards, and vineyards—then he would be guilty of breaking the commandments. When he says "I will gather all my grain," are we to assume that means "I will give nothing to the poor"? More on this momentarily. [Avoiding the Poor]

Avoiding the Poor

The starving children have been replaced by souls out on the street
We give a dollar when we pass, and hope our eyes don't meet

Mary Chapin Carpenter, "Stones in the Road," 1992, EMI April Music In. and Getarealjob Music.

The rich man continues his internal conversation: "I will say to my soul [or to myself], Soul, you have many things laid away for many years; relax, eat, drink, be happy." Luke here quotes from Ecclesiastes 8:15 (LXX): "There is nothing better for a man under the sun than to eat and to drink and to be happy, and this will accompany him in his labor all the days of his life." The similarity to the words of Scripture raises again the question of what the rich man is doing wrong: how can it be bad to follow the advice of Ecclesiastes?

Luke, at least, thinks the rich man's sin was greed. Although the parable is told as if the rich man were the only person in the world, that is only because it is told from the rich man's point of view. He had neighbors; there were poor persons living near him; there were day laborers who harvested his crops and built his new barns. One solution to the "problem" created by the bumper harvest was that he could have filled his old barns and then given away the surplus; holding the grain in the barn was not so that he would have something to eat in tough years, but so that he could sell it later, when there was no surplus and the prices were higher.[7] Also, notice the word for the rich man's property; Luke uses *chōra*, which normally is translated something like "district," rather than one of the normal words for a farm or a field. The rich man owns half the county, and so when his fields produce plentifully, it really is a problem. Where is he going to put all his stuff?

This is one of Luke's straightest jabs into the American solar plexus, and we are going to be tempted to dodge or deflect most of the blow. First sidestep: well, I'm not a rich man. I have a modest house, drive an old car, have my kids in public schools, and buy my clothes on sale from discount stores. I don't have money to buy lake houses or to invest in high-yield bonds. This is a dodge, because while we are not rich compared to the truly wealthy in our country, compared to much of the world we are. We are part of a nation that uses a disproportionate amount of the world's resources, and the fact that we can pay for it legally does not change greed into something virtuous. Our ability to pay keeps prices too high for the truly poor. Second sidestep: I give to charity. This is also a dodge, because it fails to address the real issue of greed. The rich man probably tithed, and part of that was set aside for the poor. But he had enough to feed all the hungry in his district stored up in his barns, more than he needed for his own subsistence, more even than he expected to get when he planted his crops. No doubt his old barns held enough to feed him and his household and enough to sell for a profit. Why not be satisfied with that, and give away the windfall?

When we hold the rich man in this parable against the rich man in the story about Lazarus, we can see the same emphasis on personal consumption and the same blindness to the needs of others. When we hold both of them up against Zacchaeus, or against the merciful Samaritan, we can see what behavior was expected. God's voice brings the parable to a tragic end. The rich man will die—well, we all die, so that is not necessarily a tragedy—and the things that he has worked hard to protect will be out of his control. Whose will they be? Will he leave behind an inheritance battle, like the one that introduced the parable? Will his property be confiscated by some greedy king or by a colonial power? Will there be a fire or a flood that ruins the goods stored? [Remorse]

The conclusion of the parable in v. 21 describes the rich man and his genus. The verb *thēsaurizō*, like the English word thesaurus, means to put things away or store them up; the one who does that for himself or herself and is not "rich towards God" is a fool. This is not about giving to religious causes or to the church, but about not accumulating money in the first place. Instead of being rich in accumulated things, we are directed to sell our possessions and give away the proceeds (12:33-34), and in that way put our affections and our efforts where God's heart is—with the poor. [Escaping the Lure of Avarice]

On Possessions, 12:22-34

"Don't worry," says Jesus to his disciples. These are men and women (8:1-3) who left homes, families, and professions to follow Jesus around Galilee, and are currently on the road to Jerusalem, where Jesus has already said he will be crucified. They are partly supported by the gifts of persons of substance who are members of the group (8:3), and partly supported by those to whom they minister, who provide them food and shelter (9:4; 10:7-9). They are carrying no bag for collecting contributions, so they cannot save up the bounty of good days to tide them over on the lean days (9:3; 10:4). They have no provisions—not even an extra tunic in case the weather turns cold or the one they are wearing gets ragged. "Don't worry," says Jesus—he is preaching to the choir, to one of the few groups of his followers who have taken him literally and seriously. We, on the other hand, can barely listen to this part of his teachings unless we find some loopholes. [Loopholes]

This is Q material, found in Matthew 6:19-21, 25-34, in Matthew's Sermon on the Mount. Luke's version of

Remorse

Remorse—is Memory—awake—
Her Parties all astir—
A Presence of Departed Acts—
At window—and at Door—

Its Past—set down before the Soul
And lighted with a Match—
Perusal—to facilitate—
And help Belief to stretch—

Remorse is cureless—the Disease
Not even God—can heal—
For 'tis His institution—and
The Adequate of Hell—

Emily Dickinson, 744, *The Complete Poems of Emily Dickinson*, ed. Thomas H. Johnson (Boston: Little, Brown, 1960).

Escaping the Lure of Avarice

My children, love of money leads to idolatry, because once they are led astray by money, they designate as gods those who are not gods. It makes anyone who has it go out of his mind. On account of money I utterly lost my children, and had it not been for the penitence of my flesh, the humility of my soul, and the prayers of my father, Jacob, I would have met death childless. But the God of my fathers, who is compassionate and merciful, pardoned me because I acted in ignorance.

Testament of Judah 19:1-4 (from 2d century BC).

Loopholes

A brother asked a certain old man, saying, "Wouldst thou have me keep two gold pieces for myself against some infirmity of the body?" The old man, seeing his thought, that he was wishful to keep them, said, "Even so." And the brother going into his cell was torn by his thoughts, saying, "Thinkest thou, did the old man tell me the truth or no?" And rising up he came again to the old man, in penitence, and asked him, "For God's sake tell me the truth, for I am tormented thinking on these two gold pieces." The old man said to him, "I saw that thy will was set on keeping them. So I bade thee keep them: but indeed it is not good to keep more than the body's need. If thou hadst kept the two gold pieces, in them would have been thy hope. And if it should happen that they were lost, how would God have any thought for us? Let us cast our thoughts upon God: since it is for Him to care for us."

Sayings of the Desert Fathers, xxii, in Helen Waddell, *The Desert Fathers* (Ann Arbor: University of Michigan Press, 1957), 86.

the sermon (6:20-49) also has plenty of material about possessions and charity, but Luke decided to put this section right after the parable of the rich fool as part of his Gospel-long anti-materialist theme. In the discussion that follows, we will sometimes note what Matthew has, not as a way of determining what was originally in Q, but as a way of highlighting Luke's emphatic advice on the issue of what Jesus' followers should do with their stuff.

Luke's chapter began by noting the crowds, stepping on each other as they tried to get near Jesus (12:1). Jesus ignored them at first, speaking instead to the disciples about the dangers of hypocrisy (12:1-12). Then, apropos of nothing, a member of the crowd asked Jesus to play probate judge and help settle an inheritance dispute; nope, says Jesus, and tells the parable of the rich fool to "them," which probably includes disciples as well as crowds. In v. 22, Jesus again teaches the disciples—not just the Twelve, but the larger group that has been traveling with him for some time, including men and women, and that he gave the authority to heal, to cast out demons, and to preach. The pushy, greedy crowds are in the background, still trampling each other, we suppose, and overhearing Jesus' teachings. And as Jesus refocuses on the disciples, he references the previous crowd parable with "On account of this, I say to you" (12:22).

Like the sermon on the plain, this section is built of small units with interlocking parallelism.

Don't worry,   with respect to your soul, what you may eat,
Nor   with respect to your body, what you may wear
For soul is more than food,
And body more than what's put on. (vv. 22b-23)

This four-line unit uses an ABAB pattern, repeating soul-eat//body-wear. The Greek word for soul, *psychē*, means the whole person, including the body—otherwise, it would make no sense to pair "soul" with "eat" and "food." Soul and body are two ways of thinking about what makes a live human. According to Genesis 2, God made the body out of the dirt and then breathed into it, making the whole thing—the air-filled clay-being—a living *nephesh*, the Hebrew equivalent of *psychē*. Even though food and clothing are necessary for sustaining life, a human is more.

The audience for this teaching, according to the narrative, are the disciples, but they have been living by these rules for some time. They may have needed a poverty booster shot, but it is more likely that the crowds, and Luke's audience listening in house churches and rented worship spaces, may have needed an inoculation.

Consider ravens:
They neither sow nor reap,
And God feeds them.
You are much more valuable than birds. (v. 24)

For the second time in this chapter the disciples are told that they are worth more to God than birds (see 12:7). Earlier it was sparrows, which were sold for food; in this verse, the disciples are compared to crows or ravens, which are unclean and may not be eaten (Lev 11:15). The early Christian *Epistle of Barnabas* says that "these are the only birds that do not procure their own food, but sit by idly, waiting to see how they might devour the flesh procured by others, being pestilent in their evil" (*Barn.* 10:4). Consider, then, how God takes care of these unclean, scavenging birds; they have no farms, they harvest no crops, and yet "God feeds them." Matthew's version of this saying has "the birds of the air" (Matt 6:26), so Luke either keeps (if "crows" was original to Q) or chooses a bird that his audience would not have found attractive. Crows—even crows!—God feeds them, as anyone who read their Bible would know (Ps 147:9; Job 38:41).[8] God gives these scavengers what they need to eat; do you think you count less with God than crows? [God Cares for the Birds]

God keeps up with the birds that you eat (12:7); God feeds the birds that you are not supposed to eat; you, who are sent out into the world as sheep among wolves (10:3), don't worry—God will take care of you. Why worry so much about sowing and reaping, like the rich fool whose huge estate and full barns passed out of his control in an instant?[9] But lest we try to dodge the point of the saying by making it a rich man's problem, we should recall that sowing and reaping were done by the poor, either by subsistence farmers on their own property or by day laborers on the farms of the wealthy. The images in the minds of Luke's audience were of peasants, like those in the Psalter illumination. This is not simply an exhortation to avoid conspicuous consumption, but a call to rely on God for everything.

Two Farm Workers

Two farm workers with a harrow, c.1300–c. 1340. From "The Luttrell Psalter," begun before 1340 for Sir Geoffrey Luttrell. Folio British Library, London, Great Britain. (Credit: HIP/Art Resource, NY)

God Cares for the Birds

Rain water was pouring off the children's faces. Katy's dress was stuck to her legs, and she had to keep pulling the cloth away from her skin. Louis's shoes went squelch squelch squelch when he walked. Katy's hair was slicked down on her head. They stood under the tree and listened to the rain fall through the leaves.

Katy pointed up into the boughs of the tree. She said, "See? I don't think they're waterproof." Louis looked up into the branches. His eyes took a minute to adjust, the day was so gloomy, and the shade was deep.

Then he saw them, the little birds. They were wild canaries, with greenish yellow feathers, and a fringe of brown, like little skirts. They were soaking wet. They had their eyes shut and their little bird shoulders hunched up against the weather . . . . Thirty or forty of them together, sitting in a row like children in their desks at school. . . .

The two children stood under the tree and looked at the wild birds above them.

Louis said, "Maybe God takes care of them."

Katy looked at him. She said, "I doubt it." (115–16)

[Later that night, when the rain gets worse rather than better, Katy talks Louis into sneaking out of their house to check on the birds.]

. . . Louis shined the light onto the wet ground beside them, near their feet. What he saw, he could scarcely believe. The rain-drenched canaries, all of them, thirty or more birds, lay all around them on the ground in puddles of water. They had been washed out of the tree by the rain. . . .

Katy said, "They weren't waterproof." (133–34)

[The children carry the birds home and spread them out on Katy's bed. Her bedspread has a pattern that reminds the kids of a meadow, so it seems appropriate. Katy promises to sleep without moving her legs all night. Next morning, Louis checks on them, and finds them alive, hopping around on the cloth meadow. He gets one bird to hop up on his hand.]

Louis turned slowly, slowly. He walked towards the open casement window. When he got there, he looked back at his sister.

Katy said, "Bye-bye."

Louis stuck his hand out the window and jiggled it. Suddenly, the bird's golden feathers rattled like crumpled paper, like dry leaves, like dry bones. The single bird, the wild canary lifted off Louis's hand. It sailed away, out, out into the morning light, far out from the house, beating its wings as if for dear life, or a celebration of the dearness of life, and then finally it landed in the branches of a flowering crepe myrtle bush.

As if on a signal, then, all the other birds rose up, too, only thirty or forty of them but as if there were a million, sudden and loud, up off the meadowlike comforter of Katy's bed, filling the room with their warm bodies, their gold color, their beating wings, and then they, too, sailed away, out the same window, all in a flurry of strong hearts and dropping feathers, so close to Louis's face that he believed he could smell them, their bodies washed with rain. (186)

Lewis Nordan, *The Sharp-Shooter Blues* (Chapel Hill NC: Algonquin Books, 1997).

Lewis Nordan (Credit: Barclay Burns)

But which of you by worry is able to add a cubit to his life's span? If then you are unable to do so little a thing, why worry about the rest? (vv. 25-26)

The word translated "cubit" is a measurement of length, originally measured from a man's elbow to the tip of his middle finger. In the first century, it was reckoned at about eighteen inches.[10] The word translated "life's span" really means either "height" or "a span of time."[11] Since adding one-and-a-half feet to one's height is no small feat, it makes more sense to add a metaphorical cubit to the length of one's life.

That one cannot increase one's life by worry, particularly by worrying over stuff, is obvious. The rich fool's internal mutterings over what he would do with his stuff did not make his life any longer. [George Carlin on "Stuff"] At the moment, Jesus is defining the problem that stuff creates and noting that worry is futile; just below, Jesus will address the solution to the problem.

> Consider lilies, how they grow;
> They neither toil nor spin,[12]
> But I tell you, not even Solomon in all his glory was clothed like one of these.
> So if God thus clothes the grass,
> Being in the field today
> And tomorrow thrown into the oven
> How much more you, little-faiths! (vv. 27-28)

The first unit paired soul/eat with body/clothe, and the second unit, on the ravens, explored the eating side of the parallel. Now we move from fauna to flora and from eating to wearing. The unit on lilies uses the same "how much more" logic as the unit on ravens, and likewise moves from specific (ravens/lilies) to general (birds/grass). Each unit uses two forms of work that the organism does not do, asserts that God takes care of them, and then assures the audience that God will do even more for them. But this unit introduces another element, the short-lived nature of the

George Carlin on "Stuff"

Actually this is just a place for my stuff, ya know? That's all, a little place for my stuff. That's all I want, that's all you need in life, is a little place for your stuff, ya know? I can see it on your table, everybody's got a little place for their stuff. This is my stuff, that's your stuff, that'll be his stuff over there. That's all you need in life, a little place for your stuff. That's all your house is: a place to keep your stuff. If you didn't have so much stuff, you wouldn't need a house. You could just walk around all the time.

A house is just a pile of stuff with a cover on it. You can see that when you're taking off in an airplane. You look down, you see everybody's got a little pile of stuff. All the little piles of stuff. And when you leave your house, you gotta lock it up. Wouldn't want somebody to come by and take some of your stuff. They always take the good stuff. They never bother with that crap you're saving. All they want is the shiny stuff. That's what your house is, a place to keep your stuff while you go out and get . . . more stuff!

Sometimes you gotta move, gotta get a bigger house. Why? No room for your stuff anymore.

George Carlin, "A Place for My Stuff," on *A Place for My Stuff* (CD; Atlantic, 1981).

George Carlin (Credit: Barclay Burns)

wildflowers, which connects it with the one just finished and with the parable of the rich fool.

The "lilies" are perhaps different sorts of "colorful, beautiful flowers that dot the Palestinian countryside in the spring; e.g., the scarlet anemone, the Easter daisy, the autumn crocus, ranunculi, even poppies."[13] King Solomon, legendarily impressive in all his regal finery (1 Kgs 10:4-5, 23-25), could not match them—nobody who has walked in an alpine meadow when all the wildflowers were blooming, or who strolled through woods where perennial flowers, shrubs, and trees are showing out, will call this hyperbole.

The image of blooming flowers shifts in v. 28 to grass growing in the field; the Greek word behind "field," *agros*, means a cultivated field, and if we thought "garden" or "farmland" then the sense would be clearer. While they bloom, the wildflowers are beautiful, even when they are blooming in the farmer's wheat field. But when time comes for planting, they are "grass," to be cut down, dried, and bundled as fuel for the bread-making ovens shared between households in the village. Here then is an image of something ephemeral, whose beauty, unrelated to its utility, is God's gift to humans. If God takes such care with them, how much more with you!

Hope

"Hope" is the thing with feathers—
That perches in the soul—
And sings the tune without the words—
And never stops—at all—

Emily Dickinson, 254, *The Complete Poems of Emily Dickinson*, ed. Thomas H. Johnson (Boston: Little, Brown, 1960).

The epithet "little-faith" appears often in Matthew but only here in Luke. While some interpret this as an indictment of the materialism of the audience, others see it as a sign of hope, a statement that the disciples have some faith.[14] Faith the size of a mustard seed is enough to uproot a tree, says Jesus (17:6), so a little faith is enough. [Hope]

So you must not seek what to eat or what to drink,
And you must not be haughty.
For all the nations of the world search for these things,
But your father knows that you need them.
But seek his kingdom, and these things will be added to you.
(vv. 29-31)

"Search" in v. 30 (*epizēteō*) is a more intense form of the verb "seek" in vv. 29 and 31 (*zēteō*). The verb in the second half of v. 29 is usually translated "worry," but the word literally means "be lifted up." Most assume that in context, "Don't worry" fits better,[15] but it would not explain Luke's choice of an unusual word. "Don't be haughty" would set up better, I believe, the advice that is to follow:

rather than seeking your own fortune, you must seek God's kingdom, which requires you to divest yourself of your possessions and accept what comes to you as God's gift. Greed is one obstacle to such an attitude, but so is pride.

Don't seek—since the verb tense is present, the meaning is "stop seeking."[16] Jesus' prohibition does not cover luxury items—stop buying sports cars, stop going to Aruba for spring break—but basic necessities. The disciples, who are the stated audience, have rearranged their lives so that they do not spend their days working for food, drink, clothing, and lodging. Instead, they are on the road spreading the good news of the kingdom of God, accepting the addition of "these things"—food, drink, shelter—from God by means of the hospitality of the persons to whom they minister. The fact that they are still standing there, after some indeterminate length of time moving around as itinerants, is Luke's narrative proof that Jesus' teaching is a way of life, not a path to starvation. The pushy, greedy crowds, jostling each other just out of camera range, need to hear this and to see the proof of it. [Diogenes the Cynic on Possessions]

Diogenes the Cynic on Possessions

To Apolexis, greeting. I have laid aside most of the things that weigh down my wallet, since I learned that for a plate a hollowed out loaf of bread suffices, as the hands do for a cup.

To Apolexis, greetings. I asked you about a dwelling. Thank you for undertaking to arrange one. But when I saw a snail, I found a house to keep off the wind. I mean the earthenware jug in the Metroon. So consider yourself discharged from this service and rejoice with me over my discovery of nature.

Abraham J. Malherbe, *The Cynic Epistles* (Atlanta: Scholars Press, 1977), 107–109.

> Do not be afraid, little flock, your father is well-pleased to give you
> the kingdom.
> Sell your stuff and give alms;
> Make yourselves purses that do not age,
> A treasure laid up in the heavens
> Where neither thief approaches nor moth destroys
> For where your treasure is,
> There will your heart be also. (vv. 32-34)

"Little flock" plays off "kingdom"—what use has a flock of sheep for a kingdom?; off "little-faiths"—even if their faith is small, they belong to the right shepherd, who can take care of them; and off "lambs in the midst of wolves" (10:3)—being part of a little flock can be dangerous. The disparity between a flock of sheep that needs only grass, water, and the protection of a shepherd, and a kingdom that requires taxes, bureaucracy, and an army is deliberate. Who wants to be a part of the kingdom of Rome? Their message is "pay your taxes and mind your own business, and we will refrain from squashing you." God, who gives the kingdom to sheep, requires no taxes, so the word is "Sell your stuff and give it to the poor."

For humans throughout history, but especially for Americans, this command is almost unbearable. For this reason, some commentators see the relationship between "sell your stuff" and "give alms" as a tension: "The first is divestment . . . . The second is generosity in almsgiving. In our culture, the latter has always been easier to consider than the first."[17] Early Christian interpreters like Clement of Alexandria argued that divestment alone does not prevent someone from being consumed by greed or pride:

> For . . . one, after ridding himself of the burden of wealth, may none the less have still the lust and desire for money innate and living; and may have abandoned the use of it, but being at once destitute of and desiring what he spent, may doubly grieve both on account of the absence of attendance, and the presence of regret.[18]

In addition, it is clear that complete divestment will allow the divestor to give generously to charity only so long as the proceeds from the sale of property hold out, and that a complete divestment would not provide anything for the maintenance of the divestor's family. Luke-Acts does, in fact, picture the disciples doing just exactly that—selling everything and relying on the charity of others for their support. When the number of disciples in Jerusalem grows, and when a famine hits Palestine, Christians from other parts of the world send money for relief of the poor. Acts also describes Paul and his associates working for a living in whatever city they minister. Paul himself admits that while Jesus expected ministers to be supported by those to whom they minister, he has done otherwise, for reasons he considers valid. Bottom line, then, the strategy of complete divestment and almsgiving, in Luke's understanding, was practiced by Jesus and his Galilean followers, but was not the general rule of Christian conduct.

All this is true, but it hardly then permits us to ignore the command. If we recognize that Luke understood it to have been obeyed literally only by a specific group for a specific mission, we must also take account of the double audience. Jesus' disciples, the stated audience, were living by these rules in order to bring the gospel to Palestine. But the crowds, and later generations of Christians who listen to these words read to them, must be willing to see our resistance to divestment for what it is. True, it seems impractical to us that large numbers of Christians should live this way. But we resist mostly because we like full purses and treasures laid up in our bank accounts.

Our hearts—meaning our wills, affections, and dispositions—will rest wherever our "treasure" is. If we define ourselves by our jobs, by our homes, by our club memberships, and by other status markers, then that is who we are, and we are no better off than the rich fool. If that is our self, our *psychē*, then we are lost. Seek the kingdom, says Jesus; don't worry about your stuff. The disciples, bless them, were doing that. We crowds, packed into the shadows because we want to hear Jesus but don't want to have to give up everything to follow him, have to decide whether we trust Jesus enough to obey.

Slave Parables, 12:35-48

This section strings together three slave parables:

The Master's Return, 12:35-38
The Burglar, 12:39-40
   Question of Audience, 12:41
The Faithful and Unfaithful Overseer, 12:42-46
   Implications and Concluding Proverb, 12:47-48

We cannot hear these parables in the way Luke's audience did, because we do not live with their cultural norms. Slavery as practiced in the first century differed in several respects from slavery that we know from the history of our own country. So in order to give us a shot at understanding what Luke had in mind, bear up, dear reader, for some background description of first-century slavery.

The Greek word *doulos* means a slave; English translations (for example, the NIV) sometimes translate it as "servant," which accurately describes what a slave does—serve a master, or a *kyrios*—but which inaccurately conveys the social reality of the slave. A servant, in our usage, is a paid employee, low on the social scale, to be sure, but not bound to the employer. Slavery was involuntary servitude, and so we should translate *doulos* as "slave." [Slaves in Luke]

The Greek word *diakonos*, from which we get the word "deacon," means a servant, and the verb form means to serve. The word describes a function or a job, not a state of being;

Slaves in Luke

AΩ Luke writes about slaves in several other places in the Gospel:

1:38, 42—Mary says she is the female slave of the Lord
7:2, 3, 8, 10—Jesus heals the slave of a centurion
14:17, 21, 22, 23—Slaves in the parable of the great banquet
15:22, 29—Slaves in the parable of the prodigal son
16:13—Saying: No one can be a slave to two masters
17:7-10—Teaching (parable?) about worthless slaves
19:13, 15, 17, 22—Slaves in the parable of the pounds
20:10, 11—Slaves in the parable of the wicked tenants
22:50—Slave of the high priest is wounded, and then healed

so a slave or a free person may "diakonize"—serve, or act as a servant—and because the word became the name for a specialized office among Christians, it can sometimes carry the sense of "minister." But even though Paul often called himself "slave of Jesus Christ," *doulos* never caught on as an official title or a name for a special congregational function; so when we read "slave" in Luke's parables, it is harder to hear an overtone of "minister." In 12:37, the master will "diakonize" the slaves; in 22:26-27, Jesus says he is among them as a *diakonos*, not as a *doulos*.

Slaves were property. According to Aristotle, they were part of the equipment of a household, living tools or living property. [Aristotle: What Is a Slave?] Slaves performed all sorts of duties for the household: farm and field labor, cooking and cleaning, child care and education, carrying messages and running errands, security, and personal or intimate duties (bathing, dressing, fixing hair). There was some division of labor between field hands and personal attendants, and in a large household there would often be a slave serving as *oikonomos* or overseer, who would manage the other slaves as well as the household finances. Some wealthy people preferred to hire rather than to purchase an overseer, and the handbooks on household/farm management speak of the ideal qualities of the overseer and his wife. [The Ideal Manager]

Aristotle: What Is a Slave?

Property is a part of the household, and the art of acquiring property is a part of the art of managing the household; for no man can live well, or indeed live at all, unless he be provided with necessaries. . . . Now instruments are of various sorts; some are living, others lifeless. . . . And so, in the arrangement of the family, a slave is a living possession, and property a number of such instruments; and the servant is himself an instrument which takes precedence of all other instruments.

423 I.4, trans. Benjamin Jowett in Richard McKeon, ed., *Introduction to Aristotle* (New York: Modern Library, 1947), 558.

The Ideal Manager

The Roman senator Cato, in his long treatise *On Agriculture*, described the perfect manager:

Let him keep strict discipline. Let religious festivals be observed. He must keep his hands off what doesn't belong to him, and look after what does properly. He must sort out disputes amongst the slaves. If anyone has done anything wrong, he must punish him fairly in proportion to the damage he has caused. The slaves must not be badly treated or suffer from cold or hunger. He must keep them hard at work to stop them getting involved in trouble or things that don't concern them. If the manager doesn't want them to make trouble, they won't. If he does let them make trouble, the master must not let him get away with it. He must reward good work, so that the others have an incentive to work well too. The manager must not be the kind of person who goes out a lot, he must always be sober, he must never go out to dinner. He must keep the slaves at their work and make sure that the master's orders are put into effect. He must not think that he is wiser than his master.

Cato, *On Agr.* 5, in Thomas Wiedemann, *Greek and Roman Slavery* (Baltimore: Johns Hopkins University Press, 1981), 148–49.

The wellborn counted on slave labor, but held certain negative ideas about slaves. First, with some notable exceptions, most wellborn or literate Greeks and Romans did not consider slaves to be truly or fully human. Many thought that there was a slavish type that could be recognized by appearance, and many considered the slave mentality to be animal, not human: "It is possible to make human beings more ready to obey you simply by explaining to them the advantages of being obedient;

but with slaves, the training considered to be appropriate to wild beasts is a particularly useful way of instilling obedience."[19]

Part of the training considered appropriate was corporal punishment. Most ancient writers who commented on how masters should deal with slaves advised their readers to discipline slaves, not "sparing the rod" if it was called for.

> The only girl we need is one who can weave, grind the meal, split the wood, work at wool, sweep the house, take her beatings, and cook the family's meals every day. That girl couldn't do any of this.[20]
>
> Let us consider how masters behave towards slaves of this sort [i.e., troublesome]. Is it not the case that they control any inclinations towards lechery by starving them? And stop them from stealing by locking up the places from which they might take things? Prevent them from running away by putting them in chains? Force the laziness out of them with beatings? Or what do you do when you find you have someone like that among your slaves? // I inflict every kind of punishment upon him—said Aristippos—until I can force him to serve properly.[21]

The ultimate threat for slaves was crucifixion—a messy and distasteful thing for the slave-owning population, but also considered necessary to be able to hold as a threat to keep slaves in line. "Slave owners weary of the effort [of flogging their slaves] could hire the services of professional torturers. An advertisement of one torture-and-execution business survives in an inscription from Puteoli, offering flogging and crucifixion as standard options for a flat, low rate."[22]
[Crucifixion as a Threat for Slaves]

Although people mostly agreed that slaves had to be beaten, they also recognized that treating them so did not increase the slaves' love and devotion to their masters. And since slaves were generally kept in the household, sleeping in small anterooms or in the halls (so that they would always be ready when needs arose), the threat of retaliatory violence was always in the minds of masters and mistresses:

> The slave-as-domestic-enemy expressed proverbial, gnomic wisdom circulating in the Greco-Roman milieu of ancient Christianity . . . "you may have as many enemies as you have slaves" (e.g., Seneca,

Crucifixion as a Threat for Slaves

Philocomasium (a young girl): You say that you saw me here in the house next door kissing, you rascal?

Palaestrio (a slave): You and some strange young man, he told me.

Sceledrus (another slave): Yes, I did say it, by heaven!

Philocomasium: It was me you saw?

Sceledrus: Yes, confound it! With my own eyes.

Philocomasium: You'll soon lose them, I daresay, since they see more than they see.

Sceledrus: Never, by heaven, will I be frightened out of having seen what I did see.

Philocomasium: I'm a stupid and foolish person to waste my breath on this idiot; by the powers, I'll punish him to perfection!

Sceledrus: Don't threaten me. I know the cross will be my tomb. That's where my ancestors lie, my father, my grandfather, my great-grandfather, my great-great-grandfather. You can't dig out these eyes of mine with your threats.

Plautus, *Mil. glor* (The Braggart Warrior) 363–73; in George E. Duckworth, ed., *The Complete Roman Drama* (New York: Random House, 1942), 1.562-63.

The Slave as Domestic Enemy

There is that proverb which originates from the same arrogant attitude, that we have as many enemies as we have slaves. They aren't our enemies unless we make them so. I shan't mention some other cruel and inhumane ways in which woe would be maltreating them even if they were dumb beasts instead of human beings—when, for instance, we lie down to dine, and someone has to clear up the vomit, while another stands at the bottom of the couch to remove the leavings of the drunken guests.

Seneca, *Moral Letters* 47.5, in Thomas Wiedemann, *Greek and Roman Slavery* (Baltimore: Johns Hopkins University Press, 1981), 233–34.

Epistle 47.5). The proverb pictured every slave a potential instigator of family betrayal and sedition, an "obvious" situation because of the full integration of slaves into ancient family life. The flip side of this proverbial wisdom celebrated its moral polarity—the "faithful slave" accepting the master's authority and point of view so fully as to endure torture and to give all, even life itself, to save the master's home.[23] [The Slave as Domestic Enemy]

We can only reconstruct the social standing of Luke's audience from clues in the narrative, and so cannot be dogmatic about the presence of slaves and slaveowners. Chances are, however, that Luke knew some Christians who owned slaves, some Christian slaves who served non-Christian masters, and some Christian masters who owned Christian slaves. Imagine, then, a wealthy Christian who owned a fine house and who hosted a regular Sunday worship service; let's call him Stephanas (see 1 Cor 16:17). Let's also imagine that at least one member of the congregation was one of Stephanas's employees or clients; let's name him Achaicus. Finally, let's imagine at least one of Stephanas's household slaves had been converted and regularly attended church services; in fact, let's imagine that his overseer, Fortunatus ("Lucky"), was a Christian. On the particular Sunday that this section of Luke is being read aloud to Stephanas's house church, the congregation is seated in the fine peristyle courtyard of the house. Stephanas, as befits his position as host and patron, is reclining on a dining couch; Achaicus is sitting on the ground with his back against one of the columns; Fortunatus is standing behind his master, ready to fetch him a cool drink or to begin serving the Eucharist when the time came for that part of the service.

Luke begins the parable of the master's return (12:35-38) with a quotation from Exodus 12:11 LXX: "Let your loins be belted up," which in Exodus means to tuck the long ends of your robe into your belt to leave your legs free for travel.[24] In Luke's scenario, however, the audience is to imagine preparing themselves for work, not travel; they are to think of themselves as slaves expecting the return of their master. They keep their work clothes on and the household lamps lit, even though the hour is late (v. 38), because they want to be ready, as soon as the master knocks at the door, to open it and welcome him home. Why? Because the master is returning from his wedding banquet, held at the home of his father-in-law, and he will be bringing his new bride, and the slaves' new mistress, to her new home.[25] "Blessed are those slaves whom the master, when he comes, finds watching." No doubt—and doubtless the inverse is also true, that any slave whom the master finds napping in the hallway will be in serious trouble.

But this parable has a happy ending: the narrator asks us to picture the master arriving home to a house full of ideal slaves who are hovering near the entry hall. [Good Slaves] The master brings his wife into the house; the slaves are ready to fly in and prepare whatever they request, anxious to make a good first impression. But instead, the master ties up his own long robe, tucks it in his belt, and orders/invites all the slaves to recline in the dining room. He then whips up a midnight repast and serves— "diakonizes"—all of them. It is such a bizarre image—what's the new wife doing in the meantime? Do the slaves feel embarrassed? Does the master have a clue about how to cook anything worth eating?

The image of the wedding banquet and bridegroom (5:34-35), Luke's audience knows, is a picture of the end of time and Jesus' return. That, plus the direct address in v. 35 would mean that all the audience, not just the slaves, are to take this as advice directed to them. We can imagine Stephanas and his peers resisting being put into servile roles; yes, we are disciples of Jesus, and maybe his *diakonoi*, his servants, but surely not his *douloi*, his slaves. And the master's behavior in v. 37 probably makes things worse for them, not better. The only times that masters served slaves were the days of the Saturnalia feasts, when the roles of slaves and masters were temporarily reversed, and the "slaves' holiday" on August 13.[26] No self-respecting master would otherwise act like a slave, particularly on his wedding night. Luke admits as much in 17:7-10, where the hard-working field slaves come to the house tired, but cannot eat until they have fed the master. On hearing this section, the wealthier members of Luke's audience may have wondered if Luke was trying to stir up trouble.

In fact, many commentators argue that the little vignette of 12:35-38 is designed to lampoon or to overturn the values upon which slavery rested. If the roles of master and slave can be interchanged, then in the kingdom of God—represented by the return

Good Slaves

This is your proof of a good slave who looks after his master's business, sees to it, gives it his care and consideration—when he watches over his master's business in his master's absence just as diligently as if he was present, or even more so. The fellow that's got his wits in the proper place ought to think more of his back than his gullet, more of his shanks than his belly [that is, he'll fear a beating more than he desires to steal food]. He'd better recollect how good-for-nothings, lazy, rascally fellows, are rewarded by their masters: whippings, shackles, work in the mill, exhaustion, famine, freezing stiff—these are the rewards of laziness. I'm badly afraid of such bad things, personally; that's why I've made up my mind to lead a good life rather than a bad one. . . . That's why I follow out master's orders, attend to them properly and sedately. . . . I must have a sense of fear, I must keep straight, so as to be on hand for master anywhere. (spoken by the loyal slave of a rascal)

Plautus, *Men.* 968–82.

of the bridegroom to his household—there is no real slavery at all.[27] Others are not so sure. The parable lumps all the hearers into the category of slave, urging them to wait expectantly for Jesus, and the effect of this rhetorical move on the audience may have been to make the non-slaves imagine what their slaves experienced. But Luke's argument, by praising the good slave, tends to support, rather than to undercut, the institution of slavery. Luke's good slave would have been anyone's good slave—if slaves expect to be treated well, they should work hard, stay vigilant, and keep their belts cinched for work. "Jesus' expectation that trustworthy slaves are waiting by the door for the master's return is thus entirely within the parameters of mandated servile labor."[28]

But there is more to consider. The parable of the burglar in vv. 39-40 takes the point of view of the master of the house *oikodespotēs*, is the *kyrios* in his role as head of everyone in the household, not just the slaves; the Latin equivalent is *paterfamilias*), and the slaves are left in the background. The parable takes a contrary-to-fact approach: if a householder could predict the moment a thief would arrive, he would prevent the burglary. Since he cannot, the point goes, he must be always vigilant. And so must you, says v. 40, since your Master, the Son of Man, will be arriving at some unpredictable moment. But there is a subtext to this little drama, because no householder would actually be the one to keep watch through the night against burglars; that was a slave's job. In fact, there were cases where a master was murdered, and all the household slaves crucified for failure to stop the crime. [Slave Punishments for the Master's Death] The parable of the burglar comes to the same conclusion as the parable of the master's return—since you don't know when Jesus will return, you have to keep watch constantly—but reverses the rhetorical strategy. The master's return parable makes everyone a slave, waiting for Jesus the Master, while the burglar parable makes everyone a householder taking on a slave's job while they wait for Jesus the Thief. [Jesus as a Thief]

Peter asks the question Luke's audience must have been asking by this point: Jesus, who are you addressing? Was this parable aimed at the disciples, who were neither slaves nor slave owners, or at everyone—that is, does this parable really address the Gospel's audience, sitting in someone's house listening to it read aloud?

Slave Punishments for the Master's Death

"Another requirement of Roman law, formulated in a Senate Recommendation of 10 A.D., . . . was that if an owner was killed, all the slaves within earshot at the time had to be interrogated under torture and executed." According to the Digest (ed. AD 533), the reason behind this recommendation was that "no household could be safe if slaves were not forced by the threat of danger to their own lives to protect their masters against enemies both internal and external."

Thomas Wiedemann, *Greek and Roman Slavery* (Baltimore MD: Johns Hopkins University Press, 1981), 169.

By way of answer, Jesus the *kyrios* tells a third parable, the faithful and unfaithful overseers: "Who then is the faithful, wise *oikonomos* [overseer], whom the *kyrios* will appoint over his household slaves for the purpose of distributing rations at the proper time?" As noted earlier, an overseer was sometimes a slave, sometimes not; this parable imagines a slave (vv. 43, 45 use the word *doulos*) appointed over food distribution in the household. The parable is a "two ways" teaching, like Psalm 1: there is a right way and a wrong way, a faithful, wise way and an unfaithful way. The wise, faithful overseer does what

he is appointed to do, and is rewarded for his faithfulness with . . . more work! If the master finds him doing well, the master then puts him in charge of "all his stuff"; still a slave, but higher up on the servile pecking order. The unfaithful slave deludes himself that because the master is "taking a while to come" he can get away with some high living, so he begins to "beat the male and female slaves, and to eat and to drink and to get drunk." Slaves who forget their station in life and act like fools are standard fare in ancient fiction, comedic drama, and satirical poetry, and the audience knows what to expect. There will be an accounting—the slave's foolish behavior will be discovered—and a severe punishment. Luke and Matthew both have the same word, *dichotomeō*, which means to cut in two or to dismember.[29]

Verses 47-48 read like a discussion of some of the implications of the parable's terrible ending: "The slave who knew the master's wishes but did not prepare or act according to his wishes will be beaten severely. But the one who did not know and acted in a manner worthy of blows will be beaten a little." In the first place, these verses moderate the "dismember" of v. 46; beatings are bad enough, but having one's eye gouged out for punishment is worse. [Injuries Resulting from Beatings of Slaves] In the second, the verses qualify the punishment by intent; the worst punishments are reserved for those who deliberately disobey. But wait a minute—nobody who heard these verses read aloud could claim not to know, which pushes

---

Jesus as a Thief

AΩ 1 Thess 5:2: For you yourselves know very well that the day of the Lord will come like a thief in the night.

2 Pet 3:10: But the day of the Lord will come like a thief, and then the heavens will pass away with a loud noise, and the elements will be dissolved with fire, and the earth and everything that is done on it will be disclosed.

Rev 3:3: Remember then what you received and heard; obey it, and repent. If you do not wake up, I will come like a thief, and you will not know at what hour I will come to you.

Gos. Thom. 103: Jesus said: Blessed is the man who knows in which part of the night the robbers will come in, so that he will rise and collect his [domain?] and gird up his loins before they come in.

Injuries Resulting from Beatings of Slaves

If a man adheres to the practice of never striking any of his slaves with his hand, he will be less likely to succumb [to a fit of anger] later on, even in circumstances most likely to provoke anger. . . . There are other peope who don't just hit their slaves, but kick them and gouge out their eyes and strike them with a pen if they happen to be holding one. I have seen someone strike his slave in the eye while under the influence of anger with one of the reeds we use to write with.

Galen, *The Diseases of the Mind* 4, in Thomas Wiedemann, *Greek and Roman Slavery* (Baltimore MD: Johns Hopkins University Press, 1981), 180.

everyone listening to the Gospel into the "knowing" category, eligible for the maximum sentence.

Notice how Luke has manipulated labels in this parable trifecta:

Verses 35-36: Be like slaves waiting for their master
Verses 37-38: Watchful slaves will be rewarded by having their
                       master serve them
Verses 39-40: Be like an alert householder who watches all night
                       (like a faithful slave)
Verses 42-44: Be like a wise, faithful overseer, who is rewarded with
                       more responsibility
Verses 45-48: Don't be like the unfaithful overseer, who is beaten

In v. 41, Peter wants to know who is in the crosshairs with these parables. We have imagined a typical audience sitting in a house church, listening to Luke being read aloud; that audience probably included owners, clients, and slaves. Stephanas, the host of this house church, is lord, *kyrios*, to his slaves and house master, *oikodespotēs*, to his family, clients, and slaves. The first parable makes him imagine himself as a slave waiting for his Lord Jesus to return; will he be alert and on task when Jesus arrives? The second parable puts Stephanas in his traditional role, but uncomfortably so, because he is asked to imagine himself still doing a slave's job of guarding the house while the rest of the household sleeps. The third parable asks him to imagine doing Fortunatus's job either well or poorly, and either being rewarded with more work or punished severely. While the parables assume the values of the dominant culture, they also pull and push the hearers into unaccustomed roles—a sort of "walk a mile in my shoes" strategy for getting the well-born hearers to think about what they believe and how they live. The picture of the unfaithful overseer may have been the most uncomfortable for Stephanas and his peers, because the slave is punished for acting like a master—eating and drinking to excess and beating the slaves, all of which were considered the prerogatives of the *kyrios*. Why is this behavior right for one class of people and wrong for another?

The more problematic consideration is how these parables work for the slaves in the audience. None of them take masters to task for inhumane treatment of slaves. The good slave—the attentive, wise, hard-working slave—gets rewarded, but not manumitted, while the bad slave who imitates his master gets beaten and/or mutilated. These parts of the parables simply describe the way life was, so far as we can tell, for many slaves of the first century. While the rhetorical strategy I've described above may have been intended to make the masters in the audience face up to the way they lived, we must admit that it is a subtle strategy, and that unless everyone knew this was supposed to be ironic, the parables would more likely help to reinforce prevailing cultural norms.

Compare, for example, Paul's strategy in 1 Corinthians 1:18-31. He writes, "Not many of you were wise by human standards, not many influential [lit., powerful], not many well-born. But God chose what is foolish in the world's opinion in order to shame the wise; God chose what is weak, according to the world, to shame the influential; God chose what is low-born and trashy, according to the world, even things that don't count, in order to knock down The Way Things Are" (author's translation,1:26-28). Here is a much more direct version of the same rhetorical move Luke used: Paul pushes everyone, even wealthy, influential, highborn people (of which there were some in the Corinthian church) into the same low-status, illiterate, no-count box. Paul's aim was to get them to stop fighting each other and to concentrate on what held them together. Perhaps Luke's motives were similar.

There are also other ecclesiastical overtones for these parables. Peter's question in v. 41 reminds us that the apostles in Acts, when faced with a complaint about the distribution of food, refused to take responsibility for it, passing it off to another group of church leaders (Acts 6:1-6). Scott Spencer argues that Luke's language there, when connected with these parables and with Jesus' self-definition as *diakonos* at the Last Supper, indicates Luke's disappointment with the Twelve: ". . . their reluctance to become personally involved in table-service suggests that they still have not fully accepted Jesus' holistic model of ministry."[30] These parables, especially that of the faithful and unfaithful overseer, have served as cautionary tales for church leaders for generations.

There are also christological implications from these parables. Jesus, whose return has been expected since the first generation of believers, has been delayed for quite some time. His return is described in three different images. In the first, he is the returning Master, but he acts like no master would, erasing the distinction between master and slave as he serves the whole household. In the second, he is a Thief whose return is unexpected and, to some degree, to be feared. That healthy dose of worry—will he show up today?—is supposed to keep us looking out the window. In the third, he is again a returning Master, but in this case he follows the cultural norms of the first century. He rewards faithful service with greater responsibility, and he punishes laziness and usurpation of status with beatings and torture. In both the first and third parables, the whole church is a slave of the Lord Jesus. If we follow his rules, then in the kingdom that results, the Lord Jesus serves us. But if we don't—if we act like masters in the wide world, terrorizing those whose wealth or power or education put them below us in status—then we can expect no sympathy from the Lord on the day of judgment.

Throwing Fire, Discerning Justice, 12:49-59

"One could do worse than be a swinger of birches," said Robert Frost,[31] and Jesus' choice of professions—fire-thrower and dissension-creator—does indeed sound worse. In v. 49, he sounds like an arsonist; in vv. 51-53 he is a home-wrecker, deliberately setting family members against each other. In v. 49a, he sighs as he longs for the conflagration to begin; in v. 50, the stress of waiting is torture. Yes, we thought on the basis of the angels' song that he was to bring peace, not division, to the earth (2:14), but now we find him self-described as an agitator. Jesus sounds a bit like Hazel Motes [Hazel Motes], Flannery O'Connor's evangelist for the Church Without Christ, or like the prophet Jeremiah: "I am now making my words in your mouth a fire, and this people wood, and the fire shall devour them" (Jer 5:14). [Jesus as Elijah]

Martin Luther King Jr.'s famous "Letter from the Birmingham City Jail" presents a reasoned argument for the necessity and utility of being a fire-thrower. Jailed for participating in unlawful demonstrations against discriminatory policies and the culture of violence that upheld them, Dr. King received a letter from a group of liberal white clergymen who scolded him for acting as an outside agitator, for provoking the police and civic leaders, and for being impatient. Here are selections from his rebuttal letter, setting out why he believed his role as agitator was absolutely necessary:

Hazel Motes

"Church of Christ!" Haze repeated. "Well, I preach the Church Without Christ. I'm member and preacher to the church where the blind don't see and the lame don't walk and what's dead stays that way . . . . I'm going to take the truth with me wherever I go," Haze called. "I'm going to preach it to whoever'll listen to me at whatever place." (60)

Flannery O'Connor. *Three: Wise Blood, A Good Man is Hard to Find, The Violent Bear it Away* (New York: Signet, 1962).

Martin Luther King, Jr.

(Credit: Barclay Burns)

Jesus as Elijah

Casting fire upon the earth is only one of many parallels between Jesus and the famous Israelite prophet Elijah:

In 1 Kgs 17:8-24, Elijah helps a widow who gave him hospitality and raises her son from the dead; in Luke 7:11-17, Jesus raises the only son of a widow

In 1 Kgs 18:20-40, Elijah confronts the prophets of Baal (who serve King Ahab, whose throne is in Samaria), bringing fire down from heaven to prove God is real, and then kills them all; in Luke 9:51-56, Jesus refuses to bring fire down on the Samaritans, but also (12:49) believes he has come to cast fire on the earth

In 1 Kgs 19:1-3, Queen Jezebel warns Elijah that she will kill him if she catches him; in Luke 13:31-33, the Pharisees warn Jesus that Herod Antipas wants to kill him. Elijah flees;

Jesus continues on his journey, confident that he can only die in Jerusalem at the appointed time.

In 1 Kgs 19:11-18, Elijah receives an epiphany on a mountain; in Luke 9:28-36, Jesus receives Elijah and Moses on a mountain, and Jesus becomes the epiphany for the disciples.

In 1 Kgs 19:19-21, Elijah calls Elisha to be his disciple. Elisha at first wants to say farewell to his family, but then cuts all ties and follows him. In Luke 9:57-62, Jesus makes plain to three prospective disciples that following him means abandoning family

In 1 Kgs 21:17-29, Elijah pronounces doom on Ahab and Jezebel, which later comes to pass (1 Kgs 22:29-40; 2 Kgs 9:30-37); in Luke 13:35 (and other places as well), Jesus pronounces doom on Jerusalem.

You are exactly right in your call for negotiation. Indeed, this is the purpose of direct action. Nonviolent direct action seeks to create such a crisis and establish such creative tension that a community that has constantly refused to negotiate is forced to confront the issue. It seeks so to dramatize the issue that it can no longer be ignored. . . . we must see the need of having nonviolent gadflies to create the kind of tension in society that will help men to rise from the dark depths of prejudice and racism to the majestic heights of understanding and brotherhood. . . .

We know through painful experience that freedom is never voluntarily given by the oppressor; it must be demanded by the oppressed. Frankly, I have never yet engaged in a direct action movement that was "well-timed," according to the timetable of those who have not suffered unduly from the disease of segregation. For years now I have heard the words "Wait!" It rings in the ear of every Negro with a piercing familiarity. This "Wait" has almost always meant "Never."

. . . I had also hoped that the white moderate would reject the myth of time. . . . It is the strangely irrational notion that there is something in the very flow of time that will inevitably cure all ills. Actually time is neutral. It can be used either destructively or constructively. . . . We will have to repent in this generation not merely for the vitriolic words and actions of the bad people, but for the appalling silence of the good people. . . .

You spoke of our activity in Birmingham as extreme. At first I was rather disappointed that fellow clergymen would see my nonviolent efforts as those of the extremist. . . . But as I continued to think about the matter I gradually gained a bit of satisfaction from being considered an extremist. Was not Jesus an extremist in love—"Love your enemies, bless them that curse you, pray for them that despitefully use you." Was not Amos an extremist for justice—"Let justice roll down like waters and righteousness like a mighty stream." Was not Paul an extremist for the gospel of Jesus Christ—"I bear in my body the marks of the Lord Jesus."[32]

We must investigate, then, exactly why Jesus wants the fire to start—what it will accomplish, why he wants it to begin soon, and why creating division is necessary.

This is an odd collection of verses. The lectionaries bury them deep in ordinary time and stop at v. 56,[33] but the verses are held together by the theme of judgment, and so this commentary will drive on to the end of the chapter. There are three distinct movements in this cluster:

12:49-53—Jesus' Mission and Division in Households
12:54-56—Reading the Heavens
12:57-59—Settling the Case

Some of the material sounds like verses found in Matthew but not in Mark, and so is usually assigned to Q, but Luke's wording differs substantially from Matthew's, and v. 50 sounds more like Mark 10:38 than anything in Matthew.

Verses 49-51 are connected by complicated parallel structures. Look at how the first parts of vv. 49 and 50 match up, preserving the order of the verses in Greek:

49a: Fire   I came to cast   upon the earth
50a: Baptism   I have to be baptized

The word order sets up "fire" and "baptism" as emphatic and as parallel, but the rest of the half-verses contrast, since "I came to cast" describes something Jesus will do and "I have to be baptized" something that will happen to Jesus. Both words are linked in the person of John the Baptist, who baptized in water in order to get people ready for the fire of the Day of the Lord. "The one mightier than I is coming," said John, "who will baptize with Holy Spirit and fire . . . the chaff he will burn with unquenchable fire." This fire of God's judgment Jesus refused to call down on the inhospitable Samaritans (9:51-55), but he threatens a fate worse than Sodom's for those who refuse to accept the preaching of the seventy-two (10:12). For all the threats, however, the only person in Luke consigned to the fires of judgment is Dives the rich man,

who fails to help Lazarus and winds up in torment in flames
(16:24). Fire, then, is most naturally associated with God's judgment of the Last Day, and through John, baptism can also be so
linked. [Baptism]

Notice the last halves of both verses:

| 49b: | and how | I wish that | already | it were blazing |
| 50b: | and how | I am tormented[34] | until | it has been completed |

Both of these half-verses note that the accomplishment Jesus seeks
will be brought about by God. He has been sent to initiate the fire
of God's judgment, but he must wait until God
says it is time. His baptism is yet to be accomplished, and knowing that it is on the horizon
puts him under some stress.

At this point, Luke's readers—modern and
ancient—may protest that Jesus' baptism was
narrated in 3:21; what baptism awaits him in
the future? The strong verb "tormented" would
suggest that baptism here functions as a
metaphor for Jesus' death,[35] but how would
readers guess that, unless they were familiar with
Mark 10:38—a text Luke probably had but
chose to omit? John's baptism, according to
Luke's record of John's preaching in 3:7-17, was
to rescue people from the final judgment of God. If baptism is
being used here as a parallel image for God's judgment, then Jesus
is expecting to experience it as well—perhaps through his death, if
we interpret it as part of the eschatological woes preceding the
kingdom's coming, or perhaps through his own role in baptizing
people in Spirit and fire.[36]

Verse 51 is linked both to vv. 49-50 and to verses 52-53:

| Do you think | I came to give | peace in the earth? |
| No, I tell you, | but rather | division. |

"Peace in the earth" is an antithetic parallel to "fire . . . upon the
earth," and "I came to give" and "I came to cast" are synonymous
parallels. His fire-casting mission will not bring peace, but division.
Verses 52-53 elaborate, using language drawn from Micah 7:6
(LXX). In Micah's description, the disrespect shown by younger to
elder is part of the corruption of society, part of the prophet's

Baptism

"Have you ever been Baptized?" the
preacher asked.

"What's that?" he murmured.

"If I Baptize you," the preacher said, "you'll be
able to go to the Kingdom of Christ. You'll be
washed in the river of suffering, son, and you'll go
by the deep river of life. Do you want that?"

"Yes," the child said, and thought, I won't go
back to the apartment then, I'll go under the river.

"You won't be the same again," the preacher
said. "You'll count."

Flannery O'Connor, "The River," in *The Complete Stories of
Flannery O'Connor* (New York: Farrar, Straus, and Giroux, 1971),
157–74; quote from 168.

analysis of the reasons for God's judgment. But Luke's Jesus presents this sort of division as the consequence of his ministry. Certainly this was true in Luke's day, where conversions to Christianity divided households. Paul, in 1 Corinthians 7:12-16, addresses the anxieties created by marriages between Christians and non-Christians. His advice, if we can read between the lines, seems to imply that some believers wondered whether they should, on religious grounds, divorce their non-Christian spouses, while others, whose non-Christian spouse wanted the separation, had the emotional trauma of divorce complicated by the knowledge that Jesus' teachings prohibited it. [Jesus, the Author of Discord]

Jesus, the Author of Discord

Are we to believe that he has commanded discord within families? How is he our peace, who has made both one? How does he himself say, "My peace I give to you, my peace I leave with you," if he has come to separate fathers from sons and sons from fathers by the division of households? . . . He does not say children should reject a father but that God is to be set before all. . . . You are not forbidden to love your parents, but you are forbidden to prefer them to God.

Ambrose, *Exp. Luc.* 7.134-36, cited in Arthur A. Just Jr., ed., *Luke* (ACCS: NT, vol. 3; Downer's Grove IL: Intervarsity Press, 2003), 218–19.

The kingdom is coming, and with it there is both judgment on sinners and separation of believers from nonbelievers. Jesus' words describe this as both something he wished were already done and over and as an experience of pain that cannot be anticipated happily. So if the course of his actions carried such awful consequences or collateral damage, why would he want to push forward? Why not act in the way that would preserve peace, rather than deliberately disturb the peace at such a cost? Again, Dr. King:

> In your statement you asserted that our actions, even though peaceful, must be condemned because they precipitate violence. But can this assertion be logically made? Isn't this like condemning the robbed man because his possession of money precipitated the evil act of robbery? . . . Isn't this like condemning Jesus because his unique God-consciousness and never-ceasing devotion to his will precipitated the evil act of crucifixion?
>
> You deplore the demonstrations that are presently taking place in Birmingham. But I am sorry that your statement did not express a similar concern for the conditions that brought the demonstrations into being. . . . Birmingham is probably the most thoroughly segregated city in the United States. Its ugly record of police brutality is known in every sector of this country. Its unjust treatment of Negroes in the courts is a notorious reality. There have been more unsolved bombings of Negro homes and churches in Birmingham than any city in this nation. These are the hard, brutal, and unbelievable facts . . . .[37]

So, the argument goes, actions must be taken to force the unjust society to see, clearly, its own injustice. Dr. King, like Jesus, cast fire on the earth, but did not take up the sword against evil; it is interesting that Matthew's version of the saying in Luke 12:51 reads, "Do not think that I have come to bring peace to the earth; I have not come to bring peace, but a sword" (Matt 10:34). Luke's Jesus will not use that bold metaphor, but speaks more prosaically of "dissension," removing any possibility that Jesus' saying could justify taking up arms in Jesus' name.

In v. 54, Jesus turns for the final time in this chapter to face the crowds. His attention has been divided between disciples and crowds. In 12:1, he notices the crowds but speaks to disciples; in 12:13, a member of the crowd hollers out, and Jesus tells a parable in response, but then turns back to disciples in 12:22. At 12:41, Peter wonders whether the slave parables are meant for the disciples or for everyone. So we assume that 12:49-53 is meant to be directed at the disciples and 12:54-59 to the crowds. But as usual, these categories are more fluid than that; even when he talks to one group, the other is present and is meant to overhear his words.

Verses 54-56 give a couple of examples of popular weather forecasting. Clouds in the west, coming in from the Mediterranean, mean rain; winds from the south, from the Arabian desert, mean a really hot day. Good rules of thumb, according to people who know Palestinian weather patterns.[38] If most know how to interpret these things, then why not how to interpret "this time"? Calling them "hypocrites" implies that they do know, or could know—they have the weather eye but choose not to use it to make the right choices based on what is here now.[39] Why are the crowds not as disturbed about the present moment as Jesus is? Answer: they do not recognize how close is the kingdom and its judgment, or they are blind to the injustices that demand the kingdom's arrival, or both. Again, Dr. King:

> The contemporary church is often a weak, ineffectual voice with an uncertain sound. It is so often the arch-supporter of the status quo. Far from being disturbed by the presence of the church, the power structure of the average community is consoled by the church's silent and often vocal sanction of things as they are. But the judgment of God is upon the church as never before. If the church of today does not recapture the sacrificial spirit of the early church, it will lose its authentic ring, forfeit the loyalty of millions, and be dismissed as an irrelevant social club.[40]

Luke addresses the "hypocrites" section to the crowds, but we must not forget about the disciples, standing close to him, listening to him speak. If the church acts like the crowds—if there is no separation between the values of the world and the commitment of Jesus' followers—then Jesus' polemic falls on the nearer audience as well.

The final section in this cluster begins with the question of discernment: "Why can you [all] not judge righteousness for yourselves?" Some commentators believe that 12:58-59 is a parable,[41] while others treat them as straightforward advice. In either case, the setting is a dispute between two parties, rather than an arrest, and so "judge" in v. 57 is a bit of a pun or irony—judge for yourselves what is right, or else the judge may throw you in the pokey. What is right is reconciliation (the verb *apallassō* had the root meaning of "release," and used in the passive it can mean "to settle a matter with an adversary"[42]) rather than insisting on one's day in court.

Does this advice to settle matters, to compromise, pull in the opposite direction from the two previous sections depicting Jesus as a no-compromise fire-thrower? Perhaps; one could understand it as a pragmatic section balancing the two idealistic sections that came first. Throw the fire and endure the division, because the time is close and the day of judgment at hand. But in real life, one has to negotiate and compromise—maybe that was it. Or maybe correctly interpreting "this time," as v. 56 urges the reader to do, also means knowing who the Judge is in v. 58. Some suggest that the advice in vv. 58-59 is "Get right with God now, while you are still on the road, because there will come a point when it is too late."[43]

These are both plausible attempts to connect these verses to their context. A third would reach back into the chapter and notice all the ways the author considers possessions a danger to the believer:

• 12:13-21: The rich fool—life is more than piling up possessions, and those who are not rich toward God are acting like fools.
• 12:22-31: Don't worry about possessions; consider the lilies and the crows, and trust God to give you what you need.
• 12:32-34: What you need is the kingdom of God; sell everything else and sell out for the kingdom.
• 12:41-48: The faithful and unfaithful overseer—don't get cocky, acting like a rich man, but remember that you are a slave awaiting the return of your owner.

The little narrative in vv. 58-59 imagines a court case involving debts or damages; the verdict goes against the accused, who is imprisoned until he can hand over "the last penny" (a *lepton* was 1/128th of a denarius). The accused cannot or will not pay, but the fact that he is jailed, rather than sold into slavery, implies that there are assets to be sold or relatives or a patron with deep pockets who can step forward and pay his way out of jail. [Debt-slavery] This passage then—whether we consider it a parable or non-parabolic teaching—imagines the audience in the position of a person of means that he will not admit, involved in a lawsuit that he will not settle, facing the consequences of holding out for a victory that he will not gain. All the advice of the chapter is relevant: sell your possessions and seek the kingdom; recognize that the kingdom is very close and that your only real hope is to rely on God's mercy; when you are arrested, rely on the Holy Spirit and not on the courts. What if the man, on his way to court, simply gave the accuser what he was asking for? His possessions would take a hit, but what does that matter to the disciple who is living according to Jesus' teachings?

Once again, Dr. King's experience is instructive and illustrative:

Then came the opportunity last September to talk with some of the leaders of the economic community. In these negotiating sessions certain promises were made by the merchants—such as the promise to remove the humiliating racial signs from the stores. On the basis of these promises Rev. Shuttlesworth and the leaders of the Alabama Christian Movement for Human Rights agreed to call a moratorium on any type of demonstrations. As the weeks and months unfolded we realized that we were the victims of a broken promise. The signs remained. . . . So we had no alternative except that of preparing for direct action, whereby we would present our very bodies as a means of laying our case before the conscience of the local and national community. We were not unmindful of the difficulties involved. So we decided to go through a process of self-purification. We started having workshops on nonviolence and repeatedly asked ourselves the questions, "Are you able to accept blows without retaliating?" "Are you able to endure the ordeals of jail?"[44]

Debt-slavery

Ancient Roman law allowed for a person to be sold into slavery for debt. Once a court decision about a debt was final, the debtor had thirty days to pay up or be imprisoned; once jailed, the debtor had another sixty days to arrange for payment. If at the end of the imprisonment they nor any relative or helper could pay, they could either be executed or sold into slavery, but only "across the Tiber"—that is, outside Roman territory (Table 3 of the Twelve Tables, cited in Lewis and Reinhold, *The Republic*, vol. 1 of *Roman Civilization* [New York: Columbia University Press, 1951], 103–104).

The historian Livy reports that this was changed in 326 BC because of a single case of extraordinary cruelty by a master against a recently enslaved young man:

Because of the unrestrained brutality of a single man, the powerful chains of debt were broken off on that day; the Consuls were ordered to propose to the popular assembly that no one should be held in chains or imprisoned (except those who had committed a crime, until they had paid compensation); and that the borrower's property, but not his body, should be subject to distraint for loans. So debt-bondsmen were set free, and it was forbidden for anyone to be made a bondsman in the future.

However, these laws applied to Roman citizens only, and would not have applied to citizens of other realms or to foreigners living in Rome.

Livy, *History* 8.28, in Thomas Wiedemann, *Greek and Roman Slavery* (Baltimore MD: Johns Hopkins University Press, 1981), 41.

Luke's audience, we suspect, is no more excited about the prospects of jail than we would be, and is likely to have resisted selling possessions, arguing that doing so makes life unacceptably insecure. The chapter's final vignette can then function both as a warning—if you want to hold on to your money, you may be jailed anyway—and as an exhortation—make up your mind that you will rely only on God, not on your money or your wealthy patrons.

In another place, after telling the story of the Birmingham experience in much more detail, Dr. King writes of his future hopes for the city, a reformation that he and other fire-throwers made possible by laying down their lives:

> Today Birmingham is by no means miraculously desegregated. There is still resistance and violence. The last-ditch struggle of a segregation governor still soils the pages of current events and it is still necessary for a harried president to invoke his highest powers so that a Negro child may go to school with a white child in Birmingham. But these factors only serve to emphasize the truth that even the segregationists know: The system to which they have been committed lies on its deathbed. The only imponderable is the question of how costly they will make the funeral.
>
> I like to believe that Birmingham will one day become a model in southern race relations. I like to believe that the negative extremes of Birmingham's past will resolve into the positive and utopian extreme of her future; that the sins of a dark yesterday will be redeemed in the achievements of a bright tomorrow. I have this hope because, once on a summer day, a dream came true. The city of Birmingham discovered a conscience.[45]

CONNECTIONS

"I did not have the grace or fortitude to be a servant," writes the narrator in Alice Munro's "Hired Girl."[46] In this story of a country girl who takes on a summer job cooking, ironing, and cleaning for a well-to-do family, the narrator wrestles with status issues. The daughter tells her, "You're pretty, but it doesn't count because you're the maid,"[47] and the mom lets her know, quickly and firmly, that she will eat by herself in the kitchen rather than with the family. The narrator's reactions to this are complicated. Sometimes she exaggerates the poverty that led her to this kind of work; once she remarks that her family used hired women, too; most often she holds her tongue and does the dialogue in her head.

In this chapter Luke may use a similar rhetorical strategy to get his audience to think about the issues of money and status. His central conviction is hard to swallow: "Strive for the kingdom . . . it is your Father's good pleasure to give" it to you; sell everything else and give it away. Doesn't your Father feed the birds and clothe the wildflowers? And what do possessions do for you anyway? Even if you had so much that you had to build ever-bigger storehouses, does that add to your life or increase your status with God—the only status that matters?

We know all that, just as truly as Luke's audience knew it. It wasn't news in Jesus' day. Read Proverbs, read the prophets, read Ecclesiastes: money won't make you happy, possessions drag you down, life is more than the struggle to accumulate. In the Greco-Roman world, the Cynics and Stoics taught the same things. It wasn't news, it wasn't hard to understand, but people in Luke's day found it just as hard to live by those principles as we do.

So Luke uses a series of slave parables that, like Munro's story, put us behind the eyes of a servant, trying things on for size. What does it feel like to be a slave waiting for the master to come back at any moment? What would it be like to serve a master who would take a slave's role and do the serving? What would it feel like to be a slave caught up by the desire for the master's wealth, caught out by the master's sudden return, and then beaten within an inch of his life? By putting the audience in various roles—slave waiting for a master, master guarding his house, and slave overseeing the household work—Luke may have intended to start conversations about the values that underlay his world. Whatever Luke's intent, it took a long, long time for Christians ever to come to the conclusion that slavery was simply immoral and unchristian. This should make us suspicious of our own blind spots: what is there about our current practice that will make our grandchildren ashamed? Where will they shake their heads about us, saying, "Why didn't they just say it was wrong and stop doing it?"

Jesus comes as a fire-starter, he says, and he will set people at odds with each other. Dr. King's "Letter from Birmingham City Jail" is both a descriptive account of how this works—how a prophet who calls for change will inevitably divide God's people— and a rear-view mirror showing us one of those now-obvious blind spots. Of course segregation was wrong; of course it needed to change sooner rather than later. What were we thinking? The same thing that Christians in Luke's audience were thinking when they heard the call to give up their stuff or when they were invited by the parables to think of themselves as slaves: it's too hard. You can't be serious. That's too much to change about my life.

When Munro's servant-narrator leaves at the end of the summer, the head of the house gives her a book, and the girl doesn't quite know what to think of it. "The thought of having a little corner of myself come to light, and be truly understood"—that is, to have the "master" realize that the servant was a reader—"stirred up alarm, just as much as being taken no notice of stirred up resentment." But this unease is forgotten quickly upon leaving: "In hardly any time at all I came to believe that this gift had always belonged to me."[48] That's why we must read and reread Luke, and find ways to hear it that make us uncomfortable, because real change comes only with great effort, and only after great discomfort.

NOTES

[1] Joseph A. Fitzmyer, *The Gospel According to Luke* (AB 28 and 28A; Garden City NY: Doubleday, 1981), 2.954; Bernard Brandon Scott, Hear Then the Parable: A Commentary on the Parables of Jesus (Minneapolis: Fortress, 1989), 324.

[2] Alan R. Culpepper, *The Gospel of Luke* (*NIB*, vol. 9; Nashville: Abingdon, 1995), 251.

[3] Sting, "Every Breath You Take," 1983.

[4] Pliny, *Epistles* X.96, translation in Henry Bettenson, ed., *Documents of the Christian Church* (London: Oxford University Press, 1977), 3–4.

[5] Tom Wolfe, *Bonfire of the Vanities* (New York: Farrar, Straus, & Giroux, 1987), 69–70.

[6] BAGD, 824.

[7] Joel B. Green, *The Gospel of Luke* (NICNT; Grand Rapids: Eerdmans, 1997), 490–91.

[8] Fitzmyer, *Luke*, 2.978.

[9] Green, *Luke*, 403.

[10] Fitzmyer, *Luke*, 2.978.

[11] BAGD, 435–36.

[12] Some manuscripts read "they neither spin nor weave," which is a more balanced parallel to "sew nor reap." But "neither toil nor spin" comes closer to Matt 6:28, and so the majority reading might be explained by scribal assimilation. "Toil nor spin" is printed in the latest UBS texts because it is found in the two early papyri; see Bruce Metzger, *A Textual Commentary on the Greek New Testament* (New York: United Bible Societies, 1971), 161, where it is given a "D" rating.

[13] Fitzmyer, *Luke*, 2.979.

[14] Indictment: Frederick W. Danker, *Jesus and the New Age: A Commentary on St. Luke's Gospel* (rev. ed.; Philadelphia: Fortress, 1988), 250; hope: Green, *Luke*, 493–94.

[15] Fitzmyer, *Luke*, 2.980; BAGD, 642–43.

[16] Luke Timothy Johnson, *The Gospel of Luke* (SP, vol. 3; Collegeville MN: Liturgical Press, 1991), 200; H. E. Dana and Julius R. Mantey, *A Manual Grammar of the Greek New Testament* (New York: MacMillan, 1955), 301.

[17] Culpepper, *Luke*, 261.

[18] Clement of Alexandria, "Who Is the Rich Man That Shall Be Saved?" xii; in *ANF* 2.594 (trans. William Wilson).

[19] Xenophon, *The Householder* 13.9 (cited in Thomas Wiedemann, *Greek and Roman Slavery* [Baltimore: Johns Hopkins University Press, 1981], 185).

[20] Plautus, *The Merchant* 398–402, in George E. Duckworth, ed., *The Complete Roman Drama* (New York: Random House, 1942), 1.507.

[21] Xenophon, *Memorabilia* 2.1.16-17 (cited in Wiedemann, *Greek and Roman Slavery*, 173).

[22] J. Albert Harrill, "The Domestic Enemy: A Moral Polarity of Household Slaves in Early Christian Apologies and Martyrdoms," in David Balch and Carolyn Osiek, *Early Christian Families in Context: An Interdisciplinary Dialogue* (Grand Rapids: Eerdmans, 2003), 248.

[23] Harrill, "The Domestic Enemy," 232–33.

[24] Johnson, *Luke*, 203.

[25] Arlen Hultgren, *The Parables of Jesus: A Commentary* (Grand Rapids MI: Eerdmans, 2000), 269, suggests that Luke's reference to a wedding banquet has no particular significance: "it is simply a place from which the master comes. He could just as well come home from a journey." But since Luke has Mark 13:34-35, where the master does come home from a journey, it is more plausible that Luke makes this deliberate change in order to connect this parable with the wedding banquet theme in the rest of the gospel.

[26] Harrill, "The Domestic Enemy," 236.

[27] Green, *Luke*, 501–502; many commentators note that the parable deals with the themes of Jesus' return and the church's need for watchfulness, and do not consider the slaves, except as symbols for followers of Jesus.

[28] Jennifer A. Glancy, *Slavery in Early Christianity* (New York: Oxford, 2002), 109.

[29] BAGD, 253.

[30] Scott Spencer, *Journeying Through Acts: A Literary-cultural Reading* (Peabody MA: Hendrickson, 2004), 77.

[31] From "Birches," in Louis Untermeyer, ed., *Robert Frost's Poems* (New York: Simon and Schuster, 1971), 89–90.

[32] "Letter from Birmingham City Jail," reprinted in *A Testament of Hope*, ed. James M. Washington (New York: HarperCollins, 1986), 289–302; quotes from pages 291, 292, 296–98.

[33] Year C, Proper 15, in the *New Common Lectionary*; year C, 20th Sunday after Pentecost, according to the *Book of Common Worship* (PCUSA).

[34] The verb *synechō* in the passive means "to be tormented by, distressed by something"; BAGD, 971.

[35] So Johnson, *Luke*, 208; Culpepper, *Luke*, 266, links it to his death and/or the general distress as the journey draws closer to Jerusalem and the time of his death nears.

[36] John Nolland, *Luke* (WBC, vols. 35A-C; Dallas TX: Word, 1989-93), 2.708; James D. G. Dunn, *Jesus Remembered* (Grand Rapids MI: Eerdmans, 2003), 803–804. Ancient Christian interpreters (Cyril of Jerusalem, *Catechetical Lectures* 17.8; Basil the Great, *Concerning Baptism* 1.3) sometimes connected the fire and baptism to Acts 2, where the baptism of the Holy Spirit was indicated by tongues of fire. While this might seem like a natural move, especially since Luke wrote both the Gospel and Acts, it seems less likely than the other alternatives because Luke never uses "baptism" to indicate the Spirit's descent. The faithful are "filled with the Spirit" at Pentecost and at many later moments in Acts, but never "baptized" with the Spirit.

[37] "Letter from Birmingham City Jail," 290, 295.

[38] Fitzmyer, *Luke*, 2.999-1000; Nolland, *Luke*, 2.712.

[39] Robert C. Tannehill, *The Sword of His Mouth: Forceful and Imaginative Language in Synoptic Sayings* (Missoula MT: Scholars, 1975), 129–30.

[40] "Letter from Birmingham City Jail," 300.

[41] For example, Joachim Jeremias, *The Parables of Jesus* (3rd ed.; London: SCM, 1972, 43–44; Robert C. Tannehill, *Luke* (ANTC; Nashville: Abingdon, 1996), 215.

[42] BAGD, 96.

[43] Fitzmyer, *Luke*, 2.999; Green, *Luke*, 512; Jeremias, *Parables of Jesus*, 43–44; Johnson, *Luke*, 209.

[44] "Letter from Birmingham City Jail," 291.

[45] From *Why We Can't Wait* (New York: Harper & Row, 1963), cited in *A Testament of Hope*, 554.

[46] Alice Munro, "Hired Girl," in *The View From Castle Rock* (New York: Knopf, 2006), 252.

[47] Ibid., 233.

[48] Ibid., 254.

JUDGMENT, REPENTANCE, AND HOPE

Luke 13

COMMENTARY

Better Repent!, 13:1-9

"Turn or burn/ fly or fry/ you'd better repent/ before you die." That bit of doggerel from a rural homemade billboard comes close to the in-your-face tone and message of this section on repentance. This little section continues the warning tone that began in 12:1, and continues to vary the audience being warned:

Verse	Audience	Warning
12:1	Disciples	Watch out for the hypocrisy of the Pharisees.
12:9	Disciples	Whoever denies me now will be denied on Judgment Day.
12:10	Disciples	Whoever slanders the Holy Spirit will never be forgiven.
12:15	Crowd	Beware of greed and thinking that life means possessions.
12:48	Everyone	To whom much is given, much will be required.
12:56	Crowd	Why don't you know how serious the present time is?
12:57	Crowd	Better make things right before you get thrown in jail.

Luke 13:1-9 is offered in response to a comment from bystanders who are identified not as disciples or crowds, but as people standing around while Jesus was teaching. As Peter says in 12:41, "Is this for us or for everyone?" Luke almost certainly means it for everyone.

Repentance is one of Luke's major themes. Luke uses the word far more often than any other New Testament author, and uses it to frame the Gospel between the bookends of John's preaching of repentance and the risen Jesus' commands to the church to preach repentance of sins (see the introduction for a list of passages where repentance and forgiveness appear).

Repentance, of course, has a long history in the Torah. Judges 2:11-23 summarizes what some have called the SER cycle (sin-exile-repentance/return): Israel would stop being obedient to God; God would allow them to be persecuted by other nations; they would cry to the Lord for help; and God would send them a deliverer. Occasionally, the Deuteronomic History (Deuteronomy, Joshua, Judges, 1–2 Samuel, and 1–2 Kings) identifies a moment where Israel's sin was so great that God's judgment was inevitable and catastrophic, even if repentance and righteous acts delayed it somewhat. For example, according to 2 Kings 21:10-15, Manasseh's sins were responsible for the Babylonian Exile, even though Josiah's reform gave Judah a brief reprieve (2 Kgs 22:14-20). Prophets, too, like Amos, Hosea, Isaiah, and Jeremiah, both interpret past disasters and predict future calamities as punishments for the sins of God's people.

Second Maccabees argues that great calamities always come because of sin, and that in God's mercy, they come faster to God's people than to others:

> Now I urge those who read this book not to be depressed by such calamities, but to recognize that these punishments were designed not to destroy but to discipline our people. In fact, it is a sign of great kindness not to let the impious alone for long, but to punish them immediately. For in the case of the other nations the Lord waits patiently to punish them until they have reached the full measure of their sins; but he does not deal in this way with us, in order that he may not take vengeance on us afterward when our sins have reached their height. Therefore he never withdraws his mercy from us. Although he disciplines us with calamities, he does not forsake his own people. (2 Macc 6:12-16)

This explanation for suffering does not try to account for undeserved pain or purely accidental disasters. The martyrs whose deaths are described in such detail in 2 Maccabees believe that they are dying because their nation has sinned against God, although they choose death rather than disobedience to Torah. They hope that their deaths for the sake of righteousness will help God's mercy overcome God's just anger:

> I, like my brothers, give up body and life for the laws of our ancestors, appealing to God to show mercy soon to our nation and by trials and plagues to make you confess that he alone is God, and through me and my brothers to bring to an end the wrath of the Almighty that has justly fallen on our whole nation. (2 Macc 7:37-38)

In 13:1-9, Luke takes these themes—disasters being punishments for sin; God's patience giving a reprieve but not a pardon—from

Pilate's Reaction to Protests over the Aqueduct

Josephus writes that Pilate built a much-needed aqueduct to bring in water to Jerusalem, and that he took money from the temple treasury to finance it. Note how Pilate dealt with the protestors; many were injured, and some killed as a result of the way his soldiers behaved. But the impression we get is of a man who gave the crowd a chance to disperse before he gave the signal for his troops to attack; a ruthless man, but not a man who kills without pretext.

60 But Pilate undertook to bring an aqueduct to Jerusalem, and did it with the sacred money, and took the water of the stream from the distance of twenty-five miles. However, the Jews were not pleased with what had been done about this water; and many ten thousands of the people got together, and made a clamour against him, and insisted that he should stop that design. Some of them, also, used reproaches, and abused the man, as crowds of such people usually do. 61 So he outfitted a great number of his soldiers in their clothes, who carried daggers under their garments, and sent them to a place where they might surround them. So he bade the Jews himself go away; but they boldly cast reproaches upon him, he gave the soldiers that signal which had been beforehand agreed on; 62 who laid upon them much greater blows than Pilate had commanded them, and equally punished those who were tumultuous, and those who were not, nor did they spare them in the least; and since the people were unarmed, and were caught by men prepared for what they were about to do, there were a great number of them slain by this means, and others of them ran away wounded; and thus an end was put to this sedition.

Josephus, *Ant.* 18.60-62.

---

the Bible, and uses them to stress the need for repentance. We have no information about either of the tragedies noted in vv. 1 and 4. Pilate, the Roman procurator in Judea, did all sorts of wicked and cruel things [Pilate's Reaction to Protests over the Aqueduct], but this particular episode is noted only here, and only in passing. "The Galileans whose blood Pilate mixed with their sacrifices" sounds like he may have had them killed while they were at the temple, perhaps at a festival. The second event, by contrast, sounds more like an accident; "Siloam" was the name of a fountain in the southern part of Jerusalem, and commentators guess that the tower was part of the city wall nearby.[1] [The Tower of Siloam] Perhaps it was poorly constructed or damaged, or perhaps the eighteen who died were in the process of building or repairing it; again, we don't know as much as we would like.

It is an interesting pairing of events. The interlocutors mention Pilate's victims; Jesus is the one who throws in the victims of the tower collapse. Pilate's actions were, more than likely, deliberate; he had the Galileans executed for reasons that made sense to him. We'd like to know what precipitated their deaths; why did Pilate think they should be slaughtered? We would assume that he had some reason; he probably thought he was provoked, although we might think he overreacted. The fall of the

The Tower of Siloam

Josephus writes about the wall around Jerusalem taking a turn close to the Siloam fountain. Although he mentions no tower, it would not be surprising for there to have been a tower to strengthen the wall at a place where it changed direction:

144 Now that wall began on the north, at the tower called "Hippicus," and extended as far as the "Xistus," a place so called, and then, joining to the council house, ended at the west cloister of the temple. 145 But if we go the other way westward, it began at the same place, and extended through a place called "Bethso," to the gate of the Essenes; and after that it went southward, having its bending above the fountain Siloam, where it also bends again toward the east at Solomon's pool, and reaches as far as a certain place which they called "Ophlas," where it was joined to the eastern cloister of the temple.

Josephus, *J.W.* 5.144-145; noted in Luke Timothy Johnson, *The Gospel of Luke* (SP, vol. 3; Collegeville MN: Liturgical Press, 1991), 211.

Pool of Siloam

The Pool of Siloam is located in the Lower Tyropoeon Valley, west of the City of David, at the level of the southern end of the spur on which the original city was built. The name derives from the Hebrew shiloah, which means "aqueduct" or, more literally, "the sent [of water]" (Isa 8:6). The pool was filled with water from the Gihon spring through a tunnel dug by King Hezekiah when the Assyrians were threatening Jerusalem.

Pool of Siloam excavations from northwest   (Credit: Todd Bolen, BiblePlaces.com)

tower, by contrast, was probably not deliberately caused (although, if we knew more, we might assign some responsibility to those who designed and built it), and it would be much harder to find any motive, even a cruel motive, that explained their deaths. But Jesus' rhetorical questions make no distinction between deliberate murder and accidental death; instead, both events are held up as examples of what will happen to any of us, to all of us, if we do not repent.

We would also like to know why the bystanders brought up the Galileans slain in the temple; that is, in Luke's mind, what motivates their report to Jesus? One suggestion is that, on hearing the advice about reconciling with one's accusers (12:57-59), some of the crowd tell the story of high-handed imperial "justice" to show how futile it is to try to reason with the godless Romans.[2] Another suggestion is that the bystanders are trying to justify themselves; after all the stern warnings of chapter 12, they may have been pointing fingers at those whose deaths proved them to be far worse sinners.[3] Or perhaps Luke understands this scene as a new turn in the conversation, and the bystanders' tale is simply another chance for Jesus to say "repent, or else!"

Jesus denies that disasters always indicate grave sin. Pilate's victims and those who died beneath the stones of the tower were not worse sinners than those listening to Jesus. Theologically, that's good news, because it frees us from having to explain why the victims of roadside bombs are worse sinners than those who survive the blasts, or why residents of New Orleans who died in the floods following Hurricane Katrina were worse sinners than those who were able to escape. [Hurricane Katrina as God's Judgment] But Jesus' remarks do link death and disaster to sin, and one could interpret "unless you repent, you will all perish similarly" to mean "if you do repent, you can avoid dying tragically." That reading makes no sense, however, in light of the end of the Gospel. Jesus, another Galilean, dies as Pilate's victim; could he have avoided the slaughter had he repented? Perhaps the point is much the same as in the parable of the rich fool. Death comes for all of us, often unexpectedly. Tragedy strikes the good and the evil. Therefore, you must repent while there is still time. [Hurricane Katrina as a Warning]

Luke's parable of the fig tree, while unique among the Gospels, nevertheless has intriguing connections to a couple of passages in Mark. Mark 13:28-31 uses the fig tree as metaphor for being able to discern how close is the arrival of the kingdom of God; like our current text, Mark's fig tree is a sign of imminent judgment. Even more tantalizing is Mark 11:12-14, 20, where Jesus curses a fig tree on his way into Jerusalem. He finds the fig tree "in leaf," but not yet bearing fruit, because "it was not the season for figs." He curses it, and then goes into the temple to curse it, too, overturning tables and calling it a den of thieves. Luke has a parallel to Mark 13:28-31 (Luke 21:29-33), but omits the story of the cursing of the fig tree; one wonders if this parable is his equivalent, connected as it is to stories of Pilate

Hurricane Katrina as God's Judgment

Steve Lefemine, an antiabortion activist in Columbia, S.C., was looking at a full-color satellite map of Hurricane Katrina when something in the swirls jumped out at him: the image of an 8-week-old fetus. "In my belief, God judged New Orleans for the sin of shedding innocent blood through abortion," said Lefemine, who e-mailed the flesh-toned weather map to fellow activists across the country and put a stark message on the answering machine of his organization, Columbia Christians for Life. "Providence punishes national sins by national calamities," it said. "Greater divine judgment is coming upon America unless we repent of the national sin of abortion."

In Philadelphia, Michael Marcavage saw no coincidence, either, in the hurricane's arrival just as gay men and lesbians from across the country were set to participate in a New Orleans street festival called "Southern Decadence." "We take no joy in the death of innocent people," said Marcavage, who was an intern in the Clinton White House in 1999 and now runs Repent America, an evangelistic organization calling for "a nation in rebellion toward God" to reclaim its senses. "But we believe that God is in control of the weather," he said in a telephone interview. "The day Bourbon Street and the French Quarter was flooded was the day that 125,000 homosexuals were going to be celebrating sin in the streets. . . . We're calling it an act of God."

Alan Cooperman, *Washington Post*, Sunday, 4 September 2005, A27.

Hurricane Katrina as a Warning

"We're spoiled," said Col. Joe Spraggins, the civil-defense director of the hard-hit Harrison County. "All these years we've had everything given to us. God gave us this disaster, and we've got to live with it. It might bring us back to reality."

Winston-Salem Journal, 4 September 2005.

killing innocents and of the collapse of part of the city wall of Jerusalem.

Wherever it came from, the parable imagines a landowner consulting with his gardener—more than likely, Luke imagines a slave, a field hand who is responsible, among other things, for the olives, figs, and grapes grown on the farm. Following the advice of ancient writers on agriculture, the landowner keeps careful records of the productivity of his orchards; he knows which trees are producing and which are not. After three years of fruitlessness, he orders the slave to cut down the barren fig tree and replace it with a young one being cultivated in another spot on the farm.

Again, this is an interesting grouping of images. Pilate murders Galilean pilgrims worshiping in the temple; a group dies when part of a wall falls on them; a landowner orders the death of an unproductive tree. If we connect the dots, and if the landowner is allowed, allegorically, to be God, then we are back in a theological quandary, with Pilate's victims and the accidental deaths of the eighteen being explained by their unproductivity; God struck them down because they were unprofitable, and if you don't get right, God will whack you, too. Once again, Jesus' denial saves us: the victims of those tragedies were not worse sinners, so it is wrong to try to connect their deaths to an act of God's justice. We should also be cautious about equating the landowner with the God of justice and the gardener with the merciful Savior. The point is more general: just as any orchard owner will have a limit to how long unfruitful trees are allowed to live, so our lives are limited by God. Unless we repent, we will perish without God; and lest we think we have forever to get around to repenting, we should remember the parable of the fig tree. [Sidestepping Repentance]

Sidestepping Repentance

In 1976, a major Protestant denomination narrowly defeated an attempt to destigmatize the Prayer of Confession by removing from it all guilt or guilt-oriented references: "Lord, we approach thy throne of grace, having committed acts which, we do heartily acknowledge, must be very difficult for Thee to understand. Nevertheless, we do beseech Thee to postpone judgment and to give Thy faithful servants the benefit of the doubt until such time as we are able to answer all Thy questions fully and clear our reputations in Heaven."

Garrison Keillor, "The Current Crisis in Remorse," in *We Are Still Married* (New York: Penguin, 1990), 24.

The Bent-over Woman, 13:10-17

In 13:10, Luke begins a new episode. Luke 12:1–13:9 was all teaching material, Jesus telling parables and interacting with disciples and crowds. This section takes place in a synagogue on Sabbath; Jesus heals a woman, is accosted for doing so, spars verbally with his detractors, and then tells a couple of parables. The parables of growth (mustard seed, leaven) are deliberately connected with the episode of the bent-over woman by the "therefore" of v. 18, so in the commentary on that section, we will look for Luke's connecting logic. The next pericope begins in 13:22 with the notice of Jesus' slow progress through every village as he heads toward Jerusalem.

This pericope shares common features with other Lukan healing stories. Many point to the man healed in 14:1-6, suggesting that the bent-over woman and the man with dropsy are another instance of Luke putting a man's story alongside a woman's (e.g., annunciations to Zechariah and Mary, Simeon and Anna in the temple, lost sheep [man] and lost coin [woman]). Both stories are of a Sabbath healing, both include an objection, and both end with Jesus making an argument about what is permissible on Sabbath.[4] The story also has points of connection with other synagogue appearances of Jesus (4:16-30; 4:31-37; 6:6-11); this is Jesus' last time to teach in a synagogue, and so one might expect Luke to do something to connect back to the other episodes.[5] As in the undesignated synagogue of 6:6-11, Jesus' healing on a Sabbath provokes a hostile response, but his question to them, "Is it lawful to do good or to do harm on Sabbath?" goes unanswered. As in the Capernaum synagogue, someone needs to be set free from demonic binding, and at the end of the episode, people are amazed. The reaction of the crowd at Nazareth is by far the most extreme, wanting to throw him off a cliff, and is provoked by words alone; in that setting, Jesus does not heal, but speaks of times when God's mercy was extended through prophets to persons outside Israel. By contrast, Jesus in 13:10-17 heals a "daughter of Abraham" rather than a foreigner, and still arouses the ire of the synagogue leader. Jesus' use of the language of liberation also connects this miracle to the Nazareth sermon: in healing this woman, he says, he is setting her free, which he declared to be part of his mission in 4:18.

In short: by this point in the narrative, the reader has seen Jesus operate in the synagogue, and could be expected to predict the hostile reaction, especially when he heals on Sabbath. It is in many respects a story with a set plot and a pat outcome. What sets it apart from the others Luke tells is its emphasis on liberation.

We can only guess at the root biomedical cause of this woman's stooped posture—osteoporosis, arthritis, etc.—but we can be certain that she suffered from chronic pain as a result. That sort of pain is often completely debilitating, and one woman, suffering from a back injury resulting from an automobile accident, describes her situation this way: she feels the pain as a big lump—red and hot—of muscles, nerves, tendons bunched together in my upper back. Feels as if everything has been ripped after being pulled in different directions. . . . The pain shoots up into my neck, which feels stiff sometimes and other times vulnerable, weak, like it could break off.

[The pain] controls me. It's limiting. I can only go so far and then the pain stops me. Whenever I have to do something really physical or deal with a stressful situation, the pain increases terrifically. I've had to stop thinking about decisions I need to make in my marriage and relax and get the pain under control. Can't deal with my financial and career needs when the pain is bad.[6]

No references to demons or Satan here, but the woman's choice of words is striking: the pain limits, controls, stops. A cure would feel to her, no doubt, like a liberation.

Jesus, for the last time in Luke, is teaching in a synagogue on a Sabbath. A woman, as anonymous as her village, is present. Luke describes her as "bent over," using a word that denotes the posture of humility (Sir 12:11) or grief (Sir 19:26). Her stoop is not by choice, but the result of a "spirit of sickness" that has held her for eighteen years. [Why Eighteen Years?] Jesus initiates the healing, "summoning" her; in this regard, the healing is more like the non-demonic episode in 6:6-11 than like the exorcism in 4:31-37. He says to her "Woman, be loosed from your sickness," and put his hands on her. There are three immediate results. First, she stands up straight. Second, she praises God. Third, the head of the synagogue gripes about it, telling the crowd, "There are six days on which it is necessary to work; so come on those days to be healed, and not on the Sabbath day."

To understand better the official's attitude, I refer the reader to the discussion of the nature of the Sabbath in the commentary on 6:1-11. The Sabbath was not a burden or a problem, but an important marker of Jewish identity, a chance to rest from hard physical labor, and an opportunity to worship. [Philo on the Sabbath] In order to protect its sanctity—its "set-apartness" for God—persons are commanded in Exodus 20:8-11 not to work. But Torah never precisely defines work, and so Jews debated what was permissible.

Why Eighteen Years?

AΩ Frederick Danker suggests the number 18 in 13:11, 16 "may serve as a rhetorical device to connect" this pericope with the earlier stories of judgment (13:4). He also notes that in Jdg 3:14 and 10:8, "'eighteen years' describes a long period of servitude or oppression."

Mikeal Parsons argues that the 18 may have suggested "Jesus" to Luke or to Luke's audience. The first two letters of Jesus' name in Greek, IH, when written with an overstroke (I̅H̅) was very often used as an abbreviation for "Jesus." In the 1st century, people writing in Greek were still using the letters of the alphabet for their numerals, and one way to show that you meant the letters to be read as numerals was to write them with an overstroke. When used as a number, I̅H̅ is 18. Parsons thinks that Luke gave us a clue to this by first giving the number as *dekaoktō*; in v. 11 and then as *deka kai oktō* in v. 16.

Frederick W. Danker, *Jesus and the New Age: A Commentary on St. Luke's Gospel* rev. ed. (Philadelphia: Fortress, 1988), 261.

Mikeal Parsons, *Body and Character in Luke and Acts: The Subversion of Physiognomy in Early Christianity* (Grand Rapids MI: Baker, 2006), 83–95.

Philo on the Sabbath

The fourth commandment has reference to the sacred seventh day, that it may be passed in a sacred and holy manner. Now some states keep the holy festival only once in the month, counting from the new moon, as a day sacred to God; but the nation of the Jews keep every seventh day regularly, after each interval of six days; and there is an account of events recorded in the history of the creation of the world, comprising a sufficient relation of the cause of this ordinance; for the sacred historian says, that the world was created in six days, and that on the seventh day God desisted from his works, and began to contemplate what he had so beautifully created;

therefore, he commanded the beings also who were destined to live in this state, to imitate God in this particular also, as well as in all others, applying themselves to their works for six days, but desisting from them and philosophizing on the seventh day, and devoting their leisure to the contemplation of the things of nature, and considering whither in the preceding six days they have done anything which has not been holy, bringing their conduct before the judgment seat of the soul, and subjecting it to a scrutiny, and making themselves give an account of all the things which they have said or done . . . .

Philo, *Decalogue* 20.96-98.

A man may not go out [of his house on Sabbath] with sandals shod with nails or with a single sandal if he has no wound in his foot. . . . A man may not go out with a sword or a bow or a shield or a club or a spear; and if he went out [with the like of these] he is liable to a Sin-offering. R. Eliezer says: They are his adornments. But the Sages say: They are naught save a reproach. . . . A cripple may go out with his wooden stump. So R. Meir. But R. Jose forbids it. (*m. Šabb.* 6:1-8)

The Mishnah, written about AD 200, collects earlier materials illustrating Jewish opinions on the meaning of Torah. Several passages give the clear impression that one should avoid deliberately treating non-fatal wounds and injuries on Sabbath:

• One was to avoid deliberately taking medicine, but could eat or drink things that could be either medicinal or normal food and drink: "Greek hyssop may not be eaten on the Sabbath since it is not the food of them that are in health, but a man may eat pennyroyal or drink knotgrass-water. He may eat any foodstuffs that serve for healing or drink any liquids except purgative water or a cup of root-water, since these serve to cure jaundice; but he may drink purgative water to quench his thirst, and he may anoint himself with root-oil if it is not used for healing. If his teeth pain him he may not suck vinegar through them but he may take vinegar after his usual fashion [i.e., if he drinks it at a meal], and if he is healed he is healed" (*m. Šabb.* 14:3-4).
• The urgent need of childbirth overrode the Sabbath: "They may deliver a woman on the Sabbath and summon a midwife for her from anywhere, and they may profane the Sabbath for the mother's sake and tie up the navel string [tying knots was normally forbidden]" (*m. Šabb.* 18:3).

• Injuries that could wait, should: "They may not straighten a [deformed] child's body or set a broken limb. If a man's hand or foot is dislocated he may not pour cold water over it, but he may wash it after his usual fashion, and if he is healed, he is healed" (*m. Šabb.* 22:6).

If these passages, coming as they do from the opinions of experts in Torah, are a fair approximation of the attitudes of people like the head of the synagogue, then we can see why he was upset. The woman's condition was not terminal, and not much would have changed in her condition had Jesus waited a day to heal her. Her situation did not have the urgency of something like childbirth; it was much closer to the case of the broken limb and dislocated foot. The passages also show that a coincidental healing would not have been problematic. Suppose the woman had been in the line of well-wishers after the sermon—"nice little talk, Reverend"—and had been healed when Jesus shook her hand; the "if she is healed she is healed" principle says that one cannot prevent God from graciously healing, and so no one would have been blamed. But Jesus deliberately healed her, deliberately breaking Sabbath, in the opinion of the Sages.

The head of the synagogue, angered, lectures the crowd, indirectly criticizing the woman (for coming to be healed) and Jesus (for healing) and warning away any other would-be supplicants. His "There are six days on which it is necessary to work" is also a bit indirect. Rather than saying, "The Commandments forbid work on Sabbath" or "God forbids work on Sabbath," he uses a verb (*dei*) that implies divine will or divine necessity.[7]

Jesus, however, is pretty blunt in his rejoinder. "Hypocrites" takes a whack at more than just the *archisynagogos*, anticipating the group of opponents named in v. 17.[8] Luke the narrator names Jesus "Lord," reminding the reader of Jesus' claim to be "Lord of the Sabbath" (6:5) and trumping the authority of the head of the synagogue. Jesus' argument begins with a hermeneutical point: the way everyone reads Torah, it is permissible to untie livestock on Sabbath and lead them to drink. Those actions are not considered work, or else they are considered necessary, in the category of attending a woman in labor. Luke's Jesus presumes that everyone agrees with this way of looking at things; Mishnaic passages seem to indicate that many (perhaps most) agreed, but not everyone. [Watering Animals on Sabbath] If Torah permits an animal to be loosed on Sabbath, then how much more would it permit a human to be loosed? Verse 16 then argues that since the woman was a "daughter of Abraham" and had been bound by Satan for eighteen years, it was "necessary" that she be loosed from her bondage on Sabbath. Jesus, using the same verb as the head of the synagogue, implies that the Sabbath, of all days, was the day God chose as most appropriate for this woman's liberation.

The final verse in the pericope quotes Isaiah 45:16, giving the reader a big pointer to how Luke understood this event. Isaiah 45:1-8 names Cyrus as the Lord's anointed one; according to the LXX text, "Thus says the Lord God to my 'christ' Cyrus [*Kyrios ho Theos tō christō mou Kyrō*]." God promises to open the way for Cyrus to do God's will: "I will open doors before him . . . I will break to pieces doors of brass, and bars of iron I will shatter." After the oracle to Cyrus, the narrator turns to address the people of God. Because the LXX text, the version of the Old Testament Luke most likely read, differs from the Hebrew and therefore from the translation in your Bible, I produce it here:

Watering Animals on Sabbath

Could one untie an animal on Sabbath? "These are knots for which they [that tie them on the Sabbath] are accounted culpable: camel-driver's knots and sailor's knots; as a man is culpable through the tying of them so he is culpable through the untying of them. R. Meir says: None is accounted culpable because of any knot which can be untied with one hand" (*m. Šabb.* 15:1). One presumes that if no untying was involved, or if one could undo the knot with one hand, many Torah scholars would not object.

"All beasts which wear a chain may go out with a chain and be led by a chain" (5.1), so leading the animal to water is not at issue. May one pour water into the trough? "If [a gentile] filled a trough with water to give his cattle to drink, an Israelite may give his own cattle to drink after him, but if the gentile did it for the Israelite, it is forbidden" (16.8). However, "they may not set water before bees or before doves that are in the dovecots; but they may set it before geese and fowls or Herodian doves" (24.3); Danby surmises that the difference here is between animals that can find water on their own and those that cannot (n. 1, p. 121). If that was truly the rationale, then the same principle would apply in places where a beast of burden could not walk to a stream or a well-fed watering hole.

Bottom line, no matter what the Torah experts thought: no livestock owner would take a chance on making his animals sick by not watering them.

The Mishnah, trans. Herbert Danby (Oxford: Oxford University Press, 1933), 121, n. 1.

Such a most excellent thing I have created, as a potter (from) clay! The plowman will not plow the earth forever, will he? The clay will not say to the potter, will it, "What are you doing," since it neither can work nor has hands? The thing fashioned will not talk back to the artisan, will it? Does one say to one's father, What have you begotten? Or to one's mother, What are you birthing?

For thus says the Lord, the Holy God of Israel, the one who made what is to come: Question me about my children [lit., my sons] and command me about the works of my hands. I made the earth, and humans upon it; by my hand I established the sky; I have appointed all the stars. I raised him up with righteousness as a king, and all his ways are correct. This one will build my city, and he will turn back the captivity of my people, not with ransoms nor for pay, says the Lord of Hosts (*Kyrios Sabaoth*).

Thus says the Lord of Hosts, Egypt worked, and the goods of the Ethiopians and the Sabeans, high-ranking men, passed over to you, and they are your slaves, and they will follow after you bound in chains, and will pass over to you, and worship with you, and pray with you: "God is with you [lit., is in you], and there is no God but yours. For You are God, and we did not know the God of Israel, the Savior." All who opposed him will be put to shame and will turn in shame, and they will walk in shame; O islands, consecrate yourselves to me. Israel will be saved by the Lord with eternal salvation, and they will not be ashamed, nor ever be turned in shame for eternity. (Isa 45:9-17 LXX)

The points of connection between Luke's narrative and Isaiah's oracle are many. First, God challenges anyone to question the divine will in creation or the divine purpose in liberating Israel. All who oppose God's acts of liberation will be shamed, and in Isaiah's version will themselves wind up in chains. In Luke's version, the naysayers were shamed in front of the crowd, but suffered no worse fate. Second, God speaks of "my sons"; the people of Israel are God's children, God's offspring, and God's purpose in begetting/birthing Israel is as unassailable as God's purpose in creating the earth and the sky. Luke's unusual reference to a "daughter of Abraham" probably resulted from linking Isaiah 45:11 ("question me about my children") with Isaiah 51:2, "Consider your father Abraham and Sarah who birthed you." "Daughter of Abraham" in this context does not only mean "Jew," but "child of God." Third, Isaiah's text narrates a conversion; the foreigners who enslaved the Jews, once the tables were turned, realized that the God of Israel was the only God. In Luke's version, the crowd of synagogue worshipers is convinced by Jesus rather than by the head of the synagogue, and "rejoiced in all the wonders being done by him." Fourth, Isaiah's oracle ends with a prediction of eternal salvation for Israel, brought about by the one whom God raised up. Luke's Jesus, having already announced in 4:18 that he was God's anointed one, sent to release the captives, is doing precisely that through his miracles. Finally, Isaiah's use of "kyrios sabaoth" must have been an open door for Luke's reflection on Jesus' Sabbath healings. The translators of the LXX chose to transliterate rather than translate the Hebrew word "sabbaoth," which means "armies." If Luke knew no Hebrew, he may not have known what "sabaoth" meant, and even if he did, it sounds and looks so much like "Sabbath" that it must have made it easy for him to connect Isaiah's oracle with Jesus' healings.

Christian interpreters must be careful when speaking of liberation, because too often Christians have read stories like this one to indicate that Jesus set Jews free from Sabbath worship, Torah obedience, and other aspects of Judaism. Luke is clear that Satan, not the Law, bound the woman. There are also no indications that

Luke thinks of the woman as "another person on the margins of Jewish society."[9] She is in the synagogue, apparently without objection from anyone; if other worshipers considered her demon-possessed, they were not shunning her. Jesus needs to restore her to health, but there is no need to interpret her as an outcast or an undesirable who needed to be put back into society—most of those kinds of persons do not feel welcome in village worship services. The text has also been lifted up as "a paradigm for women's liberation from all that bends them double and holds them in bondage.[10] Others, however, are not so sure, since the woman passively receives the healing and says nothing in her own defense; for some, her silence, her humble posture, and her status as victim are more troubling than liberating.[11] Again, careful treatment of the story can avoid this pitfall. The woman is not completely passive; she is in the synagogue of her own volition, she answers Jesus' invitation to come to him, and after he lays hands on her, she stands straight and praises God. She is thus far more active than the man with the withered hand in 6:6-11 or the man with dropsy in 14:1-6. She is also elevated as the naysayers are shamed; she stands straight, praising God, while they must hang their heads.[12]

How may churches help to liberate persons with physical conditions that create severe, chronic pain? Others are bent or bowed down by depression, sometimes as the by-product of some other physical or mental illness. [The Woman as a Metaphor for Humanity] Would that we could lay hands on them all and help them to walk straight! What we can do, we should, and that includes refraining from increasing their suffering by adding guilt to it; an elderly woman in steady pain from arthritis or osteoporosis does not need to be scolded for failing to attend every church service or for needing someone to listen to her complaints. Let our goal be to loosen, as much as we are able, what binds people, and so imitate our Lord.

Mustard Seed and Leaven, 13:18-21

These two parables are also paired in Matthew 13:31-33, and they both appear in the *Gospel of Thomas*. [The Mustard Seed and Leaven According to Thomas] The mustard seed parable also appears in Mark 4:30-32, complicating the issue of where

The Woman as a Metaphor for Humanity

The whole human race, like this woman, was bent over and bowed down to the ground. Someone already understands these enemies. He cries out against them and says to God, "They have bowed my soul down." The devil and his angels have bowed the souls of men and women down to the ground. He has bent them forward to be intent on contemporary and earthly things and has stopped them from seeking the things that are above. Since that is what the Lord says about the woman whom Satan had bound for eighteen years, it was now time for her to be released from her bondage on the Sabbath day. Quite unjustly, they criticized him for straightening her up. Who were these, except people bent over themselves?

Augustine, *Exposition of the Gospel of Luke* 7.174; cited in Arthur A. Just Jr., ed., *Luke* (ACCS: NT, vol. 3; Downer's Grove IL: Intervarsity Press, 2003), 226.

The Mustard Seed and Leaven According to Thomas

Mustard Seed (*Gos. Thom.* 20): The disciples said to Jesus, "Tell us what the kingdom of heaven is like." He said to them, "It is like a mustard seed. It is the tiniest of all seeds, but when it falls on prepared soil, it produces a large plant and becomes a shelter for the birds of heaven."

Leaven (Thomas 96): Jesus said, "The kingdom of the Father is like a woman. She took a little yeast, hid it in dough, and made it into large loaves of bread. Whoever has ears should hear."

Translation by Marvin Meyer in John S. Kloppenborg, et. al., *Q-Thomas Reader* (Sonoma CA: Polebridge, 1990).

Luke gets his material. Since Luke is closer to Matthew than to Mark in the mustard seed, most presume that he was copying from Q, the hypothetical document used by Luke and Matthew to supplement Mark.[13] Even if this is so, Luke presumably had Mark's version in front of him and decided to omit some of Mark's wording, and noticing this can help us zero in on Luke's interpretation of the parable.

Assuming that there was a Q, these two parables stood together in it; beyond that, we cannot know much about the Q context—perhaps Q clustered more parables together, as Mark did at 4:1-34, but we cannot know. If our source theory is correct, then Mattthew chose to expand Mark 4:1-34 by adding these two Q parables plus several others that are unique to Matthew (maybe these also come from Q, but Luke chose to omit them). Luke, by contrast, breaks up Mark's parable collection, keeping the parable of the sower, the interpretation of the sower, and the parable of the lamp together (Luke 9:4-18) but moving the mustard seed and its twin, the leaven, here. As we noted in the commentary on the bent-over woman (13:10-17), Luke intended us to connect these two parables to the healing of the woman in the synagogue and the ensuing controversy; by inserting "therefore" in v. 18, he makes these parables some kind of comment on or interpretation of the events of 13:10-17. The connection is far from obvious; Mark's context—putting these parables close to that of the sower—would keep seed-and-growth parables together. Confident, however, that Luke was not being careless, we will root for the logic that explains why the author grafted these parables onto the miracle story.

Our first clue is the movement from the beginning of the chapter until now:

13:1-5—Two stories of disaster, used to make the point "repent, or perish"
13:6-9—Fig tree: judgment is delayed to give time to bear fruit
13:10-17—A woman bound by Satan is released to stand up straight and praise God
13:18-19—Mustard seed: it grows to become host to all the birds
13:20-21—Leaven: it affects three measures of flour

The disasters and the landowner's threatened destruction of the fig tree are used to make the same point: unless you repent, you will perish. But the gardener's intervention spares the tree, giving it time to "repent" and become productive, and Jesus' liberation of the woman demonstrates that not every bent-over tree is being deliberately unproductive. In order for her to flourish, she must first be set free from what is holding her down. It is possible, then, to see the parables of growth as the happy resolution to this section that began, like the evening news, with stories of terrible disasters. Yes, all must repent; Jesus learned that from John the Baptist, and Luke agrees that it is the first step in responding to the gospel. Yes, unless you repent, there is judgment waiting. But some who would repent are being held down by larger evil forces. If you set them free, then there is potential for growth—mustard seeds can grow into trees, a pinch of leaven can make flour into bread. But as we will see, this reading may be too simple; Luke keeps us guessing whether the ending is really happy.

Luke (or Q) has structured the actions of these tiny narratives so that they parallel each other; keeping the order of the Greek words, the kingdom is like . . .

A seed of mustard, which taking a man   threw into the field
Leaven,   which taking a woman hid   into wheat flour

"Kingdom" is like seed and leaven. But as we will see, Luke avoids the most obvious metaphorical connections, leaving us with a much more nuanced set of comparisons.

Mustard is proverbial in two aspects: its seeds are very small, and it is an aggressive plant, prone to spread out, invading the spaces of other plants in a garden. The Torah prohibits sowing seeds of different kinds in the same field (Lev 19:19), raising the issue with mustard and other pushy herbs of how close one may plant them to other more genteel vegetables. The Mishnah specifies that mustard is a seed, not a vegetable, and could not be freely planted in a garden (*m. Kil.* 3:2); the rules allowed farmers to divide their small plots into patches, but warns against planting too much mustard, since "it might appear like to a field of mustard" (*m. Kil.* 2:9).[14]

Luke's mustard seed grows up rather than out, however, so the pushy character of the mustard may not have entered his thinking. Unlike Mark (whom Matthew follows), Luke makes no explicit contrast between the tiny seed and the giant tree. The surprising thing in Luke's version is that the farmer, rather than "sowing" the seed, tosses it into "his own garden."

The seed grows into a tree, home to nesting birds; here Luke blends two LXX texts. Here's Luke's Greek:

τὰ πετεινὰ τοῦ οὐρανοῦ κατεσκήωσεν ἐν τοῖς
ta   peteina   tou ournaou   kateskēōsen   en tois
the   birds   of   heaven   built homes   in   the

κλάδοις αὐτου
kladois   autou
branches   of it

Now here is the Greek of two other texts:

ἐν τοῖς κλάδοις αὐτοῦ κατῴκουν τὰ ὄρνεα τοῦ οὐρανοῦ
en tois   kladois   autou   katōkoun   ta   opnea   tou   ouranou
In   the   branches   of it   dwelt   the   birds   of   heaven
(Dan 4:12 Th)

ἐπ᾽ αὐτὰ τὰ πετεινὰ τοῦ οὐρανοῦ κατασκηνώσει
ep᾽ auta   ta   peteina   tou   ouranou   kataskēnōsei
By   them   the   birds   of   heaven   will build homes
(Ps 104:12 LXX)

Luke's version keeps Daniel's "branches" but uses κατεσκήωσεν from the psalm text, unlike Mark and Matthew, so we presume that he was deliberately strengthening the connection to the psalm. Daniel's phrase comes from Nebuchadnezzar's dream, where the king is the tree; blessed by God, his reign flourished until he grew too proud, and then God struck him down until he could learn that "the Most High rules over the kingdoms of men." Daniel, interpreting the dream to the king, urges him, "Therefore, O King, may my advice please you: atone for your sins by giving alms, and for your unrighteous deeds by acts of mercy to the poor; perhaps God will be patient with your transgressions" (4:24 LXX). That is a very Lukan sentiment; repent, give alms, and God will forgive you and take away your punishment. The psalm text is, by contrast, a hymn of praise: "Bless the Lord, O my soul," it begins. Verses 10-13 praise God for causing fountains to bring water to all the animals; "by them [that is, by the streams] the birds of the air will build homes; they give voice from between the rocks. He waters the mountain from his chambers; the earth will be satisfied from the fruit of your works" (104:12-13 LXX). This is a celebration of God's nurturing power that enables animals to live and plants to grow—also a very Lukan sentiment, and very appropriate for this setting. Luke, then, has grafted a judgment to a blessing text: Daniel's tree, which flourishes and then is chopped down (Dan 4:11) is overshadowed by the Psalm-tree growing by God's good water. The same movement takes place in Luke, as noted earlier, when sudden and violent death gives way to a threat of destruction and then to an act of healing and liberation.

The second parable compares God's kingdom to leaven. Many modern English New Testaments translate *zymē* as "yeast," but we should not think of the little foil packets you mix with warm water and work into bread dough. In Jesus' time, leaven was made of soured, spoiled dough or bread (see commentary on 12:1), and so leaven was normally a metaphor for a corruption that could spread throughout a group or a body (so at Luke 12:1; 1 Cor 5:6). Here, however, it is meant to symbolize the kingdom of God.

Some have pointed to the three *seahs* of flour in the parable, arguing that the point is that a pinch of leaven makes dough from lots of flour:

> The "three measures (RSV, NRSV) or simply "large amount" (NIV) of flour is immense. The Greek term here for "measure" is *saton*, and each such measure is about a peck and a half. The amount in question, therefore, is roughly 4.5 pecks, 1.15 bushels, or 144 cups. That would weigh about 40 pounds (a 5-pound bag of flour yields about 18 cups). Modern recipes typically call for 3.5 cups of flour to make a good-sized loaf of bread. Using that as a standard, the amount of flour in question would easily make 40 generous-sized loaves of bread—60 or even 80 small ones.[15]

This is a lot of bread, and perhaps the point is that the small amount goes a long way. But others note that in peasant households, baking was done on a clay oven outdoors, typically in the courtyard behind or between several small homes. Because fuel was scarce in Galilee, it was more efficient to bake lots of bread once the oven was hot, and it was a task that women worked at together (Luke 17:35 pictures two women grinding meal). [Communal Baking] If the baking were for several households for a week, then 40–80 loaves would not be so surprising, especially since everyone typically used a loaf of the round flat bread at every meal.[1]

Communal Baking

"Rabban Gamaliel says: Three women may knead dough at the same time and bake it in the same oven one after the other. But the Sages say: Three women may occupy themselves [at the same time] with the dough, one kneading, one rolling it out, and one baking" (*m. Pesaḥ.* 3:4). The ruling applies to Passover baking, when the women must make dough that does not rise; the question is whether the women, at Passover, may continue to use a common oven. If they do, will the loaves start to rise while they are waiting to be baked? Gamaliel's ruling is more lenient than the majority opinion. Both rulings indicate that the normal procedure was for several women to make use of the same hot oven.

Making Bread

Woman grinding grain to prepare bread. Painted wood, Egypt, Old Kingdom, 5th dynasty (2565–2420 BC). Museo Archeologico, Florence, Italy. (Credit: Nimatallah/Art Resource, NY)

Daily life and trade along the Nile. A woman shoves a bread loaf into the open-air oven. Luxor region. Luxor, Thebes, Egypt. (Credit: Erich Lessing/Art Resource, NY)

The kingdom is compared to seed and leaven, but also to what is done with them. A man takes the seed and throws it into his own field: like the falling tower of v. 4, this act seems random, except that it turns out for weal and not for woe. A woman takes the leaven and hides it in 40 pounds of flour; like Pilate's murder of the pilgrims in v. 1, this act is deliberate, but creative rather than destructive. The man's act is quick: he throws the seed and then he's done. The woman's act, by contrast, is hard work: to "hide" the leaven in the flour, she will mix it, knead it, punch it down, turn it, and repeat the process several times before letting it rise. Like the gardener of 13:8-9, the woman knows that to make bread, she must be patient, giving the leaven time to do its work.

Both parables end at an odd place. Will the man be happy to have a mustard tree filled with birds in his garden? Wouldn't he have been happier with a bunch of mustard greens ready to pick and eat? Maybe, as some suggest, we should understand the birds to be symbolic of the Gentiles who will flock to the Jesus movement; or maybe the birds are just birds, there to show the size of the tree grown from the tiny seed. Maybe—but if the point was "tiny beginnings, grand finale," then why would Luke remove Mark's language that made just that point? The woman's large quantity of dough is leavened, but that's only the first part of the task; now it must be divided, formed into loaves, and baked. We can't say "they lived happily ever after" until we know that all the loaves rose, that none burned, and that the families who ate them were satisfied. Neither parable, in fact, makes the most obvious symbolic use of the item chosen as icon for the kingdom. Luke ignored the comic possibilities of a man trying to broadcast one tiny mustard seed into his garden, and missed the chance to narrate one more meal scene—the woman's family smacking their lips over her still-warm, freshly baked bread.

So—what is the kingdom of God like? It includes God's judgment on sinners who do not repent, just as swift and unsparing as Pilate's sword or the Siloam tower. It includes God's patience to give recalcitrant trees time to repent before they are summarily executed. It includes God's grace: the mercy of God that unexpectedly relieves a woman of a pain plaguing her for eighteen years. You can never tell—maybe the kingdom is like a man who threw a single mustard seed into his yard and got a tree full of birds. But we hope the kingdom is more like the woman, feeding her family by carefully working the leaven into the flour. Maybe God will take such care with us, patiently digging around us and giving us time to bear fruit.

The Narrow Door, 13:22-30

"Knock, and it will be opened . . . to the one who knocks, it shall be opened" (11:9-10). Luke's second volume has a couple of scenes like that: the messengers from Cornelius, looking for Peter at Simon the tanner's house (Acts 10:17-18) and Peter himself, knocking at the gate to Mary's house (Acts 12:12-16). In both cases, the door was opened (in Peter's case, not immediately; Rhoda got so excited she forgot to open the door). The parable of the friend at midnight (11:5-8) works off the presumption that it is such bad manners to refuse hospitality that even in the middle of the night a householder would give a visitor food and a neighbor give the first householder the food he'd need to serve his visitor. In this section, however, Luke describes a door that is not opened to those knocking and a householder who refuses to seat extra guests at his banquet. Jesus, whose reputation is that he will eat with anybody (15:2), and whose mission to Galilee depends on being able to find hospitality in the towns and villages, describes the Judgment as an anti-hospitality event: the door shut and locked, but those excluded still able to look inside to see what they are missing.

Luke locates this episode and the one following (13:31-35) at a particular moment in Jesus' journey to Jerusalem; particular, but not

On the Journey

This second night we run between seven and eight hours, with a current that was making over four mile an hour. We catched fish, and talked, and we took a swim now and then to keep off sleepiness. It was kind of solemn, drifting down that big still river, laying on our backs looking up at the stars, and we didn't ever feel like talking loud, and it warn't often that we laughed, only a little kind of low chuckle.

Mark Twain, *The Adventures of Huckleberry Finn* (New York: Barnes and Noble Classics, 2003), 67.

especially well-identified, as we know his location by neither map nor calendar. [On the Journey] Verse 22 describes the context: "He was going through, town by town and village by village, teaching while making his journey to Jerusalem." We catch him somewhere on the road, then, when someone asks him a question and he replies—was he in one of those towns or villages, and was this days or weeks after he "set his face" for Jerusalem (9:51)? No matter—the real context is the movement toward Jerusalem and his fate, about which the reader has already heard quite a bit (8:21-22, 31, 44; 12:49-50) and about which we are about to be reminded (13:32-33). With "in that hour" (13:31) Luke connects "the narrow door" to the Pharisees' warning and Jesus' response, so that the end of the journey, named in 13:22 and predicted in 13:35, brackets the intervening material.

What sort of material is "the narrow door"? Jeremias, followed by others, thought of 13:24-30 as a parable.[17] Others (including me) think these are words of prophetic warning—not a parable, where the fictional narrative is told to illustrate something, but a figurative, cautionary description of the Day of Judgment.[18] The difference is small and the distinction fine, but important: Jesus is not telling a story, but describing part of the events of the last day. To construct this section, Luke puts together verses that have various parallels in Matthew, leading many to conclude that Luke is working from Q. Whether Matthew's or Luke's versions are more original to the hypothetical source, we cannot say, and so we will make no judgments about how Luke may have edited his material.

The section opens with an unidentified person—disciple, apostle, member of the crowd, or enemy—asking, "O Lord, the saved—will they be few?" There is no verb in the question, so "will they be few" or "are they few" are equally possible; the passive voice of the participle "saved" implies "saved by God," and the Judgment Day context of Jesus' answer pulls toward the future tense for the implied verb.[19] As commentators note, this was an open question for Jesus' audience and for Luke's. Many Jews believed that the promises to the patriarchs meant that, in the words of the Mishnah, "All Israelites have a share in the world to come" (*m. Sanh.* 10:1). Of course, the Mishnah then immediately qualifies that statement:

And these are they that have no share in the world to come: he that says that there is no resurrection of the dead prescribed in the Law, and that the Law is not from Heaven, and an Epicurean. R. Akiba says: Also he that reads the heretical books, or that utters charms over a wound . . . . Abba Saul says: Also he that pronounces the Name with its proper letters . . . .

The section goes on to list some rabbinic disputes over who would and would not be on the side of the angels at the last day.

Other Second Temple era Jewish texts likewise worry over this issue. *Fourth Ezra* famously has Ezra lament the fact that people were created at all, since so many sin and fail to repent: "O Adam, what have you done? For though it was you who sinned, the fall was not yours alone, but ours also who are your descendants" (*4 Ezra* [=2 Esd] 7:118). What good is it, the prophet asks, to have the chance of immortality if one is almost certain to lose it by one's sins? The angel answers: "The Most High made this world for the sake of many, but the world to come for the sake of only a few . . . many have been created, but only a few shall be saved" (*4 Ezra* 8:1-3). The Dead Sea Scrolls adopt a similar position, where those who join the group (after successfully completing the probationary period) are seen as the only remnant that will be saved on Judgment Day. [Will the Saved Be Few? The Dead Sea Scrolls] The Essenes, in other words, believed that because of past sins, all Israel was bound to be condemned by God, but that God had provided a way of escape through the revelation given to the Teacher of Righteousness, the founder of the Essenes.

The question of the salvation of Israel was a live one in the early church, as Paul's passionate arguments in Romans 9–11 illustrate. For Luke, the fact that most Galileans and Judeans did not follow Jesus was connected to the destruction of the temple by the Roman army (see commentary on 13:35; 19:41-44). But for Luke's mostly Gentile audience, the question of whether the redeemed would be many or few must have focused on the issue of who was truly a Christian. Luke addresses this in Acts 15, when "some" come from Judea to Antioch to teach the newly formed congregation that "unless you have been circumcised according to the custom of Moses, you cannot be saved" (Acts 15:1). The majority of the church, according to Luke, rejects that as too narrow a door, and agrees to a compromise—abstain from idol-food, from fornication,

Will the Saved Be Few? The Dead Sea Scrolls

Whoever approaches the Council of the Community shall enter the Covenant of God in the presence of all who have freely pledged themselves. He shall undertake by a binding oath to return with all his heart and soul to every commandment of the Law of Moses in accordance with all that has been revealed of it to the sons of Zadok . . . and he shall undertake by the Covenant to separate from all the men of injustice who walk in the way of wickedness. For they are not reckoned in His Covenant (1QS 5.7-11; trans. Vermes, 104).

None of the men who enter the Covenant in the land of Damascus, and who again betray it and depart from the fountain of the living waters, shall be reckoned with the Council of the people or inscribed in its book from the day of the gathering in of the Teacher of the Community until the coming of the Messiah out of Aaron and Israel (CD 8.21ff.; trans. Vermes, 134).

Geza Vermes, *The Complete Dead Sea Scrolls in English* (New York: Penguin, 1997).

The Narrow Door

He ducked down as a car came slowly past, its headlights on high beam. The preacher on the radio might be Lutheran, he didn't know. It sure wasn't the Rosary. The man was talking about sinners who had wandered away from the path, and it seemed to Florian to fit the situation. "Broad is the road that leadeth to destruction, and narrow is the path of righteousness"—that seemed to be true, too, from what he knew of freeways. The preacher mentioned forgiveness, but Florian wasn't sure about that. He wondered what this preacher would do if *he* had forgotten his wife at a truckstop and gotten lost; the preacher knew a lot about forgiveness theoretically but what would he do in Florian's situation? A woman sang, "Softly and tenderly Jesus is calling, calling for you and for me. See by the portals he's waiting and watching. Calling, O sinner, come home."

Garrison Keillor, "Truckstop," in *Leaving Home* (New York: Penguin, 1997), 64.

and from eating improperly butchered animals (Acts 15:20). Who knows what Luke's audience knew, but if they had read some of Paul's letters, they might know that Paul found nothing theologically wrong with eating food sacrificed to idols. On several grounds, then, Luke's readers might have wanted to know whether narrower or more tolerant versions of the faith were closer to Jesus' intentions.

Jesus' reply to the question, "Struggle to enter through the narrow door," goes beyond "yes, not many will be saved." "Struggle" is imperative plural: Jesus treats the interrogator as part of a larger group who needs to be warned that they may not get in. "Struggle" translates the verb *agōnizomai*, which has the root meaning of engaging in a battle or an athletic contest.[20] But against whom would the persons be fighting or competing? Matthew's version of the saying (7:13-14) has the classic "two ways" form: there's a narrow way and a broad way; the broad way leads to death, but the narrow way leads to life. The ethical imperative in Matthew's version is to choose the correct path from the two options presented: "enter through the narrow gate" (Matt 7:13). In Luke's version, the imperative is not "enter," but "struggle," and there is only one option, the narrow door. Your struggle is to fit yourself through the small opening, and most will not be able to do it. [The Narrow Door]

Once we see it this way, then 13:24 is another way of putting the familiar call to discipleship:

• If anyone wishes to come after me, let him/her deny himself/herself and take up his/her cross and follow me. (9:23)
• If anyone comes to me and does not hate his own father and mother and sister and children and brothers and sisters, even his own life, is not able to be my disciple. Whoever does not bear his own cross and come after me is not able to be my disciple. (14:26-27)
• Seek his kingdom, and these things will be added to you. . . . Sell your possessions and give alms . . . for where your treasure is, there your heart will be also. (12:31-34)

The narrow door might be compared to the needle's eye of 18:24-25; there are many factors, including possessions, that might keep a person from squeezing through.

In v. 25, the narrow door becomes a locked door,[21] reminding us of the conclusion of Matthew's wise and foolish virgins (25:1-12). The Lukan householder's "I do not know you; where are you from?"[22] is also reminiscent of the section in the Sermon on the Mount where Jesus dismisses some who claim to be his followers (7:21-23). But Luke's text, again, makes different points. At some point, the narrow door will be locked, "whenever the householder rises." As the passage continues, we realize that the householder has been reclining at dinner at the great banquet of the kingdom, attended by Abraham and Isaac and Jacob "and all the prophets." At present, then, the narrow door is open, but someday it will be closed and locked, and no amount of knocking will avail (contra 11:9-10).

The folks outside plead, "Lord, open for us," but his answer is the same: "I do not know you; where are you from?" Is the problem that they were uninvited? Probably not; Luke's meals include several surprise guests: Pharisees at Levi's house (5:30), the anointing woman at Simon the Pharisee's house (7:37), and the man with dropsy at the home of the chief Pharisee (14:2).[23] The issue is their identity: the host does not know who they are. They protest, "We ate and drank in your presence and you taught in our streets." Sounds like they might have a valid gripe—if Jesus, who ate with tax collectors and sinners, ate with them and taught them, why is he now refusing to seat them? But compare this section to 10:10-11; if he taught in their streets, it was because they would not welcome him or his emissaries into their homes. And not every meal Jesus attended was a truly hospitable event; in 7:36-50, Jesus reclines at a Pharisee's table, but was treated disrespectfully.[24] These party crashers come too late to join, so the householder orders them away, quoting Psalm 6:8 LXX, "Go away from me, all you workers of unrighteousness." The psalm's author, suffering from a protracted illness, prays for relief from God's heavy hand of judgment, and then tries to shoo his enemies away. Luke turns this around, since the householder, who stands in for God, refuses to hear the knocking and the pleas of the latecomers.

The people on the outside then weep and grind their teeth—traditional language for expressions of grief—when they see the banquet going on without them. To make matters worse, not only are the prophets and the patriarchs present, but also persons from all over the planet. "They will come from east and west and from north and south" uses the language of Isaiah 43:5-6 LXX: "Do not fear, because I am with you. I will bring my seed from the east, and I will gather you from the west. I will say to the north, Lead (them), and to the south, Stop holding back; bring my sons from far away, and my daughters from the ends of the earth." Isaiah's text describes the return of the scattered people of God, and is a word of comfort given to disconsolate survivors of the exile. But in Luke's passage, the fact that there are banqueters from every direction makes the word of judgment "where are you from?" that much more severe.

Luke is preparing the audience for the consequences of Jesus' rejection. In the parable of the great banquet in the next chapter, the invited guests will refuse the invitations and the householder will fill the banquet hall with anyone the servants can drag in. Luke 13:24-29 functions almost as a sequel to that parable; what if those who had been invited, and who had initially sent their regrets, suddenly decided to come? According to this section, there will come a time when repentance is no longer an option, when the door is locked. In the meantime, all of us who want to be at the banquet should struggle to make sure we fit through the narrow door. To overweight, overfed, overly consumerist Americans, the challenge is to divest ourselves of what would make us too large.

Prophet's Doom, 13:31-35

On April 4, 1968, Dr. Martin Luther King Jr. was murdered in Memphis, Tennessee, shot by a sniper. The day before, he had preached at the Bishop Charles Mason Temple, urging the assembled crowds to boycott various businesses in support of striking sanitation workers. In his sermon, he spoke of the dangers he had faced over the years; he referred briefly to the time he was stabbed while signing books in New York City, and how close the knife blade came to puncturing his aorta. He talked about how he and others endured beatings, hoses, prison cells, and other indignities along the way. He revealed that he knew there were serious and credible death threats against him. But he reflected on the story of the Good Samaritan, and how natural it would have been for that man to be too scared to stop and help—scared of the bandits that might be still lurking, scared that the beaten man might be part of an ambush: "And so the first question that the Levite asked was, 'If I stop to help this man, what will happen to me?' But then the Good Samaritan came by. And he reversed the question: 'If I do not stop to help this man, what will happen to him?'"[25] Dr. King, aware that there were threats against his life, went on to say that it did not matter:

> Well, I don't know what will happen now. We've got some difficult days ahead. But it doesn't matter to me now. Because I've been to the mountaintop. And I don't mind. Like anybody, I would like to live a long life. Longevity has its place. But I'm not worried about that now. I just want to do God's will. And He's allowed me to go up to the mountain. And I've looked over. And I've seen the promised land. I may not get there with you. But I want you to know tonight, that we, as a people will get to the promised land. And I'm happy, tonight. I'm not worried about anything. I'm not fearing any man. Mine eyes have seen the glory of the coming of the Lord.[26]

Here is a prophet, looking ahead to a prophet's death, knowing that it may fall at any time, dealing with it as a part of his public ministry. Luke's scene puts Jesus into the same spot: the prophet considers his doom.

This scene is unique to Luke, although it incorporates, almost verbatim, material found in Matthew 23:37-39. In Matthew the lament over Jerusalem comes at the end of Jesus' woes against the Pharisees delivered during Holy Week. Matthew's lament is thus delivered in the last week of Jesus' life, and just before the temple sermon (chapters 24–25), where he predicts that the temple will be taken apart stone by stone. Luke's pericope begins with the Pharisees warning Jesus about Herod's intention to kill him—rather a different setting than "Woe to you, scribes and Pharisees, hypocrites!"

The first exegetical task is to decide how to read the Pharisaic warning: "Leave and go from here, because Herod wishes to kill you." Is this a friendly act, or at least non-hostile—maybe the Pharisees do not appreciate Jesus' ministry, but have no interest in seeing Jesus murdered by Herod? Or are the Pharisees trying to run Jesus out of town by scaring him with a rumor that may not even be true?

First, how credible is their report? Previously, we have read that Herod Antipas arrested (3:19-20) and beheaded (9:9) John the Baptist. The narrator reports that he was confused by what was being reported about Jesus and by the opinions of some that Jesus was John *redivivus*. "Herod said, 'I beheaded John, so who is this about whom I hear such things?' And he tried to see him" (9:9). That last bit could be read straight up—Antipas wanted to meet Jesus, interrogate him, and satisfy his curiosity about these amazing things he heard. But "see him" could also be read with a cocked eyebrow: see him like he saw John, with his head in a basket. Or maybe the Pharisees don't know what they're talking about. In Luke's version of the trials, Pilate passes Jesus to Antipas because, as a Galilean, Jesus fell under Herod's jurisdiction. Luke writes, "When Herod saw Jesus, he was very happy, because he for a long time had been wishing to see him, because he had heard about him, and was hoping to see some sign performed by him" (23:8). Herod interrogated Jesus; getting no answer, he mocked him and then sent him back to Pilate. In light of the fact that Herod did not kill Jesus when he had the chance, maybe we're supposed to judge the Pharisees to be misinformed, or lying.

The Pharisees' report, then, is hard to judge. I think we can read their words in at least three ways:

- They are making this up in an attempt to scare Jesus out of Galilee.[27]
- They know, like the reader does, that Herod wants to see Jesus, but they interpret Herod's motives as suspect; their intent may not be hostile, but from the narrator's point of view, they are Nervous Nellies.[28]
- They are reading Herod's motives correctly, and give us the reliable way to interpret Herod's wish to "see" Jesus.[29]

Those who interpret the Pharisees' motives as hostile point quite appropriately to how their conduct with Jesus has mostly been hostile (6:7, 11; 11:53-54) or disrespectful (7:44-47), and how their low opinion of Jesus and John put them outside God's will (7:30; 15:1-2; 16:14). The dinners Jesus attends with Pharisees are contentious events, and the only time Jesus uses a Pharisee in a parable, it is as an example of self-deceptive self-righteousness (18:9-14). The overall hostility of the Pharisees toward Jesus makes the third option less plausible than either of the first two. The difficulty with the first reading is that Jesus is on his way out of Galilee anyway, heading to Jerusalem; if Jesus followed the advice of the Pharisees, he would only be moving toward his doom faster.

I propose reading the Pharisees as only partially informed. They know Herod wants to see Jesus, and they draw the fairly reasonable conclusion that Herod's motives cannot be good. But since they do not accept Jesus as a prophet, they do not realize that Jesus already knows how he will die and that he knows Antipas poses no credible threat to him. They play the role of the *alazōn*—the "braggart," a stock character in comic plays who thinks he knows more than he does, and who actually knows less than the audience. Perhaps they also voice a real question posed by or to Luke's audience: if Jesus was a prophet, why didn't he know he would be crucified and do something to avoid it?

The Pharisees tell Jesus to go, but since he's already going (13:22), he tells them to take their advice back to its source. "Go tell" is not meant literally, since we have no other reason in Luke (or any credible historical reason, for that matter) to think that the Pharisees were acting as Herod's agents. This is Luke's equivalent of public figures trading verbal shots in the media: "you can repeat this, because I don't care if it gets back to Herod," in other words. "Fox" is an insult. Foxes were pests that ruined vineyards (Song 2:15), scavengers that moved into ruined cities (Lam 5:18 LXX uses "foxes" rather than "jackals"; Ezek 13:4 LXX likewise) and ate the dead (Ps 62:10 LXX). Kings would like to be known as lions rather than foxes, who had to rely on cunning rather than strength to feed themselves.[30] "Go tell that little yappy-dog Herod . . ." would be a good paraphrase. [Petronius on Foxes]

Petronius on Foxes

Today, when people are at home they tend to think of themselves as lions, but in public they're just foxes.

Petronius, *Satyricon* 44, in Frederick W. Danker, *Jesus and the New Age: A Commentary on St. Luke's Gospel* rev. ed. (Philadelphia: Fortress, 1988), 265.

Jesus announces what he is doing and what he will do: "I am casting out demons and completing cures today and tomorrow" summarizes what he is up to in this part of his ministry. He could have added teaching, but that's obvious from the fact that he is talking to them. The next part is literally "I am finished on the third day," which most commentators take to mean "I reach my goal" or "I complete my journey."[31] Luke uses a present passive verb, however, which looks at the future event—Jesus' arrival in Jerusalem and all that will follow—as if it were already determined by God (taking the passive as a "divine passive"). "Third day" has inescapable connections to Jesus' death and resurrection, particularly in light of the passion predictions we have already read (9:22), so even if the primary reference is to Jesus' entry into Jerusalem, "I am finished on the third day" is hard to hear without the overtones of the cross and empty tomb.

Because the Pharisees do not accept Jesus as a prophet, he introduces v. 33 with "but." "Despite your worries that Herod may kill me, I am a prophet, and so I must go today, tomorrow, and the next day, because it is not possible for a prophet to perish outside Jerusalem." The verse uses two impersonal verbs (*dei, endechetai*) to emphasize the divine necessity to which Jesus is obedient. Prophets die in Jerusalem; I am a prophet; therefore I must keep going to meet my end.

Deaths of Prophets

Because of these visions, therefore, Beliar was angry with Isaiah, and he dwelt in the heart of Manasseh, and he sawed Isaiah in half with a wood saw. And while Isaiah was being sawed in half, his accuser, Belkira, stood by, and all the false prophets stood by, laughing and (maliciously) joyful because of Isaiah . . . . And Belkira said to Isaiah, "Say, 'I have lied in everything I have spoken; the ways of Manasseh are good and right, and also the ways of Belkira and those who are with him are good.'" . . . And Isaiah answered and said, "If it is within my power to say, 'Condemned and cursed be you, and all your hosts, and all your house!' For there is nothing further that you can take except the skin of my body." . . . And while Isaiah was being sawed in half, he did not cry out, or weep, but his mouth spoke with the Holy Spirit until he was sawed in two.

Mart. Ascen. Isa. 5:1-14, trans. M. A. Knibb, in James H. Charlesworth, *The Old Testament Pseudepigrapha* (2 vols; New York: Doubleday, 1985), 2.163-64.

Why must a prophet die in Jerusalem? It had been the site of some, but not all, prophetic deaths. At 11:50-51, Zechariah (whom Luke counts as a prophet) was said to have been killed "between the altar and the sanctuary"; not just in Jerusalem, but in the temple itself. Josephus remarks that Manasseh killed prophets on a daily basis (*Ant.* 10.38). His most famous victim, according to legend, was the prophet Isaiah. The *Martyrdom and Ascension of Isaiah* (first century AD or earlier) gives a legendary account of Manasseh having Isaiah sawn in two (*Mart. Ascen. Isa.* 5.1-16; also in the first-century *Liv. Pro.* 1.1), and the author of Hebrews perhaps has this legend in mind at 11:37. [Deaths of Prophets] There was no general belief, however, that all the prophets were killed in Jerusalem; *Lives of the Prophets* says Jeremiah was stoned by his own people in Taphnai, Egypt (2.1); Ezekiel was killed in Babylonia (3.1), etc. Nolland suggests, therefore, that the tone of v. 33 is rather cynical, setting up the oracle of v. 34; Luke's Jesus is not reporting a widely held opinion about the city, but making his own judgment on its character.[32]

Since Jesus has been operating only in Galilee so far, why does he condemn Jerusalem for a rejection that has not yet happened? This is again the prophetic stance, looking at the anticipated future as if it were present reality. The lament of v. 34 compares Jesus to a mother bird whose only desire is to gather up her chicks under her wings. He has no wish for them to be destroyed; he wants to give them peace (19:42). Jerusalem did not wish that—meaning that they chose their status as prophet-murderer and apostle-stoner and were not locked into it by God's will or Jesus' prediction. When Jesus arrives in Jerusalem, he will say "even today" things could be different (19:42), and even after his death, his apostles preach that all those who had a part in Jesus' condemnation may be forgiven (Acts 2:23, 38).

At present, however, Jesus the prophet forsees only doom for the city, just as he sees his own crucifixion there. He first predicts its destruction: "your house[hold] is left to you" means that there is no future for them; one could paraphrase "your household will be left vacant" or "your household is abandoned." Luke's readers could look back on the events of the Jewish War of 66–70 and the destruction of the temple and much of the city, and would have considered Jesus' prediction to have been fulfilled. The second prediction is fulfilled within the narrative, when Jesus arrives in the city to the shouts of "blessed is the one who comes . . . in the name of the Lord" (19:39; see commentary on that verse).

Look back now at the beginning of v. 31, where Luke indicates that the Pharisees came to him with their worries about Herod just after the question "will the saved be few" and the narrow door material. Yes, the saved will be few, at least in proportion to the numbers invited, and although there will be people at the great banquet from all over, there will be some who were excluded because they repented too late. Some of those live in Jerusalem; Jesus wants to draw them close, but they don't care for his invitation. So some who are first will be last, their household left empty.

Jesus looks at the likely fate of Jerusalem and grieves—would that everyone could be saved! But when he looks at his own fate, he is more resigned—what else may a prophet expect? [The Life of the Soul] Like Dr. King, he's not fearing any man, least of all Herod Antipas; and like Dr. King, he will not suspend his ministry just because it might be dangerous. This is how a prophet faces his death. [Pat Conroy on Facing Death]

The Life of the Soul

It is selfish of you to desire to escape, until you can take humanity with you. You are not Christlike until you demand that even after you die, your soul shall stay and help others come through to the larger life.

Frank C. Laubach, *Letters By a Modern Mystic* (Westwood NJ: Revell, 1937), 43.

Pat Conroy on Facing Death

A gypsy in Marseilles had read Tolitha's palm, studied her abbreviated, bifurcated life line, and made a prediction that Tolitha would not live past her sixtieth birthday . . . she took the gypsy's death sentence with a stoical and bemused gravity, and she began to prepare for her own demise as though it were a voyage to a fabulous country whose borders had long been closed to tourists. When it came time to purchase her casket and to make the final arrangements for her interment, she insisted that her grandchildren accompany her. Always the teacher, Tolitha wanted us to learn not to fear death. She spoke about the impending purchase of her coffin with gaiety and acted as though she were about to confirm a hotel reservation at the end of a most arduous journey.

Pat Conroy, *The Prince of Tides* (Boston: Houghton Mifflin, 1986), 174–75.

CONNECTIONS

This chapter begins with stories of disasters: a military governor kills some worshipers and a building collapses on others. This passage, like John 9:1-4, stands ready for the minister who needs to help a congregation deal with a local, national, or international tragedy. In John 9:3, Jesus says the blind man's disability was not punishment for his sins or for his parents'; in Luke 13:1-5, he tells us that those who died in Jerusalem were not worse sinners than anyone else. Both passages argue against seeing disasters as retributive justice, but neither lets God completely off the hook. "He was born blind so that God's works might be revealed in him" comes perilously close to "God has a reason for wanting you disabled," and "unless you repent, you will all likewise perish" leaves open the possibility that the victims died because they sinned, but not because they sinned worse than anyone else. There is unfortunately no New Testament passage that argues that natural disasters simply happen, outside God's control; better for the Bible interpreter to admit it than to try to squeeze something out that isn't there.

But after that stark beginning, the chapter moves into more hopeful territory. The unproductive tree will be cut down if it continues to be barren, but for now, the gardener will work with it. The bent-over woman is healed, freed from the demon that kept her stooped for eighteen years. The kingdom can grow incredibly, like a mustard seed growing into a home for the birds or a lump of leaven making a huge number of loaves. Take heart—don't let the daily news of death and disaster lead you to conclude that nothing can ever be better.

Alice Walker's story "The Welcome Table" is a good twist on the healing of the bent-over woman. In Luke's narrative, the synagogue leader has not worried about the presence of the crippled woman. If he knew she was demon-possessed, it does not seem to have bothered him. But her healing troubled him, since it seemed to break the sanctity of the Sabbath: "There are six days on which work ought to be done"; couldn't you have come tomorrow or yesterday to cure this woman? In Walker's story [Alice Walker on Being Ejected from Church], an elderly African-American woman shows up at a white church one Sunday; she's sick and confused, and the congregation is at first uncertain about what they should do. Some see her and think of their servants; others think of race riots; nobody sees her as a "daughter of Abraham" or as someone to whom they could minister. Her presence makes it impossible for them to worship, and they put her out, where she meets Jesus, walking along the highway.[33]

Alice Walker on Being Ejected from Church

It was the ladies who finally did what to them had to be done. Daring their burly indecisive husbands to throw the old colored woman out they made their point. God, mother, country, earth, church. It involved all that, and well they knew it. Leather bagged and shoed, with good calfskin gloves to keep out the cold, they looked with contempt at the bloodless gray arthritic hands of the old woman, clenched loosely, relentlessly in her lap. Could their husbands expect them to sit up in church with that? No, no, the husbands were quick to answer and even quicker to do their duty.

Under the old woman's arms they placed their hard fists (which afterward smelled of decay and musk—the fermenting scent of onionskins and rotting greens). Under the old woman's arms they raised their fists, flexed their muscular shoulders, and out she flew through the door, back under the cold blue sky. This done, the wives folded their healthy arms across their trim middles and felt at once justified and scornful. But none of them said so, for none of them ever spoke of the incident again. Inside the church it was warmer. They sang, they prayed. The protection and promise of God's impartial love grew more not less desirable as the sermon gathered fury and lashed itself out above their penitent heads.

From Alice Walker, "The Welcome Table," in *In Love & Trouble* (New York: Harcourt Brace Jovanovich, 1973), 83–84.

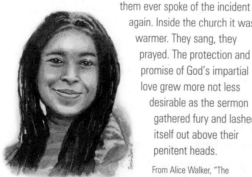

Alice Walker (Credit: Barclay Burns)

"Will the saved be few?" Jesus is asked, and he paints a picture of a great banquet from which the questioner is excluded while everyone else eats at God's Welcome Table. That's scary stuff. We who study Luke are likely to be doing it while sitting in church, assuming that we are part of the saved. Have we missed something? Well, have we missed ministry to the aged, the disabled, the poor in our midst? Are we still holding on tightly to the stuff that makes it hard for us to enter through the narrow door? There will come a time, this chapter indicates, when the door will be locked and the tree will be cut down. Make your changes now.

The chapter ends with one of Luke's many passion predictions. This one is unique to his Gospel: a warning from the Pharisees (yes, from the Pharisees!) that Herod Antipas wants to kill Jesus. We readers do not know what to make of this: Are they lying? Are they mistaken? Are they spot on? Jesus doesn't care—he isn't going to change his plans because of a rumor that Herod the Chihuahua wants to get him. He is headed for Jerusalem, where Pilate the pilgrim-killer waits to crucify him. This text, one of the Gospel lessons for Lent in Year C, is meant to make us stop and think about where we'd headed. Jesus is patiently making his way town by town, village by village, to his death. He knows he will be killed eventually; he hears that the danger may even be close at hand. But his mission—to heal, to drive out the demons, to teach, to bring life—is much more important than Pharisees's warnings or political threats. He's headed to Jerusalem, and we—we disciples, we Pharisees, we crowds?—are following him. Do we share the prophet's vision? Will we accept the prophet's fate?

NOTES

[1] Joseph A. Fitzmyer, *The Gospel According to Luke* (AB 28 and 28A; Garden City NY: Doubleday, 1981), 2.1008.

[2] Alan R. Culpepper, *The Gospel of Luke* (NIB, vol. 9; Nashville: Abingdon, 1995), 270.

[3] Joel B. Green, *The Gospel of Luke* (NICNT; Grand Rapids: Eerdmans, 1997), 514; Jo Luke Timothy Johnson, *The Gospel of Luke* (SP, vol. 3; Collegeville MN: Liturgical Press, 1991), 211.

[4] Robert C. Tannehill, *Luke* (ANTC; Nashville: Abingdon, 1996), 217–18; Culpepper, *Luke*, 272; Mary Rose D'Angelo, "Women in the Gospel of Matthew and Luke-Acts," in Ross Shepard Kraemer and Mary Rose D'Angelo, eds., *Women and Christian Origins* (New York: Oxford University Press, 1999), 182.

[5] Culpepper, *Luke*, 273; Green, *Luke*, 519–27.

[6] Arthur Kleinman, *The Illness Narratives: Suffering, Healing, and the Human Condition* (New York: Basic Books, 1988), 90–91.

[7] Charles H. Talbert, *Reading Luke: A Literary and Theological Commentary on the Third Gospel* (rev. ed.; Macon GA: Smyth and Helwys, 2002), 164.

[8] James Malcolm Arlandson, *Women, Class, and Society in Early Christianity: Models from Luke-Acts* (Peabody MA: Hendrickson, 1997), 171, argues that the plural includes the crowds, who are temporarily swayed by the synagogue leader's argument.

[9] Tannehill, *Luke*, 218.

[10] Barbara Reid, *Choosing The Better Part? Women in the Gospel of Luke* (Collegeville MN: Liturgical Press, 1996), 163. Culpepper, Luke, 273: "As in other scenes in Luke in which Jesus responds to the needs of a woman, this scene points to a new status for women in the Kingdom of God."

[11] Jane Schaberg, "Luke," in *The Women's Bible Commentary*, ed. Carol Newsome and Sharon H. Ringe (Louisville: Westminster/John Knox, 1992), 281, 291: "[Luke] hands on the tradition of the healing of the bent woman (13:10-17), while it praises the posture of female inferiority and passivity"; Reid, *Choosing The Better Part*, 167, also notes the danger of the male Jesus rescuing a woman, which can reinforce cultural attitudes of male power and female victimization.

[12] Arlandson, *Women, Class, and Society*, 170–72.

[13] Arlen Hultgren, *The Parables of Jesus: A Commentary* (Grand Rapids MI: Eerdmans, 2000), 393; Bernard Brandon Scott, *Hear Then the Parable: A Commentary on the Parables of Jesus* (Minneapolis: Fortress, 1989), 373.

[14] Some commentators understand the Mishnah to prohibit planting mustard in a garden (Joachim Jeremias, *The Parables of Jesus* [3rd ed.; London: SCM, 1972], 27, n. 11; he is followed by Scott, *Hear Then the Parable*, 375, Tannehill, *Luke*, 220). Fitzmyer reads it to say the opposite, that mustard may not be grown in a field, but must be grown in a garden (*Luke*, 2.1017). My understanding is that *m.Kilaim* 2.9 permits mustard in a grain field, but only up to two small patches: "If a man would lay out his field in patches each bearing a different kind of crop, he may lay out twenty-four patches within a seah's space, one patch to every quarter-kab's space, and sow therein what kind of seed he will; if [in a field of grain] there was but one patch or two, he may sow them with mustard seed; but if three, he may not sow them with mustard-seed, since it might appear like to a field of mustard." *m.Kilaim* 3.2 reads, "Not every kind of seed may be sown in a garden-bed, but any kind of vegetable may be sown therein. Mustard and small beans are deemed a kind of seed and large beans a kind of vegetable." This does not seem to me to prohibit planting mustard in a garden, but to make mustard subject to Torah's restrictions against mixing seeds; you can't claim an exemption by calling it a vegetable.

[15] Hultgren, *Parables of Jesus*, 406–407.

[16] Holly Hearon and Antoinette Clark Wire, "Women's Work in the Realm of God (Mt. 13.33; Lk. 13.20,21; Gos. Thom. 96; Mt. 6:28-30; Lk. 12.27-28; Gos. Thom. 36)," in Mary Ann Beavis, ed., *The Lost Coin: Parables of Women, Work and Wisdom* (Sheffield, UK: Sheffield, 2002), 139–40.

[17] Jeremias, *Parables of Jesus*, 95–96; Green, *Luke*, 530; John Nolland, *Luke* (WBC, vols. 35A-C; Dallas TX: Word, 1989-93), 2.736.

[18] Culpepper, *Luke*, 277; Johnson, *Luke*, 219–20; Fitzmyer, *Luke*, 2.1022.

[19] Johnson, *Luke*, 216, argues that the present tense of the participle implies, "Are those who are being saved few in number?"

[20] BAGD, 17.

[21] Fitzmyer's line (*Luke*, 2.1021).

[22] Luke's text is *ouk oida hymas pothen este*, lit., I do not know you whence you are. Many translations make this into one clause: I do not know whence you come. But if we punctuated it with a semicolon after *hymas* and a question mark at the end, it could be two clauses: I do not know you; whence are you?

[23] Smith, *From Symposium to Eucharist*, 22–23, notes that the uninvited guest is a frequent theme in literary accounts of meals.

[24] Smith, *From Symposium to Eucharist*, 262, also connects The Narrow Door with Luke's meals with Pharisees.

[25] Martin Luther King Jr., "I see the Promised Land," preached April 3, 1968, in Bishop Charles Mason Temple in Memphis; published in *A Testament of Hope*, ed. James M. Washington (New York: HarperCollins, 1986), 285.

[26] Ibid., 286.

[27] Johnson, *Luke*, 219–22.

[28] Green, *Luke*, 535–38, comes pretty close to the interpretation I offer below, as does David B. Gowler, *Host, Guest, Enemy, and Friend: Portraits of the Pharisees in Luke and Acts* (New York: Peter Lang, 1991), 240–41. Tannehill, *Luke*, 223, suggests the note of ironic misunderstanding.

[29] Fitzmyer, *Luke*, 2.1029-30; Nolland, *Luke*, 2.740; Gowler, *Host, Guest, Enemy and Friend*, 238, argues that Jesus accepts the threat as reliable.

[30] So Frederick W. Danker, *Jesus and the New Age: A Commentary on St. Luke's Gospel* (rev. ed.; Philadelphia: Fortress, 1988), 265. But see Mikeal Parsons, *Body and Character in Luke and Acts: The Subversion of Physiognomy in Early Christianity* (Grand Rapids: Baker, 2006), 69–71, who argues that we should also think of the fox as a predator and a destructive, dangerous pest.

[31] BAGD, 996; Fitzmyer, *Luke*, 2.1031; Culpepper, *Luke*, 281.

[32] Nolland, *Luke*, 2.741.

[33] Alice Walker, "The Welcome Table," in *In Love & Trouble* (New York: Harcourt Brace Jovanovich, 1973), 83–84.

JESUS' SYMPOSIUM

Luke 14

COMMENTARY

Dinner with Pharisees, Round Three, 14:1-24

For the third time, Jesus agrees to come to dinner at a Pharisee's house. Just to review, episode one (7:36-50) began with Simon the host refusing common courtesies to Jesus—no kiss of greeting, no water to wash his feet—and ended with an unnamed woman serving as substitute host. Simon thinks Jesus is no prophet, since he allowed the woman to touch him. Jesus exposes him for an ungracious host and praises the woman for her repentance. Episode two (11:37-54) began with the Pharisee host being surprised that Jesus has not immersed (or perhaps washed his hands) before arriving; he doesn't say anything, but Jesus knows what he is thinking, and launches into a full-scale dressingdown of the Pharisee and his friends and associates. As Jesus left the house, the Pharisees and scribes "began to act with hostility and to pester him about many things," hoping to catch him with his own words. Clearly there are hard feelings going both ways. So why is there an episode three?

Before answering that question, let us take account of the way this section is structured. The pericope just finished (13:31-35) begins with Pharisees coming to inform Jesus about Herod's plot to put him to death, and to urge him to leave Galilee. As I argued in the commentary on that section, the Pharisees may be correctly informed about Herod's intentions, but still do not understand Jesus. As prophet, he does not set his schedule according to the designs of rulers like Herod Antipas! The Pharisees do not realize that his road has been set for some time; he is on his way to Jerusalem, and he knows he will be killed there.

The presence of Pharisees in 13:31 makes 14:1 slightly less abrupt, but only slightly. In 13:35, Jesus has predicted that the people of Jerusalem will not see him until they say, "blessed is the one coming in the Lord's name." Luke 14:1 begins, "And so it was that while he was going into the house of one of the rulers of the Pharisees, to eat a meal on a Sabbath, they were watching him intently." Jesus is still on the path to Jerusalem, still willing to eat with anyone who will offer him a meal, and still under the close scrutiny of the Pharisees (this began at 11:53-54, following the second dinner).

The section includes a healing (14:2-6), a parable (14:7-11) about seating at banquets, advice to the host about his guest list (14:12-14), and a second parable (14:15-24) about a banquet. The first three sections are unique to Luke. Matthew has a version of the parable of the great banquet (Matt 22:1-14), but it is different enough from Luke's version that some have suggested Matthew and Luke were using different sources. We are to imagine this happening while Jesus and the others are at table, reclining on dining couches, eating and trading verbal darts.

Back to the question: Why, after two disastrous dinners, are the Pharisees still inviting Jesus to tie on the old feedbag? The last time they tried this, he showed up unbathed and had the gall to predict God's judgment on them for failing to attend to justice and the love of God. He called them unmarked graves, and suggested that they and their lawyers might as well have murdered the prophets. Luke must imagine that the Pharisees invited Jesus in order to humiliate him publicly. Plutarch's "The Dinner of the Seven Wise Men" includes a scene where Plutarch meets a man named Alexidemus as the latter is storming out the door. It seems the host had begged him to come to the dinner, but had assigned him to a dishonorable seat on one of the dining couches. Alexidemus interprets this as a deliberate insult to him and to his father: "It is plain that in my person he wishes to offer insult to Thrasybulus, who delegated me to come, and to put him low down to show that he purposely ignores him."[1] Luke shows us the hostility of the Pharisees with "they were watching him closely,"[2] and with their silence when Jesus asks them whether healing on Sabbath is legal.

The presence of the man with "dropsy" (a harmful accumulation of fluid someplace in the body—what is usually now called an edema[3]) is more than a little suspicious. The man just shows up—but where? Luke 14:1 locates the action "while he was going into the house," and while Jesus was under close scrutiny, so perhaps the man was not in the Pharisee's house, but in the street outside. If this is how Luke imagined it, then maybe the man's presence is God's providence. But if Luke imagines that Jesus has gone into the house and is reclining, then the presence of a man with an illness in the Pharisee's fancy dining room at dinner time on Sabbath would be due to the Pharisee's desire to start an argument.

Wherever he is, suddenly, there he is, and responding (Luke writes "answering," as if Jesus is hearing the sick man's unspoken request for help), Jesus speaks first to the lawyers and Pharisees who are (or will be) sharing dining couches with him: "Is it lawful to heal on Sabbath or not?" Put so baldly, the question had no easy answer. To judge from the Mishnah, the Sages (a term the Mishnah uses for the collective majority interpretation of the Torah over several centuries) thought one should avoid trying to cure illnesses on Sabbath unless they were life-threatening (see evidence cited in the commentary on 13:10-17). If the man was dying and needed immediate help, then yes, healing was legal. If the man could wait, then he should wait, as the synagogue ἄρχων (*archōn*, "ruler") had said (13:14). Luke imagines that this *archōn* of the Pharisees thinks the same. Jesus' answer, however, would be a straightforward "yes": if a person needed healing, then the Sabbath was actually the most appropriate day for performing it (13:16).

Their silence does not mean that they agree, but that they have no comeback; Isaiah similarly pictures Israel sitting silent before God's accusations and judgments (Isa 47:5). Jesus heals the man and sends him away, and then offers a justification for his actions. "Which of you [plural], if his son[4] or ox fell into a pit, would not immediately draw him out on the Sabbath day?" Again, Jesus' question makes it difficult to give a simple answer: a child in a pit is one thing, a beast another. A child in a pit might well need medical help immediately, and according to the majority opinion, a situation that might present a life-or-death matter overrode Sabbath or holy day restrictions (see [Dire Human Needs Override the Sabbath]). An ox or other beast in the pit is another issue entirely. On this, Jews of Jesus' day disagreed. The most restrictive view was among the Essenes, whose rule was that animals had to stay in pits until the Sabbath passed; the majority opinion is more lenient. [Animals in Ditches on Sabbath] Jesus may be reasoning from what most people actually did, however, regardless of the opinions of Torah-experts. In real life, what parent would leave a child in a pit overnight? What farmer, for that matter, would leave his valuable animal in a pit, in distress and in danger from thieves and predators? Even if the experts felt that he broke the Sabbath by raising it up, the penalty—the appropriate sacrifice at the temple the next time he was in Jerusalem—would be less costly than the loss of his ox. The Pharisees and lawyers were again silent, unable to come up with an appropriate retort.

Animals in Ditches on Sabbath

No man shall assist a beast to give birth on the Sabbath day. And if it should fall into a cistern or pit, he shall not lift it out on the Sabbath (CD 11.13-14).

They may not deliver the young of cattle on a festival day, but they may give help to the dam (*m. Šabb.* 18:3).

Banquet

(Credit: Barclay Burns)

So far, this is not a pleasant dinner party—a healing to which the host and most of the guests object, and then dead silence following unanswerable rhetorical questions. Luke most likely imagines this scene arranged much like the illustration. The dining couches are set along three sides of a rectangle, with the middle and one end open; this way, all the guests can see each other. Guests sharing dining couches were expected to carry on lively conversation with each other—a bit like our rule that if you are seated between people at a dinner, you should make a point of conversing with each in turn. [The Importance of Dinner Seating] Customarily a host would assign each guest to a couch, keeping in mind both the person's status in society and the possibility for good conversation with his neighbors. The top places, generally, were near the center of the room, although Roman and Greek customs differed slightly on which place was most desirable.

In Luke's scene, the guests are choosing their own places, and it happens that Plutarch records a debate about the merits of this practice. His brother Timon was of the opinion that allowing guests to select their own positions at the banquet was more in keeping with the egalitarian principles he believed in; the host who assigns seats

The Importance of Dinner Seating

Wherefore Chilon showed most excellent judgment when he received his invitation yesterday, in not agreeing to come until he had learned the name of every person invited. For he said that men must put up with an inconsiderate companion on shipboard or under the same tent, if necessity compels them to travel or to serve in the army, but that to trust to luck regarding the people one is to associate with at table is not the mark of a man of sense.

Plutarch, *Dinner of the Seven Wise Men* (*Moralia* 148.A).

makes himself a juryman and a judge over people who do not call upon him to decide an issue and are not on trial as to who is better than who or worse; for they have not entered a contest, but have come for dinner. Moreover, the decision is not easy, differing as the guests do in age, in influence, in intimacy, and in kinship . . . . [In making these distinctions, the host] accomplishes nothing useful, but rather transfers empty fame from market-place and theatre to social gatherings [τὴν κενὴν δόξαν ἐκ τῆς ἀγορᾶς καὶ τῶν θεάτρων εἰς τὰ συμπόσια μετσυνουσίᾳ], and, in his attempt to relax by fellowship the other passions, accidentally refurbishes a vanity which I think much more fitting for men to have washed from their soul than the mud from their feet. . . . If in other matters we are to preserve equality among men, why not begin with this first and accustom them to take their places with each other without vanity and ostentation, because they understand as soon as they enter the door that the dinner is a democratic affair and has no outstanding place like an acropolis where the rich man is to recline and lord it over meaner folk?[5]

Plutarch's father argued for the more traditional view, insisting that the host should assign spaces, since that prevents misunderstandings and acknowledges the dignity that each guest has acquired in the world. At a dinner party at Timon's house, a self-important guest looked at the seats remaining and decided to leave, saying that "he saw no remaining spot worthy of himself" (*ouk ephē ton axion eatou topon horan leipomenon*). Plutarch's father blamed his son Timon, the host, for such a gaffe:

Thus it is ridiculous for our cooks and waiters to be greatly concerned about what they shall bring in first, or what second or middle or last . . . yet for those invited to this entertainment to be fed at places selected haphazardly and by chance, which give neither to age nor to rank [ἀρχη] nor to any other distinction the position that suits it, one which does honor to the outstanding man, leaves the next best at ease, and exercises the judgment and sense of propriety of the host. For the man of quality does not have his honor and his station in the world, yet fail to receive recognition in the place he occupies at dinner.[6]

Plutarch agreed with his father about the necessity for assigned seats: his brother, "though he thinks that he avoids being offensive to his guests, he draws it down all the more upon himself to be so, for he offends each one of them by depriving him of his accustomed honor."[7]

Luke's Pharisee host is, like Timon, allowing each person judge his own station and put himself in the proper place. But the scramble for the best seats shows that Plutarch is correct: "I am afraid that, if we shut vanity out at the court-yard gate, we may seem to be letting it in by the side gate"[8]; while there may be the appearance of equality, the host and dinner guests still live by a set of values that makes the better, more honorable spots worth jostling over. Luke's Pharisees love the best seats at synagogue too (11:43), and are lovers of money (16:14); this simply makes them exemplars of the values of the larger Greco-Roman world of the first century.

Jesus' advice to the guests in vv. 7-11 is called a parable, not because he tells the guests an illustrative story, but to alert the reader that we are not to take this advice at face value. Unless we hear the ironic tone in his voice, Jesus sounds like Proverbs or Sirach or Plutarch, a first-century Miss Manners for banquet-goers:

- Do not put yourself forward in a king's presence or stand in the place of the great; for it is better to be told, "Come up here," than to be put lower in the presence of a noble. (Prov 25:6-7)
- Do not reprove your neighbor at a banquet of wine, and do not despise him in his merrymaking; speak no word of reproach to him, and do not distress him by making demands of him. If they make you master of the feast, do not exalt yourself; be among them as one of their number. . . . Among the great do not act as their equal. (Sir 31:31; 32:1, 9)
- "When we have taken our places," continued Thales, "we ought not to try to discover who has been placed above us, but rather how we may be thoroughly agreeable to those placed with us, by trying at once to discover in them something that may serve to initiate and keep up friendship, and better yet, by harboring no discontent but an open satisfaction in being placed next to such persons as these. For, in every case, a man that objects to his place at table is objecting to his neighbor rather than to his host, and he makes himself hateful to both." (Plutarch, *Dinner of the Seven Wise Men, Moralia* 149.B)

In Jesus' parable, the host has invited several guests, and either has not assigned spots on couches or has not made clear that the best seat has been reserved for someone. You go to the best seat, and prepare yourself to enjoy the wittiest conversation, the full attention of all the other guests, and the public esteem that will fall to you from eating at such an exalted spot. It was customary for the host to offer toasts to the more important guests, beginning with the person in the best place; you are mentally preparing your response as the host sees you and, with a smile, moves in your direction. But he orders you off, abruptly and rudely: "Give the spot to this one." Can you imagine how bad you'll feel to take the walk of shame down to the lowest spot? Well, of course—all Luke's readers could easily imagine it, and perhaps had even seen this done. Like Timon's guest who saw no spot worthy of himself, Luke's readers might imagine just leaving the party rather than staying and enduring the public humiliation. Jesus' "advice"—take the lowest seat, so that you can be raised to a higher one—ridicules the whole value system. In the first place, taking the lowest seat because you hope, you think, you expect to be elevated is not being humble, but hypocritical. You are still so embedded in the honor/shame culture that being called to a better seat will make you feel better about yourself; "then it will be glory for you in front of all your fellow-banqueters," says Jesus. The word translated "glory" (*doxa*) is the word Plutarch used for "fame"—public status that one accumulates in the world that is being reinforced at the dining couch. Jesus' parable shows what the real issue is—not where you sit to eat, but what determines, in your mind, whether you are valued. Why accept the notion that there are people "more honorable than you" (v. 8) based on wealth, status, or fame? If you don't, then where you sit to eat will make little difference to you. [Choosing the Lowest Seat]

Choosing the Lowest Seat

In Plutarch's *The Dinner of the Seven Wise Men*, Alexidemus, insulted because the host assigned him to a dishonorable seat, storms out. Thales, who had urged him to reconsider, upon entering the dining room, "in a louder voice than usual, said, 'Where is the place at table to which the man objected?' And when its position was pointed out to him he made his way to it, and placed himself and us there, at the same time remarking, 'Why, I would have given money to share the same table with Ardalus'" (*Moralia* 149.F). In this way, Thales showed his contempt for Alexidemus's pride and his disregard for the normal status markers in their society.

In the second place, how likely is the second scenario? If you are someone who could be unceremoniously tossed off the first chair and banished to last place, is it plausible that the host is going to move you up from last place if you start there? As some commentators note, if you are a member of Luke's audience and a Christian, your status in society has been complicated by your membership in a new and suspect religious group. Wake up—your peers, with whom you trade dinner invitations, may be more than a little embarrassed by your new religion, and you may never be top rank with them again. Does that matter to you?

Finally, Jesus' teaching about the kingdom of God is that "the last will be first and the first last" (13:30)—in other words, human status "don't mean squat" with God. The proverb that concludes the parable (14:11) is repeated at 18:14, and echoes Mary's language in 1:52. God will knock down the mighty, especially those who lift themselves up; God will exalt the lowly, especially those who humble themselves. To be a follower of Jesus means to give up the networks of family and friends that secured your place in society (14:26) and to accept a new set of values.

Inviting Rich Neighbors

The McKelveys were less than fifteen minutes late. Babbitt hoped that the Dopelbraus would see the McKelveys' limousine, and their uniformed chauffeur, waiting in front.

The dinner was well cooked and incredibly plentiful, and Mrs. Babbitt had brought out her grandmother's silver candlesticks. Babbitt worked hard. He was good. He told none of the jokes he wanted to tell. He listened to the others. He started Maxwell off with a resounding, "Let's hear about your trip to the Yellowstone." He was laudatory, extremely laudatory. He found opportunities to remark that Dr. Angus was a benefactor to humanity, Maxwell and Howard Littlefield profound scholars, Charles McKelvey an inspiration to ambitious youth, and Mrs. McKelvey an adornment to the social circles of Zenith, Washington, New York, Paris, and numbers of other places.

But he could not stir them. It was a dinner without a soul. For no reason that was clear to Babbitt, heaviness was over them and they spoke laboriously and unwillingly . . . .

At a quarter to ten McKelvey discovered with profound regret that his wife had a headache. He said blithely, as Babbitt helped him with his coat, "We must lunch together some time, and talk over the old days."

When the others had labored out, at half-past ten, Babbitt turned to his wife, pleading, "Charley said he had a corking time and we must lunch—said they wanted to have us up to the house for dinner before long."

She achieved, "Oh, it's just been one of those quiet evenings that are often so much more enjoyable than noisy parties where everybody talks at once and doesn't really settle down to—nice quiet enjoyment."

But from his cot on the sleeping-porch he heard her weeping, slowly, without hope.

Sinclair Lewis, *Babbitt* (New York: Harcourt Brace Jovanovich, 1922; citation from Signet Classics edition, 1961), 161–62.

With this, Jesus turns to his host to give him advice just as unworkable as "choose the last seat so that your host will move you up." Don't invite friends, brothers, relatives, or rich neighbors, "lest they also invite you and there would be repayment for you." *Lest*— but of course you want return invitations! Dinner invitations do several things for the host. Most importantly, they maintain the social networks that in the ancient world were the key to getting anything done (not so insignificant in our society, either). If you are part of a group that regularly eats with one another, then you and they are friends, peers, who can support each other in the world. Dinner invitations could also be a means for acquiring new status. If you invited one of your "rich neighbors" and he came, it would be a feather in your cap; maybe you and he are not friends or peers, but he deigned to eat at your table, and for a month afterward you can name-drop ("Why, that's just what Magnus said to me at dinner recently"). [Inviting Rich Neighbors]

"Instead," says Jesus, "invite the poor, the disabled, the lame, the blind; and you will be blessed, because they have no way to repay you, but it will be repaid to you in the resurrection of the righteous." This list will reappear in 14:21, and examples of persons from each category appear in Luke and in Acts, the recipients of the ministries of Jesus and his followers. The story of Tobit illustrates the presumption behind Luke 14:13-14 that the poor and the disabled (who would be assumed to be poor) had no honor to share and could only be given charity. The novella begins by describing Tobit's regular and extensive righteous deeds, and says that on Pentecost he sent his son to find a poor man to share his table (2:1-2). But when Tobit was accidentally blinded and could not be healed, his relative Ahikar had to provide for him and his wife Anna had to start selling her weaving to bring in money; the loss of status was too much for Tobit, who prayed that God would take his life so that he would have to endure no more insults (3:1-6).

The Pharisee host may well have been as charitable as Tobit, but Jesus is not asking for holiday handouts. Jesus wants the host to abandon status-confirming dinners and to invite the poor to his table regularly, instead of all the persons who would normally recline with him. True, they cannot repay you, if what you're hoping for is return invitations that will solidify or advance your status. But if what you're hoping for is to join Abraham and Isaac and Jacob and all the prophets at God's banquet table, then you should imitate God and not your rich neighbors. Invite the poor into your home and make them welcome; that's the kingdom of God.

Luke is using the Pharisees to mirror society's values—they are goodly, godly people who also crave high status—and to challenge the Christian audience to rethink their own behavior. Christians were no more likely to open their homes to the poor and the disabled than was this Pharisee; some suggest, in fact, that because they knew their peers and neighbors may have been suspicious of their new faith, Christians may have been all the more inclined to invite only the right groups to dine with them.[9] Luke spends a lot of time in Acts describing Christianity as a generous fellowship whose table is open to everyone (2:46; 4:32-34; 6:1-7; 10:23-29), but I fear that most Christians and most congregations do not truly live this way. We may assist with programs that shelter the homeless and feed the poor, but how far have we gone toward making them welcome, regular guests at our tables? Perhaps even more problematic is our treatment of the disabled or "differently" abled. Many congregations, unwittingly, have places or habits of worship that do not welcome those with physical or developmental/cognitive disabilities. Do we give them the best seats—literal and metaphorical seats—in our homes and worship spaces? God will, at the great banquet, and if we want our homes and churches to mirror God's kingdom, then we will, too.

The guest's interjection picks up on Jesus' reference to the resurrection. Pharisees were known to believe in the resurrection and the judgment (see Acts 23:8). Naturally anyone who believed in a

Excluded from the Table

Victory comes late—
And is held low to freezing lips—
Too rapt with frost
To take it—
How sweet it would have tasted—
Just a drop—
Was God so economical?
His Table's spread too high for Us—
Unless we dine on tip-toe—
Crumbs—fit such little mouths—
Cherries—suit Robins—
The Eagle's Golden Breakfast strangles—Them—
God keeps His Oath to Sparrows—
Who of little Love—know how to starve—

Emily Dickinson, 690, *The Complete Poems of Emily Dickinson*, ed. Thomas H. Johnson (Boston: Little, Brown, 1960).

future life with God would also hope that he would be included at God's table in the here-after. The Pharisee's benediction, then, is a bit like the various gospel songs celebrating owner-ship of a mansion in heaven: he expects to be one of the bread-eaters. Jesus' parable then undercuts premature house-warming parties: "everybody talking 'bout Heaven ain't getting there." [Excluded from the Table]

The plot of Luke's parable is similar to that in Matthew 22:1-14—the invitation is turned down by guests, and the host then invites a new group of guests. But Luke's banquet is not a wedding party; his guests give specific reasons for not coming; the slave is sent out twice to fill the house; and there is no Lukan parallel to the unfortunate guest who is not wearing his party clothes. The parable is also found in the *Gospel of Thomas*; the Thomas version is more like Luke's, but has a different list of excuses. [The Parable of the Great Banquet in *Gospel of Thomas*] No two of the three versions share much common wording, so instead of considering Luke's changes in a source—which we cannot reconstruct—we will instead interpret Luke's version as it sits in this chapter, in the context Luke has constructed for it.

Luke's host is an anonymous person ("a certain man"); although he is wealthy enough to have a large house that would accommo-date "many," Luke does not label him a "rich man," avoiding the nasty overtones of that moniker in this Gospel. The host of a fancy dinner would send out invitations for a certain date and time, sometimes far in advance, but then would send a slave (and some-times transportation) at the appointed time to gather in the guests.[10] Luke's readers would have assumed that the invited guests

The Parable of the Great Banquet in *Gospel of Thomas*

Jesus said: A person was receiving guests. When he had prepared the dinner, he sent his servant to invite the guests. The servant went to the first and said to that one, "My master invites you." That one said, "Some merchants owe me money; they are coming to me tonight. I must go and give instructions to them. Please excuse me from dinner." The servant went to another and said to that one, "My master has invited you." That one said to the servant, "I have bought a house, and I have been called away for a day. I shall have no time." The servant went to another and said to that one, "My master invites you." That one said to the servant, "My friend is to be married, and I am to arrange the dinner. I shall not be able to come. Please excuse me from dinner." The servant went to another and said to that one, "My master invites you." That one said to the servant, "I have bought an estate, and I am going to collect the rent. I shall not be able to come. Please excuse me." The servant returned and said to his master, "Those whom you invited to dinner have asked to be excused." The master said to his servant, "Go out on the streets, and bring back whomever you find to have dinner." Buyers and mer-chants will not enter the places of my Father.

Q-Thomas Reader, 144–45.

accepted the invitations offered in v. 16, but then, at the hour for the dinner to start, "they all as one began to decline." The excuses they offer are bogus. The first man has bought a field without ever looking at it—would you do that? (If you would, then let me talk to you about some beachfront property in Iowa.) The second man has bought beasts of burden—first-century tractors—and needs to take them for a test drive. Nope—you try out the oxen first, to make sure they are not lame, that they are broken to the plow, etc. The third man says, "I have married a wife and therefore I cannot come." This sounds almost legitimate—after all, Deuteronomy 20:7 allows newlyweds to beg off fighting in a holy war—until we remember that the husband accepted the first invitation, presumably knowing the date for his wedding, and then turned down the second one. The three speakers are examples of the sorts of excuses given by all the invited guests—so lame that the host is supposed to know that the guests are thumbing their noses at him. Somewhere between the original invitation and the dinner bell, the host has become a social pariah, and now none of his so-called friends want to attend his "great banquet."[11] Not so great if nobody comes, eh?

The slave returns to give a report to his master; "then, angry, the householder says to his slave . . . ." Note how the host changes titles: "a certain man" in v. 16, the slave's master (lord), and then "householder" in v. 21. This is his house; his slaves prepared the feast and would have served the guests, had they not refused the invitation. He then decides that if the invited guests are too good to eat with him, he will change guest lists. He sends his slave out into the streets to gather up "poor and disabled and blind and lame," the same group Jesus had recommended to the Pharisee who invited him. The slave does it, and then reports that there are still places on the dining couches. Then the master commands the slave to go outside the city and bring in people from "the roads and the hedges"—homeless people, who, like Jesus and his disciples, have no permanent place to live. Verse 24 seems to be the host's last word, but it is delivered to a plural "you": For I tell y'all that none of those men who were invited shall taste my supper. Is the host talking to all the slaves? More likely, he is speaking rhetorically to anyone who might be listening. Since those invited refused, the host in v. 24 says nothing new; this is less a curse or condemnation than a statement of fact.

The parable has often been understood to be about the history of the Jesus movement. Jesus came and offered an invitation to Israel, but they refused it, and so the church turned to the Gentiles. Such a reading is too narrow to fit Luke-Acts, where not all Israel turns down the invitation and not all the Gentiles accept it. One of Luke's consistent plot lines is that those who might be expected to respond to the gospel positively often do not, and those who do respond are often surprising; so Zechariah doubts while Mary believes. One reading of the parable is "take the invitation when it's offered, or you will be shut out when the party begins."

A second, more pointed reference for the parable is to the behavior of Luke's audience. Imagine a wealthy first-century Christian hearing Luke read aloud, being confronted with "don't invite your friends, invite the poor." He thinks to himself, "That sounds very noble, but it isn't realistic; after all, I have social obligations to uphold. If I had the city's riff-raff reclining at my table, none of my peers would ever have me over again." The parable of the great banquet is then a follow-up lesson on Christian ethics. The host of the banquet begins by ignoring Jesus' advice and inviting his friends—wealthy friends, by the sound of it, who can buy farms and lots of oxen. They all turn him down flat, inflicting public humiliation on him. The host then obeys Jesus, bringing in the poor and the disabled and the homeless, doing the right thing only after it becomes clear to him that he is high-status no longer. Reading it this way, the parable urges believers to embrace the sacrifice of status Jesus calls for in order to minister to those who need it most.

The first reading puts Luke's audience as the invited guests, and makes the parable a cautionary tale—don't presume on God's hospitality. The second reading puts the audience as the host—why not invite the poor first, and as a habit of life? A third reading situates the audience as the poor, the disabled, the homeless—they are the ones pulled into the banquet hall, "compelled to enter" by the householder's slave. These are they who, according to Mary, will be lifted up by her son's ministry, fed and satisfied when the rich are sent away with growling bellies. Read this way, the parable is an exhortation to value the kingdom more than anything else—more than farms and houses, more than oxen and crops and money, more than family. That reading is the segue into the next section, where Jesus speaks to the crowds about the demands of the cross.

Cost of Discipleship, 14:25-35

Mary Gordon's novel *Pearl* begins with a mother finding out that her daughter has "gotten herself into a little bit of an unusual situation. She's chained herself to the flagpole in front of the American embassy in Dublin. She says she hasn't eaten in six weeks, and she is refusing food and drink."[12] Pearl, her mom eventually discovers, has decided that she should give her life to protest the death of another young man, and has taken steps to make certain that she will die: she has carefully researched how a person starves, and has thought about how the authorities are likely to respond, so that once she enters the phase of public protest, she believes she will be too close to death to be rescued. While she is still lucid, she writes a letter to her mother, asking her mother to try to understand her motives. "I know that you love me," she writes. "Please know that I have loved you. You may think I should live for you, to keep you from this sorrow, but I cannot. It is better that I am not in this life. Please understand that this has nothing to do with you. There is nothing you could have done."[13]

What parent would agree that a daughter's suicide is the proper response to the unjust killing of another? How hard would it be for a parent to accept and to honor a child's choice for martyrdom, especially when the cause that transformed the child's life was outside the parent's experience—my child needs to die to honor the death of a stranger? Swap the positions of parent and child, or change the roles to spouse and spouse, or brother and sister, and the incomprehensibility of the choice is undiminished. Luke's audience—first-century Christians, mostly recent converts from other traditional religions—doubtless included men and women who had been through angry and tearful conflicts with their families over the decision to follow "the Way." In the stories of martyrs from early Christianity, family members are often pictured pleading with the martyr to change his/her mind, and responding in anger when he/she refuses. [Thecla's Family]

Never one to sugarcoat the nature of the gospel, Luke in this section presents the cost of discipleship in three stark demands for sacrifice, supported by three illustrative metaphors or parables. We interpreters must avoid making these passages easier than Luke meant them: "I know it says 'hate,' but what it really means is . . . ." But we must also find a way to make them real—to present them as real choices for the people in our audiences—

Thecla's Family

The 2d-century Acts of Paul includes a long section about a woman named Thecla who was converted by Paul's preaching. After becoming a believer, she refuses to see her non-Christian fiancé, and her mother is grieved. Thamyris, the fiancé, says to her,

"Thecla, my betrothed, why dost thou sit thus? And what is this passion that holds thee distracted? Turn to Thamyris and be ashamed." And her mother also said the same: "Child, why dost thou sit thus looking down and making no answer, but like one stricken?" And those who were in the house wept bitterly, Thamyris for the loss of a wife, Theocleia for that of a daughter, the maidservants for that of a mistress. So there was a great confusion of mourning in the house. And while this was going on all around her Thecla did not turn away, but gave her whole attention to Paul's word. (2.240-41)

In due course, Thecla was arraigned before the governor, who asks her why she is stubbornly refusing to marry her lawfully betrothed fiancé; when she does not answer, her mother condemns her: "Burn the lawless one! Burn her that is no bride in the midst of the theatre, that all the women who have been taught by this man may be afraid!" (2.242)

Acts of Paul, in Wilhelm Schneemelcher, ed., *New Testament Apocrypha,* trans. and ed. R. McL. Wilson, 2 vols (Louisville KY: Westminster/John Knox Press, 1991–1992).

something that can be done, and not just shelved with the other impossible demands from Jesus.

The setting is still the journey to Jerusalem, and the audience is the "many crowds" traveling with him. As demands to the crowds, these are entrance requirements, what one must do to move from "crowd" to "disciple." But since the Gospel is being written to be read aloud to small groups of Christians, we should also think of these demands as performance standards for disciples. If there were an annual evaluation for Jesus' disciples, these would be three of the review categories; how do we rate in these areas?

The first demand is to hate your family. It is expressed as a minimal performance goal, so that failure to meet it means one cannot be part of the group: "If someone comes to me and does not hate one's own father and mother and wife and children and brothers and sisters and even one's own life, that person is not able to be my disciple." There is a parallel in Matthew 10:37-38, and it goes a bit easier on the would-be disciple; rather than "hate," the criteria is loving the family member more than Jesus, and Matthew's list does not include wife and children. If Matthew and Luke were drawing on the same source "Q," then either Matthew has toned things down a bit or Luke has intensified the demands; however that happened, Luke's version of this demand is so unpleasant that it makes us squirm.

Luke's Jesus also commands us to love our enemies and do them good (6:35), so hating our families cannot mean actively trying to do them harm. Nevertheless, putting obedience and devotion to Jesus ahead of any family commitment may look like hate to the family and to the rest of the world. The choices one makes to follow Jesus may also feel like hating, especially if following Jesus means moving physically or emotionally farther from family. In 18:28, Peter says to Jesus, "We have followed you, abandoning our own"—their homes, their immediate and extended families, their community, their employment networks. In order to follow through with this level of social disruption and dislocation, the would-be disciple needs to face how it will be interpreted and how it will feel.

The second demand is to bear one's cross, also expressed in the negative: "Whoever does not bear his/her own cross and come after me is not able to be my disciple." In the commentary on 9:23, I argued that first-century audiences would have heard the call to bear the cross very literally. In their world, crucifixion was the punishment for rebellious slaves and for rebels against the Roman Empire. [Carrying the Cross as an Extra Warning] It was considered the most humiliating and painful way to be executed, so distasteful that educated and cultured writers often used euphemisms like "the ultimate punishment" or "the slave's death." In the bawdy comedies of Plautus, slaves and other low-class characters use "in maximam malem crucem" (lit., "in the most awful cross") as a rough equivalent to "go to hell," and are always insulting people by calling them "cross-bait."

Here's the point: when Luke's audience heard "bear your cross," they did not first think of taking on extra responsibilities or bearing up patiently under a burden, as in "Dad is living with us now—I guess that's our cross to bear." They heard it as a call to put their lives on the line as a consequence of following Jesus. As Gordon's Pearl puts it, this is not the same as a death wish or as a coming-to-terms with one's inevitable mortality:

> When you have decided that you will die—which is a different thing from knowing that you want to die and different, too, from the idea that you no longer want to live—when you've come to that point, nothing is difficult . . . you can take in anything and nothing can be taken from you.[14]

For Jesus, crucifixion was the end of the journey to Jerusalem; to follow Jesus on that road meant to accept the same fate. In the story world of the Gospel, at 14:26 that choice was still potential. Someone might have chosen to follow Jesus all the way, to do as he did and to be nailed to a cross beside him. But as Luke's audience listens to 14:26, they know that nobody did it. While Peter and the others did abandon their families, they did not go to the cross with Jesus, but instead abandoned him to his fate.

Thus the passage moves naturally to two parabolic illustrations for facing up to

Carrying the Cross as an Extra Warning

Crucifixion, as noted in the commentary, was a typical punishment for disobedient slaves. In the ancient (either 1st century BC or 1st century AD) novel Chaereas and Callirhoe, the hero Chaereas has, through a series of unfortunate incidents, been sold into slavery. Some of the other slaves working with him on the slaveowner's estate kill their overseer and try to escape, but are recaptured. "Without even seeing them or hearing their defense the master at once ordered the crucifixion of the sixteen men in the hut. They were brought out chained together at foot and neck, each carrying his own cross—the men executing the sentence added this grim public spectacle to frighten the other prisoners."

Chariton, *Chaereas and Callirhoe*, trans. B. P. Reardon, in Reardon, *Collected Ancient Greek Novels* (Berkeley CA: University of California Press, 1989), 67.

Crucified Man

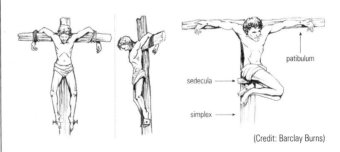

(Credit: Barclay Burns)

The only remains of a crucified person found from the 1st century are the right ankle bone of a man. The nail bent as it went into the upright part of the cross, and so when the man was buried, the nail was buried with him. The illustrations show two guesses about how he was attached to the cross. Those who heard Jesus speak about "taking up the cross" and those who heard Luke read aloud would have images like this in their minds.

the terrible choice and sacrifice of these first two demands; the would-be disciple must make an informed decision, or risk bailing out prematurely. Both parables are unique to Luke. In the first, the members of the audience are invited to imagine themselves in the narrative: "Who among you" members of the crowd, "if he/she wished to build a tower, would not first sit and calculate the cost"? The question expects the answer "yes, I'd surely do that"—before I started to build a tower in my field or vineyard[15] (a platform from which one can more easily spot two- or four-legged thieves, and from which one might sling rocks to drive them away), I'd try to estimate the materials needed, price them and the labor, and then decide if I could start. A half-finished tower is a public mistake, good for nothing except attracting ridicule.[16]

In this first parable, the negative consequence is shame, but shame from whom? The tower-builder who flakes out will be ridiculed by family, neighbors, and passers-by; if this is a parable related to deciding to follow Jesus, then those who offer ridicule are most likely the same family, friends, and neighbors whom you left behind when you became a disciple. That would be painful, but nothing like the shame that will be felt on Judgment Day when Jesus denies you before the angels (12:9). Passers-by who see and call out taunts remind us of some who watched Jesus' crucifixion: "He saved others, he cannot save himself" (23:35-36). There is shame any way one turns: humiliation for the one who follows Jesus to the cross, humiliation both now and later for the one who turns away from the cross because it is just too hard. [Cautions to Martyrs Whose Faith Fails]

The second parable begins "which king"—none of the listeners, but the parable works with typical behavior of royalty. If King A has ten thousand, he sits and thinks whether he can actually defeat King B, who has twice as many troops; if he thinks he cannot, he sends an embassy to ask for terms of peace. In this parable, the negative consequence are much more dire. King A, if he unwisely chooses to attack a superior force, may lose his life, the lives of his soldiers, and his kingdom. Generals of victorious armies often sold the losing troops as slaves. But even if he is wise, there is still not a happy ending, because the terms of peace will likely include heavy financial payments, and if he keeps his kingdom, he will certainly have to swear loyalty to King B. The only "happy"

Cautions to Martyrs Whose Faith Fails

A passage in the 2d-century *Martyrdom of Polycarp* warns about those who think they want to be martyred, but then back out:

But there was a person named Quintus, a Phrygian who had recently come from Phrygia, who was overcome with cowardice when he saw the wild beasts. This is the one who compelled both himself and several others to turn themselves in. But the insistent pleas of the proconsul convinced him to take the oath and offer a sacrifice. Because of this, brothers, we do not praise those who hand themselves over, since this is not what the gospel teaches

Mart. Pol. 4.

ending to this narrative would be King A deciding correctly that his army can win the battle, and risking all to that end.

The would-be disciple, like the king, must decide if he is up to the all-or-nothing act of committing himself and all his resources. Will he turn away from his family, even from his own life, to follow Jesus? If not, then what are his options? Jesus, on his arrival in Jerusalem, will lament that had they known the terms for peace— *ta pros eirēnēn*—then things could have been different (the phrase used in 19:42 is the same as in 14:32), but as they didn't, their destruction was certain. There are no terms for peace, in other words, other than taking up the cross and hating one's family.

[Taking up the Cross]

Oh, and poverty: "So then each of you who does not renounce all your stuff cannot be my disciple." This is not new advice: "give to everyone who asks" (6:30); "sell your stuff, and give alms" (12:33). It matches what Jesus says to the Pharisees about only inviting the poor and disabled to your banquets (14:12-14), it matches the conduct of the early church in Acts (2:44-45; 4:32, 34), and it imitates the way Jesus describes the nature of God. One could think of this third demand as a consequence of or a precondition for the first two. In Jesus' day, to abandon all one's family and social networks would be to choose poverty; yet to make a complete break with family and with one's own life and future would also require getting rid of all one's stuff. Luke's Jesus does not imagine that this means starving. The disciple who leaves everything to follow Jesus on the road will find food and shelter along the way (10:7), and will pray for daily rations, knowing that God will provide (11:3, 9-13).

> **Taking up the Cross**
>
> Earth would have been too much—I see—
> And Heaven—not enough for me—
> I should have had the Joy
> Without the Fear—to justify—
> The Palm—without the Calvary—
> So Saviour—Crucify—
>
> Emily Dickinson, 313, *The Complete Poems of Emily Dickinson*, ed. Thomas H. Johnson (Boston: Little, Brown, 1960).

The third illustrative metaphor is about salt. "Salt is good"; a simple, unqualified statement. Salt was a necessity for cooking and for preserving, as well as a condiment that made things taste better. How can salt become insipid? "Real salt cannot lose its flavor, but the complex minerals around the Dead Sea were not pure salt and could, therefore, become tasteless."[17] The unsalty salt was then good for nothing, and would be thrown out, like the unproductive tree that is cut down (13:6-9) or the worthless slave who is handed over to the torturers (12:41-48).

If this third metaphor is meant to illustrate the third demand, then it says that the call to renunciation of property is nonnegotiable. It is part of the nature of the faith, the saltiness of Jesus' disciples. In a world of profit-seekers and consumers, the followers of Jesus are expected to follow a different course. If they fail, then what good are they? If Christians become materialistic consumers just like everyone else, what will make them salty again? Nothing— if they will not follow Jesus, then they certainly will not learn renunciation of possessions from the world.

Three demands, three illustrations, all very clear, all mostly ignored or stretched beyond recognition by modern believers. Stanley Hauerwas argues that, in fact, our love of home and family often drives us to do violence; certainly we defend our nation's militarism and gross consumption because it makes our lives and property secure. He writes,

> I suspect some of us begin to have just a little sympathy with those who put Jesus to death. How dare Jesus tell me to hate my father, my mother, my spouse, and especially my children! Yet that is exactly what he said we must do if we are to be part of God's kingdom of peace and love. For any love that does not love the other in relation to the God who has loved us is now accursed.[18]

Loving our family or our enemies or ourselves, when that love takes the form of abandonment for the sake of the kingdom, will look and feel like hate. Tell your parent or your child or your spouse, "I am giving up my life for the sake of the gospel," and see what reaction you get. Tell them that you are selling all your possessions as a path to the cross, and ridicule may be the least of their responses. But it isn't shame that keeps most of us from obeying Jesus, or even attachment to family. Most of us, raised in the American church, have never seriously considered the sort of commitment that Jesus indicated was the minimum for being his disciple. Luke does not present these demands as if they were radical—although they are, and always have been—but as the lowest bar of service, things that, if not done, would render us tasteless, useless, failures. Bruce Wollenburg's advice is to admit our failure, since we can seem to do no better, and hope for terms of peace:

> We are not prepared to hate, carry, follow, or give up all our stuff. Therefore, having counted the cost and declared it excessive, we cannot be counted disciples of Jesus. Our only recourse is to the God of the cross we're incapable of carrying, to a grace that requires nothing, including discipleship. And perhaps mercy will allow us to (mis)interpret the Master's words as calling us to give up all our plans and possessions to God and let this impossible Jesus be Lord of every relationship and of every last penny.[19]

He is probably correct, or more precisely, is absolutely correct about most of us. But sometimes, for some of us at some moments, circumstances can bring us to the point where we can let go of our stuff, our networks, our loves, and ourselves, and follow Jesus:

> We forget that there are moments, public moments, what could be called moments in history that change a life. By *we* I mean those of us who have been brought up, as Pearl had been, in safety and prosperity, whose lives have been shaped by private moments, private acts. We forget, or believe it distantly, as we believe in the orbiting of the planets, the working of DNA. . . .
>
> She has never doubted that she was greatly loved. But it was not enough to let her to live in a world where her witnesses tell her there is nothing stronger than the will to harm . . . .
>
> She would give her life; she would become a witness. And what is the strongest possible witness? The witness unto death.[20]

CONNECTIONS

This chapter is absolutely packed with things we cannot or will not do: give up status markers of all sorts; invite only the poor and disabled to our dinner parties; hate our families; take up Jesus' cross; give up all our possessions. In my opinion, it is a mistake to water these things down—to say that since these things are too hard for us, Jesus must not really have meant them. In my opinion (and by this point in the commentary, you may be really tired of my opinion), we have to keep the bar as high as Jesus set it. And, as noted in the commentary section above, these are not presented in Luke as the "counsels of perfection," special vows for those who want to be special disciples. These are the minimum: if you are not willing to do these things, according to 14:26, 27, and 33, you cannot be Jesus' disciple.

But it's too hard, you and I say, it's just *too hard.* Could we not think of some intermediate steps that will at least get us started? Yes, we could, and some of you are already doing them. What we must do is think of these as steps in the direction of a goal, the goal being to come as close to obedience to Jesus' teachings as we are able.

For example, you may already give some fraction of your income to your local church (if you're a faithful tither, on behalf of your pastor, God bless you!). Why not make it your goal to increase your set-aside—not diminishing what you give to your local congregation, but decreasing what you spend on eating out, on movie rentals, on clothing, etc., until you, like righteous Tobit, are giving a second 10 percent to the local poor and a third 10 percent to relieve global poverty? You can't do this all at once, but by giving away future raises and by systematically asking what you really need, you can begin to make progress.

There are all sorts of charitable organizations in your community, and your congregation may already be partnering with them. Becoming a volunteer—building homes, feeding the hungry, spending the night with the homeless—will help you connect your gifts of money with the needs of real people. As you spend more time in face-to-face ministry, you and your values will be challenged and changed.

And then there are steps beyond changes in personal behavior. Does your church, like mine, create regular meals for the congregation? These are good and important things: they encourage busy families to make time for Bible study and mutual prayer, and they foster networks of care in the congregation. But what if large numbers of congregations started obeying Jesus and using these meals as a time to host the poor? Some churches have done this for years, and consider it simply a part of their normal ministry. Is it unreasonable to think that in every city and town, there would be enough churches willing to do this, enough so that no poor person in this country would ever have to starve? Or what if the congregations of a city decided that despite their religious differences, they could all agree that God expects God's people to minister to orphans, widows, and foreigners, and decided that every elderly person, every orphan, and every immigrant would be assigned to the ministry of a particular congregation?

One could go on and on. There are so many things we could do if it seemed important to us to do them. If ministry was valued more highly than leisure time, and if charity was more significant to us than accumulation of wealth and goods, then Christian congregations could eliminate many of our huge social problems. And if Christians would take Jesus seriously about loving our enemies . . . don't get me started about the unholy marriage of materialism and militarism in our country, and how the American church has blessed the slaughter of innocents in order to preserve our lifestyle. Let's begin where we can agree: do you agree that it's wrong for us to let the poor die if we can prevent it? Then let's do what we can, and hope for God's mercy.

NOTES

[1] Plutarch, "Dinner of the Seven Wise Men," *Moralia* 148.D (trans. F. C. Babbitt; London: Heinemann, 1928), 363.

[2] Luke Timothy Johnson, *The Gospel of Luke* (SP, vol. 3; Collegeville MN: Liturgical Press, 1991), 223, points out that the verb used here has negative connotations at Luke 6:7; 20:20; and Acts 9:24.

[3] Johnson, *Luke*, 223.

[4] Some manuscripts read "ass" instead of "son," which would make a lot more sense, and remove part of the difficulty in Jesus' question, since the cases of a child and of a beast of burden were not the same. While it is possible that "ass" was original (so John Nolland, *Luke* (WBC, vols. 35A-C; Dallas TX: Word, 1989-93), 2.744), most commentators think "son" was probably original and that later copyists wrote "ass" because they assumed "son" was an error. So Joseph A. Fitzmyer, *The Gospel According to Luke* (AB 28 and 28A; Garden City NY: Doubleday, 1981), 2.1042; Johnson, Luke, 223; Bruce Metzger, *A Textual Commentary on the Greek New Testament* (New York: United Bible Societies, 1971), 164.

[5] Plutarch, *Table Talk* I.2 (*Moralia* 616D-F).

[6] Ibid., 616B.

[7] Ibid., 617C.

[8] Ibid., 617A.

[9] Tannehill, "The Lukan Discourse on Invitations," in *The Shape of Luke's Story: Essays on Luke-Acts* (Eugene OR: Cascade, 1005), 61–69.

[10] Bernard Brandon Scott, *Hear Then the Parable: A Commentary on the Parables of Jesus* (Minneapolis: Fortress, 1989), 169; Plutarch, *Dinner of the Seven Wise Men* (Moralia 147.D), remarks on invitations being given up to a year in advance, so that women could plan their wardrobe and jewelry.

[11] So Robert C. Tannehill, *Luke* (ANTC; Nashville: Abingdon, 1996), 233; Scott, *Hear Then the Parable*, 171; Alan R. Culpepper, *The Gospel of Luke* (*NIB*, vol. 9; Nashville: Abingdon, 1995), 289; Joel B. Green, *The Gospel of Luke* (NICNT; Grand Rapids: Eerdmans, 1997), 559.

[12] Mary Gordon, *Pearl* (New York: Anchor, 2006), 6.

[13] Ibid., 18.

[14] Ibid., 13.

[15] Theoretically, the tower could also be a fortification in a city wall or in a palace, but then the "which of you" makes no sense. Arlen Hultgren, *The Parables of Jesus: A Commentary* (Grand Rapids MI: Eerdmans, 2000), 139, also argues for the likelihood of the farm tower, but notes that other sorts are not ruled out by the word chosen.

[16] The doors on my garage rotted, so I decided to build new ones myself. These were large barn-style doors hinged on either side and closing in the middle. I was taking a break from hanging them when my neighbor dropped by to check on my progress. "That's a clever design," he said. "I like how they slant towards the middle like that—is that so that all the rain comes off in one spot?"

[17] Culpepper, *Luke*, 293.

[18] Stanley Hauerwas, "Hating Mothers as the Way to Peace," in *Unleashing the Scripture: Freeing the Bible from Captivity to America* (Nashville: Abingdon, 1993), 123–24.

[19] Bruce Wollenburg, "Summoned," *ChrCent* 121/17 (24 August 2004): 17.

[20] Gordon, *Pearl*, 157, 175, 174.

THREE PARABLES OF FINDING

Luke 15

COMMENTARY

Finding the Lost, 15:1-10

This section is made of the twin parables of the lost sheep and the lost coin, along with a setting to give them a focal point. The lost sheep appears in Matthew 18:12-14, along with other teachings on the nature of the church; in the commentary below, we will take note of a couple of Lukan differences. The lost coin is found only in Luke, leading to a debate among scholars about whether Luke composed it or found it in one of his sources. The pair, like several other Lukan pairs, matches a man with a woman (Zechariah and Mary, Simeon and Anna, the centurion and widow of chapter 7); we are being encouraged to read one narrative against the other, and to read both alongside the much longer narrative that follows.

Ira Sankey, organist for Dwight L. Moody's revival meetings, found the text of "The Ninety and Nine" as a poem printed in a newspaper and, impressed by it, cut it out and put it in his musical scrapbook. ["The Ninety and Nine"] The next day, at the conclusion of a meeting where Moody and others spoke on the topic of "The Good Shepherd," Moody turned to Sankey to ask him for an appropriate solo.

> **The Ninety and Nine**
>
> There were ninety and nine that safely lay
> In the shelter of the fold
> But one was out on the hills away
> Far off from the gates of gold.
>
> "The Ninety and Nine," lyrics by Elizabeth C. Clephane, 1868.

At this moment I seemed to hear a voice saying: "Sing the hymn you found on the train!" But I thought this impossible, as no music had ever been written for that hymn. Again the impression came strongly upon me that I must sing the beautiful and appropriate words I had found the day before, and placing the little newspaper slip on the organ in front of me, I lifted my heart in prayer, asking God to help me so to sing that the people might hear and understand. Laying my hands upon the organ I struck the key of A flat, and began to sing.[1]

The hymn text merges the sheep's owner with Jesus, and the rescue with his crucifixion:

> Lord, thou hast here thy ninety-and-nine
> Are they not enough for thee?
> Said the Shepherd, I go to find the one
> That has wandered away from me . . .
> But none of the ransomed ever knew
> How deep were the waters crossed
> Nor how dark the night the Lord passed through
> E'er he found the sheep that was lost

Church art, likewise, made the parable into an allegory of Jesus' experience, with paintings reproduced in Sunday school resource packets giving the shepherd the long white robe, flowing chestnut hair, and kind face of the Sallman Jesus. In some versions, he is reaching for a lamb that stands perilously close to a cliff, about to plunge to its death; in others, he has the lamb tucked under his arm, and is about to restore it to the flock.

The lost coin, with its female protagonist, is not the stuff of gospel hymns or Sunday school paintings. Commentators from ancient times recognized that the "finding" image was the same in both parables, and that if the shepherd was an image for God or for Jesus, then the woman was as well [Cyril of Alexandria on the Lost Coin]; yet it was harder to make the straightforward identification, the woman is Christ, and so, presumably, harder to allegorize the parable quite as much. Nobody wrote, "But none of the ransomed ever knew/ how deep was the dirt he faced, / nor how dark were the corners the Lord swept up/ E'er he found the coin he misplaced."

Part of our task, then, is to rediscover the lost parable for church groups, and to read both parables together in relation to the ministry of Jesus, as Luke clearly intended by his introduction. [The Three Parables]

Jesus is still on the road to Jerusalem, although we are not told where he is or the specific setting—house, synagogue, marketplace—for these words. "All the tax collectors and sinners were approaching him to listen to him"—"all" probably meaning "in general, tax collectors and sinners responded to him," by contrast to the Pharisees and scribes (so 7:29-30). Coming near to listen, especially following Jesus' call to open ears (13:35), puts them on the road to discipleship. Tax collectors were the men who actually

---

Cyril of Alexandria on the Lost Coin

We, who had fallen and had been lost, have been found by Christ and transformed by holiness and righteousness into his image. . . . A search was made for that which had fallen, so the woman lighted a lamp. . . . By the light, what was lost is saved, and there is joy for the powers above. . . . They keep a festival over one who is saved, united with the divine purpose, and never cease to praise the Savior's goodness.

Commentary on Luke, homily 106; cited in Arthur A. Just Jr., ed., *Luke* (ACCS: NT, vol. 3; Downer's Grove IL: Intervarsity Press, 2003), 245.

The Three Parables

St. Luke did not idly present three parables in a row. By the parables of the sheep that strayed and was found, the coin which was lost and was found, and the son who was dead and came to life, we may cure our wounds, being encouraged by a threefold remedy. "A threefold cord will not be broken." Who are the father, the shepherd, and the woman? They are God the Father, Christ, and the church. Christ carries you on his body, he who took your sins on himself. The church seeks, and the Father receives. The shepherd carries. The mother searches. The father clothes. First mercy comes, then intercession, and third reconciliation. Each complements the other. The Savior rescues, the church intercedes, and the Creator reconciles. The mercy of the divine act is the same, but the grace differs according to our merits. The weary sheep is recalled by the shepherd, the coin which is lost is found, the son retraces his steps to his father and returns, guilty of error but totally repentant.

Ambrose, *Exp. Luc.* 7.207-8, cited in Arthur A. Just Jr., ed., *Luke* (ACCS: NT, vol. 3; Downer's Grove IL: Intervarsity Press, 2003), 244.

collected tolls and tariffs, who made their living by overcharging persons who passed through their booths (see commentary at 5:27-39). Sinners in Luke are persons who need to repent; in Luke, at least, it does not mean "poor" and has nothing to do with being unclean or prohibited from the temple or synagogue (more at commentary on 5:27-39).

The Pharisees "murmured" about Jesus' eating with tax collectors and sinners back at 5:30; in 15:2, Luke uses an intensified form of the same verb, the one familiar from the stories of the Israelites murmuring in the wilderness about their thirst and the boring menu (Exod 15:24, for example, uses the same verb as at Luke 15:2). The verb means that they made a public complaint; to whom? To each other, clearly, but also to the crowds, who are not named but who could be assumed from 14:25 to be still in the background to hear the parables. The disciples—the larger group of Jesus' followers, including the Twelve—are also probably assumed to be nearby, since at 16:1 Jesus addresses them without a change of venue.

Here's the scene: Jesus is tramping along the road, with a large mass of people—the crowds—in neutral colors, with no particular features. The Pharisees and scribes are along the outside of the crowd, carrying protest signs ("Jesus is a fink"), heckling ("Who'd you eat with last night, Jesus—Jack Abramoff?"), passing out flyers to the crowds exposing the real Jesus ("He claims to be a prophet, but he encourages sinful women to lick his toes"). Closest to Jesus are the tax collectors and sinners. There is at least one tax collector (5:27-28) and at least one sinner (5:8) among the apostles, who are included in the disciples; the boundaries between sinner/tax collector and disciple are thus permeable, as the parables will make clear. Imagine the group around Jesus, then, dressed in t-shirts that keep changing colors (you can do anything with special effects)— red for sinners, green for tax collectors, and white for disciples—so that the cluster of folks walking beside Jesus is constantly being transformed. When Jesus speaks "to them" in v. 3, he is addressing these multiple audiences, and as the Gospel of Luke was read to groups of first-century believers, Jesus essentially speaks to Christians far from Palestine as well.

The lost sheep in Luke's version is "lost" and does not "stray" as in Matthew's (Matt 18:12). The audience is asked to imagine themselves the owners of one hundred sheep—according to modern estimates, this would be a substantial flock and the owner therefore wealthy[2]—who "lost" one of them. In "real life," no wealthy adult man would actually tend his own sheep, but would have hired men or boys or poorer relations to do the work for him.

On Shepherds and Flocks

For herds of larger cattle older men, for the smaller [i.e., sheep and goats] even boys; but in both cases those who range the trails should be sturdier than those on the farm who come back to the steading every day. Thus on the range you may see young men, usually armed, while on the farm not only boys but even girls tend the flocks. The herdsmen should be required to stay on the range the entire day and have the herds feed together; but, on the other hand, to spend the night each with his own herd . . . . The number of herdsmen is determined differently, some having a smaller, some a larger number. My own practice is to have a herdsman to every eighty wool-bearing sheep, while Atticus has one to every hundred. If flocks of sheep are very large (and some people have as many as 1,000) you can decrease the number of shepherds more easily than you can in smaller flocks, such as those of Atticus and mine.

Varro, *On Agriculture* II.10.1-2, 11 (trans. William Davis Hooper; rev. Harrison Boyd Ash; Cambridge MA: Harvard University Press, 1967), 405, 411. Marcus Terentius Varro wrote his treatise in the late 1st century BC.

[On Shepherds and Flocks] But the parable is told in such a way that rich people could imagine the loss happening because of an employee's carelessness, and poor people could imagine it happening because they could not keep up with so many sheep at once. However the sheep is lost, the loss belongs to the owner—who is never called a shepherd—and in the story, the owner "leaves the ninety-nine in the wilderness and goes for the lost one until he finds it." Which of you, says Jesus, would not do just that?

Well, maybe nobody. In "real life," a shepherd would not leave the flock, since they could wander away, be attacked by predators, or be stolen in his absence; he would always first put them in a sheepfold or leave them with another shepherd.[3] The loss of a sheep, even if it were one out of a hundred, would be significant, but the owner acts irresponsibly to leave the ninety-nine unattended while he goes after the one.[4] Then the sheep owner, having carried the lost sheep home, throws a party, inviting his friends and neighbors: "Rejoice with me, because I found my lost sheep." The owner's joy at having found his lost property makes sense, but the banquet he puts together will quite likely require cooking animals from his flocks and herds (as at 15:23, when the prodigal returns). Nothing the sheep owner does makes economic sense: losing the sheep; risking the rest of the flock; spending money to celebrate the recovery of lost property. "Which of you would do this?" asks Jesus. Maybe none of them.

Verse 7 again speaks directly to the audiences. God's joy ("in heaven" is most likely a euphemism for God) is greater over one penitent sinner than over ninety-nine "righteous ones who need no repentance" (we set aside, for the present, the question of whether Luke imagines someone who needs no repentance). The whole scenario, then, describes the nature of God, who acts much differently than any of us. If God rejoices, then God seeks the lost. But the conclusion puts in a new wrinkle by calling the lost sheep a sinner, putting the responsibility for the "lostness" with the sinner rather than with God (more on this later also).

Change gears, change gender: "Which woman"—of you who are listening to me? Certainly, because there were women among the disciples, traveling with Jesus (8:1-3). A drachma was a small silver coin considered to be about the same value as a denarius—a day's wages for an unskilled worker, in other words.[5] The woman had ten of these; it is often plausibly suggested that they had been pierced and strung on a chain, and she wore them as a necklace; Bailey, however, points out that village peasant women do not wear jewelry for ordinary occasions,[6] and so perhaps we are to imagine that the coin had been stored somewhere—archaeologists sometimes find money buried beneath the foundations of houses—until the woman had need to check her money box.

When she realizes she has lost one of her ten coins, she lights an oil lamp—because her house is very dark and the coin is quite small—and when she cannot spot it, she begins to sweep the floor until she hears the coin ring against the floor.[7] Up to this point in the story, what she does is exactly what anyone would do: the nine coins are in no danger while she looks for the tenth; the job of caring for the coin belongs to its owner, and it is natural for the owner to want to recover it. But then the woman invites her friends and neighbors to her house to "rejoice," to have a festive meal, to celebrate the recovery of a day's wages. That hardly seems reasonable, since—like the sheep owner—she is likely to spend more than she recovered, and as a relatively poor person—she has ten drachmas—she can ill afford to act like she has money to burn. Even so, says Jesus, God celebrates the repentance of one sinner, setting out a big feed in the presence of the angels. Which of you would do this? Well, all of them could imagine doing the searching; maybe some of them could imagine giving the party. So while the first parable essentially says "God is not like you," this one makes God—and thus the godly life—more accessible. Yes, perhaps I can be like that. [Women's Work]

Thomas Merton (Credit: Barclay Burns)

Both protagonists go all out to find their lost property and go all out to celebrate its return. Each of them feels called, like Jesus, to "seek out and save the lost" (19:10), and they keep searching until they find (11:9-10). Each of them—wealthier man, poorer woman—is as much a Christ figure as the other. Christ the Good Shepherd is also Christ the Sweeping Woman; as interpreters, we can do our best to embed both images in our listeners.

The two characters are also ideal disciples. Each of them works hard to find the lost; neither of them is dissuaded by the cost of discipleship; each of them is a generous host, ready to think of their own property as a gift to be shared with others.

Neither sheep nor coin repents, and yet both narratives are explicitly said to mirror God's joy when a sinner repents. Tricky Luke: the finders work hard to find, just as Jesus did; and yet sinners must repent, just as Levi the tax collector and Peter the sinner did when they were found. [Searching as a Key to Spiritual Growth] The boundaries between sinner/tax collector and disciple turn out to be as fuzzy as the distinction between "finding" and "repenting." If they are "lost," like the sheep and the coin, then they are not really outsiders, but just temporarily misplaced. If they are "sinners" who need to repent, then they have wandered and are in danger of being excluded at the Judgment. In repenting, we find ourselves found; when we turn to go home, we discover that we are already there, God having already scooped us up. [Always Being Found]

From Luke's point of view, are there "righteous ones who need no repentance"? That seems unlikely, given 13:1-5, where the point is that everyone needs to repent, and given the parable of the Pharisee and the tax collector (18:9-14), where the self-justified are only self-deluded. Possibly the ninety-nine in 15:4, 7 would have signified for Luke those who had already repented and were part of the Jesus movement. But perhaps 15:7b is ironic; the ninety-nine who need no repentance actually do repent, and unless they do, will miss out on the joy of heaven.

> But up from the mountains, thunder-riv'n
> and up from the rocky deep
> There arose a glad cry to the gates of Heaven: Rejoice,
> I have found my sheep!
> And the angels echoed around the throne: Rejoice, for
> the Lord brings back his own!
>
> My barren black cat rubs against my legs.
> I think of the barren women
> exhorted by the Good Book
> to break into song:
> we should sing, dear cat,
> for the children who will come in our old age.
> The cat doesn't laugh,
> but I do. She rolls in dust
> as I finish sweeping.[8]

> **Always Being Found**
>
> Deep within us all there is an amazing inner sanctuary of the soul, a holy place, a Divine Center, a speaking Voice, to which we may continually return. Eternity is at our hearts, pressing upon our time-torn lives, warming us with intimations of an astounding destiny, calling us home unto Itself. Yielding to these persuasions, gladly committing ourselves in body and soul, utterly and completely, to the Light Within, is the beginning of true life. . . . In this humanistic age we suppose [the human] is the initiator and God is the responder. But the Living Christ within us is the initiator and we are the responders. God the Lover, the accuser, the revealer of light and darkness presses within us. "Behold I stand at the door and knock." And all our apparent initiative is already a response, a testimonial to His secret presence and working within us.
>
> Thomas R. Kelly, *A Testament of Devotion* (1941; New York: HarperSanFrancisco, 1992), 3–4.

The Prodigal Son, 15:11-32

This is Jesus' longest parable, and it is often characterized as the best of them all.[9] The characters are well developed and fluid, the narrator's diction is both clear and highly nuanced, and the plot provides tensions resolved and unresolved—the best of circumstances for interpreters, because there is plenty here to think about. Like many great stories, it resists titles. "The Prodigal Son" puts the focus on the younger son and his running away from home, but does not account for the second half of the story. "The Loving Father" correctly identifies the hero of the story, but fails to identify the source of the tension. "The Man and His Two Sons" is accurate enough, but bland; what if we called it "The Father and His Two Lost Boys" or "The Dysfunctional Family" or, with apologies to Tolstoy, "Unhappy Families Are All Alike"?

"There was a man who had two sons" sets up an expectation that there will be a contrast between the two boys. Luke's readers will remember Father Isaac, whose two sons Esau and Jacob fought like cats in the sack of Rachel's womb. In that story, the younger son, through his own cunning, his brother's stupidity, his father's blindness, and his mother's complicity, winds up with the elder son's right of inheritance and the parental blessing on the firstborn. If the reader is thinking of that story when this one begins, she will not be surprised to find father and sons acting in less-than-honorable ways.

The first tension comes when the younger son demands (in Greek, "give me" is an imperative, and there is no "please") his share of the inheritance. Sirach 33:20, 22 state the obvious when it cautions a father against doing this:

> To son or wife, to brother or friend, do not give authority over you while you are alive, and do not give your property to another, lest, changing your mind, you should beg from them. . . . Better that your children should beg from you than that you must look to the hand of your children.

In Jesus' culture, as in our own, land ownership was a mark of stability and security. Land was something to protect and to keep intact, if possible, so that one could pass it along to one's children. Why would a landowner put himself in the situation of having to beg, unless there were dire circumstances that forced him to sell?

The Mishnah (written around AD 200, but containing earlier traditions) includes much case law about inheritances. If we presume that it describes something close to the way that such things worked in Palestine in AD 30, then the salient facts are these:

• The elder/eldest son is supposed to have a double share of the inheritance, so that in this story, he should inherit two-thirds and his younger brother one-third of the estate.
• The father could, if he chose, sell the property that his sons were due to inherit, but "only until his death," meaning that the buyer would have to give the sons the chance to buy it back—to redeem it, in other words.
• The father could, if he chose, assign ownership of the property to his sons before his death. If he did so, he still retained the rights to use the property until he died.
• If the father assigned ownership to the sons, and the sons sold the property, the buyer could not take possession of it until after the father's death, and until that time, the father had the right to plant, to harvest, and in all ways to maintain himself. [The Mishnah on Fathers, Sons, and Property]

The last bullet comes closest to Jesus' parable, and explains why, after the father divides the property between his two sons, he can still order the servants around and host a banquet. But none of this legislation speaks to why the son feels he can demand a share of the inheritance; all of the rules delimit what a father/landowner may do, none of them what a son, particularly a younger son, might want. Our best guess is that Jesus is spinning a situation that none of his audience had ever heard of, and that they would have been shocked at the young man's disrespect and callous disregard for his father's feelings. Kenneth Bailey writes, "Any Middle Eastern son who requests his inheritance from a healthy father is understood to want his father to die. Such a son is indeed *dead* to the family."[10]

Impudent, ungrateful, and rebellious sons are not unknown in the literature of the ancient world, but when they appear, they almost always come to a bad end. The ancient story of Ahikar begins with a plot by a nephew against his uncle/adoptive father, but ends with the son being buried up to his neck in the sand while his dad quotes proverbs to him until he swells up and dies. The two sons of Eli, disobeying their father's teaching, brought down a curse upon themselves and the nation. David's son Absalom overthrew his father briefly and divided the kingdom, but was routed and killed. So the audience's presumption would have been that this boy would come to no good; maybe his father would beat him and throw him out of the house, or maybe put him on short rations until he learned his lesson. No one would have expected the father to agree, and to divide his property between the two sons, and upon hearing it, nobody would have thought this to have been a good response. You know this boy is no good—why are you giving him the means to destroy himself and your family's assets at the same time? [Being Too Nice]

In v. 13, the younger son leaves—big surprise!—after making a quick deal to get as much cash as he can out of his inheritance. In a culture where all transactions involve lengthy negotiations, and where land sales are the most involved of all, "not many days" is simply too fast to have gotten a good price. Imagine how the small town buzzed with the news:

The Mishnah on Fathers, Sons, and Property

If a man assigned his goods to his sons he must write, "From today and after my death." So R. Judah. R. Jose says: He need not do so. If a man assigned his goods to his son to be his after his death, the father cannot sell them since they are assigned to his son, and the son cannot sell them since they are in the father's possession. If his father sold them, they are sold [only] until he dies; if the son sold them, the buyer has no claim on them until the father dies. The father may pluck up [the crop of a field which he has so assigned] and give to eat to whom he will, and if he left anything already plucked up, it belongs to [all] his heirs. If he left elder sons and younger sons, the elder sons may not care for themselves [out of the common inheritance] at the cost of the younger son, nor may the younger sons claim maintenance at the cost of the elder sons, but they all share alike.

m. B. Bat. 8:7, from the Mishnah, trans. Herbert Danby (Oxford: Oxford University Press, 1933), 377–78.

Being Too Nice

I mean, you're a good guy, Ray, you have good intentions and all, but you need too much to be liked and that's a bad weakness to have. It makes you reckless. And it makes you dangerous . . . .

Richard Price, *Samaritan* (New York: Alfred Knopf, 2003), 342.

"Did you hear old man Smith's youngest boy Ralph sold off the south forty and took off for parts unknown?"

"Who bought it?"

"Well, who do you think? The Sharps have been after that land for four generations. I heard the boy was in such a hurry that he took Sharp's first offer."

"What a fool, eh?"

"Who's the bigger fool, the boy who sold the land or the daddy who gave him the deed in the first place?"

The boy goes to the "far country" and spends his money by living large; the word translated "dissolute" in the NRSV means that he was a spendthrift, but does not necessarily imply that he was carousing. Then a famine came, and the boy's money ran out, so he "hired himself out" as a day laborer to a big landowner of that region. Imagine that—he will not stay and work the land that will become his someday, but instead ends up working for pay on another man's property. This farmer was not a Jew, because he raised pigs, and he cannot have been unaware that he was sending this Jewish boy to do something against his religion. So the boy is poor, separated from his family, separated from his faith, and starving, so hungry he would have eaten the pig's food if he could. The last part of v. 16 finds him at the bottom of the pit: "and no one gave him anything." He got there by demanding everything that was coming to him, and, in fact, he got it all, far more than he expected. [Caring for the Pigs]

The expression "coming to himself" in v. 17 is a literal translation; it is used in other texts to mean something like coming to one's senses, especially when one has been under a delusion.[11] The boy thinks over his situation and decides that he can do better than this: "How many of my father's hired workers have more than enough food, while I am here perishing with hunger!" Does he truly repent? On the positive side, he says the right words and walks in the right direction; he has sinned against God and against his father, and he has started home to face the person he dishonored and damaged by leaving. On the negative side, where does he get off

Caring for the Pigs

Mrs. Turpin climbed up beside him and glowered down at the hogs inside. There were seven long-snouted bristly shoats in it—tan with liver-colored spots—and an old sow a few weeks off from farrowing. She was lying on her side grunting. The shoats were running about shaking themselves like idiot children, their little slit pig eyes searching the floor for anything left. . . . A-gruntin and a-rootin and a-groanin.

"I could quit working and take it easy and be filthy," she growled. "Lounge about the sidewalks all day drinking root beer. Dip snuff and spit in every puddle and have it all over my face. I could be nasty. . . ."

"Go on," she yelled, "call me a hog! Call me a hog again. From hell. Call me a wart hog from hell. Put that bottom rail on top. There'll still be a top and bottom!"

A garbled echo returned to her.

A final surge of fury shook her and she roared, "Who do you think you are?"

Flannery O'Connor, "Revelation," in *The Complete Stories of Flannery O'Connor* (New York: Farrar, Straus, and Giroux, 1971), 506–507.

Flannery O'Connor

(Credit: Barclay Burns)

telling his father "make me as one of your hired servants"? A truly
penitent heart might instead stop with "I am no longer worthy to
be called your son." Bailey suggests that the boy is hoping that the
father will use his influence to get him an apprenticeship somewhere so that he can earn enough to pay back the damages he has
caused.[12] But what the boy imagines asking is for the father to hire
his own son as a day laborer, and the
text suggests that the son's motive is
filling his empty stomach. Let us agree
that from the father's point of view, a
hunger-induced return is better than
nothing, and leave it at that.[13] [Returning
Home]

Returning Home

Desperado, boy, you ain't getting no younger
Your pain and your hunger, they're driving you home
Freedom, oh, freedom, that's just some people talking
Your prison is walking through this world all alone.

Don Henley and Glenn Frey, "Desperado," 1978.

The boy's interior dialogue is very life-like, as Henri Nouwen
points out. We, too, run through imaginary conversations in our
minds, snappy replies we wish we had made, retorts we might
make, and, like this boy, things we might say to get ourselves out of
a tight spot. To take this attitude with respect to God means, on
the one hand, that we think that God "demands an explanation" as
a "harsh, judgmental God." On the other, it means that we still do
not imagine ourselves coming completely home; "as a hired
servant, I can still keep my distance, still revolt, reject, strike, run
away, or complain about my pay."[14]

What do the readers expect now? Repentance, as we have already
seen, is a big part of Luke's message. Peter starts his discipleship
(5:8) by confessing, "Depart from me, for I am a sinful man," and
Jesus has said that his mission is to call sinners to repent (5:32).
Those who repent and demonstrate the fruits of repentance will no
doubt be forgiven, and the father's action at the beginning of the
story, dividing his property, keeps anyone from imagining that he is
going to be hard-nosed. The two stories just preceding this one
both involve parties at the end, so maybe the reader even expects
that there will be a celebration to welcome the prodigal home.

But the father's behavior goes beyond merciful and beyond receptive. His father sees him "still far off"—symbolically, still in the far
country, estranged from family and village and faith. Physically,
Jesus may have pictured the man sitting in the gates of the town,
where the elders usually sit, and spotting the boy walking up the
road. The old man, overcome with emotion, runs to his son,
embraces him, and begins to kiss him. Commentators agree that
this is undignified and uncharacteristic behavior for a respected
wealthy man, especially for one whom we expect to be put out with
the young man walking up the road. True enough, but then we
remember David weeping for his reprobate son Absalom; are we

sure that none of the parents listening to Jesus or reading Luke could have imagined doing the same thing?

The prodigal begins his speech, but stops before the "take me on as a hired servant" part. If this was his choice, then perhaps he has grown up a little; perhaps seeing his dad helped him realize that he could not earn forgiveness and restitution.[15] If his dad interrupted him, then the point is that the father's love overrides the boy's adolescent plans to ask a job in his father's house. Luke left no clue for what he intended, and either reading is plausible. The next part, though, clearly is all-dad, all-star, over-the-top love. The father orders a slave to run and get the best robe—the father's number-one robe—and dress him, dirty and stinky as he is. Put a ring on his finger and shoes on his feet, he orders. Imagine the father and son still standing in the road outside the town, with the other elders (who had been sitting in the gates with the father) and various townspeople watching; the slaves come running with the robe and ring and shoes, and they dress the son. So before the eyes of the town, the father restores the errant son to his status as loved, honored, and respected, making sure that the son's walk through the town to his home is not the humiliating experience he had been dreading. All the shame the son had built up was now the father's; if the townspeople were shaking their heads, it was at the landowner's foolish, soft-hearted love.[16]

To make the reunion complete, the father orders a big party: kill the fatted calf, start the music, and let's dance! The other elders may have been scandalized at their friend's behavior, but they would not turn down a party, and soon everybody in town was there, eating and drinking and singing and dancing. The father announces the theme for the party: "This, my son, was dead and is alive again, was lost and was found." Notice that the father does not assign blame; he does not say, My son destroyed himself, my son ran away. Neither does the son get credit for returning home: he is alive, he was found. And the father's only mention of himself is "my son"; "he was found" no more means "I found him" than "he was lost" means "I drove him from home."

Notice the exchange of names thus far: the younger son never calls the older man anything except "father" or "my father," even when he is suggesting that he is no longer worthy to be a son. How seriously can we take "make me as one of your day-workers"—change my status from "son" to "hired hand"—when he begins the address "father?" The boy is counting on the father-son relationship, or he would have called him *kyrios*, "Lord," the normal title of respect for a landowner, slaveowner, or potential employer. So, ironically, even though the younger son leaves the home for the far country, acting as if his father is dead, he never actually quits thinking of himself as a son to his father. In Henri Nouwen's marvelous devotional study of Rembrandt's *The Return of the Prodigal Son*, he argues that the younger son never truly gave up thinking of himself as a son, and that this self-knowledge, deeply buried and deliberately ignored, is what brought him back home. Rembrandt painted the younger boy in the welcoming arms of his father. The boy is dressed in his under-tunic, ragged and dirty; his head is shaved to look like a prisoner; his shoes are in tatters, falling from his feet; but he still wears his short sword:

The Return of the Prodigal Son

Rembrandt Harmensz van Rijn (1606–1669). *The Return of the Prodigal Son*. 1668–1669. Oil on canvas, Hermitage, St. Petersburg, Russia. (Credit: Scala/Art Resource, NY)

> Even in the midst of his debasement, he had clung to the truth that he still was the son of his father. Otherwise, he would have sold his so valuable sword, the symbol of his sonship. The sword is there to show me that, although he came back speaking as a beggar and an outcast, he had not forgotten that he was the son of his father. It was this remembered and valued sonship that finally persuaded him to turn back.[17]

By contrast, his elder brother shows a much deeper estrangement, even though he never leaves the farm. When the party begins, he is out in the field; we should imagine a typical Galilean town or village, with all the houses and shops clustered together and the fields owned by villagers all around the village. As he gets near the house, he begins to hear the sounds of the party, and he asks "one of the boys" what is going on. The word for "boy" can mean slave, but it can also mean a boy—a neighborhood kid who has been inside the party and knows what it is about. The boy/slave represents what the neighbors are saying about the event: "Your brother arrived, and your father killed the fatted calf, because he received him back whole." The verb behind "received" is active, not passive: it implies that the father has accepted him or recovered him.[18] And the word translated "whole" can mean "healthy" as well as "sound" or "correct."[19] Bailey, noting that the LXX consistently translates "*shalom*" with the Greek word in this verse, argues for "he recovered him in peace."[20] In my opinion, "whole" works better, because it catches the sense of relief that the boy was alive and well, but also the sense of restoration to the family that Bailey notes. The elder brother, then, learns all in a moment that the no-count traitor who left him with all the work of the farm is back; that the ungrateful, inconsiderate, selfish lout who sold part of the family farm to finance a free-spending lifestyle is now sitting in the dining room eating steaks from the fatted calf; and that the cold, unloving snake who as much as told his dad "You are dead to me" has been fully restored to sonship. Whole? After what this good-for-nothing did, they may never be whole; remember, somebody—somebody probably in there eating, too—holds the deed to one-third of the property, to take effect when the father dies unless he, the elder brother, can save enough to redeem the land between now and then. Whole? The elder brother's blood boils. [Unforgiving]

The brother stops outside the house, refusing to enter, standing outside in the street. The party is inside, and if Luke imagines that this was a large, wealthy man's house, he was probably thinking of one built with a central peristyle garden, the dining room facing it, with a clear line of sight from the front door through the garden to the dining room. Part of the purpose behind building houses that way was so that when the wealthy man had a party, he could leave the door open, and passersby could admire the beauty of his garden statuary and the lavish spread of his banquet, and wish they had been invited. If Luke's readers and Jesus' listeners were to imagine such a house, then the guests in the parable were no doubt watching and listening to the conversation in the street.[21] Even if we think of a more modest house, the father meets his older son in the street, just as he met his younger son in the road outside the town; this meeting, like the one just earlier that day, is public.

The elder son is, if anything, ruder than his younger brother. He will not, for sake of appearances, go in and make small talk and then have this out later behind closed doors. Instead, just when his father has restored the family, he wants to pull it apart again. He does not call his dad "father" or anything else; instead, he asserts that he has been his father's slave for many years, never once stepping out of the lines drawn by the father's commandments. That is a gross exaggeration, of course; if it were true, he would be inside the party, obedient to his father's stated wishes. He is not a slave, or he would have been hustling around killing and cooking the fatted calf, putting shoes on his younger brother and fluffing up the cushions for the guests. No, he is a son, a responsible son whose father is, with great restraint, allowing him to set his own priorities, even if it means making an ass of himself in public. The complaint about the goat—"you never gave me a goat so that I could party with my friends"—sounds as petulant as "nobody gave him anything" did in v. 16. As Bailey notes, if his friends are not in the house right then, they are completely unconnected to the family or the family's network; how likely is that? Furthermore, the farm (except for the parts the younger son sold) now belongs to the elder son. His father has the right to maintain himself on the property, but nothing would prevent the elder son from having a party if he wants. The final exaggeration is the part about the prostitutes; the elder brother has no idea how the younger brother has lived, but he imagines the worst, because that is how he thinks of his sibling. ["Who has devoured your property with prostitutes"]

The elder brother has not felt like a part of the family for some time—not his father's son, not his brother's brother. Contrast "this son of yours" with "he came to his own father" (v. 20): the younger brother left for the far country, but never stopped thinking of "my father" as the place where he could return, while the elder brother stayed put, estranged and lost, in his mind a slave with no home or family.

By the time we get to the father's last words, we may have heard enough that we are no longer surprised by the degree of his mercy. Maybe Jesus' listeners, knowing the biblical tradition of the favorite younger/youngest son, could have expected a "God loved Jacob, but

"Who has devoured your property with prostitutes"

The elder brother has no idea what the younger had been doing with the money, but the image of a young boy spending all his money on a prostitute was a typical comic plot. Plautus's play *Mercator* begins with a young man's soliloquy:

In the beginning, after I had come of age and lost my zest for childish things, I became completely captivated by a courtesan here; forthwith my father's property quietly went into exile to her. The ruthless pimp, who owned the girl, grabbed and made off with everything he could pounce on. My father denounced all this night and day, picturing the perfidy and injustice of pimps. To think that his own estate should be absolutely mangled, and that fellow's multiplied! All this at the top of his lungs; or now again he would mutter what he had to say—shake his head, and even insist that I was no son of his. All over the city he would go, bebawling and giving notice no one was to trust me when I looked for loans.

Plautus, *Mercator* 40–52, in Paul Nixon, trans., *Plautus*, vol. 3 (Cambridge MA: Harvard University, 1950), 9–11.

hated Esau" ending (Rom 9:13, quoting Mal 1:1-2). Maybe Luke's readers, members of the Gentile church, hoped that the elder brother, surrogate for the Pharisees, would be tossed out of the house for his unforgiving legalism.[22] But this father rejects no one.[23] The elder son is already dressed, already shod, already wearing the ring, but he needs to be reminded of who he is. "Child," his father says, "you are always with me." Not, "you have always been here, so you've earned your right to be son," but "you are always with me, even when you are standing out here stamping your feet in anger." "All my stuff is yours"—not "it will all be yours someday," but "it all belongs to you now." So even when the elder son does the wrong thing, the privilege of being a son is not withdrawn, and when the father does the right thing, the elder son is a part of that. The fatted calf that his brother and all the townspeople are munching is his, as is the house they are sitting in; the elder brother should be glad, the father suggests, that his stuff is being used to help restore and to bring to life. Luke carefully writes "it was necessary to celebrate and rejoice" without specifying the subject, suggesting that the father reconciles the younger son with the help of the elder brother's stuff.

Luke closes the parable before we learn if this unhappy family ever comes back together. Will the father's mercy overcome the elder brother's hard heart and transform the younger brother's irresponsible prodigality? Leaving the question open is more true to our own experiences, when sometimes there is forgiveness and reconciliation and sometimes not. In churches, in families, even within ourselves, we can always spot partially healed, partially festering wounds; we celebrate reconciliation and familial love on the one hand while maintaining cold formality or heated hostility on the other. We are each capable of acting like each of these characters simultaneously in different relationships. We can allow ourselves to repent here but to remain stiff-necked there, to run down the road to embrace some and refuse to sit at table with others. Jesus' example of eating with tax collectors, sinners, and Pharisees matches the father's choice of both his sons, and pushes us to try, again and again, to be as open-armed as he.

CONNECTIONS

Lost sheep, lost coin, lost boys; Luke wants us to think of all of them in the context of Jesus' ministry to tax collectors and sinners. In this Gospel, Jesus seeks them out and is happy to be welcomed into their houses. He justifies his behavior by arguing that God is the same way, going far beyond what most people would do to give the lost or the straying a chance to come back.

We can think of ourselves as the found objects, and that's not a bad place to start. There are various ways to be lost in these parables: misplaced, like a lost coin; inattentive and clueless, like a sheep that nibbles its way away from the flock and into a tight spot; headstrong and foolish, like the younger son; angry and unforgiving, like the older brother. In these parables, there is a savior for each kind of lost, and if we take that direction with these stories, then we can celebrate the unsurpassed love of God: ". . . a love that existed before any rejection is possible and that will still be there after all rejections have taken place . . . the love that always welcomes home and always wants to celebrate."24

We can think of ourselves as the finders, and that's also not a bad place to go. "Rescue the perishing," just as Jesus was doing: find the misplaced, the misguided, the loose-living and the stone-hearted, and try to bring them back under the love of God. The lengths to which the shepherd, the woman, and the father go to find and to retrieve the lost can inspire us to be more open, less censorious, more inviting, less judgmental.

We are actually always both finding and being found, if we are active disciples of Jesus. We lose our way, and God brings us back, often through the loving ministries of others; these others who minister to us find in turn that God is finding them in the act of ministry. What we must guard against in presenting these parables is allowing the congregation to think of themselves as spectators to this drama: We're not lost—we're sitting right here in church. But we also aren't finding the lost—that's for preachers, evangelists, social workers, that sort of thing. But it's nice to think that such things happen, isn't it?

One way to ask this question exegetically is to ask where the disciples are in this chapter. We have the Pharisees in view (15:2), and the tax collectors and sinners emerge from the crowds. But given all the stuff he says about discipleship at the end of chapter 14—you can't be my disciple if you don't hate your family, carry your cross, and give up your possessions—it isn't a bad question to ask. Are the disciples with Jesus, eating with the same tax collectors and sinners, engaging in the ministry of hospitality along with him? Let's hope so, and let's make it our aim as well.

NOTES

[1] Ira D. Sankey, *My Life and the Story of the Gospel Hymns* (New York and London: Harper and Bros., 1907), 268–71; cited by David W. Music, *Hymnology: A Collection of Source Readings* (Lanham MD: Scarecrow, 1996), 208–10.

[2] Arlen Hultgren, *The Parables of Jesus: A Commentary* (Grand Rapids MI: Eerdmans, 2000), 53. Kenneth E. Bailey, *Poet and Peasant and Through Peasant Eyes* (Grand Rapids MI: Eerdmans, 1980), 148, notes that in "real life" such a large flock might be jointly owned. But in this parable, one man is the owner.

[3] Bailey, *Poet*, 149.

[4] Bernard Brandon Scott, *Hear Then the Parable: A Commentary on the Parables of Jesus* (Minneapolis: Fortress, 1989), 415.

[5] Hultgren, *Parables*, 66; Joel B. Green, *The Gospel of Luke* (NICNT; Grand Rapids: Eerdmans, 1997), 576.

[6] Bailey, *Poet*, 157.

[7] Scott, *Hear Then the Parable*, 311, citing Joachim Jeremias, *The Parables of Jesus* (3rd ed.; London: SCM, 1972), 135.

[8] Kathleen Norris, *The Quotidian Mysteries* (New York: Paulist, 1998), 32.

[9] Joseph A. Fitzmyer, *The Gospel According to Luke* (AB 28 and 28A; Garden City NY: Doubleday, 1981), 2.1083-84.

[10] Kenneth E. Bailey, *Finding the Lost: Cultural Keys to Luke 15* (St. Louis MO: Concordia, 1992), 109.

[11] For example, in *Testament of Joseph* 3:9 Joseph "comes to himself" when he realizes that Potiphar's wife is only pretending to love him as a son when she actually wants to take him to bed with her.

[12] Bailey, *Finding the Lost*, 132.

[13] Scott, *Hear Then the Parable*, 116.

[14] Henri Nouwen, *The Return of the Prodigal Son* (New York: Doubleday, 1992), 52–53.

[15] So Bailey, *Finding the Lost*, 153.

[16] Bailey, *Finding the Lost*, 143–47, says that the father runs the gauntlet for his son.

[17] Nouwen, *The Return*, 49.

[18] *BADG*, 115.

[19] *BADG*, 1023.

[20] Bailey, *Finding the Lost*, 167–71.

[21] Ibid., 173.

[22] Scott, *Hear Then the Parable*, 105, 125.

[23] Ibid., 125: "This parable subverts a mytheme by which the kingdom decides between the chosen and the rejected. Here the father rejects no one; both are chosen."

[24] Nouwen, *The Return*, 109.

ON POSSESSIONS

Luke 16

COMMENTARY

The Unjust Overseer, 16:1-13

"This parable is often regarded as the most puzzling of all within the Synoptic Gospels."[1] The manager who cooks the books and then is praised by the CEO when the truth comes out is an odd hero for one of Jesus' stories. Luke 16:9 appears to tell us, "go thou and do likewise," and we wonder what we're being encouraged to do: cheat? lie? make free with someone else's money? pretend to have authority we don't? Yet it is a delightful tale, and the bold dishonesty of the crooked manager is meant to grab the audience's attention, making them expect something at least slightly naughty, like the minister whose sermon begins, "There was a young girl from Nantucket."

The lectionary puts the parable together with the exhortations following as the Gospel lesson for Proper 20 (25th Sunday in Ordinary Time). One could argue for including 16:14-18 also, since they include the reaction of the Pharisees to the parable and to Jesus' maxims; but then 16:19-31, the rich man and Lazarus, is also about the improper use of wealth, and will need to be related to our current passage. But dealing with the whole of chapter 16 at once makes too large a section; so we will keep the lectionary division for this section, but treat vv. 14-18 as a run-up to the rich man and Lazarus.

Jesus tells this to his disciples, says Luke: "Once there was a rich man . . . ." Boo! We know about the rich by now: they stand under God's condemnation (6:24), they can look forward to being sent empty away (1:53) and to perishing along with their wealth (12:13-21). Luke's readers know that the only proper thing to do with property is to sell it (12:33), and the only good use for money is to give it away (6:30; 14:33). If you've been looking ahead, you know that the Pharisees are labeled "money-lovers" (16:14), which links this rich man with Jesus' most vocal and persistent opponents so far. Rich men—bah! [The Rich]

The Rich

Heap up gold, amass silver, build stately prome-
nades, fill your house with slaves and the city
with your debtors; unless you lay level the emotions of your
soul, put a stop to your insatiate desires, you are but
decanting wine for a man in a fever. (Plutarch, "Virtue and
Vice," 4, *Moralia* 101.C)

A man assumes that wealth is the greatest good. This
falsehood contains venom, It feeds upon his soul, distracts
him, does not allow him to sleep, fills him with stinging
desires, pushes him over precipices, chokes him, and takes
from him his freedom of speech. (Plutarch, "Superstition,"
1, *Moralia* 165.A)

We have then before now described that wealth which is
the guard of the body . . . this kind of wealth wisdom fur-
nishes by means of rational, and moral, and natural
doctrines, and meditations from which the virtues are
derived, which eradicate luxury from the soul, engendering
in it a desire for temperance and frugality, in accordance
with the resemblance to God at which it aims. . . . But the
bad man is one of extravagant tastes, being always
thirsting for what he has not got, because of his insatiable
and unappeasable appetites which he fans and excites like
fire. (Philo, *Virtues* III.8-9)

"There's something behind it when a rich man puts on
smooth airs with a poor one. . . . When he agrees he wants
to grab! Mouth wide open to gobble down my gold! Holds
up a bit of bread in one hand and has a stone in the other! I
don't trust one of these rich fellows when he's so mon-
strous civil to a poor man. They give you a cordial
handshake, and squeeze something out of you at the same
time. I know all about those octopuses that touch a thing
and then stick." (Plautus, *Aul.* 194 ff.)

"A certain rich man had an overseer"—well, of course he did.
Wealthy people had people to do things for them, and people to
manage the people. An overseer (*oikonomos*) could be a slave or an
employee; this one is the latter, since he is being threatened with
dismissal rather than crucifixion. Since the accounts he deals with
are expressed in terms of produce rather than money, we presume
that Luke is thinking of a wealthy farmer with tenants or poorer
neighbors who borrow staples on account. Cato the Elder wrote a
long (some might say interminable), detailed account of how to
run a farm, and early on includes a section on the duties of the
overseer (Lat., *villicus*); here are some highlights:

> He must show good management. The feast days must be observed.
> He must withhold his hands from another's goods and diligently pre-
> serve his own. He must settle disputes among the slaves . . . . He
> must extend credit to no one without orders from the master, and
> must collect the loans made by the master. He must lend to no one
> seed-grain, fodder, spelt, wine, or oil. He must have two or three
> households, no more from whom he borrows and to whom he lends.
> He must make up accounts with the master often . . . . He must not
> want to make any purchases without the knowledge of the master,
> nor want to keep anything hidden from the master.[2]

It is important for our parable that the overseer collected the shares
from tenants. Cato has sample contracts for grain fields, vineyards,
olive harvesters, etc., indicating that the overseer did not set the
terms; but Cato's repeated exhortations to the overseer that he must

do exactly as the master instructs perhaps implies that sometimes overseers acted on their own, asking for kickbacks in return for favorable reports to the master. [The Dishonest Overseer]

Luke's audience would have known what was generally expected of overseers. [An Overseer's Freedom of Action] As J. Albert Harrill has shown, they also would have recognized this particular overseer as a sort of blend of two stock characters from the comedies they saw performed during some public festivals. The "parasite" was a man whose services could be bought, and who was willing to do pretty much anything. This type of character is meant to look foolish to the audience, and becomes part of whatever scheme is being cooked up in the comedy. In Plautus's play *Stichus*, the parasite is named "Gelasimus," which means "Laughter." Throughout the play, he is trying to sell his services as an entertaining party guest, and all it will cost is a meal: "I do suspect that Famine was my mother; for since I was born I have never been filled with victuals . . . . Now if any person wants a droll fellow, I am on sale, with all my equipage."[3] His constant hunger, he says, is proof of a larger social problem:

> I am in the habit of refusing no person, if anyone asks me out to eat. One form of expression has most unfortunately died away with people, and one, in faith, most beseeming and most elegant to my thinking, which formerly they employed: "Come here to dinner—do so—really, do promise—don't make any difficulties—is it convenient?—I wish it to be so, I say; I'll not part with you unless you come."

At one point in the play, he has an internal dialogue about his fate and the general cruelty of humans:

> Consider, Gelasimus, what plan you must adopt. What, I? Yes, you. What, for myself? Yes, for yourself. Don't you see how dear provisions are? Don't you see how the kindness and heartiness of men have vanished? Don't you see how drolls are set at naught, and how they themselves are sponged upon? (4.630-40)

The Dishonest Overseer

It is as though some manager responsible for an estate which should have brought in an income of 10,000 sesterces sent his master 20,000 rather than 10,000 by cutting down and selling all the trees, removing the tiles, getting rid of all the equipment and stock—and pocketed an additional 100,000 sesterces for himself. His master will at first be unaware of the damage he has suffered and will be pleased with his manager and delighted that the income from his farm has risen by such an extent; but afterwards, when he hears that all those things on which the cultivation and profits of a farm depend have been taken away and sold, he will inflict the most severe punishment on his manager and think that he has been extremely badly treated.

Cicero, *Verr.* 2,3.50, cited in Thomas Wiedemann, *Greek and Roman Slavery* (Baltimore MD: Johns Hopkins University Press, 1981), 150–51.

An Overseer's Freedom of Action

Plautus was a Roman playwright of the late 3rd to early 2d century BC (he died around 184 BC). In his comedy *Casina*, one of the main characters is the slave Olympio, who is the overseer (*vilicus*) of a wealthy man's property. His master has promised him a slave girl in marriage. Olympio has come to the city to gain his bride; when another slave accosts him for being away from his post, he replies, "I have not forgotten my duties, Chalinus; I left a manager ["prefect"] at the farm who will attend to its affairs properly, despite my absence" (1.104-105). This gives us some notion of the relative freedom that overseers of rural estates enjoyed, especially when their masters spent most of their time in the city.

Luke's overseer also has some of the traits of a second stock comedic character, the tricky slave. These characters always hoodwink their masters, always are exposed, but always get away with it somehow. In Plautus's play *Mostellaria*, the tricky slave Tranio gets pardoned at the end; the master threatens to have him crucified, and only relents when a peer acts as intercessor. But in *Epidicus*, the tricky slave Epidicus is first vilified and tied up for the tricks he has played on his master, but when it turns out he has actually done the master a favor, he gets his freedom, "shoes, a tunic, and a cloak," food, and a public apology: "I do entreat you, Epidicus, to forgive me, if unawares in fault I've done anything wrong"[4] (5.720).

Back to our story: A certain rich man—for the rest of this exegesis, we will call him Mr. Big—had an overseer—we will call him Roscoe. Someone informed on Roscoe; the word *diaballō* can mean "make a malicious accusation," so we do not know whether it is true or false.[5] The accusation said that Roscoe was "broadcasting" Mr. Big's "stuff" (*diaskorpizō*, to scatter like seed; it is the word used for what the prodigal did with his "stuff" in the far country). So Mr. Big calls Roscoe in and lowers the boom: "What is this I am hearing about you? Give me the account of your work as overseer, because you cannot still work as overseer." The English is more cumbersome than the Greek: "Give the tale [*logos*] of your oversight [*oikonomia*], for you cannot still oversee."

Now, Mr. Big is certainly within his rights to ask for his overseer to bring in the books. But he has just made two dumb mistakes. First, you should never believe every stray piece of gossip you hear about your employees. Roscoe may well be cheating you, but the informant may also be lying, so better have the facts in hand before you make an accusation. Second, and more to the point, you don't fire the bookkeeper until you have the books in your hands. So far, Mr. Big is being characterized as out of touch, quick to condemn, and not the sharpest knife in the drawer. Some of Luke's audience may have been treated like that by a real-life Mr. Big; Roscoe gets a few sympathy points.

But then he squanders them right away: "What shall I do? My master is taking the overseer's post from me. I'm not strong enough to dig, I'm ashamed to beg." Boo! Too weak to dig—who does he think he is? What he really means is that he does not want to work as hard as the tenant farmers and field hands, and the only other choice he can imagine is begging.[6] Roscoe has been working with rich people so long that he has begun to think like one. Cato warned about this: "He must see to it that he knows how to perform all the operations of the farm, and actually does perform them often. . . . He must not consider the master's friends his own friends."[7] Jesus warned about it, too, when he taught about the wicked overseer who begins to act as if he owns the joint, beating the other slaves, eating and drinking and living large (Luke 12:41-47).

So far, Roscoe has sounded like the parasite—woe is me, I might have to get a real job, the world is unfair—but next he sounds like the tricky slave: "I know what I will do, so that when I am turned out of the overseer's job they will receive me into their households." He has a plan, in other words, for getting to be overseer for somebody else. So, instead of bringing the ledger books to his master, he instead summons all the people who owe his master anything.

Picture the scene: the overseer is sitting at a desk in a small room near the front of the house, and the creditors line up at the outside gate, to be admitted one at a time. The first man comes in, hat in hand—he has no idea why all those who owe Mr. Big money have been summoned to the Big house, but he can't imagine that it means good news for him. He walks into the little office, where Roscoe sits with the ledger book on the table in front of him. "How much do you owe my master?" asks Roscoe. The first debtor starts to sweat. He's thinking, "You have the books—we both know how much I owe him—are you going to call in the loan? We have a contract!" But he says, "A hundred jugs of oil," thinking that his next move is to talk about how bad the weather has been and how sorry the olives look this year and how it will be impossible for him to pay off the whole amount. Then Roscoe says, "Take your bill, and quickly write down fifty."

"Quickly" lets the creditor know that something is up, but he doesn't care—Christmas just came early, and the creditor thinks, for the first time in a while, that he might get out of debt this year. He goes tearing out of the office, whooping, and tells everybody else in line what just happened to him. When the second guy goes in, the same thing happens; you owe 100 containers of grain? Quickly, make it 80! By the time Roscoe is through with the whole line of debtors, he has made a lot of people very happy.

Not only that, but he has put Mr. Big in an impossible bind. To round up all the debtors and force them to pay the contracted amounts would be a tremendous loss of face for the wealthy man. Not only would it be public that Roscoe put one over on him, but he would look like a tightwad. On the other hand, if he lets the trick slide, he gets credit for being generous; his prestige goes up, because now he looks so rich that he can cut bills in half and still stay rich.

In the comic tradition, the sly slave never gets crucified or whipped or any of the other things his master threatens. In the example cited above, Epidicus is freed and given a public apology. Luke's "master praised the unrighteous overseer: 'He acted shrewdly.'" Mr. Big passes the word that Roscoe is a sly one, thus preserving his own dignity (it was my idea all along), and giving a rather ambiguous employment reference for his former overseer. And there, the parable ends, with the trick against the rich man exposed and the tricky overseer heading for another house.

The second half of v. 8 offers an observation by Jesus—at least, it seems to be by Jesus, and not by Mr. Big—that is itself more than a little ambiguous. "The children of this age are more shrewd than the children of light"—that much is clear, but then there is a prepositional phrase, "for/towards/with respect to their own generation." Whose generation is meant? In 7:31 "this generation" means those, in particular the Pharisees and lawyers (7:30), who did not believe John and have not responded to Jesus. In 11:50, "this generation" again means lawyers and Pharisees who are hostile to Jesus, and who are being charged with complicity in the deaths of the prophets. "This generation is evil," according to 11:29-32, meaning those who will not pay attention to the signs around them and repent. The antecedent for "their own" is most likely "the children of this age." So, "The children of this age are more shrewd towards their own generation than are the children of light." This unrighteous—dishonest, yes, but more like amoral or undeterred by God's laws—overseer is a good example of how non-moral people may do the right thing for the wrong reason.

He helped the poor, didn't he? He scattered the rich man's stuff, just as Mary said Jesus would do (1:51); he forgave debts, just as Jesus commanded (6:30, 35; 11:4). Sure, he did it with someone else's money, and he did it to feather his own nest. But he gave away a boatload of cash, and so proves to have more wisdom than many so-called "children of light." Verse 9 then urges Jesus' followers to do the same with their own "mammon," or money. Like the overseer, it too is called "unrighteous" because it exists apart from God and God's purposes. The point is not for Christians to give away any ill-gotten gain, but that all gain that they have not yet disposed of is outside God's purposes, since Jesus has said, repeatedly, to give it all away. "Make friends" who will receive you into "eternal tents"—not so much the poor you help, but those in the kingdom of God who will welcome you to God's tent one day.[8]

Verses 10-12 continue to draw lessons from the parable. An overseer must be *pistos*, which means reliable—someone in whom the master can put faith. If the overseer proves reliable in small things, bigger responsibilities will come; but being unrighteous (*adikos*, which is a different form of the adjective used to modify the overseer in v. 8 and mammon in vv. 9 and 11) or unreliable in small things will crush your chances for the big time. Verse 11 then argues that money—unrighteous mammon—is the small time, a proving ground for bigger things to come, like the eternal kingdom of God. The message is that if we blow this one—if we can't use "filthy lucre" the way Jesus told us to—then why would he entrust us with his kingdom? Recall 12:32-33: "Don't be afraid, little flock, because your father graciously intends to give you the kingdom. Sell your stuff and give alms!"

Verse 13 switches the field of reference just a bit. "No household slave can serve two masters." Actually, in Egypt they apparently sometimes did, because Egyptian law allowed for owning shares in a slave,[9] and Jesus' elaboration demonstrates how awful an arrangement that must have been. [A Slave Owned by Two Masters] Slavery is bad enough, but to be torn between the demands of two masters would be worse. "You cannot serve God and mammon" is about as plain as it gets, and a restatement of "So then, each of you who does not renounce all your stuff cannot be my disciple" (14:33).

> **A Slave Owned by Two Masters**
>
> Plautus's comedy *Mercator* is about a young man who falls in love with a slave girl and buys her so that she can be his mistress. The young man's father sees the girl and wants her, too; neither father nor son will admit the truth to the other, so they both pretend to want to sell the girl to somebody else. Desperately the young man tries to think of a way to head his father off: "I own her in common with another man! How do I know how he feels, whether he wants her to be sold or not?"
>
> Plautus, *Mercator*, 451–52.

Moral Exhortations; Dives and Lazarus, 16:14-31

Putting these verses together is admittedly rather arbitrary, as noted in the commentary on 16:1-13. Chapter 16 is largely about money as an ethical issue for Jesus' followers, and through parable and straight exhortation, Luke's Jesus is urging his disciples to renounce their possessions. Verse 14 introduces the Pharisees as the voice of the larger culture, ridiculing Jesus, and the parable of the rich man and Lazarus closes the chapter with a cautionary tale about not using one's wealth to care for the poor. But Luke has also included three Q sayings that, to be kind, are not well integrated with the theme of the chapter; to be blunt, they look like bicycle parts left over after you've done the "some assembly required," which you then duct-taped to the frame in case they turned out to be necessary.

"All" the Pharisees reject Jesus' teaching on disposing of wealth and ridicule him, just like "all" the tax collectors and sinners stick close to Jesus (15:1). The parable of the unjust overseer was delivered to the disciples—the large group of men and women, including the twelve apostles, who were traveling with Jesus to Jerusalem. We are to imagine a large clump of people with Jesus at the head of the line, walking from village to village while Jesus and his disciples teach, heal, exorcise, preach the gospel, and accept hospitality. The Pharisees keep objecting to Jesus' conduct and opinions, "justifying themselves," in Jesus' opinion. That phrase, used of the lawyer in 10:29, gives the sense of an ongoing argument that the Pharisees keep trying to win (to justify can mean to declare someone innocent or victorious in a legal case). These verses are more salvoes in the battle for the hearts and minds of the crowds, who are always milling around Jesus, and of the disciples, whose performance on this journey has been sometimes stellar, sometimes abysmal.

"All" the Pharisees, being "money-lovers," ridicule Jesus, who has just said that one cannot serve God and mammon. Loving money was a vice in anyone's ethical literature of this period (see references in the commentary on 12:13-21). Greek ethical writers like Plutarch—himself a well-to-do person who enjoyed dining with the elite—considered money-loving a sign of poor self-discipline, and recommended the study of philosophy. Philo and Sirach had much the same idea, but recommended the study of the Law as the antidote. They all would have agreed with Jesus that the root issue was the disposition of the "heart," or the intentions: on what was one's mind fixed? They all would also have thought that a person could learn how to be rightly motivated; study of philosophy or the Torah could lead to right motivations and then to right conduct.

It is important to grasp this point: with his call to renunciation of possessions in view of the coming kingdom of God, Jesus fit within the parameters of Jewish and Greco-Roman ethical literature. Actual in-the-flesh Pharisees would have agreed that seeking God above all else was the best thing in life, and that love of possessions led one astray. Luke picks them to be the voice of caution, the voice of the cultured religious person who says, "Young man, I admire your passion, but you have a lot to learn about how the world really works. Do you think that the (temple/synagogue/church) can survive without money? Do you think that if we sell off our buildings, and that if each family sells its property, and that if we give all that to the poor, that the problem of poverty will disappear? Where will we worship? Who will teach your children the faith? Who will educate your next pastor? Sure, you can't make an idol out of mammon, but you also can't give everything away, and God doesn't expect us to do that. Give it some time—you'll lose your naiveté and come around to our point of view." Their "ridicule" of Jesus is meant to expose him before the crowds as young, foolish, wrong-headed; it is the flip side of Jesus' exposure of the way their sense of pride showed up in how they behaved at banquets (14:7-11). But Jesus sees no shame in eating with tax collectors, in showing up dirty for a dinner party, or in urging everyone to renounce all their possessions and take to the road as he has done; he has already counted the cost, including being ridiculed (14:29), and so their mocking has no effect on him.

Clarence Jordan helped to start Koinonia Farm as a Christian commune: shared property, active ministries for the poor, and racially integrated, which created much hostility in rural Georgia in the 1950s and 1960s. His "Cotton Patch" translation of Luke 16:14 reads, "Now the money-loving church members heard all this, and started booing him"; in my opinion, that's exactly what Luke had in mind. The Pharisees in 16:14 seem like outsiders, but some of them join the early church and insist that Gentiles must keep the Law of Moses if they hope to be saved (Acts 15:1-5). "We have met the enemy, and he is us," in other words; as Luke's audience listens to this part of the story, they and we must admit that nobody has resisted Jesus' call to the renunciation of wealth more vigorously than Jesus' own followers.

The word for "abomination" in v. 15 (*bdelygma*) is used for idols and their worship in Deuteronomy (e.g., Deut 7:26, "You shall not bring a *bdelygma* into your house"; Deut 18:12, "everyone who does all these things [child sacrifice, sorcery, necromancy, etc.] is a *bdelygma* to the Lord your God"). Johnson notes that the same word is used to describe remarriage of a divorced woman (Deut 24:4) and cheating the poor with two sets of weights (Deut 25:16, "Because everyone who does these things is a *bdelygma* to the Lord your God, everyone who acts unjustly [*adikon*, like being unjust in small or great things in 16:10]".[10] *Bdelygma* is such an odd word to use in v. 15 that it could be a clue to why Luke put this material together.

Verses 16-17 appear in two different contexts in Matthew. The saying on the Law and John the Baptist is in Matthew 11:12-13, along with the "what did you go into the desert to see" section that appears in Luke 7. The saying on heaven and earth and the Law appears in Matthew 5:18, in the section beginning "Don't think I have come to abolish the law or the prophets." Luke's version is not as clear as Matthew's on whether the Law remains in effect. Matthew's version of the heaven and earth saying has the emphasis on how the Law remains valid, down to jots and tittles, as long as creation remains. Luke's version:

> The law and the prophets [fill in verb] until John;
> From then, the kingdom of God is being spread as good news and everyone [is forcing/is being forced] into it.
> But it is easier for heaven and earth to disappear than for one stroke of the Law to fall.

A verb must be supplied in the first line. Many translations have something like "were" or "were in effect," which makes John the dividing line between the era of the Law and the era of the gospel.[11] But the verbs in the second line should probably influence our choice of what verb to insert into the first line. "Law and prophets" is parallel to "kingdom of God," so the verb for the first line should be something like "is being spread as good news (*euangelizetai*)." The kingdom is being preached as good news; so "the Law and the prophets were proclaimed," or something like that, until John. That does not mean that they are preached no longer, as 16:29 and the book of Acts demonstrate. In fact, since in Luke's view the Law and the prophets testify to Christ (Luke 24:26-27, 44), there is an essential continuity between what was preached before John and what came later. John marks the dividing line for when the gospel was first preached on its own terms, as a present fact, and not simply as a prediction.

It seems to me that there are at least three ways to read Luke 16:17. The first takes "fall" as the opposite of "fulfill," a meaning it sometimes has. In this reading, the verse means approximately the same thing as Luke 24:44: everything in the Law and the prophets finds its fulfillment in Christ and cannot go unfulfilled. The second reading, which seems to me the least likely for Luke, understands Luke 16:17 as if it were Matthew 5:18: no part of the Law is ever set aside. For Gentile Christians, the laws of circumcision and clean and unclean food were not binding, according to Acts 15. The third reading would understand the statement ironically: it takes an Act of Congress to get one little snip of the Law set aside.

In Acts, however, heaven and earth do move, and parts of the Law "fall," at least for the Gentile believers. No Jewish Christian, including the Pharisees who urge circumcision and Torah observance for all Gentile believers, is ever told that he or she must give up obeying Torah. (Well, God tells Peter in a dream to eat unclean animals, but he refuses.) Instead, Luke tells the story of how God prepares the way, inch by inch, for the Jewish believers to accept Gentiles without requiring full obedience to Torah. In James's compromise, the Gentiles will avoid some things that Deuteronomy would call *bdelygma*—idols, fornication, and eating blood. But although Paul delivers this word to Gentile churches, "thousands" of Torah-observant believers, all "zealous for the Law," still find Paul offensive and dangerous. In order to appease them, he follows James's advice and takes vows that demand his appearance in the temple; this leads to a riot, his arrest, and until Acts ends he is in custody. Easier to move heaven and earth, indeed!

The last bit of 16:16 is also not clear. The verb *biazō* means "to use force," and the form used in 16:16 is either passive ("being forced") or middle ("forcing oneself"). The middle sense would make this clause a version of the saying on the narrow door: "the kingdom of God is being spread as good news, and everyone is pressing themselves into it." If that's what Luke meant, then he also must have meant "every true disciple," since he has already indicated that only the few make it into the narrow door. The passive sense of the verb, which makes more sense to me, means that Jesus and his followers, who are preaching the kingdom as good news, are pressing everyone to enter it. The only drawback to this reading is that *biazō* is such a strong verb; it would almost have the sense of Jesus and his people forcing others to come into the kingdom, which would not be true to the narrative. On the other hand, the host in the parable of the great banquet, after his initial invitations are all refused, sends out his servants to compel the homeless to come to his banquet. Luke is thus capable of describing the mission in strong language, even if he does not mean it literally. All things considered, having both verbs passive keeps the parallel structure and is preferable.[12]

Verse 18 is a prohibition of remarriage after divorce. Unlike Matthew's version, there is no exception given; unlike Mark's, the second clause is about a man's conduct, not a woman's. Luke's version also does not specify who has been the victim. In the first clause, the divorcing husband must commit adultery against his wife; in the second, the man marrying the previously divorced woman must commit adultery against her first husband. But more than likely, Luke's community was less concerned about identifying the victim as about impeding divorce and remarriage, feeling that couples should either stay married or stay single once they divorced. This was Paul's view, too: they should not divorce, and if

The Vulgar Rich

I have seen Lollia Paulina . . . at an ordinary betrothal banquet covered with emeralds and pearls interlaced with each other and shining all over her head, hair, ears, neck, and fingers, their total value amounting to 40,000,000 sesterces . . . . (Pliny, *Nat.* 9.58.117)

"What am I to start with prohibiting and cutting down to the standard of old? The vast size of the country manors? The number of slaves of every nationality? The weight of silver and gold? The marvels in bronze and painting? The indiscriminate dress of men and women, or that luxury peculiar to the women alone which, for the sake of jewels, diverts our riches to foreign and even hostile peoples?

I am not unaware that at dinner parties and social gatherings these excesses are condemned and a limit is demanded. But let anyone enact a law imposing penalties, and those very same persons will clamor that the state is being subverted . . . ." (Emperor Tiberius, quoted by Tacitus, *Ann.*, 3.53-54)

Tiberius "forbade men to wear silk clothing and also forbade anyone to use golden tableware except for religious purposes." (Dio Cassius, *Roman History* 57.15.1)

"I am not a man who regards each and every acquisition of money as a blessing: plenty of people have been tainted before now by this money getting, I know that. There are even times when it certainly is more profitable to lose money than to make it. Gold! I despise it: it has led many a man into many a wrong course." (Plautus, *Capt.* 325–30)

they do, they should either stay single or be reconciled with each other.

Without any sort of introduction (such as "he told them another parable"), Jesus launches into another story about a rich man. This one sounds like the wealthy people lampooned by Juvenal and Petronius: he only wears the finest, most expensive clothes and has a sumptuous banquet every day. But the satirists were making fun of a real trend toward conspicuous displays of wealth during the first century, as the so-called Pax Romana brought unprecedented disposable income to Rome's upper crust. Romans often lamented the loss of the old values of thrift and Spartan simplicity, and some emperors tried to enact "sumptuary laws"—laws prohibiting expensive clothing or jewelry or foods. [The Vulgar Rich] Luke's rich man is thus both a recognizable type-character from satires and comedies and an icon for a whole class of real people.

The rich man with his self-indulgent lifestyle is balanced by a desperately poor man. He is so sick and weak from hunger that he cannot fight off the dogs who roam the city streets. All he wants is "to be sated from what falls from the rich man's table"—the word translated "sated" is also used at 9:17, when the great crowd ate all they wanted from the loaves and fishes; it also describes how the hungry will be filled in Luke's second beatitude (6:21). The point is that the rich man wasted enough to completely satisfy the poor man who lay at his front gate; without even changing his eating habits, he could have made Lazarus full. [The Poor at the Gate]

Interesting, isn't it, that in this story the rich man is anonymous and the poor man named? In real life, things mostly happen in the opposite way; the street people are faceless and those who starve daily nameless, but the wealthy have their faces all over the media and their names on buildings.

Both men die. The poor man is carried by angels to "Abraham's bosom"—in the great banquet in God's kingdom, Lazarus shares a dining couch with Abraham (13:28). The rich man winds up in Hades, tormented by flames. Since Luke's Jesus speaks in other places about the general resurrection of the dead, we presume that Luke thinks of the dead residing in Hades or in Paradise, either tormented or rewarded until the Day of the Lord, when all accounts will be settled permanently. In Luke's understanding, the dead cannot cross from one place to the other, but the wicked can observe the pleasures of the righteous, which adds to their torment (so also *4 Ezra* [=2 Esd] 7:76-87).

The rich man's request to Abraham shows us that he knew about Lazarus—he knows his name—and thus was aware of his predicament. It also demonstrates that being tormented has taught him little, since he still hopes to be served. His first words are not "please forgive me for my selfishness," but "send Lazarus for water." And as Abraham wryly comments, the rich man's brothers are likely as thick-headed as he—unwilling to be taught by Torah to care for the poor, they will probably also ignore the teachings of the risen Jesus.

What would have saved the rich man from his doom? If he had ordered his servants to give the leftovers to the poor, would that have been enough? Not likely. The counterpart to the selfish, willfully blind rich man is the Good Samaritan, who saw another man close to death and provided him food, shelter, clothing, and medical care. Jesus does not advocate giving scraps of charity to the poor. Instead, what he has commanded is that his followers seat the poor at their tables (14:13-14). The rich man in the parable does what most people, Christian and non-Christian, did and do: we turn our eyes away from the world's needs and spend our attention,

The Poor at the Gate

Day by day beneath the opulence of this city Wang Lung lived in the foundations of poverty upon which it was laid. With the food spilling out of the markets, with the streets of the silk shops flying brilliant banners of black and red and orange silk to announce their wares, with rich men clothed in satin and in velvet, soft-fleshed rich men with their skin covered with garments of silk and their hands like flowers for softness and perfume and the beauty of idleness, with all of these for the regal beauty of the city, in that part where Wang Lung lived there was not enough food to feed savage hunger and not clothes enough to cover bones.

Pearl S. Buck, *The Good Earth* (New York: John Day, 1931), 117.

Pearl Buck (1892–1973), American Writer. 1964. Photograph. (Credit: © Estate of Fred Stein/Art Resource, NY)

Ignoring the Poor

"You do a beggar bad service by giving him food and drink; you lose what you give and prolong his life for more misery." (Plautus, *Trin.* 338–39)

"A word of advice. Don't take up that sentimental attitude over the poor. . . . The poor are poor, and one's sorry for them, but there it is. As civilization moves forward, the shoe is bound to pinch in places, and it's absurd to pretend that anyone is responsible personally. Neither you, nor I, nor my informant, nor the man who informed him, nor the directors of the Porphyrion, are to blame for this clerk's loss of salary. It's just the shoe pinching—no one can help it, and it might easily have been worse. . . . By all means subscribe to charities—subscribe to them largely—but don't get carried away by absurd schemes of Social Reform. I see a good deal behind the scenes, and you can take it from me that there is no Social Question. . . . There are just rich and poor, as there always have been and always will be." (E. M. Forster, *Howards End* [New York: Penguin, 1980], 192–93)

E. M. Forster (Credit: Barclay Burns)

and most of our resources, on ourselves. [Ignoring the Poor]

Hank Williams's song "Tramp on the Street" caught Luke's strategy of making Lazarus a real person. After a verse that describes him as "only a poor man," the second verse makes him just like us: "He was some mother's darling/he was some mother's son/Once he was fair and/Once he was young/And some mother rocked him/her darling to sleep/But they left him to die/like a tramp on the street." Luke, by naming Lazarus, hopes to force us to look him in the eyes and see him as a human, more of a human than the spending machine that left him to die on his front steps. Then Williams's song identifies Lazarus with Christ, who was "Mary's own darling" but also left to die "like a tramp on the street." Luke saves his Christ-figuring of Lazarus to the end of the parable, in the last clause: "neither will they be persuaded if someone should rise from the dead."

CONNECTIONS

What, more stuff about money? In the middle of this chapter, we get the famous "you cannot serve God and mammon," and bookending it, the parables of the dishonest steward and the rich man and Lazarus. In the first, the steward is commended for forgiving debts, or parts of them, even though his boss, the real creditor, had no idea what his employee was doing. In the second, the rich man wakes up in torment for neglecting the needs of the poor man at his gate. The point is simple, and consistent with Luke's emphasis so far: if you have mammon—possessions, money, stuff—then use it to do good to the poor, or you'll be sorry on Judgment Day.

Luke keeps pounding us about possessions. He has tried predictions (the Magnificat), curses (the Beatitudes/woes), strings of exhortations (the Sermon on the Plain, or the material in 12:22-34), and parables using rich guys as bad examples

(12:13-21). In this chapter he tries two parables, a curveball and a nasty fastball aimed at our heads in hopes that he will get our attention.

You can't serve God and mammon, says Jesus. The Pharisees scoff: of course you can, and we probably tend to agree. You can have a lot, and still serve God, we think, and here, I'm not thinking of the mega-church pastors and televangelists who make the big, big bucks, nor about the CEOs who get razzed for throwing million-dollar birthday parties. I'm thinking about normal, everyday Christians.

We live in a time and place that teaches us that self-indulgence is good, that we have a perfect right to spend all our money on ourselves if we want, and that we're being good citizens—helping the economy—when we do. We are bombarded by psychologically sophisticated advertisements designed by clever people, ads that try to convince us that we need what they have to sell. Every year the definition of what we actually need expands. How many computers does your family own? How many cars? How many televisions? How many cell phones?

Wendel Berry puts it like this:

Love the quick profit, the annual raise,
vacation with pay. Want more
of everything ready-made. Be afraid
to know your neighbors and to die.
And you will have a window in your head.
Not even your future will be a mystery
any more. Your mind will be punched in a card
and shut away in a little drawer.
When they want you to buy something
they will call you. When they want you
to die for profit they will let you know.[13]

The curveball parable tries to get us to rethink our values by exhibiting them in the person of a crook—but a clever crook, who in Tom Sawyer fashion finds a way to turn his predicament into a way up the ladder. Whose money is it, anyway? Is it Caesar's money—does it really come to us, when we get right down to it, not only from our hard work but as a result of our privileged status in the world as Americans? Give it away! Do something crazy:

As soon as the generals and the politicos
can predict the motions of your mind,
lose it. Leave it as a sign

to mark the false trail, the way
you didn't go. Be like the fox
who makes more tracks than necessary,
some in the wrong direction.
Practice resurrection.[14]

The fastball parable tells us that we'd better beware. There are all sorts of "tramps on the street" whom we could notice if we cared enough, all sorts of sick and homeless people who die for lack of what we throw away. The rich man isn't accused of being a crook; he's accused of living well while others starve, and that should make us cringe:

Woe unto you, O rich people!
For you have put your trust in your wealth.
You shall ooze out of your riches,
For you do not remember the Most High.
In the days of your affluence, you committed oppression,
You have become ready for death, and for the day of darkness and
the day of great judgment. (*1 En.* 94:8-9)

As various groups asked John the Baptist, So what must we do? Luke provides us with at least three modes for putting our surplus at the service of those who don't have enough.

1. *Almsgiving.* The most obvious answer is that we should give from our surplus to those who have little or nothing. "Let the one with two tunics give to the one who has none, and let the one who has [more than enough] food do likewise," said John. Jesus repeats this often enough: give to whoever asks; lend, expecting nothing in return; sell your possessions and give alms; etc. The example set by the Twelve of absolute dispossession—giving up everything to follow Jesus—is the high bar. As I've argued elsewhere in the commentary, even though we are unwilling to do this, we should at least leave the bar high enough to challenge ourselves to do more than a token percentage of what's left over after we've accounted for everything we "need."

2. *Hosting the Poor.* "When you give a banquet, don't invite your friends . . . invite the poor," says Jesus. Lazarus would have liked the scraps, but setting out bags of leftovers wouldn't have gotten Dives into heaven. What he should have done was to take Lazarus into his house. In Acts 2–4, this is precisely what the early followers of Jesus do. Some sold their property to provide money for the poor, but others shared their homes with

everyone. We read about daily communal meals, and that as a consequence, "there was not a needy person among them." Almsgiving is important, because without it we citizens of the wealthiest nation in the world cannot redistribute our wealth to as many as need it. But hosting the poor enables us to share our lives together.

3. *Being Hosted by the Poor.* The missionary instructions in chapter 10 tell the disciples to be ready to accept the first invitation, even if it is from a poor person: "remain in that same house, eating and drinking whatever they provide . . . and into whatever city you enter and they welcome you, eat whatever is set before you" (10:7-8). Jesus demonstrates how this works by accepting Martha's invitation, that of a single, poor woman. No need for a grand feast, he says; don't trouble yourself on my account. If the disciples can both host and be hosted by the poor, then there is no possibility of an unequal patron-client relationship. The disciple can minister and receive ministry, and so enter the realm of family or friendship.

NOTES

[1] Arlen Hultgren, *The Parables of Jesus: A Commentary* (Grand Rapids MI: Eerdmans, 2000), 147; similar comments by Bernard Brandon Scott, *Hear Then the Parable: A Commentary on the Parables of Jesus* (Minneapolis: Fortress, 1989), 254–55; Luke Timothy Johnson, *The Gospel of Luke* (SP, vol. 3; Collegeville MN: Liturgical Press, 1991), 246; Albert J. Harrill, *Slaves in the New Testament: Literary, Social, and Moral Dimensions* (Minneapolis: Fortress, 2006), 66–67.

[2] In *Cato and Varro: On Agriculture,* trans. W. D. Hooper and H. B. Ash (Cambridge MA: Harvard University Press, 1934), 13–15.

[3] Plautus, *Stichus*, I.155, 173.

[4] Plautus, *Epidicus*, 5.720.

[5] BAGD, 226; in 4 Macc 4:1, it refers to the slanders of Simon against the godly Onias.

[6] Hultgren, *Parables*, 150, points out that full-time digging was considered very hard work, especially if it meant working in a quarry. But since those jobs were mostly for slaves, the overseer is still exaggerating.

[7] Cato, *On Agriculture*, 5.3, 5.

[8] Johnson, *Luke*, 245; Joseph A. Fitzmyer, *The Gospel According to Luke* (AB 28 and 28A; Garden City NY: Doubleday, 1981), 2.1110.

[9] "We come across slaves with multiple owners in the documentary evidence from Egypt, where we also encounter some of the problems of multiple ownership. . . . For example, a slave with multiple owners would encounter additional obstacles to manumission: what would happen if one owner was willing to manumit the slave, but the

other owner(s) opposed manumission?" (Jennifer A. Glancy, *Slavery in Early Christianity* [New York: Oxford, 2002], 107–108).

[10] Johnson, *Luke*, 250.

[11] Alan R. Culpepper, *The Gospel of Luke* (*NIB*, vol. 9; Nashville: Abingdon, 1995), 313; see Conzelmann, *Theology of St. Luke*; Fitzmyer, *Luke*, 2.1115.

[12] Culpepper, *Luke*, 313.

[13] Wendell Berry, "Manifesto: The Mad Farmer Liberation Front," in *The Selected Poems of Wendell Berry* (Washington, D.C.: Counterpoint, 1998), 87–88.

[14] Ibid.

HARD SAYINGS

Luke 17

COMMENTARY

Worthless Slaves and Other Cheery Advice, 17:1-10

> Lord, we are your worthless servants
> Doing only what we must
> And our deeds would be amazing
> If our faith were specks of dust
> But, instead, we cause to stumble
> Little ones who come to Thee
> Tie a millstone 'round our necks and
> Drown us in the deep blue sea. (Austrian Hymn)

What is the deal with Jesus? Has he never listened to Mr. Rogers? Doesn't he know that we're special? Does he think it's motivating to teach us to think of ourselves as worthless? I guess it's just one more proof, if we needed one, that Jesus never read a self-help book and never took a course in pastoral care. But even for Jesus, who can be pretty blunt, this section is a lulu.

The passage is another Lukan stew blending material from various sources:

- Verses 1-2 warn against scandalizing a little one: better you were drowned than to do that. It has some connections to Mark 9:42, especially the image of the stone around the neck.
- Verses 3-4 turn the tables: if someone sins against you, you must be ready to forgive, even if it happens seven times in one day. It is a variant, perhaps, of the "seventy times seven" passage in Matthew 18:21-22.
- Verses 5-6 speak of faith: if one had faith the size of a mustard seed, one could command trees to uproot themselves—though why one would want to uproot an innocent mulberry is not explained. The "faith like a mustard seed" is perhaps a Q saying, related to Matthew 17:20.

• Verses 7-10 are not labeled a parable, but they work like one, switching point of view from slaveowner to slave and ending with the "worthless slaves" testimonial. Neither Matthew nor Mark has anything like this.

The section is thematically connected—all the material has to do with the demands of discipleship—but the connections are pretty loose, and if we did not have boundary markers—16:31 ends the rich man and Lazarus, and 17:11 begins the episode of the ten lepers—we might not try so hard to connect the dots in these ten verses. So, with that caveat—we may find a stronger thematic connection than Luke actually intended—on we go.

The first four verses are addressed to disciples, the larger group of persons traveling with Jesus that includes the twelve apostles, the women mentioned at 8:1-3, and the seventy(-two) from 10:1-20. At v. 5 the apostles speak as a separate group, for the first time since 9:10; Peter asked a question at 12:41, but Luke has been working with the categories of crowd, Pharisees/scribes/lawyers, and disciples for most of the journey section.

"It is impossible that *ta skandala* ["scandals" or "offenses"] not come, but alas for the one through whom they come." "Scandal" is a rare word for Luke, who only uses it here and (as a verb) at 7:23; at root, it means to trip someone up by putting something in the path. Luke probably gives us some examples of what this looks like back in chapter 9. The crowd around Jesus is hungry, and the Twelve want to send them away hungry; no, says Jesus, you need to feed them (9:12-13). A father with a demon-possessed boy has asked the disciples for help, but they are not able to do anything about it; Jesus calls them faithless and obtuse, unwilling to learn (9:38-41). The disciples hear of a successful exorcist who is not part of their group, and they try to stop him; no, says Jesus, leave him alone (9:49-50). Finally, when the Samaritan village refuses to give them all a bed for the night, James and John want to ask God to roast them all; Jesus gives them another rebuke (9:51-55). To fail to be hospitable and forgiving, and to fail to minister as Jesus would—that would be like setting out a rock in the path so that someone will stub his/her toe and fall.

Luke only uses "little ones" in this verse, drawing it from Mark 9:42 ("whoever scandalizes/causes to stumble one of these little ones who believes in me"). Luke omits the "believes in me" part, and so by "little ones" Luke may well intend more than just members of the Christian community. Again, we can probably see what Luke means by considering the examples from chapter 9. By failing to feed the hungry crowd, for instance, the disciples would have given the crowd a reason to mistrust Jesus: "'blessed are the hungry,' he says, but he does nothing about it." Calling down fire on the inhospitable Samaritans would lead only to more hostilities and close out any future opportunities for ministry. Failing to minister to the demoniac boy leaves a vulnerable person helpless, subject to the forces that tormented him; he and his father may fall into despair, losing hope of God's blessing. That's probably what "causing little ones to stumble" looks like, in Luke's thinking.

The first half of v. 1 is completely realistic. It is impossible to live our lives and not fail somewhere. We will be more judgmental and less forgiving than we should be; we will be more faithless and less hospitable than we ought to be. What we would hope for, in the second half of the verse, is a fudge factor: since you can't be perfect, it will be good enough if you succeed two-thirds of the time, or if when you fail, you are really sorry about it. But instead, Jesus says that it would be better for us to drown ourselves—tie a huge grinding stone [Millstone] around our necks and be tossed into the sea. This is hyperbole meant to stress how deadly serious Jesus is about ministry. There are no times when it would be acceptable to be less than forgiving, less than compassionate, less than hospitable.

Verses 3-4 address the receiving end of the scandalizing: what if you are the one who stubs your toe on a rock that some inconsiderate twerp put right where you were bound to step? Well, tell him about it; rebuke him. And if the twerp repents, forgive, even if it happens seven times in one day. The seven times are probably not meant to be an actual limit, but another hyperbole—repeat as often as needed, in other words.

Put this together with the first set of instructions. You're bound to hurt someone else, and when you do, you'll wish you were at the bottom of the deep blue sea. But when someone else hurts you, fix it as soon as you can, even if it happens over and over again. So far, that puts all the responsibility for maintaining Christian community on me, right? I have to take great pains not to hurt someone else, but when I'm

Millstone

Millstones were huge wheels carved out of stone. They worked in pairs, one sitting on top of another. You hitched an animal to a beam attached to the top stone, and as the top wheel turned, you poured grain into a hole cut into the top stone so that it could be crushed between the two. The stones were massive, so the image of tying a millstone around one's neck is about like wearing a VW on a charm bracelet.

(Credit: Dmitry Mikhailov, iStock.com)

hurt, I'm to be brave enough to confront the scoundrel and big-hearted enough to forgive. That's hard—being appropriately confrontational and unstintingly forgiving is a hard balance to carry off. It's all too easy to be a little bit too eager to rebuke and, as a result, cause a little one to stumble. It's even easier to get your feelings hurt and say nothing to the one who hurt you, and thereby fail to forgive. And it's inevitable—if I may be so bold as to add something to the words of our Lord—that if you forgive your errant brother or sister seven times a day for things they do to hurt you, pretty soon you are going to feel like a doormat.

So the apostles, perhaps in despair, ask Jesus to increase their faith. This is just too hard, Jesus; you have to give us an extra jolt of faith if you expect us to do this. Previously in Luke, the disciples have occasionally asked for extra help. "Explain to us the parable of the sower," and Jesus does (8:9). "Teach us to pray," and Jesus does (11:1). But here, instead of giving them extra faith or telling them where they can find it, Jesus says that if they had only a speck of faith, they could go around uprooting defenseless mulberry trees and casting them in the ocean. The Twelve don't need *more* faith—they just need *some* faith (see 8:25). And since each "you" in v. 6 is plural, Jesus is saying that between them the Twelve can't come up with a grain of faith. The last time we saw the Twelve as a group, they were failing to cast the demon from the boy, arguing over who was the greatest, trying to exclude the "strange exorcist," and wanting to incinerate the Samaritans. Against that backdrop, the image of the mulberry tree sounds like a joke—if you can't handle demons, try your luck casting out this shrub—or a training exercise, like trying to catch flies with chopsticks. [If You Had Faith] At any rate, at this point in the narrative, the Twelve are unlikely to be able to do it, and so v. 6 is more a judgment than an encouragement.

The final parable[1] is the hardest part of this section. If you have a slave who has been hard at work in the field all day, when the slave comes in at dinner time, which of you would have him sit down while you serve him his supper? The answer is none of you. No master ever serves his slave, says Jesus. Instead, the slave, no matter how tired, serves the master first and eats only after the master gets up from the table. Should the slave expect that someday, the master will owe him a debt of gratitude? No; instead, the slaves should say to themselves, "we're worthless slaves, because we've done what we should." Worthless! After a hard day of tending the field or the flocks, worthless? Yes—the point is that the slave's work never adds up to anything; after a lifetime of labor, the slave is still a slave. His faithful service never puts his master in his debt. [Eating with Slaves]

If You Had Faith

In John Updike's *A Month of Sundays*, a disgraced minister has been sent by his congregation to spend a month in therapy at a facility for deranged clergy. He's supposed to be taking a break from all things religious, but can't stop himself from writing weekly sermons. In one of them, he reflects on why modern Christians can't do miracles the way Jesus could:

Well, are we not such a faithless and perverse generation? A generation of falling men, of starving men, of bleeding women, of drowning Peters? Imagine a man married to goodness, and hating the goodness as darkness hates the light; yet he cannot budge that marriage and his hate by a thumb's-width, and his spirit curses God. Why has the perfect and playful faith that Christ demonstrated in His miracles never come again, though saints have prayed in these two thousand years, and torturers have smiled?

Dearly beloved, let us open ourselves to this lesson. I feel you gathered beneath me, my docile suburban flock, sitting hushed in this sturdy edifice dedicated in the year 1883 and renovated under my canny predecessor in the year 1966. Strong its walls were built; with metal rods and extruded concrete were they reinforced. But let us pray together that its recollected and adamantine walls explode. . . . Nay, not explode, but atomize, and vanish noiselessly; nay, not that either, but may its walls and beams and mortar turn to petals, petals of peony and magnolia, carnation and chrysanthemum. . . . Let us pray for that. Let us confidently expect that. For there must be, in this sea of pinched and scrubbed Sunday faces, a single mustard seed of faith.

There is not. The walls stand. We are damned. I curse you, then, as our Lord cursed the fig tree; may you depart from this place forever sterile; may your generation wither at the roots, and a better one be fed by its rot.

John Updike, *A Month of Sundays* (New York: Alfred A. Knopf, 1975), 106–107.

John Updike (1932–). American author. 1966. Photograph. (Credit: © Estate of Fred Stein/Art Resource, NY

Let's review. It is inevitable that you cause people to stumble—that you will make it hard for someone to have faith—but that's no excuse for doing it. When others hurt you, you must forgive them every time, even if it happens repeatedly. If you had only a grain of faith, you could do small-scale miracles, so your failures can be attributed to your lack of faith. And even if you did everything perfectly, you would still be doing only what was expected of you. Being a forgiving, hospitable, diligent slave is nothing extraordinary.[2] What did you expect, gratitude? Fame? Respect? Sympathy? Nah—you've done what you were supposed to do. You're a slave. You're not going to build up some sort of treasury of merit with God or with Jesus that suddenly results in bonus points, like your frequent flyer miles that give you a first-class seat every so often. Being forgiving 99 percent of the time does not give us the right to hold out against that one stinker who really hurt us. That's hard, but it's harder still to realize that we'll never be able to do it all. So if scoring a

Eating with Slaves

That's why I find it ludicrous that there should be people who think it shameful to have dinner with their slave—what reason is there for this attitude, except for the arrogant social convention that when a master dines, he should have a crowd of slaves standing all around him? While he eats more than he can hold down, and burdens his stomach . . . meanwhile his wretched slaves aren't even allowed to move their lips in order to speak. Every sound is suppressed by the threat of a beating; and not even unintentional noises like coughing, sneezing, or hiccups are exempted from chastisement. If the silence is disturbed by any sound, it must be atoned for by a dire punishment. Throughout the night they stand there hungry and silent.

Seneca, *Letters* 47, cited in Thomas Wiedemann, *Greek and Roman Slavery* (Baltimore MD: Johns Hopkins University Press, 1981), 233.

hundred on the test makes us only a worthless slave, what does failing the test make us?

This is a section full of hard sayings. Yet Luke leaves us hints that things are not hopeless. As noted earlier, v. 2 is Luke's only use of "little ones [τῶν μικρῶν, *tōn micrōn*, where μικρῶν is the plural of μικρός], but at 12:32, he writes, "Fear not, little [μικρός] flock, because your father is pleased to give you the kingdom." We, too, are little ones whom Jesus does not wish to cause to stumble; he does not want us to goof off or expect holidays from the way of the cross, but he also does not want us to lose heart. We must forgive the offenders, sure enough; but we also know that we, too, are constantly being forgiven by God and by our brothers and sisters in the faith. We need a speck of faith, and often it must seem to us that we have none. But faith is mostly about being faithful—being found reliably working at our posts. The faithful slave, whose Master finds him or her alert and busy, will indeed be invited to sit down to table and be served (12:35-38).

Which one of you would say to your slave . . . . Does that remind you of another story? Jesus says, "Which of you, having a hundred sheep and losing one of them, would leave the ninety-nine in the wilderness and go after the one?" None of you; nobody would do that, but God does. "Which of you, after your slave came in from a hard day's work, would tell him to sit down while you served him?" None of you; but Jesus does. Yes, we are only slaves, but our master is Jesus; we don't deserve to be served, but in fact that's what he does for us.

This passage is two-sided, I think. The first side is a good strong dose of reality. You are the servants of God, the disciples of Jesus Christ. Did you think that somehow doing what you were supposed to do would add up to special perks from God? Did you think that because you've done so much good, God would look the other way while you did your secret sin; or that because you've been so faithful, God would make your life smooth and pleasant? Sorry, it doesn't work that way.

But the parable's other side is grace, reaching us in the dark places where failure and despair push us. Yes, we inevitably hurt others, even when we don't mean to, and we feel awful about it. But God loves us anyway; God loves the prodigal son and the elder brother, the penitent sinner and the unrepentant Pharisee. Yes, it is hard to be both properly confrontational and forgiving, and we are unlikely to get it right all the time. But the Lord who demands that we forgive each other seven times a day for the same offense is even more merciful than we are, and will forgive us when we are too eager to condemn or too slow to forgive. And faith? Well, my experience is that I never have the faith it takes to do miracles, but that miracles do happen. All I can figure is that somehow, between all of us, there must be at least a speck of faith; somehow God is satisfied with however much faith we have. And when I find myself pushed into that dark place in my heart by my own failures of faith, by my own unforgiving spirit, by my own careless words, when I'm ready to say "I'm worthless," then Jesus, fresh in from the fields where he has been hunting down yet another lost sheep, ties up his robe and asks me to sit down at his table, and feeds me. He does the same for all of us. [Parables]

Parables

To speak in parables implies, therefore, something other than to speak as usual; it means to choose a mode of expression in which the listener's attention is first stimulated by the surprise of something novel and then directed from the literal toward another reality. . . . Shocking, calling urgently for decision, self-realizing of is own message—this is the unique effect of the parable on those who first heard it. But its power does not cease here. Every text that has impressed us becomes our companion, and we turn to it again and again.

François Bovon, "Parable of the Gospel—Parable of the Kingdom of God," *Studies in Early Christianity* (Grand Rapids: Baker, 2003), 127, 129.

Ten Lepers, 17:11-19

This is the Gospel text for the twenty-third Sunday after Pentecost, so far into ordinary time that the minister and congregation may be forgiven for losing their place in the church year. Jesus has also been on his journey to Jerusalem since chapter 9, and the reader has no idea where he is on a map. Back in 13:22, Jesus "was going through town by town and village by village, going towards Jerusalem," and at the very outset of the journey, Jesus and the disciples had been met by an inhospitable group of Samaritans, who refused him shelter because he was dead-set on going to Jerusalem (9:53). So when the narrator tells us in v. 11 that he was still heading for Jerusalem, passing between Samaria and Galilee, we wonder if perhaps Jesus has been lost, or like the Israelites in the wilderness, he has been going in circles for some time. (Has Mary Magdalene been suggesting since chapter 10 that they stop and ask for directions? Peter: "No, it's starting to look familiar now—I know right where we are.")
[The Circuitous Journey]

The Circuitous Journey

"Every day is a winding road."
—Sheryl Crow

" . . . obstruction is in vain:
We will not be put off the final goal
We have it hidden in us to attain,
Not though we have to seize earth by the pole
And, tired of aimless circling in one place,
Steer straight off after something into space."

Robert Frost, "On a Tree Fallen Across the Road (To Hear Us Talk)," in Edward Connery Lathem, ed., *The Poetry of Robert Frost* (New York: Henry Holt, 1979), 238.

Many English versions translate v. 11 to read something like "While he was on his way to Jerusalem, he passed through the region between Samaria and Galilee." Look at a map of Palestine in Jesus' day, and you will notice that there is no territory between Samaria and Galilee. If you go south from Galilee, you enter

Map of Galilee, Samaria, TransJordan Route

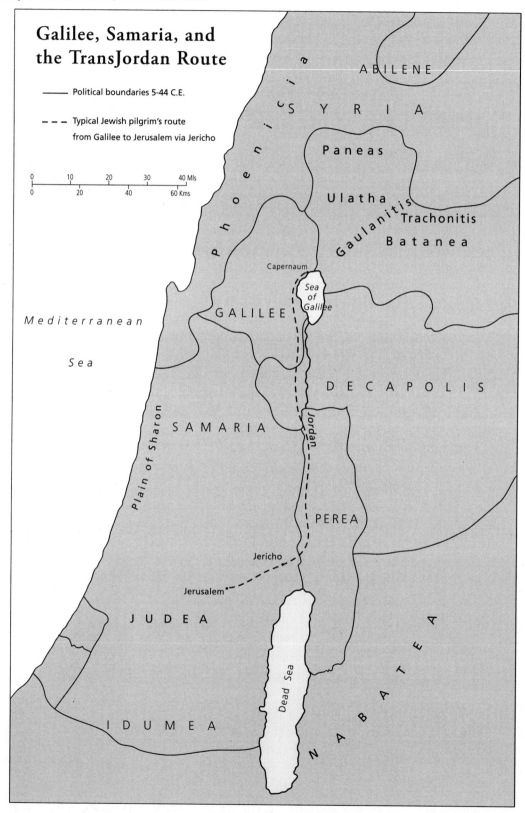

Galilee, Samaria, and the TransJordan Route

——— Political boundaries 5-44 C.E.

– – – Typical Jewish pilgrim's route
from Galilee to Jerusalem via Jericho

| 0 | 10 | 20 | 30 | 40 Mls |
| 0 | 20 | 40 | 60 Kms |

ABILENE

Phoenicia

SYRIA

Paneas

Ulatha

Gaulanitis   Trachonitis

Batanea

Capernaum

Sea of Galilee

GALILEE

Mediterranean

Sea

DECAPOLIS

Plain of Sharon

SAMARIA

Jordan

PEREA

Jericho

Jerusalem

JUDEA

Dead Sea

NABATEA

IDUMEA

Samaria, but according to Josephus, most Jews took a longer route down the east side of the Jordan, avoiding Samaria altogether. Some commentators suggest that Luke intends something like "he passed along the border between Samaria and Galilee," which would mean that he was going east, to skirt Samaria, in order to take the road most pilgrims took. Others just remark that Luke had no maps or vacation guides to sunny Galilee and so had only a dim notion of the roads Jesus would have walked.[3]

In any case, this verse tells us that in Luke's mind, Jesus has been in Galilee since the rebuff at 9:53. Perhaps the Israelites-in-the-wilderness comparison is apt: having been turned back from his road once, he is now approaching the border for a second time, facing up to the giants that blocked his path before. If the "border" explanation of v. 11 is correct, we can also know that in Luke's mind, Jesus no longer intends to go straight through Samaria, but is, like any normal Jewish traveler, trying to stay out of unfriendly territory (for details on the conflict between Jews and Samaritans, see [The Samaritans]).

Whether intentionally, because he knows more than some commentators suspect, or accidentally, because he is foggy on his geopolitical details, Luke puts Jesus into a liminal space, a twilight zone, a space where the boundaries are fuzzy. Green astutely observes that when Jesus enters the village in v. 12, the reader cannot know whether it was Jewish or Samaritan, and so cannot know, until v. 16, that the group of ten lepers included both nationalities.[4] Verse 12 also says that the lepers stood at a distance from Jesus—lepers were required to stay outside an inhabited space—so that we need to imagine Jesus, like the father in the parable of the prodigal son, standing at the edge of the village to talk to them. So in multiple ways, he is on the borderline, somewhere between Galilee and Samaria, somewhere between in and out of an unidentified village.

Leprosy is described in Leviticus 13 in some detail, so that the priests can correctly identify it: a white rash or swelling or boil that spreads, especially if it turns the body hair white, with or without itching. Leviticus does not attempt to address the cause of the disease; although there are instances of leprosy being a curse or a punishment (most famously, Miriam [Num 12:10] and Gehazi, Elisha's servant [2 Kgs 5:27]), Leviticus does not assume that all lepers are sinners cursed by God. Modern commentators agree that the levitical symptoms could arise from various sorts of causes, many of them not life-threatening. Thus the main problem with the disease was not its virulence—eczema is not contagious or deadly—but that it made the sufferer unclean to a degree beyond normal uncleanness. [More Misconceptions about Leprosy] Many things ordinary to life made men and women unclean: childbirth, menstruation, and ejaculation of semen, for instance. To be clean again, the condition had to be over, and then the person had to immerse in (ritually) clean water and wait for the sun to set; in other words, cleansing could be done in a day, by the person alone, and with no cost. The cleansing process for a newly healed leper, by contrast, took at least a week from being declared cured to being declared clean. The process also required at least two doves, the local priest, and, at the end, a trip to Jerusalem for a sacrifice at the temple (Lev 14:1-32). For whatever reason, the Law considered leprosy to be a more difficult sort of uncleanness to eradicate, and so for that cause, it had to be quarantined, lest it pollute everyone. Lepers were instructed to "wear torn clothes and let the hair of his head be disheveled; and he shall cover his upper lip and cry out, 'Unclean, unclean.' He shall remain unclean as long as he has the disease; he is unclean. He shall live alone; his dwelling shall be outside the camp" (Lev 13:45-46).

More Misconceptions about Leprosy

The "leprosy" described in Leviticus 13–14 was definitely not Hansen's disease, that is, what the modern world knows as leprosy. . . . Paleopathologists have still not fond any evidence of true leprosy . . . in human bones from the ancient Middle East that can be dated earlier than the 6th century CE!

John Pilch, "Sickness," in *The Cultural Dictionary of the Bible* (Collegeville MN: Liturgical Press, 1999), 141–42.

Luke's ten lepers were living outside the village, as required, but when they saw Jesus about to enter it, they called out, "Jesus, master, have mercy on us" (v. 13). They keep their distance as the Law required, but they do not warn him away; instead, they seem to be asking for some kind of help. Many suggest that they are asking for alms, but more likely they are asking for relief; Dives asks Abraham for mercy not too many verses earlier (16:24), and a blind man will ask for healing using this sort of address a chapter later (18:38-39). The word translated "master" is an ordinary Greek word (*despota*), but not the normal word for "Lord" (*kyrios*), and Luke is the only Gospel writer to have people address Jesus that way. The only other place where *despota* appears in Luke's writings is at Acts 4:24, where it is the initial address (to God? to Jesus? one can't tell) in the prayer of the early church for boldness. In the mouths of these lepers, it connotes respect but not discipleship.

Verse 14 pictures Jesus turning around at the sound of their voices, and upon seeing them, ordering them to go show themselves to the priests. Readers will recall from earlier discussions that in Judaism, priest was a hereditary office, and that there were thousands of priests but only one temple. Most priests lived in towns scattered throughout Palestine, and went to do their one-week stretches in Jerusalem twice annually. The inspection and the initial part of the cleansing ritual could be done anywhere, so Jesus was sending them to find the priest wherever their homes were and start the procedure for reentering society from no-man's land. Off they go, and as they go, they discover that the leprosy is gone—they are cured of their disease.

OK, freeze the frame for a minute. Up to this point, this is a great story about how ministry feels sometimes, both to the minister and to those to whom we minister. Jesus and the lepers all appear to be in the middle of nowhere. Nine chapters before, Jesus had a clear and definite mission statement, but if his goal was to get somewhere, he has literally gotten nowhere instead. And in this limbo place, not just one, but ten people come to him for help in getting back in touch with life, family, and faith. Ministry often feels like this. "Why are you asking me?" you'll want to say; "can't you see that I'm hurting, too?" But that will be precisely why they are asking, because you are in the borderlands with them; they're asking you, because you can see them and they can see you.[5] Chances are, you'll have some of your most profound experiences of ministry in those in-between times when you feel most at sea, if you will have the courage to stay there with them and invite them to experience the presence of God. [Ministry to Lepers]

Great image, isn't it? But then the story moves on. The gang of ten lepers discovers, as they go, that they aren't lepers anymore; they've been healed of their disease. Nine of them keep on going to find a priest—that's the first step in getting back into their lives, because the priest has to give them a head-to-toe physical and make sure all traces of the rash are gone. But one of them turns back, praising God, returns to where Jesus is still standing, and begins to prostrate himself at Jesus' feet, thanking him. And he was a Samaritan, adds Luke.

The Samaritan, the commentators remind us, offers an echo of the biblical story of Naaman the leper.[6] Jesus cited him in his sermon at Nazareth: many lepers lived in Israel in Elisha's day, but only Naaman the Syrian was cleansed. Naaman was a general in the Syrian army, and was indignant when Elisha told him to dip himself seven times in the Jordan. But his servant talked him into it, and he was cleansed. Naaman returned to Elisha to confess that Israel's God was the only God, and to try to give Elisha a gift. Luke's Samaritan is nobody in particular, is healed without any apparent action on Jesus' part, but does come back to praise God and to thank Jesus. This makes the Samaritans, as a group, 2 for 3

Ministry to Lepers

"In the small chapel overlooking one of the waterways that run like ribbons into the Pearl Delta in southern China, someone is playing a one-finger version of 'Jingle Bells' on the organ. It's a liturgical prelude, and those already gathered for Mass sing the Chinese lyrics with gusto. The others scurry up the hill toward the chapel. Or, to be more accurate, they limp and shuffle, the lame leading the blind. . . . Inside, the organist isn't using one finger after all: he has no fingers. He strikes the keys with a chopstick held between two stumps where his fingers used to be."

These are lepers at a leprosarium founded by Father Joseph Sweeney, who was expelled in 1953 in the cultural revolution. Even afterwards, the residents continued to recite the rosary and sing hymns "for two decades until the ban on Christianity was lifted. That is why, just now at Mass, as the organist lifts his chopsticks from the keys and rises to receive communion, the voices continue singing without hesitation. The chapel resounds with full-throated hymns. The joy inside this simple structure, filled with wasting bodies, rings to the rafters."

Sweeney went to Korea and worked with lepers there, until his death in 1966. "Recently, one of the new sisters asked a patient what he remembered about Fr. Sweeney. Did he remember the good care he'd received, the sacraments? 'He brought us food that we liked,' was the patient's reply. 'And he ate with us.'

'He ate with us.' If there is a place where the gospel has been more literally and vividly lived than Tian Muhn, I'd like to know it."

Excerpts from Mary Frances Coady, "Shunned," *Commonweal* 131 (30 January 2004): 31.

James Jacques Joseph Tissot (1836–1902). *Christ healing the lepers at Capernaum*. c. 1890. From "The Life of Our Saviour Jesus Christ," Ann Ronan Picture Library, London, Great Britain. (Credit: HIP/Art Resource, NY)

in Luke: they refuse to host Jesus (9:53), but the fictional Good Samaritan is exemplary, as is this former leper.

We start with ten lepers, right? They were living in never-neverland, in between Galilee and Samaria. Then they were healed, and when that happened, they ceased being lepers and became—what? Well, one became a Samaritan, but we don't really know about the others. Maybe we're supposed to think that the other nine lepers became Galileans, and went off to find a Jewish priest, but in truth, they just disappear. They melt back into the world Jesus left when he came into this liminal region, and we can't see them and they can't see Jesus. But the one guy—the foreigner—was an outsider even before he was a leper. When his leprosy disappears, he discovers that he's still a foreigner, and so he leaves the nine behind and instead of rejoining society, he comes to praise God, to offer himself as Jesus' servant, and to give thanks—literally, to make Eucharist. Ten were healed, as Jesus notes, but only one was really made whole; ten were cleansed, able again to enter ordinary life, but only one decided that he didn't want to fade back into the landscape. Only one, in spite of the fact that he was an outsider, or perhaps because he was an outsider, comes back to stand with Jesus in this borderland. Just as the Good Samaritan is a Christ figure, so the Samaritan leper is a church figure, embodying the essential elements of Christian worship.

That, too, is ministry. You help far more people than you see transformed, and sometimes gripe, as Jesus does, about the ingratitude and the recalcitrance and the butt-headedness of the nine. "They'll never learn," you think, when people you've pulled from the rapids walk back down to the river and start horsing around on the rocks. "I don't know why I bother," you say, when the person you've spent hours and hours counseling leaves your congregation for another one where they "really preach the word." I don't know how to make those moments feel any better, and I'm rather glad that Jesus says aloud what I thought every time I poured myself into something that most of the flock ignored: "Is this it? Where are the rest of you?"

"Where are the nine?" asks Jesus; is he addressing the disciples, invisible in this episode but mentioned in episodes preceding (17:5-10) and following (17:22-37)? If he is, he draws a circle around himself and the Twelve that omits "this foreigner," and he sounds disappointed at such a pitiful response to his miracle. The first part of v. 19, "then he said to him," probably means that Luke did not imagine that vv. 17 and 18 were directed to the Samaritan. Green's suggestion, that Luke has constructed the episode in such a way that Jesus seems to be speaking directly to the reader, makes better sense.[7] Most of Luke's readers would have been "foreigners" from Jesus' point of view; Jesus' comment, spoken to the reader, is exemplary of the sort of devotion God expects, but does not always receive, from God's people.

The final line is a familiar one in the Gospels. "Your faith has saved you" is often the conclusion to a miracle story, where "saved you" can mean "healed you" as well as "brought you God's deliverance." Here, since all ten were physically healed, the Samaritan's faith is being recognized for connecting him with the full mercy of God. His faith not only took him on the road toward the priest, where he was healed, but brought him back to the feet of Jesus. By staying in the liminal space with Jesus, on the border, outside the village, unnamed and unlocated, by choosing Jesus over reconstitution into his old life, the Samaritan had his faith affirmed and his deeds praised. By linking himself to Jesus, he becomes the canon by which the others are judged, rather than being the eternal "other."

Don't despair. Don't give up, even when you think you're lost. Don't give up, even when you don't imagine you have one more wise word or one patient response in you. Don't give up, even if 90 percent of the people you help fade away without a word of thanks. God is at work in the world, even, or maybe especially, in the unmapped places where people feel most estranged from what's holy. If you have the courage to stand in there in limbo with them, to stand where they can see you and you can see them, then you can be a part of amazing things. That's good news; that's the gospel, brothers and sisters.

The Presence and/or Coming of the Kingdom of God, 17:20-37

Verse 20 hands us an abrupt change of audience: where did the Pharisees come from? Jesus had been speaking to disciples (17:1) and apostles (17:5), and then, after traveling a bit, to the grateful Samaritan leper (17:19). The topic switches quickly, too, from the issue of gratitude over a healing to a date for the beginning of the kingdom. One can think of v. 20 as the beginning of a new episode unconnected to the healing of the lepers and at some unspecified point and time on Jesus' journey; the NRSV takes this tack ("Once Jesus was asked . . ."). But several considerations argue for the idea that Luke intends us to think of the healing story as the context for the Pharisees' question and for the instructions on the kingdom that follow. First, there are no verbal clues in v. 20 that indicate a break in context, and Luke has just given us a clear section break in v. 11. Second, Luke's assumption in the journey section is that there are always four groups around Jesus: crowds who trample each other (12:1), interrupt (12:13), give Jesus news (13:1), and react to his teaching and miracles (13:17); disciples, including men and women, tax collectors and sinners, who sometimes ask questions (11:1) but mostly receive instruction (16:1; 17:1); apostles, a subset of the disciples, who also sometimes ask questions (12:41; 17:5) in order to be singled out; and Pharisees, whose reactions to Jesus are often in response to things he has said to crowds (11:29, 37; 13:23, 31) or disciples (16:1, 14). Third, v. 20 begins a string of episodes related in one way or another to the coming of the kingdom:

17:20-21—When will the kingdom come?
17:22-37—The coming of the Son of Man
18:1-8—Don't lose heart; God will bring justice
18:9-14—Only God's judgment matters

18:15-17—Entering the kingdom as a child
18:18-30—May the wealthy enter the kingdom?

In the commentary on 17:11-19, we looked at the healing of the lepers in the context of what preceded it, thinking of it in terms of the hard comments on what is expected of Jesus' servants in 17:1-10. The story works well as a paradigm for ministry. We can also think of it as a preface for this collection of kingdom pericopes. The Samaritan—doubly an outsider as a leper and a foreigner—returns to prostrate himself before Jesus. His understanding contrasts not only with the other nine former lepers, but with the Pharisees, who quiz Jesus but do not believe. We would suspect an unfriendly question from the Pharisees, who have been dogging Jesus, trying to catch him out in his words (11:53-54), complaining about his eating habits (15:2), and making fun of his teaching on money (16:14). Luke 17:11-19 and 17:20-21 are thus inversely parallel: none praising God except a foreigner, and, at the moment, none quizzing Jesus about his eschatology except Pharisees. [The Kingdom among Enemies]

Of course, "When will the kingdom of God come" was a church question (Luke 19:11; Acts 1:6); real-live Pharisees in the first century would have been interested in it, and might have been curious about Jesus' views, but that is scarcely Luke's concern. By casting the Pharisees as the interrogators, Luke is characterizing the desire for an ETA for the kingdom as misplaced, even hostile. And he does this as a preface to the so-called Q Apocalypse, where the subject is the nature of the return of the Son of Man. Message: do not waste your time trying to predict when or where the kingdom will arrive; that's a Pharisee sort of thing to do.

> **The Kingdom among Enemies**
>
> So the Christian, too, belongs not in the seclusion of a cloistered life but in the thick of foes. There is his commission, his work. "The Kingdom is to be in the midst of your enemies."
>
> Dietrich Bonhoeffer, *Life Together*, trans. John W. Doberstein (New York: Harper, 1954), 17; Bonhoeffer is quoting Luther.

Jesus responds to their question with two negative and one positive description of the kingdom. The negatives are much easier. The kingdom "does not come with *paratērēseōs*, a word that can mean symptoms that help physicians diagnose a disease or the movements of stars and planets that were thought to help predict the future.[8] There are no reliable indicators that the kingdom is about to begin, in other words. "Nor will they say, 'Look, here!' or 'There!'" This part comes up again in vv. 23-24; the kingdom, when it arrives, will be universally obvious, and there will be no need for guides or soothsayers to point the way.

The Kingdom Is Within You

"Behold, the kingdom of God is within you." He says, "Do not ask about the times in which the season of the kingdom of heaven will again arise and come. Rather, be eager that you may be found worthy of it. It is within you. That is, it depends on your own wills and is in your own power, whether or not you receive it. Everyone that has attained to justification by means of faith in Christ and is decorated by every virtue is counted worthy of the kingdom of heaven." (Cyril of Alexandria, *Commentary on Luke*, Homily 117; cited in Arthur A. Just Jr., ed., *Luke* [ACCS: NT, vol. 3; Downer's Grove IL: Intervarsity Press, 2003], 270–71)

In fact this likeness to the divine is not our work at all; it is not the achievement of any faculty of man; it is the great gift of God bestowed upon our nature at the very moment of our birth; human efforts can only go so far as to clear away the filth of sin, and so cause the buried beauty of the soul to shine forth again. This truth is, I think, taught in the Gospel, when our Lord says, to those who can hear what Wisdom speaks beneath a mystery, that "the Kingdom of God is within you." That word points out the fact that the Divine good is not something apart from our nature, and is not removed far away from those who have the will to seek it; it is in fact within each of us, ignored indeed, and unnoticed while it is stifled beneath the cares and pleasures of life, but found again whenever we can turn our power of conscious thinking towards it. (Gregory of Nyssa, *On Virginity* 12; trans. from *NPNF²*)

Jesus said, "If your leaders say to you, 'Behold, the kingdom is in heaven,' then the birds of heaven will precede you. If they say to you, 'It is in the sea,' then the fish will precede you. Rather, the kingdom is within you and it is outside you. When you know yourselves, then you will be known, and you will understand that you are children of the living Father. But if you do not know yourselves, then you dwell in poverty, and you are the poverty." (*Gos. Thom.* Logion 3)

"The kingdom of God is not coming with indicators, nor will they say, 'Here it is!' or 'There!,' because the kingdom of God is *entos hymōn*." Luke is the only canonical Gospel to use this phrase for the kingdom, and since he only used it once, we cannot appeal to other contexts to help sort it out. Since it is used as a reason why the two negatives are true—the kingdom can't be predicted and won't need to be pointed out—we presume that Luke thought it meant something self-evident from other statements already made, and that he was not making a new claim about the kingdom's nature.

One of the oldest understandings of the verse related it to the invisible and spiritual nature of salvation. [The Kingdom Is Within You] On this reading, the kingdom is not an external physical or political thing, but lies within us, if only we will wake up and take notice. While the kingdom of God truly is spiritual, and while Jesus' teachings on the kingdom clearly require a shift in attitude to enter it, Luke's passages about it would not lead us to think of it as something purely invisible or immaterial. Luke's most frequent image for the kingdom is a banquet at which some will be seated and from which others will be excluded. Luke is quite clear that being wealthy is an impediment to entering the kingdom—being in the kingdom requires more than just an attitude adjustment. "The kingdom is right there in your hearts" would thus be a new teaching, especially directed to the Pharisees. Furthermore, the "you" in *entos hymōn* is plural. If this were addressed to disciples, then one could argue that it is similar to Paul's metaphor of the congregation as a Spirit-filled temple (1 Cor 3:16, which also uses plural "you"), but addressed to Pharisees, it makes no sense: the kingdom is an invisible reality inside the fellowship of the Pharisees?

Others interpret it as "among y'all": the kingdom is already here, among you Pharisees, so open your eyes. Recall that Jesus, reading the description of the kingdom and his work in it to the Nazareth synagogue, said, "Today this is fulfilled in your hearing" (4:21). The statement in 17:21 could mean that the kingdom itself has arrived, in the teaching and ministry of Jesus,[9] or could mean that everything necessary to recognize the kingdom is among you.[10] "The blind receive their sight, the lame walk, the lepers are cleansed, the deaf hear, the dead are raised, the poor have good news preached to them"—what more do you need to see? In the face of all that is being done through Jesus, continuing to ask for a sign or for a timetable is proof of their intransigence (11:29-32) and hypocrisy (12:54-56). Since 17:22-37 will turn to a clearly future day of the Son of Man, "you already have all the signs you need to recognize the kingdom" seems more likely to represent Luke's understanding than "the kingdom is already here."

One more option would take the last part of v. 21 as a sort of continuation of the imaginary dialogue in the first part of the verse. When the kingdom arrives, they won't say "here it is" or "there it is," because it will simply be here among you, right in plain sight. This reading would be easier if the verb in 21b were "will be" rather than "is," but it has the advantage of making v. 21 consistent with vv. 22-37.[11]

There are two collections of apocalyptic sayings in the Synoptic Gospels. [Apocalyptic] Mark 13:1-32 is often called the Temple Sermon because it is organized around Jesus' prediction of the destruction of the temple; Luke 21:5-36 appears to be Luke's version of this material. Luke 17:22-37 shares some themes with the Markan Temple Sermon—the suddenness of the last day, the false announcements of its arrival, and the hard times in store even for Jesus' followers. For the most part, however, the images and vocabulary in Luke 17:22-37 differ from the Temple Sermon; there is no attempt to sequence events (for example, "this is only the beginning of the labor pains," Mark 13:8) and there is no

Apocalyptic

AΩ The Greek word "apocalypse" means an uncovering or a revelation of something, usually by God. Modern scholars use the word "apocalyptic" to describe literature that speaks of God bringing a sudden end to ordinary time and starting up a new age. When prophets like Amos spoke of a Day of the Lord, they usually meant something within history: God would cause Israel to be attacked by another nation; thousands would perish, but some would survive and life would continue. When the New Testament speaks of the coming of the Son of Man, it means an event that will end ordinary history and begin the kingdom of God.

watershed event such as the revelation of the "desolating sacrilege" (Mark 13:14). Because some of the material in Luke 17:22-37 appears in Matthew, but not Mark, and because there is a fairly high level of verbal correspondence between Luke and Matthew, most interpreters believe that in this passage Luke is drawing from Q. In Matthew, the parallels are scattered and appear in a different order; scholars differ about the extent to which Luke has created or copied the structure of this short apocalyptic exhortation. We will approach it as it sits in Luke and leave the source questions to others.

The sermon can be divided like this:

22-25—Warnings against false sightings of the Son of Man
26-30—Warnings against complacency: two examples
31-33—Warnings against trying to hold on to things
34-35—The last day will divide
37—No advanced warnings

Verse 22 is only found in Luke, and it is a curious thing to say to the disciples. It appears to mean that at some time in the future, the disciples will want to see Jesus in his role as Son of Man, but will not be able, since he will not yet have returned.[12] "One of the days" could mean "the first of the days when the Son of Man will reign," or it might include all the days when the disciples will have seen him—all the days of his ministry plus the one day of his return (thinking of it from their perspective, expecting him to return soon). One other plausible suggestion is that Luke uses "days of the Son of Man" to parallel "days of Noah" and "days of Lot."[13]

The "they" who will tell the disciples that Jesus has returned here or there will have been believers; at various times in the history of the church, some Christians have become convinced that Jesus has returned in one form or another. Even more frequent, and just as problematic, are those who predict with great gravity and certainty that we are certainly approaching the end because of this political event or that natural disaster. Pay them no mind, says Jesus: neither leave (your home) nor pursue (them as they lead others away). The reason is that when Jesus comes back, it will be completely obvious to everyone, just as lightning shines from one half of the sky to the other.[14] Before he can return in glory, however, he must first go through really hard times. Most commentators doubt that the Q Apocalypse would have contained a passion prediction, and believe that Luke has inserted v. 25, modeling it after the Markan predictions he used at 9:22 and 9:43-44. The Lukan Jesus predicts his death frequently, and in all sorts of contexts (see the list in the commentary on 9:18-27). Here the reminder that Jesus must suffer and be humiliated before returning in glory helps to remind the disciples that they must also be prepared to suffer many things.

Being cautious about false positives could lead to complacency—also a danger for our time, when the delay has stretched to two millennia. There follow two biblical examples of sudden judgment catching people in the midst of their ordinary lives. Interestingly, the point is not that the people eating, drinking, buying, etc., were ignoring the warnings given them, but that there were no early warning signals until it was too late; once Noah entered the ark and Lot left Sodom, it was "goodnight, nurse." The day of the Son of Man will be like that (v. 30): when it happens, there will be no time to prepare, so you need to do your getting ready now.

Part of the disciples' planning should be turning loose their possessions. On that day, the person on the roof—maybe praying or napping, like Peter (Acts 10:9)—should leave by the fire escape, abandoning house and all its contents. The person working in the field should not go back into the village to pack a bag. But the disciples should have been doing this already, giving up their possessions in order to gain the kingdom of God (12:32-33; 14:33). This group, in fact, already had left homes and fields and families to follow Jesus (18:28), but perhaps they needed a warning not to turn back, like Lot's wife. Luke's audience—including us—needs to be reminded that the kingdom is given freely, but only to those who abandon everything else for its sake. Verse 33 is very similar to 9:24, but with different verbs:

9:24—Whoever wishes (*thelei*) to save (*sōsai*) . . . will lose
17:33—Whoever seeks (*zētēsē*) to preserve for oneself (*peripoēsasthai*) . . . will lose

The verbs in 17:33 fit better the situation of trying to keep one's possessions safe; the danger this verse warns against is the same mistake made by the rich fool, who confuses abundant material possessions with life and loses both. If we believe in the day of the Son of Man, we will take heed and let go of things now.

Verses 34-35 use a pair of twos to show how God's judgment falls decisively and inescapably. Two persons are either in bed or on a dining couch at dinner (*klinē* means both, which tells you something about how hard their beds were); one is taken, the other left. Same thing with two women grinding meal. Are the ones "taken" being rescued or carted off to someplace unpleasant? Are the ones left being abandoned or spared? In the cases of Noah and Lot, the ones "taken" were spared the judgment that fell on the ones left behind; yet "on that night" might be meant to put us in mind of Exodus, when those "taken" by the Destroyer perished. In fact, it does not matter which way it goes; the point is that some will be included at the kingdom banquet and others shut out, and when it happens, it will be too late to change the outcome.

Verse 36, "There will be two in a field; one will be taken and the other left," is found in a few manuscripts, but is almost universally considered to be an expansion meant to make Luke more like Matthew (see Matt 24:40). All of the earliest and most reliable manuscripts do not have this verse.

The sermon ends with v. 37, where the disciples ask, "Where?" Have they been dozing during the sermon? Jesus refused to answer the Pharisees' "when?" and warned them against false guides who would show them where the Son of Man has come back. His answer to them is rather gritty, perhaps in an effort to get them to listen: "Where the corpse is, there the eagles will be gathered." We think of eagles as noble predators, but as Benjamin Franklin pointed out, they are carrion eaters as well, quite willing to steal their dinner from some other animal; Leviticus 12:13-19 lumps all the birds of prey together as unclean, probably for this reason. Jesus' proverb means essentially the same thing as v. 24: when the Son of Man appears, you will not need to ask when or where, and you will not need any help finding him.

Two problems face the preacher or Bible teacher who tackles this passage. The first is the widespread belief, mostly confined to the United States since the late nineteenth century, that Jesus will return twice: once secretly to gather up all believers (the "rapture" of the church) and then again, openly and in glory, to judge the world. Those who have been taught that Jesus will scoop up some and leave others behind will see vv. 34-35 as confirmation of their belief; as a pop-Christian song from my youth put it, "A man and wife asleep in bed/she hears a noise and turns her head—he's gone/I wish we'd all been ready."[15]

No New Testament passage speaks of two returns of Jesus. No New Testament passage says anything about a secret or invisible return of Jesus. This passage twice says that when the Son of Man returns, it will be universally and immediately apparent. It also warns the believers, not the unbelievers, to be prepared: "I wish we'd all been ready," according to vv. 31-33, will apply to those who hold on to their stuff rather than letting it go. Verses 34-35 are not about the rapture, since there is no such thing taught by the New Testament. But I must admit that I don't believe I have ever convinced a Scofield-toting LaHaye-quoting full-fledged premillennial dispensationalist to see things my way; you may want to pick an easier argument, like how to settle the Israeli-Palestinian dispute.

The second problem is that among many Christians the "Second Coming" is a frequently anthologized Yeats poem, but not a living or vital part of their faith. Using it, as this passage does, as leverage for divesting ourselves of our possessions is wasted effort; to quote Elton John, "All this talk of Jesus/coming back to see us/couldn't fool us."[16] And to be truthful, after 2,000 years of waiting, will the prospect of Jesus' sudden return ever seem real enough to be persuasive? [Lightning and the Fear of God] I don't have an answer to this one, either. Saying, "None of us knows when we will die; even if we don't believe in a literal Second Coming, we still need to be prepared to meet God at any moment, because we do not know when that will be," doesn't help. It's true, but it isn't what Jesus was talking about in this passage; for that, we can turn to the parables of the rich fool or of the rich man and Lazarus. In this passage, as in many others in the New Testament, the return of the Son of Man will bring a universal judgment—a setting to rights what we humans have fouled up. If we do not believe that will happen someday, then a goodly portion of what Jesus meant by the kingdom of God is lost. But here I must also admit that I have never been able to convince a Borg-quoting latte-sipping liberal mainliner that he or she ought to believe in the Second Coming just because it is so fundamental to New Testament theology; they tend to say things like, "Yeah, but you're from Alabama, right?"

What this passage teaches, whether we believe it or not, is approximately what is found in the Temple Sermon, in Paul's

Lightning and the Fear of God

I got a letter from a lightning rod company this morning trying to put the fear of God in me, but with small success. Lightning seems to have lost its menace. Compared to what is going on on earth today, heaven's firebrands are penny fireworks with wet fuses.

E. B. White, "Removal," *One Man's Meat* (Gardiner ME: Tilbury House, 1997), 4.

(Credit: Jo-Hanna Wienert, iStock.com)

letters (1 Thess 4–5; 2 Thess 2; 1 Cor 15), in Revelation, and in most Christian literature prior to St. Augustine. The Son of Man will come suddenly someday, catching most people completely by surprise. When he arrives, you will not need a public service announcement, because it will be obvious—it will be the end of ordinary time as we have experienced it. Some will be prepared, others not. In the meantime, don't let anybody sell you a timetable or a script for the last days. Instead, use your time and energy to let go of stuff you have confused with real life—possessions, mostly—and to hold fast instead to your belief that one day the kingdom will come.

CONNECTIONS

"We are worthless slaves" is the conclusion to a hard ten verses, and connects us back to other slave material in Luke: Mary's word to Gabriel, "Behold, the Lord's slave-girl" (1:38), the centurion's valued slave (7:1-10), the slave parables (12:35-48), the slave-messenger in the parable of the great banquet (14:15-24). Slaves were rarely considered completely worthless. A papyrus from third-century BC Egypt documents the sale of a seven-year-old Sidonian girl for fifty drachmas; another from a hundred years later offers a reward of three copper talents for the return of an eighteen-year-old male Syrian slave.[17] But this really reinforces the point of Jesus' language: slaves are property, and can never own their own honor, and so can never be owed a favor or a debt of gratitude. Instead, we are to be everlastingly grateful to God, in the manner that the Samaritan shows us—falling down, thanking God for having brought us healing and salvation.

"The spiritual practice that undergirds a gift economy is gratitude." Our dominant economy values and rewards competence, ambition, power, and persuasiveness. "For those who prize self-sufficiency and independence, the indebtedness or obligation to respond that accompanies a gift is poison."[18] A slave cannot put the master in his/her debt, no matter how well or how hard he/she works. In our dominant economy, that sounds awful: "We are worthless slaves." We can never get on top or be in control of our own lives. The remedy is not despair, but gratitude:

> What is this practice of gratitude? A gift is given and we receive it, accept it, take it into our lives and our lives change. Our lives are transformed in the twinkling of an eye or over the course of a whole

life. The work of thanksgiving is that process of incorporation and transformation. The sign of its completion, the amen to our labor of gratitude, is in the act of passing the gift on. Generosity is born out of the work of thanksgiving.[19]

The suggestion Luke raises by the order of pericopes in this chapter is that we can move from guilt over the impossibility of ever being perfect and from despair over never fulfilling our obligations to joy and praise through the practice of gratitude.

> Before our well-being, there was your graciousness,
> before our delight, there was your generosity,
> before our joy, there was your good will.
>
> We are second and you are first . . . .
>
> Our gratitude arises out of the dailiness of our well-being,
>   of meals regularly before us, of folks regularly caring for us,
>   of homes regularly warm and safe, of sleep regularly refreshing,
>   of new days regularly given against the darkness,
>   of work regularly filling our days with order and dignity.
> And in our taken-for-granted regularity,
>   we discern your abiding and fidelity that holds our worlds
>   toward well-being.[20]

The final section of the chapter shakes up our confidence in the ceaseless regularity of everyday things. We, like Luke's audience, still await the return of the Son of Man and the resolution of this world's injustice. But many of us have experienced something like the sudden destruction of the flood or the fire-bombing of Sodom. On those days, when "the waters closed in over me, the deep surrounded me; weeds were wrapped around my head . . . I went down to the land whose bars closed upon me forever" (Jonah 2:5-6), we feel as if the millstone dragging us to the bottom was put around our necks by God. On those days—when the diagnosis is terminal; when the voice on the phone shatters your world; when the levees break and everything you own is lost—on those days, you discover that you cannot save your stuff, nor can your stuff save you. "Whoever will be on the roof with his stuff in the house, let him not go down to get them"—good advice for the crisis moment, and better advice for arranging our lives in advance of the crises. Let go of your stuff! Slaves don't need it anyway.

NOTES

[1] Most commentators agree that this is a parable, even though it is not labeled as such; Bernard Brandon Scott, *Hear Then the Parable: A Commentary on the Parables of Jesus* (Minneapolis: Fortress, 1989), 214–15; Arlen Hultgren, *The Parables of Jesus: A Commentary* (Grand Rapids MI: Eerdmans, 2000), 247–51; Joseph A. Fitzmyer, *The Gospel According to Luke* (AB 28 and 28A; Garden City NY: Doubleday, 1981), 2.1145.

[2] Luke Timothy Johnson, *The Gospel of Luke* (SP, vol. 3; Collegeville MN: Liturgical Press, 1991), 261.

[3] Alan R. Culpepper, *The Gospel of Luke* (*NIB*, vol. 9; Nashville: Abingdon, 1995), 325.

[4] Joel B. Green, *The Gospel of Luke* (NICNT; Grand Rapids: Eerdmans, 1997), 622.

[5] Culpepper, *Luke*, 327, notes how "the act of seeing plays a vital role in this story. First, Jesus sees the lepers. Then one leper sees that he has been healed . . . . In this case, 'when he saw' actually characterizes not only the recognition that he had been healed but also the recognition that the healing was the work of God that had been effected through Jesus."

[6] Culpepper, *Luke*, 325; Green, *Luke*, 620.

[7] Green, *Luke*, 625.

[8] BAGD, 771–72; Fitzmyer, *Luke*, 2.1160.

[9] Green, *Luke*, 630.

[10] Johnson, *Luke*, 263.

[11] So Nolland, *Luke*, 2.853-54.

[12] Green, *Luke*, 633.

[13] Fitzmyer, *Luke*, 2.1168.

[14] Some manuscripts lack "in his day" at the end of v. 24. Neither an omission nor an insertion changes the sense of the sentence, so one suspects that this was an accidental omission from the few but important manuscripts that do not have it; so Fitzmyer, *Luke*, 2.1170. Nolland, *Luke*, 2.859, argues that it may be an intentional insertion to connect the return of the Son of Man to the Day of the Lord. But v. 30 has "in the day the Son of Man is revealed," so "day" or "days of the Son of Man" were both already in the passage, regardless of this variant reading; a theological motive seems unnecessary and unconvincing.

[15] Larry Norman, "I Wish We'd All Been Ready," *Upon this Rock* (Capitol Records, 1969).

[16] Elton John, "Captain Fantastic and the Brown Dirt Cowboy," *Captain Fantastic and the Brown Dirt Cowboy* (MCA, 1975).

[17] Roger S. Bagnall and Peter Derow, *Greek Historical Documents: The Hellenistic Period* (Chico CA: Scholars Press, 1981), 197–98.

[18] Cathy C. Campbell, *Stations of the Banquet* (Collegeville MN: Liturgical Press, 2003), 163.

[19] Ibid., 165.

[20] Walter Brueggemann, *Awed to Heaven, Rooted in Earth: Prayers of Walter Brueggemann* (Minneapolis: Fortress, 2003), 137–38.

ON PRAYER AND POSSESSIONS

Luke 18

COMMENTARY

On Prayer, 18:1-8

The title of an article in the *Chronicle of Higher Education* caught my attention: "Study of Prayer's Healing Power on Surgery Patients Finds No Effect." The article described an experiment in having people pray, by name, for persons recovering from heart bypass surgery. [Does Prayer Work?] None of the pray-ers knew the pray-ees; some of the pray-ees knew they were being prayed for, while others were told only that it might be true for them. Would the prayers have a statistically measurable effect—would the persons prayed for suffer fewer complications than those who were not prayed for? In this test, under these conditions, not so much; "patients did just as well when church groups did not pray for them as when they did."[1] Complaints about the experiment have ranged from "why waste money trying to find objective grounds for religious beliefs?" to "it wasn't a fair test—

Does Prayer Work?

The largest medical study of the efficacy of intercessory prayer in healing has found that it has no effect on patients' recoveries from heart-bypass surgery, researchers announced in late March [2006]. Patients did just as well when church groups did not pray for them as when they did. . . . The authors said the study indicated only that the particular brand of prayer used in the project—by strangers, using a specific text—was ineffective, and that more research was necessary to determine whether other forms might work better. . . . The study was financed by the John Templeton Foundation . . . and by one of the hospitals involved in the research, the Baptist Memorial Health Care Corporation, in Memphis. The study followed 1800 heart patients at six academic medical centers for 30 days after they received heart-bypass surgery and noted whether they developed complications. . . . Three church groups (two Roman Catholic, one Protestant) prayed for two weeks for some 1200 of the 1800 patients, whom they knew by first name and last initial, after the patients were randomly assigned to one of two study groups: those who knew they were receiving prayer, and those who were told they might be prayed for. Patients in a third group received no prayers after being told they might. The two groups that did not know whether they were being prayed for fared practically the same—52 percent and 51 percent, respectively, experienced complications during recovery, after receiving prayer or no prayer from the church groups. Fifty-nine percent of the group whose members knew they were being prayed for experienced complications. "Intercessory prayer, under our restricted format, had a neutral effect," concluded Charles F. Bethea, of the Oklahoma Heart Institute, one of the authors.

Lila Guterman, "Study of Prayer's Healing Power on Surgery Patients Finds No Effect," *Chronicle of Higher Education*, 14 April 2006, A17.

people usually pray for those they know and love, and besides, this test does not measure the effect of prayer on the pray-er." I find I have mixed reactions to the finding that prayer does not always bring the desired results: (a) surely that's not news to anyone who prays regularly; (b) at least now I know that I'm not the only one, and that God isn't singling out my prayers to ignore; (c) maybe the experiment proves that there is no God who can be controlled by specific human behaviors, even if the desired outcome is unobjectionable.

Luke's parable of the unjust judge and the widow is unique to his Gospel. The little narrative about these two stock characters begins in v. 2 and ends in v. 5, and the rest is commentary. The comments pull in different directions: vv. 1 and 8 raise the possibility of a loss of faith in God's willingness to rescue the oppressed and in the near return of the Son of Man, while v. 7 pictures the people of God crying out ceaselessly for justice. Some scholars deduce from this that Luke found the parable in a source characterized by a lively hope in the immediacy of Christ's return, and that the warnings about the delay are from Luke.[2] This is plausible, but it is also possible that the two poles existed in Luke's own experience as they do in ours: moments when the reality of God's love and Christ's presence predominate, and moments when God, or Christ's return, seem very distant and of little present moment. In what follows, we will look first at the narrative and its two characters, and then puzzle over the complications introduced by Luke's commentary.

The first character is a judge in a city. Deuteronomy 1:16-17 and 16:18-20 give something of a job description/mission statement for these officials.

Listen carefully between your brothers and pronounce judgments [*krinate*] justly [*dikaiōs*] between a man and his brother, or between a man and an alien; in your judgment, do not think prejudicially, judging according to small and great; do not show favoritism to anyone, because the judgment is God's. (Deut 1:16-17 LXX)

Appoint for yourselves judges and clerks in all your cities which the Lord your God will give you tribe by tribe, and they will judge the people with just judgments [*krinousin ton laon krisin dikaion*]. They shall not turn aside from judging, nor shall they make prejudicial decisions, nor receive a bribe, for bribes blind the eyes of the wise and pervert the words of the righteous [*dikaiōn*]. He [the judge] shall justly pursue justice [*dikais to dikaion diōxē*], so that you may live and, entering, may inherit the land which the Lord your God is giving you. (Deut 16:18-20 LXX)

Because the disposition of cases depended for the most part on testimony rather than physical evidence, it was important for judges to be impartial. If there was any hint of false testimony, judges were to investigate and punish the perjurer (Deut 19:15-21). And above all, judges were to be careful to give justice to aliens, orphans, and widows (Deut 24:17-18; note the curse in 27:19).

But this judge "neither feared God nor cared for people," which makes him a dangerous person indeed. A godless judge is bad enough; the threat of Judgment Day does not hang over his head, so neither the exhortations to pursue justice nor the curses on unjust judges will slow him down. But the laws of Deuteronomy worry more about the judge caring too much for public opinion— "don't judge according to small and great" means "don't tip the scales toward those who can reward you later." A godless judge who cares nothing for what people think cannot be shamed, and so there are no constraints at all on his behavior. This is a Judge Roy Bean sort of character, the kind who will say "hang him" because he's hung over and just wants to get in out of the sun. Such a judge is profoundly "unjust"—not merely immoral, but amoral.

The widow is part of that triad of "alien, orphan, and widow" who are emblems of the most vulnerable parts of this society. Luke has already used a grieving widow to contrast with a powerful and influential centurion (7:1-17), has connected Jesus to Elijah's ministry to a widow (4:25-26), and will make ministry to widows both a point of pride and a bone of contention in the early church (Acts 6:1-6). This widow has a legal adversary, and she also has the misfortune to be under Judge Roy Bean's jurisdiction. She keeps coming to him (the imperfect tense of the verb in v. 3 implies repeated action in the past) to present her case—the implication being that there was no male relative in her city who could speak for her—and to ask the judge for a favorable verdict. Actually, she does not really ask, or even speak politely. Contrast how another biblical widow asks a wealthy man for help:

> She fell upon her face and made obeisance upon the ground, and said to him, "Why have I found favor in your eyes that you should take notice of me, even when I am a foreigner?" . . . "May I find grace in your eyes, O master, for you have encouraged me, and because you spoke to the heart of your slave, behold, I shall be as one of your house-girls." (Ruth 2:10, 13 LXX)

Even if we allow for a fair bit of eyelash-fluttering in Ruth's address to Boaz, the way she asks for help would be more expected than what Luke's widow says. Luke's widow commands without any mollifying terms of address to show that she knows her place as a petitioner: "Give me legal relief (lit., justify me, give me a favorable verdict) from my adversary!"

This goes on for a while, says Luke, until finally the judge says to himself, "Although I neither fear God nor care for people, because

"Give me a black eye"

AΩ Luke uses a colorful verb in 18:5; υπω-πιαζω (*hypōpaizō*) means to strike in the face, giving a black eye (BAGD, 1043). Because it seems so absurd for the judge to be afraid of the widow actually slugging him, many commentators assume that Luke means it metaphorically—"she will damage my reputation"—but since Luke says twice that he cares nothing about what people think of him, we should probably take this as Luke's ironic joke on the judge. Making him afraid of the widow makes him ridiculous; but since we cannot imagine actual ruthless politicians being afraid of widows, Luke's joke is a dark commentary on society.

this widow is truly giving me a hard time, I will vindicate her, lest her ceaseless coming give me a black eye." ["Give me a black eye"] Picture the judge getting up in the morning to go to his seat at the city gates. He steps out his front door, and there she is, saying, "Give me justice!" Several times each week she is the first one in line to see him: "Give me justice!" He can't even sit at the outdoor café and read the paper and sip espresso without hearing her screeching, "Give me justice!" So in the end, even though he would not do the right thing because God wants it or because he was worried about his reputation, he does it so he can have some peace.

Before we get to the commentary, let us admit that this is an improbable story. The characters are credible—we have no trouble imagining the politician so jaundiced and cynical that he cares nothing for anyone, and we have probably known some take-no-prisoners widows just like this woman. She is more like Judith than like Ruth; if she ever started sweet-talking you, you'd put on body armor. But ruthless men crush nagging widows. In real life, the judge doesn't give in to her nagging; he orders her house bulldozed,

Give Me Justice!

An AP story titled "Chinese transplant practices criticized" tells the story of Meng Zhaoping, a widow trying to get information from her government:

Clutching a bag filled with legal documents and photos of her executed son, Meng Zhaoping tries to argue her way past a guard at the provincial high court for the second day in a row. All she wants is an audience with a court officer, she says. All she has are two questions: Why was her son put to death? What happened to his body? . . . . "Let me talk to someone! Give me justice!" Meng shouts as the guard blocks her way.

"Chinese transplant practices criticized," *Winston Salem Journal*, 22 April 2007, A20.

or he turns the police dogs loose on her, or he has his goons rape and kill her. We love David and Goliath stories, but in real life, Goliath almost always wins. [Give Me Justice!]

So—commentary number one: "he told them a parable regarding how they must always pray and never lose heart." In this way of reading the parable, we make a "how much more" sort of argument: if the widow eventually received justice even from an unjust judge, how much more will we from a just and righteous God. We should then always pray—not with the mental image of nagging God into doing what we want, because God is not selfish or unconcerned like the judge. The "always" has more to do with never giving in to despair because of the world's injustice. Don't lose heart.

Commentary number two: "Will God not bring vindication for his elect who cry out to him day and night, and be patient towards them? I tell you that he will bring their vindication quickly." Some scholars, pointing to the awkwardness of "be patient," translate the last part of v. 7 as "Will God delay long in helping them?"[3] While this is possible, it seems unlikely, because it gives a very unusual sense for the verb *makrothymeō*, which otherwise means "be patient, forbear."[4] What sense does it make for God to be patient with righteous sufferers? From the widow's point of view, the judge's sloth is not patience, but wickedness; from where the suffering righteous sit, God's tardiness may be motivated by patience toward the wicked, but it feels like callousness to them. The psalms are full of this sort of thing: "How long, O Lord, will you forget me—forever? How long will you turn your face from me? . . . How long will my enemy be lifted up above me?" (Ps 13:1-2 LXX). [Praying and Not Losing Heart]

Praying and Not Losing Heart

Prayer is the little implement
Through which Men reach
Where Presence—is denied them.
They fling their Speech

By means of it—in God's ear—
If then He hear—
This sums the Apparatus
Comprised in prayer—

Emily Dickinson, 437, *The Complete Poems of Emily Dickinson,* ed. Thomas H. Johnson (Boston: Little, Brown, 1960).

But the widow asks for justice in a court case, certain that her cause is right. We may also feel as certain about our cause, but in my experience, we are better off asking for mercy than for absolute justice. Just as the God to whom we pray is far more righteous than the judge in the parable, even so we "elect" are far less righteous, generally, than we suppose this widow to have been. Are we sure than we want God's sword to fall quickly on the wicked? What if we find that we have been complicit in preventing the widow, the orphan, and the alien from receiving justice—what if we have helped Goliath crush the poor? I hope God listens to my complaints with lots of patience.

Luke's promise that God will bring their vindication quickly is problematic. If what that means is the speedy return of the Son of Man, Judgment Day, and the start of the age to come, then too much time has passed for "quickly" to stand without some modification. In fact, this passage is meant to be read in the light of the Pharisees' question and Jesus' answer (17:20-21) and Jesus' instruction to the disciples about the return of the Son of Man (17:22-37). In those passages he said clearly and repeatedly that one cannot predict the time or place when the Son of Man will return and the kingdom will begin. It will happen when it happens, and when it happens no one will need to be given an announcement. It will happen suddenly, at a time when no one is expecting it. "Quickly," then, may have the sense of "suddenly, unexpectedly."[5]

Commentary number three: "But when the Son of Man comes will he find faith on the earth?" The powerless widow vs. the corrupt judge is a biblical *topos*—a sort of stock plot and ever-present danger. The remedy is always the same: the judge and the citizen must fear God, who will hear the widow's cry and avenge her. Because of their fear of God, they must not allow the widows to be exploited. This little drama bores a hole in that line of thought: if the judge or the society does not fear God, then how will the widow ever find justice? We know that in real life the powerful are seldom worn down by the powerless. Occasionally, enough interest is mobilized in a society to change the laws to make widows less vulnerable to predatory adversaries or to unjust judges. But in the short run, this widow is going to need a community who will make certain that she is not crushed and forgotten. As we pray for justice, and while we wait for Christ to come to inaugurate the kingdom, we should also imitate the early Christian community of Acts who met the needs of the widows around them. If the poor, the orphans, the widows, and the aliens are going to have their injustices rectified quickly, then it will be by God acting through us.

Praying Up and Down, 18:9-14

This text is the Gospel reading for the 25th Sunday after Pentecost in Year C. It is the twin of 18:1-8, the parable of the widow and the unjust judge, and although the lectionary splits them up, the wise interpreter will at least consider the one when preaching on the other. Both parables appear in Luke and in no other Gospel.

The fix is in: by this point in Luke we can tell the good guys from the bad guys, and so when the two, the Pharisee and the tax collector, go into the temple to pray, we can predict that the Pharisee will come out the loser. What good is a parable if you know how it will turn out? Parables need an edge, a surprise, to work as world-expanding or presupposition-exploding events. So we read carefully, looking for the trap door.

This parable begins with the application: Jesus gave it against "those who have convinced themselves [or who are confident in themselves] that they are righteous and who despise the rest" (18:9). What an inauspicious beginning—which of us would ever admit to that? We can think of other people who fit that description, maybe, but we are not haughty or stuck up, nor do we have inflated opinions of ourselves. We know full well that only God makes us righteous, if righteous we are, and we would not dream of treating someone else with contempt. The editorial beginning, then, baits the hook: we can hardly help but think that Jesus is about to whack them, not us.

The editorial beginning also sets up an interesting relationship between this parable and the parable of the judge and the widow. The unrighteous/unjust judge had no respect for others (18:2), and this parable is told against those who despise others or treat them with disdain. The judge, whose duty it was to vindicate the righteous, was unrighteous, because he refused to do so; he had no fear of the Lord, and so did not feel compelled to give the correct verdict. One could say of him that he was amoral; he had no fear of God and no respect for others, and so he just didn't care. He is characterized by an absence of justice or righteousness—a crooked stick that could never be mistaken for anything like a straight edge. But 18:9 sets up the second parable to be told against those who are confident that they are righteous; literally, "those who have convinced themselves that they are righteous." The judge knew he was a stinker; 18:9 sets its sights on those who are clueless, who think they are guiltless when actually they are in deep trouble. The widow knew she was in the right, and demanded justice; the Pharisee knows he is right and believes God shares his point of view. Thus he demands nothing, but celebrates the God who has vindicated him and has trounced his adversary. In his self-delusion, he misses both the demands that God's justice puts on him and the extent of God's patience with sinners like the tax collector.

In Luke, the Pharisees and Jesus have a complicated relationship. Three times a Pharisee invites Jesus to dinner (7:36; 11:37; 14:1); each time, however, Jesus winds up criticizing the host—for failing to treat Jesus as an honored guest (7:44-46); for being a hand-washing, herb-tithing, praise-loving, greedy hypocrite (11:39-44); or for inviting the wrong people and seating them in the wrong places (14:7-14). The Pharisees warn Jesus that Herod Antipas wants to kill him; Jesus gives them a piece of his mind to relay to the king (13:31-32). Perhaps not surprisingly, the Pharisees are reported to have a grudge against Jesus (11:53), and are recently reported to have grumbled against him for eating with tax collectors and sinners (15:1-2, repeating 5:30). The narrator's language in 18:9 also tilts the scales against the Pharisees. In 16:14, Jesus says of them, "You are the ones justifying yourselves before humans, but

Prejudice against Pharisees

By this point in Luke, Pharisees are stock characters, almost like dictionary definitions of
"hypocrite." This excerpt from C. S. Lewis's "Screwtape
Proposes a Toast" illustrates how many of us think of
Pharisees:

But now for the pleasantest part of my duty. It falls to my lot
to propose on behalf of the guests the health of Principal
Slubgob and the Tempter's Training College. Fill your glasses.
What is this I see? What is this delicious bouquet I inhale?
Can it be? Mr. Principal, I unsay all my hard words about the
dinner. I see, and smell, that even under wartime conditions
the College cellar still has a few dozen of sound old vintage
Pharisee. Well, well, well. This is like old times. Hold it
beneath your nostrils for a moment, gentledevils. Hold it up to
the light. Look at those fiery streaks that write and tangle in
its dark heart, as if they were contending. And so they are.
You know how this wine is blended? Different types of
Pharisee have been harvested, trodden, and fermented
together to produce its subtle flavor. Types that were most
antagonistic to one another on Earth. Some were all rules and
relics and rosaries; others were all drab clothes, long faces,
and petty traditional abstinences from wine or cards or the
theatre. Both had in common their self-righteousness and the
almost infinite distance between their actual outlook and anything the Enemy really is or commands. The wickedness of
other religions was the really live doctrine in the religion of
each; slander was its gospel and denigration its litany. How
they hated each other up there where the sun shone! How
much more they hate each other now that they are forever
conjoined but not reconciled. Their astonishment, their resentment, at the combination, the festering of their eternally
impenitent spite, passing into our spiritual digestion, will work
like fire. Dark fire. All said and done, my friends, it will be an ill
day for us if what most humans mean by "religion" ever vanishes from the Earth. It can still send us the truly delicious
sins. The fine flower of unholiness can grow only in the close
neighborhood of the Holy. Nowhere do we tempt so successfully as on the very steps of the altar.

C. S. Lewis, "Screwtape
Proposes a Toast," *The
Screwtape Letters* (New
York: MacMillan, 1961),
170–72.

C. S. Lewis
(Credit: Barclay Burns)

God knows your hearts." So we do not expect too much of this
Pharisee who is going to the temple to pray. [Prejudice against Pharisees]

On the other hand, the tax collectors have responded to Jesus,
beginning with Levi and all his friends (5:27-29) and running up
to the anonymous crowd mentioned at 15:1-2. Levi, "leaving
everything, stood up and followed him" (5:28), so we are encouraged to think that this man will also do well, especially in contrast
to the Pharisee. After all, the prodigal returns, but the elder brother
stays out in the field; we predict that the tax collector will turn and
come to God with his whole heart.

We have to imagine the scene in the temple as these two guys
come in at the hour of prayer in the late afternoon (the same ceremony that opens this Gospel, when Zechariah met the angel
Gabriel—for more details, refer to the commentary on Luke
1:5-25). They come through one of the many gates into the Court
of the Gentiles—the enormous open space surrounded by colonnaded porches. They join the crowds that gather for evening
prayers and for the evening sacrifice; as the lamb, offered on the
altar for the welfare of all Jews was slaughtered, people gathered to
make their prayers. [Praying during the Daily Sacrifices] Picture a crowd

standing in the Court of Israel and in the Court of the Women, each person praying out loud in his or her own way. Most of them are standing with arms raised and faces turned toward heaven; some of them adopt the posture of mourning, with lowered heads and bent backs.

The Pharisee's prayer is by form a thanksgiving or a *berakah*, a prayer praising or blessing God for what God has done (over time, the standard beginning for one of these prayers became "Blessed art thou, O Lord our God, King of the universe, who . . ."). The two long prayers in chapter 1 are the same type, and so by contrast with them, we can see how much of a caricature the Pharisee's prayer is. Zechariah's *berakah* praises God for blessing Israel: God has raised up a savior who will save us from our enemies (1:68-79). Mary's *berakah* includes praise for how God has blessed her ("He has looked with favor on the lowliness of his servant"), praise for God's help given to the poor ("He has filled the hungry with good things, and sent the rich away empty"), and praise for mercy to Israel ("He has helped his servant Israel, in remembrance of his mercy"). Even when Mary is speaking of her own fortunate situation, she attributes everything to God's actions and mercy: "Surely from now on all generations will call me blessed, for the Mighty One has done great things for me, and holy is his name."

The Pharisee, however, first thanks God for what he is not. "God, I thank you that I am not like other people: thieves, rogues, adulterers, or even like this tax collector." He thanks God for his own righteousness in avoiding certain types of sinful lifestyles. Let us suppose that he is telling the truth, and that he is none of those things; what is wrong with giving thanks to God for avoiding sin? [Thanking God for Our Accomplishments] There are biblical precedents. Psalm 15 is an ancient entrance liturgy that asks who can stand in God's holy place, and we presume that it would have led to some kind of affirmative response from the worshipers: I have not slandered, have not done evil to a friend, have not gossiped against my neighbors, etc. Job 31:5-40 is an unforgettable list of "if I have ever done x, then let y happen to me"

Praying during the Daily Sacrifices

And for our duty at the sacrifices themselves, we ought in the first place to pray for the common welfare of all, and after that our own.

Josephus, *C. Ap.* 2.196-97.

Thanking God for Our Accomplishments

Brother Lawrence was a Carmelite lay brother whose gift for keeping God uppermost in his thoughts constantly was set down in *The Practice of the Presence of God*. The first part of the work consists of notes from conversations with him; in this section, the conversation concerned how he went about his duties in the kitchen in an attitude of prayer. Notice in the second paragraph quoted how he thanked God for the things he did well:

That when he began his business, he said to God, with a filial trust in Him, O my God, since Thou art with me, and I must now, in obedience to Thy commands, apply my mind to these outward things, I beseech Thee to grant me the grace to continue in Thy presence; and to this end do Thou prosper me with Thy assistance, receive all my works, and possess all my affections. . .

When he had finished he examined himself how he had discharged his duty; if he found well, he returned thanks to God; if otherwise, he asked for pardon, and without being discouraged, he set his mind right again and continued his exercise of the presence of God as if he had never deviated from it.

Brother Lawrence, *The Practice of the Presence of God* (Old Tappan NJ: Revell, 1958), 27–28.

statements: if I have defrauded anyone, or committed adultery, or failed to do justice to slaves, or failed to give alms to the poor . . . . We pray "lead us not into temptation," so should we not thank God for answering that prayer?

The Pharisee then thanks God for what he, the Pharisee, does: "I fast twice a week, I give a tenth of all my income." The Torah only commanded fasting on the Day of Atonement, but by the first century some Jewish groups saw fasting as a regular part of devotion to God. John the Baptist and his disciples fasted regularly, probably as a mark of their turning away from their sinful age and toward the coming kingdom of God. It is possible that Pharisees in general fasted twice weekly; a first-century Christian text, *Didache*, instructs, "Do not keep your fasts with the hypocrites. For they fast on Monday and Thursday, but you should fast on Wednesday and Friday." Whether or not this is evidence of general Pharisaic practice, a twice-weekly fast would be considered a sign of serious devotion to God. Tithing was also commanded by Torah, and Jesus says in 11:42 that the Pharisees were so scrupulous about keeping those rules that they gave a tenth of their kitchen herbs. In other words, the Pharisee thanks God that he, the Pharisee, is committed and obedient to God. Again, there are precedents; Deuteronomy 26:12-15 gives the prayer one should say after paying all one's tithes: "then you shall say before the Lord your God: I have removed the sacred portion from the house and I have given it to the Levites, the resident aliens, the orphans, and the widows, in accordance with your entire commandment that you have commanded me."

Picture the Pharisee, then, praying with his face turned up and his arms raised, thanking God for what he is and is not. It is not altogether wrong to thank God for spiritual progress made. The problem with his prayer is how he contrasts himself with the others there, especially with the tax collector. His prayer assumes that he is righteous in ways that others are not; his prayer assumes that he knows the hearts of the other worshipers; his prayer assumes God's role as all-knowing Judge. The Pharisee appears to be praying up, but he is really praying sideways, putting his attention on how he stacks up against others in the congregation. He has his face turned up, but in his mind's eye he is looking around, thinking, "I'm the only truly righteous one here."

Thomas Merton's analysis of this impulse makes it universal, and shows how dangerous it is:

There is something of this worm in the hearts of all religious [people]. As soon as they have done something which they know to be good in the eyes of God, they tend to take its reality to themselves and to make it their own. They tend to destroy their virtues by claiming them for themselves and clothing their own private illusion of themselves with values that belong to God. Who can escape the secret desire to breathe a different atmosphere from the rest of [humanity]? Who can do good things without seeking to taste in them some sweet distinction from the common run of sinners in this world?

This sickness is most dangerous when it succeeds in looking like humility. When a proud man thinks he is humble his case is hopeless. . . . The pleasure that is in his heart when he does difficult things and succeeds in doing them well, tells him secretly: "I am a saint." At the same time, others seem to recognize him as different from themselves. They admire him, or perhaps avoid him—a sweet homage of sinners! The pleasure burns into a devouring fire. The warmth of that fire feels very much like the love of God. It is fed by the same virtues that nourished the flame of charity. He burns with self-admiration and thinks: "It is the fire of the love of God." . . . And the secret voice of pleasure sings in his heart: "Non sum sicut caeteri hominess" (I am not like other men).[6]

The tax collector is praying down—he has his face turned down, his fist slowly beating his chest, in the classic posture for repentance and mourning. Just as the Pharisee would not have been the only person in the temple praying with hands raised, so the tax collector was likely not the only one to be confessing his sins. What makes his prayer noteworthy is that we know he is telling the truth. Like the Pharisees, tax collectors are stock characters in Luke. They collect import and export duties on goods transported, per-person taxes, etc. In order to make a living, they were expected to charge more than the actual tax rate and pocket the difference (see the commentary on 3:10-14). So most definitely this tax collector is a sinner: had you lived in Galilee in Jesus' day, you would have hated him. This man works to squeeze money out of you and your neighbors so that the Romans can stay in control of your country. He gets rich while your friends and neighbors have to sell their farms to pay their tax bills. He's a leech, he's a traitor, he ought to burn in hell for what he has done to the poor, and he's got a lot of nerve coming here to the temple to pray.

But he's here, and here's what he prays: "God, have mercy on me, the sinner." He prays down, head hung in shame, eyes cast down, fist beating on his chest. He's a man overcome with grief, and he is repenting. [God, Be Merciful to Me] He says what Peter said the first time

God, Be Merciful to Me

To forego self-conceit and to associate with the lowly means, in all soberness and without mincing the matter, to consider oneself the greatest of sinners. . . . If my sinfulness appears to me to be in any way smaller or less detestable in comparison with the sins of others, I am still not recognizing my sinfulness at all. My sin is of necessity the worst, the most grievous, the most reprehensible.

Dietrich Bonhoeffer, *Life Together*, trans. John W. Doberstein (New York: Harper, 1954), 96.

he saw Jesus do a miracle: O, Lord, go away from me, because I'm a sinful man. It's what the prodigal son said to his father when he returned: Father, I have sinned against God and you, and I'm no longer worthy to be called your son. It's what the thief on the cross says to Jesus as they both die: I know I'm here because I'm guilty, but this man is innocent; Jesus, remember me when you come into your kingdom. Luke's Gospel is full of sinners who repent, who turn from their sins to God and who receive God's forgiveness and blessing. If they repent, God justifies them: God declares that they are righteous. This man, says Jesus, went down to his house righteous before God.

Suppose the tax collector had said, "God, have mercy on me, because I'm a sinner, although I'm not as bad as that hypocritical Pharisee over there." Nope—that's praying sideways. Or suppose he had said, "God have mercy on me," but then went back to extorting money from the poor. Same problem: you can't ask for God's mercy if you're not willing to give it to others.

Prejudice against Hypocrites

The undertaker, Winthrop Ogletree, was waiting in the foyer of the large, rambling Victorian house at the end of the Street of Tides where he practiced his trade. He was dressed in a dark suit and his hands were folded against his stomach in an attitude of enforced piety. He was tall and thin and had a complexion like goat cheese left on the table too long. The funeral parlor smelled like dead flowers and unanswered prayers. When he wished us a good day, his voice was reptilian and unctuous and you knew he was only truly comfortable in the presence of the dead. He looked as if he had died two or three times himself in order to appreciate better the subtleties of his vocation. Winthrop Ogletree had the face of an unlucky vampire who had never received an adequate portion of blood.

Pat Conroy, *The Prince of Tides* (Boston: Houghton Mifflin, 1986), 178.

Pat Conroy
(Credit: Barclay Burns)

And that brings us back to the start of the parable. We knew before this one started who the good guys and the bad guys were going to be. The Pharisee was going to get whacked for being a self-righteous, self-satisfied, judgmental hypocrite, and we were going to thank God that we are not like him. [Prejudice against Hypocrites] Gotcha! We begin praying, "Thank you God, for the blessings of my life," and slide into, "I thank you that we are the most prosperous, most freedom-loving, most righteous people on the planet." Or we begin praying, "Lord, I'm sorry for what I did," but veer off into thinking, "but they made me, and they do it, too, worse than I do." Or start, "Lord, please bless so and so," and in the next breath, "even though I'd like to tell him where to get off." That's the trap this parable lays: we knew when the parable began that the Pharisee would get whacked, but we didn't expect that we would be the Pharisee.

Jesus told this parable against those who convince themselves that they are righteous and despise others; too often, that's us. Then let's be grateful for who God is: God is the shepherd who will search for the lost sheep. God is the woman who will hunt for the lost coin. God is the father who will welcome home the prodigal son. Any sinner, even the worst sinner in the world, can repent and find a home with our God. And God is also the father who pleads with the elder brother, urging him to quit being so judgmental and to join the party. God goes out to stand by the elder brother even when he won't admit that he has a brother or a father. God loves the tax collector and the Pharisee, the sinner and the self-righteous, the whole unlovely mass of us; God loves us all.

Did you hear the end of the parable? "All who exalt themselves will be humbled, but all who humble themselves will be exalted." That may sound like judgment, but it's grace. It's God's promise to hear all our prayers, up, down, or sideways, and to deal with us as we need. When we are broken and disconsolate, head down, eyes averted, fists beating our chests, then God in mercy will lift us up, and bring us to a place at the great banquet. When we are puffed up and proud and judgmental, then God in mercy will bring us down, down so that we can join the party with all the other sinners. Pharisee or tax collector, prodigal or elder brother, lost sheep or contented member of the flock, God wants to gather us home. That's why we should always pray and never stop. [Praying and Never Stopping]

> **Praying and Never Stopping**
>
> At least—to pray—is left—is left
> O Jesus—in the Air—
> I know not which thy chamber is—
> I'm knocking—everywhere—
>
> Thou settest Earthquake in the South—
> And Maelstrom, in the sea—
> Say, Jesus Christ of Nazareth—
> Hast thou no Arm for Me?
>
> Emily Dickinson, 502, *The Complete Poems of Emily Dickinson*, ed. Thomas H. Johnson (Boston: Little, Brown, 1960).

What They Left Behind, 18:15-30

In this section, Luke works with four episodes, all drawn from Mark and minimally edited, all having to do with what one must leave behind for the sake of the kingdom. Before we dive into it, recall lessons learned about the kingdom in the last few pericopes:

• The kingdom is not something one can predict (17:20, 23).
• The kingdom's arrival will be obvious to everyone (17:21, 24, 37).
• Only a few will find the kingdom—most will be unprepared when it comes (17:22-35).
• Jesus' followers need to keep praying for the kingdom's arrival (18:1-8).

- People need to beware of assuming they are righteous and ready for the kingdom (18:9-14).

The four scenes in 18:15-30 continue to work on the issue of who will be admitted and who will not, and what one must do in order to enter the kingdom.

In v. 15, Luke takes over Mark's "they were bringing" with its indeterminate subject. Presumably we are to imagine that as Jesus and his entourage pass through towns and villages, parents bring children to Jesus. Maybe some were sick; others were brought because the parents hoped that Jesus, the prophet who was doing so many other mighty deeds, could bless their children and keep them from harm.[7] Luke read "children" (*paidia*) in Mark and wrote "infants" instead (*brephē*)—babes in arms—and put in an extra *kai*—"they were bringing *even* infants." The disciples "were rebuking them," once again taking up the role of inhospitable persons who do not yet understand the nature of the kingdom of God. Recall the sequence in chapter 9 when they failed to heal the sick boy (9:37-43), failed to understand Jesus' predictions of his death (9:43-45), argued over who was greatest (9:46-48), tried to turn away the strange exorcist (9:49-50), and wanted to burn down the Samaritan village (9:51-56). A lot of water has gone under the bridge since then, but they are still sometimes clueless. [Confused after a Long Journey]

Mark's Jesus was angry when he saw what his disciples were doing, and spoke to them (Mark 10:14); Luke's Jesus says the same thing Mark's Jesus does, but he says it to the infants (the gender and number of the pronoun "them" makes "infants" the antecedent), and without any overt emotion: "Allow the children to come to me and stop preventing them, for the kingdom of God is of such ones as these." Interesting: the infants cannot come on their own—they must be brought, and those who are keeping them away must cease at once. But even though these are really instructions to the parents, who are bringing, and to the disciples, who are preventing, the invitation is issued to the infants, as if they are the ones who could respond.

Luke takes v. 17 straight from Mark: "Truly I tell you, whoever does not receive the kingdom of God as a child will never enter it." There are three possibilities for "as a child":

Confused after a Long Journey

Whenever [my son] is discouraged, I tell him that if I can survive on three continents, then there is no obstacle he can not conquer. While the astronauts, heroes forever, spent mere hours on the moon, I have remained in this new world for nearly thirty years. I know that my achievement is quite ordinary. I am not the only man to seek his fortune far from home, and certainly I am not the first. Still, there are times I am bewildered by each mile I have traveled, each meal I have eaten, each person I have known, each room in which I have slept. As ordinary as it all appears, there are times when it is beyond my imagination.

Jhumpa Lahiri, "The Third and Final Continent," in *Interpreter of Maladies* (Boston: Houghton Mifflin, 1998), 197–98.

- Receive the kingdom as you receive a child.
- Receive the kingdom as a child receives (as if you were a child).[8]
- Receive the kingdom as if it were a child.[9]

Each of these is contextually plausible. The first speaks directly to the nonhospitality of the disciples in v. 15, and parallels the idea of forgiving in order to be forgiven: if you fail to receive others, even infants, then you will not be received into the kingdom.[10] The verb used for "receive" in v. 17 is used elsewhere for welcoming a guest (9:5; 10:10, 38). Further, the issue of infants who were exposed, and the church's response to this, would have been a live one for Luke's audience. In this time, parents who did not want an infant could, without legal penalty, leave the child in a public place either to die or to be claimed by someone else. A second-century text, arguing that Christians were much like their neighbors, says, "They marry like everyone else and have children, but they do not expose them once they are born" (*Diog.* 5:6). Perhaps "receive the kingdom as you receive a child" was metaphorical for "as you receive anyone, even the helpless and marginalized," but perhaps also Luke meant to push his readers into taking in more of these foundlings.

The second reading asks the believer to receive the kingdom as a child receives things, or as if we were children. Commentators who go this direction often speak to child-like characteristics: openness, helplessness, humility, etc.[11] [Being Like Children] Children have no status; the infants Luke spotlights in his change of Mark's text cannot even come to Jesus on their own or speak for themselves, but must accept whatever is offered them. This reading sets up a nice contrast between the infants, who simply receive, and the ruler, who cannot receive because he cannot let go of what he already has. The infants are more like the tax collector, helpless before God; the ruler, more like the Pharisee, certain that he has already done all that is necessary to gain God's blessing. "Do not be afraid, little flock, it is your Father's good pleasure to give you the kingdom. So sell your possessions and give alms" (12:32-33).

The third reading is the most abstract: accept the kingdom as if it were a child, or you will never enter it. This interpretation also hangs on the low status of children in the ancient world: "Jesus

Being Like Children

Knowing very little or nothing at all, a baby is correctly acquitted of the charge of depravity and wickedness. It is also our duty to attempt to be like them in the very same way. We must entirely put away from us habits of wickedness, that we also may be regarded as people who do not even know the path that leads to deception. Unconscious of spite and fraud, we must live in a simple and innocent manner, practicing gentleness and a priceless humility and readily avoiding wrath and spitefulness. These qualities are found in those who are still babies.

Cyril of Alexandria, *Commentary on Luke*, Homily 121; cited in Arthur A. Just Jr., ed., *Luke* (ACCS: NT, vol. 3; Downer's Grove IL: Intervarsity Press, 2003), 281.

would be saying, then, that people cannot enter the great and glorious kingdom unless they can reject the world's values and welcome the kingdom that now appears without status and power."[12] Again, this reading leads one right into the following episodes: the ruler wants eternal life in addition to money and power, the crowds are amazed that entering the kingdom is so hard, and the disciples need to be reassured that their sacrifices are not in vain. To enter the kingdom, you must abandon the world's values.

Luke omits Mark 10:16, leaving it to the audience to imagine whether Jesus actually touched the children. Since v. 15 says that his touch was what the parents had in mind, and since in v. 16 Jesus orders the disciples to cease preventing them, maybe Luke thought it was obvious. In any event, Lucas Cranach the Elder's painting from the mid-1540s is probably more or less how we think of the episode—Jesus surrounded by mothers and children, with the frowning disciples to the side, ineffectual in their blockade.

Christ Blessing the Children

Lucas Cranach, the Elder (1472–1553). *Let the Children Come Unto Me* ("Suffer Little Children"). 1538. Hamburger Kunsthalle, Hamburg, Germany. (Credit: Bildarchiv Preussischer Kulturbesitz/Art Resource, NY)

While Jesus' teaching on entering the kingdom is still hanging in the air, he gets a question from a certain "ruler." Readers familiar with the Gospels will think of this as the "rich young ruler," but that is a conflation of the Gospel descriptions. Matthew calls him a youth (Matt 19:20); Luke is the only one who calls him "ruler," and it is unlikely that we are to think of Luke's character as young. The Greek word *archōn* is a generic term for a person in authority. Luke uses it to mean head/ruler/chief in the compounds "chief priests," "ruler of the synagogue," "chief tax collector," and "ruler of the demons." But when it appears solo, it seems to connote political authorities other than the temple leadership (23:13, 35; 24:20). This man is part of the power structure, in other words, and Luke's readers would not need to wait for the end of the story to find out that he was wealthy—of course he was. Power belongs to the wellborn and the wealthy, who use their power to stay that way. Luke's ruler does not kneel to Jesus, and Luke omits Mark's statement that Jesus loved him; Luke does nothing to make this guy a sympathetic character.

No one tries to prevent him from asking his question: "Good teacher, I will inherit eternal life by doing what?" Luke modifies

Mark's framing of the question—"what should I do so that I will inherit eternal life?"—so that it is a bit more presumptuous of the eventual outcome—"Of course I will inherit eternal life—by doing what?" Jesus refuses the address—he is nobody's pet teacher—and reminds him of the commandments that he already knows. "I have kept [lit., guarded] all these from my youth," says the ruler, echoing Psalm 119 (LXX 118):9: "By what will a youth set his way in order? By keeping [lit., guarding] your words." The babies had to be brought to Jesus, while this man comes on his own; the babies were prevented, but nobody stood in his way; the babies have no status, but he is a wealthy, pious ruler. If the kingdom belongs to babies, how much more to rich, godly power-brokers? Surprise!

Luke again makes only a slight change in his source, but it is important. Mark has Jesus say, "You are lacking one thing," using a verb that means to be missing something; Luke uses a verb that means that he left one thing out.[13] [One Thing You Lack] Luke's audience knows what this is before Jesus says it, because by this point in Luke they have heard it so many times already: "Sell all that you have and divide it among the poor, and you will have treasure in the heavens and come, follow me." According to Luke, you cannot follow Jesus unless you divest yourself of what you own (14:33; 12:32-33). Also according to Luke, Jesus' followers had trouble with this (Acts 4:32–5:11), and so we imagine Luke's audience wincing as they hear—again!—about the need to rid themselves of possessions.

The ruler's reaction may mirror the audience's: he is deeply grieved. But he apparently stays around to listen to what comes next, since Luke omits Mark's "he went away." Verse 24 begins "Looking at him"[14]; just as Jesus looked at the babies when he said, "Allow the children to come to me," he now looks at the ruler while he says, "How difficult it is for those who have possessions to enter the kingdom of God." The babies can't come—they must be brought and must not be prevented—but the ruler won't come—his possessions are preventing him. By narrative analogy, the disciples are to the babies as the ruler's possessions are to the ruler; not such a nice thing for the disciples!

Luke sets up vv. 24-27 as a conversation with the crowds, rather than with the disciples (see Mark 10:23). The babies are still there;

One Thing You Lack

One thing is lacking thee—the one thing which abides, the good, that which is now above the law, which the law gives not, which the law contains not, which is the prerogative of those who live. He forsooth who had fulfilled all the demands of the law from his youth, and had glorified in what was magnificent, was not above to complete the whole with this one thing which was specially required by the Savior, so as to receive the eternal life which he desired. . . . For he did not truly wish life, as he averred, but aimed at the mere reputation of the good choice. And he was capable of busying himself about many things, but the one thing, the work of life, he was powerless, and disinclined, and unable to accomplish. Such also was what the Lord said to Martha, who was occupied with many things . . . .

Clement of Alexandria, *Who is the Rich Man Who Can Be Saved?*, sec. 10.

the ruler is still there; and Jesus, staring at the ruler, tells the crowds that anyone but the desperately poor will find it hard to enter the kingdom; *hoi ta chrēmata echontes*, "those having stuff," would include all but the homeless. Verse 25, the famous "camel through the needle's eye" saying, is then an intensification of the general principle that people find it hard to give up their stuff: everyone finds it hard, but the rich find it impossible. As Johnson notes, "Despite all attempts to soften this saying, . . . the camel is a real camel, the needle a real needle. It is meant to be impossible, otherwise the following statement (about what is "possible" in v. 27) would have no point."[15] Because we are unwilling to give up our stuff, and because we also want to live as Christians insofar as we are able, we will probably resist this reading: one doesn't actually need to give up one's stuff so long as one is willing; it only applies to the super-rich for whom wealth is clearly an obsession; etc. Clearly, the whole New Testament does not instruct us to divest ourselves of everything we own; Paul writes in 2 Corinthians about giving that is proportional to one's income as well as sacrificial. But we should not allow our behavior or other New Testament voices to shout down Luke on this matter. God knows American Christians desperately need to be shaken awake—our materialism and consumption are ruining our faith and destroying the lives of millions around the planet. Please let Luke have his say—your stuff makes it hard for you to enter God's kingdom, and your wealth makes it impossible.

This is too hard for the crowds; if this be true, then who can be saved? Well, Luke is going to give you two examples—the disciples, who gave up their stuff, and Zacchaeus, who will give up his wealth. "What is humanly impossible is possible with God." Up speaks Peter, on cue, to remind the audience that they left their stuff (*aphentes ta idia*; lit., "leaving our own things") to follow Jesus. In response, Jesus says a curious thing. Those who leave behind everything—family, house, whatever—for the kingdom's sake will "receive in return many times more in this age, and in the age to come, eternal life." Luke makes Mark's promised recompense much less specific, but the point is most likely the same: the reward in the present is the company of believers, who are a whole new family for those who leave theirs behind.[16] For the future—well, the reward for the future is the future. To be in the age to come is to be given eternal life and to be seated at the great banquet with all the prophets and the poor and the faithful.

In the first episode, the disciples are a fence preventing some who cannot come to Jesus from being brought. We have already heard a bit about that in 17:1-10; it's probably inevitable that we will cause some to stumble, but it is a terrible thing to do; better we should tie a millstone around our necks and be thrown into the ocean. In the second episode, the rich ruler's possessions are preventing him from following Jesus. We have already heard quite a bit about that, too, and so Jesus' striking metaphor for how hard it is is not unexpected. In the third episode, the crowd says what we feel: it's hopeless, isn't it? We can't do this—we can't go through the needle, we can't avoid causing others to stumble. But then Jesus reminds us of God's power to do the impossible, and so in the fourth and final episode, the disciples are revealed as followers who really have done what Jesus asked. They left everything behind, but they gained even more. Receive the kingdom as a child; leave everything you have; with God, all things are possible; receive many times more now and eternal life on that day. That's kingdom logic for you.

Memento Mori, 18:31-43

In Muriel Spark's novel *Memento Mori*, Dame Lettie is receiving anonymous phone calls from a man who says, "Remember you must die," and then hangs up. "And quite matter-of-fact, not really threatening," she tells her brother. "Of course the man's mad." "He must be a maniac," agrees the brother. Dame Lettie, aged seventy-nine, goes to get advice from her sister-in-law's former personal assistant, herself past seventy and in a home for aging women. Miss Taylor suggests asking the police for help; that has already been tried, and nothing has come of it. "I should not answer the telephone, Dame Lettie, if I were you." That won't do, either, because

> "One must be on the phone. But I confess, I am feeling the strain. Imagine for yourself every time one answers the telephone. I never know if one is going to hear that distressing sentence. It *is* distressing." . . . "Can you not ignore it, Dame Lettie?" "No, I cannot. I have tried, but it troubles me deeply. It *is* a troublesome remark." "Perhaps you might obey it," said Miss Taylor. "What's that you say?" "You might, perhaps, try to remember you must die." She is wandering again, thought Lettie.[17]

Luke's intrepid audience, when they hear Jesus' prediction in 18:31-35, have now repeatedly heard him predict his own death (9:22, 44; 12:49-50; 13:33) and call the disciples to their deaths (9:23-24; 12:11-12; 14:26-27). It *is* distressing—no doubt about it—and hard for anyone to hear. This prediction is particularly graphic, not just a "reminder of death" but a full prediction of the events about to unfold. Why must we hear it so often? [Facing Death]

Luke follows Mark in having Jesus address this to the Twelve; he keeps Mark's progression of verbs in vv. 32-33. But Luke adds, "and everything written through the prophets about the Son of Man will be completed," setting up the post-resurrection scene where Jesus explains all this (24:44-47). On this day, on the road to Jericho, the Twelve do not understand anything, because (says Luke), it was all hidden from them. Indeed, the resurrected Jesus must "open their minds" before they can understand how Moses and the prophets predicted what happened to Jesus.

Verses 32-33 are not a precise script for Luke's Passion Narrative. Nobody spits on Jesus; nobody scourges him, although he is beaten with fists before being delivered to Pilate It is equally hard to look backward and know exactly which Scriptures Luke had in mind when he said that these events would fulfill what the prophets wrote, because there is no one passage or cluster of verses that includes all the elements Luke mentions. But because Luke quotes Isaiah 53:12 to explain why the disciples must go to the Mount of Olives armed, it is clear that he understood Jesus to be taking on the role of the servant from Second Isaiah and that some things in those poems had to be literally fulfilled. Isaiah 50:6 (LXX) mentions both scourging and spitting; perhaps that is why Luke retains them in this prediction even though he does not in the Passion Narrative itself.[18]

The twelve, then, are doubly blind—blind to the hidden interpretation of the Scriptures, and blind to the plain meanings of Jesus' words. But they are still on the road, still plodding along toward Jerusalem. In fact, they have made significant progress since we last got a GPS update; in 17:11, they were off the map, in the limbo-land between Galilee and Samaria. Now they seem to have found their way back to civilization, and are nearing Jericho, only eighteen miles or so (as the crow flies) from Jerusalem (see commentary on 10:25-36).

Luke's camera zooms in on Jesus, drawing near to the city, and then on a blind man sitting by the road begging. He hears the noise of a crowd and inquires what it might be. "They" tell him, "Jesus of Nazareth is passing through." This anonymous beggar begins to holler for mercy, just as the lepers from limbo did (17:13), only he calls Jesus "Lord [*kyrios*]," the more preferred term of address for Jesus. "They"—the ones in the front of the crowd—rebuke him,

Facing Death

I've been to the east and I've been to the west
I've traveled this whole world 'round
I've been to the river and I've been baptized
Now I'm on my hanging ground

"John Hardy," traditional.

Christ Healing the Blind at Jericho

Nicolas Poussin (1594–1665). *Christ Healing the Blind at Jericho*. Oil on canvas, Louvre, Paris, France. (Credit: Réunion des Musées Nationaux/Art Resource, NY)

telling him to be silent, but "he kept crying out all the more." The painting by Nicolas Poussin gets at some of the drama and ambiguity of this scene. Notice that Jesus has his robes pulled up in his left hand; he is on the road, only passing through Jericho. Behind the blind man whose eyes Jesus is healing is another who wants help, and behind the second blind man is a mother holding a baby; perhaps she wants to ask Jesus to bless her infant. The man standing next to the second blind man has his hand around the blind man's elbow—is he helping or trying to prevent the blind man from getting to Jesus? The three standing next to Jesus' left arm seem to be disciples, who are present, as Luke's narrative indicates, but are keeping their distance from those who need help. What is God's will for this moment? Busy ministers know all too well that they cannot help everyone who needs help; how do you know when to stop and when to move on? How do you know if you should listen to the shouts from the blind man or to the advice from those who say, "Pay him no mind—you have an appointment in twenty minutes"?

Jesus orders that the blind man be brought to him—an echo of his "allow the children to come to me and stop hindering them" (18:16)—and as the blind man "drew near"—an echo of Jesus' own approach to Jericho—Jesus asks, "What do you wish I would do for you?" Much of this chapter has been about what people must do to follow Jesus: they must receive the kingdom as a child, sell their stuff and give it to the poor, leave their homes and families. But this man has nothing to leave behind, so Jesus asks what he wants. "O Lord, that I may see again," he says. Jesus replies, "See again! Your faith has healed you." And the man, newly seeing, joins the group headed for Jerusalem, praising God—reminding us of the grateful Samaritan leper.

What if the Twelve, confused and blindly following Jesus, had asked for clarification? Or what if they, having learned the lesson of not preventing babies from getting to Jesus, had made sure this blind man had access to Jesus? What if we, noting how easily this man follows Jesus and how the wealthy ruler cannot, though it grieves him deeply, set aside our possessions and put all our hopes on God's mercy? And what if we, knowing that we will die, make up our minds to die well, free from the chains of materialistic consumerism?

> Henry Mortimer said: "If I had my life over again I should form the habit of nightly composing myself to thoughts of death. I would practice, as it were, the remembrance of death. There is no other practice which so intensifies life. Death, when it approaches, ought not to take one by surprise. It should be part of the full expectancy of life. Without an ever-present sense of death life is insipid. You might as well live on the whites of eggs."[19]

This is Stoicism, repeating advice given by ancient philosophers such as Marcus Aurelius or Epictetus. It isn't a bad idea, but it also isn't quite what Jesus meant with his repetitive predictions of death and calls for his followers to imitate him. Yes, we will all die, and if we took that seriously, then we also might take life more seriously. But the contemplation of Jesus' death, and what it means for our life and death, is different. We will die, but will we live and die as he bids us, or will we continue to ignore his calls to discipleship? Late in the novel, we learn that Dame Lettie has given up on the police catching her mystery caller and has had her telephone disconnected. In her last visit to Miss Taylor, she explains that she is at the end of her rope:

"Taylor, I cannot come here again. It is too distressing." "Go away for a holiday, Dame Lettie. Forget about the house and the phone calls." "Even the private detective whom I employed is in league with Mortimer". . . Dame Lettie was going on. Miss Taylor felt reckless. "In my belief," she said, "the author of the anonymous telephone calls is Death himself, as you might say. I don't see, Dame Lettie, what you can do about it. If you don't remember Death, Death reminds you to do so. And if you can't cope with the facts the next best thing is to go away for a holiday." "You have taken leave of your senses, Taylor," said Dame Lettie, "and I can do no more for you."[20]

CONNECTIONS

"When the Son of Man comes, will he find faith on the earth?" Faith for what, Lord? Faith in what? We don't think much of politicians, so we don't have much faith that democratic processes are going to improve things. We don't think much of the media, either; even though we spend more time than ever tuned in and wired up, we're pretty sure that it's all biased, so much so that many of us would rather listen either to parodies of news shoes or to polemicists who make no bones about their prejudices. We don't think the schools are doing what they should, so the next generation will almost certainly be underprepared for what they will face. We know that our living habits are ruining—maybe have ruined beyond repair—the climate, so that in the fairly near future the economic and political consequences of all those miles driven and forests cleared will rest on our children's heads. Faith in what? Faith for what?

Faith to keep praying for justice, praying to a just God who cares for all the world. We may not like how that justice looks when it comes, but let us keep praying that it comes. Father, let your kingdom come, where no one is privileged and where all get a place at the table.

Faith to keep praying for forgiveness, praying to a loving God who is merciful to us and to all the world. We will be tempted to sidestep God's just condemnation of us for our materialism and consumerism. We will want to pass responsibility to someone else. We will want to keep praising ourselves for all the great things we have built, for the profit margins we have kept, for the luxuries we have enjoyed. Father, forgive us our sins, and help us to see how sinful we are.

Faith to keep bringing the little ones into the kingdom, making certain that our approximations of God's realm are accessible to all the world. We love it when the rows are full of our own children and grandchildren—aren't they adorable in their choir robes up there? So wouldn't it be better still if all the world's children got the same chance? If all the world's poor and disabled were given a seat at God's welcome table? Father, give us all, day by day, the bread we need, and help those of us who have more than we need to make sure nobody starves.

Faith to let go of what keeps us out of full participation in God's kingdom—faith to be a little one, not an overloaded camel. Faith to keep praying that God will change our hearts and our behaviors, even though it is so very hard for us. It would be like dying, wouldn't it, to let go of enough that it would really change our lives, enough to make a difference to others? Father, let your name be sanctified in us; help us to be the people who exemplify the values of your kingdom.

Faith to holler, "Jesus, have mercy on me," until he does, and faith then to follow him all the way to the cross. Faith to pray, Father, we're so weak; we don't think we can stand up to this moment of trial. But let your will be done.

Have mercy on us, Lord. Amen.

NOTES

[1] Lila Guterman, "Study of Prayer's Healing Power on Surgery Patients Finds No Effect," *Chronicle of Higher Education*, 14 April 2006, A17.

[2] François Bovon, "Apocalyptic Traditions in the Lukan Special Material," *Studies in Early Christianity* (Grand Rapids MI: Baker, 2003), 51–58; Joseph A. Fitzmyer, *The Gospel According to Luke* (AB 28 and 28A; Garden City NY: Doubleday, 1981), 2.1175-77.

[3] So Fitzmyer, *Luke*, 2.1180; the NRSV translates it so as well.

[4] Luke uses the verb only here, but uses the related adverb *makrothymōs* to mean "patiently" in Acts 26:3. Fitzmyer points to the use of *makrothymeō* in Sirach 35:19 (LXX 32:19), arguing that it means "delay" in that passage, which may be part of the background to Luke's parable. But Sirach was speaking of God's actions against the wicked: "For the Lord will not be slow, nor will he be patient towards them until he has cloven the loins of the unmerciful." In Sirach's context, "delay" and "be patient" mean about the same thing, whereas in Luke's—applied to the suffering righteous—"delay" is a bad thing," but "be patient" might be a good thing.

[5] Luke Timothy Johnson, *The Gospel of Luke* (SP, vol. 3; Collegeville MN: Liturgical Press, 1991), 271.

[6] Thomas Merton, *New Seeds of Contemplation* (New York: New Directions, 1972), 48–50.

[7] Alan R. Culpepper, *The Gospel of Luke* (NIB, vol. 9; Nashville: Abingdon, 1995), 344; Joel B. Green, *The Gospel of Luke* (NICNT; Grand Rapids: Eerdmans, 1997), 650.

[8] Green, *Luke*, 651, separates these into three options, but it seems to me that receiving the kingdom as a child receives is the same as receiving the kingdom as if we were children.

[9] Robert C. Tannehill, *Luke* (ANTC; Nashville: Abingdon, 1996), 268.

[10] So Green, *Luke*, 651; Johnson, *Luke*, 276.

[11] Fitzmyer, *Luke*, 2.1194; Culpepper, *Luke*, 345.

[12] Tannehill, *Luke*, 269.

[13] Mark has *hystereō*, meaning "to be in short supply" (BAGD, 1043); Luke has *leipō*, "to fall short; to be deficient in something that ought to be present for whatever reason" (BAGD, 590).

[14] Some manuscripts read, "When Jesus saw him becoming deeply grieved," which most assume to be a clarifying insertion. Culpepper, *Luke*, 347–48, notes that it adds a depth of emotional tone to what Jesus says.

[15] Johnson, *Luke*, 278.

[16] Fitzmyer, *Luke*, 2.1206; Green, *Luke*, 659.

[17] Muriel Spark, *Memento Mori* (New York: G. P. Putnam, 1958), quotes from pp. 10, 38–39.

[18] Culpepper, *Luke*, 351–52.

[19] Spark, *Memento Mori*, 153.

[20] Ibid., 179.

ENTERING JERUSALEM

Luke 19

COMMENTARY

Zacchaeus the Camel, 19:1-10

Persons of a certain age know Zacchaeus as the "wee little man" who "climbed up in a sycamore tree/For the Lord he wanted to see" (can you do the hand motions, too?), but he is a much more complicated character. Since Zack is the last face-to-face encounter Jesus has on the journey, Luke pulls out all the stops, throwing in verbal connections and parallels to many other stories. Zacchaeus complicates most of the categories Luke has been working with through most of this Gospel.[1]

Jesus (and his disciples and the crowds and presumably the Pharisees and scribes, but none of them is mentioned yet) is passing through Jericho. He is on the move, heading toward his fate in Jerusalem, not apparently intending to stop in this village as he has in the villages of Galilee. Luke, as in the episode just before, switches quickly from Jesus to the other character, and tells us some things about Zacchaeus: his name, his occupation, and his economic status. At the beginning of the journey section, Luke gives us three persons—two want to volunteer, one receives Jesus' call—and each get rather strong statements about the nature of the kingdom and how one enters it. Zacchaeus is now the third person who, near the end of the journey, responds to Jesus. Notice how the three compare and contrast:

	Named?	Wealth?	Sinner?	Obstacle	Saved?
Ruler	No	Yes	No	Wealth	No
Blind Man	No	No	No	Crowd	Yes
Zacchaeus	Yes	Yes	Yes	Wealth/ Crowd	Yes

Luke links the episodes verbally: the ruler and Zacchaeus are rich; Jesus tells the ruler to give his money to the poor, while Zacchaeus tells Jesus that he is doing (or will do) the same; Jesus asks the ruler to follow him, while Zacchaeus seeks Jesus. The crowd is a problem for both Zacchaeus and the blind man, but in both episodes, "standing" marks the turn toward resolving the issue and "looking up/seeing again" is part of the solution.

We need first to characterize Zacchaeus correctly. He was a "chief tax collector," a word that Luke may have coined to describe the man in charge of the actual toll collectors like Levi.[2] The Romans decided how much each district would pay in tribute annually. In districts ruled by a local king (like Galilee at this time), the king bore ultimate responsibility for seeing that it was done; in districts governed by a Roman prefect (like Judea at this time), he was ultimately responsible. Commonly, the big dogs outsourced the actual collection job to others. A wealthy person would pay the tribute amount (plus bribes and commissions) and then set out to collect it—plus more, in order to make a profit. [Chief Tax Collectors and Tax Collection] If Luke means that Zacchaeus was this person—the person who bought the tax contract for the part of Judea that included Jericho—then he was not only very wealthy but also very powerful.[3] Even if Luke only means a sort of middle manager—not the franchise owner, but a person who directs the activities of the actual toll collectors in the area of Jericho—then he is still a person of considerable power.[4] If you were living in his territory, Zacchaeus was a man who could make things easier or worse for

---

Chief Tax Collectors and Tax Collection

In the first citation, two high-ranking officials discuss how to adjust the contracts offered to tax collectors (called "tax farmers" in the document) so that there will be more interest in bidding on them:

> Paniscus . . . *strategus* [lit., "general," but probably "magistrate"] of the Oxyrhynchite nome [a district in Egypt], to Asclepiades, royal secretary of the same nome, greeting. At the last auction of tax contracts held by myself and you in the presence of the customary officials, since the farmers in charge of the tax on transfers of real property and of the *agoranomus* office [officer in charge of open-air markets, who collected duties and taxes] refused to bid on the ground that they were incurring substantial losses and may even withdraw, I wrote our opinion to his Excellency the Prefect concerning the matter. He replied to the effect that I should examine the former leases and as far as possible lighten the burden of the tax farmers . . . . (Letter from Oxyrhynchus [Egypt], AD 68, cited in Lewis and Reinhold, *The Empire*, vol. 2 of *Roman Civilization* [New York: Harper and Row, 1966], 370.

In the second citation, four individuals have the tax collection contract for a region, and they contract with each other on how to make the payments to the government. Note that they have to pay the money whether they collect it or not, and that they have an armed guard for protection/leverage:

> We, Heracles, Athenodorus, Hero, and Ziolus, all four collectors of the poll tax of the village of Tebtynis, agree voluntarily and of our own free will that we have made a division [of our duties], from the 15th of the month Hathyr, the receipts of which are credited to Phaophi, of the third year of the Lord Trajan Caesar . . . and that Athenodorus and Heracles have been allotted the inhabitants of and settlers in the village, while Hero and Zoilus have for their part been allotted all the inhabitants and settlers [of Tebtynis] at other villages or in the metropolis, with the stipulation that those who have been allotted the external district shall pay each month 1,100 silver drachmas, which those who have been allotted the village shall make up the balance of the monthly quota for the poll tax, the wages of the armed guard being chargeable to those who have been allotted the village . . . . (Contract from Tebtynis [Egypt], AD 100, cited in Lewis and Reinhold, *The Empire*, vol. 2 of *Roman Civilization* [New York: Harper and Row, 1966], 371.)

you. Suppose you were a merchant who regularly brought in goods from outside the district for resale; you'd want an understanding with the man who controlled how much import tax you'd pay. Consequently, we need to be careful not to exaggerate judgments like "universally hated" and "treated as a person of low status." People thought he was a sinner—Luke makes sure we think about that in 19:7—but people also would have known he was important. People like that are often treated with extreme, even oily, courtesy to their faces, but ridiculed behind their backs. Think of Miranda Priestly in *The Devil Wears Prada*; even though she is hell on wheels, she is always invited to the best parties. Even though she always bites off their heads, service people fall all over themselves to make sure her cappuccino is the right temperature. Zacchaeus was in no sense a social outcast, except from groups like the Pharisees to which he would not care to belong anyway.

Zacchaeus was a sinner. In fact, we know what his sin was: he used his power to extort money. That's how tax collectors got rich, and that would have been the path that Zacchaeus used to become a chief tax collector. The ruler was a godly man, keeping the commandments; Zacchaeus was a sinner, breaking the commandments. But that would not have kept him from going to temple (as in the parable of 18:9-14) or to synagogue. Whatever ritual uncleanness he might have acquired by dealing with Gentiles would have been easily remedied by immersing himself in the local *mikveh* (or in his own—some wealthy people built their own immersion pools to avoid the riff-raff). Does your church ostracize wealthy people, if they show up and put money in the collection plate, because they got rich renting substandard housing to the poor? Do you refuse to serve Communion to the manager of the big box store whose company will not give proper health benefits to its minimum-wage earners? People may have hated him privately, but if Zacchaeus cared to go to synagogue, he would have been given a good seat.

So why is he up a tree? Wealthy, powerful people do not run ahead of the crowd and climb a tree if they want to see visiting preachers. They get their people to call up the preacher's road manager and set up a private lunch at their club. If they want a seat to watch the parade, they have someone arrange that, or have their goons clear a space and set up a chair and bring them a drink. The ruler has no problem getting to Jesus. He's there in the crowd, watching the parade of babies and Jesus' reaction to the disciples' role as bouncers, and when he's ready, he just asks Jesus what he wants to know. I submit that in the real world of Luke and his audience, nobody believed that the crowds could really prevent

Zacchaeus from seeing Jesus if that's what he wanted. So the fact that the crowds *are* a problem tells us something about Jesus and about Zacchaeus's frame of mind. First, Luke's Jesus is nobody's pet teacher. When the ruler calls him "good teacher," he shrugs it off; Jesus is not about swapping favors and being the grateful client to some generous wealthy patron (see the discussions of this at 7:1-10; 7:11-17; and 7:36-50). Second, Zacchaeus acts as if he knows this, and does not use his influence to get close to Jesus. He could have pushed through the crowd to ask his question, like the ruler; he could have hollered, like the blind man; instead, he sprints ahead of the crowd and shinnies up a tree, just to catch a glimpse of Jesus. Like the tax collector in the parable, he knows he needs mercy. [Up a Tree]

Up a Tree

And I can tell by the way you're searching,
for something you can't even name
That you haven't been able to come to the table

Mary Chapin Carpenter, "Jubilee," Why Walk Music, 1994.

Mikeal Parsons suggests that Luke's audience would have heard "small in height" (19:3, *hēlikia mikros*) and thought "small in spirit"—greedy, but also with low self-expectations, the opposite of "great-souled." He notes that dwarfs were exhibited as spectacles in the arenas or used as comic elements at parties. He concludes, "Luke has spared no insulting image to portray Zacchaeus as a pathetic, even despicable character. He paints a derisive and mocking picture of a traitorous, small-minded, greedy, physically deformed tax collector sprinting awkwardly ahead of the crowd and climbing a sycamore tree like an ape."[5] If Parsons is right, then Zacchaeus is Luke's way of saying, "Imagine the worst case scenario, the person most unlikely to respond to Jesus' message."

When he arrives at the spot, Jesus "looks up"—same verb translated "see again" in the blind man story—and issues a command: "Zacchaeus, hurry down, because today it is necessary for me to stay at your house." "It is necessary" is Luke's word for expressing what God says must be done. "Today" connects with the end of the story (19:9) but also with the many other times Jesus announces the arrival of good news (2:11; 4:21; 23:43) or bad (13:32-33; 19:42). Zacchaeus, for his part, hurries down and "welcomes him rejoicing." The verb "welcome" means to receive with hospitality (9:5; 10:10, 38), and was used when Jesus said that only those who "receive" the kingdom as a child will enter it. In other words, it means that Zacchaeus took Jesus home and received him hospitably: Zack gave him welcoming kisses, somebody washed his feet and hands and anointed his head with fragrant oil, and then they all sat down to eat (see 7:44-46 and the commentary in that section).

What happens next mirrors the party at Levi's house, except that the grumblers are "everyone" and not just the Pharisees and scribes. They may be part of the crowd in the dining room, grumbling about Jesus; they may have simply walked into the "public" part of Zacchaeus's house (see discussion at 5:30); maybe Luke temporarily turns the microphone toward the crowds who, until Jesus ducked into Zack's house for supper, had been walking along the road with him. This is not just about eating with small-change sinners; from the perspective of the crowds, the disciples, and the enemies, this is Jesus deliberately picking the biggest crook in the area to eat with. Has Jesus sold out? Has he decided to find some powerful friends? If he told the godly ruler to sell everything, how can he now enjoy a feast with a man getting rich by taking what he can from others?

Zacchaeus in the Sycamore

Engraving from Dover Pictorial Archive Series.

In the previous story, Jesus stood until the blind man could be brought to him. In this story, Zacchaeus stands. Some commentators see this happening outside, on the way to the house, as Zacchaeus overhears the grumbling around him.[6] That's a plausible reading, but I am opting for "he stood up from his dining couch," presuming that "welcome with rejoicing" includes the steps described above.

There are also two ways to understand what Zacchaeus says in v. 8. The verbs "I give" and "I give back" are present tense, and so it is possible to understand them either as descriptions of what he is doing or as what he is beginning to do. Some commentators, choosing the first option, see Jesus vindicating Zacchaeus in this story. He has been unfairly maligned; people think he is a sinner, when all along he has been giving generously to the poor and being careful to restore whenever he defrauds. "Jesus announces salvation 'to this house' because he sees that Zacchaeus is innocent, a true 'son of Abraham,' despite the post that he held, which branded him otherwise."[7] This reading is a helpful disruption of the categories of "sinner" and "rich," and it would make Zacchaeus the inverse of the ruler; the ruler looked godly, but his riches kept him from following Jesus; Zacchaeus looked sinful, but his willingness to disperse his riches made him eligible for salvation.

The traditional understanding is that Zacchaeus is describing what he has resolved to do, or what he is doing from this moment on, rather than what he has been doing. Luke regularly uses the imperfect tense to describe habitual past activity, so had he meant us to understand Zacchaeus as a hidden saint, he more likely would have put the verbs in the imperfect rather than the present. But I agree with those who note that Zacchaeus's repentance has already happened by the time he speaks; climbing the tree shows that he has already abandoned his power and influence and is prepared to be meeker than the blind man.

Zacchaeus says, "Half my stuff, Lord, I give to the poor, and if I have defrauded anyone of anything, I return it four-fold." Start with the last statement: if he does not defraud, he makes no profit—this was what made John the Baptist's advice to the tax collectors radical and not bourgeois. The tax-farming system was based on greed and fraud, and if tax collectors only collected what was actually owed to Rome, there would be no incentive to collect taxes, and things would grind to a halt (see commentary on 3:17). So of course Zacchaeus has defrauded people; so have all the underlings who work for him, who actually collected the taxes. If he pays each taxpayer four times more than the difference between what he collected and what they owed, then he is returning 400 percent of his profits. And if he begins his giving by disbursing half of his savings, then he is going to end up poor. [Giving Away]

Given everything Luke has said about giving up everything as the prerequisite to following Jesus, I cannot see how we can think of Zacchaeus as a poorer but still wealthy man at the end of the story.[8] But if that's correct—if this story is meant to be a corrective to the earlier imperatives to sell everything—then it is still a huge challenge for us. If you cannot imagine giving everything away, try giving away half your stuff to the poor: half the value of your house, half of your retirement, half of your clothes, half of your television sets, etc. Hmm—still no takers, eh? Not me, either.

Jesus makes three concluding remarks. First, "today, salvation has come to [or is in, or has happened in] this house." Zacchaeus's divestment of wealth was a sign that he was putting himself on the side of the angels for the coming Day of Judgment. He has received

Giving Away

There is certainly much truth in a certain saying of a philosopher, "Every rich man is either wicked or the heir of wickedness." That is why the Lord and Savior says that it is difficult for the rich to enter the kingdom of heaven. Someone may raise the objection, "how did wealthy Zacchaeus enter the kingdom of heaven?" He gave away his wealth and immediately replaced it with the riches of the heavenly kingdom.

Jerome, *Homily on Psalm 83* (84), cited in Arthur A. Just Jr., ed., *Luke* (ACCS: NT, vol. 3; Downer's Grove IL: Intervarsity Press, 2003), 290.

the kingdom as a child and is willing to live by Jesus' teachings on money. Second, "because he also is a son of Abraham." This takes us all the way back to the preaching of John the Baptist, who told the crowds coming to him that their ancestry made no difference—what counted was the fruit of their repentance (3:8). Jesus is holding up Zacchaeus as a model for faith. The ruler, although he carefully obeyed the Law, was unlikely to enter the kingdom because he could not let go of his stuff. The blind man, who had no stuff, was ready and willing to follow Jesus. Zacchaeus, a sinful rich man, could do what the pious ruler could not: he could give it all away as if he were just as poor as the blind man. And third, Jesus says, "Because the Son of Man came to seek and to save the lost." He invites all three of them—pious wealthy ruler, noisy beggarly blind man, and sinful wealthy tax collector—and will take on whoever is willing to receive him and his message about the kingdom.

The Parable of the Minas, 19:11-27

This passage is traditionally called "the parable of the pounds," because the King James Version translated the Greek word *mna* in 19:13 as "pound."[9] But a twenty-first- (or seventeenth-) century British pound is not the monetary equivalent of a first-century *mina*, so I vote for calling this story "the parable of the *minas*." A *mina* was worth a hundred *denarii*, so imagine one hundred day's wages for an unskilled day laborer, and you are as close as you will get. A really wealthy person might not miss one hundred *minas*, but a day laborer would be lucky to have saved up that much over a lifetime of work; recall that the woman in 15:8-10 had ten *denarii* and grieved the loss of one. By contrast, the very similar parable in Matthew 25:14-30 deals with talents, the largest denomination of money in the first century, equal to six thousand *denarii* or sixty *minas*. Five talents for Matthew's Slave Number One was serious cash on anyone's scale (or as Illinois senator Everett Dirksen once quipped, "a billion here, a billion there, and pretty soon you're talking about real money").

Luke's parable differs from Matthew's in several other respects, but the plot is the same: a slaveowner goes away, leaving his slaves with cash to invest. Upon his return he finds that two have done well and one has not, and hands out rewards and punishments accordingly. Gospel experts differ on whether they think there was one original parable that Matthew and/or Luke revised, or two parables, because Jesus or his early followers told it more than one way. Mark's parable of the sudden return of the master (Mark 13:32-37) and the Q parable of the trustworthy and untrustworthy slaves (Matt 24:45-51//Luke 12:41-48) show that the plot line—master goes away, master comes back, master judges slaves—was a fruitful vine with many branches.

Because Luke's parable of the *minas* is so similar to Matthew's parable of the talents, it has often been read as if it had the same "point" or interpretation. In order to disrupt this quite natural presumption, we will hold Luke's version up next to Matthew's—not because I'm confident that Luke drew from Matthew or even from a source he held in common with Matthew, but to build a case for why one might prefer to read the *minas* parable as one of Luke's twists on a standard plot. The interpretation I will offer builds on a suggestion made by R. Alan Culpepper, who shows how the king is an antitype for Jesus and how the parable is a parody of Jesus' teachings about the kingdom of God.[10] Traditionally Christian interpreters have understood Luke's parable as an exhortation to be busy in the Lord's vineyards until the Parousia; I will interpret it as part of Luke's strategy for undermining early Christian expectations that Jesus would be a king.

Matthew puts the talents in his longer version of Mark's Temple Sermon (Mark 13:1-37), in a cluster of parables about being prepared for Judgment Day.

- The householder doesn't know when the thief will arrive, and so must always be prepared (Matt 24:43-44).
- Slaves entrusted with the master's possessions must avoid thinking "my master is delayed" and living the high life, or face the consequences of the master's return (24:45-51).
- Those waiting for the bridegroom's return must keep their lamps trimmed and burning, for "you know neither the day nor the hour" (25:1-13).
- Slaves entrusted with the master's possessions need to use them according to the master's wishes (25:14-30).

All of these parables stick to the metaphor of return: the master returning after a journey, the bridegroom returning after the wedding, or the thief breaking in unexpectedly. Matthew's final "parable" speaks much more plainly: "When the Son of Man comes in his glory, and all the angels with him, then he will sit on his glorious throne" (25:31-46). In Matthew's sequence, one would be hard-pressed not to read the absent thief/master/bridegroom as the Son of Man, the Coming One.

Luke's introductory verse also puts the parable into an eschatological context: "While they were listening to these things, he put forward a parable, because he was nearing Jerusalem and it seemed to them that the kingdom of God was about to appear immediately" (19:11). Luke does not say straight out whether this presumption was true or false, or whether the parable was told to confirm or qualify or confound their belief. Most interpreters believe Luke wants the reader to come away thinking that Jesus knew the kingdom was not about to appear immediately and that he tried to warn the disciples accordingly.[11] True, the question of whether the world ended when Jesus arrived in Jerusalem had been moot for many years when Luke wrote his Gospel. But equally obvious was the answer to the question in Acts 1:6: "Lord, will you restore the kingdom to Israel at this moment?" Luke's readers knew that the kingdom had not been realized, despite the earnest hopes of the disciples; the answer to the question, "When will the kingdom come" remained "the kingdom is not something you can predict" (17:20-21).

Luke introduces "a certain man" as "well-born"—a member of the noble class—who goes away specifically to receive a kingdom; Matthew's traveler is simply called "a man going away," but the fact that he has nine talents to hand over to servants tags him as very wealthy. As he exits, Matthew's rich man "hands over his stuff" to his three servants, but in different amounts, "to each according to his ability." Luke's king-to-be gives one *mina* to each of ten servants—in other words, he does not empty his bank account, as Matthew's man does, and the sum of what he gives is one-sixth of what Matthew's guy gives to the least-able servant. Luke's aspiring ruler also gives his servants explicit instructions: "Do business with this while I'm gone [or "until I return"]," while Matthew's fellow just forks over the cash and leaves. Hmm—by contrast, Luke's nobleman seems less generous, less trusting, and more clearly interested in profit.

Matthew's parable includes nothing about receiving a kingdom, nor anything about citizens who send an embassy to protest the nobleman's elevation. Luke's audience, hearing this part, would doubtless think "typical politics." Rome installed Herod the Great as "king of the Jews" over a rival claimant. Rome refused to allow Herod's son Archelaus to rule as much territory as his father and instead put two of his brothers on thrones over parts of the kingdom. [Archelaus Goes to Rome to Receive a Kingdom] Later they deposed Archelaus altogether, replacing him with a Roman prefect; later still they deposed Archelaus's brother Antipas in favor of Agrippa I,

Archelaus Goes to Rome to Receive a Kingdom

The people assembled together, and desired of Archelaus that, in way of revenge on their account [they were protesting Herod the Great's actions just before his death], he would inflict punishment on those who had been honored by Herod; and that, in the first and principal place, he would deprive that high priest whom Herod had made, and would choose one more agreeable to the law, and of greater purity, to officiate as high priest. This was granted by Archelaus, although he was mightily offended at their importunity, because he proposed himself to go to Rome immediately, to look after Caesar's determination about him. (17.207-208)

At the same time also did Antipas, another of Herod's sons, sail to Rome, in order to gain the government . . . . (17.224)

. . . as for Archelaus, he had new sources of trouble come upon him at Rome . . . for embassage of the Jews was come to Rome, Varus [governor of Syria] having permitted the nation to send it, that they might petition for the liberty of living by their own laws. (17.299-300)

When Caesar had heard these pleadings, he dissolved the assembly; but a few days afterwards he appointed Archelaus, not indeed to be king of the whole country, but ethnarch of one-half of that which had been subject to Herod . . . but as for the other half, he divided it into two parts, and gave it to two other of Herod's sons, to Philip and to Antipas, that Antipas who disputed with Archelaus for the whole kingdom. (17.317-18)

Josephus, *Ant.*.

Antipas's nephew. These examples are all from the history of Palestine, but things worked the same way in all the small kingdoms controlled by the empire; no matter where Luke's audience lived, when they heard that the nobleman goes away to "receive his own kingdom," Luke's audience would understand "from Rome." Protests from others—either from the citizens to be ruled or from others who wished to rule—also happened regularly. Although emperors might complain publicly about the bother this caused, it was actually to Rome's benefit. Competition for the ruling spots made it clear that whoever ruled did so by the grace of the emperor, and the competitors quite naturally gave gifts to sweeten their requests.

Luke's story continues: "And so it was that upon his return, after receiving the kingdom, he ordered those slaves to whom he had given the money to be summoned to him, so that he could know what they had gained by trading." Even though there were ten servants given a *mina* each, we only hear from three of them. The first made one into ten; the second made one into five; the third hid the *mina* in a bandanna. Matthew's three slaves were working with much larger sums of money, and Matthew's parable specifies that their master was gone a long time; the two "good and faithful" slaves each doubled their stake, while the third buried his. Another interesting contrast—Luke's two "good" slaves were much more profitable than Matthew's, and his "bad" slave much more careless. Burying money under your house was a fairly common way to try to protect it, but trying to hide it in your scarf is goofy. Think about it—house-slaves typically had no private quarters, but slept in doorways and halls, so it isn't as if he could put the scarf full of coins in his underwear drawer or under his mattress. Wrapping the bag of coins in a cloth is a bit like a kid trying to hide the bag of cookies under his shirt or covering the uneaten lima beans with her napkin.

As the first act as newly installed king, Luke's nobleman wants to discover how much profit his slaves had made in his absence. Talk about your micro-manager—he owns a kingdom, but he's worried about how his penny stocks are doing. "Lord, your *mina* has earned ten *minas* more," says the first. How do you increase your capital ten-fold in a short time? Luke leaves it to the audience's imagination, but clearly something shady happened. There was no ancient stock market or buying of oil futures; ordinary money-lenders could hardly get away with charging 1,000 percent interest; no commercial venture, such as investing in shipping grain or buying property to rent to others, could have turned so large a profit without years of patience. [Ancient Money-lending Rates] Servant Number One is thus most likely a rapacious "anything for a buck" kind of guy, and his master calls him "good" and puts him in charge of ten of his new cities. Servant Number Two, because he only increased his stake five-fold, gets no "attaboy," but does get to be over five cities. So far in Luke, has there been any hint that unrestricted profit-taking was a good thing? Quite the contrary; so far in Luke, the right thing to do with one's possessions is to give them away; to lend, expecting nothing in return; to sell all, and give the money to the poor. This new king and his two trusted servants are a parody of Jesus' teaching about the kingdom.

The third slave gives his master back exactly what he was given, justifying his behavior by his fear: "I was afraid of you, because you are a strict man, withdrawing what you did not deposit, and reaping what you did not sow." The word for "strict" describes someone who is a stickler for the rules or who "practice[s] rigid personal discipline."[12] The third slave knows his master well; the new king did nothing to gain the enormous profit of Slaves One and Two, yet he receives it as his due. He has no mercy for the unprofitable; despite protests from the bystanders, he takes the one *mina* from this third slave and gives it to the one who made ten more. His explanation is choice: if the slave knew the master to be a rigid, unforgiving man, then he should have made certain to make even a little profit by putting his money with the ordinary money-lenders. The new king's low opinion of the profit margin on normal

Ancient Money-lending Rates

On Augustus 11 in the eighteenth year just past I loaned, in accordance with a public contract drawn in the record office of the said Oxyrhynchus, to Sarapias daughter of Podo . . . the sum of 900 silver drachmas at interest of one drachma per mina per month . . . . (Foreclosure notice [*Oxyrhynchus Papyrus* 485, c. AD 178]; cited in Lewis and Reinhold, *The Empire*, vol. 2 of *Roman Civilization* [New York: Harper and Row, 1966], 216. This would be an annual percentage rate of 12 percent.)

Helene, minor, daughter of Psosnaus and Eudaemonis . . . to Spartas son of Pausanias . . . I acknowledge that I have received from you the sum of 1,800 drachmas of the imperial coinage, to which nothing has been added, with interest at the rate of 3 obols per mina per month . . . or 189 drachmas altogether . . . . (Loan contract [*Oxyrhynchus Papyrus* 2134, c. AD 170]; cited in Lewis and Reinhold, *The Empire*, vol. 2 of *Roman Civilization* [New York: Harper and Row, 1966], 214–15. The APR would be 6 percent.)

money-lending underscores the rapacity of the methods employed by the "good" slaves. The master justifies his unswerving commitment to profit with a proverb: "[It] will be given to everyone who has, but from the one who has not—even what he has will be taken." The rich get more, the poor lose more—again, a parody of the values of Luke's Jesus. And instead of getting knocked off his throne—the fate Mary predicted for the powerful (1:52)—this king has all his enemies slaughtered in front of him.

There are no exemplary characters in this parable. The nobleman who goes away to receive a kingdom is neither generous nor forgiving, and his profit-taking and bloody vengeance make him more like one of the Herods or the Caesars than like Jesus. Sure, there are some features of this king that make us think of Jesus: he receives a kingdom, as Jesus says he does in 22:29; he appoints his servants to rule, as Jesus does in 22:30; he goes away and comes back to judge, as the church expected Jesus to do. But these correspondences make the king an anti-type of Luke's Jesus, a parody rather than a straightforward comparison. Jesus says lend, expecting nothing in return; this man expects his servants to lend and make a big profit, or suffer the consequences. Jesus says love your enemies; this man says slaughter my enemies while I watch. If the new king is supposed to be Jesus, then we have to suppose that this slaughtering is meant to be revenge on the citizens of Jerusalem for rejecting Jesus.[13] Some ancient Christians made precisely this interpretation [The Citizens Who Hated Him], but I doubt that Luke had this in mind. When Jesus enters Jerusalem, he does indeed predict the destruction of the city, but not as his own desire; weeping, he says, "if today even you knew the terms of peace!" That's a far cry from "slaughter them while I watch."

The Citizens Who Hated Him

It says that his citizens hated him. Likewise Christ admonishes the Jewish crowds. . . . They would not let him reign over them, and yet the holy prophets were constantly speaking predictions of Christ as a king. . . . Having denied the kingdom of Christ, they fell under the dominion of Satan and brought on themselves the yoke of sin that cannot be lifted.

Cyril of Alexandria, *Commentary on Luke*, Homily 128; cited in Arthur A. Just Jr., ed., *Luke* (ACCS: NT, vol. 3; Downer's Grove IL: Intervarsity Press, 2003), 294.

The disciples suppose that the kingdom is about to be revealed immediately; this parable exposes what surely lay in some of their hearts and, indeed, in the imaginations of Luke's audience right to the present. We want the poor to be lifted up, as long as we are the poor. We want the wealthy to be knocked down, so long as that means our enemies. We want to hear that in our economic system, everybody can get rich at nobody's expense—that the profit-taking of the two "good" servants justifies our own materialism. [Market Capitalism and the Poor] Luke's Jesus tells a dystopian story—a sort of worst-case scenario—about a greedy, ruthless man who gains a kingdom, shares power with slaves who share his values, and slaughters those who object. Do you really want more of the same empire, in other words, only with different players in place? That's not the kingdom Jesus came to proclaim. Luke offers this parable to disrupt Christian hopes for a new Christian empire—too bad Jesus' followers have had so much trouble, then and now, giving up the idea that if we ruled the world, things would go better.

According to v. 11, Jesus told this parable to the crowd who had just heard him say, "Today salvation happened in this house, because he is also a son of Abraham. For the Son of Man came to seek and to save the lost." Zacchaeus, tool of the same empire that gave the fictional king his authority, found salvation by redistributing his wealth and by opting out of the profit-taking-by-extortion system of taxation. Salvation and the kingdom are meant to improve the lot of the poor, and the Son of Man did not come to reinforce the values of the empire. When Jesus arrives in Jerusalem and they call him "king" (19:38; 23:2, 38), we should not take that at face value.

> **Market Capitalism and the Poor**
>
> In his book *Less Than Two Dollars a Day*, Kent A. Van Til argues that free market capitalism will not necessarily ensure that the poor will have what they need to survive. Those with no capital "simply don't count. The market does not change basic conditions such as inheritance, fertility of land, availability of education, and so forth. Rather, it accepts these initial endowments and then serves to distribute them efficiently through exchange" (51). Those with nothing to exchange cannot better their predicament; this requires some form of distributive justice, by providing for the poor from the surplus of the wealthy. Van Til, using various economic data, estimates that the cost of doing this—providing subsistence for the world's poor—would work out to about $100–200 per adult who lives and works in one of the developing countries (158–61). "The disturbing question is this: Why haven't we each paid the $200? Or, if we have been privileged with opportunity and wealth, why haven't we paid a multiple of the $200?" (159)
>
> Kent A. Van Til, *Less Than Two Dollars a Day: A Christian View of World Poverty and the Free Market* (Grand Rapids MI: Eerdmans, 2007)

Prophet's Arrival, 19:28-48

Finally, Jesus gets to Jerusalem! The journey that began at 9:51 comes to an end in this section. From this moment until the women discover the empty tomb, the action all takes place in or near Jerusalem. In brief outline, the story from Jesus' entry into Jerusalem through his burial is arranged like this:

19:29-48	Entry into Jerusalem, Temple
20:1–21:38	Teaching in Temple
22:1-6	Plot of Chief Priests; Judas's Complicity
22:7-38	Last Supper, on 14th Nisan
22:39-53	Prayer and Arrest on Mount of Olives
22:54-65	Jesus Beaten; Peter's Denial
22:66-71	15th Nisan: Jesus Condemned by Sanhedrin
23:1-25	Proceedings with Pilate
23:26-49	Crucifixion and Death

23:50-56   Burial: "It Was the Day of Preparation"; Rest on Sabbath

This section is often called the Passion Narrative (although some writers prefer to reserve that title for the part of the story that begins with the chief priests' plot and Judas's involvement in it), and in it, Luke mostly relies on Mark. Keeping most of Mark's episodes, and keeping them mostly in Mark's order, Luke adds a few new items:

19:41-44	Weeping over Jerusalem (Luke only)
22:3	Satan Takes Possession of Judas (Luke only)
22:24-27	Who Is the Greatest? (adapted from Mark 10:41-45//Matt 20:24-28)
22:28-30	Promise that the Twelve Will Judge Israel (This is perhaps from Q; Matthew has it at 19:28, following Peter's statement that they have left everything to follow Jesus)
22:31-32	Satan Wants to Possess Peter, but Jesus Has Prayed for Him (Luke only)
22:35-38	Arming the Disciples (Luke only)
23:6-12	Herod Antipas Interrogates Jesus (Luke only)
23:27-31	Women who Wail for Jesus (Luke only)
23:39-43	Conversation with the Two Thieves (Luke only)

Because Luke's expansions of Mark's material do not correspond to Matthew's, it is common to conclude that Q (the theoretical source or sources that Luke and Matthew shared in addition to Mark) had no Passion Narrative. This may well be correct; if Q existed, it could have been a collection mostly of Jesus' teaching materials. However, there is at least one non-Markan miracle common to Matthew and Luke that is presumed to come from Q (the healing of the centurion's son), and most commentators who work with the Q hypothesis believe that Q contained the preaching of John the Baptist and a version of Jesus' baptism. There is also at least one statement about carrying the cross in Q, so it clearly presumed, even if it did not narrate, the crucifixion. In the end, we cannot say conclusively that Q, if it existed, had no Passion Narrative, only that Matthew and Luke do not agree in their expansions of Mark's Passion Narrative.

It was Mark's Passion Narrative that gave the church its Holy Week traditions. Working backward from Mark 15:42, which identifies the day Jesus died as Friday (Sabbath starts at sundown on Friday, and Jesus dies on the Day of Preparation for Sabbath), we get the following outline:

Sunday—Jesus enters Jerusalem on the donkey, looks around in the temple, and leaves.
Monday—Next day, Jesus curses the fig tree and overturns tables in the temple.
Tuesday—Next day, the fig tree is withered; Jesus enters Jerusalem (11:27) and spends a long day dealing with accusations from chief priests, scribes, and elders. All this takes place in the temple (11:27; 12:35, 41). Jesus leaves the temple and preaches the Temple Sermon (13:1-37).
Wednesday—Two days before Passover, Jesus is anointed in Simon's house.
Thurday—Last Supper, Arrest, Trial by the Sanhedrin
Friday—Trial by Pilate, Crucifixion, Burial just before sundown

Luke keeps the references that put the Last Supper on Thursday and the crucifixion on Friday (see below), but removes the chronological references from everything earlier. Consequently, one would not know from reading Luke how long Jesus spent in Jerusalem before his arrest. Luke 19:47, "Day by day he was teaching in the temple" is matched by 21:37, "By day he was teaching in the temple, but by night he was, after leaving, spending the night on the Mount of Olives." Does Luke intend for the reader to imagine a longer period of teaching between the entry and the crucifixion? Once again, we cannot say for sure; a safer conclusion is that the length of time is less important to Luke than the pattern: Jesus is teaching every day, going back and forth undisturbed, in full view of everyone.

Everything from 22:7-65 happens on the night Passover begins, on the 14th of Nisan. Sabbath is from Friday sundown to Saturday sundown, so since Jesus was buried on "the Day of Preparation" for Sabbath, just before Sabbath began, we can assign days of the week to everything from 22:7 on:

22:7-13—Thursday before sundown, 13th Nisan, preparations for the Passover
22:14-65—Thursday after sundown, 14th Nisan, Passover begins, Last Supper, arrest, beating, Peter's denial
22:66–23:43—Friday before noon, 14th Nisan, condemnation by Sanhedrin, appearances before Pilate
23:44-56a—Friday between noon and sundown, 14th Nisan, crucifixion, burial

23:56b—Friday sundown to Saturday sundown, 15th Nisan, "They rested, according to the commandment."

The entry story is a great introduction to many of the themes or recurring questions in Luke's Passion Narrative, but as the conclusion of the journey section, it also draws on patterns set in Luke's long central section. In v. 28, Jesus is leading the way into Jerusalem, just as he "set his face" to go there when he started the trip (9:51). All along the road, he has been accompanied by a large group of disciples (including the Twelve and women), by Pharisees and their scribes, and by crowds who are not disciples. All of these appear in this scene as well. According to Luke, Jesus came to Jerusalem on the local, rather than the express, stopping in every village (13:22); fitting, then, that two more villages are named at the terminus of the journey. Bethphage is named here, but has no other role in the Gospel; Luke names Bethany as the site of Jesus' ascension (Luke 24:50). [Bethphage and Bethany]

Jesus sent two of his disciples into one of these villages with instructions to bring back a certain colt, and with instructions on what to say when they were questioned. Jesus is a prophet, after all: he knows what is coming, and prepares the disciples. They are used to being sent out by Jesus with instructions on what to do and say (9:1-6; 10:1-20), so off they go. Sure enough, they find things "just as he told them," and the colt's owners (in Greek, its "lords") ask the two why they are untying it; they repeat Jesus' words—"because the Lord needs it"—and this is apparently satisfactory. The story begins, then, by emphasizing Jesus' prophetic vocation and his disciples' obedience, and by making clear who the true Lord is.

The disciples "put Jesus upon the colt," and the story takes a turn from the prophetic toward the royal. Lifting him onto the animal and spreading their cloaks on the road are both indications of respect (see 2 Kgs 9:13, where cloaks on the ground honor the new king), and their hymn of praise celebrates him as the Coming One, the King: "Blessed in the name of the Lord is the Coming One, the King." Yet there are indications that Luke does not regard "king" as an unambiguous title for Jesus. In Mark's text, "those going before and those following" call Jesus king; Luke restricts this to disciples, giving the impression of a smaller-scale event. The royal acclamation also reinforces Jesus' status as prophet, since he predicted that Jerusalem would not see him until they said, "Blessed in the Lord's name is the Coming One" (13:35). When the disciples sing, "Peace in heaven and glory in the highest," they echo the angels who

Bethphage and Bethany

Both of these villages are located on the Mount of Olives. Bethany was on the eastern side of the Mount, and is usually identified with present-day el-Azariah. If first-century Bethphage is correctly identified as present-day et-Tur, then it is closer to Jerusalem, only about a mile from the temple.

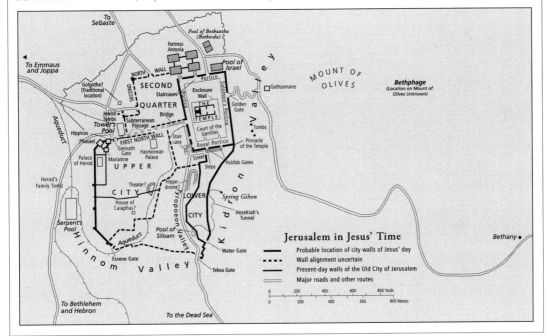

announced his birth in a manger, far from the emperor's palace. When they call him "the Coming One," they are echoing John the Baptist, who said Jesus would baptize with Holy Spirit and fire (3:16)—a Coming Prophet, not a Coming King. Yes, God has given Jesus a kingdom (22:29), but it is one in which the youngest and the slaves are most important. This Coming One has now arrived, ready to offer peace (2:14) and glory (2:32).

What happens next is about as non-regal as one can get. Luke's Jesus is mostly emotion-free, in contrast to Mark's Jesus; in the places where Mark says Jesus was angry or filled with compassion, Luke chooses to remove the descriptions of emotions. Once, Jesus is "filled with compassion" for the widow who lost her only son (7:13). Now, however, he weeps over the tragedy about to fall on Jerusalem. In the same way Elisha wept when he met Hazael, the future Syrian king, who would kill so many Israelites (2 Kgs 8:11-13).[14] Jesus' prediction of a siege against Jerusalem, ending in its destruction, would have been regarded by Luke's readers as fulfilled at the end of the 66–70 Jewish War. Look, then, how Luke has constructed a chain of prophecies. Jesus laments Jerusalem's fall in 13:34-35, and predicts that they will not see him until they say, "Blessed in the name of the Lord is the Coming

Christ's Entry into Jerusalem

Charles Le Brun (1619–1690). *Christ's Entry into Jerusalem*. Oil on canvas. Musee d'Art et d'Industrie, Saint-Etienne, France. (Credit: Réunion des Musées Nationaux/Art Resource, NY)

LeBrun's painting depicts Jesus on a single animal and has women and men in the group following him—thus far, compatible with Luke. But the young man bringing geenery, the presence of children, and the lame man in the bottom right are all elements from Matthew's version of Palm Sunday.

One!" The second part is fulfilled when Jesus arrives in the city; he then repeats the prediction of Jerusalem's doom, adding details that match what the Romans did in the siege: they built a wall around the perimeter of the city so that no defenders could escape and no reinforcements could arrive, and then they built a ramp up to the wall and used machinery to breach it. [The War of 66–70 and the Siege of Jerusalem] The third link in the chain comes in 21:20-24, where Jesus predicts the destruction of the city, the enslavement of its inhabitants, and its domination by foreigners for some unspecified period of time.

Jesus' prediction raises at least two questions. First, is it reasonable to think that he predicted the Roman siege some forty years before it happened? Is this, rather, a prophecy after the fact, a bit of history that Luke puts in Jesus' mouth in order to increase his

The War of 66–70 and the Siege of Jerusalem

Since AD 4, Judea—the southern part of Palestine that includes Jerusalem—had been governed by a Roman official who was appointed by the emperor and who reported to the governor of Syria. This local official—sometimes called "prefect" or "procurator" by the Romans, but usually called "governor" by the Gospels and by Josephus—had at his disposal a small contingent of troops, but could ask for reinforcements from Syria. In the year 66, some Jewish rebels were able to seize control of the temple and eventually the city. Josephus reports that the population of the city and the temple leaders were by no means united behind the revolutionaries, and that over the course of the war rival factions inside the city fought each other. The Romans lost a few early battles, but then the emperor Nero sent Vespasian, an experienced general, to take charge of the Roman forces in Syria. He mopped up the rebels in Galilee and was preparing to besiege Jerusalem when Nero was assassinated. For eighteen months, Rome was in crisis as first Galba, then Otho, then Vitellus tried to take the reins of power. Vespasian's army proclaimed him emperor; in due course he sailed for Rome and took control, transferring command of the army in Palestine to his son Titus.

Titus surrounded the city, clearing a space up to the walls of all trees, hedges, houses, and walls (*J.W.* 5.130-134). The Romans built siege towers and used rams to force a breach in the city wall (*J.W.* 5.302), and then built ramps to reach the walls of the temple (*J.W.* 5.356-57), but these were not immediately successful.

Titus then ordered the circumvallation of the city (encircling it with a wall; *J.W.* 5.499-511). Josephus writes, "So all hope of escaping was now cut off from the Jews, together with their liberty of going out of the city. Then did the famine widen its progress, and devoured the people by whole houses and families (*J.W.* 5.512). The Romans resumed building siege ramps, and after fierce fighting, were able to break through the walls of the Temple and into the outer courts. The sanctuary itself was burned (Josephus says accidentally) and the defenders slaughtered.

Josephus writes of the final disposition of the city,

Now when Titus was come into this upper city, he admired not only some other places of strength in it, but particularly those strong towers which the tyrants, in their mad conduct, had relinquished; for when he saw their solid attitude, and the largeness of their several stones and the exactness of their joints, as also how great was their breadth, and how extensive their length, he expressed himself after the manner following: "We have certainly had God for our assistant in this war, and it was no other than God who ejected the Jews out of these fortifications; for what could the hands of men, or any machines, do towards overthrowing these towers!" . . . To conclude, when he entirely demolished the rest of the city, and overthrew its walls, he left these towers as a monument of his good fortune, which had proved his auxiliaries, and enabled him to take what could not otherwise have been taken by him. (*J.W.* 6.409-413)

standing as a prophet? On the contrary, it is entirely likely that Jesus predicted the temple's destruction. Versions of this prediction are found in Mark 13:2 (and parallels), Mark 14:57-58 (and parallels), John 2:19, Luke (or Q) 13:34-44, Luke 19:41-44, and the *Gospel of Thomas* 71, making it one of the best-attested bits of data about the historical Jesus. The language of this particular form of the prediction is found in Old Testament texts (for example, Isa 29:3 LXX includes "encircle you" and "throw up an embankment against you"),[15] but Luke may well have shaped the language to fit the circumstances of Titus's siege of Jerusalem. [Another Jesus Predicts the Destruction of the Temple]

Second, had Jerusalem accepted Jesus' offer of peace, would that have prevented the Roman destruction of the city? Luke nowhere makes that equation; that is, Luke nowhere states that Rome crushed Jerusalem because Jerusalem handed Jesus over to be crucified. In Acts, when the apostles confront the citizens with their

Another Jesus Predicts the Destruction of the Temple

"There was one Jesus, the son of Ananus, a plebian and a husbandman, who, four years before the war began . . . began on a sudden cry aloud, 'A voice from the east, a voice from the west, a voice from the four winds, a voice against Jerusalem and the holy house, a voice against the bridegroom and the brides, and a voice against this whole people.'" [Josephus says that the temple leaders brought him before the procurator Albinus, who had him flayed.] "Yet did he not make any supplication for himself, nor shed any tears, but turning his voice to the most lamentable tone possible, at every stroke of the whip his answer was, 'Woe, woe to Jerusalem.'"

Josephus reports that Albinus decided he was insane and released him. He then repeated his prediction of woe every day until the siege began, when he was killed by a stone from one of the Roman siege machines. (*J.W.* 6.300-309)

complicity in the crucifixion, they do not threaten destruction but offer forgiveness. Jesus' focus in 19:41-44 is entirely on the fate of the city and not on his own impending death, and the good news about the kingdom of God—the things that would have made for peace—is the vision of a realm in which God rules and everyone else is safe. His message, in other words, was not "Make me king or be destroyed by Rome." It was "Be transformed by God's rule into a kingdom with no rich and no poor, no powerful and no weak." Rejecting those terms of peace meant choosing the empire instead, where inevitably the weak are crushed. Jerusalem, whose very name includes the word "peace," is ignorant of the true source of peace.

In Luke's account of the entry, Jesus enters the temple rather than the city. Omitting Mark's double entry (Mark's Jesus goes into Jerusalem on Palm Sunday, but goes back out without doing anything, and then returns on Holy Monday to turn over the tables), as well as most of the description of what Jesus did in the temple, Luke focuses the reader's eye on the prophetic statement at the end. Mark 11:17 quotes Isaiah 56:7 LXX: "My house will be called a house of prayer for all the nations"; Luke edits that down to "my house will be a house of prayer." It may seem counterintuitive that Luke, whose second volume traces the spread of the gospel to the Gentiles, should omit "for all the nations." But having just predicted the temple's demise, and looking ahead to the time when Christianity would spread around the Mediterranean, Luke chooses not to make the temple the locus of the Gentile mission, not even in Jesus' indictment of it.[16] The second part of Jesus' statement is based more loosely on Jeremiah 7:11 LXX: "My house, where my name is called upon, is not a den of bandits in your sight, is it?" Luke's Jesus takes Jeremiah's "den of bandits" phrase and applies it as an indictment. The accusation is not that the temple sales are dishonest, but that they have turned the temple into a place of safety for bandits or terrorists.

Scholars wrestle over what the historical Jesus meant by his action in the temple. Nearly everyone agrees that he really did it— why would one of his followers invent the clearest reason for thinking that Jesus was dangerous? Some imagine Jesus to have been upset over the selling of sacrificial animals in the temple itself, while others connect Jesus' deed to his prediction of destruction, understanding it as a prophetic sign/act. Luke seems to have understood Jesus' act more like an exorcism of merchants: "he began to cast out [*ekballein*, the word normally used for casting out demons] the sellers" (19:45). Luke's Jesus does not turn anything over or prevent worshipers from carrying things into the temple; Luke does not even

Christ Driving the Traders from the Temple

El Greco (Domenikos Theotokopulos) *Christ Driving the Traders from the Temple*. 1600. Canvas, National Gallery, London, Great Britain. (Credit: Erich Lessing/Art Resource, NY)

make clear that the sellers were selling sacrificial animals (although we can probably presume that his audience filled in that gap). Driving out the merchants in order to create a place for prayer fits with Jesus' anti-materialist message throughout the Gospel: give away your possessions and God will give you the kingdom.

The concluding verses show how Luke is reshaping characters a bit in the Passion Narrative. As noted above, Jesus has been traveling with disciples (including apostles), Pharisees, and crowds. In earlier parts of the commentary, I have described this as three groups that sort of mill around Jesus as he walks toward Jerusalem, interacting with him at different times, always ready to hand for the narrator. In the entry episode, the disciples are there, and they act in character. When Jesus gives them specific instructions on where to find the colt, they go and do it; but their acclamation of him as king (I have argued) is only partially correct. Typically, then, they are following Jesus and are obedient to him, but have not fully understood him.

Luke includes the Pharisees, Jesus' persistent hecklers, one more time. They also act in character, raising an objection when the disciples call Jesus king. They want Jesus to command the disciples to be silent; Jesus refuses, saying that the stones would shout if the disciples were silent. That's a great comeback. It captures the inevitability of Jesus' predictions coming true; having prophesied that the next time Jerusalem saw him, they would be saying "Blessed in the Lord's name is the Coming One," then, by golly, that's what is said. But it is also ironic, since the "stones" that would cry out in honor of Jesus are also the ones that will not be left one on another (21:6).

After 19:39, the Pharisees drop from the narrative, and their role as adversaries is taken over by "chief priests, scribes, and leaders of the people" (19:47). The Pharisees asked Jesus uncomfortable questions and invited him to hostile dinner parties. This new group of adversaries, however, wants to kill him—he's not even on the stage for a second, and already they want to do away with the hero! Luke does not explain why they want to kill Jesus, but his audience presumably would infer that they were angry because of this temple incident. Chief priests are probably the heads of priestly families and/or the advisory council for the high priest. Scribes are secretaries/lawyers who help the chief priests; just as Luke's Pharisees had their functionaries, so do Luke's temple leaders. The "leaders of the people" are other non-priestly people with power and influence in Jerusalem; in 22:66, Luke will call them "elders of the people." This troika of chief priests, scribes, and elders were the people with whom Pilate dealt when there was need to discuss the way the Romans governed the province. Luke's audience, even if they knew nothing about the history of the Roman occupation of Palestine, would know that standard Roman practice was to work through local governments as much as possible, letting them do most of the day-to-day operations on behalf of Rome. The audience could reason that the temple and civic leaders were upset because of the presence of a man who disturbed the peace of the temple, knowing that Pilate would expect them to handle it or be prepared for the consequences of Roman intervention. The audience could also have decided that these civic and temple leaders were affronted by Jesus' challenge to their authority. Most Greek and Roman cities had an official who regulated the public market; temples had officers who kept watch over the business end of sacrifices, offerings, and such. What right did Jesus have to expel the merchants? Finally, assuming that the audience knew that the merchants were selling animals for sacrifice (everybody's temples conducted animal sacrifices for various reasons, so that's a safe bet), the audience also could have figured that the priests considered Jesus' actions sacrilegious or disrespectful. The audience also had heard Jesus predict this very turn of events in 9:22; if they have been paying attention, they are not surprised, and Jesus' status as prophet is confirmed yet again.

The crowds are changing roles a bit, beginning with this scene. Along the journey, the crowds were a danger (12:1) or an interruption (12:13), and Jesus had some fairly harsh things to say to them. But starting with 19:47-48, the "crowds" (*ochloi*) often become "the people" (*laos*), and their function in the Passion Narrative is to be amazed by Jesus and to prevent him from being harmed by the temple authorities. [The People's Reaction to Jesus]

So Jesus, as when he was twelve, is in the temple, amazing people with his teaching. As when he began his ministry in Nazareth, there is a group who wants to kill him, but is being prevented from doing so. He expels the merchants in order to clear a space in the temple for his own teaching. The next few sections give us examples of what sort of things he said and did, and help to explain why the temple leadership wants to kill him.

The People's Reaction to Jesus

AΩ The last half of v. 48 can be translated "for the whole people were hanging on, listening to him" or "for the whole people were hanging onto him, listening." In the first case, they are "hanging onto his words"—a picture of a teacher who has their entire attention. In the second, they are physically close to him, crowding around in order to listen, but also preventing anyone from getting close enough to arrest him.

CONNECTIONS

The journey finally ends in this chapter, when Jesus arrives in Jerusalem. In our heads, this happens to the accompaniment of "Ride on, ride on in majesty" or "Crown him with many crowns" (insert your favorite Palm Sunday hymn if these aren't). But if we take the whole chapter together, or think about the emphases of the travel narrative, we will be skeptical of "king" as a title for Jesus in Luke. He tells the ruler to sell everything and commends wealthy Zacchaeus for courting Lady Poverty—this is not what kings or politicians do, is it? They cultivate friendships with the wealthy and powerful, looking for mutual back-scratching opportunities.

The realistically regal man is the fictional ruler in the parable of the *minas*. He demands high returns on his investments; he weeds out the deadwood efficiently; he ruthlessly suppresses dissent and eliminates his enemies. If Jesus is a king, he's nothing like that. A real king, as Jesus has pointed out earlier, counts his troops before he goes to war, and if he thinks his numbers are too few, asks for terms of peace. Jesus rides into Jerusalem at the head of a group of followers numbering somewhere between 70 and 120 and offers terms of peace. He isn't a king. Or if you want to think of it this way, he is a king, but not the sort of king (like the old joke about PhD "doctors") that does anybody any good. He wouldn't fight his enemies, he'd give the kingdom's treasury to the poor, he wouldn't promote the best producers, and he would have none of those hard men doing the hard things that we all believe are necessary for the survival of our society.

In 1971, a Stanford University psychology professor conducted an experiment with twenty-four undergraduates—all volunteers who were compensated, all mentally and physically healthy, none with any previous criminal record. The students were randomly assigned to play roles of prisoner or prison guard for what was to be a two-week stretch. The professor terminated the experiment after six days because by this point, the "guards" were systematically abusing the "prisoners": yelling obscenities at them, making them simulate intercourse with each other, depriving them of sleep, etc. The professor concludes:

> Group pressures, authority symbols, dehumanization of others, imposed anonymity, dominant ideologies that enable spurious ends to justify immoral means, lack of surveillance, and other situational forces can work to transform even some of the best of us into Mr. Hyde monsters, without the benefit of Dr. Jekyll's chemical elixir . . . . we must . . . be aware that veiled behind the power of the situation is the greater power of the system . . . .[1]

The experiment is a warning to us: we take up the power of the sword, the power of empire, with the very great probability that it will change us much more than we think possible. Well-meaning people long to use the power of the throne for good, to be a terror to bad conduct and the wrath of God against the wicked. We should think again:

> You had to be there to believe that human character could be so swiftly transformed in a matter of days—not only the traits of the students, but of me, a well-seasoned adult. Most of the visitors to our prison also fell under the spell. For example, individual sets of parents observing their son's haggard appearance after a few days of hard labor and long nights of disrupted sleep said they "did not want to make trouble" by taking their kid home or challenging the system. Instead, they obeyed our authority and let some of their sons experience full-blown emotional meltdowns later on. We had created a dominating behavioral context whose power insidiously frayed the seemingly impervious values of compassion, fair play, and belief in a just world.
>
> The situation won; humanity lost.[2]

Luke does not go as far as John the Revelator with respect to empire, and does not call on his audience to withdraw from cooperation with the Beast. I'm not at all certain that Luke would think that Rome *was* the Beast wielding the power of Satan. But the images in this chapter are enough to get us thinking about how cozy we should be with the current empire, or how easily we should adopt its values. The newly appointed king in the parable values quick, high profits and has no patience with disloyalty— sounds like good business sense to me! He rewards the highest-producing slaves, giving them the chance to rule over others, asking no questions about how they managed such an incredible return. Jesus, by contrast, sticks with his slow-witted disciples, defending them to the Pharisees even when they fail once more to understand his true nature. The parable king would have ordered the destruction of Jerusalem just as surely as Titus did, and for the same reasons: if they won't accept the imposition of imperial rule, then they must be destroyed. Jesus, on the other hand, weeps over the city, knowing that it will fall. He would have protected them, he said, if only they had been willing.

Luke's Jesus is the anti-king, who reigns over no earthly territory and whose small group of followers cannot stand up to the power of the temple, much less the power of the empire. He rides into Jerusalem not to possess it, nor to liberate it, but to predict its demise. His followers ought to watch and learn: beware of empire.

NOTES

[1] Joel B. Green, *The Gospel of Luke* (NICNT; Grand Rapids: Eerdmans, 1997), 667.

[2] The word translated "chief tax collector" is not found in any other Greek text. That may be an accident, and Luke may be using a common word (Joseph A. Fitzmyer, *The Gospel According to Luke* [AB 28 and 28A; Garden City NY: Doubleday, 1981], 2.1223); or perhaps Luke has invented a Greek word to describe a function commonly called something else.

[3] So Alan R. Culpepper, *The Gospel of Luke* (NIB, vol. 9; Nashville: Abingdon, 1995), 356–57; Frederick W. Danker, *Jesus and the New Age: A Commentary on St. Luke's Gospel* (rev. ed.; Philadelphia: Fortress, 1988), 304.

[4] Green, *Luke*, 668; Fitzmyer, *Luke*, 2.1223; Mikeal Parsons, *Body and Character in Luke and Acts: The Subversion of Physiognomy in Early Christianity* (Grand Rapids MI: Baker, 2006), 99: "He had risen to middle management in the tax system, becoming a chief tax collector."

[5] Parsons, *Body and Character*, 107.

[6] Johnson, *Luke*, 285; Fitzmyer, *Luke*, 2.1124-25.

[7] Fitzmyer, *Luke*, 2.1220-21; so also Green, *Luke*, 671–72.

[8] Contra Johnson, *Luke*, 286; Green, *Luke*, 672.

[9] This section draws from my article "The Minas Touch," in *Perspectives in Religious Studies* 35 (Spring 2008): 69–86.

[10] Culpepper, *Luke*, 361–64.

[11] Tannehill, *Luke*, 279; Fitzmyer, *Luke*, 2.1229; Johnson, *Luke*, 292–294, argues that the kingdom did arrive when Jesus arrived in Jerusalem as the King. In his view, the parable is not about the end time, but about the sense in which Jesus is King. I agree that the parable is told to contrast Jesus' understanding of kingdom with the common first-century experience of empire. But the parable can do more than one thing at once; it reaches backwards to the issues of the kingdom's timing and nature—the primary topic of 17:20–18:30—and forward to the issue of Jesus' role in establishing the kingdom, which is one of the primary issues in the Passion Narrative.

[12] BAGD, 151.

[13] Fitzmyer, *Luke*, 2.1238.

[14] Ibid., 2.1258.

[15] Fitzmyer, *Luke*, 2.1258; Green, *Luke*, 691.

[16] Culpepper, *Luke*, 374.

[17] Philip G. Zimbardo, "Revisiting the Stanford Prison Experiment: A Lesson in the Power of Situation," in *The Chronicle of Higher Education*, 30 March 2007, B7.

[18] Ibid.

JESUS IN THE TEMPLE: CONFRONTATION

Luke 20

COMMENTARY

By Whose Authority?, 20:1-19

Aristotle's classic analysis of rhetoric lists the three sources of persuasive force as logos, pathos, and ethos. *Logos* includes the arrangement and content of the arguments themselves. *Pathos* means the audience's emotions to which the speaker will try to connect. *Ethos* is the term for the persona that the speaker projects—the sort of image the persuader creates that adds to or subtracts from the power of the argument. Is the speaker coming across as desperate or confident, or as confident or arrogant? Most of the mudslinging in political campaigns is about ethos—about trying to create a negative persona for one's opponent so that even his/her best arguments will be doubted or rejected. That's the temple leaders' strategy in this episode. Jesus is preaching "good news"—a happy logos—and the people are entranced—a positive pathos—so the leaders figure that attacking Jesus' ethos is their best shot at him.

In the previous episode, Jesus exorcised the merchants from the temple and set up shop himself, teaching the people while they thronged him. Luke tells us that the chief priests, scribes, and leaders of the people want to kill him, but the crowds prevent them from moving against him. So they resort to a hearts and minds campaign—push Jesus verbally, make him look foolish, and maybe his protective screen will vanish. Their first attempt is pretty direct: "Tell us by what authority you are doing these things, or who is the one giving you this authority?"

"These things" is a little vague. It surely means at least Jesus' teaching in the temple: "What gives you the right to sit around here and pose as an expert for all these people?" If Luke is reaching back four verses instead of just one, it includes Jesus' casting out of the merchants: "Who appointed you chief of the temple police, that you roust all these vendors that we authorized?" But maybe it has the widest possible focus: "Just who do you think you are, running around the country stirring people up and then coming here, to God's house, causing trouble?"

Luke's audience knows all about Jesus' authority. It was evident to the congregation at the Capernaum synagogue that Jesus acted on God's authority to cast out unclean spirits (4:36). In order to demonstrate his authority to announce the forgiveness of sins, he healed the paralyzed man (5:24). The audience, like the crowd in the story, knows that Jesus is speaking the truth, so one function of the question is to make the temple leaders look ignorant. If they are asking a serious question, then who are they kidding? Jesus has been in the temple now for several days "spreading the good news," which Luke's audience knows is shorthand for "teaching and preaching about the kingdom of God." Duh—Jesus gets his authority from God! Even if you didn't believe it, you wouldn't need to ask him to know that's what he thinks.

So do they want him to say "God" out loud? Maybe—after all, they could certainly argue that their authority derives from God. The Torah puts the chief priest and his advisors in charge of the temple; Moses appointed elders to help govern the people. Thus if Jesus says, "God gave me my authority," and they say, "No, God gave it to us—it says so right here in the Bible—and you're an impostor who has no business meddling in our affairs," then how would he prove they were wrong? More to the point, if he enters into an argument with them on their terms, then he loses; he will have conceded too much authority to them. [Jesus Questioned by the Temple Authorities]

So Jesus uses the age-old teacher's trick of answering a question with a question. He dares them to go first—you show me yours, I'll show you mine—and then he hits them with John the Baptist. "Was the baptism of John from heaven"—that is, inspired and ordained by God, meaning that John was a true prophet—"or from humans"—that is, John was not a true prophet, but was following his own intuitions. This was a clever move from several perspectives. As the audience of Luke already knows, the crowds considered John a true prophet (7:29) and had responded to him in droves (3:7), so Jesus is choosing a topic about which the people

Jesus Questioned by the Temple Authorities

Meanwhile the chief priest droned on: "A man dies and leaves no sons, but his wife marries his brother, who has three sons by his first wife . . . [and on] The three of them leave Jericho and head south, going three point three furlongs per hour, but they are leading two donkeys, which can carry two . . . [and on] So the Sabbath ends, and they are able to resume, adding on the thousand steps allowed under the law . . . and the wind is blowing southwest at two furlongs per hour . . . [and on] How much water will be required for the journey? Give your answer in firkins."

"Five," Joshua said, as soon as they stopped speaking. And all were amazed.

The crowd roared. A woman shouted, "Surely he is the Messiah." . . .

"Five," Joshua repeated.

The priests looked around among themselves. "That's right, but that doesn't give you authority to heal in the Temple."

Christopher Moore, *Lamb: The Gospel According to Biff, Christ's Childhood Pal* (New York: HarperCollins, 2002), 375.

gathered around him will care deeply. Moreover, Jesus himself had submitted to John's baptism and had called John the greatest person ever born of a woman (7:28). Jesus' question was not a red herring, in other words, because if John was no true prophet, then neither was Jesus. But the temple leaders are unlikely to think John's authority was genuine; we have already heard that the Pharisees stayed away from John (7:30), and even before the chief priests, scribes, and elders start talking this over, we suspect that they were not Baptists.[1]

They huddle up and go over their options. To admit that John was a real prophet—something they probably don't believe—would ruin their case against Jesus. If he were, then they, too, should have repented and been baptized in view of the coming kingdom of God, the very thing that Jesus has been teaching about in their temple. But to say that he was a phony—"they'll kill us!" Luke is a master both of hyperbole and understatement; here he takes Mark's "they were afraid of the crowd" and makes it much more vivid, depicting these big shots as cowards, brave enough to kill but not brave enough to risk their lives.

"We don't know," they say, claiming ignorance, but exposing their dishonesty: had they believed John's authority came from heaven, they would have been baptized. Since they had not, it follows that they did not think John's authority came from God. "We won't say" would have been more straightforward.

That lets Jesus off the hook, but instead of withdrawing from the danger posed by his interlocutors, he counterattacks. The next item in the lesson plan is a parable, one the temple leaders "knew" that he told "against them" (20:19). The parable of the vineyard, or of the wicked tenants, is found in the *Gospel of Thomas* as well as in Mark [The Parable of the Wicked Tenants in the *Gospel of Thomas*], and is a retelling of a parable in Isaiah 5:1-7 LXX. Luke is clearly editing Mark, mostly making the parable shorter and simpler. Because Luke omits Mark's description of the vineyard's construction, Luke also makes the parable less reminiscent of Isaiah. However, Luke inserts the vineyard owner's rhetorical question to himself (20:13), bringing that part of the parable closer to Isaiah; hard to tell, then, whether Luke had Isaiah on his mind as he rewrote Mark.

The Parable of the Wicked Tenants in the Gospel of Thomas

A person owned a vineyard and rented it to some farmers, that they might work it and he might collect its produce from them. He sent his servant that the farmers might give the servant the produce of the vineyard. They seized, beat, and almost killed his servant, and the servant returned and told his master. His master said, Perhaps the servant did not know them. He sent another servant, and the farmers beat that one as well. Then the master sent his son and said, Perhaps they will show my son some respect. Because the farmers knew that he was the heir to the vineyard, they seized him and killed him. Whoever has ears should hear.

Jesus said: Show me the stone that the builders rejected; that is the cornerstone.

Gos. Thom. Logia 65–66, in *Q-Thomas Reader*, ed. John S. Kloppenborg (Sonoma CA: Polebridge Press, 1990), 145–46.

Pliny on the Growth of Large Estates

 The men of olden times believed that above all moderation should be observed in landholding, for indeed it was their judgment that it was better to sow less and plow more intensively. Vergil, too, I see agreed with this view. To confess the truth, the latifundia (large estates) have ruined Italy, and soon will ruin the provinces as well. Six owners were in possession of one half of the province of Africa at the time when the Emperor Nero had them put to death.

Pliny, *Nat.* 18.7.35, cited in Lewis and Reinhold, *The Empire*, vol. 2 of *Roman Civilization* (New York: Harper and Row, 1966), 166.

Sharecroppers' Rates

In the country around Casinium and Venafrum on good soil [the owner] should give [the share worker] the eighth part in the basket; on fairly good soil, the seventh; on third-class soil, the sixth; and if it is threshed grain that is divided by the *modius* measure, the fifth part.

Cato, *On Agr.* 136.

Tenants' Misbehavior

Pliny writes to his friend Paulinus:

I am detained by the necessity of leasing my estates so as to set them in order for several years. In which connection I am obliged to adopt new arrangements. For in the last five-year period, despite large reductions [of rent], the arrears mounted. Hence several tenants no longer have any concern to reduce a debt which they despair of ever being able to pay off; they even seize and consume whatever is produced, acting like people who think they no longer have to be thrifty since it is not their own property.

Pliny, *Letters*, book 9, number 37, cited in Lewis and Reinhold, *The Empire*, vol. 2 of *Roman Civilization* (New York: Harper and Row, 1966), 177).

The parable can be understood as a real-life story based on first-century economics. In this reading, Jesus modifies the Isaiah story to reflect the turn toward tenant farming in this period. Wealthy landowners, like the one at Luke 12:16-21, often had more than one residence and owned farms in more than one place. [Pliny on the Growth of Large Estates] Such a person could either buy enough slaves to work the fields, hiring or buying overseers to manage them, or could rent the land to sharecroppers—there were always plenty of landless poor willing to farm for shares. Such arrangements often caused strains between the owner and the tenants. The owner, who lives away from the farm most of the time, worries that his tenants are not acting responsibly, while the tenants resent having to give away the largest part of what they worked so hard to produce. [Sharecroppers' Rates] If an owner stayed away from the farm "for a long time," as Luke says (20:9), the tenants would naturally grow possessive of the land and resent having to give anything to the owner. [Tenants' Misbehavior] The part about sending slaves and then the son is also true to life; an absentee owner first tries to get his rent by sending slaves and then, suspecting that these tenants have become squatters, sends the son to straighten things out with the local magistrates.[2]

All this makes sense, and may have been in Jesus' mind or in the minds of his listeners as he told this story. But Luke and his audience could not have heard the parable without immediately identifying the "beloved son" with Jesus (3:22), the slaves with the other prophets (11:49-50), and the wicked tenants with the temple leaders.[3] This last connection is made obvious when the chief priests and scribes "knew that he told this parable against them," rather than against the people, and it squares with the LXX text of Isaiah 5:7: "For the vineyard of the Lord of hosts is the house of Israel" (*ho gar ampelōn kyriou sabaōth oikos tou Israēl*). Isaiah meant "house" in the sense of the whole people of Israel, but in Luke's setting, "house" means temple (19:46-47). According to Josephus, the front wall of the sanctuary was gold-plated and decorated with "golden vines . . . from which clusters of grapes hung as tall as a man's height";[4]—the "house of the Lord," designed to look like the Lord's own vineyard.

The vineyard owner is called "a certain man" in v. 9, but "the Lord of the vineyard" in vv. 13 and 15; like "Lord of the harvest" in 10:2, this is God. He plants the vineyard—the temple—and leases it to farmers—the temple leadership—and then goes away for a long time. God's absence from the temple is presumed by Luke in Acts 7:44-50, where Stephen points out that God does not live in houses. When the time was right, God sent a slave to the tenants "so that they would give him from the fruit of the vineyard, but they, beating him, sent him away empty" (20:10). In this and the following verse, Luke rearranged Mark's text so that we would be reminded of Mary's statement that God, through Jesus, had filled the poor with good things and "sent the rich away empty" (1:53). Luke's three slaves all receive virtually the same treatment, and after the third is thrown out of the vineyard, the Lord talks to himself about what to do. He decides to send his beloved son, thinking that it is possible that the tenants will show him respect (Luke used the same verb for "have respect" at 18:2, 4).

The tenants, when they see the son, decide to kill him so the inheritance will be theirs. At that moment in Luke's narrative, Jesus has successfully occupied the temple, making it his house in practice by virtue of the crowds that swarm him. The temple leaders want to kill him, if they can ever figure out how to get him alone. And since Jesus has already predicted that they will hand him over to death (9:21-22), it comes as no surprise that these tenants kill the vineyard owner's son. Nor is it surprising when the Lord of the vineyard kills the tenants and gives the vineyard to others: Jesus had already predicted the desolation of the temple (13:32-35; 19:41-44), and will soon predict that Jerusalem will be handed over to the Gentiles "until the times of the Gentiles are fulfilled" (21:24).

The people are aghast: "*mē genoito*" they say, "may it never be" or "God forbid" or "perish the thought." That is a very interesting reaction, since it is the people who are keeping Jesus from being seized by the temple leaders. Although they admire Jesus and soak up his teaching, they wish no ill for the temple leaders (or for the temple)—perhaps they recognize that the "others" who would most likely take control of the temple would be the Romans, which would be bad for all Jews. The temple leaders, then, have misread their own standing with the people; far from being ready to stone them (20:6), the people do not wish for the leaders to be replaced.

Jesus reminds them of Psalm 118 (LXX 117):22, a favorite text among Christians. The psalm speaks of a stone, at first set aside as unusable, but then performing a conspicuously necessary role; "head of the corner" can refer to a stone connecting two walls at a corner, or to a keystone holding together an arch.[5] The psalm celebrates how relying on God protects the righteous person: "The right hand of the Lord did a mighty deed; the right hand of the Lord lifted me; the right hand of the Lord did a mighty deed. I will not die, but I will live and narrate the works of the Lord" (vv. 15-17 LXX). The psalmist continues: "Open to me the gates of righteousness; by entering them I will confess the Lord. This is the gate of the Lord—the righteous one will enter by it. I will confess [or bless] you, because you listened to me and became my salvation. The stone which the builders rejected has become the head of the corner" (vv. 19-22). For the psalmist, the image of the rejected stone reflects his/her choice of the right path, one that brought him/her ridicule and persecution from enemies but salvation from God. For Luke's Jesus, the stone is Jesus—he is the stone, rejected by the temple leaders, but who is confident of God's vindication (see Acts 4:11).

Verse 18 is a little confusing. The stone in the first part is stationary, and people fall against it and are "dashed to pieces"; this is what the synagogue at Nazareth proposed to do to Jesus by throwing him down from a precipice. In the second part, the stone falls on and crushes someone, like the tower at Siloam (13:4). If Jesus is the rejected stone, then Jesus is probably also these two stones; those who want to destroy him will themselves be overthrown.

The section concludes by noting the reactions of the chief priests and scribes—they want to kill Jesus immediately, but fear the people—and without noting the people's reaction to Jesus' reply to their "God forbid!" Are they convinced that he is the rejected stone, and are they yet worried about the fate of the temple? Luke keeps them close to Jesus in the next few episodes, witnesses to the continuing efforts of the temple leaders somehow to catch Jesus.

Whose Head and Whose Title?, 20:20-26

"What would Jesus drive?" was a half-serious, half-mocking bumper sticker for a while, following the WWJD bracelet phenomenon. "Surely not an SUV" was the half-serious part of it;

somehow we can't picture our Lord behind the wheel of one of those gas-guzzling leather-seated sky boxes, talking on his cell phone and listening to the gospel station on his way to make pastoral calls at the hospital. Better for Christians to invest less in their rides, to opt out of the "my car reflects my personality" thing that Americans do, and to use fewer natural resources in the process. All that seems right to me, and yet I think it stops short of where Jesus might take us. If Jesus were living now, what would he have to say about a society so committed to personal mobility and so at ease with consumption that we all assume we each need a car? I rather think he might not drive at all, and choose to walk everywhere, the better to shock us into rethinking our values and our lifestyles; if we think that way, then "what would Jesus drive" becomes a much more ironic and probing question.

The famous "give to Caesar" pericope is that sort of thing, a "how deep does the irony go" sort of saying. You can read it in a way that makes Jesus a team player—pay your taxes and give your tithes—or in a much more radical way—give Caesar exactly what he deserves. Christians have often used it to urge obedience to the government; paired with Romans 13:1-7, it can support what is sometimes called the "two kingdoms" view, where we Jesus-people belong to God and to our nation. We pledge allegiance to the flag, pay our taxes, and vote our consciences as part of Caesar's world; we pray, give to the poor, and worship as part of the kingdom of God. If the two collide, then we understand that our ultimate allegiance belongs to God, but so long as Caesar does not usurp God's place, we are obliged to do as Caesar demands.

Luke has crafted a story, by clever editing of Mark 12:13-17, trickier than the two kingdoms reading indicates. The episode begins when the narrator tells us that the temple leaders, unable to get to Jesus because of the crowd and publicly humiliated in their first verbal joust with him (20:1-19), begin a program of covert surveillance. Mark makes the Pharisees ask the question about tribute (Mark 12:13), but Luke omits the Pharisees, so that the spies are agents solely for the chief priests and scribes. Luke piles on terms emphasizing the dishonesty in this approach: "And closely watching him they [the temple leaders] sent spies pretending themselves to be righteous." Their pretense will turn out to be multi-layered: they do not announce whom they represent, and their allegiances turn out to be more complicated than they might have admitted. They say flattering things about Jesus that they do not believe; they pretend to be upright with respect to the Torah, but it turns out they are not. The lawyer who asked, "Who is my

Age of Augustus: Birth of Christ

Jean Leon Gérôme (1824–1904). *Age of Augustus: Birth of Christ*. 1855. Oil on canvas, Musee d'Orsay, Paris, France. (Credit: Réunion des Musées Nationaux/Art Resource, NY)

Augustus is seated on a throne, angels over his head, subjugated nations in front of him, enemies dead at his feet. In the foreground, ignored by all but the angel of God, are the Holy Family. It is said that Gérôme painted this to flatter Emperor Napoleon III; if this is true, then the unintended irony of the painting is that this new emperor was as unworthy of eternal devotion as Augustus. What do we give to Caesar and to God?

neighbor" wanted to justify himself—to win the argument with Jesus and to be considered right with respect to God—but in his case there was no pretense (10:29). The Pharisees watched Jesus closely (14:1) but not secretly. By contrast with other interrogators, these agents of the temple leaders are less honorable opponents; it will then be fitting for them to enter into a secret pact with a Satan-possessed man in order to gain control of Jesus (22:1-6). ["So they might trap him"]

Luke tells us of the two hidden agendas behind this question. The spies want to catch Jesus by his words, "in order to hand him over to the rule and authority of the governor" (20:20). The governor is Pilate, the Roman appointed by the emperor to maintain order and to collect taxes in Judea. So although the spies work for the temple authorities, they both are ultimately hoping for a chance to cooperate with Caesar's man in putting Jesus away. Second, the spies are hoping "to catch Jesus by his words in the presence of the people" (20:26). If he could be induced to look foolish or to say something that would anger the crowds, then perhaps they would disperse, and the temple leaders could seize Jesus bodily.

So the spies approach Jesus, first with words of false praise. You only speak the truth; you never "take face," meaning that he does not defer to authority or prestige; you speak and teach correctly. All this is true, even though the spies do not believe it. Ironically, they both lie and give true testimony. Then they ask their word trap: "Is it lawful or not for us to give tribute to Caesar?"

The Romans required that all their provinces pay an annual tribute for the privilege of being ruled by the empire. There were various sorts of taxes, but the one that affected everyone was the annual head-tax of a denarius for every adult male.[6] Rome required it of the nation; the prefect Pilate was there to make certain that the taxes were paid, and professional tax collectors were used to actually do the collecting; but the Romans expected the traditional leaders of the Jews to help ensure that the collection and payment went smoothly. In other words, the Romans would expect the "chief priests, scribes, and elders of the people" to do all they could to make sure the tribute was paid.

Roman occupation and Roman tribute must have rankled the chief priests. Josephus tells about the Roman confiscation of the sacred vestments worn by the high priest on the festivals, in effect holding them hostage: if you play nicely, you can fulfill your obligations to God and to your nation. [The High Priest's Vestments] What choice did they have but to assist the Romans in the collection of tribute, when failing to do so would threaten the continued worship of God and the well-being of all the people? Had the temple leaders answered their own question to Jesus, the answer would have been "Yes, it is lawful to pay the tribute—certainly not ideal, but lawful and prudent." But to some first-century Jews, paying tribute was contrary to the Law of Moses, and the leaders who cooperated with

---

"So they might trap him"

AΩ The word translated "trap" (*epilambanō*) appears frequently in Luke and Acts. It normally has the sense of grabbing hold of someone, for good or evil purpose, in order to control the person. At Luke 23:26 the soldiers grab Simon of Cyrene to make him carry the cross; at Luke 14:4 Jesus takes the hand of the man with dropsy in order to heal him; in Acts 16:19 and 21:33, it indicates an arrest, but in Acts 18:7 it describes the action of a mob seizing Sosthenes and beating him up. Thus, the word is not always negative, but always has the sense of grabbing hold in order to deliver the person someplace—to put the person under control. The temple authorities want to be able to do that to Jesus, but because of the crowds around him, they try to gain leverage against him by his words. Once they do, they plan to deliver him to Pilate.

The High Priest's Vestments

Josephus says that Herod the Great began the custom of holding the high priest's vestments "believing that, while he had them in his custody, the people will make no innovation against him. The like to what Herod did was done by his son Archelaus, who was made king after him; after whom the Romans, when they entered on the government, took possession of these vestments of the high priest and had them reposited in a stone chamber, under the seal of the priests, and of the keepers of the temple the captain of the guard lighting a lamp there every day; and seven days before a festival they were delivered to them by the captain of the guards, when the high priest having purified them, and made use of them, laid them up again the same chamber where they had been laid up before, and this the very next day after the feast was over. This was the practice at the three yearly festivals, and on the fast day; but Vitellus [governor of Syria, who removed Pilate from office] put those garments back into our own power."

Josephus, *Ant.* 18.92-95.

Two Jewish Opinions on Tribute

[Quirinius] came himself into Judea . . . to take an account of their substance and to dispose of Archelaus' money; but the Jews, although at the beginning they took the report of a taxation heinously, yet did they leave off any farther opposition to it, by the persuasion of Joazar, who was the son of Boethus, and high priest. So they, being over-persuaded by Joazar's words, gave an account of their estates, without any dispute about it; yet there was one Judas, a Gaulonite, of a city whose name was Gamala, who taking with him Sadduc, a Pharisee, became zealous to draw them to a revolt, who both said that this taxation was no better than an introduction to slavery, and exhorted the nation to assert their liberty.

Josephus, *Ant.* 18.2-4.

the Romans were traitors. [Two Jewish Opinions on Tribute] The question, "Is it lawful?" would seem to require Jesus to choose between the temple leaders and the radicals, between those who might seem to the crowds to be collaborators, on the one hand, and liberators on the other.

But it isn't that simple to catch hold of Jesus' words. Recognizing their "craftiness," Jesus says, "Show me a denarius; whose image and inscription does it have?" The word "image" (*elkōn*, which comes into English as "icon") was a loaded word. Everyone understood that the commandment against "graven images" forbade the Jews from bringing statues or idols into the temple. Pontius Pilate had provoked public demonstrations against him by bringing the emperor's image, attached to the tops of the standards of his soldiers, into the city of Jerusalem:

> Pilate was the first who brought those images to Jerusalem, and set them up there; which was done without the knowledge of the people, because it was done in the nighttime but as soon as they knew it, they came in multitudes to Caesarea [where the official residence of the procurator was], and interceded with Pilate many days, that he would remove the images; and when he would not grant their requests, because it would tend to the injury of Caesar, while yet they persevered in their request, on the sixth day he ordered his soldiers to have their weapons privately, while he came and sat upon his judgment seat, which seat was so prepared in the open place of the city, that it concealed the army that lay ready to oppress them; and when the Jews petitioned him again, he gave a signal to the soldiers to encompass them round, and threatened that their punishments should be no less than immediate death, unless they would leave off disturbing him, and go their ways home. But they threw themselves upon the ground, and laid their necks bare, and said they would take their death very willingly, rather than the wisdom of their laws should be transgressed; upon which Pilate was deeply affected with their firm resolution to keep their laws inviolable, and presently commanded the images to be carried back from Jerusalem to Caesarea.[7]

However accurate the story may or may not be in its particulars, it illustrates how the people of Jerusalem, including its leading citizens, would not bear to have the emperor's image brought into the Holy City. Yet these spies for the temple leaders have at least one image of Caesar they can show to Jesus—in the temple! There, on the denarius, is the same image that Pilate snuck into the city, with an inscription that read, "Tiberius Caesar, the divine Augustus, son of the divine Augustus"—in case there was any doubt that it was the image of a god! Before Jesus even gets to his pronouncement he has already shown them to be much less than "righteous," if that word is taken to mean "zealous for keeping the Law."

A denarius was considered then a day's wage for a day laborer. For the wealthy, it did not amount to much, but of course, taxes and tribute fell much harder on the poor. Jesus—who presumably has no denarius in his pocket[8]—has been preaching steadily against accumulated wealth. "Give Caesar's things to Caesar and God's things to

Denarius

Photo courtesy of EdgarLOwen.com

God" simply cannot mean, "make your living, pay your taxes, give your tithe, and then spend the rest however you like"—not in this Gospel, anyway. "You cannot serve God and possessions"; "none of you can be my disciple if you do not give up all your stuff"; "never fear, little flock, it is your Father's pleasure to give you the kingdom. Sell your possessions, and give alms." Luke's Jesus expects his followers to have given their denarii to the poor, so for him and for his people, the question of paying Caesar is moot. But notice that the spies ask, "is it lawful for *us* . . . ." To them, Jesus issues a challenge: give Caesar his coin—it has his name and face on it, and you shouldn't have brought it into the temple in the first place—and then give God what belongs to God—namely, your entire self in love and obedience.

The spies are silenced by his answer. Completely unable to grab hold of him by his words, they are also exposed by their own behavior to be dishonorable. Nothing to do but walk off quietly and let Jesus resume his teaching.

So, Jesus, should we pay our taxes? Paul gives a straight answer ("pay to all what is due them—taxes to whom taxes are due . . ." Rom 13:7), but not Jesus. It seems to me that by following Jesus' teachings elsewhere in the Gospel of Luke, we would reduce our income and our property to the point that we would not owe taxes. Giving God's stuff to God, however—that's a debt that can never be met. [Prayer for Forgiveness]

Whose Wife Will She Be?, 20:27-40

The Sadducees' riddle introduces a hypothetical woman, married and widowed seven times, never able to bear any children. Those familiar with the apocryphal Tobit will think of Sarah, the virtuous—virginal!—seven-time widow:

> Sarah, the daughter of Raguel, was reproached by one of her father's maids. For she had been married to seven husbands, and the wicked demon Asmodeus had killed each of them before they had been with her as is customary for wives. So the maid said to her, "You are the one who kills your husbands! See, you have already been married to seven husbands and have not borne the name of a single one of them. Why do you beat us? Because your husbands are dead? Go with them! May we never see a son or daughter of yours."
>
> On that day she was grieved in spirit and wept. When she had gone up to her father's upper room, she intended to hang herself. But she thought it over and said, "Never shall they reproach my father, saying to him, 'You had only one beloved daughter but she hanged herself because of her distress.' And I shall bring my father in his old age down in sorrow to Hades. It is better for me not to hang myself, but to pray the Lord that I may die and not listen to these reproaches anymore." (Tob 3:7-10)

Luke's story also reminds one of another apocryphal widow who lost seven sons in one day, tortured to death before her eyes because they refused to eat pork. The martyrs' mother in 4 Maccabees not only urges her sons to die rather than disobey God's law, but in order to protect her own virtue, throws herself on the flames (4 Macc 16:4–17:1), enduring the contest to gain the prize of "immortality in endless life" (4 Macc 17:11).

Tobit's Sarah and 4 Maccabees' mother of the martyrs show us just how flat a character is the widow in the Sadducees' riddle. Sarah and the martyr's mother are both ideal followers of God—righteous, brave, pious, ready to face death rather than do anything not in line with Torah. We are also allowed to see some of the pain of their circumstances. By contrast, the Sadducees' widow, who endures seven deaths and years of childlessness before her own death, is simply a legal prop, a hypothesis so ridiculous that it disproves the resurrection. We'll return to this at the end of our consideration of the section.

Jesus is still in the temple teaching the people, who surround him so that the temple authorities cannot seize him (19:47–20:1; 20:19). The temple leaders tried once to confront him directly; Jesus dodged the question about where his authority came from and told a parable implying that God would soon remove them from their leadership positions. They next sent spies to ask about the legality of taxes; another swing, another whiff, as Jesus publicly demonstrated their duplicity. Next up are the Sadducees, the sect to which the high priest and his close associates all belong, according to Luke (Acts 5:17). This, then, is the third attempt by the temple leadership to trap Jesus with his words and to damage his reputation with the crowds he has attracted.

One identifying mark of the Sadducees, according to Josephus and the New Testament, was that they did not believe in the resurrection: that is, they believed that there was no future day when the dead would be raised. [The Sadducees] We cannot say for certain how many other first-century Jews agreed with them about the

---

The Sadducees

We do not know a lot about the Sadducees. Their name probably derives from Zadok, one of David's priests (2 Sam 8:17). Many commentators, on the basis of Acts 4–5, consider the Sadducees to have been an elite group with membership mostly from the upper classes and the priesthood. This fits with what Josephus writes about them in a couple of places:

> But the doctrine of the Sadducees is this: That souls die with the bodies; nor do they regard the observation of anything besides what the law enjoins them; for they think it an instance of virtue to dispute with those teachers of philosophy whom they frequent; but this doctrine is received but by a few, yet by those still of the greatest dignity. (Josephus, *Ant.* 18.16-17)

> . . . the Sadducees, whose notions are quite contrary to those of the Pharisees . . . the Pharisees have delivered to the people a great many observations by succession from their fathers which are not written in the law of Moses; and for that reason it is that the Sadducees reject them and say that we are to esteem those observances to be obligatory which are in the written word, but are not to observe what are derived from the tradition of our forefathers; and concerning these things it is that great disputes and differences have arisen among them, while the Sadducees are able to persuade none but the rich, and have not the populace obsequious to them, but the Pharisees have the multitude of their side . . . . (Josephus, *Ant.* 13.293, 297–98)

In another place, however, Josephus writes as if it were unusual for the high priest to be a Sadducee: "This younger Ananus . . . was a bold man in his temper, and very insolent; he was also of the sect of the Sadducees, who are very rigid in judging offenders, above all the rest of the Jews, as we have already observed . . . ." Josephus gives as an illustration that Ananus, after the death of Festus the procurator in 62, and before Albinus, his replacement, could arrive, took it upon himself to arrest and kill James, Jesus' brother, for which he was removed from office. (*Ant.* 20.197-203)

Josephus writes about the Sadducees as if they were a philosophical school or sect, one of several varieties of Judaism in the Second Temple period:

> But the Sadducees . . . take away fate entirely, and suppose that God is not concerned in our doing or not doing what is evil; and they say, that to act what is good, or what is evil, is at men's own choice, and that the one or the other belongs so to every one, that they may act as they please. They also take away the belief in the immortal duration of the soul, and the punishments and rewards in Hades. (Josephus, *J.W.* 2.164-65)

In the Mishnah, the Sadducees are likewise defined by their interpretation of the Law of Moses, most often in argument with the Pharisees; since those who collected and arranged the Mishnah considered themselves to be the descendants of the Pharisees, it is no surprise that in the Mishnaic arguments between the two groups, the Pharisees always win.

resurrection, but the impression given by our sources is that the Sadducees were in the minority on this, and that most people believed in some form of life after death. The Old Testament has only one clear reference to God bringing the dead back to life (Dan 12:1-4), and there are many passages that take the point of view that the dead are gone, forgotten even by God. We can therefore think of the Sadducees' position on this issue as more conservative or more traditional.

They make their only appearance in Luke in this episode, but they come back in Acts 4–5 and in Acts 23. In the early parts of Acts, the Sadducees are "annoyed because [Peter and John] were teaching the people and proclaiming in Jesus the resurrection from the dead" (Acts 4:2), and doing so in the temple precincts. In the latter part of Acts, Paul claims that his persecution by the temple authorities is all about his belief in the resurrection from the dead, and he starts an argument between Pharisees and Sadducees over this point (23:6-9). This episode is therefore not only Jesus' third and climactic argument with the temple leadership, but serves as a pattern for how the apostles and Paul will relate to the same group after Jesus' resurrection.

Luke makes few changes in Mark, his source, in vv. 27-33. The riddle set out by the Sadducees involves the hypothetical story of a woman who married seven brothers in succession, in obedience to the law of levirate marriage: "If brothers live together, and if one of them dies but has no progeny [lit., seed], the dead man's wife shall not become the wife of a man outside the immediate family; her husband's brother shall go in to her and shall take her to himself as wife and shall be intimate with her [lit., live in the house with her]. And the child which she may bear shall be appointed by the name of the dead man, and his name will not be erased from Israel" (Deut 25:5-6 LXX). The levirate law says that its purpose is to make certain that a man's name is not lost in Israel (Deut 25:6), but presumably it also had the effect, and perhaps the purpose, of providing for the widow's well-being. If her former brother-in-law married her and raised children to inherit the dead husband's property, then the widow's future would also be more assured. Suppose this happened seven times, said the Sadducees, but with no children ever born. If all eight former spouses were raised from the dead, whose wife would the woman be? [Levirate Marriage]

Levirate Marriage

The law requiring a brother to marry his brother's widow is called "levirate marriage" (the Latin word for "brother-in-law" is *levir*). The story of Ruth supposes that there was a man more closely related to Naomi's husband than Boaz, and that he had to relinquish the right (or the duty) to marry Ruth before Boaz could do so. Deut 25:7-10 addresses the issue of a widow who wants to be remarried to her brother-in-law, but who can't get him to do his duty; in the end, the reluctant bridegroom does not have to go through with it, but at the cost of shame attaching to him and to his family. The story of Tamar in Gen 38 illustrates how a father might be reluctant to pledge a son to marry his widowed daughter-in-law. Josephus, in his long paraphrase and summary of the Law of Moses, includes a section parallel to the levirate law in Deut 25:5-10 (*Ant.* 4.254-56).

The riddle rests on three presuppositions:

1. The Law of Moses is eternal; if there were to be an age to come, the Torah would still be in effect. Based on statements like Deuteronomy 11:1, 12:1, that's not a bad assumption.
2. A resurrected body would be pretty much just like the one previously alive, so that resurrected men and women would want/need to be married.
3. Nobody would answer, "She'd be married to all seven"; the Torah contemplated a man having more than one wife, but considered the reverse an "abomination."

The Sadducees believed they had found an iron-clad argument against the resurrection, and since the levirate law presumes that the dead man's memory and heritage can only be kept alive through his children, one must admit that this is a good case.[9] That is, if there were a resurrection of the dead, why would there need to be laws promoting levirate marriage?

Luke edits Jesus' answer fairly extensively. He deletes Mark's opening salvo about knowing neither the Scriptures nor the power of God (Mark 12:24), so that this becomes a much more civilized exchange. He also takes Mark's fairly simple "For whenever they are raised from the dead, they neither marry nor are given in marriage" and makes it much more complicated: "The children [lit., sons] of this age marry and are given in marriage, but those considered worthy to attain that age and the resurrection of the dead neither marry nor are given in marriage, because they are unable to die; for they are angel-like and are children [lit., sons] of God, being children [lit., sons] of the resurrection." Luke's more cumbersome "considered worthy to attain" emphasizes how one's presence in the kingdom is at God's invitation, and that not everybody will be chosen (13:22-30; 14:23-24).[10] "Sons of this age" and "sons of the resurrection" means people belonging to those periods, and everyone in the latter group was first a member of the former group. God moves them from one to the other by the act of resurrection. "Sons of God" means "belonging to God," but it is also a typical phrase from the Old Testament for "angels," and Luke's use of it reinforces his assertion that resurrected people are like angels. "Sons of God" also connects resurrected people with Jesus, whose resurrected appearance probably gives us a good notion of what Luke thinks the resurrection implies.

Those who belong to this age marry and are given in marriage— a simple statement about how most people in Jesus' day behaved.

Marriages were arranged by parents, so the "given" part could be taken to refer equally to men and women, although "married" might also be understood to refer to men and "given in marriage" to women. Those whom God grants to be part of the resurrection do not marry—that's clear enough, but what follows can be read in different ways: "because they are unable to die, because they are angel-like." Angels were regarded as immortal, so "because they are angel-like" could be a reason supporting "they are unable to die"; but then why would "unable to die" be a reason explaining why the resurrected ones do not marry? One supposes that since marriage in antiquity was primarily viewed as a way to produce legitimate children who could inherit property and carry on the family name, immortality would remove the need for marriage.[11] Explained this way, Luke's Jesus undermines the Sadducees' argument by attacking the second presupposition listed above.

Another way of reading the answer is to begin with "like the angels" and to connect it to a belief that angels are spirits—incorporeal, or bodiless, beings who can look human sometimes but who do so only to accommodate human sensibilities (cf. LXX Ps 103:4: he makes his angels spirits, and his ministers a flame of fire).[12] Some of these "sons of God" did take women for themselves, according to Genesis 6:1-4, and produced offspring—the giants, who plagued Israel, and who, according to *1 Enoch*, themselves produced the demons who plague the whole world. Based on these texts, the logic would not be that angels cannot marry or have sex, but that they should not; angelic life is supposed to be focused on heavenly matters and not on the things of the flesh. [*1 Enoch* on the Life of Angels] Some commentators go farther: Luke's Jesus is promoting celibacy, not only for godly angels, but for those who hope to attain to the resurrection.[13] In support of this view, recall that Luke adds "wife" to the list of things that faithful disciples have left to follow Jesus (Luke 18:29; cf. Mark 10:29). But while it is possible to read "neither marry nor are given in marriage" as characteristics of the present life, it is not possible to think that Luke meant "they are unable to die" as referring to the current followers of Jesus, and so this reading seems to me implausible.

---

1 Enoch on the Life of Angels

In the following passage from *1 Enoch* 15 (dated 3rd or 2d century BC), Enoch is being instructed on how to admonish the Watchers—the angels from Genesis 6:1-4 who consorted with human women:

For what reason have you abandoned the high, holy, and eternal heaven; and slept with women and defiled yourselves with the daughters of the people, taking wives, acting like the children of the earth, and begetting giant sons? Surely you, you used to be holy, spiritual, the living ones, possessing eternal life; but now you have defiled yourselves with women, and with the blood of the flesh begotten children, you have lusted with the blood of the people, like them producing blood and flesh, which die and perish. On that account, I have given you wives in order that seeds might be sown upon them and children born by them, so that the deeds that are done upon the earth will not be withheld from you. Indeed you, formerly you were spiritual, having eternal life, and immortal in all the generations of the world. That is why formerly I did not make wives for you, for the dwelling of the spiritual beings of heaven is heaven.

1 Enoch 15:3-7, trans. E. Isaac, in James H. Charlesworth, *The Old Testament Pseudepigrapha* (2 vols; New York: Doubleday, 1985), 1.21.

Another interpretive issue is whether Luke's Jesus here defends the resurrection of the dead only, or a belief in immortality as well as the resurrection. In the first case, Luke's Jesus, like the Pharisees and Essenes, teaches that there will be a day when God will raise the dead, and until then, they are dead.[14] In the second case, Luke's Jesus teaches that the righteous are always alive and with God, even between the present time and the day of resurrection.[15] Jesus' citation of the episode of Moses at the burning bush seems to support both "that the dead are raised" and that "all are alive to [God]." In that last phrase, Luke sounds like the Jewish first-century writing 4 Maccabees 7:18-19; speaking of those who are willing to face death rather than disobey God's law, the author says, "they believe that to God they do not die, for just as our patriarchs Abraham, Isaac, and Jacob, they live to God." [4 Maccabees on Eternal Life]

Part of the difficulty in settling this issue is that our texts were much less concerned to be precise about it than we would like. Fourth Maccabees has the martyrs say (repeatedly and vigorously) that the wicked Antiochus will roast eternally while they will be granted life with God. But the text never addresses whether this happens immediately or at Judgment Day. Luke, for his part, gives us texts that we can read in support of some kind of existence

---

4 Maccabees on Eternal Life

4 Maccabees is a Jewish document written in Greek, usually dated to the 1st century AD. It expands on the stories of the martyrdoms of the elderly priest Eleazar, seven brothers, and their mother, found in 2 Maccabees 6–7. Before they die, each of the martyrs make lengthy speeches about how they gladly give their lives for the sake of the law, and they often profess their confidence that God will punish Antiochus Epiphanes, who was conducting the tortures, and that God will reward all of them with eternal life. Here are some representative quotes:

9:8-9: For we, through this severe suffering and endurance, shall have the prize of virtue and shall be with God, on whose account we suffer; but you, because of your bloodthirstiness toward us, will deservedly undergo from the divine justice eternal torment by fire.

10:9-11: When he was about to die, he said, "We, most abominable tyrant, are suffering because of our godly training and virtue, but you, because of your impiety and bloodthirstiness, will undergo unceasing torments."

10:14-15: But he said to them, "You do not have a fire hot enough to make me play the coward. No—by the blessed death of my brothers, by the eternal destruction of the tyrant, and by the everlasting life of the pious, I will not renounce our noble family ties."

13:14-17: "Let us not fear him who thinks he is killing us, for great is the struggle of the soul and the danger of eternal torment lying before those who transgress the commandment of God. Therefore let us put on the full armor of self-control, which is divine reason. For if we so die, Abraham and Isaac and Jacob will welcome us, and all the fathers will praise us."

16:24-25: By these words the mother of the seven encouraged and persuaded each of her sons to die rather than violate God's commandment. They knew also that those who die for the sake of God live to God, as do Abraham and Isaac and Jacob and all the patriarchs.

18:23-24: But the sons of Abraham with their victorious mother are gathered together into the chorus of the fathers, and have received pure and immortal souls from God, to whom be glory forever and ever. Amen.

Last Judgment

Fra Angelico (1387–1455). *Last Judgment*. c. 1431. Museo di S. Marco, Florence, Italy. (Credit: Scala/Art Resource, NY)

This lively altarpiece illustrates the final resurrection of the dead. Christ, in the center, is surrounded by seraphim and angels. His right hand is raised in blessing; the Virgin is on his right, and the newly resurrected souls there are being welcomed into Paradise. His left hand is lowered in judgment. John the Baptist sits there, and the souls of the damned are being herded by demons into great torments. The two seated groups include Old Testament figures as well as modern saints.

immediately upon death: the parable of the rich man and Lazarus, Jesus' statement to the penitent thief, and this passage. But Luke is also pretty clear about expecting a day when God will raise the dead (Acts 3:21; 17:31), and so one can always argue that the dead are always alive to God in the sense that God sees all times in light of God's final disposition of things.

In the end, we must admit that Luke's Jesus definitely believes that the dead are raised, and may also believe that they live on after death in a temporary place of blessing or punishment, while they await the final disposition at the last day. The latter view is that of *1 Enoch* and some other Jewish writings from this period, so it is not an impossible position for Luke to have held. We can also look at Luke's descriptions of the resurrected Jesus in Luke 24 and Acts 1 to gain some understanding of what Luke meant by "the resurrection of the dead." Jesus famously eats fish to prove that he is no ghost and that he has flesh and bones (24:42-43), and yet he could appear and vanish as though he were a spirit (24:13, 36). If the "children of the resurrection" are like the resurrected Son of God, they will be corporeal, able to sit down to a real table with the patriarchs and all the prophets, and yet their *corpus* will be the new and improved model Jesus demonstrated.

Some of the scribes are impressed with his answer and tell him so. "Scribe" describes a profession rather than a religious point of view; Luke uses the word to mean a legal expert or a secretary. Luke may have thought that these scribes worked for the Sadducees, but he also might have meant some who worked for the temple authorities, who have been hanging around for all three of the confrontations over Jesus' authority (20:1). In either case, Luke probably did not think that the scribes belonged to the sect of the Sadducees. Their "attaboy, Jesus!" previews the support Paul will get from fellow Pharisees when he argues for the resurrection (Acts 23:6-9).

Before we leave this pericope, consider again the widow imagined in it. The Sadducees' riddle deals with a hypothetical widow, and we should not assume that it tells us anything about how the sect felt about actual widows; but taken on its face, their conundrum imagines a life of perpetual tragedy for a woman adding up to a denial of any sort of eternal life—no children, no resurrection—as if God thought like Sarah's rebellious maid in Tobit. Luke's Jesus never addressed the question about the widow—whose wife will she be?—because he believed that in the age to come, there was no marriage and no death. In the kingdom that is coming, men and women will live as children of God, alive to God as are the angels, the great patriarchs, and the Son of God. No need for protection of widows; no need for childless women to wish for death; no need for any mother to watch her children die. May that day come soon, and may God's people work to make this age more like the age to come!

Whose Son, Who's Lord?, 20:41-47

> So Gollum hissed: "What has roots as nobody sees, is taller than trees, up, up it goes, and yet never grows?"
> "Easy!" said Bilbo. "Mountains, I suppose."
> "Does it guess easy? It must have a competition with us, my preciouss! If precious asks, and it doesn't answer, we eats it, my preciousss. If it asks us, and we doesn't answer, then we does what it wants, eh? We shows it the way out, yes!"[16]

In Bilbo's contest in the dark with Gollum, the contestants take turns asking each other riddles; after several rounds, Bilbo wins, sort of, when he asks Gollum, "What have I got in my pockets?" Gollum protests that it is not a fair riddle—he has a point—but when he cannot guess in three tries, the game is over. Jesus' contest with the temple authorities takes place in the temple, in full view of the crowds; they or their stalking horses have been bested and silenced three times, and v. 40 says nobody any longer dared to ask him anything.

So Jesus asks "them" a stumper: the antecedent of "them" is most likely the scribes of v. 39, even though when they last spoke, they were praising him for trouncing the Sadducees. They may agree with him that the dead will be raised, but they are hardly Jesus' allies, since they are also associated with the temple leadership (20:1). Jesus will flay them in vv. 45-47, so we can think of v. 41 as the beginning of his offensive.

Jesus' riddle assumes several things:

1. The Messiah was commonly regarded as a descendant of David. [Messianic Expectations in the Second Temple Period] According to 2 Samuel 7:12-14, God promised David that one of his progeny

---

Messianic Expectations in the Second Temple Period

 Some documents predict a Messiah from the line of David:

T. Jud. 24: A man shall arise from my posterity like the sun of righteousness, walking with the sons of men in gentleness and righteousness [assuming this is not a Christian interpolation, *T. Jud.* is from the 2d century BC]

Ps. Sol. 17:21: See, Lord, and raise up for them their king, the son of David, to rule over your servant Israel [1st century BC or AD]

4 Ezra 12:32: This is the Messiah whom the Most High has kept until the end of days, who will arise from the offspring of David, and will come and speak with them. He will denounce them for their ungodliness . . . for first he will bring them alive before his judgment seat, and when he has reproved them, then he will destroy them. But in mercy he will set free the remnant of my people. [1st century AD]

At least some of the Dead Sea community expected a messiah from the line of David plus a messianic priest from the line of Levi:

1QSa 11 ff: When God engenders (=begets) the Priest-Messiah, he shall come with them at the head of the whole congregation of Israel with all his brethren, the sons of Aaron

the priests, those called to the assembly, the men of renown; and they shall sit before him, each man in the order of his dignity. And then the Messiah of Israel shall come, and the chiefs of the clans of Israel shall sit before him, each in the order of his dignity, according to his place in their camps and marches . . . . And when they shall gather for the common table, to eat and to drink new wine, when the common table shall be set for eating and the new wine poured for drinking, let no man extend his hand over the first-fruits of bread and wine before the Priest . . . thereafter, the Messiah of Israel shall extend his hand over the bread, and all the congregation of the Community shall utter a blessing, each man in the order of his dignity.

1QS 9:10 ff: They shall depart from none of the counsels of the Law . . . but shall be ruled by the primitive precepts in which the men of the Community were first instructed until there shall come the Prophet and the Messiahs of Aaron and Israel.

Some Jews hoped for God to save their people and do not mention a Messiah at all:

T. Mos. 10:3, 7: For the Heavenly One will arise from his kingly throne. Yea he will go forth from his holy habitation with indignation and wrath on behalf of his sons . . . . For God Most High will surge forth, the Eternal One alone. In full view will he come to work vengeance on the nations. [1st century AD] would always occupy the throne. But following the Babylonian Exile, this was no longer true. Since God cannot lie, the reasoning went, the promise will one day be restored, and a king from David's line will rule Israel once again. Gabriel promised Mary that Jesus would be that very person in 1:32-33, so by "how can they say that the Messiah is David's son" Luke cannot mean, "They say it, but they are wrong."

2. David wrote the psalms, and some of them—including Psalm 110 (109 in the LXX)—contained predictions of the Messiah. The way Luke's Jesus reads the text, "The Lord said to my lord" means "God spoke to the Messiah." Luke makes clear in Acts 2:32-36 that he understands Jesus' ascension to be with God to fulfill the prediction contained in the verse quoted in Luke 20:42-43.

3. It would be unthinkable for a progenitor—the great-great-great-however-many-great-grandfather of the Messiah—to call his progeny "lord." Children respect their elders, and the elders do not call the children "master."

Thus, Jesus has noted a tension, if not a contradiction, between two common readings of the Old Testament. If the Messiah comes from David's line, then how can David call him "lord"?

This question is a bit like "where did Cain get his wife"; it's an imponderable, the sort of thing one might bring up at a dinner party to get some appreciative "hmms," or in a riddle contest as the coup de grace. There is no evidence that anyone in ancient times really worried about it.[17] Luke has no difficulty believing both that Jesus was descended from David and that God appointed him Lord over everyone, including King David (who, with the rest of the prophets, could be expected to be in the kingdom of God). In fact, it is only a riddle to those who do not believe that God raised Jesus from the dead and then took him into heaven until time for his return. Peter gives the answer that "they" would have known, had they been Jesus' followers: "This Jesus God raised up . . . being therefore exalted at the right hand of God . . . . David did not ascend into the heavens" (Acts 2:32-34). Since God has made Jesus "both Lord and Messiah" by virtue of the resurrection and ascension, David's prophetic confession of Jesus as Lord makes perfect sense.

Nobody answers; following Mark, Luke goes directly into Jesus' harangue against the scribes. Luke adds some stage directions: "While all the people were listening, he said to the disciples . . . ." The disciples have been silent by-standers since the Pharisees complained about their calling Jesus king (19:29-40). Throughout Jesus' prediction of Jerusalem's destruction, his entry into the temple, and his contest of wits with the temple leaders, the disciples have had no role. Now, however, they are the audience for Jesus' warnings; as we will see in 22:24-38, the disciples do not completely absorb the lesson.

Jesus' complaint about the scribes is that they act like wealthy people. They wear "long, flowing robes" that were only practical for someone who did no physical labor. They "love greetings in the marketplace and first chairs in the synagogues and first couches at dinners"; that is, they enjoy having other people accord them markers of high status. Synagogues normally had rows of benches around three sides of the room; we can guess that the seats on the bottom row, nearest the speaker, may have been considered prime. Formal dinners in this period were done with the diners reclining on couches arranged in a U-shape. A spot near the host in the center of the "U" was especially desirable (see discussion at 14:1-24).

So far, this is all just petty stuff: the scribes act like the wealthy people who employ them—so what else is new? The more serious charges are in v. 47. They "devour the houses of widows" and "as a pretext [or for appearance's sake] they pray a lot [or long]." "Widows' houses" are their income, their subsistence; the vivid metaphor of gobbling down their property becomes clear in the next episode, when the widow puts her whole life into the collection bin at the temple (21:1-4).[18] The scribes are part of the bureaucracy that would take a widow's last two bits; by contrast, Jesus wants wealthy people like these guys to sell all their stuff and give the money to the poor (12:33), and according to Acts, that's just what his followers do.

Do his followers still? Not often, unfortunately. We dress like the wealthy trendsetters if we are able; we cherish the markers of success and status in our world; we plug into an economic system that grinds the poor and go to church and pray; and except for token charitable contributions or activities, most of us do very little to keep the widows off the streets. Our programs take a lot of money to run, after all.

"The greater judgment"—greater than what? Maybe greater than the praise and wealth they sought.[19] Or greater than whose? Maybe greater, as a part of the temple leadership, than the destruction coming on the whole city.[20]

CONNECTIONS

The war of words between Jesus and the chief priests, scribes, and elders is the public version of the quieter, deadlier, struggle. These leaders of Jerusalem and the temple "kept looking for a way to kill him" (19:47), "wanted to lay hands on him" the moment they heard the parable of the wicked tenants, and tried to find a pretext to "hand him over to the power and authority of the governor" (20:20). For them, any means will do: a straightforward challenge (20:2), a delegation of flatterers (20:20-21), or a scriptural conundrum (20:27-33).

Jesus' answers to their questions are indirect. "Who gives you the authority to do what you do?" The answer is "God," but that perhaps would only have started another argument about whether the temple leaders or Jesus were truly sent from God, and God knows nobody would win that fight. Don't we worship as we do because we think God approves of it? So does every church, synagogue, mosque, and temple; arguments over which religion or which form of any specific religion has God's approval are futile. Jesus' answer—"I claim the same authority as John; where do you think his came from?"—showed that the temple leaders were not as sure of their own authority as their question sounded, since they would not speak their opinions for fear of what the crowds would do. That's worth remembering: sometimes fear is the source of hostility, and the wise teacher or minister, rather than responding directly to the anger, will instead address the fear.

The question about paying tribute gets a very slippery answer. "Give to Caesar what's Caesar's and to God what's God's" can be read as "obey all of Caesar's commands," if we believe that "whoever resists authority resists what God has appointed" (Rom 13:2). It can also be read as "let Caesar keep his stupid coins—they only get you in trouble anyway—and give your whole self to God." Note that Luke, alone among the Gospels, says that one of the charges against Jesus was that he forbade paying tribute to Caesar (23:2). Pilate, Caesar's representative, did not exercise his lawful (if not God-given) authority in defense of justice, but gave the order to crucify an innocent man and to release a murderer and insurrectionist. Clearly Luke does not think that trust is something one can safely give to Caesar; we religious folk should take warning.

The question about the resurrection is an attempt to draw Jesus into a sectarian debate. Jesus' answer marks him, like the Pharisees, the Essenes, and the followers of John the Baptist, as a believer in the resurrection. He believed that those worthy of the age to come would be raised to live forever, and that none of the dead is lost to

God, who is God of the living. While this does not answer all our questions about the future life, it speaks forcefully to the deep human fear of dying and becoming nothing, not even a memory. "To God, all are alive"—Jesus' faith is in a life-affirming God.

Jesus' riddle to his interlocutors about how to interpret Psalm 110:1 goes unanswered; not surprising, because in Luke's scheme, nobody comprehended God's plan for Jesus' resurrection until after it happened. Rather than explain things now, Luke leaves Jesus' question hanging until Peter unpacks it in his Pentecost sermon, but we can read ahead to see that Luke understands "sit at my right hand" to be fulfilled in Jesus' resurrection and ascension. In Luke's reading, Jesus' only throne is at God's right hand; he will not be a new improved Caesar, but inaugurates a whole different kind of kingdom.

In the final section of the chapter, Jesus engages in polemic against the scribes. The tone and content are not too different from 11:38-52, the woes against the Pharisees and lawyers. One presumes that Luke finds these sections compatible with Jesus' command "Love your enemies . . . bless those who curse you" (6:27-28), but the tension should give us pause. Jesus' complaints about the scribes are significant: they like to act like the wealthy, and in doing so help to destroy the poor. We, too, align ourselves too quickly and too naturally with the wealthy and powerful, adopting their values and their measures of success and self-worth.

By whose authority do we do what we do? This chapter shows us how claims for divine backing may mask our dependence on popular opinion, on government support, on sectarian truth-claims, or on the patronage of the wealthy. It's hard to picture ourselves as Jesus' opponents, but do we form the public statements of our faith around what we think people's reactions will be? Do we give to Caesar what's rightfully God's? Do our lifestyles advance justice for the poor, or do we live as much like the rich as we can afford? Dangerous questions, but worthy of straight answers.

NOTES

[1] "Baptists" in this sentence means "first-century disciples of John the Baptist." I hate to explain jokes, but there are some twenty-first-century Baptists who believe (mistakenly, in my opinion) that the Baptist denomination started with John the Baptist and continued in unbroken succession as the true faith down to the present.

[2] See William R. Herzog II, *Prophet and Teacher: An Introduction to the Historical Jesus* (Louisville: Westminster/John Knox, 2005), 200–203, who reads it as a protest

against the oppression of the poor by the temple leaders and "the architects of colonial occupation and Herodian client rule."

[3] See John Nolland, *Luke* (WBC, vols. 35A-C; Dallas TX: Word, 1989-93), 3.950; Alan R. Culpepper, *The Gospel of Luke* (NIB, vol. 9; Nashville: Abingdon, 1995), 380–81; Joseph A. Fitzmyer, *The Gospel According to Luke* (AB 28 and 28A; Garden City NY: Doubleday, 1981), 2.1279-82; Arlen Hultgren, *The Parables of Jesus: A Commentary* (Grand Rapids MI: Eerdmans, 2000), 351–78. All these note the details of the story that fit the first-century context, but agree that Luke understands it as an allegory of God's judgment on the temple leaders.

[4] Josephus, *J.W.* 5.210.

[5] Nolland *Luke*, 3.953.

[6] Joel B. Green, *The Gospel of Luke* (NICNT; Grand Rapids: Eerdmans, 1997), 711.

[7] *Ant.* 18.56–59.

[8] Fitzmyer, *Luke*, 2.1291.

[9] Green, *Luke*, 719–20.

[10] Fitzmyer *Luke*, 2.1305; Green, *Luke*, 720; Luke Timothy Johnson, *The Gospel of Luke* (SP, vol. 3; Collegeville MN: Liturgical Press, 1991), 313.

[11] Johnson, *Luke*, 313; Fitzmyer, *Luke*, 2.1305.

[12] Johnson, *Luke*, 313; Fitzmyer, *Luke*, 1.1305.

[13] Halvor Moxnes, *Putting Jesus in His Place* (Louisville: Westminster/John Knox, 2003), 94; Dale Allison, *Jesus of Nazareth* (Minneapolis: Fortress, 1998), 208–209.

[14] Green, *Luke*, 721–22.

[15] Fitzmyer, *Luke*, 2.1307.

[16] J. R. R. Tolkien, *The Hobbit* (rev. ed.; New York: Ballantine, 1965), 73.

[17] Fitzmyer, *Luke*, 2.1311.

[18] Nolland, *Luke*, 3.976, and Fitzmyer, *Luke*, 2.1318, list several possible ways scribes may have been taking from widows, but both note that the lack of specifics in the text makes all the suggestions equally iffy. Thus it seems to me that whatever scribes in Jerusalem may have done to widows in Jesus' day, we should assess Luke's understanding by how this condemnation leads into the episode in 21:1-4.

[19] So Green, *Luke*, 728.

[20] So Culpepper, *Luke*, 393; Nolland, *Luke*, 3.977.

JESUS IN THE TEMPLE: PREDICTION

Luke 21

COMMENTARY

The Widow: Prelude to the Temple Sermon, 21:1-4

"Take my life, and let it be consecrated, Lord to thee . . . . Take my silver and my gold, not a mite would I withhold."[1] "Savior, thy dying love thou gavest me, nor should I aught withhold, dear Lord, from thee; in love my soul would bow, my heart fulfill its vow, some offering bring thee now, something for thee."[2] And so forth—all churchgoers know that moment in the service when we are going to hear, in exhortations from the pulpit and/or from the words of hymns, the call to give to the Lord. And many of us have heard this very story on Stewardship Sunday interpreted thus: the widow gave all she had to God, and Jesus blessed her generosity. You can't be expected to do the same thing she did, but surely you can do better than you've done. Dig deeper, cough it up, fork it over, and let's meet our budget for the year, or send the teenagers on the mission trip, or help support the missionaries in Nairobi. If Jesus had truly been encouraging people to empty their bank accounts in support of the temple, one wonders why the temple leaders wanted to kill him: "Jesus is out there yelling at the wealthy to give more to the temple!" "Yeah? Hey, how much more do we need in the building fund? Maybe we should rethink arresting him . . . ."

Luke takes the story from Mark (Matthew leaves it out, interestingly enough), making only a few changes. In Mark's scene, the rich are part of crowds making offerings; Luke zooms in on the wealthy, so that the contrast with the poor widow is more starkly drawn. Luke also makes sure that the audience will connect the widow pericope with the critique of the scribes (20:45-47) and with the prediction of the temple's destruction (21:5-6). Jesus' polemic against the scribes was spoken "to the disciples" but "while all the people were listening" (20:45); so at the beginning of this scene, Luke has Jesus "looking up," moving his eyes away from his audience first to the rich ("he saw," v. 1) and then to the widow ("he saw," v. 2).

The temple—that is to say, the upkeep of priests and Levites who worked in the temple, the costs for the daily sacrifices of lambs and incense that benefited the whole nation, costs associated with holy days (for example, the many sacrifices required by the Day of Atonement)—was supported by the contributions of Jews throughout the world. Some contributions, including some of the tithes, were collected in villages and towns by Levites, who lived on some of it and brought the rest to the temple. There was an annual half-shekel temple offering required of every adult male (see Exod 30:11-16); according to the Mishnah, it was announced on the first day of Adar and then collected beginning on the 15th of that month, with collection centers outside Palestine as well as in the temple. In addition to these regular payments specified by the Torah, people made other offerings as part of vows: "Lord, if you help me out, I promise to make an offering of wood to the temple." According to the Mishnah, there were thirteen collection devices in the temple, almost certainly spaced out around the Court of the Gentiles, labeled for the collection of different things: "There were thirteen Shofar-chests in the Temple, whereon was inscribed: 'New Shekel dues,' 'Old Shekel dues,' 'Bird-offerings,' 'Young birds for the Whole Offering,' 'Wood,' 'Frankincense,' 'Gold for the Mercy-seat,' and on six of them, 'Freewill-offerings'" (*m. Šeqal.* 6:5). The name "shofar-chests" suggests that the collection boxes were funnel-shaped, like the shofar (the ram's horn trumpet), or that there was a funnel leading into a box. The two "shekel dues" boxes were for collecting either this year's or last year's half-shekel temple offering, which implies that people regularly needed to promise to pay later what they could not afford at present.

In Luke's scene, Jesus has just raked the scribes over the coals for acting like wealthy people—wearing long robes, craving the perks of high status—and for gobbling down the income of widows. Looking up, he then notices rich people making their gifts into these collection spaces. Maybe some are paying off temple dues and others are making freewill gifts. Then he sees the widow—a poor widow, who is first described as "needy (verse 2)" and then "destitute (verse 3)"—put in two *lepta*, each of which makes up 1/128th of a denarius.[3] The denarius, recall, was considered the average pay for one day's work for a day laborer; four denarii make one shekel.[4] Her gift, then, is 1/64th as much as an adult male would hope to make by working in the fields for a day, and 1/128th of the annual temple dues for an adult male. Not so much, in other words.

But Jesus the prophet knows her circumstances: she put in "more than all," because "all of these [rich folks] threw in their gifts out of their abundance, but she, out of her lack, threw in what she had—all her life." By repeating the word "all" three times, Luke hammers on the difference between what the widow did and what every other rich person did: she gave it all. [Not the Amount, but the Proportion]

The connection between the widow throwing in her whole life and the scribes who scarf down widows' houses is intentional. Luke's scribes dress and act like the wealthy who are spotlighted in 21:1. Surely part of the critique is that they do so little in comparison to her whole-life sacrifice; after all, the Lukan Jesus has been telling people to divest themselves of their wealth, to give generously, to lend and expect nothing in return. The rich righteous man of 18:18-25 goes away sad because he cannot give away everything as this widow has done; the rich tax collector of 19:1-10 enters salvation joyfully because he does give away everything. So "give sacrificially," it seems to me, is a correct understanding of this story and consistent with the rest of Luke.

However, the point made at the beginning of this passage is still valid: if Jesus had joined the development staff of the temple, then we cannot account for their hostility against him, nor for his sharp words against the scribes, who in this part of Luke are the allies of the chief priests, the temple leadership. Scribes who "gobble down widows' houses" are located in the temple, and their long robes and prime seats at synagogue are by virtue of the prestige they derive from their service to the temple hierarchy. Connect the dots: some scribes praised Jesus' answer to the Sadducees (20:39-40); Jesus asked them a riddle (20:41-44) and then blasted them in the hearing of all the people (20:45-47); and then, lifting his eyes, he watches how rich people and one poor widow behave. Why aren't these rich scribes noticing the poor widow and making sure that, having given everything to the temple, she will not starve? [Nice Things] As noted in the commentary on 20:41-47, there is an implied contrast between how the chief priests and scribes run the temple and how the followers of Jesus will run their congregation in Jerusalem, where people sell land in order to feed the widows (Acts 4:32-37; 6:1).

Not the Amount, but the Proportion

One's generosity is to be evaluated in terms of one's resources. Generosity is not measured in terms of the amount given; it depends on the attitude of the donor. People who are truly generous give in proportion to what they actually have. It is possible, therefore, that a person who gives a little out of small resources is more generous than another.

Aristotle, *Eth. nic.* 4.1.19; cited in Frederick W. Danker, *Jesus and the New Age: A Commentary on St. Luke's Gospel* rev. ed. (Philadelphia: Fortress, 1988), 328.

Nice Things

Who would want to get in on something where you're miserable, poor, broke and ugly and you just have to muddle through until you get to heaven? . . . I believe God wants to give us nice things.

Joyce Meyer, television preacher, quoted in "Does God Want You to Be Rich?" *Time* 168/12 (18 September 2006): 52.

Mammon

George Frederic Watts (1817–1904). *Mammon*. 1884–85. Oil on canvas, Tate Gallery, London, Great Britain. (Credit: Tate, London/Art Resource, NY)

In this allegorical painting, King Mammon sits with the money in his lap, crushing the man, abusing the woman.

True, in Luke-Acts the temple is a place of revelation (Luke 1:5-23; 2:22-51), and Jesus has essentially occupied the temple in order to teach the people (19:47-48; 21:38). After Jesus' resurrection, the apostles chose the temple as their primary spot to preach about Jesus (2:46; 3:1, 11; 5:12, 25, 42), and keep returning until the persecution begins (8:1). But "the Most High does not dwell in houses made with human hands" (Acts 7:48), and in the long Temple Sermon following this story, Jesus will explain how the temple will be dismantled (21:6). Furthermore, when Jesus exhorts his followers to give everything, he does not say "to the temple," but "to the poor" (6:30; 12:33; 18:22). It is therefore not inconsistent for Luke's Jesus to praise the widow for her willingness to give everything, but condemn the receiving institution, or its leaders, for being blind to her condition.

This, then, is indeed a superlative text to use when speaking to church people of stewardship of resources. Most of us, like the wealthy donors Jesus watched, give from our abundance and give far less than the all that he asked for. So, indeed, cough it up and fork it over; you and I will probably have to rethink our spending and living habits in order to do that, but that would be a good thing. But then there's another level of critique in this story, a critique of the way sacred institutions can absorb resources just as easily as rich individuals. Certainly, the church has bills to pay and salaries to award; but there is no excuse for us when we ask people to "give to the Lord" and then shut our institutional eyes to the needs of the poor. We rich Americans spend too much on ourselves and give too little to God, and we do the same when we organize ourselves into churches. Of course, truly to "give to the Lord" we churches have to rethink our spending patterns; to give more away, we'll need to think outside the box of American business practices, but that would be a good thing. [Christian Prosperity]

The Temple Sermon, Part 1, 21:5-24

The Temple Sermon (Luke 21:5-36) is a literary unit, but the lectionary breaks it into two sections: vv. 5-19, the Gospel lesson for the next-to-last Sunday in ordinary time in Year C, and 21:25-36, the Gospel lesson for the first Sunday in Advent in Year C. As a consequence of this arrangement, churches following the lectionary will hear the last part of the sermon on the first Sunday of the ecclesial year and the first part almost at the last; or to think of it another way, we hear the first part of the sermon on one Sunday and the final part about three years and two weeks later. Well, the last will be first and the first last, according to Jesus.

Because the sermon is rather long, and for the sake of making the divisions of this commentary useful to those who teach and preach the Bible in church, I am treating vv. 5-24 in this section and 25-38 in the next. But let us first take note of the arrangement of the sermon as a whole. I suggest the following outline:

5-6, Observation: Jesus responds by predicting the temple's destruction.
7-11, Question: Jesus begins by warning against quickly assuming that the End is close.
12-19, Flashback: Persecution of Jesus' followers
20-24, Destruction of the temple and aftermath
25-28, Signs of the coming of the Son of Man
29-36, Concluding parable and exhortations: be alert
37-38, Conclusion to Jesus' days of teaching in the temple

Throughout the sermon, Luke is editing Mark—sometimes lightly, sometimes extensively—and the aims of his editing are pretty clear. First, Luke separates, more clearly than Mark, the end of the temple from the end of time. To this end, Luke slightly changes the wording of the question in 21:7, completely rewrites Mark's "desolating sacrilege" section, and inserts a whole new open-ended period—the "times of the Gentiles"—into Mark's sequence of events.

Second, Luke wants to show how Jesus predicted many things that the early church experienced, as laid out in Acts. This both confirms Jesus' status as prophet and gives an important interpretation of the suffering that Jesus and his followers went through; as horrible as those things were, they were predicted and fell within the plan of God.

Third, Luke chooses to make Jesus' final teaching be a warning against the dangers of materialism. "Keep awake" in the final section of Mark's sermon is about being prepared for Christ's sudden return; Luke doesn't drop that, but instead overlays it with the need to beware of being sucked in by the habits of the wealthy.

Luke's "some were saying about the temple" (21:5) and "they asked him" (21:7) are much less specific than Mark's introduction to the sermon, where "one of his disciples" praised the temple's beauty and Peter, James, John, and Andrew asked Jesus about the time of its destruction (Mark 13:1, 3-4). While Luke could have meant us to assume "disciples" from 20:45, those asking Jesus the question address him as "teacher"—something only people who have not become his followers call him (7:40; 8:49; 9:38; 10:25; 11:45; 12:13; 18:18; 19:39; 20:21, 28, 29).[5] More probably, Luke means the question to come from some of the "people" gathered to hear him (20:45; 21:38). This fits with how Luke's Jesus does not leave the temple to preach this sermon, nor deliver it to disciples "alone" (Mark 13:3; Matt 24:3). It is not private or secret instruction about the end of time, but a public warning about the fate of Israel's most important religious institution, the temple.

While the identity of those remarking on the temple's beauty is more vague, their observation is more precise. Mark's nameless disciple says, "Teacher, look what sorts of stones and what sorts of buildings!" Luke's group comments "that the stones and votive offerings erected were beautiful." They were, indeed; see Josephus's remarks about the façade of the sanctuary (the tall building inside the court of the priests containing the "holy place" and the "holy of holies"). [The Beauty of the Temple] "Votive offerings" were adornments donated by wealthy people, often in gratitude for God's blessings. Second Maccabees 9:16-17 describes Antiochus IV Epiphanes, cursed by God with a fatal illness for his persecutions of God's people, repenting and vowing to set up beautiful votive offerings (using the same phrase Luke has). Recall the scenes that immediately precede this one: Jesus scourges the scribes for loving the luxurious life of the wealthy and for destroying widows' houses; a widow then contributes two small coins in contrast to the

The Beauty of the Temple

Now the outward face of the temple in its front wanted nothing that was likely to surprise either men's minds or their eyes, for it was covered all over the plates of gold of great weight, and, at the first rising of the sun, reflected back a very fiery splendor, and made those who forced themselves to look upon it to turn their eyes away, just as they would have done at the sun's own rays. But this temple appeared to strangers, when they were at a distance, like a mountain covered with snow; for as to those parts of it that were not gilt, they were exceeding white.

Josephus, *J.W.* 5.222-23.

gifts of the wealthy. The gifts of the wealthy made possible the gold-plated front of the temple; lovely and impressive, to be sure, but Jesus holds them culpable for their ignorance of the fate of a godly widow and predicts that this will all be demolished.

"These things you see—days are coming in which a stone will not be left upon a stone that will not be torn down." This is now Jesus' third prediction of the demise of the city and the temple:

• "Behold, your household is abandoned" (13:35)
• "Days are coming upon you when your enemies will throw up ramparts against you and encircle you and press on you from all sides, and throw down you and your children in you, and they will not leave a stone upon a stone within you" (19:43-44)

One more prediction is coming in the sermon (vv. 20-24), and yet another as he is on his way to be crucified (23:28-31). Yet the accusation that he threatened the temple is missing from Luke's trial narrative (22:66–23:5; cf. Mark 14:58). Luke treats Jesus' prophecies only as proofs that he was truly inspired by God, since Luke's audience knows that what he predicted came true.

The second question is in two parts. "When will these things be, and what is the sign when these things are about to happen?" is not very different from Mark 13:4. But Luke, by substituting "these things are about to happen" for Mark's "all these things are about to be completed," makes it easier to think of "these things" as the destruction of the temple and nothing more.[6] The predictions of false representatives of Jesus, of wars and insurrections, and of terrifying signs from heaven all belong to this first period—the period leading up to the destruction of the temple—and not to the period before the end of time. It was a bold interpretive strategy, accomplishing several things at once. Between the date when Jesus preached this sermon (say, AD 30, give or take a year or two) and the date the temple fell (AD 70), there were certainly wars, insurrections, famines, earthquakes, etc., in various parts of the empire. A Christian preacher could certainly have named specific places and times as fulfillments of these predictions. Furthermore, Luke's Jesus says plainly that these events are not the prelude to the end; his non-return and the continuation of history into the audience's present are then validations, or at least not disconfirmations, of Jesus' status as prophet.

"When will these things be?" Jesus never answers that, but instead lists several kinds of phenomena that do not indicate that his prediction of "not one stone on another" was about to be fulfilled.

- The appearance of false prophets is no sign, says Jesus. There will be some who try to convince you that "the time is near," says Jesus; they will come in my name and say, "I am"—Luke's predicted false predictors say *egō eimi*, without specifying who they claim to be. Maybe "I am the Messiah," or "I am the return of Jesus," or "I am the prophet sent by Jesus to tell you that his return is close"; any of those is possible.[7] Do not follow them, warns Jesus, and do not conclude that their appearance means the end is nigh.

- Wars and rebellions are also not indicators of anything; they must happen, but don't expect the end soon thereafter (vv. 9-10). "Don't be terrified" can only mean "by those who say that these events are signs of the end." If one is unlucky enough to live in a place overrun by invasion or insurrection, terror is largely unavoidable.

- Likewise, upheavals in the natural order—earthquakes, famines, and plagues, which were often predicted in apocalyptic writings—will happen, but the end is not close (v. 11). These are "portents and great signs from heaven," but signs of what? In Luke's understanding, of nothing in particular; he uses these words because it was inevitable that people would interpret things like comets, meteors, unruly sacrificial animals, or strange weather patterns as signs of an impending disaster. [Josephus on Portents of the Temple's Destruction]

Mark 13 had likewise listed false teachers, "wars and rumors of wars," earthquakes, and famines as "only the beginning" and not the end (Mark 13:5-8). Mark's next section describes how Jesus' followers will be persecuted by various groups, and encourages the audience to think of it both as a chance to spread the gospel and as something that simply must be endured (Mark 13:9-13). Luke, in another bold interpretive move, makes the persecution section a prelude to the wars and earthquakes section: "But before all these things, they will lay their hands on you and persecute you" (21:12). Thus, since wars, famines, earthquakes, and false prophets are not signs of the end, the persecution of Christians is even less a sign, since those kinds of things must happen first.

Luke's description links Jesus' experiences in the Gospel to those of the apostles and Paul in Acts:[8]

- "They will lay hands upon you": Jesus (Luke 20:19); apostles (Acts 4:3, 5:18); Paul (Acts 21:27).

Josephus on Portents of the Temple's Destruction

Josephus includes a section of signs preceding the fall of the temple, which he says the inhabitants of Jerusalem ignored to their peril.

Thus were the miserable people persuaded by these deceivers, and such as belied God himself; while they did not attend nor give credit to the signs that were so evident, and did so plainly foretell their future desolation; but, like men infatuated, without either eyes to see or minds to consider, did not regard the denunciations that God made to them.

Thus there was a star resembling a sword, which stood over the city, and a comet, that continued a whole year. Thus also, before the Jews' rebellion, and before those commotions which preceded the war, when the people were come in great crowds to the feast of unleavened bread, on the eighth day of the month of Xanthikos and at the ninth hour of the night, so great a light shone around the altar and the holy house, that it appeared to be bright daytime; which lasted for half an hour. This light seemed to be a good sign to the unskilful, but was so interpreted by the sacred scribes as to portend those events that followed immediately upon it. At the same festival also, a heifer, as she was led by the high priest to be sacrificed, brought forth a lamb in the midst of the temple. Moreover, the eastern gate of the inner [court of the] temple, which was of brass, and extremely heavy, and had been with difficulty shut by twenty men, and fastened with iron-bound bars, and had bolts sunk very deep into the firm floor, which was there made of one entire stone, was seen to be opened of its own accord about the sixth hour of the night.

Josephus, *J.W.* 6.288-293; cited by Frederick W. Danker, *Jesus and the New Age: A Commentary on St. Luke's Gospel* rev. ed. (Philadelphia: Fortress, 1988), 331.

- "handing you over to synagogues and prisons": Jesus is "handed over" to the "chief priests, officers of the temple police, and elders of the people" (Luke 22:48, 52), and held in the high priest's house (22:54); Saul, acting for the chief priests, "hands over" Christians throughout Palestine to prison (Acts 8:3); Paul claims he was "handed over" to the Romans (Acts 28:17).
- "leading you before kings and governors": Jesus appears before Herod and Pilate (the first a tetrarch, or "quarter-king," and the second a governor, according to Luke 3:1); Paul appears before two governors, Felix and Festus, and before King Agrippa (Herod Agrippa II). The apostles and the rest of the early followers in Judea are hauled up before the temple authorities, but for them Acts narrates no appearances before kings and governors.

As many interpreters observe, Luke uses Jesus' experiences as a template for the apostles and then for Paul. All of them heal and cast out demons; all of them preach the good news in the face of opposition; all of them are violently opposed by the temple leadership. First Jesus, then Stephen, then James the son of Zebedee, and finally Paul (although Acts does not narrate the story of his martyrdom) are killed, each suffering a prophet's death for the sake of the word of God. This strategy pulls two ways: Jesus' identity as prophet is further validated by his correct predictions, and the trajectory from Jesus through the apostles to Paul is also validated by how much the later representatives resemble Jesus.

But some of the material in 21:12-19 seems to speak more directly to the audience, since it does not match material in Acts. Jesus is betrayed by Judas, a traveling and table companion who could be described as a friend, but neither Paul nor any of the apostles are handed over by close associates (21:16); and although all of them encounter hostility, especially from the chief priests, Acts never specifies that the apostles or Paul are hated (21:17). Depending on when and where Luke was written, some of its original audience may have known Christians who were killed after being identified as Christians by their neighbors. Pliny, the governor of Bithynia, wrote a famous letter to the Emperor Trajan around 112 explaining what he did when Christians were exposed:

> Meanwhile, this is the course that I have adopted in the case of those brought before me as Christians. I ask them if they are Christians. If they admit it I repeat the question a second and a third time, threatening capital punishment; if they persist I sentence them to death. For I do not doubt that, whatever kind of crime it may be to which they have confessed, their pertinacity and inflexible obstinacy should certainly be punished. There were others who displayed a like madness and whom I reserved to be sent to Rome, since they were Roman citizens.
>
> Thereupon the usual result followed; the very fact of my dealing with the question led to a wider spread of the charge, and a great variety of cases were brought before me. An anonymous pamphlet was issued, containing many names. All who denied that they were or had been Christians I considered should be discharged, because they called upon the gods at my dictation and did reverence, with incense and wine, to your image which I had ordered to be brought forward for this purpose, together with the statues of the deities; and especially because they cursed Christ, a thing which, it is said, genuine Christians cannot be induced to do.[9]

Most interpreters think Luke wrote in the 80s or 90s, before the practices Pliny describes became widespread; others, dating Luke to the first quarter of the second century, would take Luke 21:16-17 as a reflection of the dangers faced by Luke's original audience. In either case, second-century Christians faced exposure by those who knew them best. In the second-century *Acts of Paul and Thecla*, Thecla's fiancé brings her before the governor[10]; in the second-century *Martyrdom of Polycarp*, the aged bishop is arrested after one of his household slaves confessed under torture: "for it was impossible for him to keep in hiding, since the ones who betrayed him [lit., those handing him over] were members of his own household."[11] Whether or not these martyrologies preserve historical memories, they certainly illustrate what many Christians feared might be their fate. Jesus' advice, then, would have been especially helpful for many of Luke's early readers: persecution is not a sign of the end, but it is something that many of you may need to endure, so here is how to do it.

Luke's Jesus orders his followers not to prepare for martyrdom by rehearsing their last words: "so set down in your hearts not to prepare your apology ahead of time." An apology was a speech given by the defendant or his advocate explaining things from his point of view. Jesus' followers need not rehearse anything, since Jesus (or the Holy Spirit, according to 12:11-12) would teach them what to say, and would give them irrefutable arguments. [Jesus Will Teach You What to Say] Interestingly, Jesus himself is largely silent before his accusers, while the apostles, Stephen, and Paul have plenty to say, but all of them share an innocence before which the accusers can only hurl threats and insults.

Second-century readers of Luke might also think of another reason not to prepare their speeches ahead of time. The *Martyrdom of Polycarp* warns against the overzealous who invite martyrdom:

> For Polycarp waited to be betrayed, as also did the Lord, that we in turn might imitate him, thinking not only of ourselves, but also of our neighbors. For anyone with true and certain love wants not only himself but also all the brothers to be saved.
>
> But there was a person named Quintus, a Phrygian who had recently come from Phrygia, who was overcome with cowardice once he saw the wild beasts. This is the one who compelled both himself and several others to turn themselves in. but the insistent pleas of the proconsul convinced him to take the oath and offer a sacrifice. Because of this, brothers, we do not praise those who hand themselves over, since this is not what the gospel teaches.[12]

Like Mark, Luke urges the readers to think of persecution both as a chance to give testimony (21:13) and as an ordeal to be endured (21:16-19). The second-century martyr texts make the most of both of these themes. Polycarp, ordered to insult Christ, instead praises him: "For eighty-six years I have served him, and he has done me no wrong. How can I blaspheme my king who has saved me?"[13] Having received a vision that he would be burned

Jesus Will Teach You What to Say

The *Martyrdom of Polycarp* describes the deaths of believers in Smyrna in the second century:

> For who would not be astounded by their nobility, endurance, and love of the Master? For they endured even when their skin was ripped to shreds by whips, revealing the very anatomy of their flesh, down to the inner veins and arteries, while bystanders felt pity and wailed. But they displayed such nobility that none of them either grumbled or moaned, clearly showing us all that in that hour, while under torture, the martyrs of Christ had journeyed far away from the flesh, or rather, that the Lord was standing by and speaking to them.

Mart. Pol. 2.2, from *The Apostolic Fathers*, ed. and trans. Bart D. Ehrman, 2 vols. (Cambridge MA: Harvard University Press, 2003), 1.369.

alive, Polycarp asks that he not be nailed to the stake: "Leave me as I am; for the one who enables me to endure the fire will also enable me to remain in the pyre without moving, even without the security of your nails."[14]

Verses 18-19, "Not a hair from your head will perish; by your endurance you will gain your souls," would at first glance seem to promise that those who remained faithful under torture would be able to walk away unscathed. This is the way the story goes with Thecla—thrown to the beasts, she is protected by a lioness; thrown to hungry seals, she is spared while they are killed by a lightning bolt; tied to the feet of bulls, she is saved from being trampled to death—and her invulnerability leads to her eventual release.[15] As Luke knows well, many brave witnesses to Christ die (21:16), and so some interpret the promise in vv. 18-19 as the assurance of God's remembrance and eternal life for the martyrs.[16] However, if we leave vv. 16 and 18-19 in tension, then the passage exhorts all believers to stay faithful under persecution, promising that while some will be killed, others will not be harmed. This, in fact, is the way things happen in Acts, where Saul's persecution leads to death for Stephen and prison for many others, but where the apostles remain in Jerusalem, for the moment untouched by the storm around them (Acts 8:1-3).

In vv. 20-24, Luke thoroughly reworks his source. Mark's "whenever you see the desolating sacrilege set up where it should not be" (Mark 13:14) becomes "whenever you see Jerusalem surrounded by armies, then know that its desolation is close (or has come)." Mark's phrase "the desolating sacrilege" quotes Daniel 9:27 (also 11:31; 12:11); in Daniel, the phrase describes how Antiochus IV Epiphanes, the Syrian king who ruled Palestine, in 167 BC deliberately polluted the temple by setting up an altar to Zeus and sacrificing on it. Here is how 1 Maccabees 1:54-63 describes those events:

> Now on the fifteenth day of Chislev, in the one hundred forty-fifth year, they erected a desolating sacrilege on the altar of burnt offering. They also built altars in the surrounding towns of Judah, and offered incense at the doors of the houses and in the streets. The books of the law that they found they tore to pieces and burned with fire. Anyone found possessing the book of the covenant, or anyone who adhered to the law, was condemned to death by decree of the king. They kept using violence against Israel, against those who were found month after month in the towns.
>   On the twenty-fifth day of the month they offered sacrifice on the altar that was on top of the altar of burnt offering. According to the

decree, they put to death the women who had their children circumcised, and their families and those who circumcised them; and they hung the infants from their mothers' necks.

But many in Israel stood firm and were resolved in their hearts not to eat unclean food. They chose to die rather than to be defiled by food or to profane the holy covenant; and they did die.

The 1 Maccabees text illustrates what Mark's Jesus appears to expect: something like Antiochus's altar set up in the temple, provoking a terrible time of persecution. Luke's Jesus, on the other hand, expects what Luke's audience knows to have been the case—an invading army surrounding the city and eventually laying it waste. By the time you see the army, says Jesus, there will be no hope of salvation for the city. Head for the hills, he urges: anyone inside the city should try to leave (before the army builds the siege walls), and anyone on the outside should keep far away.

In vv. 22-24 Luke strings together phrases from several Old Testament passages dealing with the destruction of Jerusalem, giving us some clue about how he understood the siege and fall of the city to be "a fulfillment of all that has been written." In v. 22, Luke takes the phrase "days of vengeance" from Hosea 9:7 LXX; the larger context in Hosea predicts an inevitable punishment coming on Israel for their sins: they will go into exile and be buried there; their silver will perish; thorns will take over their dwellings; God "will remember their

The Capture of Jerusalem

Marc Chagall. (1887–1985). *The Capture of Jerusalem*. 1957. (Credit: Artist Rights Society, NY)

unrighteousness and take vengeance on their sins." Luke takes v. 23 from Mark, "woe to the pregnant and the nursing mothers in those days," but notice that Hosea 9:14 LXX asks, "Give them, Lord—what will you give them? A miscarrying womb and dry breasts." Verse 24 samples from at least four different prophetic sections:

- "they will fall by the sword's edge": Jeremiah 21:7 LXX, where God promises to give King Zedekiah and the remnant of the inhabitants of Jerusalem over to the Babylonians, who will "cut them down with the sword's edge"
- "and they will be taken as exiles into all the nations": Zechariah 14:1-2 LXX, in which God promises to gather "all the nations" to war against Jerusalem, with the result that half the city is taken into exile
- "And Jerusalem will be trampled under by the nations": Zechariah 12:3 LXX: "And it shall be on that day that I will set Jerusalem as a stone to be walked upon by all the nations." Recall the end of Jesus' parable of the wicked tenants? His testimony, the word of God, is like a rejected stone that nevertheless crushes those who stand against it (20:17-18); Jerusalem, however, will be dismantled, stone by stone, and used as paving stones by the nations who will dominate the city.
- "until the times of the nations are fulfilled": Tobit 14:4-5 LXX (BA text): "Go into Media, child, because I am persuaded that everything that Jonah the prophet spoke concerning Nineveh will come to pass, but in Media there will be peace yet for a time, and then our brothers in the Land will be taken as exiles from the good Land, and Jerusalem will be a desert, and the house of God in her shall be burned down and shall be deserted for a time. But then God will again have mercy upon them and will return them to the Land, and they will build the house, not like the first, until the times of the ages are fulfilled."

The city will fall, then, and the temple with it—not one stone left on another—and this ravaged condition will persist for some indeterminate time, the "times of the nations" or "times of the Gentiles." Thus, not only are there no clear indicators for when the temple will fall, but its fall will inaugurate an open-ended period where "the nations"—read Rome—will have sway over the holy city and the house of God. [Another Prediction of Jerusalem's Fall]

Luke pictures Jesus delivering these woes to the crowds and to his disciples while standing in the temple. "Great misery upon the Land (Judea, in other words) and wrath for this people" is not good news at all, particularly when the prophet delivering the blow indicates no means of escape. Jesus didn't give them any sort of timetable or early warning signs; wars, famines, celestial disturbances, etc., would not help them know the temple's doom was near. In the story Luke has created, Jesus' sermon is pretty fatalistic—this is going to happen, and when you see it, do your best to stay out of the way.

Read aloud in Luke's own time to a group of Christians in some part of the empire, this scene would have a completely different tone. The destruction of the temple was old news; Jesus' description of how things would happen fit the way they turned out. That bolsters Jesus' reputation as a prophet. Throughout the Temple Sermon, Jesus stresses how there are no sure signs that the end is near and no reliable forecasters of the coming judgment. That, Luke probably hoped, would cut down on useless speculation and endless speculators about the end. Mostly the sermon tells us what not to do: don't believe anyone who tells you that the end is close; don't follow anyone who wants to use Jesus' name and authority to sell books and videos and charts and game systems and television networks and evangelistic crusades, all with the aim of telling you when and how the world will end. Don't listen to them, don't buy from them, don't believe them, and don't be frightened by them.

When the sermon gets around to positive instruction, it tells us to endure. When we are hated, arrested, or betrayed, endure. In other words, there will be hard times that befall Christians because they bear Christ's name. Use this as an opportunity to tell your story, says Jesus, and stick it out—notice that he makes no promise to snatch you away before the bad times come. The "times of the nations" have to go on for a while, and then things will happen, but in the meantime, "by your endurance you will gain your souls."

Another Prediction of Jerusalem's Fall

Sibylline Oracle 4 is generally considered to have been written not long after the death of Alexander the Great and then revised in the late 1st century AD. It is a Jewish document, with little or no Christian overwriting. The passage on the fall of Jerusalem is thus probably approximately contemporaneous with Luke. Note how the author moves quickly from the events of the fall to the larger politics of Rome; note how vague, by contrast, Luke's "times of the nations" appears. The "great king" who flees is Nero, who killed his own mother; this author is one of many ancients who believed that Nero fled Rome rather than being assassinated. After his death/disappearance, there were three emperors in eighteen months, and then Vespasian, who had been sent to Syria to deal with the Jewish revolt, was acclaimed emperor with the support of the armies. The "leader of Rome" who burns the temple is Vespasian's son Titus.

An evil storm of war will also come upon Jerusalem .
From Italy, and it will sack the great Temple of God,
Whenever they put their trust in folly and cast off piety
And commit repulsive murders in front of the Temple.
Then a great king will flee from Italy like a runaway slave
Unseen and unheard over the channel of the Euphrates,
When he dares to incur a maternal curse for repulsive murder
And many other things, confidently, with a wicked hand.
When he runs away, beyond the Parthian land,
Many will bloody the ground for the throne of Rome.
A leader of Rome will come to Syria who will burn
The Temple of Jerusalem with fire, at the same time slaughter
Many men and destroy the great land of the Jews with its broad roads.
Then indeed an earthquake will destroy at once Salamis and Paphos
When the dark water overwhelms Cyprus, which is washed by many waves.

Sibylline Oracle 4.115-129.

Temple Sermon, Conclusion, 21:25-38

Doubtless, gentle reader, you have not been drawn by my compelling arguments and sparkling prose to read this commentary from beginning to end; if I'm wrong, then please forgive me repeating some of the introduction from the previous unit. The Temple Sermon (Luke 21:5-36) is a literary unit, but the lectionary breaks it into two sections: vv. 5-19, the Gospel lesson for the next-to-last Sunday in ordinary time in Year C, and 21:25-36, the Gospel lesson for the first Sunday in Advent in Year C. If you are reading this part to get ready for Advent, I'd urge you also to read the preceding section, to see how this second part fits with the first.

After Jesus predicted that the temple would be taken apart stone by stone, "someone"—probably someone from the crowds who had been listening to Jesus' daily instruction sessions in the temple since 19:47—asked Jesus when it would happen. Rather than telling when, Jesus gave a list of events that, he said, were not signs for when the temple would fall: wars, famines, false Christian teachers, and cosmic disturbances would all happen, but none of this meant anything. Jesus predicted that his followers would be persecuted, and some even put to death. This, he said would happen *before* all the non-indicators, so that his listeners should not interpret oppression and martyrdom as proof that the time was short. If anybody tells you otherwise, he says—if anybody tells you "the time is near," even if they come in Jesus' name—do not believe them and do not go after them. The first "sign" that really counts is the appearance of the army camps surrounding Jerusalem, and by then it will be too late to do anything but run.

The destruction of the city and the temple had happened at least a couple of decades, if not longer, before Luke wrote. For Luke's audiences, 21:5-24 mostly functioned to validate Jesus as a prophet, to urge them not to pay attention to those who predicted the end of the world, and to encourage them to endure hard times, using them as a chance to testify to their faith. Luke closes that part of the Temple Sermon by predicting that Jerusalem would be trodden under by the nations until the "times of the nations are fulfilled." How long would that take? Who knows; better not worry about it—just keep your mind on what you're supposed to be doing.

With so much effort going into saying "it's not the end—don't listen to anyone who tells you that the end is close—there are no signs that can tell you that the end is close," one wonders why Luke didn't just omit the whole apocalyptic sermon. Mark 13, his source, also emphasized how the periods of tumults and persecutions were only the beginning, but at least Mark gave one sign—the appearance of the desolating sacrilege in the temple—that believers could think of as the knot on the well-rope that lets you know you're almost at the end. In Luke's version, that gets transformed into the destruction of the city—twenty or more years in the past, for Luke's first readers—and then the nebulous "times of the nations." But then, beginning with v. 25, we read what does sound like signs that predict the return of Christ and the coming of the end.

All ancient peoples thought that cosmic events, particularly unusual ones, were harbingers of something. [Romans and Heavenly Signs] For example, here are two passages, the first from from *Sibylline Oracle* 3.796-806, and the second from *4 Ezra* (=2 Esdras) 6:17-24, both Jewish documents roughly contemporary with Luke:

> I will tell you a very clear sign, so that you may know
> When the end of all things comes to pass on earth:
> When swords are seen at night in starry heaven
> Toward evening and toward dawn,
> And again dust is brought forth from heaven
> Upon the earth and all the light of the sun
> Is eclipsed in the middle from heaven, and the rays
> Of the moon appear and return to the earth.
> There will be a sign from the rocks, with blood and drops of gore.
> You will see a battle of infantry and cavalry in the clouds,
> Like a hunt of wild beasts, like a mist.

When I heard this, I got to my feet and listened; a voice was speaking, and its sound was like the sound of mighty waters. It said, "The days are coming when I draw near to visit the inhabitants of the earth, and when I require from the doers of iniquity the penalty of their iniquity, and when the humiliation of Zion is complete. When the seal is placed upon the age that is about to pass away, then I will show these signs: the books shall be opened before the face of the firmament, and all shall see my judgment together. Children a year old shall speak with their voices, and pregnant women shall give birth to premature children at three and four months, and these shall live and leap about. Sown places shall suddenly appear unsown, and full storehouses shall suddenly be found to be empty; the trumpet shall sound aloud, and when all hear it, they shall suddenly be terrified. At that time friends shall make war on friends like enemies, the earth and those who inhabit it shall be terrified, and the springs of the fountains shall stand still, so that for three hours they shall not flow."

Romans and Heavenly Signs

One of Augustus's many campaigns was the reform of official state religion in Rome. Suetonius writes that after Augustus became *pontifex maximus*—high priest of the official cult of Rome—"he collected whatever prophetic writings of Greek or Latin origin were in circulation anonymously or under the names of irresponsible authors and burned more than 2,000 of them, retaining only the Sibylline Books and making a selection even among these; and he deposited them in two gilded cases under the pedestal of the Palatine Apollo" where they would be used under his guidance to interpret unusual events as "signs" of what policy decisions should be made.

Quote from Suetonius, *Life of Augustus* 31, cited in Lewis and Reinhold, *The Empire*, vol. 2 of *Roman Civilization* (New York: Harper and Row, 1966), 55–56.

Compared to the signs listed by these two passages, or even compared to Mark 13:24-25, Luke's signs are vague. "Signs in the sun and moon and stars"—what signs? Mark is fairly specific: the stars fall, the sun goes dark, and the moon turns to blood (Mark 13:24, citing Joel 3:4 LXX). While that is happening among the heavenly bodies, on the earth there will be "distress of nations in confusion" and "roaring of seas and wave."[17] Huh? When does the sea not roar? And since Jesus had already predicted wars and revolutions among the nations (21:9-11), how is the addition of "confusion" going to mark a noticeable change? ("According to a recent poll, 65 percent of the member nations of the UN say they don't understand what's going on in the world, so the end must be close. More from our reporter in New York . . . .")

Verse 26 is a bit more specific: " . . . while people are fainting from fear and expectation of the things coming upon the earth, for the powers of the heavens will be shaken." Luke takes the part after the comma from Mark 13:25, who may have taken it from a variant text of Isaiah 34:4 LXX, where some manuscripts have "all the powers of the heavens will be dissolved.[18] The image of large groups of people fainting from dread of what is about to happen is reminiscent of the scene in 2 Maccabees 3:13-21, where the city of Jerusalem is in great distress because Heliodorus, servant of King Seleucus of Antioch, had been sent by the king to pilfer the temple treasury:

> But Heliodorus, because of the orders he had from the king, said that this money must in any case be confiscated for the king's treasury. So he set a day and went in to direct the inspection of these funds. There was no little distress throughout the whole city. The priests prostrated themselves before the altar in their priestly vestments and called toward heaven upon him who had given the law about deposits, that he should keep them safe for those who had deposited them. To see the appearance of the high priest was to be wounded at heart, for his face and the change in his color disclosed the anguish of his soul. For terror and bodily trembling had come over the man, which plainly showed to those who looked at him the pain lodged in his heart. People also hurried out of their houses in crowds to make a general supplication because the holy place was about to be brought into dishonor. Women, girded with sackcloth under their breasts, thronged the streets. Some of the young women who were kept indoors ran together to the gates, and some to the walls, while others peered out of the windows. And holding up their hands to heaven, they all made supplication. There was something pitiable in the prostration of the whole populace and the anxiety of the high priest in his great anguish. (2 Macc 3:13-21)

The similarity between this account and Luke's also points up, again, Luke's lack of specificity. The people of Jerusalem have plenty of reason to tremble when Heliodorus shows up; he "set a day" when everyone knew what was about to happen. But in Luke's scheme, there are no time markers: the destruction of Jerusalem is followed by an elastic "times of the Gentiles," which comes to a close accompanied by the same kinds of things that, according to vv. 7-11, in an earlier period did not mean that the end was close. How is a person to be able to spot the real end of time when it happens?

You can't—that's the point. This is consistent with what Luke's Jesus said earlier, when asked when the kingdom of God would arrive: it isn't the sort of thing that comes in a predictable manner, and when it gets here, you won't need anyone to point it out to you (17:20-37). Signs are useless as predictors of its near arrival, and unnecessary as indicators of its presence—the kingdom is already near, and when it arrives, you'll know. Just as the only "sign" that showed when Jerusalem was about to fall was the appearance of the Roman legions encircling the city, the only "sign" of Jesus' coming that amounts to anything is his appearance. Luke 21:27 repeats Mark 13:26, in turn adapted from Daniel 7:13 LXX. "They will see"—i.e., everyone, including his enemies, will see—Jesus coming with the power of heaven. When this happens, according to 21:28, stand up straight and lift your head, because your rescue has drawn close. [Redemption or Rescue?]

Luke follows Mark in placing the parable of the fig tree next (although in Luke, it is the parable of the fig tree and all other trees). The appearance of leaves is an obvious sign that summer is near. True—leaves come out in the spring, so they show that summer is just around the bend. "So it is with you" (v. 31)—just as you can see the leaves and know what season it is, so

Redemption or Rescue?

AΩ The word here translated "rescue" is *apolytrōsis*, which is often translated "ransom" or "redemption" in other contexts. Mark 10:45, to which Luke has no parallel, uses the root word *lytron*, "ransom," to describe the purpose or effect of Jesus' death. Here, "rescue" is more appropriate, and the circumstances of how Jesus' followers will be rescued at his coming will be amplified in vv. 34-36.

"whenever you see these things happening, you know that the kingdom of God is near." Well, yes: when you see the buzzards, you know the location of the corpse (17:37). When you see the armies around Jerusalem, you know its desolation is only a matter of time (21:20). When you, and all the rest of the world, see Jesus coming on the clouds, then you know that the kingdom of God finally will replace the kingdoms of this world.

Thus by the time Luke arrives at Mark 13:30-31—the promise that Jesus would return within a generation—he has redirected, if not subverted, its force. In Mark, "this generation" was probably meant to describe the audience for the saying—Jesus' apostles, in other words. And even if that is not how Mark understood it, other New Testament passages show that many early Christians believed that Jesus promised to return within the lifetime of the Twelve (see John 21:23, 2 Pet 3:3-4; both passages are attempts to reinterpret this belief). But in Luke, "this generation" means those who see what is predicted in vv. 25-28, where the only clear predictor of Jesus' return is—well, Jesus swooping out of heaven on the clouds.[19]

By this time, we begin to wonder is Luke is pulling our legs, because he has given us a series of non-indicators (21:7-11); then a prequel to the non-indicators (21:12-19); then the destruction of Jerusalem—already old news when Luke wrote (21:20-23); then a nonspecific period when the Gentiles control Jerusalem (21:24); then a time of general confusion (21:25-26); and then Jesus appears. Think of the marketplace scene in *Life of Brian* where one of the prophets predicts, in a mumbly way, "There shall be in that time rumors of things going astray, and there shall be a great confusion as to where things really are." Perhaps it goes too far to call Luke 21:5-33 a satire on the typical apocalyptic sermon, but it surely seems to be designed to give no traction for those who want a clear timetable for the future; if it isn't satire, it's prophetic Jell-O.

But with vv. 34-36, Luke is back to comfortable terrain, and his rhetoric becomes much more specific. The Temple Sermon closes with material he has used before. Don't let your hearts be weighed down with dissipation and drunkenness and life's worries: witness the rich fool who thought he had nothing to do but eat, drink, and celebrate (12:13-21), and Dives, who ate sumptuously every day while Lazarus starved on his doorstep (16:19-31). The parable of the sower warned that "life's worries" were like thorns that can choke the growth of the word of God in a person's heart (8:11-15). The remedy, as Jesus has said several times in Luke, is to divest oneself of stuff: sell it, give it away, and seek only the kingdom of God. Otherwise, the day—the day when Jesus returns and the Judgment commences, or the day of one's death, as in the parables of the rich fool and Dives and Lazarus—will catch you napping.

The path to salvation is hard work, as Luke describes it. Materialism is a hard demon to shake. Which of us can obey his commands to "sell your stuff and give to charity" (12:33) or to "give to everyone who asks, and if anyone takes away your stuff, don't ask for it back" (6:30)? The thorns of materialism are what we have to flee, it seems to me, in order to be able to stand before the Son of Man when he comes. Some Christians in other times and in other parts of the world now face hatred and potential martyrdom for their faith; for them, the appearance of Jesus would be a rescue and an escape from the powers of evil. But for most of us reading this commentary, in order truly to obey our Lord and stand before him on that day, we'd need to be ripped up out of the briar patch of possessions, the pursuit of profit, and the profligate consumption of our world's resources. Do we really want to be rescued, if it means giving up our affluent lifestyles?

The sermon ends, and Luke closes the scene with a summary description of Jesus' time between the entry into Jerusalem and the Last Supper. Every day—however long Luke imagines that to have been—Jesus taught in the temple precincts, surrounded by crowds. Every night he would exit and sleep on the Mount of Olives. The summary, reaching back to 19:47-48, encloses Jesus' temple teaching ministry and draws this section to a close. It also emphasizes, again, that the presence and earnest attention of the people to Jesus' teaching prevented his early arrest by the temple authorities (19:48; 22:2), and sets up his remark in 22:52-53 that they could only arrest him because of Satan's involvement. Finally, it sets up the exegetical puzzle of chapter 23, where the people, who have risen early to hear him teach, also take part in his condemnation.

CONNECTIONS

According to tradition, the temple fell on the ninth day of the Jewish month of Ab, a date that quickly became a time of fasting and mourning: "In the week wherein falls the 9th of Ab it is forbidden to cut the hair or wash the clothes . . . . On the eve of the 9th of Ab let none eat of two cooked dishes, let none eat flesh, and let none drink wine" (*m. Ta'an.* 4:7). Josephus wrote that "the multitude of those that therein [in Jerusalem] perished exceeded all the destructions that either men or God ever brought upon the world" (*J. W.* 6.429); his hyperbole gets at how awful an event it was. So, too, for Jesus, who longed to protect the city (13:34) and who wept at his clear vision of its destruction (19:41-44). When we read about Jerusalem "surrounded by armies," we should think about the misery that the Roman siege created; when we read of the citizens of Jerusalem being slain by the sword or being led captive, we should know that this really happened:

> Together with those whom they had orders to slay, they slew the aged and the infirm; . . . as for the rest of the multitude that were above

seventeen years old, he put them into bonds, and sent them to the Egyptian mines. Titus also sent a great number into the provinces, as a present to them, that they might be destroyed upon their theaters, by the sword and by the wild beasts; but those that were under seventeen years of age were sold for slaves. (Josephus, *J. W.* 6.415-18)

Unfortunately, ancient believers often held up the tragedy of the fall of Jerusalem as God's vengeance on Jerusalem for killing Jesus:

For He forewarned them, that however worthy the temple might be accounted by them of all admiration, yet at its season it would be destroyed from its foundations, being thrown down by the power of the Romans, and all Jerusalem burnt with fire, and retribution exacted of Israel for the slaughter of the Lord. For after the Savior's crucifixion, such were the things which it was their lot to suffer.[20]

Notice that Luke 21 says not a word about this. It would be more in keeping with Luke's Jesus for Christian interpreters to lament the death and destruction of AD 70 than to use it as proof of God's displeasure with ancient Israel.

The chapter urges its Christian audience to hold on and to bear up. "They will persecute you . . . by your endurance you will gain your souls." Jesus' followers are to expect tough going, and counseled that when people generally are falling out from their terror of the chaos around them, they should "stand up and raise your heads." When times are hard, then, be steadfast, and take the opportunities that come to give witness.

The chapter also warns the same audience about the dangers of prosperity, about how their hearts might be "weighed down" by overindulgence and worries about money. For Christians like that—like most of us—the day of the Lord will seem less like a rescue and more like a surprise IRS audit. Pray, says Jesus; pray that you will be strong enough to flee from these things—not just the unpleasant consequences of Judgment Day, but flee also the materialist lifestyle that will sink our lives.

When Luke wrote this chapter, at least fifty years had passed since Jesus had preached that the coming of the kingdom of God was near. When we read it in church, two millennia have come and gone; we cannot hope to hear "near" in the same way Luke's audience did. We can make the same exegetical move as 2 Peter 3:8-10 and redefine "near" as taking into account God's eternity—what does "soon" mean to God, to whom past, present, and future are all the same? Or we can think of Christ's return as a variant of the promise that even when we die, we are not lost to God, and that

Christ will gather us to our eternal home. There are many options, including insisting on the ethical necessity of believing that Jesus could return at any moment; ethical, that is, in the sense that 21:34-36 uses Jesus' return as the threat that keeps us focused on living by his teachings. The important point, I think, is that we retain Jesus' conviction that the present age, full of wars and famines and plagues, characterized both by persecution and corruption of the faithful, is not permanent, and does not represent a full experience of God's justice. Stand firm; hold fast; give in neither to hard times nor to prosperity, for your redemption is coming.

NOTES

[1] Frances R. Havergal, "Take My Life," 1874 (public domain).

[2] Sylvanus Dryden Phelps, "Savior, Thy Dying Love" 1862 (public domain).

[3] BAGD, 592.

[4] John J. Rousseau and Rami Arav, *Jesus and His World* (Minneapolis MN: Fortress, 1995), 57.

[5] So Joel B. Green, *The Gospel of Luke* (NICNT; Grand Rapids: Eerdmans, 1997), 734; Alan R. Culpepper, *The Gospel of Luke* (*NIB*, vol. 9; Nashville: Abingdon, 1995), 399; contra Luke Timothy Johnson, *The Gospel of Luke* (SP, vol. 3; Collegeville MN: Liturgical Press, 1991), 320, who takes it to be disciples.

[6] Joseph A. Fitzmyer, *The Gospel According to Luke* (AB 28 and 28A; Garden City NY: Doubleday, 1981), 2.1331.

[7] Culpepper, *Luke*, 400, "I am the Christ"; so also John Nolland, *Luke* (WBC, vols. 35A-C; Dallas TX: Word, 1989-93), 3.991, although he also notes that "I am speaking for Christ, who has secretly returned" is possible. Fitzmyer, *Luke*, 2.1336, opts for "I am Christ's representative." Frederick W. Danker, *Jesus and the New Age: A Commentary on St. Luke's Gospel* (rev. ed.; Philadelphia: Fortress, 1988), 330, opts for "false prophets."

[8] Culpepper, *Luke*, 400–01; Green, *Luke*, 736–37; Robert C. Tannehill, *Luke* (ANTC; Nashville: Abingdon, 1996), 303–304.

[9] Pliny, *Epistles* X.96; translation in Henry Bettenson, ed., *Documents of the Christian Church* (London: Oxford University Press, 1977), 3–4.

[10] *Acts of Paul and Thecla* 27; *New Testament Apocrypha* 2.244.

[11] *Mart. Pol.* 6:2 from *The Apostolic Fathers*, ed. and trans. Bart D. Ehrman, 2 vols. (Cambridge MA: Harvard University Press, 2003), 1.375.

[12] *Mart. Pol.* 1, 4; Ehrman, *Apostolic Fathers*, 1.367-69, 373.

[13] *Mart. Pol.* 9:3; Ehrman, *Apostolic Fathers*, 381.

[14] *Mart. Pol.* 13:3; Ehrman, *Apostolic Fathers*, 385–87.

[15] *Acts of Paul and Thecla* 32–38; *New Testament Apocrypha*, 2.245-46.

[16] Green, *Luke*, 737–38; Tannehill, *Luke*, 304; Danker, *Jesus and the New Age*, 332.

[17] Luke's syntax is not clear in this section. Johnson, *Luke*, 327, understands the fainting of v. 26 to be as the result of the sea's roaring; Fitzmyer, *Luke*, 2.1349, and many others take the roaring as the cause of the confusion of the nations. I understand v. 25 to be giving signs in three quadrants: heavens, earth, and sea.

[18] So Fitzmyer, *Luke*, 2.1350; Johnson, *Luke*, 328.

[19] So Fitzmyer, *Luke*, 2.1353; Culpepper, *Luke*, 408; Johnson, *Luke*, 330.

[20] Cyril of Alexandria, *Commentary on the Gospel of Saint Luke* (trans. R. Payne Smith; New York: Studion, 1983), homily 139.

THE SUPPER, BETRAYAL, AND ARREST

Luke 22

COMMENTARY

Plots and Preparations, 22:1-13

Earlier, at the comments on 19:28-48, I noted how the material in chapters 22–23 fit into Luke's story of Jesus in Jerusalem. For whatever reasons, Luke chose not to retain Mark's chronological markers of a Passion Week. Instead, chapters 20 and 21 take place over an unspecified period of time. But while we do not know what day it is, we do know—because Luke tells us more than once—where Jesus is; namely, in the temple. And we know what he is doing throughout that section: he is teaching the crowds, the "people," who gather around him from early morning until evening to listen to him teach.

In this section, several things change. First, we begin to get chronological notations: "The feast of unleavened bread, also called 'Passover,' was getting close." In v. 7, the first day of the feast arrives, which would be Maundy Thursday in the church calendar. Everything from 22:7 through 23:56 happens between Thursday evening and Friday evening—a much more concentrated pace than in the rest of the Gospel. Second, Luke tells us how Jesus' enemies were powerless to seize him until Satan possessed Judas. Satan, whom Jesus resisted in 4:1-13 and saw fall from heaven in 10:18, now reappears, and Jesus will admit in 22:53 that this period is Satan's hour. Third, Jesus leaves the temple for good. The disciples are sent into the city to arrange for a room for the paschal meal, so on the basis of 21:37, we are probably to imagine Jesus, in v. 8, giving his instructions from the Mount of Olives.

The Festival of Unleavened Bread, commemorating the Israelites' exodus from Egypt, begins with the Passover meal. All leaven, and all products made with it, were removed from the house. A special meal was prepared, traditionally with a roasted lamb as the main course. For those lucky enough (and physically and financially able) to make

Luke 22

the pilgrimage to Jerusalem, the lamb would be slaughtered in the temple. For any of Luke's readers familiar with the holiday, 22:1 would convey a sense of expectation—thousands of Jews from all over the empire making the trek to Jerusalem; millions of Jews, wherever they were, busily making preparations for the big meal and the weeklong celebration to follow; people buying, traveling, and gathering, all to celebrate God's mighty act of freeing Israel from bondage.

The chief priests would have had plenty to do, one expects, to prepare for the holidays and its influx of worshipers—making sure there would be enough priests to take care of the multitudes, making sure that all the cleansing preparations had been done, etc. But Luke depicts them "searching," along with their secretaries and advisors (the scribes), to find a way to kill Jesus. Why not just grab him and do it? "They feared the people"—the same factor that had prevented their arresting him since he entered the city.

At this point, Mark has the story of Jesus' anointing by an anonymous woman while he sat at table in the house of Simon the leper in Bethany. Luke has already used a variant on that story—the one where Jesus, in the house of Simon the Pharisee, had his feet washed and anointed by another nameless woman (7:36-50). In Mark's arrangement, the anointing is sandwiched between the wish of the chief priests for a way to destroy Jesus and Judas's offer of help. This sandwiching, or intercalation, offers Mark's reader a chance to contrast the way one woman "does what she could" to respond to Jesus' imminent death, with how Judas and the chief priests are conspiring to cause his death, and with the rest of the apostles, who do nothing except complain about the woman's gift. But Luke prefers to move right to how Judas came to hand Jesus over. Perhaps, as many commentators suggest, Luke omits the story here because he does not generally repeat material. But Luke also seems to want to diminish the guilt heaped on Jesus' followers for their failures surrounding Jesus' crucifixion.

In any case, Satan entered Judas Iscariot (in case you forgot, Luke reminds you that he was one of the Twelve). He then went to converse with the chief priests and the "temple officers" about how to hand Jesus over to them. [Officers of the Temple] They "rejoiced" and made a deal with

Officers of the Temple

$A\Omega$ Luke uses a word that often means "generals" in other Greek writers (*stratēgoi*). In Acts 16, he uses it to mean the chief officials of Philippi; here, he cannot mean the people in charge of the temple, because that would be the chief priests. Because of the military background of the term, and because we know from other sources that the temple had Jewish guards or sergeants-at-arms to keep order and to guard the money, most people assume that Luke is here meaning the officers in charge of the guards. So the term is sometimes translated "officers of the Temple police" (so Green, 751). Others suggest that these were the people in charge of the money—the head accountants or bursars or business managers—appropriate since the contract with Judas involves payment (so Fitzmyer, 2.1375).

Joel B. Green, *The Gospel of Luke* (NICNT; Grand Rapids: Eerdmans, 1997).

Joseph A. Fitzmyer, *The Gospel According to Luke* (AB 28 and 28A; Garden City NY: Doubleday, 1981).

him: they would give him money, and he would take over their "search" for a chance to nab Jesus when the crowds were not present.

Judas presented something of a riddle for the evangelists. Mark 14:10-11 gave no motive at all for his decision to conspire with the chief priests, and the offer of money came after they struck a deal. Mark 14:21 explains that the betrayal was forecast in Scripture, but aside from that, there is no explanation. Matthew plays up the money. In Matthew 26:14-16, Judas goes to ask the chief priests how much he can get for handing Jesus over, and they agree on the famous "thirty pieces of silver." Both John (in 13:2) and Luke go an extra step; only the agency of Satan could explain how one of Jesus' closest associates acted in such a way. He was possessed, and not just by a mere demon; Satan took him over. Luke, in fact, understands all the Twelve to be under satanic attack on this night (22:31), and only Jesus' intercession protected them (22:32). Like Mark, Luke believes that Judas was at the table when Jesus conducted the supper (22:21), so we are to understand that final night as a spiritual battle between Satan and Jesus, of which the possession in 22:3 is the opening salvo.

Like Mark, Luke believed that Scripture predicted Judas's betrayal, but also that Judas still bore the guilt for his perfidy (22:23). Unlike Matthew, who includes a scene where Judas repents and attempts to make restitution for his crime by recanting his testimony and returning the money (Matt 27:3-10), Luke's Judas moves on with his life, using his ill-gotten gain to buy a field. There's no repentance or possible absolution for him in Luke—while inspecting his new property, he fell and "burst open in the middle and all his bowels gushed out" (Acts 1:18). Gruesome! So Luke's Judas becomes the tool of the devil, and instead of leaving everything to follow Jesus, he hands Jesus over for pay and invests the money in real estate. Luke's Judas is another version of the rich fool or Dives

Judas's Betrayal

Canavesio, Giovanni and Giovanni Baleison. *Judas Receiving Money from the High Priest*. 1492. Fresco. Chapelle Notre Dame des Fontaines, La Brigue, Alpes Maritimes, France. (Credit: © François Guenet / Art Resource, NY)

Judas in the *Gospel of Judas*

The recent discovery of the *Gospel of Judas*—a Gnostic text in Coptic, probably composed around the middle of the 2d century—gives us yet another version of Christianity's premier villain. The author of the text believed that the physical body was corrupt, and that Jesus needed to shed it in order to ascend back to the true, hidden God. So, along with a full explanation about the nature of the cosmos, Jesus tells Judas to betray him: "But you [Judas] will exceed all of them [i.e., the other apostles who, by sticking to Judaism, are worshiping false gods]. For you will sacrifice the man that clothes me."

Text in Rudolphe Kasser, Marvin Meyer, and Gregor Wurst, *The Gospel of Judas* (Washington, D.C.: National Geographic, 2006), 43.

(the rich man who ignored Lazarus). [Judas in the *Gospel of Judas*]

According to the Jewish lunar calendar, Passover fell on the first full moon after the spring equinox, on the 14th day of the month Nisan. Each day started at sundown, so 22:7 refers to the daylight hours of the 13th of Nisan, when Jews in Jerusalem would be taking their lambs to the temple to be slaughtered, as well as preparing the rest of the food for the Passover meal: unleavened bread, bitter herbs, salt water, and a sweet fruit mixture, along with other vegetables and salad that were eaten without being part of the ceremony. [The Passover Meal] So, according to Luke, Jesus orders Peter and John to go into Jerusalem and get everything ready; they ask him where, and he tells them how to find a hospitable host. This changes Mark in two ways; Mark has the disciples ask Jesus first, but does not specify which two disciples. The first change is in the service of Luke's characterization of Jesus as a prophet; Jesus knows what to do without being asked, and knows what they will find when they go into Jerusalem. His detailed prediction of what they will see and how the person will respond reminds us of 19:30-31, where he also sent two disciples into Bethany to borrow the colt.

The second change, spotlighting Peter and John, previews the two of the Twelve who will have the biggest role in the early chapters of Acts. Jesus' choice of them to make all the necessary preparations for Jesus' final meal before the cross helps pave the way for their leadership in the second volume of Luke's work. Jesus tells them, "As you are going into the city, a man carrying a water jar will meet you; follow him . . . ." Commentators discuss whether the sight of a man carrying water would have been unusual;[1] not necessarily, since slaves often prepared and served meals, and since some male slaves worked both in the fields and in the kitchen (see Luke 17:7-8).[2] The water-bearer simply leads the disciples to the house, where they meet the owner, who shows them the place they will use. As we have seen earlier, slaves are often almost invisible in Luke, and Luke copies this slave from Mark, but his presence heightens an ironic (perhaps unintentionally so) contrast. The disciples "follow" him, just as they have followed Jesus, who will describe himself as a servant (22:27). They will prepare the Passover meal (v. 13), just as the water-carrying servant is almost certainly doing for his master's household; at this moment, they are most

The Passover Meal

Josephus says that once Cestius, legate of Syrian when Nero was emperor, asked the chief priests to estimate how many Jewish pilgrims came to Jerusalem for Passover. They counted lambs slaughtered rather than people, and multiplied by ten, as a sort of average size of each group sharing a lamb; there were "two hundred and fifty-six thousand five hundred lambs," so Josephus estimates "two million seven hundred thousand and two hundred persons" (*J.W.* 6.422-427). Most think his numbers were inflated, but agree that between 300,000 and half a million people crammed into Jerusalem for the festivals.

At one lamb for ten persons, that's still a lot of lambs to kill in one afternoon. The Mishnah says that the people came in three groups; when the first group filled up the temple court, a shofar sounded, the gates were shut, and the priests got to work slaughtering the lambs. "The priests stood in rows and in their hands were basins of silver and basins of gold . . . An Israelite slaughtered his own offering and the priest caught the blood. The priest passed the basin to his fellow, and he to his fellow, each receiving a full basin and giving back an empty one. The priest nearest to the altar tossed the blood in one action against the base" (*m. Pesah.* 5:5-6). After the blood was drained, the lamb would need to be flayed and eviscerated, and the internal organs given to the priest to be burned on the altar. Imagine, then, an assembly line of sorts, with men and lambs coming in one side of the Court of Israel and leaving by the other with the carcasses ready to take home and cook. The other possibility is that the priests consecrated part of the outer courts in order to conduct so many sacrifices in so short a space of time.

Exod 12:1-20 specifies a roasted lamb eaten with unleavened bread and bitter herbs. Philo, in the fragmentary *Questions and Answers on Exodus*, book 1, discusses these rules: roasted, for speed and for simplicity (he says you add spices to boiled meat but not to roasted); unleavened bread and bitter herbs, as a sign of repentance: "And so we who desire repentance eat the unleavened bread with bitter herbs, that is, we first eat bitterness over our old and unendurable life, and then (we eat) the opposite of overboastful arrogance through meditation on humility, which is called reverence" (*QE*, 1.14-15). Exod 12:26 and 13:8 speak to questions that children will ask on that night; at some point, this developed into the ritual of the "four questions" that the youngest person at the table asks of the host. *M. Pesah.* 10 gives the following outline for the meal: "A first cup, over which the host says a benediction for the Passover day and one for the wine; this is shared around the table, and then everyone eats the bitter herbs dipped in *haroseth*" (a sweet fruit sauce; see *m. Pesah.* 10:3).

Then when the second cup is ready, "here the son asks his father (and if the son has not enough understanding his father instructs him), 'Why is this night different from other nights? For on other nights we eat seasoned food once, but this night twice; on other nights we eat leavened or unleavened bread, but this night all is unleavened; on other nights we eat flesh roasted, stewed, or cooked, but this night all is roasted'" (*m. Pesah.* 10:4). Then the father recites Deut 26:5-11, "A wandering Aramean was my father . . ." and the first part of the Hallel (Pss. 113–114); R. Akiba adds a benediction to the recitation of the psalms. The second cup is passed, the host breaks bread and gives some to everyone, and then the meal is served.

Then comes the third cup, over which the host says the benediction for the meal. "Over a fourth cup he completes the Hallel (through the end of Psalm 118) and says after it the Benediction over song" (*m. Pesah.* 10:7).

like the slave and most like their Lord. But when they are in charge of the Lord's followers, they and the rest of the Twelve will refuse to prepare tables any longer (Acts 6:2).

"Where is the *katalyma*?" they ask the householder; attentive readers will remember this word from 2:7, where it is usually translated "inn" but more likely means, as here, a spare room. The *oikodespotēs* has a nice large house with at least two floors, and so he shows the disciples "a large furnished [or "paneled," or maybe "carpeted"[3]] room on the upper floor," where they prepare the meal. Mary and Joseph found no room in a Bethlehem *katalyma*, but the adult Jesus finds one already set up and at his disposal. As he has told his disciples, they should go and ask, expecting that someone will provide them shelter (10:5-7; 11:9-10); this will now be the sixth banquet Jesus has attended in someone else's home, but this will be the first one at which he is the stated host.

Last Supper, 22:14-23

Before plunging into commentary, we must clarify what text we are interpreting, because there are two major versions of Luke 22:14-23 in the early manuscripts. At the end of this argument, I will explain why I think the whole passage is original; readers who are not interested in issues of text criticism [Text Criticism] may want to skip the next few paragraphs. The vast majority of ancient manuscripts of Luke, including the oldest and most reliable texts, have the whole passage as it is printed in most Bibles, including vv. 19b-20 ("which is given for you . . . shed for you."). A few manuscripts—one major Greek text (Codex Bezae, dated to the fifth or sixth century) and several Latin ones—omit 19b-20. The longer text has

15-16, Vow to abstain from eating until the kingdom's banquet begins

17-18, Cup passed around; vow to abstain from drinking until the kingdom's banquet begins

19, Bread broken, shared: "This is my body given for you"; command to celebrate in his memory

20, Cup "after supper," shared: "This cup is the new covenant in my blood, shed for you"

The shorter text, by stopping at "This is my body," omits the second cup and the more traditional form of the words of institution; all that remains are the vows not to eat and drink and the use of bread to symbolize Jesus' death.[4] The issue is complicated by the fact that Codex Bezae is characterized by "the free addition (and occasional omission) of words, sentences, and even incidents."[5] Thus, because the codex that normally conflates readings omits this one, text critics pause over it.

Text Criticism

The books of the New Testament were copied by hand from the time of their composition until the invention of the printing press. For every verse of every book—no exaggeration—there exist multiple different versions. Text criticism is the subfield of biblical studies that tries to catalog all the variant readings and then from them tries to decide what was originally written. The New Testament documents were written in Greek between the late 40s or early 50s (some of Paul's letters) and 125–150 (2 Peter is usually dated to this period). There are fragments in Greek dating to 150–300, and mostly complete manuscripts from that point forward; there are also translations into Latin, Copic, Syriac, and other ancient languages, and quotations of verses and phrases in the writings of early Christians.

Study Bibles in English often footnote some of the more puzzling textual variants, usually with a note such as "other ancient versions read . . . ." Critical editions of the Greek New Testament summarize the most important data for making decisions about the variants that, in the opinions of the editors, are the most significant or the most difficult to resolve. A good introduction to the theory and practice of New Testament text criticism is by Bruce Metzger and Bart Ehrman: *The Text of the New Testament: Its Transmission, Corruption, and Restoration* (4th ed.; New York: Oxford, 2005).

Both the longer and the shorter texts differ from the other Gospels. Luke either had cup-bread or cup-bread-cup, which does not match the bread-cup of Matthew, Mark, and 1 Corinthians 11:23-26. Mark and Matthew have a vow of abstinence after the cup, and therefore after the bread; both the longer and shorter texts of Luke have this vow after the first cup and before the bread. Therefore, although some regard either the longer or shorter texts as an attempt to square Luke with the "official" order of the words of institution,[6] this seems implausible to me, since Luke is different from the others on either reading. It is plausible, however, to imagine a scribe adding vv. 19b-20 in order to add more of the familiar words of institution.[7] It is also plausible to imagine that scribes, in order to combat heretical views of Jesus, would add these verses to Luke. A follower of Marcion or some other Christian with a docetic understanding of Jesus [Marcion and Docetics] might fasten onto the shorter text as evidence that Jesus only seemed human and never actually shed blood on the cross; perhaps some early "proto-orthodox scribes . . . altered their text of Luke in order to counter" such views.[8] However, it is just as plausible that someone—a Marcionite, perhaps, or another docetic Christian—shortened the text of Luke in order to make it more compatible with their views. Either way, the presence or absence of 19b-20 was probably motivated by the issue of a docetic Christology. The text was not added or omitted accidentally, nor added or omitted over a concern for harmonization with the other Gospels.

If this is true, then we should consider other passages that bear on the issue.

Marcion and Docetics

Marcion was a native of Pontus, born somewhere in the second half of the 1st century AD. He was called a shipowner by one of his opponents, but mostly he is known for beliefs that most Christians judged to be heretical, and for creating an alternative network of congregations with its own leadership structure. He believed that the God of the Old Testament was not the God who was the Father of Jesus Christ, and he rejected both the Old Testament and its use in the New. He also believed that Jesus only appeared to be human, and that he did not truly die on the cross; these last two points of view are called "docetic," from the Greek verb "to seem."

- Luke 22:43-44, the description of Jesus' praying in agony until his sweat turned to blood, is omitted by the oldest and best manuscripts of Luke, but included in the majority of texts, including Bezae. Justin Martyr, writing around 150, used the verses to argue that Jesus was truly human, so the reading existed very early.[9] Most argue, as I will, that the verses are not original to Luke, since they spoil the parallelism of the passage and go against Luke's tendency to portray Jesus as placid and unworried.[10] This being so, it is clearly plausible that 22:19b-20 were early anti-docetic additions to Luke's text.

- Luke 24:40, "And saying this, he showed them his hands and feet," is included by the majority but omitted by Bezae. It is almost superfluous, since Jesus orders them to "behold my hands and feet" at the beginning of v. 39. A docetic Christian might be happy for its omission, but since v. 39 argues that Jesus did have real flesh and bone, omitting v. 40 does not go far enough; a docetic Christian would probably want to chuck the whole pericope. Adding it, however, would only slightly strengthen the orthodox view.
- Luke 24:42-43, wherein Jesus eats some fish, is included (with some manuscripts adding "and [a portion from] a honeycomb") in all major manuscripts.
- Luke has no exact parallel to Mark 10:45, "The Son of Man came not to be served [διακονηθῆναι] but to serve [διακονῆσαι] and to give his life as a ransom for many." Luke does not object to the notion that Jesus was a servant: "Who is greater, the one who reclines [to eat] or the one who serves [ὁ διακονῶν]? Is it not the one who reclines? But I am in your midst as one who serves" (Luke 22:27). Thus Luke probably omitted Mark 10:45 because the "ransom" explanation of Jesus' death was not his view. But 22:19b-20 does not suggest a ransom-type atonement, and it is not precisely true that Luke nowhere links Jesus' death to salvation.[11] It is his view that Jesus, as Messiah, was required to suffer and die and be raised (24:25-27, 46-47) and that faith in this dying and rising Messiah is the key to salvation. The theology behind 22:19b-20 is compatible with the Lukan understanding of Jesus' death, as I will argue shortly.

To sum up, it is plausible that the shorter text is original, and that verses 19b-20 were added by orthodox scribes who wanted to remove a potentially useful text for docetic Christians. It is just as plausible that a docetic Christian removed the verses to create a more congenial form of the words of institution. Since Luke has unquestionably original material that sounds anti-docetic, the anti-docetic utility of these verses does not by itself prove that they were added. Luke does not understand Jesus' death to have been a ransom, but that does not rule out the originality of 22:19b-20, since they offer a different understanding of Jesus' death.

In my opinion, the more plausible case is that the longer text is earlier. First, it has the best manuscript support. Second, the longer text has a nice parallel structure, as noted above, which the shorter text lacks. Third, as I will argue below, the effect of the longer text is to strengthen the connections between the Passover meal, the Lord's Supper, Jesus' death, and the great banquet in the age to come. All of this seems to me entirely congenial with Luke's theology. My guess is that the shorter text arose from a heterodox scribe's efforts to create words of institution that had less to do with the flesh-and-blood nature of Jesus' death.

"When the hour had come" sounds a bit like the Gospel of John, which uses "my hour has not yet come" in the first half of the Gospel in order to foreshadow Jesus' death and then opens the Passion Narrative with "Before the festival of Passover, Jesus, knowing that his hour had come . . ." (John 13:1). But Luke frequently uses "hour" as a way of signaling a particular time: "All the multitude of the people were outside praying at the hour of the incense-offering" (1:10); "at that hour [i.e., while Mary and Joseph were still in the temple with baby Jesus] Anna, coming in, praised God" (2:38; see also 7:21; 10:21; 12:12; 13:31).[12] Luke 22:1 said that the paschal meal was near; 22:7 says that it was the day of the meal, and shows us the preparation for the meal; 22:14 means that the moment had come to recline and eat.

The NRSV translates v. 14, "he took his place at table"; "he reclined to eat" is surely closer to what Luke had in mind.[13] That is, we should try to erase the memory of da Vinci's *The Last Supper* and the image of Jesus and the disciples sitting at a table. Instead, think of the banqueting practices of Luke's day: dining couches arranged in a U-shape around the outside of the room, with small tables in front of each one. Jesus, as host, would be near the center of the U.

His first words are unique to Luke: "I have deeply desired to eat this Passover with you before I suffer." His first two words are literally "with desire I have desired," wherein Luke uses a grammatical form common in the Septuagint to express intense emotions (see Gen 31:30 LXX, where Laban uses it to characterize Jacob's desire to go back to his homeland). Since Luke mostly avoids attributing intense emotions to Jesus and only rarely describes

Bassano's *Last Supper*

Jacopo Bassano (1515–1592). *The Last Supper.* Galleria Borghese, Rome, Italy. (Credit: Alinar /Art Resource, NY)

Bassano's painting has a European-style seating, rather than having Jesus and the disciples recline to eat. But his lively composition can help us to imagine the level of conversation Luke depicts in his version of the Last Supper, and his apostles are clearly peasants.

his interior state of mind, we should take this verse seriously: why does Luke stress Jesus' desire to share this particular meal with the apostles?

The meal draws together several threads that have been running through the narrative. First, and most obviously, Jesus has been predicting his death, characterizing it as a prophet's death that must happen in Jerusalem (see the entire list in the commentary section on 9:18-27). His death is near, and in Luke's version of the Last Supper Jesus will continue to work as a prophet, preparing his disciples for what is about to happen. Second, Luke's Jesus will use the supper to explore further how Jesus' role as servant helps to explain why his death must happen, according to God's plan. Third, Luke's Jesus has attended three banquets hosted by Pharisees and two hosted by tax collectors, and the issue of Jesus' willingness to eat with anyone has been part of the discussion on every occasion. The meals with enemies and sinners have given Jesus a chance to practice what he preaches about loving enemies and forgiving sinners, but beyond that, the meals have been illustrations of what Luke's Jesus believes about the kingdom of God. In this Last Supper, Jesus eats with his betrayer (22:21) and the rest of the sinners (22:37), but offers all of them his body and blood, as well as his vow to eat and drink with them in the kingdom. Fourth, Luke's version of the meal gives another pass at themes such as prayer (22:32), renunciation of status (22:24-27), the presence/coming of the kingdom (22:16, 18, 29-30), and the duty to suffer with Jesus (22:28). Thus, we can understand the "deep desire" on at least a couple of levels. Luke's Jesus "set his face" to get to Jerusalem and go to the cross in 9:51, and has been pursuing the destiny God set for him; this is the climactic moment. But "deep desire" also points to what this meal means to Luke. This moment has also been a long time coming, in terms of narrative pacing; Luke is going to make the most of it.

The two vows (verses 16 and 18) are parallel in structure:

Λέγω γὰρ ὑμῖν ὅτι οὐ μὴ φάγω αὐτὸ
   ἕως ὅτου πληρωθῇ ἐν βασιλείᾳ τοῦ θεοῦ
Legō gar hymin hoti ou mē phagō auto
   heōs houtou plērōthē en basileia tou theou
For I say to you (pl) that I will certainly not eat it
   Until it may be fulfilled in the kingdom of God

Λέγω γὰρ ὑμῖν ὅτι οὐ μη πίω ἀπὸ τοῦ γενήματος τῆς ἀμπελου
   ἕως οὗ ἡ βασιλεία τοῦ θεοῦ ἔλθῃ

*Legō gar hymin hoti ou mē piō apo tou genēmatos tēs
ampelou*
   heōs hou hē basileia tou theou elthē
For I say to you (pl) that I will certainly not drink from the fruit of
the vine
   Until the kingdom of God may come.

As Luke has set things up, both vows apply to elements of Passover.
In v. 16, the antecedent of the pronoun *auto* (it) is either the whole
Passover meal or the lamb. Since v. 18 specifies "the fruit of the
vine," using language from the standard blessing offered for wine
("Blessed art thou, O Lord our God, King of the Universe, who
creates the fruit of the vine," *m. Ber.* 6:1), we should probably
understand "it" in v. 16 to refer to the lamb.

Jesus' first vow has sometimes been understood to mean "I am
not going to eat with you guys now, and will not eat until we can
eat together in the kingdom of God."[14] This is possible, but one
would expect an adversative conjunction ("but" or "instead")
between "I have deeply desired to eat" and "I will certainly not
eat"; the *gar* ("for") offers a reason in support of Jesus' deep desire,
not a contradiction of it. Jesus vows to abstain from eating "it," the
Passover; given that he eats fish in 24:42-43, Luke cannot understand him to mean he was giving up eating until the Second
Coming. The vow means "I will not eat the Passover again until it
is fulfilled in the kingdom," and gives us an insight into how Luke
understood the great banquet. Passover celebrated God's act of
deliverance in the exodus, making a people from a group of slaves.
In Luke's thinking, the great banquet *is* the kingdom, a hall filled
with "the poor, the crippled, the blind and the lame" as well as all
the homeless from the roads (14:21-23); a place where a poor sick
beggar gets a spot on the couch next to Abraham (16:23); a place
where there will be no first and last, no status markers, and where
the master will serve the slaves (12:37). Jesus' own "exodus" has to
happen first (9:31 uses this word to predict Jesus' death in
Jerusalem), but the vow is an assurance that the fulfillment will
come; down the road, past Jesus' death, there will be a time to celebrate in the kingdom.

The second vow of abstinence begins by Jesus taking a cup—one
of the first three of the four cups of the Passover meal, and most
likely the second cup, which is accompanied by the "four questions" and the recitation of the exodus story.[15] He pronounces the
blessing over it and then, following normal practice for this meal,
takes a sip and passes it to the others so that each in turn may take

Drinking in Moderation at Banquets

Most people in imperial times believed that merrymaking was to be expected at banquets, and that this involved drinking wine. But most moral writers of the period also encouraged moderation, especially when there was something important to be decided. Sirach's advice is to avoid drinking to excess but also to avoid criticizing the person on the neighboring couch if he drank too much:

Wine drunk at the proper time and in moderation is rejoicing of heart and gladness of soul. Wine drunk to excess leads to bitterness of spirit, to quarrels and stumbling. Drunkenness increases the anger of a fool to his own hurt, reducing his strength and adding wounds. Do not reprove your neighbor at a banquet of wine, and do not despise him in his merrymaking; speak no word of reproach to him, and do not distress him by making demands of him. (Sir 31:28-31)

Plutarch's *Table Talk* includes a discussion of whether a group could profitably discuss something serious if they had been drinking. The majority believed that it was unwise:

Over a glass of wine men should make only ridiculous slips, and not such as may prove tragical, lamentable, or of any considerable concern. Besides, in serious debates, it is chiefly to be considered, that persons of mean understanding and unacquainted with business should be guided by the wise and experienced; but wine destroys this order . . . for none over a glass of wine thinks himself so noble, beauteous, or rich (though he fancies himself all these), as wise; and therefore wine is babbling, full of talk, and of a dictating humor; so that we are rather for being heard than hearing, for leading than being led. (Plutarch, *Table Talk*, book 7, question 10)

a sip. Whereas the first vow probably means "I'm not going to eat the Passover again until it is fulfilled in the kingdom," this one probably means "I'm not going to drink any more wine until the kingdom arrives," meaning that Jesus was planning to abstain from the rest of the cups at the supper.[16] This is appropriate: the cup symbolizes his own death, which he will drink in a way unshared by the disciples. For Luke's Greco-Roman audience, Jesus' decision to drink only a small amount of wine with dinner would also have shown his seriousness and self-discipline in the face of all that was to come that night. [Drinking in Moderation at Banquets]

Following the two vows, Luke presents the words of institution. Jesus, taking a piece of the unleavened bread on the table, having pronounced the blessing over it ("Blessed art Thou, O Lord our God, King of the Universe, who bringest forth bread from the earth," *m. Ber.* 6:1), broke it into pieces and gave a piece to each person at the table.[17] The sequence of "took-blessed-broke-gave" reminds us of the miracle at Luke 9:16, and is found in Mark 14:22 and (omitting the "gave") in 1 Corinthians 11:23-24. Jesus' words as he passed out the bread are very similar, but not identical in the three Synoptics and in 1 Corinthians (assuming that we know what each one originally said—there are many variants for each reading).

Mark 14:22	Take;	this is my body.
Matt 26:26	Take, eat	this is my body
Luke 22:19		this is my body given for you; do this for my memorial.
1 Cor 11:24		this is my body for you; do this for my memorial.

We presume that each writer has been influenced by the way he is accustomed to hearing or saying the words of institution—by the practice(s) of his local congregation(s). Paul's version, written twenty years or more before Mark's Gospel, shows that Luke's version could preserve old, traditional wording used in some churches. But we also presume that each writer might hope to influence practice. For instance, Luke might have omitted "take" from Mark and might have added "given for you; do this for my memorial," even if his own congregation normally did things as Mark describes them, because he felt those were helpful changes in practice.

"Given for you," as noted above, means that Luke does have an understanding of Jesus' death functioning to bring forgiveness of sins (again presuming that the longer text is original to Luke). But—preachers and teachers need to make this clear—this does not imply "substitutionary" or penal atonement theories. Some Jews in the Second Temple period believed that the deaths of persons who were killed because they were trying to obey God's law could perhaps lead God to forgive the rest of the sinful nation; God could accept the unjust suffering of the innocents in lieu of punishment justly due to the whole people of Israel (2 Macc 7:37-38; 4 Macc 6:27-29, "Make my blood their purification, and take my life in exchange for theirs."). The theology behind these passages is not that the martyrs were somehow laden with the sins of the nation, or that they suffered all the agonies due to come upon the rest of the sinners. Instead, the idea is that God, being just, will want to balance things, and so if some have to die unjustly, then that should count toward increasing God's mercy toward others. Luke understood Jesus to be the Servant of the Lord spoken of in Isaiah 40–55, who was "wounded for our iniquities" (Isa 53:4; see Acts 8:32-35 and the discussion of Luke 22:24-27 below). But (and after Mel Gibson's *The Passion of the Christ*, one has to make this plain) it is extremely unlikely that Luke believed Jesus' sufferings were in proportion to our sins, or even that Luke thought of Jesus' death as a sacrifice. Luke's understanding of Jesus as Servant gave him an important way to explain why Jesus had to die: Isaiah 53:8 says the servant had to die, and so Luke can write that "it was necessary" (Luke 24:26, 46). Luke already had one explanation to hand—Jesus also had to die because he was a prophet, and all true prophets are rejected and killed for their message (Luke 11:47-51; 13:33). But adding the category of servant to prophet gave him a way to explain how Jesus' death could have been a good thing: "upon him was the punishment that made us whole" (Isa 53:5).

"Do this for my memorial"

AΩ A memorial (*anamnēsis*) is a reminder of something. Lev 24:7-8 LXX uses the word to describe the twelve loaves of "the bread of the Presence" which were baked weekly and laid on the table "for a memorial laid before the Lord. On every Sabbath they shall be set in front of the Lord, in the presence of the sons of Israel, as an eternal covenant"—a reminder, perhaps, for God and for Israel of the covenant with the twelve tribes. Josephus uses it for verbal reminders (*Ant.* 19.218, 318) or for things that bring memories to mind (*Ant.* 11.82-83, where the postexilic temple creates differing reactions in the young and the old). Most significantly, the word appears in LXX Exod 12:14: "And this day shall be to you a memorial, and you shall celebrate it as a feast to the Lord for all your generations."

"Do this for my memorial" or "as my memorial" means that the ritual of bread and cup is to keep Jesus, his ministry and teachings, in the forefront of the minds of the participants. Just as the Passover meal is to help the participants not only remember the exodus but (as much as possible) experience it, so the Eucharist will be one of the ways the church experiences the living Jesus (see Luke 24:28-35). ["Do this for my memorial"]

The "cup after supper" could mean the third or fourth cup of the Passover seder, since both followed the main meal. Again, Jesus' words are transmitted with slight variations:

Mark 14:24   This   is my blood of the covenant which is shed for many

Matt 26:28   For this   is my blood of the covenant which is shed for many for forgiveness of sins

Luke 22: 20 This cup is the new covenant in my blood shed for you

1 Cor 11:25 This cup is the new covenant in my blood

"New covenant" perhaps quotes Jeremiah (Jer 31:31 [LXX 38:31]), who predicted a covenant that Israel would not break because God would "write the laws upon their hearts," giving them the will to obey God. But since Luke does not elsewhere take up Jeremiah's potent language, perhaps "new" means only "different from the covenant represented by the Passover." "Blood of the covenant," which Luke presumably read in Mark, quotes Exodus 24:8 LXX; there, following the reception of the Law, Moses sprinkled the people with sacrificial blood and said, "Behold the blood of the covenant, which the Lord made with you concerning all these commandments [lit., "words"]." Luke makes it "the new covenant in my blood," corresponding to no Old Testament text and to no Old Testament understanding of sacrifice; no sacrificial victim ever said, "this is a covenant in my blood." The verb for "shed" was used in the LXX for sacrificial blood poured out by the priest at the base of the altar (Lev 4:18),[18] but also for murder (Gen 9:6; Num 35:33; Isa 59:7).[19] Luke uses the verb in this latter sense elsewhere (Luke 11:50; Acts 22:20; in Acts 1:18, the word describes how Judas's insides spill out, and in Luke 5:37 how fermenting wine bursts old wineskins and spills out). I suggest, then, that for Luke, "shed" connotes Jesus' death as murder, rather than sacrifice; that Jesus was a righteous man who was murdered is the burden of the apostolic preaching in Acts 2–7. For Luke, "shed" also invites connection to the gift of the Spirit (it is used of the "pouring out" of the Spirit at Acts 2:17-18, 33; 10:45). In Acts 2:17-36, Peter argues, "You murdered Jesus, according to God's preset plan. God raised him from the dead, and Jesus has now poured out the Spirit on us. If you repent, you can be forgiven and receive the same gift."

So murder is not the last word on Jesus' death. Because he is willing to drink the cup of suffering (Luke 22:42; see commentary for that section), and because a merciful God is willing to overlook the sins of those who repent, his death begins a new covenant between God and anyone who repents (Acts 3:19-20). His death is "for you"—for those sitting around the table, who would shortly fail to live up to the demands of discipleship.

The penal or substitutionary understanding of the atonement is so often read into the New Testament that, at the risk of beating a hole in the drum, let me be perfectly clear:

- Luke does not think of Jesus' death as a sacrifice. Paul sometimes writes of Jesus' death that way, but Luke never does. Luke never uses the technical language of "sin offering" or "ransom" or anything of the sort, never compares Jesus to the lamb (Paul, John, and Revelation do, but not Luke) but only to the bread and the cup. "Given for you" means "given for your benefit," but not "given as a sacrifice for you."
- Luke does not think that Jesus' physical sufferings produced the forgiveness of our sins. In fact, compared to Mark, Luke decreases the reader's focus on Jesus' suffering and instead describes a much more placid death.
- Luke does not think that as Jesus died, God "turned His back on His Son" or anything of that sort. In Luke's version, all Jesus' words from the cross indicate that his relationship with his Father and his ability to conduct his ministry continued until he died.
- Luke thought that Jesus had to be killed in order to follow the plan of God revealed in Scripture. Luke thought that Jesus had to be killed because all prophets had to be killed. Luke did not think that Jesus had to be killed in order for God to forgive sins;

The Treachery of Supposed Friends

It is cruel to discover friends that are no friends at a crucial time which calls for friends, since there is then no exchanging one that is untrustworthy and spurious for the true and trustworthy. But one's friend, like a coin, should have been examined and approved before the time of need, not proved by the need to be no friend.

Plutarch, *How to Tell a Flatterer from a Friend*, 49.

Why Is this Night Different from All Other Nights?

Kyrie eleison: Night
like no other night, plotted
and palmed,
omega of terror,
packed like a bullet
in the triggered chamber.

Stanley Kunitz, from "Around Pastor Bonhoeffer," in
Passing Through: The Later Poems New and Selected
(New York: Norton, 1995), 48.

forgiveness was a part of John's preaching before Jesus began and a part of Jesus' preaching from the sermon in Nazareth up to his words from the cross.

Without any pause, Jesus moves right into an announcement that one of them would betray him; by moving the prediction of betrayal from the beginning of the meal (Mark 14:18-21) to the end, Luke makes it plain that he imagines Judas sitting through the whole meal with all the others.[20] This dramatically raises the level of treachery involved [The Treachery of Supposed Friends], but also means that Jesus practices what he preaches about loving one's enemies—he is treating Judas as a friend and a trusted associate. Luke, like Mark, does not picture Jesus identifying Judas directly, and so preserves Mark's sense that Jesus could have meant any or all of them. Verse 22 states the paradox of the betrayal from the perspective of Christian theology. From one point of view, the betrayal had to happen (Luke writes, "the son of man goes according to what has been determined"); Isaiah 53:12 LXX reads, " . . . on their account his life was handed over [the same verb translated "betrayed" in Luke 22:22] to death and he was reckoned with the lawless, and he bore the sins of the many, and he was handed over because of their lawlessness." Jesus, the Servant of God, had to be handed over "in order to fulfill all that was written of him," and so somebody had to do it. But from the other point of view, it was a terrible thing to betray Jesus. Luke, you recall, explained Judas's actions as the result of being possessed by Satan (22:3), and will describe the betrayer's gruesome death in Acts 1:18. Here, then, is another prophetic woe announced by Jesus and fulfilled within the narrative of Luke-Acts, further reinforcing Jesus' status as prophet. [Why Is this Night Different from All Other Nights?]

The apostles react to Jesus' announcement by arguing (*syzēteō* means to dispute or to debate) over which of them might be about to do this. Interesting—Luke's phrasing implies that they do not doubt the truth of Jesus' prediction and so assume that one of them is "he who is about to do this," and start wrangling with each other over who it will be. But they don't stay at it long; v. 24 has them arguing over who is greatest. Luke has a real gift for the absurd: "I'll bet you're the booger who's going to hand Jesus over." "Not me—I'm better than all you lot—it's you, isn't it?"

After dinner, the table talk continues, as Luke's readers would have expected for a group of friends at a banquet. We should imagine Jesus and the guys still reclining, as Luke takes us through a range of types of discourse: dispute and argumentation, instruction, affirmation and promises, prophetic oracles of woe, words of consolation, and then a most puzzling command just before they exit the room.

Table Talk, 22:24-38

David James Duncan's novel *The Brothers K* explores the life of a family—dad, mom, four sons, two daughters—whose religious habits are all over the map. The dad mangled his thumb in a work accident, cutting short his professional baseball career, but with the fourth son's encouragement, he has built a shed in the backyard and is pitching again as a way to lift himself from depression. He does his pitching just after work, while the others are sitting down to dinner, and the narrator comments on how the father's absence creates an opening for family conflict:

> But any gathering of eight human beings has an astounding potential for complication. Picture a toy castle made of alphabet blocks . . . consider how a single block down at the base of an alphabet-block castle is visually just an insignificant detail. Its removal might pass unnoticed. But stomp hard on the floor after such a block removal and the whole edifice may well go tumbling.
>
> Well, Papa's presence at the Chance family suppertable—or, more specifically, the anemic little grace he'd mutter every night before we fell upon our food—turned out to be such a block. . . . all our lives Papa had deployed the same *Book of Common Prayer* standby, and had invariably uttered it in exactly the same way: speaking so swiftly and monotonally that he sounded more like a bashful auctioneer than a supplicant, he'd mumble *Giveusgratefulheartsour Father andmakeusevermindfuloftheneedsofothersthroughChristourLord, Amen,* and that was that. . . . the whole holy diphthong spilled out of him so fast that there was no time for Freddy to clown or for Bet to fuss or for Mama to genuflect or Everett to apostasize or Peter to celebrate or Irwin to guffaw or me to lust after my dinner. Papa's prayer was a three-and-a-half second masterpiece—a rustic but reliable footbridge that led us so blithely over the deadly crevasse of our religious differences that we scarcely realized the crevasse existed—until the night he left us alone . . . .[21]

Jesus and the Twelve are reclining in a well-appointed guest room of a house in Jerusalem. It is the night of the Passover meal, and the group has already eaten it, and has heard solemn instructions from Jesus. First, he vows that this will be his last Passover meal until it is fulfilled in the great banquet of the kingdom of God; he also vows not to drink any more wine until the kingdom comes. Then, taking a piece of the unleavened bread from the table, he breaks it and hands a piece to everyone, saying, "This is my body given for you—do this for my memorial." After they have finished the whole meal, he passes around a cup of wine, asking each one to take a sip, saying, "This cup is the new covenant in my blood which is shed for you." As the cup is still making its way from one dining couch to another, Jesus predicts that one of his dinner guests will hand him over; this saying incites an argument among the disciples about which one of them might do such a thing.

A Quarrel Arose

AΩ Luke used a word for "quarrel" (*philoneikia*) that literally means "love of strife" (Fitzmyer, *Luke*, 2.1416). His choice to make this an impersonal phrase—"a quarrel arose" rather than "each began to quarrel with the other"—implicates all of them, but identifies this vice as the problem rather than the apostles themselves. Satan had taken possession of Judas (22:3) and was trying to grab all of them (22:31-32); the appearance of *philoneikia* in the room was a symptom of the larger struggle between Jesus and evil.

We begin to get a glimpse of what might happen to the Twelve and to the nascent movement Jesus has begun once he is removed from them. As noted in the commentary in the previous section, Luke's wording in 22:23 implies that the apostles did not doubt that one of them "was the one about to do this thing"; not exactly "all for one and one for all." But as they "begin to argue" over which one of them might be the traitor, "a quarrel arose among them, namely, which of them appeared to be greatest." [A Quarrel Arose] Oh, this is rich—not "they started to quarrel," but "a quarrel arose," as if nobody started it; not "which one *is* greatest," but "which one *seems* to be greatest," as if the real issue on this night was appearances (think of George Clooney's character in *O Brother, Where Art Thou*, waking up to the sound of a sheriff's bullhorn and the threat of being burned alive, saying "My hair!"). Not only is this a completely inappropriate moment for a round of "who's the greatest," but they've already been through this once, back in Galilee (9:46-48). Jesus told them who was greatest: none of them, since they had not yet learned that in God's kingdom, only the humble, the least, are great.

The first argument over who was greatest followed Jesus' second passion prediction; this one follows Jesus' introduction of the body-and-blood meal that the disciples are to continue as Jesus' memorial. Jesus is trying to teach his apostles something about how leadership will function in his group after he is dead; the apostles, as suggested in the commentary on 9:43b-50, probably remind Luke's audience of rival claimants to thrones, like Herod the Great's sons (see [Succession Struggles]).

Jesus' response begins by describing The Way Things Are—the prevailing cultural norms, which the apostles and Luke's audience all know well. "The kings of the nations rule them" is one way to translate the first half of v. 25; the more pejorative translation is "the kings of the nations lord it over them." "Nations" can be translated "Gentiles," meaning "any ethnic group other than the Jews," and since Jesus and the apostles are all Jews, that is appropriate. But the point is not the ethnicity of the rulers, but their predictable habits—wherever you find a king, you find someone who acts like a master, a *kyrios*. The verb alternately translated "rule" or "lord it over" is the verbal form of *kyrios*, meaning to "act as master." The *kyrios* of a household—the husband/father/master/homeowner—had some absolute rights over the lives of the other members of the household. In the same way, a king was *kyrios* of his realm, having the power to enforce his will on them. If we translate "lord it over," we get the sense of the illegitimate use of authority, but this is not the situation Jesus sets up. A king rules the kingdom—that is The Way Things Are.

But kings also normally like public attention to be on their acts of beneficence rather than on their exercises of power: "their great ones are called [or call themselves] 'benefactors.'" [King Prefers to be Called Benefactor] The title "benefactor" (*euergetai*, "good deed doers," as the Wizard of Oz has it) was commonly used by emperors, kings, and various other rulers across the empire. In his list of accomplishments as emperor, Augustus details many benefactions: money given at various times to all citizens of the city; cash bonuses and gifts of land to retired soldiers; gifts of money to the treasury; times when he personally bought grain for the public dole; buildings he erected and repaired in Rome (prompting the line in Suetonius's biography that "he had found it a city of brick and left it a city of marble"). The bit about land for soldiers is worth noting: "I reimbursed municipalities for the lands which I assigned to my soldiers in my fourth consulship . . . . The sums involved were about 600 million sesterces which I paid for Italian estates and about 260 million sesterces which I paid for provincial lands."[22] The benefaction to his retired legionnaires came after he had exercised his right of eminent domain over the estates of people who were not his allies or clients; the largesse of an emperor always comes at someone's expense, but the emperor will always claim that he did it for the public good.

> **King Prefers to be Called Benefactor**
>
> Dio Cassius wrote in his *Roman History* that Augustus, the first of the emperors, preferred titles other than "king" or "dictator"—*princeps*, or "first citizen"; consul or proconsul, which were titles given to senators elected by the citizens to lead the government; even "father of his country." But, as he notes, "By virtue of these Republican titles they have clothed themselves with all the powers of the government, so that they actually possess all the prerogatives of kings without the usual title."
>
> Dio Cassius, *Roman History* 53.21.3.

For Luke's audience, this was The Way Things Are. Unless you were born into wealth and power, the only way to get ahead was to become a client to a powerful patron. The patron would expect the client's service, even obedience; in return, the client would hope for the patron's benefactions to pave the way for a better future. There is no doubt that early Christians listening to the Gospel of Luke being read aloud lived by those standards, whether in dealings with other Christians or non-Christians. Wealthy believers, of whom Luke knew a few, acted as patrons for the poorer believers, and expected to be rewarded with the proper respect. Several times already, Luke has tried to disrupt the patron-client pattern:

- The least one living among all of you is "the great" (9:48)—Jesus used a child as the model disciple, and urged the others not only to be "least," but also to welcome "the least," rather than giving preferential treatment to the powerful.
- Blessed are those slaves whom the master finds watchful when he comes (12:37; cf. 12:43)—Luke's Jesus forces all his listeners to think of themselves as slaves who are blessed if they do the master's bidding even when the master isn't around. In 17:7-10, he notes that slaves who faithfully do all that is expected of them never put their master in their debt, never build up "brownie points" for good behavior.

Now he has Jesus tell the apostles that the greatest among them should be like the youngest and the leader like "one who serves" (*ho diakonōn*). Even in our youth-oriented society, we would be reluctant to let the youngest person in a group be the leader; Jesus is inverting the normal values of his society, as he did with the example of a child in 9:46-48. Even in our society that espouses equal rights for all, the "one who serves" is considered inferior to the one who is served. Jesus makes the obvious point that the ones reclining to eat are superior in status to the slaves or servants who bring them their food. "But I am among you as one who serves"— he may mean that during the meal, Jesus did all the table service; he certainly served them bread and wine, and so perhaps we should take this first as a description of the way the meal has gone.[23] Be that as it may, Jesus certainly means for "as one who serves" to describe his life among them generally.

Mark 10:41-45, Luke's probable source for this section, has "whoever wishes to be great among you will be your *diakonos* [servant], and whoever wishes to be first among you will be everyone's *doulos* [slave]." Luke's "the greatest among you" rather than "whoever wishes to be great" puts the onus on those who already have status rather than those who hope for it. He swaps "youngest" for Mark's "servant," and then puts "servant" in the second line in place of "slave." As noted earlier, Luke has no problems asking Christians to think of themselves as slaves, but perhaps did hesitate to call Jesus a *doulos*, a slave. Christians who wanted to present their religion as a viable option for Greeks and Romans had to contend with the characterization of Christianity as a religion for slaves—not just because it was attractive to the lower classes, but because crucifixion was widely used as the ultimate punishment for disobedient slaves and was commonly called a servile death. [Elite Romans Characterize Christianity] In addition, by the time of Luke's writing, *diakonos* was already being used as the name of an office or responsibility within Christian congregations (Phil 1:1), and the verb *diakoneō* ("act as servant") appears several times in Acts to describe specific ministries (notably in Acts 6:1-6, where the apostles reject table-waiting in preference to the "ministry of the word"). Switching to "servant" created resonances with Acts and with current church practice.

The disciples, and Luke's readers, are to think of themselves as servants and slaves of their *kyrios* Jesus. But their *kyrios* acts like a *diakonos*, a servant. The distance between master and slave thus collapses, if only in the ideal world of perfect obedience to Jesus' teaching. In the real world, the group of early believers listening to this part of Luke included wealthy masters and their slaves, patrons and their clients. "Not so among you!" says Jesus, but they and we find it hard to hear and obey.

In vv. 28-30 the image takes a sudden turn from a band of servants led by a servant, all striving to be least, to a prince and his companions [The Companions of the King], enjoying the bounty of the royal table and dividing the realm between them. "You are those who have remained with me" uses a verb that means "stay [in the same place or in the same condition] throughout," which Luke uses in Luke 1:22 for Zechariah's loss of speech (it "remained" until

Elite Romans Characterize Christianity

". . . a group hated for their abominations, whom the populace called Christians. Christus, from whom the name had its origin, had been condemned to death in the reign of Tiberius by the procurator Pontius Pilate, and the pernicious superstition, thus suppressed for the moment, was breaking out again not only in Judaea, the original source of this evil, but even in Rome, where all things horrible or shameful from all parts of the world collect and become popular." (Tacitus, *Ann.* 15)

"Accordingly, I judged it all the more necessary to find out what the truth was by torturing two female slaves who were called deaconesses. But I discovered nothing else but depraved, excessive superstition." (Pliny to Trajan, *Letters* 10.96)

"Is it not deplorable that a faction . . . of abandoned, hopeless outlaws makes attacks on the gods? They gather together ignorant persons from the lowest dregs, and credulous women, easily deceived as their sex is, and organize a rabble of unholy conspirators . . . . To say that a man put to death for a crime and the lethal wooden cross are objects of their veneration is to assign altars suitable for abandoned and impious men." (Minucius Felix, *Oct.* 8.)

The Companions of the King

Alexander the Great had an elite band of troops called "companions" who were given special privileges—eating and drinking with the king, calling him by name rather than by title—and who in return were given the most dangerous and arduous assignments. Josephus frequently refers to the companions of a royal person, often meaning "comrades in arms" (*Ant.* 7.312, 12.302, 13.26, 13.311). Luke's audience, hearing Jesus say that these twelve men had stood with him in all his trials, would likely have made that association.

John was born and named) and in Acts 10: 48 for Cornelius's invitation for Peter to "remain" at his house for several days. Luke does not credit the apostles with a faultless performance; they have, in the past and just a few moments earlier, failed to live up to Jesus' expectations, and Jesus is about to predict Peter's denial. But Luke omits Mark's damning "All of them deserted him and fled" (Mark 14:50; cf. Luke 22:53-54) and probably means for us to imagine the Twelve watching the crucifixion from a distance (Luke 23:49). In one sense, then, since they do not desert him, the eleven "remain with" him even in the period of testing/trial that is to come. In another sense, however, Jesus' words are an indictment; sure, they are "with him," if remaining silent and watching from afar counts. Jesus' pronouncement is best seen as a standard that they are not currently meeting, but that they will in Acts, when they endure their own testing/trials for the sake of bearing witness to Jesus.

Because Jesus counts these twelve as true companions, he bestows on them not "a kingdom" but "the kingdom," the same kingdom that his Father gave him—"my kingdom," he says. These twelve will be his close associates in the glory times to come, eating and drinking with him in the kingdom, as he has just promised (22:15, 18). The privilege of being able to eat and drink at the king's table was a famous image in the ancient world for gaining ultimate status. But then Jesus takes it another step: "you will sit upon thrones judging the twelve tribes of Israel." Notice that Matthew's version has "you will sit upon twelve thrones" (Matt 19:28); Luke's version gives a little space to account for Judas's defection. "Judging" might refer to heroes like Gideon, Samson, and Deborah, who delivered Israel in the days before the kings,[24] but probably here is synonymous with "ruling."[25]

This is not the first time that Jesus has promised the kingdom to the disciples: "Fear not, little flock, it is your Father's good pleasure to give you the kingdom," provided that you make yourself poor in order to enter it (12:32-33). But the dark hour is fast approaching, and so it is appropriate for Jesus to renew the promise.

In 22:24-30, we get, in a nice compact paragraph, Luke's paradoxical understanding of how kingship and kingdom apply to Jesus and his followers. Among the nations, kings rule and call it benefaction; not so among you! At the same time, here is your share of my kingdom, along with the privileges of eating at the royal table and sharing the responsibility of ruling. I am among you as a servant; I also have a kingdom; be youngest, be least, be a servant; be a co-regent and rule with me. It is the same paradox that began the Gospel. Gabriel tells Mary that her son will sit on David's throne and will reign over the house of Jacob forever (1:32-33), and Mary, inspired by the Spirit, says that her son will bring down the powerful from their thrones and lift up the lowly (1:52). There are ways to resolve the paradox. One can think temporally: upending the powerful and living as the least is for now, while ruling in the kingdom is for later, when God inaugurates the kingdom in power.[26] One can think spiritually or metaphorically: Jesus is king (and the Twelve with him) over those who swear allegiance to him; in Acts, the Twelve exercise Jesus' authority over this new version of the twelve tribes and so fulfill the predictions of Gabriel and Jesus.[27]

As we interpret the paradox, we should keep in mind that Jesus is defining "kingdom" and "ruling" in terms of service—vv. 24-27 are pretty clear about that. The apostles are not supposed to replicate The Way Things Are, with figures who rule and exercise kingly authority, even if they do so with motives of benefaction. Jesus never says "I am among you as a king," but "I am among you as a servant." Contrast, for example, the behavior of the nobleman who went to get a kingdom (19:11-27). He, too, receives a kingdom; he returns and shares it with others. But he is no servant, and he does not treat his slaves as if they were his friends. He is unforgiving toward the slave whose conduct does not come up to standard, and orders that his enemies be slaughtered while he watches. Jesus, by contrast, makes himself and all the others servants as a prelude to his kingly largesse; the apostles are praised for standing with him and are not censured for failures; Peter and Judas do not lose their places at the table; and Jesus does not condemn those who do not wish him to be their king. Servant-kingship is an oxymoron, but that seems to be what Luke is driving at—one can only "rule" or "judge" if one does it as Jesus does, by an open invitation to the table.

Again, without pause, Luke switches directions. Imagine Jesus and the Twelve, still reclining on their dining couches, with the Twelve relishing the prospect of doing this in the future, when they will be known as the friends of the King. Jesus then looks Peter in the eye, and says, in the hearing of all the rest, "Simon, Simon, Satan has asked for you [plural] in order to sift you as if you were wheat, but I have prayed for you [singular], lest your faith give out." [Satan Has Asked for You] Satan, who took possession of Judas, wants all the apostles. When this comes just after Jesus' praise of the Twelve as stalwart in the face of testing, one is reminded of

Satan Has Asked for You

There is an interesting parallel to Jesus' statement in the *Testament of Benjamin* (2d century BC) 3.3: "Fear the Lord, and love your neighbor, and if the spirits of Beliar should ask for you [same verb Luke uses] for tribulations unto all wickedness, he will never rule over you with any wicked tribulations, as he also never did Joseph my brother."

Jesus' Intercession

A woman who sometimes seemed like Job to me, for all that she had come through with her faith in God intact—the accidental death of one of her children, her own ill health, a husband whose recovery from alcoholism and verbal abuse of his family had come slow and hard—told me that her favorite Bible verse was [Luke 22:31-32] . . . . The woman told me that it had made all the difference to her that Jesus knew that Peter would deny him; he predicts it two verses later. She said that she often wanted to deny her troubles, and that she turned away from God in anger when things seemed unbearable. "But then I remember that Jesus himself has promised to pray for me, and this church is his gift. And if I need the people here so much, someone else might need me. So, like Peter, I turn back."

Kathleen Norris, *Amazing Grace: A Vocabulary of Faith* (New York: Riverhead, 1998, 136.

God's praise of Job and Satan's retort that he could make him cry "uncle" (Job 1:8-12; 2:2-5).[28] "Sifting" is always an image of separating the good from the worthless; Satan's tempting/testing will test whether Jesus is correct about how the disciples will remain with him. Satan wants all of the Twelve—thus the plural "you"—but Jesus singles out Peter as the one "standing in the need of prayer." Why not pray for all of them? Praying for Peter doesn't rule this out, but the tradition as it came to Luke names Peter as the one who openly denies Jesus, and so the narrative dictates why he would be especially in need of Jesus' intercession. [Jesus' Intercession] Why not pray for Judas, too? Again, the narrative has Judas's role fixed as the betrayer, and the meta-narrative behind that, in Luke's understanding, is the story of the servant who was handed over (Isa 53:12 LXX; see commentary in the previous section). "When you have returned" implies what Jesus says explicitly in v. 34—Peter, "the rock," will fail by denying that he knows Jesus. But he will return, and when he does, he should strengthen the rest. Peter thinks he's ready to go to prison or to die with Jesus—echoing Jesus' "you are those who have remained with me in my testing/trials." For now, he's wrong, but later in Acts he will go to jail and face the threat of death.

The final zigzag is the most puzzling of all. Jesus first reminds the Twelve of their earlier missionary work, when Jesus sent them out "without purse and bag and sandals." "You didn't go without anything, did you?" he asks them, and they agree. Now he reverses field: "Let the one who has a purse take it—likewise a bag—and let the one who has no sword sell his cloak and buy one."[29] The "purse" is for money; the "bag" is for provisions; the "sword" is a long knife or short sword. Wait—he wants us to carry swords now? Well, we can't go buy any right this minute, after sundown on the night of the Passover feast; how many can we scrounge between us? "Lord, look, we have two swords here with us." "That's enough," he says.

Our question here is what Luke most likely thought Jesus meant by this. If there was no mention of swords, then one might think that Luke is trying to account for the difference between the missionary commands in Luke 9:1-5 and 10:1-16 and the actual practice of the apostles in Acts. But "sell your cloak and buy a sword," particularly in view of "love your enemies" and "sell your possessions and give to the poor," is hard to take literally. Some have therefore suggested that it is a warning about the dangers ahead for Jesus' followers, the equivalent of "You thought things were bad? You ain't seen nothing yet." The disciples take Jesus too literally; "that's enough" is his "exasperated termination of this discussion."[30] A slight variation makes "purse, bag, and sword" symbolic of the kind of spiritual preparation needed to be successful apostles, like the "armor of the Lord" in Ephesians 6:11-17.[31] Another angle would make Jesus' words ironic. First he gets them to admit that his teachings about voluntary poverty and nonviolence actually worked—they needed nothing when they were being obedient. Then he gives them an ironic contradictory command—go and do the opposite of what I told you—a command that, because it was Passover, they could not actually obey—and what do you know, it turns out they already have two swords, proving that that they have not actually been living by his teachings after all. "I give up," we might paraphrase Jesus' last remark.

Something like one of these options—Jesus is being figurative or ironic—may be the only way to make sense of the episode. However, the tradition as it reached Luke included the scene where, as Jesus was being arrested, one of those with him drew a sword and used it to wound the high priest's slave (Mark 14:47). Why would one of Jesus' close associates be armed, especially in view of his teachings on nonretaliation (6:27-29) and of his instructions to the apostles to carry not even a staff (9:3)? Luke inserts this puzzling scene to explain why the disciples had swords—Jesus ordered them to get some. And why would Jesus command such a thing? Luke tells us: "the thing which has been written must be fulfilled in me, 'And he was reckoned with the lawless'; for even this has an end concerning me." Here "end" has the sense of "goal" as well as "termination"; this thing written will be wrapped up in that night's events. Just as before, the back story is what happened to the servant of the Lord in Isaiah 53. Jesus' quotation is from Isaiah 53:12 LXX, the same passage that speaks of the servant being handed over. Luke's understanding is that everything written about Jesus must be fulfilled (24:44). Jesus is a prophet (7:16) and so must die a prophet's death in Jerusalem (13:33). Jesus is a servant (22:27), and so what is written about the servant must be completed by his experience. Possibly this is how Luke makes sense of the sword play in the garden. But by calling them "lawless," Luke means not to exonerate the armed apostles;

Duccio's *Last Supper*

Duccio (di Buoninsegna) (c.1260–1319). *The Last Supper*. Panel from the back of the Maesta altarpiece. Museo dell'Opera Metropolitana, Siena, Italy. (Credit: Scala/Art Resource, NY)

Although Duccio's painting of the Last Supper puts Jesus and the Twelve seated at a table (rather than reclining, as Luke presumes), it does suggest the table talk of Luke's narrative, and also where the "swords" might have come from.

they are "lawless" because they already had the swords, proving yet again that they have not given up everything to follow Jesus.

What an amazing bunch of twists and turns. Don't be like the kings of the nations, ruling their subjects and telling everyone it is for the public good. Instead, try to be like the youngest or the servant. Here, I'm giving you a share of my royal table—you will all rule over Israel. You are all my close companions during my trials; but Satan wants you all, and Peter will deny he knows me three times, so I will pray for you that your faith won't fail. You did fine when you hit the road with nothing in your hand, didn't you? Well, now make sure you have your moneybag, your knapsack, your walking shoes, and a sword. The apostles, too, are all over the place. Judas is possessed by Satan. Peter thinks he is ready to die with Jesus, but his faith will falter, and he will need to repent. Each still thinks he might be the greatest; none has grasped the significance of Jesus' teachings about service; two of them have swords, in contravention of Jesus' nonviolent principles. Soon Jesus will be taken away from them—will they come apart at the fissures this discourse reveals?

Not so, according to Luke's Jesus. He has prayed for them, and even though Peter will fall away, he will return to strengthen the rest. Jesus is still at work: teaching, correcting, predicting, forgiving, consoling, and challenging this motley crew at the table. That's our Lord, who rules by serving, whose kingdom is a table where all—traitors, apostates, lawless—are welcome.

Jesus' Prayer and Arrest, 22:39-53

My mental image of Jesus praying on the night of his arrest was formed early, because the Sallman painting *Christ in Gethsemane* (1940–1950), reproduced on folio-sized cardstock, hung in the children's classroom in the church I attended. Jesus is kneeling, his arms resting on an altar-like rock shelf, his hands clasped, his face turned up in prayer. The background is dark, naturally—it is late at night, after the dinner and the post-dinner conversation—and in the middle distance, just past Jesus' head, you can see a clump of apostles sleeping under a tree. There are olive branches all around Jesus and in the far distance, on the next ridge, what looks like the dome of the temple. So far, not a bad representation of how Luke constructs the scene: dozing disciples, Jesus on the Mount of Olives opposite the temple mount, Jesus in prayer. But Sallman pictures Jesus more as Mark does, "distressed and agitated . . . deeply grieved" (Mark 14:3-34): Jesus' brow is furrowed, his eyebrows raised as if he were pleading, the tension from his clenched hands evident in his arms. The fifteenth- or sixteenth-century carved Jesus, is by contrast, much more com- posed and calm, at peace with what is about to happen to him. This Jesus is more like Luke's, praying but not agonizing, and to read Luke correctly, we must first put Mark out of our minds.

Mark describes Jesus' very strong emotions as he enters the garden: "he began to be distressed [ἐκθαμβέω, *ekthambeō*, "to be moved to a relatively intense emotional state because of something causing great surprise or perplexity"[32]] and agitated [ἀδημονέω, *adēmoneō*, "to be in anxiety, be distressed, trou- bled"[33]], and he says to them, 'My soul is grieved to the point of death'" (Mark 14:33-34). Luke tells us nothing about Jesus' inner emotional state as he arrives at the Mount of Olives; his concern is

Christ Praying

Christ Praying. Fragment from Christ on the Mount of Olives. ca. 1500. Linden wood with polychrome traces. From Ulm (?), Swabia, Germany. Louvre, Paris, France. (Credit: Réunion des Musées Nationaux/Art Resource, NY).

for the apostles, whom he orders to pray lest they enter into temptation. Mark's Jesus "fell upon the earth" (14:35), whereas Luke's "knelt." Luke shifts the emotion of grief from Jesus to the apostles (22:45), and as we will note below, softens the request to remove the cup by making it conditional on God's plan—"if you desire."

Most study editions of the English New Testament will have a note about the textual problem of vv. 43-44. The oldest and most reliable manuscripts of Luke and several early translations omit these, and some later manuscripts include them with marks indicating that the verses were not present in the text they were copying, but were inserted from another source. In addition, these verses appear after Matthew 26:39 in some ancient lectionaries (selected Gospel texts arranged for reading in worship services). Because the manuscripts and versions without the verses are early and from many different parts of the empire, and because the verses "wander" as they are transcribed, it seems more plausible to me that they were not originally part of Luke.[34] The scene was known to Justin Martyr (*Dial.* 103.8), who died around 150, so it is very old. [Justin Martyr on Jesus' Prayer] Perhaps, as some theorize about the pericope of the adulterous woman (John 7:43–8:11), it was an old tradition repeated orally as a part of Christian preaching. At some point—probably in the fourth or fifth century—it needed a home in a gospel, which eventually became this spot in Luke. The omission of the verses preserves Luke's non-emotional Jesus as well as the chiastic structure of the passage (see below), and I will first interpret the passage without them. But because the verses are so much a part of the popular image of Jesus' prayer on that night, at the end of these comments I will read the longer passage and comment on how that changes Luke's presentation of Jesus.

Luke begins the scene by describing Jesus' exit: "And coming out [of the house? of the city? both, perhaps] he went to the Mount of Olives, as he had been doing." "As was his custom" reminds the audience of 21:37, where Luke tells us that Jesus had been leaving the city every night to sleep on the mount. Luke writes only that Jesus went to "the spot" (22:40), meaning the spot of his nightly bivouac; Mark and Matthew say "the region called Gethsemani" (Mark 14:32; Matt 26:36), whereas John calls the place a "garden" located "beyond the Kidron." The Kidron Valley lay between the temple mount and the Mount of Olives, so John means that the garden is on the Mount of Olives. "Gethsemani" appears to be derived from the Hebrew words for "olive press," and since in Jesus' day the hill was covered with olive groves, there surely would have been at least one olive press there. [The Mount of Olives] Quite probably, then, all four evangelists imagine Jesus leaving the meal to go to a place on the Mount of Olives; Luke's choice of words is intended to show that even though Jesus knew what was about to happen, he went to his accustomed place, making no attempt to hide.

"His disciples also followed him." Does this imply that more than the twelve apostles were present at the arrest? Luke specifies that the apostles were with him at the supper (22:14), and that Judas was there for the meal (22:21); like Mark, Luke does not tell the reader when Judas slipped away from the rest of them (Matthew implies that it happens just before Jesus broke the bread; John has Jesus dismiss Judas after handing him a piece of bread). Perhaps the switch from "apostles" to "disciples" is to indicate the moment when Judas left, so that they are no longer twelve; notice that 24:9 calls them "the eleven." But the group that came with him from Galilee was larger than the twelve and included women (23:55); Acts 1:15 estimates 120 persons, too large for one Passover meal. Luke may presume that the larger group has been waiting for Jesus and follows him out of the city back to their spot. That would be consistent with how Luke identifies those who watched Jesus die: "all who knew him, including the women who had followed him from Galilee" (23:49). Notice also that Luke does not have Jesus pick out Peter, James, and John to stick closer to him; all the disciples present, however many that was, were commissioned to pray along with him, but none of them does.

As noted earlier, the scene of Jesus' prayer is a chiasm, where the first element is like the last one, the second one like the next to last, and so forth:

A. He said to them, "Pray lest you enter into temptation." (40)
  B. And he withdrew from them about a stone's throw (41a)
    C. Knelt down and prayed (41b)
      D. Father . . . your will be done (42)
    C'. And rising from prayer (45a)

The Mount of Olives

    Josephus, *J.W.* 6.5-7, states that before the siege of Jerusalem during the War of 66–70, the hills around Jerusalem were full of trees and gardens:

And now the Romans, although they were greatly distressed in getting together their materials, raised their banks in twenty-one days, after they had cut down all the trees that were in the country that adjoined to the city, and that for about twelve miles all around, as I have already related. And truly, the very view itself of the country was a melancholy thing; for those places which were before adorned with trees and pleasant gardens, were now become a desolate country all over, and its trees were all cut down: nor could any foreigner that had formerly seen Judea and the most beautiful suburbs of the city, and now saw it as a desert, but lament and mourn sadly at so great a change.

B'. Coming to the disciples he found them sleeping from grief (45b)

A'. And he said to them, "Why do you sleep? Rise, pray, lest you enter into temptation." (46)[35]

It is relatively unusual for Luke to repeat something precisely, and to repeat "pray lest you enter into temptation" in just a few verses is meant to draw our attention both to this structure and to Luke's understanding of this scene as the moment just before the big temptation/testing. Jesus' double command echoes the last phrase of Luke's version of the model prayer, "do not lead us into temptation." But the prayer, at this moment in time, cannot be granted by God; the disciples are there, with Jesus, and the arresting party is on its way. This moment belongs to those under Satan's control, Jesus will say (22:53), and so the disciples will have to face their own testing/temptations. Thus Luke's Jesus asks the disciples to pray essentially the same prayer he prayed—let this moment pass, but only if that conforms to Your will.

Had they prayed this way, rather than falling asleep, how might things have gone at the arrest? Given Jesus' teachings about nonviolent responses to persecution, one suspects Luke imagined that the disciples should have reacted more like Jesus, denouncing the motives of his persecutors but not trying to harm them physically. [Praying with Jesus in the Garden]

The Synoptic Gospels transmit Jesus' prayer differently. Paying close attention to the variations will help us to notice the nuances that Luke has in mind.

Mark 14:36	Abba, Father, all things are possible for you;
Luke 22:42	O Father, if you desire,[36]
Matthew 26:39	My Father, if it is possible,

Mark has Jesus address God as "abba," which he then translates for the reader (*ho patēr*, "the father"). Matthew and Luke both drop the Aramaic and change the Greek "father" to a form of direct address.[37] Luke and Matthew also change Mark's wording slightly in order to make Jesus' request conditional, and thus give the reader a way to understand why it was not granted by God. Luke

---

Praying with Jesus in the Garden

Lord, help me to persist when I want to give up.
Lord, help me to keep trying although I can't see what good it does.
Lord, help me to keep praying although I'm not sure you hear me.
Lord, help me to keep living in ways that seek to please you.
Lord, help me to know when to lead and when to follow.
Lord, help me to know when to speak and when to remain silent.
Lord, help me to know when to act and when to wait.

Marian Wright Edelman, *Guide My Feet* (New York: HarperCollins, 1995), 65.

also uses a different verb; *boulein* connotes God's will in the sense of a plan or preset course of action. Thus, Jesus is asking for God to take the cup away only if it is part of the larger plan.[38]

Mark 14:36	Take this cup from me
Luke 22:42	Take this cup from me
Matthew 26:39	Let this cup depart from me

Luke keeps Mark's very direct request for God to take the cup away; "take" is second-person imperative. Matthew substitutes a slightly more indirect third-person imperative. The "cup" is a symbol for a person's or group's destiny as determined by God. Often in the Old Testament it is the "cup of God's wrath" (LXX Ps 74:8; Isa 51:17; Hab 2:16; Jer 25:15; Lam 4:21; Ezek 23:31-33; Rev 14:10), but it can also stand for salvation (LXX Pss 15:5; 115:13). Jesus' destiny, as he has already predicted several times, is to be handed over to the Gentiles and killed. "Take this cup from me" asks God to do something different—provided it is within God's plan, God's *boulē*. [Let this Cup Pass] Since we know what God's plan is, we know as well as Jesus does that he cannot avoid the cross. So why pray at all? The example of the sleeping disciples may answer the question. They, too, could not avoid entering temptation/testing; but had they stayed awake, praying that God keep them from it, they would have had their minds focused in the right place. Jesus' prayer shows the way forward for someone who might be paralyzed by fear or overcome by sorrow: pray, using it as a way both to express your fears to God and to submit to God's wise guidance. [Thomas More on Jesus' Prayer in the Garden]

Let this Cup Pass

Dear God, with you everything is possible. Let the cup of war, killing, and destruction, the cup of bloodshed, human anguish and desolation, the cup of torture, breakage in human relationships and abandonment . . . Dear God, let this cup pass us by. We are afraid. We are trembling in the depths of our being. We feel the sweat and tears of thousands of people all over the world, people who are afraid—afraid to fight, afraid to kill, afraid of being killed, afraid of an uncertain future.

Henri J. M. Nouwen, in *Prayers for Healing*, ed. Maggie Oman (Berkeley CA: Conari Press, 1997), 122.

Thomas More on Jesus' Prayer in the Garden

Therefore, since he foresaw that there would be many people of such a delicate constitution that they would be convulsed with terror at any danger of being tortured, he chose to enhearten them by the example of his own sorrow, his own sadness, his own weariness and unequalled fear, lest they should be so disheartened as they compare their own fearful state of mind with the boldness of the bravest martyrs that they would yield freely what they fear will be won from them by force. To such a person as this, Christ wanted his own deed to speak out (as it were) with his own living voice: "O faint of heart, take courage and do not despair. You are afraid, you are sad, you are stricken with weariness and dread of the torment with which you have been cruelly threatened. Trust me . . . be content to have me as your shepherd, follow my leadership; if you do not trust yourself, place your trust in me. See, I am walking ahead of you along this fearful road."

From Thomas More, *The Sadness of Christ* (trans. Clarence Miller, ed. Gerard Wegemer; cited in Matthew Levering, ed., *On Christian Dying*; New York: Rowan and Littlefield, 2004), 86.

Mark 14:36	But not what I wish but what you [wish]
Luke 22:42	But let not my will but yours be done
Matthew 26:39	But not as I wish but as you [wish]

The Prayer and the Divinity of Jesus

The prayer to let the cup pass also raised lots of questions among ancient Christians about the divinity of Christ. According to some, "the passion of grief or affliction or sore distress as we may call it, cannot have reference to the divine nature of the Word, which is not able to suffer" (Cyril of Alexandria, *Commentary on Luke*, homily 146; cited in Just, 341). But for others, the mystery of the incarnation meant that God was willing to suffer in Christ: "When he begged to be spared death he did so naturally, with his divine will wanting and permitting. He was thus in agony and afraid. Then, when his divine will wanted his human will to choose death, it freely accepted the passion. He did not freely deliver himself over to death as God alone but also as man" (John of Damascus, *Orthodox Faith* 3.18; cited in Just, *Luke*, 342).

Arthur A. Just Jr., ed., *Luke* (ACCS: NT, vol. 3; Downer's Grove IL: Intervarsity Press, 2003).

Luke's statement is slightly broader than either Mark's or Matthew's: "let . . . your will be done" rather than "as you wish" covers everyone's actions, not just God's. In other words, Luke's Jesus prays not just that God will do as God wills, but that everyone will act according to God's will. [The Prayer and the Divinity of Jesus]

Rising from his prayer, Jesus goes to find the disciples asleep "from grief." In Mark, the disciples are awakened three times, making Jesus something of a snooze button and highlighting the disciples' lack of discipline and self-control. Luke reduces their naps from three to one, so perhaps "from grief" is also meant to excuse them.[39] However, in Luke's culture, grief-stricken persons do not normally fall asleep; they wail, tear their clothes, pull out their hair, and weep bitterly (see Sir 38:16-23; Jdt 7:23-29; 2 Macc 3:14-21; 2 Esd 9:38–10:4). Sleeping while the master may be approaching is not admirable behavior (Luke 12:35-38), nor is allowing grief to master one's self-control (2 Macc 7:20-38; 4 Macc 15–18). Fourth Maccabees 1:18-30 LXX identifies grief as an emotion created by pain that reason, instructed by the Torah, can hold in check. The mother of the seven martyrs is called "defender of the Law" (15:29 LXX) because she bewailed none of them in death, "nor did she grieve for them as for those who died" (16:12 LXX). In the minds of Luke's audience, as Jesus' close associates the disciples should have been encouraging him rather than letting negative emotions like fear and grief overmaster them. [Jesus as a Model for Martyrs]

Jesus' command to the disciples to get up and pray still rings in the audience's ears when Judas arrives—"one of the twelve," just to remind us of his perfidy—leading a "crowd." Both Mark and Matthew use this word, too, and say that the crowd was "from" the chief priests, scribes, and elders; Luke saves the identification until Jesus speaks to them in v. 52, so that at the moment, the "crowd" could have been anyone.

Jesus as a Model for Martyrs

Ancient Christians turned to this scene as a model for how to face persecution and possible martyrdom. The *Martyrdom of Polycarp*, written to show its audience "a martyrdom in conformity with the gospel" (*Mart. Pol.* 1:1), describes how Polycarp allowed others to talk him into leaving the city of Smyrna for "a small country house," but that while he was there he continued his work as bishop, "night and day doing nothing but pray for everyone and for the churches throughout the world, as was his custom" (*Mart. Pol.* 5:1). He had a vision that let him know he would be burned, and when the police converged on the house "fully armed as if pursuing a bandit," the aged bishop made no attempt to escape. "He could have fled elsewhere even from there, but he chose not to, saying, 'Let the will of God be done'" (*Mart. Pol.* 7:1).

Judas "drew near to Jesus in order to kiss him," but Luke skips the actual kiss (Mark 14:45), reminiscent of how he also avoided saying that John baptized Jesus (3:21). One can assume it happened or not, and translate v. 48 as either "And Jesus said to him, 'Judas, are you handing over the Son of Man with a kiss?'" or "But Jesus said to him, 'Judas, would you hand over the Son of Man with a kiss?'"[40]

Picture the scene: Jesus and Judas are at the center, standing close together, and just behind Judas, a crowd. Around Jesus are his followers, who only a moment before were sleeping. They "see what was coming" and ask, "Lord, should we strike with the sword?" Without waiting for a reply one of them strikes the high priest's slave, cutting off his right ear (a left-handed disciple, most likely, although that is hardly the point Luke is making). Jesus warned them earlier that they should pray lest they fall into temptation; sure enough, the moment of crisis has caught them unprepared, and they react, not like their Lord, but like any other armed person might if he felt threatened. Luke leaves the identification of the sword-wielder completely ambiguous; we know there were at least two swords among the Twelve, and only one struck the blow. It could have been any of them—that's the point. It takes a lot of self-control to maintain a stance of nonviolence in a crisis; Jesus' disciples should have been praying rather than napping. And what did the blow accomplish? The violent disciple wounded a slave, whom Luke's audience would have assumed was unarmed and probably carrying a torch or a lantern. "Enough of this!" says Jesus, and heals the slave's ear.

Now Luke chooses to do a close-up on the crowd. "Jesus said to those who came out for him, the chief priests and officers of the temple and elders . . . ." "Chief priests" are the heads of the priestly families or divisions, serving as advisors to the high priest; the "officers" are perhaps the heads of the temple guards or police; the "elders" are the heads of the leading Jewish families in Jerusalem. In other words, Luke's "crowd" includes the big shots with whom Judas made a bargain in 22:3-6. They are armed with swords and clubs "as if for a bandit"; he is no brigand, but by disobeying his teachings on nonviolence, his disciples have given the big shots some justification for coming with weapons. Jesus reminds them that he was in public view for days in the temple—right in their headquarters—and yet they chose instead to seize him in secret. If their cause is just, why must it be carried out in the dark?

Jesus is thus surrounded by people who reject his teachings. The crowd of authorities, armed as if to seize a dangerous warlord; the disciple who, under Satan's prompting, has conspired with them to arrest him; the rest of his disciples who sleep rather than praying and who strike out rather than accepting God's will—nobody is following him now. "This is your hour," he says, "and the authority of darkness." They asked him, in the temple, where his authority came from; now he exposes where theirs originates.

Reading 22:39-53 without vv. 43-44, we meet a Jesus who is the eye of the hurricane. He prays for another way, but only if it is God's will. When the disciples sleep, he wakes them up and warns them, but with none of the scolding and sarcasm of Mark's account (14:37-38). When the disciples panic, he halts the scuffle and heals the injured person. He denounces the methods and motives of those who arrest him, but offers no resistance. And nobody flees, as in Mark—neither the young man nor the rest of the disciples—so that the end of the scene is not the chaos of scattering disciples, but the clarity of Jesus' prophetic word.

If we add in vv. 43-44, then we must alter our picture of Jesus somewhat. These verses, if included in the story, depict him wrestling with strong emotions. The angel appears, strengthening him, as he has commissioned Peter to do for other believers (22:32). There have been angels in Luke already, and there will be more, but these others function as messengers (Gabriel to Zechariah and Mary; the two angels at the tomb and at the ascension). An angel comes to let Peter out of jail (Acts 12:6-11), but there is no other example in Luke-Acts of an angel assisting someone in prayer or giving comfort to someone in distress. (Interestingly, Mark has angels who minister to Jesus at the end of Satan's temptation, but Luke omits them.) By that measure, then, Jesus' distress was great: "being in agony" (v. 44) makes this explicit. "Agony" transliterates a Greek word that means a struggle; in different contexts, this could be an athletic contest, a battle, a gladiatorial fight, or the human struggle for self-mastery. Jesus is pictured struggling in prayer until his sweat "became as drops of blood falling upon the ground." Although some ancient writers took this to mean he literally sweated blood, the verses only compare his sweat to blood drops; he was sweating as if he was wounded, in other words, as if the crucifixion were already underway. As Brown points out, the martyrs in 4 Maccabees are described struggling as they are tortured: bathed in sweat (4 Macc 6:11), dripping blood (4 Macc 10:8), etc., but never submitting to the demands that they transgress the Law. I agree that this is the context from which the image comes: Jesus as martyr-to-be, fully imagining what is about to happen, wrestling with it in prayer, and then rising from prayer, prepared to face his destiny. But because Luke takes steps, as we have seen and will continue to see, to reduce or eliminate Mark's references to Jesus' emotional responses to his arrest, these verses still seem to me to be out of place in Luke's account.

Jesus and Peter on Trial, 22:54-71

This is one of the most dramatic scenes in the Gospel. Jesus, after being grabbed by the crowd of chief priests, temple officers, and elders, was led by them to the house of the high priest. Like Mark, Luke does not give his name; Matthew 26:57 and John 18:13 correctly identify him as Caiaphas, son-in-law of the former high priest Annas; Luke 3:1 speaks of "the high priesthood of Annas and Caiaphas" and Acts 3:5 calls Annas the high priest, so it is possible that Luke was not certain which of the two was high priest during Jesus' trial. Others think these double references were due to the ongoing influence of Annas and his descendants, who controlled the high priesthood during the first half of the first century. [Josephus on the High Priest]

Caiphas's house was no doubt in the "Upper City" part of Jerusalem where the mansions of the nobility were. Although Christians as far back as the fourth century have identified a certain place as Caiaphas's house, the tradition must be taken with a grain of salt. The Upper City was looted and then burned when the Roman army entered the city in 70, and there is no evidence that Christians venerated the spot continuously. However, based on excavations of first-century mansions, we can get an idea of what Caiaphas's house may have been like. The "Palatial Mansion," for instance,

Josephus on the High Priest

Caiaphas was appointed high priest by Valerius Gratus, just before Pilate came to replace him as procurator.

[Nero] was now the third emperor; and he sent Valerius Gratus to be procurator of Judea, and to succeed Annius Rufus. This man deprived Ananus [i.e., the Annas of the New Testament] of the high priesthood, and appointed Ismael, the son of Phabi, to be high priest. He also deprived him in a little time, and ordained Eleazar, the son of Ananus, who had been high priest before, to be high priest: which office, when he had held for a year, Gratus deprived him of it, and gave the high priesthood to Simon, the son of Camithus; and, when he had possessed that dignity no longer than a year, Joseph Caiaphas was made his successor. When Gratus had done those things, he went back to Rome, after he had tarried in Judea eleven years, when Pontius Pilate came as his successor.

Josephus, *Ant.* 18.33-35.

Reconstructed Upper-class Home

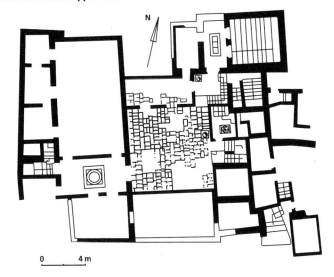

0   4 m

has living spaces on three sides of a central courtyard, as well as a large, beautifully decorated hall. It was thirty-five feet long, with a mosaic floor and painted plaster panels on the walls.[41] Other houses in the neighborhood followed the same pattern:

> Avigad's excavations in the Upper City revealed a well-planned city whose residents lived an aristocratic lifestyle. There were remains of magnificent houses some two or more stories high, built around a central court. Mosaic flooring, frescoes, and painted plaster adorned the homes of many Jerusalem residents . . . . Painted pottery of superior quality, well-crafted furnishings, and beautiful stone objects, including tables, bowls, and purification jars, reflected the wealth of Jerusalem in the Herodian period.[42] [Stone Kitchenware]

Stone Kitchenware

Stone furniture or tableware was much more expensive than ordinary wooden furniture or ceramic tableware, but could not become impure, so the stone stuff indicates not only wealth but concern for purity.

A single- or multi-storied home built around a "courtyard" (*aulē*) seems to be the kind of architecture Luke has in mind for this scene. Jesus is brought "into the house of the high priest" and yet he can see Peter, who is sitting in the *aulē*. The scene works whether we imagine Jesus also in the courtyard (which is part of the house) or in one of the many rooms that opened onto it in the typical floor plan of such a house. The courtyard, even though it was in the center of the house, was more or less public space in an insula (a multi-storied, multi-family house with separate living units around a central courtyard) or in a peristyle house (a multi- or single-story, normally single-family house with the rooms situated so that many of them have openings and sight-lines to the colonnaded courtyard, often decorated with statuary and plants). Clients of the householder or persons who claimed to have some business with another member of the household could be admitted to the courtyard to wait their turn. According to John 18:16, Peter had to wait on the street until the "disciple whom Jesus loved" vouched for him; Luke assumes that Peter, who followed Jesus "at a distance," could walk in unchallenged.

Peter's location is integral to the story. He begins on the Mount of Olives, with Jesus, Judas, the arresting crowd of chief priests, temple officers, and elders, and the rest of the larger group of disciples. Jesus is led away by the arresting crowd; Judas and the rest of the disciples disappear from view for a while; only Peter "follows at a distance." That's as close as he will get to Jesus until after the resurrection. He, with all the rest who know Jesus, watch him die "from a distance" (23:49). They (as Acts 1:21-22 notes) are witnesses to everything from John's baptism until the ascension; witnesses, but not yet participants.

"After they lit a fire in the middle of the courtyard and were sitting down together, Peter sat in their midst" (22:55). Most likely, Luke imagines that the "crowd" of big shots and their servants who have seized Jesus enter the house, and some of them—servants, no doubt—start a fire; it's going to be a long night. Where's Jesus? Luke waits until the most dramatic moment to spring that on us (22:61). Peter, who has told Jesus that he was prepared to go with him both to prison and to death, follows them in, and once the fire is going, sits down with the group. Is he gathering intelligence, waiting for his chance to speak on Jesus' behalf, or hoping for an opportunity to help Jesus escape? It was brave to walk into hostile territory and sit down by the fire with the enemy's servants; but his courage and whatever plans he had in mind blew away with the smoke as soon as the slave girl spoke: "When she noticed him sitting by the light and when she had stared at him, she said, 'This one was with him, too.'" The implication is that she had seen Peter with Jesus before—maybe she was with the arresting party that night—and that she speaks to someone else and not to Peter. Peter's first test is thus not a direct accusation but a form of corridor talk between slaves and clients. "He denied, saying, 'I do not know him, woman.'" "Denied" was one of the standard terms used for repudiating Christ (Shepherd of Hermas, *Visions* 2.2.8; *Diogn.* 7.7; *2 Clem.* 17:7; *Mart. Pol.* 9:2), so "denied," meaning "denied what she said," carries overtones of "denied him" as well.

The second one to identify Peter was an unnamed man, who after a bit noticed him and said to him, "You are also of them"— one of "them," the group attached to that unfortunate man. This second test is a direct statement, apparently unconnected to the first—just a separate observation. "But Peter said, 'Man, I am not.'" But then an hour later someone else "began to insist, saying, 'Truly this one was also with him, for he is also a Galilean.'" The three identifications are meant to increase in intensity: first, a remark about Peter that he overhears; second, a statement directly to him; third, another statement about him, but stated firmly, with supporting evidence—his Galilean accent gives him away. Peter maintains his denials: "I do not know him, woman"; "Man, I am not"; "Man, I do not know what you are talking about." He does not curse, as in Mark 14:71, but, like a well-trained

Denials

"In the closing days of the 1932 campaign, Franklin Roosevelt promised a crowd in Pittsburgh that he'd balance the federal budget while cutting 'government operations' by 25 percent. Wisely, he attempted neither, but four years later as he prepared for another campaign trip to western Pennsylvania, he asked his speechwriter Sam Rosenman what he should say if his earlier vow came up. 'Deny you were ever in Pittsburgh,' Rosenman replied."

Carl M. Cannon, "Untruth and Consequences," *The Atlantic* 299/1 (January/February 2007) 59.

politician, sticks to his denial even in the face of growing public opinion against him. [Denials]

Many early Christians from at least the 110s, if not earlier, faced the issue of what to do when they were identified as believers. Pliny, governor of Bithynia, wrote a letter to the Emperor Trajan in 112 describing how he had put some Christians to death when they would not curse Christ and offer incense to the emperor's statue. He states that once word of the executions got out, "the usual result followed; the very fact of my dealing with the question led to a wider spread of the charge, and a great variety of cases were brought before me. An anonymous pamphlet was issued, containing many names."[43] The *Martyrdom of Polycarp* shows the same range of ways that Christians were exposed, some by their aggressive public witness, but some by neighbors or slaves. Peter's experience demonstrated how one's allegiance to Christ might come to light as gossip or as a public denunciation. He is the negative example, a cautionary tale for how not to respond. The more appropriate thing to say is, like Polycarp, "Eighty-six years I have served him, and he never harmed me; how then can I slander my king and my savior?" (*Mart. Pol.* 9:2) [The Martyr Blandina]

As Peter was speaking his third denial, the rooster crowed, "and turning, the Lord looked hard at Peter." The easiest way to explain this is to imagine that Jesus was being held in the courtyard while the dignitaries discussed things inside.[44] This makes the drama even more intense: Jesus in one corner of the courtyard, Peter and a crowd around a fire in the center, and each of Peter's three "accusers" pointing or nodding to the "him" with whom they say Peter is associated. We could imagine, as noted earlier, that Jesus is in one of the rooms with a line of sight to the courtyard. But since Luke does not include any pre-trial interrogations, the scenario with Jesus in the courtyard is more plausibly how he imagined it. Did Peter think Jesus wouldn't hear what he was saying? In the hour between the second and third "outing," did he turn things over in his head, wondering whether he should admit that he lied and that he did belong to the captive? Or was he hoping that nobody else would try to expose him? At any rate, after

---

The Martyr Blandina

Blandina was a Christian, the house-slave of a Christian woman, who was arrested with many others in Gaul in the 3rd century. Eusebius, quoting from an earlier account of these martyrdoms, writes,

For while we all trembled, and her earthly mistress, who was herself also one of the witnesses, feared that on account of the weakness of her body, she would be unable to make bold confession, Blandina was filled with such power as to be delivered and raised above those who were torturing her by turns from morning till evening in every manner, so that they acknowledged that they were conquered, and could do nothing more to her. And they were astonished at her endurance, as her entire body was mangled and broken; and they testified that one of these forms of torture was sufficient to destroy life not to speak of so many and so great sufferings. But the blessed woman, like a noble athlete, renewed her strength in her confession; and her comfort and recreation and relief from the pain of her sufferings was in exclaiming, "I am a Christian and there is nothing vile done by us."

Eusebius, *Hist. eccl.* 5.1.17-19.

the cock's crow, Jesus turns and under his steady gaze, Peter remembered "the Lord's word" about how he would deny knowing Jesus three times, and "going out, he wept bitterly." Most of us know all too well how he felt; ever failed to speak up for the faith when you had the chance?

Peter thought he was ready to go with Jesus to prison and to death; he was not ready even to be identified as one of Jesus' associates. Nobody had threatened him, nobody put a knife to his throat, but as Jesus predicted, he folded the first time anyone suggested he knew Jesus. Jesus' gaze at the end of the scene is meant to be intense; the verb means to look at someone straight on, like our sense of looking someone in the eyes. Peter's bitter weeping as he turns to go, realizing the full extent of his failure, is probably also supposed to signify the beginning of his turn back to faith and to his responsibility to strengthen others (22:31-32).

Now that Peter is offstage, attention turns back to Jesus. "The men holding him" are not identified precisely. One could assume they were the same group of chief priests, officers, and elders that arrested him (22:52), but it seems more likely that Luke's audience would think that these important men left Jesus with their slaves or bodyguards, or with temple guards under the command of the "officers."[45] Luke describes a mocking scene rather than a real beating or scourging; Jesus was blindfolded, and then his captors hit him and asked him to use his prophetic powers to identify who struck him.[46] In Luke's account of Jesus' arrest and trial, there is never a scourging, although Pilate twice says that he will order it done to Jesus. The point of the "blind man's bluff" is to hold up to ridicule the notion that Jesus is a prophet, but ironically, it only proves that he is, since he predicted that he would be mocked (18:32).[47]

On the next morning, the "council of elders of the people" was gathered. The *presbyterion* was a normal feature of city government across the Mediterranean during imperial times, where the leading citizens met to discuss things and make decisions. In this verse, Luke specifies "chief priests and scribes"; in 23:13, "chief priests and rulers"; in Acts 4:5-6, "rulers, elders, scribes, with Annas the high priest and Caiaphas and John and Alexander and others of the high priest's family"; in Acts 5:21, "the high priest and those with him . . . convened the Sanhedrin and all the tribal leaders of the sons of Israel." In other words, Luke presumes that there was in Jerusalem a council of the most important people, including the high priest and all the chief priests, other members of the high priest's family, scribes, and the elders. This would bring together all the leaders of the significant families, both priestly and non-priestly, plus their secretaries and legal advisors. The term *presbyterion* meant the group who met, and would have been a familiar term to Luke's audience. "Sanhedrin" is derived from the Greek word *synedrion*, which in Luke 22:66 appears to mean the room where the *presbyterion* met, but in Acts 5:21 appears to mean the group that was meeting. According to Josephus, the "council house" was near the temple, abutting the old wall around the temple mount (*J. W.* 5.144); according to the Mishnah, the meeting room was inside the temple, in the forecourts (*m. Mid.* 5:4).

In Luke's version of the trial, they meet in daytime; Mark's version has them meeting at night, on the night of Passover, which may not have seemed proper to Luke. He also dispenses with Mark's statement that the council was looking for testimony that would lead to a death sentence (Mark 14:55), and omits the parade of false testimony against Jesus (Mark 14:56-59). Their first question is "If you are the Messiah, tell us." This is one of the charges they lay against him when they hand him over to Pilate (23:2), and anyone in Luke's audience would know that Roman procurators are expected to be merciless when dealing with would-be kings. The question thus has teeth to it, even if it sounds benign.

Jesus' answer is indirect. "If I tell you, you will not believe"—Jesus presumes, correctly, that their minds are already made up that he is not the real Messiah but a messianic pretender. "If I question [you], you will not answer"—Jesus has had this experience before, in the exchange in the temple about where his authority came from. He asked them to take a position on John the Baptist, and they refused (20:1-8), so he does not expect them to act differently now that they have him in custody. These two statements also square with how nobody in the narrative, not even the disciples, understands that Scripture mandates Jesus' sufferings. Everyone is in the dark until after the resurrection, when Jesus opens their minds to understand the Scriptures. "But from now on the Son of Man will be seated on the right of the power of God"—rather than answer their question straight out, Luke's Jesus makes another prediction. The "son of man" is his characteristic phrase for himself; so he is claiming that he will be elevated to sit at God's right—the position of power—"of the power of God," which connotes the all-encompassing rule of God. In other words, they can believe what they will, but he will have the power position next to the Almighty. In Luke's theology, the resurrection and ascension is the event proving that "God has made him both Lord and Messiah, this Jesus whom you crucified" (Acts 2:36).

Notice how Jesus' statement in Luke differs from what he says in Mark; in answer to the question, "Are you the Messiah, the Son of the Blessed?" Mark's Jesus says, "I am, and you will see the Son of Man seated at the right hand of Power and coming with the clouds of heaven." From Luke's point of view, the high priest and his associates will not see Jesus enthroned; Stephen the martyr will (Acts 7:55), but not these guys. From Luke's point of view, it is more correct to focus on Jesus' enthronement, rather than his return, as the event validating his status as God's chosen one. And from Luke's point of view, it is important that Jesus never answers the question about being Messiah in the affirmative. "You [plural] say that I am" (22:70) means the same thing as "You [singular] say" (in 23:3): those are your words; I never said them.

Jesus thus dodges the first question, "If you are the Messiah, tell us." They then ask another: "So, then, you are the Son of God?" His answer, "You say that I am" is even slipperier. It isn't a denial, but it is also not an affirmation.[48] Pilate asks him, "Are you the king of the Jews?" and when Jesus replies, "You say," Pilate dismisses the charge against him (23:3-4). But the council of elders takes it as an admission: "Why do we still need witnesses? We ourselves have heard from his mouth." Luke is being very careful here. Jesus never says he is Messiah, so he cannot be justly condemned for claiming to be a king. Luke thus avoids putting Jesus in the unsympathetic role of a non-Roman lower-class person who claimed to be a king and was crucified for it. On the other hand, he is called "Jesus the Christ," and his followers are known as "Christians." Luke does not have Jesus deny the title, which was so firmly embedded in the tradition. Instead, Luke has been trying to undercut the connection between the messianic promise to David, that Gabriel declares Jesus will fulfill, and kingship as typically practiced in his world. Jesus' father gave him a kingdom (22:29), but that does not make Jesus a king; instead, Jesus is a servant, a "deacon" (22:27), whose kingdom is a table to which everyone is invited.

Christian preachers and teachers must be direct in how they treat this passage, which is one of those that has done so much damage by misuse. The accounts of Jesus' arrest and handling by the temple authorities range in tone from Matthew, who accuses the high priest and the council of trying to encourage false testimony during an illegal night meeting, to John, which says Jesus was interrogated by Annas and then handed over to Pilate. Luke is in the middle; no night meeting, no false testimony, but also an official meeting of the council to bring about a foregone conclusion. Church members who already think "Pharisee" means "hypocrite" have no problem believing that the Sanhedrin was nothing but a kangaroo court providing a show trial before sentencing Jesus to death. This is a dangerous path; anti-Jewish attitudes are not Christ-like, and ministers should avoid reinforcing them.

CONNECTIONS

Throughout Christian history, the Communion meal has been both a divisive and a unifying ritual. Think of the reasons why persons have been excluded from the table: because they were not members of that particular denomination; because they were judged to be living in ways contradictory to church doctrine; because they were members of the wrong ethnic group; etc. Some Baptist congregations have refused to serve Communion to members of other Baptist churches. When I was a teenager, my youth director got in hot water for serving Communion to the youth on a retreat—many in the congregation felt that Communion was only to be served in the sanctuary. During the oral examination for my ordination, I was asked about the propriety of a bunch of ministers at a pastors' conference serving Communion to each other. "Sounds like a good idea to me," I said, forgetting that Landmarkism—the view that the local church is the only church, and that Communion should be shared only between members of a local church—was particularly strong in that part of the country. We debated that for a while; eventually they decided to ordain me anyway, reasoning that I was young and had plenty of time to come around to the truth.

Luke's presentation of Jesus' last supper is, it seems to me, a strong argument for letting Communion be as inclusive as possible. "The one who betrays me is with me, and his hand is on the table"—a hand, remember, that was currently possessed by Satan! If Jesus didn't exclude Judas, knowing full well what he was about to do, then what business do we have excluding others? I know that other New Testament passages argue for a stricter policy. Paul urged the Corinthians to exclude the unrepentant man who shacked up with his stepmother; the epistles of John warn the recipients to refuse to eat with anyone who does not confess that Jesus was a real human being. All the same, Luke's description of Jesus' practice should weigh heavily in our own calculations.

The after-dinner talk revolves around the nature of the church and the nature of its leadership. Which one of them could betray him? Any of them; but Jesus will pray for them, and they will eat at the great banquet of the kingdom of God. Which one of them is the greatest? Wrong question: Jesus' followers are not to judge themselves by normal standards of greatness. Jesus is among them as a servant, and his followers should imitate him. Jesus was surrounded by sinners, by people like us who wanted status and security; but despite the fact that they continued to demonstrate that they had not understood him and had not completely obeyed his commands, he accepted them, encouraged them, warned them, and trusted them. That's the church—a bunch of sinners loved by Jesus into being more than they could otherwise be.

In the last part of this chapter, Jesus enters the dark hour when Satan's authority seems to prevail. From 19:47 through 22:2, the temple authorities and elders cannot seize Jesus because they fear the crowds that are always around him. They hoped for a way to be able to "hand Jesus over to the rule and the authority of the governor" (20:20), and when Satan entered Judas, they found that way. Luke satirizes the arrest and interrogation. The chief priests, scribes, and elders—the most important Jewish men in Jerusalem—arm themselves with clubs and swords to arrest Jesus, as if he were a bandit. Yet the posse cannot prevent the injury to the high priest's slave; it's Jesus who stops the violence and heals the slave. The council of big shots ask Jesus to tell them whether he is Messiah or Son of God. They get two non-answers—"if I tell you, you will not believe" and "you say that I am"—and one straightforward prediction that they are not able to understand—"from now on the Son of Man will be seated at the right hand of God's power." But they act as though they have an admission of guilt, and then hand Jesus over, charging him with things they have not discussed. It's all absurd, and Luke's explanation—"this is your hour, and the authority of darkness"—makes Satan the root cause of the injustice being done.

"The devil made them do it?" Maybe that sounds too facile an explanation. But it allows Luke, in the early chapters of Acts, to give all who participated in condemning Jesus a chance, like the prodigal son, to come to their senses and realize they made a terrible mistake. "You rejected the Holy and Righteous One and asked to have a murderer given to you . . . repent therefore, and turn to God so that your sins may be wiped out" (Acts 3:14, 19).

Chapter 22 thus promotes inclusion of all sorts. Yes, allow the traitor to sit at the Lord's table. Yes, assure the apostate not only that he will be included in the great banquet, but that he will help to restore others to the faith. Yes, forgive those who are treating you unjustly; do not construe them as so far from God that they could not repent. That's the gospel as Luke understands it.

NOTES

[1] Yes, since carrying water was women's work: Alan R. Culpepper, *The Gospel of Luke* (*NIB*, vol. 9; Nashville: Abingdon, 1995), 416; Joseph A. Fitzmyer, *The Gospel According to Luke* (AB 28 and 28A; Garden City NY: Doubleday, 1981), 2.1383; John Nolland, *Luke* (WBC, vols. 35A-C; Dallas TX: Word, 1989-93), 3.1033, who notes that the man/person meets the disciples, rather than the other way around, so that the issue is moot.

[2] Richard Saller, "Women, Slaves, and the Economy of the Roman Household," in David L. Balch and Carolyn Osiek, eds., *Early Christian Families in Context* (Grand Rapids MI: Eerdmans, 2003), 196, describes the use of male slaves in meal service as "a form of conspicuous consumption," since male slaves were more expensive and since female slaves could do this sort of work just as well.

[3] See the discussion in BAGD, 949. The root meaning of the word is "spread," but without any clue for what is spread, any of the guesses seem plausible. 22:14 indicates that Jesus and the Twelve reclined to eat, so "furnished"—with dining couches and small tables—seems the most plausible.

[4] There are other readings "which appear to be compromises between the two principal forms"; because of their more obvious secondary nature, I am not discussing them. Interested readers can consult Bruce M. Metzger, *A Textual Commentary on the Greek New Testament* (New York: United Bible Societies, 1971), 174.

[5] Bruce Metzger, *The Text of the New Testament: Its Transmission, Corruption, and Restoration* (3rd ed.; New York: Oxford, 1992), 50.

[6] See the discussion in E. E. Ellis, *The Gospel of Luke* (London: Oliphants, 1974), 254–55, and I. Howard Marshall, *The Gospel of Luke* (Grand Rapids MI: Eerdmans, 1978), 799–800; both consider arguments about whether a scribe might have made the short text long or the long text short in order to make it more like the Mark-Matthew-Paul order.

[7] Metzger, *Textual Commentary*, 174, lists this as one possible reason for preferring the shorter text.

[8] Bart Ehrman, *Misquoting Jesus: The Story Behind Who Changed the Bible and Why* (New York: HarperSanFrancisco, 2005), 166–67.

[9] Justin Martyr, *Dial.* 103.8: "For in the memoirs which I say were drawn up by His apostles and those who followed them, [it is recorded] that His sweat fell down like drops of blood while He was praying, and saying, 'If it be possible, let this cup pass:' His heart and also His bones trembling; His heart being like wax melting in His belly: in order that we may perceive that the Father wished His Son really to undergo such sufferings for our sakes, and may not say that He, being the Son of God, did not feel what was happening to Him and inflicted on Him."

[10] Ehrman, *Misquoting Jesus*, 164–65; Culpepper, *Luke*, 433; Fitzmyer, *Luke*, 2.1443-44; Nolland *Luke*, 3.1080-81. However, Green, "Jesus on the Mount of Olives (Luke 22.39-46): Tradition and Theology," *JSNT* 26 (1986): 35–36, argues for their

originality, as does Luke Timothy Johnson, *The Gospel of Luke* (SP, vol. 3; Collegeville MN: Liturgical Press, 1991), 351.

[11] As Ehrman argues, *Misquoting Jesus*, 164–67.

[12] Johnson, *Luke*, 337, who suggests that "hour" gives "a more solemn tone" to the time references.

[13] Nolland, *Luke*, 3.1049; Fitzmyer, *Luke*, 2.1384; Johnson, *Luke*, 337.

[14] See the discussion in Fitzmyer, *Luke*, 2.1396.

[15] Johnson, *Luke*, 337.

[16] So Nolland, *Luke*, 3.1050, who nevertheless objects to calling this a vow of abstinence.

[17] Frank C. Senn, *Christian Liturgy: Catholic and Evangelical* (Minneapolis: Fortress, 1997), 56.

[18] Johnson, *Luke*, 339, argues strongly for a sacrificial understanding of the words of institution.

[19] Nolland, *Luke*, 3.1055; Green, *Luke*, 763.

[20] So Nolland, *Luke*, 3.1059; Fitzmyer, *Luke*, 2.1409.

[21] David James Duncan, *The Brothers K* (New York: Bantam, 1993), 166–67.

[22] *Res Gestae Divi Augusti*, section 16; cited in Naphtali Lewis and Meyer Reinhold, *The Empire*, vol. 2 of *Roman Civilization* (New York: Harper and Row, 1966), 14.

[23] Fitzmyer, *Luke*, 2.1418.

[24] Frederick W. Danker, *Jesus and the New Age: A Commentary on St. Luke's Gospel* (rev. ed.; Philadelphia: Fortress, 1988), 351.

[25] Fitzmyer, *Luke*, 2.1419; Green, *Luke*, 770.

[26] Green, *Luke*, 770; Fitzmyer, Luke, 2.1415; Culpepper, *Luke*, 426; Nolland, *Luke*, 3.1066.

[27] Johnson, *Luke*, 345–46.

[28] Culpepper, *Luke*, 427.

[29] The last part of v. 36 literally reads, "and the one who has not, let him sell his cloak and buy a sword." Most assume that "sword" functions as the object of both "has" and "buy," but it is also possible to read "and the one who has nothing" or "and the one who does not have purse or bag." "Let the one who has nothing sell his cloak" makes no sense. "Let the one who has neither purse nor bag sell his cloak and buy a sword" would be a call to banditry; if this is what Luke meant, then the case for an ironic reading is even stronger.

[30] Johnson, *Luke*, 347; so also Culpepper, *Luke*, 429–30.

[31] Fitzmyer, *Luke*, 2.1432.

[32] BAGD, 303.

[33] BAGD, 19.

[34] Metzger, *Commentary*, 177, argues this way; the UBS text prints the verses in double brackets to indicate that they were not original but were of ancient origin. So also Fitzmyer, *Luke*, 2.1443-44; Culpepper, *Luke*, 433. But Brown, *Death*, 179–90; Green, "Mount of Olives," 35–36; Johnson, *Luke*, 351, all argue that the verses were original to *Luke*.

[35] Culpepper, *Luke*, 432, and Nolland, *Luke*, 2.1081, agree on this chiastic structure. Brown, *Death*, 182, calls this "another example of the exaggerated chiasm detection that plagues modern scholarship." But Brown admits that the passage is bounded by the repeated "pray lest you enter into temptation" and that this is meant to set off Jesus' own prayer in the middle, so his objection has less force than it sounds.

[36] For readers of the Greek New Testament, this form is a little puzzling. Luke has *boulei*, which in Koine Greek is a third-person singular verb: "He/she/it desires." Most interpreters take this to be a rare New Testament use of an Attic second-person singular verb ending: "you desire." So Nolland, *Luke*, 3.1048.

[37] Mark's "father" is in the nominative case; Luke's and Matthew's "father" is vocative, the case of direct address in Greek.

[38] Brown, *Death*, 1.171.

[39] Nolland, *Luke*, 2.1084; Culpepper, Luke, 432; Green, Luke, 781.

[40] Green, *Luke*, 783, and Culpepper, *Luke*, 435, think Jesus prevented the kiss; Raymond E. Brown, *The Death of the Messiah: From Gethsemane to the Grave* (2 vols.; Garden City NY: Doubleday, 1994), 252–59, thinks that Luke has subtly implied that Jesus accepted the kiss; Nolland, *Luke*, 3.1088, thinks the verse can be read either way.

[41] John J. Rousseau and Rami Arav, *Jesus and His World* (Minneapolis MN: Fortress, 1995), 170–71.

[42] Philip J. King, "Jerusalem," *ABD* 3.759.

[43] Pliny, *Epistles* X.96, translation in Henry Bettenson, ed., *Documents of the Christian Church* (London: Oxford University Press, 1977), 3–4.

[44] Fitzmyer, *Luke*, 2.1465.

[45] So Nolland, *Luke*, 3.1099. Johnson, *Luke*, 358, opts for the temple leaders themselves; Culpepper, *Luke*, 440, allows for either reading.

[46] Nolland, *Luke*, 3.1099, suggests that there were ancient games like the one here described: "in κολλαβισμός a player with eyes covered has to guess which hand another player has used to strike him; in χαλκῆ μυῖα a blindfolded player tries to find other players while being struck by them with papyrus husks."

[47] Culpepper, *Luke*, 440–41.

[48] Fitzmyer, *Luke*, 2.1468, calls it "a half-yes answer," but Brown, *Death*, 493, calls it "a full affirmative." Brown reasoned that since Luke includes Mark's "I am" in the answer and since it is clear that Luke regards Jesus as Son of God, this is meant to be an affirmation. But, as Brown notes, what Jesus says to the council is only the plural form of what he says to Pilate, and there it is clearer that he is not the King of the Jews.

THE TRIAL, CRUCIFIXION, DEATH, AND BURIAL

Luke 23

COMMENTARY

The Trial Before Pilate, 23:1-25

Pontius Pilate was appointed by Emperor Tiberius to be the prefect of Judea. The traditional date for the beginning of his term is AD 25 or 26, but recently scholars have argued that he took office in AD 19.[1] All agree that his term ended when he was ordered to return to Rome in AD 37, to answer a charge that he needlessly killed innocent civilians. A prefect is a military governor; later the Roman officials in Judea were called procurators, and Tacitus (*Ann.* 15.44) calls him by that title. Josephus sometimes calls Pilate by the Greek equivalent of procurator (*epitropos*) and sometimes, like the Gospels, calls him governor (*hēgemōn*). We presume that like most prefects or procurators, Pilate was a member of the equestrian order, and so from a good family and having a personal fortune of at least 400,000 sesterces (=100,000 denarii, or 16 2/3 talents). To qualify for the senate, a man had to be worth at least a million sesterces, so an *eques* tended to look upon a provincial governorship as a chance to impress his superiors, especially his patron; as a chance to collect clients of his own, increasing his prestige; and as a chance to increase his personal fortune. Non-Romans

> **Pilate's Inscription**
>
> Pilate left this inscription to mark a public work of some sort. The top line reads STIBERIEUM—"something Tiberieum," either a temple to Tiberius, or some other structure named for him; the next line reads TIUSPILATUS—"[Pon]tius Pilatus"; the third line reads ECTUSIUDA . . E—"[Praef]ectus Iuda[ea]e," Prefect of Judea; the final line has only an E, which could be part of "DEDIT," dedicates, or "REFECIT," restores, or almost anything.
>
>
>
> Inscription dedicated to and honoring Emperor Tiberius, with the name of Pontius Pilate, prefect of Judea (26–36 CE). Stone, from Caesarea, Israel, Israel Museum (IDAM), Jerusalem, Israel. (Credit: Erich Lessing/Art Resource, NY)

Prefects and Tax Collectors

 From a 2d-century AD papyrus from Egypt:

... Prefect of Egypt declares: I am informed that the tax farmers have employed exceedingly clever devices against those passing through the country and, in addition, are fraudulently demanding charges not due them and are laying hold of those who are in haste, so that some may buy from them a speedier departure. I therefore order them to desist from such greed.

Lewis and Reinhold, *The Empire*, vol. 2 of *Roman Civilization* (New York: Harper and Row, 1966), 145.

Procurators Making Legal Decisions

And now Archelaus's part of Judea was reduced into a province, and Coponious, one of the equestrian order among the Romans, was sent as a procurator, having the power of life and death put into his hands by Caesar. (Josephus, *J.W.* 2.117)

The following is the first part of a petition to the procurators of a section of Egypt for the right to plant vacant land owned by the emperor. The Mancian Law, dating from the late 1st century AD, offered tenant farmers the chance to increase the size of their farms by cultivating vacant properties; the emperor retained ownership of the land, but the tenant farmer did not have to pay rent for the first few years and, so long as he continued to grow crops, could make use of the property. The document dates to 117, and demonstrates that procurators made decisions about the uses of imperial lands:

... we ask, procurators, that through the foresight which you exercise in the name of Caesar, you be minded to have regard for us and for his advantage, and grant us the land which is swampy and wooded to plant with olive orchards and vineyards on the terms in force on the neighboring Neronian estate in accordance with the Mancian Law

Lewis and Reinhold, *The Empire*, vol. 2 of *Roman Civilization* (New York: Harper and Row, 1966), 182.

living in the provinces were very much at the mercy of the emperor and the Senate, and many were willing to enrich the prefect if he would use his influence on behalf of his clients.

Pilate's authority in Judea was broad, always subject to review by the governor of Syria or by the emperor. Prefects/procurators oversaw the collection of taxes and tax-collectors [Prefects and Tax Collectors], made legal decisions of all sorts [Procurators Making Legal Decisions], put down disturbances with the troops at their disposal [A Prefect's Inscription Honoring Himself for Military Victories], and hoped to gather glory and funds enough to become a bigger player [A Prefect's Clients Celebrate His Accomplishments]. What we know about Pilate as an individual comes from Josephus and Philo. Philo clearly hated him, accusing him of "corruption . . . acts of insolence, and his rapine, and his habit of insulting people, and his cruelty, and his continual murders of people untried and uncondemned, and his never-ending, and gratuitous, and most grievous inhumanity . . . a man of most ferocious passions" (*Embassy* 302). Josephus is not as negative; he holds Pilate responsible for using unnecessary force when he put down the mob protesting the aqueduct (see commentary on 3:1-17 and [Pilate's Reaction to Protests over the Aqueduct]), but uses none of Philo's polemical language.

It is unlikely that Luke or any of his audience would know anything about the personality or career of the prefect of Judea from some forty to fifty years before; thus, while Josephus's information and Philo's opinions are interesting, they are not relevant for understanding Luke's account. Luke knows what he read in Mark, and he has a sense of how Roman civil and military officials act when performing their duties in the provinces. Drawing on these resources, he tries to present a credible and compelling account of Jesus' death, with the aims of explaining why Jesus was crucified and how such a person could be considered admirable, even divine.

> **A Prefect's Inscription Honoring Himself for Military Victories**
>
> Gaius Cornelius Gallus son of Gnaeus, Roman eques, first prefect of Alexandria and Egypt after the overthrow of the kings by Caesar, son of a god—having been victorious in two pitched battles in the fifteen days within which he suppressed the revolt of the Thebaid, capturing five cities—Boresis, Coptus, Ceramice, Diospolis Magna, and Ophieum—and seizing the leaders of these revolts; having led his army beyond the Nile cataract, a region into which arms had not previously been carried either by the Roman people or by the kings of Egypt; having subjugated the Thebaid, the common terror of all the kings; and having given audience at Philae to envoys of the king of the Ethiopians, received that king under [Roman] protection and installed a prince over the Triacontaschoenus, a district of Ethiopia—dedicated this thank offering to his ancestral gods and to the Nile his helpmate. (29 BCE) [Note: the part about being the first to take an army beyond the first cataract is nonsense, since the pharaohs ruled both upper and lower Egypt for centuries.]
>
> Lewis and Reinhold, *The Empire*, vol. 2 of *Roman Civilization* (New York: Harper and Row, 1966), 45.

Note the elements Luke omits from Mark's account:

- There is no mention of Jesus being bound (Mark 15:1b).
- Pilate does not ask Jesus to respond to the accusations of the chief priests (Mark 15:3-4).
- There is no mention of Pilate's custom of releasing a prisoner for whom the crowd asked (Mark 15:6).
- Pilate never asks the crowd, "Do you want me to release for you the King of the Jews?" (Mark 15:9, 12).
- There is no statement that Pilate knew Jesus had been handed over out of jealousy (Mark 15:10).
- Luke does not say that the chief priests incited the crowd to ask for Barabbas (Mark 15:11).
- Luke does not say that Pilate wishes to satisfy the crowd (Mark 15:15).
- Luke never narrates a flogging (Mark 15:15).

In Mark's account, Pilate says three things to the crowd:

Do you want me to release for you the King of the Jews?
What do you wish me to do with the man you call the king of the Jews?
Why, what evil has he done?

Luke retains the structure of three public pronouncements, but Pilate has different lines, as we will see. Luke also has a three-part examination: first by Pilate, then by Herod, and finally by the crowd—the chief priests, leaders, and people.

> **A Prefect's Clients Celebrate His Accomplishments**
>
> To Marcus Petronius Honoratus son of Marcus, of the Quirine tribe; prefect of the first Cohort of the Raetians; military tribune of the dutiful and faithful Legion I Minervia; prefect of the dutiful and faithful Augustan Company of the Thracians; procurator of the mint; procurator of the five-percent tax on inheritances; procurator of the provinces of Belgium and the two Germanies; financial secretary to the emperor; prefect of the grain supply; prefect of Egypt; minor pontiff. The oil merchants from Baetica [dedicated this to him], their patron.
>
> Lewis and Reinhold, *The Empire*, vol. 2 of *Roman Civilization* (New York: Harper and Row, 1966), 126.

The Accusation (vv. 1-2)

Luke described the group of chief priests, officers, and elders who arrested Jesus as a "crowd" (22:47). Jesus appeared before the same group acting in their official capacity as the "council of elders of the people, both chief priests and scribes" (22:66). Now Luke calls the group a "multitude" (*plēthos*) that rose as one to lead him to Pilate. Here is the first hint of how this story will turn out—it will be the sheer force of their voices, rather than truth or justice, that carries the verdict. They lay three specific charges against Jesus.

(1) Perverting our *ethnos*: the verb *diastrephō* often has the sense of diverting someone from what is proper or right (in Acts 13:10, Paul accuses the magician Elymas of doing this). The *ethnos* are the Jews; not a "nation" in the modern sense of a sovereign country, but an organized group with a common heritage and common religion who have been granted certain rights within the empire. The accusation, then, is that Jesus is a threat that the Romans should take seriously, because he is a bad influence on the Jewish *ethnos*. Pilate ignored this completely in his interrogation. Luke's audience, remembering all the times that an episode ended with the people praising God, will conclude that Jesus, instead of turning people from God, brought them closer to God.

(2) Forbidding giving tribute to Caesar: Judea owed Caesar an annual tribute payment, mostly in return for the privileges of being governed by the Romans and of having Roman troops quartered in Judea. Failure to pay would have been an act of rebellion, a direct challenge to Caesar and his representative the prefect. If Jesus were urging such a rash course of action, especially if he were doing it in the name of God, then it would have been something to take seriously. Pilate ignored this charge, too; the audience knows it is spurious, because of Jesus' statement about giving to Caesar and giving to God (20:25).

(3) Claiming he is Christ, a king: Josephus writes about other persons who claimed to be king. He lists two, Simon and Athronges, who style themselves kings after the death of Herod the Great; both were caught and killed by troops loyal to Herod. Others appeared during the war of 66–70; Menachem's attempt to be king was thwarted by Eleazar and the other rebels, and the rest, we presume, were dispersed or killed by the Romans. The point is that in Josephus's account, no standing government, Jewish or Roman, tolerated a rival king. Luke's audience knows this charge is also false. Jesus has never claimed to be king. Others have said it about him (19:38); in 9:20 Peter called him "The Messiah of God," and Jesus' response was sternly to order them never to repeat

this (9:21). He has spoken about the coming kingdom as "my kingdom" (22:30), but the only titles he uses for himself are "servant" (22:27) and "son of man" (22:69). But Luke's audience would also not be surprised that the only one of the charges that interests Pilate is this last one.

The Interrogation (v. 3)

Pilate's question to Jesus is direct: "Are you the king of the Jews?" In Greek, one can phrase the question so as to expect a positive or negative reply; Pilate's is phrased so as to be neutral. Pilate's question is exactly the same in all four Gospels (Mark 15:2; Matt 27:11; John 18: 33). Jesus' answer is also identical in the three Synoptic Gospels, and is ambiguous: "You say." In Luke's account, this cannot mean "yes" for three reasons.

First, it isn't true; in fact, it is a ridiculous question that can only be answered in the negative. That there is a Roman prefect in Jerusalem acting as judge over a Galilean Jew is proof that there is no king of the Jews. Had Pilate asked, "Do you think you are king of the Jews?" then it could be a question about Jesus' mental state. "Would you like to become king of the Jews?" would be about Jesus' criminal intent. But "Are you king of the Jews?" is about the nature of politics in first-century Palestine. If there was a "king of the Jews" at that moment, it was Caesar.

Second, according to Luke's theology, Jesus would "rule over the house of Jacob forever" (1:33) as "Lord and Messiah" after the resurrection and ascension, when he was enthroned at God's right hand (22:69; Acts 2:25-36). At this moment, standing before Pilate, Jesus was not yet king; and later, enthroned in heaven, his title would be much broader than "king of the Jews."

Third, "you say" cannot mean "yes," because according to Luke's understanding of things, Jesus was not guilty of the charge against him. His death was a grave error for which the population of Jerusalem and temple leaders needed to repent (Acts 2:36-38, 3:14-19; 5:28).

So why not have Jesus say "no"? In part, because he certainly was "the Christ," a title that quickly became part of his name; but also in part, because Luke is spoofing the veneer of legal process that produced such a miscarriage of justice. "You say" must mean "those are your words, not mine,"[2] and constitute a non-answer, just as Luke's Jesus also never answered the questions of the council of elders (22:67-68). But Pilate jumps on it, just as the Sanhedrin did, although he interprets "you say" to mean exactly the opposite of what the Sanhedrin understood.

Pilate Dismisses the Charges (v. 4)

Pilate has no further questions for the accused. To the "chief priests and the crowd," he says, "I find no cause in this man." "Cause" (*aition*) means the precipitant cause—the thing that leads directly to something else happening. In a legal situation, it means a charge that if proven would result in punishment (so in Josephus, *Ant.* 7.362, 16.268, 17.164). "I find no cause" means "there is nothing here that would require punishment." Pilate is acting well within the authority of his office. The accusing group has offered no witnesses and no evidence other than their own opinions ("we found this one . . ."). Pilate asks the accused whether he is king, which is ludicrous; of course he isn't. Where is his army? Where is his palace? He poses no credible threat to Pilate's job of maintaining the emperor's control of this little part of the empire.

Because Luke so stresses Jesus' innocence in the trial and crucifixion narratives, we perhaps are too quick to take Pilate's snap decision as reasonable; after all, his "there is no cause" is Luke's view, too. But to Luke's audience, "It would have been difficult for a Roman citizen familiar with Roman judicial practice . . . to understand Pilate's quick judgment. . . . Why was Pilate so superficial in his investigation of the serious charges against a suspected rebel? Jesus was not even 'examined by torture.'"[3]

This is the first mention of the "crowd," who will have a part in deciding the verdict; in 23:13, Luke calls them "the people." Because "the people" gathered to hear him every morning (21:38) and were persuaded by his teachings (19:48), the chief priests, scribes, and elders had been prevented for a time from arresting Jesus. Now the crowd has joined their leaders and will be part of the group condemning Jesus to crucifixion. Luke's explanation for this: the "hour" belongs to Satan (22:53) and is under the authority of darkness. Satan has caught more than just Judas in his sieve.

New Charge (v. 5)

They—the chief priests and the crowd—"grew strong" or "remained persistent," not giving up on their case, claiming that "He incites the people, teaching all around Judea, beginning from Galilee and all the way here [to Jerusalem]." "Incite" is a throw-down word, like "organizing a terrorist cell" would be these days. It literally means "brandish a shield" (so Josephus, *J. W.* 5.120), the age-old act of soldiers to raise their own courage or to frighten the enemy. The new charge is that Jesus has been roaming around Judea stirring up an insurrection—it's no truer than the others, but it gives Pilate a new stratagem for disposing of the case.

The prefect had announced his decision, but the chief priests and the crowd were able to prevent his acting on it by "growing strong." This would not be flattering to any Roman civic leader hoping to make a name for himself. Take, for example, the case of a procurator accused of abuse of power when Commodus was emperor. The complaints against him included using soldiers to arrest and torture the plaintiffs, who say that even Roman citizens were unjustly beaten with rods and clubs. The emperor's response says only that the procurator will make certain that the sharecroppers will not be forced to do labor beyond the terms set down in Hadrianic law. [Complaint against a Procurator] In other words, heavy-handed prefects/procurators seem to have been par for the course, and Luke's audience would have been surprised that Pilate did not simply do what he wanted without regard for the opinions of the chief priests.

Complaint against a Procurator

From an Egyptian inscription dated 180/183:

. . . that you may know of the collusion which your procurator has practiced without limit not only with Allius Maximus, our adversary, but with practically all the chief lessees, in violation of our right and to the detriment of your fisc. . . . to the point of sending soldiers into the said Burunitan estate and ordering some of us to be seized and tortured, others fettered, and some, including even Roman citizens, beaten with rods and cudgels; and the only thing we did to deserve this was that, in the face of injury so palpable and so oppressive in relation to the measure of our insignificance, we had resorted to sending a letter of complaint beseeching your majesty's aid . . . .

The Emperor Caesar Marcus Aurelius Commodus Antoninus Augustus Sarmaticus Germanicus Maximus to Lurius Lucullus and the others represented by him: In view of established tradition and my order, procurators will see to it that nothing more than three periods of two days' work per man is unjustly exacted from you in violation of established practice.

Lewis and Reinhold, *The Empire*, vol. 2 of *Roman Civilization* (New York: Harper and Row, 1966), 183–84.

Change of Venue (vv. 6-7)

In Luke's account, Pilate knew nothing of Jesus, not even that he was a Galilean. This would make sense to Luke's audience: no Roman could be expected to tell one Jew from another (Jesus and his followers could be recognized as Galileans, 22:59). Pilate had executed some Galileans in Jerusalem at some earlier time (13:1), but on this occasion, he decided to send Jesus to Herod Antipas, "knowing that [this man] was under the authority of Herod" and that Herod was in Jerusalem during those [festival] days. Rhetorical handbooks recommended a motion for a change of venue as a stratagem for legal advocates facing a prejudiced judge or jury.[4] But Pilate *is* the judge; unlike the judge in the parable (18:1), he cares what people think of him. So, acting more as Jesus' advocate than as the hanging judge, Pilate sends Jesus to Herod, implicitly granting him the authority to decide the case.

No other Gospel gives a hint of Antipas's involvement in Jesus' trial. Because of its singularity, and because it fits Luke's heavy emphasis on Jesus' innocence, many scholars conclude that Luke invented the episode; some argue that Luke's motive was to exonerate the Romans as much as possible in order to make Christianity seem less dangerous to Rome.[5] Whether Luke found this story written down (or heard someone talk about it and wrote it up himself) or invented it is impossible to say. Sometimes Luke is very free in rewriting Mark, and that this episode fits smoothly in Luke's narrative proves only that he keeps his material well in hand. Whether the episode is historical is also impossible to say for certain. We can conclude, however, that since none of the other early witnesses to the story of Jesus' arrest, trial, and death show any knowledge of it, the tradition either began with Luke or was not widely known among Christians until he reported it.

Luke's supposed pro-Roman apologetic is not consistent with all the evidence. There were, of course, limits to what Luke could have done with the story had he wanted to exonerate the Romans and blame the temple authorities for Jesus' death. Since everyone knew Jesus died by crucifixion, Luke could not plausibly remove Pilate completely; nobody would have believed a story in which Jesus was crucified without Roman approval. But Luke's Pilate is far from being the ideal Roman procurator. Mark's Pilate asks the crowd what they would have him do with Jesus; Luke, writing not so much for Romans as for citizens of other places ruled by the Romans, knows that no Roman procurator/prefect would do such a thing. Similarly, Mark's report about granting the crowd at Passover the choice of a prisoner to release probably strained Luke's imagination. I suggest Luke made these changes to make the story sound more credible. But once Pilate starts saying "I will do x" and then allows the crowd to override him, from the Roman point of view, he has failed in his duty. The point of crucifying someone is to use the unfortunate's body as a billboard advertising Rome's power and the will to use it. Pilate "hands him over to their wishes" (23:25); nobody in Rome's ladder of power would be flattered by such a picture or motivated to treat Christians more humanely.

Interrogation by Herod Antipas; return to Pilate (vv. 8-12)
Herod was "very glad" to see Jesus, because (a) he had wanted to see him for a long time (9:9; 13:31); (b) he hoped to hear about him, having had questions and having heard rumors for a while (9:7-9); and (c) he hoped to see a sign from him, like some of the crowd back in Galilee (11:16). But although Herod questioned him "with many words," Jesus made no reply.

Verses 10 and 11 depict two different negative responses to Jesus. In v. 10, the chief priests and scribes, who have apparently followed Jesus to Herod's palace in Jerusalem and have been admitted to the interrogation, stand by vehemently accusing Jesus. Herod and his soldiers, however, think Jesus and the charges against him are ridiculous, so in order to mock him, they dress Jesus in a "gleaming" robe. Luke's audience might think of the *toga candida*, the dazzling-white garment worn on election day by candidates so that all the voters could spot them easily, and as symbols of spotless reputations. But they might also think of the "shining robes" worn by the two angels on Jesus' resurrection day (Luke 24:4), or by the angel who appeared to Cornelius (Acts 10:30). In either case, the reference is ironic. Herod does not think of Jesus as a candidate for anything; he does not think that Jesus is guilty of the charges, but has no respect for him. Luke's audience knows that Jesus' true identity, which the transfiguration prefigured (9:29), will be proven by the resurrection. So even if Herod is mocking Jesus by dressing him in gleaming clothes, he is telling the truth.

Herod sends Jesus back to Pilate; in v. 15, Pilate interprets this action as a declaration of Jesus' innocence. If Jesus had been tearing around Herod's Galilee stirring up insurrection, then certainly Herod would know and would put Jesus to death. Instead, he sent him back, a courteous way of treating Pilate as the ultimate authority in Judea, even over residents of Galilee. Luke observes that after this, Herod and Pilate were friends; each had respected the authority of the other.

Christ Before Pilate

Mihaly Munkacsy (1844–1909). *Christ before Pilate*. 1881. Oil on canvas, Musee d'Orsay, Paris, France. (Credit: Erich Lessing/Art Resource, NY)

Most church paintings of Christ before Pilate include either the crown of thorns (from Mark, Matthew, and John) or Pilate's washing his hands (from Matthew). This one has neither of those elements, but shows Christ in a gleaming robe before a very Roman-looking Pilate, while the temple authorities argue for his condemnation.

As noted above, we cannot prove that Antipas's interrogation of Jesus did not happen. Whether it did or didn't, we can wonder why Luke, of all New Testament sources, thought it important to include. Acts 4:25-28 suggests a link to Psalm 2:1-2 LXX: "Why did the *gentiles* rage and *the peoples* imagine vain things? The kings of the earth stood, and the rulers *gathered themselves together* against the Lord and *against his Messiah.*" Luke probably considered this one of the things "written about [Jesus] in the law of Moses, the prophets, and the psalms" that needed to be fulfilled.[6] In Acts 4, after citing the psalm, Luke writes, "For truly in this city they *'gathered together against'* your holy son Jesus *Christ* whom you *anointed,* both Herod and Pontius Pilate with *'gentiles'* and *'the peoples'* of Israel, to do whatever your hand and your will had pre-ordained." Jesus' appearance before Pilate and Herod also gives two witnesses for Jesus' innocence; Luke has doubled the angels at the tomb possibly for the same reason. Jesus' appearance before Herod and Pilate also parallels Paul's appearances before Felix the procurator and Agrippa the king. And in addition to all of this, it must have seemed appropriate to Luke, who knew that Antipas's formal authority covered Galilee, to have Pilate ask him for a ruling. In this way, no one could claim that Pilate was simply uninformed about seditious things Jesus had done in the rural parts of Galilee.

Pilate Declares Jesus Free of Guilt; Sentences Him to Flogging (13-16)

Pilate then summons "the chief priests and rulers and the people"—the group who arrested Jesus plus the general crowd who joined the scene in v. 4—to report on his findings. "You presented this man to me as one who 'perverted the people,' and after interrogating him in your presence, I found in this man nothing of the cause of which you accuse him. Neither did Herod, for he sent him back to us; so nothing worthy of death has been done by him. Therefore after beating him, I shall release him."

A summary of the charge, review of investigations done so far, and the judge's conclusion—sounds like Luke has listened to a judge's summary before. "Nothing worthy of death" is the first time anyone has mentioned a capital sentence, but that was the only real option if Jesus were really trying to create an insurrection or to install himself as a king or to prevent the tribute payment. No evidence was discovered to corroborate the charges; thus, there is no "cause"—no case against Jesus. So why beat him? Pilate's decision here shows that Luke understands how the Romans viewed corporal punishment. Jesus had done nothing worthy of death, but somehow he had drawn attention to himself and had created trouble. A beating would warn not only him but anyone else that peasants should always try to be invisible.

Mob Scene: Demand for Release of Barabbas, Crucifixion of Jesus (vv. 18-21)

Things get out of hand. Luke uses a word that means a crowd acting in unison (*pamplēthei*, lit., "all of a multitude"), and says they "shouted . . . saying, 'Take this one, but give us Barabbas.'" Again, there is a close parallel between this scene and one involving Paul. In Acts 21:27-36, a crowd seizes Paul, suspecting him of something he did not do; they are prevented from killing him by the intervention of the Roman officer, but even as he takes Paul away, the "multitude of the people" is following and "shouting, 'Take him!'" No government likes a mob,[7] but aristocratic governments trust them not at all. Josephus, even when writing about Roman misconduct, has no sympathy for unruly multitudes, even Jewish ones. [The Abuse of a Mob] Luke's account of the mob scene in Ephesus (Acts 19:23-41) and in Jerusalem (Acts 21:27-36) shows that he also thinks mobs are as dangerous to Jesus' followers as to civic order.

The crowd has no say in Pilate's verdict on Jesus, but since they brought the accusation, one could understand their anger. But why do they think Pilate should release Barabbas? Since Luke omits Mark's bit about a Passover tradition, there is nothing reasonable about their request, particularly when Luke informs us that

---

The Abuse of a Mob

But Pilate undertook to bring an aqueduct Jerusalem, and did it with the sacred money, and took the water of the stream from the distance of twenty-five miles. However, the Jews were not pleased with what had been done about this water; and many ten thousands of the people got together, and made a clamor against him, and insisted that he should stop that design. Some of them, also, used reproaches, and abused the man, as crowds of such people usually do. (Josephus, *Ant.* 18.60)

When that feast which is called the Passover was at hand, at which time our custom is to use unleavened bread, and a great multitude was gathered together from all parts to that feast, Cumanus was afraid lest some attempt of sedition should then be made by them; so he ordered that one regiment of the army should take their arms, and stand in the temple cloisters, to repress any attempts of sedition, if perchance any such should begin; and this was no more than what the former procurators of Judea did at such festivals. But on the fourth day of the feast, a certain soldier let down his breeches, and exposed his privy members to the multitude, which put those who saw him into a furious rage, and

made them cry out that this impious action was not done to approach them, but God himself; nay, some of them reproached Cumanus, and pretended that the soldier was set on by him, which, when Cumanus heard, he was also himself not a little provoked at such reproaches laid upon him; yet did he exhort them to stop such seditious attempts, and not to raise a tumult at the festival. But when he could not induce them to be quiet, for they still went on in their reproaches to him, he gave orders that the whole army should take their entire armor, and come to Antonia, which was a fortress, as we have said already, which overlooked the temple; but when the multitude saw the soldiers there, they were frightened by them, and ran away hastily; but as the passages out were but narrow, and as they thought their enemies followed them, they were crowded together in their flight, and a great number were crushed to death in those narrow passages; nor, indeed, was the number fewer than twenty thousand that perished in this tumult. So, instead of a festival, they had at last a mournful day of it; and they all forgot their prayers and sacrifices, and betook themselves to lamentation and weeping; so great an affliction did the impudent obscenity of a single soldier bring upon them. (Josephus, *Ant.* 20.106-12)

Barabbas was in prison for sedition (for creating a *stasis*—a riot or rebellion—in the city) and murder. Luke also, by taking out Mark's note that the temple leadership "incited" the crowds to ask for Barabbas, makes this sound like the craziness of a large group—as if the idea occurred to all of them at once, so they started shouting for it.

Pilate, "wishing to release Jesus [see Acts 3:13]," tries to "address" them (*prosphōneō*), but they are all "yelling" (*epiphōneō*), "Crucify, crucify him." Pilate is losing control; the crowd is acting irrationally; but because Luke has specified that this is Satan's hour and that things are happening under his authority, in Acts 3:17 Peter can declare that the people of Jerusalem and their leaders (not "rulers"; Luke uses *archontes*, the same word used in Luke 23:13 for the non-priestly members of the council of elders) acted in ignorance.

Pilate Repeats—Jesus Is Not Guilty, and Will Be Beaten and Released (v. 22)

For "the third time," Pilate states what he is going to do. "For what evil (thing) he did?"—in other words, "You want me to crucify him—for what crime that he committed?" Pilate's line is pretty much the same as in Mark 15:14, but Luke has changed its meaning. Mark's Pilate asks the crowd a real question; Luke's Pilate is asking a rhetorical question, ridiculing the suggestion that Jesus be crucified, because there is no cause worthy of death. Luke then repeats, verbatim, v. 16—unusual for Luke to repeat himself like that, so he is making the point that Pilate was being very clear, even redundant, about what he intended.

The Mob Overrules Him (v. 23)

The crowd "confronted" or "pushed" Pilate "with large voices, requesting that he be crucified, and their voices defeated him." It was not unprecedented for a prefect/procurator to be confronted with an implacable multitude and to decide to go with what they wanted. In the episode of the standards, when Pilate tried to bring images of Caesar into Jerusalem and provoked public protests, Josephus writes that Pilate, "deeply affected with their firm resolution to keep their laws inviolable," ordered that the images be taken back to Caesarea. [Pilate and Caesar's Images] But this was after Pilate surrounded the crowd with armed soldiers, and after the crowd proved willing to die rather than disperse; it is not as if the crowd's shouting made him change his mind. Luke's choice of verbs at the end puts the episode from a Roman perspective; if this is the way it happened, it was a defeat for Pilate and therefore for Rome.

Pilate Accedes to the Demands of the Mob (vv. 24-25)

Pilate gave his judgment for their request: "he released the one who had been thrown into prison for insurrection and murder, but he handed Jesus over to their wishes."

If we are keeping score, several parts of Jesus' predictions about how he would die have now come true.

- "The son of man must undergo great suffering, and be rejected by the elders, chief priests, and scribes, and be killed, and on the third day be raised" (9:22)
- "The son of man is about to be handed over into human hands" (9:44)
- "It is impossible for a prophet to be killed outside Jerusalem" (13:33)
- "See, we are going up to Jerusalem, and everything written about the son of man by the prophets will be accomplished. For he will be handed over to the Gentiles; and he will be mocked and insulted and spat upon. After flogging him they will kill him, and on the third day he will rise" (18:31-33)

> **Pilate and Caesar's Images**
>
> But now Pilate, the procurator of Judea, moved the army from Caesarea to Jerusalem, to take their winter quarters there, in order to abolish the Jewish laws. So he introduced Caesar's effigies, which were upon the ensigns, and brought them into the city; whereas our law forbids us the very making of images; on which account the former procurators were wont to make their entry into the city with such ensigns as had not those ornaments. Pilate was the first who brought those images to Jerusalem, and set them up there; which was done without the knowledge of the people, because it was done in the night time; but as soon as they knew it, they came in multitudes to Caesarea, and interceded with Pilate for many days that he would remove the images; and when he would not grant their requests, because it would tend to the injury of Caesar, while yet they persevered in their request, on the sixth day he ordered his soldiers to have their weapons secretly, while he came and sat upon his judgment seat, which seat was so prepared in the open place of the city, that it concealed the army that lay ready to oppress them; and when the Jews petitioned him again, he gave a signal to the soldiers to surround them, and threatened that their punishment should be no less than immediate death, unless they would stop disturbing him, and go their ways home. But they threw themselves upon the ground, and laid their necks bare, and said they would take their death very willingly, rather than the wisdom of their laws should be transgressed; upon which Pilate was deeply affected with their firm resolution to keep their laws inviolable, and presently commanded the images to be carried back from Jerusalem to Caesarea.
>
> Josephus, *Ant.* 18.55-59.

Jesus has been "rejected" by the elders, chief priests, and scribes; he was handed over to Pilate, and thus to the Gentiles, but then handed back to the desires of the people and their leaders. He has been mocked and insulted, and there will be more of that once he is crucified. Only the spitting and flogging do not happen here in Luke.

This last point deserves a little attention. Luke's Jesus is preeminently a prophet, and it is unlike Luke to allow something Jesus predicted to go un-narrated. Moreover, the flogging was right there in Mark 15:15; it isn't as if the detail slipped Luke's mind; he had to choose not to reproduce it in his own account. Furthermore, because Isaiah's Servant of the Lord endured spitting and scourging (Isa 50:4 LXX), including that in the account would have enhanced the identification between Jesus and the Servant—an identification that Luke surely had in mind, given the citations of Isaiah 53:12 in 22:14-38 and the use of "servant" images in Luke 22:24-27 and Acts 3:11-26. Luke's omission of spitting and beating, or any other graphic descriptions of Jesus' physical pain, results from Luke's decision to make his account of Jesus' execution different from most Jewish or Christian martyr texts. The deaths of Eleazar, the seven martyrs and their mother (2 Macc 7; 4 Macc 6–17) are full of grisly details—blood dripping, body parts severed, innards spilling out—as are most Christian martyr texts. The voyeuristic appeal is pretty obvious—"ooh, isn't that awful—show me more"—and perhaps targeted a public used to bloody spectacles in the arenas. Luke's account is even less like that than Mark's; Luke wants to impress the audience with Jesus' firm and quiet resolve, but will not do it by intense descriptions of how much flesh Jesus lost when the whips dug into his back. So Luke has no whipping, no spitting, and no crown of thorns; if a crucifixion can be more or less dignified, Luke's Jesus loses less dignity.

Luke's trial illustrates what is wrong with empires. Even though Pilate has ultimate authority, he cannot or will not use it to do what is right, even when he knows what "right" should look like. Far from being an exoneration of Pilate or an attempt to placate the Romans, Luke's account of Jesus before Pilate makes nobody except Jesus look good. The prefect does not act as he says he will. The crowds and temple leaders prefer a violent sinner to the righteous man. For his part, Jesus does not plead for his life and does not try to curry favor by doing miracles at Herod's request. He is quiet, except for his "so you say" to Pilate, but not because he is afraid; we will see him continue to act as a prophet as he is led away to his death.

The Crucifixion of Jesus, 23:26-56

How does a just man or woman face an unjust death? Peter Lake, in Mark Helprin's *Winter's Tale*, has outrun his enemies time and again. But one day, out of pity and mercy, he allows one to get close enough to wound him fatally. When he knows his death is close, he waits for his nemesis Pearly Soames to catch up with him. Pearly tries to convince him that Athansor, Peter's magic white horse, has been captured and killed. Peter drops to his knees in despair; Pearly puts a sword to his neck and gloats:

"You have come to the common and inevitable end, though you struggled hard to get to it. In a moment, you will be forever mute and forgotten. There will be no one to remember you. Nothing. It was all in vain." . . .

As Pearly, too, strained to listen, the tip of the sword left Peter Lake's shoulder and hung in the air. From the north came a sound like rolling thunder that grew louder and louder as it approached. It was steady and electrifying. Then it swept by them—hoofbeats drumming the ground. The whole island was shaking . . . .

"That's the white horse," Peter Lake declared, his outstretched right arm pointing toward the thunder. "And the way he's running, he's going to make it."

Pearly hadn't changed his stance. Peter Lake took the tip of the sword and replaced it above his collarbone. "And so am I, Pearly, so am I, although in a way that will never be clear to you. . . . Only love . . ." he said. "Drive hard."

The sword was driven into him until its hilt came to rest on his shoulder and he was dead.[8]

Jesus never runs in Luke—just continues about his business in Galilee, secure in the knowledge that no prophet can die outside Jerusalem. And for a time, even there the crowds keep his enemies at bay. But on the night of the Passover meal, his own apostle leads his enemies to the spot where he can be arrested quietly. At his trial, neither Pilate nor Antipas think he is guilty of anything; but the crowds join the chief priests and elders in shouting for Jesus' crucifixion. Jesus has been handed over by Judas to the council of elders, by the council to Pilate, by Pilate to Herod, by Herod back to Pilate, and then, finally, by Pilate to "their wishes"—the wishes of the council and the crowd. Luke knows perfectly well that the Romans carried out the crucifixion, and so the "they" who lead Jesus away in 23:26 are soldiers under Pilate's command.

After Jesus answers (or doesn't, depending on how you look at it) Pilate's question, "Are you the king of the Jews?" (23:3), Jesus has nothing to say throughout the rest of his trial. But Luke quickly assures the audience that Jesus has not despaired; he will need no heavenly intervention or supporting angel to get him through these next few hours. In fact, Luke's death scene is composed to show Jesus still ministering, still in communication with his Father up to his last moments.

Luke's crucifixion scene includes:

• Procession (23:26-32): involving Simon of Cyrene, "a great multitude of the people and women," and the other criminals

- Crucifixion (23:33-38): involving the people, their leaders, and the soldiers
- Conversation (23:39-43): involving the two criminals and Jesus
- Death (23:44-46): Jesus' final word
- Recession (23:47-49): involving the centurion, the crowds, and "all those who knew him"
- Burial (23:50-56): involving Joseph of Arimathea, Pilate, and the women

The Procession (vv. 26-32)

All three Synoptic Gospels name Simon of Cyrene as the person who carried Jesus' cross. But Luke edits Mark's verse a bit; he omits the identification "the father of Alexander and Rufus"—perhaps those names mean nothing to Luke or to his audience—and switches Mark's "they requisitioned a certain by-stander . . . so that he would carry his cross" (Mark 15:21) to "they laid the cross on him for him to bear behind Jesus." Simon thus fulfills Jesus' demands for disciples to bear the cross and follow after him (9:23; 14:27),[9] even though he is not designated as a disciple and carries the cross only by compulsion. Simon's forced "discipleship" contrasts both with the disciples' passive "watching from a distance" (23:49) and Joseph's voluntary act of burying Jesus, forcing the reader to wonder who comes closest to Jesus' ideal.

No other Gospel includes an encounter like the one between Jesus and the women in 23:27-31. Characteristically, Luke has several things going on at once. First, a "great multitude of the people" was following him as he walked toward his crucifixion. They will be witnesses to Jesus' death and take the first step toward repentance and restitution at the end of the scene. Second, there were women grieving for him, weeping and beating their breasts. These are two typical signs of grief (Mic 1:8 LXX uses the same two verbs together); Luke leaves us puzzling over how much sympathy we are to imagine that these women have for Jesus. Do they disapprove of the decision to put him to death? If so, is Luke indicating that some of the crowd who shouted "crucify, crucify him" already regret what they did?

John Irving's novel *A Prayer for Owen Meany* ends with the hero sacrificing himself to save the lives of some children, Vietnamese orphans who are being threatened by a teenager whose brother had been killed in Vietnam. The teenager is about to throw a grenade, when Owen Meany speaks to the children:

"*DOONG SA*," Owen Meany told them. "DON'T BE AFRAID," Owen told the children. "*DOONG SA, DOONG SA*," he said. It was not only because he spoke their language; it was his voice that compelled the children to listen to him—it was a voice like their voices. That was why they trusted him, why they listened. "*DOONG SA*," he said, and they stopped crying.[10]

"Daughters of Jerusalem, don't weep for me," Jesus said. Save your tears for yourselves and your children, he meant, because the destruction he had predicted for the city was certainly going to come, and like all disasters, it would fall hardest on the weakest. It isn't comfort or protection he offers them, but one more prophetic word that the hard times were coming and that they had better get ready. The point of the proverb in v. 31 is debatable. "Green wood," hard to light, is compared to dry wood, easily set ablaze. Perhaps Jesus is comparing his fate (the green wood) to what will happen later when his predictions came true; you are weeping now, but wait until the terrible days of the war—how will you be able to make it? [Green Wood, Dry]

> **Green Wood, Dry**
>
> How did this happen? When the war came on the country of the Jews, they all totally perished, small and great. Infants with their mothers and sons with their fathers were destroyed without distinction.
>
> Cyril of Alexandria, *Commentary on Luke*, Homily 152; cited in Arthur A. Just Jr., ed., *Luke* (ACCS: NT, vol. 3; Downer's Grove IL: Intervarsity Press, 2003), 358.

There were two other "evil-doers" crucified along with Jesus; all four Gospels include this detail. Mark and Matthew call them "bandits"; Luke uses this word in 22:52, when Jesus confronts the chief priests, temple officers, and elders with their cowardice: "Have you come out with swords and clubs as if against a bandit?" But possibly because of the political connotations of the word—it can have the sense of "terrorist"—Luke uses it for none of the three men crucified that day.

Crucifixion (vv. 33-38)

They crucified Jesus and the two "evil-doers" at the placed named "Skull"; Luke saves this detail from Mark, but ditches the word "Golgotha" as he did "Gethsemane," perhaps to save his audience hard-to-pronounce, foreign-sounding words. The place name may refer to the shape of the hill, but if it had been used for executions for any length of time, "skull hill" could have been an acquired nickname. Since, so far as I know, there are no texts or inscriptions predating the Gospels that give that name to any place in or just outside Jerusalem, it seems to me that the second theory is the more plausible.[11] Of the traditional sites, the one inside the Church of the Holy Sepulchre is generally thought to have the best chance of being authentic, but this depends on whether the site of the church was outside the city walls in Jesus' day (a place of

Father, Forgive Them

📖 Mary Gordon's *Pearl* is about an American girl who tries to starve herself to death in Dublin as a public protest over the police shooting of a boy. (Caution: In what follows, I'm giving away much of the ending of the novel.) The dead boy's mother, Breeda, blames Pearl for involving Stevie, her son, a young man of diminished mental capacities, in life-threatening activities. Pearl is involuntarily hospitalized, so weak that it is not clear that she will live, and until she can be assured of Breeda's forgiveness, she isn't sure she wants to live. In the following passage, Pearl's mother, Maria, returns to Pearl's hospital room after conversation with Breeda:

> She runs into Pearl's room.
> "What did she say?"
> "She said there was nothing to forgive. She said you weren't yourself. She said you spoke out of the heat of anger as she spoke out of the heat of grief. . . . And she needs you to mourn with her, to be with her in the work of mourning, of remembering. I think she blames Stevie's father for not mourning. For wanting to forget their son. That she finds unforgivable."
> "Then some things are unforgivable. How do we know what they are?"
> "We know if we're forgiven."
> "And then what?"
> "And then we live our lives."

Mary Gordon, *Pearl* (New York: Anchor, 2006), 336–37.

execution and burial had to be outside the walls, or the city would have been unclean).[12]

Verse 34 is one of the most significant features of Luke's narrative. No other early Christian source suggests that Jesus asked God to forgive those who were executing him, making this verse one of the most profound examples of how Jesus' teachings on nonviolence, nonretaliation, and forgiveness are to be lived out. [Father, Forgive Them] In 2006 we saw an unforgettable example of how a Christian group imitates the Lukan Jesus:

> The blood was barely dry on the floor of the West Nickel Mines School when Amish parents sent words of forgiveness to the family of the one who had slain their children . . . . Their forgiveness was more than words. Fresh from the funerals where they buried their own children, grieving Amish families attended the October 7 burial of the 32-year-old non-Amish killer . . . . Of the 75 in attendance, at least half were Amish. The Amish families greeted [the killer's wife and their three children] . . . . Plans were set to continue the conversation between the families of killer and killed. And forgiveness was more than a graveside presence: the Amish helped to establish a fund for the assassin's family.

As Anabaptists, the Amish take the life and teachings of Jesus seriously. . . . Their model is the suffering Jesus . . . who, hanging on the cross, extended forgiveness to his tormentors: Father, forgive them, for they know not what they do.[13]

Ironically, Luke 23:34 is also a thorny textual variant, omitted by a handful of very ancient manuscripts and, for that reason, printed in double brackets in some editions of the Greek New Testament. Yet the verse was known to second-century Christians such as Justin Martyr, and the support for it is not confined to just one geographical area. The issue comes down to Lukan style and scribal probabilities: does the verse fit Luke's theology? That one is easy: of course, since Jesus urged his followers to forgive their enemies, since the early sermons in Acts also explain the crucifixion as an act of ignorance (Acts 3:17), and since Stephen, the first Christian martyr in Acts, prays the same prayer (Acts 7:60, where there are no significant textual variants). Is it more likely that the verse was removed or inserted? Culpepper summarizes reasons why it might have been removed:

(1) Tension between Christians and Jews led Christian scribes to delete Jesus' prayer for forgiveness of the Jewish leaders. (2) Scribes may have deleted the prayer after the destruction of Jerusalem so that it would not appear that his prayer had not been answered. (3) Scribes may have found the prayer (with its presumption of ignorance) morally unjustifiable.[14]

These seem to me to be plausible reasons for some early scribe removing it. Others, unconvinced by this, propose that it was a saying of Jesus that was remembered in preaching and inserted into Luke later, when it needed a home.[15] But in my opinion, it is unlikely that Luke would have written Acts 3:17 and 7:60 without having first written 23:34—there's no way that Luke would allow Stephen's death to be more Christ-like than Jesus', and no way that Luke would have had Peter attribute the crucifixion to ignorance unless Jesus had done so first.

The other participants in this scene have various reactions to what was going on. One group, presumably the soldiers, "divvied up his clothes" by "casting lots"—the words in quotations were in Mark's Gospel, and come originally from Psalm 21:18 LXX (Ps 22:18 in English Bibles). The implication is that Jesus was naked as he died—a deliberate humiliation that went along with the Roman purpose for crucifixion, proving that the condemned was no match for mighty Rome. The "people" (*ho laos*) stood watching. Their "leaders" or "rulers" (*hoi archontes*, lit., "first ones") mock Jesus' inability to remove himself from the cross: "he saved others, let him save himself, if this one is the Messiah of God, the chosen one." The soldiers repeat "save yourself," but use the title "King of the Jews" that had also been posted over his head. [Save Yourself] The offer of "dry wine" or "vinegary wine" was perhaps also meant as part of the mocking; the sweeter wines were more expensive,[16] and this sort—the kind of stuff the poor and common soldiers drank—was hardly what one would offer a king.[17] This detail, too, is found in a psalm (69:21; LXX 68:21).

Save Yourself

In the ancient (1st century BC or 1st century AD) novel Chaereas and Callirhoe, the hero Chaereas is about to be crucified unjustly, due to a series of mishaps. His friend Polycharmus manages to get the attention of someone who can change the outcome:

Before [Polycharmus] had finished [speaking], Mithridates cried, "Is it Chaereas you mean?" "He is my friend," said Polycharmus. "Sir, please tell the executioner not to separate even our crosses." This story was greeted with tears and groans, and Mithridates sent everybody off to reach Chaereas before he died. They found the rest nailed up on their crosses; Chaereas was just ascending his. So they shouted to them from far off. "Spare him!" cried some; others, "Come down!" or "Don't hurt him!" or "Let him go!" So the executioner checked his gesture, and Chaereas climbed down from his cross . . . .

Chariton, *Chaereas and Callirhoe*, trans. B. P. Reardon, in Reardon, *Collected Ancient Greek Novels* (Berkeley: University of California Press, 1989), 69.

The charge over Jesus' head, called the *titulus* in Latin, was apparently a regular feature of crucifixions, a sign affixed to the crosses of the dying that spelled out the nature of the offense.[18] In Luke's account, the title agrees with one of the charges made against Jesus by the council: "he says that he is the Messiah, a king" (23:2). Of the three charges (the other two, recall, are that he led the people astray and forbade paying taxes to the emperor), this is the only one that Pilate takes seriously. He immediately asks Jesus, "Are you the king of the Jews?" and Jesus replies, "You say," which (see the earlier discussion) means "Those are your words." Pilate dismissed the charge, saying, "I find no grounds [for condemnation] in this man."

But here he is being crucified under that title, although Pilate and Herod Antipas both agreed that he was not a king. The spectators, those who had hollered, "Crucify him!" also do not seem to think he is a king. The chief priests mock him, saying, "he saved others, let him save himself if he is the Christ, God's chosen one." The soldiers crucifying him mocked him: "If you are the king of the Jews, save yourself!" One of the other criminals being executed also insulted him, saying, "Aren't you the Christ? Save yourself and us!" Since Luke has already signaled that in this Roman setting "Christ" means "king," and since Jesus is being killed under the heading "King of the Jews," all three taunts are the same: if he were the real king, he could save himself and others, but he can't, so he isn't.

Note their presupposition: a real king could save himself and others. What king have they ever had who did that? Caesar Augustus was widely celebrated as a savior, but what had he ever done for these people except station soldiers on their land and make them pay for it? Herod the Great had been king of the Jews, and had built many beautiful buildings and completely remodeled the temple, but nobody in this crowd would have considered him a savior. His semi-competent son Herod Antipas was a "quarter-king" up in Galilee. Not long after Jesus' death he asked for a promotion to rule over more territory and instead was removed from what he had; he could not save himself.

Did Luke think that Jesus could have saved himself—that he could have taken himself down from the cross had he wanted to? In Matthew, the answer is a bit more clear-cut: "Do you think I cannot appeal to my Father, and he will at once send me more than twelve legions of angels?" (Matt 26:53). Luke's Jesus makes no such claims, and so one suspects that Luke thought that Jesus, like any other human, would have been powerless to remove himself once he was affixed to the cross. [A Crucified Man Saved by the Gods] The three-fold taunt, "Save yourself!" is met with only silence. He cannot, if "save" here means "heal" as it often does. He could have avoided Jerusalem altogether, and saved himself that way; he could have left Jerusalem after the temple incident rather than spending the week teaching in full view of the authorities. But once he was on the cross, which he came to voluntarily, he could not take himself down nor keep himself from dying.

Conversation (vv. 39-43)

Luke now focuses the audience's attention on the three men hanging on crosses. One of the other men says, echoing the taunts from below, "Aren't you the Messiah? Save yourself and us!" That Luke means this to be sarcastic is evident from his use of the verb "slander, blaspheme" to name this malefactor's speaking, but it also has a hint of desperation, since the question "Aren't you the Messiah" is framed so as to expect a positive answer. The other man "rebukes" him, asking if he does not fear God even at the moment of his death. This man admits his own guilt and the presumed guilt of the other—"we indeed [are being judged] justly since we are receiving [a sentence] worthy of what we did." How he knows that Jesus is innocent is not explained; perhaps Luke's audience is meant to assume that these criminals heard the public trial of Jesus before Pilate.

His request is for Jesus, whom he is certain will truly be king someday, to remember him. Like biblical Joseph who asks the butler to remember him when he gets out of jail (Gen 40:14), this man wants a friend in high places, and given his current circumstances, he is hoping for a good verdict on Judgment Day and a merciful entrance into the kingdom of God.

The evildoer has said "whenever"; Jesus, as he did in his Nazareth sermon, says "today" (4:21). Luke's view of the afterlife appears to be that one moves either to torment or to the blessings symbolized

A Crucified Man Saved by the Gods

In the 2d-century AD Greek novel *An Ephesian Tale*, the hero Habrocomes has been falsely accused of murdering an Egyptian.

Meanwhile Habrocomes came before the prefect of Egypt. The Pelusians had made him a report of what had happened, mentioning Araxus' death and stating that Habrocomes, a household slave, had been the perpetrator of so foul a crime. When the prefect heard the particulars, he made no further effort to find out the facts but gave orders to have Habrocomes taken away and crucified. . . . The prefect's agents brought him to the banks of the Nile, where there was a sheer drop overlooking the torrent. They set up the cross and attached him to it, tying his hands and feet tight with ropes; that is the way the Egyptians crucify. Then they went away and left him hanging there, thinking that their victim was securely in place. But Habrocomes looked straight at the sun, then at the Nile channel, and prayed, "Kindest of the gods, ruler of Egypt, revealer of land and sea to all men; if I, Habrocomes, have done anything wrong, may I perish miserably and incur an even greater penalty if there is one; but if I have been betrayed by a wicked woman, I pray that the waters of the Nile should never be polluted by the body of a man unjustly killed; nor should you look on such a sight, a man who has done no wrong being murdered in your territory." The god took pity on his prayer. A sudden gust of wind arose and struck the cross . . . .

Habrocomes is blown, still attached to the cross, into the river, where he floats unharmed straight back into the hands of the authorities. They next try to burn him, but Habrocomes prays again and the Nile puts out the flames of the pyre.

Xenophon of Ephesus, *An Ephesian Tale* 4.2, trans. Graham Anderson, in Reardon, *Collected Ancient Greek Novels* (Berkeley: University of California Press, 1989), 155–56.

Crucifixion

This painting of the crucifixion has a crowd below the cross, as Luke indicates, although Luke would have positioned the followers of Jesus farther away. Gaddi conventionally locates Mary Magdalene at the base of the cross, holding on to it, and the Beloved Disciple standing looking up. The fainting Virgin is being supported by three other female followers of Jesus.

Agnolo Gaddi. *Crucifixion*. (c.1350–1396)/
Private Collection.
(Credit: © Bonhams, London, UK/
The Bridgeman Art Library.)

by the great banquet in the presence of the patriarchs and the prophets (16:19-31; 13:28-29). Such a view is compatible with a belief in the general resurrection of the dead, which Luke also seems to accept (20:35); the places of reward or torment could have been understood as divided spaces within Sheol, where the dead wait for the Day of Judgment (so at *1 En.* 60–61). Other interpreters argue strongly that Luke's view is of an immediate entrance into either eternal torment or blessing, i.e., heaven or hell (so *Apoc. Ab.*).[19]

Luke's Jesus, as he dies, is preaching salvation, just as he has done since his first sermon. His first audience rejected him and tried to kill him (4:16-30); his second received him gladly, with the result that many were healed (4:31-41). Both of the evildoers could have asked for his help, and he would have granted it; why does one respond favorably and one sarcastically? Jesus' followers should expect that many will refuse to hear the gospel, even when they seem to need it most.

Near the conclusion of Leif Enger's *Peace Like a River*, a father and his son have both been shot, the father fatally; while he lies apparently dead, the son has a vision of himself and his father on the outskirts of Paradise, both healed and healthy and running like crazy, just for the pleasure of it:

We attained a pass where the stream sang louder than ever, for it swelled with depth and energy the farther it rose. Dad reached it first; I saw him mount a shelf of spraysoaked stone and stand waiting for me, backlit, silverlined, as though the sky had a sun after all and it was just beyond this mountain.

But it wasn't a sun. It was a city. . . .

Then Dad pointed to the plains below, at movement I took at first to be rivers . . . . They're people, Dad said. And looking again, looking harder, I could see them on the march, pouring forth from vast distances: People like I'd seen everywhere and others like I'd not seen, whole tributaries of people with untamed faces you would fear as neighbors; and most were afoot, and a few were horseback, and many bore standards with emblems strange to me. And even those who were wild were singing a hymn that rose up to us on the mountain . . . .

We listened a long time. Dad held my hand, and I felt the music growing in his fingers.

Take care of Swede, he said. . . .

I thought, Lord, can't I be among them? Can't I come in too?

Please, I said.

Soon, he replied, which makes better sense under the rules of that country than ours. Very soon! He added, clasping my hands; then, unable to keep from laughing, he pushed off the rock like a boy going for the first cold swim of spring . . . .[20]

Death (vv. 44-46)

The sixth hour is noon, halfway through the twelve hours of daylight. The three-hour span of darkness and the tearing of the temple veil (the passive "it was torn" almost certainly means "by God") are both symbolic, but of what? The failure of the sun is a cosmic sign of God's approaching judgment (Joel 2:10, 31; cf. Amos 5:18), and the tearing of the veil could be a premonition of the temple's destruction.[21] Others, however, link the darkness to Jesus' word about "the authority of darkness" (22:53) and interpret the tearing as God's rejection of the temple as the means of salvation.[22] A third possibility is that the tearing of the veil is a symbol of revelation; as Stephen dies, he sees the heavens opened and Jesus standing at God's right hand (Acts 7:56), and Jesus has told the council that he would be elevated to that station.[23]

While the world is in darkness and the temple veil is being torn, Jesus dies, his last words indicating his complete trust in God. Luke's Jesus quotes Psalm 30:5 LXX (31:5 English). Since only Luke has Jesus say this, it is worth looking at the wider text from which he selected Jesus' last words:

Upon you, O Lord, I hoped; do not let me be ashamed for eternity. In your righteousness rescue me and lead me out. Turn your ear towards me, in order to release me quickly. Be to me a protecting God and a house of refuge in order to save me. For you are my strength and my refuge, and on account of your name you will lead me in the Way and maintain me. You will release me from this snare which they hid for me, because you are my defender, O Lord. Into your hands I entrust my spirit; you ransomed me, O Lord, the God of truth. (Ps 30:1-5 LXX)

They cast lots for his clothes, but "my lots are in your hands" (Ps 30:15 LXX). He "became a thing of reproach" for all his enemies and a "fearful thing" for "those who knew" him (Ps 30:11 LXX), and he "heard the slander of many who dwelt all around"(Ps 30:13 LXX). "But I hoped in you, O Lord. I said, 'You are my God, in your hands are my lots; rescue me from the hand of my enemies and from those who persecute me. Let your face shine upon your slave; save me in your mercy. O Lord, do not let me be ashamed, because I called upon you" (Ps 30:14-17 LXX).

In short, Jesus' death conforms to the model of the psalm text and is Luke's model for how believers should die (see Acts 7:59, where Stephen says something very close). Or as the hero of Marilynne Robinson's *Gilead* says, "I'll pray, and then I'll sleep."[24]

Recession (vv. 47-49)

Up to the moment of Jesus' death, the bystanders have either been passive (the people stand and watch) or mocking (the leaders and the soldiers) or acquisitive (the soldiers cast lots to divide his clothes). But his death and the cosmic signs accompanying it make an impact on at least some of the group. The centurion "glorified" or praised God, saying, "Surely this man was righteous." Centurions were often the most experienced and most senior of the soldiers; this one, Luke's audience assumed, probably had command of the soldiers carrying out the crucifixion and had seen many criminals die before. "Righteous" certainly includes "innocent," but given its use in Psalm 30 LXX, Luke probably means a bit more by it. It is God's righteousness that makes the psalmist certain of rescue; the wicked have set a trap and "speak lawlessness against the righteous person" (Ps 30:18 LXX), but God will vindicate him. The soldiers mocked Jesus as one who could not save himself, but the centurion is declaring Jesus to be innocent, not only because he heard Pilate, but because he interpreted the events of the day to mean God found Jesus righteous.[25]

The crowd—"all those who had gathered for this spectacle"— after they saw what happened, "returned beating their breasts." This is what the bereaved do as well as those mourning their own sins (18:13). It is a sign that they now regret what has happened; this helps to explain why the crowd on Pentecost is so easily "cut to the heart" (Acts 2:37). There is no mention of the "leaders" at this point. In Acts, the chief priests are implacable enemies of Jesus' followers, but "a great crowd of priests" joined the movement.

Finally, we hear about Jesus' followers. The last mention of them was just before Jesus' arrest, when "his disciples followed him" (22:39). After his arrest, we lose sight of the bigger group for a while, but Peter follows at a distance (22:54) until he denies Jesus, and then leaves the high priest's house for an undisclosed location. Where were they while the trial was going on—that is, where does Luke want us to imagine them? Possibly we are to think of them offstage, as it were, hanging about somewhere in the city while other people act, until they reappear just after Jesus' death. Possibly, however, we are to imagine them as a group in the throng that heard Pilate declare him guiltless, that followed the soldiers and the condemned to "Skull," and that watched the whole spectacle. There is precedent for this: during the journey section, Luke appears to imagine that there are always crowds, disciples, apostles, and Pharisees close by Jesus, ready to pop up to speak their lines. In my opinion, Luke pictures the larger group of disciples—"all who knew him . . . and the women who had followed him from Galilee" standing far off, watching the whole business. As noted earlier, this makes them all witnesses, if not fellow sufferers.

So, one of his enemies confesses that he is righteous; the crowd that wanted him dead is now mourning; and his followers stand at a distance, watching. Which comes closest to the ideal response?

Burial (vv. 50-56)

Joseph of Arimathea appears in all four Gospels at the end, when it is time to bury Jesus. Mark 15:43 calls him "a well-respected member of the council, who was also himself expecting the kingdom of God." By this, Mark may have intended to hint that Joseph was already a disciple of Jesus, but since the whole council voted to put Jesus to death (Mark 14:65), it is also possible that Mark meant Joseph to be a member of the council converted after Jesus' death. Luke clarifies this: Joseph did not consent to the council and to their action. Other than that, Luke calls him a "good and righteous man"—certainly not a rich man (Matt 27:57), since in Luke rich people are only good if they give their money to the poor, and also not "a secret disciple for fear of the Jews" (John 19:38). "From the Jewish city of Arimathea" and "who was expecting the kingdom of God" completes Luke's identification; like Simon of Cyrene, he is from out of town; like the rest of the disciples, he hopes that Jesus will inaugurate the kingdom soon. In the meantime, however, he is not sitting around. He gets permission from Pilate to bury Jesus—Luke omits the part about Pilate's amazement that Jesus was already dead—and does so. Joseph takes down the corpse, wraps it in a piece of linen, and lays it in a previously unused rock tomb. John 19:41 also calls this an unused tomb, so it is possible that Luke drew this detail from Christian preaching about Jesus' death and burial. Perhaps "unused" is meant as a gesture of respect, like the "colt upon which no one has ever sat (Luke 19:30, 38); in contrast to the shining robe and sour wine, given to Jesus to mock him, Luke means for Joseph's gift of a tomb to be a token of esteem.[26]

Last to be mentioned are the women. They followed him from Galilee, where they had been an important part of his movement (8:1-3); they stood at a distance and watched him die; now they follow behind Joseph, and take note of the tomb where he was buried. They are the only part of the Galilean disciples who are said to see Jesus buried. Apparently, Luke followed Mark in thinking that Joseph and the women did not know each other; that may account for Luke's "from the Jewish town of Arimathea," to explain that Joseph came from somewhere else. So, since it was getting close to sundown and the beginning of the Sabbath, the women went back home—like the crowd in 23:48, but with a different purpose, since these women intend to return with spices and ointments to anoint Jesus' body.

Here's the scorecard, at the end of the story:

• Simon of Cyrene: bears Jesus' cross behind him, but only involuntarily
• The people: some weep on the way to the cross; all watch and then mourn on the way home
• The women of Jerusalem: follow Jesus to the cross, weeping; Jesus tells them to stop and warns them that times in the future will be hard
• The soldiers: crucify Jesus; cast lots for his clothes; mock his helplessness; but their commander, watching Jesus die, calls him a righteous man
• The leaders: mock Jesus
• Jesus' companions: watch the crucifixion from a distance
• The Galilean women: watch the crucifixion from a distance, and follow behind all the way to the tomb
• Joseph of Arimathea: asks Pilate for the body and buries Jesus respectfully

There are thus various levels of hostility, passivity, and activity, inviting the reader to think about what the proper response should be.

Jesus' death in Luke is the death of a righteous man, one who forgives his enemies, who offers salvation to others, and who never waivers in his belief that God will deliver him. Each of the Gospels has its own important contribution to make to our understanding of the cross, but without Luke, it is hard to see how we would associate the cross with forgiveness.

CONNECTIONS

Jesus, who never called himself "Messiah" or "King," is accused, convicted, and executed for claiming to be "King of the Jews." This is a farce—a satire—since nothing about the process goes in normal ways and since in the end none of the participants seem to believe it.

The Sanhedrin wants to hand Jesus over to the authority of the empire (20:20), so they accuse Jesus of things Luke's narrative demonstrates to be false. Pilate asks Jesus only one question: "Are you the king of the Jews?" Pilate takes "you say" as proof, without any other evidence, of Jesus' innocence; he takes Herod Antipas's mockery as a declaration of innocence; he announces three times that there is no basis for the charges against Jesus, and says that he will release him. But the people and the Sanhedrin, who handed Jesus over to Pilate's authority, then overmaster the governor, forcing him to agree to their wish to have Jesus crucified.

In *Amphitryon*, a comedy by the second-century BC playwright Plautus, Jupiter impersonates Amphitryon in order to seduce his wife. After taking over his house and servants, humiliating him publicly several times, and impregnating his wife, Jupiter tells his victim to thank his lucky stars that his wife gets to bear a god's offspring. Luke's trial narrative lampoons the empire in approximately the same way—it's a system that exploits you over and over and then tells you to count your blessings. That's why, according to Luke's Jesus, "it is not to be so among you." No top-down systems of power, no measuring authority by wealth or status, no fights over who's on top; if only we would truly listen! The enduring symbol of our religion is a cross, a sign to the empire of its ability to repress and to overmaster, but to us of God's choice to lift up the humble. Be a slave; carry the cross; sell your possessions; nothing in any of that sounds like "structure your churches according to the best business practices" or like "thank God that you can enjoy the highest quality of life on the planet."

As noted in the commentary above, without Luke's crucifixion narrative we'd be hard-pressed to connect the cross with forgiveness. Each Gospel makes its own contribution to how we interpret Jesus' death. Mark's account emphasizes how Jesus is betrayed, abandoned, and ridiculed, crying out, "My God, my God, why have you forsaken me?" Mark keeps us from ever romanticizing the crucifixion or forgetting how awful it was. Matthew's account connects the moment of Jesus' death to cosmic events: the temple veil was torn, there were earthquakes, and some of the dead rose. His Gospel wants us to take note of how Jesus' death and resurrection marked the turn of the ages. John's account of Jesus' death, like Luke's, presents Jesus as calm and under control. John's Jesus makes certain that his mother will be cared for, takes a drink in order to fulfill a Scripture, and then, saying, "it is finished," dies. John's Gospel is also the only one to interpret the cross as a demonstration of God's love for the world.

Luke's Jesus gives one more prophetic warning about the danger to Jerusalem, forgives his executioners, offers salvation to one more penitent, and dies entrusting his spirit to God. He dies as he lived and taught, matching Luke's audience's expectations for a noble death. Luke's narrative challenges us to rise above our natural human inclinations and to forgive our enemies, to bless those who curse us, to do good to those who mistreat us.

NOTES

[1] The dating depends on how one interprets Josephus. Pilate came to Judea as a replacement for Valerius Gratus, and Josephus says that Gratus's term was eleven years long. But he also gives conflicting data that could make Gratus's term shorter. For instance, Josephus writes that Pilate went to Judea at about the same time as a scandal in Rome involving four Jews who took large sums of money from a Roman matron, telling her that it was for the temple in Jerusalem (*Ant.* 18.81-84); Tacitus writes about the same event (*Ann.* 2.85), dating it to about AD 19. See Daniel R. Schwartz, "Pontius Pilate," *ABD* 5.396-97; Craig A. Evans, "Excavating Caiaphas, Pilate, and Simon of Cyrene," in Charlesworth, ed., *Jesus and Archaeology* (Grand Rapids MI: 2006), 336–37.

[2] Joseph A. Fitzmyer, *The Gospel According to Luke* (AB 28 and 28A; Garden City NY: Doubleday, 1981), 2.1473: "It is you who say this!"

[3] Paul Walaskay, *"And So We Came To Rome": The Political Perspective of St. Luke* (Cambridge: Cambridge University Press, 1983), 41. The testimony of ignoble people— slaves, foreigners, persons suspected of violent crimes—had to be tested and corroborated by torture; see J. Albert Harrill, *Slaves in the New Testament: Literary,*

Social, and Moral Dimensions (Minneapolis: Fortress, 2006), 158–59. Scenes in which torture or the threat of it induce a criminal to tell the truth appear in the Greek novels *Chaereas and Callirhoe* and *Leucippe and Clitophon*, and although these scenes tend toward melodrama, they illustrate how normal it would have been for Pilate to flog Jesus after his "testimony" in order to ensure that he was telling the truth.

[4] For example, *Rhetorica ad Herennium* I.12.22 gives as an example a plaintiff who, when arrested for embezzlement, argues that his case should be tried instead as theft, and therefore in a different court under a different praetor. The author admits the stratagem is only occasionally of any use.

[5] Robert Funk et al., eds., *The Acts of Jesus* (San Francisco: HarperSanFrancisco, 1998), 358–59.

[6] Frederick W. Danker, *Jesus and the New Age: A Commentary on St. Luke's Gospel* (rev. ed.; Philadelphia: Fortress, 1988), 365.

[7] Cf. Sirach 26:5: Of three things my heart is frightened, and of a fourth I am in great fear: Slander in the city, the gathering of a mob, and false accusation—all these are worse than death.

[8] Mark Helprin, *Winter's Tale* (Orlando: Harcourt, 1985), 741–42.

[9] Luke Timothy Johnson, *The Gospel of Luke* (SP, vol. 3; Collegeville MN: Liturgical Press, 1991), 372; Fitzmyer, *Luke*, 2.1497.

[10] John Irving, *A Prayer for Owen Meany* (New York: Random House, 1989), 612.

[11] Contra Fitzmyer, *Luke*, 2.1503; Johnson, *Luke*, 378; Alan R. Culpepper, *The Gospel of Luke* (*NIB*, vol. 9; Nashville: Abingdon, 1995), 454. Raymond E. Brown, *The Death of the Messiah: From Gethsemane to the Grave* (2 vols.; Garden City NY: Doubleday, 1994), 2.937, thinks the shape determined the name but mentions the other option as a possibility.

[12] According to James Charlesworth, "There also seems to be a consensus among archaeologists that Jesus was possibly, and perhaps probably, crucified" on the white stone inside the Church of the Holy Sepulchre. Citing the work of Dan Bahat, Charlesworth is confident that the crucifixion site lay outside the city at the time of Jesus' crucifixion, since the wall that enclosed it was built by Agrippa, ca. 41–44; see Charlesworth, "Jesus Research and Archaeology: A New Perspective," in Charlesworth, ed., *Jesus and Archaeology* (Grand Rapids: Eerdmans, 2006), 31–36. So also Virgilo C. Corbo, "Golgotha," *ABD* 2.1072-73. John J. Rousseau and Rami Arav, *Jesus and His World* (Minneapolis MN: Fortress, 1995), 112–17, examine the same evidence and come to the conclusion that there is no proof that the site on which the church sits was outside the walls in Jesus' day.

[13] Donald B. Kraybill, "Forgiveness Clause," *ChrCent* 123/22 (31 October 2006): 8. For a fuller discussion of the tragedy and Amish understandings of forgiveness, see Kraybill, Steven M. Nolt, and David L. Weaver-Zercher, *Amish Grace: How Forgiveness Transcended Tragedy* (San Francisco: Wiley, 2007).

[14] Culpepper, *Luke*, 455.

[15] Bruce Metzger, *A Textual Commentary on the Greek New Testament* (New York: United Bible Societies, 1971), 180, judges that the verse was omitted by so many early manuscripts from so wide a geographical spread that it cannot be explained as a deliberate excision, and proposes that it was a floating dominical saying inserted into Luke by the second century.

[16] BAGD, 715.

[17] So Joel B. Green, *The Gospel of Luke* (NICNT; Grand Rapids: Eerdmans, 1997), 821; Brown, *Death*, 2.997; Culpepper, *Luke*, 456.

[18] Brown, *Death*, 2.963, states, "Sometimes the *titulus* was carried before the condemned as he went to be crucified or was marched around the amphitheater; other times it was hung around his neck."

[19] Brown, *Death*, 2.1009-13.

[20] Leif Enger, *Peace Like a River* (New York: Grove, 2001), 303–304.

[21] Culpepper, *Luke*, 460.

[22] Green, *Luke*, 825–26; Fitzmyer, *Luke*, 2.1519.

[23] John Nolland, *Luke* (WBC, vols. 35A-C; Dallas TX: Word, 1989-93), 3.1156-57.

[24] Marilynne Robinson, *Gilead* (New York: Farrar, Straus, and Giroux, 2004), 247.

[25] Johnson, *Luke*, 382.

[26] Brown, *Death*, 2.1255.

THE RESURRECTION

Luke 24

COMMENTARY

Discovery of the Empty Tomb, 24:1-12

The oldest written tradition about Jesus' resurrection is found in 1 Corinthians 15:3-8:

> For I passed on to you among the first things [I told you] what I also had received [from those who passed the tradition along to me], that Christ died for our sins according to the scriptures; and that he was buried; and that he was raised on the third day according to the scriptures; and that he appeared to Cephas, then to the twelve; then he appeared to upwards of 500 "brethren" at once, of whom most are alive but some have died; then he appeared to James, then to all the apostles; finally, as to one born out of time, he appeared to me.

Note that "he was buried," but not "and his empty tomb was seen by many," was part of this ancient catechism. And note that no women are named, although some might be hidden in the "brethren" to whom Christ appeared in a bunch. It makes us wonder, then, why the Gospels tell the story the way they do—because all four have a woman or women discover the empty tomb—when it was possible for Christians to transmit the essence of their faith without this story. In other words, set aside for a moment the issue of "what really happened," and ask yourself what is gained theologically or narratively by telling this story.

"He was buried" in the tradition Paul learned may signify "he was really dead," to counter possible objections that the resurrection was simply a failed execution. But it also might signify "somebody buried him, instead of leaving his body for the vultures or the dogs, and somebody knew where the place was." We cannot know for certain, because Paul never narrates the crucifixion or burial, but it is possible that "he was buried" condenses a story like the one found in Mark 16:1-8, the story Luke edits in this section. This seems to me more plausible than the other possibility, that Mark expanded "he was buried" into the story of the women at the tomb. Mark's story is particularly ill-suited if he wanted to convince people that Jesus was really alive: Jesus never appears; the only witnesses are women; the "young man" points to what isn't there; and the women run away in fear. Wow—impressive, eh?

So Mark, I think, is repeating ancient testimony, not filling a gap in the catechism. But we still want to know why he, and Luke following him, told the story. Even if that's the way it really happened, it still isn't very convincing as a proof of Jesus' resurrection. Why not move straight to the appearances, as Paul's catechism does, leaving out the fearful women who see nothing and are convinced of something?

Luke begins his story at dawn on Sunday ("the first day of the week"). Jesus' female disciples, who had followed him from Galilee and had watched his crucifixion and burial, had gone home as the Sabbath began (at sundown on Friday) and had prepared burial spices and ointments (23:56). Mark's account named two women who watched his burial and three who went to anoint him; my opinion is that Luke thinks it was a much larger group than that. Acts 1:12-15 numbers the total group of disciples in Jerusalem at about 120, and names the eleven plus "women and Mary the mother of Jesus and his brothers." Of this group of women, we know the names of seven: Mary the mother of Jesus (8:21 indicates she was a disciple in Galilee); Mary Magdalene, Joanna (both named at 24:11 and 8:2-3); Susanna (8:3); Mary the mother of James (24:11); and Mary and Martha (10:38-42, whom Luke associates with a Galilean village, not with Bethany). But of 120 Galileans, surely there were more than seven women; "all who knew him" watched him die (23:49), and then the women in the group stayed around to watch him be buried—this may have been a large group indeed in Luke's mind. In fact, the way 24:9-10 is phrased, it sounds like all the women ("Mary Magdalene and Joanna and Mary the mother of James and the rest of the women with them") told all the men ("the eleven and all the rest") about their experiences.

Unlike Mark's women, Luke's are not worrying about the stone as they approach the tomb. Since Luke never says "it was very large," his audience can assume it wasn't, or that the women felt sufficient to handle it. Like Mark's women, Luke's find the stone moved and go into the tomb [Jesus' Tomb], but Luke specifically says "they did not find the body of the Lord Jesus." While they were puzzling over this, "behold—two men dressed in dazzling clothes were standing by them." The "behold" is meant to signal that the two suddenly appeared. Angels? Probably, but we should notice that at the transfiguration, the two men were Moses and Elijah, and allow for the possibility that Luke thinks those two returned to remind Jesus' followers about what he'd said about his "exodus" (9:31). Why two? The usual answer is that according to the Law of Moses, two witnesses are required to establish anything. And so there are pairs of witnesses in several places: at Jesus' birth (Simeon and Anna), at the transfiguration (Moses and Elijah), at his trial (Pilate and Herod Antipas), and at his crucifixion

> ### Jesus' Tomb
>
> Luke specifies a tomb cut into rock. Rock tombs have been excavated in Jerusalem and in Jericho, and those dating from close to Jesus' lifetime (the loculi type, also called *kokhim* in Hebrew) consist of a chamber, tall enough that a person could stand, with niches or tubes cut into the walls of the chamber. The entrance to the chamber would be sealed with a large stone; these were often round, like a millstone, to make them easier to move. The corpse could be prepared for burial in the chamber, which often had a bench for that purpose cut into the side of one wall, and then interred in the niche, sometimes in a wooden coffin. During the Second Temple period, sometimes the bones of the departed were collected a year after death and re-interred in a stone ossuary (a bone-box).
>
> Rachel Hachlili, "Burials, Ancient Jewish," *ABD* 1.789-94; John J. Rousseau and Rami Arav, *Jesus and His World* (Minneapolis MN: Fortress, 1995), 164–69.

(one of the evildoers and the centurion both said Jesus was guilt-free). But these two are angels or saints, testifying to Jesus' resurrection; if the women were going to be like Zechariah and doubt the word of one angel, would two make any difference? Possibly Luke has been influenced by Zechariah 4:11-14, with its "two 'sons of fatness' who stand by the Lord of all the earth" (4:14 LXX), or possibly the pattern of two angels (continued in Acts 1) is a carry-over from the transfiguration story.

The women certainly act as if they are seeing angels; they become frightened and lower their faces to the earth (or lie facedown on the earth). The angels, uncharacteristically, do not say, "Don't be afraid," but begin by rebuking the women: "Why do you seek the living among the dead?" The implication is "you should know better than that";[1] the angels treat the women as if they should already have known what was going to happen, since Jesus had predicted it. What the women need, then, is to be reminded of lessons already learned but perhaps forgotten momentarily.

The angels first point out what the women already know—"he is not here"—and then interpret his absence—"he has been raised." "He is risen" is such familiar language, and is a possible translation of *ēgerthē*, but "has been raised" more perfectly conveys "raised by God," which Luke certainly means.[2] The angels then repeat some of the main points of Jesus' many predictions of his death and resurrection, which "he spoke . . . while he was still in Galilee":

- "it is necessary for the son of man": this repeats all the words of the first part of 9:22, but in a slightly different order; in all three predictions of Jesus' death that Luke takes over from Mark, he uses "son of man" (see the list in the commentary on 9:18-27). "It is necessary" means to Luke that this series of events was part of God's plan recorded in Scripture, and so things had to go this way.
- "to be handed over into the hands of sinful men": 9:44 has "handed over into the hands of men," 18:32 has "handed over to the Gentiles," and 22:37, quoting Isaiah 53:12, has "reckoned with the lawless." So what the angels say is not unprecedented, but it does reflect how Luke will begin speaking of the crucifixion from this point forward: it was a sinful act for which the perpetrators had better repent.
- "and crucified": Luke does not have this word in any of the three predictions he took from Mark; there he says "and killed" (9:22) and "they will kill him" (18:33). Note that Paul's catechism also says "Christ died" rather than "Christ was crucified." One suspects that for many believers, the nature of Jesus' death was not something to which they wanted to draw immediate attention. Crucifixion was such an ignoble means of death and so firmly associated with slaves that many early formulations of the faith do not use the word "crucify." But Luke's Jesus has prepared the disciples for the cross: 9:23 and 14:27 both call for disciples to imitate Jesus by bearing the cross.
- "and on the third day arise": almost word for word from the end of 18:33.

The angels thus summarize Jesus' previous teachings about his death, drawing on various expressions from various parts of the Gospel. All this presumes that the women were present for all of it and could be expected to remember it. Although they were initially confused by the crucifixion, once they remembered Jesus' teachings, they understood. Just as Mary and Elizabeth served as prototypes for the prophet-leaders that their sons and their sons' followers would be, so this group of women—who may include Mary—serves as prototypes for the way Luke thinks people come to faith. God—in this case through angels, but perhaps in most cases through the Spirit—brings one to understand the teachings of Jesus that one has already heard.

The women do remember his words, and, in sharp contrast to Mark's women, do not run from the tomb in fear, but return home to share their experiences with the rest of the community. Mark's angel tells Mark's women to go and tell the apostles and Peter; these women need no prompting, but "announce these things to all the eleven and to all the rest." At this point, let us remind ourselves that Luke imagines not just a few women, but a bunch, and that Luke has told the reader early on that these women were part of the group from the beginning, and that their ministry and their providing of their means kept things going. Why, then, do the guys ignore them? They heard the same predictions the women did; Peter, James, and John knew that two heavenly messengers appeared with Jesus before, and so the testimony of the women should have been credible. They know these women; James and John are doubting the word of their sainted mother, for crying out loud. Like Zechariah, they are not thinking straight when they dismiss the testimony of their wives, mothers, sisters, and companions in the faith as "foolish chatter." [The Women and "Foolish Chatter"]

Peter, however, has second thoughts. "Jumping up, he ran to the tomb and peering in, saw only the wrappings, and went away by himself amazed [or wondering] at what happened." Just as earlier he followed Jesus into the courtyard, but remained "at a distance," so now he follows the women to the tomb, but is too late to hear the angels. Peter's amazement is somewhere between the men's disbelief and the women's faith; he is essentially where the women were when they first saw the tomb and had not yet been reminded of Jesus' words by God's messengers.

The Women and "Foolish Chatter"

It is well documented that many 1st-century men thought that women were not as reliable as men as witnesses, being more emotional. For instance, Josephus, writing on the requirement of two witnesses in Torah, states,

Let not a single witness be credited, but three, or two at the least, and those such whose testimony is confirmed by their good lives. But let not the testimony of women be admitted, on account of the levity and boldness of their sex; nor let servants be admitted to give testimony, on account of the ignobility of their soul; since it is probable that they may not speak truth, either out of hope of gain, or fear of punishment. (*Ant.* 4.219)

The Mishnah shows that rabbis were divided on the matter of whether women's testimony was trustworthy in certain situations. For example, suppose a man married a woman and found that she was not a virgin,

And she said, "After thou didst betroth me I was forced and thy field was laid waste," and he said, "Not so, but [it befell] before I betrothed thee, and my bargain was a bargain made in error," Rabban Gamaliel and R. Eliezer say: She may be believed. But R. Joshua says: We may not rely on her word; but she must be presumed to have suffered intercourse before she was betrothed and to have deceived her husband unless she can bring proof for her words. (*m. Ketub.* 1:6)

Philo also thought women were naturally inclined to be deceitful; writing about why the Essenes were celibate, he says this was wise, because

. . . woman is a selfish creature and one addicted to jealousy in an immoderate degree, and terribly calculated to agitate and overturn the natural inclinations of a man, and to mislead him by her continual tricks; for as she is always studying deceitful speeches and all other kinds of hypocrisy, like an actress on the stage, when she is alluring the eyes and ears of her husband, she proceeds to cajole his predominant mind after the servants have been deceived. (*Hypothetica* 11.14-15)

Luke's audiences, ancient and modern, face many of the same issues illustrated by the divided responses of the early followers of Jesus. We have the testimony of early believers; according to some traditions, we could even visit Jesus' tomb and like Peter note that it is empty. But our experience will be different from the women's. Had the rest of the apostles gotten off their keisters early that morning, maybe they all could have heard the angels; but they didn't, and we can't. We either accept their testimony or we don't.

I think it is significant that both in this episode and in the next one, where Jesus appears incognito to the two disciples on the road, Jesus' words can make "our hearts burn within us" when we are given a chance to hear them, remember them, and then have those memories stirred by an agent of God. The angels speak to the women; Jesus will speak to the two on the road and to the rest in Jerusalem; the Spirit will speak to the crowd in Jerusalem on Pentecost. It is a mystery how and when God raises Jesus' words in our consciousness, why sometimes they lie dormant and other times they change our lives. But thank God that it happens—it's Easter, and he lives, and we live with him!

First Appearance: The Emmaus Story, 24:13-35

The Emmaus story brings together so many themes from Luke's Gospel that one can think of it as a narration of Luke's under-standing of the resurrection of Jesus. It is unique to Luke's Gospel; Mark, Matthew, and John have nothing exactly like this, and Paul's listing of resurrection appearances also has nothing about "he appeared to Cleopas and the other one." However, there are inter-esting parallels between Luke's appearances and the list in 1 Corinthians 15:3-8: "he appeared to Cephas, then to the twelve; then he appeared to upwards of 500 'brethren' at once, of whom most are alive but some have died; then he appeared to James, then to all the apostles; finally, as to one born out of time, he appeared to me." If you skip this story, Luke's list would go "he appeared to Peter, then to the eleven and to the rest of the approximately 120 'brethren,' including James; finally, he appeared to Paul [Acts 9]."

As others have observed, Luke's audience would recognize this story as a "recognition" scene (*anagnōrisis*), where literary characters suddenly discover the true identity of someone else.[3] Homer's *Odyssey*, with which Luke's audience would surely have some famil-iarity, has several of these recognition moments, all intertwined. When Odysseus comes home at last from his travels, he finds that his house has been overrun with suitors for his wife Penelope, and he knows he will have to fight to regain his rightful place. So he disguises himself as a beggar, to scout things out, to find out who is still loyal to him, to discover weaknesses he can exploit, etc. His disguise fools everybody: the wicked suitors, various household servants and field hands, his wife, and his son all interact with him without knowing him.

The swineherd Eumaeus does not know the beggar is his master, but offers him gracious hospitality anyway. Odysseus reveals his true identity to his loyal servant by showing him a scar from a boar-hunting incident. His old nurse Eurycleia spots the same scar as she is washing his feet, and is about to reveal him to Penelope, but "Penelope was not prepared to meet her glance or understand it, for Athene had distracted her attention."[4] Odysseus nearly throttles Eurycleia and threatens to kill her if she reveals him; the old nurse harrumphs that he need not threaten her in order to make certain of her help.

Odysseus's son Telemachus also does not recognize his father the first time he sees him. The moment of recognition is further complicated by the appearance of the goddess Athene, who comes to insist that Odysseus make himself known to Telemachus; but Athene is also in disguise, and Odysseus (and the dogs) know her true identity, but not Telemachus. So Athene touches Odysseus with her wand, changing his appearance and his clothing. Telemachus is amazed, and thinks his father is a god; but then Odysseus says, "Why do you take me for an immortal? . . . I am no god. But I am your father, on whose account you have endured so much sorrow and trouble and suffered persecution at men's hands."[5]

The same sorts of plot devices appear in Greek drama, and Aristotle discussed them in his *Poetics*, writing that in his opinion, the best dramatic plots connected reversal ("a change to the opposite direction of events") and recognition ("a change from ignorance to knowledge, leading to friendship or to enmity, and involving matters which bear on prosperity or adversity").[6] In Aristotle's opinion, recognition scenes like the one where Odysseus shows his scar to the swineherd are less artistic than the bath scene, where the moment is more complicated; the nurse discovers the truth for herself, but is prevented from passing it on, and the narrative tension is continued rather than released. "Best of all is recognition ensuing from the events themselves, where the emotional impact comes from a probable sequence [Aristotle means a sequence of plausible events, not something contrived] . . . for only such recognitions do without contrived tokens."[7] As we move through this story, I will refer back to the Homeric scenes and to Aristotle's opinions of them, to show how "artistic" Luke's narrative is.

Luke puts the story "on that same day," Easter Sunday, the day of the discovery of the empty tomb (24:1-12). Two of Jesus' followers are leaving Jerusalem for Emmaus, which Luke says lies 60 stadia or about 7 miles away. We cannot identify Emmaus. Josephus writes of one town by that name, but it is about 20 miles away, too far for the two disciples to go there and back on the same day. Another village named Ammaous (modern Qaloniyeh) was about 3.5 miles from Jerusalem (Josephus, *J. W.* 7.217, says "thirty stadia from Jerusalem"). Maybe Luke meant that place, but it's impossible to say. As commentators note, the main point is that Emmaus lies close to Jerusalem—close enough for the two to get there and back in a day, but more importantly, close enough that Jesus' command for them to remain in Jerusalem makes sense (24:47-49). Who are the two? Cleopas is otherwise unknown, and the anonymous fellow traveler (his wife? a friend or neighbor?) is a complete blank. But they are not apostles—we know all their names, and Cleopas is not one of them. So Luke, who began this chapter with a story of women hearing and believing what the eleven failed to hear and believe now has Jesus reveal himself first to persons other than the eleven. Since Luke's definition of "apostle" is "a witness of everything from the baptism of John to the ascension [Acts 1:22]," he is carefully noting how not only did people other than the twelve see the risen Jesus, but that maybe they saw him first.

As the two walk along, they are having conversation about (*homileō*) and discussing, maybe even arguing about (*syzēteō*, can mean either), what had happened. You can picture them trudging home, trying to get the sequence of things straight, wondering why this person did that or didn't say something else, speculating about what might come next. Like the women in the tomb, they are confused, and they are trying to talk it all out. While they are walking and talking, "Jesus himself, drawing near, began to walk with them"—he overtakes them from behind, in other words, and they walk together. "But their eyes were prevented [lit., were being held back] so that they would not recognize him." Jesus is not in disguise, in other words; Luke uses a passive verb ("were prevented" or "were being held back") to indicate that God was preventing them from being able to know Jesus. [Angels in Disguise] That's curious, is it not? Luke understood the resurrection/ascension to be God's validation of Jesus' status as Lord and Messiah (Acts 2:32-36), so if this story was to function as evidence for Jesus' resurrection and therefore for his honored status, wouldn't it work better if people knew who he was?

But, in fact, the Emmaus story is not so much about proving that Jesus was raised, but about interpreting his death and resurrection for the church. The nonrecognition means that like Odysseus, Jesus can scope things out, to find out whether these disciples remember anything he taught them. But unlike Odysseus, Jesus does not need to disguise his identity; he goes unrecognized for the same reason Athene could appear to Telemachus to be "a tall, beautiful, and accomplished woman . . . since it is by no means to everyone that the gods grant a clear sight of themselves."[8]

Jesus pulls up even with them and asks them what words they had been exchanging; this "stops them in their

Angels in Disguise

The angel Raphael appears incognito in the book of Tobit. Tobit sends his son Tobias to deal with some finances in a distant city, but requires Tobias to find an experienced guide. Tobias "found the angel Raphael standing in front of him; but he did not perceive that he was an angel of God" (Tob 5:4). The disguise holds, and nobody suspects anything until the end, when Tobias is about to pay him and send him on his way. Raphael explains that he is one of the seven angels of the presence, and was sent to test them (12:14-15). He reminds them that he never ate or drank anything in front of them; even when he seemed to be doing so, it was a vision (14:19). After blessing them, Raphael ascends into heaven.

Titian (Tiziano Vecellio) (c.1488–1576). *Young Tobit and the Archangel Raphael.* Accademia, Venice, Italy. (Credit: Cameraphoto/Art Resource, NY)

tracks, overcome with sorrow" (taking *estathēsan* as an ingressive aorist, focusing on their beginning to stand). The first part of Cleopas's reply can be understood different ways: "Are you the only visitor to Jerusalem who does not know . . ."; "You are a solitary visitor [or "only a visitor"] to Jerusalem, so you do not know . . . .[9]" However we read it, Cleopas believes that he knows more than this guy who just popped up—even though he asks no questions about who the man is or what he has been doing for the past few days.

The Way to and Supper at Emmaus

The Way to and Supper at Emmaus. Codex Egberti (Ms. 24), folio 87 recto. 10th C. Stadtbibliothek, Trier, Germany. (Credit: Foto Marburg/Art Resource, NY)

This illumination from a 10th-century Gospel manuscript identifies Luke as Cleopas's unnamed companion.

Cleopas is taking another familiar dramatic role, that of the "know it all," or *alazōn*.[10] Aristotle again commended Homer for complicating recognition scenes like this by allowing a character to make a false inference that takes him, and potentially the audience, down the wrong road.[11] Jesus takes the part of the "iron," the character who knows the truth but is hiding it: "What things?" he says, perhaps with a puzzled look on his face.

The recitation by Cleopas and friend in vv. 19-21a is a pretty good summary of the least that one should have been able to conclude about Jesus from Luke's narrative—absent faith. Cleopas thus represents approximately the position of "the people" at this point in the story. Jesus was a great prophet sent by God (7:16, reported as popular opinion about Jesus), "powerful in word and deed" (4:36; 19:48). Blaming "our chief priests and leaders" for handing Jesus over to death reminds the audience that although the people also called for Jesus' crucifixion, they had been grief-stricken before and after the crucifixion (23:27, 48), while the leaders had mocked Jesus on the cross (23:35). The people, then, were already on the way to repentance, but their leaders had not changed their minds. Finally, "we were hoping that he is the one about to redeem Israel." This was Zechariah's interpretation of the births of John and Jesus (1:68), which he elaborated as "salvation from our enemies and from the hands of all who hate us" (1:71). Luke notes that there were others looking forward to this day (2:38), hoping for the appearance of the Messiah (3:15); the disciples more specifically hoped that Jesus was a king (19:38) and that he would restore Israel's self-rule (Acts 1:6).

But Cleopas and his walking buddy are not just "the people"; they're members of the group of Jesus' followers. Why is their understanding no clearer than the crowds'? Has the Son of Man returned only to find no faith among his disciples (18:8)? These two remark that "in addition to these things, this, the third day from everything that happened, has come"; it is not clear that they know the significance of "the third day," and thus fail to remember Jesus' prediction to be raised (18:33). They do remember the experience and testimony of the women, and report that some of the men then went to see the tomb, finding it as empty as the women said. But nothing seems to have twigged their memory of how Jesus predicted all this, and thus they are unprepared to recognize Jesus even though he stands next to them.

Odysseus, in his beggar's costume, meets his wife Penelope and tells her that he entertained her husband in Crete. She asks him to describe Odysseus; he does, down to the clothes he was wearing, and she weeps as she admits that she prepared those very robes for her departed beloved. Now Odysseus tells her to dry her tears, and assures her that he knows that her husband is not dead, but waiting to learn "how he should approach his own island of Ithaca after so long an absence, whether to return openly or in disguise. So you see that he is safe and will soon be back. Indeed, he is very close. His exile from his friends and his country will be ended very soon."[12]

Jesus is less tender with his two disciples: "O fools and slow in heart to believe everything the prophets said!" "Slow in heart" might mean either "slow-witted" or "reluctant," since the ancients considered the heart the spot where one thought and made decisions.[13] Jesus' reference to "what the prophets said" is expanded in v. 27 to "Moses and all the prophets" and in v. 44 to "everything written about me in the Law of Moses, the prophets, and the psalms." Clearly in v. 27 and in vv. 46-47, Jesus is interpreting Scripture, and so the primary reference for "prophets" in v. 25 is probably the Bible in its entirety. But we should probably also include Jesus' own predictions of his death, since the two disciples admit that he was a prophet; and I wonder if Luke would include the male disciples' slowness to believe the words of the women, who brought them the word of God's having raised Jesus?

Luke believed that according to Scripture, "it was necessary for the Messiah to suffer and [then] to enter his glory" by being raised from the dead and given a seat at God's right. The Servant Songs from Isaiah as well as some of the psalms of lament speak of how a just man, rejected by others and numbered with the lawless, is handed over to death but then rewarded by God (Isa 53:12 LXX; Ps 30:5 LXX [Eng 31:4]—note that the next verse is "into your hands I commit my spirit"). "It was necessary," then, because God's plan, revealed in Scripture, had to be fulfilled. So Jesus had to be "handed over" from Judas to the chief priests to Pilate to death; because it was all pre-scripted, Jesus could with confidence predict it (9:22; 18:31-33). But the disciples failed to understand it when he predicted it (18:34), for the same reason they are clueless in this scene: "this matter was hidden from them and they did not understand what was being said."

OK—why would God prevent the disciples from understanding Jesus' predictions of his death, if that would have helped them deal with the shock of his death? And why call them foolish and dull-witted/reluctant for failing to understand what God had hidden from them? This is another example of the kind of paradox that Jesus' Passion Narrative presented for Luke. Take Judas, for instance; one of Jesus' own disciples handed him over—that was in the tradition Luke inherited and had to explain. If it happened that way, it must have been part of God's plan, yet the one who betrayed Jesus cannot be held guiltless (22:22). Luke's received tradition also made it clear that despite Jesus' predictions of the cross, his death stunned his closest followers; Luke's source Mark has the disciples flee in 14:50 and the women run from the tomb, saying nothing to anyone (Mark 16:8). This, too, must be part of God's plan, in Luke's way of thinking—"God must have prevented their comprehension" would make sense to Luke's audience. But just as Judas should be blamed for his crime, even though it was "necessary" and even though he was under Satan's control, so the disciples really should have remembered Jesus' predictions and the words of the prophets. Looking backwards, Luke can reason that all went according to God's plan, but he cannot completely excuse Judas's treachery or the disciples' failures to comprehend; they were all called to a much higher standard, to bearing their cross and following Jesus.

It is worth noting that although Luke's Gospel spends almost no time amplifying which Scriptures Jesus had in mind, "beginning from Moses and all the prophets" probably indicates that in the congregations Luke frequented, Christians read the whole Old Testament christologically. We see some particular examples of how this is done in the speeches of Acts. "David spoke of the resurrection of the Messiah" in Psalms 16 and 110 (Acts 2:31, 34); Moses predicted Jesus in Deuteronomy 18 (Acts 3:22); etc. Luke's audience, very familiar with this style of scriptural interpretation, could well imagine what passages Jesus interpreted to his two disciples on the road.

In v. 28, Jesus continues acting; as they drew near Emmaus, he "pretended[14] that he was going farther." The two disciples may have forgotten Jesus' teachings, but they remember their manners and invite him to stay with them, and he accepts their offer—keeping alive the pattern that Jesus never turns down an invitation to dinner! Even though he is the guest, he acts as host, and Luke repeats language from the Last Supper. "When he had reclined with them, taking a loaf, he blessed it, and breaking it, he gave it to them." At this moment, "their eyes were opened and they recognized him"; "were opened" means that God did it, just as God "held their eyes back" at the beginning of the pericope. And then he was gone, vanished.

They did not know him when they saw him; they were being prevented, most plausibly because they were not ready to believe. They did not know him as he was interpreting the Scriptures for them, but upon reflection, they felt something powerful: "Didn't our heart [sic] burn while he spoke to us on the road?" [Hearts Burning within Us] Luke writes "our heart," singular, rather than "our hearts," which would be more expected; his point is that the two were experiencing the same thing. The heart that was slow to believe nevertheless was inspired and lit by understanding. But the real moment of recognition and reversal was the moment when Jesus broke the bread. Not only is this the fitting recognition moment for this Gospel, since Jesus spent so much time at table and used the great banquet as a primary metaphor for God's kingdom, but it foreshadows the life of the church that Luke will narrate in the next volume, where the company of Jesus' followers broke bread daily and held all things in common. Aristotle would approve: their recognition of Jesus came from the events themselves, from his repetition of a familiar act in a plausible setting, and the moment of recognition was also a reversal of their state of mind. They go from deep grief to joy, from confusion to understanding, and most importantly from disbelief to faith, and the crucial moment is the breaking of the bread. What a brilliant pastoral theologian! Had Luke put the moment of recognition on the road, when they saw Jesus, or at some point in his exposition of the Scripture, then subsequent believers could only wish they could have been present.

Hearts Burning within Us

The image of a burning heart is not always a positive thing. Note the following passage in Philo, where he describes God's voice emerging from a flame of fire:

It is therefore with great beauty, and also with a proper sense of what is consistent with the dignity of God, that the voice is said to have come forth out of the fire . . . . Since the property of fire is partly to give light and partly to burn, those who think fit to show themselves obedient to the sacred commands shall live for ever and ever as in a light which is never darkened . . . , But all those who are stubborn and disobedient are forever inflamed, and burnt, and consumed by all their internal appetites, which, like flame, will destroy all the life of those who possess them. (*The Decalogue* 48–49)

Luke's usage may have been influenced by Ps 38:4 LXX: "My heart is heated within me, and in my meditation a fire burns."

Supper At Emmaus

This contemporary painting captures the moment of recognition, and invites us, the viewers, to sit at table with Jesus.

He Qi. *Supper at Emmaeus.* 2000. www.heqigallery.com

Like those who went to look at the empty tomb after hearing the testimony of the women, we might have been able only to testify to what we had not seen. But "he had been made known to them in the breaking of the bread"; all of us who repeat the meal as he commanded can have this experience.

The two disciples hurry back to Jerusalem and find the whole crowd gathered together, talking about how Jesus had appeared to Simon Peter. Luke chooses not to narrate this appearance, if in fact he knew any of the details of how Peter first saw the Lord. Luke instead lifts up the experiences of the women and these two disciples, emphasizing the memory of Jesus' teachings, the feeling of inspiration when the Scriptures are interpreted as referring to Christ, and the recognition of Jesus that believers have when they share meals together, especially the Eucharist. The presence of the risen Lord, mediated through memory, teaching, and ritual, belongs to the whole community of faith.

Second (Third?) Appearance: In Jerusalem, 24:36-53

Easter Sunday was a busy day, according to Luke: the women discover the tomb empty, and see two angels who tell them that Jesus has been raised. They report this to the disciples; Peter goes to check it out for himself, but none but the women believe. Later that day, two disciples are walking home when Jesus appears to them. They do not know him by his appearance or by his teaching, but when he breaks the bread with them at suppertime, they recognize him. Off they go, back to Jerusalem, where they discover that Jesus has also appeared to Peter, convincing the larger group that

Jesus was alive indeed. The two then tell about their own encounter with the risen Lord, and while they are still speaking, Jesus appears. After presenting them with evidence that he had been physically raised, he commissions them and then ascends into heaven.

The two earlier stories in this chapter, the empty tomb and the road to Emmaus, both deal with how the believers should have been expecting Jesus' crucifixion and resurrection, since he had predicted it (24:6-7) and since the Old Testament confirms that such was God's plan (24:25-27). In the first story, Jesus isn't present; angels remind the women of what he had said in Galilee. In the second, Jesus isn't recognized at first, and then, as soon as he is, he vanishes. Neither story spends much time, then, on any proof that he was truly alive or on the nature of his resurrected body. The second story, in fact, would sound to Luke's audience more like an encounter with a ghost, the shade of the departed Jesus, and Luke needed to clarify this impression for at least two reasons.

First, not all early Christians believed in an actual bodily resurrection of Jesus. Some, for whatever reason, did not believe that the dead were raised bodily (1 Cor 15:12-19); these may have believed that Jesus truly died and was now alive, but only as a spirit or Spirit. Others who adopted a docetic Christology (see [Marcion and Docetics]) believed that as the Son of God, Jesus only had the appearance of human flesh and thus only appeared to die on the cross. Crucifixion was a most dishonorable way to die; it was regarded as a punishment for rebellious slaves or as a counter-terrorist measure. Perhaps not surprisingly, then, some early Christians preferred to believe that Jesus was not truly crucified. For Luke, Jesus' actual death is a theological necessity as well as a well-established part of the story. His strategy for making the crucifixion meaningful was to argue that it was a "must" within God's plan and that it was a noble act by Jesus. By stressing the physical nature of the risen Lord, Luke tries to block docetic interpretations of the resurrection. [Ignatius against Docetic Christians]

Second, Luke's audience would have known other ghost stories—stories of famous people who died and whose shades were seen by others, or whose spirits spoke through prophets. The process of the divinization of the emperors, where someone testified that he saw the spirit of the emperor rising to heaven, followed by a vote of the Senate proclaiming that the departed ruler was now divine, was also known to Luke's audience. Luke takes pains in this episode to rule out a "ghost story" interpretation of Jesus' resurrection—nope, he was really dead and then really came back to life. [Justin Martyr on Resurrected Spirits]

Ignatius against Docetic Christians

Ignatius, bishop of Antioch, wrote about Christians who believed that Jesus only seemed to be human, calling them unbelievers and warning the faithful to have nothing to do with them. In his letter to the Smyrneans, he refers to this passage from Luke:

In the time of Pontius Pilate and the tetrarch Herod, he was truly nailed for us in the flesh—we ourselves come from the fruit of his divinely blessed suffering—so that through his resurrection he might eternally lift up the standard for his holy and faithful ones, whether among Jews or Gentiles, in the one body of his church.

For he suffered all these things for our sake, that we might be saved; and he truly suffered, just as he also truly raised himself—not as some unbelievers say, that he suffered only in appearance. They are the ones who are only an appearance; and it will happen to them just as they think, since they are without bodies, like the daimons.

For I know and believe that he was in the flesh even after the resurrection. And when he came to those who were with Peter, he said to them, "Reach out, touch me and see that I am not a bodiless daimon." And immediately they touched him and believed, having been intermixed with his flesh and spirit. For this reason they also despised death, for they were found to be beyond death. And after his resurrection he ate and drank with them as a fleshly being, even though he was spiritually united with the Father

Ignatius, *Smyr* 1.2-3.3.

Justin Martyr on Resurrected Spirits

Justin's *Apology*, written in the mid-2d century, is an argument for a more tolerant Roman policy toward Christians. In one part he is arguing that a belief in the resurrection of Jesus is not ridiculous, since Greeks and Romans have plenty of stories and institutions that testify to a belief in life after death:

For the oracles of the dead and the revelations of innocent children, the invoking of departed human souls, the dream senders and guardians of the magi, and what is done by those who know about such things—all this should convince you that souls are still conscious after death. Then there are the men who are seized and torn by the spirits of the dead, whom everyone calls demon-possessed and maniacs, and the oracles so well-known among you, of Amphilocus and Dodona and Pytho, and any others of that kind and the teaching of writers, Empedocles and Pythagoras, Plato and Socrates, and the ditch in Homer and the descent of Odysseus to visit the dead, and other stories like this. Treat us at least like these; we believe in God not less than they do, but rather more, since we look forward to receiving again our own bodies though they be dead and buried in the earth, declaring that nothing is impossible to God.

Justin, *1 Apol.* 18, in Cyril C. Richardson, ed., *Early Christian Fathers* (New York: MacMillan, 1970), 253–54.

But beyond the apologetic or doctrinal features of this story, it also serves to reconnect the reader to some of the earliest scenes of the Gospel. Luke uses language that reminds the reader of how the story began and of Jesus' teaching and ministry, drawing his narrative to an artistic close.

Resetting the scene, the two who saw him at Emmaus have rushed back to Jerusalem to find that Peter has already seen him. We want to know when and where—Luke either does not know or chooses not to narrate this story, with the result that Jesus' appearance to the Eleven is also his appearance to all his disciples. He shows up while they are talking—meaning either while the two are telling their story or during a general conversation among the approximately 120 people Luke says were gathered in Jerusalem (Acts 1:15). "He stood in their midst," meaning that nobody saw him enter; in that way the angels appeared to the women at the tomb (24:4, "behold, two men in shining clothes stood next to them") and Gabriel appeared to Zechariah (1:11, "and the angel of the Lord appeared to him, standing by the right of the incense altar"). Jesus' greeting, "Peace to you [it is a plural "you"]," is at once a typical greeting for speakers of Hebrew or Aramaic, a reminder of his command to his disciples that they greet everyone in peace (10:5-6), and a connection to the expectation that Jesus' advent will mean peace for those whom God favors (1:79; 2:14). In fact, Jesus has brought peace to some (2:29; 7:50; 8:48; 19:38), but those who would not recognize him have lost a chance for peace (19:42).[15]

These disciples, in fact, do not yet know peace; they are "terrified and fearful" (*ptoēthentes de kai emphoboi*). The women seeing the angels "became fearful" (*emphobōn de genomenōn autōn*) and Zechariah, seeing the angel, was "terrified" (*etarachthē*) and "fear fell upon him" (*phobos epepesen ep' auton*). Fear is not an unusual reaction to the sudden appearance of the divine, but the explanation "they thought they saw a ghost" means that despite the experiences of the community so far and their confident assertion "the Lord has been truly raised" (24:34), they still do not believe. That is, Luke wants to label "they thought they were seeing a *pneuma*" (a spirit or a ghost), as confusion caused by fear rather than as an acceptable Christian belief. Jesus' words to them, "Why are you terrified," use a form of the verb describing Zechariah's reaction to Gabriel—less than ideal, that is—and "why are reasonings arising in your hearts?" hearkens back to Simeon's prediction that Jesus would expose such "reasonings" as he divided belief from unbelief, rising from falling (2:34-35).[16] Their "reasonings"—*dialogismos* can mean "opinion" or "argument," and is often translated "doubts" in this context—are their incorrect conclusions that they were seeing a ghost. Mostly Jesus has been exposing the inner debates and errant suppositions of those opposed to him, but here he uncovers the roots of an argument between believers in Luke's day.

Jesus' first offer of proof is that they can see from his hands and feet that he is himself. If Luke was thinking of the wounds or scars from the crucifixion, he does not say so; but it is hard to imagine his audience not making that leap.[17] He next invites them to touch him: no *pneuma* has the solidity of flesh and bone. If v. 40 is original to Luke,[18] Jesus next shows them his hands and feet. After three tries, the disciples are still confused. We are not told whether any of them actually touched him, and some early Christians assumed that they had (see [Ignatius against Docetic Christians] above). But I rather imagine that Luke wants us to think of the 120 disciples crowded around Jesus, wide-eyed, mouths agog, in a deer-in-the-headlights sort of pose: "and while they were still disbelieving from joy and amazed" (24:41). Jesus then turns to another sort of evidence: he eats a piece of broiled fish in front of them, since everyone knew that spirits like angels never ate (Tob 12:19, where the angel Raphael tells Tobit and Tobias that he only appeared to eat).

Still no response from the disciples, and in my opinion, this is not accidental. The women at the tomb are not convinced by seeing nothing, but believe when they are reminded to remember Jesus' words. The two disciples on the road have their hearts strangely warmed as they listen to Jesus, but only recognize him in the breaking of the bread. The larger company of disciples sees Jesus, has the chance to touch him, and watches him pull up his sleeves ("Look, arms! Real hair! Scars!"), chew, and swallow. But the coin doesn't drop for them until he "opens their minds," reminding them of his teaching and interpreting the Scriptures for them. "Disbelieving from joy" may let them off the hook a little—happy, but confused?—but disbelief for any reason is not acceptable, and must be addressed. So Jesus reminds them, chides them, and gives them supernatural help.

Before turning to the commissioning scene, we should review. The disciples were afraid because they thought they saw a *pneuma*. Jesus did show and tell. Did they now believe that he was alive as a physical being, not just as a shade? We presume Luke thinks so, because in the apostolic preaching, Peter and the rest insist that while King David's body lies a-moldering in the grave, Jesus' body saw no corruption but was raised (Acts 2:25-32). We presume that's also what Luke believes and what he considers to be the correct belief for his audience—Jesus was raised bodily, which probably also means that's how he imagined the general resurrection.

The first part of Jesus' commission to the disciples repeats the testimony of the two angels (24:6-7) and what he told the two disciples on the road (24:25-27): the crucifixion was necessary, was predicted by Jesus, and is a fulfillment of God's plan revealed in Scripture (see commentary on 24:13-35). "The law of Moses and the prophets and the psalms" is meant to cover the whole Bible, at least as it was known to Luke or to his audience.[19] This way of reading the Bible, according to Luke, was part of Jesus' instructions to his followers as well as the result of Jesus' "opening their minds to comprehend the Scriptures." Luke admits, then, that the way Jesus and his followers understand the Bible, interpreting it all in light of Jesus' experience, is more the result of following Jesus than the precondition for it; not everyone will be convinced that this is the correct way to read Moses, the prophets, and the psalms.

The second part of Jesus' instructions focuses on what the disciples are to tell the world. In this version of their commission, Jesus keeps everything in a "divine must" format: the Christ had to suffer and be raised from the dead on the third day; repentance for the forgiveness of sins had to be preached in his name to all the nations, beginning from Jerusalem. That, as many others have pointed out, is a good summary of the apostolic preaching in Acts, and not a bad summary of the core of the gospel in Paul's letters.[20] "You are witnesses of these things," according to v. 48: they have been with Jesus since Galilee, and have witnessed everything from his baptism through his death and resurrection (Acts 1:21-22). Now it is time for them to do more than simply watch from a distance, as Peter did in the courtyard and all did while he died. They have a role to play in the divine "must"; Christ has fulfilled his part, and now they must preach his message of repentance and forgiveness. But not quite yet—they must wait in Jerusalem until they are "clothed with power from on high," with the descent of the Spirit at Pentecost.

Without yet signaling how the disciples respond to all this, Luke moves straight to the final moment of the Gospel—a scene that overlaps with the one in the first chapter of Luke's second volume, Acts. Jesus leads the group out of Jerusalem, toward Bethany—still Easter Sunday night, so far as we know. Bethany is close to Jerusalem (19:29), and what Luke may have in mind is that the group went far enough that they were by themselves, so that none but the disciples witnessed the ascension. Jesus blesses them, just as the angel Raphael blessed Tobit and Tobias before he ascended (Tob 12:6-22), or as Moses blessed Israel before he died (Deut 33:1-29). "Raising his hands, he blessed them," and that is his posture as he moves away from them and ascends—it is the last image we see of Jesus in Luke. Now Luke draws our attention to the disciples: they are worshiping him. When they are done, they return to Jerusalem as ordered "with great joy and were constantly in the temple blessing God." This looks back to when Mary and Joseph brought their infant son to the temple and were blessed by Simeon and Anna (who also never left the temple); it also looks forward to Acts 1–6, when the early community was constantly in the temple as witnesses to precisely those things Jesus listed.

CONNECTIONS

Jesus is alive, we say; on what basis do we make that claim? Well, there is the testimony of those who saw him raised or who saw his empty tomb. But Luke's narrative shows that such testimony can be discounted, even by members of Jesus' own movement. There are the Scriptures that testify to his resurrection, but Luke's story includes Jesus explaining the Scriptures to disciples who remain skeptical. Some are gifted by visions of the Lord; Luke's narrative shows us how some could walk and talk with Jesus and not know him, or watch him suddenly appear in a room and disbelieve. The two kinds of convincing evidence offered by this chapter are the memories of Jesus' teachings, especially as interpreted by someone else who truly believes, and the experience of Jesus in meals shared with fellow believers, especially the Communion meal. The women were confused until the two heavenly witnesses reminded them of what Jesus had said. The two on the way to Emmaus were confused until Jesus blessed and broke the bread. The apostles and disciples were confused even after Jesus ate in front of them until he "opened their minds to understand the scriptures."

Thus does Luke instruct us that our experience of the resurrection, two millennia after the event, is not second-rate or defective. When we experience the risen Christ in Communion, he is truly present. And the experience of a Lukan Jesus present with us at Communion would be a good thing for the church. This is the man who accepted two dinner invitations from tax collectors and three from Pharisees, who broke bread with his betrayer and with his quarrelsome disciples. He refused to be bullied into rejecting the hospitality of Levi, Zacchaeus, or the woman who anointed his feet; he instructed his disciples, likewise, to accept whatever was put before them from whoever would receive them peaceably. If we conducted our Communions the way Luke's Jesus conducted his meals, then they'd be full of surprising guests and uncomfortable revelations about our values and conduct, and there would almost certainly be some moments to make the respectable folks cringe. Are we brave enough to welcome that Jesus to our meals, or better yet, to sit at the table that Jesus hosts?

Luke's resurrection narrative also shows us how memory and reflection, guided by wise interpreters, are part of how we come to know the risen Lord. The angels remind the women; Jesus opens the minds of the disciples; and in Acts, the Spirit fills the believers, giving them boldness and insight. But there is also the actual work of learning, thinking, meditating: chapter 24 pictures the disciples sharing their experiences with each other and talking things over, and Acts continues the theme of the whole church gathering regularly to eat, to worship, and to be instructed. Our experience of the risen Jesus is thus not only a moment in worship but a process of formation under the guidance of the Spirit and in the teachings of Jesus.

Luke ends with a teaser—"stay in Jerusalem until you have been clothed with power from on high"—and thus points us firmly to Acts. Wise students of Luke will continue the story in its second installment.

NOTES

[1] Luke Timothy Johnson, *The Gospel of Luke* (SP, vol. 3; Collegeville MN: Liturgical Press, 1991), 387; Frederick W. Danker, Jesus and the New Age: A Commentary on St. Luke's Gospel (rev. ed.; Philadelphia: Fortress, 1988), 388. Note the parallel with Acts 1:11, where the apostles are rebuked for standing around looking up into the air after Jesus ascends.

[2] Joseph A. Fitzmyer, The Gospel According to Luke (AB 28 and 28A; Garden City NY: Doubleday, 1981), 2.1545; Alan R. Culpepper, The Gospel of Luke (NIB, vol. 9; Nashville: Abingdon, 1995), 468.

[3] Culpepper, *Luke*, 479–81; Charles H. Talbert, *Reading Luke: A Literary and Theological Commentary on the Third Gospel* (rev. ed.; Macon GA: Smyth and Helwys, 2002), 259; Johnson, *Luke*, 398.

[4] *Odyssey*, 19.479-81.

[5] Ibid., 16.186–89.

[6] Aristotle, *Poetics* 11.20-30.

[7] Ibid., 17.15-20.

[8] *Odyssey*, 16.160-61. Note also the bath scene described above, where Athene prevents Penelope from paying attention to her nurse's discovery of Odysseus's true identity.

[9] Culpepper, *Luke*, 477. The NRSV has the first, the NIV the second; both make it a rhetorical question. The New Jerusalem has "You must be the only person staying in Jerusalem who does not know . . . ."

[10] Culpepper, *Luke*, 477.

[11] Aristotle, *Poetics* 24.15-25: "It is above all Homer who taught other poets the right way to purvey falsehoods: that is, by false inference. When the existence or occurrence of *b* follows from *a*, people suppose that if *b* is the case, *a* too must exist or be occurrent; but this is false. So, if the antecedent is false, but were it true some further fact would necessarily exist or occur, the poet should supply the latter: because it knows the truth of the consequent, our mind falsely infers the truth of the antecedent too. One example of this comes from the Bath Scene"—namely, the scene from the *Odyssey* where the nurse identifies Odysseus but Penelope does not. Penelope has been convinced by Odysseus's deceptive speech that he truly is a beggar, but that he has seen her husband alive and well.

[12] *Odyssey*, 19.296-302.

[13] Fitzmyer, *Luke*, 2.1595, opts for "slow of wit"; Johnson, *Luke*, 395, opts for "reluctant."

[14] BAGD, 884, s.v. προποιέω.

[15] Johnson, *Luke*, 400–401; Culpepper, *Luke*, 485.

[16] Johnson, *Luke*, 401; Green, *Luke*, 854.

[17] Fitzmyer, *Luke*, 2.1576, argues that Luke presupposes the nails; Johnson, *Luke*, 401, and Culpepper, *Luke*, 485, note that since Luke does not mention nails or nailing, one can read this to mean that the disciples should recognize that the parts of Jesus' body visible to them were made of real flesh.

[18] The majority of manuscripts have it. A few omit it, and so the argument is whether it was omitted because it seems superfluous, or added either to strengthen the case against docetic interpretations or to make Luke's story more like John 20:19-23. In my opinion, the verse is most likely original, due to the age and widespread geographical spread of the manuscripts that contain it. But see Bruce Metzger, *A Textual Commentary on the Greek New Testament* (New York: United Bible Societies, 1971), 187.

[19] We cannot be confident of the extent of Luke's "Old Testament canon," to use an anachronistic phrase. "The Law of Moses" is clearly the Pentateuch, but would Luke think that "prophets" covered Samuel-Kings as well as Isaiah, Jeremiah, Ezekiel, and the Twelve? Would Luke include everything else under "psalms"? We simply cannot say, because there are parts of our canon Luke never quotes or alludes to.

[20] Most famously, C. H. Dodd, *The Apostolic Preaching and Its Developments* (Ann Arbor MI: Baker, 1980); Culpepper, *Luke*, 486–87.

BIBLIOGRAPHY

À Kempis, Thomas. *The Imitation of Christ*. Translated by Betty I. Knott. London: Collins, 1963.

Ahlstrom, Sydney E. *A Religious History of the American People*. 2 volumes. New York: Doubleday, 1975.

Alexander, Loveday. *Acts in Its Ancient Literary Context*. London: T & T Clark, 2007.

———. *The Preface to Luke's Gospel: Literary Convention and Social Context In Luke 1.1-4 and Acts 1.1*. Cambridge: Cambridge University Press, 1993.

Allison, Jr., Dale C. "The Eye Is the Lamp of the Body (Matthew 6.22-23=Luke 11.34-36)," *NTS* 33 (1987): 61–83.

———. *Jesus of Nazareth: A Millenarian Prophet*. Minneapolis: Fortress, 1998.

Arlandson, James Malcolm. *Women, Class, and Society in Early Christianity: Models from Luke-Acts*. Peabody MA: Hendrickson, 1997.

Arnal, William E. *Jesus and the Village Scribes*. Minneapolis: Fortress, 2001.

Atkinson, Gordon. *RealLivePreacher.com*. Grand Rapids: Eerdmans, 2004.

Bagnall, Roger S., and Peter Derow. *Greek Historical Documents: The Hellenistic Period*. Chico CA: Scholars Press, 1981.

Bailey, Kenneth E. *Finding the Lost: Cultural Keys to Luke 15*. St. Louis MO: Concordia, 1992.

———. *Poet and Peasant and Through Peasant Eyes*. Grand Rapids MI: Eerdmans, 1980.

Balch, David, and Carolyn Osiek, editors. *Early Christian Families in Context: An Interdisciplinary Dialogue*. Grand Rapids MI: Eerdmans, 2003.

Barrett, C. K., editor. *The New Testament Background: Writings from Ancient Greece and the Roman Empire*. Revised edition. New York: Harper and Row, 1987.

Beard, Mary, et al., editors. *Religions of Rome*. 2 volumes. Cambridge: Cambridge University Press, 1998.

Beavis, Mary Ann, editor. *The Lost Coin: Parables of Women, Work and Wisdom*. Sheffield, UK: Sheffield Academic, 2002.

Berry, Wendell. "Manifesto: The Mad Farmer Liberation Front." In *The Selected Poems of Wendell Berry*. Washington, D.C.: Counterpoint, 1998.

Bettenson, Henry D. *Documents of the Christian Church*. 2d edition. New York: Oxford, 1977.

Betz, Hans Dieter, editor. *The Greek Magical Papyri in Translation*. Chicago: University of Chicago, 1986.

———. *The Sermon on the Mount*. Minneapolis: Fortress, 1995.

Birnbaum, Philip, editor. *The Daily Prayer Book*. New York: Hebrew Publishing, 1949.

Bishop, Marilyn E., editor. *Religion and Disability*. Kansas City: Sheed and Ward, 1995.

Block, Jennie Weiss. *Copious Hosting: A Theology of Access for People with Disabilities*. New York: Continuum, 2002.

Bock, Darrell. *Luke.* Grand Rapids MI: Baker, 1994.

Bonhoeffer, Dietrich. *Life Together.* Translated by John W. Doberstein. New York: Harper, 1954.

Boring, M. Eugene, et al., editors. *Hellenistic Commentary to the New Testament.* Nashville: Abingdon, 1995.

————, and Fred Craddock. *The People's New Testament Commentary.* Louisville: Westminster/John Knox, 2004.

Bovon, François. *Luke The Theologian.* 2d revised edition. Waco TX: Baylor University Press, 2006.

————. *Luke 1: A Commentary on the Gospel of Luke 1:1–9:50.* Hermeneia. Ed. Helmut Koester. Minneapolis: Fortress, 2002.

————. *Studies in Early Christianity.* Grand Rapids MI: Baker, 2003.

Brown, Raymond E. *The Birth of the Messiah: A Commentary on the Infancy Narratives in the Gospels of Matthew and Luke.* Garden City NY: Doubleday, 1993.

————. *The Death of the Messiah: From Gethsemane to the Grave.* 2 volumes. Garden City NY: Doubleday, 1994.

————. *Gospel According to John.* New York: Doubleday, 1970.

Brueggemann, Walter. *Awed to Heaven, Rooted in Earth: Prayers of Walter Brueggemann.* Minneapolis: Fortress, 2003.

Bryson, Bill. *A Walk in the Woods.* New York: Broadway, 1998.

Buck, Pearl S. *The Good Earth.* New York: John Day, 1931.

Buechner, Frederick. *Peculiar Treasures: A Biblical Who's Who.* New York: Harper and Row, 1979.

————. *Wishful Thinking: A Theological ABC.* New York: Harper and Row, 1973.

Campbell, Cathy C. *Stations of the Banquet.* Collegeville MN: Liturgical, 2003.

Cannon, Carl M. "Untruth and Consequences." *The Atlantic* 299/1 (January/February 2007): 56–67.

Chabon, Michael. *The Yiddish Policemen's Union.* New York: HarperCollins, 2007.

Charlesworth, James H. "Forgiveness (Early Judaism)." *ADB* 2.833-35.

————, editor. *Jesus and Archaeology.* Grand Rapids MI: Eerdmans, 2006.

————. "Jesus Research and Archaeology: A New Perspective." In James H. Charlesworth, editor, *Jesus and Archaeology.* Grand Rapids: Eerdmans, 2006.

————, editor. *The Old Testament Pseudepigrapha.* 2 volumes. Garden City NY: Doubleday, 1983.

Christ, Karl. *The Romans.* Berkeley: University of California Press, 1984.

Coady, Mary Frances. "Shunned." *Commonweal* 131 (30 January 2004): 31.

Codrescu, Andrei. *The Devil Never Sleeps and Other Essays.* New York: St. Martins, 2000.

Cohen, Shaye J. D. "The Temple and the Synagogue." In William Horbury et al., editors, *The Cambridge History of Judaism.* Volume 3. Cambridge: Cambridge University Press, 1999.

Coleridge, Mark. *The Birth of the Lukan Narrative: Narrative as Christology in Luke 1–2.* Sheffield, UK: Sheffield Academic Press, 1993.

Conroy, Pat. *The Prince of Tides*. Boston: Houghton Mifflin, 1986.

Corbo, Virgilo C. "Golgotha." *ABD* 2.1071-73.

Corley, Kathleen E. *Private Women, Public Meals: Social Conflict in the Synoptic Tradition*. Peabody MA: Hendrickson, 1993.

Craddock, Fred B. *Craddock Stories*. Edited by Mike Graves and Richard F. Ward. St. Louis: Chalice, 2001.

————. *Luke*. Interpretation. Louisville: Westminster/John Knox, 1990.

Crossan, John Dominic, and Jonathan L. Reed. *Excavating Jesus*. San Francisco: HarperSanFrancisco, 2001.

Crossan, John Dominic. *The Historical Jesus*. San Francisco: HarperSanFrancisco, 1991.

Culpepper, R. Alan. *The Gospel of Luke*. The New Interpreter's Bible. Volume 9. Nashville: Abingdon, 1995.

Cunningham, Michael. *The Hours*. New York: Farrar, Straus, and Giroux, 1998.

Curzon, David. *The Gospels in Our Image: An Anthology of Twentieth-Century Poetry Based on Biblical Texts*. New York: Harcourt Brace, 1995.

Dana, H. E., and Julius R. Mantey. *A Manual Grammar of the Greek New Testament*. New York: MacMillan, 1955.

D'Angelo, Mary Rose. "(Re)Presentations of Women in the Gospel of Matthew and Luke-Acts." In Ross Shepard Kraemer and Mary Rose D'Angelo, editors, *Women and Christian Origins*. New York: Oxford University Press, 1999.

Danker, Frederick W. *Jesus and the New Age: A Commentary on St. Luke's Gospel*. Revised edition. Philadelphia: Fortress, 1988.

Dickinson, Emily. *The Complete Poems of Emily Dickinson*. Edited by Thomas H. Johnson. Boston: Little, Brown, 1960.

Dillard, Annie. *Pilgrim at Tinker Creek*. New York: Harper and Row, 1974.

Dodd, C. H. *The Apostolic Preaching and Its Developments*. Ann Arbor MI: Baker, 1980.

Duncan, David James. *The Brothers K*. New York: Bantam, 1993.

Dunn, James D. G. *Jesus Remembered*. Grand Rapids MI: Eerdmans, 2003.

Edelman, Marian Wright. *Guide My Feet: Prayers and Meditations for Our Children*. New York: HarperCollins, 2000.

Ehrman, Bart D. *Misquoting Jesus: The Story Behind Who Changed the Bible and Why*. New York: HarperSanFrancisco, 2005.

Eiesland, Nancy L. *The Disabled God: Toward a Liberatory Theology of Disability*. Nashville: Abingdon, 1994.

Elliott, J. K., editor. *The Apocryphal Jesus*. New York: Oxford University Press, 1996.

Ellis, E. E. *The Gospel of Luke*. London: Oliphants, 1974.

Enger, Leif. *Peace Like a River*. New York: Grove, 2001.

Epp, E. J., and Gordon D. Fee. *New Testament Textual Criticism*. Oxford: Clarendon, 1981.

Evans, Craig A. "Excavating Caiaphas, Pilate, and Simon of Cyrene." In James H. Charlesworth, editor, *Jesus and Archaeology*. Grand Rapids MI: Eerdmans, 2006.

Farris, Stephen. *The Hymns of Luke's Infancy Narratives: Their Origin, Meaning and Significance.* Sheffield, UK: Sheffield, 1985.

Fee, Gordon. "One Thing is Needful?" In E. J. Epp and Gordon D. Fee, *New Testament Textual Criticism.* Oxford: Clarendon, 1981.

Finegan, Jack. *Encountering New Testament Manuscripts.* Grand Rapids: Eerdmans, 1974.

Fitzmyer, Joseph A. *The Gospel According to Luke.* Anchor Bible, volumes 28 and 28A. Garden City NY: Doubleday, 1981.

———. "The Virginal Conception of Jesus in the New Testament." *Theological Studies* 34 (1973): 541–75.

Forster, E. M. *Howards End.* New York: Penguin, 1980.

Frazier, Charles. *Cold Mountain.* New York: Atlantic Monthly, 1997.

Frost, Robert. *The Poetry of Robert Frost: The collected poems, complete and unabridged.* Edited by Lathem, Edward Connery. New York: Henry Holt, 1979.

Funk, Robert W., et al., editors. *The Acts of Jesus.* San Francisco: HarperSanFrancisco, 1998.

———. *The Five Gospels.* New York: MacMillan, 1993.

Gamble, Harry. *Books and Readers in the Early Church: A History of Early Christian Texts.* New Haven: Yale University Press, 1995.

Gordon, Mary. *Pearl.* New York: Anchor, 2006.

Gowler, David B. *Host, Guest, Enemy, and Friend: Portraits of the Pharisees in Luke and Acts.* New York: Peter Lang, 1991.

Glancy, Jennifer A. *Slavery in Early Christianity.* New York: Oxford, 2002.

Green, Joel B. *The Gospel of Luke.* The New International Commentary on the New Testament. Grand Rapids: Eerdmans, 1997.

———. "Jesus on the Mount of Olives (Luke 22.39-46): Tradition and Theology," *Journal for the Study of the New Testament* 26 (1986): 29–48.

Grisham, John. *The Last Juror.* New York: Bantam, 2004.

Guterman, Lila. "Study of Prayer's Healing Power on Surgery Patients Finds No Effect." *Chronicle of Higher Education* 52 (14 April 2006): A 17.

Hachlili, Rachel. "Burials, Ancient Jewish." *ABD* 1.789-94

Harrill, J. Albert. "The Domestic Enemy: A Moral Polarity of Household Slaves in Early Christian Apologies and Martyrdoms." In David Balch and Carolyn Osiek, *Early Christian Families in Context: An Interdisciplinary Dialogue.* Grand Rapids MI: Eerdmans, 2003.

———. *Slaves in the New Testament: Literary, Social, and Moral Dimensions.* Minneapolis: Fortress, 2006.

Harris, Joanne. *Chocolat.* New York: Viking, 1999.

Hauerwas, Stanley. *Unleashing the Scripture: Freeing the Bible from Captivity to America.* Nashville: Abingdon, 1993.

Hearon, Holly, and Antoinette Clark Wire. "Women's Work in the Realm of God (Mt. 13.33; Lk. 13.20,21; Gos. Thom. 96; Mt. 6:28-30; Lk. 12.27-28; Gos. Thom. 36)." In Mary Ann Beavis, editor, *The Lost Coin: Paables of Women, Work and Wisdom.* Sheffield, UK: Sheffield, 2002.

Heinemann, Joseph, editor, and Jakob J. Petuchowski. *Literature of the Synagogue.* New York: Behrman House, 1975.

Heinemann, Joseph. *Prayer in the Talmud: Forms and Patterns.* New York: de Gruyter, 1977.

Helprin, Mark. *Winter's Tale.* Orlando: Harcourt, 1985.

Hengel, Martin. *Crucifixion.* Philadelphia: Fortress, 1977.

Herzog II, William R. *Prophet and Teacher: an introduction to the historical Jesus.* Louisville KY: Westminster/John Knox, 2005.

Hornik, Heidi J., and Mikeal C. Parsons. *Illuminating Luke: The Infancy Narrative in Italian Renaissance Painting.* Harrisburg PA: Trinity, 2003.

————. *Illuminating Luke: The Public Ministry of Christ in Italian Renaissance and Baroque Painting.* New York: Trinity, 2005.

Hultgren, Arlen. *The Parables of Jesus: A Commentary.* Grand Rapids MI: Eerdmans, 2000.

Irving, John. *A Prayer for Owen Meany.* New York: William Morrow, 1989.

Jeremias, Joachim. *The Parables of Jesus.* 3rd edition. London: SCM, 1972.

Johnson, Luke Timothy. *The Gospel of Luke.* Sacra Pagina 3. Collegeville MN: Liturgical Press, 1991.

Just, Jr., Arthur A., editor. *Luke.* Ancient Christian Commentary on Scripture: New Testament, volume 3. Downer's Grove IL: Intervarsity Press, 2003.

Kasser, Rudolfe, Marvin Meyer, and Gregor Wurst. *The Gospel of Judas.* Washington, D.C: National Geographic, 2006.

Kay, James F. "Mary's Song—And Ours." *ChrCent* 114 (10 Dec 1997): 1157.

Kee, Howard Clark. *Miracle in the Early Christian World.* New Haven: Yale University, 1983.

Keillor, Garrison. *Lake Woebegone Days.* New York: Penguin, 1985.

————. *Leaving Home.* New York: Penguin, 1997.

————. *We Are Still Married.* New York: Penguin, 1990.

Kelly, Thomas R. *A Testament of Devotion.* New York: HarperSanFrancisco, 1992; originally published 1941.

Kennedy, George. *New Testament Interpetation through Rhetorical Criticism.* Chapel Hill: University of North Carolina Press, 1984.

Kierkegaard, Søren. *Purity of Heart Is to Will One Thing.* Translated by Douglas Steere. New York: Harper and Row, 1956.

Kiley, Mark, editor. *Prayer from Alexander to Constantine: A Critical Anthology.* London: Routledge, 1997.

Kimmel, Haven. *The Solace of Leaving Early.* New York: Random House, 2002.

King, Philip J. "Jerusalem." *ABD* 3.747-766.

Kleinman, Arthur. *The Illness Narratives: Suffering, Healing, and the Human Condition.* New York: Basic Books, 1988.

Kloppenborg, John S. "The Theodotos Synagogue Inscription and the Problem of First-Century Synagogue Buildings." In James H. Charlesworth, editor, *Jesus and Archaeology.* Grand Rapids MI: Eerdmans, 2006.

Kraybill, Donald. B. "Forgiveness Clause: The Amish Clause." *ChrCent* 123/22 (31 October 2006): 8–9.

Kraybill, Donald, Steven M. Nolt, and David L. Weaver-Zercher. *Amish Grace: How Forgiveness Transcended Tragedy.* San Francisco: Wiley, 2007.

Kunitz, Stanley. *Passing Through: The Later Poems New and Selected.* New York: Norton, 1995.

Lahiri, Jhumpa. *Interpreter of Maladies.* Boston: Houghton Mifflin, 1998.

Laubach, Frank C. *Letters by a Modern Mystic.* Westwood NJ: Revell, 1937.

Brother Lawrence, *The Practice of the Presence of God.* Old Tappan NJ: Revell, 1958.

Levering, Matthew, editor. *On Christian Dying.* New York: Rowan and Littlefield, 2004.

Lewis, C. S. *The Screwtape Letters.* New York: MacMillan, 1961.

Lewis, Naphtali, and Meyer Reinhold. *Roman Civilization.* Volume 1: *The Republic.* New York: Columbia University Press, 1951.

Lewis, Naphtali, and Meyer Reinhold. *Roman Civilization.* Volume 2: *The Empire.* New York: Harper and Row, 1966.

Lewis, Sinclair. *Babbitt.* New York: Harcourt Brace Jovanovich, 1922; citation from Signet Classics edition, 1961.

Lodge, David. *Changing Places.* New York: Penguin, 1975.

McKeon, Richard, editor. *Introduction to Aristotle.* New York: Modern Library, 1947.

Malherbe, Abraham J. *The Cynic Epistles.* Atlanta: Scholars Press, 1977.

Malina, Bruce, and Richard L. Rohrbach. *Social Science Commentary on the Synoptic Gospels.* Minneapolis: Fortress, 1992.

Malone, Michael. *Time's Witness.* New York: Little, Brown, and Co., 1989.

Marshall, I. Howard. *The Gospel of Luke.* Grand Rapids MI: Eerdmans, 1978.

Martz, Louis L., editor. *George Herbert and Henry Vaughan: A Critical Edition of the Major Works.* New York: Oxford University Press, 1992.

Meeks, Wayne. "Assisting the Word by Making (Up) History: Luke's Project and Ours." *Interpretation* 57 (April 2003): 151–62.

Meier, John P. *A Marginal Jew.* New York: Doubleday, 1994.

Melville, Herman. *Moby-Dick.* Edited by Harrison Hayford and Hershel Parker. New York: Norton, 1967.

Merton, Thomas. *The Climate of Monastic Prayer.* Spencer MA: Cistercian, 1969.

———. *Life and Holiness.* New York: Doubleday, 1963; citation from 1996 edition.

———. *New Seeds of Contemplation.* New York: New Directions, 1972.

Metzger, Bruce M. *The Text of the New Testament: Its Transmission, Corruption, and Restoration.* 3rd edition. New York: Oxford, 1992.

———. *A Textual Commentary on the Greek New Testament.* New York: United Bible Societies, 1971.

Moody, Anne. *Coming of Age in Mississippi.* New York: Delta, 2004; originally published 1968 by Doubleday.

Moore, Christopher. *Lamb: The Gospel According to Biff, Christ's Childhood Pal.* New York: HarperCollins, 2002.

Moule, C. F. D. *An Idiom Book of New Testament Greek*. Cambridge: Cambridge University Press, 1959.

Moxnes, Halvor. *Putting Jesus in His Place*. Louisville KY: Westminster/John Knox, 2003.

Music, David W. *Hymnology: A Collection of Source Readings*. Lanham MD: Scarecrow, 1996.

Munro, Alice. *The View From Castle Rock*. New York: Knopf, 2006.

Nordan, Lewis. *The Sharp-Shooter Blues*. Chapel Hill NC: Algonquin Books, 1997.

Norris, Kathleen. *Amazing Grace: A Vocabulary of Faith*. New York: Riverhead, 1998.

———. *The Quotidian Mysteries*. New York: Paulist, 1998.

Nouwen, Henri. *The Return of the Prodigal Son*. New York: Doubleday, 1992.

O'Connor, Flannery. *The Complete Stories of Flannery O'Connor*. New York: Farrar, Straus, and Giroux, 1971.

Oman, Maggie, editor. *Prayers for Healing*. Berkeley CA: Conari Press, 1997.

Osiek, Carolyn, and David Balch. *Families in the New Testament World*. Louisville: Westminster/John Knox, 1997.

Parsons, Mikeal C. *Body and Character in Luke and Acts: The Subversion of Physiognomy in Early Christianity*. Grand Rapids MI: Baker, 2006.

———. *Luke: Storyteller, Interpreter, Evangelist*. Peabody MA: Hendrickson, 2007.

Perkins, Pheme. "Patched Garments and Ruined Wine: Whose Folly?" In Mary Ann Beavis, editor, *The Lost Coin: Parables of Women, Work, and Wisdom*. Sheffield: Sheffield Academic Press, 2002.

Piercy, Marge. *To Be of Use*. New York: Alfred A. Knopf, 1982.

Pilch, John. *The Cultural Dictionary of the Bible*. Collegeville MN: Liturgical, 1999.

———. *Healing in the New Testament: Insights from Medical and Mediterranean Anthropology*. Minneapolis: Fortress, 2000.

Price, Richard. *Samaritan*. New York: Alfred Knopf, 2003.

Reid, Barbara A. *Choosing the Better Part? Women in the Gospel of Luke*. Collegeville MN: Liturgical, 1996.

Reif, Stefan C. "The Early Liturgy of the Synagogue." In William Horbury et al., editors, *The Cambridge History of Judaism*. Volume 3. Cambridge: Cambridge University Press, 1999.

Richardson, Cyril C., editor. Early Christian Fathers. New York: MacMillan, 1970.

Ringe, Sharon. *Luke*. Louisville KY: Westminster/John Knox, 1995.

Robinson, Barbara. *The Best Christmas Pageant Ever*. New York: Harper and Row, 1972.

Robinson, Marilynne. *Gilead*. New York: Farrar, Straus, Giroux, 2004.

Robinson, Spider. *God Is an Iron and Other Stories*. Waterville ME: Gale Group, 2002.

Rousseau, John J., and Rami Arav. *Jesus and His World*. Minneapolis: Fortress, 1995.

Saller, Richard. "Women, Slaves, and the Economy of the Roman Household." In David L. Balch and Carolyn Osiek, editors, *Early Christian Families in Context*. Grand Rapids MI: Eerdmans, 2003.

Sanders, E. P. *Jesus and Judaism*. Philadelphia: Fortress, 1985.

———. *Judaism: Practice and Belief, 63 BCE–66 CE*. Philadelphia: Trinity, 1992.

Schaberg, Jane. "Luke." In the Women's Bible Commentary, edited by Carol Newsome and Sharon H. Ringe. Louisville: Westminster/John Knox, 1992.

———. *The Resurrection of Mary Magdalene: Legends, Apocrypha, and the Christian Testament*. New York: Continuum, 2002.

Scheffler, Eben. *Suffering in Luke's Gospel*. Zürich: Theologischer Verlag, 1993.

Schneemelcher, Wilhelm, editor. *New Testament Apocrypha*. Translated and edited by R. McL. Wilson. 2 volumes. Louisville KY: Westminster/John Knox Press, 1991–1992.

Schottrof, Luis. *The Parables of Jesus*. Translated by Linda M. Maloney. Minneapolis: Fortress, 2006.

Schwartz, Daniel R. "Pontius Pilate." *ABD* 5.395-401.

Schweitzer, Albert. *The Quest of the Historical Jesus*. 2d edition. Translated by W. Montgomery; London: Black, 1931.

Scott, Bernard Brandon. *Hear Then the Parable: A Commentary on the Parables of Jesus*. Minneapolis: Fortress, 1989.

Seim, Turid Karlsen. *The Double Message: Patterns of Gender in Luke-Acts*. Nashville: Abingdon, 1994.

Senior, Donald. "Beware of the Canaanite Woman: Disability and the Bible." In Marilyn E. Bishop, editor, *Religion and Disability*. Kansas City: Sheed and Ward, 1995.

Senn, Frank C. *Christian Liturgy: Catholic and Evangelical*. Minneapolis: Fortress, 1997.

Shiner, Whitney. *Proclaiming the Gospel: First-Century Performance of Mark*. Harrisburg PA: Trinity, 2003.

Skrade, Kristofer, editor. *The Christian Handbook*. Minneapolis: Augsburg, 2005.

Smith, Dennis. *From Symposium to Eucharist*. Minneapolis: Fortress, 2003.

Spark, Muriel. *Memento Mori*. New York: G. P. Putnam, 1958.

Spencer, F. Scott. *Dancing Girls, Loose Ladies, and Women of the Cloth*. New York: Continuum, 2004.

———. *Journeying Through Acts: A Literary-cultural Reading*. Peabody MA: Hendrickson, 2004.

———. *What Did Jesus Do*. Harrisburg PA: Trinity, 2003.

Stevenson, Kenneth W. *The Lord's Prayer: A Text in Tradition* (Minneapolis: Fortress, 2004.

Talbert, Charles H. *Reading Luke: A Literary and Theological Commentary on the Third Gospel*. Revised edition. Macon GA: Smyth and Helwys, 2002.

Tannehill, Robert C. *Luke*. Abingdon New Testament Commentaries. Nashville: Abingdon, 1996.

———. *The Narrative Unity of Luke-Acts: A Literary Intepretation*. Volume 1: *The Gospel According to Luke*. Philadelphia: Fortress, 1986.

———. *The Shape of Luke's Story: Essays on Luke-Acts*. Eugene OR: Wipf and Stock, 2005.

———. *The Sword of His Mouth: Forceful and Imaginative Language in Synoptic Sayings.* Missoula MT: Scholars, 1975.

Taylor, John V. *The Incarnate God.* New York: Continuum, 2004.

Tolkien, J. R. R. *The Hobbit.* Revised edition. New York: Ballantine, 1965.

———. *The Lord of the Rings.* Boston: Houghton Mifflin, 1994.

Twain, Mark. *The Adventures of Huckleberry Finn.* New York: Barnes and Noble Classics, 2003.

———. *The Adventures of Tom Sawyer.* New York: Barnes and Noble Classics, 2003.

Tyson, Joseph B. *Marcion and Luke-Acts: A Defining Struggle.* Columbia: University of South Carolina, 2006.

Updike, John. *A Month of Sundays.* New York: Alfred A. Knopf, 1975.

Van Til, Kent A. *Less Than Two Dollars a Day: A Christian View of World Poverty and the Free Market.* Grand Rapids MI: Eerdmans, 2007.

Volf, Miroslav. *The End of Memory: Remembering Rightly in a Violent World.* Grand Rapids MI: Eerdmans, 2006.

von Balthasar, Hans Urs. *Prayer.* Translated by A. V. Littledale. New York: Paulist, 1961.

Waddell, Helen. *The Desert Fathers.* Ann Arbor: University of Michigan Press, 1957.

Walaskay, Paul. '*And So We Came To Rome*': *The Political Perspective of St. Luke.* Cambridge: Cambridge University Press, 1983.

Walker, Alice. "The Welcome Table." *In Love & Trouble.* New York: Harcourt Brace Jovanovich, 1973. 83–84.

Washington, James M., editor. *A Testament of Hope: The Essential Writings of Martin Luther King, Jr.* San Francisco: Harper & Row, 1986.

Webb-Mitchell, Brett. *Dancing with Disabilities: Opening the Church to All God's Children.* Cleveland OH: United Church Press, 1996.

Weisberger, Bernard. *They Gathered at the River.* Boston: Little, Brown, and Co, 1958.

White, E. B. *One Man's Meat.* Gardiner ME: Tilbury House, 1997.

Wiedemann, Thomas. *Greek and Roman Slavery: A Sourcebook.* Baltimore MD: Johns Hopkins University Press, 1981.

Wink, Walter. *Unmasking the Powers.* Philadelphia: Fortress, 1986.

Wolfe, Tom. *Bonfire of the Vanities.* New York: Farrar, Straus, & Giroux, 1987.

Wollenburg, Bruce. "Summoned." *ChrCent* 121/17 (24 August 2004): 17.

Zimbardo, Philip G. "Revisiting the Stanford Prison Experiment: A Lesson in the Power of Situation." *The Chronicle of Higher Education* 53 (30 March 2007): B6.

INDEX OF MODERN AUTHORS

INDEX OF SIDEBARS AND ILLUSTRATIONS

Illustration Sidebars

INDEX OF SCRIPTURES

INDEX OF TOPICS